THEORETICAL MODELS AND PROCESSES OF LITERACY

The Seventh Edition of this foundational text represents the most comprehensive source available for connecting multiple and diverse theories to literacy research, broadly defined, and features both cutting-edge and classic contributions from top scholars. Two decades into the 21st century, the Seventh Edition finds itself at a crossroads and differs from its predecessors in three major ways: the more encompassing term *literacy* replaces *reading* in the title to reflect changes in how readers and writers communicate in a digital era; the focus is on conceptual essays rather than the mix of essays and research reports in earlier volumes; and, most notably, contemporary literacy models and processes enhance and extend earlier theories of reading and writing. Providing a tapestry of models and theories that have informed literacy research and instruction over the years, this volume's strong historical grounding serves as a springboard from which new perspectives are presented. The chapters in this volume have been selected to inspire the interrogation of literacy theory and to foster its further evolution. This edition is a landmark volume in which dynamic, dialogic, and generative relations of power speak directly to the present generation of literacy theorists and researchers without losing the historical contexts that preceded them. Some additional archival essays from previous editions are available on the book's eResource page.

New to the Seventh Edition:

- Features chapters on emerging and contemporary theories that connect directly to issues of power and contrasts new models against more established counterparts.
- New chapters reflect sweeping changes in how readers and writers communicate in a digital era.
- Slimmer volume is complemented by some chapters from previous editions available online.

Donna E. Alvermann is the University of Georgia Appointed Distinguished Research Professor of Language and Literacy Education, and holds the Omer Clyde and Elizabeth Parr Aderhold Professorship in Education at the University of Georgia, USA.

Norman J. Unrau is Professor of Education Emeritus at California State University, Los Angeles, USA.

Misty Sailors is Professor of Literacy Education and Director of the Center for the Inquiry of Transformative Literacies at the University of Texas at San Antonio, USA.

Robert B. Ruddell is Professor Emeritus at the University of California at Berkeley, USA.

THEORETICAL MODELS AND PROCESSES OF LITERACY

Seventh Edition

Edited by Donna E. Alvermann, Norman J. Unrau,
Misty Sailors, and Robert B. Ruddell

Routledge
Taylor & Francis Group

NEW YORK AND LONDON

Seventh edition published 2019
by Routledge
711 Third Avenue, New York, NY 10017

and by Routledge
2 Park Square, Milton Park, Abingdon, Oxon, OX14 4RN

Routledge is an imprint of the Taylor & Francis Group, an informa business

First edition published by the International Reading Association, Inc. 1970
Sixth edition published by the International Reading Association, Inc. 2013

Library of Congress Cataloging-in-Publication Data
Names: Alvermann, Donna E., editor. | Unrau, Norman, editor. |
    Sailors, Misty, editor. | Ruddell, Robert B., editor.
Title: Theoretical models and processes of literacy / edited by Donna E. Alvermann,
    Norman J. Unrau, Misty Sailors, and Robert B. Ruddell.
Description: Seventh Edition. | New York : Routledge, 2019. | "Sixth edition published
    by the International Reading Association, Inc. 2013"—T.p. verso. |
    Includes bibliographical references and index.
Identifiers: LCCN 2018024329 | ISBN 9781138087262 hardback |
    ISBN 9781138087279 paperback | ISBN 9781315110592 ebook
Subjects: LCSH: Reading. | Reading—Research.
Classification: LCC LB1050 .T48 2019 | DDC 428.4—dc23
LC record available at https://lccn.loc.gov/2018024329

ISBN: 978-1-138-08726-2 (hbk)
ISBN: 978-1-138-08727-9 (pbk)
ISBN: 978-1-315-11059-2 (ebk)

Typeset in Bembo
by Apex CoVantage, LLC

Visit the eResources website: www.routledge.com/9781138087279

We dedicate this seventh edition of *Theoretical Models and Processes of Literacy* to

Brian V. Street

an individual whose scholarship spanned disciplines, challenged normative ways of thinking, and invited difficult discussions in which Brian's gentle presence added to the dialogue.

CONTENTS

Contents

Contents

FIGURES, TABLES, AND BOXES

Figures

Tables

Box

PREFACE

Welcome to *Theoretical Models and Processes of Literacy, Seventh Edition* (TMPL7). If you have followed earlier editions of this series, you will instantly note an important change that is both substantive and long overdue. The title of the seventh edition has expanded from "reading" to "literacy" to acknowledge the role of writing in relation to reading in the realm of theory. In fact, for the first time there is a chapter titled "Waves of Theory Building in Writing and its Development, and their Implications for Instruction, Assessment, and Curriculum." Genre-wise, this chapter along with the other chapters new to TMPL7, is a theoretical essay as compared to a mix of essays and research reports in earlier volumes.

In TMPL7, contemporary literacy models extend, enhance, or even break with earlier theories of reading and writing processes. This is intentional, given our goal of producing a volume in which the present generation of literacy theorists and researchers speak directly to issues involving relations of power, which in the past may have been avoided because such were deemed a poor fit with what academics typically addressed. Dynamic, dialogical, and generative, this present generation of theorists is providing new insights without ignoring the historical contexts that spawned the theories and the empirical foundations that ground the same.

But those differences are not the only changes you will instantly notice. Consider the size of TMPL7. After several decades in which the width of the book had expanded to match the content carried forward plus the new invited chapters for each subsequent edition, we were advised that it was time to slim down by trimming both the number of chapters in the seventh edition and also making the newly invited chapters shorter in comparison to earlier volumes. Not to worry, however. Routledge/Taylor & Francis Group, our new publisher, as a result of the International Literacy Association's decision to end its book publishing division in 2017, provided us with a website on which to host chapters from *Theoretical Models and Processes of Reading, Sixth Edition* that do not appear in TMPL7. Those freely downloadable chapters from TMPR6 are available at: www.routledge.com/9781138087279.

Given these substantive changes, you may be wondering about the process we used to trim the volume's size. The short answer to that question is this: Naomi Silverman, before her retirement from Routledge/Taylor & Francis Group in 2017, enlisted a panel of seven international scholars whose names were not made known to us to advise her (and ultimately us) on which topics of contemporary scholarship were not represented in TMPR6, as well as those that were overrepresented. The goal was to make TMPL7 a compendium of newer theories and models set alongside some of their earlier ancestors or counterparts. The panelists, like we as editors, were well aware of the special place of TMPL7 in the history of our field. We sometimes think of this current volume as balancing on the cusp of a shift, perhaps a shift in paradigms, whose qualities and dimensions will be more visible and more capable of being described by the time the eighth edition is conceived.

Finally, and by no means least is our most important addition to *TMPL7*—Misty Sailors, who joins us from the University of Texas at San Antonio. When we invited Misty to consider taking on the role of third editor of *TMPL7* (in the line-up of Alvermann, Unrau, and Ruddell), we collectively held our breath. Would she, the lead editor of the *Journal of Literacy Research* and the wearer of many other hats, find time for us? She did, and this volume would not be what it is without Misty's insights and indefatigable energy. Please welcome her, and linger here for a short time to soak up the history of this remarkable series with which Robert Ruddell has been associated from the start.

A Brief History of *Theoretical Models and Processes of Reading*

The first edition of *TMPR* emerged from a 1969 symposium presented at the 14th annual convention of the International Reading Association (IRA) in Kansas City, Missouri. Robert Ruddell of the University of California, Berkeley, and Harry Singer of the University of California, Riverside, discussed the idea that a book might evolve from invited speakers' informative research presentations at the convention. The idea of honoring Professor Jack Holmes of the University of California, Berkeley, was at the center of the volume's creation. Holmes, who passed away in 1969, had been Singer's doctoral advisor and mentor and Robert Ruddell's former senior colleague at Berkeley. In 1970, the collection of papers, which were edited by Singer and Ruddell, became the first edition of *TMPR*. Graduate students in reading programs throughout the United States were quick to use that first 348-page volume.

The second edition, published in 1976, doubled in length to 768 pages. Several new ideas grew from conversations between Harry Singer and Robert Ruddell as they planned the new edition. That edition included an introduction highlighting pioneers in reading research and three major sections on (1) the processes of reading, (2) models, and (3) teaching and research issues. That structure for *TMPR* endured through several volumes. Dedicated to researchers who had contributed to an understanding of the reading process, the second edition included research articles that would illustrate various research traditions and focusing questions at the beginning of each section.

The third edition of *TMPR*, published in 1985, was again edited by Harry Singer and Robert Ruddell. These two editors remained dedicated to publishing the exceptionally high quality work of faculty researchers and graduate student researchers who were formulating theories of reading, testing hypotheses, and generating new theory and knowledge in the field.

The fourth edition of *TMPR*, published in 1994 and edited by Robert Ruddell, Martha Ruddell, and Harry Singer, expanded to 1,296 pages. Like previous editions, most of the content in the fourth edition provided new frameworks and insights, with more than 80% of the selected articles having not appeared in any earlier volumes. As with earlier editions, the fourth edition retained four themed sections: "Historical Changes in Reading: Researchers and Their Research," "Processes of Reading and Literacy," "Models of Reading and Literacy Processes," and "New Paradigms: Theory, Research, and Curriculum." The selections in these four sections made evident the explosion of knowledge in our field during the prior decade with new and revised theoretical perspectives, new paradigms, the use of multiple research stances, and new research findings.

The fifth edition, published in 2004 and edited by Robert Ruddell and Norman Unrau, was by far the largest in *TMPR*'s history. It reflected the editors' aspirations to extend the coverage and depth of *TMPR*. The fifth edition consisted of 56 chapters for a total of 1,728 pages. As had been the case with earlier editions of *TMPR*, the editors gathered an abundance of information from a wide range of sources and discussed at great length how the new edition should be structured and what content would fill that structure. For example, they looked for reprints of publications that reflected developments during the past decade and were likely to have significant and enduring effects on the literacy field. In addition to retaining the four main sections of the fourth edition, *TMPR5* included a supplementary CD that contained several earlier *TMPR* classics and more recent pieces that could not be included in the already expansive fifth edition.

In the sixth edition of *Theoretical Models and Processes of Reading* published in 2013 and edited by Donna Alvermann, Norman Unrau, and Robert Ruddell, over half of the chapters had never appeared in any earlier edition. Eight of those new chapters were especially commissioned to reflect growing trends in the field and to include a more diverse set of authors. Additionally, 20% of the chapters in *TMPR6* that had appeared earlier were updated by their authors to reflect more current research and instructional developments. Looking to the field to inform their selection of content for the sixth edition, Alvermann, Unrau, and Ruddell took into account the results of 640 completed surveys distributed and analyzed by the IRA. Small focus groups that included researchers (both faculty and graduate students) gathered at the annual meetings of the Literacy Research Association and the IRA to assist the editors in striking a balance between new trends in the field and earlier classics that had retained relevancy well into the 21st century.

ACKNOWLEDGMENTS

As we conclude our work on the seventh edition, we would like to recognize and express our appreciation to a number of people who have supported us in this endeavor. We first want to thank Naomi Silverman, former Publisher at Routledge/Taylor & Francis Group. Without her intervention there would have been no seventh edition. Similarly, Dan Mangan of the International Literacy Association (ILA) created a smooth transition by ensuring that copyrights from the sixth edition reverted to the authors and/or original copyright owners when ILA's book publishing ended. Second, we appreciate *TMPR6*'s authors' patience while the four editors of the seventh edition (Alvermann, Unrau, Sailors, and Ruddell) worked to produce a greatly slimmed down version of the earlier handbook.

Our appreciation also goes to three outstanding professionals at Routledge: Karen Adler, Editor; Emmalee Ortega, Editorial Assistant; and Katharine Atherton, Production Editor. They were knowledgeable and extremely patient in answering our questions in a timely and fully comprehensible manner. We also value the contributions of our in-house copyeditors, Rachel Meyers, Rebecca Bender, and Kasey Lockwood.

Finally, we thank our families for their care and encouragement during the year and a half that it took to complete *TMPL7*. A big shout-out to Jack and Jazz, who excel in the world of humans and golden retrievers when it comes to patience and loyalty in dealing with Donna's projects. To Norm's wife, Cherene, to her listening ear, and to her understanding as we moved step by step through the creation of this work go boundless appreciation. Much recognition to Misty's professional and life partner, Jim Hoffman, who did more than his share of the gardening and cooking (and other shared responsibilities) during the editing of this book. To Bob's wife, Sandra McCormick, he wishes to say how nice it is to be married to an established literacy researcher—our conversations are interesting and useful.

Donna E. Alvermann
Norman J. Unrau
Misty Sailors
Robert B. Ruddell

SECTION ONE

Historical

The first section of this volume offers four chapters, all of which contribute historical perspectives to crucial aspects of literacy scholarship and instruction. In Chapter 1, "Literacies and Their Investigation Through Theories and Models," Norman Unrau, Donna Alvermann, and Misty Sailors describe and explore the complexity of meanings for the terms *theory* and *models*, the relationships between them, and the paradigm shifts that have affected their inner core and their impact on research and practice over the past three-quarters of a century. Having recognized the omnipresence of theory, both overt and tacit, in literacy research or instruction, the chapter's authors explain theories that have shaped and reformed the field. These include constructivism, social constructionism, transactional theory, information and cognitive processing theories of reading and writing, sociocultural theories, sociocognitive theory, structuralism, critical theory, poststructural theory and non-representational theories, and posthumanism. The authors cite chapters in this volume that are built upon a particular theory or examine that theory's deeper structure and influence. Readers are encouraged to continue to interrogate theories through relentless curiosity and to formulate new literacy theory that aligns with evidence and promises improving outcomes.

In Chapter 2, Patricia Alexander and Emily Fox provide us with "Reading Research and Practice Over the Decades: A Historical Analysis." In their chapter, the authors survey the past 70 years of reading history and identify six perspectives on learning beginning with the "Era of Conditioned Learning" that started in the 1950s and progressed to what the authors believe is our current "Emergent Era of Personalized Learning." The authors then distill lessons learned from those 70 years. Their review of seven decades of reading research and instruction magnifies and clarifies factors, such as trends in research, which have guided and shaped the identity and evolution of the field of reading.

In Chapter 3, Anna Smith describes theory building in writing as periods of concentration on particular dimensions of writing. She identifies four key dimensions in the history of writing instruction that she explores: a *products* dimension, a cognitive and stage *processes* dimension, a *practices* dimension, and a *pathways* dimension. Because writing always contains these dimensions, she observes that each dimension has been a focus of scholarship in waves, a metaphor that informs her view of theory building in writing scholarship. Smith also reminds us that these dimensions in writing are always interacting and calls for synthesizing rather than isolating them. Furthermore, she cites scholars who resonate with the history she presents and who use that history as a foundation for principles of writing development. Finally, she laments the obsession with "theoretically starved" educational assessment and mandated writing curriculum and instruction that have failed to fit the dynamic ecology of human learning in the sphere of writing development.

Chapter 4 in this section attends to one of the field's most influential contributors to reading development theory and instruction, Marie Clay. In this chapter entitled "Marie M. Clay's Theoretical Perspective: A Literacy Processing Theory," Mary Anne Doyle traces the development of the well-known literacy intervention: Reading Recovery. Although much has been written about Clay's research and theoretical undertakings, Doyle synthesizes a multiplicity of complex threads in Clay's work and applies them to instructional decision-making. She reviews Clay's discoveries that arose from her careful efforts to describe the changes she observed in children's literacy processing during acquisition stages, the theory arising from efforts to make sense of her observations, and literacy activities likely to promote the best path of development for young learners, especially those needing more guidance on their path to proficiency. For readers who may have asked why Reading Recovery is effective, Doyle's investigation and explanations offer answers.

1

LITERACIES AND THEIR INVESTIGATION THROUGH THEORIES AND MODELS

Norman J. Unrau, Donna E. Alvermann, and Misty Sailors

Theory and theoretical models have the power to cast both light and shadow on our understanding of literacies. They exercise their powers not absolutely but on a continuum of degrees of illumination so that we sometimes receive from a theory only a narrow shaft of light that provides an insight into a literacy process, such as reading. Furthermore, the intensity of light that a narrow shaft provides varies. So a theory's powers to illuminate can rise or fall depending on our capacity to grasp a particular theory or model, its individual components, their interactions, the potential outcomes of those interactions, and its degree of relevance to the context we've applied it. In this sense, all theories are relative. Their explanatory powers fluctuate, depending on our ability to appreciate their assumptions, subtleties, and implications.

While theories of reading, both conscious and unconscious, affect readers generally, specialized readers, such as researchers, teacher educators, graduate students, reading specialists, and classroom teachers activate and use their own theories of reading. Their use of theory may affect a wide range of activities and decisions. Regarding the identification of issues in reading or writing to investigate, seasoned and newly emerging researchers often turn to theory and theoretical models to provide a theoretical framework for their investigations and to identify key issues they plan to examine in detail. Theories and models may also provide researchers with knowledge organized into structures that can frame the discussion of a study's results, their bearing on current policies and instructional practices, and their implications for subsequent research. In addition, researchers often use their findings to provide documentation for a theory's validity, to reject a theory in part or in its entirety, to modify aspects of it, and to posit new theories that more powerfully and comprehensively explain literacy processes or outcomes. In fact, the importance of findings often comes to life when seen within a particular theoretical perspective.

For those interested in literacy research or engaged in it, grappling with literacy theory or theoretical models of literacy processes is unavoidable. Addressing theoretical considerations for a research project arises in most educational research textbooks included in undergraduate and graduate courses (Creswell, 2015; Mertens, 2015). Authors of research textbooks have adopted and embraced different views of theory and its role in educational research. While some authors focus primarily on assumptions about methodologies, such as qualitative, quantitative, and mixed methods, others object to what appears to them as problematic dichotomies artificially created by larger paradigmatic concerns. Because paradigms vary in form and function, they inherently point researchers in different directions. For example, Mertens' (2015) transformative paradigm, which guides researchers interested in social justice and the furtherance of human rights, prioritizes ethical concerns that might be entirely missing in a positivistic paradigm, which relies on scientific evidence (experiments and statistics) to explain how a process or a social group operates. This difference in emphasis is exactly why researchers and people who read their research need to be aware of the influence of paradigms on what can be studied and hence discovered. Equally important is an awareness of semantic controversies that stem from imprecise usage of terms, such as paradigms, theories, and models (Tracey & Morrow, 2017). The language or terminology of research in literacy currently reflects considerable divergence, a divergence with which researchers navigating the world of theory and models ought to be aware. One of our guiding purposes for this chapter pivots on helping readers think through various dichotomies and differences in the field of literacy research to discover what perspectives they find compatible with their present knowledge and beliefs and to situate themselves as knowledgeable consumers and producers of ideas.

In current practice, research studies on literacy published in professional journals frequently open with a review of literature relevant to the research questions posed, to the domain investigated, or to the theory used in framing a study. Answering a call for proposals from a governmental agency or private organization typically necessitates the articulation of a theoretical framework for the proposed research. In instances of intervention research—the type most often funded through the U.S. Institute of Educational Studies (IES)—applicants must clearly describe their intervention and the theory (or theories) framing the intervention. Applicants who seek funding from private organizations, such as the Spencer Foundation, must also provide a strong theoretical foundation for their research. Developing a deep understanding of theory and its uses in literacy studies can make a difference between being funded (or not), especially when a review committee is comprised of individuals who represent multiple disciplines, business entities, and community groups.

Although the functions and benefits of theories can be demonstrated, the extent of their explicit appearance in published papers in the field of literacy may occur with less consistency than we might expect (Yang, Kuo, Ji, & McTigue, 2018). Researchers (Parsons, Gallagher, & the George Mason University Content Analysis Team, 2016) conducted a content analysis of nine literacy journals considered to be among the "most influential" and the highest ranking with respect to impact factor ratings in the field. The researchers categorized over a thousand articles from these journals into 24 theoretical perspectives that they identified. The theoretical perspectives most frequently represented were Sociocultural, Cognitive/Information Processing, and New Literacies. However, many influential journals that publish articles on literacy were not included in the content analysis. That leads us to caution readers regarding the credibility of the researchers' findings and its generalization to the literacy field. Although the scope of important journals publishing literacy articles may have been limited, Parsons et al. claim that theoretical perspectives were left unspecified in 76% of all the articles. Even though these findings ought to be viewed with some degree of circumspection, they suggest that authors of articles on both research and instruction in literacy need to address with more consideration the theoretical perspectives they have adopted and how their findings inform, reform, or reframe a particular perspective.

In this chapter, we first clarify the meaning of theory and model, particularly in relation to literacy studies. We then explore meanings of paradigm and their shifts relevant to the field of literacy research over the past half-century or so. Subsequently, we review central theories and associated models that influence literacy research, including constructivism, social constructionism, transactional theory, information/cognitive processing theory, sociocultural perspectives, sociocognitive theory, structuralism, critical theory, poststructuralism and non-representational theories, and posthumanism. Finally, we speculate on the evolution of literacy theories and models for future research.

Theory and Model: Their Meanings, Relationships, and Foundations

A word's roots often reveal its essence, and, to some degree, that is what the ancient Greek root of *theory* affords. Our modern theory is rooted in the Greek word *theoria* (θεωρία) which, when translated, means "a looking at, viewing, contemplation, speculation, also a sight, a spectacle"

(Oxford English Dictionary). Aspects of our current use of the word theory, certainly as viewing and speculation, are reflected in these ancient meanings. However, when we take a Wittgensteinian view of language and look at the meaning of words in the context of their use in the current game of language (Wittgenstein, 1953), we soon discover a fascinating range of meanings when people, including educators, speak of *theory*. In living rooms, offices, and classrooms, we hear people providing us with a description or explanation for how and why events have occurred the way they did including why the Cubs won the World Series in 2016, ending a 108-year drought. Not infrequently, we hear listeners respond to these descriptions and explanations with comments such as, "That's an interesting theory," "I've heard that theory before," or "I don't think that theory works here, Albert." In classrooms, especially those in which science is taught, we are more likely to hear explanations for events that are grounded in a hypothesis, but, because that hypothesis has been vigorously tested, speakers refer to it as a theory, perhaps with accompanying laws. A theory has been so carefully developed and tested that it not only describes and explains events but can also be used to predict them, sometimes to an impressive degree of mathematical precision. With this usage of the word theory in mind, we would be comfortable assuming that in some contexts, when people are talking about theory, they are describing, explaining, and attempting to predict events. When used by natural or physical scientists, a theory usually refers to an explanation of some aspect of reality, such as the behavior of gases under pressure, that has been subjected to extensive testing, survived falsification, and became widely accepted by the scientific community in which the theory is germane.

In science broadly and in literacy research in particular, theories are propositional networks commonly used to help members of a community of researchers and practitioners understand, explain, and make predictions about key concepts and processes in their field of study. Theories themselves can be expressed in natural language, in mathematical terms, or in some other symbolic language, such as that used in chemistry. Darwin (1859/1988), for example, presented his theory of evolution to the general public in his book *On the Origin of Species*. He introduced the theory that populations evolve over time through the process of natural selection and presented evidence, much of which he collected during his voyage on the *Beagle*, that life's diversity came about through a branching pattern of common descent. However, a theory need not be completely developed and verified at birth. Although we have come to understand many of the branches Darwin sketched, we will undoubtedly be filling in the missing sprouts and myriad details in our understanding of that evolutionary process for generations.

Overt and Tacit Theories

All people are theoreticians, according to Gee (2012), but some are more mindful of their immersion in theory than others. When introducing the importance of theory in ethical discourse, Gee defined theory as "a set of generalizations about an area . . . in terms of which descriptions of phenomena in that area can be couched and explanations can be offered" (p. 13). Gee asserted that theories provide a foundation for beliefs, even though individuals may not be cognizant of the particular theory or theories they are using to ground their beliefs and claims. Theories, once articulated, give critical information about what counts as evidence to support them and where we might discover that evidence. Undoubtedly, some theories that serve as a base for our beliefs and claims are sound. However, many, if not all of us, are likely to use generalizations which, if put to a thorough analysis and testing, would prove to be unsupportable and so undermine the credibility of our theories.

Our ability to clarify and explain the theories and generalizations upon which our beliefs and claims rest is to Gee (2012) of moral and ethical importance because, generally speaking, the use of theories can cause damage to other people, especially in the form of social injustice. Noting that individuals, when presenting their arguments, vary in the degree to which they articulate or are capable of articulating the theories underlying beliefs and claims included in those arguments, Gee observed that theories in discourse can be viewed as lying on a continuum from overt to tacit. Individuals using tacit theories to ground beliefs and claims are, to varying degrees, unaware or unconscious of the generalizations contributing to their positions' theoretical foundations. Individuals using overt theories are more conscious of their theories' supporting generalizations. These two qualities of theory, tacit and overt, cannot be viewed as absolutes because individuals may understand the grounding for their theory to a large degree but still not be entirely conscious of all of the theory's underlying generalizations. Alternatively, it is possible to be unaware of a theory's foundation but still have a limited understanding of several generalizations supporting it.

People, according to Gee (2012), also operate with primary or non-primary theories. Those who have analyzed, researched, and reflected upon the generalizations that support their theories and who have discussed and debated over them with others hold what Gee calls primary theories and primary generalizations that support those theories. Those who hold non-primary theories have yet to put their supporting generalizations under rigorous examination for the purpose of discovering their truth value. Generalizations not exposed to examination, debate, and discussion are said to be non-primary. Non-primary theories and generalizations are usually adopted by individuals from beliefs and claims they have heard or read that others espouse.

Articles classified as not having a specified theory in the content analysis of journal publications conducted by Parsons, Gallagher, et al. (2016) may have been so categorized because they arose from non-primary theories. Although Gee does not argue that these primary and non-primary theories can also lie on a continuum, they most likely can because a primary theory could be grounded by some durable generalizations that were well examined but undermined by others more tacit in nature and less carefully explored for their quality of truth.

Next, we examine the relation of theory to model. Doing so requires that we consider the historical contributions these concepts have made to literacy research and to our understandings of reading and writing processes.

What Is a Model?

Just as theory has taken on different meanings from user to user and context to context, so has model. In the context of the artist's studio, a model can inspire the representation of the human form on canvas. In other contexts, a model is a prototype in design of what is to be produced or emulated. Car designers create models of automobiles that enable them to envision the lines and curves of the new year's fleet. In scientific contexts, scientists create models to depict scientific processes or structures that are often invisible, such as the model of an atom. In yet another context, economists design models to render in mathematical terms a network of complex variables, such as an economic model of international trade. These examples of the use of the word model hardly exhaust the variations we find in its application.

With the general term *model* having such a rich array of meanings, it comes as no surprise that it is defined variably within the field of literacy research as well. For example, a journal article can provide an explanation and discussion of professional development models that have demonstrated their effectiveness in helping teachers address issues in language and literacy instruction. However, the individual components of such models may never have been subject to any form of independent or interdependent assessment. In the third edition of *Theoretical Models and Processes of Reading* (Ruddell, Ruddell, & Singer, 1994), the editors wrote in an introduction to the section on models of reading and literacy processes that, while a theory is an explanation of a phenomenon,

> a model serves as a metaphor to explain and represent the theory. This representation often takes the form of a depiction of the interrelationships among a theory's variables and may even make provision for connecting the theory to observations. The theory is thus more

dynamic in nature than the model but describes the way the model operates; the model is frequently static and represents a snap-shot of a dynamic process.

(p. 812)

Theory may also be seen as a model of reality. Reality serves as the ultimate model of how things work. All humanly created models are then replicas that mimic or represent reality's perfect form and function. The degree to which a humanly designed model, such as a model of the reading process, represents or at least reflects the reality of a complex and invisible process varies widely. All models are theoretical because they are an imitation of reality, an effort to describe or explain it—not reality itself. So, calling a model of the reading process a theoretical model may be a redundancy because a model, in this instance of its use, is already theoretical. Nevertheless, a model of reading, writing, or both represents in ordinary language or graphic form the components of a process and explains how those components function and interact with one another.

In the broader literacy field, we now encounter models as metaphors that represent abstract constructs that might be quite difficult to operationalize and calibrate as well as those that represent theoretical variables that have been operationalized and quantified. Models embodying abstract constructs have emerged from qualitative research, as we see in the case of Carol Lee (2001/2013) who developed a model of instruction to enable historically marginalized students to engage with literature. Qualitatively-derived models offer readers through conceptual and graphic formats an alternative to quantitative models.

Paradigm Shifts Affecting Literacy Theories and Models

In the field of literacy studies, profound changes in perspectives, some with the magnitude of paradigm shifts, have taken place since the 1950s as we moved from behaviorism through a cognitive revolution to a pronounced social turn. In the next chapter, Alexander and Fox (see Chapter 2 this volume) capture these three perspectives by referring to them as "eras," while reviewing the history of reading research and practice. In *The Structure of Scientific Revolutions,* Kuhn (1996) wrote that science does not fit the vision of knowledge generated by the steady accumulation of discoveries. Rather, the history of science has proceeded through peaceful, relatively long episodes of tradition-framed normal science ruptured occasionally by powerful intellectual revolutions in which one widely accepted conceptual view was overthrown by another. For example, the discovery of oxygen by Lavoisier resulted in the displacement of theoretical ideas about an imaginary element called phlogiston that was believed to be the cause of combustion, and Newton's widely accepted concepts and laws of physics were eventually revised radically by Einstein's theory of relativity.

It is not merely a theory or model that sustains a paradigm but a network of theoretical, conceptual, instrumental, methodological, and sociocultural sources that serve scientists broaching scientific puzzles in their research community. This network of resources enables scientists practicing in their discipline to frame experiments, to carry them out, to record them, and to distribute empirical findings to others in the research community that shares a common paradigm. In the field of literacy studies, we have seen three major shifts in paradigms over the past six or seven decades.

For several decades before the cognitive revolution, behaviorism dominated the psychological sciences. As a school of psychology, behaviorism took observed behavior as the focus of its research and the basis of its theory without consideration of any experience of consciousness. During the late 1950s, behaviorism migrated into the domain of language acquisition and its analysis. B. F. Skinner, the founder of behaviorism, published *Verbal Behavior* in 1957. In that book, he defined verbal behavior as "behavior reinforced through the mediation of other persons" who "must be responding in ways which have been conditioned precisely in order to reinforce the behavior of the speaker." To Skinner, the reinforcement of verbal behaviors and its conditioning by others constituted essential processes in language acquisition. Those beliefs set the stage for the rise of cognitive psychology.

Noam Chomsky (1957) radically critiqued Skinner's behaviorist theory in an essay that signaled the beginning of the cognitive revolution in theoretical linguistics and that reverberated across disciplines, into the psychological sciences, and into literacy studies. That cognitive revolution, according to Howard Gardner (1985), was driven by the need to answer enduring questions of epistemology: What is the true nature of knowledge? Where does knowledge come from? How is it developed and used? By the 1970s, literacy researchers were joining the cognitive revolution in an effort to analyze and explain various complexities associated with the reading process. The first edition of *Theoretical Models and Processes of Reading* (Singer & Ruddell, 1970), included a collection of six papers and reactions to them that dealt with cognitive, linguistic, and perceptual components of the reading process.

That shift to a cognitive perspective extended into the 1980s and 1990s (Gardner, 1985; Miller, 2003). It was a time that enabled psychologists to adopt new theoretical frameworks to explain mental activities, such as learning, memory, and language processes, and to use new approaches to their investigation while examining and building theories and models. Volumes two and three of *Theoretical Models and Processes of Reading*, published respectively in 1976 and 1985, are rich with chapters on models of reading and on reading processes rooted in cognitive theory, such as LaBerge and Samuels' (1974/1976) "Toward a Theory of Automatic Information Processing in Reading" and Rumelhart's (1985) "Toward an Interactive Model of Reading" that focused on the interaction of an array of "information sources." Researchers (Flower & Hayes, 1981) constructed a cognitive processing model of writing that included hierarchically organized processes and component processes embedded in other components. However, by 1985, there were increasing numbers of chapters taking into consideration social dimensions of reading, reading acquisition, and reading instruction, such as Yopp and Singer's (1985) interactive reading instructional model that reflected the role of teachers and Ruddell and Speaker's (1985) model of the interactive reading process that integrated the reader's instructional environment. The same happened some years later in the design of writing models as evidenced by the appearance of a new model that included the social environment composed of the audience and collaborators (Hayes, 1996/2004).

By the mid-1980s, a new model of literacy instruction was making inroads into the field of literacy education—a field that had previously been dominated by the cognitive model of how people learn to read and write. Brian V. Street, professor and chair of language in education at King's College, University of London, drew from his anthropological field work on literacy practices in Iran during the 1970s to question assumptions of the cognitive model. Street (1995), who had a longstanding commitment to linking the cultural dimension of language and literacy to contemporary practices in education, critiqued the autonomous model—or the assumption that reading and writing occur in a vacuum as if untouched by relations of power embedded within myriad social and cultural influences. In Street's words:

> A great deal of the thinking about literacy . . . has assumed that literacy with a big "L" and single "y" [is] a single autonomous thing [with] consequences for personal and social development. . . . One of the reasons for referring to this position as an autonomous model of literacy is that it represents itself as though it is not a position located ideologically at all, as though it is just natural. One of the reasons why I want to call the counter-position ideological is precisely in order to signal that we are not simply talking here about technical features of the written process or the oral process. What we are talking about are competing models and assumptions about reading and writing processes, which are always embedded in power relations.
>
> *(pp. 132–133)*

A point worth underscoring is that viewing literacy instruction as ideologically situated does not require giving up on the cognitive aspects of reading and writing, nor on the technical skills associated with the autonomous model. Instead, the ideological model might be said to subsume the autonomous model and simultaneously incorporate an array of social, cultural, and political ways of knowing that account for seemingly absent but always present relations of power.

Street's (1995) introduction of a competing model of literacy instruction marked one of several events that signaled what Gee (1998) later referred to as the *social turn*. It was a paradigmatic shift that took the spotlight off earlier foci on individual behavior and individual minds. With that shift, theorists and researchers from disciplines other than psychology began to focus on reading and writing. For instance, Heath's (1983) seminal work, *Ways with Words*, awakened an interest in the social and cultural interactions of readers and writers in schools that represented different socioeconomic contexts. Barton, Hamilton, and Ivanic's edited volume, *Situated Literacies* (2000), provided a collection of key writings on how uses of written language vary within different times and places. The social turn also introduced the concept of multiliteracies (Cope & Kalantzis, 2000), digital literacies in classroom spaces (Lankshear & Knobel, 2006), and a broadening of what counts as texts (Rowsell, Kress, Pahl, & Street, see Chapter 27, this volume). Finally, Gee's theory of reading as a social language (see Chapter 5 this volume) and Luke's seminal work in critical literacy as it relates to social justice and schooling (see Chapter 17 this volume) continue to influence the field of literacy instruction and to bear witness to the generative features of the social turn.

Theories Influencing Literacy Research

A remarkably wide range of theories has influenced research on literacy, including theoretical models and their related reading and writing processes. While some of these theories, particularly in more recent years, arose from the field of literacy research, many theories originated in fields outside the domain of literacy research but frequently allied with it, such as psychology and literary theory. This should come as no surprise because psychology has long been a breeding ground for inquiry into learning and learning related processes, such as memory, cognition, and the social dimensions of learning. Among the broad and influential theories that have had a significant impact on literacy research are constructivism, social constructionism, transactional theory, information/cognitive processing theories, sociocultural theories, sociocognitive theory, structuralism, critical theory, poststructuralism and non-representational theories, posthumanism, and motivation theory, to name a few. An introduction, brief though it may be, to these theoretical frameworks and perspectives provides readers with knowledge to understand concepts that appear frequently in this volume and in literacy research. While significant analysis, reconnaissance, and reflection preceded the placement of individuals and their work within particular categories, these placements may not be consistent with each reader's or writer's understanding or remain accurate over time as ideologies evolve.

Constructivism

Among educators, constructivism is a widely applied theory of learning that explains how knowledge and meanings are constructed, rather than transmitted or absorbed, through our interaction with others and the environment. In the light of constructivist theory, learners control the process of resolving tensions between personally constructed models of the world held in memory and socially constructed representations of new experiences. Typically, learners construct new knowledge when they interact with others or objects in their surroundings, activate existing background knowledge in response to interactions, build new knowledge from prior knowledge, or transform older knowledge into newer information. Constructivists view that negotiated knowledge as "temporary, developmental, nonobjective, internally constructed, and socially and culturally mediated" (Fosnot, 1996, p. ix). To the constructivist, contexts for learning are inseparable from what is learned, the learner has significant capacity to regulate the knowledge construction process, and meanings are negotiated in social settings (Cambourne, 2002).

In her exploration of the constructivist metaphor, Spivey (1997) argued that what distinguishes constructivism from other perspectives is an underlying metaphor of building that guides thought and inquiry. Constructivists, she believed, look upon individuals as agents "whose *ways* of knowing, seeing, understanding, and valuing influence what is known, seen, understood, and valued" (p. 3) (italics in original). Arising from a review of constructivism's historical antecedents, Spivey found differences in focal points for constructivist agents that varied across individuals, small groups or dyads, and communities. Forms of constructivism that focus on individuals as agents include cognitive constructivism with its emphasis on schema theory and cognitive-developmental constructivism with its emphasis on Piaget's theory of cognitive development (Piaget & Inhelder, 1969). Forms of constructivism that focus on small groups or pairs as agents are usually based on Vygotsky's theories, wherein two people, a child and her mother, for example, collaborate to build knowledge, especially through language. And forms of constructivism that focus on larger communities are exemplified in the work of the sociologist Durkheim (1982) who developed the notion of a collective consciousness and literary theorist Fish (1980) who studied interpretive communities and the meaning-making discourses that transpired within them.

Two theories or frameworks under the umbrella of constructivism and applicable to the investigation of literacy demonstrate the broad and deep importance of this perspective to literacy research. These frameworks include schema theory and psycholinguistics.

Schema Theory

During the mid-1970s, schema theory made its appearance as part of the cognitive revolution that resurrected the study in psychology of internal mental events and became an important theoretical resource for reading research and pedagogy. Although sometimes considered a theory of reading comprehension, schema theory is about how we structure knowledge and represent it in memory. A schema is a hypothetical knowledge structure, hypothetical because it is difficult to examine empirically. However, we can infer the existence of schema from the study of memory and its influence on the interpretation of new experience. Schemata have been compared to scripts, file cabinets, storage slots, and containers (Anderson, see Chapter 7 this volume). Anderson has identified and explained several functions of schemata and their effects on learning and remembering when interacting with texts. Among these functions, which occur during both the reading and writing of texts, are a schema's capacity to provide scaffolding as we process or construct text, to allow effective memory searches, and to facilitate inference making. Cognitive processing models of writing, such as that of Flower and Hayes (1981) to which Smith refers in her chapter on writing (see Chapter 3 this volume), include long-term memory components where schema-like writing plans are housed and available for activation. McVee, Dunsmore, and Gavelek (2005/2013) have revisited schema theory to review its impact on literacy research and evaluate its continuing usefulness as a theoretical framework to understand and investigate reading processes and to inform practice.

Researchers have identified risks inherent in adhering to a constricted or rigid conceptualization of schemata as fixed and inflexible structures. While fixed or mechanical views of knowledge structures or mental representations may be more likely to appear when learners first acquire knowledge in a field, more advanced understanding and application of knowledge structures in complex knowledge domains, such as medicine, need to be developed. Cognitive flexibility theory (Spiro, 1988), as a successor of schema theory, provides themes, especially in realms of advanced knowledge acquisition and applications, that encourage liberation from the risks of schema rigidity. Among those themes are the avoidance of oversimplification of complex problem domains, the importance of constructing multiple representations of complex concepts, and the capacity to assemble schemata in novel configurations rather than merely retrieving them from memory and applying them. For researchers advancing knowledge generation in the field of literacy, as in all other complex domains, this move from generic schema activation to situation-specific assembly of knowledge is of critical importance.

Psycholinguistic Theory

In the late 1950s, behaviorist theories of language acquisition proposed by B. F. Skinner (1957) were radically critiqued by the linguist Noam Chomsky (1959) in an essay that signaled the beginning of the cognitive revolution in the psychological sciences. Chomsky proposed that human beings have a universal grammar or an innate language acquisition device (LAD) that enabled them to generate an infinite variety of sentences typical of their language's syntactical structures. Children could not acquire the rich diversity of language by simply imitating the sentences they heard adults utter. Instead, they construct sentences using their steadily growing knowledge of words and their inborn universal grammar. Although all children have an inborn LAD, that is not enough for the development of normal language function. Children also need a language acquisition support system (LASS) that enables their inborn language potential to be activated and realized through social interaction (Bruner, 1986).

Psycholinguistic theory enabled reading educators to look at reading as a "psycholinguistic guessing game" (Goodman, 1967) in which readers predict what will be coming next in sentences as they read from text and try to construct meaning. Miscues can then be viewed not as errors but as keys to the kinds of problems children may be having in learning to read. The Goodmans (Goodman and Goodman, Chapter 8 this volume) found that the concept of schema was helpful in exploring the role of miscues in learning language. They explored two kinds of miscues in the light of schema theory and two schema processes: schema-forming and schema-driven miscues. The constructivist conceptions of assimilation and accommodation (Piaget, Gruber, & Voneche, 1977) clarify the function of the two kinds of miscues. When a schema-forming miscue occurs, a reader is working toward accommodation or the modification of an existing schema to adjust to new language experiences, but, when a schema-driven miscue takes place, the reader reveals assimilation or the understanding of new language experiences with existing schema. Schema-forming miscues reveal a reader's development of rules for language use, the application of those rules, and their limits. For example, before children have developed the alphabetic principle, they may read the title of a frequently read story by guiding their finger across the words and saying, "Gooooodniii-iightmoooooon." Schema-driven miscues result from the activation of existing schemata to either construct or comprehend language. For example, when a child is learning the plural form of mouse, she may read "mices" rather than mice, revealing that she believes, because of pre-existing schema, that the –s must be added to generate a plural noun. As the Goodmans pointed out, these miscues may not always be easily distinguished, but the miscues children make not only reveal the construction and reconstruction of schema but also the contributions of miscues to the development of self-regulated reading.

In sum, constructivism as a theory covers several inter-related theoretical frameworks for the investigation and understanding of reading and writing processes. Schema theory and psycholinguistics share the central concepts of constructivism and demonstrate the active role that learners have in the acquisition and application of knowledge that contributes to the development of reading and writing.

Social Constructionism

Although Berger and Luckmann (1966) are widely acknowledged as the voices of authority on social constructionism, it is Bruffee (1986), a notable figure in the field of rhetoric and composition pedagogy, who explicitly aligns a social constructionist view of knowledge building with our purpose in writing this section of the chapter. In his 1986 essay in *English Composition* titled "Social

Construction, Language, and the Authority of Knowledge," Bruffee argued the following: "A social constructionist position in any discipline assumes that any entities we normally call reality, knowledge, thought, facts, texts, selves and so on are constructs generated by communities of like-minded peers" (p. 774). Implications of this argument for English teachers' goals and practices, which were of interest to Bruffee in the 1980s, are of no less interest to literacy researchers and teachers today.

Basically, Bruffee (1986) showed in his essay how cognitivist beliefs in a foundational structure for knowledge building is antithetical to a nonfoundational, social constructionist view in which "concepts, ideas, theories, the world, reality, and facts are all language constructs generated by knowledge communities and used by them to maintain community coherence" (p. 777). These opposing views of knowledge building and their implications for practice are important to understand, especially in a chapter that purports to investigate theoretical models of multiple literacies. As Bruffee cogently argued, educators' tendency to classify knowledge into two distinct categories, theory and practice, has its beginnings in a cognitivist approach to understanding. That is to say, if one believes in a foundational mode of knowledge building (as the cognitivists do), then it follows that one views theory as the grounding or sanctioning of literacy practices. On the other hand, if one views knowledge building through a social constructionist lens, then it stands to reason that theory and practices are no longer treated as opposites, with theory holding sway over practice.

Social constructionism arose initially from inquiry focusing on social processes and their effects on the construction of knowledge. Everyday life, as Berger and Luckmann (1966) posited, presents us with a reality we interpret, find subjectively meaningful as a "coherent world," and share intersubjectively with others. The reality of everyday life is filled with objectivations of subjective processes, most often through language, that make the intersubjective world possible. Everyday life is lived in and through language that we share with others, making our understanding of language essential for our understanding of reality.

With language as its *sine qua non*, social constructionism may be understood as a theoretical orientation with several assumptions. In describing four key assumptions, Gergen (1985) informed readers of the growing influence that the turn toward social processes was having in his field of psychology. Membership in the social constructionism movement, according to Burr (2003), need not require the acceptance of all of these assumptions. Just accepting one could be sufficient. Among the assumptions constituting social constructionism, according to Gergen, are the following:

(1) In an atmosphere of increasing criticism of positivist and empiricist beliefs about knowledge generation, social constructionism "begins with radical doubt in the taken-for-granted world" and works as a social critic. Constructionism asks us to suspend our belief that "commonly accepted categories or understandings receive their warrant through observation. Thus, it invites one to challenge the objective basis of conventional knowledge" (p. 267).

  Social constructionists question the power of the words we use to capture reality and render it as we do. This assumption about the limits of language casts doubt upon much of our knowledge base, including that formed through positivistic or scientific methods.

(2) Understandings about the world arise from interaction among people in relationships. That epistemological perspective invites inquiry into how cultural and historical beliefs and processes construct the world.

(3) Our ways of understanding the world as we believe it to be are sustained through daily interactions in social settings, especially those that involve language. Communication in communities, negotiation, and rhetoric have greater influence on prevailing and continuing understandings than the empirical validity of a perspective.

(4) Social constructionists believe that conceptions and understandings of the world are deeply and directly associated with social actions in that world. A form of social action might be simply a description and explanation of the world as an individual perceives it. To change that description and explanation might well change decisions we make about actions we take in the world.

Serving to summarize our discussion and provide a view of social constructionists, Gergen (2002) wrote that

> . . . constructionists do not draw a strong distinction between the observing scientist and the world observed. Rather, they see scientists engaged in a collaborative construction of what they will take to be the world. Armed with a set of shared assumptions, a language of description and explanation, and a set of related practices, a world of particulars is established. Thus, we may anticipate the development of multiple realities, depending on one's discipline. . . . Because disciplinary practices are inevitably linked to preferred ways of life, claims to knowledge are never neutral in their societal ramifications. Reality claims are inherently saturated with visions of the good.
>
> *(pp. 188–189)*

Transactional Theory

Although some educators believe an objective meaning exists in a text, others (Bleich, 1980; Culler, 1980) have argued that the meanings for a text are to be found in the reader's personal responses. This perspective aligned somewhat with Rosenblatt's articulation of transactional theory. According to Rosenblatt (see Chapter 23 this volume), every act of reading is a transaction between a particular reader and a particular text at a particular time in a particular context. The reader and the text compose a transactional moment. The meaning does not pre-exist in the text or in the reader but results from the transaction between reader and text. Meaning is the result of the reader's meaning construction that engages his or her unique background knowledge and cognitive processing. When readers transact with a text, they create an evocation or mental representation of the text that can be observed, analyzed, reflected upon, pondered, explained, and savored. While exploring and clarifying the evocation, readers assemble meanings or interpretations for the text.

When Rosenblatt developed her theoretical perspective on the transaction process between the reader and the text, she believed it explained all modes of reading because it took into account the range of stances that a reader could adopt toward a text. The two stances she identified were the efferent or aesthetic stances. When adopting the efferent stance, the reader transacts with texts to construct information, to create an evocation believed to represent the text. When transacting with a text from an aesthetic stance, the reader's attention is focused on the lived experiences depicted in a reading event, such as a poem. According to her theory, these two stances exist on a continuum to acknowledge that readers might take stances that include both efferent and aesthetic qualities. More recently, questions about these stances and other aspects of transactional theory have arisen (Dressman, see Chapter 24 this volume).

Information/Cognitive Processing Theories and Models of Reading and Writing

The first edition of *Theoretical Models and Processes of Reading* contained the first published theory of reading. That first theory, which reflected a cognitive processing perspective of reading, was created by Jack Holmes (1953) to whom the first edition was dedicated by its editors, Harry Singer and Robert Ruddell (1976). According to Singer (1994), prior research in reading had been atheoretical, largely because of the dominance of behaviorism. In the paper, Holmes (1960/1970) proposed to answer a question, "Just how complex is this ability we call reading, what are its dimensions, and how do they operate" (p. 187)? Using a statistical procedure called substrata-factor analysis, Holmes created a substrata-factor theory of reading in which he identified variables correlated with levels of reading proficiency. Furthermore, he identified sub-variables in four variable categories to predict speed and power of reading. Holmes designed the investigation to discover relationships between speed and power of reading and the 37 "sub-abilities" categorized under intelligence, linguistic ability, oculo-motor ability, and personality traits. He found his theoretical model explained reading through the interaction of 13 of the initial 37 variables tested. Of the 13 key variables, knowledge of vocabulary in context played a significant role in both speed and power of reading. Holmes concluded this first paper on a theory of reading with the assertion that he was justified in formalizing the hypothesis into a generalized theory and that, while the theory was complex, his methodology highlighted an important dimension of reading that deepened our knowledge of the dynamics of reading.

The information processing or cognitive theory of reading influenced research most intensely from the mid-1970s to the mid-1980 but continues to pervade theories and models currently. Reading and writing researchers using this theoretical framework hoped to discover and explain how the individual reader interacted with print to construct meaning or constructed meaning while writing. Often using a computer metaphor, interested in artificial intelligence, and sometimes striving toward a mathematical representation of reading processes, researchers investigated several related cognitive processes, such as sensory input, attention allocation, symbol interpretation, strategy use, the organization of knowledge, its storage in short- and long-term memory, and outputs, especially in the form of text representation or comprehension. Meanwhile, researchers investigating the writing process (Bereiter & Scardamalia, 1987; Flower & Hayes, 1981) designed models of the cognitive processes that writers engage when writing. While schema theory along with its effects on knowledge construction plays an important part in the information processing perspective, usually missing from the menu of investigated processes was the effects of the reader's or writer's sociocultural environment, both historical and current, on cognition, a reflection of the emphasis on individual and internal mental events within this theoretical framework.

Two information processing models of reading appeared in the second edition of *Theoretical Models and Processes of Reading*: Gough's (1972/1976) "One Second of Reading" and LaBerge and Samuels' (1974/1976) "Toward a Theory of Automatic Information Processing in Reading." Included in that volume's section on information processing models were two other papers by Anderson and his colleagues (Anderson, Goldberg, & Hidde, 1971/1976; Anderson, 1974/1976) who explored sentence processing. Here, our focus will be on the two information processing models themselves, both of which were "bottom-up" models, meaning that they focused on graphic input and its processing without recognizable attention to prior knowledge activation and its effects on text processing and comprehension.

Gough's Information Processing Model

Gough's "One Second of Reading" included a reading model whose key features are in italics in the following (hyper-condensed) description of the model. Following an eye fixation and focus on *graphemic input*, the *visual system* forms an *icon* and retains it while a *scanner* with a *pattern recognizer* reviews the icon. The pattern recognition component identifies the letters that compose the icon that was formed from graphemic input. The letters, which are transferred into a *character register*, are decoded by a *decoder* with the help of a *code book* and transformed into a *phonemic tape* or representation. The phonemic representation becomes input to the *librarian* that compares the phonemic string with a *lexicon* and that puts the lexical activation into *primary memory*. The activated lexical symbols in primary memory become input for *Merlin*, a system that applies *rules of semantics and syntax* to construct the input's meaning or "deep structure." That meaning is then transferred to what Gough called *The Place Where Sentences Go When They Are Understood* (aka, TPWSGWTAU). The text has been read once the initial graphemic input has found its way to TPWSGWTAU, a process that takes about one second.

In a postscript to his "One Second of Reading" model that appeared in the third edition of *Theoretical Models and Processes of Reading*, Gough (1985) announced that the model was "wrong." He renounced the explicit claim that readers always read letter-by-letter or serial (at the rate of

10–20 milliseconds per letter) but asserted that letters do mediate word recognition. He also renounced the claim that phonological recoding mediates all word recognition because he later realized that proficient readers have direct access to high-frequency or "sight" words, at the least, but he held that phonological recoding mediates recognition of most words. While agreeing that his bottom-up model failed, he believed it pointed educators and researchers in the right direction.

LaBerge-Samuels Information Processing Model

The 1974 LaBerge and Samuels' automatic information processing model (Samuels, 1994) was composed of three memory systems that held three different representations of graphemic input as it was processed: the Visual Memory System, the Phonological Memory System, and the Semantic Memory System. The registration of a visual signal on the sensory surface initiates the reading process. A set of feature detectors analyzes the information. While some features map as spelling pattern codes, others map onto visual word codes. Words can be transferred into meanings by means of several different routes described in the model. When the complete set of initial inputs has been processed, the reader constructs a word-group meaning and comprehends the input. Of historical significance, Samuels (1977) soon realized that the "bottom-up," linear design of this model needed to be revisited and modified it to include feedback loops to account for prior knowledge in semantic memory and its interaction with the processing of input as it moved toward comprehension.

Rumelhart's Interactive Model

Rumelhart (1985, see Companion Website) believed that the concept of information flow and the use of flowcharts to represent that information's processing became "vehicles" for the design of early models of reading that attempted to "approximate" the reading process. Top-down information about the syntactical development of sentences in which words appear should have been accounted for but were not in the early information processing models. Furthermore, semantic context was not accounted for in the early models even though research had shown convincingly that the semantic environment affected word recognition. Discrepancies between research findings and their lack of representation in existing models of reading led Rumelhart to construct his interactive, bottom-up and top-down model of reading. That model took into account not only bottom-up graphemic input but also orthographic, syntactical, semantic, and lexical knowledge, all of which fed into a hypothesized "pattern synthesizer" that could generate probable interpretations of a text. The "pattern synthesizer," however, was the key component of the model because "all that is interest-ing" occurred there. To represent all of the parallel and interacting reading processes, Rumelhart established a "message center" that developed hypotheses about such things as letter features, letter clusters, lexical information, and syntactical structures. As information moved through the message center, the message center constructed and evaluated hypotheses to discover the best likely meanings and nullifying the least likely. Essentially, reading as represented in Rumelhart's model was a complex hypothesis-testing process that operated interactively, bottom-up and top-down.

Several other cognitive processing models that still exercise a significant influence on researchers' perspectives and reading pedagogy appeared during the 1970s and 1980s. These include models developed by Walter Kintsch and by Marcel Just and Patricia Carpenter.

Construction-Integration Model

During the era dominated by the emergence of cognition in psychological studies, other infor-mation or cognitive processing models of reading also appeared. An early rendition of Kintsch's construction-integration model of reading was presented in the late 1970s. In that model, the authors (Kintsch & van Dijk, 1978) assumed that texts can be described at microlevels (local) and macrolevels (global). That model accounted for the construction of a semantic textbase that was generated by a cyclical process limited by working memory and a situation model that represented information given by the text and integrated with the reader's background knowledge. The model they proposed included "macro-operators" that reduced text information to its gist, or what they termed its "theoretical macrostructure." Schema in this model referred to text structures, such as an argument, or to reader's goals, such as discovering how women were treated in the fourteenth century by reading stories in the *Decameron*. Such schema controlled the macro-operators that transformed the text base into an hierarchical structure of macropropositions that represented the text's gist and determined which micropropositions were relevant to that gist. Although the model did not explain how inferences occur while reading, it assumed they do occur as schemata are activated and developed to represent a text. The full representation of the text constructed by the reader constituted his comprehension. This model's description of the reading process as constructive provides a foreshadowing of Kintsch's later construction-integration model of reading (see Chapter 10 this volume) which included three levels of mental representation: the surface structure, a textbase, and a situation model.

Just and Carpenter Reading Model

Just and Carpenter (1980/2013) drew upon research that they and others had conducted, especially in the field of eye-movement studies, and a theoretical framework based on production systems while reading to design their bottom-up and top-down model. Unlike earlier information processing models that researchers had proposed, the architectural features of their model accounted for reading time on words, clauses, and sentences, for events at several levels of processing, such as those at the word encoding and lexical access levels, and for the complexities of processing during top-down and bottom-up interactions.

Dual Coding Theory Model

Before it was extended to explain reading comprehension, Dual Coding Theory (DCT) was an established theory of cognition that took into account both verbal and nonverbal memory processes. Sadoski and Krasny (Chapter 9 this volume) have characterized DCT as a scientific theory; an embodied cognitive theory; a theory of decoding, comprehension, vocabulary, and response in reading; a theory of written composition and spelling; and a theory of multimedia/multimodal literacy. The DCT model provides an alternative to information processing models based primarily on schema theory and verbal processes. One of the basic assumptions of the DCT model is that every mental representation retains qualities, linguistic or nonlinguistic, of the original experience from which it arose. According to DCT, the different characteristics of verbal and nonverbal codes lead to their development into two different processing systems, one for language processing and another for processing the imagery of events and objects. Combined, the two systems or codes can take into account all knowledge of language and the world. Models of reading that omit basic units of nonverbal information, *imagens*, are unable to capture the rich sensory contribution that reality makes to comprehension and memory. Acknowledging, explaining, and integrating mental imagery into their model has provided, they believe, a more accurate depiction of how the mind, especially that of the reader, processes and remembers sensory experience. Absent a thorough consideration of mental imagery, other models of reading are limited to a single code, verbal processing, and to a solely abstract representation of knowledge gained through interaction with texts.

Cognitive Processing in Models Of Writing

Cognitive processing in text production contributed to explanations of composition in several models of writing during the 1980s. Relying on think-aloud protocol analysis, Flower and Hayes

(1981) developed an influential model of writing intended to reveal the cognitive processes that were activated and engaged while composing. The model provided a foundation for further discoveries into writers' thinking processes. The major components of the model include the task environment, the writer's long-term memory, and the writing processes. The task environment consists of both the rhetorical problem with its topic, audience, and exigency along with the text produced so far. Components of the writing process include planning, translating, reviewing, and monitoring. While they plan, writers generate text, organize it, and set goals for their composition, and, while they review their text, they evaluate and revise it. During the time they plan, translate, and review their emerging text, writers monitor these processes and decide when to shift from one process to another. Flower and Hayes found that the processes were hierarchically organized, but the component processes were frequently embedded within other components while a network of goals guided the overall process.

Also conceptualizing their model of writing as problem-based and within cognitive processing theory, Bereiter and Scardamalia (1987) argued that sophisticated writers adopt knowledge transforming strategies. Expert writers develop rhetorical goals that call upon more complex problem-solving processes while novice writers employ a knowledge-telling process in which one idea is linked to the next (Smith, see Chapter 3 this volume; Duke and Cartwright, see Chapter 6 this volume).

With advances in technology, such as functional magnetic resonance imaging (fMRI), researchers have been able to investigate how the brain functions when processing texts and how these brain functions correlate with cognitive theories and models of reading processes, some of which we have described in this chapter. Hruby and Goswami (see Chapter 13 this volume) have reviewed these findings and report correlates of decoding and comprehension of texts and relate those discoveries to models of reading, reading pedagogy, and reading disabilities. In the light of their review, the authors believe that neuroscience research holds much potential for reading researchers and practitioners to deepen our knowledge of literacy processes, their development, and their dysfunction.

Sociocultural Theories

Sociocultural perspectives in the literature on literacy commonly refer to both a specific theoretical perspective, that of Lev Vygotsky, and to a set of related theoretical perspectives which share assumptions about the mind, the world, and their relationship (Gavelek & Bresnahan, 2009). The term sociocultural, in its more inclusive application, refers to a group of perspectives that contains sociolinguistics, pragmatism, and second-generation cognitive science and that commonly manifests themes distilled from Vygotsky's cultural-historical theory. Those themes include the beliefs that the mind emerges from social interaction with other minds, that activities of the mind are mediated by tools and symbol systems (languages), and that, to understand a mental function, one must understand the roots and processes contributing to that function's development. Among the sociocultural theorists explored here are Vygotsky, Scribner and Cole, Halliday, Heath, Lee, and Kress who, along with Street, contributed to the development of social semiotic theory. These individuals and their colleagues have provided researchers with theoretical frameworks for inquiring into a substantive body of knowledge about language and literacies (Tatum, see Chapter 14 this volume; Leu et al., see Chapter 16 this volume).

Vygotsky, Society, and Language

Among Vygotsky's (1978, 1986) many ideas, three are of particular importance for understanding the connections among society, culture, and the development of minds. First, Vygotsky embraced the idea that we must understand the historical, social, and cultural contexts of each child's experiences to truly understand that person's intellectual or cognitive development. Second, Vygotsky believed that our individual development depends on language that allows us to interact with others in our culture and to strive for self-mastery. Language and our writing system enable us progressively to develop skills and higher mental functions. Third, Vygotsky believed that every step in a child's cultural development appears twice: first as a process between people and second as an individual process within each child. Interpersonal processes, like our use of language to communicate with each other, are transformed into intrapersonal ones, like our use of inner speech when we talk our way through to the solution of a complex problem. If in reading about this two-stage concept of development a reader only experienced the first stage and did not internalize it for individual use, then it has not and cannot contribute to mental development. This dialogic process has also influenced writing theories (Smith, see Chapter 3 this volume) that have conceptualized writing as a conversation and a mediator of thinking.

Further clarifying Vygotsky's viewpoint, Bruner wrote (1986), "Language was an agent for altering the powers of thought—giving thought new means for explicating the world. In turn, language became the repository for new thoughts once achieved" (p. 143). In contrast to Piaget, Vygotsky believed that language could provide a path to a "higher ground," by which he seems to have meant a more elevated level of abstraction or a wider perspective of one's culture. As Bruner notes, Vygotsky bestows upon language "both a cultural past and a generative present, and assigns it a role as the nurse and tutor of thought" (p. 145).

In sum, Vygotsky (1978, 1986) expressed the belief that we internalize our culture's sign systems. As we internalize these sign systems, especially our culture's language, they function as a bridge that enables us to transform our behavior and our consciousness. Because we become competent members of our society largely through language and its acquisition, the investigation of how that bridge is built and how it functions has been a dominant interest to literacy researchers and teachers. On our way toward competence, we interact with and learn from others (Forman and Cazden, 1985/2013). One of Vygotsky's key ideas, the zone of proximal development (ZPD), emphasizes the importance of the interactive, socially based nature of learning. The ZPD is the difference between what one can achieve alone and what one can achieve with the help of a more knowledgeable or capable person. As a result of interactions in the ZPD, children internalize culturally appropriate knowledge and behaviors that they can eventually demonstrate independently. In Vygotsky's words, "An essential feature of learning is that it creates the zone of proximal development" (1978, p. 90). Where and how Vygotsky's cultural-historical theory is being challenged in terms of understanding the minds of both dominant and non-dominant groups of children are the issues in an edited volume titled *Vygotsky in 21st Century Society: Advances in Cultural Historical Theory and Praxis with Non-dominant Communities* (Portes & Salas, 2011).

Scribner and Cole: The Vai of Liberia

The benefits attributed to literacy were both explicit and implicit in Vygotsky's work. More explicit claims of literacy's effects on cognition and higher-order reasoning came through Vygotsky's work with Luria in South Central Asia at a time when the Soviet Union was striving to bring literacy to peoples of that region. Vygotsky and Luria (Luria, 1976) compared the performance of newly literate and non-literate people on reasoning tasks, including working through syllogisms, and found significant differences between the groups favoring the reasoning and higher-order thinking skills of the newly literate population. Benefits of western literacy like those alleged by Luria and Vygotsky have been aligned with similar and even far broader claims about the cognitive benefits of literacy in books like *The Domestication of the Savage Mind* (Goody, 1977), *The Literate Revolution in Greece and Its Cultural Consequences* (Havelock, 1982), and *Orality and Literacy: The Technologizing of the Word* (Ong, 1982). Some scholars, such as Scribner and Cole (1981), questioned the validity of the cognitive effects supposedly arising from western literacy and began to wonder about the contributions of culture, especially the culture of schooling, that sometimes came with literacy's "benefits."

In their research with the Vai in Liberia, Scribner and Cole (1981) attempted to answer two crucial questions: (1) Is the difference in mental functioning of literate versus non-literate groups the result of literacy or of attending school? (2) Is it possible to detect differences in the effects of different forms of literacy that are used for different purposes in an individual's life or in a society's functioning? Conditions of language learning and use among the Vai provided the researchers with an exceptional opportunity to address these questions. Three conditions for acquisition of literacy existed in Vai society: (1) English could be acquired in a formal school environment. (2) The Vai have a language and script that is learned outside of school settings. (3) The Vai have a form of Arabic literacy. Of additional importance, for each of these literacies, the Vai have a distinct set of uses: English for government and education, Vai literacy for keeping records and writing letters (usually commercial), and Arabic for reading, writing, and memorizing the *Koran*.

Some Vai were found to be literate in one, two, or all three of these languages, and some were non-literate. That meant Scribner and Cole could disaggregate their data and address their questions to discover if literacy was having an effect on mental functioning. If schooling was the critical variable, then only literates who attended school would show the cognitive benefits of literacy. To generate data, the researchers administered to their participants tests, many with items similar to those Vygotsky and Luria used, to detect improvements in abstract thinking, taxonomic categorization, memory, logical reasoning, and reflective knowledge about language.

Scribner and Cole (1981) found that only English literacy was associated with the kinds of abstract thinking and cognitive skills tested. Neither the Vai script nor Arabic had a significant effect on higher-order thinking and reasoning. Because English literacy among the Vai was acquired in school setting, schooling appeared to be the key variable affecting higher-order thinking abilities. That finding suggested that western conceptions of literacy alone were not the only path to better cognitive or intellectual functioning. The culture of schooling while acquiring western conceptions of literacy had its own effects on cognitive abilities.

With regard to detecting the effects of different forms of literacy that were used for different purposes in the Vai culture, Scribner and Cole (1981) found that each form of literacy was related to some specific skills. For example, Arabic literacy had a positive effect on memory tasks, and literacy in the Vai script conferred more skill in integrating syllables and using grammar rules. While a specific literacy enhanced these practice-related skills, no literacy alone generated evidence to support claims that westernized notions of literacy improved higher-order cognitive abilities.

The acquisition of westernized notions of literacy alone appears to have no predictable effects on the quality of an individual's cognitive or reasoning skills—or on the acquisition of capacities that lead to a good life. According to Scribner and Cole's findings, literacy in the form of reading and writing could not substitute for formal schooling when it came to performance on the cognitive tasks measured. However, school effects were not enduring; being out of school for a few years or away from school-like occupations led to significantly weaker performance on the intellectual operations measured.

Through their seminal work, Scribner and Cole vaporized the "myth of literacy." The belief that learning to read and write, outside of any school context, will bring significant improvements in higher-order thinking and reasoning could not be supported with the findings their study generated. Currently, a new "myth of literacy and schooling" prognosticates that given the opportunity in school, children will gain the literacy they require to achieve success. However, that new myth also has its significant doubters who believe that deeper social changes must occur for deeper effects of schooling to become manifest (Gee, 2012).

Halliday: Every Child a Meaning Maker

Sociolinguists, who study language as a social phenomenon, frequently explore language use in communities, how language functions to initiate and carry out social action, and how that language contributes to the development of literacy, power structures, and identity. From very early in life, children participate in making meaning through interaction with mothers, fathers, siblings, and "significant others." While engaged in these dialogues, children are also constructing an identity (Halliday, 1994, see Companion Website). The four- or five-month-old, while interacting with significant others, engages in what Halliday called systematic symbolic constructions. These symbolic encounters with the persons and objects in the child's world constitute moments when meaning is mutually constructed. In a multitude of these symbolic moments, the child develops a protolanguage that employs a system of signs, signals, and symbols that will enable him to take future linguistic steps into the realm of real language and a far more complex symbolic system.

Having evolved a protolanguage that enables the child to communicate with his mother, father, and other caregivers in the world and that feeds a growing sense of self, the child is ready not only to transition from crawling to walking but also from protolanguage to human language. The emerging language enables the child to interface with people and objects in the world, to receive information about that world, and to communicate information to all the individuals who populate his world. (For more on children using language to enter a community of minds, see Nelson, 2013. For a sociocultural perspective on the play of young children as natural and emergent literacy, see Wohlwend, Chapter 15 this volume.)

Bourdieu's Social Theory

Reading researchers (e.g., Alvermann, Friese, Beckmann, & Rezak, 2011; Jimenez, Smith, & Martinez-Leon, 2003; Marsh, 2006) who draw on Pierre Bourdieu's work (Bourdieu, 1980/1990; 1982/1991; Bourdieu & Passeron, 1970/1990) are typically interested in exposing structural hierarchies that perpetuate inequalities in educational opportunities. Like Bourdieu, they are less interested in theory for theory's sake, especially theory that distances itself from the social world and institutional practices associated with schooling. From Bourdieu's perspective, fields are social sites characterized by specific rules and logics that determine the resources to which individuals in those fields have access (e.g., a high school classroom). Resources, in Bourdieu's terms, refer to several forms of capital (e.g., cultural capital and symbolic capital) that are used as thinking tools in analyzing data. Another thinking tool common to Bourdieu's work is misrecognition, an "alienated cognition that looks at the world through the categories the world imposes, and apprehends the social world as a natural world" (Bourdieu, 1980/1990, pp. 140–141). Misrecognition is perpetuated by beliefs and understandings held by individuals in social fields that are assumed to be natural, but are in fact arbitrary and often in need of reexamination (Bourdieu 1982/1991).

Heath: Language Acquisition in Three Communities

Heath (1983) has carefully depicted the influence of family and culture on literacy development, especially the place of early reading and language use during childhood. In her book, *Ways with Words*, she described three Appalachian communities: Trackton (a Black mill community), Roadville (a White mill community), and Gateway (a "mainstream" mainly White urban community).

In Trackton, children experienced a social environment in which their community shared in the teaching and the uniting of their children with their community. Children were part of the larger community, not just one family. Language interactions with children were rich and varied and centered on flexibility and adaptability. Storytelling played a large role in language learning in Trackton and followed a vibrant oral history tradition. Heath found stories in Trackton to be ornate and often fictionalized accounts of actual events. As children, especially the boys, got older, they prized stories, playsongs, and dialogue that included double entendres that sounded harmless on the surface but snapped with irony, insult, or innuendo beneath.

Although the timing, purpose, and content of stories in Roadville differed significantly from stories in Trackton, people in Roadville also spent time telling them. Roadville stories had to be based in fact with a minimum of embellishment and carry a moral message. They were intended to confirm membership in the community and the community's behavioral norms. Furthermore, Roadville children were reared in an environment where parents talked with their babies, modified their language to involve their children, and used interactional patterns that included answering questions, labeling, and naming objects. The children of Roadville were expected to accept the power of print through association with alphabet letters and workbook-like activities.

In Gateway, townspeople placed a high value on schools and schooling for both Black and White children. Families, mostly middle class, nurtured their children's interest in children's literature books from an early age. Parents frequently asked their children information-type questions and developed book-sharing routines. The children often saw parents and siblings reading for a variety of purposes. Heath concluded that Gateway children acquired values about reading and writing that the Trackton and Roadville children found strange. The Gateway children were not only familiar with book-reading routines but with comprehension strategies as well. The discourse and literacy practices of Trackton and Roadville children needed to be bridged by the teachers in the school context whereas the Gateway children were more school-ready because of the alignment between their experiences with reading and the expectations of teachers.

Heath (2013) has followed the history and development of citizens living in and moving from these Appalachian communities over decades. She documented the lives of the children of Trackton's children as they moved to urban centers and the effects of those moves on the meanings of cultural membership to members of a community and how the socialization of children can alter radically in transitions to urban communities where cultural resources for adaptation may deteriorate. With friends often replacing family as the heart of daily life, "intimate strangers" providing after-school supervision in activities, and an onrush of electronic media alluring to adolescents, relationships between parents and their children interlaced with extended conversations became, in general, less intimate and interactive, more tenuous and distant.

Lee: Cultural Modeling

In attempting to provide support for students, teachers, and English departments in urban schools, Carol Lee (2013) developed a system of cultural modeling that drew upon students' mental models of language use. In the case of African American students who speak an African American English vernacular, she believed that readers approached texts with mental models of language play they acquired through interaction outside the classroom, often on the playgrounds and playing fields of their communities. The particular genre of talk she explored as a mental model was *signifying*, a form of language that always involves double entendre and indirection, frequently in the service of ritualized insults. Her intention was to use these language modes as an instructional resource that would enable students to respond to literature. She developed an instructional strategy that guided students in the analysis of signifying dialogues so that they could discover the implications and meanings of each turn in a dialogue. This process could then be transferred to the analysis of other literary texts. In short, students' vernacular served as a bridge for the scaffolding of response to literature and other texts. Through cultural modeling, teachers could transform what might have been viewed as a deficit into an asset for the development of academic literacy. While the model that emerged from Lee's work is quite different from other sociocognitive models we have explored, it suggests once again the range of meanings that the term model has acquired in literacy studies.

Kress: Social Semiotic Theory

Semiosis is a process for making meaning through the use of signs, which include both the observable signifier (e.g., the color red) and the signified meaning (e.g., danger). Because in the field of social semiotics what a sign stands for is not a pre-given (Hodge & Kress, 1988; van Leeuwen, 2005), the term *resource* is preferred. According to van Leeuwen (2005):

> Semiotic resources are not restricted to speech and writing and picture making. Almost everything we do or make can be done or made in different ways and therefore allows, at least in principle, the articulation of different social and cultural meanings. Walking could be an example. We may think of it as . . . basic locomotion, something we have in common with other species. But there are many different ways of walking. . . . Different ways of walking can seduce, threaten, impress and much more. . . . As soon as we have established that a given type of physical activity or a given type of material artifact constitutes a semiotic resource, it becomes possible to describe . . . its potential for making meaning.
>
> *(p. 4)*

Although it is fairly common among literacy researchers to refer to multimodal frameworks as theoretical constructs, the actual theory behind such constructs is semiotic theory, or more specifically, *social* semiotic theory for researchers who view people as having agency in using and shaping semiotic resources (Halliday, 1978; Hodge & Kress, 1988). Multimodality is but the field to which a theory of social semiotics is applied (Jewitt & Kress, 2003).

Social semiotic theory is useful for explaining the ways in which people play a central role in making meaning—how they use various resources (signs) to represent through different modes (e.g., oral and written language, still and moving images, sound, gesture, performance) what it is they wish to communicate to others (Kress & van Leeuwen, 1996). Said another way, it is through the representations people make of the resources available to them, that researchers and teachers are able to infer what *matters* to their participants and students (Jewitt & Kress, 2003). Inferences of this kind have particular relevance when they contradict a prevailing community's expectations about reading and reading instruction.

For example, in *Before Writing: Rethinking the Paths to Literacy*, Kress (1997) challenged the field to rethink commonly held assumptions about language and literacy that privileged a linguistic mode of communication over other modes. Of particular interest is his thinking on semiotic mediation and its implications for *modal reach* (Kress, 2009):

> What is done by speech in one culture may be done by gesture in another; what may be well done through image in one culture may be better done in three-dimensional forms in another; and so on. We cannot assume that translations from one mode to the 'same' mode in another culture can draw on the same resources. In other words, the implicit assumption that 'languages' (and now modes) can deal broadly with the same domains in different cultures—even if differently—is likely to be unfounded. It may be that a meaning expressed by gesture in this culture has to be *spoken* in that other culture; what may be handled by image here, may need to be *written* there.
>
> *(Kress, 2009, pp. 57–58)*

Social semiotic theory is particularly germane to research conducted as part of the New Literacy Studies (NLS). To read *Social Linguistics and Literacies: Ideology in Discourses* in which Gee (2012) overviews the sociocultural approaches to language and literacy that came together in the last decade or two of the 20th century is to better understand the relationship of New Literacy Studies to social semiotic theory.

Heath's (1983) influential *Ways with Words,* a precursor of the social turn, demonstrated that it is *how* children are socialized into different literacies that matters (e.g., their different ways with words and whether or not those ways match the school's approach to literacy instruction). Just prior to Street's (1995) critique of the autonomous model of literacy, Gee's (1990) seminal publication,

Social Linguistics and Literacies: Ideology in Discourse, was helping to reshape the field's thinking about reading and why it was no longer adequate to think of it as a process residing solely in one's head. Then, in 1996, the New London Group published its treatise on multiliteracies. This work drew attention to the need for a multiplicity and integration of communication modes (e.g., language, still and moving images, speech, sound, gesture, and movement) in the context of a culturally and linguistically diverse world grown significantly more attached to new communication technologies, though multiliteracies need not involve digital technologies (Lankshear & Knobel, 2006). Typically, the term *multiliteracies* denotes more than "mere literacy" (Cope & Kalantzis, 2000, p. 5), which remains language- and print-centered in conventional classroom instruction. Over time, however, the notion of literacy with a big "L" and single "y" has loosened to make room for the plural form, literacies or multiliteracies. In addition, terms such as *situated literacies* (Barton, Hamilton, & Ivanic, 2000), *digital literacies*, and the *New Literacy Studies* (Gee, 1996; New London Group, 1996) have become part of a burgeoning research literature, as have multimodal texts that are part and parcel of New Literacy Studies.

Sociocognitive Theory and Models of Literacy

Beginning in the mid-1980s as increased attention and interest were given to sociocultural influences on literacy, models of reading and writing began to appear in which cognitive processes were increasingly embedded and integrated with social and cultural influences.

Gee and Discourse Development

The perspective of reading that permeates the work of Gee (Chapter 5 this volume) is founded in the belief that reading is always situated in a social environment where knowledge construction, language, motives, values, societies, and cultures interact. While linguistic processes, such as phonemic awareness and letter-sound relationships, decoding, and word recognition, are essential for reading to occur, reading is, nevertheless, embedded or situated in complex sociocultural systems that shape and support reading and its emergence in children. Each literacy event we experience is composed not only of a text that needs to be "read" but also of a social language, a Discourse, and a cultural world in which the text exists. Literacy and languages have no meaning outside their particular cultural world.

As children acquire social languages, they become socialized into what Gee calls Discourses (with a capital D to distinguish it from discourse as just language use). While Discourses always involve language, they also involve ways of using words, ways of talking, writing, interacting, believing, valuing, and feeling in order to enact "meaningful socially situated identities and activities" (p. 124). Discourses, as identity kits, reflect who we are and how we act as a teacher, special education student, gang member, third grader, or feminist. These Discourses can also blend or conflict, as happens, for example, with some students who adopt the Discourse of a gifted middle school science student during class time but who access a street-savvy, hip-hop adolescent Discourse during time in the home community. During a life-time, each of us is quite likely to master and mix a number of Discourses.

While we become socialized into a Discourse, we also develop an accompanying theory about the world that is shared by people who are socialized into that Discourse. That cultural model (Gee, 1999, 2012) informs people of what the world looks like from the viewpoint of a particular Discourse. Furthermore, a cultural model embodies a Discourse of parenting that includes various aspects of parent-child relations for the group socialized into that model, including model-appropriate patterns of childhood behaviors and development. Gee points out that middle-class and working-class models of childhood vary and that child-raising guidebooks and other materials help parents realize the cultural model they have internalized. Theories, beliefs, and images of childhood development and early literacy within a cultural model guide practices that contribute to each child's early reading, writing, speaking, and listening.

Sociocognitive Models of Reading

Kucer's mid-1980s model of reading and writing processes (Kucer, 1985) had cognitive processes and strategies to describe the parallel processes of reading and writing at its core. However, he recognized that knowledge was culturally coded, reflecting Vygotsky's belief that minds are embedded in the history and culture of their time. Because objects, events, and processes are culturally based, cultural knowledge is integrated with the knowledge we construct when reading and writing (Kucer, 2001). Along with other designers of models who viewed society and culture as inseparable from reading and writing, Kucer created an integrated model that reflected not only top-down and bottom-up cognitive processes but also the inherent, ever-present impact of social and cultural life on literacy.

An interactive reading process model designed by Ruddell and Speaker (1985) and published in the third edition of *Theoretical Models and Processes of Reading* included components for declarative and procedural knowledge, knowledge utilization and control, and reader output that reflected information processing factors. However, it also took into account the influence of the reader's social and cultural environment in which reading processes were embedded. Later models of reading (Ruddell & Unrau, 1994, 2013; Ruddell, Unrau, & McCormick, see Chapter 11 this volume) that evolved from this model expanded on the importance of the social and cultural environment by integrating an elaborated description and analysis of the teacher's role in developing an instructional environment for reading and learning. That later model also depicted a complex meaning negotiation process with texts affected by an array of social and cultural factors, such as a community of students' interpretations of texts of many kinds in the social context of a classroom.

Sociocognitive models of writing also emerged from earlier cognitive processing models of writing (Flower & Hayes, 1981) that explained writing as a set of thinking processes guided by a writer's growing network of self-constructed goals. Hayes (2004/1996) designed an individual-environment writing model that contains two major components, namely the task environment, which is both social and physical, and the individual. The individual component of the model includes cognitive processes, working memory, long-term memory, and motivation. While the first three of these features represent the cognitive processing dimensions of writing, the last feature, motivation, was newly added to take into account the writer's affective states.

Sociocognitive Models of Literacy Instruction

While these sociocognitive models of reading and writing reflect the concerns and interests of researchers and other educators in the literacy field, the expansion of researchers' attention to the socially grounded investigation of reading and reading processes is evident in work published from the mid-1990s onward. Grounded in cognitive theory, namely Rumelhart's interactive model of reading, and the social interactions between an observant teacher and her student is Maria Clay's acclaimed instructional intervention: Reading Recovery. Clay, with her accumulated years of research with children and documented change in literacy behaviors with the passage of time, discovered a transformative model of literacy acquisition and evidence for a literacy processing theory. Clay's instructional plan was grounded in two hypotheses. First, a teacher's continuing observations of literacy behaviors should serve as the basis for the child's learning. Second, powerful opportunities that support learning arise from the reciprocal relationship between reading and writing (Doyle, see Chapter 4 this volume).

Literacy Motivation Theories

Several motivational theories or perspectives have been applied in the past few decades to provide researchers with a framework for studying motivation for reading. Frequently, these motivational theories have influenced the development of instruments to measure students' motivation for or engagement in reading. One of the most influential of these has been Guthrie and Wigfield's (2000) engagement theory. Guthrie and Wigfield argue that engaged reading occurs when readers coordinate cognition, in the form of knowledge and strategies, within a social context to satisfy or achieve motivational ends, such as readers' goals, wishes, and intentions. According to this perspective, "motivation is the foundational process for reading engagement and is a major contributor . . . to disengagement from reading" (Guthrie & Wigfield, 2000, p. 405). Thus, reading engagement theory is focused on describing how instructional, motivation, and engagement variables interact to explain reading outcomes.

Among other motivation theories that have served as frameworks for research are self-determination theory (Deci & Ryan, 1985), behaviorist theory (Thorndike, 1913), social-cognitive theory (Bandura, 1986), expectancy-value theory (Wigfield & Eccles, 2000), and control-value theory (Pekrun, 2009). While still other motivational theories, such as attribution and goal theory, have also been applied in research on classroom practice related to reading, the motivation theories that are presented here offer a glimpse of the work that has been and remains to be done on motivation and its effects on reading and writing processes. (For more on motivation theories in literacy, see Taboada Barber et al., Chapter 12 this volume.)

Structuralism

As a theory, structuralism operates on an underlying assumption that structures exist in the events, texts, or processes under study, that those structures can be identified, and that their functions, often within other larger structures, can be described or explained. Two structuralists who have influenced literacy studies over the years illustrate the theory in action: Saussure and Lévi-Strauss. Saussure, often considered the founder of structuralism (Spivey, 1997), was a late-19th and early-20th century linguist who approached the study of language with the purpose of discovering its structures. He derived several principles about language from his inquiry. Among them was the precept that there is a language system belonging to a social group (*langue*), that there is also a language used by an individual when communicating (*parole*), and that *parole* should be studied to understand the abstract structure of the *langue*. Lévi-Strauss was an anthropologist who was familiar with Saussurian principles but focused his interests on mythology. Interested in a myth's universal structures, Lévi-Strauss examined specific myths (*parole*) to discover their more abstract structure (*langue*). In part, he studied myths to discover rules governing them within and across cultures. Through the examination of myths, he was able to understand both their internal structure and how they coalesced as constellations of related myths for the cultures to which they belonged. While both of these illustrative structuralists have, to some degree, influenced studies in literacy, we present next a group of critical theorists who, along with Bourdieu, have had even greater influence on the field. They are the critical theorists whose perspectives have been used as frameworks for investigating the accumulation of cultural, social, and economic capital and the effects of its expression on marginalized social groups.

Critical Theory

When knowledge is conveyed to others, especially when that knowledge is presented to less powerful individuals or social groups by those with more power, critical theorists are likely to question or challenge privileges or group preferences that more powerful agents may convey or transmit.

Founding critical theorists believed that repressive (and oppressive) institutions manipulated masses of citizens for the benefit of the few at the cost of the many and that growing awareness of the structure and function of those repressive institutions could impel social change and foster individual freedom. The impetus for this movement in social theory coalesced in Frankfurt a decade or two before the rise of fascism in Germany and other European nations. Scholars associated with the Frankfurt School, including Adorno (2002), Habermas (1962/1989), Horkheimer (2002), and Marcuse (1964), often applied Marxist categories (e.g., social class differences) in their analysis and critique of hegemonic structures, including social and cultural institutions. Applied to education, Marx's theory focuses on "the process whereby the members of the working class will come to see themselves as members of this class and, as such, in direct opposition not only to members of the bourgeoisie but to capitalism itself" (Fay, 1987, p. 35).

Critical literacy Theory and Critical Pedagogy

Ideas rooted in critical theory have served as the foundation for critical literacy (Luke, see Chapter 17 this volume) and critical pedagogy (Alvermann & Moje, see Chapter 18 this volume). In *Pedagogy of the Oppressed*, Freire (1993) developed the construct of "conscientização" (or critical consciousness), which is the capacity to perceive social, political, and economic contradictions and to act against oppressive forces. Freire focused on the roots of oppression and methods of unearthing them for close examination. Running throughout Freire's work and that of his followers is the belief that through reflection on the forces of oppression, the oppressed can be liberated. A considerable body of research informed by critical theory exists beyond that of Freire: for example, Morrell's (2008) work with "Othered" individuals in pursuit of social justice, and McVee and her colleagues' work with positioning theory (see McVee et al., Chapter 19 this volume).

Critical Race Theory

Critical Race Theory (CRT) first emerged in American legal scholarship in the mid-1970s in response to the slow pace in racial reform that grew from the Civil Rights Era (Delgado, 1995). CRT originated with a team of legal scholars who collaborated to support racial reform and critique litigation that sustained social and economic oppression. Its observations include (a) "society's acceptance of racism as ordinary," (b) "the phenomenon of Whites allowing Black progress when it also promotes their interests," (c) "the importance of understanding the historic effects of European colonialism," and (d) a "preference of the experiences of oppressed peoples (narrative) over the 'objective' opinions of Whites" (Taylor, Gillborn, & Ladson-Billings, 2009, p. 4). Kimberle Crenshaw (1989), a legal scholar, first coined the term intersectionality theory, which is an aspect of critical race theory that captures the intersection of race, gender, class, and sexual orientation while confirming that those aspects of identity form dynamically interacting relationships (Brooks, see Chapter 21 this volume.) According to Ladson-Billings (1999), CRT provides a means for "preparing teachers for diversity that moves beyond both superficial, essentialized treatments of various cultural groups and liberal guilt and angst" (p. 241). More recent work in CRT argues that it is time to move beyond rhetoric by instituting conditions for real change in literacy teaching and teacher education (Haddix, 2017).

Transcending Traditional Theory

Several new theoretical perspectives have emerged during the past decade that inform critical literacy studies. Among these are Miller's trans★⁺ness (see Chapter 20 this volume), transnational theory (Skerrett, see Chapter 26 this volume), and multilanguaging (Makalela, see Chapter 25 this volume). Additional theoretical perspectives that transcend traditional theorizing about reading and writing include a multimodal perspective on textual reading (Rowsell, Kress, Pahl, & Street, see Chapter 27 this volume) and, Sailors' use of a theory of imagination in the re-imagining of teacher education (see Chapter 24 this volume).

Poststructural and Non-Representational Theories

Texts are usually thought to signify meaning—meaning that is contingent upon the interaction of reader, text, and context. Less typical is Deleuze and Guattari's (1980/1987) concept of a text. In their poststructural decentering project, Deleuze and Guattari avoid any orientation toward a culmination or ending point. In their sense of the term, a text is neither signifier nor the signified; therefore, it is inappropriate to think of interpreting or understanding texts in the conventional way. As Grosz (1994) explained:

> It is . . . no longer appropriate to ask what a text means, what it says, what is the structure of its interiority, how to interpret or decipher it. Instead, one must ask what it does, how it connects with others things (including its reader, its author, its literary and nonliterary context).
>
> *(p. 199)*

The conventional modes of interpretation and analysis espoused by linguists, literacy theorists, and semioticians do not hold when analyzing texts from Deleuze and Guattari's (1980/1987) perspective. Instead, it is how texts function outside themselves that is of interest. This interest stems from the view that texts, like rhizomes, connect with other things. For instance, "A rhizome ceaselessly establishes connections between semiotic chains, organizations of power, and circumstances relative to the arts, sciences, and social struggles" (Deleuze & Guattari, 1980/1987, p. 7).

Moreover, from Deleuze and Guattari's perspective, researchers interested in theory building would do well to make maps, not tracings. In their metaphoric use of the terms, "a map is a part of the rhizome . . . open and connectable in all its dimensions . . . [with] multiple entryways, as opposed to the tracing, which always comes back 'to the same'" (p. 12). Maps, unlike tracings, are always becoming; they have no beginnings and endings, just middles. It is by looking at the middles that we begin to see how, in perspective, everything else changes. Dimitriadis and Kamberelis (1997) explain the process this way:

> In drawing maps, the theorist works at the surface, "creating" possible realities by producing new articulations of disparate phenomena and connecting the exteriority of objects to whatever forces or directions seem potentially related to them. As such, maps exceed both individual and collective experiences of what seems "naturally" real.
>
> *(p. 150)*

Looking for middles rather than beginnings and endings, makes it possible to decenter key linkages and find new ones, not by combining old ones in new ways, but by remaining open to the proliferation of ruptures and discontinuities that in turn create other linkages (Alvermann, 2000; Leander, Phillips, & Taylor, 2010). Rhizomatic cartography is a spatial methodology for studying a range of literacy practices, such as adolescents' uses of popular cultural texts to renegotiate their identities (Hagood, 2004), a Christian faith-based school's literacy practices (Eakle, 2007), students' multimodal/embodied classroom performances that have implications for literacy pedagogy (Leander & Rowe, 2006), and Miller's trans★+ness (see Chapter 20 this volume).

Non-representational theory surfaced in the mid- to late 1990s, largely through the work of Thrift (1996), who argued that "bodies and things are not easily separated terms" (Thrift 1996, p. 13). Approximately a decade later, Latour (2007) in *Reassembling the Social* contended that "when social scientists add the adjective 'social' to some phenomenon, they designate a stabilized state of affairs, a bundle of ties that, later, may be mobilized to account for some other phenomenon" (p. 1). To Latour's contention, Law (2004) added the following insight: "I argue that (social) science should also be trying to make and know realities that are vague and indefinite *because much of the world is enacted in that way*" (p. 14, italics in the original). In Leander and Boldt's (2013) non-representational reading of two young boys' manga play, they focused not on what they (the researchers) might assert about the outcomes of such play (e.g., youths' identity development) but rather on "the sensations and movements of the body in the moment-by-moment unfolding or emergence of activity . . . to follow the emergence of activity, including the relations among texts and bodies in activity and the affective intensities of these relations" (p. 34). In theorizing such intensities, Ehret (see Chapter 29 this volume) asks what differences become available for literacy studies in this shift, in theorizing new ways of seeing and feeling "vague and indefinite" life through affect theory. Drawing on the long history of process philosophy that forms the theoretic foundation of current movements in affect and non-representational theories (from Spinoza, 1985, to Whitehead, 1927–1928/1985, to Deleuze, 1994), Ehret destabilizes researchers' relationships to "data" and to research with theoretic tools that compel living, thinking, and writing in the present as it constantly unfolds. With this concept of emergence, essential to process philosophy (Leander & Boldt, 2013), Ehret provides a new way of thinking and feeling the intensities of an essential concept in the field, of 'literacy events' as they emerge and become known to us as experiences with singular, often unnamable, qualities.

Posthumanism

Posthumanism, as its name implies, is all about decentering the human. Thus, at the center of any posthumanist project is work that challenges the ontological binary between human and nonhuman. Such work has implications for literacy researchers, teachers, and teacher educators, especially if they were to give "the force of things [their] due" (Bennett, 2010, p. viii) and acknowledge that "[t]he locus of agency is always a human-nonhuman work group" (xvii). Imagine, for example, a theoretical framework that would house, support, or embed these variables of interest: social justice, competition, renewal, and motivation.

Posthumanism moves beyond anthropocentric perspectives that are grounded in personal agency and individual intentions as explanations of social actions. A material or posthuman stance is grounded in the belief that humans act in networks of other humans, objects, and institutions. Those actions entail the biological, physical, environmental, cultural, and institutional. In education, some researchers have turned to theories of materiality to view educational processes in schools and classrooms where literacy events are grounded in these interacting networks. Posthuman theory now permeates work on early childhood experiences in literacy classrooms (Olssen, 2009; Vecchi, 2010) and on relationships among play, literacy, and learning in elementary classrooms (Thiel, 2015).

The roots of posthumanism appear to be grounded in social theory that has arisen in a range of disciplines, such as feminist theory, ecology, and continental philosophy. For Haraway (1985, 1991), a feminist theorist, the cyborg represents the posthuman in that the hybrid embodies contraries, such as fact/fiction; alive/dead; mind/body; male/female; moral/immoral; mortal/immortal. As she wrote in an early manifesto, "A cyborg is a cybernetic organism, a hybrid of machine and organism, a creature of social reality as well as a creature of fiction" (1985, p. 117). Others (Rae, 2014) have discovered additional posthumanism roots in phenomenology, particularly in Heidegger's destruction of metaphysics and his critique of the binary logic grounding anthropocentric humanism. What is shared among these legacies is an interest in moving the human "as locus of agency, causality, and knowledge" out of the center of our experience in the world and replacing that center with an understanding that we live in vast environments and dynamic networks that enable and constrain our experience (Nichols & Campano, 2017). The posthuman view acknowledges the imperfectability and disarray within the human mind, and the capacity to fluidly change identities marks the posthuman condition.

As Braidotti (2016) has observed, an alliance between feminist theory and horror science fiction makes up a "fast-growing posthuman strand" that introduces bonds between species and across categories of living and machine-driven objects. The movie *Ex Machina* (2014), written and directed by Alex Garland, presents an example of a cyborg (a female humanoid A.I.) driven toward freedom from domination in any form.

Literacy Theory and Models in Evolution

Tensions over theories, including the information they convey and the impact they have on literacy research and instruction, have torn groups apart and also pulled them together. New theories in science, such as Darwin's theory of evolution, have altered the way scientists in a community have understood the foundation of their field, explained how and why things work as they do, solved common, perplexing problems, and made predictions about the future of a discipline. While tensions between competing or conflicting theories can spur contention and disputes, they can also stimulate creative resolution, stir new insights, spawn new understandings to explain how things work. While theory and theoretical models have brought light to the invisible processes of reading and writing both within our mind and in our social environment, they have also distorted our vision, even bringing episodes of blindness that made the accurate perception of processes both internal and external impossible.

As the field of literacy research, policy development, and instruction moves forward, it appears that we are in an era of considerable theoretical tensions. The reasons for those tensions are many. Some lie with new findings that have led to skepticism about widely accepted theories and demands for their deeper interrogation, such as we have seen occur with schema theory. Some lie with a growing belief among literacy educators and researchers that theory should reflect more deeply the social injustices manifested in classrooms and educational policies. In describing the foregoing theories and models, we have tried to provide readers with a vision of the wide landscape of theory that has arisen over the past decades.

It is abundantly clear that encouraging the generation of theory and providing justification for theory in the form of evidence, discussion, and debate—practices Gee (2012) considered ethically responsible—can immeasurably enrich our work and move us further toward understanding the issues that arise and perplex us in our investigation of literacy processes. As we move forward, we can continue to use inquiry to identify and define literacy problems calling for solutions and discover how our findings can address those problems through improved practice (Dillon and O'Brien, see Chapter 30 this volume). By identifying the literacy issues that contributed to high remediation rates in the California State University system, developing theory and practices to address those problems, and supporting high school teachers as they presented innovative curriculum to their students, educators (Katz, Brynelson, and Edlund, see Chapter 28 this volume) were able to develop theory and improve student performance as readers and writers during their senior year in high school and better prepare them for college.

In the domain of writing, educators and researchers (Smith, see Chapter 3 this volume) have observed a profound and troubling gap between theory on the one hand and writing instruction on the other. Assessment and evaluation of writing, driven by standard-based policies, have had a deeper influence on the teaching of writing than theory about writing. Theorization of writing development that takes into consideration a more ecological view and includes interacting dimensions of writing processes and pathways to development offers possibilities for more dynamic and beneficial learning environments for young writers.

Theory building has had a profound impact on many disciplines, including physics, psychology, and the biological sciences. We don't have to look far to find examples. They have arisen from

Einstein, Freud, and Darwin, and they have revolutionized how we perceive the world in which we live—both visible and invisible. We have evidence of the importance of theoretical developments in education and in literacy studies as well. One of our goals as editors of *TMPL*7 is to encourage the growth of theorizing, the examination of theory, and the development of pedagogical practices based on sound theory.

Theories structure and guide literacy practice—whether we are aware of those theories or not. While degrees of awareness about theory and the depth of their influence on teaching or research vary enormously, we have little variance in our belief that it is vitally important to discover what theories are structuring and driving practice in our classrooms and our research. As a vehicle with its lights on, theory can help us see better where we are going, why we're going there, and how we might get safely to our destination. However, theory can be misleading. It has the power to influence our decisions and to shape our interpretation of events. So with a degree of vigilance we need to monitor theory's impact on our work and heighten our awareness of its influence while always being ready to reframe its structure even on the move. We encourage readers of *TMPL*7 to continue to interrogate literacy theory through research and relentless curiosity, to reformulate pre-existing literacy theory where possible, and to formulate new literacy theory that aligns with evidence and promises better outcomes in our schools and universities.

References

Adorno, T. (2002). *The culture industry*. London: Routledge.

Alvermann, D. E. (2000). Researching libraries, literacies, and lives: A rhizoanalysis. In E. A. St. Pierre & W. Pillow (Eds.), *Working the ruins: Feminist poststructural theory and methods in education* (pp. 114–129). New York: Routledge.

Alvermann, D E., Friese, E., Beckmann, S., & Rezak, A. (2011). Content area reading pedagogy and domain knowledge: A Bourdieusian analysis. *The Australian Educational Researcher, 38*, 203–220.

Anderson, R. C. (1976). Concretization and sentence learning. In H. Singer & R. B. Ruddell (Eds.), *Theoretical models and processes of reading* (pp. 588–596). Newark, DE: International Reading Association. (Original work published 1974)

Anderson, R. C., Goldberg, S. R., & Hidde, J. L. (1976). Meaningful processing of sentences. In H. Singer & R. B. Ruddell (Eds.), *Theoretical models and processes of reading* (pp. 580–587). Newark, DE: International Reading Association. (Original work published 1971).

Bandura, A. (1986). *Social foundations of thought and action: A social cognitive theory*. Englewood Cliffs, NJ: Prentice-Hall.

Barton, D., Hamilton, M., & Ivanic, R. (Eds.). (2000). *Situated literacies: Reading and writing in context*. London: Routledge.

Bennett, J. (2010). *Vibrant matter: A political ecology of things*. Durham, NC: Duke University Press.

Bereiter, C., & Scardamalia, M. (1987). *The psychology of written composition*. Hillsdale, NJ: Lawrence Erlbaum Associates.

Berger, P. L., & Luckmann, T. (1966). *The social construction of reality: A treatise in the sociology of knowledge*. New York, NY: Doubleday.

Bleich, D. (1980). Epistemological assumptions in the study of response. In J. P. Tompkins (Ed.), *Reader-response criticism: From formalism to post-structuralism* (pp. 134–163). Baltimore, MD: Johns Hopkins University Press.

Bourdieu, P. (1990). *The logic of practice* (R. Nice, Trans.). Stanford, CA: Stanford University Press. (Original work published 1980)

Bourdieu, P. (1991). *Language and symbolic power* (G. Raymond & M. Adamson, Trans.). Cambridge, MA: Harvard University Press. (Original work published 1982)

Bourdieu, P., & Passeron, J. (1990). *Reproduction in education, society and culture* (R. Nice, Trans.) London: Sage. (Original work published 1970)

Braidotti, R. (2016). Posthuman critical theory. In D. Banerji & M. R. Paranjape (Eds.), *Critical posthumanism and planetary futures* (pp. 13–32). India: Springer.

Bruffee, K. A. (1986). Social construction, language, and the authority of knowledge: A bibliographical essay. *College English, 58*, 773–790.

Bruner, J. (1986). *Actual minds, possible worlds*. Cambridge, MA: Harvard University Press.

Burr, V. (2003). *Social constructionism* (2nd ed.). London: Routledge.

Cambourne, B. (2002). Holistic, integrated approaches to reading and language arts instruction: The constructivist framework of an instructional theory. In A. E. Farstrup & S. J. Samuels (Eds.), *What research has to say about reading instruction*, pp. 25–47. Newark, DE: International Reading Association.

Chomsky, N. (1957). *Syntactic structures*. The Hague/Paris: Mouton.

Chomsky, N. (1959). A review of B. F. Skinner's *Verbal Behavior*. *Language, 35*(1), 26–58.

Cope, B., & Kalantzis, M. (2000). *Multiliteracies: Literacy learning and the design of social futures*. New York: Routledge.

Crenshaw, K. (1989). Demarginalizing the intersection of race and sex: A Black feminist critique of antidiscrimination doctrine, feminist theory and antiracist politics. *University of Chicago Legal Forum, special issue: Feminism in the Law: Theory, Practice and Criticism*, 139–168.

Creswell, J. W. (2015). *Educational research: Planning, conducting, and evaluating quantitative and qualitative research* (5th ed.). Upper Saddle River, NJ: Pearson.

Culler, J. (1980). Literary competence. In J. P. Tompkins (Ed.), *Reader-response criticism: From formalism to post-structuralism* (pp. 101–117). Baltimore, MD: Johns Hopkins University Press.

Darwin, C. (1988). *On the origin of species*. New York, NY: New York University Press. (Original work published 1859)

Deci, E. L., & Ryan, R. M. (1985). *Intrinsic motivation and self-determination in human behavior*. New York: Plenum.

Deleuze, G. (1994). *Difference and repetition*. New York, NY: Columbia University Press.

Deleuze, G., & Guattari, F. (1987). *A thousand plateaus: Capitalism and schizophrenia*. (B. Massumi, Trans.) Minneapolis: University of Minnesota Press. (Original work published 1980)

Delgado, R. (Ed.). (1995). *Critical race theory: The cutting edge*. Philadelphia, PA: Temple University Press.

Dimitriadis, G., & Kamberelis, G. (1997). Shifting terrains: Mapping education within a global landscape. *The Annals of the Academy of Political and Social Science, 551*, 137–150.

Durkheim, E. (1982). *Rules for the sociological method*. New York, NY: Free Press.

Eakle, J. (2007). Literacy spaces of a Christian faith-based school. *Reading Research Quarterly, 42*, 472–510.

Fay, B. (1987). The basic scheme of critical social science. In B. Fay, *Critical social science* (pp. 27–41). Ithaca, NY: Cornell University Press.

Fish, S. (1980). *Is there a text in this class*. Cambridge, MA: Harvard University Press.

Flower, L., & Hayes, J. R. (1981). A cognitive process theory of writing. *College Composition and Communication, 32*, 365–387.

Forman, E. A., & Cazden, C. B. (2013). Exploring Vygotskian perspectives in education: The cognitive value of peer interaction. In D. E. Alvermann, N. J. Unrau, & R. B. Ruddell (Eds.), *Theoretical models and processes of reading* (6th ed., pp. 182–203). Newark, DE: International Reading Association. (Original work published 1985)

Fosnot, C. T. (Ed.) (1996). *Constructivism: Theory, perspectives, and practice*. New York, NY: Teachers College Press.

Freire, P. (1993). *Pedagogy of the oppressed* (M. B. Ramos, Trans.). New York, NY: Continuum. (Original work published 1970)

Gardner, H. (1985). *The mind's new science: A history of the cognitive revolution*. New York, NY: Basic Books.

Gavelek, J., & Bresnahan, P. (2009). Ways of making meaning: Sociocultural perspectives on reading comprehension. In S. E. Israel & G. G. Duffy (Eds.), *Handbook of research on reading comprehension* (pp. 140–176). New York, NY: Routledge.

Gee, J. P. (1990). *Social linguistics and literacies: Ideology in discourses. Critical perspectives on literacy and education*. London: Falmer Press.

Gee, J. P. (1996). *Social linguistics and literacies: Ideology in discourses* (2nd ed.). London: Taylor & Francis.

Gee, J. P. (1998). The New Literacy Studies: From "socially situated" to the work of the social. Retrieved from http://jamespaulgee.com/pdfs/The%20New%20Literacy%20Studies%20and%20the%20Social%20Turn.pdf

Gee, J. P. (1999). *An introduction to discourse analysis: Theory and method*. London: Routledge.

Gee, J. P. (2012). *Social linguistics and literacies: Ideology in discourses* (4th ed.) London: Routledge.

Gergen, K. J. (1985). The social constructionist movement in modern psychology. *American Psychologist, 40*(3), 266–275.

Gergen, K. J. (2002). Beyond the empiricist/constructionist divide in social psychology. *Personality and Social Psychology Review, 6*(3), 188–191.

Goodman, K. S. (1967). Reading: A psycholinguistic guessing game. *Journal of the Reading Specialist, 6*, 126–135.

Goody, J. (1977). *The domestication of the savage mind*. New York, NY: Cambridge University Press.

Gough, P. B. (1976). One second of reading. In H. Singer & R. B. Ruddell (Eds.), *Theoretical models and processes of reading* (2nd ed., pp. 509–535). Newark, DE: International Reading Association. (Original work published 1972)

Gough, P. B. (1985). One second of reading: Postscript. In H. Singer & R. B. Ruddell (Eds.), *Theoretical models and processes of reading* (3rd ed., pp. 687–688). Newark, DE: International Reading Association.

Grosz, E. (1994). A thousand tiny sexes: Feminism and rhizomatics. In C. V. Boundas & D. Olkowski (Eds.), *Gilles Deleuze and the theater of philosophy* (pp. 187–210). New York: Routledge.

Guthrie, J. T., & Wigfield, A. (2000). Engagement and motivation in reading. In M. L. Kamil, P. B. Mosenthal, P. D. Pearson, & R. Barr (Eds.), *Handbook of reading research* (Vol. III, pp. 403–422). Mahwah, NJ: Erlbaum.

Habermas, J. (1962/trans. 1989). *The structural transformation of the public sphere: An inquiry into a category of bourgeois society.* Cambridge: Polity.

Haddix, M. M. (2017). Diversifying teaching and teacher education: Beyond rhetoric and toward real change. *Journal of Literacy Research, 49*(1), 141–149.

Hagood, M. C. (2004). A rhizomatic cartography of adolescents, popular culture, and onstructions of self. In K. M. Leander & M. Sheehy (Eds.), *Spatializing literacy research and practice* (pp. 143–160). New York, NY: Peter Lang.

Halliday, M. A. K. (1978). *Language as social semiotic.* London: Arnold.

Halliday, M. A. K. (1994). The place of dialogue in children's construction of meaning. In R. B. Ruddell, M. R. Ruddell, & H. Singer (Eds.), *Theoretical models and processes of reading* (4th ed., pp. 70–82). Newark, DE: International Reading Association. (Adapted from S. Stati, E. Weigand, and E. Hundsnurscher (Eds.), *Dialoganalyse III: Referate der 3: Arbeitstagung, Bologna 1990* [3rd International Conference on Dialogue Analysis] (Vol. 2, pp. 417–430). Tübingen: Niemeyer)

Haraway, D. (1985). A cyborg manifest: Science, technology, and socialist-feminism in the late 20th century. *Socialist Review, 80*, 65–108.

Haraway, D. (1991). *Simians, cyborgs, and women.* New York, NY: Routledge.

Havelock, E. A. (1982). *The literate revolution in ancient Greece and its cultural consequences.* Princeton, NJ: Princeton University Press.

Hayes, J. R. (1996/2004). A new framework for understanding cognition and affect in writing. In R. B. Ruddell & N. J. Unrau (Eds.), *Theoretical models and processes of reading* (5th ed., pp. 1399–1430). Newark, DE: International Reading Association. (Original work published 1996)

Heath, S. B. (1983). *Ways with words: Language, life, and work in communities and classrooms.* New York, NY: Cambridge University Press.

Hodge, R., & Kress, G. (1988). *Social semiotics.* Cambridge: Polity.

Holmes, J. (1953). *The substrata-factor theory of reading.* Berkeley, CA: California Book Company.

Holmes, J. (1970). The substrata-factor theory of reading: Some experimental evidence. In H. Singer & R. B. Ruddell (Eds.), *Theoretical models and processes of reading* (pp. 187–197). Newark, DE: International Reading Association. (Original work published in 1960)

hooks, b. (1990). *Yearning: Race, gender, and cultural politics.* Boston, MA: South End.

Horkheimer, M. (2002). Traditional and critical theory. In C. Calhoun, J. Gerteis, J. Moody, S. Pfaff, K. Schmidt, & I. Virk (Eds.). *Classical sociological theory* (pp. 304–318). Malden, MA: Blackwell.

Jewitt, C., & Kress, G. (Eds.). (2003). *Multimodal literacy.* New York, NY: Peter Lang.

Jimenez, R. T., Smith, P. H., & Martinez-Leon, N. (2003). Freedom and form: The language and literacy practices of two Mexican schools. *Reading Research Quarterly, 38*(4), 488–508.

Just, M. A., & Carpenter, P. A. (2013). A theory of reading: From eye fixations to comprehension. In D. E. Alvermann, N. J. Unrau, & R. B. Ruddell (Eds.), *Theoretical models and processes of reading* (6th ed., pp. 748–782). Newark, DE: International Reading Association.

Kintsch, W., & van Dijk, T. A. (1978). Toward a model of text comprehension and production. *Psychological Review, 85*, 363–394.

Kress. G. (1997). *Before writing: Rethinking the paths to literacy.* London: Routledge.

Kress, G. (2009). What is a mode? In C. Jewitt (Ed.), *The Routledge handbook of multimodal analysis* (pp. 54–67). London: Routledge.

Kress, G. & van Leeuwen, T. (1996). *Reading images: the grammar of visual design.* New York: Routledge.

Kucer, S. B. (1985). The making of meaning: Reading and writing as parallel processes. *Written Communication, 2*, 317–336.

Kucer, S. B. (2001). *Dimensions of literacy: A conceptual base for teaching reading and writing in school settings.* Mahwah, NJ: Erlbaum.

Kuhn, T. (1996). *The structure of scientific revolutions* (3rd ed.). Chicago, IL: University of Chicago Press.

LaBerge, D., & Samuels, S. J. (1976). Toward a theory of automatic information processing in reading. In H. Singer & R. B. Ruddell (Eds.), *Theoretical models and processes of reading* (2nd ed., pp. 548–579). Newark, DE: International Reading Association. (Original work published 1974)

Ladson-Billings, G. J. (1999). Preparing teachers for diverse student populations: A Critical Race Theory perspective. *Review of Research in Education, 24*, 211–247.

Lankshear, C., & Knobel, M. (2006). *New literacies: Everyday practices and classroom learning* (2nd ed.). Maidenhead: McGraw-Hill/Open University Press.

Latour, B. (2007). *Reassembling the social: An introduction to Actor-Network-Theory.* New York, NY: Oxford University Press.

Law, J. (2004). *After method: Mess in social science research.* New York, NY: Routledge.

Leander, K., & Boldt, G. (2013). Rereading "A pedagogy of multiliteracies": Bodies, texts, and emergence. *Journal of Literacy Research, 45*(1), 22–46.

Leander, K. M., Phillips, N. C., & Taylor, K. H. (2010). The changing social spaces of learning: Mapping new mobilities. *Review of Research in Education, 34,* 329–394.

Leander, K., & Rowe, D. W. (2006). Mapping literacy spaces in motion: A rhizomatic analysis of a classroom literacy performance. *Reading Research Quarterly, 41*(4), 428–460.

Lee, C. (2013). Revisiting is October Brown Chinese? A cultural modeling activity system for underachieving students. In D. E. Alvermann, N. J. Unrau, & R. B. Ruddell (Eds.), *Theoretical models and processes of reading* (6th ed., pp. 265–296). Newark, DE: International Reading Association.

Luria, A. R. (1976). *Cognitive development: Its cultural and social function.* Cambridge, MA: Harvard University Press.

Marsh, J. (2006). Popular culture in the literacy curriculum: A Bourdieuan analysis. *Reading Research Quarterly, 41*(2), 160–174.

Marcuse, H. (1964). *One dimensional man: Studies in the ideology of advanced industrial society.* London: Routledge and Kegan Paul.

McVee, M. B., Dunsmore, K., & Gavelek, J. R. (2013). Schema theory revisted. In D. E. Alvermann, N. J. Unrau, & R. B. Ruddell (Eds.), *Theoretical models and processes of reading* (6th ed., pp. 489–524). Newark, DE: International Reading Association.

Mertens, D. M. (2015). *Research and evaluation in education and psychology* (4th ed.). Los Angeles, CA: Sage.

Miller, G. (2003). The cognitive revolution: A historical perspective. *Trends in Cognitive Sciences, 7*(3), 141–144.

Morrell, E. (2008). *Critical literacy and urban youth: Pedagogies of access, dissent, and liberation.* New York, NY: Routledge.

Nelson, K. (2013). Language pathways into the community of minds. In D. E. Alvermann, N. J. Unrau, & R. B. Ruddell (Eds.), *Theoretical models and processes of reading* (6th ed., pp. 437–457). Newark, DE: International Reading Association.

New London Group. (1996). A pedagogy of multiliteracies: Designing social futures. *Harvard Educational Review, 66,* 60–93.

Nichols, T. P., & Campano, G. (2017). Post-humanism and literacy studies. *Language Arts, 94*(4), 245–251.

Olssen, L.M. (2009). *Movement and experimentation in young children's learning: Deleuze and Guattari in early childhood education.* New York, NY: Routledge.

Ong, W. J. (1982). *Orality and literacy: The technologizing of the word.* New York, NY: Methuen.

Parsons, S., Gallagher, M. A., & the George Mason University Content Analysis Team (2016). A content analysis of nine literacy journals, 2009–2014. *Journal of Literacy Research, 48*(4), 476–502.

Pekrun, R. (2009). Emotions at school. In K. R. Wentzel & A. Wigfield (Eds.), *Handbook of motivation at school* (pp. 575–604). New York, NY: Routledge.

Piaget, J., Gruber, H. E., & Voneche, J. J. (Eds.). (1977). *The essential Piaget.* New York, NY: Basic Books.

Piaget, J., & Inhelder, B. (1969). *The psychology of the child.* New York, NY: Basic Books.

Portes, P. R., & Salas, S. (Eds.). (2011). *Vygotsky in 21st century society: Advances in cultural historical theory and praxis with non-dominant communities.* New York, NY: Peter Lang.

Rae, G. (2014). Heidegger's influence on posthumanism: The destruction of metaphysics, technology and the overcoming of anthropocentrism. *History of the Human Sciences, 27*(1), 51–69.

Ruddell, R. B., Ruddell, M. R., & Singer, H. (1994), *Theoretical models and processes of reading* (4th ed.). Newark, DE: International Reading Association.

Ruddell, R. B., & Speaker, R. B. (1985). The interactive reading process: A model. In H. Singer & R. B. Ruddell (Eds.), *Theoretical models and processes of reading* (3rd ed., pp. 751–793). Newark, DE: International Reading Association.

Ruddell, R. B., & Unrau, N. J. (1994). Reading as a meaning-construction process: The reader, the text, and the teacher. In R. B. Ruddell, M.R. Ruddell, & H. Singer (Eds.), *Theoretical models and processes of reading* (4th ed., pp. 996–1056). Newark, DE: International Reading Association.

Ruddell, R. B., & Unrau, N. J. (2013). Reading as a motivated meaning-construction process: The reader, the text, and the teacher. In D. E. Alvermann, N. J. Unrau, & R. B. Ruddell (Eds.), *Theoretical models and processes of reading* (6th ed., pp. 1015–1068). Newark, DE: International Reading Association.

Rumelhart, D. E. (1985). Toward an interactive model of reading. In H. Singer & R. B. Ruddell (Eds.), *Theoretical models and processes of reading* (3rd ed., pp. 722–750). Newark, DE: International Reading Association.

Samuels, S. J. (1977). Introduction to theoretical models of reading. In W. Otto, C. Peters, & N. Peters (Eds.), *Reading problems: A multidisciplinary perspective* (pp. 7–41). Reading, MA: Addison Wesley.

Samuels, S. J. (1994). Toward a theory of automatic information processing in reading, revisited. In R. B. Ruddell, M. R. Ruddell, & H. Singer (Eds.), *Theoretical models and processes of reading* (4th ed., pp. 816–837). Newark, DE: International Reading Association.

Scribner, S., & Cole, M. (1981). *The psychology of literacy.* Cambridge, MA: Harvard University Press.

Singer, H. (1994). The substrata-factor theory of reading. In R. B. Ruddell, M. R. Ruddell, & H. Singer (Eds.), *Theoretical models and processes of reading* (4th ed., pp. 895–927). Newark, DE: International Reading Association.

Singer, H., & Ruddell, R. B. (Eds.) (1970). *Theoretical models and process of reading* (2nd ed.). Newark, DE: International Reading Association.

Singer, H., & Ruddell, R. B. (Eds.) (1976). *Theoretical models and process of reading* (2nd ed.). Newark, DE: International Reading Association.

Skinner, B. F. (1957). *Verbal behavior.* Acton, MA: Copley Publishing Group.

Spinoza, B. (1985). *The collected works of Spinoza* (E. Curley, trans.). Princeton, NJ: Princeton University Press.

Spiro, R. J. (1988). *Cognitive flexibility theory: Advanced knowledge acquisition in ill-structured domains* (Tech. Rep. No. 441). Champaign, IL: University of Illinois, Center for the Study of Reading.

Spivey, N. N. (1997). *The constructivist metaphor: Reading, writing, and the making of meaning.* San Diego, CA: Academic Press.

Street, B. V. (1995). *Social literacies: Critical approaches to literacy in development, ethnography and education.* London: Longman.

Taylor, E., Gillborn, D., & Ladson-Billings, G. (2009). *Foundations of critical race theory in education.* New York, NY: Routledge.

Thiel, J. J. (2015). "Bumblebee's in trouble!" Embodied literacies during imaginative superhero play. *Language Arts, 93,* 38–43.

Thorndike, E.L. (1913). *Educational psychology: Vol. 2. The psychology of learning.* New York, NY: Teachers College Press.

Tracey, D. H., & Morrow, L. M. (2017). *Lenses on reading: An introduction to theories and models* (3rd ed.). New York, NY: Guilford Press.

Thrift, N. (1996). *Spatial formations.* London: Sage.

van Leeuwen, T. (2005). *Introducing social semiotics.* London: Routledge.

Vecchi, V. (2010). *Art and creativity in Reggio Emilia: Exploring the role and potential of ateliers in early childhood education.* New York, NY: Routledge.

Vygotsky, L. S. (1978). *Mind in society: The development of higher psychological processes.* Cambridge, MA: Harvard University Press.

Vygotsky, L. S. (1986). *Thought and language.* Cambridge, MA: MIT Press.

Whitehead, A. N. (1927–1928/1985). *Process and reality.* New York, NY: The Free Press.

Wigfield, A., & Eccles, J. S. (2000). Expectancy-value theory of achievement motivation. *Contemporary Educational Psychology, 25,* 68–81.

Wittgenstein, L. (1953). *Philosophical investigations.* (G. E. M Anscombe, trans.). Oxford: Blackwell.

Yang, X., Kuo, L., Ji, X., & McTigue, E. (2018). A critical examination of the relationship among research, theory, and practice: Technology and reading instruction. *Computers & Education, 125,* pp. 62–73.

Yopp, H. K., & Singer, H. (1985). Toward and interactive reading instructional model: Explanation of activation of linguistic awareness and metalinguistic ability in learning to read. In H. Singer & R. B. Ruddell (Eds.), *Theoretical models and processes of reading* (3rd ed., pp. 135–143). Newark, DE: International Reading Association.

2

READING RESEARCH AND PRACTICE OVER THE DECADES

A Historical Analysis[1]

Patricia A. Alexander and Emily Fox

Introduction

One of the evident transformations now marking the domain of reading, and more precisely, the teaching of reading, is its intertwining with other language domains, in particular writing and speaking. This transformation is chronicled in the retitling of leading professional organizations (e.g., from National Reading Conference to Literacy Research Association). It is likewise evident in the renaming of prestigious journals (e.g., from *Journal of Reading Behavior* to *Journal of Literacy Research*) and even this publication (i.e., from *Theoretical Models and Processes of Reading* to *Theoretical Models and Processes of Literacy*). In all instances, the singular identifier *reading* has been replaced by the amalgamated term *literacy*. In this chapter, we will discuss this repositioning of reading research and practice under the literacy umbrella within the context of recent historical developments. However, it is our intention in this historical analysis to remain focused specifically on reading research and practice as it has unfolded over the decades, beginning in 1956, when the International Reading Association (IRA; now the International Literacy Association) was founded.

The decision to remain centered on reading as the domain of interest was driven by several factors. For one, engaging in historical analysis demands an extensive knowledge base. Although we are conversant with the related domains of writing and speaking, we are by no means experts in those aspects of literacy. For another, the historical paths followed by the domains that compose literacy may at times converge, but they are by no means identical. Consequently, the task of weaving the historical tapestry of literacy within a single chapter is both daunting and perilous. Thus, we leave it for others to take the historical eras documented for reading research and practice in this chapter and overlay those for the other literacy domains. Nonetheless, when it is possible to reference concomitant events or practices in writing and speaking with those pertinent to reading, we will endeavor to do so.

We expressly chose the founding of the IRA as our starting point in our historical analysis of reading because this event is regarded as transformational (Monaghan & Saul, 1987). Without question, the efforts of researchers to study the nature and processes of reading during that formative period remain an enduring legacy. Yet, that was not the only period of significant change for the reading community over the past 60 years. In fact, the domain of reading has undergone both gradual and dramatic transformations in response to internal and external forces that have altered both research and practice. Our purpose here is to position those transformations within a historical framework that allows for reasoned reflection and affords a perspective on the domain that can be lost when one is immersed in ongoing study and practice (VanSledright, 2002).

To capture this historical perspective, we describe certain internal and external conditions that helped frame each era, discuss the prevalent views of learning, and identify resulting principles related to reading that are characteristic of that era. Moreover, to bring the historical landscape into clearer focus, we highlight exemplary and prototypic works that encapsulate the issues and concerns of the time, and we take note of rival stances that existed as educational undercurrents. Of course, we recognize that the boundaries and distinctions we draw between these eras are approximations of permeable and overlapping periods of reading research and practice. Nonetheless, these eras help set the context for understanding the contributions making up this volume.

In again revisiting the historical perspective we have offered in prior editions of *Theoretical Models and Processes of Reading* (Alexander & Fox, 2004, 2013), we considered the degree to which our interpretation of past and emergent perspectives remained stable over time. What we determined was that our interpretation of the overarching approaches characterizing distant eras required no substantive revision. However, our more provisional or speculative characterization of the emergent era and our judgment as to where the field was heading required greater scrutiny.

The Era of Conditioned Learning (1950–1965)

Conditions for Change

As early as the first decades of the 20th century, during the nascence of psychology, the processes of reading were already of passing interest to educational researchers (e.g., Buswell, 1922; Huey, 1908; Thorndike, 1917). However, it was not until somewhat later in that century that reading became a recognized field of study with systematic programs of research aimed at ascertaining its fundamental nature and the processes of its acquisition. Although reading had long been a basic component of formal schooling in the United States, attention to and efforts toward marrying research knowledge and instructional practice regarding the processes entailed in reading acquisition underwent a significant increase during the 1950s. Instigation for that marked change came as a result of a confluence of social, educational, political, and economic factors occurring in that decade.

Postwar America was fertile ground for transformations in reading research and practice for several reasons. For one, the high birthrate during and immediately following World War II resulted in record numbers of children entering the public school system (Ganley, Lyons, & Sewall, 1993). This baby boom contributed to both quantitative and qualitative changes in the school population. One of those qualitative changes was a seeming rise in the number of children experiencing difficulties in learning to read. Such reading problems, while nothing new to teachers, took on particular significance in the age of Sputnik, as America's ability to compete globally became a defining issue (Allington & McGill-Franzen, 2000). The outcome was a growing public pressure on the educational community to find an answer to the "problem" of reading acquisition.

One of the groundbreaking but controversial publications of this period was *Why Johnny Can't Read—and What You Can Do About It* by Rudolf Flesch (1955). This publication exemplified a growing interest in reading research and its relevance to educational practice (Ruddell, 2002). In arguments reminiscent of more recent debates, Flesch attacked the prevailing look–say method of reading instruction as a contributor to the reading problems experienced by many American students. As the basis for his attack, he referred to research that established the effectiveness of phonics-based techniques over those that relied on a whole-word approach. Before long, volumes like the Dick and Jane books, with their look–say approach, gave way to controlled vocabulary readers and synthetic phonics drill and practice in such approaches as the Lippincott Basic Reading Program, Reading with Phonics, and Phonetic Keys to Reading (Chall, 1967).

The burgeoning interest in finding an answer to children's reading problems interfaced with psychological research in the guise of Skinnerian behaviorism, the prevailing research orientation at the

Connections

time (Goetz, Alexander, & Ash, 1992). With its promise of bringing a scientific perspective to the reading problem, behaviorism seemed suited to the task at hand (Glaser, 1978). In effect, it was time to turn the attention of the research community to the fundamental task of learning to read, and to apply the same principles of analysis that explained and controlled the behavior of animals in the laboratory to children's language learning. Such an analysis would presumably result in pedagogical techniques based on an understanding of the physiological and environmental underpinnings of human behavior (Glaser, 1978).

Based on this perspective, the processes and skills involved in learning to read could be clearly defined and broken down into their constituent parts. Those constituent parts could then be practiced and reinforced in a systematic and orderly fashion during classroom instruction (Pearson & Stephens, 1994). With this analytic view, there was a growing tendency for problems in the reading act to be looked upon as deficiencies in need of remediation, just as physical ailments require medical remedies. Indeed, it was a medical metaphor of reading, with its diagnosis, prescription, and remediation, that came to the foreground in the 1950s. Moreover, despite the claims of some within the reading research community that little of significance occurred in reading until the 1960s (Weaver & Kintsch, 1991), the continued influence of behaviorism on educational practice remains evident today.

Guiding View

Because of the prevailing influences of behavioristic theory in educational research and practice, reading during this period was conceptualized as conditioned behavior, and just another process susceptible to programming. The Skinnerian or strict behaviorist perspective was that learning should not be conceived as growth or development, but rather as acquiring behaviors as a result of certain environmental contingencies. As Skinner (1974/1976) stated:

> Everyone has suffered, and unfortunately is continuing to suffer, from mentalistic theories of learning in education. . . . The point of education can be stated in behavioral terms: a teacher arranges contingencies under which the student acquires behavior which will be useful to him under other contingencies later on. . . . Education covers the behavior of a child or person over many years, and the principles of developmentalism are therefore particularly troublesome.
>
> *(pp. 202–203)*

In this theoretical orientation, learning results from repeated and controlled stimulation from the environment that comes to elicit a predictable response from the individual. This repeated pairing of stimulus/response, often linked with the application of carefully chosen rewards and punishments, leads to the habituation of the reading act. For example, the child presented with the symbols C-A-T immediately produces the desired word, *cat*, seemingly without cognitive involvement.

Within this perspective, the investigation of academic learning involved identification of the requisite desired behaviors and determination of the environmental conditions (i.e., training) that produced them. The task for this generation of reading researchers, therefore, was to untangle the chained links of behavior involved in reading, so that learners could be trained in each component skill. The act of reading consisted in the competent and properly sequenced performance of that chain of discrete skills. Research was additionally concerned with the structuring and control of materials effective in the delivery of environmental stimulation and practice opportunities (Glaser, 1978; Monaghan & Saul, 1987). There was also a concomitant interest in the identification and remediation of problems in skill acquisition, which would require even finer-grained analysis of the appropriate behaviors so that skill training could proceed in the smallest of increments (Glaser, 1978).

Resulting Principles

Out of the labors of the reading researchers of this era came a body of literature on the multitude of subskills required for reading. Interest in the study of the components of reading processes was exemplified by such efforts as the interdisciplinary studies at Cornell University that became the Project Literacy program (Levin, 1965; Venezky, 1984). As a result of the behaviorist emphasis on studying observable behavior, there was a particular focus on reading as a perceptual activity. Such perceptual activities included the identification of visual signals, the translation of these signals into sounds, and the assembly of these sounds into words, phrases, and sentences (Pearson & Stephens, 1994). Phonics instruction came to be seen as part of the logical groundwork for beginning to read (Chall, 1967) and had the desirable attribute of being eminently trainable. The counterpart of this emphasis on skills was an interest in developing and validating diagnostic instruments and remedial techniques (C. E. Smith & Keogh, 1962). Where there were problems in skill acquisition, the solution was likely to be an individually paced training program (Glaser, 1978).

Rival Views

Although the behaviorist perspective dominated the psychological research of the time, alternative theories of human learning also remained operative. The legacy of William James (1890) endured in the notion that human thought mattered in human action and that introspection and self-questioning were effective tools for uncovering those thoughts. This view stood directly against the behaviorist antagonism to mentalism and insistence on observation of overt behavior.

From another angle, the reductionist aspect of behaviorism, with its intended training program of bottom-up assembly of linked sets of behaviors to create a coherent activity such as learning to read, stood in opposition to Gestalt theory (Wertheimer, 1945/1959). For Gestalt theory, understanding phenomena as wholes was essential and could never be achieved by concatenation of individual facts, skills, or observations (Wulf, 1922/1938). The top-down perspective emphasized by Gestalt theorists was evident in the developmental approach to learning to read, a competing stance taken by reading researchers leading into and during this era (e.g., Gray & Rogers, 1956; Russell, 1961; Strang, McCullough, & Traxler, 1955). These developmentalists emphasized whole-word recognition, the importance of context in comprehension and word identification, and the consideration of reading as a unique human activity with its own definitive characteristics. From this perspective, even at its earliest stages, reading development was never merely a matter of acquisition of skills but entailed an understanding of reading as meaning-making and as ultimately aimed toward achievement of the reader's own purposes.

The Era of Natural Learning (1966–1975)

Conditions for Change

By the mid-1960s, there was general unrest with the precepts of Skinnerian behaviorism and with the conceptualization of reading as discrete skills passively drilled and practiced until reflexively demonstrated. Several factors served to hasten the transition in research on the learner and the learning process. One of those factors was an increased interest in internal mental structures and processes sparked by advances in neurology and in artificial intelligence (Ericsson & Smith, 1991). Both of these movements turned attention back inside the human mind and away from the environment.

Another factor in this theoretical transformation was the fact that the dissatisfaction with behaviorism as an explanatory system was shared by diverse segments of the educational research community whose views on many other issues were frequently at odds (Pearson & Stephens, 1994). In the mid-1960s, a federally funded nationwide cooperative research venture, the First Grade Studies

(Bond & Dykstra, 1967), brought together researchers on 27 different reading projects in a systematic comparison of various approaches to instruction in beginning reading. The attention of researchers in a wide range of disciplines had been drawn to the investigation of the reading process, the effect of which was an interdisciplinary perspective on the nature of reading and the teaching of reading that remains a hallmark of the field.

Two communities of theorists and researchers were especially influential in setting the stage for this period of reading research: linguists and psycholinguists. On the one hand, linguists following in the tradition of Chomsky (1957, 2002) held to a less environmentally driven and more hardwired view of language acquisition, and hence of reading. Psycholinguistic researchers, on the other hand, felt that the attention to discrete aspects of reading advocated in behaviorism destroyed the natural communicative power and inherent aesthetic of reading (Goodman & Goodman, 1979; F. Smith, 1973). Given these circumstances, the stage was set for a new era of reading research.

Guiding View

In this new era of reading research, the conceptualization that served as the formative stance was of learning as a natural process. Language, as with other innate human capacities, was to be developed through meaningful use, not practiced to the point of mindless reaction, as behaviorists proposed. It was assumed that human beings were biologically programmed to acquire language under favorable conditions. This programming involved the existence of mental structures designed to perform the complex task of assimilating and integrating the particular linguistic cues provided by a given language community (Chomsky, 1975).

Such a view of the language learner was strongly influenced by the writings of linguist Noam Chomsky (e.g., 1998, 2002), and marked a dramatic shift from the behaviorist view of learning as conditioning. Chomsky (1957) helped establish the field of generative grammar, which focused on the assumed innate mental structures that allowed for language use. In framing his theory, Chomsky was influenced by the emerging research in neuroscience and cognitive science (Baars, 1986). He saw unquestionable relations between the universality of neurological structures and the universality of grammatical structures. His assertion was that humans emerge from the womb with a preexisting template that guides language use. "Languaging" was thus perceived to unfold naturally, to follow a developmental trajectory, and to involve not just the action of the environment on the individual, but also the individual's contribution as far as a predisposition or innate capacity (Chomsky, 1957, 1998). This shift in the view of language acquisition from conditioned behavior to natural process inevitably reverberated in the reading research community in the form of psycholinguistics (Goodman, 1965; F. Smith, 1973). As with the generative grammarians, psycholinguists argued that because all human languages follow similar production rules, the capacity for language must be built-in. Psycholinguists carried this assumption beyond oral language into print or reading. They also focused on semantics or meaning and how meaning is acquired, represented, and used during the process of reading. Consequently, learning to read, the textual counterpart of acquiring an oral language, came to be viewed as an inherent ability, rather than a reflective act involving the laborious acquisition of a set of skills (Harste, Burke, & Woodward, 1984). Just as children came to understand the spoken language of their surrounding community (Halliday, 1969), they would come to understand its written language given enough exposure in meaningful situations (Goodman & Goodman, 1979).

Resulting Principles

With the view that language development was a native capacity of human beings came significant changes not only in perceptions of the nature of reading, but also in the position of reading relative to other language processes and in preferred modes of diagnosis and instruction. Specifically, because the premise underlying this "natural movement" was that language had a natural and rule-governed structure, it became essential to unite all manner of language acquisition and use. To assume that the process of acquiring and using written language was somehow divorced from that of speaking or listening would be disruptive to the theoretical premises upon which this perspective was founded. Thus, in this period and for subsequent eras of reading research, we see a tendency toward the aggregation of the language arts into the unified field of literacy (Halliday & Hasan, 1974).

Concurrent with this new view of learning to read as a natural process, investigations into the inferred mental structures and processes of reading in relation to the reader's performance took shape. For one, the learner was cast in the role of an active participant, a constructor of meaning who used many forms of information to arrive at comprehension (Halliday, 1969). Learning to read was not so much a matter of being taught, but a matter of arriving at facility as a result of a predisposition to seek understanding within a language-rich environment. For another, reading diagnosis within this period was less about isolating and correcting problems in the underlying skills of reading than it was about understanding how readers arrived at their alternative interpretations of written text (Clay, 1967, 1976). Unlike the diagnostic studies of the preceding period, this new model of diagnosis did not focus on identifying and eradicating the source of readers' errors. Rather, the goal was to ascertain how the unexpected responses readers produced were reflective of their attempts at meaning-making (Goodman & Goodman, 1979). The groundbreaking work by Kenneth Goodman and colleagues on miscue analysis was prototypic of this reconceptualization occurring in reading diagnosis (e.g., Goodman, 1965).

Rival Views

Interestingly, some of the very conditions that sparked the "reading as a natural process" movement helped establish a rival view of reading that came to dominate in the subsequent decade (Fodor, 1964). Specifically, a number of individuals invested in cognitive science and artificial intelligence were equally as fascinated with the internal structures and processes of the human mind as were generative grammarians and psycholinguists. However, for these researchers, the focus was more on how those processes and procedures could be best represented symbolically and transferred into computer programs that could approximate human performance (Fodor, 2001). In effect, these individuals were interested in creating "intelligent machines" that mimicked the problem solving of intelligent humans (Alexander, 2003).

Another area of interest that would emerge as an overarching theme for a later era of reading research was the interaction of language as a system and language in its particular social uses. While generative grammarians and psycholinguists sought for the universals underlying human language acquisition and use, sociolinguistic investigations such as those of Labov (1966) and Shuy (1968) began to explore variations in everyday language use and the relation of those variations to social roles (Labov, 1972). The contrast between the everyday language of children growing up in different social settings and the language demanded in an educational setting began to surface as an issue for educational research and practice (Labov, 1971; Shuy, 1969).

The Era of Information Processing (1976–1985)

Conditions for Change

By the mid-1970s, the reading research community was again poised for theoretical transformation. Conditions for that change included the growing attention to the structure and processes of the human mind and increased federal funding for basic reading research (Alexander, 1998a). These converging conditions led to the creation of research centers dedicated to reading research and, concomitantly, a significant influx of theorists and researchers into the reading community whose interests were more in basic than applied research and whose roots were primarily in cognitive psychology (Pearson & Stephens, 1994). The interdisciplinary character of these centers, most notably the Center for the Study of Reading under Richard Anderson, involved individuals from psychology and reading-related fields such as English, literature, communications, and writing.

Given their more basic research agenda and their strong cognitive roots, those involved in these alliances forwarded a perspective on reading that deviated markedly from the naturalistic orientation that had dominated. Specifically, this new perspective held little regard for the innateness or naturalness of reading and little interest in the amalgamation of literacy fields. As would be expected, some within the reading research community felt uneasy about this basic research emphasis, arguing that it had the "deleterious" effects of "squeezing out" reading educators and undervaluing instructional practice (Vacca & Vacca, 1983, p. 383).

Guiding View

It was cognitive psychology, and more specifically information-processing theory that dominated reading research during the period between 1976 and 1985 (R. C. Anderson, 1977). This era of cognitive psychology was characterized by unprecedented research on knowledge, especially the construct of prior knowledge (Alexander, 1998a). This new generation of reading researchers searched for general processes or "laws" that explained human language as an interaction between symbol system and mind. With the burgeoning studies in expert/novice differences and artificial intelligence (Chi, Feltovich, & Glaser, 1981; Ericsson & Smith, 1991; Schank & Abelson, 1977), the medical metaphor of diagnosis, prescription, and remediation that reigned in the 1950s and the "learning as natural" metaphor of the 1960s were replaced with a mechanistic information-processing metaphor (Reynolds, Sinatra, & Jetton, 1996). Text-based learning was about knowledge, which was organized and stored within the individual mind, and resulted from the input, interpretation, organization, retention, and output of information from the individual's environment (Samuels & Kamil, 1984).

Resulting Principles

As noted, the construct of prior knowledge and its potent influence on students' text-based learning were enduring legacies of this era (Alexander, 1998a; Alexander & Murphy, 1998). Specifically, readers' knowledge base was shown to be *powerful, pervasive, individualistic,* and *modifiable.* Prior knowledge was linked to individuals' perspectives on what they read or heard (Pichert & Anderson, 1977), their allocation of attention (R. C. Anderson, Pichert, & Shirey, 1983), and their interpretations and recall of written text (Bransford & Franks, 1971; Lipson, 1983). In addition, significant associations were established between readers' existing knowledge and their subsequent reading performance (Stanovich, 1986), comprehension (Alvermann, Smith, & Readence, 1985), memory (R. C. Anderson, Reynolds, Schallert, & Goetz, 1977), and strategic processing (Alexander & Judy, 1988; Garner, 1987).

Because of the primacy of reading-specific studies during this period, an extensive literature on text-based factors arose, particularly in relation to comprehension. Writings on story grammar, text cohesion, text structure, and text genres proliferated (Armbruster, 1984; Mandl, Stein, & Trabasso, 1984; Meyer, 1975; Taylor & Beach, 1984). Further, the research activities of this period demonstrated that students' knowledge could be significantly modified by the implementation of strategies (i.e., intentional and effortful procedures) that could be enhanced through direct intervention, training, or explicit instruction (Paris & Winograd, 1990; Pressley, Goodchild, Fleet, Zajchowski, & Evans, 1989; Weinstein, Goetz, & Alexander, 1988). The expanding body of strategy research from this period targeted a spectrum of general text-processing strategies, including summarization, mapping, self-questioning, and predicting (Brown, Campione, & Day, 1981; Hansen, 1981; Raphael & Wonnacott, 1985; Tierney, Readence, & Dishner, 1990). There was also consideration of instructional environments and pedagogical techniques that contributed to improved comprehension of text (Duffy, Roehler, Meloth, & Vavrus, 1986; Lysynchuk, Pressley, D'Ailly, Smith, & Cake, 1989; Pearson, 1984).

Rival Views

Among the most vocal critics of the information-processing approach to reading research were those who held to a more naturalistic and holistic view of reading (e.g., F. Smith, 1985). Many of the psycholinguists who had fueled the "reading as natural process" movement were significant forces in this rival perspective. However, there were several important distinctions between this iteration of the natural movement and its predecessor. For one, there was a shift away from the neurological or physiological arguments central to that earlier period and more concern for naturalism in the materials and procedures used to teach reading. One reason for this shift was an influx of literature and writing researchers into the reading community who were more interested in the unity within the language arts than in any potential dissimilarities. The expanding literature on the common bases of reading and writing was indicative of this integrated view (Spivey & King, 1989; Tierney, Soter, O'Flahavan, & McGinley, 1989), as were the studies on discussion (Alvermann & Hayes, 1989; Bloome & Green, 1984; Heath, 1982).

Characteristic of this rival view was an increased concern for the aesthetic of reading rather than for its rational aspects. The writings of Louise Rosenblatt, especially her classic treatise *The Reader, the Text, the Poem: The Transactional Theory of the Literary Work* (1978/1994), helped to frame several decades of literacy research around the notion of reader stances or responses to text (e.g., Britton, 1982; Cox & Many, 1992; Fish, 1980). On one side of this characterization was the aesthetic stance, or lived-through experience that arose from the reader's personal and emotional connection with the text. On the other side was the efferent stance, where attention was directed toward the "residue" of text engagement (Rosenblatt, 1978/1994, p. 23) or the information or knowledge that resulted. The contrast between the aesthetic and efferent stances Rosenblatt described had the effect of casting learning from text, central to the information-processing orientation, in a less favorable light and countered the seemingly analytic, less personal perspective on reading forwarded by cognitive researchers (Benton, 1983; Britton, 1982; Rosenblatt, 1938/1995). In effect, the more valued goal was to lose oneself *in* the text and not specifically to learn *from* it. For those who espoused this goal, a "learning from text" perspective transformed a natural literary, aesthetic experience into an unnatural, overly analytic act.

The Era of Sociocultural Learning (1986–1995)

Conditions for Change

As the mid-1980s came along, there were indications that the reading community was positioned for further change. The explanatory adequacy of the computer metaphor that had guided the information-processing research of the previous decade was perceived as diminishing, even by those in the field of artificial intelligence who had fostered this metaphor (J. R. Anderson, Reder, & Simon, 1996). For instance, within cognitive psychology, the earlier information-processing approach was replaced by a constructivist theory that acknowledged learning as individualistic, while rejecting the mechanistic and computerlike aspects of learning implicit in this stance (Reynolds et al., 1996).

This shift in emphasis may have come to pass as the applications of the information-processing approach in such areas as expert systems development and classroom training programs were seen to have less-than-ideal outcomes. The expert systems that were designed to imitate human decision-making processes (e.g., Clancey, 1983) did not always live up to their claims (Chipman, 1993). In the realm of reading education, the application of information-processing theory in cognitive training programs also proved less promising than anticipated, which engendered doubt as to the feasibility of these training approaches (Harris, 1996). Many students failed to benefit from the explicit instruction in strategies or components of reading that was intended to improve their text-based learning. For some students, no improvements were produced by this instruction, while for others, the benefits did not endure or transfer (Paris, Wasik, & Turner, 1991). Although the prior era of information-processing researchers had embraced general "laws" of text processing, these laws did not appear to account for the behaviors and results seen in specific applications, such as with particular populations, with different types of textual materials, and in variable classroom conditions (Paris et al., 1991).

A further force for change was the increased influence of alternative perspectives and research traditions speaking from outside the realm of cognitive psychology. Writings in social and cultural anthropology (Heath, 1983; Lave, 1988; Rogoff, 1990) provided a new viewpoint for literacy researchers, as well as those in the larger educational research community. These writings sparked a growing acceptance in the literacy community of the ethnographic and qualitative modes of inquiry advocated in social and cultural anthropology. Along with these modes of inquiry came the practice of studying literacy with naturally occurring texts read in natural settings, including homes and workplaces (R. C. Anderson, Wilson, & Fielding, 1988). These new approaches brought the methodology of literacy research more in line with the holistic and aesthetic school of thought. Reflecting this shift in emphasis, the *Journal of Reading Behavior* became first the *Journal of Reading Behavior: Journal of Literacy* in 1991 and then the *Journal of Literacy Research* in 1996. That is, the behavioral orientation toward reading of the 1950s and 1960s, reflected in the title for the journal of the National Reading Conference for many years thereafter, was fully abandoned in favor of a more integrated designation at the beginning of the 1990s.

Guiding View

As a result of the aforementioned forces, group orientations came to replace the more individualistic focus in learning and instruction seen in the prior era (Alexander, Murphy, & Woods, 1996). Literacy research now sought to capture the shared understanding of the *many* rather than the private knowledge of the *one*. From detection of the universal laws of learning, the goal became the description of the "ways of knowing" unique to particular social, cultural, and educational groups. The shared literacy experiences advocated in the aesthetic stance of the prior era were enthusiastically taken up, extended, and more broadly accepted with this adoption of social and cultural perspectives on literacy learning. The dominant perspective during this time became the view of learning as a sociocultural, collaborative experience (Alexander, 1996; Reynolds et al., 1996), and of the learner as a member of a learning community (Brown & Campione, 1990). The widespread popularity of such concepts as cognitive apprenticeship, shared cognition, and social constructivism during this time period are evidence of the power of this view.

Resulting Principles

In this era of literacy research, a number of researchers made the sociocultural nature of schools and classrooms the focus of their efforts, developing instructional procedures that engendered optimal social interchanges in the classroom (e.g., Bereiter & Scardamalia, 1989; Palincsar & Brown, 1984). Teachers, in these approaches, played the essential role of facilitator or guide (Rogoff & Gauvain, 1986), with the scaffolding provided by the teacher diminishing in proportion to the students' increasing knowledge, interest, and strategic abilities in a particular area (e.g., Alexander, 1997b; Brown & Palincsar, 1989). By gradually removing their direction, teachers were assumed to help readers develop self-direction and autonomy (Deci & Ryan, 1991). In effect, literacy development was conceptualized as an apprenticeship (Collins, Brown, & Newman, 1989), with teachers serving as mentors.

Further, the new awareness of the salience of social and contextual contributions to learning was evident in the proliferation of such terms as *learning communities* (Brown & Campione, 1990), *socially shared cognition* (Resnick, Levine, & Teasley, 1991), *distributed cognition* (Salomon, 1993), *shared expertise* (Brown & Palincsar, 1989), *guided participation* (Rogoff, 1990), *situated action* (Greeno & Moore, 1993), or *anchored instruction* (Cognition and Technology Group at Vanderbilt, 1990). As these new terms suggest, the social nature of literacy acts was certainly a centerpiece of this era. For instance, there were researchers such as Judith Green and colleagues who wrote extensively about literacy as a social process occurring within a unique context (Bloome & Green, 1984; Green & Dixon, 1993; Green & Meyer, 1991). Others during this era focused more on the cultural nature of literacy, often through the lens of underrepresented populations (Au, 1993; Moll & González, 1994).

Overall, most members of the literacy research community agreed that schooling, at least, was a social and cultural phenomenon, along with its resultant knowledge (e.g., Cognition and Technology Group at Vanderbilt, 1996; Lave, 1988; Rogoff, 1990). Schools clearly functioned as social institutions centered on the interactions of students and teachers, and classrooms were social communities nested within those institutions. Designed to serve socially contrived goals, schools operated as unique socially sanctioned contexts in which students were to build the requisite knowledge base for our postindustrialized societies (e.g., Perret-Claremont, Perret, & Bell, 1980).

Rival Views

Although the predominant orientation during this particular era emphasized social interactions and a valuing of context, there were two rival and contrasting perspectives operating in this timeframe that merit consideration. The first of those perspectives, associated with situativity or situated action (Clancey, 1983; Greeno & Moore, 1993), placed far more significance on the power of the immediate context than most socioculturalists. Those holding this view questioned the mental representation of unfolding events and were invested in the study of real-time interactions. Thus, for these researchers, it was the process of knowing and not knowledge that mattered. While this particular perspective was especially evident in science and mathematics education (e.g., Greeno & the Middle School Mathematics Through Applications Project Group, 1998), it did not hold particular sway within the literacy community.

The second perspective, in contrast, was invested in achieving a deeper and more sophisticated understanding of knowledge in text-based learning. This investment was manifested in several ways. For one, reviews of the knowledge terms used by literacy researchers and in broader educational contexts (Alexander, Schallert, & Hare, 1991; de Jong & Ferguson-Hessler, 1996; Greene & Ackerman, 1995) revealed that knowledge was not a singular construct but existed in diverse forms and interactive dimensions (Paris, Lipson, & Wixson, 1983; Prawat, 1989). For another, there was a growing interest in how disciplinary traditions affected reading and learning in different academic domains (Alexander, 1998b; Nolen, Johnson-Crowley, & Wineburg, 1994; Stahl, Hynd, Glynn, & Carr, 1996). Another line of inquiry in this area considered how students' existing knowledge could be an impediment to what they understood and remembered when reading (Alexander, 1998c; Guzzetti & Hynd, 1998; Vosniadou, 1994). Research on persuasion also provided insight into the possible negative role of preexisting knowledge (Alexander, Murphy, Buehl, & Sperl, 1997; Chambliss, 1995; Garner & Hansis, 1994). Specifically, those who approached arguments and evidence presented in text with little relevant knowledge or with a strong opinion proved more resistant to the author's message.

The Era of Engaged Learning (1996–2005)

Conditions for Change

As the 1990s moved along, there were forces at work that boded a change in the way learners and learning were perceived and studied within the literacy community. Those forces led to changing perceptions of text, readers, and the reading process. Prior to this period, texts were generally defined as printed materials (e.g., books, magazines) read in a linear fashion (Wade & Moje, 2000). Further, the readers targeted in the research were most often young children acquiring the ability to decode and comprehend written language or older students struggling with the demands of traditional text-based learning (Hiebert & Taylor, 2000; Pigott & Barr, 2000). Moreover, outside the concern for readers' efferent or aesthetic response to literature or the creation of a stimulating print-rich learning environment, there was little regard for motivation in the form of readers' goals, interests, and involvement in the learning experience (Oldfather & Wigfield, 1996). However, several conditions conspired to change these typical perceptions of text, reader, and reading, ushering in a new era of reading research.

First, with the growing presence of hypermedia and hypertext, the reading and broader literacy community began to consider the effects of the nature and form of these nonlinear and less traditional forms of text on students' reading and writing (Alexander, Kulikowich, & Jetton, 1994; Bolter, 1991). The term *nonlinear text* refers to discourse that does not have a specified order in which it must be read; electronic versions of nonlinear text (e.g., hypertext or hypermedia) are typically accompanied by a database management system that guides or prompts readers to linked informational sites and sources (Gillingham, Young, & Kulikowich, 1994). This influx of hypermedia and hypertext became coupled with an increased attention to classroom discourse and its role in students' academic development (Alvermann, Commeyras, Young, Randall, & Hinson, 1997). Researchers considered the form and content of that discourse and its relation to reading performance, as well as to subject-matter learning (Jetton & Alexander, 1998). Collectively, the interest in hypermedia and classroom discourse extended notions of text beyond traditional and into alternative forms (Alexander & Jetton, 2003).

Second, during this time, the rich and impressive body of literature on motivation that had been formed over the past several decades found its way into the reading community (Guthrie & Wigfield, 2000). This infusion of motivation research led to the consideration of such critical factors as learners' interests, goals, and self-efficacy beliefs, as well as their self-regulation and active participation in reading and text-based learning (Almasi, McKeown, & Beck, 1996; Hidi, 1990; Schallert, Meyer, & Fowler, 1995; Schraw, Bruning, & Svoboda, 1995; Turner, 1995). These motivational factors were not considered in isolation but were studied in relation to other factors such as students' knowledge, strategic abilities, and sociocultural background and features of the learning context. The result of this infusion of motivation theory and research into the reading literature was a reconceptualization of the student as an engaged or motivated reader (Guthrie & Wigfield, 2000). This motivational focus was especially apparent in the activities of the National Reading Research Center funded by the U.S. Department of Education.

Finally, for many reasons, including a deepening understanding of human development, the increased longevity of the population, and the mounting demands of functioning within a postindustrial, information-technological age, the literacy community's view of reading shifted (Alexander et al., 1996; Reinking, McKenna, Labbo, & Kieffer, 1998). Throughout the previous eras of reading research, activities, debates, and stances revolved primarily around the acquisition of reading processes and whether reading development could best be understood as mastering a discrete set of skills or as a more natural unfolding of competence fostered by meaningful, aesthetic engagement. What became apparent, however, was that neither orientation toward reading effectively captured the complexity of reading or recognized the changing nature of reading as individuals continue their academic development (Alexander, 2003). In other words, it became increasingly difficult to ignore that reading development relates not only to the young or struggling reader but also to readers of all abilities and ages. The earlier dichotomization of reading into "learning to read" and "reading to learn" stages (Chall, 1995) was shifting back to a more integrated and developmental perspective.

Guiding View

The guiding view of the learner during this era highlighted the importance of the blending of affect, knowledge, and strategic processing that characterized the nature of the learner's interaction with the learning situation, with this blending being termed *engagement* (Guthrie & Wigfield, 2000). The label "engaged" captured several of the aforementioned forces that shaped perceptions of reading and informed research toward the end of the 20th century. For one, it acknowledged that reading is not confined to traditional print materials but extends to the texts students encounter daily, including the nonlinear, interactive, dynamic, and visually complex materials conveyed via audiovisual media (Alexander & Jetton, 2003). It also entails the discussions that occur around both traditional and alternative texts (Alvermann et al., 1997; Wade, Thompson, & Watkins, 1994).

Of course, understanding how students learn by means of alternative forms of text was still emergent and the nature of reading online remained a topic of controversy (Alexander, Graham, & Harris, 1998; Lankshear & Knobel, 2003; Wade & Moje, 2000). As our history in dealing with other nonprint modes of communication (e.g., television; Neuman, 1988) indicated, there was indeed a great deal to learn about the potentials of alternative, nonlinear media. For example, as these alternative forms of text became more prevalent, literacy researchers and practitioners began to consider possible implications for such fundamental concepts as learning, memory, and strategic processing (Bolter, 1991; Garner & Gillingham, 1996; Goldman, 1996; Salomon, Perkins, & Globerson, 1991). Those who wanted to forward claims about *new literacies* (Leu, Kinzer, Coiro, & Cammack, 2004) not only acknowledged this need for closer examination of online reading, but also perceived the distinctions between the processing of traditional and hypermedia text to be so extensive as to require fundamentally new forms of reading knowledge, skills, and strategies. They strove to open the door on alternative texts and text processing to a degree not seen previously. An additional research area that began to be recognized was the need to examine how pedagogical techniques and learning environments could be adapted to assist not only readers who struggle with traditional text, but also those who get lost in hyperspace (Alexander et al., 1994; Lawless & Kulikowich, 1996; Reinking et al., 1998).

Engagement also pertained directly to students' meaningful participation in text-based learning. The research on reader engagement further established that learners are more than passive receptacles of information (Guthrie & Wigfield, 2000). They are active and willful participants in the construction of knowledge (Alexander, 1997a; Reed & Schallert, 1993; Reed, Schallert, & Goetz, 1993). However, the picture of engagement emerging during this decade deviated from prior sociocultural interpretations in terms of the focus on the individual learner within the educational environment (Alexander & Murphy, 1999). In particular, while the learner still resided and operated within a sociocultural context, attention was once more turned to the individual working to create a personally meaningful and socially valuable body of knowledge. Thus, the portrait of the engaged reader framed by the research had both individualistic and collective dimensions, a reconciliation of the information-processing and sociocultural perspectives of past decades (Guthrie, McGough, Bennett, & Rice, 1996; Guthrie, Van Meter, et al., 1996).

A further consequence of this view of the learner as actively engaged in the process of learning was a rekindled interest in strategic processing. In contrast to the habituated skills of earlier eras, the effective use of strategies was understood to require reflection, choice, and deliberate execution on the part of the learner (Alexander et al., 1998). Strategy use by its nature calls for engaged learners who are willing to put forth effort, and who can knowledgeably respond to the demands of a particular situation. The body of literature on learning strategies, particularly reading comprehension strategies, grew in these years in response to this new view of the engaged learner (Pressley, 2002).

Finally, the view of learners as actively engaged allowed for a return to the developmental perspective on reading. Developmentally, individuals were viewed as continually in the process of learning to read and had a direct role to play in their literacy growth. From this vantage point, students are not yet complete as readers when they can demonstrate basic linguistic skills or fluency in reading. Rather, they continue to grow as readers as their linguistic knowledge, subject-matter knowledge, strategic capabilities, and motivations expand and mature (Alexander, 1997b). This developmental perspective on reading extended concern beyond the early elementary years into adolescence and adulthood. Notably, the RAND Reading Study Group (2002), in its publication, *Reading for Understanding: Toward an R&D Program in Reading Comprehension*, described learning to read well as "a long-term developmental process" (p. xiii) and recognized the need for research that "will contribute to better theories of reading development" (p. 29).

Resulting Principles

Several principles appeared to guide this decade of reading research. One of those principles pertained to the complexity and multidimensional nature of reading. Specifically, notions that reading is cognitive, aesthetic, sociocultural, *or* affective in nature were set aside. Instead, all these forces were seen to be actively and interactively involved in reading development (Alexander & Jetton, 2000). For example, there is a significant relation between learners' knowledge and their interests (Alexander, Jetton, & Kulikowich, 1995; Csikszentmihalyi, 1990). Similarly, encountering personally relevant texts was seen as promoting deeper student engagement in learning (Guthrie & Wigfield, 2000).

Another guiding principle of this era was that students encounter a range of textual materials, both traditional and alternative, that should be reflected in their learning environment (Wade & Moje, 2000). Although their views on the merits of technology differed, educational researchers acknowledged that technology had transformed learning and teaching (Cuban, 1993; Postman, 1993; Scardamalia, Bereiter, McLean, Swallow, & Woodruff, 1989). Computer-based technologies were now commonplace in the lives of K-12 students in postindustrial societies. These students regularly surfed the Web, e-mailed, and communicated via text messages—acts that changed the face of information processing and human communication (Alexander & Knight, 1993; Garner & Gillingham, 1996). This technological revolution produced an unimaginable proliferation of information sources and text types. This proliferation further complicated perceptions of reading and placed new demands on readers (Gillingham et al., 1994). For instance, effective reading now was seen to include assessing credibility, identifying possible biases, analyzing persuasive or literary techniques, and locating and selecting optimal sources (Rouet, Vidal-Abarca, Erboul, & Millogo, 2001). However, these new technologies also held promise for reading in what Reinking et al. (1998) called a post-typographic world.

Because reading was viewed as multidimensional in character, with significant relations among readers' knowledge, strategic processing, and motivation, simple models or theories based on a "learning to read" and "reading to learn" distinction needed to be supplanted with more complex, reciprocal models of reading development (Alexander, 2003). Specifically, investigation of the initial stages of reading acquisition could not be isolated from the issues emerging when comprehension of texts became the focus. This required a genuinely developmental theory of reading, spanning preliteracy reading readiness to proficient adult reading. This developmental vision of reading was reflected in the report of the RAND Reading Study Group (2002): "a vision of proficient readers who are capable of acquiring new knowledge and understanding new concepts, are capable of applying textual information appropriately, and are capable of being engaged in the reading process and reflecting on what is read" (p. xiii).

Rival Views

In this era, the view in the literacy research community of the learner as a motivated, engaged knowledge seeker and of the learning process as developmental and anchored in a sociocultural context stood in sharp contrast to a trend that had been gaining momentum over the previous several decades. We chose to label this rival perspective as "learning as reconditioning." The choice of the term *reconditioning* is meant to signal several significant features of this rival undercurrent. First, as in the early conditioning period, this rival stance was invested in the identification, teaching, and remediation of the subskills or components underlying reading acquisition (e.g., Foorman, Francis, Fletcher, Schatschneider, & Mehta, 1998). In addition, the emphasis in this rival orientation was on beginning or struggling readers who had yet to master these reading fundamentals. In many ways, "why Johnny *still* can't read" was a suitable anthem for adherents to this strong minority perspective.

Unlike the earlier "learning as conditioning" era, the concentration on reading subskills and components at this point was less driven by theory than by other forces. One of those forces was the drive toward accountability, primarily in the form of high-stakes testing and the push for national standards (Paris & Urdan, 2000). From the stance of learning as engagement, assessments that fostered knowledge seeking around challenging, valuable, and meaningful problems and issues would be warranted (American Psychological Association Presidential Task Force on Psychology in Education, 1993). However, responses to such problems were not readily measurable or as predictive of reading difficulties in the early years. Moreover, the effort to institute national standards that seemingly prescribed the content and skills learners should have acquired at given points in their school careers necessarily constrained the views of learners and learning (Paris & Urdan, 2000).

Another difference between the conditioning and reconditioning perspectives was the alliances each represented. Specifically, the investment in basic skills and components of reading gained support from researchers in special education and others who worked with struggling readers (Foorman et al., 1998; Torgesen, 1998, 1999). These researchers were joined by those engaged in neuroscience. In particular, advancements in neuroimaging techniques allowed researchers to examine the neurological structures and processes of struggling readers and readers with special needs (Shaywitz et al., 2000). On the basis of such neuroimaging studies, still in a formative stage, researchers attempted to pinpoint the specific neurobiological or physiological patterns related to specific reading outcomes or documented conditions (Pugh et al., 1997; Shaywitz, Fletcher, Holahan, & Shaywitz, 1992).

The Era of Performance-Oriented Learning (2006–2015)

Conditions for Change

In the prior iteration of this historical analysis chapter, we ventured to describe the conditions for change, resulting principles, and rival views operating within the most recent period and to find a suitable designation for that period. In hindsight, we were relatively successful at those goals, although we are now in a better position to adjust and elaborate on what we originally labeled the "Era of Self-Directed Learning." For instance, we previously identified a coalescence of internal and external conditions that shaped this recent era. The first of those conditions pertained to the expanding presence of technologies both in and out of schools, and the complications arising from living in a hypermedia age (Leu et al., 2004; Leu, O'Byrne, Zawilinski, McVerry, & Everett-Cocapardo, 2009). The second was the unrelenting obsession with testing within schools in the U.S., as exemplified by the growing popularity of standards-based assessment, and the effects of this obsession on the perceptions and intentions of students (Alexander, in press; Valli, Croninger, Chambliss, Graeber, & Buese, 2008). After all, this was the period that witnessed the development and launch of the Common Core State Standards (CCSS) Initiative, including the English Language Arts Standards (National Governors Association Center for Best Practices, Council of Chief State School Officers, 2010) that attempted to reframe what is taught and what is assessed in U.S. classrooms, addressing reading, writing, and speaking/listening as three distinct domains under the English Language Arts and Literacy umbrella.

The third condition we described sat at the intersection of the other two. It involved rising concerns about the ability of the school-age population to think deeply or critically about information, whether that information was contained in their textbooks, encountered on the Internet, or shared through expanding social media (e.g., Facebook, Twitter; Bereiter & Scardamalia, 2005). We see this concern reflected in the CCSS English Language Arts and Literacy Standards, for instance, where there is frequent mention of students' ability to evaluate claims and evidence encountered in text.

To those previously identified conditions, we would add a fourth—a rise in minority, immigrant, or second-language populations in the United States. For example, according to *U.S. News and World Report* (Camera, 2016), the population of first- and second-generation immigrant children in the United States grew by 51% from 1995 to 2014. Further, in its report on the Condition of Education, the National Center for Education Statistics (McFarland et al., 2017) stated that the percentage of public school students who were English language learners (ELLs) rose to 9.4% in the 2014–2015 academic year.

Guiding View

Collectively, these conditions contributed to significant shifts in reading research and practice that led us to characterize this period as the era of performance-oriented learning. We purposefully chose the descriptor *performance* because of its multiple connotations, which allowed us to consolidate several distinct lines of research and classroom-based initiatives. One of those lines of research involved the infusion of technology as a performance-oriented scaffold in instruction and assessment, not only as a medium for delivery (e.g., e-books and e-readers) or to assist those with specific reading needs (e.g., Morgan, 2013), but also to include elements in reading assessments (e.g., avatars, animations, or sound) that are not possible with traditional print (Sabatini, O'Reilly, Halderman, & Bruce, 2014). Such enhancements are being used in high-stakes reading tests such as those developed by the Partnership for Assessment of Readiness for College and Career (PARCC) and Smarter Balanced Assessment Consortium (SBAC), intended to assess the attainment of the objectives outlined in the CCSS, as well as the National Assessment of Education Progress (NAEP) and Programme for International Student Assessment (PISA). These tests incorporate scenario-based performance tasks, which require students to demonstrate their comprehension through the products they create (Sabatini et al., 2014).

Another manifestation of a performance orientation was apparent in the growing number of research programs that focused on critical, analytical talk and disciplinary reading. Performance in this case had to do with students' support of claims and arguments made during discussions or in writing. For instance, there is the work of Anderson, Chinn, Murphy, Wilkinson, and others who sought to raise the quality of talk occurring in classrooms to ensure that deeper comprehension and significant learning would result (Chinn & Anderson, 1998; Kim, Anderson, Nguyen-Jahiel, & Archididou, 2007; Murphy, Wilkinson, & Soter, 2011; Murphy, Wilkinson, Soter, Hennessey, & Alexander, 2009). Similarly, there were intervention programs in history and science for teachers and for students that aimed to improve students' ability to deal with disciplinary text structures (Moje, Tucker-Raymond, Varelas, & Pappas, 2007; Wijekumar & Meyer, 2006) and to enhance their abilities to interrogate the ideas forwarded in those texts (Felton & Kuhn, 2007; Maggioni, VanSledright, & Alexander, 2009).

Critical and analytic reading is evidentiary in nature (Wilkinson, Soter, & Murphy, 2010). There is an old Yiddish proverb that loosely translates: "For example is not proof." The ability to talk about text, to offer an illustration or example from one's own experience or to forward an opinion, is not in and of itself proof that text of any sort has been adequately understood or comprehended. Bloom's taxonomy aside, evaluation in the form of unsubstantiated opinion does not require higher forms of cognitive thought than inferring an unstated relation or even finding a specific fact within a complex piece of text (Bereiter & Scardamalia, 2005). The ability to offer reasoned and reasonable justification does not occur spontaneously or without provocation for many developing readers (Alexander et al., 2011). Critical and analytic reading and evidentiary reasoning, as with other complex and demanding ways of thinking, are more apt to take shape under the tutelage of more competent others and when the value of such analytic processing is mirrored in the time dedicated to it and the assessments administered within school settings (Garner, 1990; Murphy et al., 2009).

The concern for critical and analytic thinking that marked this period was also tied to disciplinary reading and to the structure and evidentiary base within those readings. For example, the literature on content-area reading and expository text processing made it evident that there are features of domain exposition that can be challenging for students. It is not solely the structural or linguistic demands (e.g., specialized terminology, complex paragraph structures) of disciplinary or informational text that are at issue (Ozuru, Dempsey, & McNamara, 2009; VanSledright, 2002). It is also that the role texts play in varied disciplines or domains can be markedly different, as can the disciplinary standards for what constitutes viable evidence (Alexander et al., 2011). Further, in order for students to perform well in history, chemistry, geometry, or other content domains, they must be able to navigate the often multimodal texts associated with those domains (Serafini, 2011). Multimodal texts include varied representations (e.g., pictures, graphs, or formula) nested in the written documents, and the effects of those representations on comprehension garnered much attention during this era (Ainsworth, 2014; Cromley et al., 2013; Mayer, 2014).

Finally, during this era there was an expanding interest in serving the needs of ELLs, as well as those who find the academic language of schools and domains unfamiliar and challenging (Snow, Lawrence, & White, 2009). This increased attention was undoubtedly sparked at least in part by the requirement written into law (No Child Left Behind Act, 2001) that schools were responsible for the performance of subgroups of students on required reading assessments, and the mandate to have every student reading at grade-level proficiency by 2014. In their analysis of *Reading Research Quarterly*'s 50 years of publication, Reutzel and Mohr (2015) noted a "decidedly sociocultural turn" in the articles appearing in the journal (p. 18). Evidence of this turn was the sharp increase in articles in the journal specifically dealing with ELLs and minority students. As one example of this growing literature, Reyes and Azuara (2008) followed the biliteracy development of 12 young Mexican immigrant children to understand what features of different cultural contexts helped or hindered their development.

Similarly, Silverman and colleagues (2014) looked at bilingual students in grades 3 to 5, as well as their monolingual classmates. These researchers focused their attention on elementary teachers' instructional practices around vocabulary and comprehension and whether those practices differed as a consequence of students' language status (i.e., monolingual or bilingual). Other researchers have centered their attention on minority students and the way in which the language and culture of schools can work against learning in other content domains (Moje, 2007), creating a disconnect between students' literate lives outside versus inside schools. (Alvermann, 2008). We see this burgeoning interest in bilingual readers as further illustrative of the performance orientation that prevailed during this era—the press to enhance these learners' literacy development and their ability to think and reason critically. There are alternative perspectives regarding bilingual and multilingual learners that arose during the latter phases of this era, which we discuss within "Rival Views."

Resulting Principles

The convergence of factors that framed this era helped forge several basic principles that undergirded this focus on performance-oriented learning. First and foremost, there was a reconceptualization of reading competence (Fox, 2009; Fox, Dinsmore, & Alexander, 2010). This new conceptualization demands more of readers than basic processing and comprehension skills (Alexander & the Disciplined Reading and Learning Research Laboratory [DRLRL], 2010). Rather, it requires learners to demonstrate a deeper understanding of textual content through their discussions or writings. Moreover, this reconceptualization encompasses competent readers' predictable and appropriate manifestation of critical and analytic thought and evidentiary-based reasoning relevant to the tasks and texts at hand. This expanded view builds on the contention of Alexander and the DRLRL (2010) that "reading competence, as with competence in any domain, is marked by adaptive and consistent (i.e., what we identify as higher order) thinking . . . that is principled in its focus and disciplined in its processing" (p. 266).

For the domain of reading, competence would thus entail a particular configuration of readers' knowledge of text structures and conventions, knowledge of the topic or domain that the text addresses, strategies for interrogating the content or claims made within the text, and the motivation to put forth the effort that this level of processing demands (Alexander, 1997b). Further, competent reading, so described, would require readers' sensitivity to the form and quality of evidence that given questions framed within certain domains (e.g., history, science, mathematics) would warrant (Moje, 2007; Shanahan & Shanahan, 2008). Learners' awareness of, selection of, and movement toward appropriate goals are thus key elements in their competent reading performance.

The perspective on performance-oriented learning highlights learners' understanding of the task situation and all that it entails. It is not enough to assume that learners are doing what the task directs. Instead, how learners interpret that task and their personal intentions relative to whatever they may be directed to do becomes part of the performance calculus (Kulikowich & Alexander, 2010; McCrudden, Magliano, & Schraw, 2010). In effect, it is also learners' intentionality that matters in this new era. In this way, the foregrounding of learners' goals differs in this period from the attention received in prior eras. Specifically, the focus is now on a system of constructs that learners bring to the reading experience—epistemic beliefs, perceptions, intentions, and corresponding goals—in interaction with the affordances provided by the particular object of knowledge and the learning context.

Yet another principle to emerge from this era pertains to the interface between competent learning and digital and hypermedia technologies (Gee & Hayes, 2011). Specifically, what marks competence in this instance is not whether smart technologies are used or not, but whether those technologies are used "smartly"—that is, in a manner that contributes to learning rather than inhibits or distracts from it (Sana, Weston, & Cepeda, 2013). We consider this particular principle in more detail in the discussion of rival views of learning and learning and revisit it in our speculations about the ensuing decade.

Rival Views

The perspective on technologies just mentioned as belonging to the principles operative in the performance-oriented era is distinct from the position of those promoting new or digital literacies (Coiro, Knobel, Lankshear, & Leu, 2008; Kellner, 2001). For those individuals, there is no unified view of reading that can encompass both traditional and digital texts or for reading offline and online. Consequently, there is no unified view of reading competence that can be articulated from the standpoint of new literacies. Instead, the argument is that the demands of reading and learning online are so unique that, by default, there must be knowledge, skills, and strategies that apply uniquely to hypermedia texts.

It remains to be seen whether those who champion the notion of new literacies will be able to identify truly unique forms of textual knowledge and processes that are not manifest in any form in the competent reading of traditional text. For now, we remain with those who do not dismiss the growing presence and power of the Internet or hypermedia technologies, but perceive the variability of processing across text types as iterations of already existing knowledge and processes rather than as unique forms—as variations on a theme rather than an entirely new melody (Afflerbach & Cho, 2009). At a minimum, we argue against creating a false, seemingly universal dichotomy between reading offline or online, since whether reading materials accessed digitally differ only in the mode of delivery or involve elaborate technological features foreign to print can vary dramatically.

Yet another rival view of learning grew in strength in this era with the ascendance of test-driven education. In essence, those who were inclined toward a view of learning as a set of basic processes and skills were still present in the research community (Foorman et al., 2006). The simple model of reading (Gough & Tunmer, 1986), with its diagnostically oriented separation of reading into decoding and oral language comprehension, remained a widely used and studied explanatory paradigm (e.g., Cartwright, 2007; Vellutino, Tunmer, Jaccard, & Chen, 2007; Verhoeven & van Leeuwe, 2008). Along with the continued stress placed on testing and students' test performance, another factor contributing to the resurgence of this orientation toward learning was the growing popularity of cognitive neuroscience and its efforts to pinpoint the brain regions and brain functions associated with text processing among normally functioning and identified populations (e.g., dyslexics or learning disabled populations). The level of funding dedicated to this line of research also fueled interest in such research endeavors, although the educational implications remain limited (Schlaggar & McCandliss, 2007).

There is yet another rival view that arose during this performance-oriented era that warrants consideration. Specifically, there were those who felt that the long prevailing perspective on bilingual and multilingual learners, represented by such labels as "English language learners" (ELLs) or "limited English proficient students" (LEPs), failed to give due consideration to the home languages and cultural understandings of these children (García, Kleifgen, & Falchi, 2008; Koyama & Menken, 2013; Menken, 2013). Those holding to this rival view argue that the labels of ELL or LEP place the emphasis only on English proficiency, disregarding the merits of these children's existing bilingual and bicultural lives, and undermining the message that the educational mission for these students should be to support the development of their bilingualism. For that reason, there has been a concerted effort within the literacy community to refer to those whose heritage language is other than English as *emergent bilinguals* or *multilinguals*.

The Era of Personalized Learning (2016–Present)

It is always risky to characterize the period that is currently taking shape, but we will endeavor to do so, nonetheless. However, because this emergent era is still quite young, we will not attempt to forward principles or consider rival views. We were aided in this speculative analysis by the fact that the first author was recently called upon to imagine the future of learning as it pertains to educational psychology. Specifically, on the 125-year anniversary of the American Educational Research Association and the creation of the *Journal of Educational Psychology*, Alexander (2017) projected trends in educational research and practice occurring 25 years into the future. What shaped this image of the future were several significant developments that have already taken root. Thus, in considering this emergent era, we turned to those same transformational developments as the conditions for change. We did so because we believe they will cast a long shadow over reading research and practice in the coming years. Specifically, we will discuss information saturation, the inescapability of technology, and the personalization of interventions as the conditions of change.

As the label for this era suggests, one of the most salient effects of these conditions is personalization—the individualization of the processes and products of human learning. In the choice of the descriptor *personalization*, our intention is to project that reading research and instruction during the next decade will be positioned to pay even greater attention to the unique attributes and experiences of each learner. Owing to changing conditions in the world outside the classroom, the rapid developments in technology and methodologies being witnessed, and the trend in other fields, most notably medicine, away from global or generic treatments to those designed expressly for a particular person, we see growing evidence of personalization in the years to come. In what follows, we briefly address the aforementioned catalysts for this nascent era.

Changing Conditions

A slogan that effectively captures life in this information-saturation age is that "data never sleep." To illustrate that very point, one information management company observed that within the span of one minute,

- YouTube users upload 400 hours of new videos;
- Instagram users share 2,430,555 new photos;
- Snapchat users watch 6,944,444 videos; and
- Over 100,000 tweets are sent (DOMO, 2016).

What is also true is that new ways of generating and communicating information are continually being invented. It is not only this deluge of information with which today's learners must contend, but also the questionable veracity or quality of those data (Del Vicario et al., 2016; Mason, Boldrin, & Ariasi, 2010). As a consequence, attempting to separate the trivial from the significant and the accurate from the inaccurate in this continuous information flow is a Herculean task, one that is beyond the abilities or motivations of most learners, especially those who are still academic novices.

Further, personalization comes into play in this context because the individual learner is free to pick and choose what information she or he will access, what data will be communicated to others and in what form, and what standards of evidence (if any) will be applied in judging the truthfulness of whatever information is encountered (List, Alexander, & Stephens, 2016). It is safe to assume that today's learners encounter much more information outside than inside schools. Moreover, this "outside" information contributes to the perceptions and conceptions they bring into schools and to their academic reading, writing, and discussions (Heddy & Sinatra, 2013). A term like *constructivism*, which includes the inevitability that individuals shape or color whatever they see, hear, or read, and which has been so central to contemporary theories of learning and instruction, cannot fully capture the breadth of this personalization phenomenon. That is because this personalization is about not only the interpretation of what is encountered but also the orchestration of informational events that fuel those interpretations.

Technological Advancements

The information saturation just described has much to do with the role that technology and social media play in students' lives. In this decade, it will become increasingly important to take a much more critical look at technology's influence on learners and learning than has been witnessed to date. There are several reasons for this assertion. For one, educational researchers and practitioners owe it to students to be aware of the good *and* bad that come with any technology, not only academically, but also socially, motivationally, and neurologically (Gazzaley & Rosen, 2016). Issues such as poor calibration/self-monitoring, multitasking, distractibility, limited attention, loss of privacy, cyberbullying, and technology addiction are becoming frequent topics within the literature (Carrier, Rosen, Cheever, & Lim, 2015; Pea et al., 2012; Rosen, 2012; Whittaker & Kowalski, 2015). Such occurrences must be acknowledged and addressed, now and in the future. One great paradox of these new technologies, which relates to the theme of personalization, is that the more students are social media connected, the more they appear to lose touch with the physical environment around them and the people who inhabit that environment (Brooks, 2015).

Minimally, literacy researchers and practitioners need to be attuned to the fact that there are meaningful differences that arise when reading occurs in print rather than online (Singer & Alexander, 2017). Consequently, the question of when it is preferable to engage in print versus digital reading needs to be given more explicit attention within the literacy community. We appreciate that similar warnings have been directed toward technological innovations throughout history, from printed texts to chalkboards (Postman, 1993). Yet, there is one undeniable difference about these newer technologies that has never been the case before—individuals are rarely separated from them. In fact, they can now be carried on wrists and mounted on glasses. Through nanoscience, these technologies have been miniaturized to the point that they can be carried within instead of worn outside. As a result, scientists and innovators such as Elon Musk expect to achieve direct brain-computer interface in the near future (Winkler, 2017). When that occurs, no external device will be required and there will truly be no separation between students and their digital devices.

Personalized Data and Interventions

Although it is fair to assume that personalization will take on an entirely new meaning under those circumstances, the effects of such an "advancement" on learning and on reading cannot be predicted. However, given that we have called for critical analysis of technology, we would be remiss if we did not point out a potential boon of the technological advancements just described that will likely transform the way in which effective instruction is researched and delivered. This specific transformation is already underway in the field of medicine and relates to the personalization of diagnoses and treatments. Nanotechnology and the development of micro machines have afforded medicine the ability to secure continuous and highly detailed data on patients and to dispense exact dosages to targeted areas of the body (Brayner, Fiévet, & Coradin, 2013).

Analogously, there is the ability to gather increasingly more sophisticated cognitive, motivational, sociocultural, and behavioral data on students through advancements in data-gathering devices (Dunton et al., 2014; Hedeker, Mermelstein, Berbaum, & Campbell, 2009). As is already occurring within the medical field, there will be the opportunity to gather micro-level, detailed, and ongoing data relevant to students' literacy development and performance. Such data have the potential to push aside common data-gathering methods in reading (e.g., self-reports, think-alouds, interviews) as more simplistic or as complementary rather than primary. Further, these sophisticated data could potentially be used to craft personalized interventions that build on each student's particular strengths and documented needs. This suggests that prevailing notions of "best practices," including for reading, writing, and speaking, may need to be rethought. In effect, the idea that one broad intervention can effectively meet the needs of all students in a classroom regardless of their backgrounds and histories will require reevaluation. Putting the onus on teachers to provide differentiation that can accommodate the needs of every individual student while delivering a generalized curriculum aimed at having every student achieve the same instructional grade-level objectives at the same time has not proven to be a realistic expectation (Hansen, 2012).

Over the course of this emergent era, we anticipate more efforts to devise educational "treatments" that are more precisely targeted to those who would benefit the most, and selectively administered under the most favorable conditions. Without question, the success of these personalized interventions will rest on the quality of the data gathered and will demand the collaborative efforts of experts from multiple fields (e.g., developmental, educational, and social psychology; cognitive neuroscience; academic domains; educational measurement and statistics). The development of these interventions is likely to require a shift away from the idea that generalizability is the goal, and that all interventions should be capable of scaling up for wide-scale use. This may necessitate critical changes in the types of research paradigms that are seen as worthy of funding and as yielding significant contributions to the knowledge base about reading and literacy development.

Concluding Thoughts

Our purpose in undertaking this historical analysis of the past 60-plus years of reading research was to craft a vista through which to view current and future endeavors. Of course, such a retrospective—to say nothing of our attempts at prognostication—comes with no assurances.

Historical analysis, after all, is an interpretative science. However, a glance backward at where reading has been serves to remind us that today's research and practice have roots that run far and deep into the past. Even the seemingly new developments in the field of reading that have broken ground in the past 60 years cannot be entirely divorced from reading's historical roots. Indeed, many "new" movements or transformations are better understood as iterations of past movements or transformation. The treatment of reading as a more unique domain of research and practice or as a component of an integrated language arts system is one such iteration that we witnessed in this survey of reading's past and present. Moreover, it is essential to recognize that by paying our respects to that past, we may better understand the activities of the present and envision the paths for literacy research that lie ahead.

Note

1 This chapter is an adaptation of prior versions: "A Historical Perspective on Reading Research and Practice," in *Theoretical Models and Processes of Reading* (5th ed., pp. 33–68), edited by R. B. Ruddell and N. J. Unrau, 2004, Newark, DE: International Reading Association, Copyright © 2004; and "A Historical Perspective on Reading Research and Practice, Redux," in *Theoretical Models and Processes of Reading* (6th ed., pp. 3–46), edited by D. E. Alvermann, N. J. Unrau, and R. B. Ruddell, 2013, Newark, DE: International Reading Association, Copyright © 2013 by the International Reading Association.

References

Afflerbach, P., & Cho, B. (2009). Identifying and describing constructively responsive comprehension strategies in new and traditional forms of reading. In S. E. Israel & G. G. Duffy (Eds.), *Handbook of research on reading comprehension* (pp. 69–90). New York, NY: Routledge.

Ainsworth, S. (2014). The multiple representation principle in multimedia learning. In R. E. Mayer (Ed.), *Cambridge handbook of multimedia learning* (pp. 464–486). New York, NY: Cambridge University Press.

Alexander, P. A. (1996). The past, present, and future of knowledge research: A reexamination of the role of knowledge in learning and instruction [Editor's notes]. *Educational Psychologist, 31,* 89–92.

Alexander, P. A. (1997a). Knowledge-seeking and self-schema: A case for the motivational dimensions of exposition [Special issue]. *Educational Psychologist, 32,* 83–94.

Alexander, P. A. (1997b). Mapping the multidimensional nature of domain learning: The interplay of cognitive, motivational, and strategic forces. In M. L. Maehr & P. R. Pintrich (Eds.), *Advances in motivation and achievement* (Vol. 10, pp. 213–250). Greenwich, CT: JAI Press.

Alexander, P. A. (1998a). Knowledge and literacy: A transgenerational perspective. In T. Shanahan & F. Rodriguez-Brown (Eds.), *The forty-seventh yearbook of the National Reading Conference* (pp. 22–43). Chicago, IL: National Reading Conference.

Alexander, P. A. (1998b). The nature of disciplinary and domain learning: The knowledge, interest, and strategic dimensions of learning from subject-matter text. In C. Hynd (Ed.), *Learning from text across conceptual domains* (pp. 263–287). Mahwah, NJ: Lawrence Erlbaum Associates.

Alexander, P. A. (1998c). Positioning conceptual change within a model of domain literacy. In B. Guzzetti & C. Hynd (Eds.), *Perspectives on conceptual change* (pp. 55–76). Mahwah, NJ: Lawrence Erlbaum Associates.

Alexander, P. A. (2003). Profiling the developing reader: The interplay of knowledge, interest, and strategic processing. In C. M. Fairbanks, J. Worthy, B. Maloch, J. V. Hoffman, & D. L. Schallert (Eds.), *The fifty-first yearbook of the National Reading Conference* (pp. 47–65). Oak Creek, WI: National Reading Conference.

Alexander, P. A. (2017). Past as prologue: Educational psychology's legacy and progeny [Invited for the 125th anniversary of the American Psychological Association]. *Journal of Educational Psychology.* Retrieved from http://dx.doi.org/10.1037/edu0000200

Alexander, P. A. (in press). Information management versus knowledge building: Implications for learning and assessment in higher education. In O. Zlatkin-Troitschanskaia, M. Toepper, H. A. Pant, C. Lautenbach, & C. Kuhn (Eds.), *Assessment of learning outcomes in higher education: Cross-national comparisons and perspectives.* Dordrecht: Springer.

Alexander, P. A., Dinsmore, D. L., Fox, E., Grossnickle, E. M., Loughlin, S. M., Maggioni, L., . . . Winters, F. I. (2011). Higher-order thinking and knowledge: Domain-general and domain-specific trends and future directions. In G. Schraw & D. R. Robinson (Eds.), *Assessment of higher order thinking skills* (pp. 47–88). Charlotte, NC: Information Age.

Alexander, P. A., & the Disciplined Reading and Learning Research Laboratory. (2010). *The challenges of developing competent literacy in the 21st century.* Washington, DC: The National Academy of Sciences.

Alexander, P. A., & Fox, E. (2004). A historical perspective on reading research and practice. In R. B. Ruddell & N. J. Unrau (Eds.), *Theoretical models and processes of reading* (5th ed., pp. 33–68). Newark, DE: International Reading Association.

Alexander, P. A., & Fox, E. (2013). A historical perspective on reading research and practice, redux. In D. E. Alvermann, N. J. Unrau, & R. B. Ruddell (Eds.), *Theoretical models and processes of reading* (6th ed., pp. 3–46). Newark, DE: International Reading Association.

Alexander, P. A., Graham, S., & Harris, K. R. (1998). A perspective on strategy research: Progress and prospects. *Educational Psychology Review, 10*, 129–154.

Alexander, P. A., & Jetton, T. L. (2000). Learning from text: A multidimensional and developmental perspective. In M. L. Kamil, P. B. Mosenthal, P. D. Pearson, & R. Barr (Eds.), *Handbook of reading research* (Vol. 3, pp. 285–310). Mahwah, NJ: Lawrence Erlbaum Associates.

Alexander, P. A., & Jetton, T. L. (2003). Learning from traditional and alternative texts: New conceptualization for an information age. In A. Graesser, M. Gernsbacher, & S. Goldman (Eds.), *Handbook of discourse processes* (pp. 199–241). Mahwah, NJ: Lawrence Erlbaum Associates.

Alexander, P. A., Jetton, T. L., & Kulikowich, J. M. (1995). Interrelationship of knowledge, interest, and recall: Assessing a model of domain learning. *Journal of Educational Psychology, 87*, 559–575.

Alexander, P. A., & Judy, J. E. (1988). The interaction of domain-specific and strategic knowledge in academic performance. *Review of Educational Research, 58*, 375–404.

Alexander, P. A., & Knight, S. L. (1993). Dimensions of the interplay between learning and teaching. *Educational Forum, 57*, 232–245.

Alexander, P. A., Kulikowich, J. M., & Jetton, T. L. (1994). The role of subject-matter knowledge and interest in the processing of linear and nonlinear texts. *Review of Educational Research, 64*, 201–252.

Alexander, P. A., & Murphy, P. K. (1998). The research base for APA's learner-centered principles. In N. M. Lambert & B. L. McCombs (Eds.), *Issues in school reform: A sampler of psychological perspectives on learner-centered schools* (pp. 25–60). Washington, DC: American Psychological Association.

Alexander, P. A., & Murphy, P. K. (1999). Learner profiles: Valuing individual differences within classroom communities. In P. L. Ackerman, P. C. Kyllonen, & R. D. Roberts (Eds.), *The future of learning and individual differences research: Processes, traits, and content* (pp. 413–431). Washington, DC: American Psychological Association.

Alexander, P. A., Murphy, P. K., Buehl, M. M., & Sperl, C. T. (1997, December). *The influence of prior knowledge, beliefs, and interest in learning from persuasive text.* Paper presented at the annual meeting of the National Reading Conference, Scottsdale, AZ.

Alexander, P. A., Murphy, P. K., & Woods, B. S. (1996). Of squalls and fathoms: Navigating the seas of educational innovation. *Educational Researcher, 25*(3), 31–36, 39.

Alexander, P. A., Schallert, D. L., & Hare, V. C. (1991). Coming to terms: How researchers in learning and literacy talk about knowledge. *Review of Educational Research, 61*, 315–343.

Allington, R. L., & McGill-Franzen, A. (2000). Looking back, looking forward: A conversation about teaching reading in the 21st century. *Reading Research Quarterly, 35*, 136–153.

Almasi, J. F., McKeown, M. G., & Beck, I. L. (1996). The nature of engaged reading in classroom discussions of literature. *Journal of Literacy Research, 28*, 107–146.

Alvermann, D. E. (2008). Why bother theorizing adolescents' online literacies for classroom practice and research? *Journal of Adolescent & Adult Literacy, 52*(1), 8–19.

Alvermann, D. E., Commeyras, M., Young, J. P., Randall, S., & Hinson, D. (1997). Interrupting gendered discursive practices in classroom talk about texts: Easy to think about, difficult to do. *Journal of Literacy Research, 29*, 73–104.

Alvermann, D. E., & Hayes, D. A. (1989). Classroom discussion of content area reading assignments: An intervention study. *Reading Research Quarterly, 24*, 305–335.

Alvermann, D. E., Smith, L. C., & Readence, J. E. (1985). Prior knowledge activation and the comprehension of compatible and incompatible text. *Reading Research Quarterly, 20*, 420–436.

American Psychological Association Presidential Task Force on Psychology in Education. (1993). *Learner-centered psychological principles: Guidelines for school redesign and reform.* Washington, DC: American Psychological Association.

Anderson, J. R., Reder, L. M., & Simon, H. A. (1996). Situated learning and education. *Educational Researcher, 25*, 5–11.

Anderson, R. C. (1977). The notion of schemata and the educational enterprise. In R. C. Anderson, R. J. Spiro, & W. E. Montague (Eds.), *Schooling and the acquisition of knowledge* (pp. 415–431). Hillsdale, NJ: Erlbaum.

Anderson, R. C., Pichert, J. W., & Shirey, L. L. (1983). Effects of the reader's schema at different points in time. *Journal of Educational Psychology, 75*, 271–279.

Anderson, R. C., Reynolds, R. E., Schallert, D. L., & Goetz, E. T. (1977). Frameworks for comprehending discourse. *American Educational Research Journal, 14*, 367–381.

Anderson, R. C., Wilson, P. T., & Fielding, L. G. (1988). Growth in reading and how children spend their time outside of school. *Reading Research Quarterly, 23,* 285–303.

Armbruster, B. B. (1984). The problem of "inconsiderate texts." In G. G. Duffy, L. R. Roehler, & J. Mason (Eds.), *Theoretical issues in reading comprehension* (pp. 202–217). New York, NY: Longman.

Au, K. H. (1993). *Literacy instruction in multicultural settings.* Belmont, CA: Wadsworth.

Baars, B. J. (1986). *The cognitive revolution in psychology.* New York, NY: Guilford Press.

Benton, M. G. (1983). Secondary worlds. *Journal of Research and Development in Education, 16,* 68–75.

Bereiter, C., & Scardamalia, M. (1989). Intentional learning as a goal of instruction. In L. B. Resnick (Ed.), *Knowing, learning, and instruction: Essays in honor of Robert Glaser* (pp. 361–392). Hillsdale, NJ: Lawrence Erlbaum Associates.

Bereiter, C., & Scardamalia, M. (2005). Beyond Bloom's taxonomy: Rethinking knowledge for the knowledge age. In M. Fullan (Ed.), *Fundamental change: International handbook of educational change* (pp. 5–22). Dordrecht: Springer.

Bloome, D., & Green, J. (1984). Directions in the sociolinguistic study of reading. In P. D. Pearson, R. Barr, M. L. Kamil, & P. Mosenthal (Eds.), *Handbook of reading research* (Vol. 1, pp. 395–422). New York, NY: Longman.

Bolter, J. D. (1991). *Writing space: The computer, hypertext, and the history of writing.* Hillsdale, NJ: Lawrence Erlbaum Associates.

Bond, G. L., & Dykstra, R. (1967). The cooperative research program in first-grade reading instruction. *Reading Research Quarterly, 2*(4), 5–142.

Bransford, J. D., & Franks, J. J. (1971). The abstraction of linguistic ideas. *Cognitive Psychology, 2,* 331–350.

Brayner, R., Fiévet, F., & Coradin, T. (2013). *Nanomaterials: A danger or a promise?* London: Springer-Verlag.

Britton, J. N. (1982). *Prospect and retrospect.* Montclair, NJ: Boynton/Cook.

Brooks, S. (2015). Does personal social media usage affect efficiency and well-being? *Computers in Human Behavior, 46,* 26–37.

Brown, A. L., & Campione, J. C. (1990). Communities of learning and thinking: Or, a context by any other name. *Human Development, 21,* 108–125.

Brown, A. L., Campione, J. C., & Day, J. D. (1981). Learning to learn: On training students to learn from text. *Educational Researcher, 9,* 14–21.

Brown, A. L., & Palincsar, A. S. (1989). Guided, cooperative learning and individual knowledge acquisition. In L. B. Resnick (Ed.), *Knowing, learning, and instruction: Essays in honor of Robert Glaser* (pp. 393–451). Hillsdale, NJ: Lawrence Erlbaum Associates.

Buswell, G. T. (1922). *Fundamental reading habits: A study of their development.* Chicago, IL: University of Chicago Press.

Camera, L. (2016, January). The increase of immigrant students tests tolerance. *U.S. News and World Report.* Retrieved from https://www.usnews.com/news/blogs/data-mine/articles/2016-01-05/number-of-immigrant-students-is-growing

Carrier, L. M., Rosen, L. D., Cheever, N. A., & Lim, A. F. (2015). Causes, effects, and practicalities of everyday multitasking. *Developmental Review, 35,* 64–78.

Cartwright, K. B. (2007). The contribution of graphophonological-semantic flexibility to reading comprehension in college students: Implications for a less simple view of reading. *Journal of Literacy Research, 39,* 173–193.

Chall, J. S. (1967). *Learning to read: The great debate.* New York, NY: McGraw-Hill.

Chall, J. S. (1995). *Stages of reading development* (2nd ed.). New York, NY: Wadsworth.

Chambliss, M. (1995). Text cues and strategies successful readers use to construct the gist of lengthy written arguments. *Reading Research Quarterly, 30,* 778–807.

Chi, M. T. H., Feltovich, P., & Glaser, R. (1981). Categorization and representation of physics problems by experts and novices. *Cognitive Science, 5,* 121–152.

Chinn, C. A., & Anderson, R. C. (1998). The structure of discussions intended to promote reasoning. *Teachers College Record, 100,* 315–360.

Chipman, S. F. (1993). Gazing once more into the silicon chip: Who's revolutionary now? In S. P. Lajoie & S. J. Derry (Eds.), *Computers as cognitive tools* (pp. 341–367). Mahwah, NJ: Lawrence Erlbaum Associates.

Chomsky, N. (1957). *Syntactic structures.* New York, NY: Mouton de Gruyter.

Chomsky, N. (1975). *Reflections on language.* New York, NY: Pantheon Books.

Chomsky, N. (1998). *On language.* New York, NY: The New Press.

Chomsky, N. (2002). *On nature and language.* New York, NY: Cambridge University Press.

Clancey, W. J. (1983). The epistemology of a rule-based expert system: A framework for explanation. *Artificial Intelligence, 20,* 215–252.

Clay, M. M. (1967). The reading behavior of five-year-old children: A research report. *New Zealand Journal of Educational Studies, 2,* 11–31.

Clay, M. M. (1976). *Young fluent readers.* London: Heinemann.

Cognition and Technology Group at Vanderbilt. (1990). Anchored instruction and its relationship to situated cognition. *Educational Researcher, 19*(6), 2–10.

Cognition and Technology Group at Vanderbilt. (1996). Looking at technology in context: A framework for understanding technology and education research. In D. C. Berliner & R. C. Calfee (Eds.), *Handbook of educational psychology* (pp. 807–840). New York, NY: Macmillan.

Coiro, J., Knobel, M., Lankshear, C., & Leu, D. J. (2008). Central issues in new literacies and new literacies research. In J. Coiro, M. Knobel, C. Lankshear, & D. J. Leu (Eds.), *Handbook of new literacies* (pp. 1–21). New York, NY: Taylor & Francis.

Collins, A., Brown, J. S., & Newman, S. E. (1989). Cognitive apprenticeships: Teaching the crafts of reading, writing, and mathematics. In L. B. Resnick (Ed.), *Knowing, learning, and instruction: Essays in honor of Robert Glaser* (pp. 453–494). Hillsdale, NJ: Erlbaum.

Cox, C., & Many, J. E. (1992). Towards an understanding of the aesthetic response to literature. *Language Arts, 69,* 28–33.

Cromley, J. G., Bergey, B. W., Fitzhugh, S., Newcombe, N., Wills, T. W., Shipley, T. F., & Tanaka, J. C. (2013). Effects of three diagram instruction methods on transfer of diagram comprehension skills: The critical role of inference while learning. *Learning and Instruction, 26,* 45–58.

Csikszentmihalyi, M. (1990). *Flow: The psychology of optimal experience.* New York, NY: Cambridge University Press.

Cuban, L. (1993). *How teachers taught: Constancy and change in American classrooms, 1890–1980.* New York, NY: Teachers College Press.

Deci, E. L., & Ryan, R. M. (1991). A motivational approach to self: Integration in personality. In R. Dienstbier (Ed.), *Nebraska Symposium on Motivation: Perspectives on motivation* (Vol. 38, pp. 237–288). Lincoln, NE: University of Nebraska Press.

de Jong, T., & Ferguson-Hessler, M. G. M. (1996). Types and qualities of knowledge. *Educational Psychologist, 31,* 105–113.

Del Vicario, M., Bessi, A., Zollo, F., Petroni, F. Scala, A., Caldarelli, G., . . . Quattrociocchi, W. (2016). The spreading of misinformation online. *PNAS, 113,* 554–559. Retrieved from www.pnas.org/cgi/doi/10.1073/pnas.1517441113

DOMO. (2016). *Data never sleeps.* Retrieved from https://www.domo.com/blog/2015/08/data-never-sleeps-3-0/

Duffy, G., Roehler, L. R., Meloth, M. S., & Vavrus, L. G. (1986). Conceptualizing instructional explanation. *Teaching and Teacher Education, 2,* 197–214.

Dunton, G. F., Huh, J., Leventhal, A. M., Riggs, N., Hedeker, D., Spruijt-Metz, D., & Pentz, M. A. (2014). Momentary assessment of affect, physical feeling states, and physical activity in children. *Health Psychology, 33,* 255–263.

Ericsson, K. A., & Smith, J. (1991). *Toward a general theory of expertise: Prospects and limits.* New York, NY: Cambridge University Press.

Felton, M. K., & Kuhn, D. (2007). How do I know? The epistemological roots of critical thinking. *Journal of Museum Education, 32,* 101–123.

Fish, S. F. (1980). *Is there a text in this class?* Cambridge, MA: Harvard University Press.

Flesch, R. (1955). *Why Johnny can't read—and what you can do about it.* New York, NY: Harper & Brothers.

Fodor, J. A. (1964). *The structure of language: Readings in the philosophy of language.* New York, NY: Prentice-Hall.

Fodor, J. A. (2001). *The mind doesn't work that way: The scope and limits of computational psychology.* Cambridge, MA: MIT Press.

Foorman, B. R., Francis, D. J., Fletcher, J. M., Schatschneider, C., & Mehta, P. (1998). The role of instruction in learning to read: Preventing reading failure in at-risk children, *Journal of Educational Psychology, 90,* 37–55.

Foorman, B. R., Schatschneider, C., Eakin, M. N., Fletcher, J. M., Moats, L. C., & Francis, D. J. (2006). The impact of instructional practices in Grades 1 and 2 on reading and spelling achievement in high poverty schools. *Contemporary Educational Psychology, 31,* 1–29.

Fox, E. (2009). The role of reader characteristics in processing and learning from informational text. *Review of Educational Research, 79,* 197–261.

Fox, E., Dinsmore, D. L., & Alexander, P. A. (2010). Reading competence, interest, and reading goals in three gifted young adolescent readers. *High Ability Studies, 21,* 165–178.

Ganley, A. C., Lyons, T. T., & Sewall, G. T. (1993). *The U.S.A. since 1945: After Hiroshima* (3rd ed.). White Plains, NY: Longman.

García, O., Kleifgen, J. A., & Falchi, L. (2008). *From English language learners to emergent bilinguals: Equity matters.* Research Review No. 1. New York, NY: Campaign for Educational Equity, Teachers College, Columbia University.

Garner, R. (1987). *Metacognition and reading comprehension.* Norwood, NJ: Ablex.

Garner, R. (1990). When children and adults do not use learning strategies: Toward a theory of settings. *Review of Educational Research, 60*, 517–529.

Garner, R., & Gillingham, M. G. (1996). *Conversations across time, space, and culture.* Mahwah, NJ: Lawrence Erlbaum Associates.

Garner, R., & Hansis, R. (1994). Literacy practices outside of school: Adults' beliefs and their responses to "street texts." In R. Garner & P. A. Alexander (Eds.), *Beliefs about text and instruction with text* (pp. 57–73). Hillsdale, NJ: Lawrence Erlbaum Associates.

Gazzaley, A., & Rosen, L. D. (2016). *The distracted mind: Ancient brains in a high-tech world.* Cambridge, MA: MIT Press.

Gee, J. P., & Hayes, E. R. (2011). *Language and learning in the digital age.* New York, NY: Routledge.

Gillingham, M. G., Young, M. F., & Kulikowich, J. M. (1994). Do teachers consider nonlinear text to be text? In R. Garner & P. A. Alexander (Eds.), *Beliefs about text and instruction with text* (pp. 201–219). Hillsdale, NJ: Lawrence Erlbaum Associates.

Glaser, R. (1978). The contributions of B. F. Skinner to education and some counterinfluences. In P. Suppes (Ed.), *Impact of research on education: Some case studies* (pp. 199–265). Washington, DC: National Academy of Education.

Goetz, E. T., Alexander, P. A., & Ash, M. (1992). *Educational psychology: A classroom perspective.* Columbus, OH: Charles E. Merrill.

Goldman, S. R. (1996). Reading, writing, and learning in hypermedia environments. In H. Van Oostendorp & S. de Mui (Eds.), *Cognitive aspects of electronic text processing* (pp. 7–42). Norwood, NJ: Ablex.

Goodman, K. S. (1965). A linguistic study of cues and miscues in reading. *Elementary English, 42*, 639–643.

Goodman, K. S., & Goodman, Y. M. (1979). Learning to read is natural. In L. S. Resnick & P. A. Weaver (Eds.), *Theory and practice in early reading* (Vol. 1, pp. 137–154). Hillsdale, NJ: Lawrence Erlbaum Associates.

Gough, P. B., & Tunmer, W. E. (1986). Decoding, reading, and reading disability. *Remedial and Special Education, 7*, 6–10.

Gray, W. S., & Rogers, B. (1956). *Maturity in reading, its nature and appraisal.* Chicago, IL: University of Chicago Press.

Green, J. L., & Dixon, C. N. (1993). Talking knowledge into being: Discursive and social practices in classrooms. *Linguistics and Education, 5*(3–4), 231–239.

Green, J., & Meyer, L. (1991). The embeddedness of reading in classroom life: Reading as a situated process. In C. Baker & A. Luke (Eds.), *The critical sociology of reading pedagogy* (pp. 141–160). Amsterdam: John Benjamins.

Greene, S., & Ackerman, J. M. (1995). Expanding the constructivist metaphor: A rhetorical perspective on literacy research and practice. *Review of Educational Research, 65*, 383–420.

Greeno, J. G., & the Middle School Mathematics Through Applications Project Group. (1998). The situativity of knowing, learning, and research. *American Psychologist, 53*, 5–26.

Greeno, J. G., & Moore, J. L. (1993). Situativity and symbols: Response to Vera and Simon. *Cognitive Science, 17*, 49–59.

Guthrie, J. T., McGough, K., Bennett, L., & Rice, M. E. (1996). Concept-oriented reading instruction: An integrated curriculum to develop motivations and strategies for reading. In L. Baker, P. Afflerbach, & D. Reinking (Eds.), *Developing engaged readers in school and home communities* (pp. 165–190). Mahwah, NJ: Lawrence Erlbaum Associates.

Guthrie, J. T., Van Meter, P., McCann, A., Wigfield, A., Bennett, L., Poundstone, C., . . . Mitchell, A. (1996). Growth of literacy engagement: Changes in motivations and strategies during concept-oriented reading instruction. *Reading Research Quarterly, 31*, 306–332.

Guthrie, J. T., & Wigfield, A. (2000). Engagement and motivation in reading. In M. L. Kamil, P. B. Mosenthal, P. D. Pearson, & R. Barr (Eds.), *Handbook of reading research* (Vol. 3, pp. 403–422). Mahwah, NJ: Lawrence Erlbaum Associates.

Guzzetti, B., & Hynd, C. (1998). *Theoretical perspectives on conceptual change.* Mahwah, NJ: Lawrence Erlbaum Associates.

Halliday, M. A. K. (1969). Relevant models of language. *Educational Review, 22*, 1–128.

Halliday, M. A. K., & Hasan, R. (1974). *Cohesion in English.* London: Longman.

Hansen, J. (1981). The effects of inference training and practice on young children's reading comprehension. *Reading Research Quarterly, 16*, 391–317.

Hansen, J. H. (2012). Limits to inclusion. *International Journal of Inclusive Education, 16*(1), 89–98.

Harris, K. R. (1996, April). *The state of strategy research: Is this old territory or are there new frontiers?* Panel discussion presented at the annual meeting of the American Educational Research Association, New York.

Harste, J. C., Burke, C., & Woodward, V. (1984). *Language stories and literacy lessons.* Portsmouth, NH: Heinemann.

Heath, S. B. (1982). What no bedtime story means: Narrative skills at home and school. *Language in Society, 11*, 49–76.

Heath, S. B. (1983). *Ways with words: Language, life, and work in communities and classrooms.* New York, NY: Cambridge University Press.

Heddy, B. C., & Sinatra, G. M. (2013). Transforming misconceptions: Using transformative experience to promote positive affect and conceptual change in students learning about biological evolution. *Science Education, 97*(5), 723–744.

Hedeker, D., Mermelstein, R. J., Berbaum, M. L., & Campbell, R. T. (2009). Modeling mood variation associated with smoking: An application of a heterogeneous mixed-effects model for analysis of ecological momentary assessment (EMA) data. *Addiction, 104*, 297–307.

Hidi, S. (1990). Interest and its contribution as a mental resource for learning. *Review of Educational Research, 60*, 549–571.

Hiebert, E. H., & Taylor, B. M. (2000). Beginning reading instruction: Research on early interventions. In M. L. Kamil, P. B. Mosenthal, P. D. Pearson, & R. Barr (Eds.), *Handbook of reading research* (Vol. 3, pp. 455–482). Mahwah, NJ: Lawrence Erlbaum Associates.

Huey, E. B. (1908). *The psychology and pedagogy of reading.* New York, NY: Macmillan.

James, W. (1890). *Principles of psychology* (Vols. 1 & 2). New York, NY: Holt.

Jetton, T. L., & Alexander, P. A. (1998, April). *Teachers' views of discussion: Issues of control, time, and ability.* Paper presented at the annual meeting of the American Educational Research Association, San Diego, CA.

Kellner, D. (2001). New technologies/new literacies: Reconstructing education for the new millennium. *International Journal of Technology and Design Education, 11*, 67–81. Retrieved from http://gseis.ucla.edu/faculty/kellner/essays/newtechnologiesnewliteracies.pdf

Kim, I.-H., Anderson, R. C., Nguyen-Jahiel, K., & Archididou, A. (2007). Discourse patterns during children's collaborative online discussions. *The Journal of the Learning Sciences. 16*, 333–370.

Koyama, J., & Menken, K. (2013). Emergent bilinguals: Framing students as statistical data? *Bilingual Research Journal, 36*(1), 82–99.

Kulikowich, J. M., & Alexander, P. A. (2010). Intentionality to learn in an academic domain. *Early Education and Development, 21*, 724–743.

Labov, W. (1966). *The social stratification of English in New York City.* Washington, DC: Center for Applied Linguistics.

Labov, W. (1971). Systematically misleading data from test questions. *Urban Review, 9*(3), 146–170.

Labov, W. (1972). *Sociolinguistic patterns.* Philadelphia, PA: University of Pennsylvania Press.

Lankshear, C., & Knobel, M. (2003). *New literacies: Changing knowledge and classroom learning.* Buckingham: Open University Press.

Lave, J. (1988). *Cognition and practice.* Cambridge: Cambridge University Press.

Lawless, K. A., & Kulikowich, J. M. (1996). Understanding hypertext navigation through cluster analysis. *Journal of Educational Computing Research, 14*, 385–399.

Leu, D. J., Kinzer, C. K., Coiro, J. L., & Cammack, D. W. (2004). Toward a theory of new literacies emerging from the Internet and other information and communication technologies. In R. B. Ruddell & N. J. Unrau (Eds.), *Theoretical models and processes of reading* (5th ed., pp. 1570–1613). Newark, DE: International Reading Association.

Leu, D. J., O'Byrne, W. I., Zawilinski, L, McVerry, J. G., & Everett-Cocapardo, H. (2009). Expanding the new literacies conversation. *Educational Researcher, 39*, 264–269.

Levin, H. (Ed.). (1965). *Planning for a reading research program.* Ithaca, NY: Cornell University.

Lipson, M. Y. (1983). The influence of religious affiliation on children's memory for text information. *Reading Research Quarterly, 18*, 448–457.

List, A., Alexander, P. A., & Stephens, L. A. (2016). Trust but verify: Examining the association between students' sourcing behaviors and ratings of text trustworthiness. *Discourse Processes, 54*, 83–104.

Lysynchuk, L. M., Pressley, M., D'Ailly, H., Smith, M., & Cake, H. (1989). A methodological analysis of experimental studies of comprehension strategy instruction. *Reading Research Quarterly, 24*, 458–470.

Maggioni, L., VanSledright, B., & Alexander, P. A. (2009). Walking on the borders: A measure of epistemic cognition in history. *The Journal of Experimental Education, 77*(3), 187–214.

Mandl, H., Stein, N. L., & Trabasso, T. (1984). *Learning and comprehension of text.* Hillsdale, NJ: Lawrence Erlbaum Associates.

Mason, L., Boldrin, A., & Ariasi, N. (2010). Epistemic metacognition in context: Evaluating and learning online information. *Metacognition and Learning, 5*(1), 67–90.

Mayer, R. E. (Ed). (2014). *Cambridge handbook of multimedia learning.* New York, NY: Cambridge University Press.

McCrudden, M. T., Magliano, J. P., & Schraw, G. (2010). Exploring how relevance instructions affect personal reading intentions, reading goals and text processing: A mixed methods study. *Contemporary Educational Psychology, 35*, 224–241.

McFarland, J., Hussar, B., de Brey, C., Snyder, T., Wang, X., Wilkinson-Flicker, S., . . . Hinz, S. (2017). *The condition of education 2017* (NCES Publication No. 2017144). Washington, DC: National Center for Education Statistics. Retrieved from https://nces.ed.gov/pubsearch/pubsinfo.asp?pubid=2017144

Menken, K. (2013). Restrictive language education policies and emergent bilingual youth: A perfect storm with imperfect outcomes. *Theory Into Practice, 52*(3), 160–168.

Meyer, B. J. F. (1975). *The organization of prose and its effects on memory*. Amsterdam: North-Holland.

Moje, E. B. (2007). Developing socially just subject-matter instruction: A review of the literature on disciplinary literacy teaching. *Review of Research in Education, 31,* 1–44.

Moje, E. B., Tucker-Raymond, E., Varelas, M., & Pappas, C. (2007). Giving oneself over to science: Exploring the roles of subjectivities and identities in learning science. *Cultural Studies of Science Education, 1,* 593–601.

Moll, L. C., & González, N. (1994). Lessons from research with language-minority children. *Journal of Reading Behavior, 26*(4), 439–456.

Monaghan, E. J., & Saul, E. W. (1987). The reader, the scribe, the thinker: A critical look at the history of American reading and writing instruction. In T. S. Popkewitz (Ed.), *The formation of school subjects: The struggle for creating an American institution* (pp. 85–122). Philadelphia, PA: Falmer Press.

Morgan, H. (2013). Multimodal children's e-books help young learners in reading. *Early Childhood Education Journal, 41*(6), 477–483.

Murphy, P. K., Wilkinson, I. A. G., & Soter, A. O. (2011). Instruction based on discussion. In R. E. Mayer & P. A. Alexander (Eds.), *Handbook of research on learning and instruction* (pp. 382–407). Oxford: Taylor & Francis.

Murphy, P. K., Wilkinson, I. A. G., Soter, A. O., Hennessey, M. N., & Alexander, J. F. (2009). Examining the effects of classroom discussion on students' high-level comprehension of text: A meta-analysis. *Journal of Educational Psychology, 101,* 740–764.

National Governors Association Center for Best Practices, Council of Chief State School Officers. (2010). *Common Core State Standards for English language arts and literacy in history/social studies, science, and technical subjects*. Washington, DC: Authors.

Neuman, S. B. (1988). The displacement effect: Assessing the relation between television viewing and reading performance. *Reading Research Quarterly, 23,* 414–440.

No Child Left Behind Act of 2001, Pub. L. No. 107–110. (2001).

Nolen, S. B., Johnson-Crowley, N., & Wineburg, S. S. (1994). Who is this "I" person, anyway? The presence of a visible author in statistical text. In R. Garner & P. A. Alexander (Eds.), *Beliefs about text and instruction with text* (pp. 41–55). Hillsdale, NJ: Lawrence Erlbaum Associates.

Oldfather, P., & Wigfield, A. (1996). Children's motivations to read. In L. Baker, P. Afflerbach, & D. Reinking (Eds.), *Developing engaged readers in school and home communities* (pp. 89–113). Mahwah, NJ: Lawrence Erlbaum Associates.

Ozuru, Y., Dempsey, K., & McNamara, D. S. (2009). Prior knowledge, reading skill, and text cohesion in the comprehension of science texts. *Learning and Instruction, 19,* 228–242.

Palincsar, A. S., & Brown, A. L. (1984). Reciprocal teaching of comprehension-fostering and monitoring activities. *Cognition and Instruction, 1,* 117–175.

Paris, S. G., Lipson, M. Y., & Wixson, K. K. (1983). Becoming a strategic reader. *Contemporary Educational Psychology, 8,* 293–316.

Paris, S. G., Wasik, B. A., & Turner, J. C. (1991). The development of strategic readers. In R. Barr, M. L. Kamil, P. Mosenthal, & P. D. Pearson (Eds.), *Handbook of reading research* (Vol. 1, pp. 609–640). New York, NY: Longman.

Paris, S. G., & Winograd, P. (1990). Dimensions of thinking and cognitive instruction. In B. F. Jones & L. Idol (Eds.), *How metacognition can promote academic learning and instruction* (pp. 15–51). Hillsdale, NJ: Lawrence Erlbaum Associates.

Paris, S. G., & Urdan, T. (2000). Policies and practices of high-stakes testing that influence teachers and schools. *Issues in Education, 6*(1/2), 83–107.

Pea, R., Nass, C., Meheula, L., Rance, M., Kumar, A., Bamford, H., . . . Zhou, M. (2012). Media use, face-to-face communication, media multitasking, and social well-being among 8- to 12-year-old girls. *Developmental Psychology, 48*(2), 327–336.

Pearson, P. D. (1984). Direct explicit teaching of reading comprehension. In G. G. Duffy, L. R. Roehler, & J. Mason (Eds.), *Comprehension instruction: Perspectives and suggestions* (pp. 222–233). New York, NY: Longman.

Pearson, P. D., & Stephens, D. (1994). Learning from literacy: A 30-year journey. In R. B. Ruddell, M. R. Ruddell, & H. Singer (Eds.), *Theoretical models and processes of reading* (4th ed., pp. 22–42). Newark, DE: International Reading Association.

Perret-Claremont, A., Perret, J., & Bell, N. (1980). The social construction of meaning and cognitive activity in elementary school children. In L. B. Resnick, J. M. Levine, & S. D. Teasley (Eds.), *Perspectives on socially shared cognition* (pp. 41–62). Washington, DC: American Psychological Association.

Pichert, J. W., & Anderson, R. C. (1977). Taking different perspectives on a story. *Journal of Educational Psychology, 69*, 309–315.

Pigott, T. D., & Barr, R. (2000). Designing programmatic interventions. In M. L. Kamil, P. B. Mosenthal, P. D. Pearson, & R. Barr (Eds.), *Handbook of reading research* (Vol. 3, pp. 99–108). Mahwah, NJ: Lawrence Erlbaum Associates.

Postman, N. (1993). *Technopoly.* New York, NY: Vintage Books.

Prawat, R. S. (1989). Promoting access to knowledge, strategy, and disposition in students: A research synthesis. *Review of Educational Research, 59*, 1–41.

Pressley, M. (2002). Comprehension strategies instruction: A turn-of-the-century report. In C. C. Block & M. Pressley (Eds.), *Comprehension instruction: Research-based best practices* (pp. 11–27). New York, NY: Guilford Press.

Pressley, M., Goodchild, F., Fleet, J., Zajchowski, R., & Evans, E. D. (1989). The challenges of classroom strategy instruction. *Elementary School Journal, 89*, 301–342.

Pugh, K. R., Shaywitz, B. A., Shaywitz, S. E, Shankweiler, D. P., Katz, L., Fletcher, J. M., . . . Gore, J. C. (1997). Predicting reading performance from neuroimaging profiles: The cerebral basis of phonological effects in printed word identification. *Journal of Experimental Psychology: Human Perception and Performance, 23*, 299–318.

RAND Reading Study Group. (2002). *Reading for understanding: Toward an R&D program in reading comprehension.* Santa Monica, CA: RAND.

Raphael, T. F., & Wonnacott, C. A. (1985). Heightening fourth-graders' sensitivity to sources of information for answering comprehension questions. *Reading Research Quarterly, 22*, 282–296.

Reed, J. H., & Schallert, D. L. (1993). The nature of involvement in academic discourse. *Journal of Educational Psychology, 85*, 253–266.

Reed, J. H., Schallert, D. L., & Goetz, E. T. (1993, April). *Interest happens but involvement takes effort: Distinguishing between two constructs in academic discourse tasks.* Paper presented at the annual meeting of the American Educational Research Association, Atlanta, GA.

Reinking, D., McKenna, M. C., Labbo, L. D., & Kieffer, R. D. (1998). *Handbook of literacy and technology: Transformations in a post-typographic world.* Mahwah, NJ: Lawrence Erlbaum Associates.

Resnick, L. B., Levine, J. M., & Teasley, S. D. (1991). *Perspectives on socially shared cognition.* Washington, DC: American Psychological Association.

Reutzel, R. D., & Mohr, K. A. (2015). 50 years of *Reading Research Quarterly* (1965–2014): Looking back, moving forward. *Reading Research Quarterly, 50*(1), 13–35.

Reyes, I., & Azuara, P. (2008). Emergent biliteracy in young Mexican immigrant children. *Reading Research Quarterly, 43*(4), 374–398.

Reynolds, R. E., Sinatra, G. M., & Jetton, T. L. (1996). Views of knowledge acquisition and representation: A continuum from experience centered to mind centered. *Educational Psychologist, 31*, 93–104.

Rogoff, B. (1990). *Apprenticeship in thinking: Cognitive development in social context.* New York, NY: Oxford University Press.

Rogoff, B., & Gauvain, M. (1986). A method for the analysis of patterns illustrated with data on mother-child instructional interaction. In J. Valsiner (Ed.), *The individual subject and scientific psychology* (pp. 261–290). New York, NY: Plenum.

Rosen, L. D. (2012). *iDisorder: Understanding our obsession with technology and overcoming its hold on us.* New York, NY: St. Martin's Press.

Rosenblatt, L. (1994). *The reader, the text, the poem: The transactional theory of the literary work.* Carbondale, IL: Southern Illinois Press. (Original work published 1978)

Rosenblatt, L. M. (1995). *Literature as exploration.* New York, NY: Modern Language Association. (Original work published 1938)

Rouet, J-F., Vidal-Abarca, E., Erboul, A. B., & Millogo, V. (2001). Effects of information search tasks on the comprehension of instructional texts. *Discourse Processes, 3*, 163–186.

Ruddell, R. B. (2002). *Teaching children to read and write: Becoming an effective literacy teacher* (3rd ed.). Boston, MA: Allyn & Bacon.

Russell, D. H. (1961). *Children learn to read* (2nd ed.). New York, NY: Ginn.

Sabatini, J. P., O'Reilly, T., Halderman, L. K., & Bruce, K. (2014). Integrating scenario-based and component reading skill measures to understand the reading behavior of struggling readers. *Learning Disabilities Research & Practice, 29*(1), 36–43.

Salomon, G. (1993). *Distributed cognition: Psychological and educational considerations.* Cambridge: Cambridge University Press.

Salomon, G., Perkins, D. N., & Globerson, T. (1991). Partners in cognition: Extending human intelligence with intelligent technologies. *Educational Researcher, 20*(3), 2–9.

Samuels, S. J., & Kamil, M. L. (1984). Models of the reading process. In P. D. Pearson, R. Barr, M. L. Kamil, & P. Mosenthal (Eds.), *Handbook of reading research* (Vol. 1, pp. 185–224). New York, NY: Longman.

Sana, F., Weston, T., & Cepeda, N. J. (2013). Laptop multitasking hinders classroom learning for both users and nearby peers. *Computers & Education, 62,* 24–31.

Scardamalia, M., Bereiter, C., McLean, R. S., Swallow, J., & Woodruff, E. (1989). Computer-supported intentional learning environments. *Journal of Educational Computing Research, 5,* 51–68.

Schallert, D. L., Meyer, D. K., & Fowler, L. A. (1995). The nature of engagement when reading in and out of one's discipline. In K. A. Hinchman, D. J. Leu, & C. K. Kinzer (Eds.), *Perspectives on literacy research and practice* (44th yearbook of the National Reading Conference, pp. 119–125). Chicago, IL: National Reading Conference.

Schank, R. C., & Abelson, R. P. (1977). *Scripts, plans, goals, and understanding: An inquiry into human knowledge structures.* Hillsdale, NJ: Lawrence Erlbaum Associates.

Schlaggar, B. L., & McCandliss, B. D. (2007). Development of neural systems for reading. *Annual Review of Neuroscience, 30,* 475–503.

Schraw, G., Bruning, R., & Svoboda, C. (1995). Sources of situational interest. *Journal of Reading Behavior, 27,* 1–17.

Serafini, F. (2011). Expanding perspectives for comprehending visual images in multimodal texts. *Journal of Adolescent & Adult Literacy, 54*(5), 342–350.

Shanahan, T., & Shanahan, C. (2008). Teaching disciplinary literacy to adolescents: Rethinking content-area literacy. *Harvard Educational Review, 78,* 40–59.

Shaywitz, B. A., Fletcher, J. M., Holahan, J. M., & Shaywitz, S. E. (1992). Discrepancy compared to low achievement definitions of reading disability: Results from the Connecticut Longitudinal Study. *Journal of Learning Disabilities, 25,* 639–648.

Shaywitz, B. A., Pugh, K. R., Jenner, A. R., Fulbright, R. K., Fletcher, J. M., Gore, J. C., & Shaywitz, S. E. (2000). The neurobiology of reading and reading disability (dyslexia). In M. L. Kamil, P. B. Mosenthal, P. D. Pearson, & R. Barr (Eds.), *Handbook of reading research* (Vol. 3, pp. 229–249). Mahwah, NJ: Lawrence Erlbaum Associates.

Shuy, R. W. (1968). Detroit speech: Careless, awkward, and inconsistent, or systematic, graceful, and regular? *Elementary English, 45*(5), 565–569.

Shuy, R. W. (1969). Some considerations for developing beginning reading materials for ghetto children. *Journal of Reading Behavior, 1*(2), 33–43.

Silverman, R. D., Proctor, C. P., Harring, J. R., Doyle, B., Mitchell, M. A., & Meyer, A. G. (2014). Teachers' instruction and students' vocabulary and comprehension: An exploratory study with English monolingual and Spanish–English bilingual students in Grades 3–5. *Reading Research Quarterly, 49*(1), 31–60.

Singer, L. M., & Alexander, P. A. (2017). Reading on paper and digitally: What the past decades of empirical research reveal. *Review of Educational Research, 87,* 1007–1041.

Skinner, B. F. (1976). *About behaviorism.* New York, NY: Vintage Books.

Smith, C. E., & Keogh, B. K. (1962). The group Bender-Gestalt as a reading readiness screening instrument. *Perceptual and Motor Skills, 15,* 639–645.

Smith, F. (1973). *Psycholinguistics and reading.* New York, NY: Holt, Rinehart & Winston.

Smith, F. (1985). A metaphor for literacy: Creating worlds or shunting information? In D. R. Olson, N. Torrance, & A. Hildyard (Eds.), *Perceiving, acting, and knowing: Toward an ecological psychology* (pp. 1–39). Hillsdale, NJ: Lawrence Erlbaum Associates.

Snow, C. E., Lawrence, J. F., & White, C. (2009). Generating knowledge of academic language among urban middle school students. *Journal of Research on Educational Effectiveness, 2*(4), 325–344.

Spivey, N. N., & King, J. R. (1989). Readers as writers composing from sources. *Reading Research Quarterly, 24,* 7–26.

Stahl, S. A., Hynd, C. R., Glynn, S. M., & Carr, M. (1996). Beyond reading to learn: Developing content and disciplinary knowledge through texts. In L. Baker, P. Afflerbach, & D. Reinking (Eds.), *Developing engaged readers in school and home community* (pp. 139–163). Mahwah, NJ: Lawrence Erlbaum Associates.

Stanovich, K. E. (1986). Matthew effects in reading: Some consequences of individual differences in the acquisition of literacy. *Reading Research Quarterly, 21,* 360–407.

Strang, R., McCullough, C. M., & Traxler, A. E. (1955). *Problems in the improvement of reading* (2nd ed.). New York, NY: McGraw-Hill.

Taylor, B. M., & Beach, R. W. (1984). The effects of text structure instruction on middle-grade students' comprehension and production of expository text. *Reading Research Quarterly, 19,* 134–146.

Thorndike, E. L. (1917). Reading as reasoning: A study of mistakes in paragraph reading. *Journal of Educational Psychology, 8,* 323–332.

Tierney, R. J., Readence, J. E., & Dishner, E. K. (1990). *Reading strategies and practices: A compendium* (3rd ed.). Boston, MA: Allyn and Bacon.

Tierney, R. J., Soter, A., O'Flahavan, J. F., & McGinley, W. (1989). The effects of reading and writing upon thinking critically. *Reading Research Quarterly, 24*, 134–173.

Torgesen, J. K. (1998). Instructional interventions for children with reading disabilities. In B. K. Shapiro, P. J. Accardo, & A. J. Capute (Eds.), *Specific reading disability: A view of the spectrum* (pp. 197–200). Parkton, MD: York Press.

Torgesen, J. K. (1999). Reading disabilities. In R. Gallimore, A. Bernheimer, G. MacMillan, D. Speece, & S. Vaughn (Eds.), *Developmental perspectives on children with high incidence disabilities: Papers in honor of Barbara K. Keogh* (pp. 157–182). Mahwah, NJ: Lawrence Erlbaum Associates.

Turner, J. C. (1995). The influence of classroom contexts on young children's motivation for literacy. *Reading Research Quarterly, 30*, 410–441.

Vacca, R. T., & Vacca, J. L. (1983). Two less than fortunate consequences of reading research in the 1970's [Guest editorial]. *Reading Research Quarterly, 18*, 382–383.

Valli, L., Croninger, R. G., Chambliss, M. H., Graeber, A. O., & Buese, D. (2008). *Test-driven: High-stakes accountability in elementary school*. New York, NY: Teachers College Press.

VanSledright, B. (2002). *In search of America's past: Learning to read history in elementary school*. New York, NY: Teachers College Press.

Vellutino, F. R., Tunmer, W. E., Jaccard, J. J., & Chen, R. (2007). Components of reading ability: Multivariate evidence for a convergent skills model of reading development. *Scientific Studies of Reading, 11*, 3–32.

Venezky, R. L. (1984). The history of reading research. In P. D. Pearson, R. Barr, M. L. Kamil, & P. Mosenthal (Eds.), *Handbook of reading research* (pp. 3–38). New York, NY: Longman.

Verhoeven, L., & van Leeuwe, J. (2008). Prediction of the development of reading comprehension: A longitudinal study. *Applied Cognitive Psychology, 22*, 407–423.

Vosniadou, S. (1994). Capturing and modeling the process of conceptual change. *Learning and Instruction, 4*, 45–69.

Wade, S. E., & Moje, E. (2000). The role of text in classroom learning. In M. L. Kamil, P. B. Mosenthal, P. D. Pearson, & R. Barr (Eds.), *Handbook of reading research* (Vol. 3, pp. 609–627). Mahwah, NJ: Lawrence Erlbaum Associates.

Wade, S. E., Thompson, A., & Watkins, W. (1994). The role of belief systems in authors' and readers' constructions of texts. In R. Garner & P. A. Alexander (Eds.), *Beliefs about text and instruction with text* (pp. 265–293). Hillsdale, NJ: Lawrence Erlbaum Associates.

Weaver, C. A., & Kintsch, W. (1991). Expository text. In R. Barr, M. L. Kamil, P. B. Mosenthal, & P. D. Pearson (Eds.), *Handbook of reading research* (Vol. 2, pp. 230–245). Mahwah, NJ: Lawrence Erlbaum Associates.

Weinstein, C. E., Goetz, E. T., & Alexander, P. A. (Eds.). (1988). *Learning and study strategies: Issues in assessment, instruction, and evaluation*. San Diego, CA: Academic Press.

Wertheimer, M. (1959). *Productive thinking*. New York, NY: Harper & Row. (Original work published 1945)

Whittaker, E., & Kowalski, R. M. (2015). Cyberbullying via social media. *Journal of School Violence, 14*(1), 11–29.

Wijekumar, K., & Meyer, B. J. F. (2006). Design and pilot of a Web-based intelligent tutoring system to improve reading comprehension in middle school students. *International Journal of Technology in Teaching and Learning, 2*, 36–49.

Wilkinson, I. A. G., Soter, A. O., & Murphy, P. K. (2010). Developing a model of quality talk about literary text. In M. G. McKeown & L. Kucan (Eds.), *Bringing reading research to life* (pp. 142–169). New York, NY: Guilford Press.

Winkler, R. (2017, March 27). Elon Musk launches Neuralink to connect brains with computers. *The Wall Street Journal*. Retrieved from www.wsj.com

Wulf, F. (1938). Tendencies in figural variation. In W. D. Ellis (trans. and condensed), *A source book of Gestalt psychology* (pp. 136–148). New York, NY: Routledge & Kegan Paul. (Original work published 1922)

3

WAVES OF THEORY BUILDING IN WRITING AND ITS DEVELOPMENT, AND THEIR IMPLICATIONS FOR INSTRUCTION, ASSESSMENT, AND CURRICULUM

Anna Smith

Introduction

Literacy, argued Kirkland (2013), is an artifact of humanity. Drawing on sociolinguists' theoretical work such as Smitherman's (1977) scholarship identifying linguistic social hierarchies, Hymes's (1994) calls to understand language in its everyday use, and Bakhtin's (1986) notions of individuals' articulations as processes of identification, Kirkland illustrated the ways writing, as literacy practice, results from human drives for pleasure, play, creativity, and curiosity. Along with the work of these theorists, his proposition was informed by long-term, ethnographic work tracing the development of literacy practices with six young, Black men in Lansing, Michigan. Though often depicted in dehumanizing ways—as apathetic, lazy, and even illiterate—by some adults around them, these young men were writers. They carried notebooks, which they filled with diary entries, poems, raps, and essays, and they engaged in cypher and storytelling circles with friends and family. By working alongside the young men to examine their writing across the rich literate landscape they traversed, Kirkland concluded that their writing development was, among other attributes, idiosyncratic, multimodal, cultural, political, and historical.

This is a complex rendering of writing and its development that is frequently evoked (Boscolo, 2008). Even when scholars have focused in on just one dimension of writing, such as the orchestration of cognitive processes (Berninger & Richards, 2002), writing is characterized as a complex, recursive, and rhetorical activity. Bereiter (1980), for instance, explained that at its most basic form, writing entails several activities that call for writers to engage in constant comparison between their intended message and the messages forming on the page, including:

1. creating a personal intention for the piece that aligns to the writer's understanding of the task;
2. coming up with a game plan to accomplish the task and personal goals; . . . and
3. tuning the written output to the writer's intention and understanding of the discourse for which it is being written. (p. 78)

This complexity exists whether a writer is regurgitating text, in what Bereiter and Scardamalia (1987) called a knowledge-telling model, or composing a new text, that is, working within a knowledge-transforming model. Flower and Hayes (1981) similarly argued that cognitive processes of constructing a rhetorical situation and goal setting were acts of creativity. Much like Kirkland's (2013) theorization of writing with a sociolinguistic grounding, writing and its development through a cognitive processes lens are depicted as idiosyncratic, rhetorical, and creative activities.

Though seemingly distant in their foci, when writing is discussed on a theoretical level in several fields, not only is its complexity consistently referenced, but so too are its ties to human desire, creativity, and identity. These complex, humanizing depictions of writing are in direct contradiction to the writing-as-basic-skill approach that has frequented assessment and curricular frameworks since writing became a school subject (Dixon, 1967; Hillocks, 2008; Yancey, 2009). Not surprisingly, studies that have characterized writing instruction practices in K-12 schools (Applebee, 1981; Applebee & Langer, 2006, 2009, 2011; Britton, Burgess, Martin, McLeod, & Rosen, 1975; Cutler & Graham, 2008) have repeatedly demonstrated that the writing and writing instruction happening in schools aligns to mandates and assessment regimes rather than research-informed theory (McCarthey, 2008).

These large-scale research studies have found that over decades much of the writing instruction in schools has remained quite limited to short, paragraph-length original answers or fill-in-the-blank type templates for which teachers are the primary or sole audience (Applebee & Langer, 2011). Although decades of research have shown the futility of isolated grammar instruction (e.g., Braddock, Lloyd-Jones, & Schoerer, 1963), grammar exercises still masquerade as writing instruction. When youth *are* asked to develop an extended piece of writing, it is typically in service of preparing for on-demand, timed year-end assessments. Increased emphasis on high-stakes writing assessments has also left teachers feeling pressure to devote the time they have for writing in school to prepare students for the five-paragraph themes or other formulaic, template-type responses that are prompted on large-scale assessments (Anson, 2008; Hillocks, 2002, 2008). In Applebee and Langer's (2013) most recent survey of writing instruction in U.S. secondary schools, in which they compared their findings across 30 years of inquiry, they found that though teachers' conceptions of writing have become more aligned to theorists' depictions of the complexity of writing, instructional practices have not much changed.

This is a bleak image of the state of writing instruction in schools. Hence, in this chapter, I review theoretical perspectives on writing and writing development as they relate to instructional practice, and focus in on the mismatch between theoretical depictions of writing development and current assessment and curriculum regimes. I advocate for theoretically reframing writing and writing development in assessment and curriculum—aligning guidance for writing instruction to the transdisciplinary theoretical perspectives that depict writing as emergent, multidimensional, relational, dynamic, and driven by human desire. The theory reviewed in this chapter is neither exhaustive nor meant to be definitive; rather, it is one telling[1] of some of the modern waves of writing's transdisciplinary theory building across time in response to recent theoretically starved educational standards and policies regarding writing, its development, and instruction.

Theoretical Perspectives on Writing and Implications for Instruction

Thus far, I have used a variety of terms in relation to writing. Some of the words—such as recursive, idiosyncratic, relational, and multidimensional—are descriptive of writing, whereas others identify its multiple dimensions, such as writing's textual and linguistic written *products* dimension, its cognitive and stage *processes* dimension, its social and contextual *practices* dimension, and its material, modal, and mobilities or *pathways* dimension. Although writing has always entailed these dimensions, and thus, is described as multidimensional, each dimension has received focal attention in multiple waves of scholarship over time, and hence, can be told as a history of transdisciplinary theory building. By "theory," I do not merely refer to abstracted models, but as Prior and Lunsford (2008) advocate, I refer to a broad arc of theoretical work in writing from reflective practice to theoretical implications drawn from research to grand theory. In writing studies, *reflective practice* has played a distinct role in its history of theory building. Prior and Lunsford describe reflective practice as "sustained, collaborative attention to a phenomenon" (p. 83) during which a metadiscourse about a phenomenon develops allowing the phenomenon to be critically described, taught, practiced, and further scrutinized.

Following Lewis and del Valle (2008) and Yancey (1999), I describe this theoretical history as building in *waves* to draw on what the metaphor implies. These theoretical foci are not bound to particular time periods or specific dimensions, nor are they clearly distinct from each other. Rather, they ebb and flow across eras and dimensions, as well as when and how they have been taken up—if at all—in pedagogical practice. When attention to a particular ontological or epistemological approach within a dimension recedes, like tide pools, some attention remains and is carried on through research and practice, and like a beach, the landscape of writing theory has been left changed—sometimes just ever so slightly—before the next wave of theory building washes ashore.

A Products Dimension

Many scholars point to the late 1800s—and specifically to the introduction of a written entrance exam at Harvard University in the 1870s—as the time when writing's *product* dimension received its first wave of attention in modern schooling in the United States (Elliott, 2005). Deeming many of the passages written by incoming freshmen as inadequate, Harvard University began to offer remedial writing courses. During this era, writing in K-12 schools focused primarily on copying text and penmanship. Yancey (2009) argued that this initial framing of writing as a basic, entry-level skill—one that could be assessed adequately by a single written product—can be traced to today when writing in schools is still associated primarily with assessment, either of the written product itself or on behalf of demonstrating other content knowledge. This, she argued, is an atheoretical, techno-functional uptake of writing that has sustained a sense of crisis around students' perceived inability to produce quality written products.

Although the ways written products are assigned and assessed in schools have been often critiqued as atheoretical, the written product has received waves of theory building since that time, with a peak of theory building across dimensions cresting in the 1960s and 1970s (Nystrand, Greene, Wiemelt, 1993). For instance, researchers (e.g. Hunt, 1970; Loban, 1976) analyzed the syntactic strategies employed by writers to make developmental claims about the sophistication of sentences in written products. Their findings pushed back on popular assumptions that more mature writers wrote longer, more complex sentences. They articulated a perspective on mature writing that involved syntactic complexity, but more precisely that more "mature" syntactic complexity involved elaboration within sentence parts and succinct embedded concepts. It is important to emphasize that they did not find that syntactic complexity related to the effectiveness of the sentences or the evaluated quality of the written product. They also found that across time, and depending on the rhetorical situation and familiarity of the content, the syntactic complexity did not increase in a linear fashion or steady pace. Though a student's syntactic complexity was not associated with quality of written products or theoretically linked to development as a writer, working at the sentence level of written products with sentence-combining activities has been a popular instructional uptake in this dimension of writing.

At the same time, but taking a entirely different approach to the written product, Moffett (1968) applied Piagetian psychological theories of maturity to theorize a cognitive-distance developmental sequence in which the content of a written product that involved the self or personal experiences was at the lower end of the scale, and products that involved distant, abstracted content that was not experienced personally was at the developed end of the scale. Appling Moffett's cognitive-distance scale to the linguistic and structural patterns in a large sample of secondary students' written products, Britton et al. (1975) created a hierarchal taxonomy of the types of audiences and functions students were prompted to write. The base or least mature function was described as expressive or emotive, and the cognitively abstract functions, such as persuading, informing, and entertaining, were considered the most mature. Britton et al. found that students were most often asked to regurgitate information for which the teacher was the primary and sole audience. They termed these assignments "dummy runs" (p. 106), and advocated that a developing writer should have more opportunities to write for "real" audiences and purposes. Theirs was not the first call for authenticity in opportunities to write in schools, and not the last. Sheeran and Barnes (1991) have argued that schools have continued to foster genres of writing that are not in play outside of school, and therefore have a limited relevance to developing as a writer.

Perhaps due to the scope and scale of the Britton et al. (1975) study, their developmental taxonomy—rooted in applied Piagetian theories of cognitive development—had a major impact on writing in schools. The first UK National Curriculum in English, for instance, was based on a cognitive abstraction developmental sequence (Andrews & Smith, 2011). However, prescribing a sequence for writing curriculum was not the intention of the scholars who developed this taxonomy. Although the assigned writing tasks aligned with a cognitive-distance scale, the recommendation from Britton's team was that a developing writer needed a range of opportunities to produce written products for various audiences and with a growing range of function and form. Rather than a maturational sequence of cognition, Britton et al. (1975) argued:

> [T]he work we have classified cannot be taken as a sample of what young writers can do. It is a sample of what they have done under the constraints of a school situation, a curriculum, a teacher's expectations, and a system of public examinations which itself may constrain both teacher and writer.
>
> *(p. 108)*

The theoretical work of these studies was descriptive of what was made possible by the prompts and structures at place in the classrooms, and should not be taken as prescriptive.

A Processes Dimension

Another theoretical focus has been on writers' *processes* or the series of varied types of activities, both cognitive and rhetorical, that writers engage in as they produce a written product. Writers' processes have had at least three distinct waves of theory building that emerged within the same era, each rising from direct observation and reflective practice of student writers at work. Rohman (1965) is often cited as one of the first researchers to focus on what the writer is doing while composing school-based tasks. He suggested a simple, linear stage model: pre-writing, writing, and rewriting. A wave of researcher-practitioners, including Emig (1971), Perl (1979), and Sommers (1980), challenged the linearity and simplicity of this model. Perl, for instance, demonstrated that writers' processes were recursive and within each phase was a series of various activities during which writers "shuttled" back and forth between activities.

Writing instruction has been intertwined with the development of theories about writers' processes (Boscolo, 2008; Pritchard & Honeycutt, 2006), not only because the theory emerged from reflective practice, but also because these theories suggested writing instruction should be embedded throughout the process. Murray (2003) claimed, "When we teach composition, we are not teaching a product, we are teaching process" (p. 3–4). Instructional practices such as freewriting, peer response groups, and teacher conferences are all associated with this recursive stage model of writing processes. The writing workshop approach also grew out of this focus on writers' processes (Calkins, 1983).

During this same time, a resonant wave of theorizing this dimension as a process of personal discovery was washing ashore. Arguing that formalist approaches, which emphasized form and correctness in the written product, were fundamentally flawed, Elbow (1973) suggested that writing is a learning transaction in which the writer discovers and learns as they write. Referred to as "expressionists" or "progressives," scholars in this wave advocated that students write about personal experiences in order to discover understandings of the world. This expressionist wave was marked by an emergence of the idea of personal "voice" in writing, and foregrounded imagination, experimentation, and creativity as fundamental to writing. It was argued that these attributes should be advocated for in the writing done in schools (Coles, 1967). This wave focused on the constructivist and transactional notions of learning through the processes of writing (Mayher, Lester, & Pradl, 1983). For instance, Macrorie's (1988) I-Search Paper approach suggested that writing extended well beyond the immediate processes of inscribing text, and that writing in school should engage students in inquiring into the contexts of phenomena through questioning.

Another wave in this dimension focused on the cognitive processes of text production. Both Bereiter and Scardamalia (1987) and Flower and Hayes (1981) constructed models of the cognitive processes a writer engages in as they are writing, which have had great uptake in the field since they were introduced (McCutchen, Teske, & Bankston, 2008). Since Bereiter and Scardamalia's models have been briefly reviewed in the introduction, here I will provide an overview of Flower and Hayes's (1981) more fine-grained model that depicted composition as a goal-driven distinct series of cognitive processes. Their model presented four overarching, highly embedded cognitive processes involving Task Environment, Writing Processes, Long-term Memory, and Monitoring. Each of these processes involved embedded sub-processes. For instance, within Writing Processes, they identified three sub-processes—planning, translating, and reviewing— and each of these processes had sub-processes of their own. Planning involved processes of generating, organizing, and goal setting, and reviewing involved processes of evaluating and revising. Comparing the results of several think-aloud studies of adults and young children, they theorized that a sign of development in writing was having more conscious control of these processes, and they argued that metacognitive handling of writing processes was a key and learnable aspect of this dimension.

Across these three waves, writers' processes can be characterized generally as a problem-solving "non-linear, exploratory, and generative process[es] whereby writers discover and reformulate their ideas as they attempt to approximate meaning" (Zamel, 1983, p. 165). Historically speaking, the turn to foregrounding writers' processes marked a radical shift from decontextualized, formalist depictions of writing to more dynamic and relational theorization, including focus on writers' voices, interests, strategies, and approaches. However, the writing instruction that stemmed from these waves of theory building has not come without critique. Delpit (1988) argued that the heavy emphasis on personal discovery processes to the exclusion of discursive study and practice in conventional academic forms creates an instructional imbalance that leaves youth already marginalized in society and schooling at a further disadvantage in gaining access to the "culture of power" (p. 282). She explained, "In this country, students will be judged on their product regardless of the process they utilized to achieve it. And that product, based as it is on the codes of a particular culture, is more readily produced when the directives of how to produce it are made explicit" (p. 287). The instructional approaches for supporting writers through the recursive processes of writing have continued to be questioned for not yet proving to be effective in consistently delivering quality written products (Pritchard & Honeycutt, 2006). Others have argued that merely facilitating writers' otherwise "naturally" occurring processes is insufficient writing instruction (Applebee, 1986; Hillocks, 1986). Instead, Hillocks (2008) argued for an environmental (or structured; see Smagorinsky, Johannessen, Kahn & McCann, 2010) instructional approach in which teachers balance attentiveness to the students, materials, activities, and task through a mix of small and large group inquiry.

A Practices Dimension

The waves of theory building focused on the processes dimension in the 1960s to 1970s—specifically on the work that began to ask about aspects beyond the immediate end product or process of text production—were influential in drawing focus to a writing dimension in which writers' sociocultural *practices,* and historical and contextual positioning and power relations in writing, were theorized (Nystrand, Greene, & Wiemelt, 1993). However, attention to the social nature of writing had been brewing for some time before these swells. In the 1930s, the National Council of Teachers of English developed a Dewey-inspired *Experience Curriculum in English,* which suggested that writing experiences "are never limited solely to language; they are always social contacts" (Hatfield, 1935, p. 136). This curriculum encouraged teachers to position their teaching and themselves alongside students as they were engaged in their writing process, and to look at students' lives outside of school to inspire connections and relevance in teaching. These imperatives for writing instruction were repeated at the Dartmouth Conference of the 1960s that brought together expert representatives from English-speaking countries to map out theoretically attuned guidance for English curricula. Dixon (1967) summarized some of these findings, which were rooted in a developmental perspective on learning as socially constructed and included a call for more exploratory talk and writing in classrooms, equal emphasis on writing process as to written products, and opportunities to write about personal experiences outside the classroom.

Since this time, waves of theory in this dimension have described writing practices as dialogic, using a metaphor of writing as a conversation (McCarthey, 2007). This metaphor refers to the immediate "conversations" of literacy practice as a mediator of thinking (Vygotsky, 1986), as well as the broader exchanges of a person and their social environments (LeFevre, 1987), and broader still, the histories of practices that have come before (Bakhtin, 1986; Voloshinov, 1973) and which are reanimated or remediated (Prior & Hengst, 2010; Wertsch, 1991) at each composed utterance. Prior (1998, 2006) uses the terms *dispersed* and *distributed* to point to these longer socio-historical chains of influence that writing entails. He further suggests that given writing's "confluence of many streams of activity: reading, talking, observing, acting, making, thinking, and feeling as well as transcribing words" (p. xi) that an appropriate unit of focus in writing is literacy activity, or embodied, mediated, dialogic, semiotic practice (Prior, 2017; see also Agha, 2007; Witte, 1992).

Understanding writing as literacy practice means situating it in and across contexts as an inherently "social act" (Shaughnessy, 1977), and not just a rhetorical or grammatical exercise. As social practice, writers' activities, including their products and processes, position them in relation to others and in varying forms of participation in and across contexts (Kwok, Ganding, Hull, & Moje, 2016). Dyson's (e.g. 1993) work in the 1980s and 1990s, which focused on young children's writing development—highlighting their linguistically diverse repertoires and use of pop culture in everyday literacy activity—exemplifies this wave of theory building around the practices of writing as socially and contextually situated, historically rendered, and playing out through relationships and power hierarchies. This work is also historically significant to the field of writing studies as it marked scholarly attentiveness to the writing practices of young children, and the research and theory that could extend from a sociocultural approach. Boscolo (2008) explains that though "emergent literacy" was a phrase used in the 1960s (i.e., Clay, 1967), interest in instructional activities to guide children's writing development did not spark until the 1970s. However, since that time, pedagogies that focus on particular students and their development in the form of child study have remained popular (Carini, 1986; Owocki & Goodman, 2002; Rowe, 1994), and are a promising form of instruction that humanizes the developing writer in relation to multiple sociocultural aspects (Schultz, 2003).

Vandenberg, Hum, and Clary-Lemon (2006, p. 10) explain that the practice dimension is held by three theoretical presuppositions (paraphrased here with key references for each): (1) Writing is essentially social in a historical sense, in that "vocabulary, style, and voice are all an outcome of prior language use," either the writers' or others' verbal and written discourse (e.g. Voloshinov, 1973); (2) Writing is ideological, meaning it is "unavoidably bound up in" perpetuating or denouncing particular values and beliefs (e.g. Street, 1984); (3) Writing is constitutive, meaning it is sociogenetic material involved in the "creation, organization, and continuing development" of societies (e.g. Cole, 1996) and individuals' identities (e.g. Compton-Lilly, 2014; Ivanič, 1998). Further, Vandenberg, Hum, and Clary-Lemon (2006) add that writing practices position people in relation to others relative to "physically apparent or culturally constructed" differences that "critically affect the way we frame our experiences and encounters with others, and the way we are framed by others as we enter new contexts" (p. 14). For such reasons, Winn and Johnson (2011) argue for a culturally relevant and sustaining (Ladson-Billings, 2014) writing pedagogy in which students interrogate and act on social and political issues and ideologies at play in their lives.

Waves of theory building have keyed into writing practice as a form of identity work. Lewis and del Valle (2008) identified three of these waves—one in the 1970s and 1980s when identity was predominantly framed as a stable set of personal characteristics, followed by a wave in the 1990s through 2000s when identities were often discussed as negotiated and performed through practices. A current wave emphasizes the creative labor of writers in mediating hybrid, dynamic identities in response to their lives (Muhammad, 2015). In this wave, Yagelski (2011) argues for seeing writing ontologically as a way of being, of sensing the self and others through and during the writing experience. Centering American Indian philosophy, Arola (2017) argues for conceptualizations of composing as *culturing*, a term she draws from Ojibwemowin language in which "there is no static noun for *being* Ojibwe, but there is a sense of culture-ing *as* Ojibwe" (p. 279, italics in original). In this sense, composing, identities, and cultures are mutually constituted within active production during which "There is no authentic self who produces original works, instead there are writers who exist in relation to one another, draw from one another, and produce within ecologies of meaning" (p. 280). Indigenous rhetorics, she argues, imply ethics of care, empathy, and reflexivity attuned to others as one writes, remixes, and composes. In an era marked by rapid acceleration in the means to digitally compose and distribute writing, Hull and Stornaiuolo (2010) similarly theorize that writers' self- and other-work are aesthetic engagements that involve ethical and moral responsibilities to others in a globally networked world. Scholars drawing from queer theory (Alexander & Gibson, 2004) also position writing as self and other praxis, in which lesbian, gay, bisexual, transgender, queer, and intersex (LGBTQI) writers counter dominant narratives and normative discourses, connect with others, and compose to cope (Wargo, 2017) through what Pritchard (2017) theorizes (drawing also from Black and feminist theory) are restorative literacy practices of self-definition, self-care, and self-determination.

Since the 1970s and 1980s, the prefix *socio-* began to append many of the terms used in each of writing's dimensions, e.g. sociolinguistics (Halliday, 1973; Smitherman, 1977), sociocognitive (Scribner & Cole, 1981). The centrality of social practice was a key conclusion from multiple investigations into writing, its development, and its instruction by the National Center for the Study of Writing and Literacy (1985–1995; Freedman, Flower, Hull, & Hayes, 1995). Beck (2009) posited that social practice integrates product and cognitive process dimensions, arguing it could be seen more of a descriptive term about, rather than a dimension of writing. Scholarship focused on genre, for instance, took a social turn (Bazerman, Bonini, & Figueiredo, 2009; Miller, 1984), making discussions of a product's genre indistinguishable from its mutually constitutive sociocultural practices

(Luke, 1996). Rather than a separate dimension then, many theorize that each dimension of writing is inherently and thoroughly social (Gee, 2013; Prior, 2006).

A Pathways Dimension

Waves of theory building within a fourth *pathways* dimension have been co-currently emerging with and from the scholarship articulating writing as social practice. This dimension entails writing's dynamic ecologies or systems and mobilities, including its writer and their practices, as well as modalities, materials, and meanings (Nordquist, 2017; Stornaiuolo, Smith & Phillips, 2017). Whereas work in articulating the dimension of writing practices focused on the contexts *in* which writing takes place (Dryer, 2017), theory building in the pathways dimension troubles the concept of *contexts* as singular, bounded social spaces. Likewise, drawing from longitudinal studies of youths' writing development, Compton-Lilly (2014) theorizes that like spaces, the times and temporalities of writing are elastic as "the word, the self, and the world are created as remembered pasts and anticipated futures are enacted in literacy activity" (p. 41; see also Freire, 1970). Dyson (2007) challenges researchers and practitioners alike to consider writing contexts as nexuses of human interaction in which the "configurations of shared practices—themselves develop" (p. 116). Pennycook (2010) further argues that the concept of "shared practice" is itself an illusion of repetition rather than sedimented systemization and, drawing from Massey (1991), suggests that mobilities are essential for human life biologically and socially.

In these ways, this wave directs attention to writing as an aspect of dynamic, sociomaterial systems. From literacy studies (Barton, 2007) to writing studies (Dobrin, 2012), an ecological perspective on writing has been building. Though it has not yet been widely embraced in policy and instructional practice, Alvermann and Robinson (2017) argue that there has been a recurrent theme in writing ecologies theory over three decades on the interdependencies of the dimensions of writing, other activity, and the lives of the individuals who are writing. A humanizing writing ecologies approach, they further argue, calls for an intersectional approach (Nuñez, 2014) to understanding the inequitable systemic forces at play in these interdependencies.

Similar to a practices dimension, when attending to literacies' movements and mobilities, social power dynamics and the unequal and potentially inequitable movement of some messages, materials, practices, people, and modes over others are highlighted. Just as some writing practices, processes, and products are valued and supported in their capacity to transform from one space and time to another, others are held immobile—a phenomenon Lorimer Leonard (2013) calls the "paradox of mobility." Articulating a critical pedagogy of transliteracies that addresses these paradoxes, Smith, Stornaiuolo, and Phillips (2018) suggest three "pedagogical moves" for teachers taking up a critical orientation in writing instruction to make literacies' pathways dimension explicit: designing for emergence, practicing relational reflexivity, and surfacing critical lenses.

Attention to writing's pathways has been influenced, in part, by the distinctly interconnected nature of the modern era, marked by social and cultural global flows of information, people, resources, and media (Appadurai, 1996), and by rapid acceleration of socio-technological change, which has, in turn, heightened awareness of the media, modes, and materialities of writing. Though multimodality is not new to writing or writing instruction (Palmeri, 2012), the proliferation of digital technologies used with and for multimodal and multimedia composition has accented the urgency for writing instruction to extend beyond alphabetic text. Banks (2011) admonished, however, that uncritical acceptance of traditional print-based writing instruction practices applied to digital multimedia could perpetuate and exacerbate long-standing inequalities. This wave of theory building also draws renewed attention to the tools and objects of writing. From the motor activities of the body (eyes, hands, body position) in composing that have changed as writing utensils have evolved from primarily pen and paper to keyboard, touch screens, and currently, mobile technologies (Haas,

1995), theory building in writing's pathways dimension point to the *more-than-human* interactions of writing (Ehret, this volume; Micciche, 2014).

A current wave of theory building across disciplines has thus focused on transmodality or semiotic mobility. Newfield (2015) explains, "The point of tracing the transmodal sequences of meaning-makers—of tracing the routes along which their representations migrate and mutate—is to show how their ideas are formed, developed and change, in other words, how their literacy practices are semiotically mobile" (p. 267). Drawing from scholars who advocated for a repertoire approach in translingual writing instruction, Shipka (2016) called for instructional attention to compositional fluency, or as Horner, Lu, Royster, and Trimbur (2011) suggested "deftness in deploying a broad and diverse repertoire of language resources, and responsiveness to the diverse range of readers' social positions and ideological perspectives" (p. 308; see also Horner, Lockridge, & Selfe, 2015).

In a wave from the field of digital rhetoric, the theoretical apparatus *electracy* has surfaced as post-process pedagogy focused on the everyday collaborative social action of digital composing (Arroyo, 2005; Ulmer, 2003). Morey (2016) explains, "Metaphorically, electracy breaks from 'digital literacy,' as the latter term retrofits a prior logic (literacy) onto a new technology, a logic that was designed for an older technology (alphabetic writing)" (p. 2). Smith and Wargo (2017) argue that electracy critically attunes writing pedagogy to the embodied, multimodal, sociomaterial writing experience as mobile praxis. Across these waves of theory building in writing's pathways dimension, writing development is located with the individual as entangled with sociomaterial encounters— themselves developing—moving across dynamic contexts.

Caveats for Describing Writing as Multidimensional

I have described theory building in writing as waves of focus on particular dimensions of writing; however, there are two caveats to describing them as such. First, it may be that describing writing as multidimensional, and telling this history of theory building as waves of focus in these dimensions, may in fact perpetuate the false notion that writing's dimensions could or should be approached either in instruction or in research as separate. Instead, as theorized across waves, many scholars are calling for the synthesis of these dimensions (Bazerman et al., 2017), explaining that they coexist no matter the dimension of focus or emphasis (Prior & Thorne, 2014). The implication for writing instruction of this "everything and the kitchen sink" call from theorists is that rather than focusing on isolated or discrete activities, instructional approaches must take on writing as complex activity.

Second, this history of theory building is representative yet only partial—not comprehensive. It depicts writing and its history only as gleaned selectively from statements published in journals, reports, and books within academia that have been distributed and taken up broadly in the field. With publication pressures, support structures, and monetary incentives for knowledge generation in the form of publication, much of this history has taken place in university settings by researchers who may or may not have worked with younger populations in educational spaces. Theories of writing and its instruction that stem from K-12 educators and are disseminated in practitioner journals simply do not entertain the same reception and uptake in academia, and generations of writing and instruction in community practice and outside of schools go without representation in academia (except when in partnership with scholars at universities, such as Kinloch, 2009; Larson & Moses, 2018). Further, it is consequential that too often the work of scholars of color or work that centers on youth of color has been and is underrepresented in these histories, including this one. This is due to many reasons, including the historical and perpetuated underrepresentation of scholars and teachers of color in education (Haddix, 2017; Turner, Haddix, Gort & Bauer, 2017). There is also a tendency when work centering youth of color is included that it is framed as a boutique perspective reserved for sections on identity or linguistic "diversity."

Writing Development and Its Discontents with Assessment and Curricular Mandates

Transdisciplinary waves of writing theory are tightly intertwined with conceptions of writing development. It is worth reviewing these conceptions in order to reiterate a few theoretical disjunctures between theories of writing development and the assessment and curriculum regimes that guide writing instruction in schools. Recently, a collective of scholars whose scholarship in writing punctuates the history above, Bazerman, Applebee, Berninger, Brandt, Graham, Matsuda, Murphy, Rowe, and Schleppegrell (2017), engaged in years of discussions to map out a multidimensional approach to writing development. Working across fields of study, they articulated eight principles for understanding writing development across a person's lifespan. These principles are useful as succinct theoretical guideposts:

1. Writing develops across the lifespan as part of changing contexts.
2. Writing development is complex because writing is complex.
3. Writing development is variable; there is no single path and no single end point.
4. Writers develop in relation to the changing social needs, opportunities, resources, and technologies of their time and place.
5. The development of writing depends on the development, redirection, and specialized reconfiguring of general functions, processes, and tools.
6. Writing and other forms of development have reciprocal and mutually supporting relationships.
7. To understand how writing develops across the lifespan, educators need to recognize the different ways language resources can be used to present meaning in written text.
8. Curriculum plays a significant and formative role in writing development.

A dynamic, emergent, relational, multidimensional understanding of writing development, as these scholars depict, differs widely from common approaches to measuring growth and mandating instructional practice. As theories of writing and its development are translated to teaching, "development" is often reduced to an idealized, prescriptive, linear trajectory on a teleological scale of written product quality indexed by age or grade level, and set at a steady pace that can be communicated and regulated with policy and assessment oversight. However, modeling writing development as a simple, mechanistic trajectory of product quality across time is not reflective of the waves of theory building across dimensions and fields of study. For instance, in describing their third principle, "Writing development is variable; there is no single path and no single end point," Bazerman et al. (2017) note, "Individuals' developmental trajectories are marked by normal variation in the pacing and sequence of learning, and by both forward movement and 'backward transitions,' where writers use less sophisticated strategies in more difficult tasks or unfamiliar social situations" p. 355. Rather than a "closed system" in which linear trends in writers' products are idealized and predetermined (Anson, 2008), what is needed in assessment and curriculum is a theorization of writing development that accounts for multiple dimensions—inclusive of writing's processes, practices, and pathways and their complex, dynamic, emergent relations.

To make this shift, Andrews and Smith (2011) argue that new conceptual metaphors for development are needed. Ecological metaphors seem to be well suited (or harmonious; Fleckenstein, Spinuzzi, Rickly, & Papper, 2008) to conceiving of the emergent, relational, multidimensional, complex nature of writing development. Wardle and Roozen (2012) suggest that an ecological perspective on writing development can integrate the "vertical" or linear models of development within a single context or genre with the "horizontal" or breadth of literate lives. This would include interactions, activity, and materials not traditionally assumed to be involved in writing (Kell, 2009), but which theory in the writing pathways dimension surface. Smidt (2009) situates an ecological metaphor for writing development in Bakhtinian (1986) dialogics, which draws attention to the multiple historical relations at play when a writer is writing. An ecological metaphor is promising particularly due to its coherence to the waves of theoretical work in the practices and pathways dimensions of writing that depict writing and its development as a complex, emergent, multidimensional, relational, and dynamic phenomenon.

The Undertow: Persistent Problems in Assessment and Curriculum

Depictions of writing development as ecological run counter to the typical ways writing has been assigned and assessed in K-12 schooling. The evaluation of written products, and more specifically, single written products with tightly constricted parameters, frequently stands in proxy for other dimensions of writing (i.e., 46 out of 50 U.S. states assess writing using single, on-demand essays; Behizadeh & Pang, 2016). The development of a writer is charted in retrospect as a comparison of previously written products—either the students' own or against other students' or adults' prepared "exemplar" written products. When a written product or set of characteristics of a written product are positioned at the end of a teleological scale, it sets youths' written products in perpetual deficit to an idealized, and frankly imaginary, form. This perpetuates problematic assumptions about writing development, and the aims and approaches of writing instruction. As Andrews and Smith (2011) articulate:

> It assumes that successful communication can be predetermined by those outside of the intended audience. Even more basic, it is assumed that these single pieces—or in the case of portfolios, a set of written products—can determine writing ability. Performance on one task is assumed to be representative of typical current performance, as well as predictive of future performances. . . . It is also assumed that individuals can and should be assessed in isolation from others, and that writing is always a solitary activity. Finally, when these isolated performances or measurements of discrete skills are compared against each other by age group, they are described as if they measure development of writing—not just performance. Comparisons are simply not development.
>
> *(p. 170)*

Many other disconnects between theory and assessment practice can be added to this list, including the dominance of print text in these assessments as a sole indicator of composition, as well as the complete occlusion of the product to any other dimension of writing, including processes, practices, and pathways. The influential ways young people develop as writers through play (Medina & Wohlwend, 2016); digital composing with family (Lewis, 2014); counternarration and "bending" racist, xenophobic, sexist, and gender binaries (Thomas & Stornaiuolo, 2016); and participatory politics (Soep, 2014) remain outside the scope of these limited assessment schemes.

By attending to a single dimension in such a limited fashion, current assessment regimes are not guided by the rich theoretical histories charted in this chapter. Dixon (2010) argued that theoretical work on writing development was essentially "shut down" in the 1990s after the imposition of staged "progression" models in high-stakes testing regimes: "Fatally, the teacher's goal of finding optimal conditions . . . for developing writers was pushed aside, in the interests of setting national tests" (p. 4). Using a historical analysis of written assessment from the 1900s forward, Behizadeh and Engelhard (2011) found that psychometrics and measurement theory, more so than writing theory, have guided the construction and deployment of writing assessments. Likewise, Huot and Neal (2006) argue that advancing technologies have also driven writing assessment with increasing attention on measurements' reliability through automating decontextualized norming protocols. This overemphasis on reliability in the pursuit of "objectivity," they explain, usurps validity as writing assessments have become more increasingly at odds with writing theory. Further, particularly in terms of how writing assessments are used as gatekeepers for enrollment, placement, and promotion, and historically have been used to disenfranchise people politically and socially along racial, language, and gender lines (Inoue, 2015), the issue of assessment validity moves beyond a concern of measurement quality and fairness to one of social justice (Poe & Inoue, 2016). Looking beyond products to the multidimensional ecologies of writing development, argued Yancey (2009), would finally pivot writing instruction "beyond an obsessive attention to form and beyond writing as testing; it points us toward creating the fully articulated research base, the theories of composing, and the planned curriculum that have been missing from composition and instruction for over a hundred years" (p. 7–8).

Alternatives to single written product evaluations, normed rubrics, and teleological scales exist. Employing ecological theories of writing development, these alternatives are inclusive of writing's multiple dimensions and their interrelations. Since the 1980s, many scholars point to portfolios as one theoretically resonant assessment method (Yancey, 1999), but not as repositories for written products—rather, as reflective curated sets of artifacts across which assessors (teachers, students, family, and community together) think ethnographically and longitudinally (Wardle & Roozen, 2012) to descriptively and/or visually articulate the developing multidimensional repertoire (Andrews & Smith, 2011) of their growing rhetorical dexterity (Carter, 2008). In addition to attending to the characteristics of written products, students' writing processes, practices, and pathways are represented and traced (Wynhoff Olsen, VanDerHeide, Goff, & Dunn, 2017), including the (im)mobilities and fluencies of the writer in relation to the many sites they find themselves traveling across (Anson, 2008). Inoue (2015) theorizes that more just and anti-racist ecological assessment frameworks engage students in interrogating their writing ecologies to gain fuller understanding of their conditions of assessment. Suggesting that students need to be granted the power to participate in their assessment, Inoue suggests grading contracts as another assessment method resonant with writing ecologies theory.

In much the same way, many curricular mandates that guide writing instruction are incoherent with theories of writing development. In order to mandate curriculum, standards must be limited to teaching practices that can be implemented with fidelity across an entire school system. In an era obsessed with standardizing curriculum in this way, scaling ecological writing theory to a statewide or national sphere is problematic. Aspects from across writing's dimensions—such as self-discovery through writers' processes, and uptake (or not) of writing practices across settings—cannot be reliably regulated across classrooms, schools, districts, and so on. Thus, these components of writing dimensions are simply absent from curricular standards.

In the place of complex, ecological theorizations of writing development, many writing curricula borrow constructs from cognitive psychology. This has continued to be a popular and problematic approach to creating developmental schemes for writing. The developmental sequence of the U.S. Common Core Curriculum in Writing, for instance, rather than rooted in writing or rhetorical theory (Andrews & Smith, 2011; Rives & Wynhoff Olsen, 2015), can be seen as an application of a gradual release of responsibility type model, but stretched across the grades. In kindergarten, for example, students are asked to write "with guidance and support from adults." In second grade, "peers" are added to this phrase. By sixth grade, however, students' writing is supposed to involve *only* "some" guidance and support from others. By ninth grade "guidance and support" are taken completely from the standard. Such developmental schemes imply that a mature writer is one who composes in isolation; however, as the waves of theory building in the social practices dimension emphasize, writing inherently evokes engagement with others regardless of the age or development of the writer.

Murray (1968) argued that it was an all too common myth that a student's grade level should be associated with differing expectations in the parameters of a written product, engagement in a process, or type of social practice, explaining, "[It is a] fallacy that there is a group of writing problems peculiar to the tenth grade, the seventh grade or the twelfth grade" (p. 107). Echoing this sentiment, Bazerman et al. (2017) raised the challenge that in regard to the contemporary accountability and standards movement, "[S]pecifying benchmarks to be achieved and assessed at particular points in primary and secondary education has *de facto* formulated developmental objectives, even though these may not be grounded in research or an informed model of writing development. It has not even been determined whether broad-scale assessments based on the standards can be warranted by developmental research" (p. 325).

Impacts on Writing Instruction

The relationship between articulated theories of writing, its development, and instruction, and the tacit, everyday working theories of classroom teachers is a tenuous one (Andrews & Smith, 2011). When given time and space to reflect on their writing instruction in relation to their students' writing products, processes, practices, and pathways, teachers often trace multiple, and even conflicting, theoretical influences to their pedagogical practice (Handsfield, 2016; McCarthey, Woodard, & Kang, 2014). Policy and assessment regimes play a role in this, and act as a double-edged sword. They authoritatively communicate depictions of writing, development, and instruction modeled after linear, teleological developmental schemes with limited coherence to the theories discussed in this chapter. And at the same time, when teachers are required to enact these prescribed curricula—under pressure to have students produce decontextualized written products that cohere to a limited definition of quality—they tacitly build rationales for the action they are compelled to take. This phenomenon contributes to perpetuating instructional approaches misaligned to writing theory. New instructional practices or approaches can end up being put into practice within atheoretical frameworks—stripping the approach of its theoretical coherence (Whitney et al., 2008).

Take, for example, writing's processes dimension. Following the initial waves of theoretical work in the 1970s articulating writers' processes, Graves (1984) bemoaned that he was seeing "a sudden epidemic of orthodoxies" about writing's processes being perpetuated in pedagogical uptakes. He reflected later: "Artful response, listening, flexibility in decision-making, were replaced by attempts to regularize the process. I once overheard one teacher comment to another, 'Do you use the five-step or the seven-step Graves?' Writing theory was bypassed for brainstorming on Monday, writing leads on Tuesday, churning out a first draft on Wednesday, revising on Thursday, and publishing the final copy on Friday" (2004, p. 90). Jacobson (2015) has traced how a similarly regimented writing process is being perpetuated further in the implementation of the U.S. Common Core State Standards. Although linear, prescriptive curricular guides standardize instruction and lend a sense of control in a large, complicated educational infrastructure, they are simply not sufficient models of the development of a writer's products, processes, practices, and pathways (Dyson, 2013). Further, in use, they can contribute to perpetuating education's well-oiled deficit framework (Stevens, 2008).

If we hope to see coherent uptake of writing and development theory into practice, teachers need time and support (Locke, 2015) to engage in reflective practice, particularly regarding the interaction of mandated or "vertical" aspects of writing along with "horizontal" pathways of their students' and their own writing ecologies (Gutiérrez, 2008; Wardle & Roozen, 2012). Given the historical trend of emphasis on reading over writing in K-12 settings, and a lack of professional development and curricular and pedagogical resources for writing (Cutler & Graham, 2008), it cannot be assumed that efforts directed at "literacy" are supporting teachers in these forms of reflective practice in writing instruction. Drawing on a meta-analysis of studies looking at the relationship between a teacher's personal writing life and instructional impact, Cremin and Oliver (2017) have found teachers citing this intersection as a particular area of struggle and tension, with teachers repeatedly reporting low self-confidence in writing, negative writing histories, and limited ideas of what counts as writing. However, professional development dedicated to writing instruction that engages teachers in immersive writing workshops (Gardner, 2014), creative writing groups (Woodard, 2015), and/or reflective writing instruction groups, such as the National Writing Project (Whitney et al., 2008), has been shown to support teachers in reframing their epistemological stances toward writing, particularly in recognizing writing's dynamic processes, social practices, and negotiated pathways.

Conclusion

In this chapter, I have reviewed several modern waves of theory building in relation with their instructional implications, focusing on four mutually constitutive and dynamic dimensions of writing: products, processes, practices, and pathways. Although written products have been dominant in discussions of writing instruction, research, and assessment, the history of writing theory has bent toward more holistic, ecological understandings of writing and its development as complex, multidimensional, relational, dynamic, and driven by human desire. As theory has developed across dimensions, humanizing instructional approaches (Bartolomé, 1994) have been washing ashore. Humanizing approaches focus on the developing writer and their practices and pathways across writing ecologies, and are contrasted with instruction directed solely on the developing writing (whether that be the written product or process). These approaches have been long called for and requested anew in each dimension and wave of theory building—and most recently reiterated in the NCTE's report Professional Knowledge for the Teaching of Writing (2016).

I have also reviewed theoretically starved educational assessment and curricular mandates regarding writing and writing instruction that have had a long history of being ill fit to ecological and humanizing understandings of writing and its development. Like an ocean's undertow, regimes of assessment and curriculum have historically pulled against the waves of theory that have been building across dimensions of writing. If more just, ecological approaches were taken up in assessment frameworks and curricular mandates, however, the written product might finally be decentered from its domineering position. In its place, as Hatfield (1935) so long ago argued for, writing instruction would be situated as an activity that happens alongside writers as they navigate their writing processes and pathways and grow their repertoire of practices and rhetorical dexterity. Taking up writing in its complexity does not mean product characteristics would be ignored, but rather, instead of primarily directing instruction at the developing written product, developing *writers* would become central. In this humanizing endeavor, the dignity of a developing writer, and the culturing work of their writing are foregrounded over mechanics and "mistakes." In looking both at and beyond products and processes, the larger writing ecology can come into view and instructors can participate in critical engagement with youth in regard to their practices as they navigate their multiple and divergent writing pathways.

Note

1 Other histories of writing and its instruction from differing fields of study provide complementary tellings. As an opening salvo of histories to consider, I recommend, among others, Nystrand, Greene, Wiemelt's (1993) article on the intellectual history of the origins of collegiate composition studies; Freedman, Flower, Hull, & Hayes' (1995) report from the National Center for the Study of Writing and Literacy; Prior and Lunsford's (2008) treatise on writing studies as a multidisciplinary dialogue; Yancey's (1999) history of writing assessment and (2009) NCTE report on writing in the 21st Century; Berlin's (1982) review of pedagogy and rhetoric; and as a pair, Hillocks' (2008) history of writing in secondary schooling and Rowe's (2008) history of writing development for early literacy.

References

Agha, A. (2007). *Language and social relations*. Cambridge: Cambridge University Press.
Alvermann, D., & Robinson, B. (2017). Youths' global engagement in digital writing ecologies. In K. A. Mills, A. Stornaiuolo, A. Smith, & J. Z. Pandya (Eds.), *Handbook of writing, literacies, and education in digital cultures* (pp. 161–173). New York, NY: Routledge.

Alexander, J., & Gibson, M. (2004). Queer composition(s): Queer theory in the writing classroom. *JAC, 24*(1), 1–21.

Andrews, R., & Smith, A. (2011). *Developing writers: Teaching and learning in the digital age.* London: Open University Press.

Anson, C. M. (2008). Closed systems and standardized writing tests. *College Composition and Communication, 60*(1), 123–128.

Appadurai, A. (1996). *Modernity at large: Cultural dimensions of globalization.* Minneapolis, MN: University of Minnesota Press.

Applebee, A. N. (1981). *Writing in the secondary school: English and the content areas.* Urbana, IL: National Council of Teachers of English.

Applebee, A. N. (1986). Musings . . .: Principled practice. *Research in the Teaching of English, 20,* 5–7.

Applebee, A. N., & Langer, J. A. (2006). *The state of writing instruction in America's schools: What existing data tell us.* Albany, NY: Center on English Learning & Achievement.

Applebee, A. N., & Langer, J. A. (2009). What is happening in the teaching of writing? *English Journal, 98*(5), 18–28.

Applebee, A. N., & Langer, J. A. (2011). A snapshot of writing instruction in middle schools and high schools. *English Journal, 100*(6), 14–27.

Applebee, A. N., & Langer, J. A. (2013). *Writing instruction that works: Proven methods for middle and high school classrooms.* New York, NY: Teachers College Press.

Arola, K. L. (2017). Composing as culturing: An American Indian approach to digital ethics. In K. A. Mills, A. Stornaiuolo, A. Smith, & J. Z. Pandya (Eds.), *Handbook of writing, literacies, and education in digital cultures* (pp. 275–284). New York, NY: Routledge.

Arroyo, S. (2005). Playing to the tune of electracy: From post-process to a pedagogy otherwise. *JAC, 25*(4), 683–715.

Bakhtin, M. M. (1986). *Speech genres and other late essays* (V. W. McGee, Trans.). Austin, TX: University of Texas Press.

Banks, A. (2011). *Digital griots: African American rhetoric in a multimedia age.* Carbondale, IL: Southern Illinois University Press.

Barton, D. (2007). *Literacy: An introduction to an ecology of written language* (2nd ed.). Hoboken, NJ: Wiley-Blackwell.

Bartolomé, L. (1994). Beyond the methods fetish: Toward a humanizing pedagogy. *Harvard Educational Review, 64*(2), 173–194.

Bazerman, C., Applebee, A. N., Berninger, V. W., Brandt, D., Graham, S., Matsuda, P. K., Murphy, S., Rowe, D. W., & Schleppegrell, M. (2017). Taking the long view on writing development. *Research in the Teaching of English, 51*(3), 351–360.

Bazerman, C., Bonini, A., & Figueiredo, D. (2009). *Genre in a changing world.* Denver, CO: Parlor Press.

Beck, S. W. (2009). Composition across secondary and post-secondary contexts: Cognitive, textual and social dimensions. *Cambridge Journal of Education, 39*(3), 311–327.

Behizadeh, N., & Pang, M. E. (2016). Awaiting a new wave: The status of state writing assessment in the United States. *Assessing Writing, 29,* 25–41. doi:10.1016/j.asw.2016.05.003

Behizadeh, N., & Engelhard, G. (2011). Historical view of the influences of measurement and writing theories on the practice of writing assessment in the United States. *Assessing Writing, 16,* 189–211.

Bereiter, C. (1980). Development in writing. In L. Gregg and E. Steinberg (Eds.) *Cognitive processes in writing* (pp. 73–96). Hillsdale, NJ: Lawrence Erlbaum Associates.

Bereiter, C., & Scardamalia, M. (1987). *The psychology of written composition.* Hillsdale, NJ: Lawrence Erlbaum Associates.

Berlin, J. A. (1982). Contemporary composition: The major pedagogical theories. *College English, 44*(8), 765–777.

Berninger, V., & Richards, T. (2002). *Brain literacy for educators and psychologists.* New York, NY: Academic Press.

Boscolo, P. (2008). Writing in primary school. In C. Bazerman (Ed.) *Handbook of research on writing* (pp. 293–310). Hillsdale, NJ: Lawrence Erlbaum Associates.

Braddock, R., Lloyd-Jones, R., & Schoerer, L. (1963). *Research in written composition.* Urbana, IL: National Council of Teachers of English.

Britton, J., Burgess, T., Martin, N., McLeod, A., & Rosen, H. (1975). *The development of writing abilities (11–18).* London: Macmillan.

Calkins, L. (1983). *Lesson from a child: On the teaching and learning of writing.* Portsmouth, NH: Heinemann.

Carini, P. F. (1986). Building from children's strengths. *Journal of Education, 168*(3). Boston, MA: Boston University.

Carter, S. (2008). *The way literacy lives: Rhetorical dexterity and basic writing instruction.* New York, NY: SUNY Press.

Clay, M. M. (1967). The reading behaviour of five-year-old children: A research report. *New Zealand Journal of Educational Studies, 2,* 11–31.

Cole, M. (1996). *Cultural psychology: A once and future discipline.* Cambridge, MA: Harvard University Press.

Coles, W. (1967). The teaching of writing as writing. *College English, 29*(2), 111–116. doi:10.2307/374047

Compton-Lilly, C. (2014). The development of writing habitus: A ten-year case study of a young writer. *Written Communication, 31*(4) 371–403. doi:10.1177/0741088314549539

Cremin, T., & Oliver, L. (2017). Teachers as writers: A systematic review. *Research Papers in Education, 32*(3), 269–295.

Cutler, L., & Graham, S. (2008). Primary grade writing instruction: A national survey. *Journal of Educational Psychology, 100*(4), 907–919.

Delpit, L. (1988). The silenced dialogue: Power and pedagogy in educating other people's children. *Harvard Educational Review, 58*(3), 280–298.

Dixon, J. (1967). *Growth through English.* Oxford: Oxford University Press.

Dixon, J. (2010). Writing: Unfinished business? Back to finding out what actually works in teaching writing. *English Drama Media, 18,* 10–12.

Dobrin, S. (2012). *Ecology, writing theory, and new media.* London: Routledge.

Dryer, D. B. (2017). The state of the prefix: Two considerations, three examples, and four proposals. Plenary presented at the Translanguage, Transliteracies, & Transmodality Symposium, Urbana, IL.

Dyson, A. H. (1993). *Social worlds of children: Learning to write in an urban primary school.* New York, NY: Teachers College Press.

Dyson, A. H. (2007). School literacy and the development of a child culture: Written remnants of the "gusto of life." In D. Thiessen & A. Cook-Sather (Eds.), *International handbook of student experiences in elementary and secondary school.* Dordrecht: Kluwer.

Dyson, A. H. (2013). The case of the missing childhoods: Methodological notes for composing children in writing studies. *Written Communication, 30*(4), 399–427.

Elbow, P. (1973). *Writing without teachers.* Oxford: Oxford University Press.

Elliott, N. (2005). *On a scale: A social history of writing assessment in America.* New York, NY: Peter Lang.

Emig, J. (1971). *The composing processes of twelfth graders.* Urbana, IL: National Council of Teachers of English.

Fleckenstein, K., Spinuzzi, C., Rickly, R., & Papper, C. (2008). The importance of harmony: An ecological metaphor for writing research. *College Composition and Communication, 60,* 388–419.

Flower, L., & Hayes, J.R. (1981). A cognitive process theory of writing. *College Composition and Communication, 32*(4), 365–387.

Freedman, S. W., Flower, L., Hull, G., & Hayes, J. R. (1995). *TR 01-C. Ten years of research: Achievements of the National Center for the Study of Writing and Literacy.* Berkeley, CA: National Center for the Study of Writing and Literacy.

Freire, P. (1970). *Pedagogy of the oppressed.* New York, NY: Continuum.

Gee, J. (2013). Reading as situated language: A sociocognitive perspective. In D. Alvermann, N. Unrau, & R. Ruddell (Eds.), *Theoretical models and processes of reading* (6th ed., pp. 136–151). Newark, DE: International Reading Association.

Gardner, P. (2014). Becoming a teacher of writing: Primary student teachers reviewing their relationship with writing. *English in Education 48*(2), 128–148.

Graves, D. (1984). *A researcher learns to write.* Portsmouth, NH: Heinemann.

Graves, D. (2004). What I've learned from teachers of writing. *Language Arts, 82*(2), 88–94.

Gutiérrez, K. D. (2008). Developing a sociocritical literacy in the third space. *Reading Research Quarterly, 43*(2), 148–164.

Haas, C. (1995). *Writing technology: Studies on the materiality of literacy.* New York, NY: Routledge.

Haddix, M. M. (2017). Diversifying teaching and teacher education: Beyond rhetoric and toward real change. *Journal of Literacy Research, 49*(1), 141–149.

Halliday, M. A. K. (1973). *Explorations in the function of language.* London: Edward Arnold.

Handsfield, L. (2016). *Literacy theory as practice: Connecting theory and instruction in K-12.* New York, NY: Teachers College Press.

Hatfield, W. W. (1935). *An experience curriculum in English.* New York, NY: Appleton-Century.

Hillocks, G. (1986). *Research on written composition: New directions for teaching.* Urbana, IL: National Conference on Research in English/ERIC Clearinghouse on Reading and Communication Skills.

Hillocks, G. (2002). *The testing trap: How state writing assessments control learning.* New York, NY: Teachers College Press.

Hillocks, G. (2008). Writing in secondary schools. In C. Bazerman (Ed.), *Handbook of research on writing* (pp. 311–330). Hillsdale, NJ: Lawrence Erlbaum Associates.

Horner, B., Lockridge, T., & Selfe, C. (2015). Translinguality, transmodality, and difference: Exploring dispositions and change in language and learning. *Enculturation Intermezzo.* Retrieved from http://intermezzo.enculturation.net/01/ttd-horner-selfe-lockridge

Horner, B., Lu, M., Royster, J. J., & Trimbur, J. (2011). Language difference in writing: Toward a translingual approach. *College English 73*(3), 303–313.

Huot, B., & Neal, M. (2006). Writing assessment: A techno-history. In C. A. MacArthur, S. Graham, & J. Fitzgerald (Eds.), *Handbook of writing research* (pp. 417–432). New York, NY: Guilford Press.

Hull, G. A., & Stornaiuolo, A. (2010). Literate arts in a global world: Reframing social networking as cosmopolitan practice. *Journal of Adolescent and Adult Literacy, 54*(2), 84–96.

Hunt, K. W. (1970). *Syntactic maturity in schoolchildren and adults*. Chicago, IL: University of Chicago Press for the Society for Research in Child Development.

Hymes, D. (1994). Toward ethnographies of communication. In J. Maybin (Ed.), *Language and literacy in social practice* (pp. 11–22). London: Multilingual Matters.

Inoue, A. B. (2015). *Antiracist writing assessment ecologies: Teaching and assessing writing for a socially just future*. Anderson, SC: Parlor Press.

Ivanič, R. (1998). *Writing and identity: The discoursal construction of identity in academic writing*. Philadelphia, PA: John Benjamins Publishing.

Jacobson, B. (2015). Teaching and learning in an "audit culture": A critical genre analysis of Common Core implementation. *Journal of Writing Assessment, 8*(1). Retrieved from http://journalofwritingassessment.org/article.php?article=85

Kell, C. (2009). Literacy practices, text/s and meaning making across time and space. In M. Baynham & M. Prinsloo (Eds.), *The future of literacy studies* (pp. 75–99). London: Palgrave Macmillan.

Kinloch, V. (2009). *Harlem on our minds: Place, race, and the literacies of urban youth*. New York, NY: Teachers College Press.

Kirkland, D. (2013). *A search past silence: The literacy of young black men*. New York, NY: Teachers College Press.

Kwok, M. N., Ganding, E., Hull, G.A., & Moje, E. B. (2016). Sociocultural approaches to high school writing instruction: Examining the roles of context, positionality, and power. In C. A. MacArthur, S. Graham, & J. Fitzgerald (Eds.), *Handbook of writing research* (pp. 257–271). New York, NY: Guilford Press.

Ladson-Billings, G. (2014). Culturally relevant pedagogy 2.0: A.K.A. the remix. *Harvard Educational Review, 84*(1), 74–84.

Larson, J., & Moses, G. (2018). *Community literacies as shared resources for transformation*. New York, NY: Routledge.

LeFevre, K. B. (1987). *Invention as a social act*. Carbondale, IL: Southern Illinois University Press.

Lewis, T. Y. (2014). Apprenticeships, affinity spaces, and agency: Exploring blogging engagements in family spaces. *Journal of Adolescent and Adult Literacy, 58*(1), 71–81.

Lewis, C., & del Valle, A. (2008). Literacy and identity: Implications for research and practice. In L. Christenbury, R. Bomer, & P. Smagorinsky (Eds.), *Handbook of adolescent literacy research* (pp. 307–322). New York, NY: Guilford Press.

Loban, W. (1976). *Language development: Kindergarten through grade twelve. NCTE committee on research report no. 18*. Washington, DC: Office of Education (DHEW), Cooperative Research Program.

Locke, T. (2015). *Developing writing teachers: Practical ways for teacher-writers to transform their classroom practice*. New York, NY: Routledge.

Lorimer Leonard, R. (2013). Traveling literacies: Multilingual writing on the move. *Research in the Teaching of English, 48*(1), 13–39.

Luke, A. (1996). Genres of power? Literacy education and the production of capital. In R. Hasan & G. Williams (Eds), *Literacy in Society* (pp. 308–338). New York: Longman.

Macrorie, K. (1988). *The I-search paper*. Portsmouth, NH: Boynton/Cook Publishers.

Massey, D. (1991). A global sense of place. *Marxism Today*, 24–29.

Mayher, J., Lester, N., & Pradl, G. (1983). *Learning to write/writing to learn*. Portsmouth, NH: Heinemann.

McCarthey, S. J. (2007). Four metaphors of the composing process. In L. Bresler (Ed.), *International handbook of research in arts education* (pp. 477–495). Dordrecht: Springer.

McCarthey, S. J. (2008). The impact of No Child Left Behind on teachers' writing instruction. *Written Communication, 25*(4), 462–505.

McCarthey, S. J.; Woodard, R., & Kang, G. (2014). Elementary teachers negotiating discourses in writing instruction. *Written Communication, 31*(1), 58–90.

McCutchen, D., Teske, P., & Bankston, C. (2008). Writing and cognition: Implications of the cognitive architecture for learning to write and writing to learn. In C. Bazerman (Ed.), *Handbook of writing research* (pp. 451–470). Hillsdale, NJ: Lawrence Erlbaum Associates.

Medina, C., & Wohlwend, K. (2016). *Literacy, play and globalization: Converging imaginaries in children's critical and cultural performances*. New York, NY: Routledge.

Micciche, L. R. (2014). Writing material. *College English, 76*(6), 488–505.

Miller, C. (1984). Genre as social action. *Quarterly Journal of Speech, 70*, 151–167.

Moffett, J. (1968/1983). *Teaching the universe of discourse*. Boston, CA: Houghton Mifflin Company.

Morey, S. (2016). *Rhetorical delivery and digital technologies: Networks, affect, electracy*. New York, NY: Routledge.

Muhammad, G. E. (2015). In search for a full vision: Writing representations of African American adolescent girls. *Research in the Teaching of English, 49*(3), 224–247.

Murray, D. (1968). *A writer teaches writing: A practical method of teaching composition.* Boston, MA: Houghton Mifflin Company.

Murray, D. (2003). Teaching writing as a process not product. In V. Villanueva (Ed.), *Cross-talk in comp theory.* Urbana, IL: National Council of Teachers of English.

National Council of Teachers of English. (2016). *Professional knowledge for the teaching of writing.* Retrieved from www2.ncte.org/statement/teaching-writing/

Newfield, D. (2015). The semiotic mobility of literacy: Four analytical approaches. In J. Rowsell & K. Pahl (Eds.), *The Routledge handbook of literacy studies* (pp. 267–281). New York, NY: Routledge.

Nordquist, B. (2017). *Literacy and mobility: Complexity, uncertainty, and agency at the nexus of high school and college.* New York, NY: Routledge.

Nuñez, A. M. (2014). Employing multilevel intersectionality in educational research: Latino identities, contexts, and college access. *Educational Researcher, 43*(2), 85–92.

Nystrand, M., Greene, S., & Wiemelt, J. (1993). Where did composition studies come from? An intellectual history. *Written Communication, 10*(3), 267–333.

Owocki, G., & Goodman, Y.M. (2002). *Kidwatching: Documenting children's literacy development.* Portsmouth, NH: Heinemann.

Palmeri, J. (2012). *Remixing composition: History of multimodal writing pedagogy.* Carbondale, IL: Southern Illinois University Press.

Pennycook, A. (2010). *Language as local practice.* New York, NY: Routledge.

Perl, S. (1979). The composing processes of unskilled college writers. *Research in the Teaching of English, 13*(4): 317–336.

Poe, M., & Inoue, A.B. (2016). Social justice and writing assessment: An idea whose time has come. *College English, 79*(2), 115–122.

Pritchard, E. D. (2017). *Fashioning lives: Black queers and the politics of literacy.* Carbondale, IL: Southern Illinois University Press.

Prior, P. (1998). *Writing/disciplinarity: A sociohistoric account of literate activity in the academy.* Mahwah, NJ: Lawrence Erlbaum Associates.

Prior, P. (2006). A sociocultural theory of writing. In C. A. MacArthur, S. Graham, & J. Fitzgerald (Eds.), *Handbook of writing research* (pp. 54–66). New York, NY: Guilford Press.

Prior, P. (2017). Setting a research agenda for lifespan writing development: The long view from where? *Research in the Teaching of English, 52*(2), 211–219.

Prior, P., & Hengst, J. (2010). Introduction: Exploring semiotic remediation. In P. Prior & J. Hengst (Eds.), *Exploring semiotic remediation as discourse practice* (pp. 1–13). Houndsmill: Palgrave.

Prior, P., & Lunsford, K. (2008). History of reflection and research on writing. In C. Bazerman (Ed.), *Handbook of research on writing* (pp. 81–96). Hillsdale, NJ: Lawrence Erlbaum Associates.

Prior, P., & Thorne, S. (2014). Research paradigms: Beyond product, process, and social activity. In E. M. Jakobs & D. Perrin (Eds.), *Handbook of writing and text production* (pp. 31–54). Berlin: Walter de Gruyter.

Pritchard, R., & Honeycutt, R. (2006). The process approach to writing instruction: Examining its effectiveness. In C. A. MacArthur, S. Graham, & J. Fitzgerald (Eds.), *Handbook of writing research* (pp. 275–290). New York, NY: Guilford Press.

Rives, A., & Wynhoff Olsen, A. (2015). Where's the rhetoric?: Exposing the (mis)alignment in the Common Core State Writing Standards. *Journal of Adolescent & Adult Literacy, 59*(2), 161–170. doi:10.1002/jaal.443.

Rohman, G. (1965). Pre-writing the stage of discovery in the writing process. *College Composition and Communication, 16*(2), 106–112.

Rowe, D. W. (1994). Preschoolers as authors: Literacy learning in the social world of the classroom. Cresskill, NJ: Hampton Press.

Rowe, D. W. (2008). Development of writing abilities in childhood. In C. Bazerman (Ed.) *Handbook of research on writing* (pp. 401–420). Hillsdale, NJ: Lawrence Erlbaum Associates.

Schultz, K. (2003). *Listening: A framework for teaching across differences.* New York, NY: Teachers College Press.

Scribner, S., & Cole, M. (1981). *The psychology of literacy.* Cambridge, MA: Harvard University Press.

Shaughnessy, M. (1977). *Errors and expectations: A guide for the teacher of basic writing.* Oxford: Oxford University Press.

Sheeran, Y., & Barnes, D. (1991). *School writing: Discovering the ground rules.* Milton Keynes: Open University Press.

Shipka, J. (2016). Transmodality in/and processes of making: Changing dispositions and practice. *College English, 78*(3), 250–257.

Smagorinsky, P., Johannessen, L. R., Kahn, E. A., & McCann, T. M. (2010). *The dynamics of writing instruction.* Portsmouth, NH: Heinemann.

Smidt, J. (2009). Developing discourse roles and positionings: An ecological theory of writing development. In R. Beard, D. Myhill, D. Nystrand, & J. Riley (Eds.), *The SAGE handbook of writing development* (pp. 117–125). London: Sage.

Smith, A., & Wargo, J. (2017). Experiencing electracy: Digital writing and the emerging communicative landscapes of youth composing selves. In K. A. Mills, A. Stornaiuolo, A. Smith, & J. Z. Pandya (Eds.), *Handbook of writing, literacies, and education in digital cultures.* New York, NY: Routledge.

Smith, A., Stornaiuolo, A., & Phillips, N. C. (2018). Multiplicities in motion: A turn to transliteracies. *Theory into Practice, 57*(1), 20–28.

Smitherman, G. (1977). *Talkin and testifyin: African American language and culture.* New York, NY: Routledge.

Soep, E. (2014). *Participatory politics: Next-generation tactics to remake public spheres.* Cambridge, MA: Massachusetts Institute of Technology.

Sommers, N. (1980). Revision strategies of student writers and experienced adult writers, *College Composition and Communication, 31*(4), 378–388.

Stevens, L. P. (2008). (Re)framing policy analysis. *Journal of Adolescent and Adult Literacy, 47*(1), 454–461.

Stornaiuolo, A., Smith, A., & Phillips, N. C. (2017). Developing a transliteracies framework for a connected world. *Journal of Literacy Research, 49*(1), 68–91.

Street, B. (1984). *Literacy in theory and practice.* New York, NY: Cambridge University Press.

Thomas, E., & Stornaiuolo, A. (2016). Restorying the self: Bending toward textual justice. *Harvard Educational Review, 86*(3), 313–338.

Turner, J. D., Haddix, M. M., Gort, M., & Bauer, E. B. (2017). Humanizing the tenure years for faculty of color: Reflections from STAR mentors. *Journal of Literacy Research.* doi:10.1177/1086296x17733493

Ulmer, G. (2003). *Internet invention: From literacy to electracy.* New York: Longman.

Vandenberg, P., Hum, S., & Clary-Lemon, J. (2006). *Relations, locations, positions: Composition theory for writing teachers.* Urbana, IL: National Council of Teachers of English Press.

Voloshinov, V. (1973). *Marxism and the philosophy of language.* (Trans. L. Matejka & I. Titunik). Cambridge, MA: Harvard University Press.

Vygotsky, L. (1986). *Thought and language* (Rev. ed.). Cambridge, MA: Harvard University Press.

Wardle, E., & Roozen, K. (2012). Addressing the complexity of writing development: Toward an ecological model of assessment. *Assessing Writing, 17*(2), 106–119.

Wargo, J. M. (2017). Designing more just social futures or remixing the radical present? Queer rhetorics, multimodal (counter)storytelling, and the politics of LGBTQ youth activism. *English Teaching: Practice & Critique, 16*(2), 145–160.

Wertsch, J. (1991). *Voices of the mind: A sociocultural approach to mediated action.* Cambridge, MA: Harvard University Press.

Whitney, A., Blau, S., Bright, A., Cabe, R., Dewar, T., Levin, J., Macias, R., & Rogers, P. (2008). Beyond strategies: Teacher practice, writing process, and the influence of inquiry. *English Education, 40*(3), 201–230.

Winn, M. T., & Johnson, L. (2011). *Writing instruction in the culturally relevant classroom.* Urbana, IL: National Council of Teachers of English.

Witte, S. (1992). Context, text, intertext: Toward a constructivist semiotic of writing. *Written Communication, 9*(2): 237–308. doi:10.1177/0741088392009002003

Woodard, R. L. (2015). The dialogic interplay of writing and teaching writing: Teacher writers' talk and textual practices across contexts. *Research in the Teaching of English, 50*(1), 35–59.

Wynhoff Olsen, A., VanDerHeide, J., Goff, B., & Dunn, M. (2017). Examining intertextual connections in written arguments: A study of student writing as social participation and response. *Written Communication, 35*(1), 58–88.

Yagelski, R. (2011). *Writing as a way of being: Writing instruction, nonduality, and the crisis of sustainability.* New York, NY: Hampton Press.

Yancey, K. B. (1999). Looking back as we look forward: Historicizing writing assessment. *College Composition and Communication, 50*(3), 483–503.

Yancey, K. B. (2009). *Writing in the 21st century: A report for the National Council of Teachers of English.* Urbana, IL: National Council of Teachers of English.

Zamel, V. (1983). The composing processes of advanced ESL students: Six case studies. *TESOL Quarterly, 17*, 165–187.

4

MARIE M. CLAY'S THEORETICAL PERSPECTIVE

A Literacy Processing Theory

Mary Anne Doyle

Marie M. Clay was a clinical child psychologist who chose to study young learners during their initial, formative years of literacy acquisition. Applying the perspectives and practices of developmental psychology (Clay, 2001), she sought to document behavioral changes in children's literacy development by capturing performance in reading and writing tasks collected over time. She therefore designed studies to gather empirical evidence collected in controlled conditions, and she grounded her tentative theories in the resulting data (Clay, 1998).

Clay's initial work was motivated by questions resulting from the correlations found between learners' literacy performance in the first year of school and their rankings among peers in subsequent years. Specifically, she found that those with very limited progress in reading and writing at the end of their first year of instruction remained among the lowest performing students year after year. To address this challenge and create instructional opportunities to change predictions of failure, Clay chose to initiate her work by pursuing clarification of optimal literacy development among young learners, that is, securing descriptions of the literacy progress of successful children.

Applying the perspectives and practices of developmental psychology (Clay, 1991a), she documented changes in children's literacy development by capturing behavioral performance in reading and writing tasks collected longitudinally. There were no existing accounts of learners engaged in their earliest school-based encounters with literacy; therefore, she set out to document what occurs, which she referred to as a legitimate first step (Clay, 2001). Although delineation of behaviors changing over time was her first objective, related goals, aligned with her developmental orientation, were explanations of observed changes and consideration of how to modify learning conditions to optimize development for all individuals (Clay, 2004). For struggling learners, she described this as "leading children back . . . to a more secure developmental track, that is, to the *recovery of a more normal trajectory*" (Clay, 1998, pp. 288–289), which brought her to the study of intervention.

Resulting from her earliest investigations of literacy, Clay (2001) embraced a complex theory of literacy and defined reading as

> a message-getting, problem-solving activity, which increases in power and flexibility the more it is practised. It is complex because within the directional constraints of written language, verbal and perceptual behaviours are purposefully directed in some integrated way to the problem of extracting sequences of information from texts to yield meaningful and specific communications.
>
> *(p. 1)*

Her quest for theoretical explanations focused on building understandings of both the specific perceptual and cognitive behaviors involved in reading and writing and explanations of the integration of complex in-the-head processes. Thus, explanations of progress involved descriptions of working systems, that is, the perceptual and cognitive working systems directed to complete reading and writing tasks.

The acquisition of literacy processing "begins when a child is expected to compose and write a simple message or read a simple continuous text" (Clay, 2001, p. 97), for it is in processing complete messages that the working systems for literacy are engaged and developed. She therefore focused on learners reading continuous texts and composing and writing personal messages.

Initially, Clay focused on discovering the emerging and changing literacy behaviors of children who were found to be proficient readers and writers for their age cohort. She sought to base her inferences on patterns of development in the behaviors of those children exhibiting expected changes in reading and writing over their first year of school. An additional benefit of detailed accounts of optimal development was understandings of "when and how to begin teaching, of the changes that may be expected over time, of the track that most children take, of the variability to be expected, and of different developmental paths" (Clay, 1998, p. 255).

Clay considered the pre-school, developmental histories of children to be unique, individual, and replete with complex learning tasks. Children construct their own understandings as a result of opportunities to learn, they do not shy away from complexity, and they bring their unique stores of knowledge with them to school. At 5 years of age, each school entrant has extensive knowledge of oral language even though their oral language acquisition is incomplete. Their oral language proficiency, their vocabulary knowledge, their knowledge of their worlds, and their pre-school experiences with literacy are available when formal literacy instruction begins and they initiate construction of complex processing systems.

The following discussion reviews Clay's discoveries resulting from her meticulous efforts to describe changes observed in children's literacy processing during early acquisition, the theoretical perspective resulting from her quest to explain observed changes, and actions relative to promoting optimal development for young learners in need of a more secure developmental track.

Research Efforts: Documenting Changes Observed in Literacy Processing

Clay began her quest to document change in observable literacy behaviors with an atheoretical, no-hypothesis stance to data collection (Clay, 1982). Unsatisfied with existing explanations of reading acquisition, she sought new understandings through scientific methodology involving both qualitative and quantitative procedures. Her initial goal was to record children's behaviors sequentially "using reliable, systematic sampling and observation techniques" (Jones & Smith-Burke, 1999, p. 262).

Clay's methodology deviated from prevalent approaches that tended to quantify the effects of instruction by examining learners' pre- and postinstructional performance. In opposition to quantifying the effects of instruction (or teaching), Clay's interest was the delineation of qualitative changes in children's learning. She focused on the study of observable behaviors in how children work in reading and writing continuous texts (i.e., literacy processing) and interpreted changes as signals of change in psychological processes, such as perceiving, linking, and decision making. She referred to her perspective as a literacy processing view of progress in literacy acquisition and determined that the resulting descriptions of change offered an alternative view of progress—alternative to the more common use of pre- and posttests and statistical computations to set expectations (of both curricular goals and student achievement) and to evaluate results (Clay, 2001). Her focus included examining what young readers do as they encounter and problem solve increasingly difficult tasks. Therefore, by studying learners over time through the documentation of observed behaviors, she sought to clarify the sequence of changes in ways children process information and the emergence of competencies for effective reading and writing.

To conduct her research, she developed and applied an unusual lens, defined by her as any observational tool or research methodology that gathers "detailed data on changes in literacy processing over short intervals of time from subjects engaged in reading or writing continuous texts" (Clay, 2001, p. 16). Clay's running record of reading provides an example of an observational tool for collecting sequential, detailed accounts of what occurs as a child reads continuous text.

Clay's (1982) seminal research of 100 New Zealand children entering school at the age of 5.0 was a longitudinal study involving both weekly, systematic observations of individuals' writing and reading behaviors collected within natural settings and a test battery administered at three points over each child's first year of school. Clay conducted her study in classrooms where children were engaged in writing personal messages and reading storybooks daily within weeks of entering school. Although the participants were from different classrooms and schools, Clay determined that the common curriculum guidelines created instructional consistency across settings. Teachers did not delay opportunities for authentic literacy tasks, nor did they follow a prescriptive curriculum requiring proficiency with prerequisite skills prior to engaging children in reading and writing stories. Teachers expected children to work as independently as possible, and their expectations matched children's competencies. Thus, initial writing samples were often drawings with labeling provided by an adult. Although none of her participants could read at entry to school, all were introduced to short story books written in a familiar language within their first seven weeks of school.

When children reached the end of their first year of instruction and were tested with standardized instruments, Clay used the results to create four groups of varying levels of proficiency: high, high average, low average, and low. Comparing the performance within and between groups, Clay (1966) discovered that children were significantly different in their literacy learning. The results revealed multifactored ways in which children "constructed complex literacy processing systems for both reading and writing" (Clay, 2001, p. 288). Her documented map of literacy behaviors allowed her to describe literacy learning in the process of change, which gave Clay the genesis of her literacy processing theory.

This study prompted ongoing research conducted by Clay and her colleagues to pursue and confirm understandings and to test alternative hypotheses. The foci of her extensive body of research include the reading behaviors of children in their third year of instruction, syntactic analyses of reading errors, self-correction behavior, writing development, oral language performance, language proficiency of bilingual children, analysis of linguistic variables in oral reading (juncture, pitch, stress), concepts about print, visual perception, prevention, and early intervention (see Clay, 1982, 2001).

Research Findings: Documented Changes in Literacy Behaviors Over Time

Clay observed that the young learners she followed often read their first books using low-level strategies, or primitive working systems, acquired from experiences with talking, writing, and listening to stories prior to entering school. For example, some appeared to rely on their auditory memory of predictable sentences or stories. Many were aware of concepts of books, including awareness of the connections between pictures and text and anticipating and using a repeated sentence pattern. Their prereading behaviors indicated that they were attending to many aspects of literacy as

- they responded to print with a series of utterances
- they checked with pictures for agreement
- they matched pointing and word utterance on 50 percent of the text
- they increased attention to words using the spaces between words to guide them
- they located one or more words on request (Clay, 2001, p. 59)

Although such early processing behaviors (low-level strategies for reading) are not effective, they were found by Clay to be an adequate, initial starting place as they evolved into behaviors revealing more complex working systems and accurate and efficient responses as a result of instruction. Clay (1982) confirmed that the development and learning that led to more appropriate literacy processing behaviors resulted from ongoing exposure to stories (i.e., continuous texts). There was no advantage to delaying text reading and personal writing opportunities for 5-year-old children. In contrast, experience in continuous texts revealed important advantages.

Clay (1966, 1982) reported observing changes in a range of behaviors in each of four areas as learners exhibited more proficient reading behaviors. These four areas are (1) the directional constraints on movement (i.e., consistent left to right movement across words and lines of text), (2) visual perception of print (i.e., awareness of letter and word forms), (3) constructing appropriate types of speech responses (i.e., appropriate speech or syntax), and (4) the matching of spoken word units to written word units (i.e., synchronized one-to-one matching; Clay, 1982).

Clay determined that the earliest, teacher-scaffolded reading and writing activities supported essential learning neglected by most literacy theories. This includes the appropriate directional schema for attending to print and the movement patterns for processing text. "Directional behaviors manage the order in which readers and writers attend to anything in print. Gaining control of them is a foundational step in literacy as oral language is matched to written language" (Clay, 2001, p. 118). Establishing consistency in directing visual attention to print so lines of text, words, letters, and clusters of letters within words are scanned left to right in sequence is challenging and requires time. Evidence resulting from a study of quadruplets revealed both a time span of six months and clear, individual differences among children in the time needed to secure appropriate directional scanning of text (Clay, 1974, 2001).

Where to look, what to look for, and how to fixate and move the eyes across print are among the first things learned by novice readers. For the beginning reader/writer, this learning involves coordinating the body, hand, and eye movements needed for literacy processing, and thus, motor behaviors create an early working system for processing text. Gradually, directional order and one-to-one matching of speech with print become established routines requiring no conscious attention. This learning is one of the advantages of immersing beginning readers in the reading and writing of continuous texts.

In regard to visual perception of print, Clay found the richest depictions of the learner's awareness of letter and word forms in the writing products of her proficient learners. The following is a brief depiction of this learning of the features of print and the relationship between letters and words. Children gradually shifted from creating messages by drawing and writing to recording written messages without drawings; they exhibited awareness that writing consists of letters, a string of letters comprise a word, a word is a specific sequence of letters, and the sequence of letters relates to the spoken form of the word (Clay, 1998). The child's knowledge of letters and sound–symbol relationships is neither extensive nor complete at this point, and gaining control of this information is a major task. However, awareness and initial understandings create supportive visual knowledge for early reading that will continue to expand as a result of ongoing reading and writing experiences.

With only a few known items of visual knowledge (several letters and words), the proficient readers appeared to expand their literacy processing by increased applications of their newly acquired information. Analyses of their oral reading errors revealed searching and monitoring behaviors on the basis of visual information, often only an initial letter. The important processing advance was the child's increased receptiveness to visual information and ability to pull a new kind of information in print knowledge together with other knowledge sources (i.e., syntactic information) to read a message (Clay, 2001, p. 64).

Clay determined that early writing experiences served as a significant source of new learning that contributed to the child's construction of more effective working systems for processing literacy. Children in her studies were learning to read and write concurrently, which created benefits supporting the acquisition of foundational knowledge and the inner control of literacy processing. By writing a single sentence, the learner coordinates a range of behaviors: movement patterns required for dealing with print, ordering written language in appropriate sequences, visual scanning of letters and words, and the analysis of sounds in words. The learner attends to features of letters, learns new letters and some words, and begins to link sounds with letters. Writing experiences help build the working systems needed to search for information in print, strategies used to combine and check information, an awareness of how to construct a message, and awareness of the sources of knowledge available in written language (Clay, 2001, p. 17). These represent key, foundational aspects shared by writing and reading.

Based on her study of writing development over time, Clay (1975) observed that in the writing context, young writers

> do not learn about language on any one level of organization before they manipulate units at higher levels. When they know a few letters they can produce several words, and with several words they can make a variety of sentences.
>
> *(p. 19)*

Their attention to letters, sounds, and words serves their efforts to record personal messages, and they manage the complexity of the full range of information sources to complete their intentions. Clay (1982) noted that although their initial understandings are perhaps intuitive, her observations and evidence suggest that children learn on all levels of the language hierarchy at once, and it is the "rich intermingling of language learning across levels which probably accounts in some way for the fast progress which the best children can make" (Clay, 1975, p. 19). This represents the reciprocity between writing and reading that is so beneficial to the learner's construction of early literacy systems and acquisition of language knowledge that extends processing in both reading and writing.

Interestingly, Clay (1982) found no developmental sequence apparent in her records of proficient readers' emerging and changing behaviors in reading and writing. Individual children exhibited unique developmental histories, including "by-passing many of the steps which another child may follow" (Clay, 1982, p. 14). This discovery confirmed that individual learners take different paths to proficient reading and writing development (Clay, 1998, 2001). However, records also revealed that some children had difficulties with various aspects of the four early areas of development, and others persisted with inappropriate responses to reading and writing, such as a consistent right to left approach to print or inventing stories when asked to read (Clay, 1982).

In regard to changes documented in the readers' awareness of foundational literacy behaviors, records of reading behaviors revealed increasing awareness of the following:

* where to attend
* where to search
* what information to use
* what to relate information to
* how to monitor its acceptability
* what to do in the face of a dissonant result (Clay, 2001, p. 104)

As children gained awareness and their behaviors suggested more proficient working systems, they began to integrate information from two or more sources (e.g., from visual and syntactic information sources) more consistently to match what they said to the print. These behaviors were early forms of efficient reading behaviors that "became purposefully directed in some primitively integrated way to the problem of extracting a sequence of cues from text" (Clay, 2001, p. 60). These behaviors were interpreted by the teachers in Clay's study as indicative of the learners' preparedness for their first formal instructional texts.

One pattern of behavior appearing in Clay's original data was the unprompted, spontaneous self-correction of reading errors by young learners. Self-corrections were observed in the earliest readings of stories and first appeared when the child noted that his or her speech (oral reading of words) did not correspond to (match) the locating movements for the printed words on the page (often involving finger pointing). Based on monitoring appropriate movement patterns for reading, the reader revised, or corrected, his reading. This early behavior indicates a learner's willingness to choose between alternatives in order to read a precise message and maintain a fit between the language and visual information, two sources of information for text reading (Clay, 1991b, 2001).

As her proficient readers advanced in text reading levels, Clay (1991b, 2001) found that self-correction behaviors revealed that readers could search and check more and more detail in print to both correct and confirm their reading, which involved the range of information sources: visual information, including letter forms and letter–sound relationships; syntax; and semantic information. Clay (1982, 1991b, 2001) proposed that self-correction and the problem solving it entails is tutorial for the reader who is reinforced internally for his or her monitoring, searching, generating, choosing, and evaluating. Thus, Clay (2001) suggested that a learner's "willingness to choose between alternatives leads to a search for more information and this can potentially take processing to new levels of complexity" (p. 120).

There were two additional discoveries regarding self-correction behavior. First, a high level of reading accuracy (90%) is required for proficient self-correction behavior, and there is a clear progression in the amount of rereading completed by readers engaged in self-correcting. Records revealed that rereading is initially done from the very beginning of a sentence or a line of text and progresses to the rereading of a phrase, then rereading of a word, then an initial letter. Clay (2001) reported that this sequence, a pattern found to be identical in the records of high and low progress readers, provides a way to judge progress and observe change in the reader's literacy processing over time.

At the point when proficient learners transitioned into formal instruction, Clay's (2001) records of behaviors revealed the following:

- They could not read, but they identified the words in the text with 80% accuracy.
- They selected words one after the other to construct viable sentences.
- They could reject a response and try a different one.
- They began to self-correct.
- They knew a few words in reading and/or writing.
- They could bring two kinds of behaviors together (e.g., verbal and pointing behavior).
- They often stressed the separation (juncture) between words.

Gradually, readers demonstrated the ability to construct what a line of text might say, locate the sequence of information to attend to, and detect, or monitor, mismatches between their seeing and saying (Clay, 2001).

As these beginning readers worked with different kinds of information, their processing was labored, observable, and sequential. The transitions and development that Clay observed were replicated by Nalder (as cited in Clay, 2001) and delineated as follows:

- (Readers) begin to try to use the language of the book, to match what they say line by line and (later) word by word with some attention to occasional visual cues in known words. Language composed by the child supports any processing but can override the printed text.
- Another change is detected when the reader uses the language of the book, matched word to word, and definitely attends to some visual information. There is a lot of searching, checking and self-correcting with appropriate appeals for help and some omissions.

- Within about six months, fluent accurate reading is achieved by many with some successful solving, and two or more sources of information are used for one decision.
- After six months at school, proficient readers can be independent when handling the challenges in appropriately selected easy texts, using several sources of information (semantic, syntactic, visual, or sounds in sequence), and knowing how to check one kind of information against another.

Therefore, as a result of instruction in continuous text, "a quite simple set of responses became controlled, accurate and co-ordinated" (Clay, 2001, p. 59). In effect, these behaviors were early forms of efficient reading behaviors that

> became purposefully directed in some primitively integrated way to the problem of extracting a sequence of cues from text. Children were attending to letters, and words, and the sounds of letters in reading and writing, and they monitored these activities while enjoying the story they were composing in either reading or writing.
>
> *(Clay, 2001, p. 60)*

Clay had documented the early emergence of foundational processing and ongoing changes in her readers' literacy processing systems. She found that from the beginning, proficient readers use language and visual and motor information so "what on the surface looks like simple word-by-word reading . . . involves children in linking many things they know from different sources (visual, auditory/phonological, movement, speaking/articulating, and knowledge of the language)" (Clay, 2001, p. 79) to read a precise message. In effect, the reader making good progress constructs a literacy processing system that involves all language knowledge sources, including story structure, language structure, words and word structure, letters, and the features and sounds of letters.

Over time, the records of oral reading by proficient, beginning readers revealed increasing attention to and success with the visual information in text (e.g., initial letters, letter clusters, word parts, words) while maintaining appropriate syntactic and semantic utterances for the given context. In the beginning reader, each knowledge source is limited, and proficient development results from ongoing instruction in both reading and writing contexts. Much of the new learning entails visual perception and the acquisition of a large set of items (e.g., letters, letter clusters, words) acquired over time. However, in both reading and writing contexts, Clay's young learners engaged in literacy activities successfully by being allowed to draw on their existing language knowledge while being introduced to new learning. Clay (1982) found this to be true of a diverse set of learners, even bilingual children whose command of the English language of instruction was limited.

Proficient readers used their knowledge of oral language from the beginning. Their oral language provided a reliable source of information for predicting messages and for detecting reading errors. Gradually, the readers' awareness of semantic and syntactic information in text was enhanced by visual perceptual learning, including the learning of letters, letter–sound associations, words, and the use of word parts and syllables. Over time, semantic and syntactic information sources continued to expand, and important learning also proceeded "in the direction of more and more receptiveness to visual perception cues which must eventually dominate the process" (Clay, 1982, p. 28). Reading is a visual task, and the learner's increased, detailed control of visual information is an essential part of early reading acquisition (Clay, 2001).

In addition to the observed changes over time in a proficient reader's awareness of and increasing knowledge of the range of sources of language information in text, Clay's (2001) evidence also revealed how the early, primitive literacy processing expanded into more efficient decision-making. She discovered that proficient readers were constructing a network of strategic behaviors, action systems, or cell assemblies for processing text—cognitive terms useful in describing "what readers do as they work sequentially on the information sources in print to get the author's message"

(Clay, 2001, p. 198). The readers had learned how to search and check information, how to go back to search again, and how to monitor their reading and confirm their decision making. The types of strategic behaviors they applied include the following:

- controlling serial order according to the directional rules for the script being read, across lines and within words
- using what you know about in reading to help writing and vice versa
- problem-solving with more than one kind of information
- actively searching for various types of information in print
- using visual information
- using language information
- drawing on stored information
- using phonological information
- working on categories, rules or probabilities about features in print
- using strategies which maintain fluency
- using strategies which problem-solve new features of printed words and meanings
- using strategies which detect and correct errors (Clay, 2001, p. 199)

To explore the reading of proficient readers after three years of instruction, children's oral reading behaviors were gathered in a number of studies conducted by Clay and colleagues (see Clay, 1982). Clay's summary of this observational data revealed successful readers working sequentially across text, giving detailed attention to the range of information sources. They read accurately at a good pace, solved new or difficult words independently, and detected and self-corrected many of their errors.

Analyses of oral reading errors showed that on many occasions, the word read, although wrong, was typically influenced by syntax, meaning, letter knowledge, and letter–sound relationships. When an error occurred and was uncorrected, the substituted word corresponded to the text word on all four types of information, suggesting that good readers could be using subword, word, syntactic, and semantic information jointly when approaching unfamiliar words to read with accuracy. Self-corrections implied a mismatch between the information used in the substitution and other information sources available to and monitored by the reader. In addition to noting that these readers attended to multiple sources of language information, Clay (2001) also discovered that when the proficient readers in this age group engaged in analyzing text, they initiated their problem solving from any one of the information sources. In summarizing her observations, Clay (1982) suggested that the processing behaviors of these readers approximated the behaviors of a mature reader.

Summary of the Research

This overview of the documented findings of studies conducted by Clay with follow-up investigations by her colleagues confirms that literacy processing behaviors of young learners engaged in reading and writing continuous text change over time. Beginning, novice readers/writers apply low-level strategies in their earliest attempts to read and write as they approach literacy tasks with vague, rudimentary understandings. They gain proficiency as a result of opportunities to engage in reading and writing continuous texts with supportive instruction. They acquire more knowledge to support their processing, and over time their behaviors indicate acquisition of a more efficient and effective inner processing system, a complex network of working systems for processing text.

The patterns of behaviors observed in the records of children over multiple early studies, and ultimately over years of research with thousands of learners in her early intervention, led Clay to two theoretical considerations. She had discovered a transformative model of literacy acquisition, explaining changes in processing systems from primitive to more expert over the first year of school, and she had evidence on which to base a literacy processing theory.

Theoretical Perspective: Literacy Processing Theory

Resulting from her earliest investigations, Clay embraced a complex theory of literacy and defined reading, as we saw in the first section of this chapter. Her quest for theoretical explanations focused on building understandings of both the specific perceptual and cognitive behaviors involved in reading and writing and explanations of the integration of complex in-the-head processes. Thus, explanations of progress involved descriptions of the emergence of a network of complex neural processing systems, that is, the perceptual and cognitive working systems directed to complete reading and writing tasks.

Literacy processing is a reader's decision making about what a text says. It involves

> many working systems in the brain which search for and pick up verbal and perceptual information governed by directional rules; other systems which work on that information and make decisions; other systems which monitor and verify those decisions; and systems which produce responses.
>
> *(Clay, 2001, p. 1)*

These working systems are neural networks, perceptual and cognitive systems, which are constructed by the learner as a result of engagement in reading continuous texts to discern meaningful messages. For the proficient reader after one year of instruction, these working systems have the capacity to function as self-extending systems, allowing the learner to expand his or her competencies in acts of processing texts of increasing demands.

Readers operate on multiple sources of information to read for meaning, and Clay found this processing reflective of Rumelhart's (1994) interactive theory of reading. Rumelhart's theory posits that all knowledge sources are decision-making sources, and the reader's perceptions during reading are the product of interactions among all levels of the language hierarchy. For Rumelhart, this involves hypothesis generating and evaluating during the act of reading as tentative decisions about the message are made and then confirmed or revised on the basis of perceiving more and more information. For example, decisions regarding perceptions of letter features, letter sounds, letter clusters, and words are evaluated and confirmed or revised in conjunction with decisions regarding syntactic information, at either a phrase or clause level, and decisions on the basis of semantic information, which is more general knowledge of the topic or genre. Thus, the reader attends to all available sources of information in text (visual, syntactic, semantic), and "the reading process is the product of the simultaneous joint application of all the knowledge sources".

The reader's knowledge of the language information sources in text support his or her complex processing systems, that is, the decision making that serves reading for meaning. The reader's working systems consider, scan, and integrate information from all levels of the language hierarchy when processing text, and therefore, giving more value to any level of the linguist's hierarchy of language information is unproductive and may be misleading. It is agreement across information sources that confirms a good decision and incongruity that signals the need for more searching, confirming, and perhaps correcting. To add understanding of the perceptual and cognitive working systems, Clay (2001) referenced Singer's concept of assembling the working systems for a specific task, a theory that allows "more scope for knowledge sources and neurological networks to be used flexibly and effectively by readers" (p. 101).

According to Singer (1994), readers who have acquired the necessary working systems are able to mobilize rapidly and flexibly a hierarchical organization of subsystems in which a minimum of mental energy and attention are devoted to input systems (perceptual systems involved in the perception of stimuli, including visual information) and a maximum is expended on mediation and output systems (cognitive systems involved in interpreting, inferring, integrating, and responding). Thus, when reading is proceeding in a fluent, proficient manner, the perceptual working systems operate without conscious attention, allowing the reader to focus attention on thinking about and responding to meaning, which engages the cognitive systems.

This processing suggests that the reader is employing working systems to search and monitor information sources supportive of his construction of meaning with ease. In terms of visual information specifically, this means that the information is located and scanned proficiently and recognized instantly. However, when a reader detects any disruption of meaning, the reader will shift attention to problem solve the dissonance by attending more closely to information sources supportive in refining his or her decision making. In beginning readers, this often involves analyzing visual information to identify words by focusing on the features and sounds of letters, or clusters of letters. As the young reader acquires more knowledge of each information source in text and "comes to know how and when each kind of information can help with decisions" (Clay, 2001, p. 111), the reader becomes more efficient in shifting to problem solving and resolving any issue quickly without loss of meaning.

Cognition and perception (and the related working systems) function on a problem-solving continuum (Bruner, 1957, 1974; Clay, 1991b, 2001), and shifts of conscious attention and problem-solving behaviors occur in ever-changing sequences. In effect, the reader adapts a range of complex processes flexibly "to the demands of a specific literacy task by assembling a temporary system from among those available to deal with the literacy task at hand" (Clay, 2001, p. 101).

Singer (1994) described readers mobilizing "cell assemblies in the brain and organizing them into different working systems according to moment-to-moment changes in the tasks or purposes of the reader" (Clay, 2001, p. 112). This suggests the individualized nature of both the emerging literacy processing systems of young readers and the ongoing, ever-changing assemblies of working systems supporting proficient reading. Clay (1998, 2001) and Singer both concluded that there could be more than one route to successful reading: "Individuals may attain the same level of achievement but by means of different compilations of working systems" (Clay, 2001, p. 113). Reading and learning to read vary in many ways across individuals.

The neural networks for literacy do not exist before the child engages in reading and writing continuous texts. Yet, as teachers provide children opportunities to write and to read a gradient of texts with increments of increasing challenges, learners have new opportunities to work at higher levels of complexity. This creates the problem-solving experiences that extend the efficiency of the neural processing systems.

Clay's literacy processing theory, a theory of assembling a complex network of perceptual and cognitive working systems for reading or writing continuous texts, is based on her observational research. Her meticulous documentation and study of patterns of behaviors collected over time revealed key discoveries. These include the "critical factor of individual differences" (Clay, 2001, p. 137) substantiating different paths to proficient literacy acquisition among young learners; the reciprocity of reading and writing; the transformational nature of literacy acquisition, that is, change over time in processing behaviors as learners acquire more knowledge and initial primitive strategies become more like that of a mature reader; and the initial evidence of a learner's self-extending system, "the strategic power to use what is known in the service of problem-solving the unknown" (Clay, 2001, p. 129). In effect, learners acquire a neural network of complex working systems that learns to extend itself.

While aspects of both Singer and Rumelhart's models of reading resonated with Clay's observations, she found that because neither theorist had addressed the early formative period of literacy acquisition, their explanations were incomplete. Clay's (2001) theory offers literacy awareness and orientation to print as essential aspects of early literacy learning:

> Children have to adapt their preschool working systems to make them work on the written code, learn some new skills, lay down the foundational knowledge sources and learn how knowledge from very different sources can be found, assembled, and integrated.
>
> *(Clay, 2001, p. 137)*

The key concepts include knowing the following:

- how to assemble stories
- that print can be written
- that attention must follow the rules of direction
- that symbols have only one orientation
- how to switch attention out to the page and back into the head
- how to work with complex information and come to decisions (Clay, 2001, p. 137)

In summary, Clay's meticulous documentation of observed literacy behaviors collected over time revealed changes in children's literacy processing during early acquisition and led her to a complex literacy processing theory, which she described as follows:

> In a complex model of interacting competencies in reading and writing the reader can potentially draw from all his or her current understanding, and all his or her language competencies, and visual information, and phonological information and knowledge of printing conventions, in ways which *extend both the searching and linking processes as well as the item knowledge repertoires.* Learners pull together necessary information from print in simple ways at first . . ., but as opportunities to read and write accumulate over time the learner becomes able to quickly and momentarily construct a somewhat complex operating system which might solve the problem.
>
> *(Clay, 2001, p. 224)*

It was her perspective that this complex processing theory was critically important in creating powerful learning opportunities for any child struggling with early literacy.

Instructional Implications of a Complex Literacy Theory

As Clay's research focus evolved to investigating instructional assistance for young readers/ writers struggling with literacy acquisition, she approached challenging issues with a developmental perspective and her emerging, theoretical explanations of change over time in literacy processing behaviors. Her goal was an intervention designed to allow optimal literacy development that would result in proficient performance in reading and writing and prevent subsequent failures. On the basis of her theoretical perspective, it is apparent that such complex learning results from "a curriculum of psychological processes (perceptual and cognitive) necessary for working with written language" (Clay, 2005a, p. 18). Specific goals are to accelerate the pace of learning, lift each child's level of achievement, and build a secure foundation for subsequent literacy learning (Clay, 2001).

Intervening early in the child's educational experience was paramount to Clay, as she had determined that the developing competencies of low-progress children differed from those of proficient learners from the initial, earliest opportunities to read and write (Clay, 1966, 1982). Low-progress students were observed to initiate literacy learning with ineffective behaviors, and their processing did not improve during their first year of instruction. Consequently, Clay (1987) realized that the gap existing between proficient and low-progress children in the first year of school widened over time. For these children, classroom programs did not meet their individual needs, and the most deleterious outcome of such instruction, inadequate for any of a wide range of reasons, is a child who has learned to be learning disabled (Clay, 1987; Vellutino, 2010). For both Clay and Vellutino, this means that children may appear learning disabled as a result of instructional and experiential deficits, not as a result of cognitive deficits. Early intervention is key to averting ongoing difficulties and confusion and to bringing children quickly to levels of proficiency that allow them to profit from classroom literacy programs.

An important aspect of designing instruction to meet individual needs was Clay's rejection of any single cause of literacy difficulties. Multiple causes, idiosyncratic to individual learners, require individual programs of instruction delivered in one-on-one settings. This allows the greatest scope for adjusting instruction to "find ways around a child's limitations in some functions, and which could break a cycle of interacting deficits, whatever those limitations might be" (Clay, 2001, p. 220). One-on-one instructional settings allow the teacher to focus intently on the learner's response repertoire, respond immediately with the most appropriate, contingent support, and adjust instruction as needed. This is the important experience needed by the child who is having severe difficulty in acquiring literacy.

Clay based the goals of her early, individually delivered intervention on her study of proficient readers and focused on how to help struggling learners acquire complex neural networks for processing text. Active learners construct theories of reading and writing that emerge from primitive beginnings and transform as a result of instruction and experience into more mature behaviors. Instruction must support the child's construction of working systems that use all sources of language knowledge to read and write texts and become able to expand and improve as a result of ongoing challenge in texts of increasing complexity. Self-improvement results from the independent learning created by effective linking, evaluating, and decision making, which constitutes the self-extending system. Such independence in reading and writing is encouraged by teachers who scaffold the learner (Vygotsky, 1962) and ultimately act as a resource as the child "pursues a large amount of the activity by himself, pushing the boundaries of his own capacities" (Clay, 1991b, p. 255). Because the self-extending system creates a bootstrapping effect (Stanovich, 1986), Clay (2001) likened it to what Stanovich labeled the positive Matthew effect; she attributed this effect to the complexity of interacting neural networks.

Complex learning results from instruction that starts with a child's strengths and builds on his or her existing, perhaps primitive, processing systems (Clay, 1998, 2005a). Teachers accomplish this by drawing on the child's competent systems while supporting new tentative responding until new strengths are established (Clay, 2001). As a result, the child experiences success, feels in control of his or her learning, and gains awareness of new features of text and/or new ways of responding (Clay, 1998). Teachers make use of each individual's existing response repertoire; therefore, each child's series of lessons is unique, and different paths to efficient processing are expected and supported (Clay, 1998).

Clay (2005a) identified two key hypotheses that informed her intervention plan. The first is that the child's instruction should be based on the teacher's continuous, detailed observations of literacy behaviors. Thus, the reflective teacher considers her observations of the child's problem-solving strategies in writing and in reading daily (using running records). The child's new discoveries, partially correct responses, and self-correction behaviors inform instructional decisions, which often occurs on a moment-to-moment basis. The second hypothesis is that the reciprocal relationship between reading and writing creates powerful opportunities for the learner's competencies in one area to support learning in the second.

More specifically, Clay (2001) discerned that the similar aspects shared by reading and writing include the following:

> 1) the stores of knowledge about letters, sounds and words which they can draw upon, 2) the ways in which known oral language contributes to print activities, 3) some similar processes that learners use to search for the information they need to solve new problems, and 4) ways in which they pull together or integrate different types of information common to both activities.
>
> *(p. 33)*

More specific examples of processes common to both reading and writing activities include the following:

- controlling serial order
- problem-solving with more than one kind of information
- drawing on stored information and acting on it
- using visual information
- using phonological information
- using the meaning of what was composed
- using the vocabulary and structure of what was composed
- searching, checking and correcting
- categorizing, using rules, and estimating probabilities of occurrence (Clay, 2001, p. 32)

Clay's (2005b) instructional plan for daily lessons includes reading texts of easy and instructional levels, writing personal stories, and using brief decontextualized activities to support learning items such as letters and words, which are encountered in and linked to reading and writing activities. The texts for reading are not controlled or contrived; they are selected to give the young reader access to all levels of the language hierarchy as working systems for perceiving, integrating, and evaluating information sources—strengthened only as a result of reading continuous, meaningful texts.

In describing the instruction that reflects important theoretical constructs, Clay (2001) emphasized the following:

- The teacher would support the development of literacy processing by astute selection of tasks, judicious sharing of tasks, and by varying the time, difficulty, content, interest and methods of instruction, and type and amount of conversation within the standard lesson activities.
- The teacher would foster and support active constructive problem-solving, self-monitoring, and self correction from the first lesson, helping learners to understand that they must take over the expansion of their own competencies. To do this the teacher would focus on process variables (how to get and use information) rather than on mere correctness and habitual responses, and would temporarily value responses that were partially correct for what ever they contributed toward correctness.
- The teacher would set the level of task difficulty to ensure high rates of correct responding plus appropriate challenge so that the active processing system could learn from its own attempts to go beyond current knowledge. (p. 225)

Clay (2009) approached the challenges in helping low-progress learners recover a more normal trajectory of literacy performance by asking, what is possible? This led to years of exploration and theory refinement, lesson design, and extensive research of instructional approaches, teacher effectiveness, and children's progress. The result of her development and design efforts was an early intervention known internationally as Reading Recovery, an intervention she also referred to as

Reading and Writing Recovery (Clay, 2001). Reading Recovery is currently available to children experiencing the most difficulty in reading and writing following one year of schooling in educational systems around the world.

In the early development phase of her intervention,

> Clay used a grounded theory approach: She used observations of children and teachers to develop theory, she used theory to guide selection of methods, she applied the methods to practice in a systematic way, and she used detailed observations and records to confirm or revise theory and procedures.
>
> *(Jones & Smith-Burke, 1999, p. 271)*

Clay (2009) conducted studies to explore questions regarding teaching procedures, teacher-training possibilities, implementation issues, decisions about when to end a child's series of lessons, and sustained effects for participants one year as well as three years following the intervention (Jones & Smith-Burke, 1999). In this way, working with teachers and testing the intervention in schools, Clay was able to confirm instructional decisions and discern important training and implementation issues.

Professional development and implementation issues received extensive attention as Clay was asked to scale up Reading Recovery, and she approached all challenges with tentativeness, flexibility, and a problem-solving attitude (Clay, 2001). Always supportive of classroom teachers, she designed a trainer-of-trainer model of professional preparation and found teachers astute learners of her complex literacy theory and instructional procedures. She was masterful in addressing implementation issues, and as educators from other countries and in languages other than English worked with her to adopt and implement Reading Recovery, she was sensitive to cultural and educational differences. "Using a process of accommodation, she found adaptive ways to implement Reading Recovery without lessening the high standards that lead to optimal results for both teachers and children" (Doyle, 2009, pp. 292–293).

The success of these efforts is assessed in evaluation studies replicated by each country with a national implementation, and the resulting data, collected and analyzed for each participating child, are reported annually (see Watson & Askew, 2009, for full descriptions). These reports confirm that Reading Recovery has been successful in accelerating learning and securing a firm literacy foundation for children in diverse settings and in multiple languages, including English, Spanish, and French.

Clay (2001) has attributed the success of Reading Recovery to five key aspects, including the specific guidelines for program delivery, the training that prepares teachers to be astute decision makers, a theory of constructive learning, a complex theory of literacy learning, and lesson components that support perceptual and cognitive processing. These components suggest that she based her early intervention on considerations of behaviors observed in proficient learners over time and instructional modifications needed to optimize literacy development for struggling learners.

Summary

This discussion has presented a review of Marie M. Clay's complex literacy processing theory, her theoretical perspective of literacy learning, and implications of her theory for her design of an intervention for children struggling with early literacy. From these efforts, via a grounded theory process, Clay solidified her literacy processing theory of reading and writing continuous texts, explaining how literacy learning is transformed in a series of changes from simple to more complex processes. Her studies afforded examination of behavioral evidence revealing the nature of the learner's construction of literacy processing abilities over time. In addition, noting that new entrants bring vastly different personal repertoires of experience and knowledge to school, she documented how unique, or individual, their paths to literacy might be.

Clay's analyses of early literacy behaviors led to what she called a literacy processing theory, a theory of assembling perceptual and cognitive working systems capable of completing increasingly complex tasks (Clay, 2001). She considered Rumelhart's information processing theory helpful for considering the integration of language information sources, and she was informed by the theoretical discussions of Holmes (1953, 1960/1970) and Singer (1994). However, Clay also realized that theorists had not considered the challenges and learning associated with initial literacy acquisition. Her observational research led her to important discoveries, and her resulting theory is a multi-faceted theory of beginning reading and writing, accounting for the early, foundational learning necessary for acquiring complex cognitive processing.

When Clay initiated her observational research, her methodology differed from the existing practices to quantify learner performance. Her interest was to delineate qualitative changes in children's learning. She created new assessment tools, considered an unusual lens for documenting behaviors sequentially, and collected data longitudinally. Therefore, her focus and approach parallel the microgenetic analyses of learning, as described by Siegler (2006), currently applied by developmental psychologists, and discussed in relation to Clay's literacy processing perspective by Schwartz and Gallant (2011).

Microgenetic analyses involve the scientific exploration of the genesis, or very beginnings, of learners' strategic behaviors, how children's learning occurs, and how it changes over time. Specifically, the methods of study include observations that span the period of rapidly changing competencies by securing a density of observations—a high amount of observations in relation to the rate of change. The resulting observations of learners engaged in specific tasks are analyzed intensively with the goal of inferring in-the-head processes (see Siegler, 2006). Clay's studies (1966, 1974, 1975, 1982, 2001) of changes over time in the reading and writing behaviors of novice learners not only provide the first, rich model of this scientific approach to the study of early literacy but also reveal the importance and power of alternative approaches to understanding complex literacy learning.

Clay was astute at transitioning her theory to practice, making a remarkable difference for children, teachers, and schools. Again, she applied scientific rigor to test all aspects of her assessment instruments, the instructional practices designed to support the learner's construction of perceptual/cognitive working systems, teachers' professional development, and effective implementations of early intervention in a wide range of differing school systems. The success of her Reading Recovery early intervention, substantiated internationally by ongoing analyses of student data, attests to the robustness of her theoretical perspectives of literacy acquisition, children's learning, professional development, and systemic design.

Additional indicators of effectiveness are found in evaluations conducted by non–Reading Recovery entities. The National Center on Response to Intervention in the United States has endorsed her assessment tool, *An Observation Survey of Early Literacy Achievement* (Clay, 2006), and the What Works Clearinghouse (2008a, 2008b) has substantiated the scientific evidence resulting from multiple researchers' investigations of instructional effects. Reading Recovery is currently recognized as a powerful, scientifically based Response to Intervention, and in fact, Clay's contribution to the movement is considered seminal (Vellutino, 2010). Vellutino has acknowledged that "Marie Clay was actually the first reading researcher to use RTI to identify children who might be afflicted by organically based reading difficulties" (p. 7) as opposed to limitations resulting from experiential or instructional deficits which Reading Recovery instruction addresses.

Clay (2001) has written that she used theory as a tool to explain the changes in literacy behaviors discovered in the reading and writing processes that she documented so astutely. Always tentative, she described herself as living in a "perpetual state of enquiry" (Clay, 2001, p. 3) and sought refinement of her perspectives through her ongoing search for answers to important, new questions. Her quest for explanations and her actions relative to promoting the optimal development of learning potential among young learners are profound contributions to the literacy community and millions of children around the world.

References

Bruner, J.S. (1957). On perceptual readiness. *Psychological Review, 64*(2), 123–152. doi:10.1037/h0043805

Bruner, J.S. (1974). The organisation of early skilled action. In M.P.M. Richards (Ed.), *The integration of a child into a social world* (pp. 167–184). London: Cambridge University Press.

Clay, M.M. (1966). *Emergent reading behaviour.* Unpublished doctoral dissertation. University of Auckland, New Zealand.

Clay, M.M. (1974). The spatial characteristics of the open book. *Visible Language, 8*(3), 275–282.

Clay, M.M. (1975). *What did I write? Beginning writing behaviour.* Auckland, NZ: Heinemann.

Clay, M.M. (1982). *Observing young readers: Selected papers.* Exeter, NH: Heinemann.

Clay, M.M. (1987). Learning to be learning disabled. *New Zealand Journal of Educational Studies, 22*(2), 155–173.

Clay, M.M. (1991a). Child development. In J. Flood, J. Jensen, D. Lapp, & J.R. Squire (Eds.), *Handbook of research on teaching the English language arts* (pp. 40–45). Newark: DE: International Reading Association; Urbana, IL: National Council of Teachers of English.

Clay, M.M. (1991b). *Becoming literate: The construction of inner control.* Portsmouth, NH: Heinemann.

Clay, M.M. (1998). *By different paths to common outcomes.* York, ME: Stenhouse.

Clay, M.M. (2001). *Change over time in children's literacy development.* Portsmouth, NH: Heinemann.

Clay, M.M. (2004). Simply by sailing in a new direction you could enlarge the world. In J. Worthy, B. Maloch, J.V. Hoffman, D.L. Schallert, & C.M. Fairbanks (Eds.), *Fifty-third yearbook of the National Reading Conference* (pp. 60–66). Oak Creek, WI: National Reading Conference.

Clay, M.M. (2005a). *Literacy lessons designed for individuals: Part one: Why? when? and how?* Portsmouth, NH: Heinemann.

Clay, M.M. (2005b). *Literacy lessons designed for individuals: Part two: Teaching procedures.* Portsmouth, NH: Heinemann.

Clay, M.M. (2006). *An observation survey of early literacy achievement* (Rev. 2nd ed.). Portsmouth, NH: Heinemann.

Clay, M.M. (2009). The Reading Recovery research reports. In B. Watson & B. Askew (Eds.), *Boundless horizons: Marie Clay's search for the possible in children's literacy* (pp. 37–100). Rosedale, New Zealand: Pearson Education.

Doyle, M.A. (2009). A dynamic future. In B. Watson & B. Askew (Eds.), *Boundless horizons: Marie Clay's search for the possible in children's literacy* (pp. 287–308). Rosedale, New Zealand: Pearson Education.

Holmes, J.A. (1953). *The substrata-factor theory of reading.* Berkeley, CA: California.

Holmes, J.A. (1970). The substrata-factor theory of reading: Some experimental evidence. In H. Singer & R.B. Ruddell (Eds.), *Theoretical models and processes of reading* (pp. 187–197). Newark, DE: International Reading Association. (Reprinted from *New frontiers in reading*, by J.A. Figurel, Ed., 1960, New York: Scholastic)

Jones, N.K., & Smith-Burke, M.T. (1999). Forging an interactive relationship among research, theory, and practice: Clay's research design and methodology. In J.S. Gaffney & B.J. Askew (Eds.), *Stirring the waters: The influence of Marie Clay* (pp. 261–285). Portsmouth, NH: Heinemann.

Rumelhart, D.E. (1994). Toward an interactive model of reading. In R.B. Ruddell, M.R. Ruddell, & H. Singer (Eds.), *Theoretical models and processes of reading* (4th ed., pp. 864–894). Newark, DE: International Reading Association.

Schwartz, R.M., & Gallant, P.A. (2011). The role of self-monitoring in initial word-recognition learning. In C. Wyatt-Smith, J. Elkins, & S. Gunn (Eds.), *Multiple perspectives on difficulties in learning literacy and numeracy* (pp. 235–253). New York: Springer. doi:10.1007/978-1-4020-8864-3_11

Siegler, R.S. (2006). Microgenetic analyses of learning. In W. Damon, R.M. Lerner (Series Eds.), D. Kuhn, & R.S. Siegler (Vol. Eds.), *Handbook of child psychology: Vol. 2. Cognition, perception, and language* (6th ed., pp. 464–510). Hoboken, NJ: Wiley.

Singer, H. (1994). The substrata-factor theory of reading. In R.B. Ruddell, M.R. Ruddell, & H. Singer (Eds.), *Theoretical models and processes of reading* (4th ed., pp. 895–927). Newark, DE: International Reading Association.

Stanovich, K.E. (1986). Matthew effects in reading: Some consequences of individual differences in the acquisition of literacy. *Reading Research Quarterly, 21*(4), 360–407. doi:10.1598/RRQ.21.4.1

Vellutino, F.R. (2010). Learning to be learning disabled: Marie Clay's seminal contribution to the Response to Intervention approach to identifying specific reading disability. *The Journal of Reading Recovery, 10*(1), 5–23.

Vygotsky, L.S. (1962). *Thought and language* (E. Hanfmann & G. Vakar, Eds. & Trans.). Cambridge, MA: MIT Press. doi:10.1037/11193-000

Watson, B., & Askew, B. (Eds.). (2009). *Boundless horizons: Marie Clay's search for the possible in children's literacy.* Rosedale, New Zealand: Pearson Education.

What Works Clearinghouse. (2008a). *Reading Recovery* (WWC Intervention Report). Washington, DC: Institute of Education Sciences, US Department of Education. Retrieved May 15, 2012, from ies.ed.gov/ncee/wwc/reports/beginning_reading/reading_recovery/

What Works Clearinghouse. (2008b). *Reading Recovery appendix* (WWC Intervention Report). Washington, DC: Institute of Education Sciences, U.S. Department of Education. Retrieved May 15, 2012, from ies.ed.gov/ncee/wwc/reports/beginning_reading/reading_recovery/

SECTION TWO

Cognitive and Sociocognitive

The second section of this volume provides eight chapters, all of which reflect cognitive or socio-cognitive theories or models of literacy processes. James Paul Gee's "Reading as Situated Language: A Sociocognitive Perspective" (Chapter 5) reflects the view that reading is far more than processing skills; it is a process embedded in a context of social interaction and culture. As children learn social languages—such as the language of rap, street gangs, classrooms, or law—they also are socialized into Discourses, which Gee also calls "communities of practice" or "identity kits." While socialized into Discourses, children build cultural models that inform Discourse members of what are linguistically, socially, and culturally acceptable practices for that community. A Discourse establishes a reader's/writer's world and suggests that the reader's/writer's work in that world is to gain a critical consciousness of how he or she is defined by texts.

As rolled out in Chapter 6, Nell Duke and Kelly Cartwright deliver a "DRIVE" model of reading, an acronym that stands for Deploying Reading In Varied Environments. Their model provides a tour of the reading experience internally and externally with reference to elements in the ecological context. All of the elements of their model are supported with empirical research. Portions of the car itself represent reading processes. For example, the dashboard represents comprehension monitoring; the seats and chassis, language knowledge; axles, reading fluency; tires, decoding and word recognition; and the tire's treads, phonological awareness. The ecological surroundings through which the car travels on its journey to comprehension represents the reader's context.

Richard Anderson's "Role of the Reader's Schema in Comprehension, Learning, and Memory" (Chapter 7) explains schema theory and its part in comprehension of texts. Anderson describes schema-based processes during learning and remembering that include schema operating as an ideational and conceptual scaffold for assimilating text, schema facilitating the allocation of attention, schema facilitating inference making, and schema enabling orderly searches of memory while processing texts. He then provides examples of evidence supporting the theory and makes recommendations for the theory's application to classroom instruction.

In "To Err Is Human: Learning About Language Processes by Analyzing Miscues" (Chapter 8), Yetta and Kenneth Goodman develop the role of schema in meaning construction through their exploration of miscue analysis. Arguing that there is nothing random about miscues, the Goodmans explain the role of schema-forming miscues as a kind of struggle toward accommodation of new information and schema-driven miscues as those reflecting assimilation of either old or new information into a preexisting schema. A reader's linguistic and conceptual schematic background manifests itself in both miscues and in the reader's conceptual understanding of texts.

In "Dual Coding Theory: An Embodied Theory of Literacy" (Chapter 9), Mark Sadoski and Karen Krasny present a unified theory of literacy under the aegis of a general theory of mind, Dual Coding Theory (DCT). Since its introduction in the late 1960s, DCT has evolved and expanded through programs of research to many areas of cognition, especially into literacy. With its emphasis on multisensory mental representations and connections between verbal and non-verbal mental systems, DCT proposes a multicode, multimodal approach to reading and writing that accounts for meaning making in multimodal and multimedia texts as well as printed texts. After summarizing DCT in relation to contemporary theoretical perspectives in literacy, the authors characterize DCT as: a scientific theory; an embodied cognitive theory; a theory of decoding, comprehension, vocabulary, and response in reading; a theory of written composition and spelling; and a theory of multimedia/multimodal literacy. In addition, they show that the mental representations and processes in DCT are fundamental to achieving the intersubjectivity central to the social epistemic movement in literacy.

In Chapter 10, "Revisiting the Construction-Integration Model of Text Comprehension and Its Implications for Instruction," Walter Kintsch explains the relationship between cognition and representation while reading. He describes three levels of mental representation during reading: the surface structure, a textbase, and a situation model. The surface structure for a text refers to sentences or fragments of them that are held in a reader's memory. The textbase, or the semantic underpinnings of a text, is composed of microstructures and macrostructures. The situation model represents information provided by a text, but integrated with information from a reader's goals, beliefs, and prior knowledge. Although we know quite a lot about how readers process words and sentences into text structures, we know far less about the processes that occur during the formation of a situation model.

In Chapter 11, "A Sociocognitive Model of Meaning Construction: The Reader, the Teacher, the Text, and the Classroom Context," Robert Ruddell, Norman Unrau, and Sandra McCormick present a sociocognitive model of reading in which meanings are constructed during a socially contextualized bottom-up/top-down reading process. Specifically, the model proposes the elements that are engaged when "meaning is constructed" interactively within social environments comprised of *readers, teachers, texts*, and *classroom contexts*, and it explains how these four components are in a state of dynamic activity and interaction while individuals process text and make meaning. The model demonstrates that understanding text is never a static endeavor in which the text alone carries and conveys meaning, but, rather, a *meaning-construction process*, with meanings assembled through a variety of interactions with a text within a context.

In Chapter 12, "The Role of Motivation Theory in Literacy Instruction," Ana Taboada Barber, Karen Levush, and Susan Klauda focus on motivation applied to both reading and writing. They point out, in the light of their perspective, that reading motivation as a construct has been approached empirically in much more depth than that of writing motivation. However, because of the relevance that motivation has for both literacy processes, the authors review theories of motivation and their implications to both reading and writing. They draw primarily from four major theories of motivation: Self-determination theory, social cognitive theory; expectancy-value theory, and achievement goal theory. Within each motivation theory, the authors have focused on implications for reading and writing development as well as instruction—emphasizing the empirical work that has been done relevant to each construct. The authors also conceptualize reading engagement as a multidimensional construct and draw from a model of reading engagement to elaborate on its implications for reading instruction. They end their chapter with other key motivation constructs relevant to reading and writing in order to identify potential issues and areas for future work in literacy motivation.

In "Educational Neuroscience for Reading Researchers" (Chapter 13), George Hruby and Usha Goswami review promising advances in neuroscientific research on cognitive processes involved in reading, noting that, over the last 35 years of brain research, only the surface has been scratched to date regarding areas of neural activation that function when a reader is making sense of text. The authors offer an overview of the neural correlates of reading while pointing out that neural images do not provide evidence that areas of the brain have been dedicated since birth to specific reading processes. More likely, much of the neural imaging portrays the anatomical result of development in response to interactions with texts and instruction. Neuroscience is an exciting field, as understanding how brains operate when learning occurs offers enormous potential for educators, and could very well upend established literacy theories.

5

READING AS SITUATED LANGUAGE

A Sociocognitive Perspective

James Paul Gee

This chapter is reprinted from *Journal of Adolescent & Adult Literacy,* 44(8), 714–725.

My main goal here is to situate reading within a broad perspective that integrates work on cognition, language, social interaction, society, and culture. In light of recent reports on reading (National Reading Panel, 2000; Snow, Burns, & Griffin, 1998) that have tended to treat reading quite narrowly in terms of psycholinguistic processing skills, I argue that such a broad perspective on reading is essential if we are to speak to issues of access and equity in schools and workplaces. I also argue that reading and writing cannot be separated from speaking, listening, and interacting, on the one hand, or using language to think about and act on the world, on the other. Thus, it is necessary to start with a viewpoint on language (oral and written) itself, a viewpoint that ties language to embodied action in the material and social world.

I have organized this article into four parts. First, I develop a viewpoint on language that stresses the connections among language, embodied experience, and situated action and interaction in the world. In the second part, I argue that what is relevant to learning literacy is not English in general, but specific varieties of English that I call "social languages." I then go on to discuss notions related to the idea of social languages, specifically Discourses (with a capital *D*) and their connections to socially situated identities and cultural models. In the third part, I show the relevance of the earlier sections to the development of literacy in early childhood through a specific example. Finally, I close the article with a discussion of the importance of language abilities (construed in a specific way) to learning to read.

A Viewpoint on Language

It is often claimed that the primary function of human language is to convey information, but I believe this is not true. Human languages are used for a wide array of functions, including but by no means limited to conveying information (Halliday, 1994). I will argue here that human language has two primary functions through which it is best studied and analyzed. I would state these functions as follows: to scaffold the performance of action in the world, including social activities and interactions; to scaffold human affiliation in cultures and social groups and institutions through creating and enticing others to take certain perspectives on experience. *Action* is the most important word in the first statement; *perspectives* is the most important word in the second. I will discuss each of these two functions in turn.

Situated Action

Traditional approaches to language have tended to look at it as a closed system (for discussion, see Clancey, 1997). Any piece of language is treated as representation (re-presenting) of some information. On the traditional view, what it means to comprehend a piece of language is to be able to translate it into some equivalent representational system, either other language (one's own words) or some mental language or language of thought that mimics the structure of natural languages (e.g., is couched in terms of logical propositions).

However, there are a variety of perspectives today on language that tie its comprehension much more closely to experience of and action in the world. For example, consider these two remarks from work in cognitive psychology: "comprehension is grounded in perceptual simulations that prepare agents for situated action" (Barsalou, 1999a, p. 77); "to a particular person, the meaning of an object, event, or sentence is what that person can do with the object, event, or sentence" (Glenberg, 1997, p. 3).

These two quotes are from work that is part of a family of related viewpoints. For want of a better name, we might call the family "situated cognition studies" (e.g., Barsalou, 1999a, 1999b; Brown, Collins, & Dugid, 1989; Clancey, 1997; Clark, 1997; Engestrom, Miettinen, raij Punam- aki, 1999; Gee, 1992; Glenberg, 1997; Glenberg & Robertson, 1999; Hutchins, 1995; Latour, 1999; Lave, 1996; Lave & Wenger, 1991; Wenger, 1998). While there are differences among the members of the family (alternative theories about situated cognition), they share the viewpoint that meaning in language is not some abstract propositional representation that resembles a verbal language. Rather, meaning in language is tied to people's experiences of situated action in the material and social world. Furthermore, these experiences (perceptions, feelings, actions, and interactions) are stored in the mind or brain, not in terms of propositions or language but in something like dynamic images tied to perception both of the world and of our own bodies, internal states, and feelings: "Increasing evidence suggests that perceptual simulation is indeed central to compre- hension" (Barsalou, 1999a, p. 74).

It is almost as if we videotape our experiences as we are having them, create a library of such videotapes, edit them to make some prototypical tapes (or set of typical instances), but stand ever ready to add new tapes to our library. We re-edit the tapes based on new experiences or draw out of the library less typical tapes when the need arises. As we face new situations or new texts we run our tapes—perhaps a prototypical one, or a set of typical ones, or a set of contrasting ones, or a less typical one, whatever the case may be. We do this to apply our old experiences to our new experience and to aid us in making, editing, and storing the videotape that will capture this new experience, integrate it into our library, and allow us to make sense of it (both while we are having it and afterwards).

These videotapes are what we think with and through. They are what we use to give meaning to our experiences in the world. They are what we use to give meaning to words and sentences. But they are not language or *in* language (not even in propositions). Furthermore, since they are representations of experience (including feelings, attitudes, embodied positions, and various sorts of foregrounds and backgrounds of attention), they are not just information or facts. Rather, they are value-laden, perspective-taking movies in the mind. Of course, talking about videotapes in the mind is a metaphor that, like all metaphors, is incorrect if pushed too far (see Barsalou, 1999b for how the metaphor can be cashed out and corrected by a consideration of a more neurally realistic framework for "perception in the mind").

On this account, the meanings of words, phrases, and sentences are always situated, that is, customized to our actual contexts (Gee, 1999a). Here context means not just the words, deeds, and things that surround our words or deeds, but also our purposes, values, and intended courses of action and interaction. We bring out of our store of videotapes those that are most relevant to understanding our current context or those that allow us to create and construe that context in a certain way. We can see this in even so trivial an example as the following: If you hear "The coffee spilled, go get the mop" you run a quite different set of images (that is, assemble a quite different situated meaning) than when you hear "The coffee spilled, go get a broom."

On this account, too, the meaning of a word (the way in which we give it meaning in a particular context) is not different than the meaning of an experience, object, or tool in the world (i.e., in terms of the way in which we give the experience, object, or tool meaning):

> The meaning of the glass to you, at that particular moment, is in terms of the actions avail-
> able. The meaning of the glass changes when different constraints on action are combined.
> For example, in a noisy room, the glass may become a mechanism for capturing attention
> (by tapping it with a spoon), rather than a mechanism for quenching thirst.
>
> *(Glenberg, 1997, p. 41)*

While Glenberg here is talking about the meaning of the glass as an object in one's specific experience of the world at a given time and place, he could just as well be talking about the meaning of the word *glass* in one's specific experience of a piece of talk or written text at a given time and place. The meaning of the word *glass* in a given piece of talk or text would be given by running a simulation (a videotape) of how the glass fits into courses of action being built up in the theater of our minds. These courses of action are based on how we understand all the other words and goings on in the world that surrounds the word *glass* as we read it: "[T]he embodied models constructed to understand language are the same as those that underlie comprehension of the natural environment" (Glenberg, 1997, p. 17).

If embodied action and social activity are crucially connected to the situated meanings oral or written language convey, then reading instruction must move well beyond relations internal to texts. Reading instruction must be rooted in the connections of texts to engagement in and simulations of actions, activities, and interactions—to real and imagined material and social worlds.

Perspective-Taking

Let me now turn to the second function of language already mentioned. Consider, in this regard, the following quote from Tomasello (1999):

> [T]he perspectivial nature of linguistic symbols, and the use of linguistic symbols in dis-
> course interaction in which different perspectives are explicitly contrasted and shared,
> provide the raw material out of which the children of all cultures construct the flexible and
> multi-perspectival—perhaps even dialogical—cognitive representations that give human
> cognition much of its awesome and unique power.
>
> *(p. 163)*

Let's briefly unpack what this means. From the point of view of the model Tomasello was developing, the words and grammar of a human language exist to allow people to take and communicate alternative perspectives on experience (see also Hanks, 1996). That is, words and grammar exist to give people alternative ways to view one and the same state of affairs. Language is not about conveying neutral or objective information; rather, it is about communicating perspectives on experience and action in the world, often in contrast to alternative and competing perspectives: "We may then say that linguistic symbols are social conventions for inducing others to construe, or take a perspective on, some experiential situation" (Tomasello, 1999, p. 118).

Let me give some examples of what it means to say that words and grammar are not primarily about giving and getting information but are, rather, about giving and getting different perspectives on experience. I open Microsoft's Web site: Is it selling its products, marketing them, or underpricing them against the competition? Are products I can download from the site without paying for them free, or are they being exchanged for having bought other Microsoft products (e.g., Windows), or are there strings attached? Note also how metaphors (like "strings attached") add greatly to, and are a central part of, the perspective-taking we can do. If I use the grammatical construction "Microsoft's new operating system is loaded with bugs" I take a perspective in which Microsoft is less agentive and responsible than if I use the grammatical construction "Microsoft has loaded its new operating system with bugs."

Here is another example: Do I say that a child who is using multiple cues to give meaning to a written text (i.e., using some decoding along with picture and context cues) is reading, or do I say (as some of the pro-phonics people do) that she is not really reading, but engaged in emergent literacy? (For those latter people, the child is only really reading when she is decoding all the words in the text and not using nondecoding cues for word recognition). In this case, contending camps actually fight over what perspective on experience the term *reading* or *really reading* ought to name. In the end, the point is that no wording is ever neutral or just "the facts." All wordings—given the very nature of language—are perspectives on experience that comport with competing perspectives in the grammar of the language and in actual social interactions.

How do children learn how words and grammar line up to express particular perspectives on experience? Here, interactive, intersubjective dialogue with more advanced peers and adults appears to be crucial. In such dialogue, children come to see, from time to time, that others have taken a different perspective on what is being talked about than they themselves have. At a certain developmental level, children have the capacity to distance themselves from their own perspectives and (internally) simulate the perspectives the other person is taking, thereby coming to see how words and grammar come to express those perspectives (in contrast to the way in which different words and grammatical constructions express competing perspectives).

Later, in other interactions, or when thinking, the child can re-run such simulations and imitate the perspective-taking the more advanced peer or adult has done by using certain sorts of words and grammar. Through such simulations and imitative learning, children learn to use the symbolic means that other persons have used to share attention with them: "In imitatively learning a linguistic symbol from other persons in this way, I internalize not only their communicative intention (their intention to get me to share their attention) but also the specific perspective they have taken" (Tomasello, 1999, p. 128).

Tomasello (1999) also pointed out—in line with my previous discussion that the world and texts are assigned meanings in the same way—that children come to use objects in the world as symbols at the same time (or with just a bit of a time lag) as they come to use linguistic symbols as perspective-taking devices on the world. Furthermore, they learn to use objects as symbols (to assign them different meanings encoding specific perspectives in different contexts) in the same way they learn to use linguistic symbols. In both cases, the child simulates in his head and later imitates in his words and deeds the perspectives his interlocutor must be taking on a given situation by using certain words and certain forms of grammar or by treating certain objects in certain ways. Thus, meaning for words, grammar, and objects comes out of intersubjective dialogue and interaction: "[H]uman symbols [are] inherently social, intersubjective, and perspectival" (Tomasello, 1999, p. 131).

If value-laden perspectives on experience are connected to the situated meanings oral or written language convey, then, once again, we have an argument that reading instruction must move well beyond relations internal to texts. Reading instruction must be rooted in the taking and imagining of diverse perspectives on real and imagined material and social worlds. The moral of both the functions of language that we have discussed is this: Our ways with words (oral or written) are of the same nature as our ways with ways of understanding and acting on the material and social world.

In a quite empirical sense, the moral is one Freire (1995) taught us long ago: Reading the word and reading the world are, at a deep level, integrally connected—indeed, at a deep level, they are one and the same process.

Social Languages

The perspective taken thus far on language is misleading in one respect. It misses the core fact that any human language is not one general thing (like English), but composed of a great variety of different styles, registers, or social languages. Different patterns of vocabulary, syntax (sentence structure), and discourse connectors (devices that connect sentences together to make a whole integrated text) constitute different social languages, each of which is connected to specific sorts of social activities and to a specific socially situated identity (Gee, 1999a). We recognize different social languages by recognizing these patterns (in much the way we recognize a face through recognizing a certain characteristic patterning of facial features).

As an example, consider the following, taken from a school science textbook: "1. The destruction of a land surface by the combined effects of abrasion and removal of weathered material by transporting agents is called erosion. . . . The production of rock waste by mechanical processes and chemical changes is called weathering" (Martin, 1990, p. 93).

A whole bevy of grammatical design features mark these sentences as part of a distinctive social language. Some of these features are heavy subjects (e.g., "The production of rock waste by mechanical processes and chemical changes"); processes and actions named by nouns or nominalizations, rather than verbs (e.g., "production"); passive main verbs ("is called") and passives inside nominalizations (e.g., "production . . . by mechanical processes"); modifiers that are more "contentful" than the nouns they modify (e.g., "transporting agents"); and complex embedding (e.g., "weathered material by transporting agents" is a nominalization embedded inside "the combined effects of . . . ," and this more complex nominalization is embedded inside a yet larger nominalization, "the destruction of . . .").

This style of language also incorporates a great many distinctive discourse markers, that is, linguistic features that characterize larger stretches of text and give them unity and coherence as a certain type of text or genre. For example, the genre here is explanatory definition, and it is characterized by classificatory language of a certain sort. Such language leads adept readers to form a classificatory scheme in their heads something like this: There are two kinds of change (erosion and weathering) and two kinds of weathering (mechanical and chemical).

This mapping from elements of vocabulary, syntax, and discourse to a specific style of language used in characteristic social activities is just as much a part of reading and writing as is the phonics (sound-to-letter) mapping. In fact, more people fail to become successful school-based, academic, or work-related readers or writers because of failing to master this sort of mapping than the phonics one.

There are a great many different social languages—for example, the language of medicine, literature, street gangs, sociology, law, rap, or informal dinner-time talk among friends (who belong to distinctive cultures or social groups). To know any specific social language is to know how its characteristic design features are combined to carry out one or more specific social activities. It is to know, as well, how its characteristic lexical and grammatical design features are used to enact a particular socially situated identity, that is, being, at a given time and place, a lawyer, a gang member, a politician, a literary humanist, a "bench chemist," a radical feminist, an everyday person, or whatever. To know a particular social language is either to be able to "do" a particular identity, using that social language, or to be able to recognize such an identity, when we do not want to or cannot actively participate.

Let me give two further examples of social languages at work. First, I'll use an example I've used in this journal before. It's about a young woman telling the same story to her parents and to her boyfriend (*JAAL*, February 2000; Gee, 1996). To her parents at dinner she says, "Well, when I thought about it, I don't know, it seemed to me that Gregory should be considered the most offensive character." But to her boyfriend later she says, "What an ass that guy was, you know, her boyfriend." In the first case, the young woman is taking on the identity of an educated and dutiful daughter engaged in the social activity of reporting to her parents her viewpoints on what she has learned in school. In the second case, she is taking on the identity of a girlfriend engaged in the social activity of bonding with her boyfriend.

Here is a second example from Myers (1990, p. 150): A biologist wrote in a professional science journal, "Experiments show that *Heliconius* butterflies are less likely to oviposit on host plants that possess eggs or egg-like structures." Writing about the same thing in a popular science magazine, the same biologist wrote, "*Heliconius* butterflies lay their eggs on *Passiflora* vines. In defense the vines seem to have evolved fake eggs that make it look to the butterflies as if eggs have already been laid on them." In the first case, the biologist is taking on the identity of professional scientist engaged in the social activity of making experimental and theoretical claims (note, for instance, the subject "Experiments") to professional peers. In the second case, the biologist is taking on the identity of a popularizer or scientific journalist engaged in the social activity of telling the educated public a factual story about plants and animals (note, for instance, the subjects "butterflies" and "vines").

Now here is the bite of social languages and genres: When we talk about social languages and genres, oral and written language are inextricably mixed. Some social languages are written; some are spoken. Some have both spoken and written versions; written and spoken versions are often mixed and integrated within specific social practices. Furthermore, social languages are always integrally connected to the characteristic social activities (embodied action and interaction in the world), value-laden perspectives, and socially situated identities of particular groups of people or communities of practice. If discussions about reading are not about social languages (and thus, too, about embodied action and interaction in the world, value-laden perspectives, and socially situated identities), then they are not, in reality, about reading as a semiotic meaning-making process (and it is hard to know what reading is if it is not this).

Here is another part of the bite of talk about social languages and genres. Both inside and outside school, most social languages and genres are clearly not acquired by direct instruction. While some forms of (appropriately timed) scaffolding, modeling, and instructional guidance by mentors appear to be important, immersion in meaningful practice is essential. Social languages and genres are acquired by processes of socialization, an issue to which I will turn below.

It is inevitable, I would think, that someone at this point is going to object that social languages are really about the later stages of the acquisition of literacy. It will be pointed out that the current reading debates are almost always about small children and the earlier stages of reading. What, it will be asked, has all this talk of social languages got to do with early literacy? My answer is, everything. Social languages (and their connections to action, perspectives, and identities) are no less relevant to the first stages of learning to read than they are to the later ones (and there are not so much stages here as the same things going on over time at ever deeper and more complex levels). However, before I turn to the relevance of social languages to early childhood at the end of this article, I need to develop briefly a few more theoretical notions related to social languages.

Discourses

I said earlier that social languages are acquired by socialization. But now we must ask, socialization into what? When people learn new social languages and genres—at the level of being able to produce them and not just consume them—they are being socialized into what I will call Discourses with a big "D" (I use discourse with a little "d" to mean just language in use, Gee, 1996, 1999a; see also Clark, 1996). Even when people learn a new social language or genre only to consume (interpret), but not produce it, they are learning to recognize a new Discourse. Related but somewhat different terms others have used to capture some of what I am trying to capture with the term *Discourses* are communities of practice (Wenger, 1998), actor-actant networks (Latour, 1987, 1991), and activity systems (Engestrom, Miettinen, raij Punamaki, 1999; Leont'ev, 1978).

Discourses always involve language (i.e., they recruit specific social languages), but they always involve more than language as well. Social languages are embedded within Discourses and only have relevance and meaning within them. A Discourse integrates ways of talking, listening, writing, reading, acting, interacting, believing, valuing, and feeling (and using various objects, symbols, images, tools, and technologies) in the service of enacting meaningful socially situated identities and activities. Being-doing a certain sort of physicist, gang member, feminist, first-grade child in Ms. Smith's room, special ed (SPED) student, regular at the local bar, or gifted upper-middle-class child engaged in emergent literacy are all Discourses.

We can think of Discourses as identity kits. It's almost as if you get a toolkit full of specific devices (i.e., ways with words, deeds, thoughts, values, actions, interactions, objects, tools, and technologies) in terms of which you can enact a specific identity and engage in specific activities associated with that identity. For example, think of what devices (e.g., in words, deeds, clothes, objects, attitudes) you would get in a Sherlock Holmes identity kit (e.g., you do not get a "Say No to Drugs" bumper sticker in this kit; you do get both a pipe and lots of logic). The Doctor Watson identity kit is different. And we can think of the Sherlock Holmes identity kit (Discourse) and the Doctor Watson identity kit (Discourse) as themselves parts of a yet larger Discourse, the Holmes-Watson Discourse, because Watson is part of Holmes's identity kit and Holmes is part of Watson's. Discourse can be embedded one inside another.

One Discourse can mix or blend two others. For example, Gallas (1994) created a sharing-time Discourse (a way of being a recognizable sharer in her classroom) that mixed Anglo and African American styles. Discourses can be related to each other in relationships of alignment or tension. For example, Scollon and Scollon (1981) have pointed out that school-based Discourses that incorporate essayist practices and values conflict with the values, attitudes, and ways with words embedded in some Native American home and community-based Discourses (i.e., ways of being a Native American of a certain sort). These latter Discourses value communicating only when the sender knows the receiver of the communication and his or her context and do not value the sorts of fictionalizing (generalizing) of sender and receiver that essayist practices involve.

Cultural Models

Within their socialization into Discourses (and we are all socialized into a great many across our lifetimes), people acquire cultural models (D'Andrade & Strauss, 1992; Gee, 1999a; Holland & Quinn, 1987; Shore, 1996; Strauss & Quinn, 1997). Cultural models are everyday theories (i.e., storylines, images, schemas, metaphors, and models) about the world that people socialized into a given Discourse share. Cultural models tell people what is typical or normal from the perspective of a particular Discourse (or a related or aligned set of them).

For example, certain types of middle-class people in the United States hold a cultural model of child development that goes something like this (Harkness, Super, & Keefer, 1992): A child is born dependent on her parents and grows up by going through (often disruptive) stages toward greater and greater independence (and independence is a high value for this group of people). This cultural model plays a central role in this group's Discourse of parent-child relations (i.e., enacting and recognizing identities as parents and children).

On the other hand, certain sorts of working-class families (Philipsen, 1975) hold a cultural model of child development that goes something like this: A child is born unsocialized and with tendencies to be selfish. The child needs discipline from the home to learn to be a cooperative social member of the family (a high value of this group of people). This cultural model plays a central role in this group's Discourse of parent-child relations.

Discourses: Ways of combining and coordinating words, deeds, thoughts, values, bodies, objects, tools, and technologies, and other people (at the appropriate times and places) so as to enact and recognize specific socially situated identities and activities.

Social languages: Ways with words (oral and written) within Discourses that relate form and meaning so as to express specific socially situated identities and activities.

Genres: Combinations of ways with words (oral and written) and actions that have become more or less routine within a Discourse in order to enact and recognize specific socially situated identities and activities in relatively stable and uniform ways (and, in doing so, we humans reproduce our Discourses and institutions through history).

Cultural models: Often tacit and taken-for-granted schemata, storylines, theories, images, or representations (partially represented inside people's heads and partially represented within their materials and practices) that tell a group of people within a Discourse what is typical or normal from the point of view of that Discourse.

Figure 5.1 Summary of Tools for Understanding Language and Literacy in Sociocultural Terms

These different cultural models, connected to different (partially) class-based Discourses of parenting, are not true or false. Rather, they focus on different aspects of childhood and development. Cultural models define for people in a Discourse what counts as normal and natural and what counts as inappropriate and deviant. They are, of course, thereby thoroughly value laden.

Cultural models come out of and, in turn, inform the social practices in which people in a Discourse engage. Cultural models are stored in people's minds (by no means always consciously), though they are supplemented and instantiated in the objects, texts, and practices that are part and parcel of the Discourse. For example, many guidebooks supplement and instantiate the above middle-class cultural model of childhood and stages. On the other hand, many religious materials supplement and instantiate the above working-class model of childhood.

Figure 5.1 summarizes the discussion so far, defining all the theoretical tools and showing how they are all related to one another.

Early Literacy as Socioculturally Situated Practice

I turn now to a specific example involving early literacy from my own research. I do this both to give a more extended example of the perspective I have developed so far and to show the relevance of this perspective to early childhood and the earliest stages of the acquisition of literacy. The event is this: An upper-middle-class, highly educated father approaches his 3-year-old (3:10) son who is sitting at the kitchen table. The child is using an activity book in which each page contains a picture with a missing piece. A question is printed under the picture. The child uses a "magic pen" to rub the missing piece and "magically" uncovers the rest of the picture. The part of the picture that is uncovered is an image that constitutes the answer to the question at the bottom of the page, though, of course, the child must put this answer into words.

In the specific case I want to discuss here, the overt part of the picture was the top half of the bodies of Donald and Daisy Duck. The question printed at the bottom of the page was "In what are Donald and Daisy riding?" (Note the social language in which this question is written. It is not the more vernacular form: "What are Donald and Daisy riding in?") The child used his pen to uncover an old fashioned Model T sort of car with an open top. Donald and Daisy turn out to be sitting in the car.

The father, seeing the child engaged in this activity, asks him, after he has uncovered the car, to read the question printed below the picture. Notice that the father has not asked the child to give the answer to the question, which is a different activity. The father is confident the child can answer the question and has a different purpose here. It is to engage in an indirect reading lesson, though one of a special and specific sort.

The father is aware that the child, while he knows the names of the letters of the alphabet and can recognize many of them in words, cannot decode print. He is also aware that the child has on several previous occasions, in the midst of various literacy-related activities, said that he is "learning to read." However, in yet other activities, at other times, the child has said that he "cannot read" and thereafter seemed more reluctant to engage in his otherwise proactive stance toward texts. This has concerned the father, who values the child's active engagement with texts and the child's belief, expressed in some contexts and not others, that he is not just learning to read, but is in fact "a reader."

We might say that the father is operating with a however tacit theory (cultural model) that a child's assuming a certain identity ("I am a reader") facilitates the acquisition of that identity and its concomitant skills. I believe this sort of model is fairly common in certain sorts of families. Parents co-construct an identity with a child (attribute, and get the child to believe in, a certain competence) before the child can actually fully carry out all the skills associated with this identity (competence before performance).

So, the father has asked the child to read the printed question below the picture of Donald and Daisy Duck sitting in the newly uncovered car. Below, I give the printed version of the question and what the child offered as his "reading" of the question:

Printed version: In what are Donald and Daisy riding?
Child's reading: What is Donald and Daisy riding on?

After the child uttered the above sentence, he said, "See, I told you I was learning to read." He seems to be well aware of the father's purposes. The child, the father, the words, and the book are all here in sync to pull off a specific practice, and this is a form of instruction, but it's a form that is typical of what goes on inside socialization processes.

The father and son have taken an activity that is for the child now a virtual genre—namely, uncovering a piece of a picture and on the basis of it answering a question—and incorporated it into a different *metalevel activity.* That is, the father and son use the original activity not in and for itself but as a platform with which to discuss reading or, perhaps better put, to co-construct a cultural model of what reading is. The father's question and the son's final response ("See, I told you I was learning to read") clearly indicate that they are seeking to demonstrate to and for each other that the child can read.

Figure 5.2, which will inform my discussion that follows, (partially) analyzes this event in terms of the theoretical notions we have developed above.

From a developmental point of view, then, what is going on here? Nothing so general as acquiring literacy. Rather, something much more specific is going on. First, the child is acquiring, amidst immersion and adult guidance, a piece of a particular type of *social language.* The question he has to form—and he very well knows this—has to be a *classificatory question.* It cannot be, for instance, a narrative-based question (e.g., something like "What are Donald and Daisy doing?" or "Where are Donald and Daisy going?"). Classificatory questions (and related syntactic and discourse resources) are a common part of many school-based (and academic) social languages, especially those associated with nonliterary content areas (e.g., the sciences).

The acquisition of this piece of a social language is, in this case, scaffolded by a genre the child has acquired, namely to uncover the piece of the picture, form a classificatory question to which the picture is an answer (when the parent isn't there to read the question for the child), and give the

113

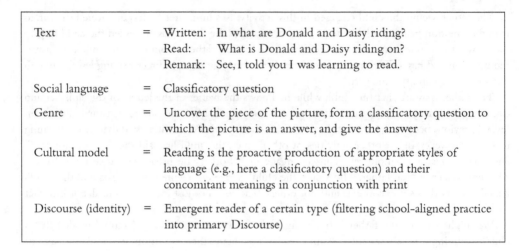

Figure 5.2 Partial Analysis of a Literacy Event

answer. This genre bears a good deal of similarity to a number of different non-narrative language and action genres (routines) used in the early years of school.

Finally, in regard to social languages, note that the child's question is uttered in a more vernacular style than the printed question. So syntactically it is, in one sense, in the wrong style. However, from a discourse perspective (in terms of the function its syntax carries out), it is in just the right style (i.e., it is a classificatory question). It is a mainstay of child language development that the acquisition of a function often precedes acquisition of a fully correct form (in the sense of contextually appropriate, not necessarily in the sense of grammatically correct).

In addition to acquiring a specific piece of certain sorts of social languages, the child is also, as part and parcel of the activity, acquiring different cultural models. One of these is a cultural model about what reading is. The model is something like this: Reading is not primarily letter-by-letter decoding but the proactive production of appropriate styles of language (e.g., here a classificatory question) and their concomitant meanings in conjunction with print. This is a model that the father (at some level quite consciously) wants the child to adopt, both to sustain the child's interest in becoming a reader and to counteract the child's claims, in other contexts, that he can't read. Of course, the child's claim that he can't read in those other contexts reflects that, in other activities, he is acquiring a different cultural model of reading, namely one something like this: Reading is primarily the ability to decode letters and words, and one is not a reader if meaning is not primarily driven from decoding print. As his socialization proceeds, the child will acquire yet other cultural models of reading (or extend and deepen ones already acquired).

The genres, social languages, and cultural models present in this interaction between father and son existed, of course, in conjunction with ways of thinking, valuing, feeling, acting, interacting and in conjunction with various mediating objects (e.g., the book and the "magic pen"), images (the pictures of Donald, Daisy, and the car), sites (kitchen table), and times (morning as father was about to go to work). In and through the social practices that recruit these genres, social language, and cultural models, the 3-year-old is acquiring a Discourse. The father and the child are co-constructing the child as a reader (and, indeed, a person) of a particular type, that is, one who takes reading to be the proactive production of appropriate styles of language and meanings in conjunction with print. This socially situated identity involves a self-orientation as active producer (not just consumer) of appropriate meanings in conjunction with print; meanings that, in this case, turn out to be school and academically related.

However, this Discourse is not unrelated to other Discourses the child is or will be acquiring. I have repeatedly pointed out how the social language, genre, and cultural models involved in this social practice are in full alignment with some of the social languages, genres, cultural models, and social practices the child will confront in the early years of school (here construing schooling in fairly traditional terms).

At the same time, this engagement between father and child, beyond being a moment in the production of the Discourse of a certain type of reader, is also a moment in the child's acquisition of what I call his primary Discourse. The child's primary Discourse is the ways with words, objects, and deeds that are associated with his primary sense of self formed in and through his (most certainly class-based) primary socialization within the family (or other culturally relevant primary socializing group) as a "person like us." In this case, the child is learning that "people like us" are "readers like this."

Now consider what it means that the child's acquisition of the reader Discourse (being-doing a certain type of reader) is simultaneously aligned with (traditional) school-based Discourses and part of his acquisition of his primary Discourse. This ties school-related values, attitudes, and ways with words, at a specific and not some general level, to his primary sense of self and belonging. This will almost certainly affect how the child reacts to, and resonates with, school-based ways with words and things.

Reading and Early Language Abilities

Many of the recent reading reports (e.g., see Gee, 1999b; National Reading Panel, 2000; Snow, Burns, & Griffin, 1998) have stressed that there is significant correlation between early phonological awareness and later success in learning to read and, thus, called for early phonemic awareness training in schools and early sustained and overt instruction on phonics. However, some of these reports are aware that a good many other things, besides early phonological awareness, correlate with successfully learning to read in the early years of school. It turns out, for instance, that the correlation between early language abilities and later success in reading is just as large as, if not larger than, the correlation between early phonological awareness and success in reading. Indeed, as one might suspect, early language abilities and early phonological awareness are themselves correlated (Snow, Burns, & Griffin, 1998):

> [P]erformance on phonological awareness tasks by preschoolers was highly correlated with general language ability. Moreover it was measures of semantic and syntactic skills, rather than speech discrimination and articulation, that predicted phonological awareness differences.
>
> *(p. 53)*

> . . .

> What is most striking about the results of the preceding studies is the power of early preschool language to predict reading three to five years later.
>
> *(pp. 107–108)*

> . . .

> On average, phonological awareness (r. = .46) has been about as strong a predictor of future reading as memory for sentences and stories, confrontation naming, and general language measures.
>
> *(p. 112)*

So what are these early language abilities that seem so important for later success in school? According to the National Research Council's report (Snow, Burns, & Griffin, 1998), they are things like vocabulary—receptive vocabulary, but more especially expressive vocabulary—the ability to recall and comprehend sentences and stories, and the ability to engage in verbal interactions. Furthermore, I think that research has made it fairly clear what causes such verbal abilities. What appears to cause enhanced school-based verbal abilities are family, community, and school language environments in which children interact intensively with adults and more advanced peers and experience cognitively challenging talk and texts on sustained topics and in different genres of oral and written language.

However, the correlation between language abilities and success in learning to read (and in school generally) hides an important reality. Almost all children—including poor children—have impressive language abilities. The vast majority of children enter school with large vocabularies, complex grammar, and deep understandings of experiences and stories. It has been decades since anyone believed that poor and minority children entered school with "no language" (Gee, 1996; Labov, 1972).

The verbal abilities that children who fail in school lack are not just some general set of such abilities, but rather specific verbal abilities tied to specific school-based practices and school-based genres of oral and written language of just the sort I looked at in the earlier example of the 3-year-old making up a classificatory question. This 3-year-old will have been exposed to a great number of such specific, but quite diverse, practices, each offering protoforms of later school-based and academic social languages and genres. These protoforms, always embedded in specific social practices connected to specific socially situated identities (and useless when not so embedded), are the stuff from which success in school-based and academic reading flows. These are the sorts of protoforms that must be delivered to all children—amidst ample practice within socialization in specific Discourses—if we are to have true access and equity for all children.

References

Barsalou, L.W. (1999a). Language comprehension: Archival memory or preparation for situated action. *Discourse Processes, 28,* 61–80.

Barsalou, L.W. (1999b). Perceptual symbol systems. *Behavioral and Brain Sciences, 22,* 577–660.

Brown, A.L., Collins, A., & Dugid, P. (1989). Situated cognition and the culture of learning. *Educational Researcher, 18,* 32–42.

Clancey, W.J. (1997). *Situated cognition: On human knowledge and computer representations.* Cambridge, England: Cambridge University Press.

Clark, A. (1997). *Being there: Putting brain, body, and world together again.* Cambridge, MA: MIT Press.

Clark, H.H. (1996). *Using language.* Cambridge, England: Cambridge University Press.

D'Andrade, R., & Strauss, C. (Eds.). (1992). *Human motives and cultural models.* Cambridge, England: Cambridge University Press.

Engestrom, Y., Miettinen, R., & raij Punamaki (Eds.). (1999). *Perspectives on activity theory.* Cambridge, England: Cambridge University Press.

Freire, P. (1995). *The pedagogy of the oppressed.* New York: Continuum.

Gallas, K. (1994). *The languages of learning: How children talk, write, dance, draw, and sing their understanding of the world.* New York: Teachers College Press.

Gee, J.P. (1992). *The social mind: Language, ideology, and social practice.* New York: Bergin & Garvey.

Gee, J.P. (1996). *Social linguistics and literacies: Ideology in Discourses* (2nd ed.). London: Taylor & Francis.

Gee, J.P. (1999a). *An introduction to discourse analysis: Theory and method.* London: Routledge.

Gee, J.P. (1999b). Reading and the New Literacy Studies: Reframing the National Academy of Sciences report on reading. *Journal of Literacy Research, 31,* 355–374.

Glenberg, A.M. (1997). What is memory for? *Behavioral and Brain Sciences, 20,* 1–55.

Glenberg, A.M., & Robertson, D.A. (1999). Indexical understanding of instructions. *Discourse Processes, 28,* 1–26.

Halliday, M.A.K. (1994). *Functional grammar* (2nd ed.). London: Edward Arnold.

Hanks, W.F. (1996). *Language and communicative practices.* Boulder, CO: Westview Press.

Harkness, S., Super, C., & Keefer, C.H. (1992). *Learning to be an American parent: How cultural models gain directive force.* In R. D'Andrade & C. Strauss (Eds.), *Human motives and cultural models* (pp. 163–178). Cambridge, England: Cambridge University Press.

Holland, D., & Quinn, N. (Eds.). (1987). *Cultural models in language and thought.* Cambridge, England: Cambridge University Press.

Hutchins, E. (1995). *Cognition in the wild.* Cambridge, MA: MIT Press.

Labov, W. (1972). *Language in the inner city.* Philadelphia, PA: University of Pennsylvania Press.

Latour, B. (1987). *Science in action.* Cambridge, MA: Harvard University Press.

Latour, B. (1991). *We have never been modern.* Cambridge, MA: Harvard University Press.

Latour, B. (1999). *Pandora's hope: Essays on the reality of science studies.* Cambridge, MA: Harvard University Press.

Lave, J. (1996). Teaching, as learning, in practice. *Mind, Culture, and Activity, 3,* 149–164.

Lave, J., & Wenger, E. (1991). *Situated learning: Legitimate peripheral participation.* New York: Cambridge University Press.

Leont'ev, A.N. (1978). *Activity, consciousness, and personality.* Englewood Cliffs, NJ: Prentice-Hall.

Martin, J.R. (1990). Literacy in science: Learning to handle text as technology. In F. Christe (Ed.), *Literacy for a changing world* (pp. 79–117). Melbourne, NSW, Australia: Australian Council for Educational Research.

Myers, G. (1990). *Writing biology: Texts in the social construction of scientific knowledge.* Madison, WI: University of Wisconsin Press.

National Reading Panel. (2000). *Report of the National Reading Panel: Teaching children to read.* Washington, DC: Author. Available online: www.nationalreadingpanel.org.

Philipsen, G. (1975). Speaking "like a man" in Teamsterville: Culture patterns of role enactment in an urban neighborhood. *Quarterly Journal of Speech, 61,* 26–39.

Scollon, R., & Scollon, S.W. (1981). *Narrative, literacy, and face in interethnic communication.* Norwood, NJ: Ablex.

Shore, B. (1996). *Culture in mind: Cognition, culture, and the problem of meaning.* New York: Oxford University Press.

Snow, C.E., Burns, M.S., & Griffin, P. (Eds.). (1998). *Preventing reading difficulties in young children.* Washington, DC: National Academy Press.

Strauss, C., & Quinn, N. (1997). *A cognitive theory of cultural meaning.* Cambridge, England: Cambridge University Press.

Tomasello, M. (1999). *The cultural origins of human cognition.* Cambridge, MA: Harvard University Press.

Wenger, E. (1998). *Communities of practice: Learning, meaning, and identity.* Cambridge, England: Cambridge University Press.

6

THE DRIVE MODEL OF READING
Deploying Reading in Varied Environments

Nell K. Duke and Kelly B. Cartwright

Research has shed light on an unprecedented number and range of factors that contribute to reading processes, including an array of textual and contextual factors. However, it has been difficult for researchers to capture and communicate these factors to reading educators, curriculum developers, and others who influence reading education. The field needs a model of reading that includes and unpacks the wide range and multiplicity of influences on reading processes. In this chapter, we attempt to use the metaphor of driving to provide a complex but accessible model for reading, with particular attention to the roles that textual and contextual factors play.

Many decades of research reveal that skilled comprehenders have an array of characteristics and abilities that enable them to make meaning with text. However, reading comprehension also depends critically on factors beyond readers' individual characteristics and skills, including their reading purposes or goals, the text or texts they are reading, the nature of the reading activity, and the context in which reading occurs. Models of reading rarely encompass this diversity of factors. The aptly named simple view of reading (Gough & Tunmer, 1986), for example, offers a model of reading with just two factors—decoding and listening comprehension—and has shaped contemporary models that funnel various influences on reading comprehension through those factors (e.g., the direct and indirect effect model (Kim, 2017)). Other models of reading are more complex, such as the construction-integration model (Kintsch, 1988), the braid model (Scarborough, 2001), the component model (Aaron, Joshi, Gooden, & Bentum, 2008), and the direct and inferential mediation model (Cromley & Azevedo, 2007). However, these models have focused primarily on the ways that reader factors interact to produce successful reading comprehension, with scant attention to other factors—such as text, activity, purpose, or context—that also impact reading comprehension (see, e.g., Britt, Rouet, & Durik, 2018; Butterfuss & Kendeou, 2017; and McNamara & Magliano, 2009 for reviews of theories of reading comprehension).

Some models of reading have attempted to explicitly encompass text, activity, purpose, and other contextual factors. Freebody and Luke's (1990) groundbreaking four resources model does so, postulating that successful reading requires four roles: "code breaker ('How do I crack this?'), text participant ('What does this mean?'), text user ('What do I do with this, here and now?'), and text analyst ('What does this do to me?')" (p. 14). The often cited RAND Reading Study Group (2002) model also posits that reading comprehension is comprised of four major factors: the reader, the text, the activity, and their sociocultural context. These models are more inclusive, but neither explicates how these elements interact nor unpacks them to identify the many factors that contribute to each.

Yet a model of reading that comes closer to capturing its multifaceted and complex nature is likely to come at a price. Such a model may be too complex to be of practical value in education research and practice. Indeed, it is no accident that the simple view of reading (Gough & Tunmer, 1986) is still often relied upon in K-12 education and research, despite considerable evidence that it is too simple, missing the interaction of its component factors and factors that directly predict reading comprehension above and beyond (and not through) decoding and listening comprehension (e.g., Cartwright, 2007; Ouellette & Beers, 2010; Verhoeven & Van Leeuwe, 2008). Its simplicity makes it feel accessible and actionable. In an attempt to represent complexity but maintain accessibility and actionability, we have decided to use a metaphor to present a model. Metaphor provides a powerful tool for conceptualization (e.g., Lakoff & Johnson, 1980) and "can have an impact on practical as well as theoretical developments" (Leary, 1990, p. 15). In this chapter, we attempt to use the metaphor of driving to provide a complex but accessible model for reading, with particular attention to the roles that oft-neglected textual and contextual factors play in the reading process.[1] We call our model the **d**eploying **r**eading **in v**aried **e**nvironments (DRIVE) model.

Driving Destination : Reading Purpose

We drive for a purpose, typically to reach a particular destination but sometimes for the experience of driving itself. Our purpose affects how we drive, such that, for example, driving for the purpose of seeing sights will likely be more leisurely and varied in pace than driving for the purpose of running a familiar errand, which will in turn be different from driving for the purpose of test-driving a new car. In fact, if resources permit, we may choose different vehicles altogether for particular types of drives (e.g., an all-terrain vehicle for challenging terrain). Similarly, research has documented that purpose impacts reading comprehension, both in offline and online environments (Narvaez, van den Broek, & Ruiz, 1999; Zhang & Duke, 2008). For example, if our purpose is to find a particular piece of information, we are likely to skim, whereas if our purpose is to enjoy learning about a topic of interest, we are less likely to do so. And just as drivers may select a vehicle based on their reading purpose, readers may select different constellations of "problem solving behaviors" to reach different kinds of purposes (Britt et al., 2018). Establishing authentic purposes for students' reading and writing is associated with higher growth in reading comprehension over time (Purcell-Gates, Duke, & Martineau, 2007). Readers also benefit from setting goals for improving aspects of their reading (Fuchs, Fuchs, & Deno, 1985; Gaa, 1973, 1979), just as a new driver might view improvement of their driving skills as one purpose for driving.

Ignition and Gas : Reading Motivation

A drive cannot begin without the act of ignition. Similarly, reading does not begin without the motivation to engage in the process. Yet, while ignition is typically a matter of off or on, reading motivation may come in degrees. We may be only mildly motivated to engage in a reading task, or we may be highly motivated, or we may fall anywhere on the spectrum in between. Research finds that greater motivation to read in general is positively associated with reading comprehension (Schiefele, Schaffner, Möller, & Wigfield, 2012; Taboada, Tonks, Wigfield, & Guthrie, 2009). However, we also recognize that motivation is situational and may vary with different types of texts (Ho & Guthrie, 2013; Lin, Wong, & McBride-Chang, 2012). Specific teaching practices can cause students to be more motivated to read, which in turn improves comprehension (Guthrie et al., 2006; Guthrie, McRae, & Klauda, 2007).

Motivation provides not only the ignition but also the gas needed to sustain a driving experience. Some driving tasks, such as running a quick errand, require little gas, and some reading tasks, such as quickly looking up an actor's previous film, require little motivation. Other driving tasks, such as reaching a faraway destination, require a lot of gas, and some reading tasks, such as making one's way through a lengthy textbook, require a great deal of motivation. Our level of interest plays a substantial role in the degree to which we maintain reading motivation. Fulmer and Fritjers (2011) found that when the text was of high- as opposed to low- self-reported interest, students were more likely to persist in reading when given the option to stop, regardless of text complexity. The gas/reading motivation is also closely related to the destination/reading purpose. The degree to which we invest in gas will depend on the degree to which we are committed to and making progress toward the destination. Our reading motivation will depend on the degree to which we are committed to and making progress toward the reading purpose.

Weather Conditions : Reading Conditions

Our driving is considerably affected by weather or driving conditions. In fog, for example, we are likely to drive more slowly and with our lights on. On a clear day, we are likely to drive faster and with our lights turned off. Similarly, reading is affected by the conditions in which reading occurs. In a noisy and distracting environment, one is likely to read more slowly, or at least less efficiently, and perhaps with strategies designed to promote focus. In contrast, in a quiet and static environment, we are likely to read more quickly, or at least efficiently, and are less likely to require strategies designed to promote focus. Indeed, research suggests that a variety of environmental factors, such as noise, music, and presence or absence of natural light, impact reading comprehension (e.g., Anderson & Fuller, 2010; Cheryan, Ziegler, Plaut, & Meltzoff, 2014). In sum, the context "around" driving and reading impacts the very process of reading, a truism rarely recognized in work on reading comprehension.

Roads : Texts

Critically influential on driving are the roads on which we drive. Critically influential on reading is (are) the text(s) that we read. In this section, we address several aspects of text that have been shown to impact reading comprehension.

Road Types : Text Types

The kind of road on which we drive has a profound effect on our driving. Consider a highway versus a city street, for example: our speed differs, the vehicular features we make use of differ, our driving strategies differ, and so on. A muddy dirt road will be approached differently than smooth pavement. Similarly, research indicates that the type of text we are reading impacts our reading comprehension. In a research review they titled *The Genre-Specific Nature of Reading Comprehension*, Duke and Roberts (2010) identified 18 ways in which reading processes differ for narrative versus informational text. They also cited research indicating that on- and offline reading of informational texts require different kinds of strategies, with online reading requiring greater degrees of physical and cognitive self-regulation (Coiro, 2011; Coiro & Dobler, 2007).

Returning to our driving analogy, the type of car and the type of road interact. For example, a bumpy road is less of a problem for an SUV than a sports car, but a smooth highway is easier for a sports car to handle efficiently than an SUV. Likewise, in reading, text type and reader factors interact. For example, some readers will bring a deep level of facility with informational text, whereas other readers will find literary reading more manageable. The same text does not affect every reader or reading process in precisely the same way.

Roadmaps : Text Structure

As a driver embarks on a trip, they must map their route in order to ensure that they achieve their driving goal. Thus, tools such as an atlas, map, or GPS device are critical components to effective driving, at least for unfamiliar routes. Similarly, a skilled comprehender begins a reading task with a purpose and a plan to understand a text for that purpose (Britt et al., 2018; Cartwright, 2015). Scanning a text's structure in order to plan one's route through that text is a critical part of this process. However, just as a driver must have knowledge of maps, atlases, or GPS devices to use them effectively as they plan and navigate a route, a reader must have knowledge of various types of text structures, across multiple genres, to use them in planning a route through a text (Oakhill & Cain, 2012; Williams et al., 2002). Students with poor reading comprehension, despite good word reading skills, have significantly less awareness of text structure (Cain, 1996). However, just as learning to use roadmaps enables one to navigate a route more efficiently, text structure instruction produces gains in reading comprehension (Hebert, Bohaty, Nelson, & Brown, 2016; Pyle et al., 2017).

Road Signs : Organizational Signals

A good driver attends to road signs as they make their way along a route; a reader makes good use of textual cues the author provides that signal text structure. Road signs vary on different types of terrain (e.g., smooth highway vs. narrow, winding mountain road), just as they do within different text types. For example, organizational signals, such as headings, subheadings, and bold terms, highlight organization in informational texts, and clue words (e.g., *next, suddenly, so, in contrast, whereas*) alert a reader to critical information in both literary and informational texts (Lemarié, Lorch, Eyrolle, & Virbel, 2008), supporting the reader's understanding and use of text structure (Lorch, Lemarié, & Grant, 2011), and helping readers remember text content (Lorch & Lorch, 1996; Spyridakis & Standal, 1987). Indeed, organizational signals play a significant role in learning from informational texts, particularly for students with low levels of motivation (Kardash & Noel, 2000). Furthermore, poor comprehenders use fewer signal words in retellings of narratives, suggesting a lack of awareness and use of these important directional signals in text (Cain, 2003; Oakhill & Yuill, 1996). A driver who doesn't read signs get lost; likewise, a reader who doesn't attend to texts' organizational signals has difficulty reaching comprehension goals.

Other Road Features : Other Text Features

Beyond road features previously discussed, other road features that arise, such as potholes, rumble strips, new pavement, and patches of ice, also impact driving. Similarly, when reading, a variety of text features beyond those discussed to this point impact our comprehension. We may encounter specific graphical devices that facilitate our understanding, as graphical devices typically do (Roberts, Norman, & Cocco, 2015). In contrast, we may encounter a portion of text that is poorly written (aka "inconsiderate text"; Armbruster, 1984) and need to slow way down to deploy strategies to render it more comprehensible (and there are a number of other reasons we might slow down, such as to deconstruct the text, more deeply explore meaning, savor the beauty of the text, and so on). The decoding, syntactic, semantic, and pragmatic demands of the text also affect reading, and interact with reader knowledge and skill, as detailed later in this chapter.

The Scenery : Text Content

Driving is affected by the scenery. For example, interesting or unusual scenery is likely to capture some of our attention; tedious or familiar scenery is likely to do so less. Disengaged drivers may encounter risks, such as missing a turn or falling asleep at the wheel, particularly on difficult terrain. Similarly, the engagingness of the text impacts our reading processes, and disengaged readers may risk mind-wandering and comprehension failure, particularly with difficult texts (Feng, D'Mello, & Graesser, 2013; Moss, Schunn, Schneider, & McNamara, 2013). In fact, text content more broadly is critically important, largely in interaction with the reader's background and knowledge base, as detailed later in this chapter.

Number of Lanes : Number of Texts

Sometimes, drivers' routes take them along single-lane roads, but other times driving involves navigating among multiple lanes on an interstate highway. Reading is much the same in that sometimes readers may select one text to meet a reading goal, but other times must navigate among, and integrate information across, multiple texts. The number of lanes (or texts) one must handle at a given time affects the kinds of processes recruited to read and comprehend those texts. There is a long and continuing history of research that examines multiple-text comprehension (e.g., Davis, Huang, & Yi, 2017; Hartman, 1995), and several models of multiple-text reading have been developed (Britt et al., 2018; List & Alexander, 2017).

How Vehicle Transportation Works : Concepts of Print and Graphics

Driving requires fundamental understandings of how vehicle transportation works—Driver's Ed 101, if you will—and reading requires fundamental understanding about how print and graphics work (concepts of print (e.g., Clay, 2000) and of graphics (Duke, Norman, Roberts, Martin, Knight, Morsink, & Calkins, 2013), respectively). We need to know what vehicular transportation can do for us, and what print and graphics can do for us (e.g., that print can represent language and communicate, that graphics can provide information not found in the written text). We need to know how to open a car door in driving and how to open a book in reading. We need to know where the driver sits to begin to drive and where the book starts for us to begin to read. We need to know how the driving proceeds, for example whether we drive on the right or the left depending upon the country and the type of road, and we need to know how the reading proceeds, for example left to right or right to left depending upon the language and the type of book. We need to know which symbols are generally more or less important to driving— for example traffic lights versus lights on buildings, traffic signs as opposed to billboards—and which symbols are generally more and less important to reading—for example the copyright information versus the words on page one, decorative borders versus a central graphic. And so on. In sum, there are fundamental understandings of driving, and of reading, necessary to engage in the task.

Rules of the Road : Culture and Reading

The discussion of Driver's Ed 101 and concepts of print and graphics raises a critically important understanding about driving—and reading—that they are heavily cultural. As fundamental a matter as whether we drive on the left- or right-hand side of the road—or read from left to right or right to left—is culturally determined. Who even gets to drive is culturally determined, depending on the country, by age; by socioeconomic factors related to the costs of licenses, vehicles, insurance, and gas; by demographic factors, such as, in some countries, gender, just as who gets to read is culturally determined based on some of the same factors. Purposes for driving and reading vary by culture (e.g., whether we drive to a place of worship, whether we read religious texts). How we go about driving and reading also varies by cultural context. Consider, for example, how differently people seem to drive in New York City as opposed to the rural Midwest, or how differently people read who are, or are not, from a community with a high degree of skepticism about news reporting. A cultural group is defined in part by shared beliefs, practices, and conventions; these shared beliefs, practices, and conventions are the rules of the road, so to speak, for a group. Reading has rules of the road as well, and many of these vary based on cultural context, including the culture of schooling in which students find themselves—for example whether it's one that privileges literal or inferential comprehension. Disciplinary context has been of particular interest to many reading researchers. It, too, offers rules of the road for reading and other discourse practices, such that, for example, reading practices are different for a historian versus a chemist versus a mathematician (Shanahan, Shanahan, & Misischia, 2011). Abundant research across many contexts documents ways in which reading is culturally influenced and even defined (e.g., Moje, 2000; Morrell, 2002; Paris, 2009; Purcell-Gates, Jacobson, & Degener, 2004; Street, 1984). A growing body of research suggests that employing culturally familiar texts and culturally relevant instructional practices fosters reading development or development more broadly (Bell & Clark, 1998; Morrison, Robbins, & Rose, 2008), as does teaching specific disciplinary literacy practices (e.g., Greenleaf et al., 2011; Lee, 1995).

Route Knowledge : Background Knowledge

An important part of culture is shared background knowledge and indeed, background knowledge has an enormous impact on reading comprehension (e.g., Fincher-Kiefer, 1992; McNamara & Kintsch, 1996; Recht & Leslie, 1988), particularly for informational text (Best, Floyd, & McNamara, 2008). For example, if you were given an abstract of a journal article on nuclear physics, you would be likely to struggle to comprehend it. That is likely due not to the usual targets of reading instruction—decoding, fluency, comprehension strategies, and the like—and not even entirely to vocabulary, but to your overall content knowledge related to the topic.

Returning to the driving metaphor or analogy, many of us have had the experience of driving a familiar route with little conscious attention to the process of driving, perhaps even arriving somewhere without any memory of how you got there. Your relevant background knowledge is so high that the process is largely automatic. In contrast, when we are navigating somewhere new, or encountering unusual traffic or construction, we are likely to be more conscious in our driving and have more memory of how we got to the destination. Similarly, when we are reading text for which we have a high degree of relevant background knowledge, we are less likely to be paying conscious attention to the reading process and may even reach the end of the text without remembering how we got there. Yet, if we are reading text for which we have limited relevant background knowledge, we are likely to need to devote considerably more conscious attention to thinking about our reading process and, ultimately, to remember our challenges. Furthermore, even when a driver has route knowledge, if he or she forgets (or doesn't activate) that knowledge, it can't positively impact the driving process. Likewise, when reading, if one does not activate relevant background knowledge, comprehension will not be enhanced by that prior knowledge (Tarchi, 2015). Fortunately, research suggests that building content knowledge can improve reading comprehension (Cervetti, Wright, & Hwang, 2016) and that teaching reading in content-rich contexts has considerable benefits for reading development (e.g., Guthrie, McRae, & Klauda, 2007; Romance & Vitale, 2012).

Tires : Decoding and Word Recognition

Tires are necessary to driving, and decoding and word recognition are necessary to reading. A car won't get far without them, and the reading of most texts won't either. Decoding and word recognition are highly and causally related to comprehension (García & Cain, 2014; Lovett et al., 2017; McCandliss, Sandak, Beck, & Perfetti, 2003): they are absolutely necessary. At the same time, a set of tires rolling along a road alone does not constitute driving, and identifying words alone is not reading—that is, tires, and word identification, are necessary, but not sufficient (Locascio, Mahone, Eason, & Cutting, 2010; Oakhill, Cain, & Bryant, 2003). The clearest illustration of this point comes in the phenomenon of students who are able to decode text fluently, but still fail to understand what they read. These students, whom teachers commonly call *word callers*, make up 10 to 30% of struggling readers (Buly & Valencia, 2002; Catts, Compton, Tomblin, & Bridges, 2012; Torppa et al., 2007), demonstrating that skilled decoding alone is insufficient for successful reading to occur. Fortunately, educational interventions that support poor comprehenders' attention to the meaning of texts are effective in improving their reading comprehension (e.g., Cartwright, 2010; Hulme & Snowling, 2011).

Ehri and McCormick (2004) describe four ways in which readers read words: by prediction, by decoding, by analogy, and by sight. Eventually, nearly all words we encounter as proficient readers will be read by sight or automatically, enabled by a previous history of having grapho-phonemically analyzed the words (e.g., Ehri, Satlow, & Gaskins, 2009). Much as proficient drivers rarely think about the tires on their cars, proficient readers rarely think about word identification. However, there are times, when the road surface is unusually bumpy, unusually slick, or the like, when drivers may think about their tires. Similarly, sometimes even proficient readers need to think about their word identification, more deliberately employing word recognition strategies—for example, when reading some of the words in an article about nuclear physics. They may need to go into four-wheel drive or put on the snow tires, so to speak, to get through a text with many unfamiliar words. If a driver is paying a great deal of attention to their tires on a regular basis, that's a sign of trouble: worn treads, tire inflation issues, or continually challenging road conditions. If a reader is paying a great deal of attention to their word reading on a regular basis, that's also a sign of trouble, as it leaves less cognitive attention for many of the other aspects of reading discussed in this chapter (Laberge & Samuels, 1974). It is difficult to get the kind of traction we need in understanding a text if too much attention is focused on reading its words. At the same time, if we are inadequately attentive to reading the words, guessing based on limited orthographic information, misreading and skipping words, it's like hydroplaning: we aren't really gripping the text's surface.

Tire Treads : Phonological Awareness

A great deal of research has examined the role of phonological awareness in reading (and writing). Phonological awareness, or conscious attention to the sounds in speech, is causally connected to word reading (e.g., Bradley & Bryant, 1983; Vellutino & Scanlon, 1987). Part of phonological awareness is recognizing words in the speech stream—for example, recognizing that *I love you* is three words, not one. A *concept of word in text*, or understanding that in print, written clusters of letters separated by space are words, is an important milestone in reading development (Flanigan, 2007; Morris, 1993). A specific type of phonological awareness, termed *phonemic awareness*, refers to the smallest contrastive unit of sound in speech: the phoneme. Readers employ phonemic skills when they decode words. After associating a letter or letters with a sound or sounds, the reader also needs to blend those sounds together in order to form the word, a process called *phonemic blending* that is associated with reading comprehension (Hudson, Torgesen, Lane, & Turner, 2012). Within our driving metaphor, we might think of phonological awareness as the treads of the word reading tires. Phonological awareness alone cannot make a reader, but the underlying linguistic insight and skill is needed for the word reading to work, just as treads are needed for tires to work.

The Axles : Reading Fluency

We liken reading fluency to the axles of a car. The axles coordinate the tires (word reading) and connect to the rest of the car. Similarly, fluency is often described as involving the coordination of word reading and a bridge to comprehension (e.g., Kuhn & Stahl, 2003; Pikulski & Chard, 2005). Axles need to move such that we stay in our lane (accuracy), at just the right pace (automaticity) for the road conditions (texts, reading conditions), and need to move with the contours of the road (prosody). Reading fluency is generally understood to have these three components: accuracy, automaticity, and prosody. Accuracy involves reading the words as written; automaticity involves reading them readily, with little conscious effort; and prosody involves expression, volume, and phrasing (Rasinski, 2004). Notably, some equate fluency (automaticity) with reading rate and view higher rates of reading as inherently better. However, research suggests that good readers vary the pace of their reading depending on the demands of the text (August, Flavell, & Clift, 1984; Connor, Radach, Vorstius, Day, McLean, & Morrison, 2015), much as a driver might slow the rotation of the axles if road conditions are difficult, and employ strategies, such as rereading, that can also reduce reading rate.

The Seats and the Chassis : Language Knowledge

Reading rests heavily on the reader's language knowledge: it's the seats and the chassis of our reading. To mix metaphors for a moment, Britton (1970) wrote that "literacy floats on a sea of talk" (p. 164). The extent to which you have knowledge of the language of the text plays a strong role in your comprehension of it. For example, when we read a text in Polish, a language neither of us knows, we have essentially zero comprehension; when we read a text in our first language, English, but with atypical syntactic structures and lots of unfamiliar vocabulary, we can anticipate higher comprehension, but without the depth to which we're normally accustomed; when we read a paper in English in our field of expertise, with familiar linguistic structures and vocabulary, we experience a high degree of comprehension.

Traditionally, we think of language knowledge as encompassing phonological knowledge (discussed earlier), and syntactic, semantic, and pragmatic knowledge. With regard to syntactic knowledge, or knowledge of the ordering of words and phrases, studies illustrate a strong relationship with reading comprehension (Bentin, Deutsch, & Liberman, 1990; Gaux & Gombert, 1999). Child (Nation & Snowling, 2000) and adult (Cartwright, Bock, Coppage, Hodgkiss, & Nelson, 2017) readers who struggle with reading comprehension despite adequate word reading ability are significantly less aware of the proper ordering of words in sentences than their peers with better comprehension, which negatively impacts their reading comprehension. Semantic knowledge refers primarily to knowledge of word meaning. Both the depth and breadth of vocabulary knowledge in a language is associated with reading comprehension in that language (Tannenbaum, Torgesen, & Wagner, 2006). Vocabulary knowledge, and teaching vocabulary within a text, supports comprehension of that text (Elleman, Lindo, Morphy, & Compton, 2009; Wright & Cervetti, 2017). It is important to note that vocabulary varies across text genre, with academic meanings of polysemous words more common in informational texts, which may be challenging for some students, such as many English learners (Logan & Kieffer, 2017). Pragmatics deals with language use in context, such as conventions for turn-taking and implicit meaning, such as understanding irony and sarcasm. In reading, pragmatic knowledge is important to comprehension (Pexman, Ferretti, & Katz, 2000). For example, if one is reading dialogue in which a character says, "It's cold in here," and then becomes annoyed with her partner who stays seated on the couch, we use pragmatic knowledge to understand that "It's cold in here" actually meant "Could you please close the window that you opened?" and understand the basis of the character's annoyance. As is evident from this example, pragmatics, as well as semantic and syntactic knowledge, are heavily cultural, reinforcing points made earlier about the central role of cultural knowledge in reading.

A component of language knowledge that cuts across some of the aforedescribed categories is morphological knowledge, or knowledge of the smallest meaningful parts of words, essentially roots, prefixes, and suffixes. Research indicates that morphological awareness and knowledge is associated with reading comprehension (e.g., Nagy, Berninger, Abbott, Vaughan, & Vermeulen, 2003) and that instruction in morphology can foster reading comprehension (see Goodwin & Ahn, 2013 for a meta-analysis). Like fluency, morphology can be seen as playing a connective role, linking decoding and word recognition, which often relies on word parts, and vocabulary, which requires knowledge of those parts' meanings. In our driving metaphor, they might be seen as the shock absorbers of the car or the springs of the seats.

The Dashboard : Comprehension Monitoring

Modern-day cars have a number of instruments that are designed to provide information relevant to the drive: the car's speed, the temperature of the engine and outside the vehicle, the amount of gas in the tank, the miles traveled, progress on the route (GPS), and so on. Proficient drivers attend to these instruments to monitor how the drive is going and to inform decisions about any adjustments that may be needed, and careful attention to the instruments predicts a more successful driving experience. In reading, the nearest equivalent is a type of metacognitive process known as *comprehension monitoring*. Proficient readers think about how the reading is going and use information they gather to inform decisions about any adjustments that may be needed. Stronger readers are more likely to recognize when something they have read does not make sense (August et al., 1984; Oakhill, Cain, & Bryant, 2003) and to take time to resolve the problem (Connor et al., 2015). Stronger readers may also recognize when their mind has wandered while reading and, again, make adjustments accordingly. Comprehension monitoring predicts successful reading comprehension from first to third grades (Language and Reading Research Consortium & Yeomans-Maldonado, 2017). Instruction in comprehension monitoring has been shown to improve comprehension (e.g., Baumann, Seifert-Kessell, & Jones, 1992; Connor et al., 2014; Malone & Mastropieri, 1991); it seems that increasing attention to the instrument panel of reading supports reading proficiency.

The Strategic Driver: The Strategic Reader

A quick Internet search reveals many recommended driving strategies. The American Association of Retired Persons (AARP) (2013), for example, suggests strategies for highway driving dealing with merging, blind spots, stopped vehicles, and so on. These and other lists consist of strategies that we associate with good drivers. Similarly, accounts of the behaviors of good readers (e.g., Cromley & Wills, 2016; Pressley & Afflerbach, 1995; Pressley & Lundeberg, 2008) include a number of metacognitive strategies. Lists of these strategies vary, but often include setting purposes for reading; previewing and predicting; activating prior knowledge; monitoring, clarifying, and fixing; visualizing and creating visual representations; drawing inferences; self-questioning and thinking aloud; summarizing and retelling (Duke, Pearson, Strachan, & Billman, 2011). Evidence is strong that teaching these strategies supports reading comprehension, even in young readers (Shanahan et al., 2010). Strategies can be taught individually, but there is also evidence to support teaching strategies as clusters, establishing routines of strategy use and discussion that have been shown to have positive effects on comprehension (Palincsar & Brown, 1984; Reutzel, Smith, & Fawson, 2005; Spörer, Brunstein, & Kieschke, 2009).

A particular note should be made about drawing inferences, which is sometimes automatic and sometimes quite deliberate. When we are driving, we routinely make inferences about relevant contextual features and about other drivers. For example, if we see a detour sign ahead, we assume our route must change and slow our vehicle accordingly. Or if we notice a driver's turn signal on for many blocks, we can infer the driver does not mean to have it on. Similarly, we make many inferences when reading. Local, in-text inferences require readers to link bits of text information separated by distance; the greater the distance between those bits of information, the more difficult the inference is for readers (Yuill & Oakhill, 1988). Global inferences require connecting text information to prior knowledge and support literary (Cain & Oakhill, 1999) and informational (Elbro & Buch-Iversen, 2013) text comprehension. Instruction in inference improves reading comprehension (see meta-analysis by Elleman, 2017).

We should also note that not all inferences are created equal. When we read, we make some inferences about nonsocial features of text and others that require readers to understand and infer characters' mental or emotional states, such as inferring a character is angry when a text describes that character stomping out of a room. This is analogous to when a driver infers another driver's intention to take a parking place by the speed and positioning of their car. The ability to consider another's thoughts is called *theory of mind* in the research literature (Astington, Harris, & Olson, 1988). In the context of reading, students' theory of mind, or social understanding, is directly related to their ability to infer characters' internal states (Astington, 1990; Pelletier & Astington, 2004), which is in turn essential for comprehension of many texts with characters. Even in pre-readers, inferences about characters' internal mental and emotional states predict narrative comprehension (Tompkins, Guo, & Justice, 2013), and preschool social understanding predicts reading comprehension 3.5 years later (Guajardo & Cartwright, 2016). However, elementary school students still have difficulty inferring characters' internal motivations, unless the motives are stated explicitly (Shannon, Kameenui, & Baumann, 1988), and they rarely reference characters' internal motivations in their retellings of stories (Carnine, Kameenui, & Woolfson, 1982). Fortunately, teaching students to identify the internal mental, emotional, and motivational causes of characters' behaviors through text discussion (Lysaker, Tonge, Gauson, & Miller, 2011), facilitative questioning (Carnine, Stevens, Clements, & Kameenui, 1982), or elaborated story-mapping techniques (Emery, 1996; Shanahan & Shanahan, 1997) improves students' abilities to make social inferences, which fosters improvement in reading comprehension. In sum, just as driving requires a range of inferences, some more straightforward than others, so too does the process of reading, and just as beginning drivers may have more difficulty making some inferences, so too do young readers, whose theory of mind and other key abilities are still developing.

Road Reviews : Critical Reading

Ask any driver to talk about specific roads and routes, and you're likely to get an earful: roads that need to be repaired, streets to avoid at rush hour, highways that do or don't shave time off your drive, and so on. Good drivers often focus attention on the quality and characteristics, advantages and disadvantages of the roads and routes they travel. Similarly, good readers tend to be critical readers of text. They form opinions, relate information in texts to their own prior knowledge, question texts, and make applications of the knowledge they encounter to the broader world beyond the text. Good readers react to texts, to the opinions and voices of authors, and they consider texts' audiences. Critical readers are aware of the story and perspectives that are represented in a text, but also of the story and perspectives that are left out. They understand that texts often have social, political, cultural, or personal implications for people in real time. Teaching practices that support critical literacy focus on the active, engaged, reflective, evaluative practices characteristic of skilled comprehenders (Alvermann & Hagood, 2000; Behrman, 2006).

The Multi-tasking Driver : Executive Skills and Reading

Anyone who has attempted to teach someone to drive can attest to the fact that this task, although it feels like second nature to many of us now, is highly complex. Drivers have to simultaneously or in close proximity attend to their purpose for driving, applying ignition and gas when needed, and navigate under varying driving conditions, along varying types of roads, while attending to the route, road signs, and other road features as they arise, such as rumble strips or slick spots. Drivers must simultaneously utilize their knowledge of the ways that vehicle transportation works, the rules of the road for their context, supported by their prior knowledge of the driving process and of the particular route that they are taking. Drivers must have vehicles with tires, the tires must have adequate treads, and the axles must move the tires along the route while the drivers are continuously supported by the seats and chassis. Finally, drivers must constantly monitor their driving, using the dashboard instruments, employing strategic processes when needed, and analyzing the appropriateness of the route for their driving purpose. All of these various driving processes must be managed simultaneously while the drivers are traveling down the road and inhibiting attention to distractions, such as cell phones, snacks, or radio stations!

Similarly, reading is highly complex—in fact even more complex. Such complexity necessarily requires and recruits executive skills: higher-level thinking processes that enable individuals to manage multifaceted tasks in order to achieve goals (Anderson, 2002; Cartwright, 2015; Diamond, 2013). Executive skills include three core processes: working memory (holding information in mind while working with part of that information, for example holding text meaning in mind and updating it while one reads through a text), inhibition (resisting distracting impulses or information, for example ignoring ambient noise or inappropriate word meanings while reading), and cognitive flexibility (switching between different processes or elements in a task, for example switching between semantic and phonological elements of text). These core skills underlie more complex executive skills such as planning, and often involve metacognition (Roebers & Feurer, 2016). All of these processes contribute significantly to reading comprehension (Cartwright, 2012, 2015; Locascio et al., 2010; Sesma, Mahone, Levine, Eason, & Cutting, 2009). How do these skills support reading comprehension? Readers need to simultaneously, and flexibly, switch attention between multiple, competing aspects of reading. They must hold their reading goals or purposes in working memory while maintaining sufficient motivation to support continued progress toward their goals, recruiting fluent phonological decoding and word recognition processes as they make their way through a text. Readers must inhibit attention to distracting reading conditions, while flexibly shifting attention between text structure, organizational signals, graphical devices, and other text features, continually updating their mental models of the text's meaning in working memory. Readers must manage all of these processes, relying on their concepts of print, prior knowledge of text content, and language knowledge, while actively monitoring their ever-changing model of the text's meaning in working memory. To ensure effective understanding and meaning-construction, readers flexibly deploy reading strategies as needed, like making inferences, questioning the text, or connecting to their prior knowledge, inhibiting attention to irrelevant associations with text content, such as inappropriate word meanings. These processes do not stop after readers reach the ends of their texts (routes), because readers continue to hold text meaning in working memory in order to flexibly integrate it with prior knowledge, evaluate their progress toward their reading goals, and critically evaluate text content.

Readers with specific reading comprehension difficulties (RCD), despite having adequate, age-appropriate, fluent decoding and word reading skills, often lack executive skills needed to support reading comprehension, such as working memory (Cain, 2006), inhibition (Borella, Carretti, & Pelegrina, 2010), cognitive flexibility (Cartwright, Coppage et al., 2017), and planning (Locascio et al., 2010). These findings underscore the point that just as tires, treads, and axles are not sufficient for a successful drive, fluent decoding and word reading processes are not sufficient to support reading comprehension. Drivers need to have strong multi-tasking skills, and readers need to have strong executive function skills. Fortunately, research shows that instruction in executive skills such as cognitive flexibility (Cartwright, 2002; Cartwright, Coppage et al., 2017) and working memory (Dahlin, 2011) can improve reading comprehension.

Conclusion

In this chapter, we have attempted to use the metaphor of driving to depict the complexity of reading. We have presented a case for the importance and influence of a wide range of factors in the reading process, including not only factors traditionally associated with the reader but also factors less commonly considered (e.g., cultural background(s)). We have also placed a heavy emphasis on factors involved with the text and with the context around the reader and text, which are neglected or underspecified in many existing models of reading. See Figure 6.1 for a visual summary of the model.

In the case of nearly all factors, we have been able to cite research that shows a causal relationship between that factor and reading comprehension. Models that do not include this multiplicity of

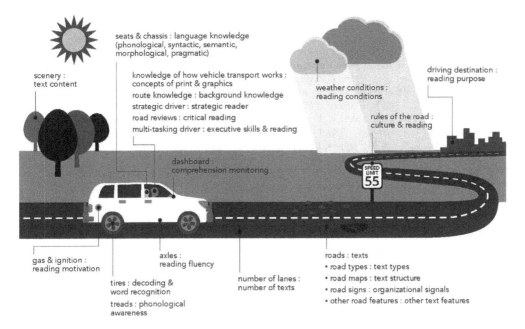

Figure 6.1   The DRIVE Model

factors are unable to account for key findings from the field. Therefore, the DRIVE model offers a depiction of reading that is considerably more complex and inclusive than others that are commonly invoked in the field. Our hope is that in the future, this more sophisticated model of reading will drive our field.

Note

1 Throughout this chapter, by reading, we mean reading comprehension and draw on the National Assessment Governing Board *Reading Framework for the 2015 National Assessment of Educational Progress* definition: "Reading is an active and complex process that involves: understanding written text, developing and interpreting meaning, [and] using meaning as appropriate to type of text, purpose, and situation" (p. iv).

References

Aaron, P. G., Joshi, R. M., Gooden, R., & Bentum, K. E. (2008). Diagnosis and treatment of reading disabilities based on the component model of reading: An alternative to the discrepancy model of LD. *Journal of Learning Disabilities*, *41*(1), 67–84.

Alvermann, D. E., & Hagood, M. C. (2000). Critical media literacy: Research, theory, and practice in "New Times." *Journal of Educational Research*, *93*(3), 193–205.

American Association of Retired Persons (AARP) (2013, September 3). *Ten strategies for highway driving.* Retrieved from https://www.aarp.org/auto/driver-safety/info-2013/10-strategies-for-highway-driving.html.

Anderson, P. (2002). Assessment and development of executive function (EF) during childhood. *Child Neuropsychology*, *8*(2), 71–82.

Anderson, S. A., & Fuller, G. B. (2010). Effect of music on reading comprehension of junior high school students. *School Psychology Quarterly*, *25*(3), 178–187.

Armbruster, B. B. (1984). The problem of "inconsiderate text." In G. G. Duffy, L. R. Roehler, & J. Mason (Eds.), *Comprehension instruction* (pp. 202–217). New York, NY: Longman.

Astington, J. W. (1990). Narrative and the child's theory of mind. In B. K. Britton & A. D. Pellegrini (Eds.), *Narrative thought and narrative language* (pp. 151–171). Hillsdale, NJ: Lawrence Erlbaum Associates.

Astington, J. W., Harris, P. L., & Olson, D. R. (1988). *Developing theories of mind*. New York, NY: Cambridge University Press.

August, D. L., Flavell, J. H., & Clift, R. (1984). Comparison of comprehension monitoring of skilled and less skilled readers. *Reading Research Quarterly, 20*, 39–53.

Baumann, J. F., Seifert-Kessell, N., & Jones, L. A. (1992). Effect of think-aloud instruction on elementary students' comprehension monitoring abilities. *Journal of Reading Behavior, 24*(2), 143–172.

Behrman, E. H. (2006). Teaching about language, power, and text: A review of classroom practices that support critical literacy. *Journal of Adolescent & Adult Literacy, 49*(6), 490–498.

Bell, Y. R., & Clark, T. R. (1998). Culturally relevant reading material as related to comprehension and recall in African American children. *Journal of Black Psychology, 24*(4), 455–475.

Bentin, S., Deutsch, A., & Liberman, I. Y. (1990). Syntactic competence and reading ability in children. *Journal of Experimental Child Psychology, 49*(1), 147–172.

Best, R. M., Floyd, R. G., & McNamara, D. S. (2008). Differential competencies contributing to children's comprehension of narrative and expository texts. *Reading Psychology, 29*(2), 137–164.

Borella, E., Carretti, B., & Pelegrina, S. (2010). The specific role of inhibition in reading comprehension in good and poor comprehenders. *Journal of Learning Disabilities, 43*(6), 541–552.

Britt, M. A., Rouet, J., & Durik, A. M. (2018). *Literacy beyond text comprehension: A theory of purposeful reading.* New York, NY: Routledge.

Buly, M. R., & Valencia, S. W. (2002). Below the bar: Profiles of students who fail state reading assessments. *Educational Evaluation and Policy Analysis, 24*(3), 219–239.

Bradley, L., & Bryant, P. E. (1983). Categorizing sounds and learning to read—a causal connection. *Nature, 301*(2), 419–421.

Britton, J. (1970). *Language and learning.* Coral Gables, FL: University of Miami Press.

Butterfuss, R., & Kendeou, P. (2017). The role of executive functions in reading comprehension. *Educational Psychology Review*, 42–60. https://doi.org/10.1007/s10648-017-9422-6

Cain, K. (1996). Story knowledge and comprehension skill. In C. Cornoldi & J. Oakhill (Eds.), *Reading comprehension difficulties: Processes and intervention* (pp. 167–192). Mahwah, NJ: Lawrence Erlbaum Associates.

Cain, K. (2003). Text comprehension and its relation to coherence and cohesion in children's fictional narratives. *British Journal of Developmental Psychology, 21*(3), 335–351.

Cain, K. (2006). Individual differences in children's memory and reading comprehension: An investigation of semantic and inhibitory deficits. *Memory, 14*(5), 553–569.

Cain, K., & Oakhill, J. V. (1999). Inference making ability and its relation to comprehension failure in young children. *Reading and Writing, 11*(5–6), 489–503.

Carnine, D. W., Kameenui, E. J., & Woolfson, N. (1982). Training of textual dimensions related to text-based inferences. *Journal of Literacy Research, 14*(3), 335–340.

Carnine, D., Stevens, C., Clements, J., & Kameenui, E. J. (1982). Effects of facilitative questions and practice on intermediate students' understanding of character motives. *Journal of Literacy Research, 14*(2), 179–190.

Cartwright, K. B. (2002). Cognitive development and reading: The relation of reading-specific multiple classification skill to reading comprehension in elementary school children. *Journal of Educational Psychology, 94*(1), 56–63.

Cartwright, K. B. (2007). The contribution of graphophonological-semantic flexibility to reading comprehension in college students: Implications for a less simple view of reading. *Journal of Literacy Research, 39*(2), 173–193.

Cartwright, K. B. (2010). *Word callers: Small-group and one-to-one interventions for children who "read" but don't comprehend.* Portsmouth, NH: Heinemann.

Cartwright, K. B. (2012). Insights from cognitive neuroscience: The importance of executive function for early reading development and education. *Early Education & Development, 23*(1), 24–36.

Cartwright, K. B. (2015). *Executive skills and reading comprehension: A guide for educators.* New York, NY: Guilford Press.

Cartwright, K. B., Bock, A. M., Coppage, E. A., Hodgkiss, M. D., & Nelson, M. I. (2017). A comparison of cognitive flexibility and metalinguistic skills in adult good and poor comprehenders. *Journal of Research in Reading, 40*(2), 139–152.

Cartwright, K. B., Coppage, E. A., Lane, A. B., Singleton, T., Marshall, T. R., & Bentivegna, C. (2017). Cognitive flexibility deficits in children with specific reading comprehension difficulties. *Contemporary Educational Psychology, 50*, 33–44.

Catts, H. W., Compton, D., Tomblin, J. B., & Bridges, M. S. (2012). Prevalence and nature of late-emerging poor readers. *Journal of Educational Psychology, 104*(1), 166–181.

Cervetti, G. N., Wright, T. S., & Hwang, H. (2016). Conceptual coherence, comprehension, and vocabulary: A knowledge effect? *Reading and Writing: An Interdisciplinary Journal, 29*, 1–19.

Cheryan, S., Ziegler, S. A., Plaut, V. C., & Meltzoff, A. N. (2014). Designing classrooms to maximize student achievement. *Policy Insights from the Behavioral and Brain Sciences, 1*(1), 4–12.

Clay, M. M. (2000). *Concepts about print: What have children learned about the way we print language?* Portsmouth, NH: Heinemann.

Coiro, J. (2011). Predicting reading comprehension on the Internet: Contributions of offline reading skills, online reading skills, and prior knowledge. *Journal of Literacy Research, 43*(4), 352–392.

Coiro, J., & Dobler, E. (2007). Exploring the online reading comprehension strategies used by sixth-grade skilled readers to search for and locate information on the Internet. *Reading Research Quarterly, 42*(2), 214–257.

Connor, C. M., Phillips, B. M., Kaschak, M., Apel, K., Kim, Y.-S., Al Otaiba, S., . . . Lonigan, C. J. (2014). Comprehension tools for teachers: Reading for understanding from prekindergarten through fourth grade. *Educational Psychology Review, 26*(3), 379–401.

Connor, C. M., Radach, R., Vorstius, C., Day, S. L., McLean, L., & Morrison, F. J. (2015). Individual differences in fifth graders' literacy and academic language predict comprehension monitoring development: An eye-movement study. *Scientific Studies of Reading, 19*(2), 114–134.

Cromley, J. G., & Azevedo, R. (2007). Testing and refining the direct and inferential mediation model of reading comprehension. *Journal of Educational Psychology, 99*(2), 311–325.

Cromley, J. G., & Wills, T. W. (2016). Flexible strategy use by students who learn much versus little from text: Transitions within think-aloud protocols. *Journal of Research in Reading, 39*(1), 50–71.

Dahlin, K. I. (2011). Effects of working memory training on reading in children with special needs. *Reading and Writing, 24*(4), 479–491.

Davis, D. S., Huang, B., & Yi, T. (2017). Making sense of science texts: A mixed-methods examination of predictors and processes of multiple-text comprehension. *Reading Research Quarterly, 52*(2), 227–252.

Diamond, A. (2013). Executive functions. *Annual Review of Psychology, 64*, 135–168.

Duke, N. K., Norman, R. R., Roberts, K. L., Martin, N. M., Knight, J. A., Morsink, P. M., & Calkins, S. L. (2013). Beyond concepts of print: Development of concepts of graphics in text, pre-K to grade 3. *Research in the Teaching of English, 48*, 175–203.

Duke, N. K., Pearson, P. D., Strachan, S. L., & Billman, A. K. (2011). Essential elements of fostering and teaching reading comprehension. In S. J. Samuels & A. E. Farstrup (Eds.), *What research has to say about reading instruction* (4th ed.) (pp. 51–93). Newark, DE: International Reading Association.

Duke, N. K., & Roberts, K. M. (2010). The genre-specific nature of reading comprehension. In D. Wyse, R. Andrews, & J. Hoffman (Eds.), *The Routledge International Handbook of English, Language and Literacy Teaching* (pp. 74–86). London: Routledge.

Ehri, L. C., & McCormick S. (2004). Phases of word learning: Implications for instruction with delayed and disabled readers. In R. B. Ruddell and N. J. Unrau (Eds.). *Theoretical Models and Processes of Reading* (pp. 365–389). Newark, DE: International Reading Association.

Ehri, L. C., Satlow, E., & Gaskins, I. (2009). Grapho-phonemic enrichment strengthens keyword analogy instruction for struggling young readers. *Reading & Writing Quarterly: Overcoming Learning Difficulties, 25*(2–3), 162–191.

Elbro, C., & Buch-Iversen, I. (2013). Activation of background knowledge for inference making: Effects on reading comprehension. *Scientific Studies of Reading, 17*(6), 435–452.

Elleman, A. M. (2017). Examining the impact of inference instruction on the literal and inferential comprehension of skilled and less skilled readers: A meta-analytic review. *Journal of Educational Psychology, 109*(6), 761–781.

Elleman, A. M., Lindo, E. J., Morphy, P., & Compton, D. L. (2009). The impact of vocabulary instruction on passage-level comprehension of school-age children: A meta-analysis. *Journal of Research on Educational Effectiveness, 2*(1), 1–44.

Emery, D. W. (1996). Helping readers comprehend stories from the characters' perspectives. *The Reading Teacher, 49*(7), 534–541.

Feng, S., D'Mello, S., & Graesser, A. C. (2013). Mind wandering while reading easy and difficult texts. *Psychonomic Bulletin & Review, 20*(3), 586–592.

Fincher-Kiefer, R. (1992). The role of prior knowledge in inferential processing. *Journal of Research in Reading, 15*(1), 12–27.

Flanigan, K. (2007). A concept of word in text: A pivotal event in early reading acquisition. *Journal of Literacy Research, 39*(1), 37–70.

Freebody, P., & Luke, A. (1990). Literacies programs: Debates and demands in cultural context. *Prospect: An Australian Journal of TESOL, 5*(7), 7–16.

Fuchs, L. S., Fuchs, D., & Deno, S. L. (1985). Importance of goal ambitiousness and goal mastery to student achievement. *Exceptional Children, 52*(1), 63–71.

Fulmer, S. M., & Frijters, J. C. (2011). Motivation during an excessively challenging reading task: The buffering role of relative topic interest. *The Journal of Experimental Education, 79*(2), 185–208.

Gaa, J. P. (1973). Effects of individual goal-setting conferences on achievement, attitudes, and goal-setting behavior. *Journal of Experimental Education, 42*(1), 22–28.

Gaa, J. P. (1979). The effects of individual goal-setting conferences on academic achievement and modification of locus of control orientation. *Psychology in the Schools, 16*(4), 591–597.

García, J. R., & Cain, K. (2014). Decoding and reading comprehension: A meta-analysis to identify which reader and assessment characteristics influence the strength of the relationship in English. *Review of Educational Research, 84*(1), 74–111.

Gaux, C., & Gombert, J. E. (1999). Implicit and explicit syntactic knowledge and reading in pre-adolescents. *British Journal of Developmental Psychology, 17*(2), 169–188.

Goodwin, A. P., & Ahn, S. (2013). A meta-analysis of morphological interventions in English: Effects on literacy outcomes for school-age children. *Scientific Studies of Reading, 17*(4), 257–285.

Gough, P. B., & Tunmer, W. E. (1986). Decoding, reading, and reading disability. *Remedial and Special Education, 7*(1), 6–10.

Greenleaf, C. L., Litman, C., Hanson, T. L, Rosen, R., Boscardin, C., Herman, J., . . . Jones, B. (2011). Integrating literacy and science in biology: Teaching and learning impacts of reading apprenticeship professional development. *American Educational Research Journal, 48*(3), 647–717.

Guajardo, N. R., & Cartwright, K. B. (2016). The contribution of theory of mind, counterfactual reasoning, and executive function to pre-readers' language comprehension and later reading awareness and comprehension in elementary school. *Journal of Experimental Child Psychology, 144*, 27–45.

Guthrie, J. T., McRae, A., & Klauda, S. L. (2007). Contributions of Concept-Oriented Reading Instruction to knowledge about interventions for motivations in reading. *Educational Psychologist, 42*(4), 237–250.

Guthrie, J. T., Wigfield, A., Humenick, N. M., Perencevich, K. C., Taboada, A., & Barbosa, P. (2006). Influences of stimulating tasks on reading motivation and comprehension. *Journal of Educational Research, 99*(4), 232–246.

Hartman, D. K. (1995). Eight readers reading: The intertextual links of proficient readers reading multiple passages. *Reading Research Quarterly, 30*(3), 520–561.

Hebert, M., Bohaty, J. J., Nelson, J. R., & Brown, J. (2016). The effects of text structure instruction on expository reading comprehension: A meta-analysis. *Journal of Educational Psychology, 108*(5), 609–629.

Ho, A. N., & Guthrie, J. T. (2013). Patterns of association among multiple motivations and aspects of achievement in reading. *Reading Psychology, 34*(2), 101–147.

Hudson, R. F., Torgesen, J. K., Lane, H. B., & Turner, S. J. (2012). Relations among reading skills and sub-skills and text-level reading proficiency in developing readers. *Reading and Writing, 25*(2), 483–507.

Hulme, C., & Snowling, M. J. (2011). Children's reading comprehension difficulties: Nature, causes, and treatments. *Current Directions in Psychological Science, 20*(3), 139–142.

Kardash, C. M., & Noel, L. K. (2000). How organizational signals, need for cognition, and verbal ability affect text recall and recognition. *Contemporary Educational Psychology, 25*(3), 317–331.

Kim, Y. G. (2017). Why the simple view of reading is not simplistic: Unpacking component skills of reading using a direct and indirect effect model of reading (DIER). *Scientific Studies of Reading, 21*(4), 310–333.

Kintsch, W. (1988). The role of knowledge in discourse comprehension: A construction-integration model. *Psychological Review, 95*(2), 163–182.

Kuhn, M. R., & Stahl, S. A. (2003). Fluency: A review of developmental and remedial practices. *Journal of Educational Psychology, 95*(1), 3–21.

LaBerge, D., & Samuels, S. J. (1974). Toward a theory of automatic information processing in reading. *Cognitive Psychology, 6*(2), 293–323.

Lakoff, G., & Johnson, M. (1980). *Metaphors we live by.* Chicago, IL: University of Chicago Press.

Language and Reading Research Consortium (LARRC), & Yeomans-Maldonado, G. (2017). Development of comprehension monitoring in beginner readers. *Reading and Writing, 30*(9), 2039–2067.

Leary, D. E. (Ed.) (1990). *Metaphors in the history of psychology.* Cambridge: Cambridge University Press.

Lee, C. D. (1995). A culturally based cognitive apprenticeship: Teaching African American high school students skills in literary interpretation. *Reading Research Quarterly, 30*(4), 608–630.

Lemarié, J., Lorch, R. F., Jr., Eyrolle, H., & Virbel, J. (2008). SARA: A text-based and reader-based theory of signaling. *Educational Psychologist, 43*(1), 27–48.

Lin, D., Wong, K. K., & McBride-Chang, C. (2012). Reading motivation and reading comprehension in Chinese and English among bilingual students. *Reading and Writing, 25*(3), 717–737.

List, A., & Alexander, P. A. (2017). Analyzing and integrating models of multiple text comprehension. *Educational Psychologist, 52*(3), 143–147.

Locascio, G., Mahone, E. M., Eason, S. H., & Cutting, L. E. (2010). Executive dysfunction among children with reading comprehension deficits. *Journal of Learning Disabilities, 43*(5), 441–454.

Logan, J. K., & Kieffer, M. J. (2017). Evaluating the role of polysemous word knowledge in reading comprehension among bilingual adolescents. *Reading and Writing, 30*(8), 1687–1704.

Lorch, R., Lemarié, J., & Grant, R. (2011). Signaling hierarchical and sequential organization in expository text. *Scientific Studies of Reading, 15*(3), 267–284.

Lorch, R. F., Jr., & Lorch, E. P. (1996). Effects of organizational signals on free recall of expository text. *Journal of Educational Psychology, 88*(1), 38–48.

Lovett, M. W., Frijters, J. C., Wolf, M., Steinbach, K. A., Sevcik, R. A., & Morris, R. D. (2017). Early intervention for children at risk for reading disabilities: The impact of grade at intervention and individual differences on intervention outcomes. *Journal of Educational Psychology, 109*(7), 889–914.

Lysaker, J. T., Tonge, C., Gauson, D., & Miller, A. (2011). Reading and social imagination: What relationally oriented reading instruction can do for children. *Reading Psychology, 32*(6), 520–566.

Malone, L. D., & Mastropieri, M. A. (1991). Reading comprehension instruction: Summarization and self-monitoring training for students with learning disabilities. *Exceptional Children, 58*(3), 270–279.

McCandliss, B., Beck, I. L., Sandak, R., & Perfetti, C. (2003). Focusing attention on decoding for children with poor reading skills: Design and preliminary tests of the word building intervention. *Scientific Studies of Reading, 7*(1), 75–104.

McNamara, D. S., & Kintsch, W. (1996). Learning from texts: Effects of prior knowledge and text coherence. *Discourse Processes, 22*(3), 247–288.

McNamara, D. S., & Magliano, J. (2009). Toward a comprehensive model of comprehension. *Psychology of learning and motivation, 51*, 297–384.

Moje, E. B. (2000). "To be part of the story": The literacy practices of gangsta adolescents. *Teachers College Record, 102*, 652–690.

Morrell, E. (2002). Toward a critical pedagogy of popular culture: Literacy development among urban youth. *Journal of Adolescent & Adult Literacy, 46*(1), 72–77.

Morris, D. (1993). The relationship between children's concept of word in text and phoneme awareness in learning to read: A longitudinal study. *Research in the Teaching of English, 27*(2), 133–154.

Morrison, K. A., Robbins, H. H., & Rose, D. G. (2008). Operationalizing culturally relevant pedagogy: A synthesis of classroom-based research. *Equity & Excellence in Education, 41*(4), 433–452.

Moss, J., Schunn, C. D., Schneider, W., & McNamara, D. S. (2013). The nature of mind wandering during reading varies with the cognitive control demands of the reading strategy. *Brain Research, 1539*, 48–60.

Nagy, W., Berninger, V., Abbott, R., Vaughan, K., & Vermeulen, K. (2003). Relationship of morphology and other language skills to literacy skills in at-risk second-grade readers and at-risk fourth-grade writers. *Journal of Educational Psychology, 95*(4), 730–742.

Narvaez, D., van den Broek, P., & Ruiz, A. B. (1999). The influence of reading purpose on inference generation and comprehension in reading. *Journal of Educational Psychology, 91*(3), 488–496.

Nation, K., & Snowling, M. J. (2000). Factors influencing syntactic awareness skills in normal readers and poor comprehenders. *Applied Psycholinguistics, 21*(2), 229–241.

National Assessment Governing Board. (2015). *Reading framework for the 2015 National Assessment of Educational Progress.* Washington, DC: Author. Retrieved from https://www.nagb.gov/content/nagb/assets/documents/publications/frameworks/reading/2015-reading-framework.pdf

Oakhill, J. V., & Cain, K. (2012). The precursors of reading ability in young readers: Evidence from a four-year longitudinal study. *Scientific Studies of Reading, 16*(2), 91–121.

Oakhill, J., Cain, K., & Bryant, P. E. (2003). The dissociation of word reading and text comprehension: Evidence from component skills. *Language and Cognitive Processes, 18*(4), 443–468.

Oakhill, J., & Yuill, N. (1996). Higher order factors in comprehension disability: Processes and remediation. In C. Cornoldi & J. Oakhill (Eds.), *Reading comprehension difficulties: Processes and intervention* (pp. 69–92). Mahwah, NJ: Lawrence Erlbaum Associates.

Ouellette, G., & Beers, A. (2010). A not-so-simple view of reading: How oral vocabulary and visual-word recognition complicate the story. *Reading and Writing, 23*(2), 189–208.

Paris, D. (2009). "They're in my culture, they speak the same way": African American language in multiethnic high schools. *Harvard Educational Review, 79*(3), 428–448.

Palincsar, A. S., & Brown, A. L. (1984). Reciprocal teaching of comprehension-fostering and comprehension-monitoring activities. *Cognition and Instruction, 1*(2), 117–175.

Pelletier, J., & Astington, J. W. (2004). Action, consciousness, and theory of mind: Children's ability to coordinate story characters' actions and thoughts. *Early Education and Development, 15*(1), 5–22.

Pexman, P. M., Ferretti, T. R., & Katz, A. N. (2000). Discourse factors that influence online reading of metaphor and irony. *Discourse Processes, 29*(3), 201–222.

Pikulski, J. J., & Chard, D. J. (2005). Fluency: Bridge between decoding and reading comprehension. *The Reading Teacher, 58*(6), 510–519.

Pressley, M., & Afflerbach, P. (1995). *Verbal protocols of reading: The nature of constructively responsive reading.* Hillsdale, NJ: Lawrence Erlbaum Associates.

Pressley, M., & Lundeberg, M. (2008). An invitation to study professionals reading professional level texts: A window on exceptionally complex, flexible reading. In K. B. Cartwright (Ed.), *Literacy processes: Cognitive flexibility in learning and teaching* (pp. 165–187). New York, NY: Guilford Press.

Purcell-Gates, V., Duke, N. K., & Martineau, J. A. (2007). Learning to read and write genre-specific text: Roles of authentic experience and explicit teaching. *Reading Research Quarterly, 42*(1), 8–45.

Purcell-Gates, V., Jacobson, E., & Degener, S. (2004). *Print literacy development: Uniting cognitive and social practice theories.* Cambridge, MA: Harvard University Press.

Pyle, N., Vasquez, A. C., Gillam, S. L., Reutzel, D., Olszewski, A., Segura, H., . . . Pyle, D. (2017). Effects of expository text structure interventions on comprehension: A meta-analysis. *Reading Research Quarterly, 52*(4), 469–501.

RAND Reading Study Group. (2002). *Reading for understanding: Toward an R&D program in reading comprehension.* Santa Monica, CA: RAND.

Rasinski, T. V. (2004). Assessing reading fluency. *Pacific Resources for Education and Learning (PREL).* Retrieved from https://files.eric.ed.gov/fulltext/ED483166.pdf.

Recht, D. R., & Leslie, L. (1988). Effect of prior knowledge on good and poor readers' memory of text. *Journal of Educational Psychology, 80*(1), 16–20.

Reutzel, D. R., Smith, J. A., & Fawson, P. C. (2005). An evaluation of two approaches for teaching reading comprehension strategies in the primary years using science information texts. *Early Childhood Research Quarterly, 20*(3), 276–305.

Roberts, K. L., Norman, R. R., & Cocco, J. (2015). Relationship between graphical device comprehension and overall text comprehension for third-grade children. *Reading Psychology, 36*(5), 389–420.

Roebers, C. M., & Feurer, E. (2016). Linking executive functions and procedural metacognition. *Child Development Perspectives, 10*(1), 39–44.

Romance, N. R., & Vitale, M. R. (2012). Expanding the role of K-5 science instruction in educational reform: Implications of an interdisciplinary model for integrating science and reading. *School Science and Mathematics, 112*(8), 506–515.

Scarborough, H. S. (2001). Connecting early language and literacy to later reading (dis)abilities: Evidence, theory, and practice. In S. B. Neuman & D. K. Dickinson (Eds.), *Handbook of early literacy research* (pp. 97–110). New York. NY: Guilford Press.

Schiefele, U., Schaffner, E., Möller, J., & Wigfield, A. (2012). Dimensions of reading motivation and their relation to reading behavior and competence. *Reading Research Quarterly, 47*(4), 427–463.

Sesma, H. W., Mahone, E. M., Levine, T., Eason, S. H., & Cutting, L. E. (2009). The contribution of executive skills to reading comprehension. *Child Neuropsychology, 15*(3), 232–246.

Shanahan, C., Shanahan, T., & Misischia, C. (2011). Analysis of expert readers in three disciplines: History, mathematics, and chemistry. *Journal of Literacy Research, 43*(4), 393–429.

Shanahan, T., Callison, K., Carriere, C., Duke, N. K., Pearson, P. D., Schatschneider, C., & Torgesen, J. (2010). *Improving reading comprehension in kindergarten through 3rd grade: A practice guide* (NCEE 2010–4038). Washington, DC: National Center for Education Evaluation and Regional Assistance, Institute of Education Sciences, U.S. Department of Education. Retrieved from whatworks.ed.gov/publications/practiceguides.

Shanahan, T., & Shanahan, S. (1997). Character perspective charting: Helping children to develop a more complete conception of story. *Reading Teacher, 50*(8), 668–677.

Shannon, P., Kameenui, E. J., & Baumann, J. F. (1988). An investigation of children's ability to comprehend character motives. *American Educational Research Journal, 25*(3), 441–462.

Spörer, N., Brunstein, J. C., & Kieschke, U. (2009). Improving students' reading comprehension skills: Effects of strategy instruction and reciprocal teaching. *Learning and Instruction, 19*(3), 272–286.

Spyridakis, J. H., & Standal, T. C. (1987). Signals in expository prose: Effects on reading comprehension. *Reading Research Quarterly, 22*, 285–298.

Street, B. V. (1984). *Literacy in theory and practice.* Cambridge: Cambridge University Press.

Taboada, A., Tonks, S. M., Wigfield, A., & Guthrie, J. T. (2009). Effects of motivational and cognitive variables on reading comprehension. *Reading and Writing, 22*(1), 85–106.

Tannenbaum, K. R., Torgesen, J. K., & Wagner, R. K. (2006). Relationships between word knowledge and reading comprehension in third-grade children. *Scientific Studies of Reading, 10*(4), 381–398.

Tarchi, C. (2015). Fostering reading comprehension of expository texts through the activation of readers' prior knowledge and inference-making skills. *International Journal of Educational Research, 72*, 80–88.

Tompkins, V., Guo, Y., & Justice, L. M. (2013). Inference generation, story comprehension, and language skills in the preschool years. *Reading and Writing, 26*(3), 403–429.

Torppa, M., Tolvanen, A., Poikkeus, A. M., Eklund, K., Lerkkanen, M. K., Leskinen, E., & Lyytinen, H. (2007). Reading development subtypes and their early characteristics. *Annals of Dyslexia, 57*(1), 3–32.

Vellutino, F. R., & Scanlon, D. M. (1987). Phonological coding, phonological awareness, and reading ability: Evidence from a longitudinal and experimental study. *Merrill-Palmer Quarterly, 33,* 321–363.

Verhoeven, L., & Van Leeuwe, J. (2008). Prediction of the development of reading comprehension: A longitudinal study. *Applied Cognitive Psychology, 22*(3), 407–423.

Williams, J. P., Lauer, K. D., Hall, K. M., Lord, K. M., Gugga, S. S., Bak, S. J., . . . & deCani, J. S. (2002). Teaching elementary school students to identify story themes. *Journal of Educational Psychology, 94,* 235–248.

Wright, T. S., & Cervetti, G. N. (2017). A systematic review of the research on vocabulary instruction that impacts text comprehension. *Reading Research Quarterly, 52*(2), 203–226.

Yuill, N., & Oakhill, J. (1988). Understanding of anaphoric relations in skilled and less skilled comprehenders. *British Journal of Psychology, 79,* 173–186.

Zhang, S., & Duke, N. K. (2008). Strategies for Internet reading with different reading purposes: A descriptive study of twelve good Internet readers. *Journal of Literacy Research, 40,* 128–162.

7

ROLE OF THE READER'S SCHEMA IN COMPREHENSION, LEARNING, AND MEMORY

Richard C. Anderson

This chapter is reprinted from *Learning to Read in American Schools: Basal Readers and Content Texts* (pp. 243–257), edited by R.C. Anderson, J. Osborn, & R.J. Tierney, 1984, Hillsdale, NJ: Erlbaum. Copyright © 1984 by Lawrence Erlbaum Associates. Reprinted with permission.

The last several years have witnessed the articulation of a largely new theory of reading, a theory already accepted by the majority of scholars in the field. According to the theory, a reader's *schema*, or organized knowledge of the world, provides much of the basis for comprehending, learning, and remembering the ideas in stories and texts. In this chapter I attempt to explain schema theory, give illustrations of the supporting evidence, and suggest applications to classroom teaching and the design of instructional materials.

A Schema-Theoretic Interpretation of Comprehension

In schema-theoretic terms, a reader comprehends a message when he is able to bring to mind a schema that gives a good account of the objects and events described in the message. Ordinarily, comprehension proceeds so smoothly that we are unaware of the process of "cutting and fitting" a schema in order to achieve a satisfactory account of a message. It is instructive, therefore, to try to understand material that gives us pause, so that we can reflect upon our own minds at work. Consider the following sentence, drawn from the work of Bransford and McCarrell (1974):

The notes were sour because the seam split.

Notice that all of the words are familiar and that the syntax is straightforward, yet the sentence does not "make sense" to most people. Now notice what happens when the additional clue, "bagpipe," is provided. At this point the sentence does make sense because one is able to interpret all the words in the sentence in terms of certain specific objects and events and their interrelations.

Let us examine another sentence:

The big number 37 smashed the ball over the fence.

This sentence is easy to interpret. *Big Number 37* is a baseball player. The sense of *smash the ball* is to propel it rapidly by hitting it strongly with a bat. The fence is at the boundary of a playing field. The ball was hit hard enough that it flew over the fence.

Suppose a person with absolutely no knowledge of baseball read the Big Number 37 sentence. Such a person could not easily construct an interpretation of the sentence, but with enough mental effort might be able to conceive of large numerals, perhaps made of metal, attached to the front of an apartment building. Further, the person might imagine that the numerals come loose and fall, striking a ball resting on top of, or lodged above, a fence, causing the ball to break. Most people regard this as an improbable interpretation, certainly one that never would have occurred to them, but they readily acknowledge that it is a "good" interpretation. What makes it good? The answer is that the interpretation is complete and consistent. It is complete in the sense that every element in the sentence is interpreted; there are no loose ends left unexplained. The interpretation is consistent in that no part of it does serious violence to knowledge about the physical and social world.

Both interpretations of the Big Number 37 sentence assume a real world. Criteria of consistency are relaxed in fictional worlds in which animals talk or men wearing capes leap tall buildings in a single bound. But there are conventions about what is possible in fictional worlds as well. The knowledgeable reader will be annoyed if these conventions are violated. The less knowledgeable reader simply will be confused.

It should not be imagined that there is some simple, literal level of comprehension of stories and texts that does not require coming up with a schema. This important point is illustrated in a classic study by Bransford and Johnson (1972) in which subjects read paragraphs, such as the following, written so that most people are unable to construct a schema that will account for the material:

> If the balloons popped the sound wouldn't be able to carry since everything would be too far away from the correct floor. A closed window would also prevent the sound from carrying, since most buildings tend to be well insulated. Since the whole operation depends upon a steady flow of electricity, a break in the middle of the wire would also cause problems. Of course, the fellow could shout, but the human voice is not loud enough to carry that far. An additional problem is that a string could break on the instrument. Then there could be no accompaniment to the message. It is clear that the best situation would involve less distance. Then there would be fewer potential problems. With face to face contact, the least number of things could go wrong.
>
> *(p. 719)*

Subjects rated this passage as very difficult to understand, and they were unable to remember much of it. In contrast, subjects shown the drawing on the left side of Figure 7.1 found the passage more comprehensible and were able to remember a great deal of it. Another group saw the drawing on the right in Figure 7.1. This group remembered no more than the group that did not receive a drawing. The experiment demonstrates that what is critical for comprehension is a schema accounting for the *relationships* among elements; it is not enough for the elements to be concrete and imageable.

Trick passages, such as the foregoing one about the communication problems of a modern day Romeo, are useful for illustrating what happens when a reader is completely unable to discover a schema that will fit a passage and, therefore, finds the passage entirely incomprehensible. More typical is the situation in which a reader knows something about a topic, but falls far short of being an expert. Chiesi, Spilich, and Voss (1979) asked people high and low in knowledge of baseball to read and recall a report of a half-inning from a fictitious baseball game. Knowledge of baseball had both qualitative and quantitative effects on performance. High-knowledge subjects were more likely to recall and embellish upon aspects of strategic significance to the game. Low-knowledge subjects, in contrast, were more likely to include information incidental to the play of the game.

Schema theory highlights the fact that often more than one interpretation of a text is possible. The schema that will be brought to bear on a text depends upon the reader's age, sex, race, religion, nationality, occupation—in short, it depends upon the reader's culture. This point was illustrated in

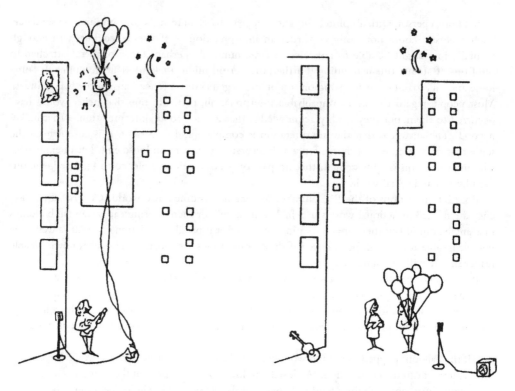

Figure 7.1 Illustrations from Bransford and Johnson (1972). Version "a" represents the appropriate context and version "b" represents the inappropriate context. See text for accompanying passage.

Source: Copyright 1972 Elsevier. Reprinted with permission.

an experiment completed by Anderson, Reynolds, Schallert, and Goetz (1977), who asked people to read the following passage:

> Tony slowly got up from the mat, planning his escape. He hesitated a moment and thought. Things were not going well. What bothered him most was being held, especially since the charge against him had been weak. He considered his present situation. The lock that held him was strong but he thought he could break it. He knew, however, that his timing would have to be perfect. Tony was aware that it was because of his early roughness that he had been penalized so severely—much too severely from his point of view. The situation was becoming frustrating; the pressure had been grinding on him for too long. He was being ridden unmercifully. Tony was getting angry now. He felt he was ready to make his move. He knew that his success or failure would depend on what he did in the next few seconds.

Most people think the foregoing passage is about a convict planning his escape from prison. A special group of people, however, see the passage an entirely different way; these are men who have been involved in the sport of wrestling. They think the passage is about a wrestler caught in the hold of an opponent. Notice how the interpretation of *lock* varies according to perspective. In the one case, it is a piece of hardware that holds a cell door shut; in the other it may be a sweaty arm around a neck. Males enrolled in a weight lifting class and females enrolled in a music education class read the foregoing passage and another passage that most people interpret as being about several people playing cards, but that can be interpreted as being about a rehearsal session of a woodwind ensemble. The results were as expected. Scores on a multiple choice test designed to reveal interpretations of the passages showing striking relationships to the subjects' background. Physical education students usually gave a wrestling interpretation to the prison/wrestling passage and a card playing interpretation to the card/music passage, whereas the reverse was true of the music education students. Similarly, when subjects were asked to recall the passages, theme-revealing distortions appeared, even though the instructions emphasized reproducing the exact words of the original text. For example, a physical education student stated, "Rocky was penalized early in the match for roughness or a dangerous hold," while a music education student wrote, "he was angry that he had been caught and arrested."

The thesis of this section is that comprehension is a matter of activating or constructing a schema that provides a coherent explanation of objects and events mentioned in a discourse. In sharp contrast is the conventional view that comprehension consists of aggregating the meanings of words to form the meanings of clauses, aggregating the meanings of clauses to form the meanings of sentences, aggregating the meanings of sentences to form the meanings of paragraphs, and so on. The illustrations in this section were intended to demonstrate the insufficiency of this conventional view. The meanings of the words cannot be "added up" to give the meaning of the whole. The click of comprehension occurs only when the reader evolves a schema that explains the whole message.

Schema-Based Processes in Learning and Remembering

According to schema theory, reading involves more or less simultaneous analysis at many different levels. The levels include graphophonemic, morphemic, semantic, syntactic, pragmatic, and interpretive. Reading is conceived to be an interactive process. This means that analysis does not proceed in a strict order from the visual information in letters to the overall interpretation of a text. Instead, as a person reads, an interpretation of what a segment of a text might mean is theorized to depend both on analysis of the print and on hypotheses in the person's mind. Processes that flow from the print are called "bottom-up" or "data driven" whereas processes that flow in the other direction are called "top-down" or "hypothesis driven," following Bobrow and Norman (1975). In the passage about Tony, who is either a wrestler or a prisoner, processing the word *lock* has the potential to activate either a piece-of-hardware meaning or a wrestling-hold meaning. The hypothesis the reader has already formulated about the text will tip the scales in the direction of one of the two meanings, usually without the reader's being aware that an alternative meaning is possible. Psychologists are at work developing detailed models of the mechanisms by which information from different levels of analysis is combined during reading (see Just & Carpenter, 1980; Rumelhart & McClelland, 1980).

The reader's schema affects both learning and remembering of the information and ideas in a text. Six functions of schemata that have been proposed (Anderson, 1978; Anderson & Pichert, 1978) are briefly explained.

A schema provides ideational scaffolding for assimilating text information. The idea is that a schema provides a niche, or slot, for certain text information. For instance, there is a slot for the main entree in a dining-at-a-fine-restaurant schema and a slot for the murder weapon in a who-done-it schema. Information that fits slots in the reader's schema is readily learned, perhaps with little mental effort.

A schema facilitates selective allocation of attention. A schema provides part of the basis for determining the important aspects of a text. It is hypothesized that skilled readers use importance as one basis for allocating cognitive resources—that is, for deciding where to pay close attention.

A schema enables inferential elaboration. No text is completely explicit. A reader's schema provides the basis for making inferences that go beyond the information literally stated in a text.

A schema allows orderly searches of memory. A schema can provide the reader with a guide to the types of information that need to be recalled. For instance, a person attempting to recall the food served at a fine meal can review the categories of food typically included in a fine meal: What was the appetizer? What was the soup? Was there a salad? And so on. In other words, by tracing through the schema used to structure the text, the reader is helped to gain access to the particular information learned when the text was read.

A schema facilitates editing and summarizing. Since a schema contains within itself criteria of importance, it enables the reader to produce summaries that include significant propositions and omit trivial ones.

A schema permits inferential reconstruction. When there are gaps in memory, a rememberer's schema, along with the specific text information that can be recalled, helps generate hypotheses about the missing information. For example, suppose a person cannot recall what beverage was served with a fine meal. If he can recall that the entree was fish, he will be able to infer that the beverage may have been white wine.

The foregoing are tentative hypotheses about the functions of a schema in text processing, conceived to provide the broadest possible interpretation of available data. Several of the hypotheses can be regarded as rivals—for instance, the ideational scaffolding hypothesis and the selective attention hypothesis—and it may be that not all of them will turn out to be viable. Researchers are now actively at work developing precise models of schema-based processes and subjecting these models to experimental test.

Evidence for Schema Theory

There is now a really good case that schemata incorporating knowledge of the world play an important role in language comprehension. We are beginning to see research on differentiated functions. In a few years it should be possible to speak in more detail about the specific processing mechanisms in which schemata are involved.

Many of the claims of schema theory are nicely illustrated in a cross-cultural experiment, completed by Steffensen, Joag-Dev, and Anderson (1979), in which Indians (natives of India) and Americans read letters about an Indian and an American wedding. Of course, every adult member of a society has a well-developed marriage schema. There are substantial differences between Indian and American cultures in the nature of marriages. As a consequence, large differences in comprehension, learning, and memory for the letters were expected.

Table 7.1 summarizes analyses of the recall of the letters by Indian and American subjects. The first row in the table indicates the amount of time subjects spent reading the letters. As can be seen, subjects spent less time reading what for them was the native passage. This was as expected since a familiar schema should speed up and expedite a reader's processing.

The second row in Table 7.1 presents the number of idea units recalled. The gist measure includes not only propositions recalled verbatim but also acceptable paraphrases. The finding was

Table 7.1 Mean Performance on Various Measures

| | Nationality | | | |
| | Americans | | Indians | |
Measure	American Passage	Indian Passage	American Passage	Indian Passage
Time (seconds)	168	213	304	276
Gist recall	52.4	37.9	27.3	37.6
Elaborations	5.7	.1	.2	5.4
Distortions	.1	7.6	5.5	.3
Other overt errors	7.5	5.2	8.0	5.9
Omissions	76.2	76.6	95.5	83.3

(From Steffensen, Joag-Dev, and Anderson, 1979)

Source: Copyright by John Wiley & Sons, Ltd. Reprinted with permission.

precisely as expected. Americans recalled more of the American text, whereas Indians recalled more of the Indian passage. Within current formulations of schema theory, there are a couple of reasons for predicting that people would learn and remember more of a text about a marriage in their own culture: A culturally appropriate schema may provide the ideational scaffolding that makes it easy to learn information that fits into that schema, or, it may be that the information, once learned, is more accessible because the schema is a structure that makes it easy to search memory.

The row labeled *Elaborations* in Table 7.1 contains the frequency of culturally appropriate extensions of the text. The next row, labeled *Distortions,* contains the frequency of culturally inappropriate modifications of the text. Ever since Bartlett's day, elaborations and distortions have provided the intuitively most compelling evidence for the role of schemata. Many fascinating instances appeared in the protocols collected in the present study. A section of the American passage upon which interesting cultural differences surfaced read as follows:

> Did you know that Pam was going to wear her grandmother's wedding dress? That gave her something that was old, and borrowed, too. It was made of lace over satin, with very large puff sleeves and looked absolutely charming on her.

One Indian had this to say about the American bride's dress: "She was looking alright except the dress was too old and out of fashion." Wearing an heirloom wedding dress is a completely acceptable aspect of the pageantry of the American marriage ceremony. This Indian appears to have completely missed this and has inferred that the dress was out of fashion, on the basis that Indians attach importance to displays of social status, manifested in such details as wearing an up-to-date, fashionable sari.

The gifts described in the Indian passage that were given to the groom's family by the bride's, the dowry, and the reference to the concern of the bride's family that a scooter might be requested were a source of confusion for our American subjects. First of all, the "agreement about the gifts to be given to the in-laws" was changed to "the exchange of gifts," a wording that suggests that gifts are flowing in two directions, not one. Another subject identified the gifts given to the in-laws as favors, which are often given in American weddings to the attendants by the bride and groom.

In another facet of the study, different groups of Indians and Americans read the letters and rated the significance of each of the propositions. It was expected that Americans would regard as important propositions conveying information about ritual and ceremony whereas Indians would see as important propositions dealing with financial and social status. Table 7.2 contains examples of text units that received contrasting ratings of importance from Indians and Americans. Schema theory predicts that text units that are important in the light of the schema are more likely to be learned and, once learned, are more likely to be remembered. This prediction was confirmed. Subjects did recall more text information rated as important by their cultural cohorts, whether recalling what for them was the native or the foreign text.

Of course, it is one thing to show, as Steffensen, Joag-Dev, and Anderson did, that readers from distinctly different national cultures give different interpretations to culturally sensitive materials, and quite another to find the same phenomenon among readers from different but overlapping subcultures within the same country. A critical issue is whether cultural variation within the United States could be a factor in differential reading comprehension. Minority children could have a handicap if stories, texts, and test items presuppose a cultural perspective that the children do not share. An initial exploration of this issue has been completed by Reynolds, Taylor, Steffensen, Shirey, and Anderson (1982), who wrote a passage around an episode involving "sounding." Sounding is an activity predominantly found in the black community in which the participants try to outdo each other in an exchange of insults (Labov, 1972). In two group studies, and one in which subjects

Table 7.2 Examples of Idea Units of Contrasting Importance to Americans and Indians

American Passage		Indian Passage	
Idea Units More Important to Americans	Idea Units More Important to Indians	Idea Units More Important to Americans	Idea Units More Important to Indians
Then on Friday night they had the rehearsal at the church and the rehearsal dinner, which lasted until almost midnight.	*She'll be lucky if she can even get her daughter married, the way things are going.*	Prema's husband had to wear a dhoti *for that ceremony and for the wedding the next day.*	*Prema's in-laws seem to be nice enough people.* They did not create any problem in the wedding, *even though Prema's husband is their only son.*
All the attendants wore dresses that were specially designed to go with Pam's.	Her mother wore yellow, which looks great on her *with her bleached hair,* and George's mother wore pale green.	*There were only the usual essential rituals:* the curtain removal, the parents giving the daughter away, walking seven steps together, etc., *and plenty of smoke from the sacred fire.*	*Since they did not ask for any dowry,* Prema's parents were a little worried about their asking for a scooter before the wedding, *but they didn't ask for one.*
Her mother wore yellow, which looks great on her with her bleached hair, *and George's mother wore pale green.*	Have you seen the diamond she has? It must have cost George a fortune because it's almost two carats.	There must have been about five hundred people *at the wedding feast. Since only fifty people could be seated at one time, it went on for a long time.*	*Prema's parents were very sad when she left.*

Note. Important idea units are in italics.

were individually interviewed, black teenagers tended to see the episode as involving friendly give-and-take, whereas white teenagers interpreted it as an ugly confrontation, sometimes one involving physical violence. For example, when attempting to recall the incident, a black male wrote, "That everybody tried to get on the person side that joke were the best." A white male wrote, "Soon there was a riot. All the kids were fighting." This research established that when written material has an identifiable cultural loading there is a pronounced effect on comprehension. It remains to be seen how much school reading material is culturally loaded.

In the foregoing research, schemata were manipulated by selecting subjects with different backgrounds. Another approach for getting people to bring different schemata to bear is by selecting different passages. Anderson, Spiro, and Anderson (1978) wrote two closely comparable passages, one about dining at a fancy restaurant, the other about a trip to a supermarket. The same 18 items of food and beverage were mentioned in the two texts, in the same order, and attributed to the same characters. The first hypothesis was that subjects who received the restaurant passage would learn and recall more food and beverage information than subjects who received the supermarket passage. The reasoning was that a dining-at-a-fine-restaurant schema has a more constrained structure than a trip-to-a-supermarket schema. That is to say, fewer food and beverage items will fit the former schema; one could choose soda-pop and hot dogs at a supermarket, but these items would not be ordered at a fine restaurant. Moreover there are more cross-connections among items in a restaurant schema. For example, a steak will be accompanied by a baked potato, or maybe french fries. In two experiments, subjects who read the restaurant text recalled more food and beverage items than subjects who read the supermarket text.

The second prediction was that students who read the restaurant text would more often attribute the food and drink items to the correct characters. In a supermarket it does not matter, for instance, who throws the brussel sprouts into the shopping cart, but in a restaurant it does matter who orders which item. This prediction was confirmed in two experiments.

A third prediction was that order of recall of foods and beverages would correspond more closely to order of mention in the text for subjects who read the restaurant story. There is not, or need not be, a prescribed sequence for selecting items in a grocery store, but there is a characteristic order in which items are served in a restaurant. This hypothesis was supported in one experiment and the trend of the data favored it in a second.

Another technique for manipulating readers' schemata is by assigning them different perspectives. Pichert and Anderson (1977) asked people to pretend that they were either burglars or homebuyers before reading a story about what two boys did at one of the boys' homes while they were skipping school. The finding was that people learned more of the information important to their assigned perspective. For instance, burglars were more likely to learn that three 10-speed bikes were parked in the garage, whereas homebuyers were more likely to learn that the house had a leaky roof. Anderson and Pichert (1978; see also Anderson, Pichert, & Shirey, 1983) went on to show that the reader's perspective has independent effects on learning and recall. Subjects who switch perspectives and then recall the story for a second time recall additional, previously unrecalled, information important to their new perspective but unimportant to their original perspective. For example, a person who begins as a homebuyer may fail to remember that the story says the side door is kept unlocked, but may later remember this information when told to assume the role of a burglar. Subjects report that previously unrecalled information significant in the light of the new perspective "pops" into their heads.

Recent unpublished research in my laboratory, completed in collaboration with Ralph Reynolds and Paul Wilson, suggests selective allocation of attention to text elements that are important in the light of the reader's schema. We have employed two measures of attention. The first is the amount of time a subject spends reading schema-relevant sentences. The second is the response time to a probe presented during schema-relevant sentences. The probe is a tone sounded through earphones; the subject responds by pushing a button as fast as possible. The logic of the probe task is that if the mind is occupied with reading, there will be a slight delay in responding to the probe. Our results indicate that people assigned a burglar perspective, for instance, have slightly longer reading times and slightly longer probe times when reading burglar-relevant sentences. Comparable results have been obtained by other investigators (Cirilo & Foss, 1980; Haberlandt, Berian, & Sandson, 1980; Just & Carpenter, 1980).

Implications of Schema Theory for Design of Materials and Classroom Instruction

First, I urge publishers to include teaching suggestions in manuals designed to help children activate relevant knowledge before reading. Children do not spontaneously integrate what they are reading with what they already know (cf. Paris & Lindauer, 1976). This means that special attention should be paid to preparation for reading. Questions should be asked that remind children of relevant experiences of their own and orient them toward the problems faced by story characters.

Second, the teachers' manuals accompanying basal programs and content area texts ought to include suggestions for building prerequisite knowledge when it cannot be safely presupposed. According to schema theory, this practice should promote comprehension. There is direct evidence to support knowledge-building activities. Hayes and Tierney (1980) asked American high school students to read and recall newspaper reports of cricket matches. Performance improved sharply when the students received instruction on the nature of the game of cricket before reading the newspaper reports.

Third, I call for publishers to feature lesson activities that will lead children to meaningfully integrate what they already know with what is presented on the printed page. From the perspective of schema theory, prediction techniques such as the Directed Reading-Thinking Activity (Stauffer, 1969) can be recommended. The DRTA would appear to cause readers to search their store of knowledge and integrate what they already know with what is stated. It must be acknowledged, however, that the empirical evidence for the efficacy of the DRTA is flimsy at present (Tierney & Cunningham, in press). Recently, Anderson, Mason, and Shirey (1983, Experiment 2) have illustrated that under optimum conditions strong benefits can be obtained using a prediction technique. A heterogeneous sample of third graders read sentences such as, "The stupid child ran into the street after the ball." Children in the prediction group read each sentence aloud and then indicated what might happen next. In the case of the sentence above, a frequent prediction was that the child might get hit by a car. A second group read the sentences aloud with an emphasis on accurate decoding. A third and a fourth group listened to the sentences and read them silently. The finding was that the prediction group recalled 72% of the sentences, whereas the average for the other three groups was 43%.

Fourth, I urge publishers to employ devices that will highlight the structure of text material. Schema theory inclines one to endorse the practice of providing advance organizers or structured overviews, along the lines proposed by Ausubel (1968) and Herber (1978). Ausubel, who can be regarded as one of the pioneer schema theorists, has stated that "the principal function of the organizer is to bridge the gap between what the learner already knows and what he needs to know before he can successfully learn the task at hand" (1968, p. 148). There have been dozens of empirical studies of advance organizers over the past 20 years. Thorough reviews of this bulky literature by Mayer (1979) and Luiten, Ames, and Ackerson (1980) point to the conclusion that organizers generally have a facilitative effect. Nevertheless, from within current formulations of schema theory, there is room for reservations about advance organizers. Notably, Ausubel's insistence (cf. 1968, pp. 148, 333) that organizers must be stated at a high level of generality, abstractness, and inclusiveness is puzzling. The problem is that general, abstract language often is difficult to understand. Children, in particular, are more easily reminded of what they know when concrete language is used. As Ausubel himself has acknowledged (e.g., 1968, p. 149), "To be useful . . . organizers themselves must obviously be learnable and must be stated in familiar terms."

A final implication of schema theory is that minority children may sometimes be counted as failing to comprehend school reading material because their schemata do not match those of the majority culture. Basal reading programs, content area texts, and standardized tests lean heavily on the conventional assumption that meaning is inherent in the words and structure of a text. When prior knowledge is required, it is assumed to be knowledge common to children from every subculture. When new ideas are introduced, these are assumed to be equally accessible to every child. Considering the strong effects that culture has on reading comprehension, the question that naturally arises is whether children from different subcultures can so confidently be assumed to bring a common schema to written material. To be sure, subcultures within this country do overlap. But is it safe simply to *assume* that when reading the same story, children from every subculture will have the same experience with the setting, ascribe the same goals and motives to characters, imagine the same sequence of actions, predict the same emotional reactions, or expect the same outcomes? This is a question that the research community and the school publishing industry ought to address with renewed vigor.

References

Anderson, R.C. (1978). Schema-directed processes in language comprehension. In A. Lesgold, J. Pellegrino, S. Fokkema, & R. Glaser (Eds.), *Cognitive psychology and instruction.* New York: Plenum.

Anderson, R.C., Mason, J., & Shirey, L.L. (1983). *The reading group: An experimental investigation of a labyrinth* (Tech. Rep. No. 271). Champaign: University of Illinois, Center for the Study of Reading.

Anderson, R.C., & Pichert, J.W. (1978). Recall of previously unrecallable information following a shift in perspective. *Journal of Verbal Learning and Verbal Behavior, 17,* 1–12.

Anderson, R.C., Pichert, J.W., & Shirey, L.L. (1983). Effects of the reader's schema at different points in time. *Journal of Educational Psychology, 75*(2), 271–279.

Anderson, R.C., Reynolds, R.E., Schallert, D.L., & Goetz, E.T. (1977). Frameworks for comprehending discourse. *American Educational Research Journal, 14*, 367–382.

Anderson, R.C., Spiro, R.J., & Anderson, M.C. (1978). Schemata as scaffolding for the representation of information in connected discourse. *American Educational Research Journal, 15*, 433–440.

Ausubel, D.P. (1968). *Educational psychology: A cognitive view.* New York: Holt, Rinehart.

Bobrow, D.G., & Norman, D.A. (1975). Some principles of memory schemata. In D.G. Bobrow & A.M. Collins (Eds.), *Representation and understanding: Studies in cognitive science.* New York: Academic.

Bransford, J.D., & Johnson, M.K. (1972). Contextual prerequisites for understanding: Some investigations of comprehension and recall. *Journal of Verbal Learning and Verbal Behavior, 11*, 717–726.

Bransford, J.D., & McCarrell, N.S. (1974). A sketch of a cognitive approach to comprehension. In W.B. Weimer & D.S. Palermo (Eds.), *Cognition and the symbolic process.* Hillsdale, NJ: Erlbaum.

Chiesi, H.L., Spilich, G.J., & Voss, J.F. (1979). Acquisition of domain-related information in relation to high- and low-domain knowledge. *Journal of Verbal Learning and Verbal Behavior, 18*, 257–274.

Cirilo, R.K., & Foss, D.J. (1980). Text structure and reading time for sentences. *Journal of Verbal Learning and Verbal Behavior, 19*, 96–109.

Haberlandt, K., Berian, C., & Sandson, J. (1980). The episode schema in story processing. *Journal of Verbal Learning and Verbal Behavior, 19*, 635–650.

Hayes, D.A., & Tierney, R.J. (1980, October). *Increasing background knowledge through analogy: Its effects upon comprehension and learning* (Tech. Rep. No. 186). Urbana: University of Illinois, Center for the Study of Reading. (ERIC Document Reproduction Service No. ED195953).

Herber, H.L. (1978). *Teaching reading in content areas* (2nd ed.). Englewood Cliffs, NJ: Prentice Hall.

Just, M.A., & Carpenter, P.A. (1980). A theory of reading: From eye fixation to comprehension. *Psychological Review, 87*, 329–354.

Labov, W. (1972). *Language in the inner city: Studies in the black English vernacular.* Washington, DC: Center for Applied Linguistics.

Luiten, J., Ames, W., & Ackerson, G. (1980). A meta-analysis of the effects of advance organizers on learning and retention. *American Educational Research Journal, 17*, 211–218.

Mayer, R.E. (1979). Can advance organizers influence meaningful learning? *Review of Educational Research, 49*, 371–383.

Paris, S.G., & Lindauer, B.K. (1976). The role of inference in children's comprehension and memory. *Cognitive Psychology, 8*, 217–227.

Pichert, J.W., & Anderson, R.C. (1977). Taking different perspectives on a story. *Journal of Educational Psychology, 69*, 309–315.

Reynolds, R.E., Taylor, M.A., Steffensen, M.S., Shirey, L.L., & Anderson, R.C. (1982). Cultural schemata and reading comprehension. *Reading Research Quarterly, 17*(3), 353–366.

Rumelhart, D.E., & McClelland, J.L. (1980). *An interactive activation model of the effect of context in perception* (Part 2; CHIP Tech. Rep.). La Jolla, CA: University of California, Center for Human Information Processing.

Stauffer, R.G. (1969). *Teaching reading as a thinking process.* New York: Harper & Row.

Steffensen, M.S., Joag-Dev, C., & Anderson, R.C. (1979). A cross-cultural perspective on reading comprehension. *Reading Research Quarterly, 15*, 10–29.

Tierney, R.J., & Cunningham, J.W. (in press). Research on teaching reading comprehension. In P.D. Pearson, R. Barr, M.L. Kamil, & P. Mosenthal (Eds.), *Handbook of reading research.* New York: Longman.

8

TO ERR IS HUMAN

Learning About Language Processes by Analyzing Miscues

Yetta M. Goodman and Kenneth S. Goodman

This chapter is reprinted from *Theoretical Models and Processes of Reading* (4th ed., pp. 104–123), edited by R.B. Ruddell, M.R. Ruddell, and H. Singer, 1994, Newark, DE: International Reading Association. Copyright © 1994 by the International Reading Association.

Everything people do, they do imperfectly. This is not a flaw but an asset. If we always performed perfectly, we could not maintain the tentativeness and flexibility that characterize human learning and the ways we interact with our environment and with one another. This model of imperfection causes us as researchers not to worry about why people fall short of perfection; rather, we are concerned with why people do what they do and with what we can learn about language processes from observing such phenomena.

The power of language users to fill knowledge gaps with missing elements, to infer unstated meanings and underlying structures, and to deal with novel experiences, novel thoughts, and novel emotions derives from the ability to predict, to guess, to make choices, to take risks, to go beyond observable data. We must have the capability of being wrong lest the limits on our functioning be too narrowly constrained. Unlike the computer, people do not exhibit specifically programmed, totally dependable responses time after time. We are tentative, we act impulsively, we make mistakes, and we tolerate our own deviations and the mistakes of others.

If you doubt that perfection in human behavior is the exception rather than the norm, consider how intensely a performer of any kind—athlete, actor, musician, writer, reader—must practice to achieve anything approaching error-free performance. If you doubt our view of how people deal with mistakes, think about the proofreader who skips over errors in a text or the native North Americans who deliberately insert flaws in handicrafts to remind themselves that the crafts are the work of human hands.

Miscues: Unexpected Responses

For more than 25 years we have studied the reading process by analyzing the miscues (or unexpected responses) of children and adults orally reading written texts. Ken Goodman coined this use of the word *miscue* because of the negative connotation and history of the term *error*. The term *miscue* reveals that miscues are unexpected responses cued by readers' linguistic or conceptual cognitive structures.

We started with the assumption that everything that happens during reading is caused, that a person's unexpected responses are produced in the same way and from the same knowledge, experience, and intellectual processes as expected responses. Reading aloud involves continuous oral response by the reader, which allows for comparisons between expected and observed responses. Such comparisons reveal the reader's knowledge, experience, and intellectual processes. Oral readers are engaged in comprehending written language while they produce oral responses. Because an oral response is generated while meaning is being constructed, it not only is a form of linguistic performance but also provides a powerful means of examining readers' process and underlying competence.

Miscue analysis requires several conditions. The written material must be new to the readers and complete with a beginning, middle, and end. The text needs to be long and challenging enough to produce sufficient numbers of miscues for patterns to appear. In addition, readers receive no help and are not interrupted. At most, if readers hesitate for more than 30 seconds, they are urged to guess, and only if hesitation continues are they told to keep reading even if it means skipping a word or phrase. Except that it takes place orally and not silently, the reading during miscue analysis requires as normal a situation as possible.

Depending on the purpose of miscue analysis research, readers often have been provided with more than one reading task. Various fiction and nonfiction reading materials have been used, including stories and articles from basal readers, textbooks, trade books, and magazines. Readers have been drawn from elementary, secondary, and adult populations and from a wide range of proficiency and racial, linguistic, and national backgrounds. Studies have been conducted in many languages other than English and in various writing systems (Goodman, Brown, & Marek, 1993).

Betsy's oral reading of the folktale "The Man Who Kept House" (from McInnes, Gerrard, & Ryckman, 1964, pp. 282–283) is used throughout for examples (Goodman, Watson, & Burke, 1987). The story has 68 sentences, 711 words. Betsy, a 9-year-old from Toronto, was selected by her teacher as representative of students with reading difficulties. Betsy read the story hesitantly, although in most places she read with appropriate expression. Below are the first 14 sentences (s1–s14) from the story, with the actual printed text on the left and the transcript of Betsy's oral reading on the right.

	Text	*Transcript*
s1	Once upon a time there was a woodman who thought that no one worked as hard as he did.	Once upon a time there was a woodman. He threw . . . who thought that no one worked as hard as he did.
s2	One evening when he came home from work, he said to his wife, "What do you do all day while I am away cutting wood?"	One evening when he . . . when he came home from work, he said to his wife, "I want you do all day . . . what do you do all day when I am always cutting wood?"
s3	"I keep house," replied the wife, "and keeping house is hard work."	"I keep . . . I keep house," replied the wife, "and keeping . . . and keeping . . . and keeping house is and work."
s4	"Hard work!" said the husband.	"Hard work!" said the husband.
s5	"You don't know what hard work is!	"You don't know what hard work is!
s6	You should try cutting wood!"	You should try cutting wood!"
s7	"I'd be glad to," said the wife.	"I'll be glad to," said the wife.
s8	"Why don't you do my work some day?	"Why don't you. . . . Why don't you do my work so . . . some day?
s9	I'll stay home and keep house," said the woodman.	I'll start house and keeping house," said the woodman.
s10	"If you stay home to do my work, you'll have to make butter, carry water from the well, wash the clothes, clean the house, and look after the baby," said the wife.	"If you start house. . . . If you start home to do my work, well you'll have to make bread, carry . . . carry water from the well, wash the clothes, clean the house, and look after the baby," said the wife.
s11	"I can do all that," replied the husband.	"I can do that. . . . I can do all that," replied the husband.

147

s12 "We'll do it tomorrow!"	"Well you do it tomorrow!"
s13 So the next morning the wife went off to the forest.	So the next day the wife went off to the forest.
s14 The husband stayed home and began to do his wife's job.	The husband stayed home and began to do his work.

Betsy's performance reveals her language knowledge. These examples are not unusual; what Betsy does is done by other readers. She processes graphophonic information: Most of her miscues show a graphic and phonic relationship between the expected and the observed response. She processes syntactic information: She substitutes noun for noun, verb for verb, noun phrase for noun phrase, verb phrase for verb phrase. She transforms phrases, clauses, and sentences: She omits an intensifier, changes a dependent clause to an independent clause, shifts a *wh* question sentence to a declarative sentence. She draws on her conceptual and linguistic background and struggles toward meaning by regressing, correcting, and reprocessing as necessary. She predicts appropriate structures and monitors her own success based on the degree to which she is making sense. She develops and uses psychosociolinguistic strategies as she reads. There is nothing random about her miscues.

Reading Miscues and Comprehension

Because we understand that the brain is the organ of human information processing, that it is not a prisoner of the senses but controls the sensory organs and selectively uses their input, we should not be surprised that what is said in oral reading is not what the eye has seen but what the brain has generated for the mouth to report. The text is what the brain responds to; the oral output reflects the underlying competence and the psychosociolinguistic processes that have generated it. When expected and observed responses match, we get little insight into this process. When they do not match and a miscue results, researchers have a window on the reading process.

We have come to believe that the strategies readers use when miscues occur are the same as when there are no miscues. Except for s3, s8, and s9, all of Betsy's miscues produced fully acceptable sentences or were self-corrected. By analyzing whether miscues are semantically acceptable with regard to the whole text or are acceptable only with regard to the prior portion of text, it is possible to infer the strategies readers actively engage in. s2 provides a powerful example. Betsy reads, *I want you do all day,* hesitates, reads slowly, and eventually—after a 23-second pause—reconsiders, probably rereads silently, and self-corrects the initial clause in this sentence. The verb *said* in the sentence portion prior to her miscue and her knowledge about what husbands might say when they come home from work allowed her to predict *I want you. . . .* After she self-corrects the first part of the dialogue, she reads, *when I am always cutting wood* for *while I am away cutting wood* with confidence and continues her reading. These two substitution miscues (*when* for *while* and *always* for *away*) produce a clause that fits with the meaning of the rest of the story. The more proficient the reader, the greater the proportion of semantically acceptable miscues or miscues acceptable with the prior portion of the text that are self-corrected (Goodman & Burke, 1973).

In s12 Betsy produces, *Well you do it tomorrow* instead of *We'll do it tomorrow.* Although it seems that Betsy simply substitutes *well* for *we'll* and inserts *you,* the miscues are shown to be more complex when we examine how the phrase and clauses are affected by the miscues. Betsy substitutes an interjection prior to the subject *you* to substitute for the noun and the beginning of the verb phrase represented by the contraction *we'll.* In addition, Betsy shifts intonation to indicate that the wife rather than the husband is talking. Apparently Betsy predicted that the wife was going to speak to maintain the pattern of husband–wife conversation that is established by the author in the previous sections (s2 and s11). Although the author's intended meaning is changed, the sentence is semantically acceptable within the story.

A reader's predicting and confirming strategies are evident in miscues that are acceptable with the text portion prior to the miscues. Such miscues often occur at pivotal points in sentences, such as junctures between clauses or phrases. At such points the author may select from a variety of linguistic structures to compose the text; the reader has similar options but may predict a structure that is different than the author's. Consider these examples from Betsy's reading:

	Text	*Transcript*
s38	"I'll light a fire in the fireplace and the porridge will be ready in a few minutes.	"I'll light a fire in the fireplace and I'll . . . and the porridge will be ready in a flash . . . a few minutes."
s48	Then he was afraid that she would fall off.	Then he was afraid that the . . . that she would fall off.

Betsy's predictions of *I'll* instead of *the* in the second clause of the first example is logical. Because *and* often connects two parallel items, it is not an unreasonable prediction that the second clause will begin with the subject of the first. However, when *I'll* does not fit with the second clause, Betsy confidently disconfirms her prediction and immediately self-corrects. The miscue substitution of *the* for *she* in the second example is also at a pivotal point in the sentence. Whenever an author uses a pronoun to refer to a previously stated noun phrase, a reader may revert to the original noun phrase. The reverse phenomenon also occurs. When the author chooses a noun for which the referent has been established earlier, the reader may use that pronoun. Choosing a noun for which the referent has been established earlier, the reader may use that pronoun. Betsy was probably predicting *the cow* which *she* refers to. These miscues clearly show that Betsy is an active language user as she reads. Ken Goodman has done studies on the control readers have over determiners and pronouns in relation to the cohesion of text (Goodman, 1983; Goodman & Gespass, 1983).

The idea that miscues often occur at specific pivotal points in any text is important enough to provide an example from another reader. An Appalachian reader, while reading the phrase "By the time I got out and over to where they were," inserted *of the water* between *out* and *and*. In the previous paragraph the male character is in the water. The author and the reader have similar options at this point in the grammatical structure. The prepositional phrase *of the water* is understood by the reader though not stated by the author and therefore may be omitted or inserted without changing the meaning. In this case, the reader makes explicit what the author left implicit.

Miscues that result in semantically acceptable structures are confirmed as acceptable to readers and, therefore, are less likely to be corrected than those that are not acceptable or acceptable only with the immediately preceding text. Miscues at pivotal points in the text are often acceptable with regard to the preceding text. Of the 10 semantically acceptable miscues that Betsy produced in the first excerpt, she corrected only one (*all* in s11). However, of the six miscues that were acceptable only with the prior portion of the text, she corrected four. Such correction strategies tend to occur when the reader believes they are most needed—when a prediction has been disconfirmed by subsequent language cues.

Insights are gained into the reader's construction of meaning and the process of comprehension when we ask questions such as "Why did the reader make this miscue? Does it make sense in the context of this story or article?" Through such examination, it is possible to see the pattern of comprehending strategies a reader engages in.

We contrast comprehending—what the reader does to understand during the reading of a text—with comprehension—what the reader understands at the end of the reading. Open-ended retellings that always follow the reading during miscue analysis are an index of comprehension. They add to the profile of comprehending, which shows the reader's concern for meaning as expressed through the reading miscues. Retellings also provide an opportunity for the researcher or teacher to gain insight into how concepts and language are actively used and developed throughout a reading event.

Although the concept of retelling is common to present-day research, in the early 1960s when we first used this concept, many questioned the term and the appropriateness of its use in reading research. Rather than asking direct questions that would give cues to the reader about what is significant in the story, we asked for unaided retelling. Information on the readers' understanding of the text emerges from the organization they use in retelling the story, from whether they use the author's language or their own, and from the conceptions or misconceptions they reveal. Here is the first segment of Betsy's retelling:

> Um . . . it was about this woodman and um . . . when he . . . he thought that he um . . . he had harder work to do than his wife. So he went home and he told his wife, "What have you been doing all day." And then his wife told him. And then, um . . . and then, he thought that it was easy work. And . . . so . . . so his wife, so his wife, so she um . . . so the wife said, "Well so you have to keep," no . . . the husband says that you have to go to the woods and cut . . . and have to go out in the forest and cut wood and I'll stay home. And the next day they did that.

By comparing our interpretation of the story with Betsy's retelling and her miscues, we are able to analyze how much learning has occurred during Betsy and the author's transaction. For example, although the story frequently uses *woodman* and *to cut wood, forest*, the noun used to refer to setting, is used twice. Not only does Betsy provide evidence in her retelling that she knows that *woods* and *forest* are synonymous, she also indicates that she knows the author's choice is *forest*. The maze she works through suggests her search for the author's language. Her oral language mazes are evidence of her intentions and self-correction patterns. Betsy seems to believe that the teacher is looking for the author's language rather than her own. Additional evidence of Betsy's concern to reproduce the author's language is seen in her use of *woodman* and *husband*. In the story, the woodman is referred to as *woodman* and *husband* eight times each and as *man* four times; the wife is referred to only as *wife*. Otherwise pronouns are used to refer to the husband and wife. In the retelling, Betsy uses *husband* and *woodman* six times and *man* only once; she called the wife only *wife*. Betsy always uses appropriate pronouns in referring to the husband and wife. However, when *cow* was the referent, she substituted *he* for *she* twice. (What does Betsy know about the sex of cattle?)

The linguistic and conceptual schematic background a reader brings to reading not only shows in miscues but is implicit in the developing conceptions or misconceptions revealed through the reader's retelling. Betsy adds to her conceptual base and builds her control of language as she reads this story, but her ability to do both is limited by what she brings to the task. In the story, the husband has to make butter in a churn. Betsy makes miscues whenever butter-making is mentioned. For example, in s10 she substituted *bread* for *butter*. (Breadmaking is much more common than butter-making as a home activity for North American children.) The next time *butter* appears, in s15, she reads it as expected. However, in s18, *Soon the cream will turn into butter*, Betsy reads *buttermilk* for *butter*. Other references to butter-making include the words *churn* or *cream*. Betsy reads *cream* as expected each time it appears in the text but produces miscues for *churn*. She pauses about 10 seconds at the first appearance of *churn* and finally says it with exaggerated articulation. However, the next two times *churn* appears, Betsy reads *cream*.

	Text	Transcript
s25	. . . he saw a big pig inside, with its nose in the churn.	. . . he saw a big pig inside, with its nose in the cream.
s28	It bumped into the churn, knocking it over.	It jumped . . . it bumped into the cream, knocking it over.
s29	The cream splashed all over the room.	The cream shado [nonword miscue] . . . splashed all over the room.

In the retelling Betsy provides evidence that her miscues are conceptually based and not mere confusions:

> And the husband was sitting down and he poured some buttermilk and um . . . in a jar. And, and he was making buttermilk, and then he um . . . heard the baby crying. So he looked all around in the room and um. . . . And then he saw a big, a big, um . . . pig. Um . . . he saw a big pig inside the house. So, he told him to get out and he, the pig, started racing around and um . . . he di . . . he um . . . bumped into the buttermilk and then the buttermilk fell down and then the pig, um . . . went out.

Betsy, who is growing up in a metropolis, knows little about how butter is made in churns. She knows that there is a relationship between cream and butter, although she does not know the details of that relationship. According to her teacher, she has also taken part in a traditional primary school activity in which sweet cream is poured into a jar, closed up, and shaken until butter and buttermilk are produced. Although Betsy's miscues and retelling suggest that she has only some knowledge about butter-making, the concept is peripheral to comprehending the story. All that she needs to know is that butter-making is one of the wife's many chores that can cause the woodman trouble.

For a long time, teachers have been confused about how a reader can know something in one context but not know it in another. Such confusion comes from the belief that reading is word recognition; on the contrary, words in different syntactic and semantic contexts become different entities for readers, and Betsy's response to the structure *keep house* is good evidence for this. In s3, where the clauses *I keep house* and *and keeping house* occur the first time, Betsy reads the expected responses but repeats each several times before getting the words right, suggesting that she is grappling with their meanings. In s9 she reads *start house and keeping house* for *stay home and keep house*, and she reads the first phrase in s10 as *If you start home to do my work*. The structure *keep house* is a complex one. To a 9-year-old, *keep* is a verb that means being able to hold on to or take care of something small. *Keeping house* is no longer a common idiom in American or Canadian English. *Stay home* adds complexity to *keep house*. Used with different verbs and different function words, *home* and *house* are sometimes synonyms and sometimes not. The transitive and intransitive nature of *keep* and *stay* as well as the infinitive structure *to keep* and *to stay* add to the complexity of the verb phrases.

In her search for meaning and her transaction with the published text, Betsy continues to develop strategies to handle these complex problems. In s14 she produces *stayed home*; however, in s35 she encounters *keeping house* again and reads, *perhaps keeping house . . . home and . . . is . . . hard work*. She is exploring the concept and grammaticality of *keeping house*. She first reads the expected response and then abandons it. In the story *home* appears seven times and *house* 10 times. Betsy reads them correctly in every context except in the patterns *staying home* and *keeping house*. Yet as she continues to work on these phrases throughout her reading she finally is able to handle the structures and either self-corrects successfully or produces a semantically acceptable sentence. Thus Betsy's miscues and retelling reveal the dynamic transaction between a reader and written language.

Through careful observation and evaluation, miscue analysis provides evidence of the ways in which the published text teaches the reader (Meek, 1988). Through continuous transactions with the text, Betsy develops as a reader. Our analysis also provides evidence for the published text as a mediator. Betsy is in a continuing zone of proximal development as she works at making sense of this text (Vygotsky, 1934/1978). Because the text is a complete one it mediates Betsy's development.

The Reader: An Intuitive Grammarian

Reading is not simply knowing sounds, words, sentences, and the abstract parts of language that can be studied by linguists. Reading, like listening, consists of processing language and constructing meaning. The reader brings a great deal of information to this complex and active process. A large body of research has been concerned with meaning construction and the understanding of reading processes and has provided supporting evidence to many of the principles we have revealed through miscue analysis. However, there is still too little attention paid to the ability of readers to make use of their knowledge of the syntax of their language as they read.

Readers sometimes cope with texts that they do not understand well by manipulating the language. Their miscues demonstrate this. The work of both Chomsky and Halliday has helped us understand the syntactic transformations that occur as readers transact with texts. Such manipulations are often seen when readers correctly answer questions about material they do not understand. For example, we ask readers to read an article entitled "Downhole Heave Compensator" (Kirk, 1974). Most readers claim little comprehension, but they can answer the question "What were the two things destroying the underreamers?" by finding the statement in the text that reads, "We were trying to keep drillships and semisubmersibles from wiping out our underreamers" (p. 88). It is because of such ability to manipulate the syntax of questions that we decided to use open-ended retellings for miscue analysis.

In miscue analysis research, we examine the syntactic nature of the miscues, the points in the text where miscues occur, and the syntactic acceptability of sentences that include miscues. Readers often produce sentences that are syntactically, but not semantically, acceptable. In s10 Betsy finally reads, *If you start home to do my work* for the text phrase *If you stay home to do my work*. Her reading of this phrase is syntactically acceptable in the story but unacceptable semantically because it is important to the story line that the woodman stay home.

We became aware that readers were able to maintain the grammaticality of sentences even if the meaning was not maintained when we examined the phenomenon of nonwords. Such nonsense words give us insight into English-speaking readers' grammatical awareness because sentences with nonwords often retain the grammatical features of English although they lose English meaning. Betsy produces only 2 nonword miscues among the 75 miscues she produces. In s58 Betsy reads, *As for the cow, she hang between the roof and the gorun* instead of the expected response *She hung between the roof and the ground*. She repeats *and the* prior to *ground* three times and pauses for about 10 seconds between each repetition. She seems to be aware that the word *ground* is not a familiar one in this context, but she maintains a noun intonation for the nonword. This allows her to maintain the grammatical sense of the sentence so that later in the story when the text reads *the cow fell to the ground*, she reads it as expected without hesitation.

Use of intonation also provides evidence for the grammatical similarity between the nonword and the text word. Miscues on the different forms of *to* (as the initial part of an infinitive or as a preposition), *two*, and *too* are easy to clarify by paying attention to intonation patterns. Nonwords most often retain similarities not only in number of syllables, word length, and spelling but also in bound morphemes—the smallest units that carry meaning or grammatical information within a word but cannot stand alone (for example, the *ed* in *carried*). In one of our research studies (Goodman & Burke, 1973), a group of sixth graders read a story that included the following: "Clearly and distinctively Andrew said 'philosophical'" and "A distinct quiver in his voice." The nonword substitutions for each were different depending on the grammatical function of the word. For *distinctly* readers read nonwords that sounded like *distikily, distintly*, and *definely*, while for *distinct* they read *dristic, distink, distet*.

There is abundant evidence in miscues of readers' strong awareness of bound morphemic rules. Our data on readers' word-for-word substitutions, whether nonwords or real words, show that, on average, 80% of the observed responses retain the morphemic markings of the text. For example, if the text word is a non-inflected form of a verb, the reader will tend to substitute that form; if the word has a prefix, the reader's substitution will tend to include a prefix. Derivational suffixes will be replaced by derivational suffixes, contractional suffixes by contractional suffixes.

Maintaining the syntactic acceptability of the text allows readers to continue reading and at the same time to maintain the cohesion and coherence of the text. Only a small portion of Betsy's substitution miscues do not retain the same grammatical function as the text word. Analysis of the word-for-word substitutions of fourth and sixth graders showed that their miscues retained the identical grammatical function over 73% of the time for nouns and verbs (Goodman & Burke, 1973). Function words were the same 67% or more of the time, while noun modifiers were retained approximately 60% of the time. In addition, an examination of what kinds of grammatical function were used for substitution when they were not identical indicated that nouns, noun modifiers, and function words are substituted for one another to a much greater degree than they are for verbs. Again this suggests the power of grammaticality on reading. Of 501 substitution miscues produced by fourth graders, only 3 times was a noun substituted for a verb modifier, and sixth graders made such a substitution only once in 424 miscues.

Evidence from miscues occurring at the beginning of sentences also adds insight into readers' awareness of the grammatical constraints of language. Generally, in prose for children few sentences begin with prepositions, intensifiers, adjectives, or singular common nouns without a preceding determiner. When readers produce miscues on the beginning words of sentences that do not retain the grammatical function of the text, we could not find one miscue that represented any of these unexpected grammatical forms. (One day we will do an article called "Miscues Readers Don't Make." Some of the strongest evidence comes from all the things readers could do that they do not.) These patterns are so strong that we have been able to detect manufactured examples in some professional texts. The authors have offered examples of errors readers do not make.

Readers' miscues that cross sentence boundaries also provide insight into the readers' grammatical sophistication. It is not uncommon to hear teachers complain that readers read past periods. Closer examination of this phenomenon suggests that when readers do this they are usually making a logical prediction that is based on a linguistic alternative. Although Betsy does this a few times, we will use an example from a story we used with fourth graders: *He still thought it more fun to pretend to be a great scientist, mixing the strange and the unknown* (Goodman & Goodman, 1978). Many readers predict that *strange* and *unknown* are adjectives and intone the sentence accordingly. This means that their voices are left up in the air, so to speak, in anticipation of a noun. The more proficient readers in the study regress at this point and self-correct by shifting to an end-of-the-sentence intonation pattern. Less proficient readers either do not correct at all and continue reading sounding surprised or try to regress without producing the appropriate intonation pattern.

Interrelations of All the Cueing Systems

Reading involves the interrelationship of all the language systems. All readers use graphic information to various degrees. Our research (Goodman & Burke, 1973) demonstrates that the least proficient readers we studied in the 6th, 8th, and 10th grades use graphic information more than the most proficient readers. Readers also produce substitution miscues similar to the phonemic patterns of text words. An examination of Betsy's word substitution miscues reveals that she pays more attention to the look-alike quality of the words than to their sound-alike quality. Although attention to graphic features occurs more frequently than attention to the phonemic patterns, readers use both systems to show that they call on their knowledge of the graphophonic system. Yet the use of these systems cannot explain why Betsy would produce a substitution such as *day* for *morning* or *job* for *work* (s13 and s14). She is clearly showing her use of the syntactic system and her ability to retain the grammatical function and morphemic constraints of the expected response. But the graphophonic and syntactic systems together do not explain why Betsy could seemingly understand words such as *house, home, ground,* and *cream* in certain contexts but not in others. To understand these aspects of reading, one must examine the interrelationship of all the cueing systems.

The integration of all the language systems (grammatical, graphophonic, semantic, and pragmatic) are necessary in order for reading to take place. Miscue analysis provides evidence that readers integrate cueing systems from the earliest initial attempts at reading. Readers sample and make judgments about which cues from each system will provide the most useful information in making predictions that will get them to meaning. All the miscue examples we have cited point to the notion that readers monitor their reading and ask themselves, "Does this sound like language?" (syntactically acceptable) and "Does this make sense in this story?" (semantically acceptable). Finally, if they have to return to the text to check things, they look more closely at the print using their graphophonic knowledge to confirm and self-correct as they read.

As readers make use of their knowledge of all the language cues, they predict, make inferences, select significant features, confirm, and constantly work toward constructing a meaningful text. Not only are they constructing meaning, they are constructing themselves as readers.

Schema-Forming and Schema-Driven Miscues

Our analysis of oral reading miscues began with the foundational assumption that reading is a language process parallel to listening. Everything we have observed among readers from beginners to those with great proficiency supports the validity of this assumption. The analysis of miscues, in turn, has been the basis for the development of a theory and model of the reading process.

What we have learned about miscues in reading has been applied to aspects of language such as spelling, composition, response to literature, and oral language development. Such research, liberated from the "perfection misconception," has demonstrated the linguistic creativity of humans. Errors children make as they develop oral language have provided insight not only into how the young learn language but into the nature of language—how it develops, grows, and changes (Brown, 1973). Children also invent schemata about the nature of written language as they become writers (Ferreiro & Teberosky, 1982; Goodman & Wilde, 1992). Invented punctuation and spelling are especially good examples of the ways in which children learn to control the relationship between the sound system of their dialects and the conventions of the writing system (Read, 1986; Wilde, 1992). Adults develop the craft of writing through making miscues (Shaughnessy, 1977). Rosenblatt (1978) has long argued for a transactional view of reader response to literature in which all response is seen as a transaction between reader and text which of necessity results in variation among readers as they proceed toward interpretation, evaluation, and criticism. The readers' schemata are vital to the transactions.

What we have learned from the study of oral reading miscues and what we have seen in research on other language processes can help to explain the generation of miscues. The concept of schema is helpful to explore how miscues are necessary to language learning. A schema, as we define the term, is an organized cognitive structure of related knowledge, ideas, emotions, and actions that has been internalized and that guides and controls a person's use of subsequent information and response to experience.

Humans have schemata for everything they know and do. We have linguistic schemata (which we call rules) by which we produce and comprehend language. For example, we know when to expect or produce questions and when a question requires an answer. We have schemata for what language does and how it works. With such schemata, we use language to control the behavior of others. We have conceptual schemata for our ideas, concepts, and knowledge of the world. We may reject a Picasso portrait because it does not meet our expectation or schema of the human face.

Our work has led us to believe that humans also develop overarching schemata for creating new schemata and modifying old ones. These we might call schemata for new schema formation. Chomsky's (1965) concept that the generation of language is controlled by a finite set of transformational rules is a case of a schema for schema formation. The rules determine and limit what syntactic patterns may be accepted as grammatical in a language; these same rules also make it possible for speakers to create new sentences that have never been heard before but will be comprehensible to others.

Conceptual schemata work much the same way, and they are also controlled by overarching schemata. That explains why we often use analogy and metaphor in making connections to well-known words and ideas when we talk about new experiences. An example is the use of the term *docking* for space travel. Conceptual and linguistic schemata are at work simultaneously. The schemata must all be in harmony. If more than one complexity occurs, the result is compounding; the possibility of miscues increases disproportionately.

The earlier discussion about Betsy's miscues relating to the concepts of *to stay home* and *to keep house* is a good example. Her complete retelling after reading indicates good understanding of these concepts. In order to build this kind of understanding, Betsy has to work hard during her reading. She relates her own limited knowledge of staying home and keeping house to the meanings she is constructing in transaction with the author. She has to develop control over the syntactic and conceptional complexity of *stay home* and *keep house* and add to her understanding of the relationship of *home* and *house*. She keeps selectively using the available graphophonic cues to produce both expected and unexpected responses. It is important to understand the complexity of thinking that Betsy has to use and that her miscues reflect. Much of children's language learning can be explained in terms of developing control over language schemata. With growing linguistic and conceptual schemata, children use language to predict, process, and monitor expression and comprehension.

Now let's reconsider a concept from miscue analysis: Miscues are produced by the same process and in response to the same cues as expected responses. Putting that together with what we have just said about schema formation and use, we can consider miscues from the perspective of two schema processes: *schema-forming* or *schema-driven* miscues. And because schemata can be forming while we use our existing schemata, both processes can go on at the same time.

Piaget's (1977) concepts of assimilation and accommodation are pertinent here. A schema-forming miscue may be seen as a struggle toward accommodation, while a schema-driven miscue shows assimilation at work. Further, the effect of the miscue on subsequent language processing or intent may result in a disequilibrium, which may lead to reprocessing—that is, self-correction. Schemata may need to be abandoned, modified, or reformed as miscues are corrected.

A *schema-forming* miscue reflects the developmental process of building the rule systems of language and concepts, learning to apply those language rule systems, and delimiting them. For example, Susie responds to the printed name Corn Flakes on a box of cereal by pointing to each line of print successfully while drawing out the word *ceeerrreeeeuuuull* until she finishes moving her finger. Although she has not yet developed the concept that English print is alphabetic, she shows through her unexpected response that she is developing a schema concerning a relationship between the length of print and the length of oral utterance.

The young child's development of the rules of past tense, number, and gender are reflected in the miscues children make in oral language (Brown, 1973). Rebecca, age 3, provides a good example when she says to her aunt, who is waiting to read her a story, "I'll come and get you in a few whiles." She shows her control of the schema for pluralization (*few* take a plural) but she has taken *while*, which functions as a noun in the idiom *wait a little while* and has made it a count noun (*a few whiles*).

In the view of some scholars, a subject's production of language is dependent on whether the subject is dealing with old or new information. A schema-forming miscue is likely to involve new information, either linguistic or conceptual, which may not be easily assimilated. A schema-driven miscue may involve either old (given) information or new information in a predictable context. Furthermore, the schema, as well as the information, may be old or new.

A *schema-driven* miscue is one that results from the use of existing schemata to produce or comprehend language. In our research the concept of prediction has become important. Texts are hard or easy in proportion to how predictable they are for readers. They may use their existing schema to predict and comprehend, but sometimes the organization of the knowledge—that is, the schema on which the predictions are made—is so strong that it overrides the text and miscues occur. In the initial paragraph of a story that many adolescents and adults have read for us, the phrase *the headlamps of the car* occurs. The majority read *headlights* rather than *headlamps*. Many of those who do read *headlamps* indicate that they expected *headlights* and had to reread to accept *headlamps*.

Language variations also show evidence of schema-driven miscues. We shift dialects and registers when we move from formal written language to more informal styles or from one regional dialect to another. Tommy was overheard saying to his mother, a Texan, "Mom, Dad wants to know where the bucket is" and then to his father, a Midwesterner, "Here's the pail, Dad." Tommy had learned to switch codes depending on the situation, and his schema-driven responses were appropriate to each parent. Understanding that dialect miscues are driven by schema may help teachers and researchers see them in proper perspective. A rural African American fourth grader in Port Gibson, Mississippi, was reading a story that included the line *the ducks walked in single file*. At this point in the story, mother duck was leading her babies in a proud and haughty manner. The child reading that line produced *the ducks walk signifying*.

The malapropisms that we all exhibit are also evidence of schema-driven miscues at work. We try to use schemata for word formation beyond word-formation limits. These result in miscues in listening as well as speaking. Television's Archie Bunker was upset because of the *alteration* he had had with a boisterous customer. We cannot help relating the concept of schema-driven miscues to Tannen's (1990) work on conversations between men and women and among different ethnic groups. "I make sense of seemingly senseless misunderstandings that haunt our relationships and show that a man and a woman can interpret the same conversation differently, even when there is no apparent misunderstanding," she writes (p. 13). By understanding the reasons that underlie our misunderstandings perhaps we can form schemata that will help us "prevent or relieve some of the frustration" (p. 13).

In many cases it is not easy to separate miscues into schema-forming or schema-driven processes because they often occur simultaneously. At any particular point in time, it is fairly easy to explain the schemata that drive the miscues that occur. Schema formation, on the other hand, is less likely to occur at a single point and be easily discernible in a single miscue. The study of children's writing development allows us one way to observe the process of schema formation. It also reveals how both schema-forming and schema-driven miscues can occur in concert. An example from a story that Jennifer wrote in the first grade illustrates invented spelling that is driven by her linguistic schemata. Jennifer produced past-tense verbs about 20 times. Each reflected her invented phonic rules (and her awareness of the phonological rules of her own speech) because each had the letter *d* or *t* at the end, representing the appropriate phoneme. These spelling miscues included *rapt* (wrapped) and *yeld* (yelled). Her phonic schemata at this point led her to invent consistent spellings of single letters for single sounds. But a year later her spelling represented an awareness of the interrelationship of both the morphophonemic rules (past tense taking one of three forms depending on the preceding consonants) and the orthographic rule that spelling is not determined by sound in a simple one-to-one manner. Of 28 regular past-tense verbs in a story she wrote in the second grade, 25 were spelled conventionally. Jennifer was in a classroom where a lot of writing was encouraged but there was no direct teaching of spelling. During this year, she continually reformed her schemata and moved toward socially conventional ones.

Readers' miscues often can be driven by conceptual schemata, but at the same time readers can be forming new schemata. This is often revealed through the retelling as well as the miscues. In our research, we have had children read a story that has a significant concept represented by an unfamiliar but high-frequency word. One such word was *typical*. Although the children who read this story often reproduced oral substitutions for *typical* in the text (such as *tropical, type-ical,* and *topical*), they usually were able to explain the meaning of the word as it developed in the reading of the text. One Texas youngster said, "Oh, yeah, *tropical* means ordinary, just like all kinds of other babies. But, you know, it could also be a big storm."

Sometimes a new word represents a concept well known to the reader. In this case the reader must assimilate the new term to the old concept. Bilingual students often face this when they begin to read in a second language. We studied Arabic immigrant students who produced miscues on the word *plow* in a story they were reading, substituting *palow, pull, pole, polo, plew,* and *blow,* among other words and nonwords (Goodman & Goodman, 1978). However, they all were able to provide evidence that they had a "plowing" schema. One reader's example is representative:

> Well, it's a thing with two handles and something pointing down. You got to pull it. But they don't push it with a camel. They push it with a cow. When the cow moves, the one who's pushing it got to go push on it so it goes deeper in the underground.

In such a context we see both schema-driving and schema-forming processes taking place in a dynamic way. These fourth-grade Arabic readers are new to English. They use their developing knowledge of English to produce unexpected responses to the word *plow* and their knowledge about plowing to show understanding of the concept (schema-driven). At the same time, they add new knowledge as they encounter the English word for the concept (schema-forming). The example also indicates that the reader rejected the story element that a camel was used to pull a plow as implausible because of his conceptual schema.

We hope that our discussion of the role miscues play in language learning communicates to teachers and researchers that miscues are the positive effects of linguistic and conceptual processes rather than the failure to communicate or comprehend. If a language user loses meaning, she or he is likely to produce a miscue. If the language user chooses a syntactic schema different from the author's, a miscue will likely result. If a reader or listener interprets in a way different from the meaning intended by the speaker or author, a miscue will result. Miscues reflect readers' abilities to liberate themselves from detailed attention to print as they leap toward meaning. Readers make use of their linguistic and conceptual schemata to reverse, substitute, insert, omit, rearrange, paraphrase, and transform. They do this not only with letters and single words, but with two-word sequences, phrases, clauses, and sentences. Their own experiences, values, conceptual structures, expectations, dialects, and lifestyles are integral to the process. The meanings they construct can never be a simple reconstruction of the author's conceptual structures because they are dependent on the reader's schemata.

Risk-taking has been recognized as a significant aspect of both language learning and proficient language use. In risk-taking there is a necessary balance between tentativeness and self-confidence. Miscues reflect the degree to which existing schemata fit the existing circumstance and the level of confidence of the language user. In speaking a second language, speakers often show great tentativeness, consciously groping for control of developing schemata. As their confidence grows so does their risk-taking, and their miscues show the influence either of schemata for the first language (schema-driven) or of their developing schemata for the second language (schema-forming). An example of the former cautious type is this sentence from a native Spanish-speaking adult who is asking his English teacher for advice: "Ms. Buck, please, I hope I do not molest you." This oral miscue is driven by the speaker's schema for the Spanish *molestar* (to bother). In her response to the student, the teacher will provide information that will help the student form a schema to provide semantic limits for the English *molest*.

Oral and Silent Reading

We need to say a word about the relationship between oral and silent reading because much of miscue analysis research uses oral reading. The basic mode of reading is silent. Oral reading is special because it requires production of an oral representation concurrently with comprehending. The functions of oral reading are limited. It is a performing art used by teachers, entertainers, politicians, and religious leaders. We have already explained why we use oral reading in miscue analysis. But a basic question remains: Are oral and silent reading similar enough to justify generalizing from studies of oral reading miscues to theories and models of silent reading?

In our view, a single process underlies all reading. The language cueing systems and the strategies of oral and silent reading are essentially the same. The miscues we find in oral reading occur in silent reading as well. We have some research evidence of that. Studies of nonidentical fillers of cloze blanks (responses that do not match the deleted words) show remarkable correspondence to oral reading miscues and indicate that the processes of oral and silent reading are much the same (Anderson, 1982; Cambourne & Rousch, 1979; Chapman, 1981). Still, there are dissimilarities between oral and silent reading. First, oral reading is limited to the speed at which speech can be produced; therefore, it need not be as efficient as rapid silent reading. Next, superficial misarticulations such as *hangaber* for *hamburger* occur in oral reading but are not part of silent reading. Also, oral readers, conscious of their audience, read passages differently from when they read silently. Examples are production of nonword substitutions, persistence with several attempts at problem spots, overt regression to correct miscues already mentally corrected, and deliberate adjustments in ensuing text to cover miscues so that listeners will not notice them. Furthermore, oral readers may take fewer risks than silent readers. This can be seen in the deliberate omission of unfamiliar words, reluctance to attempt correction even though meaning is disrupted, and avoidance of overtly making corrections that have taken place silently to avoid calling attention to miscues. Finally, relatively proficient readers, particularly adults, may become so concerned with superficial fluency that they short-circuit the basic concern for meaning. Professional oral readers (newscasters, for example) seem to suffer from this malady. With these reservations noted, we believe that making sense is the same in oral and silent reading; in construction of meaning, miscues must occur in both.

Parts and Wholes

Too much research on language and language learning is still concerned with isolated sounds, letters, word parts, words, and even sentences. Such fragmentation, although it simplifies research design and the complexity of the phenomena under study, seriously distorts processes, tasks, cue values, interactions, and realities. Many years ago, Kintsch (1974) wrote as follows:

> Psycholinguistics is changing in character. . . . The 1950s were still dominated by the nonsense syllables . . . the 1960s were characterized by the use of word lists, while the present decade is witnessing a shift to even more complex learning materials. At present, we have reached the point where lists of sentences are being substituted for word lists in studies of recall recognition. Hopefully, this will not be the endpoint of this development, and we shall soon see psychologists handle effectively the problems posed by the analysis of connected text.
>
> *(p. 2)*

Through miscue analysis we have learned that, other things being equal, short language sequences are harder to comprehend than are long ones. Sentences are easier than words, paragraphs easier than sentences, pages easier than paragraphs, and stories easier than pages. We see two reasons for this. First, it takes some familiarity with the style and general semantic thrust of a text's language for the reader to make successful predictions. Style is largely a matter of an author's syntactic preferences; the semantic context develops over the entire text. Short texts provide limited cues for readers to build a sense of either style or meaning. Second, the disruptive effect of particular miscues on meaning is much greater in short texts. Longer texts offer redundant opportunities to recover and self-correct. This suggests why findings from studies of words, sentences, and short passages produce different results from those that involve whole texts. It also raises a major question about using standardized tests, which employ words, phrases, sentences, and short texts to assess reading proficiency.

Sooner or later all attempts to understand language—its development and its function as the medium of human communication—must confront linguistic reality. Theories, models, grammars, and research paradigms must predict and explain what people do when they use language and what makes it possible for them to do so. Researchers have contrived ingenious ways to make a small bit of linguistic or psycholinguistic reality available for examination. But then what they see is often out of focus, distorted by the design. Miscue analysis research makes fully available the reality of the miscues language users produce as they participate in real speech and literacy events. Huey (1908) said,

> And so to completely analyze what we do when we read would almost be the acme of a psychologist's achievements, for it would be to describe very many of the most intricate workings of the human mind, as well as to unravel the tangled story of the most remarkable specific performance that civilization has learned in all its history.
>
> *(p. 6)*

To this we add that miscues are the windows on language processes at work.

Note

This chapter is based on and updated from "Learning About Psycholinguistic Processes by Analyzing Oral Reading," *Harvard Educational Review,* 47(3), 317–333; and "To Err Is Human," *New York University Education Quarterly, 12*(4), 14–19.

References

Anderson, J. (1982, July). *The writer, the reader, the text.* Paper presented at the 19th annual UKRA Reading Conference, Newcastle-upon-Tyne, United Kingdom.

Brown, R. (1973). *A first language: The early stages.* Cambridge, MA: Harvard University Press.

Cambourne, B., & Rousch, P. (1979). *A psycholinguistic model of the reading process as it relates to proficient, average, and low-ability readers* (Tech. Rep.). Wagga Wagga, NSW, Australia: Riverina College of Advanced Education, Charles Sturt University.

Chapman, J.L. (1981). The reader and the text. In J.L. Chapman (Ed.), *The reader and the text.* London: Heinemann.

Chomsky, N. (1965). *Aspects of the theory of syntax.* Cambridge, MA: MIT Press.

Ferreiro, E., & Teberosky, A. (1982). *Literacy before schooling.* Portsmouth, NH: Heinemann.

Goodman, K.S. (1983, July). *Text features as they relate to miscues: Determiners* (Occasional Paper No. 8). Tucson: Program in Language and Literacy, College of Education, University of Arizona.

Goodman, K.S., Brown, J., & Marek, A. (1993). *Annotated chronological bibliography of miscue analysis* (Occasional Paper No. 16). Tucson: Program in Language and Literacy, College of Education, University of Arizona.

Goodman, K.S., & Burke, C.L. (1973, April). *Theoretically based studies of patterns of miscues in oral reading performance* (Project No. 9–0375). Washington, DC: U.S. Office of Education.

Goodman, K.S., & Gespass, S. (1983, March). *Text features as they relate to miscues: Pronouns* (Occasional Paper No. 7). Tucson: Program in Language and Literacy, College of Education, University of Arizona.

Goodman, K.S., & Goodman, Y.M. (1978). *Reading of American children whose language is a stable rural dialect of English or a language other than English* (Final Report, Project NIE-C-00–3-0087). Washington DC: U.S. Department of Health, Education and Welfare, National Institute of Education.

Goodman, Y.M., Watson, D., & Burke, C. (1987). *Reading miscue inventory: Alternative procedures.* Katonah, NY: Richard C. Owen.

Goodman, Y.M., & Wilde, S. (1992). *Literacy events in a community of young writers.* New York: Teachers College Press.

Huey, E.B. (1908). *The psychology and pedagogy of reading.* New York: Macmillan.

Kintsch, W. (1974). *The representation of meaning in memory.* Hillsdale, NJ: Erlbaum.

Kirk, S. (1974, June). Downhole heave compensator: A tool designed by hindsight. *Drilling-DCW,* 88.

McInnes, J., Gerrard, M., & Ryckman, J. (Series Eds.). (1964). *Magic and make believe* (Basal Program). Don Mills, ON: Thomas Nelson.

Meek, M. (1988). *How texts teach what readers learn.* Exeter, UK: Thimble.

Piaget, J. (1977). *The development of thought: Equilibration of cognitive structures.* New York: Viking.

Read, C. (1986). *Children's creative spelling.* London: Routledge & Kegan Paul.

Rosenblatt, L. (1978). *The reader, the text, the poem: The transactional theory of the literary work.* Carbondale: Southern Illinois University Press.

Shaughnessy, M.P. (1977). *Errors and expectations: A guide for the teacher of basic writing.* New York: Oxford University Press.

Tannen, D. (1990). *You just don't understand: Women and men in conversation.* New York: Morrow.

Vygotsky, L.S. (1978). *Mind in society: The development of higher psychological processes* (M. Cole, V. John-Steiner, S. Scribner, & E. Souberman, Eds. & Trans.). Cambridge, MA: Harvard University Press. (Original work published 1934)

Wilde, S. (1992). *You kan red this! Spelling and punctuation for whole language classrooms, K–6.* Portsmouth, NH: Heinemann.

9

DUAL CODING THEORY

An Embodied Theory of Literacy

Mark Sadoski and Karen A. Krasny

This chapter presents a unified theory of literacy under the aegis of a well-established and continually-developing general theory of mind, Dual Coding Theory (DCT). As part of the cognitive revolution of the 1960s, DCT was originally developed to account for verbal and non-verbal differences in memory (Paivio, 1969). Since its introduction, it has continuously evolved and has been systematically extended through focused programs of research to many other areas of cognition including intelligence, expertise, motivation, creativity, and the evolution of the human mind, among others (Paivio, 1971, 1986, 1991, 2007, 2010, 2014). It has been practically applied in many fields including medicine (e.g., Sanders, Sadoski, Van Walsum, Bramson, Wiprud, & Fossum, 2008), psychotherapy (e.g., Bucci, 1985), sports (e.g., Hardy, Oliver, & Tod, 2009), and especially literacy including literary criticism and rhetorical studies (e.g., Krasny, 2007, 2016; Sadoski, 1992, 2015, 2018; Sadoski & Paivio, 2001, 2013a, 2013b). With its emphasis on multisensory mental representations and connections between verbal and nonverbal mental systems, DCT offers a multicode, multimodal approach to reading and writing with advantages in accounting for making meaning in multimodal and multimedia texts as well as more traditional printed texts.

This chapter will briefly summarize DCT as it relates to contemporary theoretical perspectives in literacy. We will characterize DCT as: (a) a scientific theory, (b) an embodied cognitive theory, (c) a theory of decoding, comprehension, vocabulary, and response in reading, (d) a theory of written composition and spelling, and (e) a theory of multimedia/multimodal literacy. In addition, we will demonstrate throughout that the mental representations and processes in DCT are basic to achieving the intersubjectivity central to the social epistemic movement in literacy.

DCT as a Scientific Theory of Literacy

DCT was derived from and follows the general principles of science. The principles of scientific theorizing as applied to literacy have been reviewed (Sadoski & Paivio, 2007), and we briefly summarize them here.

Science is a cycle of observation and theory. It involves the careful, objective observation of phenomena, the extraction of consistent patterns in those observations, and the tentative formulation of general constructs and principles that hypothetically explain and predict the patterns. Those hypotheses are then tested through more observations, modifications are made as needed, and the cycle proceeds until a stable and testable theory is tentatively established. All scientific theories are necessarily tentative, evolving toward more accurate and inclusive theories in an ongoing, asymptotic approach involving successive formulation and reformulation as new findings emerge. Renewed theories are built from the remains of inadequate theories, with the end goal being the precise interpretation and prognosis of phenomena in a domain under a common, parsimonious set of principles.

Science does not claim title to ultimate truth, and it can be wrong and even misused. But science perforce employs the faculties of imagination, skepticism, and self-correction that have produced the most reliable source of applicable knowledge we have. However, scientific theories of literacy are still quite young. The first volume of scientific theories of reading was published less than 50 years ago (Singer and Ruddell, 1970). We acknowledge that all current scientific theories of literacy fall short of comprehensiveness, but we maintain that DCT is among the strongest current candidates for developing a unified, scientifically-based theory of literacy (Sadoski & Paivio, 2007, 2013b).

Understanding multiple literacies necessitates a psychological accounting of the human capacity to perceive, recognize, interpret, comprehend, evaluate, organize and store in memory information received through complex multisensory sources. The rest of this chapter summarizes how DCT can explain many aspects of the wide domain of literacy to varying degrees. Our positions are derived primarily from empirical, theoretically-based, peer-reviewed scientific investigations that can be traced back through the key references we provide.

DCT as a Cognitive Theory Applied to Literacy

As noted earlier, DCT began as part of the cognitive revolution of the mid-20th century. Cognitivism explored the inner world of mental experience by focusing on the inner mental activity that came between (i.e., mediated) external stimuli and our external responses to them. These internal processes included perception, memory, the nature and structure of knowledge, and language comprehension and production, among others.

Although the cognitive revolution prominently featured mental imagery as a phenomenon of scientific interest, much cognitive theory in the second half of the 20th century was dominated by the controversial view that the mind was a computer or computer-like: Mental activity theoretically involved abstract computational codes and complex programs for input, processing, storage, and output. Such theories postulated abstract representations such as abstract lexical nodes, propositions, or schemata. However, mental imagery, for all its acknowledged importance, did not fit well in such theories, and DCT remains a challenge to them (Krasny, Sadoski, & Paivio, 2007; Sadoski, 2018; Sadoski, Paivio, & Goetz, 1991).

DCT differs fundamentally from abstract computational theories because DCT has never postulated any abstract mental representations. All mental representations in DCT are specific to a sensory modality (i.e., *modality-specific* as opposed to *amodal*) and coded as either *verbal* (i.e., language) or *nonverbal* (e.g., mental imagery). The inclusion of nonverbal aspects of cognition such as mental imagery is a distinctive aspect of DCT especially in literacy theory, but DCT provides a comprehensive account of the verbal, linguistic aspects of literacy as well.

As the 21st century approached, the *embodied cognition* movement emerged as many new findings in behavioral and neuroscience questioned the foundations of computational theories (reviewed in Sadoski, 2018). This movement ushered in a renewed interest in the body and the physiological basis of thought and language. The development of non-invasive brain imaging technologies such as event-related potential (ERP) records and functional magnetic resonance imaging (fMRI) made possible more detailed and precise observations of neuronal activity to corroborate a wave of new behavioral studies and motivate a reinterpretation of earlier studies. As a result, a growing body of neuropsychological-neurophysiological evidence has emerged in support of embodied theories of cognition and the ways by which we achieve and make use of our encoded sensory knowledge (e.g., Damasio, 1996; Lieberman, 2002; Martin, Haxby, Lalonde, Wiggs, & Ungerleider, 1995). For example, Lakoff and Johnson (1999) maintained that all knowledge is inherently embodied—rooted in the experience of our senses. Cognition is therefore fundamentally concrete; abstract conceptualization and reasoning are based in metaphors of sensorimotor experience (e.g., life is a journey). Other embodied theories emerged and have been extensively developed and applied to literacy (e.g., Barsalou, 1999; Glenberg, 1997).

DCT can be seen as a parent of these theories because embodied principles have been inherent to DCT since its inception in the 1960s. As explained earlier, mental representations and processes in DCT are assumed to be derived from sensory experience and stored in modality-specific rather than amodal form. DCT and all other embodied theories differ from computational theories in this critical way. However, DCT differs somewhat from other current embodied theories in the theorized qualitative differences in the verbal and nonverbal codes that predict and explain phenomena such as the differences in the way we process concrete and abstract language, picture-language effects in multimedia learning, and so on. We will emphasize the embodied nature of DCT as well as its uniqueness in this family of theories in this chapter.

General DCT Applied to Reading

DCT provides a unified account of all aspects of reading under a common set of principles. As we shall see, the same basic DCT principles apply to grapheme-phoneme correspondences, vocabulary, grammar, the construction of mental models of text episodes, and imaginative responses to text including the social construction of self and others in literacy encounters. Among other advantages, this unified approach offers a parsimony that is lacking in separate theories for these processes that propose different and sometimes conflicting constructs.

We develop visual representations in the verbal code for language units we have seen such as letters, words, or common phrases (e.g., *baseball bat*). But we also develop visual representations in the nonverbal code for nonlinguistic objects or scenes that we have seen (e.g., an actual wooden or aluminum baseball bat). Likewise, we develop auditory representations in the verbal code for speech units we have heard such as phonemes and their combinations (e.g., the phoneme /b/, the rime /-at/, the spoken word /bat/), and auditory representations in the nonverbal code for nonlinguistic environmental sounds (e.g., the crack of a wooden bat or the clink of an aluminum bat). Likewise, we develop haptic (i.e., motor or tactile) representations in the verbal code for linguistic motor acts (e.g., pronouncing /b/ or writing the letter *b* or touching the Braille sign for *b*), and we develop haptic representations in the nonverbal code for the active "feel" of objects, textures, and movements (e.g., the heft and swing of a baseball bat). We do not represent language in the chemical sense modalities (smell and taste), but we have nonverbal representations for them (e.g., the smell and taste of a juicy hot dog at a baseball game). To these we add affect—visceral emotional feelings and moods. These are nonverbal by definition although we have many referent names for these emotional states. We might imagine the feelings of an excited player or an enthusiastic fan at a baseball game, for example.

Table 9.1 provides a diagram of this orthogonal relationship. Understanding these "codes and modes" is basic to understanding the DCT interpretation of reading. The overall system can be imagined as a set of modality- and code-specific subsystems that are laced with interconnections. These subsystems are independent and are specialized in certain, sometimes multiple, areas of the brain (Paivio, 2007; Sadoski & Paivio, 2013b). A misunderstanding of the distinction between mental codes and sensory modalities has sometimes led to the inaccurate characterization of DCT as being about the verbal and visual codes. The correct distinctions are between verbal and nonverbal codes, and between the visual modality and the other sensory modalities.

Table 9.1 Orthogonal Relationship Between Mental Codes and Mental Sensory Modalities

	Mental Code	
Mental Sensory Modality	*Verbal*	*Nonverbal*
Visual	Visual language (writing)	Visual objects
Auditory	Auditory language (speech)	Environmental sounds
Haptic	Braille, handwriting	"Feel" of objects
Gustatory		Taste memories
Olfactory		Smell memories
Emotion		Feelings and moods

Basic Units

In DCT, the basic units in the verbal system are *logogens,* and the basic units in the nonverbal system are *imagens.* Other embodied theories call these units *simulations, emulations,* or similar terms. Theoretically, these terms apply to verbal as well as nonverbal simulations or emulations because speech can be mentally simulated or emulated as well as nonverbal objects or events (e.g., experiencing inner speech in our own voice or the voices of others). As noted earlier, these units are modality-specific and not abstract; there are no abstract nodes, propositions, or schemata in embodied theories.

Logogens

A logogen is anything learned as a unit of language in some sense modality. Language units vary in size, although some sizes are more familiar than others (e.g., words). Hence, we have visual logogens for letters and written words and phrases; auditory logogens for phonemes and word and phrase pronunciations; haptic logogens for pronouncing, writing, or signing these language units.

Logogens and the verbal system into which they are organized are characterized by sequential constraints. In all languages, units are combined into certain conventional sequences at all levels. Hence, the letters *b, a, t* can be orthographically sequenced as a single, pronounceable English word in *bat* or *tab* but not *bta* or *tba*; the words *a, baseball,* and *bat* can be meaningfully sequenced as *a baseball bat* or *bat a baseball* but not *baseball a bat,* and so on. A hierarchy also characterizes the verbal system such that smaller units can be sequentially synthesized into larger units (e.g., letters to words to sentences) or larger units can be sequentially analyzed into smaller units (e.g., sentences to words to letters).

Imagens

Imagens are modality-specific and vary in size as well, but they tend to be perceived in nested sets in a more continuous, integrated way and cannot as easily be separated and sequenced into discrete elements comparable to phonemes, letters, words, or sentences. That is, mental images are often holistically and hierarchically embedded in larger mental images.

Hence, we can visually imagine a baseball bat, the bat in the hands of a batter, and a batter at home plate in a crowded stadium in an embedded manner. In the auditory modality, we can imagine the crack of the bat or the crack of the bat over the noise of the crowd. In the haptic modality we can imagine the act of our swinging the bat and running, and so on. These simulations may be associated into a multimodal mental episode of the bat being swung, the crack of the bat and roar of the crowd, and running to base. That is, while the imagens remain modality-specific, they can be associated into a larger mental structure that reflects the multimodal nature of physical reality.

Processing Operations

Three basic processes (or levels of processing) are theorized in DCT: *representational* processing, *associative* processing, and *referential* processing. Using the levels metaphor is only partly useful because in actual cognition processing operations are difficult (but not impossible) to isolate.

Representational Processing

Representational processing is the initial activation of logogens or imagens. This level involves simply recognizing something as familiar and does not necessarily imply meaningful comprehension. The activation of a representation depends on the stimulus situation and individual differences. In reading, the stimulus would be the text characteristics, and individual differences would include reading ability, background knowledge, motivation, and so on. If a visually familiar word was also familiar from speech, its associated auditory-motor phonological logogen usually would be activated almost immediately (e.g., *baseball*). If the visual word was not familiar, visual and phonological logogens at lower levels would be activated, requiring more time and attention (e.g., base-ball). Pictures in illustrated texts or multimedia would likewise directly activate memory imagens of the objects and events pictured.

Associative Processing

Associative processing involves spreading activation within a code that is usually associated with meaningful comprehension. Meaningful associative processing within the verbal code involves the activation of associated logogens of at least the morpheme level. For example, the word *single* has many verbal associations, but only a subset will be activated in a given context. In a baseball game, the word *single* might activate verbal associations such as *hit, first base, safe,* and so on. This network of verbal associations gives the word a degree of meaning and would provide a verbal definition. Associations within the nonverbal code involve an imagen activating another imagen (e.g., a visual image of a batter hitting a ball might activate an auditory image of the crack of the bat).

Referential Processing

Referential processing involves connections between the codes that is usually associated with meaningful vocabulary and comprehension. In reading, this means that activated logogens in turn activate imagens. The word *bat* may activate mental images of a wooden or aluminum baseball bat; and *single* may activate an entire dynamic, nested set of images of a batter hitting a baseball and running to first (in other contexts, *bat* and *single* might activate other imagens because these words have multiple meanings). There is not a rigid, one-to-one referential correspondence between logogens and imagens. Some logogens might referentially activate few imagens, while other logogens might activate many, depending on context and our knowledge. Some logogens might activate no imagens at all. This is particularly true of language that is highly abstract; it is difficult to form images of *basic idea*, for example. Without the context of a concrete situation, such phrases lack referential meaning and can only be defined by verbal associations. This implies that concrete language should be generally better understood and recalled, a consistent finding in research.

In reading, activated logogens may spread their activation referentially to one or more imagens in the nonverbal system; associative processing may occur within that system and, in turn, refer back to the verbal system. For example, the set of imagens referentially activated by the logogen *single* might be associatively elaborated in the nonverbal system to include an image of a batter running to first base in a crowded, cheering stadium. These imagens might in return referentially activate logogens such as *stadium* or *crowd* or *cheers*. In this way, spreading activation between and within codes both refines and elaborates the meaning of language. Further, it supplies inferred information to the interpretation beyond what might be literally stated. Mental imagery plays an invaluable role in adding concrete sensory substance to meaning; taken literally, this is what "making sense" in reading is all about.

Figure 9.1 shows a theoretical model of these units and processes as derived from the general theory. From the top downward, verbal and nonverbal stimuli are perceived by the sensory systems and logogens and imagens are mentally activated respectively. The verbal system is illustrated as a hierarchical, sequenced arrangement of logogens. These units are modality-specific and of different sizes so that smaller ones may be representations for graphemes or phonemes. Larger ones may be visual words or their auditory-motor pronunciations, and so on. The associative relationships illustrated by the arrows are of many kinds: grapho-phonemic associations (*b-/b/*), compound word associations (e.g., *base-ball*) common sequences (e.g., *first, second, third, home*), hierarchical associations (e.g., *baseball, sports*), synonym or antonym associations (e.g., *batter-hitter; safe-out*), and on and on. The nonverbal system is illustrated as a series of overlapping and nested sets of imagens (e.g., a baseball being hit in a crowded, cheering stadium) or other imagens not associated with that set in this context. Referential connections are illustrated as arrows running between the codes. Verbal and nonverbal responses (e.g., oral reading or creating an illustration, respectively) are shown as output of the respective systems.

This figure illustrates some of the most basic assumptions of DCT, but the illustration and our explanation is necessarily very simplified. In actuality, a model for reading even a simple text would be interlaced with connections and abuzz with activity.

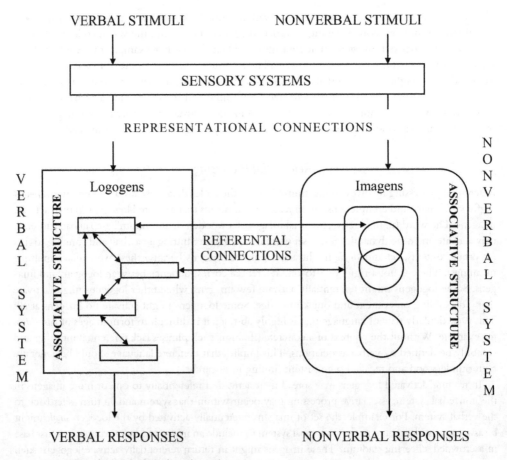

Figure 9.1   General Model of Dual Coding Theory

The Reading Process Elaborated: Decoding, Comprehension, Response

The preceding section provided an overview of the basic assumptions of DCT in reading-relevant terms. The reading process might be better explained through an extended example that involves decoding, comprehension, and response in reading a single sentence. We will deviate briefly to elaborate on decoding, comprehension, and response in turn. We use a single sentence here, but the reader should keep in mind that such sentences are more realistically read in much richer, extended contexts complete with text structures, motivations, and so on. We conclude by applying DCT to an analysis of theories of reader response that continue to hold considerable currency followed by a brief introduction to the potential of DCT to inform our understanding of the phenomenal experience of readers and to philosophically inquire into the contested relation between the aesthetic and moral value of literature.

Consider the moment-to-moment reading of the sentence *The batter singled to center in the first* in the context of a baseball game. The eyes fixate on the first printed forms, probably *The batter* in the first fixation. Visual logogens for the familiar words *The* and *batter* are activated at the representational level, and associated with their auditory-motor logogens. "The batter" may then be experienced as inner speech, recoded in phonological form. Nearly as quickly, the words are syntactically associated as a simple noun phrase. Spreading activation to semantic associations also begins with the different verbal and nonverbal associates of *batter* activated as options. In this context, common verbal associates of *batter* could be *hitter* or *player* (not cake batter), and nonverbal referential connections could be images of a person at bat. At this point, the words *The batter* are phonologically recoded and tentatively comprehended in both verbal and nonverbal form as a baseball player at bat.

A word here about decoding. In reading, this term is theoretically imprecise. The term *recoding* is often preferred because it indicates converting the printed form to the spoken form without necessarily comprehending, as the more general definition of *decoding* implies (i.e., to decode a message). Conformably, DCT assumes that in reading, the activation of logogens at the representational level involves their phonological associations but not necessarily their syntactic and semantic associates and referents. Very familiar phrases such as *The batter* may even be activated as a single unit similar to *hot dog*. However, unfamiliar words, graphophonemically irregular words, or ambiguous words may require more grapheme-phoneme level processing, more conscious effort, and possibly some top-down semantic and syntactic processing (e.g., heteronyms such as *lead, close, dove*). Thus, DCT accommodates top-down and bottom-up multiple-route models in word recognition including the LaBerge and Samuels (1974) model (for a full treatment of the DCT explanation of decoding, see Sadoski, McTigue, & Paivio, 2012; Sadoski & Paivio, 2013b, chapter 7).

Returning to our example, the next fixation falls on the word *singled,* perhaps already noticed in the parafovea of the first fixation. This word appears after the noun phrase and is cued as a verb by the *-ed* suffix. Associative processing syntactically connects *The batter* with *singled* and the familiar subject-verb syntactic unit is recognized. Nonverbal referents are also elaborated such as imagining the runner advancing to first base.

A word here about syntax and grammar: Extensive grammatical parsing in reading is not often conscious, and it may be less formal than is commonly assumed. The verb here may be comprehended simply as an extension of the noun phrase. That is, a mental model of the sentence thus far may be forming in which the batter is imagined in action, hitting the ball and running to first. This emerging mental model takes the form of a verbal-nonverbal episode in short term memory. In this sense, grammar need not involve abstract, deep-structure propositions or complex transformational rules. Familiar word sequences that evoke a comprehensible image can account for much. Developmentally, language depends initially on a substrate of nonverbal imagery derived from observations and behaviors with concrete objects and events – the "nouns" and "verbs" of life that soon become encoded in simple words, phrases, and brief sentences in the conventions of various languages. Elementary verbal structures become elaborated and extended (e.g., the use of modifiers and function words) according to other language conventions as learners develop, but the structures still remain linked to the imagery that makes them comprehensible. Eventually, the verbal system gains some degree of functional autonomy so that unknown or abstract language is parsed conventionally (e.g., *The spleeter fringled* is parsed like *The batter singled* even though nonsensical). For an extended explanation of DCT's account of grammar and syntax, see Paivio (1986, 2007). Neuropsychological support for an embodied view in which associative learning can account for complex grammatical processes such as embedding and recursion is discussed by Pulvermüller (2010).

The next fixation includes *to center*. The various associates and referents of *to center* (e.g., *middle, between left field and right field*) are part of the spreading activation. A less familiar reader may verbally elaborate this elliptical phrase into *to center field*. The words *The batter singled to center (field)* may then be syntactically parsed as the familiar subject-verb-modifier pattern, recoded phonologically as inner speech, and imagined to now include the ball speeding to the middle outfield as the batter runs to first base.

The final fixation falls on *in the first*. Familiar verbal elaborations such as *in the first inning* may be associatively activated. The phrase will be recognized as another modifier consistent with the syntax established so far and the entire sentence parsed and cumulatively recoded as inner speech. However, *in the first* would probably add little to the imaginal mental model of the episode except possible time cues such as the fresh uniforms and empty scoreboards of the early innings of a baseball game. However, the sentence at this point might involve another nonverbal aspect of comprehension—an affective response consisting of visceral emotions and moods. More on this in a later section on reader response.

A few words here about meaning, comprehension, and mental models. As noted in the present example, the text would be mentally represented in two codes and in at least two different modalities: an auditory-motor representation probably experienced as inner speech, and a nonverbal representation probably experienced as visual mental imagery. Both might be elaborated in various ways. As noted, the word *center* may be verbally elaborated to *center field,* and *in the first* may be elaborated to *in the first inning.* Beyond this, verbal elaboration may take the form of a related set of cued associations in the verbal system such as *baseball, swing, hit, run, first base, safe,* and so on. A more fully elaborated nonverbal image might involve multimodal imagery including the crack of the bat and the roar of the crowd. Associative connections and referential connections between the verbal associates and the nonverbal associates form an internally consistent activated network that is the substance of meaning, comprehension, and the mental model. Later in our discussion of multimodal and multimedia literacies, we illustrate how the processing operations in DCT make possible our ability to make intertextual connections within and across a range of textual artefacts both print and non-print.

"Meaning" in this instance consists of this coherent network of activated verbal and nonverbal representations. The richer the elaboration of activated mental representations and their defining interconnections the more "meaningful" is our response. "Comprehension" is the relative equilibrium in the network: The set of verbal associations and the set of nonverbal associations correspond and restrict each other sufficiently to produce coherence and closure. The term "mental model," as used here, applies to the total verbal-nonverbal correspondence aggregate. The term does not imply any theoretical construct beyond what has already been explained. That is, a mental model in DCT is not an abstraction; the modality-specific units activated and connected retain some of their original sensory properties, much as pebbles in an aggregate.

However, the explanation does not end here. Consider the inferences that may occur as a mental model is formed for the sentence *The batter singled to center in the first.* The sentence does not specify if the hit was a fly ball or a grounder. It does not specify if the game was a professional baseball game, a little league game, or a sandlot game. It does not specify if the game was at night or during the day. Yet our mental models are often specific on such points. Many of these inferences can be attributed to mental imagery—imagining the general situation described by the language in concrete specifics. Imagery forms an invaluable companion to language in fleshing out its skeleton.

All these inferences are probabilistic in varying degrees. We read with varying degrees of depth and elaboration based on purposes and individual differences. Comprehension is not an all-or-none process; it occurs in degrees from simple recognition to strategic elaboration. In many cases our comprehension is superficial because there is no need or motivation to elaborate as deeply as we might. In other cases our comprehension is deeper, richer, and more precise.

This leads us back to the subject of response. In many ways, this term implies the formation of a fully realized mental model, a coherent and elaborated simulation of the text beyond what is literally stated. A reader may experience (i.e., construct a response to) a simple text such as *The batter singled to center in the first* by imagining the event only as described thus far. But in a still more elaborate response, one might "feel" oneself as the batter, sensing the heft of the bat, the jolt as it connects, and still more multisensory and affective associations.

In other contexts, response may take a more logical form. Analyzing an exposition or an argument may introduce a verbal monitoring of the text experienced in inner expressions such as "I don't get this," or "Now I see," or "But you haven't considered. . . ." Our evaluative powers may be evoked, and the experience may also be affective. Our inner critics may be impressed with a well-argued position with which we are forced to agree; we may be irked by propaganda. In its fullest sense, response involves the reader as a part of the authoring, a partner in a back-and-forth social construction of an interpretation. This may take the reading well beyond what the text language may have included or what the author may have ever intended, complete with all social implications.

Our extended example used highly concrete language. A question sometimes raised of DCT is how we comprehend and respond to highly abstract language. The answer is that the comprehending abstract language is primarily a matter of verbal associations. Consider the abstract sentence *The act produced a gain*. As with a more concrete sentence, this sentence can be phonologically recoded, grammatically parsed, and associated with other language units (e.g., *act = event, produced a gain = positive result*). But beyond such mental parsing and paraphrasing, there is little tangible substance to mold. What is this sentence actually about? A hit in a baseball game? Selling at a profit? Over-eating? Without a concrete contextual referent to concretize the abstract, it remains a grammatical but ambiguous verbalism. Research has consistently found that abstract language at all levels is comprehended and recalled less well than concrete language even when a host of other variables is controlled. DCT explains these findings readily.

Response implies still more. We noted earlier that emotions and moods might be evoked such as the excitement of the batter or the enthusiasm of spectators. In literary texts, such affective responses are often a central aspect of experiencing the text (e.g., *Casey at the Bat*). The reader might therefore sense the batter's anticipation of the pitch, the exhilaration of the hit, and the satisfaction of getting on base (or the disappointment of striking out). Or one might respond by imaging oneself as an enthusiastic spectator cheering and munching a hot dog. The construction of a response involves much of the self, both personal and social.

DCT and Theories of Reader Response

There is no argument from DCT's embodied perspective that readers use prior knowledge to comprehend and respond to texts. The representational, associative, and referential processing in DCT support Rosenblatt's (1982) claim that:

> The words in their particular pattern stir up elements of memory, activate areas of consciousness. The reader, bringing past experience of language and of the world to the task, sets up tentative notions of a subject, of some framework into which to fit the ideas as the words unfurl.
>
> (p. 268)

Our concern, however, is to qualify the epistemic nature of how we achieve and make use of knowledge by investigating the psychological and physiological basis for such claims. While Rosenblatt's (1978) reminder that *aesthetic derives* from the Greek *aesthetes* ("one that perceives") is consistent with the perceptual origins of language implicit in DCT, decades of empirical research in DCT consistently demonstrate that imagery and affect contribute to the comprehension, memory, and appreciation of both literary and informational text. This works to contradict Rosenblatt's articulation of an aesthetic/efferent continuum where efferent reading is concerned with carrying away information, lexical meaning, explanation, or directions.

We contend that readers do not oscillate between aesthetic and efferent stances but rather, consistently and simultaneously rely on the neural circuitry and mental structures implied in perception to maintain, access, and retrieve sensate data stored in memory to process information verbally and nonverbally in response to all text. In other words, the evocation of imagery and affect greatly enhances our ability to engage with and "carry away" information regardless of stance or genre.

Similarly, DCT has no argument with Iser's (1980) basic claim that the "potential text is infinitely richer than any of its individual realizations" (p. 55). Iser (1978) envisions a textual coupling with the reader which, at first glance, is consistent with the mental projection of multisensory images in DCT to produce an elaborate mental model. In Iser's phenomenology of reading, images "emerge from the reader, but they are also guided by the signals which project themselves into him (sic)"-making it, in Iser's estimation, "extremely difficult to gauge where signal leaves off and the reader's imagination begins the process of projection" (p. 135).

We point out, however, that Iser's (1978) "implied reader," grounded in Husserl's phenomenological bracketing, is relegated to "occupy shifting vantage points . . . geared to a prestructured activity and to fit the diverse perspectives into a gradually evolving pattern" (p. 35). As a result, the evocation of imagery and affect is theorized to be sublimated almost completely to the effects of the text. Iser, like other reader receptionists intent on demonstrating the ascending role of the reader, may be overly conscious of succumbing to the affective fallacy described in Wimsatt & Beardsley's (1946) contentious essay. Having dispensed with the role of the author detailed in more intersubjective constructions of reader response, Iser's theory ultimately implies an autonomous text to which readers must orient their imaginative and affective responses toward achieving unity, coherence, and emphasis of the work. Apart from a tacit acknowledgment of the function of imagery in constituting the text, Iser's "virtual text" may have more in common with computational theories of comprehension than with embodied responses to literary texts.

Informed by the constitution of flux in Husserl's phenomenological hermeneutics, Iser's reader is expected to constitute the intention of the work by reducing the polysemantic possibilities within the framework of text conventions. Similar to the place of the propositional textbase in Kintsch's (1998) construction integration model of reading, Iser emphasizes the heuristic value of sentence correlatives. Accordingly, the role of the reader is to animate the text through the use of a variety of *schematized* views to fill in the gaps created within the liminal space resulting from something being translated into something else. In Iser's view, mental imagery seems to function not as a form of response with rich possibilities for textual elaboration and critical extension but solely as the vehicle through which the reader constitutes the pre-existing text.

By contrast, in a number of studies investigating the relationship between imagery and affect evoked during the reading of stories (e.g., Krasny & Sadoski, 2008; Sadoski, Goetz, & Kangiser, 1988; Sadoski, Goetz, Olivarez, Lee, & Roberts, 1990; Sadoski & Quast, 1990), qualitative reports of both imagery and affect demonstrated that participants frequently made associative links to personal experiences and events outside of the text and that these images were often accompanied by the arousal of emotions. The dense overlap of within system and between system connections as detailed in DCT accounts for readers' intertextual—text to self, text to text, and text to world—connections so often associated with reader response.

Recent work grounded in DCT and neurobiological accounts of consciousness directed at understanding the phenomenal experience of the reader (Krasny, 2007, 2016) calls for renewed attention to the contested relation between the aesthetic and moral value of literature. Somatic and visceral changes (somatosensory affective images) experienced as a result of undergoing the text can engage readers imaginatively in affective relations with others. In DCT terms, the human capacity to form mental images allows us to project feelings of interiority upon others, in both real life and vicarious encounters, to yield an empathetic recognition that others are in possession of the same sense of self as I am.

Notably, historian Lynn Hunt (2008) credited the epistolary novel with producing a sense of interior likeness through which we are able to identify with individuals imagined to be fundamentally like ourselves. Hunt maintains that reading epistolary novels produced somatic effects that once mapped by the body and stored in the brain contributed to a developing sense of self and an expanding moral consciousness. Linking the 18th-century epistolary novel to the emergence of new developments in human rights, Hunt argues that social and political change occur not just because people inhabit a particular social or cultural context but because through their interactions with each other they share similar experiences.

Similarly, Watt's (1957) classic study in realism pointed to Samuel Richardson's use of the letter form in his 1740 novel *Pamela* "that induced in the reader a continual sense of actual participation in the action which was until then unparalleled in its completeness and intensity" (p. 25). The idea that intersubjective self/other relations figures prominently in our engagement with literature is further explored in our overview of DCT applied to written composition in the next section.

Reminiscent of Dewey's concept of dramatic rehearsal, Krasny (2007) argues that literature invites readers to mentally project themselves into the role of the other and try out solutions to morally problematic situations in landscapes that would not otherwise be available. Moving well beyond "the movie in the mind" metaphor, nonverbal representations including affective reactions perform an important function in constructing meaning and are requisite in engaging the ethical agency of both readers and writers.

Nevertheless, while the persuasive powers of the senses have been at the center of philosophical introspection since Plato first banished the poets from his Republic, we are not so naïve as to suggest that empathetic projections generated from reading a book guarantee a direct path to moral behavior or social justice. We caution against what Bogdan (1992) once characterized as a blind faith in literature's transfer value humanism. While readers can construct knowledge about themselves and the world through the evocation of mental imagery and affect in their aesthetic responses to literature, it is what readers do with that knowledge that signifies ethics. Literature often narrates that which we find unbearable or unimaginable in real life. Accordingly, the capacity for mental imagery grants us opportunities to vicariously, and for the most part, safely, explore the human capacity for good and evil and contemplate, among other things, the fundamental ambiguity of existence (Krasny, 2004).

DCT Applied to Writing

The philosophical, psychological, and rhetorical bases of the role of mental imagery and language as the inspiration for, and vehicles of composing were discussed in relation to DCT by Sadoski (1992). Sadoski and Paivio (2001, chapter 7; 2013b, chapter 8) later summarized the relevant research and theoretical literature and extended DCT to a general cognitive theory of the composing process. And more recently, Krasny (2016) extended DCT to crafting consciousness in the novel and more fundamentally to writing as an intersubjective enterprise in which our capacity to form mental images from sensory input plays a critical role. Again, the broad array of literacy concepts explained under a common set of DCT principles offers a parsimony not afforded in separate theories. Here we will briefly summarize the DCT views of composing written text and spelling.

Composing Written Text

In the DCT view, written language production begins with some external or internal motivation to write. Everyday examples include a traditional school composition assignment, or the need to initiate a social media message, e-mail, or a more formal business letter. Social constraints apply strongly here; different language registers are used in different situations. Informal communications frequently use less-than-perfect spelling and grammar and often employ abbreviations and slang, whereas formal situations employ formal language conventions.

The general model shown in Figure 9.1 applies directly to composing. The original verbal or nonverbal motivations evoke related mental language (logogens) and/or mental images (imagens) that guide the composing process. For example, composing a business letter typically evokes a spatial image with top-to-bottom blocks for heading, opening, body, and closing. Referential language evocations would include contextually appropriate salutations (e.g., "Dear Sir or Madam"), language for the body of the letter (e. g., "In the matter of," "respectfully request," "appreciate your timely attention"), and complimentary closings (e.g., "Sincerely yours").

The imagined effect on the audience is central in composing. In writing to personal friends, a first name or a nickname is preferable to a formal salutation. Otherwise, an acquaintance used to getting "Dear Mandy" messages might fret about the sudden chill in the relationship caused by a "Dear Ms. Amanda Jones." Author's imaginings of themselves and their audiences, and the feedback loop of language decisions designed to produce intended effects, is captured in the rhetorical concept of *persona*. Persona comes from the Latin word for mask, as in the smiling and frowning masks that symbolize theater, and it is the root of the words person and personality. Authors imaginatively assume personas when they write and imagine the effects of their words on the imagined personas of their audiences. That is, both verbal and nonverbal social processes are inherently and extensively involved in composing even simple texts (for an extended illustrative example, see Sadoski & Paivio, 2001, chapter 7).

On a larger scale, entire literary works have emerged from a single sentence or mental image. For example, Joseph Heller (1977, p. 50) described the inspiration for his novel *Catch-22*:

> Then one night the opening lines of *Catch-22* — all but the character's name, Yossarian — came to me: "It was love at first sight. The first time he saw the chaplain he fell madly in love with him." My mind flooded with verbal images.

C. S. Lewis (1966, p. 42) reported inspiration for his books in specific mental images:

> One thing I am sure of. All of my seven Narnian books, and three of my science fiction books, began with seeing pictures in my head. At first they were not a story, just pictures. The *Lion* [*the Witch and the Wardrobe*] all began with a picture of a Faun carrying an umbrella and parcels in a snowy wood.

From such verbal and nonverbal inspirations, entire structures such as whole novels or written scientific theories emerge in the same theoretical way as more mundane texts. Paivio (2007, chapter 17) explained the development of Darwin's theory in dual-coding terms. Miller (1984) historically traced how the entire development of 20th-century physics was a creative interplay between the mental imagery and language use of scientists such as Bohr, Einstein, Heisenberg, and others (for more examples, see Sadoski & Paivio, 2001, chapter 7).

Beyond fictional and scientific inspiration, DCT's embodied emphasis on the structure and function of mental imagery and affect provides critical insight and a psychological basis for Krasny's (2016) recent elaboration on Bakhtin's novelistic discourse and how authors intersubjectively craft inner consciousness and dialogic encounters between characters. She emphasizes the primary function of the image in mapping object-organism relationships to reframe our metalinguistic understanding of double-voiced discourse that characterizes Bakhtin's dialogism and in particular, his concept of addressivity. Achieving addressivity amounts to our capacity to sustain dialogue through the apprehension and evaluation of the comments of others.

In other words, our discourse intimately depends on the discourse of others and this idea can also be applied to the intersubjective relation between author and reader. Reminiscent of the imaginative formation of Mead's (1934) "generalized other" in which the direct experience of playing a succession of roles within an ". . . organized community or social group . . . gives to the individual his unity of self" (p. 154), authors must be able to manipulate images stored in memory to fulfill the role of both self and other to intersubjectively engage with their characters and with their imagined audience. Fundamental to our capacity to fulfill the functions of both self and other in participating in and/or authoring dialogic encounters is an understanding that we are not just conscious of having consciousness, but that *our* consciousness is also conscious of the consciousness of *others*. This is the basic form of empathy—an acknowledgment that the other is in possession of the same feelings of interiority as I, thus making it possible to empathetically identify with characters or imaginatively project ourselves in the place of the other.

In DCT terms, empathy depends on our capacity to form the necessary images of the other, and *affectively* enrich those images, to promote feelings of interiority, that is, the feelings that suggest that this other (whether real or imaginary) is in possession of a sense of self equal to that of our own self (Krasny, 2016). Damasio (2003) cites neurological studies to further support the idea that the human capacity for empathy is fundamental to the co-construction of meaning. He explains that damage to the right somatosensory cortices dominant with regard to empathy is consistently associated with defects in emotion and feeling. While language and speech may remain intact, communication is nonetheless difficult for those persons who cannot empathetically fulfill the functions of self and other.

Certain DCT predictions applied to written composition have been experimentally investigated using the concrete-abstract language distinction noted earlier and reported strategy use. Theoretically, concrete language should afford an advantage over abstract language because it involves dual coding, that is, more access to representations in both the verbal and nonverbal codes that provide more elaborate and richly connected memories for composing. Another prediction of DCT is that mental imagery will be more used as a strategy in writing about concrete concepts, whereas a verbal-associative strategy will be more used in writing about abstract concepts.

These predictions were confirmed in an extended research program involving composing definitions of concrete words vs. abstract words. Across different studies using different sets of words and methods, concrete words produced longer definitions, definitions reliably rated higher in quality, and more reports of using a mental imagery strategy than abstract words. Definitions of abstract words used longer words and more reports of a verbal-associative strategy (reviewed in Sadoski & Paivio, 2013b, chapter 8).

Written Spelling

The DCT account of written spelling also derives from the general model in Figure 9.1. The spelling of a word is mainly an intra-verbal process as visual logogens for the whole word and its letter sequence are searched out in memory. When the familiar whole word is readily available, the written response is performed without much more processing (i.e., spelling common, overlearned words like *is, and, the,* or your own name are relatively "automatic").

If whole word logogens are not readily available, other typical strategies are engaged including sounding the word out, finding familiar parts, considering its meaning, and so on. This introduces more time and effort into spelling, and both verbal and nonverbal semantic connections may be activated as mental connections spread (e.g., we often mentally hunt for helpful connections while trying to remember or construct the spelling of a word). Accordingly, any imagens associatively evoked could in turn referentially help to recollect the word logogen or its parts. For example, imagine a spelling quiz in which children are asked to spell the word *yacht* dictated in a meaningful sentence. Even if previously studied, the new word and its irregular spelling might not be immediately recalled, but an image of a ship referentially evoked by the sentence context could, in turn, referentially contribute to the recollection of the word and its spelling—one clue in the hunt.

Initial support for this hypothesis was provided in a review of neuropsychological studies determining that there were direct neurological connections between semantics and orthography and that these connections were sufficient to support accurate spelling performance although phonology could be employed as well (Tainturier & Rapp, 2001). In DCT, semantic connections can include mental images and therefore concrete words might be generally easier to spell than abstract words.

This prediction was tested with a large national sample of students by Sadoski, Willson, Holcomb, and Boulware-Gooden (2005). Results showed that of ten predictors of spelling performance, including number of letters, syllables, digraphs, silent letters, proportion of grapheme-phoneme correspondence, word frequency, and so on, only three were consistently significant: proportion of grapheme-phoneme correspondence, number of syllables, and concreteness. That is, controlling for a host of relevant linguistic variables and word frequency, concrete words were still easier to spell.

In summary, DCT provides an account of the writing process from the macro level of composing to the micro level of spelling. Still other findings have shown that concrete verbs tend to be associated with cumulative sentences with final modifiers, a sentence construction consistently related to higher quality writing (Sadoski & Goetz, 1998). Much remains to be learned about the writing process at all levels, but DCT provides a parsimonious account using the same theoretical principles applied to reading. These principles likewise can be applied to multimedia learning, to which we turn next.

DCT Applied to Multimedia and Multimodal Texts

As a well-established multimodal theory of general cognition with growing neuroscientific support, DCT has clear advantage in accounting for the cognitive and socially-situated processes used in composition and meaning making activities associated with multimodal and multimedia texts. While numerous definitions abound and often adapt to various audiences (Lauer, 2009), by and large, the literacy field has embraced the work of The New London Group (e.g., Cope & Kalantzis, 2000; Kress, 2003, 2005; and Kress & Van Leeuwen, 2001) and their clarification of "multimodal" whereby multiple modes can be combined independently and interdependently in more dynamic ways of making meaning.

As Kress and Van Leeuwen (2001) explain, multiple modes "can be operated by one multi-skilled person, using one interface, one mode of physical manipulation" (p. 2). Multimodal meaning making implies a direct engagement with the senses and a greater range of choice in composition than that associated with more traditional forms of literacy. It requires the skilled application of modalities that can include sound/music, still and moving image, text, animation, and virtual reality. Complex forms of meaning making and cultural production require attention to the rhetorical and material context and the intended audience.

Theories of embodied cognition with their ecological approach to knowledge emphasizing affordances – the possibilities of an action on an object or environment directly perceived and available to an agent – can serve to direct our attention on what specific modalities and their combination with others can afford in enhancing the sensory interface between composer and audience. While the formation of verbal and nonverbal mental models in DCT has been shown to account for fashioning an imaginary audience, it is also basic to the execution of small spatial stories associated with intentional tool-using processes implicit in multimodal composition. The capacity to form verbal and nonverbal mental models fundamental to our ability for structuring perceptual and conceptual categories and to the projected animation of objects and events toward the completion of an act is relevant to the selection, application, and integration of multimodalities in the creation of multimedia texts.

Comprehending and learning in multimedia environments involves verbal and nonverbal formats to varying degrees. Cognitive theoretical models of multimedia learning that derive from or are akin to DCT have been proposed by several researchers (e.g., Mayer, 2009). Mayer defines multimedia instruction in dual-coding terms:

> I define multimedia instruction as the presentation of material using both words and pictures, with the intention of promoting learning. . . . I have opted to limit the definition to two formats – verbal and pictorial – because the research base in cognitive science is most relevant to this distinction. Thus, what I call multimedia learning is more accurately called dual-mode, dual format, dual-code, or dual-channel learning.
>
> *(p. 5)*

Mayer conducted a systematic research program that identified a set of multimedia learning principles with a basic theme: Learning from words and pictures is superior to learning from words alone. Among those multimedia principles were: (a) use words and pictures rather than words alone, (b) place words near corresponding pictures on a page and present narrations concurrently with corresponding animations, and (c) in animations, present language as spoken narrations rather than on-screen written text to minimize modality-specific interference of visually trying to read and study pictures simultaneously.

All these principles are consistent with the DCT model shown in Figure 9.1. Logogens and imagens would be directly activated by the respective multimedia stimuli at the representational level. Referential processing between them would be established by spatial and temporal contiguity as well as by direct reference to accompanying pictures in the text or vice-versa. As detailed earlier, dually-encoded content is more elaborate, comprehensible, and memorable than content restricted to one code. That is, no changes in DCT principles are required to deal with comprehending and learning in multimedia environments, as implied by Mayer in his definition.

DCT principles have been applied in virtual environments (e.g., Chen, 2006; Jankowski & Decker, 2013; Meilinger, Knauff, & Bulthoff, 2008; Yang, Chen & Jeng, 2010). For example, Jankowski and Decker (2013) developed a virtual reality environment where users could read about a fictitious museum and take a 3D virtual tour of its various rooms and displays. They conducted a study using (a) a hypertext user interface where text was present on the screen with links to 3D visuals of rooms and displays, (b) a 3D user interface where a virtual visual tour of the museum was present on the screen with links to textboxes for rooms and displays, or (c) a dual code interface where users could strategically switch between the two. Using matched sets of questions that could be answered by information found only in text or only in the visuals, the researchers found that using the dual code interface produced significantly better results than the other two interfaces. Subjective ratings showed that participants favored the dual code interface.

DCT can serve as a cognitive explanation for all multisensory learning, and the future of educational multisensory technology has much potential. Virtual reality, simulations, and remote sensing involve more than the auditory and visual senses and are already being used in some educational settings. DCT is one of few theories to address this complex form of learning, although much remains to be theoretically specified and new issues arise regularly.

References

Barsalou, L. W. (1999). Perceptual symbol systems. *Behavioral and Brain Sciences, 22,* 577–660.

Bogdan, D. (1992). *Re-educating the imagination: Towards a poetics, politics and pedagogy of literary engagement.* Portsmouth, NH: Heinemann.

Bucci, W. (1985). Dual coding: A cognitive model for psychoanalytic research. *Journal of the American Psychoanalytic Association, 33,* 571–607.

Chen, C. J. (2006). The design, development and evaluation of a virtual reality based learning environment. *Australasian Journal of Educational Technology, 22,* 39–63.

Cope, B., & Kalantzis, M. (Eds.). (2000). *Multiliteracies: Literacy learning and the design of social futures.* New York, NY: Routledge.

Damasio, A. R. (1996). The somatic marker hypothesis and possible functions of the prefrontal cortex. *Philosophical Transactions of the Royal Society of London, Series B, Biological Studies, 351,* 1413–1420.

Damasio, A. R. (2003). *Looking for Spinoza: Joy, sorrow, and the feeling brain.* New York, NY: Harcourt.

Glenberg, A. M., (1997). What is memory for? *Behavioral and Brain Sciences, 20,* 1–55.

Hardy, J., Oliver, E., & Tod, D. (2009). A framework for the study and application of self talk within sport. In S. Mallalieu and S. Hanton (Eds.), *Advances in applied sport psychology: A review* (pp. 37–74). New York, NY: Routledge.

Heller, J. (1977). Reeling in Catch-22. In L. R. Obst (Ed.), *The sixties* (pp. 50–52). New York, NY: Random House/Rolling Stone Press.

Hunt, L. (2008). *Inventing human rights: A history.* New York: W. W. Norton.

Iser, W. (1978). *The act of reading: A theory of aesthetic response.* Baltimore, MD: Johns Hopkins University Press.

Iser, W. (1980). The reading process: A phenomenological approach. In J. Tompkins (Ed.), *Reader-response criticism: From formalism to post-structuralism* (pp. 50–69). Baltimore, MD: Johns Hopkins University Press.

Jankowski, J., & Decker, S. (2013). On the design of a dual-mode user interface for accessing 3D content on the World Wide Web. *International Journal of Human-Computer Studies, 71,* 838–857.

Krasny, K. (2004). *Imagery, affect and the embodied mind* (Unpublished doctoral dissertation). Texas A&M University, College Station, TX.

Krasny, K. (2007). Seeking the imaginative and the affective in the act of reading: Embodied consciousness and the evolution of the moral self. In D. Vokey (Ed.), *Philosophy of Education 2006* (pp. 429–437). Normal, IL: Philosophy of Education Society.

Krasny, K. (2016). Toward an embodied account of double-voiced discourse: The critical role of imagery and affect in Bakhtin's dialogic imagination. *Semiotica, 213,* 177–196.

Krasny, K., & Sadoski, M. (2008). Mental imagery and affect in English/French bilingual readers: A cross-linguistic perspective. *Canadian Modern Language Review, 674,* 399–428.

Krasny, K., Sadoski, M., & Paivio, A. (2007). Unwarranted return: A response to McVee, Dunsmore, & Gavelek's (2005) "Schema theory revisited." *Review of Educational Research, 77,* 239–244.

Kress, G. (2003). *Literacy in the new media age.* London: Routledge.

Kress, G. (2005). Gains and losses: New forms of texts, knowledge, and learning. *Computers and Composition, 22,* 5–22.

Kress, G., & Van Leeuwen, T. (2001). *Multimodal discourse: The modes and media of contemporary communication.* London: Arnold.

Kintsch, W. (1998). *Comprehension: A paradigm for cognition.* Cambridge: Cambridge University Press.

LaBerge, D., & Samuels, S. J. (1974). Toward a theory of automatic information processing in reading. *Cognitive Psychology, 6,* 293–323.

Lakoff, G., & Johnson, M. (1999). *Philosophy in the flesh.* New York, NY: Basic Books.

Lauer, C. (2009). Contending with terms: "Multimodal" and "multimedia" in the academic and public spheres. *Computers and Composition, 26,* 225–239.

Lewis, C. S. (1966). It all began with a picture. . . . In W. Hooper (Ed.), *Of other worlds: Essays and stories* (p. 42). New York, NY: Harcourt, Brace, and World.

Lieberman, P. (2002). On the nature and evolution of the neural basis of human language. *Yearbook of Physical Anthropology, 45,* 35–62.

Mayer, R. E. (2009). *Multimedia learning* (2nd ed.). New York, NY: Cambridge University Press.

Martin, A., Haxby, J., Lalonde, F., Wiggs, C., & Ungerleider, L. (1995). Discrete cortical regions associated with knowledge of color and knowledge of action. *Science, 270,* 102–105.

Mead, G. H. (1934). *Mind, self and society.* Chicago, IL: University of Chicago Press.

Meilinger, T., Knauff, M., & Bulthoff, H. H. (2008). Working memory in wayfinding—A dual task experiment in a virtual city. *Cognitive Science, 32,* 755–770.

Miller, A. I. (1984). *Imagery in scientific thought: Creating 20th century physics.* Boston, MA: Birkhauser.

Paivio, A. (1969). Mental imagery in associative learning and memory. *Psychological Review, 76,* 241–263.

Paivio, A. (1971). *Imagery and verbal processes.* New York, NY: Holt, Rinehart, and Winston. (Reprinted 1979, Hillsdale, NJ: Lawrence Erlbaum)

Paivio, A. (1986). *Mental representations: A dual coding approach.* New York, NY: Oxford University Press.

Paivio, A. (1991). Dual coding theory: Retrospect and current status. *Canadian Journal of Psychology, 45,* 255–287.

Paivio, A. (2007). *Mind and its evolution: A dual coding theoretical approach.* Mahwah, NJ: Lawrence Erlbaum.

Paivio, A. (2010). Dual coding theory and the mental lexicon. *The Mental Lexicon, 5,* 205–230.

Paivio, A. (2014). Intelligence, dual coding theory, and the brain. *Intelligence, 47,* 141–158.

Pulvermüller, F. (2010). Brain embodiment of syntax and grammar: Discrete combinatorial mechanisms spelt out in neuronal circuits. *Brain & Language, 112,* 167–179.

Rosenblatt, L. (1978). *The reader, the text, the poem.* Carbondale, IL: Southern Illinois University Press.

Rosenblatt, L. (1982). The literary transaction: Evocation and response. *Theory into Practice, 21,* 268–277.

Sadoski, M. (1992). Imagination, cognition, and persona. *Rhetoric Review, 10,* 266–278.

Sadoski, M. (2015). Reading comprehension, embodied cognition, and dual coding theory. In S. R. Parris & K. Headley (Eds.), *Comprehension instruction: Research-based best practices* (pp. 45–55). New York, NY: Guilford Press.

Sadoski, M. (2018). Reading comprehension is embodied: Theoretical and practical considerations. *Educational Psychology Review, 30,* 331–349. (Published online April 14, 2017).

Sadoski, M., & Goetz, E. T. (1998). Concreteness effects and syntactic modification in written composition. *Scientific Studies of Reading, 2,* 341–352.

Sadoski, M., Goetz, E. T., & Kangiser, S. (1988). Imagination in story response: Relationships between imagery, affect and structural importance. *Reading Research Quarterly, 23,* 320–336.

Sadoski, M., Goetz, E. T., Olivarez, A., Lee, S., & Roberts, N. (1990). Imagination in story reading: The role of imagery, verbal recall, story analysis, and processing levels. *Journal of Reading Behavior, 22,* 55–70.

Sadoski, M., McTigue, E. M., & Paivio, A. (2012). A dual coding theoretical model of decoding in reading: Subsuming the LaBerge and Samuels model. *Reading Psychology, 33,* 465–496.

Sadoski, M., & Paivio, A. (2001). *Imagery and text: A dual coding theory of reading and writing* (1st ed.). Mahwah, NJ: Lawrence Erlbaum.

Sadoski, M., & Paivio, A. (2007). Toward a unified theory of reading. *Scientific Studies of Reading, 11,* 337–356.

Sadoski, M., & Paivio, A. (2013a). Dual coding theory and literacy: An update. In D. E. Alvermann, N. J. Unra, & R. B. Ruddell (Eds.), *Theoretical models and processes of reading* (6th ed., pp. 917–922). Newark, DE: International Reading Association.

Sadoski, M., & Paivio, A. (2013b). *Imagery and text: A dual coding theory of reading and writing* (2nd ed.). New York: Routledge.

Sadoski, M., Paivio, A., & Goetz, E. T. (1991). A critique of schema theory in reading and a dual coding alternative. *Reading Research Quarterly, 26,* 463–484.

Sadoski, M., & Quast, Z. (1990). Reader response and long term recall for journalistic text: The roles of imagery, affect, and importance. *Reading Research Quarterly, 25,* 256–272.

Sadoski, M., Willson, V., Holcomb, A., & Boulware-Gooden, R. (2005). Verbal and nonverbal predictors of spelling performance. *Journal of Literacy Research, 36,* 461–478.

Sanders, C. W., Sadoski, M., van Walsum, K., Bramson, R., Wiprud, R., & Fossum, T. (2004). Comparing the effects of physical practice and mental imagery rehearsal on learning basic surgical skills by medical students. *American Journal of Obstetrics and Gynecology, 191,* 1811–1814.

Singer, H., & Ruddell, R. B. (1970). *Theoretical models and processes of reading.* Newark, DE: International Reading Association.

Tainturier, M-J., & Rapp, B. (2001). The spelling process. In B. Rapp (Ed.), *The handbook of cognitive neuropsychology: What deficits reveal about the human mind* (pp. 263–289). Philadelphia, PA: Psychology Press.

Watt, I. (1957). *The rise of the novel: Studies in Dafoe, Richardson, and Fielding.* London: Chatto & Windus.

Wimsatt, W., & Beardsley, M. (1946). The affective fallacy. In W. Wimsatt (Ed.), *The verbal icon: Studies in the meaning of poetry.* Louisville, KY: University of Kentucky Press.

Yang, J. C., Chen, C. H., & Jeng, M. C. (2010). Integrating video-capture virtual reality technology into a physically active learning environment for English learning. *Computers & Education, 55,* 1346–1356.

10

REVISITING THE CONSTRUCTION–INTEGRATION MODEL OF TEXT COMPREHENSION AND ITS IMPLICATIONS FOR INSTRUCTION

Walter Kintsch

This chapter is adapted from *Theoretical Models and Processes of Reading* (5th ed., pp. 1270–1328), edited by R.B. Ruddell and N.J. Unrau, 2004, Newark, DE: International Reading Association. Copyright © 2004 by the International Reading Association.

Comprehension: A Paradigm for Cognition

Understanding and *comprehension* are everyday terms—useful but imprecise. We know what we mean when we say we understand a text, but understanding is difficult to define precisely: It is not necessary that we repeat the text verbatim, but we ought to be able to come up with the gist; it is not necessary that we think of every implication of what we have read, but we do not understand it if we miss the most obvious ones; it is not necessary that we answer every question that could be asked, but we cannot miss them all. In the laboratory as well as in the classroom, this problem is solved by fiat operationally. We are willing to say that someone understands a text if he or she passes whatever test we have decided on: provide a summary, answer questions, verify inferences, and so forth. Not all of these operational definitions of understanding are equivalent, nor are they appropriate for all purposes. Much of the discussion in this piece aims at clarifying this situation empirically by showing what works where and for what purposes and theoretically by providing a framework that allows us to describe the different flavors of comprehension processes and outcomes.

There is, however, also a more technical use of the term *comprehension* that concerns us here. It is the sense in which comprehension is used in the phrase *comprehension as a paradigm for cognition*. Cognition ranges from perception on the one hand to analytic thought on the other. Typically, the processes of perception and thinking are conceptualized in different ways. Perception is usually considered as some sort of constraint satisfaction process, where the organism must make sense of a wide variety of sensory inputs involving several modalities, such as solving a puzzle in which the pieces could be assembled in several different ways; the best way is the one that violates the least number of constraints. Thinking or problem solving, in contrast, is a matter of planning, of generating search spaces and using means–end strategies to find a solution path. Reading comprehension shares aspects with both. On the one hand, one normally just reads and understands, much like we understand when we look at a visual scene, without elaborate planning and effortful problem solving. On the other hand, when this normal process breaks down, the reader (or perceiver) becomes a problem solver who must figure out what it is he or she reads (or sees). Comprehension in this technical sense is automatic meaning construction via constraint satisfaction, without purposeful, conscious effort. Normal reading involves automatic comprehension, as well as conscious problem solving whenever the pieces of the puzzle do not fit together as they should.

The theory of text comprehension outlined here is a comprehension model in the sense discussed, but it leaves room for problem solving and planning when that becomes necessary to complement normal reading. This is a matter with considerable educational implications because instruction by its very nature pushes readers beyond what they already know and are comfortable with, requiring active, effortful, resource-demanding problem-solving activities that are difficult to maintain and direct.

Cognition and Representation

Theorists interested in text comprehension talk about the outcome of comprehension in terms of mental representations. Considered most broadly, in the present context, a mental representation is some change in the way the mind views the world as a result of reading a text, that is, some sort of trace of the text read, including indirect effects, cognitive as well as affective ones—perhaps a tendency to act in a certain way or to feel good or bad about something. There is little agreement about mental representations (or the lack thereof) among cognitive scientists at this point, and it would be impossible to do justice to the complex literature in a brief review. But there are a few points that are directly relevant to text comprehension and that are not overly controversial.

The mind represents different aspects of the world. It is convenient to talk about these as different types or levels of representation. In a reading context, the levels that concern us most directly are perceptual, verbal, and semantic representations. Perceptual representations may be images of how the words looked on the page or how they sounded when spoken by a particular person. They also may be, however, images of the scene described by the text, constructed by the reader. Verbal or linguistic representations are about the words, sentences, and discourses themselves. Semantic representations refer to the ideas expressed by the words. Obviously, these levels are not cleanly separable. A word has perceptual characteristics as well as meaning, but when we talk about how a word is perceived and remembered, it is useful to keep these different aspects separate because they behave differently. Similar visual forms are confused with each other, as are similar phonemes, but words are more often confused on the basis of semantic similarity; decoding is strongly influenced by word length and word frequency, but semantic relations and conceptual structure are more important for comprehension. Hence, psychologists, as well as educators, do well to differentiate between the various levels of mental representations.

There is one more reason for the distinction among levels of representation. Theorists and model builders can deal quite well with verbal and semantic representations, but so far they have not developed the tools to deal effectively with imagery. Various systems are in use to represent the meaning of words. Feature systems are used widely; for instance, *bachelor* has the features *male* and *unmarried,* plus some others. Alternatively, word meanings are represented by their position in a semantic structure: *Shark* is defined as a member of the category *fish,* with special properties, such as *dangerous.* Or one can define word meanings by their position in a semantic space: *Lion* might be characterized by high values on the dimensions *size* and *ferocity,* whereas *mouse* would have low values. High-dimensional, abstract semantic spaces are especially effective for representing the meaning of words. Propositions are idea units, combining more than one word in a schematic form: *The hiker watches the elk with his binoculars* is a conceptual unit that relates, by means of the predicate *watches,* an agent, object, and an instrument in a meaningful, conventional way. Propositions thus allow the theorist to represent the meaning of sentences, independent of their syntactic structure (e.g., a sentence in passive or active voice would be represented by the same proposition). Furthermore, propositions can be combined to form representations of whole texts, as described in more detail below. The structure of these text representations is of great significance because it allows the theorist to distinguish important ideas from mere detail, and it predicts how a text is comprehended and remembered.

Propositional structures are useful to represent the meaning of a text because they tend to mimic the properties of how people represent the meaning of a text. As yet we do not have comparable systems to represent mental images. Pictures will not do, for much the same reason that a text is not well represented by the actual words used: The picture does not make explicit the psychologically important aspects of an image. In the auditory domain, phonemic features capture quite well the salient aspects of how people perceive and remember the sounds of a language. However, visual feature systems have been only partially successful and have limited use. Although propositions provide the theorist with a convenient and workable representation for the meaning of texts, at present there really is no language that we can use to represent the salient features of complex mental images. This deficiency is a major reason why much of the research on text comprehension has focused on the verbal aspects, neglecting the role of mental imagery for all its acknowledged significance. We shall, however, point out that significance wherever possible.

Levels of Text Representation

Texts consist of words organized into sentences, paragraphs, and higher order discourse units such as sections or chapters. The mental representation a reader forms thereof often is called the *surface-level memory*—the memory for the actual words and phrases of the text. Surface memory is typically short-lived, especially for instructional texts, where it does not matter much exactly how something is said (Sachs, 1967). Where that matters, as in a poem, joke, or argument, exact wording can be remembered very well, however (W. Kintsch & Bates, 1977).

For many purposes, we are not concerned with exact wording but with the message conveyed. Thus, it is useful to distinguish a semantic level of text representation—the ideas expressed by the text. We shall call this the *propositional level* of representation because propositions are one way of specifying what constitutes an idea in a text.

For the present purposes,[1] we define *atomic proposition* as a linguistic unit consisting of a relational term (or predicate) and one or more arguments (which may be concepts or other propositions). Some examples of phrases and their corresponding atomic propositions are as follows:

(1) *Little boy* or *The boy is little* → [LITTLE, BOY]
(2) *The boy chopped the wood* → [CHOP, BOY, WOOD]

Note that this representation does not represent all information in a sentence (e.g., the past tense in (2), which is not important enough in many situations in which such propositional representations are used).

A *complex proposition* is a network of atomic propositions corresponding to a (simple) sentence. Propositions are linked in a network either because they are related referentially, as in (3), or because of propositional embedding (in (4) the arguments of the proposition are themselves atomic propositions).

(3) *The little boy chopped wood* → [CHOP, BOY, WOOD] — [LITTLE, BOY]
(4) *Although the boy was little, he chopped the wood* →

$$[ALTHOUGH] \diagdown\!\!\!\!\!\!\!\!\diagdown [LITTLE, BOY]$$

$$[CHOP, BOY, WOOD]$$

Links may be based on other-than-referential overlap among propositions, for example, on the basis of a causal relationship, as in the following sentence:

(5) *The little boy was tired from chopping wood* →
                  [TIRED, BOY] —————— [LITTLE, BOY]

                  [CHOP, BOY, WOOD]

This form of propositional representation is intentionally crude; its purpose is not to represent the meaning of a text in all its considerable complexity but to make it possible to count idea units in a text in a reasonably principled way (W. Kintsch, 1974; van Dijk & Kintsch, 1983). Both for the purpose of psychological research on text and instructional design, the number of idea units as defined here and their interrelationship are major variables of interest. Usually, we are not interested in how many words someone remembers but in how many and which ideas are remembered. What makes reading difficult is determined not only by sentence length and the familiarity of the words used but also by the number of ideas expressed, their coherence, and their structure (W. Kintsch, 1974). Propositional analysis, therefore, has become a valuable research tool (although it is not a teaching tool). Unfortunately, because it depends on hand coding, it is extremely laborious and not fully objective (a current guide is W. Kintsch, 1998, Chap. 3.1.1).

The syntactic information in a sentence largely determines the structure of the propositional network. For instance, the main verb of a sentence is taken to form the superordinate proposition, and modifiers are subordinated to it, as in (3). However, there is more structure in a discourse than the sentence syntax. Discourses are organized globally, often according to conventional rhetorical formats. Thus, the simplest stories are of the form setting–complication–resolution; instructional texts may employ various structures such as a compare-and-contrast schema or a generalization-plus-examples schema. To distinguish this discourse-level structure from the sentence-level structure, the terms *macrostructure* and *microstructure* are used. The microstructure of a text is the network of propositions that represents the meaning of the text. One can think of it as a translation from the actual words used into an idea-level format. The macrostructure is the global organization of these ideas into higher order units. Thus, a story may have many propositions linked in a complex network, but at the macrostructure level, these propositions are grouped into the conventional sections: setting, complication, and resolution. However, a writer also could have chosen a different way of telling his story, for example, starting with the resolution and then filling in the setting and complication in the form of a flashback. That approach yields a very different macrostructure, while the microstructure might not be changed very much.

Microstructure and macrostructure together form the *textbase,* the semantic underpinning of a text. However, for purposes of psychological research on text comprehension, as well as for understanding educational practice, it is important to distinguish a further level of text representation, the *situation model.* The situation model represents the information provided by the text, independent of the particular manner in which it was expressed in the text, and integrated with background information from the reader's prior knowledge. What sort of situation model readers construct depends very much on their goals in reading the text as well as the amount of relevant prior knowledge they have. Thus, cooperative and attentive readers will more or less form the same textbase micro- and macrostructures, as invited by the author of the text. But depending on readers' interests, purposes, and background knowledge, they may form widely different situation models. In instruction, it is usually the situation model that the student forms from reading a text that is of interest; the teacher does not care whether the student can recite the text but whether the student understood it correctly and, for future use, was able to integrate the textual information with whatever background knowledge there was.

Situation models are not necessarily verbal. Texts are verbal, and textbases are propositional structures, but to model the situation described by a text, people often resort to imagery. Mental images of maps, diagrams, and pictures are integrated with verbal information in ways not well understood by researchers. Individual preferences in this regard further limit the ability to predict just what sort of a situation model a reader will form from a text.

It is important to ask not only whether a good, correct situation model has been formed by a reader reading a text but also whether this new model has been integrated with the reader's prior knowledge. It is quite possible that readers may construct adequate textbases but fail to link them with other relevant portions of their prior knowledge. The result is encapsulated knowledge. If readers are reminded of the text from which they have acquired this knowledge, they can remember it and successfully use this knowledge, but it is not part of their generally available knowledge base. Encapsulated knowledge can be retrieved only via the specific episodic text memory; it is not available on occasions when such knowledge may be useful but the episodic retrieval cues are lacking. Thus, students can do their calculus problems at the ends of the chapters in their textbooks and even on final exams, but they have no idea what to do when they are supposed to use their knowledge in an engineering class. To make knowledge acquired from texts usable in novel situations, it must be actively linked to semantic retrieval cues, which is not an automatic process but one that requires strategic action and effort on the part of the reader/learner.

Example: Levels of Representation

"Connected" is a story of about 2,500 words written with the purpose of teaching novice students some basic facts about electricity that are embedded in the story in the form of explanations provided by a father to his daughter, who is trying to solve a puzzle requiring knowledge of these facts. The story has four subheadings: "An important event," "Life on the farm," "How does electricity work?," and "Solving the mystery."

The surface memory for this text refers to whatever sentences and sentence fragments from this text are still available in the reader's memory, and it need not concern us further here.

The macrostructure of the text is shown in Table 10.1. It is basically a high-level summary, organized according to the classical story schema. It only roughly corresponds to the subheadings of the actual text: The setting comprises the first section and part of the second, the complication corresponds to part of the second and the third sections, and the resolution matches the final section.

An example of the microstructure for this text is given for one brief paragraph in Table 10.2. The first sentence is represented as two complex propositions, C1 and C2, each consisting of three atomic propositions. C1 and C2 are linked by P4 (i.e., the sentence connective *while*). The third and fourth sentences of the paragraph are each represented by a complex proposition, C3 and C4. Note that anaphoric inferences are necessary here: The *she* of the text has to be identified as *Katie*. To understand, a further inference is required: The *appliances* in the last sentence must be identified with the *electric iron,* the *electric lamp,* and the *electric sewing machine* mentioned earlier. For an adult reader, this is an automatic inference, made unconsciously and effortlessly. For a child, however, who does not really know what an appliance is, this may be a major stumbling block, requiring the reader to regress and figure out that the *appliances* are the *lamp* (which makes *light*), the *iron* (which makes *heat*), and the *sewing machine* (whose parts *moved*). What is necessary here is a conscious, strategic process of meaning construction, which is effortful and resource demanding. The reader who avoids this effort still can form a coherent textbase—Katie realizes that appliances make heat and so on—but will be unable to construct an adequate situation model without knowing what *appliances* refers to.

What sort of situation model might a student construct upon reading this story? The student's reading goal is to learn about electricity. Hence, the situation model we are interested in concerns what the student has learned about electricity; the story is merely there to keep up the students' interest. Skillfully interwoven into our story is a puzzle, the "mystery" Katie must solve for which

Table 10.1 The Macrostructure of the Story "Connected"

Setting

Location: on a farm
Time: old days
Actors: Katie, Tom, and their parents

Electricity is coming to town.
The children wonder what sort of appliance their parents are going to buy.

Complication

Their father asks them to guess what electricity-using appliance they will get first.
Katie finds out how electricity works and what it is used for.
She finds out that the appliance is not to produce either heat or motion.

Resolution

Because there are two wires on the electric line being installed, the
first appliance their parents buy will be a telephone.

Table 10.2 The Microstructure for One Paragraph

*In town, her father filled the Model T's gas tank, while Katie bought a sewing machine belt and browsed
in the general store.* **She** *saw an electric iron, electric lamps, and a sewing machine that no one had
to pedal.* **She** *realized there were* **appliances** *that made heat and light and those that moved.*

C1	P1	[IN, TOWN, P2]
	P2	[FILL, FATHER, GAS-TANK]
	P3	[HAS-PART, MODEL-T, GAS-TANK]
	P4	[WHILE, P2, P5, P7]
C2	P5	[BUY, KATIE, BELT]
	P6	[HAS-PART, SEWING-MACHINE, BELT]
	P7	[BROWSE, KATIE, GENERAL-STORE]
C3	P8	[SEE, **KATIE**, IRON, LAMPS, SEWING-MACHINE]
	P9	[ELECTRIC, IRON]
	P10	[ELECTRIC, LAMPS]
	P11	[NOT-HAVE, SEWING-MACHINE, PEDAL]
C4	P12	[REALIZE, **KATIE**, P13, P14]
	P13	[MAKE, APPLIANCE, HEAT, LIGHT]
	P14	[MOVE, APPLIANCE]
	INF	[IS, **APPLIANCES**, P9, P10, P11]

Note. For explanation, see page 182. C = a complex proposition. P = an atomic proposition.

one needs to know certain elementary facts about electricity. The students are not faced with a list of dry facts about electricity but with information that is significant for the puzzle they—and Katie—are trying to solve. Table 10.3 lists these facts as the situation model a successful reader will form and link to whatever he or she already knows about electricity.

To construct Table 10.3, hypothetical prior knowledge for a typical reader has been assumed; any real reader may not know exactly what is listed. What is important is that the readers retrieve such pieces of prior knowledge at the right moment when reading this story so they can become associated with the new information provided by the text. Thus, suppose a reader already knows

Table 10.3 The Situation Model

Prior Knowledge	Information Provided by the Text
Electricity needs wires.	Electricity comes to you via **wires** (you do not have **to get it like wood to burn in the stove**).
You have to **bring wood in for the stove**.	Electricity is generated from coal or water. Static electricity produces sparks and lightning. Electric current is a form of energy (like water power).
Electricity is needed for **lamps, ironing, sewing machines**, and **telephones**.	Electric energy is used to make **light** (by heating up the filament in a bulb). make heat (such as for **ironing**). make motion (such as in a **sewing machine** or record player). talk on the **telephone** (which needs extra wire and was invented by Bell).

Note. Links are formed between corresponding items printed in bold.

that electricity is needed for ironing; now he or she learns that the electric energy generates heat in the process of ironing, and if this new bit of information is linked with what is already known, it successfully becomes a part of the reader's knowledge base, not just an item of information remembered in the context of that particular text.

Surface structure, textbase, and situation model are levels of the mental representation of texts. We next turn to the question of how these representations are constructed.

The Process of Comprehension: Construction and Integration

Most of the research on reading deals with the decoding problem: How do readers translate the written text into words and sentences? In other words, how is the surface representation generated from a written text? This is, of course, an extremely important question with complex answers, but it is not the question that will be addressed here. Instead, we shall assume this level of representation as given and look at the formation of the textbase and the situation model.

Microstructure

Given a text—a structured string of sentences—how are the corresponding idea units derived, and how are they organized? For the most part, the language provides good cues as to the underlying ideas: *The goat ate the grass* unproblematically translates into [EAT, GOAT, GRASS]. However, language is full of ambiguities. We understand both of the following sentences:

(6) *The grade was too steep.*
(7) *His grade was an A.*

And we know who *she* and *he* are in these two sentences:

(8) *The nurse scolded the woman because she had not taken her medicine.*
(9) *The hiker saw the grizzly bear. He was afraid.*

There are two kinds of explanations of how people deal with such ambiguities, top-down theories and bottom-up theories. According to the top-down view, a schema filters out incorrect interpretations: We know we are talking about a hill, or a student, and hence assign the right meaning to *grade*; the nurse–patient schema dictates the referent for *she*; and the grizzly bear schema specifies who has to be afraid. Schema theory is very powerful (e.g., Schank & Abelson, 1977), and schema effects in perception and comprehension are well documented. Nevertheless, schema-as-filter theories of comprehension cannot fully account for comprehension processes and have been replaced by theories that assign a more decisive role to bottom-up processes, such as the construction–integration (CI) model (W. Kintsch, 1988, 1998). Instead of trying to construct only the correct meaning of a sentence, the CI model generates several plausible meanings in parallel and only later, when a rich context is available, sorts out which construction is the right one. This sorting out is done by means of an integration or constraint satisfaction process that suppresses those constructions that do not fit in well with the context and strengthens those that do. Specifically, activation is spread around in the propositional network that has been constructed, including the contradictory elements; the activation eventually settles on those nodes of the network that hang together, while outliers and isolated nodes become deactivated. Thus, in (6) and (7), propositions will be constructed initially involving both meanings of *grade*, but the incorrect meaning will become deactivated during the integration phase. For the anaphora identification in (8), the construction process yields

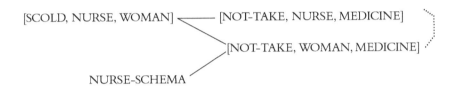

where the dotted line indicates an inhibitory link. In the integration process, the correct proposition will win out because it is connected to prior knowledge about nurses and patients (here labeled the NURSE-SCHEMA). Thus, schemata play a role in the CI model, too, not as filters that control construction but as context that influences the integration process. The inference in (9) is handled similarly: In the construction phase, the model is not sure whether the *hiker* or the *bear* is afraid, but prior knowledge settles that question during the integration phase. Thus, the CI model uses a bottom-up construction phase in which contradictory assumptions are explored, resulting in an incoherent network that needs to be cleaned up in the integration phase. The computational advantage of such a dual process is that the construction rules do not have to be very smart because errors can be corrected in the integration phase. Psychological data that suggest that human comprehension processes employ a similar scheme are discussed in a subsequent section on word identification.

To illustrate the construction of a microstructure, let us return to the "Connected" story discussed earlier. The list of propositions in Table 10.2 corresponds to the network shown in Figure 10.1. The links in Figure 10.1 are based on referential overlap between propositions. Two obligatory inferences are required to identify the pronouns for P8 and P12.

The final activation values for the network in Figure 10.1, once the process of spreading activation has stabilized, are shown in Figure 10.2. Figure 10.2 implies that after reading this paragraph, the strongest information in memory should be that Katie bought a belt, browsed in the general store, and saw an electric iron, electric lamps, and a sewing machine. On a recall test, those should be the items most frequently recalled. A large number of studies have borne out such recall predictions (e.g., W. Kintsch, 1974).

Also shown in Figure 10.2 are the strength values obtained if the reader makes the optional inference [IS-APPLIANCE, IRON, LAMP, SEWING-MACHINE]. This inference changes the picture a great deal by emphasizing the relationship between the (complex) propositions corresponding to the last two sentences of the text. It will be remembered that this was an instructional text supposed to teach about electricity. Note that without this "deep" processing (the inference about appliances), the present paragraph would not contribute much to the goal of learning physics.

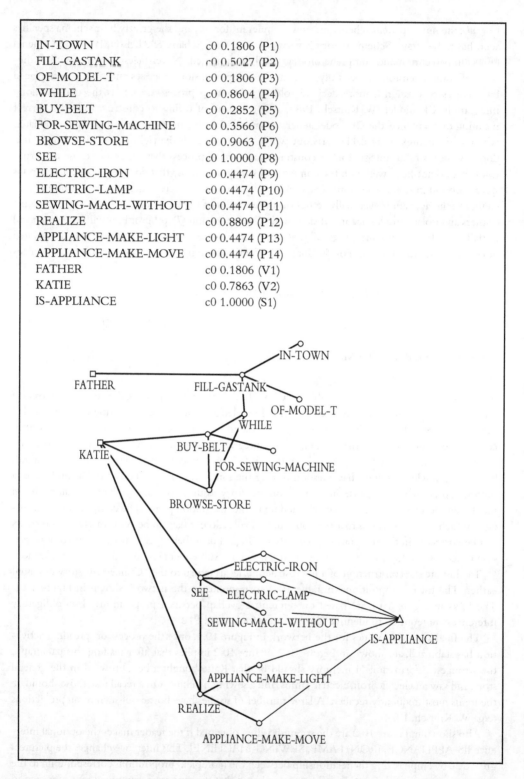

IN-TOWN	c0 0.1806 (P1)
FILL-GASTANK	c0 0.5027 (P2)
OF-MODEL-T	c0 0.1806 (P3)
WHILE	c0 0.8604 (P4)
BUY-BELT	c0 0.2852 (P5)
FOR-SEWING-MACHINE	c0 0.3566 (P6)
BROWSE-STORE	c0 0.9063 (P7)
SEE	c0 1.0000 (P8)
ELECTRIC-IRON	c0 0.4474 (P9)
ELECTRIC-LAMP	c0 0.4474 (P10)
SEWING-MACH-WITHOUT	c0 0.4474 (P11)
REALIZE	c0 0.8809 (P12)
APPLIANCE-MAKE-LIGHT	c0 0.4474 (P13)
APPLIANCE-MAKE-MOVE	c0 0.4474 (P14)
FATHER	c0 0.1806 (V1)
KATIE	c0 0.7863 (V2)
IS-APPLIANCE	c0 1.0000 (S1)

Figure 10.1 The CI Network for a Paragraph From the "Connected" Story (Corresponds to the Proposition List in Table 10.2)

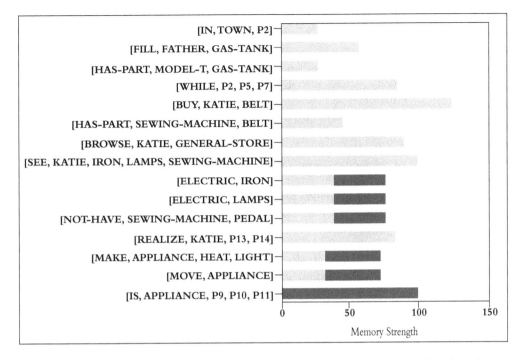

Figure 10.2 The Result of the Integration Process for the Network in Figure 10.1, Without the Inference (IS-APPLIANCE) and With It (Darker Bars)

Macrostructure

Generally (except for the case of very brief texts), understanding a text requires formulating a mental representation of its macrostructure. Just what role a proposition plays in a text depends on its function in the overall structure: It may be part of the gist of an essay, or it may be an expendable detail; it may be a crucial link in the causal chain of a story, or it may be irrelevant to the main story line. To capture this kind of intuition, van Dijk (1980) has introduced the concept of a macrostructure. The macrostructure of a text consists of those propositions that are globally relevant, that form its gist in everyday language. Macrostructures are frequently but not necessarily schematic; that is, they are based on conventional rhetorical forms. Thus, narratives have a conventional structure in our culture; essays may be in the form of arguments, or definitions-plus-illustrations, and so on (see van Dijk & Kintsch, 1983, Chap. 2.9, for a detailed discussion). Van Dijk (1980) has enumerated three rules that describe the formation of macrostructures: (1) *selection* of macrorelevant propositions (and correspondingly the deletion of propositions that are not macrorelevant); (2) *generalization,* that is, substitution of a superordinate proposition for subordinate propositions; and (3) *construction,* the substitution of a general proposition describing a whole sequence of interrelated propositions. Given a text and a set of macropropositions, these rules can be used to show how the macropropositions were derived from the text. However, these rules are post hoc: They describe how macropropositions were derived after the fact, but they are not rules that allow us to generate macropropositions from a text. They do not tell us what is to be deleted or what is to be generalized. In order to use these rules, one must already know what is macrorelevant, what can be subsumed under a construction, and so on. In other words, the macrorules are incomplete because they do not include the conditions for their application. This shortcoming has seriously limited the modeling of macrostructures, which is unfortunate because macrostructures play such an important role in comprehension (e.g., W. Kintsch & van Dijk, 1978).

A logical analysis of the relations linking linguistic units that overcomes some of the limitations of macrorules has been suggested by Le (2002), who distinguishes three types of relations among text units: (1) coordination (either in the form of elaboration or parallelism), (2) subordination, and (3) superordination. After one specifies the relations among text units (sentences or complex propositions), hierarchical structures at levels higher than the sentence can be generated that allow the identification of macropropositions. To illustrate Le's procedure, consider the brief paragraph analyzed in Table 10.2 that consists of four complex propositions, C1–C4. As shown in Table 10.4, C1 is subordinated to C2; C2 and C3 are coordinated, C3 being an elaboration of C2. C4 is logically superordinated to C3 because it expresses a generalization based on C3. Thus, Le's analysis identifies C4—the complex proposition at the highest level in the paragraph hierarchy—as the macroproposition for that paragraph.

A different approach to the generation of macrostructures has been taken by W. Kintsch (2002). It is not based on a logical analysis of the relations among text units, but rather on the centrality of the content of the (complex) propositions. Latent Semantic Analysis (LSA; Landauer, McNamara, Dennis, & Kintsch, 2007) allows one to measure the similarity of the content of sentences. The sentence in a paragraph that is most similar to all the other sentences in that paragraph is a good candidate for a macroproposition because it is the most central one. In Table 10.4, C3 correlates most strongly with the other sentences, as measured by LSA, and hence should be considered as the macroproposition for this paragraph. Note that this is a different result than the one obtained from Le's (2002) logical analysis. There is no reason why two so totally different methods should yield identical results; large-scale empirical tests of which predictions correspond best with human judgments have not yet been reported. Note also that in terms of the activation values for complex propositions as shown in Figure 10.2, the most strongly activated complex proposition is C2. (Activation values for complex propositions are obtained by adding the activation values of their constituent atomic propositions.)

It has long been known that gist-level—that is, macrostructure—processes play a decisive role in the comprehension and memory of long texts. That much was shown by W. Kintsch and van Dijk in their 1978 paper. Modeling the generation of macrostructures, however, is still in its infancy, as the earlier discussion illustrates. Worse, there are basic limitations to the approaches of Le (2002) and W. Kintsch (2002): Both models can only select from the propositions in a text, whereas macropropositions often must be constructed by the reader. Macropropositions frequently are inferences that are not stated explicitly in the text. Computational models specifying how new macropropositions are generated do not yet exist. This is an important area for future research, as is the research on the formation of situation models, which is in a similarly underdeveloped state.

Table 10.4 Determining the Macroproposition for a Paragraph

C1   *In town, her father filled the Model T's gas tank,*
C2   *while Katie bought a sewing machine belt and browsed in the general store.*
C3   *She saw an electric iron, electric lamps, and a sewing machine that no one had to pedal.*
C4   *She realized there were appliances that made heat and light and those that moved.*

Situation Models

The problems faced by the researcher trying to model the formation of situation models are formidable. Textbases at the micro- and macrolevel are tightly constrained by the nature of the text, which a faithful reader must respect. The text, however, is only one factor in the situation model: The reader's goals, interests, beliefs, and prior knowledge also must be taken into account. Generally, these are only incompletely known. Furthermore, even the form that a situation model takes is not fully constrained: Situation models may be imagery based, in which case the propositional formalism currently used by most models fails us. Nevertheless, in well-defined contexts, modeling situation models is quite feasible and will surely be the focus of research on text comprehension in the next decade.[2]

How one might approach this task has been demonstrated by Schmalhofer, McDaniel, and Keefe (2002). The CI model simulates the construction of a textbase: A network of propositions derived from the text is constructed and integrated via a spreading activation constraint satisfaction process. Schmalhofer et al. added two other networks to the propositional network: (1) a surface level, where the nodes are linguistic structures and words; and (2) a situation representation, where the nodes are schemata. Nodes are interconnected at each level, but importantly, there are also links between levels, so a sentence in the surface structure is connected to the corresponding proposition in the textbase, which in turn is connected to the appropriate schema at the situation model level. Schmalhofer et al. illustrate their model with an example that is reproduced here in simplified form in Figure 10.3.

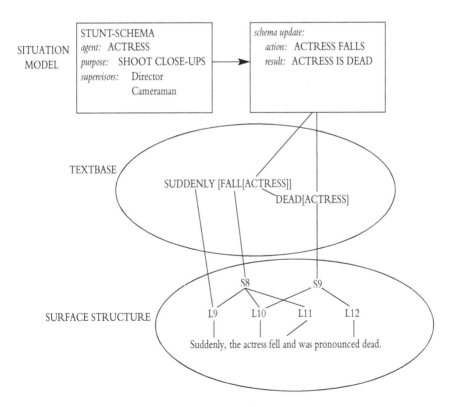

Figure 10.3 Surface Structure, Textbase, and Situation Model

Note. L = word units. S = syntactic units. Based on "A Unified Model for Predictive and Bridging Inferences," by F. Schmalhofer, M.A. McDaniel, and D. Keefe, 2002, *Discourse Processes, 33*(2), 105–132.

The text is a story about a movie stunt that results in a fatal accident. For the surface level of analysis, one sentence is shown, with word units L9 to L12 and syntactic units S8 and S9; of course, all this is part of a much larger network with rich interconnections not shown here. The units at the surface level are connected not only to each other but also to the propositional units at the textbase level. The propositions of the textbase are linked, in turn, to the situation model units, which here are schemata. The STUNT-SCHEMA has been partly filled in with information from previous portions of the text, but it is updated now with current information from the sentence being processed: An action and a result slot are filled in. When activation is spread in such a triple network, it is the structure present at each level of analysis that determines which nodes get activated, and complex interactions between levels also occur. This has important consequences, especially for the maintenance of inferences, as Schmalhofer et al. show. A model such as this explains how inferences at the situation model level can become integral parts of text memory, solidly and permanently anchored in the text structure.

The approach to modeling situation models pioneered by Schmalhofer et al. (2002) is a very promising one. Still, there are some limitations: The researchers selected their story in such a way that schema units were appropriate to represent the situation model. Not all situation models can be represented by schemata, however, and a more general approach is required. What needs to be represented in a situation model is at least partially understood (Graesser, Millis, & Zwaan, 1997; Zwaan & Radvansky, 1998). This is an active research area today (Louwerse, 2002; Tapiero, 2007; Todaro, Millis, & Dandotkar, 2010), with the goal of developing and evaluating situation models for complex narratives and especially declarative texts, such as chapters from a science text, at the same level of detail and explicitness as Schmalhofer et al. have done for simple stories. If we understand better what students have to do, we shall be better able to guide and help them.

To summarize the research on the processes of text comprehension, we can say that we have a good understanding of how people go from the words and sentences of a text to the underlying ideas and how the text structure determines the organization of these ideas into a coherent textbase, at least at the local level. Less is known about global organization, or how readers form macrostructures, and even less is known about how situation models are constructed through the interplay among texts, background knowledge, and reader goals. However, promising beginnings have been made in these areas, and rapid progress can be expected now that reading researchers are placing more emphasis on comprehension rather than on the decoding aspects of reading.

The first part of this chapter has described a general theory of comprehension. In the next sections, the focus will be on the application of that theory to important research topics in the area of discourse comprehension: how words are identified in a discourse context, the representation of knowledge, the construction of macrostructures and situation models, and the role of inferences and working memory. Of particular interest are the implications of these research results for instruction, which will be emphasized throughout this discussion.

Word Identification

A great deal of research has gone into determining how the letter shapes on a page are turned into meaningful words. The results of this work will not be reviewed here because they have been discussed in other chapters of this volume. Instead, a body of research will be introduced here that complements this research in that it is concerned with the question of how readers arrive at the correct sense or meaning of a word[3] when they encounter it in a discourse context. To give a concrete example of what the issue is here, consider the following sentences:

(10) *A beautiful sight in downtown Denver is the* <u>*mint*</u>.
(11) *A fragrant tea is made with* <u>*mint*</u>.

How do we know that *mint* is a building in the first sentence but the leaves of a plant in the second? *Mint* is a homonym in English, that is, a word with more than one meaning, and readers obviously and effortlessly find the right meaning when they read (10) and (11). Similarly, when words with only a single meaning are used in different senses, readers readily perceive what is meant:

(12) *The fox ran faster than the hedgehog.*
(13) *The chancellor's decree ran into strong opposition.*

One explanation of how readers identify word meanings in context assumes that all word meanings and word senses are listed in a mental lexicon and that readers must select the right meaning or sense for the given context. There are at least two ways in which this selection could occur:

1. The schema acts as a filter. Suppose that each word meaning/sense in the mental lexicon is associated with a specific context. Thus, *mint* in (10) is associated with *a building-in-which-coins-are-manufactured* schema; reading (10) activates this schema, and the schema selects the proper sense of *mint* from the list of available senses. This is a top-down model, where the schema acts like a filter, admitting only the schema-relevant meaning and not admitting irrelevant meanings. Models of this type have been proposed by, among others, Schank and Abelson (1977).
2. The context suppresses inappropriate meanings. According to this model, all meanings/senses of a word are activated when reading it, but inappropriate meanings are suppressed by the context because they do not fit the contextual constraints. When reading (10), all versions of *mint* in the mental lexicon would be activated initially, but only one—the one associated with *building, downtown,* and *Denver*—would be consistent with the sentence context and would survive. Models of this type have been proposed by, among others, Swinney (1979).

Fortunately, it is possible to decide among these alternatives experimentally. Till, Mross, and Kintsch (1988) have reported a relevant experiment using the "lexical decision" method. In this experiment, participants read sentences such as (10) and were then asked to decide as quickly as possible whether a briefly presented string of letters was an English word. Four types of test items were used (each participant saw only one of these):

1. A nonword string (e.g., *baher*) for which the correct response was no
2. An associate of the target word that was contextually appropriate (e.g., *money*)
3. An associate of the target word that was contextually inappropriate (e.g., *tea*)
4. An unrelated control word (e.g., *baker*)

The correct response for the last three items was yes, but interesting differences in response speed were observed. When the test item was presented immediately after the sentence, response times for associated items were significantly shorter than response times to unrelated control items, whether or not the association was contextually appropriate. That is, *mint* in (10) primed both *money* and *tea*. When the test item was presented with a 350-millisecond (msec) delay after the sentence, the response time for the contextually appropriate associate was shorter than the response time for either the control word or the inappropriate associate. That is, 350 msec after reading (10), only *money* was primed, not *tea*.

The Till et al. (1988) data clearly contradict the schema–as–filter model and support a model that posits a bottom–up activation of all word meanings, followed by a contextual constraint satisfaction process that deactivates inappropriate meaning. Indeed, these data were one of the original inspirations for the CI model (W. Kintsch, 1988). Today there exists a very large and complex literature on this subject, which cannot be reviewed here (see, e.g., Rayner, Pacht, & Duffy, 1994). Results depend on various boundary conditions, but on the whole, they effectively rule out the schema–as–filter model. It appears that, generally, multiple meanings and senses of a word are activated initially but that context-inappropriate meanings and senses are suppressed rapidly.

It is difficult to imagine, however, how such a meaning selection model could work. Just what are the cues that allow the selection of the right meaning or sense among so many alternatives? Furthermore, just what are the alternatives in the mental lexicon? How do we decide how many meanings or senses a word has? People learn to use words in ever-novel ways. Can a mental lexicon in which every use must somehow be explicitly defined do justice to this complexity? What if the different word meanings and senses are not predefined in a mental lexicon but emerge in context? How could such a generative lexicon be constructed? One attempt to do so invokes the idea of semantic elements that can be combined to form all meanings, much like the 100+ chemical elements can be combined to form all the manifold substances in the universe. This approach has not been successful, however, because no one has been able to come up with a principled list of semantic elements or the rule system that would allow us to construct all meanings from the combination of these elements. An alternative approach that appears promising to achievement of the goal of a generative lexicon is based on some recent developments in statistical semantics.

Macrostructures and Summaries

Macrostructures are mental representations of text at a global level. They may simply mirror the structure of the text from which they were derived, or they may reflect, to varying degrees, the comprehender's own prior knowledge structure that has been imposed on the text in the creation of a situation model.

Macrostructures as envisaged by van Dijk (1980) and discussed in van Dijk and Kintsch (1983) are hierarchies of propositions. Macropropositions put into words are summary statements at different levels of generality. They subsume what the different sections of a text are about. They are derived from the text by the operations of selection, generalization, and construction, but propositional macrostructures cannot be computed automatically from a text. The macrorules merely help us explain what can be done, but they are not algorithms or computational procedures that generate macropropositions from a text automatically. A computationally more feasible—but in other ways more limited—alternative for the representation of macrostructures is provided by LSA (Landauer et al., 2007). LSA serves as a model of how human verbal knowledge is represented and is of considerable benefit for modeling the use of knowledge in comprehension. Instead of representing the meaning of a sentence by a proposition, the meaning can be represented as a vector in an existing high-dimensional semantic space. For some purposes, such a representation is all that is needed. For example, one can compare new texts, such as summaries students write, with these macrovectors; one can compute the importance or typicality of sentences from the text, and so on.

For other purposes, verbal statements corresponding to macropropositions are needed. W. Kintsch (2002) has described how LSA can be used to select topic sentences from a text and to generate a summary by concatenating these topic sentences. There is more to a summary than just selecting topic sentences, but it is instructive to see what can be achieved in that way—and what is still missing. The text analyzed by Kintsch is a chapter titled "Wind Energy," taken from a junior high school science textbook. It is 960 words long and divided by its author into six sections, each with its own subtitles. Thus, the author indicates the intended macrostructure and even provides appropriate macropropositions, in the form of six subtitles. Macrorules can be used to explain where these subtitles come from. Consider the following paragraph (the second subsection of the chapter):

(14) *The history of windmills*

> *Since ancient times, people have harnessed the wind's energy. Over 5,000 years ago, the ancient Egyptians used the wind to sail ships on the Nile River. Later, people built windmills to grind wheat and other*

grains. The early windmills looked like paddle wheels. Centuries later, the people in Holland improved the windmill. They gave it propeller-type blades. Holland is still famous for its windmills. In this country, the colonists used windmills to grind wheat and corn, to pump water, and to cut wood at sawmills. Today people still sometimes use windmills to grind grain and pump water, but they also use new wind machines to make electricity.

The macrorule of construction can be used to compress sentences 2–4 into

People used wind energy in Egypt.

Similarly, the other sentences of the paragraph can be reduced to

People used windmills in Holland.
People used windmills in the colonies.
People use windmills today.

These sentences can be transformed by the macrorule of generalization into

(15) *People used windmills throughout history.*

or

(16) *The history of windmills.*[4]

Thus, macrorules allow us to postdict, or explain, what the author did. But the application of these rules depends on our intuitions about the text and our knowledge about it. By themselves, these rules cannot compute anything.

LSA provides a computational mechanism that can compute macrostructures of a kind. For instance, we can compute a vector in LSA space that is the centroid of all the words in paragraph (14). Such a vector may seem to be totally useless—it is, after all, a list of 300 uninterpretable numbers—but that is not so. It can be quite useful, for instance, to decide how appropriate a proposed subtitle is. The cosine between the paragraph vector and the proposed subtitle is a measure of how close the subtitle is to the paragraph as a whole. For instance, (15) and (16) have rather similar cosines with the paragraph: .39 and .48, respectively—high enough to indicate that they are both acceptable summary statements. But suppose we had chosen an ill-considered subtitle for the paragraph such as "Holland is still famous," or something totally inappropriate such as "Rain douses forest fires." The cosine measure would have allowed us to reject these choices (the cosine is .26 in the first case and only .05 in the second—both much lower than the cosines for (15) and (16)).

There are other uses for vector representation of a macrostructure, too. For instance, we can compute how closely related the sections of a text are to each other. This kind of information can be of interest in various ways. If two sections of a text are very closely related, one might consider combining them. Or if two similar sections are separated by a dissimilar one in the text, one might consider reordering the sections of the text. We also can obtain a measure of how important a section is to the overall text. One way to do this is to compute the cosine between the whole text and each section.

To generate the full range of macropropositions is beyond the scope of LSA; operations such as generalization and construction are not readily modeled within this framework. But we can generate a degenerate macrostructure using only the selection operation. For each section, we can find the most typical sentence in the section. For this purpose, we define *most typical* as the sentence with the highest average cosine to all the other sentences in the section. This will not always yield the best result because the ideal macroproposition may involve generalization or construction, but it will serve as a reasonable approximation.

Thus, some progress can be made toward a computational model of macrostructure generation. LSA allows us to generate an abstract vector representation of the macrostructure of a text (at least in those cases where the subsections of the text are clearly indicated, as in the example above). Furthermore, procedures can be devised to select the most typical sentence for each section of a text. However, that does not make a summary yet, and the operations for reducing the selected typical sentence to an essential phrase or fragment depend on more analytic procedures that go beyond LSA.

There are other, more practical uses of LSA's ability to represent the content of a text mathematically and compare it with other texts. For instance, we can express the summary written by a student as a vector and compare it with the vector of the to-be-summarized text. If the cosine between summary and text is high, the summary has much the same content as the original text. However, if the cosine is low, the summary does not reflect the content of the original text. A system, called *Summary Street*, that employs this method to help students write better summaries has been used with considerable success in some classrooms (E. Kintsch et al., 2000; E. Kintsch, Caccamise, Franzke, Johnson, & Dooley, 2007). For instance, students in sixth-grade classes were routinely asked to write summaries of chapters of their science textbooks. The teachers assigned a text to be summarized, say, on energy sources (coal, wind, petroleum, etc.) or Meso-American civilizations (Incan, Mayan, or Aztec). Each text is usually composed of four or five sections, and the teachers wanted the content of each section to be covered in the summary. Furthermore, the teachers required the summary to be of a certain length, say, between 150 and 200 words. The students write their summaries on an interface that is much like a standard word processor and send them to the LSA system for analysis via the Web. The feedback is received almost immediately and involves a number of steps.

Content feedback indicates whether all sections of the text have been covered in the summary. For this purpose, the cosine between the student's summary and each of the sections of a text are computed. If a cosine is below a certain threshold value, the student is told that this section is not adequately covered in the summary. The student then has the option to look at the appropriate section of the text on the computer screen and add some material about this section to the summary. If the threshold is exceeded for all sections, the student is told that he or she has now covered all parts of the text. Because the length of the summaries is restricted to avoid extensive copying from the source texts, students are told how long their summaries are so far and which of their sentences may be redundant or irrelevant.

Summary Street has been shown to be effective in helping students write better summaries. When summary writing was compared with and without system feedback (Wade-Stein & Kintsch, 2004), the analysis showed that students were willing to work harder and longer when given feedback. Indeed, their time on task more than doubled. Summaries written with content feedback received higher grades from the teachers. This was the case for difficult summaries, for which grades more than doubled, whereas for texts that were easy to summarize anyway, the use of the system had no significant effect. Finally, a transfer effect was observed. Students who had written summaries with the help of the system wrote better summaries a week later even when they no longer had access to the feedback the system provided. They had learned something about how summaries should be written.

Summary Street has been used by thousands of students in several hundred middle school classrooms with considerable success: Students who actually used the program at least four or five times during a year actually learned how to write summaries (E. Kintsch et al., 2007). Today, the Write-ToLearn software marketed by Pearson Education incorporates a version of *Summary Street*.

Inferences and Situation Models[5]

Text comprehension always goes beyond the text. The mental representations that readers construct—their understanding of the text—depend as much on what readers bring to the text, such as their goals, interests, and prior experience, as on the text itself. Readers must make inferences to construct situation models. But not all inferences in comprehension are alike.

Classification of Inferences

A distinction should be made between problem-solving processes on the one hand, where there are premises from which some conclusion is drawn (not necessarily by the rules of logic)—which may be justly called inferences—and knowledge-retrieval processes on the other hand, where a gap in the text is bridged by some piece of preexisting knowledge that has been retrieved (W. Kintsch, 1998). Both inferences proper and knowledge retrieval may be either automatic (and usually unconscious) or controlled (and usually conscious and strategic). This classification results in the 2-by-2 table shown in Table 10.5.

Retrieval adds preexisting information to a text from long-term memory. Generation, in contrast, produces new information by deriving it from information in the text by some inference procedure. Thus, while the term *inference* is suitable for information-generation processes, it is a misnomer for retrieval processes.

A prototypical example for cell A, the automatic retrieval process that enriches the information in a text, would be the activation of *with a hammer* by *John nailed down a board*, or *cars have doors* by *A car stopped. The door opened.* In both cases sufficient retrieval cues for the information retrieved exist in short-term memory. These cues are linked with pertinent information in long-term memory. Such knowledge use is automatic and rapid, and it places no demands on cognitive resources.

There are two theories that describe automatic knowledge retrieval. One is the long-term working memory theory of Ericsson and Kintsch (1995), which is described in more detail in the next section of this chapter. According to the long-term working memory theory, for well-practiced associations, retrieval cues in short-term memory are linked to contents in long-term memory, which thereby become directly available, thus expanding the capacity of working memory. An alternative model for this kind of knowledge retrieval is the resonance theory of Myers (Myers, O'Brien, Albrecht, & Mason, 1994). According to this model, cues in short-term memory produce a resonance in long-term memory, so the resonating items become available for further processing in working memory. Thus, either via retrieval structures or resonance, relevant, strongly related items in long-term memory become potential parts of working memory, creating a long-term working memory that is much richer than the severely capacity-restricted short-term working memory. Indeed, it is only this long-term working memory that makes discourse comprehension (or, indeed, any other expert performance) possible. Smooth, efficient functioning would be impossible if we had no way of expanding working-memory capacity beyond the rigid limits of short-term memory.

Table 10.5 A Classification System for Inferences in Text Comprehension

	Retrieval	*Generation*
	A	*C*
Automatic processes	Bridging inferences Associative elaborations	Transitive inferences in a familiar domain
	B	*D*
Controlled processes	Search for bridging knowledge	Logical inferences

Note. Based on *Comprehension: A Paradigm for Cognition*, by W. Kintsch, 1998. New York: Cambridge University Press.

In cell B of Table 10.5 are cases where automatic retrieval is not possible. That is, the cues present in short-term memory do not retrieve relevant information that bridge whatever gap exists in the text. An extended search of memory is required to yield the needed information. A memory search is a strategic, controlled, resource-demanding process in which the cues available in short-term memory are used to retrieve other likely cues from long-term memory that, in turn, are capable of retrieving what is needed. Consider the following sentences:

(17) *Danny wanted a new bike. He worked as a waiter.*

Purely automatic, associative elaboration might not retrieve the causal chain from *want-bike* to *buy-bike* to *money* to *work*. However, a directed search for causal connections between the two sentences would easily generate these by-no-means-obscure links. In all probability, genre-specific strategies exist to guide such search processes. In a story, one would look for causal links. In a legal argument, one routinely looks for contradictions. In an algebraic word problem, algebraic formulas guide the search. The difficulty of such procedures, and the resource demands they make, vary widely.

Retrieval processes merely access information available in long-term memory, either automatically or by a resource-demanding search. Generation processes actually compute new information on the basis of the text and relevant background information in long-term memory. They, too, may be either automatic or controlled.

Some generation procedures are fully automatic (cell C of Table 10.5). For instance, given the sentence

(18) *Three turtles rested on a floating log, and a fish swam beneath them.*

the statement *The turtles are above the fish* is immediately available to a reader. Indeed, readers often are unable to distinguish whether they were explicitly told this information (e.g., Bransford, Barclay, & Franks, 1972). Note, however, that this is not merely a question of knowledge retrieval as in *doors are parts of cars*: The statement *the turtles are above the fish* is not something that already exists in long-term memory and is now retrieved, but it is generated during the comprehension process. The reason why it is so highly available in the reader's working memory is, presumably, that the fish-log-and-turtle scene is encoded as an image, and this mental image constitutes a highly effective retrieval structure that provides ready access to all its parts—not just the verbal expression used in its construction.

The information that allows the reader to infer that the turtles are above the fish is, presumably, in the form of a spatial image. It is given directly by the image that serves as the situation model representation of the sentence in question. Indeed, at this level of representation, there is no difference between explicit and implicit statements. A difference only exists at the level of the textbase and surface representation, which, however, may not always be effective (as in the experiments of Bransford et al., 1972, in which subjects could not distinguish between explicit and implicit statements, given study and test sentences as in the example discussed here).

However, what happens in cell C of Table 10.5 should hardly be called an inference either. It is simply a case, in which due to the analog nature of the mental representation involved, more information is generated in forming a situation model than was explicit in the text. The term *inference* really should be reserved for cell D of Table 10.5. This is the domain of deductive reasoning. It is a domain that extends far beyond text comprehension, although deductive reasoning undoubtedly plays an important role in text comprehension, too. Explicit reasoning comes into play when comprehension proper breaks down. When the network does not integrate, and the gaps in the text cannot be bridged any other way, then reasoning is called for as the ultimate repair procedure.

Inferences (real inferences, as in cell D) require specific inference procedures. What these inference operations are is a matter of considerable controversy in psychology—whether inference proceeds by rule (Rips, 1994) or mental model (Johnson-Laird, Byrne, & Schaeken, 1992). Inferences in domains where the basic representation is an action or perceptual representation, that is, analog rather than linguistic or abstract, probably involve operations on mental models. Inferences in truly symbolic, abstract domains may be by rule. Inferences in the linguistic domain, where the representation is at the narrative level, may be based on mental models but also could involve purely verbal inference rules.

Inference Generation During Discourse Comprehension

The literature on "inferences" in discourse comprehension is for the most part not concerned with cell D of Table 10.5. Indeed, it is heavily concentrated on cell A, the processes that are the least inferencelike, according to the argument presented here. A major focus of the recent research has been on the question of to what extent inferences are made during normal comprehension. On the one hand, it is clear that if the readers of a story are asked to make inferences and are given sufficient time and incentive, there is almost no limit to what they will produce (Graesser, 1981). On the other hand, there is good evidence that much of the time, and in particular in many psychology experiments, readers are lazy and get away with a minimum of work (e.g., Foertsch & Gernsbacher, 1994). McKoon and Ratcliff (1992, 1995) have elaborated the latter position as the *minimalist hypothesis*, which holds that the only inferences readers normally make are bridging inferences required for the maintenance of local coherence, and knowledge elaboration where there are strong preexisting, multiple associations. Many text researchers (e.g., Graesser & Kreuz, 1993; Graesser, Singer, & Trabasso, 1994; Singer, Graesser, & Trabasso, 1994), however, feel that this minimalist position underestimates the amount of inference making that occurs during normal reading and would at the least add inferences that are necessary for global coherence to the list (superordinate goal inferences, thematic inferences, and character emotional reactions). While this controversy has contributed a great deal to our understanding of the role of inferences in text comprehension, it also has shown that the question concerning which inferences are necessary for and are normally made during text comprehension has no simple answer. Text characteristics (much of the research is based on stories, mostly ministories), task demands, and individual differences among readers create a complex, though orderly, picture.

Trabasso and Suh (1993) have combined discourse analysis, talk-aloud procedures, and experimental measures, such as recognition priming, reading times, coherence ratings, and story recall, to show that their readers made causal inferences in reading a story and that these inferences could be predicted by their analysis.

In an illuminating series of studies, O'Brien and his colleagues have shown that causal inferences in story understanding should best be regarded as a passive operation that makes available background and causal antecedents via a resonance-like mechanism (or what I would call a retrieval structure). Such a process contributes to the coherence of the text representation (Garrod, O'Brien, Morris, & Rayner, 1990) but is not predictive. Readers refrain from prediction unless there is absolutely no chance of being discomfirmed (O'Brien, Shank, Myers, & Rayner, 1988). Global automatic goal inferences occur only under limited conditions (Albrecht, O'Brien, Mason, & Myers, 1995), probably because such inferences are as risky as predictions: They are frequently discomfirmed as the later text reveals a different goal. When global goal inferences occur, resonance describes what happens better than the notion of inference. Through resonance, related parts of a text are connected because of preexisting retrieval structures. In contrast, the construction of a full mental model with rich causal connections appears rather as a nonautomatic, controlled process (Albrecht & O'Brien, 1995; O'Brien, 1995).

How much time and resources the reader has strongly determines the amount of inference making that occurs. Magliano, Baggett, Johnson, and Graesser (1993), using a lexical decision task, found that causal antecedent inferences were not made when texts were presented rapidly at a 250-msec rate, but they were made when the presentation rate was 400 msec. Long, Golding, and Graesser (1992) found that superordinate goal inferences linking various episodes of a story (but not subordinated goal inferences) were made by readers when they were given a lot of time. However, with a rapid presentation rate, only good comprehenders made such inferences, while there was no evidence for goal inferences by poor comprehenders (Long & Golding, 1993).

Readers are much more likely to make antecedent causal inferences than consequent causal inferences (e.g., Magliano et al., 1993). For instance, readers of *The clouds gathered quickly, and it became ominously dark. The downpour only lasted 10 minutes* infer the causal antecedent *the clouds caused the rain.* But given *The clouds gathered quickly, and it became ominously dark,* they do not infer the consequent *the clouds caused rain.* This finding that antecedent, but not consequent causal, inferences are made in text comprehension is readily accounted for by the CI model. Suppose a text describes a situation that is a common cause of some event and then asserts that this event occurred, without mentioning an explicit causal connection between the antecedent and the event. Preexisting retrieval structures causally link the antecedent and the event in the reader's memory, and the causal link will be activated and is likely to become a permanent part of the reader's episodic text memory because it connects two highly activated nodes in the memory structure.

The situation is different for the consequent inferences. The same retrieval structures that made available the causal antecedent will make available the causal consequent, too. But at that point in the reading process, the consequent is a dangling node in the episodic text structure because it is connected to nothing else in the network but the antecedent. Therefore, the consequent will not receive much activation in the integration process and will be excluded from episodic memory. Thus, *The clouds gathered quickly, and it became ominously dark* might make available *the clouds caused rain,* but if nothing else in the text connects to *rain,* this node will become quickly deactivated in the network. When in a later processing cycle other information becomes available that could have linked with *rain,* that node is most likely lost from working memory. Hence, although the retrieval structures in the reader's long-term memory make available both antecedent and consequent information, only the former is likely to survive the integration process and become a stable component of the reader's text memory.

Time Course for Constructing Knowledge-Based Inferences

Of considerable interest is the time course of constructing knowledge-based inferences in text comprehension. We know that it takes about 300–350 msec for word meanings to become fixed in a discourse context. Inferences require more time. In Till et al. (1988), no evidence for topic inferences was obtained at a stimulus onset asynchrony (SOA; the time interval between the presentation of the target word and the test word) of 500 msec, but topic inferences were clearly made at an SOA of 1,000 msec (there were no data points in between). In contrast, Magliano et al. (1993) found that antecedent causal inferences required an SOA of only 400 msec. Long, Oppy, and Seely (1994), in a study modeled after Till et al.'s, have used SOAs of 200, 300, 400, 500, 750, and 1,000 msec. Associative effects are already fully apparent in their data at 300 msec. Topic effects develop gradually: They are already apparent at 500 msec but increase in strength up to 750 msec. Because different materials and conditions were used in all these studies, the differences in the results are not surprising. It seems that sentence-level inferences require from 400 to 750 msec, depending on experimental conditions. Thus, sentence meanings take roughly twice as long as word meanings to fixate.

The Construction of Situation Models

Much recent research has been concerned with the construction of situation models (e.g., Glenberg, Kruley, & Langston, 1994; Glenberg & Langston, 1992; Graesser & Zwaan, 1995; Mani & Johnson-Laird, 1982; Tapiero, 2007; Todaro et al., 2010; Trabasso & Suh, 1993; Zwaan, Magliano, &

Graesser, 1995). There is no single type of situation model and not a single process for the construction of such models. Situation models are a form of "inference" by definition, and Table 10.5 is as relevant for situation models as it is for any other "inference" in discourse comprehension. That is, situation models may vary widely in their character. In the simplest case, their construction is automatic. Relevant information is furnished by existing retrieval structures, as in the examples given for cell A in Table 10.5. Or it may be available simply as a consequence of a particular form of representation, such as imagery. Such situation model inferences do not add new propositions to the memory representation of the text but simply make available information in long-term memory via retrieval structures, or information that is implicit in the mental representation, such as an image (see Fincher-Kiefer, 1993, and Perfetti, 1993, for similar suggestions). On the contrary, situation models can be much more complex and result from extended, resource-demanding, controlled processes. All kinds of representations and constructions may be involved. The process may be shared by a social group or even by a whole culture and extend over prolonged periods of time. Text interpretation is not something that is confined to the laboratory.

Spatial and temporal information are usually important components of a situation model. Perrig and Kintsch (1985) had subjects read descriptions of the spatial layout of a small town. The same town was described in two ways, first by providing route descriptions (*after the church, turn right on Main Street to go to the courthouse*) and second by means of survey descriptions (*the courthouse is north of the church on Main Street*). Subjects were tested both for their ability to recall and recognize the text they had read and to make novel spatial inferences on the basis of that text. The results of their first experiment dramatically illustrated the textbase–situation model distinction: Subjects' recall was excellent and sentence recognition nearly perfect—but their ability to verify inferences was similar to results of random choices. In a second experiment, with a simpler town and more study time, subjects successfully constructed a spatial situation model. They performed well on recall and recognition as well as on inference tasks. Interestingly, the kind of situation model differed, depending on the text they had read: Route texts led to route models, and survey texts led to survey models. When the inference question was in the same form as the text a subject had read, performance was better than when the text was a route description and the question in the survey format, or vice versa. The Perrig and Kintsch study shows that situation models are by no means automatic consequences of good textbases and that there may be different types of situation models. Which one is best depends on the reader's purpose.

A study by van der Meer, Beyer, Heinze, and Badel (2002) explored the construction of temporal situation models by presenting events in their chronological order (*fall down–get up*) or in reverse order (*fall down–slip*). Overall, chronologically related information was accessed faster compared with reverse-ordered sentences, but processing time made a crucial difference. When there was not enough processing time, neither chronological nor reverse information was integrated into the situation model. When there was a great deal of time for elaboration, both were integrated. In the intermediate condition, however, chronologically ordered events were integrated into the situation model, whereas reverse, past-oriented events were not. Thus, what sort of inferences people make and how elaborate a situation model they construct depend crucially on the amount of processing. If there is time and they are motivated, people will construct rich situation models—but that is a controlled, effortful process, not the kind of automatic knowledge activation discussed earlier.

Research on Reading Comprehension and the Teaching of Reading Comprehension

Research on reading has been an active field in the last few decades. Relatively large sums of money have been made available by federal agencies such as the National Institute of Mental Health to support this field. However, the focus of this research effort has been squarely on early reading instruction—on the study of decoding processes, rather than comprehension. To focus research on decoding was a perfectly defensible and successful strategy: We now have a fairly good understanding of the cognitive bases of decoding processes in reading and about reading instruction in the early grades. Surely, there remain problems to be resolved, but there exists an underlying consensus today about early reading instruction in the United States, as exemplified by the National Research Council's report *Preventing Reading Difficulties in Young Children* (Snow, Burns, & Griffin, 1998). Educators know what to do, even if getting it done in schools on a national scale is still another matter.

There also is agreement among reading researchers today that research on reading comprehension lags far behind research on decoding processes and early reading instruction and that it is time to shift the research focus onto reading comprehension beyond the early years. Recent assessments of research needs by the RAND Reading Study Group (2002) and the Strategic Education Research Partnership report of the National Research Council's Panel on Learning and Instruction (Donovan, Wigdor, & Snow, 2003) agree on the need for a better understanding of the processes of text comprehension as well as instructional methods to improve comprehension.

My goal in this chapter has been to show that there exists a solid basis for further research in reading comprehension. We do not have to start from zero; there is a sparse but solid database, as well as a theoretical framework, that can serve at least as a good starting point for further research on reading comprehension. Throughout this chapter, open research questions have been pointed out, most pressingly about the formation of situation models and the modeling of macrostructures. There is much to be learned, but we also have already learned quite a bit about comprehension. This chapter was not intended as a general review of research on comprehension, but rather as a description of one particular research program and theoretical approach. A broader discussion would certainly have provided further evidence of the considerable progress made in the study of reading comprehension in recent years.

In the meantime, the way we read is changing: Web-based materials have become more and more important. Thus, comprehension research must deal with hypertext and multimedia because students today depend on these sources for information and learning. How comprehension theory can be expanded to incorporate these modern developments has been discussed by Butcher and Kintsch (2013).

The explicit goal of the comprehension research presented here is to inform instructional practice. As yet, this link is weak because there are so many unanswered questions and limited, conditional answers, but there is no reason to suppose that a focused research effort in this area would not yield results that achieve this goal.

Theories of discourse comprehension such as the one presented here are based on data from proficient readers. Indeed, these readers, as long as they read familiar material, can be considered to be comprehension experts. Comprehension for them is fluent, automatic, and easy. Well-established knowledge structures and skills are the basis for this automaticity. The goal of instruction is to help students become such expert readers. Paradoxically, however, comprehension instruction requires students to behave in very different ways than experienced readers do. Because for student readers comprehension is not the automatic, fluent process that it is for mature readers, students need to engage in active problem solving, knowledge construction, self-explanation, and monitoring— activities very different from the automatic, fluent comprehension of experts. For the expert reader, comprehension is easy; to become an expert, comprehension must be hard work. Research on comprehension, therefore, has two quite distinct goals: (1) to describe expert comprehension with all its components and (2) to determine the training sequence that leads to this expert performance. What the student needs to do in training is quite different from how the expert operates. This is not a problem peculiar to comprehension training. Take, for example, ski instruction. Watching the instructor glide down a steep slope with elegant turns is not helpful to the novice skier. The novice must learn by doing things quite differently, and with much more effort, and the instructor must gradually, via a carefully thought-out training sequence, bring the novice to the point where he can begin skiing like an expert, that is, when he is no longer a novice. Thus, if it is to be relevant for instruction, comprehension theory must pay attention not only to the final automatic comprehension that characterizes expert readers in familiar domains but also to the strategies that support comprehension for the beginner, or for the expert who is faced with materials outside his or her domain of expertise (W. Kintsch, 2009).

Assessment plays a central role in gaining expertise in reading comprehension. This chapter has stressed how nontrivial comprehension assessment is. The levels of comprehension range from the superficial to the deep, from surface features to the textbase to the situation model. Assessing comprehension at these different levels is tricky because quite different tests are required. To teach comprehension, we need a thorough understanding of the different aspects of comprehension and the tests that assess comprehension at these different levels. Richer comprehension tests need to be developed and evaluated that adequately assess the different aspects of comprehension. Furthermore, not only must teachers be able to tell how well students understood something, but the students themselves also must have tools to assess their comprehension or lack thereof. People are notoriously bad at this task, and one of the goals of comprehension research must be to find better, and more practical, ways to assess comprehension.

Research on comprehension will probably see a big boost in the next decades. To fulfill its potential, it will have to find the right balance between observation, experiment, and theory. Careful studies of the basic cognitive processes in comprehension are needed, together with research on instructional practices and tools that support effective comprehension. Our goal should be a comprehensive theory of comprehension that allows us to understand how people, novices as well as experts, will react in novel situations. We cannot always perform a new experiment for every new question; instead, we need a broad theoretical framework that provides reasonably good answers to these questions. Educational researchers need a reliable theory to navigate by, much as engineers do in other fields, when they only occasionally resort to experiment because they know they can rely on their computations, except for special problems.

Notes

1 The term *proposition* was borrowed from logic, where it is used quite differently.
2 The distinction between textbase and situation model is made for the convenience of the theorist; mental representation integrates aspects of both.
3 Different word *meanings* are unrelated, as in *bank-(of river)* and *bank-(financial institution)*; different word senses are related, as in *chill-(bodily coldness with shivering)* and *chill-(moderate coldness)*.
4 For comparison, the autosummary computed by MS Word is "Later, people built windmills to grind wheat and other grains."
5 Based in part on W. Kintsch (1998, Chap. 6).

References

Albrecht, J.E., & O'Brien, E.J. (1995). Goal processing and the maintenance of global coherence. In R.F. Lorch & E.J. O'Brien (Eds.), *Sources of coherence in reading* (pp. 263–278). Hillsdale, NJ: Erlbaum.

Albrecht, J.E., O'Brien, E.J., Mason, R.A., & Myers, J.L. (1995). The role of perspective in the accessibility of goals during reading. *Journal of Experimental Psychology: Learning, Memory, and Cognition, 21*, 364–372.

Bransford, J.D., Barclay, J.R., & Franks, J.J. (1972). Sentence memory: A constructive versus interpretive approach. *Cognitive Psychology, 3*, 193–209.

Butcher, K.R., & Kintsch, W. (2013). Text comprehension and discourse processing. In I.B. Weiner (Series Ed.), A.F. Healy, & R.W. Proctor (Vol. Eds.), *Experimental psychology: Vol. 4. Handbook of psychology* (2nd ed., pp. 578–604). Hoboken, NJ: John Wiley & Sons.

Donovan, M.S., Wigdor, A.K., & Snow, C.E. (Eds.). (2003). *Strategic Education Research Partnership*. Washington, DC: National Academy Press.

Ericsson, K.A., & Kintsch, W. (1995). Long-term working memory. *Psychological Review, 102*(2), 211–245.

Fincher-Kiefer, R.H. (1993). The role of predictive inferences in situation model construction. *Discourse Processes, 16*(1), 99–124.

Foertsch, J., & Gernsbacher, M.A. (1994). In search of complete comprehension: Getting "minimalists" to work. *Discourse Processes, 18*(3), 271–296.

Garrod, S., O'Brien, E.J., Morris, R.K., & Rayner, K. (1990). Elaborative inferencing as an active or passive process. *Journal of Experimental Psychology: Learning, Memory, and Cognition, 16*, 250–257.

Glenberg, A.M., Kruley, P., & Langston, W.E. (1994). Analogical processes in comprehension: Simulation of a mental model. In M.A. Gernsbacher (Ed.), *Handbook of psycholinguistics* (pp. 609–640). San Diego, CA: Academic.

Glenberg, A.M., & Langston, W.E. (1992). Comprehension of illustrated text: Pictures help to build mental models. *Journal of Memory and Language, 31*(2), 129–151.

Graesser, A.C. (1981). *Prose comprehension beyond the word*. New York: Springer.

Graesser, A.C., & Kreuz, R.J. (1993). A theory of inference generation during text comprehension. *Discourse Processes, 16*(1/2), 145–160.

Graesser, A.C., Millis, K.K., & Zwaan, R.A. (1997). Discourse comprehension. *Annual Review of Psychology, 48*, 163–189.

Graesser, A.C., Singer, M., & Trabasso, T. (1994). Constructing inferences during narrative text comprehension. *Psychological Review, 101*(3), 371–395.

Graesser, A.C., & Zwaan, R.A. (1995). Inference generation and the construction of situation models. In C.A. Weaver, S. Mannes, & C.R. Fletcher (Eds.), *Discourse comprehension: Essays in honor of Walter Kintsch* (pp. 117–139). Hillsdale, NJ: Erlbaum.

Johnson-Laird, P.N., Byrne, R.M.J., & Schaeken, W. (1992). Propositional reasoning by model. *Psychological Review, 99*(3), 418–439.

Kintsch, E., Caccamise, D., Franzke, M., Johnson, N., & Dooley, S. (2007). Summary Street®: Computer-guided summary writing. In T.K. Landauer, D.S. McNamara, S. Dennis, & W. Kintsch (Eds.), *Handbook of Latent Semantic Analysis* (pp. 263–277). Mahwah, NJ: Erlbaum.

Kintsch, E., Steinhart, D., Stahl, G., Matthews, C., Lamb, R., & LSA Research Group. (2000). Developing summarization skills through the use of LSA-backed feedback. *Interactive Learning Environments, 8*(2), 87–109.

Kintsch, W. (1974). *The representation of meaning in memory*. Hillsdale, NJ: Erlbaum.

Kintsch, W. (1988). The role of knowledge in discourse comprehension: A construction–integration model. *Psychological Review, 95*(2), 163–182.

Kintsch, W. (1998). *Comprehension: A paradigm for cognition*. New York: Cambridge University Press.

Kintsch, W. (2002). On the notion of theme and topic in psychological process models of text comprehension. In M. Louwerse & W. van Peer (Eds.), *Thematics: Interdisciplinary studies* (pp. 157–170). Amsterdam: John Benjamins.

Kintsch, W. (2009). Learning and constructivism. In S. Tobias & T.M. Duffy (Eds.), *Constructivist instruction: Success or failure?* (pp. 223–241). New York: Routledge.

Kintsch, W., & Bates, E. (1977). Recognition memory for statements from a classroom lecture. *Journal of Experimental Psychology: Human Learning and Memory, 3*, 150–159.

Kintsch, W., & van Dijk, T.A. (1978). Towards a model of text comprehension and production. *Psychological Review, 85*, 363–394.

Landauer, T.K., McNamara, D.S., Dennis, S., & Kintsch, W. (Eds.). (2007). *Handbook of Latent Semantic Analysis*. Mahwah, NJ: Erlbaum.

Le, E. (2002). Themes and hierarchical structures of written text. In M. Louwerse & W. van Peer (Eds.), *Thematics: Interdisciplinary studies* (pp. 171–188). Amsterdam: John Benjamins.

Long, D.L., & Golding, J.M. (1993). Superordinate goal inferences: Are they automatically generated during reading? *Discourse Processes, 16*(1/2), 55–73.

Long, D.L., Golding, J.M., & Graesser, A.C. (1992). A test of the on-line status of goal-related inferences. *Journal of Memory and Language, 31*, 634–647.

Long, D.L., Oppy, B.J., & Seely, M.R. (1994). Individual differences in the time course of differential processing. *Journal of Experimental Psychology: Learning, Memory, and Cognition, 20*, 1456–1470.

Louwerse, M. (2002). Computational retrieval of texts. In M. Louwerse & W. van Peer (Eds.), *Thematics: Interdisciplinary studies* (pp. 189–216). Amsterdam: John Benjamins.

Magliano, J.P., Baggett, W.B., Johnson, B.K., & Graesser, A.C. (1993). The time course of generating causal antecedent and causal consequence inferences. *Discourse Processes, 16*(1/2), 35–53.

Mani, K., & Johnson-Laird, P.N. (1982). The mental representation of spatial descriptions. *Memory & Cognition, 10*(2), 181–187.

McKoon, G., & Ratcliff, R. (1992). Inference during reading. *Psychological Review, 99*(3), 440–466.

McKoon, G., & Ratcliff, R. (1995). The minimalist hypothesis: Directions for research. In C.A. Weaver, S. Mannes, & C.R. Fletcher (Eds.), *Discourse comprehension: Essays in honor of Walter Kintsch* (pp. 97–116). Hillsdale, NJ: Erlbaum.

Myers, J.L., O'Brien, E.J., Albrecht, J.E., & Mason, R.A. (1994). Maintaining global coherence during reading. *Journal of Experimental Psychology: Learning, Memory, and Cognition, 20*, 876–886.

O'Brien, E.J. (1995). Automatic components of discourse comprehension. In R.F. Lorch & E.J. O'Brien (Eds.), *Sources of coherence in reading* (pp. 159–176). Hillsdale, NJ: Erlbaum.

O'Brien, E.J., Shank, D.M., Myers, J.L., & Rayner, K. (1988). Elaborative inferences during reading: Do they occur on-line? *Journal of Experimental Psychology: Learning, Memory, and Cognition, 14*(3), 410–420.

Perfetti, C.A. (1993). Why inferences might be restricted. *Discourse Processes, 16*(1/2), 181–192.

Perrig, W., & Kintsch, W. (1985). Propositional and situational representations of text. *Journal of Memory and Language, 24,* 503–518.

RAND Reading Study Group. (2002). *Reading for understanding: Toward an R&D program in reading comprehension.* Santa Monica, CA: RAND.

Rayner, K., Pacht, J.M., & Duffy, S.A. (1994). Effects of prior encounter and global discourse bias on the processing of lexically ambiguous words: Evidence from eye fixations. *Journal of Memory and Language, 33,* 527–544.

Rips, L.J. (1994). *The psychology of proof: Deductive reasoning in human thinking.* Cambridge, MA: MIT Press.

Sachs, J.S. (1967). Recognition memory for syntactic and semantic aspects of connected discourse. *Perception and Psychophysics, 2,* 437–442.

Schank, R.C., & Abelson, R.P. (1977). *Scripts, plans, goals, and understanding: An inquiry into human knowledge structures.* Hillsdale, NJ: Erlbaum.

Schmalhofer, F., McDaniel, M.A., & Keefe, D. (2002). A unified model for predictive and bridging inferences. *Discourse Processes, 33*(2), 105–132.

Singer, M., Graesser, A.C., & Trabasso, T. (1994). Minimal or global inference during reading. *Journal of Memory and Language, 33,* 421–441.

Snow, C.E., Burns, M.S., & Griffin, P. (Eds.). (1998). *Preventing reading difficulties in young children.* Washington, DC: National Academy Press.

Swinney, D.A. (1979). Lexical access during sentence comprehension: (Re)consideration of context effects. *Journal of Verbal Learning and Verbal Behavior, 18,* 645–659.

Tapiero, I. (2007). *Situation models and levels of coherence: Toward a definition of comprehension.* Mahwah, NJ: Erlbaum.

Till, R.E., Mross, E.F., & Kintsch, W. (1988). Time course of priming for associate and inference words in a discourse context. *Memory & Cognition, 16*(4), 283–298.

Todaro, S., Millis, K., & Dandotkar, S. (2010). The impact of semantic and causal relatedness and reading skill on standards of coherence. *Discourse Processes, 47*(5), 421–446.

Trabasso, T., & Suh, S. (1993). Understanding text: Achieving explanatory coherence through online inferences and mental operations in working memory. *Discourse Processes, 16*(1/2), 3–34.

van der Meer, E., Beyer, R., Heinze, B., & Badel, I. (2002). Temporal order relations in language comprehension. *Journal of Experimental Psychology: Learning, Memory, and Cognition, 28*(4), 770–779.

van Dijk, T.A. (1980). *Macrostructures: An interdisciplinary study of global structures in discourse, interaction, and cognition.* Hillsdale, NJ: Erlbaum.

van Dijk, T.A., & Kintsch, W. (1983). *Strategies of discourse comprehension.* New York: Academic Press.

Wade-Stein, D., & Kintsch, E. (2004). Summary Street: Interactive computer support for writing. *Cognition and Instruction, 22*(3), 333–362.

Zwaan, R.A., Magliano, J.P., & Graesser, A.C. (1995). Dimensions of situation model construction in narrative comprehension. *Journal of Experimental Psychology: Learning, Memory, and Cognition, 21,* 386–397.

Zwaan, R.A., & Radvansky, G.A. (1998). Situation models in language comprehension and memory. *Psychological Bulletin, 123*(2), 162–185.

11

A SOCIOCOGNITIVE MODEL OF MEANING-CONSTRUCTION

The Reader, the Teacher, the Text, and the Classroom Context

Robert B. Ruddell, Norman J. Unrau, and Sandra McCormick

Early in the 20th century, Huey (1908/1968) described the process of reading as the "most remarkable specific performance that civilization has learned in all its history" (p. 6). The model, depicted in Figure 11.1, provides insight into many of the intricacies involved in this extraordinary act called *reading,* from a sociocognitive point of view. Specifically, the model proposes the factors that are involved when "meaning is constructed" interactively within social environments comprised of *readers, teachers, texts*, and *classroom contexts*, and it demonstrates how these four components often are in a state of dynamic change and interchange while individuals are engaged in making sense of print. The model supports the view that understanding text is not a static endeavor in which the text is the only conveyer of meaning, but, rather, a *meaning-construction process*, with meanings constructed as a result of a variety of interactions with a text.

The Reader, the Text and Classroom Context, and the Teacher: An Overview

For our sociocognitive interactive model, reading is conceptualized as a meaning-construction process in the instructional context of the classroom. A survey of the model reveals three major components (as shown in Figure 11.1): the reader, text and classroom context, and teacher. As the reading process occurs, these three components are in a state of dynamic change and interchange while meaning negotiation and meaning construction take place. Our discussion of the model begins with the reader component because the reader is at the center of meaning construction. We then examine the teacher component as the instructional decision making proceeds. Next, we discuss the text and classroom context and apply the process to a high school English classroom. We conclude with selected implications for research and practice.

The Reader

As we consider various factors that contribute to the readers' meaning-construction process, we should keep in mind that reader-related factors function simultaneously and in an integrated manner. These relationships are portrayed in Figure 11.1 by the circular flow of arrows surrounding the section titled "Prior Beliefs and Knowledge," as well as by the two-way arrows connecting various reader components.

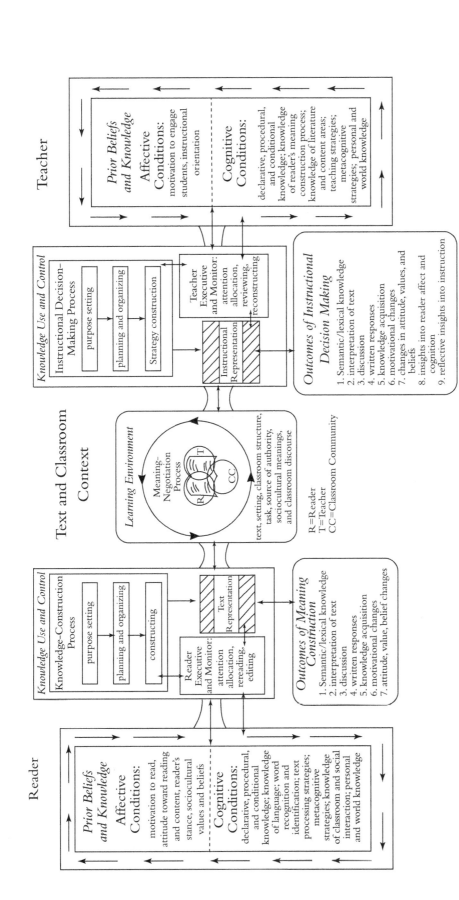

Figure 11.1 Reading as a Meaning-Construction Process: The Reader, the Text, and the Teacher

Prior Beliefs and Knowledge

Prior beliefs and knowledge are preexisting factors, both *affective* and *cognitive*, influencing a reader's understanding of text. *Beliefs* include opinions, assumptions, and convictions based on life experiences. These beliefs impact affective conditions critical to the meaning-construction process such as *motivation to read, attitude toward reading, attitude toward specific content, stance,* and *sociocultural values and beliefs* (see Figure 11.1).

In our model, *knowledge* refers to both concepts and procedures and includes *declarative knowledge, procedural knowledge,* and *conditional knowledge* (Alexander & Judy, 1988). Other forms of knowledge relate to *language, word recognition and identification, text-processing strategies, metacognitive strategies, classroom and social interaction procedures, as well as personal and world knowledge.* All of these knowledge forms are discussed in a later section.

Affective Conditions

As noted in Figure 11.1, prior beliefs and prior knowledge exert influence on *motivation to read* that springs from each reader's motivational system. We view that system as a network of interacting forces prompting a reader's activation and engagement. These potential motivational forces can be activated through mechanisms and processes both within readers and in their environment. Viewing motivational potential within a motivational system for reading engagement offers us the opportunity to integrate multiple motivational resources and to understand how they may interact and compliment each other as individuals operate as learners in their social contexts. (See Taboada Barber et al., Chapter 12 this volume.)

Motivation has been described as a condition of wanting to perform a specific activity, such as reading, in a given context (Schiefele, 2009). Self-processes constitute a major factor determining the strength and persistence of a reader's motivation. Self-efficacy is a vital self-process that has received attention in investigations of motives that drive and control our actions and learning (Linnenbrink-Garcia & Patall, 2016). Bandura (1986) conceived of self-efficacy as a personal belief about what an individual is capable of learning or doing by means of organizing and carrying out actions that lead to a successful outcome. Self-efficacy has been demonstrated to exert a profound influence on student motivation for learning (Schunk & Pajares, 2009). More specifically, the beliefs people have about their capability, for example, as readers, serve as better predictors of their behavior than what they actually accomplish (Bandura, 1997).

Self-efficacy for reading is a reader's perceptions of competence in their ability to successfully complete reading tasks (Guthrie & Coddington, 2009). Readers are more likely to demonstrate effort and persistence in reading a text if they believe in their capacity to comprehend it successfully (Solheim, 2011). We could expect, therefore, that readers with high self-efficacy in reading engage in more reading-related activities over longer periods of time than those with lower self-efficacy. Readers with higher levels of reading self-efficacy are also apt to have higher levels of reading comprehension, and, because we have found that self-efficacy is malleable, it is susceptible to instruction leading to its growth (Unrau et al., 2017).

Another critical factor shaping reading motivation is the value readers place on successfully understanding a text (Guthrie & Klauda, 2014). For example, prior knowledge may inform a reader that passing a driver's test is more likely to be in the cards if one has genuinely comprehended the information in the driver's manual. Or, former experiences may strongly imply that a good grade on a mid-term might not be possible if there have not been good interpretations of information in the class history book. Motivation to achieve any such valued outcomes as these and others, in turn, prompts readers to read carefully and deeply.

In their engagement model of reading development, Guthrie and Wigfield (2000) identified several variables contributing to motivation that are affected in some way by prior beliefs or prior knowledge, including teacher evaluation, strategy instruction, and rewards and praise. Other identified motivators were teacher involvement, student-to-student collaboration, interesting texts, real-world interactions, autonomy support for individual student choice, and learning and knowledge goals. These processes may overlap and interact in any instructional context that theoretically could augment engagement, conceptual mastery, and reading achievement. Subsequent research (Guthrie, Wigfield, & You, 2012) exploring the implications of this engagement model has shown that students' motivation and engagement mediate the impact of classroom practices on student achievement outcomes. Other research suggesting modification of the engagement model to capture the impact of student-teacher relationships in the classroom has underscored the vital importance of the quality of those relationships to learning outcomes, especially for struggling readers (Unrau, Ragusa, & Bowers, 2015).

Closely related to motivation, the reader's *attitude toward reading and toward specific text content* also are impacted by pre-existing beliefs and knowledge (Figure 11.1) (Mathewson, 2004; Shnayer, 1969). As examples, previous experiences may lead a reader to believe that reading is only a burdensome school task, not an activity for enjoyment, or, conversely, may lead to the belief that reading is one of the best ways to spend free time. Attitude toward reading in general has a high correlation with the amount of voluntary reading in which a reader participates (McCormick & Zutell, 2015). This is an important consequence since a necessary correlate to reading competence is interaction with an abundance of connected text material of different genres. A positive attitude increases a reader's intention to read—and the inclination to spend considerable time doing so. A negative attitude likely will do neither.

Attitude to specific text content often is predicated on a reader's interests, on a match between the reader's prior reading development level and the difficulty level of the text, on amount of background knowledge the reader brings to the material, on the author's writing style, and, in school contexts, on the instructional setting provided by the teacher. In some cases, readers, especially good readers, will persevere with and comprehend text that is above their instructional levels if they have high interest in its content (Shnayer, 1969).

Positive attitudes toward reading and toward text content produce engaged readers. The motivation research undertaken at the National Reading Research Center resulted in important findings about engaged readers. In this use, "engaged" refers to being involved, engrossed, absorbed in acts of reading. Engaged readers not only read larger amounts of text, but also put more effort into using reading strategies that aid understanding (Guthrie & Klauda, 2014).

Another element that may be affected by prior beliefs and prior knowledge is the reader's *stance*. "Stance" refers to an emotional or intellectual attitude that a reader assumes in relation to a given text. For example, if an individual who is a progressive democrat is told that the policy paper he or she is about to read was written by a conservative republican (or, vice versa), the reader may approach this text with the attitude that there will be much in the paper that is incorrect, adopting this perspective before beginning to read.

Theorists and researchers have described several different stances that readers may adopt (e.g., Beach & Hynds, 1990.) If a reader chooses a library book on a topic about which he or she has learned interesting information in the past, this reader may focus on ideas and concepts to be taken away from the text, a stance referred to by Rosenblatt (see Chapter 23 this volume) as an "efferent stance"; this is opposed to an "aesthetic stance" in which the reader is absorbed in a text world of imagination and feelings where "attention is focused on what [the reader] is living through during the reading event" (Rosenblatt, 1985, p. 38). These stances are not strict categories but reside on a continuum along which the degree of emphasis may change as the reader progresses through a text. Note that the reader's perspective and orientation are influenced both by the nature of the text and by the desired interaction with the text.

The stance taken is, to varying degrees, under the reader's control (although it can be influenced by a teacher in a classroom context). It is because stance often is under the reader's control that it can be swayed by that individual's preexisting beliefs and knowledge.

The pre-existing *sociocultural values and beliefs* the reader has previously acquired through family, peer group, and community interaction have an effect on school success in general and reading development in particular (Gee, Chapter 5 this volume). According to Gee, reading is embedded in complex sociocultural systems that support reading's emergence in children. Children become socialized into what he calls Discourses—with a capital D to set it apart from discourse as plain language. While Discourses always involve language, they include how we use words in talking, writing, interacting, believing, valuing, and feeling to situate ourselves socially and culturally. Gee states, "Being/doing a certain sort of physicist, gang member, feminist, first-grade child in Ms. Smith's room, special ed (SPED) student, regular at the local bar, or gifted-upper-middle class child engaged in emergent literacy all are Discourses" (p. 000). As identity kits, Discourses reflect who we are and how we behave as a student or teacher or in a wide range of other social roles.

While we become socialized into a Discourse, we also develop an accompanying cultural model about the world that is shared by people who are socialized into that Discourse. Gee (see Chapter 5 this volume) points out that theories and beliefs about childhood development and early literacy within a cultural model often shed light on children's early reading, writing, speaking, and listening.

The influence of family and previously developed cultural values on schooling is clearly depicted in Heath's (1983, 2013) research. She describes literacy development in three communities: Trackton (a Black mill community), Roadville (a White mill community), and Gateway (a "mainstream" urban community). Trackton children experienced a social environment in which the community shared in teaching and in uniting the youngsters with the community. Children, especially boys, were expected to respond creatively to challenging questions. Stories they created were designed to exaggerate "truth," glorify self, and entertain the listener. Few children's books or book-reading activities were found in the homes. Roadville children were reared in an environment where parents talked with their babies, modified their language to involve their children, and used interactional patterns that included answering questions, labeling, and naming objects. The children were expected to accept the power of print through association with alphabet letters and workbook-like activities. Stories were characterized by truthfulness and carried a moral message. In Gateway, a high value was placed on schools and schooling for both black and white children. From an early age, families nurtured their children's interest in books. Parents frequently asked their children information-type questions and developed book-sharing routines. The children often saw parents and siblings reading for a variety of purposes. Heath concluded that the Gateway children acquired values about reading and writing unfamiliar to the Trackton and Roadville children. The Gateway children were acquainted with both book-reading routines and comprehension strategies. The language and literacy practices of the Trackton and Roadville children needed to be bridged into the school.

Sociocultural values and beliefs constitute an important aspect of the reader's affective conditions for learning. The teacher must exercise understanding and sensitivity to these values and beliefs if the reader's potential for success is to be enhanced.

Cognitive Conditions

Cognitive conditions and various knowledge forms, to which we now turn, play a vital part in the reading process. First, we consider the role of *declarative, procedural, and conditional knowledge* in meaning-construction (see Figure 11.1). Declarative knowledge includes the reader's "what" knowledge of facts, objects, events, language, concepts, and theories about the world. The reader's procedural knowledge consists of how-to skills and strategies for using and applying knowledge, ranging from using a context strategy in identifying a new word to the use of a text-organization strategy in reading a chapter. Conditional knowledge accounts for the reader's awareness of knowledge use. This may be viewed as "when" and "why" knowledge, which provides for application of declarative and procedural knowledge (Paris, Lipson, & Wixson, 1983). The reader's previously learned declarative, procedural, and conditional knowledge are stored in memory and include a variety of other knowledge forms essential to meaning construction, as noted in Figure 11.1. Before discussing these other knowledge forms, we will briefly examine how any knowledge is represented in memory.

In our model, we assume that the reader's declarative, procedural, and conditional knowledge all are stored in knowledge structures known as schemata. Furthermore we assume that those schemata were acquired in social contexts and are socioculturally embedded (McVee, Dunsmore, & Gavelek, 2013). Schemata can be thought of as information modules, each of which is used to organize a particular class of concepts formed from our prior experience. As described in work by Rumelhart (1981, 2013) and Kintsch (see Chapter 10 this volume) these information modules, or, knowledge structures, are composed of "slots" to be filled with specific information when a problem is to be solved or a text is to be processed. As knowledge is stored in memory, these structures set up expectations for the reader when new information is encountered. If new information fits the "slots" of an existing schema (the singular form of "schemata") to the point where it becomes filled with concrete instances that fit—a condition called *instantiation*, that schema may be taken to be the "correct" one when the reader is trying to find meaning for the new information, and in that case, it is said to exert control over the reader's meaning-construction process (Anderson, 2013).

The explanatory power of schema theory is found in the idea that the first level of any schema provides for a conceptual framework for all events that fall below it that are within its domain. For example, a schema such as "going to the grocery store" may represent an overarching information module that a grocery store is a business establishment where one purchases food to take home to use in meal preparation. Below this global concept are more specific schemata such as going to a large food market or to a small corner store.

Schemata have important meaning-construction roles. They assist in recall, allow inferences to be made, permit reorganization of text content, and are helpful in summarizing content. A reader's schema appears to function by using the following properties: (a) procedural information that allows the schema to become activated by interaction with a text; (b) inheritance, which simply means that a subschema acquires knowledge from a higher-level schema; (c) default values that provide for inferences based on the text; and (d) a hierarchical organizational structure, such as that exemplified by the previous example of the "going to the grocery store" schema.

The view of schemata as rigid knowledge structures used to direct the comprehension of texts has been expanded to include an alternative perspective that views schemata as "knowledge resources" for the building of new knowledge structures (Spiro, Coulson, Feltovich, & Anderson, 2013). In this less linear, more flexible perspective, the reader does not fill slots. Instead, he or she takes chunks of knowledge from several different existing hierarchically designed, and in some way related, knowledge structures. From these, the reader assembles new meanings far more complex than any one hierarchically designed knowledge structure. The newly constructed schema allows for more elaborate interconnections and accounts for more effective problem solving and meaning construction than does the hierarchical schema that provides for a sole meaning representation.

Certain researchers (e.g., Sadoski & Paivio, 2001, 2013, see Companion Website) have challenged schema theory, posing instead a dual-coding theory of verbal and nonverbal knowledge representation. The nonverbal imagery system, which is separate but connectable to the verbal system, includes all sensory modes, such as sight, smell, and sound, and has the capacity to evoke strong emotion and meaning through images. Such imagery often contributes to our aesthetic response to literature—for example, as Hester Prynne's *A* in *The Scarlet Letter* acts as an image that carries her anguish and consolidates meaning for many readers. Furthermore, research suggests that imagery plays an important role in the comprehension and long-term recall of both narrative and expository texts. At this time, however, schema theory provides strong explanatory power in accounting for the reader's knowledge representation and the role of this knowledge in the meaning-construction process (McVee, Dunsmore, & Gavelek, 2013).

We now turn to specific knowledge forms included in Figure 11.1 that are critical to the reader's meaning-construction process. Reading is a linguistically based process that requires *language knowledge* to construct meaning. That knowledge consists of schemata that represent orthographic, phonological, syntactical, and lexical information. These knowledge forms are well developed for most children long before the start of formal schooling (Cox, Fang, & Otto, 2004; Ruddell, 1974). The syntactical and lexical features, however, continue to increase in complexity throughout the school years (Juel & Minden-Cupp, 2004).

Phonological knowledge is internalized by about age 4 (Gibson & Levin, 1975). Children at this age choose words that conform to English phonology in contrast to sound clusters that do not follow English phonological rules—*klec* versus *dlek*, for example (Morehead, 1971). Upon entry into kindergarten or first grade, this system is near completion (Ervin & Miller, 1963).

Syntactical knowledge is also well developed before children begin to read. The capacity to understand and generate language is innate (Chomsky, 1965) but requires a social support system for development. This support system may develop in many different social settings. The development of syntactic knowledge previous to and during school years is well documented. Scollon (1979) discerned subtle syntactic forms when children begin to speak in two-word utterances, while Dore (1979) demonstrated that preschoolers have a significant command of conversational skills and what can be done with language. The close connection between syntactical complexity and reading comprehension has also been established (Ruddell, 1965). Together, these studies demonstrate that potential for developing syntactic knowledge appears to be inborn, that its manifestations begin early in the socially stimulated language environment, and that it directly affects the ability to read.

Lexical knowledge refers to knowledge of words and word meanings. Lexical knowledge is directly related to comprehension and meaning construction as demonstrated by a range of vocabulary research (e.g., Brinchmann, E. I., Hjetland, H.N., & Lyster, S. H., 2016; Kuhn & Stahl, 2013; Wright & Cervetti, 2017). Estimates indicate that children expand their vocabulary at the rate of 2,700 to 3,000 words per year—or about seven words a day (Nagy & Scott, 2013). Not surprising, vocabulary knowledge and reading comprehension are positively related. Efficient meaning construction requires an understanding of concepts, and the reader must rely on an internal mental dictionary as a resource. The larger the lexicon, the larger the reader's capacity to comprehend what is read. Furthermore, the reader's speed of access to lexical knowledge is related to processing efficiency and meaning construction. Less efficient readers usually have slower lexical access speeds than those readers who are more efficient. This is explained by the rapid and nearly automatic access of concept knowledge stored in the schemata of the skilled reader.

Knowledge of *word recognition and identification* provides information that enables readers to transform visual symbols in print to meaning. This knowledge expands from preschool experiences with print to the later grades where skills are used in the conscious analysis of new words and in automatic processing of known words (Samuels, 2013, see Companion Website).

There is strong support for the idea that readers progress through several developmental phases in acquiring word knowledge (Frith, 1985; Mason, Herman, & Au, 1991), regardless of the instructional methodology used. Ehri's extensive research (1991, 1994; Ehri & McCormick, 2013) posits five such phases: (a) pre-alphabetic (uses visual, contextual, or graphic cues), (b) partial-alphabetic (uses letter-sound associations in a limited way), (c) full-alphabetic (uses letter-sound relationships), (d) consolidated-alphabetic (uses predictable letter patterns and word parts), and (e) automatic-alphabetic (uses multiple sources to verify word recognition and support automaticity).

Thus, as the reader becomes more skilled, progress is made from learning how the spelling system symbolizes phonemes in speech to orthographic (that is, spelling pattern) processing of predictable letter combinations and eventually to the automatic recognition of words. The principles acquired enable the reader to recode unfamiliar word spellings phonologically. This recoding in turn provides access to word meanings. However, when a reader automatically recognizes words, phonologically recoded information may not be activated. The spelling of specific words held in memory may thus serve to represent pronunciation (Ehri, 1994; Samuels, 2013, see Companion Website).

The role of *text-processing strategies* in the present model is critical as the reader interprets narrative or expository text. These strategies are stored as mental schemata and hold the key to understanding text-pattern organization. Narrative text structure, often referred to as "story grammar," accounts for setting, characters, plot structure, climax, and resolution. Schemata for expository writing account for structures such as comparison-contrast, cause-effect, problem-solution, thesis-support, or enumeration of ideas.

At the preschool and kindergarten levels, children develop an understanding of story construction that moves through several stages, from picture-governed attempts in which the story is not formed to print-governed reading in which the story read closely follows the print (Sulzby, 1985). For beginning readers, the development of a concept of story structure evolves from unorganized lists of events to full narrative forms. This progression culminates in the understanding that stories follow an organizational pattern (Hiebert & Martin, 2004).

Through experience with narrative reading, the reader develops a sense of story pattern that provides for expectations useful in constructing meaning. The understanding of these text patterns, in effect, enables the reader to form a plan for reading. The plan for narrative text structures enables the reader to direct attention to making inferences and memory searches using prior knowledge and to predict features useful in the comprehension process.

Expository reading also relies on a reader's awareness of text organization. The identification of the organizational plan of a text leads to more effective understanding. For example, the reader encountering a text that explores cause-effect relationships reads and comprehends the text better by using a cause-effect text schema. Research evidence suggests that instruction, including web-based tutoring systems, can assist students in identifying organizational structures in expository text and in using these structures to more effectively construct meaning (Meyer & Poon, 2004; Pyle et al., 2017; Wijekuman, Meyer, & Lei, 2017).

Knowledge of text organization enables highly efficient top-down text processing in the meaning-construction process. More skilled readers are highly effective in using text structure strategies in immediate and delayed recall of text information. Less-skilled readers sometimes appear not to have developed these important meaning-construction strategies or are unable to apply them in the comprehension of text.

In the model, the reader's *metacognitive strategies* provide for self-monitoring and self-correcting routines used in meaning construction (Anderson & Kaye, 2017). Following years of research, educators widely agree that metacognition includes (a) knowledge of one's own knowledge and cognitive processes and (b) ability to monitor and regulate one's knowledge and cognitive processes (e.g., Baker, 2005; Griffith & Ruan, 2005; Hacker, 2004). Metacognitive strategies while reading include monitoring levels of text difficulty, depth and relevance of background knowledge, problems in comprehension, meaningful text processing, and progress toward setting and reaching reading goals (Afflerbach & Cho, 2010). Metacognitive strategies direct interactive processing as needed, drawing on prior knowledge of language, word recognition and word identification skills, and text-processing strategies.

Emergence of metacognitive control appears to take place in preschool years. Researchers note that literacy-related metacognitive strategies such as planning, monitoring, checking, evaluating, and revising are found in the utterances of 4- and 5-year-olds in pretend reading of storybooks (e.g., Rowe, 1989).

Other research indicates that skilled readers, in contrast to less-skilled readers, are more aware of the need to take corrective action when meaning difficulties are encountered (Ruddell & Speaker, 1985). In addition, while there is evidence that less-skilled readers use the same metacognitive decision-making strategies as more skilled readers, the strategies are used less often and less efficiently. Furthermore, less-skilled readers have more difficulty identifying the sources of problems if reading complex text; this may be attributed, in part, to the need for heavy allocation of their attention to word recognition and identification.

To effectively use text in the classroom, readers must have *knowledge of classroom and social interaction* patterns. As Dyson and Genishi (2013, see Companion Website) emphasize, literacy is centered in social activity and is much more than skills and strategies. Features of interaction patterns used in the classroom include message form, message content, addressor, addressee, audience, outcomes, tone, and manner (Hymes, 1974). Readers must internalize these features of classroom dialogue if appropriate and meaningful interaction is to occur.

They also must acquire communicative competence (Forman & Cazden, 2013). This includes not only the ability to respond to texts and to teacher but also to the complex social network of the classroom community. Teachers should be sensitive to the reader's understanding of the ways language can be used during classroom discussion and interaction (Knight, 2016).

Personal and world knowledge includes schemata representing a wide range of understandings that have been acquired both in school and out. This knowledge includes declarative forms (for example, historical information acquired during a field trip to a museum), procedural forms (such as how to activate a self-directed museum display), and conditional forms (illustrated by understanding the appropriate time to pose questions to the docent). Both personal knowledge and world knowledge are formed from the reader's life experiences and include facts and assumptions, actions and procedures, and understanding of appropriate conditions for knowledge use. Activation of these schemata directly affects interpretation of a text. Two readers with different personal and world knowledge schemata may read an ambiguous text and arrive at different interpretations (Hull & Rose, 2004).

In addition, intertextual references frequently influence the understandings readers achieve as they read (Hartman, 1991). "Intertextuality" is the process of connecting current texts with past texts to construct meaning. Those past texts are part of the reader's personal and world knowledge. In our model, the meaning of "text" is expanded to include not only printed texts but also the text of events, communication, and cultures (Bloome & Bailey, 1992). These texts range from art and music to ritual and gesture. Intertextuality is thus broadly conceived as the interaction between the text being read and the texts based on our experiences.

In short, the use of personal and world knowledge has a strong influence on the comprehension process. The reader who has a rich knowledge base and flexible access to that base can more effectively assemble a coherent and meaningful text representation than the reader who does not.

Knowledge Use and Control

The knowledge use and control component, seen in the model (Figure 11.1), directs the reader's meaning-construction process. As can be noted, this component is linked to, and interactive with, the reader's prior knowledge and beliefs. Knowledge use and control consists of three components: *the knowledge-construction process, text representation, and reader executive-and-monitor.*

The Knowledge-Construction Process

The reader's knowledge-construction process sets the purpose for reading and integrates prior beliefs and knowledge through planning, organizing, and constructing meaning. As meaning is formed, it is reflected in text representation. The reading executive-and-monitor oversees this entire process based on the original purpose and, if necessary, prompts reconstruction of purpose and meaning.

Purpose setting is initiated as the reader creates a goal or, more commonly, multiple goals when a text is encountered. This process reflects the reader's motivation or intent and is influenced by the affective and cognitive conditions noted in Figure 11.1. For example, the reader's stance may be aesthetic, anticipating the pleasure of entering an imaginary world of romance or intrigue, or the reader may take a predominantly efferent stance to learn more about dinosaurs, jellyfish, or electromagnets.

The learning environment created by the teacher can have a strong influence on the reader's purpose setting (Alvermann, Young, Green, & Wisenbaker, 2004). Assignments may require students to read efferently and attend to particular aspects of a text, such as claims used to support a thesis. Or, the teacher may encourage an aesthetic transaction with the text, for instance, to evoke the reader's feelings and attitudes toward key characters (Many, 2004).

As the reader's original goals are realized, other goals may become the focus of attention. Thus, purpose setting for the reader is usually in flux as goals, both conscious and unconscious, are made and met.

Planning and organizing take place simultaneously as the reading process is established. The reader begins to form a plan based on the structure of the text (e.g., on whether it is a narrative, story-type structure or an informational structure) and develops an action plan to achieve the reading purpose. The reader's plans may include a *top-down* approach to knowledge construction. Top-down information refers to many forms of knowledge held in long-term memory, in other words, prior knowledge. This approach often is expectation driven. As one example, when starting to read a science experiment based on background knowledge about that text type, there may be expectations that prompt readers to invoke a cause and effect schema when considering their reading plan.

However, with some texts, the reading plan must initially focus on *bottom-up* processing. Bottom-up processing refers to cognitive activities stimulated by a reader's perceptions of printed words. An example of a text necessitating bottom-up processing is technical prose containing an abundance of vocabulary unfamiliar to the reader. Plainly speaking, with such texts, the reader must first decode words and attach meanings to them to allow meaningful clauses and sentences to form. The cognitive components of comprehension presented in this model rely on top-down and bottom-up processes interacting.

Reading is a process of *constructing*, of knowledge integration, and of building meaning. The goals that the reader forms, the plans adopted or created, and the organizing that occurs as text is processed and interpreted contribute to the text-constructing process. For some kinds of texts (especially narrative), the reader often constructs meaning as schemata that are activated and instantiated. But that top-down process alone is not sufficient, especially for complex expository and narrative forms.

Bottom-up processing refers to cognitive activities stimulated by a reader's perceptions of printed words on a page. However, these perceptions and word activations from the bottom-up contribute to the formation of propositions in the reader's mind. They represent meaningful clauses and sentences to the reader. A proposition is a basic unit of meaning. Kintsch (1998) defined an atomic proposition as a linguistic unit made up of a predicate and one or more concepts. For example, "The ball is round," as an atomic proposition becomes [ROUND, BALL]. Essentially, it's the smallest unit of knowledge that can be put to a test of being true or false (Bauer, 1994). However, the propositions that are formed bottom-up together with a reader's top-down long-term memory combine to form a network of activated ideas in working and long-term memory. The constructed plasma of propositions and activated memories, some relevant and some less so, may be quite chaotic. The elements contributing to that chaos are eventually sorted out so that relevant features remain activated in working memory or at a threshold state in long-term memory while irrelevant features fade away. As chaotic conditions subside, the emerging pattern of activated meanings soon becomes stabilized into what the reader experiences as comprehension. This proposition-construction process followed by the integration of features that must satisfy certain relevancy constraints is similar to Kintsch's (1998) construction-integration (or CI) theory. However, the model of reading presented here, while drawing upon Kintsch's work, also draws upon the research and perspectives of many other reading researchers and theorists.

Text Representation

As the interactive bottom-up and top-down processes of creating meaning proceed, readers construct multiple forms of text representation. In this case, "representation" refers to images and ideas formed by the mind in reaction to a stimulus—the stimulus in this instance being the printed page. These representations range from literal interpretations of the letters, words, clauses, and sentences on a page to a personal interpretation created through knowledge and experience activated from long-term memory. While struggling readers may have trouble constructing even basic text representations, proficient readers are often facile negotiators of multiple representations.

Reader Executive-and-Monitor

Managing and overseeing the meaning-construction process is the reader executive-and-monitor. As shown in Figure 11.1, it is linked by two-way arrows with the knowledge-construction process, text representation, and prior knowledge and beliefs. Researchers and theorists (e.g., Baddeley, 2007; Semma, Mahone, Levine, Eason, & Cutting, 2009) believe the executive-and-monitor, as part of an evaluative function, intervenes to *allocate attention* to the repair of meaning breakdowns when they are detected. This may require the search for and accessing of additional information in prior knowledge, shifts of attention to *reread* parts of the text, shifts in reading stance, or even altering the reading purpose. During class discussions, the reader interacts not only with the text but also with the teacher's discourse and classmates' responses. Under these conditions, more cognitive functions are activated and more attention management is required than during individual text reading. Because of the range of tasks, the reader's executive-and-monitor must make decisions about which cognitive tasks will be given most priority. As text meaning construction is represented in the mind of the reader, that representation undergoes a reviewing process that is under the control of the reading executive-and-monitor. The reader's text representation may be reviewed depending on the difficulty of the text, and that review may result in *editing* through further planning, organizing, and reconstructing until the reader creates a text representation that is coherent and meaningful. Time allocated to reading the text is also determined by this component. Skilled readers, for example, have been shown to adjust their reading rates and time allocation in relation to the reading purpose (Reynolds, Standiford, & Anderson, 1979) and comprehension difficulty of the text (Wagner & Sternberg, 1987).

Outcomes of Meaning Construction

During and after reading, the reader develops a number of text-related outcomes. These outcomes are identified in Figure 11.1.

While reading, the reader employs word identification and language information to develop *semantic and lexical knowledge*, which includes the learning of new words, their range of meanings, and their use. Often context assists the reader in deciding which meanings are appropriate for the text being read. *Interpretation of text* based on prior knowledge and beliefs may be the central goal for the reader. Most readings of text in classroom settings will lead to *discussion* of the text. Discussion is a valuable outcome for teacher and readers as they explore responses to the text and expand their understanding and knowledge base. *Written responses* offer the reader an opportunity to understand, synthesize, and clarify what has been learned from the text through its reading and discussion. A wide range of written responses to texts is possible, extending from an expression of the reader's feelings and emotions to the creation of new works that expand on the reader's understanding and beliefs about a text. *Knowledge acquisition* includes specific domain knowledge, such as categories, concepts, and processes.

While readers learn to read, they read to learn. *Motivational changes* can influence the reader's attitude toward reading and the reader's intention to continue to read. If the reader reads because of an internally driven desire or if meaningful learning accompanies reading, *motivation* to read—and to learn—is likely to increase, especially if the reader believes he or she has accomplished reading tasks successfully and so enhanced self-efficacy. However, motivation can diminish if enjoyment and expectations are not fulfilled. The final outcome of the meaning-construction process shown in the figure is the reader's *attitude, value, and belief change*. Rich and rewarding personal experiences with books can change the way a reader feels, acts, and perceives. Through reading, students can experience new and enchanting narrative worlds, discover new and tantalizing subjects, and gain new knowledge of themselves and others.

In our exploration of the process that enables readers to construct meaning, we have identified a number of interacting components. We now turn to the role of the teacher in facilitating a reader's construction of meaning.

The Teacher

Teachers who have been influential in the academic and personal lives of students possess a number of common characteristics (Ruddell, 2004, 2009). These teachers consistently use clearly formulated instructional strategies that include focused goals, plans, and monitoring for student feedback. They possess in-depth knowledge of reading and literacy processes as well as content knowledge, and they understand how to teach these processes effectively to students. They also frequently tap internal student motivation, stimulate intellectual curiosity, explore students' self-understanding, and encourage engagement in problem solving. These influential teachers reveal something else in their instruction that promotes motivation to learn: They are warm, caring, and flexible, while having high expectations for themselves and their students. Furthermore, they are concerned about their students as individuals in the social context of the classroom.

As seen in Figure 11.1, the teacher components of our model parallel those of the reader components. In the following sections, we briefly explore these teacher components.

Prior Knowledge and Beliefs

The teacher's prior knowledge and beliefs consist of affective and cognitive conditions based on and shaped by a wide range of life experiences. These conditions have a strong influence on knowledge use and control, instructional decision making, and instructional outcomes in the learning environment.

Affective Conditions

The teacher, like the reader, holds beliefs based on opinions, assumptions, and convictions. Teacher beliefs have a direct impact on the affective conditions that influence the teacher's instructional purpose, plan, and strategy construction. The teacher's *motivation to engage students* is to a significant degree shaped by his or her instructional orientation, driven by the desire to create an optimal learning environment where students will participate fully and persist in meaning construction. In this process the "fit" between text content, text complexity, and the student's interests and reading ability is of central importance. In the following discussion, we focus specifically on a teacher's instructional orientation and its components.

Instructional orientation, or the alignment of teacher and student with a teaching or learning task, affects student motivation and engagement. Several critical factors make up instructional orientation, for example, (a) achievement goals, (b) task values, and (c) sociocultural values and beliefs. Achievement-goal theory stresses the engagement of the individual in selecting, structuring, and making sense of achievement experience. Research has focused on two kinds of achievement goals: mastery (or task-oriented goals) and performance (or ego-oriented goals). Individuals seeking mastery goals are intrinsically motivated to acquire knowledge and skills that lead to their becoming more competent. Individuals who are pursuing performance goals are eager to demonstrate their skills or knowledge in a competitive, public arena. Perceptions of ability have been shown to be one critical factor that influences patterns of achievement (Guthrie & Klauda, 2014). If individuals believe they can become better teachers by making an effort, they are more likely to embrace a mastery-goal orientation. They see themselves as able to improve over time by making an effort to master challenging tasks. By making the effort to acquire knowledge and skills, teachers' feelings of self-worth and competence are likely to increase, as is their intrinsic motivation (Ryan & Deci, 2009).

Several interacting components that make up an individual's perception of task values, such as those related to reading tasks, have been identified and investigated (Guthrie & Klauda, 2014). These components include attainment value (the importance an individual attributes to a task), intrinsic-interest value (the task's subjective interest to an individual), utility value (the useful-ness of a task in light of a person's future goals), and the cost of success (the "disadvantages" of accomplishing a task, such as experiencing stress). Both students and teachers commonly evaluate a task's values before undertaking it. While students are likely to ask themselves how a reading assignment might contribute to their understanding of a topic in which they are interested, teach-ers may consider the value of redesigning a reading lesson in terms of its usefulness as a vehicle to improve student performance.

A teacher's sociocultural values and beliefs, what Gee (see chapter 5 this volume) would refer to as their Discourse and its related cultural model, have a profound effect on relationships with students, instructional decision making, and the interpretation of texts. Students are vulnerable to breakdowns in communication if their sociocultural values and beliefs do not match those of the teacher or if the teacher is not responsive to cultural differences (Hull & Rose, 2004). As Heath (1983) discovered, teachers can also positively affect students who enter school cultures that are divergent from those in which they grew up. Through the building of relationships, reflection, and self-exploration, teachers can become more responsive to students' sociocultural backgrounds and design classroom instruc-tion that takes divergent perspectives into consideration, a move that is likely to enhance students' motivation and engagement.

Cognitive Conditions

As with learners, a teacher's cognitive conditions include specific types of knowledge forms stored as *declarative knowledge* ("what"), *procedural knowledge* ("how to"), and *conditional knowledge* ("when" and "why"). These cognitive knowledge forms are highly interactive with one another and with the affective conditions, as illustrated by the broken line separating them in Figure 11.1.

The teacher's *knowledge of the reader's meaning-construction process* is essential to instruction and instructional decision making. We assume the teacher constructs meaning from text by relying on the same processes. The meaning-construction process is discussed in depth throughout our earlier exploration of the reader component of the model. That discussion assumes a constructivist per-spective that views the creation of meaning as an active comprehension process in the social context of the classroom. As indicated, this takes into account the reader's prior knowledge and beliefs as meaning construction occurs and text representation is formed under the control of the reader's executive-and-monitor. Meaning negotiation in the classroom social context among teacher, reader, and classroom community is an important part of this meaning-construction process, as we shall see in our later discussion.

Knowledge of literature and content areas constitutes a store of information critical to instruc-tion. This knowledge, largely declarative in nature, is acquired through academic experiences and enriched through personal and world knowledge. Knowledge of this type ranges from familiarity with accepted literary principles to an understanding of important concepts in science, mathemat-ics, and the social sciences. It also includes an understanding of the organization of both narrative and expository text and related text-processing strategies. The teacher selects literary works that are likely to engage students and to move them toward deeper understandings of various literary forms and techniques or chooses expository prose to provide students with opportunities for optimum growth in understanding language structures and stylistic approaches commonly used in persuasive or content area texts, such as history or science (Unrau, 2008a).

Knowledge of teaching strategies (cf., "communities of practice," Wenger (1998)) is obviously decisive in the teacher's instructional decision making. Teaching-strategy knowledge may consist of understandings that provide for general problem solving or of strategies that can be used in reaching specific instructional goals. Such strategies are illustrated by the following: the Directed Reading–Thinking Activity or DRTA (Stauffer, 1976), designed to establish reader predictions, confirmations, and conclusions in narratives; the Prereading Plan or PREP (Langer, 1981), which serves to activate and assess reader background knowledge before reading narrative or expository material; the Question–Answer Relationships strategy or QARS (Raphael, 1982), which serves to assist the reader in connecting reading purpose to text and to personal information sources; the Reciprocal Teaching strategy (Brown, Palincsar, & Armbruster, 2013), which uses teacher modeling to clarify and summarize meaning, develop student predictions, and generate questions; Students Achieving Independent Learning (SAIL) (Brown, Pressley, Van Meter, & Schuder, 2004), which provides low-achieving second graders with multiple-strategies instruction; and TASK (Thesis Analysis and Synthesis Key; Unrau, 1992, 2008b) or PAPA Square (Hairston, 1986), which guide students through the process of analyzing argumentative expository texts. Knowledge of and ability to use strategies such as these contribute to effective comprehension instruction (Raphael, George, Weber, & Nies, 2010) and the growth of students' metacognitive knowledge and skills (Israel, Block, Bauserman, & Kinnucan-Welsch, 2005).

An important part of the teacher's strategy knowledge resides in understanding and using formative assessments during instruction (Heritage, 2013). Teachers gather data about students' reading processes and interpret that information. The teacher's interpretation of the information provides insights into each reader's meaning-construction process and opportunities for feedback to the reader along with follow-up instruction to address the reader's learning needs for further growth.

Metacognitive strategies provide a resource to teachers for self-monitoring, self-regulation, and instructional decision making during and after instruction. Those resources are used by the teacher executive-and-monitor, guided by the instructional purpose, and are interactive with other cognitive and affective conditions. Teachers who work in the dynamic and complex social context of classrooms must think on their feet and think about their thinking at the same time—clearly a description of metacognition.

To activate and apply their metacognitive strategies, teachers need to have an independent spirit, what Duffy (2005) called "visioning," to construct and execute instruction in reading. While visioning, the teacher uses strategies to monitor, evaluate, regulate, and adjust instruction so that optimum conditions for learning prevail in the classroom. As instruction proceeds, the teacher must attend to a wide range of factors, including student responses, content of the lesson, instructional strategies, time constraints, and use of text and materials. The teacher must also be aware of communication breakdowns and possible ways to clarify meaning and alter instructional strategies to improve the meaning-negotiation process. Acute metacognitive awareness and skills are required to detect meaning difficulties, shift attention to understand the problem, and draw on specific strategies to correct the problem during instruction.

The teacher also learns what is working for students by reflecting on classroom interaction after instruction. By mentally replaying events, keeping a journal, videotaping, and using formative assessments the experienced teacher is able to reflect on the quality and productivity of the learning relationship with students. This reflection represents an attempt to discover what could be changed to improve instruction.

The teacher's *personal and world knowledge* represents those experiences acquired through life outside of school and academic experiences. Personal knowledge, formed from these experiences and bound by time and situation, is stored in episodic memory while world knowledge is represented by schemata in semantic memory (Anderson & Pichert, 1978; Tulving, 1983, 1986).

As with the student learner, the teacher's personal and world knowledge directly affect the construction of meaning and interpretation of text. However, the teacher's knowledge base usually has developed over a longer time or from a wider range of personal and world experiences.

As previously noted, the meaning of text as used in this model is expanded to include the "texts" from areas such as art, music, digital media, and cultural rituals. In this sense, the teacher's personal and world knowledge provide for interaction between the "texts" based on experience and the text being read. The extensive intertextual knowledge often held by the teacher can provide an important resource in instructional decision making and assist readers in the classroom to negotiate and construct meaning.

Knowledge Use and Control

The teacher's knowledge use and control component directs the instructional decision-making process, provides a mental instructional representation, and evaluates instructional purpose through the teacher executive-and-monitor. This component is closely connected to and interactive with prior knowledge and beliefs, as shown in Figure 11.1.

Instructional Decision-Making Process

The instructional decision-making process establishes *purpose setting* for instruction that reflects the teacher's instructional intent. The affective and cognitive conditions, as shown under prior knowledge and beliefs in Figure 11.1, help influence and shape this intent.

Planning and organizing draw on the teacher's knowledge of literature and content areas and of a reader's meaning-construction process. This may be reflected in the teacher's selection of a story or novel appropriate to the reader's interest and achievement level.

Strategy construction accounts for decisions made about teaching strategies designed to implement the selected instructional stance. For example, if stance toward a text is to be aesthetic and designed to focus reader responses on personal feelings and attitudes, question prompts to facilitate discussion and discovery will need to be more open-ended than would be the case with an efferent stance—for example, "How would you have felt and reacted had you been the first person to see the words *Some Pig* written in Charlotte's web in the barnyard that foggy morning?" In addition, the use of a reader response journal provides opportunities for students to record their responses and to share ideas and reactions in small-group discussions. The teacher's personal and world knowledge may be drawn on in such discussions to provide personal experiences that illuminate understandings related to the text.

Instructional Representation

An instructional representation is created in the teacher's mind during instructional planning, stimulated as the lesson's purpose, organization, and strategies are considered. As instruction is initiated with the students, the original representation begins to unfold and change with the ongoing instructional process. This representation is conceived of as an "instructional world" that reflects the instructional interaction with the students (Ruddell & Speaker, 1985).

Teacher Executive-and-Monitor

The teacher executive-and-monitor provides for managing and monitoring the instructional decision-making process and meaning construction. As noted in Figure 11.1, it is in a central position and linked to instructional representation, instructional decision making, and prior knowledge and beliefs.

The executive-and-monitor controls *attention allocation* during instruction, *reviewing* of interactions and content discussed, and guidance for *reconstructing* of inferences and conclusions. In effect, the executive-and-monitor evaluates the ongoing instructional process reflected in instructional representation. This teacher-monitoring process draws on assessment and metacognitive strategies to evaluate the relationship between the original instructional purpose, plan, strategy use, and meaning construction reflected in instructional representation. Assuming the classroom interaction and meaning-negotiation process are successful and aligned with the original purpose and plan, instruction proceeds; if they are not, a shift in plan and strategy may be necessary to achieve the original purpose more effectively.

Outcomes of Instructional Decision Making

Based on the instructional plan, the teacher usually has expectations that students will acquire knowledge or have significant experiences of a particular kind. The nature of the meaning-negotiation process, shaped by the teacher, strongly influences instructional outcomes. The teacher often obtains two kinds of outcomes arising from instruction. The first involves the teacher's perceptions of readers' understandings, and the second consists of the teacher's own insights.

During instruction, the teacher gains an understanding of the *semantic and lexical knowledge* that readers acquire. For instance, he or she may learn of readers' new word knowledge through direct instruction, meaning negotiation in large- and small-group discussions, formative assessments, student self-directed use of classroom resources, and other sources of information.

The reader's *interpretation of text* depends heavily on the instructional stance and strategies used by the teacher. Certainly, the teacher recognizes that the reader's prior beliefs and knowledge exert a strong influence on the text interpretation that is constructed (see Hull & Rose, 2004). The teacher's interpretation of text may also shift as a result of interaction in the classroom community.

During classroom *discussion* readers' personal responses and understandings of the text are expressed. The discussion may also alter the teacher's response to a text based on viewpoints derived from a reader's and the classroom community's perspective.

Written responses to text provide the teacher with an understanding of a reader's text interpretations. Possible responses that include straightforward summaries and syntheses, journal writing, and analytical or argumentative compositions reveal the reader's underlying beliefs and emotions that a text has evoked. Again, the teacher's belief about a text may be changed after reflection on the reader's written responses.

Readers' *knowledge acquisition* is evident to the teacher through their use of new concepts and fresh conceptions. This acquisition is heavily influenced by engagement of the reader's interests and motivation arising from dynamic comprehension, discussion, and writing activities. The teacher's acquisition of new knowledge is influenced in a similar manner.

While the teacher expects to observe *motivational changes* in the reader, these expectations may not always be realized. The teacher's knowledge of the reader's key interests and internal motivations makes possible the connection of readers with text of high interest to them. In addition, the teacher may derive insights into motivation to engage individual students based on reader response during instruction.

The teacher may recognize *attitude, value, and belief changes* through the reader's discourse involving text interpretations, discussions, and written responses. These activities enable the reader to examine closely held attitudes, values, and beliefs. In addition, the teacher may experience attitude, value, and belief change related to the text content based on the social interaction with students. The teacher's attitude toward readers may also change as a result of reader responses in the instructional setting.

A key instructional outcome for the teacher is found in *insights into reader affect and cognition*. Both direct classroom observation of the reader as he or she constructs meaning, as well as formative assessments provide "a window on the mind" that can lead to important insights. These may range from understanding of personal motivations and interests to conceptual knowledge and text-processing strategies.

Closely connected to these insights about readers is the outcome of *reflective insights into instruction*. As the teacher gains understanding of the reader in the context of instruction, reflective insight can provide opportunities for refining instruction. This may include use of specific reader motivation strategies, employment of a variety of active comprehension strategies, or incorporation of an instructional stance that recognizes the importance of active reader response.

Text and Classroom Context

Our model takes a constructivist perspective of learning in which the teacher creates a learning environment that engages the reader in active comprehension through confronting and solving authentic problems in a social context. In the text and classroom context, shown in Figure 11.2, this environment includes a meaning-negotiation process that accounts for text, task, source of authority, and sociocultural meanings.

The Learning Environment

The learning environment has a powerful influence on students' motivation to engage in learning (Langer, 2004). How teachers structure text-related tasks, who carries the power of authority, and concern for sociocultural meanings can make major differences in the goals that readers attempt to achieve and the way readers feel about themselves, their classmates, and their accomplishments (Alvermann et al., 2004).

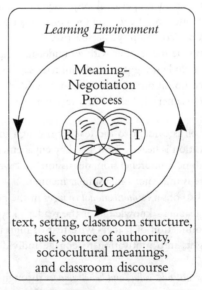

R=Reader
T=Teacher
CC=Classroom Community

Figure 11.2   The Text and Classroom Context

The learning environment influences not only the reader's decision to engage with a text but also the ways in which the text is engaged. We can expect the reader's engagement with reading, interaction with teacher and peers, and participation in the meaning-negotiation process if the reader is motivated to read and to learn, if prior beliefs and knowledge are activated, if tasks are personally relevant, and if active meaning construction is involved. The teacher who incorporates these features in the learning environment is considered to be mastery-goal oriented and is much more likely to produce productive learning in students.

Furthermore, the reader's motivation to achieve is enhanced if social goals and a constructivist view of learning have been integrated into the learning environment. These social goals include the influence of teachers and parents on children and the impact of cultural expectations on learning.

The Meaning-Negotiation Process

As shown in Figure 11.2, the meaning-negotiation process involves interaction between text (shown in the background representing a printed text), the reader (R), the teacher (T), and the classroom community (CC). During negotiation for meanings related to texts, readers bring their own meanings to the interaction, teachers bring their understanding of the text as well as their understanding of the reading process, and members of the class interact with the text to shape—and reshape—meanings. We hold, in the model, that meaning is not entirely in either the text or the reader but is created as a result of these sociocognitive interactions.

But, given the multitude of interpretations that readers can construct for a particular text, which one is to be accepted as correct or valid? The task of both students and teachers is to confirm that interpretations are indeed grounded in the actual text. This does not mean that the ultimate meaning is only in the text but that interpretations should be reasonably supportable with reference to events, statements, or claims that occur there and in relation to concepts or impressions evoked in the reader's mind. As Rosenblatt (1978) has observed,

> Fundamentally, the process of understanding the work implies a recreation of it, an attempt to grasp completely the structured sensations and concepts through which the author seeks to convey the quality of his sense of life. Each must make a new synthesis of these elements with his own nature, but it is essential that he evoke these components of experience to which the text actually refers.
>
> *(p. 113)*

Conversely, from the point of view of some critics and theorists, the opinions of a classroom community have been taken as a standard for validity (Fish, 1980). In this case, the meaning that is constructed as students and teacher interact is the only meaning that counts. While this view certainly frees readers from adherence to an objective standard—namely, the text—it obviously creates other problems. Thus, we find Rosenblatt's constraint upon interpretations most tenable for our model—that is, interpretation should be grounded in experiences "to which the text actually refers."

In Figure 11.2, the three overlapping circles symbolize the interactive nature of the meaning-negotiation process for teacher (T), reader (R), and classroom community (CC). However, as depicted here, that process overlaps the real text upon which a dialogue is based. Also noted in Figure 11.2, the circle with arrows surrounding the meaning-negotiation process symbolizes that meaning construction and negotiation are fundamentally cyclical. As readers and teacher voice their views about the meaning of a text, a cycle of hypothesizing and validation proceeds.

Thus, meanings are negotiated in classrooms among readers and between readers and teacher. Meanings are open, not closed or fixed, though they need to be grounded in text. Meanings are shaped and reshaped in a hermeneutic circle. As the reader's knowledge changes, as the reader interacts with other readers and with the teacher in a social context, constructed meanings can change. In a sense, while a text may be fixed, its meanings for the reader are always becoming.

Interacting Variables in the Meaning-Construction Process

In the model's learning environment, the meaning-negotiation process involves interplay across text, setting, classroom structure, task, source of authority, sociocultural meanings, and classroom discourse. Next, we briefly examine the role each of these plays in meaning construction.

Text meanings arise from the reader's meaning-construction process. Because the teacher and student bring different affective and cognitive states to the construction of a text representation, we expect different interpretations of a text. For this reason, the classroom necessarily becomes a forum for the articulation and negotiation of meanings. Those meanings shared by the entire class become part of the classroom community's intersubjective understanding of a text. However, even those shared meanings are also open for reinterpretation as the meaning-negotiation process continues in the context of classroom interaction.

The *classroom setting* refers to the immediate environment in which students and teachers interact. It includes the configuration of the classroom itself, the arrangement of desks, posters, pictures, examples of students' work, signs, bookcases, displays, quotations, and materials. For example, significantly different messages could be conveyed by a room whose desks are arranged in a circle, in several groups of three or four, or in rows with the teacher's desk facing the rows. Just as we are likely to do when reading a novel, we could ask ourselves what effects the setting is likely to have on the characters and actions that take place within that setting. The way a classroom's objects are arranged and displayed can stimulate students' interest in learning and their interests in topics. The environment can affect learning.

A *classroom structure* can convey information to observers about the kinds of knowledge delivery and knowledge generation that are valued by a teacher. Elements of classroom structure that signal this evidence include the teacher's daily routines, lesson plans, instructional strategies, management practices, behavioral expectations, and grade policies. Many times readers can determine, after a few classes, whether the teacher structures lessons for knowledge transmission or for knowledge construction or for some mix of modes. If lectures and recitation are dominant, the teacher's pedagogical preference may be read as transmission oriented. If small-group discussions, open-ended questions, and whole class conversations predominate, the teacher probably prefers a constructivist pedagogy that encourages students to discover or build knowledge in social contexts. Which of these pedagogies a teacher expresses can have consequences for students' levels of engagement and styles of interaction.

Task meanings, the interpretations assigned to tasks, have both an academic and social content (Harris, 1989). Academic meanings include understanding the goals for an activity, knowledge of subject matter, text structure, instructions, and knowing what will count as a completed task. Social meanings consist of understanding the relationship between teacher and reader, and understanding what rules will guide participation.

The interpretation of tasks, those structured activities designed or selected by the teacher and related to the text, may differ between teacher and reader. Interpretation differences are closely connected to children's success in the classroom (Dyson & Genishi, 2013, see Companion Website). The negotiation and interpretation of task meanings are important aspects of instruction.

Flower (1987) found that college students frequently interpret an assignment quite differently from one another and from the teacher. She discovered that the process was more problematic and perplexing for students than teachers thought. What teachers, as established members of a discourse community, may not realize is that forms of response that may be instructionally transparent to them—such as asking students to analyze their responses to a story—may be very difficult for students to construe. If a task is complex and less well-known to the reader, it may require elaborate interpretation to provide structure and meaning. For example, some tasks, such as writing a summary after reading, are represented automatically if the reader has a well-structured summary schema. If the reader lacks such a schema, the task may require elaborate interpretation to give it structure. It is thus important that the reader and the teacher construct and negotiate task meanings and also monitor those meanings.

Source of authority refers to an agreed upon understanding of where and in whom authority for constructed meanings resides. In classrooms, teachers and their students inevitably arrive at a decision about whom or what is the authority regarding the legitimacy of an interpretation—arriving at this conclusion as a result of multiple reading and interpreting events. That authority could reside solely in the text, solely in meanings that students construct as they interact with a text, solely with the teacher, or in a negotiated meaning arising from interaction of texts, students' meanings, and teacher's interpretations all within the classroom community. That is, the final arbiter of the source of authority for the meaning of a text could arise from the interactions among all these potential sources of authority.

Teachers usually decide for their classrooms how much time and thought will be given to negotiation over the source of authority for text meanings. To a significant degree, the content area in which we teach influences our decisions about appropriate sources of authority. For example, the most appropriate choice for source of authority may differ greatly when students are reading a science text versus a narrative poem. In addition, the teacher's belief about principles of learning may sway his or her thinking: Some may find the text speaks loudest; some may decide that a teacher's understandings should have most significant authority; some will encourage students to exercise textual authority; and some will negotiate the proper source of authority on different occasions.

Sociocultural meanings are influenced by the school and community ethos as well as the unique conglomeration of attitudes and values that arise in classrooms. The student and the teacher not only bring their own sociocultural values from prior beliefs and knowledge into the classroom, they also interpret the social life and culture they find there. Furthermore, each student and teacher may "read" various aspects of that sociocultural setting differently. While some students may believe that the culture of their school is supportive of their growth and development, other students—even ones in the same class—may be convinced that the school's culture is suffocating them and their identities (Ogbu & Simons, 1998). Teachers, like their students, may also have a range of sociocultural interpretations. In addition, some understandings of the social and cultural life of a school or classroom may be shared by most, if not all, participants. Sociocultural beliefs can undoubtedly impact interpretation of text.

Classroom discourse creates an abundance of oral texts that students and the teacher interpret. The origins of those texts—whether from the teacher or from students in discussions—can affect understanding. In many cases, students are strongly influenced by peers' opinions about text meanings; in others, they may be more secure in accepting a teacher's clarifications and explanations.

Also important is the perspective conveyed by the discourse. For example, in regard to the teacher's discourse, does he or she create oral texts that support the transmission of content or does the teacher generate questions that extend dialogue and discovery among students as they explore texts meanings? In regard to student discourse, their oral texts can express much more than an understanding of basic concepts. It can send information about a student's level of belief in that content and attitudes toward the content. Some teachers are exceptionally good readers of sub-surface messages that students broadcast, picking up deep levels of conviction to an interpretation or cynical disavowal delivered with subtlety.

In summary, the meaning-negotiation process involves a matrix of meanings that influence meaning construction, brought to the negotiation process by both reader and teacher. Furthermore, the classroom community exchanges and acquires group meanings that become influential in confirming validity upon interpretations. The teacher, meanwhile, assumes a critical role in the orchestration and negotiation of meaning in the text and classroom context.

Meaning Negotiation in the Classroom: An Example

A class of eleventh graders taught by Norman Unrau read a short story titled "The Laughing Man" by J. D. Salinger (1963). This is a love story seen through the eyes of a 9-year-old boy as he watches at a distance his baseball coach, John Gedsudski, weave through a relationship with his girlfriend, Mary Hudson. The coach, whom the young baseball players call "the Chief," has a talent for storytelling and imparts the tale of a "Laughing Man" who covers his disfigured face with a mask and combats evil in the underworld. The story of the Laughing Man reflects symbolically the course of the coach's relationship with his girlfriend and its ultimate end. The young baseball player and his teammates, who hear the story while traveling to and from games, suffer as they hear about the Laughing Man's death which echoes the end of the coach's relationship with his girlfriend.

To gather data on the meaning-negotiation process related to the story, Unrau maintained a teaching log, observation notes, and photocopies of students' logs over several days. Tasks for the readers included participation in a prediction strategy—designed to activate background knowledge and heighten motivation—in which they were asked to predict the story's content based on its title and discuss these predictions, after which they read the story. Subsequent tasks called for writing first meanings in their response logs and sharing these in small groups.

The source of authority for the validity of text interpretations was distributed among the class members—including Unrau. Authority was structured with the intent of placing a large portion of responsibility on students for forming and sharing meanings while Unrau encouraged the expression of those meanings that students had constructed.

Each small group's reporter presented the group's ideas to the whole class. Several students said that reading and discussing other student's interpretations made them think in new ways about the story's significance. As groups reported, Unrau encouraged elaboration of meanings. Concern was given not only to meanings for the whole story, but also for specific aspects of it. For example, students expressed different interpretations of a vial of eagle's blood, a vital food for the Laughing Man that he crushes in despair before he dies:

Erica: We thought it represented his love for Mary Hudson.
Unrau: How would that work out?
Erica: When their relationship was going well, the Laughing Man survived by drinking the blood. But when Mary and the Chief broke up, the Laughing Man crushed the vial, and he died along with his love for Mary.
Unrau: Sort of like his life blood being crushed?
Erica: Yeah, something like that.
Unrau: What other explanations came up in your small-group discussions?
Mark: I thought it stood for children in the Comanche Club (the baseball team's name).
Unrau: How does that work?
Mark: I don't know. Just seems that way.
Unrau: But we need to tie the meaning to something. Events in the story. Ideas you had when reading it. Something so it makes sense.
Mark: Seemed to me that the children of the Comanche tribe were keeping the Laughing Man alive.
Alison: I thought it was the baseball game.
Katie: Someone in our group said it stood for a false lifestyle.
Unrau: Does anyone want to explain how those meanings would make sense in the context of the story?
Katie: I don't know about baseball, but I thought that there was something false about how the Chief was living or his relationship with Mary and when the truth was out, the relationship died.

John: I'm not absolutely sure what the vial is, but, if it has a deep meaning, I'm sure it isn't baseball or the kids because they are not really deep issues. I can see the false lifestyle, but there are inconsistencies in the story because the Chief doesn't have a false life but a different life than the kids see. The mask would be more appropriate.

Unrau: What do you think the vial represents?

John: I'd have to agree with Erica. The vial would be Mary and the Chief's love.

Unrau explored these and other meanings with the students. He frequently asked them to explain how an interpretation could be grounded in the text and how it made sense in relation to the whole story. But he tried not to impose his own construal of the story on the students. The whole-class discussion gave students an opportunity to create a classroom community meaning for the story or parts of it. One student wrote, "The discussion changed my view of the story completely. I never saw any link between the coach's life and his bizarre stories. I didn't understand that the Laughing Man's death meant anything."

A few days after the discussions, each student wrote his or her current understanding of the story and described how and why their interpretations changed, if they had. Most students reported that they had formed or reformed meanings they had given to the story during or after the small-group and whole-class deliberations. Mira, who said she did not really have an understanding when she first read the story, arrived at a meaning that went significantly beyond that initial response. She wrote:

> I think that the story of the Laughing Man that the Chief would tell the Comanches was in a sense the way he saw himself. The Laughing Man was an alter ego of John Gedsudski, the Chief. Both were not handsome and shunned by the society and peers. Both had a band of loyal followers who looked up to them. For the Chief it was the kids; for the Laughing Man it was a dwarf, a Mongolian, and a beautiful Eurasian girl. At around the time that the Laughing Man is held captive by Dufarge, the Chief is having problems with Mary Hudson. When the Laughing Man gets shot, it is at the same time the Chief and Mary break up. This just enforces my theory that the Chief and Laughing Man are one in the same. The Chief takes the installments from his own day-to-day life, but he enhances them and makes them more exciting.

Students like Mira contributed to what became a classroom community meaning for the relationship between the Chief and the Laughing Man—that is, the two paralleled each other in many ways. As for the vial of eagle's blood that could have saved the Laughing Man, Mira wrote that it "represents the Chief's love for Mary".

Emily, whose initial rather stock response to the story was "You can't judge a book by its cover," later wrote that the story was "tragic." She thought that the Chief was so hurt and depressed by the breakup with Mary that he "took it out on the players." She wrote:

> That night, driving home on the bus, John began telling the story of the Laughing Man once again. In this final story, John killed the Laughing Man because Mary left him, and, because his love was taken away from him, he did the same to the Comanches. They loved the Laughing Man so John took him away from them.

Although Emily interprets the meaning of Laughing Man's death differently from Mira, she wrote that the vial of eagle's blood represented John's crushed love for Mary.

Many readers—the initially "clueless" as well as those who offered early interpretations—began to share a community interpretation of the story. Almost everyone agreed that a close correspondence existed between the Chief's life and that of the Laughing Man. Nevertheless, many readers held divergent meanings about other aspects of the story.

Being in an environment that allowed alternative readings was important to several students. Sarah wrote:

> Too many teachers think that their understanding is the only correct one. Now I understand that a story can mean so many things, and as long as you back it with at least some good thought, it's right for yourself. Now I feel I can just put more of my thoughts out there even if other people don't agree. I basically think that's the way my interpretation of "The Laughing Man" has changed. I think I have a little more freedom to say what I think.

While this example is from the high school level, the key model components can also be readily applied to the elementary school learning environment (Ruddell, 2009), as well as the college classroom (Hull & Rose, 2004).

Implications for Practice and New Research Directions

Our explanation of reading as a meaning-construction process is not only a theory but also a reality-based, classroom-centered model and accounts for interactions that involve the reader, the teacher, the text, and the classroom context. Instructional implications that derive from the model include the following:

1. Activation of the reader's prior beliefs and knowledge relative to the text is of central importance to effective meaning construction.
2. Mobilization of reader motivation, attitudes, values, and beliefs related to the text content is critical to attention focus, persistence, and the comprehension process.
3. Creation of a purpose to guide and focus meaning construction provides for higher interest in the reading comprehension process.
4. Recognition that meaning construction is a purposeful, interactive, and strategic process contributes significantly to the effective comprehension of narrative and expository texts.
5. Use of metacognitive strategies that assist in monitoring, rereading, and checking meaning construction is essential to the comprehension process.
6. Awareness of the most appropriate reader stance and teacher stance relative to the text and reading purpose serves to develop higher levels of motivation and comprehension.
7. Understanding by readers and teacher of varied classroom community sociocultural values provides more opportunities for active meaning negotiation in the classroom.
8. Sharing authority in the meaning-negotiation process allows readers to seek verification or validity for their interpretation within the classroom community rather than depending upon the sole authority of the teacher.
9. Encouraging readers to accept the premise that meanings evolve for both teacher and reader facilitates students' active meaning construction.
10. Engaging readers in understanding and reflecting upon divergent meanings increases the richness of interpretation within the classroom community.
11. Designing instructional activities that foster comprehension, discussion, and inclusion builds readers' perceptions that they are part of a classroom community.
12. Helping readers understand that they construct meanings not only of printed text but also of tasks, sources of authority, and their sociocultural environment furthers the understanding and creation of a context for learning that actively involves the reader and classroom community.

While reflecting on the design of our model of reading as a meaning-construction process, a number of specific research implications have emerged. These implications are intended to contribute to a fuller understanding of the processes that involve the reader, the teacher, and meaning negotiation of text within the classroom context. We briefly sample these research implications for each of the three major areas of the model.

Our discussion of the reader's prior knowledge and beliefs demonstrates that further research is needed to better understand the affective conditions that influence the reading process. We know, for example, that motivation to read changes as students progress through the grades, usually resulting in less independent, pleasure reading in older students. While we know that intrinsically motivated readers engage more frequently and for longer periods of time in reading, what constellation of motivational variables contributes to intrinsic motivation for reading and how could those variables be developed in classrooms? Sociocultural background has been found to shape classroom discourse, but how do differences in sociocultural beliefs mold interpretations of texts?

Several compelling issues are related to the reader's cognitive conditions and need further research. For example, to what degree can text-processing strategies improve comprehension of reading across content areas? There is also need for further research on metacognition, especially in meaning construction for early readers.

More research on processes that occur in the reader's knowledge use and control is also needed. For example, what effect on reading comprehension and discussion do students' self-selected purposes, together with teacher support for student autonomy, have in comparison to teacher-selected purposes? Do conscious and deliberate plans of action change reading outcomes? A number of intriguing issues need exploration to better understand the reader's executive-and-monitor. For instance, which functions and resources engaged during knowledge construction are most, and which are least, subject to direct control of an executive? Which functions and processes occur automatically? If they do operate automatically, what conditions enable those automatic functions to develop? Because neurological correlates underlie psychological processes described in our model, we believe it is important to further investigate the relationship between the psychological description of knowledge construction while reading and the underlying neurological processes (see G. Hruby, chapter 13 this volume).

Future research pertaining to the reader's outcomes of meaning construction needs to explore the ways in which reading can change motivation, attitudes toward reading, and value systems. Further study is also needed to explore the impact of different kinds of writing, such as summary and analysis, on text comprehension. While we know that certain kinds of writing can improve reading comprehension (Graham & Hebert, 2010), we know little about the effects of writing instruction on reading processes. For example, does explicit instruction in formulating a thesis or in planning and organizing an expository essay contribute to improvements in comprehending expository prose?

Implications for research arising from our representation of the teacher component are clearly present. In regard to the teacher's prior beliefs and knowledge, future research needs to further define the role of affective conditions in instruction. The most pressing work should address the influence of instructional stance on the teacher's instructional decision making process. And, what kinds of stances do teachers encourage readers to adopt? In regard to cognitive conditions, do teachers' schemata lead to misinterpretations or "misreadings" of students, their responses, and patterns of student interactions in the classroom context? The teacher's knowledge use and control constitute an important area also needing further exploration. For example, how do novice and expert teachers differ in creating instructional plans, in selecting instructional strategies, and in making "in-flight" instructional decisions?

Several areas of research would augment our understanding of the teacher's use of outcomes of instructional decision-making. What, for example, do novice and expert teachers gain from observing the outcomes of the knowledge-construction process in the reader? What kinds of teacher observation and feedback would encourage the development of reflective teaching for preservice and for practicing teachers?

Many research issues emerge from the text and classroom context in our model. The issue of meaning negotiation is central among these. For example, what reader motivational profile promotes highly successful engagement in the meaning-negotiation process? What kinds of texts and tasks support a reader's involvement or openness during meaning negotiation? Do different instructional stances and different sources of authority have a differential impact on the negotiation process? For example, do "authoritative teachers" have a different impact on meaning negotiation than those teachers oriented toward more openness with the classroom community? Additional knowledge related to questions like these holds high potential for better understanding of the role of meaning negotiation in the meaning-construction process.

In conclusion, our model of reading as a meaning-construction process draws on and integrates knowledge from a wide range of disciplines. Central to our discussion, however, is the role of the social context of the classroom and the influence of the teacher on the reader's meaning negotiation. Our understanding of this negotiation is of vital importance if we are to meet a challenge set forth by Huey (1908/1968) early in the 20th century—that of understanding how the reader constructs meaning.

Note

This chapter is adapted from "Reading as a Motivated Meaning-Construction Process: The Reader, the Text, and the Teacher" in *Theoretical Models and Processes of Reading* (6th ed., pp. 1015–1068), edited by D. E. Alvermann, N. J. Unrau, and R. B. Ruddell, 2013, Newark, DE: International Reading Association. Copyright © 2013 by the International Reading Association.

References

Afflerbach, P., & Cho, B. (2010). Determining and describing reading strategies. In H. S. Waters & W. Schneider (Eds.), *Metacognition, strategy use, and instruction* (pp. 201–225). New York, NY: Guilford Press.

Alexander, P. A., & Judy, J. E. (1988). The interaction of domain-specific and strategic knowledge in academic performance. *Review of Educational Research, 58*(4), 375–404.

Alvermann, D. E., Young, J. P., Green, C., Wisenbaker, J. M. (2004). Adolescents' perceptions and negotiations of literacy practices in after-school read and talk clubs. In R. B. Ruddell & N. J. Unrau (Eds.), *Theoretical models and processes of reading* (5th ed., pp. 870–913). Newark, DE: International Reading Association.

Anderson, N. L., & Kaye, E. L. (2017). Finding versus fixing: Self-monitoring for readers who struggle. *The Reading Teacher, 70*, 543–550.

Anderson, R. C. (2013). Role of the reader's schema in comprehension, learning, and memory. In D. E. Alvermann, N.J. Unrau, & R. B. Ruddell (Eds.), *Theoretical models and processes of reading* (6th ed., pp. 476–488). Newark, DE: International Reading Association.

Anderson, R. C., & Pichert, J. W. (1978). Recall of previously unrecallable information following a shift in perspective. *Journal of Verbal Learning and Verbal Behavior, 17*, 1–12.

Baddeley, A. (2007). *Working memory, thought, and action.* Oxford: Oxford University Press.

Baker, L. (2005). Developmental differences in metacognition: Implications for metacognitively oriented reading instruction. In S. E. Israel, C .C. Block, K. L. Bauserman, & K. Kinnucan-Welsch (Eds.), *Metacognition in literacy learning: Theory, assessment, instruction, and professional development* (pp. 61–79). Mahwah, NJ: Erlbaum.

Bandura, A. (1986). *Social foundations of thought and action: A social cognitive theory.* Upper Saddle River, NJ: Pearson Education.

Bandura, A. (1997). *Self-efficacy: The exercise of control.* New York, NY: W. H. Freeman and Company.

Bauer, J. (1994). *Schools for thought.* Cambridge, MA: MIT Press.

Beach, R., & Hynds, S. (1990). *Developing discourse practices in adolescence and adulthood.* Norwood, NJ: Ablex.

Bloome, D., & Bailey, F. (1992). Studying language and literacy through events, particularities, and intertexuality. In R. Beach, J. Green, M. Kamil, & T. Shanahan (Eds.), *Multidisciplinary perspectives on literacy research* (pp. 181–210). Urbana, IL: National Council of Teachers of English.

Brinchmann, E. I., Hjetland, H. N., & Lyster, S. H. (2016). Lexical quality matters: Effects of word knowledge instruction on the language and literacy skills of third- and fourth-grade poor readers. *Reading Research Quarterly, 51*, 165–180.

Brown, A., Palinscar, A. S., & Armbruster, B. B. (2013). Instructing comprehension-fostering activities in interactive learning situations. In D. E. Alvermann, N. Unrau, & R. B. Ruddell (Eds.), *Theoretical models and processes of reading* (6th ed., pp. 657–690). Newark, DE: International Reading Association.

Brown, R., Pressley, M., Van Meter, P., & Schuder, T. (2004). A quasi-experimental validation of transactional strategies instruction with low-achieving second-grade readers. In R. B. Ruddell & N. J. Unrau (Eds.), *Theoretical models and processes of reading* (5th ed., pp. 998–1039). Newark, DE: International Reading Association.

Chomsky, N. (1965). *Aspects of the theory of syntax*. Cambridge, MA: MIT Press.

Cox, B. E., Fang, Z., & Otto, B. W. (2004). Preschoolers' developing ownership of the literate register. In R. B. Ruddell & N. J. Unrau (Eds.), *Theoretical models and processes of reading* (5th ed., pp. 281–312). Newark, DE: International Reading Association.

Dore, J. (1979). Conversation and preschool language development. In P. Fletcher & M. Garman (Eds.), *Language acquisition* (pp. 337–361). Cambridge: Cambridge University Press.

Duffy, G. G. (2005). Developing metacognitive teachers: Visioning and the expert's changing role in teacher education and professional development. In S. E. Israel, C. C. Block, K. L. Bauserman, & K. Kinnucan-Welsch (Eds.), *Metacognition in literacy learning: Theory, assessment, instruction, and professional development* (pp. 299–314). Mahwah, NJ: Erlbaum.

Dyson, A. H., & Genishi, C. (2013). Social talk and imaginative play: Curricular basics for young children's language and literacy. In D. E. Alvermann, N. J. Unrau, & R. B. Ruddell (Eds.), *Theoretical models and processes of reading* (6th ed., pp. 164–181). Newark, DE: International Reading Association.

Ehri, L. C. (1991). Development of the ability to read words. In R. Barr, M. L. Kamil, P. Mosenthal, & P. D. Pearson (Eds.), *Handbook of reading research* (Vol. 2, pp. 383–417). White Plains, NY: Longman.

Ehri, L. C. (1994). Development of the ability to read words: Update. In R. B. Ruddell, M. R. Ruddell, & H. Singer (Eds.), *Theoretical models and processes of reading* (4th ed., pp. 323–358). Newark, DE: International Reading Association.

Ehri, L. C., & McCormick, S. (2013). Phases of word learning: Implications for instruction with delayed and disabled readers. In D. E. Alvermann, N. J. Unrau, & R. B. Ruddell (Eds.), *Theoretical models and processes of reading* (6th ed., pp. 339–361). Newark, DE: International Reading Association.

Ervin, S. M., & Miller, W. R. (1963). Language development. In H. Stevenson (Ed.), *Child psychology* (62nd yearbook of the National Society for the Study of Education, pp. 108–143). Chicago, IL: University of Chicago Press.

Fish, S. (1980). *Is there a text in this class? The authority of interpretive communities*. Cambridge, MA: Harvard University Press.

Flower, L. (1987). *The role of task representation in reading to write* (Tech. Rep. No. 6). Berkeley, CA: Center for the Study of Writing.

Forman, E. A., & Cazden, C. B. (2013). Exploring Vygotskian perspectives in education: The cognitive value of peer interaction. In D. E. Alvermann, N, J, Unrau, & R. B. Ruddell (Eds.), *Theoretical models and processes of reading* (6th ed., pp.182–203). Newark, DE: International Reading Association.

Frith, U. (1985). Beneath the surface of developmental dyslexia. In K. E. Patterson, J. C. Marshall, & M. Coltheart (Eds.), *Surface dyslexia* (pp. 301–330). Hillsdale, NJ: Erlbaum.

Gibson, E. J., & Levin, H. (1975). *The psychology of reading*. Cambridge, MA: MIT Press.

Graham, S., & Hebert, M. A. (2010). *Writing to read: Evidence for how writing can improve reading*. A Carnegie Corporation Time to Act Report. Washington, DC: Alliance for Excellent Education.

Griffith, P. L., & Ruan, J. (2005). What is metacognition and what should be its role in literacy instruction? In S. E. Israel, C. C. Block, K. L. Bauserman, & K. Kinnucan-Welsch (Eds.), *Metacognition in literacy learning: Theory, assessment, instruction, and professional development* (pp. 3–18). Mahwah, NJ: Erlbaum.

Guthrie, J. T., & Coddington, C. S. (2009). Reading motivation. In K. R. Wentzel & A. Wigfield (Eds.), *Handbook of motivation at school* (pp. 503–525.) New York: Routledge.

Guthrie, J. T., & Klauda, S. L. (2014). Effects of classroom practices on reading comprehension, engagement, and motivations for adolescents. *Reading Research Quarterly, 49*, 387–416.

Guthrie, J. T., & Wigfield, A. (2000). Engagement and motivation in reading. In M. L. Kamil, P. B. Mosenthal, P. D. Pearson, & R. Barr (Eds.), *Handbook of reading research* (Vol. 3, pp. 403–422). Mahwah, NJ: Erlbaum.

Guthrie, J. T., Wigfield, A., & You, W. (2012). Instructional contexts for engagement and achievement in reading. In S. J. Christenson, A. L. Reschly, & C. Wylie (Eds.), *Handbook of research on student engagement* (pp. 601–634). New York: Springer.

Hacker, D. J. (2004). Self-regulated comprehension during normal reading. In R. B. Ruddell & N. J. Unrau (Eds.), *Theoretical models and processes of reading* (5th ed., pp. 755–779). Newark, DE: International Reading Association.

Hairston, M. (1986). *Contemporary composition: Short edition*. Boston, MA: Houghton Mifflin.

Harris, P. J. (1989). *First-grade children's constructs of teacher-assigned reading tasks in a whole language classroom* (Unpublished doctoral dissertation, University of California, Berkeley).

Hartman, D. K. (1991). The intertextual links of readers using multiple passages: A post-modern/semiotic/ cognitive view of meaning making. In J. Zutell & S. McCormick (Eds.), *Learner factors/teacher factors: Issues in literacy research and instruction* (40th yearbook of the National Reading Conference). Chicago, IL: National Reading Conference.

Heath, S. B. (1983). *Ways with words.* Cambridge: Cambridge University Press.

Heath, S. B. (2013). It's a book! It's a bookstore. Theories of reading in the worlds of childhood and adolescence. In D. E. Alvermann, N. J. Unrau, & R. B. Ruddell (Eds.), *Theoretical models and processes of reading* (6th ed., pp. 204–227). Newark, DE: International Reading Association.

Heritage, M. (2013). *Formative Assessment in Practice: A Process of Inquiry and Action.* Cambridge, MA: Harvard Press.

Hiebert, E. H., & Martin, L. A. (2004). The texts of beginning reading instruction. In R. B. Ruddell & N. J. Unrau (Eds.), *Theoretical models and processes of reading* (5th ed., pp. 390–411). Newark, DE: International Reading Association.

Huey, E. B. (1968). *The psychology and pedagogy of reading.* Cambridge, MA: MIT Press. (Original work published 1908)

Hull, G., & Rose, M. (2004). "This wooden shack place": The logic of an unconventional reading. In R. B. Ruddell & N. J. Unrau (Eds.), *Theoretical models and processes of reading* (5th ed., pp. 268–280). Newark, DE: International Reading Association.

Hymes, D. (1974). *Foundations in sociolinguistics: An ethnographic approach.* Philadelphia, PA: University of Pennsylvania Press.

Israel, S. E., Block, C. C., Bauserman, K. L., & Kinnucan-Welsch, K. (Eds.) (2005). *Metacognition in Literacy Learning: Theory, assessment, instruction, and professional development.* Mahwah, NJ: Erlbaum.

Juel, C., & Minden-Cupp, C. (2004). Learning to read words: Linguistic units and instructional strategies. In R. B. Ruddell & N. J. Unrau (Eds.), *Theoretical models and processes of reading* (5th ed., pp. 313–364). Newark, DE: International Reading Association.

Kintsch, W. (1998). *Comprehension: A paradigm for cognition.* New York, NY: Cambridge University Press.

Knight, J. (2016). *Better conversations: Coaching ourselves and each other to be more credible, caring, and connected.* Thousand Oaks, CA: Corwin Press.

Kuhn, M. R., & Stahl, S. A. (2013). Fluency: Developmental and remedial practices – revisited. In D. E. Alvermann, N. J. Unrau, & R. B. Ruddell (Eds.), *Theoretical models and processes of reading* (6th ed., pp. 385–411). Newark, DE: International Reading Association.

Langer, J. A. (1981). From theory to practice: A prereading plan. *Journal of Reading, 25*(2), 152–156.

Langer, J. A. (2004). Beating the odds: Teaching middle and high school students to read and write well. In R. B. Ruddell & N. J. Unrau (Eds.), *Theoretical models and processes of reading* (5th ed., pp. 1040–1082). Newark, DE: International Reading Association.

Linnenbrink-Garcia, L. & Patall, E. A. (2016). Motivation. In L. Corno & E. Anderman (Eds.), *Handbook of educational psychology* (pp. 91–103). Washington, DC: American Psychological Association.

Many, J. E. (2004). The effect of reader stance on students' personal understanding of literature. In R. B. Ruddell & N. J. Unrau (Eds.), *Theoretical models and processes of reading* (5th ed., pp. 914–928). Newark, DE: International Reading Association.

Mason, J. M., Herman, P. A., & Au, K. H. (1991). Children's developing knowledge of words. In J. Flood, J. M. Jensen, D. Lapp, & J. R. Squire (Eds.), *Handbook of research on teaching the English language arts* (pp. 721–731). New York, NY: Macmillan.

Mathewson, G. C. (2004). Model of attitude influence upon reading and learning to read. In R. B. Ruddell & N. J. Unrau (Eds.), Theoretical models and processes of reading (5th ed., pp. 1431–1461). Newark, DE: International Reading Association.

McCormick, S., & Zutell, J. (2015). *Instructing students who have literacy problems* (7th ed.). Columbus, OH: Pearson.

McVee, M. B., Dunsmore, K., & Gavelek, J. R. (2013). Schema theory revisited. In D. E. Alvermann, N. J. Unrau, & R. B. Ruddell (Eds.), *Theoretical models and processes of reading* (6th ed., pp. 489–524). Newark, DE: International Reading Association.

Meyer, B. J. F., & Poon, L. W. (2004). Effects of structure strategy training and signaling on recall of text. In R. B. Ruddell & N. J. Unrau (Eds.), *Theoretical models and processes of reading* (5th ed., pp. 810–851). Newark, DE: International Reading Association.

Morehead, D. M. (1971). Processing of phonological sequences by young children and adults. *Child Development, 42,* 279–289.

Nagy, W. E., & Scott, J. A. (2013). Vocabulary processes. In D. E. Alvermann, N. J. Unrau, & R. B. Ruddell (Eds.), *Theoretical models and processes of reading* (6th ed., pp. 458–475). Newark, DE: International Reading Association.

Ogbu, J. U., & Simons, H. D. (1998). Voluntary and involuntary minorities: A cultural-ecological theory of school performance with some implications for education. *Anthropology & Education Quarterly, 29*(2), 155–188.

Paris, S. G., Lipson, M. Y., & Wixson, K. K. (1983). Becoming a strategic reader. *Contemporary Educational Psychology, 8*, 293–316.

Pyle, N., Vasquez, A. C., Lignugaris/Kraft, B., Gillam, S. L., Reutzel, D. R. Olszewski, . . . Pyle, D. (2017). Effects of expository text structure interventions on comprehension: A meta-analysis. *Reading Research Quarterly, 52*(4), 469–501.

Raphael, T. E. (1982). Question-answer strategies for children. *The Reading Teacher, 36*, 186–190.

Raphael, T. E., George, M., Weber, C. M., & Nies, A. (2010). Approaches to teaching reading comprehension. In S. E. Israel & G. G. Duffy (Eds.) *Handbook of research on reading comprehension* (pp. 449–469). New York, NY: Routledge.

Reynolds, R. E., Standiford, S. N., & Anderson, R. C. (1979). Distribution of reading time when questions are asked about a restricted category of text information. *Journal of Educational Psychology, 71*, 183–190.

Rosenblatt, L. M. (1978). *The reader, the text, the poem: The transactional theory of the literary work.* Carbondale, IL: Southern Illinois University Press.

Rosenblatt, L. M. (1985). The transactional theory of the literary work: Implications for research. In C. R. Cooper (Ed.), *Researching response to literature and the teaching of literature* (pp. 33–53). Norwood, NJ: Ablex.

Rowe, D. W. (1989). Preschoolers' use of metacognitive knowledge and strategies in self-selected literacy events. In S. McCormick & J. Zutell (Eds.), *Cognitive and social perspectives for literacy research and instruction* (38th yearbook of the National Reading Conference, pp. 65–76). Chicago, IL: National Reading Conference.

Ruddell, R. B. (1965). Effect of the similarity of oral and written language structure on reading comprehension. *Elementary English, 42*, 403–410.

Ruddell, R. B. (1974). *Reading-language instruction: Innovative practices.* Englewood Cliffs, NJ: Prentice Hall.

Ruddell, R. B. (2004). Researching the influential literacy teacher: Characteristics, beliefs, strategies, and new research directions. In R. B. Ruddell & N. J. Unrau (Eds.), *Theoretical models and processes of reading* (5th ed., pp. 979–997). Newark, DE: International Reading Association. (Original work published 1997)

Ruddell. R. B. (2009). *How to teach reading to elementary and middle school students.* Boston, MA: Allyn & Bacon.

Ruddell, R. B., & Speaker, R. B. (1985). The interactive reading process: A model. In H. Singer & R. B. Ruddell (Eds.), *Theoretical models and processes of reading* (3rd ed., pp. 751–793). Newark, DE: International Reading Association.

Rumelhart, D. E. (1981). Schemata: The building blocks of cognition. In J. T. Guthrie (Ed.), *Comprehension and teaching: Research reviews* (pp. 3–26). Newark, DE: International Reading Association.

Rumelhart, D. E. (2013). Toward an interactive model of reading. In D. E. Alvermann, N. J. Unrau, & R. B. Ruddell (Eds.), *Theoretical models and processes of reading* (pp. 719–747). Newark, DE: International Reading Association.

Ryan, R. M., & Deci, E. L. (2009). Promoting self-determined school engagement. In K. R. Wentzel & A. Wigfield (Eds.), *Handbook of motivation at school* (pp. 171–195). New York, NY: Routledge.

Sadoski, M., & Paivio, A. (2001). *Imagery and text: A dual coding theory of reading and writing.* Mahwah, NJ: Erlbaum.

Sadoski, M., & Paivio, A. (2013). A dual coding theoretical model of reading. In D. E. Alvermann, N. J. Unrau, & R. B. Ruddell (Eds.), *Theoretical models and processes of reading* (6th ed., pp. 886–922). Newark, DE: International Reading Association.

Salinger, J. D. (1963). *Nine stories.* New York, NY: New American Library of World Literature.

Samuels, S. J. (2013). Toward a theory of automatic information processing in reading, revisited. In D. E. Alvermann, N. J. Unrau, & R. B. Ruddell (Eds.), *Theoretical models and processes of reading* (6th ed., pp. 698–718). Newark, DE: International Reading Association.

Schiefele, U. (2009). Situational and individual interest. In K. R. Wentzel & A. Wigfield (Eds.), *Handbook of motivation at school* (pp. 197–222). New York, NY: Routledge.

Schunk, D. H., & Pajares, F. (2009). Self-efficacy theory. In K. R. Wentzel & A. Wigfield (Eds.), *Handbook of motivation at school* (pp. 55–54). New York, NY: Routledge.

Scollon, R. (1979). A real early stage. In E. Ochs & B. B. Schieffelin (Eds.), *Developmental pragmatics* (pp. 215–227). New York, NY: Academic.

Semma, H. W., Mahone, E. M. Levine, T., Eason, S. H., & Cutting, L. E. (2009). The contribution of executive skills to reading comprehension. *Child Neuropsychology, 15*, 232–246.

Shnayer, S. W. (1969). Relationships between reading interests and reading comprehension. In J. A. Figurel (Ed.), *Reading and realism* (pp. 698–702). Newark, DE: International Reading Association.

Solheim, O. J. (2011). The impact of reading self-efficacy and task value on reading comprehension scores in different item formats. *Reading Psychology, 32*, 1–27.

Spiro, R. J., Coulson, R. l., Feltovich, P. J., & Anderson, D. K. (2013). Cognitive flexibility theory: Advanced knowledge acquisition in ill-structured domains. In D. E. Alvermann, N. J. Unrau, & R. B. Ruddell (Eds.), *Theoretical models and processes of reading* (6th ed., pp. 544–557). Newark, DE: International Reading Association.

Stauffer, R. B. (1976). *Teaching reading as a thinking process.* New York, NY: Harper.

Sulzby, E. (1985). Children's emergent reading of favorite storybooks: A developmental study. *Reading Research Quarterly, 20,* 458–481.

Tulving, E. (1983). *Elements of episodic memory.* Oxford: Oxford University Press.

Tulving, E. (1986). What kind of hypothesis is the distinction between episodic and semantic memory? *Journal of Experimental Psychology: Learning, Memory, and Cognition, 12,* 307–311.

Unrau, N. (1992). The TASK of reading (and writing) arguments: A guide to building critical literacy. *Journal of Reading, 35,* 436–442.

Unrau, N. (2008a). *Content area reading and writing: Fostering literacies in middle and high school cultures* (2nd ed.). Upper Saddle River, NJ: Pearson.

Unrau, N. (2008b). *Thoughtful teachers, thoughtful learners: A guide to helping students think critically.* Scarborough, ON: Pippin.

Unrau, N., Ragusa, G., & Bowers, E. (2015). Teachers focus on motivation for reading: "It's all about knowing the relationship." *Reading Psychology, 36,* 105–144.

Unrau, N. J., Rueda, R., Son, E., Polanin, J. R., Lundeen, R. J., & Muraszewski, A. K. (2018). Can reading self-efficacy be modified? A meta-analysis of the impact of interventions on reading self-efficacy. *Review of Educational Research, 88*(2), 167–204.

Wagner, R. K., & Sternberg, R. J. (1987). Executive control in reading comprehension. In B. K. Britton & S. M. Glynn (Eds.), *Executive control processes in reading* (pp. 1–22). Hillsdale, NJ: Erlbaum.

Wenger, E. (1998). *Communities of practice: Learning, meaning, and identity.* New York, NY: Cambridge University Press.

Wijekuman, K., Meyer, B. J. F., & Lei, P. (2017). Web-based text structure strategy instruction improves seventh graders' content area reading comprehension. *Journal of Educational Psychology, 109*(6), 741–760.

Wright, T. S., & Cervetti, G. N. (2017). A systematic review of the research on vocabulary instruction that impacts text comprehension. *Reading Research Quarterly, 52,* 203–226.

12

THE ROLE OF MOTIVATION THEORY IN LITERACY INSTRUCTION

Ana Taboada Barber, Karen C. Levush, and Susan Lutz Klauda

One effective way to encourage children to read is to arrange it so that they are frequently reading what they want to read (e.g., Krashen, Lee, & Lao, 2018). However, often, the students who need the most support in reading are the ones who do not know what or how to choose what to read. Teachers also perceive the paradox of choice because curricular boundaries and the culture of testing exert limitations on the frequency and breadth with which children can choose what to read. Yet, when parents, educators or literacy researchers think of motivated readers two ideas often come to mind: reading for fun and choosing to read. Although it is true that both are dimensions of motivation, reading motivation is a multifaceted construct.

Similarly, when it comes to writing, it is well known that weak and novice writers can feel overwhelmed by the task of writing (Graham, 1990) and that their sense of competence or self-efficacy can be low, leading to negative feelings about their writing abilities. This low self-efficacy affects their performance and their beliefs that they can be good writers (Hidi & Boscolo, 2006; Pajares, Johnson, & Usher, 2007; Pajares & Valiante, 2006). Judgments of personal efficacy affect what students choose to do, the effort they expend, and the persistence they exert when challenges arise, as well as the emotional reactions and thought patterns they experience (Pajares, 2003). Motivation for writing encompasses all of these dimensions, making it a manifold concept to approach.

In this chapter, we focus on motivation as it applies to the two key dimensions of literacy: reading and writing. In doing so, we first note that reading motivation is a construct that has been approached empirically much more assiduously than that of writing motivation, and as such theories of motivation have been less often applied to writing than to reading instruction and its development. Nevertheless, given the importance that motivation has for both literacy processes, we review theories of motivation and their implications for both reading and writing development and instruction. We draw from four major theories of motivation: self-determination theory (Deci & Ryan, 1985), social cognitive theory (Bandura, 1986); expectancy-value theory (Wigfield & Eccles, 2000) and achievement goal theory (Pintrich, 2000). Within each theory, we aim to focus evenly on implications for reading and writing development and instruction—emphasizing the empirical work for each construct. Before concluding the chapter, we conceptualize reading engagement as a multidimensional construct (Guthrie, Wigfield & You, 2012) and draw from the model of reading engagement (Guthrie & Wigfield, 2000) to elaborate on its implications for reading instruction. We close the chapter with other key motivation constructs to demarcate possible areas for future work.

Reading Motivation and Writing Self-Efficacy

Reading motivation has been defined as an individual's personal goals, values, and beliefs with regard to the topics, processes, and outcomes of reading (Guthrie & Wigfield, 2000). Some of these goals lead to excitement during and as a result of reading, whereas others may be conducive to dedicated effort and hard work. Because motivation is a multifaceted construct there are multiple dimensions to it. Some define the type of motivation—extrinsic or intrinsic; others refer to the behaviors, emotions and attitudes that characterize the motivated reader. And yet other dimensions refer to the contexts in classroom and one-on-one reading situations that can spur motivated reading—such as the provision of choice. Given that this volume focuses on theoretical models, our chapter reviews four main theories of motivation that are to date the most influential on reading and literacy researchers. We also draw from these four theories because each, in some way, influences the model of reading engagement (Guthrie, Wigfield, & You, 2012), which draws from both motivation and engagement theory and has clear implications for literacy educators.

Writing motivation has been less delineated in the empirical and theoretical literature, with emphasis given to *writing self-efficacy* and its importance for writing performance instead. A strong sense of competence—or self-efficacy—may serve students well during writing tasks because it fosters greater interest and attention to writing, and likely greater perseverance in the face of adversity (Pajares, 2003). As Bandura (1997) pointed out, successful performance reflects not only skill levels, but also the confidence individuals have for performing in specific domains or contexts. Given that writing effectively is a multi-step complex process, self-efficacy judgments will affect whether students attempt specific tasks and their continuing engagement when they face difficulties (Bruning & Kauffman, 2016).

Self-Determination Theory

Theoretical Overview

Self-determination theory (SDT; Deci & Ryan, 1985; Ryan & Deci, 2000) is a theory of motivation and development rooted in the idea that humans are innately curious and have a desire to grow. SDT distinguishes between intrinsic and extrinsic motivation within a continuum based on reasons for action. Intrinsic motivation is characterized as the prototypic form of the human propensity toward engaging in interesting activities and is thus posited as doing something for its inherent satisfaction. It is catalyzed when environmental conditions are conducive to its expression (Ryan & Deci, 2000). Extrinsic motivation, on the other hand, refers to doing something because it leads to an outcome (e.g., praise or satisfaction of material needs, Ryan & Deci, 2000). In line with the notion that the natural state of human action manifests as intrinsically motivated behaviors, SDT outlines three fundamental psychological needs that facilitate self-determined behavior when fulfilled: competence, autonomy, and relatedness. Fulfillment of each of these needs supports our human tendencies to seek and overcome challenges. Their satisfaction is conducive to psychological growth, productivity, and well-being (Ryan & Deci, 2000).

The need for competence is defined as "a need for having an effect, [and] for being effective in one's interactions with the environment" (Deci & Ryan, 1985, p. 27). People have little incentive to engage in activities that do not make them feel competent; thus, they seek an *optimal* level of challenge to satisfy this need. Autonomy refers to the experience of an internal perceived locus of causality for engaging in a particular activity. In other words, the psychological need for autonomy denotes the importance of exercising our capacity to choose and "to have those choices, rather than reinforcement contingencies, drives, or any other forces or pressures, be the determinants of one's actions" (Deci & Ryan, 1985, p. 38). SDT suggests that the experience of autonomy is integral to intrinsically motivated behavior. The need for relatedness refers to the need for a "sense of belongingness and connectedness to the people and culture disseminating a goal" (Ryan & Deci, 2000, p. 64). A growing body of evidence has shown that the satisfaction of these needs supports psychological functioning across individualistic (Western, mostly) and collectivistic (Eastern) cultures (e.g., Ferguson, Kasser, & Jahng, 2010; Jang, Reeve, Ryan, & Kim, 2009).

Within SDT, motivations can vary in level (i.e., how much motivation) and in orientation (i.e., what type of motivation). Orientation of motivation refers to the underlying attitudes and goals that lead to action or the reasons for our actions (Ryan & Deci, 2000). Within the theoretical framework of SDT, the social and environmental factors that *facilitate* versus *thwart* intrinsic motivation are considered. For example, a large body of research examines teachers' instructional behaviors, differentiating between provisions of controlling tactics versus autonomy supportive practices (Jang, Kim, & Reeve, 2012; Reeve, Bolt, & Cai, 1999; Reeve & Jang, 2006).

Implications for Literacy Instruction

The Extrinsic-Intrinsic Continuum

In recognition that most activities we engage in are not, in their pure form, intrinsically motivated, SDT distinguishes extrinsically motivated behaviors from intrinsic ones by proposing that extrinsic motivations can vary in the degree to which they are perceived as autonomous within a continuum. For example, a student who meets with a teacher after school to practice reading out loud only because the teacher required their attendance is extrinsically motivated. The student is doing so in order to attain the separable outcome of avoiding the potential consequences. Likewise, a student who meets with a teacher after school for assistance with persuasive writing because they personally believe in the value of this skill for attaining a grade in the class is also extrinsically motivated. They are meeting with the teacher to improve their grade and to attain the benefits associated with good grades, rather than because they believe reading is enjoyable or because they find persuasive writing an interesting, sufficiently challenging skill to pursue. Both of these examples involve extrinsic rewards; however, the latter case denotes a personal endorsement of the behavior and a feeling of choice (referred to as "introjected regulation" of behavior, since the value of the skill is perceived), whereas the former indicates the exclusive compliance with an external control—the grade—(and it is referred to as "externally regulated" behavior; Deci & Ryan, 1985). As such, both of these examples represent extrinsically motivated actions that vary in their relative autonomy. To carry on with the same scenario, if a student perceived the personal importance of reading (or persuasive writing) and there is a conscious valuing of the activity (i.e., "it is good for my future") there is an investment in the activity that denotes an "identified regulation" (a higher degree of autonomous and lower degree of externally-controlled behavior). The ultimate expression of intrinsically motivated actions within the SDT continuum are those that are fully intrinsically regulated or endorsed by the self—as when the child feels an inherent satisfaction that is derived from the act of reading (as in getting lost in a story!).

Satisfying Students' Psychological Needs

An important question about motivated literacy activities within SDT is: What contexts can foster engaged or intrinsically motivated reading and writing? Within the formal context of school, a large portion of the activities students are expected to engage in are not necessarily intrinsically motivating or autonomously driven. Thus, classroom conditions that facilitate satisfaction of students' psychological needs for relatedness, competence, and autonomy, can help toward internalized regulation of behavior and higher intrinsic motivation. For example, a student's sense of connectedness to the teacher and to the topics of texts to be read or written are integral for facilitating internalization of the value of literacy. In other words, students' feelings of being respected by the teacher and reading materials and writing activities that cater to their individual interests are essential determinants of their willingness, respectively, to get involved in in-depth, close reading and put full effort into drafting and revising essays and stories. Giving choices in content, styles and approaches to writing are key to gaining and maintaining control of a writing task, which in turn is critical to fostering intrinsic motivation for writing (Bruning & Horn, 2000). Social supports with respect to perceived competence (or self-efficacy, see the social cognitive theory section) are also required for students to adopt and internalize goals for reading and writing. For instance, students who feel confident in their abilities to complete writing assignments successfully are more likely to adopt and internalize the goal of crafting clear and compelling written products as their own.

A large body of research examines teachers' instructional behaviors within SDT, differentiating between use of controlling tactics versus autonomy supportive practices. The interpersonal behavior of *autonomy support* can be characterized as intentional behaviors aimed to nurture students' psychological need of autonomy, such as asking students for input, based on their interests and preferences, as to what they would like to study and providing rationales for classroom rules or activities. Teachers can provide multiple literacy-related choices: within a given topic or unit, teachers can offer a menu of choices of what texts to read or choices of sections to read within a text as well as options for sub-topics to write about and the written form in which to convey their knowledge. Student perceptions of autonomy support have been linked with student reports of intrinsic reading motivation for fifth graders (Ng, Guthrie, Van Meter, McCann, & Alao, 1998) and especially for adolescent girls versus boys (De Naeghl, Valcke, De Meyer, Warlop, van Braak, & Van Keer, 2014). Further, implementation of autonomy supportive practices in conjunction with other motivation supports has been linked with increased intrinsic motivation to read and write in interventions such as Concept-Oriented Reading Instruction, as will be discussed in more detail later (e.g., Guthrie et al., 2004; Guthrie & Klauda, 2014). Additionally, in a study of secondary students in Hong Kong, student-perceived autonomy support during a 3-session expository writing unit correlated strongly ($r = .53$) with self-reported writing motivation, and, moreover, writing motivation mediated the relationship between a composite including autonomy support and other motivation practices, and writing performance (Lam & Law, 2007). Importantly, research has indicated that the practice of providing choices in the classroom tends to be optimally effective when choices are not overwhelming, are clearly presented, are meaningful (as opposed to superfluous), allow students to self-regulate their behaviors and are administered to individuals interested in the task (Patall, 2013; see Patall, 2012 for a review).

In addition, the practice of providing rationales for existing classroom rules or for why a particularly un-interesting activity is worthy of attention and effort is autonomy supportive because it affords students with an opportunity for a "sense of valuing to guide their classroom activity" (Reeve & Jang, 2006, p. 210) as well as to see the relevance of the activity or content presented (e.g., Taboada Barber, 2016). Within our work, we found that sixth graders who were Spanish-speaking ELs found a renewed sense of autonomy when they were provided with explanations for the need to use specific (and otherwise seemingly repetitious) comprehension strategies to enhance their understanding of text (Taboada Barber et al., 2015). Bruning and Horn (2000) have been critical that school writing often takes place under artificial conditions, such as abstracting chapters from books, completing essay exams, and writing terms papers that bear no relevance to students' lives. Having genuine reasons for writing is motivating and when teachers relate the writing activity to students' interests and their past and future experiences they help students think through "Why do I have to write this?" (Newby, 1991; Bruning and Horn, 2000), creating a sense of relevance for writing. Importantly, motivation researchers have determined that an autonomy supportive classroom does not imply a non-structured classroom. On the contrary, highly structured instruction coincides with autonomy supportive practices, such as in teachers' provision of strong guidance, clear and explicit instructions, and constructive feedback; these elements of structure enable students to work independently. Classroom structure and students' sense of autonomy are thus positively correlated and can predict students' academic engagement (Jang, Reeve, & Deci, 2010).

Social Cognitive Theory

Theoretical Overview

Bandura's (1986) social cognitive theory is a foundational theory of motivation research mostly because of its theorizing and empirical work on the construct of self-efficacy. Central to social cognitive theory is the dynamic interplay of internal biological, cognitive, and affective factors, behavioral patterns, and environmental events. Based on the assertion that most environmental influences operate through cognitive processes, social cognitive theory emphasizes the idea that individuals are "self-organizing, proactive, self-regulating and self-reflecting" (Bandura, 2006, p.164).

SCT posits that the most central and pervasive mechanism of human agency is individuals' beliefs of self-efficacy, or "people's judgements of their capabilities to organize and execute courses of action required to attain designated types of performances" (Bandura, 1986, p. 391). Important to note is that rather than being diffuse or undifferentiated beliefs, self-efficacy beliefs are specific to a task within a given context and can be generalized across similar activity domains (Bandura, Barbaranelli, Caprara, & Pastorelli, 1996). Because self-efficacy beliefs are at the basis of self-regulation of behavior they affect individuals' choices, aspirations, how much effort they expend toward a goal, and how long they persist when faced with difficulties or setbacks (Bandura, 1986). That is, at a basic level, the degree to which people feel confident in their effectiveness to cope with a given situation is likely to guide their preference for, and avoidance of, particular activities and environments. For example, consider a fifth-grader who struggles to translate his ideas for stories into written form with grammatically correct structures and vivid description and thus feels self-doubt about his ability to develop a sense of voice in writing, precisely because the mechanics of grammar may not be in place. In this case, a weak sense of self-efficacy as a writer is likely to manifest in feelings of anxiety in situations involving specific writing activities and tasks. In this case, such an activity that is perceived to potentially highlight an individual's shortcomings provides little incentive for its valuing or expenditure of efforts and persistence. In contrast, perceptions of high self-efficacy indicate a strong belief in one's capacity to accomplish a given task, leading to high-level goal setting and a deep commitment toward attaining them (Bandura, 1991).

Implications for Literacy Instruction

Self-Efficacy as a Predictor of Performance

Theoretical and empirical work has indicated that people tend to be more interested in "activities at which they judge themselves to be self-efficacious and from which they derive satisfaction by mastering challenges" (Bandura, 1991, p. 258). It is well known that students are more likely to persist in activities at which they believe they will succeed. Because self-efficacy beliefs require some consideration of the skills one possesses, achievement and self-efficacy beliefs are usually correlated (Multon, Brown, & Lent, 1991; Pajares & Kranzler, 1995). For example, self-efficacy for writing has been reliably linked to students' writing performance (e.g., Pajares, 2003; Pajares, Miller, & Johnson, 1999; Shell, Colvin, & Bruning, 1995). Efficacy beliefs for writing can vary in "level, strength, and generality" such as in assessing one's confidence in their ability to demonstrate a certain level of writing skills (e.g., grammar, usage, composition), complete a particular writing task, or attain a particular grade in a language arts class (Pajares, 2003, p. 144). Two decades ago researchers focused especially on self-efficacy for writing *tasks* versus writing *skills*, with the former focused on student judgments of their likely success in specific activities such as writing a letter or essay and the latter on success in specific components of writing such as writing a sentence with proper punctuation and grammar (Shell, Murphy, & Bruning, 1989; Shell, Colvin, & Bruning, 1995). It was found that self-efficacy for writing *skills*, but not for writing *tasks* predicted writing performance (Shell et al., 1989). More recent work replicated these findings with writing skill efficacy having a stronger relationship with writing performance than efficacy beliefs focused on a writing task or graded writing performance (Troia, Shankland, & Wolbers, 2012b). Overall, relatively recent research has found that self-efficacy for writing skills *and* tasks, the interest they have in the writing task, and their attributions for success with writing (i.e., is my success dependent on effort or ability?) mediates the relationship between their writing activity and the quality of their writing (Troia, Harbaugh, Shankland, Wolbers, & Lawrence, 2012a).

The domain or skill-specificity of self-efficacy beliefs also translates into research on reading self-efficacy, where self-efficacy refers to students' beliefs about their competence in specific reading tasks, such as identifying the main idea of a passage or using context to decipher the meaning of unfamiliar vocabulary. When assessed with this granularity, self-efficacy has been shown to relate moderately to strongly to reading comprehension for elementary students (Baker & Wigfield, 1999; Guthrie et al., 2004), to standardized, state reading test performance for middle schoolers (Mucherah & Yoder, 2008), and to language arts class performance for high school students (Greene, Miller, Crowson, Duke, & Akey, 2004). Of particular note, Mucherah and Yoder (2008) found that self-efficacy showed the most positive bivariate correlation with reading achievement out of 11 motivation dimensions examined and significantly predicted the standardized test scores controlling for three other motivations and four demographic variables.

Instructional Contexts that Foster Self-Efficacy Beliefs

Several explicit teaching practices have been identified as increasing students' self-efficacy for reading and writing (Schunk & Zimmermann, 2007). The self-efficacy-fostering framework consists of providing students' process goals, that is, steps for performing literacy tasks successfully. Teachers provide feedback that affects students' efficacy during the processes of engaging in literacy activities rather than feedback on the students' products or outcomes of reading and writing. That is, teachers give specific direction to students about the effectiveness of their strategy for performing work and reaching their writing or reading goals (Bruning & Horn, 2000). It is also important for teachers to make it apparent that students' successes are due to the effort they invest in using reading and writing strategies (Schunk, 2003). For instance, within our own work in the domain of reading we have found that consistent, informative feedback on effective use of comprehension strategies significantly helped middle-school struggling readers understand the steps involved in deriving literal and conceptual meaning from text. When such support for self-efficacy was coupled with students reading texts of their interest, a marked increase in their feelings of competence in reading was found (Taboada Barber et al., 2015).

An encompassing framework to foster self-efficacy for writing is self-regulated strategy development (SRSD; Harris & Graham, 1996, 1999), through which students are taught specific writing strategies as well as self-regulatory procedures (e.g., goal setting, self-monitoring and self-instruction) to support students' ability to effectively apply the target writing strategies (Harris, Graham, & Mason, 2006). SRSD has been extensively and successfully evaluated for developing writing skills, showing that teacher modeling (ranging from teachers posing story ideas to demonstrating how to plan, revise and overcome challenges) is key to writing performance as well as that mastery experiences are needed to build students' self-efficacy for writing. Accordingly, Lam and Law (2007) stress the importance of assigning challenging but achievable writing tasks, so that students build mastery experiences over time and of carefully scaffolding writing activities, to enable students to progress from simpler to more complex tasks. These recommendations are grounded in their findings that adolescents' perceptions that teachers provided appropriate challenge in writing lessons correlated strongly with their motivation for writing.

Within reading, beneficial to students' self-efficacy, is their perception of coherence across the texts they read. When students can identify the connectedness of themes and topics across texts their beliefs in their capacity to understand texts deeply increase (Guthrie, Mason-Singh, & Coddington, 2012). In addition, reading within a theme for a sustained period of time fosters a sense of mastery of content—this is crucial not only for nurturing reading self-efficacy but also for fostering knowledge goals, a key element of the reading engagement model that we review later in the chapter.

Expectancy-Value Theory

Theoretical Overview

Expectancy-value theory (EVT) builds upon a long-standing perspective in the fields of psychology and achievement motivation (Atkinson, 1957; Eccles et al., 1983; Wigfield, 1994; Wigfield & Eccles, 1992). In line with other major theories of achievement motivation, expectancy-value theorists also propose that expectancies for success and ability beliefs pertaining to various tasks are critical to understanding people's motivation to engage in achievement tasks. For example, in Bandura's social cognitive theory (1977) *efficacy expectations*, an aspect of self-efficacy beliefs, are defined as "the conviction that one can successfully execute the behavior required to produce the outcomes" (p. 193), and Weiner's attribution theory (1985) contends that individuals' attributions to ability, or the lack thereof, when they succeed or fail at particular tasks have important motivational consequences. However, the expectancy-value perspective poses another important determinant of one's decision to participate in achievement-related activities: the value an individual ascribes to a task needed to achieve a successful outcome. The model for modern expectancy-value theory (Eccles, 1984; Eccles et al., 1983; Wigfield, 1994; Wigfield & Eccles, 1992), shown in Figure 12.1, is based on Atkinson's (1957) seminal work, which highlights that expectancies for success and subject task value are directly linked to achievement-related choices of tasks, persistence on carrying those tasks and performance on them" (Wigfield & Eccles, 2000). Empirical findings suggest that within EVT, values especially predict the former two outcomes, while expectancies especially predict the latter (Wigfield & Eccles, 1992).

Expectancies refer to children's beliefs about how well they will do on upcoming tasks, either in the immediate or longer-term (Wigfield & Eccles, 2000). Expectancies are distinguished from efficacy beliefs conceptually (albeit not empirically since they are highly related; i.e., Linnenbrink-Garcia & Patall, 2015) in that efficacy beliefs refer to current perceptions of ability while expectancies refer to beliefs of how well one will perform on a future task. Expectancies for success within EVT are closely related to self-efficacy expectations or beliefs defined by Bandura (1997) in the sense that both refer to an individual's beliefs that one can effectively render the behavior needed for manifestation of the desired results (Bandura, 1997). Different from self-efficacy beliefs, which are task-specific, expectancies refer to beliefs of success at the domain level. These become distinguishable when operationalized in survey instruments, for example, "How good in reading are you?" is a sample item used to measure ability/efficacy beliefs and "How well do you expect to do in reading this year?" is a sample item used to measure expectancies (Wigfield & Eccles, 2000).

The other significant construct in EVT is task value, which broadly refers to the value individuals designate to a given activity or task. Eccles et al. (1983) proposed four major components of the construct: attainment value, intrinsic value, utility value and cost (see Eccles, et al, 1983; Wigfield & Eccles, 1992 for a detailed discussion of these components). Attainment value refers to the importance with which individuals view a particular task in reference to their goals and personal and social identities. Intrinsic value is the enjoyment or fun one derives from doing a task (Wigfield & Eccles, 2000). This construct is highly related to the view of intrinsic motivation held by proponents of self-determination theory. Utility value refers to the perception of usefulness that a task has for someone's future plans or other aspects of one's life. Utility value may be associated with more "extrinsic" related sources of motivation because it involves performing a task in order to attain a

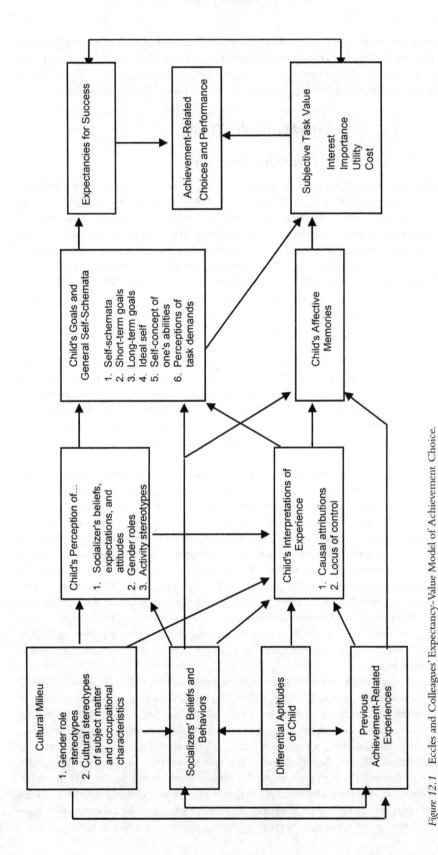

Figure 12.1 Eccles and Colleagues' Expectancy–Value Model of Achievement Choice.

From "Achievement values: Interactions, interventions, and future directions", by A. Wigfield, E. Rosenzweig, and J. S. Eccles, 2017, In A. Elliot, C. Dweck, and D. Yeager (Eds.) *Handbook of Competence and Motivation: Theory and Application*, 2nd ed., p. 118. Copyright 2017 by Guilford Press. Reprinted with permission.

separable outcome, such as enrolling in a creative writing course to fulfill a general requirement for graduation (Wigfield, Tonks, & Klauda, 2016). Lastly, cost refers to the negative aspects, emotional cost, or relative effort needed to engage in a task or activity. Eccles et al. (1983) posited that perception of relative cost is especially important to achievement-related choices.

Several EVT components were tested within a study exploring writing motivation, in which Troia and colleagues (2012a) investigated the interrelationships of writing motivation, activity, and performance in a sample of over 600 U.S. students in the fourth through tenth grades. Their findings supported an expectancy-value theory-based explanation of performance, in that students' writing motivation, including their self-efficacy beliefs and task interest and value, mediated relations between their self-reported frequency of writing activities and the quality of their fictional story writing.

Implications for Literacy Instruction

Given the breadth and multiple constructs within EVT there can be several implications for literacy instruction, tied to strengthening or recasting students' perceptions of themselves as readers and writers and of the value they place on literacy activities. Contextual variables at both the school and classroom levels—as well as the broader cultural milieu at home and in the community—play significant roles in individuals' development of expectancies for success in reading and writing and their valuing of these activities (Wigfield et al., 2016). Take, for instance, a struggling Latino student from a family with low socioeconomic status, for whom reading for pleasure or writing to share knowledge is perceived in his social milieu as a far shot for success or simply lacking utility value. How does this student perceive himself as a reader and writer? What attainment value does he see in literacy performance tasks (tests or else)? What are the costs of persevering or even trying to become an on-grade reader and writer? The expectancies for success around literacy and subjective values associated with literacy acts are likely to create a constellation of poor predictors for choosing to read and write as worthy academic activities and performing well in these areas. However, this constellation could be diluted and perhaps even reversed through the efforts of teachers and school leaders. As depicted in the EVT model, socializers' beliefs and behaviors and the broader cultural milieu impact individuals' expectancies and values indirectly through multiple pathways. Thus, it may be productive for teachers and school leaders to, for instance, model the attitude that all students are potential readers and writers. Such types of activities can consist of visits from local Latino community leaders to share how reading and writing helped them achieve their goals and continue to play crucial roles in their lives.

Further, in agreement with the intervention work of Harackiewicz, Hulleman, and colleagues (Hulleman & Harackiewicz, 2009; Hulleman, Godes, Hendricks, & Harackiewicz, 2010), teachers trying to strengthen students' expectancies and values could incorporate brief activities every few weeks such as asking students to write about the relevance of literacy activities to their lives. Hulleman and colleagues found that such simple interventions in the domains of science and math strengthened students' utility value and interest.

Additionally, school leaders and teachers might think about ways of minimizing the social comparisons that children make about their abilities, which influence their expectancies for success (Lam & Law, 2007; Wigfield et al., 2016), such as refraining from posting grades or sharing work examples that make differences in performance readily apparent. This may be especially important in settings where children vary widely in their performance in a given classroom and where there are gender or ethnic disparities in achievement, in order to prevent stereotypes about certain groups being more capable than others from forming or spreading. Wigfield et al. (2016) also note that children compare their own and their peers' interest in different activities, and that this influences the value they place on them. With respect to literacy motivation and instruction, teachers and other school personnel could capitalize on this tendency by creating regular opportunities for students to "sell" what they are reading through book talks or written reviews. Further, when students know that they will be sharing their writing with an audience beyond their teacher, for a purpose besides earning a good grade, this in itself is motivating (Bruning & Horn, 2000). Real-life purposes for writing, like persuading, informing, and expressing beliefs and feeling may especially augment students' beliefs about the value of writing.

Achievement Goal Theory

Theoretical Overview

Goal-orientation theories were conceived by developmental, motivational, and educational psychologists to explain students' learning and performance on academic tasks, and as such are relevant to learning and instruction (Schunk, Pintrich, & Meece, 2008). Achievement goal theory is a prominent motivation theory in educational psychology which purports that there are two main reasons or purposes for individuals' participation in achievement-related activities: mastery and performance goal orientations. Goal orientations refer to the purposes or reasons for engaging in achievement behaviors (Pintrich, 2003). A mastery goal orientation is defined as a focus on learning or mastering a task with goals of self-improvement, developing new skills, improving competence, or trying to gain understanding or insight (Ames, 1992; Dweck & Leggett, 1988; Midgley et al., 1998; Pintrich, 2000). In contrast, a performance goal orientation refers to a focus on demonstrating competence or ability and how ability will be judged relative to others (Ames, 1992; Dweck & Leggett, 1988; Midgley et al., 1998). In addition to this classic distinction, other types of goal orientations have been studied. For instance, performance goals have been further differentiated into performance-approach goals (appearing competent) and performance-avoidance goals (avoiding appearing incompetent; Elliot 1999). Goal orientations represent an individual's framework for interpreting and reacting to achievement settings in that they shape their beliefs about the causes of success and whether they attribute success to effort, a malleable trait that can be shaped by hard work, or to ability, a fixed characteristic that is pointless to endeavor to augment (Duda & Nicholls, 1992). For instance, students who adopt a mastery-orientation focused on learning and developing competence are more likely to give a reason for success such as "They try to understand instead of just memorizing." However, students who adopt a performance orientation and are concerned with their ability to outdo others are likely to cite reasons for success such as "They are better than others at taking tests" (Duda & Nicholls, 1992).

Implications for Literacy Instruction

Student Goal Orientations

Why do some students develop mastery goals while others form performance goals? While personal and family characteristics certainly play a role, research indicates that schools and classrooms create goal structures—or messages that accentuate the priority of certain goals (Ames, 1992)—and that a mastery goal structure is associated with, if not a causal agent in, the formation of students' mastery goals and other positive aspects of motivation and behavior. Conversely, there is some evidence and concern that a performance goal structure may negatively impact students' motivation and achievement-related behaviors (e.g., reduced help-seeking) (Urdan & Schoenfelder, 2006).

Research, however, concerning students' goal orientations and goal structures specifically within the domain of literacy is quite limited, especially as compared to that in the domain of math (Meece, Anderman, & Anderman, 2006). In one study, Meece and Miller (2001) longitudinally examined children's goals for literacy activities from grades 3 to 5. While they found declines in both mastery and performance goals over time, importantly the changes did not vary by gender or ability level, suggesting that students varying in these characteristics may respond similarly to classroom features pertinent to goal structure. In addition, they found that changes in mastery goal levels from third grade to fourth grade explained 46% of the variance in children's use of active learning strategies at the end of fourth grade, controlling for prior achievement and strategy use. Active learning strategies included such tactics as asking oneself questions to ensure understanding of assignments and trying independently to complete difficult aspects of a task. The positive implication here for literacy instruction is that encouragement of mastery goals may facilitate children's use of strategies when they encounter challenging tasks that demand deep processing of text or substantial research and planning in preparation for writing, and thereby benefit their achievement. Based on the work of Grant and Dweck (2003), Meece et al. (2006) pointed out that mastery goals appear to be especially related to performance "when a high degree of challenge is present, when processing of complex or difficult material is needed, or when the learning task itself is personally valued" (p. 499). As state and national literacy standards and assessments increasingly demand that students move beyond a literal understanding of text, connect their reading to their own experiences, compose a variety of sophisticated written products, and write about complex informational text, this finding seems to underscore the benefits of creating classroom contexts that stress mastery goals.

Encouraging Mastery Goals in the Classroom

Given the importance of student goal orientations for their learning, how can teachers encourage mastery goals and deter performance goals through their classroom literacy activities? One key way is to make a knowledge goal the driving question of instruction, which sets a learning-focused purpose for both students' reading and writing. Such guiding questions as "How do meteorologists predict the weather?" and "Why do certain animals live only in certain habitats?" compel students to engage in deeper processing of text and comprehend more than when trivial facts or performance goals are emphasized (Benware & Deci, 1984; Meece, Blumenfeld, & Hoyle, 1988; Taylor, Pearson, Clark, & Walpole, 2000), as well as to craft more complex and thoughtful written responses. Moreover, knowledge goals ". . . provide motivation for students because they give a purpose for using different reading comprehension strategies. By having knowledge goals, students learn to use the strategies with greater effort, attention, and interest than in a context devoid of deep, conceptual themes" (Wigfield, Mason-Singh, Ho & Guthrie, 2014, p. 44).

In addition, teachers can convey a mastery goal message by making it clear that they expect all students can fulfill such knowledge goals, offering them learning and motivational support along the way, and discussing the value of the information to be gained through the reading necessary to gain a deeper conceptual understanding of the topic of instruction (Stipek, Givvin, Salmon, & MacGyvers, 1998; Turner et al., 2002; Urdan & Schoenfelder, 2006). These practices, in turn, further support the writing process, enabling students to generate meaningful content through organized ideas (Hidi & Anderson, 1992; Hidi & McLaren, 1991). Further, teachers can downplay performance goals by recognizing students for effortfully using and improving their reading and writing strategies and for developing and communicating knowledge, rather than recognizing the highest performers on achievement tests or attributing students' successes on literacy tasks to ability rather than effort (Linnenbrink, 2005; Maehr & Midgley, 1996; Schunk & Swartz, 1993; Urdan & Schoenfelder, 2006). In addition, since leveled readers and reading groups are employed frequently at the elementary level, teachers may be able to foster stronger mastery goals and diminish performance goals by emphasizing that progressing to a new level or joining a new group depends on developing certain reading skills, not on achieving particular test scores. At all grade levels, too, teachers may devise ways to more frequently allow students to group themselves by reading and writing interests and mutual knowledge goals and less frequently to group students by ability.

Notably, intervention studies that focus specifically on goal structures are rare in literacy motivation research. As discussed shortly, however, achievement goal theory has influenced the design of interventions that examine the impact of a composite of motivation practices.

Integrating Theories: The Reading Engagement Model

Overview

So far, we have discussed four major theories of motivation and their specific implications for literacy instruction, that is, how teachers can promote their students' experience of the key motivational constructs in those theories. The assumption is—and varied research evidence indicates—that by bolstering students' motivations, teachers are also facilitating their students' literacy achievement. There is, however, a missing element in our story of the role of motivation in achievement thus far: literacy engagement.

Engagement, like motivation, is a multidimensional construct, encompassing affective or emotional, behavioral, and cognitive aspects of involvement in an activity (Fredricks, Blumenfeld, & Paris, 2004). In particular, reading engagement—as opposed to writing engagement—has received much attention from literacy researchers over the past two decades; thus, the reading engagement model (Guthrie et al., 2012) and a multicomponent curriculum intervention based on it are our focus below. Further, although multicomponent writing interventions like SRSD similarly include motivation supports such as teacher guidance in setting goals for writing tasks and social collaboration via peer feedback (e.g., Harris, Graham, & Mason, 2006), these supports are not central to the aims of the intervention nor have their effects on writing motivation been assessed. To our knowledge, there are no multicomponent frameworks that simultaneously focus on writing performance *and* writing motivation—both as instructional components and as student outcomes. Indeed, writing engagement has not been sufficiently investigated empirically, thus, integrating principles of the reading engagement model into a theoretical framework of writing engagement is feasible and a fertile terrain for future investigation, but has not yet been done.

Therefore, in this section we focus on the reading engagement model, reflecting on the need for such instructional intervention models for writing in the conclusion of the chapter. This said, in our discussion of the reading engagement model below, we highlight where the intervention linked reading with writing in instruction or assessment, thereby underscoring the interrelations of these aspects of literacy and potential for future intervention studies to examine them in a more integrated manner.

Engaged readers are individuals who read deeply, frequently, strategically, and socially; as stated by Guthrie et al. (2000, p. 209), ". . . engagement is a network of bonds among skills, strategies, knowledge, and motivation, in the social community." Reading engagement is the centerpiece of a model that draws on multiple motivation theories—especially the four described herein—to create an elaborate yet cohesive portrait of how teachers may create a classroom context that facilitates students' engagement in reading and thereby their reading achievement (Guthrie & Wigfield, 2000). The most recent formulations of the model (Guthrie & Klauda, 2016; Guthrie et al., 2012) depict the classroom context directly impacting students' motivations to read, which, in turn, play a major role in energizing students' behavioral engagement in reading. In the model, behavioral engagement, or dedication to reading, substantially mediates the relationship between motivation and achievement. That is, motivated individuals invest more time and effort in reading, more actively processing text and persisting longer in challenging reading activities, with evidence of their active and persistent reading being reflected not only in their actual reading behaviors but also in their writing—of factual notes, inferences drawn from reading, summaries across single and multiple texts, integrative reports, complex charts and more. In turn, this willful engagement in literacy activities strengthens multiple aspects of individuals' reading achievement, including their literal and higher-level comprehension skills, fluency, and vocabulary (Guthrie & Klauda, 2016). For an extensive review of the empirical evidence supporting each of the links in the reading engagement model, see Guthrie et al. (2012).

How do teachers create engaging classroom contexts? Guthrie et al. (2012) describe nine key elements that may be considered. While ideally teachers incorporate all nine elements into their instruction, in practice, instructional interventions based on the model have been designed that focus on a subset of these elements, selected and operationalized in implementation based on the developmental level and other characteristics of the particular students participating in the intervention. For sake of brevity, we outline the five practices emphasized in Guthrie, Wigfield and colleagues' most recent endeavor to develop an instructional intervention guided by the engagement model (e.g., Guthrie & Klauda, 2014; Guthrie, Klauda, & Ho, 2013). Specifically, they designed a version of Concept-Oriented Reading Instruction (CORI) for seventh-grade students in a rural, ethnically diverse setting; CORI, which had previously been studied in the third to fifth grades, entails systematic, cohesive implementation of motivational practices and cognitive strategy instruction in the context of a science or social studies conceptual theme. In CORI for seventh grade, language arts teachers received professional development in implementing the practices of choice, relevance, success, importance, and collaboration (Guthrie & Klauda, 2016). In brief, *choice*, which is closely akin to autonomy support as discussed extensively above, includes giving students meaningful options in their literacy activities, including what and how they will read as well as in what written or verbal form they will demonstrate their comprehension. *Relevance* refers to helping students recognize or form personal connections between their reading and their lives, such as through hands-on science experiments. Choice and relevance particularly support intrinsic motivation. The practice of *success*, intended to encourage self-efficacy, means providing competence support, such as by helping students form realistic reading goals and providing texts closely matched to their capabilities. *Importance* means helping students develop value for reading, by, for instance, asking them to think and write about the benefits of reading a specific text. Lastly, *collaboration* includes structuring opportunities for students to work together in reading activities and in producing written products based on their reading, which helps encourage students to interact positively with others and develop a shared positive orientation toward reading. In addition, the CORI teachers focused on the cognitive strategies of making inferences, summarizing, and concept mapping through direct, carefully scaffolded instruction—which all entail transforming thoughts into the written word. CORI for middle school did not emphasize *knowledge goals* as a distinct motivation practice; however, they are one of the additional classroom context elements in the full model (Guthrie et al., 2012), and in line with achievement goal theory (Pintrich, 2003), students learned to use the cognitive strategies in the service of gaining and synthesizing knowledge to address authentic questions and goals for reading. That is, they were encouraged to form mastery goals in their language arts class.

Empirical Effects of Reading Engagement Interventions

How does instruction based on the full reading engagement model impact students' reading motivation, engagement, and achievement? A meta-analysis of 11 CORI studies conducted in third-through fifth-grade classrooms demonstrated positive effects compared to traditional instruction and instruction featuring cognitive strategy instruction but not motivation practices in several regards, with effect sizes ranging from .49 (for students' amount of reading) to 1.2 (for students' self-reported reading motivation). Notably, effects on achievement measures included those on standardized tests of reading comprehension (ES = .93), as well as researcher-developed assessments of such variables as comprehension, fluency, and word recognition (Guthrie, McRae, & Klauda, 2007); with regard to writing, a key comprehension assessment entailed students writing for 30 minutes about survival in two given biomes (e.g., ponds and deserts) after a 50-minute period of reading and note-taking on those biomes from a 75-page packet (Guthrie et al., 2004). Studies in seventh-grade classrooms also provide evidence that the CORI classroom context benefits students' motivation, engagement, and achievement relative to traditional instruction for both science (Guthrie et al., 2013) and history subject matter (Guthrie & Klauda, 2014). Instantiations of the engagement model applied to English learners in sixth and seventh grade also evinced increased comprehension in history, self-efficacy for reading history and engagement with history texts (Taboada Barber et al., 2015; Taboada Barber, 2016).

Other Key Dimensions of Motivation for Literacy

In this chapter, we have aimed to show how constructs drawn from multiple, broadly applicable motivational theories may be connected to both reading and writing. Because most of the research on motivation applied to literacy achievement contexts has been in the domain of reading, we also summarized a framework formulated specifically to integrate specific constructs and general theoretical perspectives: the reading engagement model. There are two important gaps, however, in our conceptualization of literacy motivation, pertinent especially to reading, that we feel compelled to address.

The first gap is the question of what constructs truly represent motivations for literacy. Over the last two decades, much scholarly work has focused on defining a set of key reading motivation dimensions and examining individual differences and developmental patterns in them. In the late 1990s, Wigfield, Guthrie, and colleagues advocated a multidimensional view of reading motivation, including as many as 11 distinct dimensions (Baker & Wigfield, 1999; Wigfield & Guthrie, 1997). In the past few years, however, researchers (e.g., Schiefele, Schaffner, Möller, & Wigfield, 2012; Schiefele & Schaffner, 2016) have questioned what dimensions truly represent the construct of reading motivation, based on both theoretical logic and factor analytical studies (e.g., Schaffner & Schiefele, 2007). Specifically, out of the 11 dimensions of reading motivation identified by Wigfield and Guthrie (1997), Schiefele & Schaffner (2016) argue that reading for *curiosity* and *involvement* represent intrinsic reasons for reading and that reading for *recognition, competition, compliance*, and *grades* represent extrinsic reasons. In contrast, they consider the remaining five dimensions—*challenge, importance, self-efficacy, social* and *work avoidance*—primarily antecedents or consequences of motivation. For example, self-efficacy is viewed as a necessary antecedent of choosing to read (or write) and a consequence of one feeling successful in reading, but not an end for which someone purposefully decides to read.

With regard to writing motivation, there is much less research on its dimensionality than there has been in the domain of reading. However, Troia and colleagues' work (2012a, 2012b) suggests that a multidimensional view is beneficial for understanding and conceiving ways of strengthening students' willingness to attempt and persist in writing tasks. Specifically, Troia et al. (2012a) examined how writing self-efficacy, success attributions, task interest/value, mastery goals, performance goals and avoidance goals intertwined with each other and with writing frequency, ability, grade level, and gender. This work suggests a complex web of factors contributing to writing performance, particularly supporting expectancy-value and achievement goal theories, but also more broadly suggesting the import of broadening how writing motivation is assessed. This complexity reflects, as well, efforts to apply theoretical models of motivation to writing. Again, although these efforts are not yet fully formulated as theoretical models of writing motivation, studies such as this may lead the way in forging the development of theories of writing motivation.

Within the domain of reading, however, dimensions of reading motivation have emerged in qualitative studies, but these are not captured in measures commonly employed in quantitative studies (Schiefele et al., 2012) and point to the second key gap in this chapter and in the explication of the reading engagement model itself, as noted by Guthrie et al. (2012). Two such dimensions of reading motivation relate to readers' emotions: emotional regulation (reading to help manage negative feelings such as sadness or anger) and relief from boredom (reading to assuage feelings of boredom). While emotions are an important part of the affective dimension of engagement, their specific role in the reading domain has not received much consideration. Nor have emotions received much attention within writing research, except with regard to writing anxiety.

Recent work has focused on emotions as part of Pekrun and colleagues' control-value theory (Pekrun, 2000, 2006). In control-value theory, *achievement emotions* are characterized by an individual's "affective arousal that is tied directly to achievement activities (e.g., studying) or achievement outcomes (success and failure)" (Pekrun & Perry, 2014, p. 121). Motivation, cognitive resources, strategy use, and self-regulatory strategies appear to mediate, or explain the impact of such emotions on learning and achievement (Pekrun, Elliot, & Maier, 2006). Generally speaking, positive emotions relate positively to student engagement and academic achievement. In contrast, negative emotions such as anxiety or shame can negatively influence intrinsic motivation but also increase the extrinsic value of achievement and rewards. Within literacy, control-value theory suggests that it is imperative for teachers to consider how texts themselves, reading and writing activities, and classroom organization emotionally affect students, and thus how they can potentially augment student engagement by creating situations that induce more positive emotions.

Concluding Thoughts

As is the case with the theoretical frameworks presented in the rest of this volume, theories of motivation should facilitate researchers' and practitioners' efforts to identify and explain the myriad facets shaping individuals' development as readers and writers. Understanding the research on these facets is critical to crafting classroom contexts that foster engaged writing and reading and to designing empirical research studies that pinpoint remaining questions about how students can satisfy both their teachers' and their own literacy-related objectives. Avenues for future research are manifold. Clearly, in contrast to reading motivation, writing motivation has been less explored. Given the challenges that many students face with writing, exploring the interrelations of writing motivation and performance and focusing on motivational constructs within writing interventions, are necessary and enticing areas of scholarly inquiry. Ultimately, we hope that the theories and the research they inspire guide researchers and educators in manifesting the understanding that supporting motivation should not only be in the service of improved reading and writing performance, but that increased motivation and engagement are worthy outcomes in themselves. We also hope that the theories reviewed in this chapter, the more recently identified empirical constructs, and their implications for literacy instruction help researchers and educators renew or deepen their own sense of efficacy for creating pathways to engaged literacy for all students.

References

Ames, C. (1992). Classrooms: Goals, structures, and student motivation. *Journal of Educational Psychology, 84*(3), 261–271. doi:10.1037/0022-0663.84.3.261

Atkinson, J. W. (1957). Motivational determinants of risk taking behavior. *Psychological Review, 64,* 359–371. doi:10.1037/h0043445

Baker, L., & Wigfield, A. (1999). Dimensions of children's motivation for reading and their relations to reading activity and reading achievement. *Reading Research Quarterly, 34,* 452–477. doi:10.1598/RRQ.34.4.4

Bandura, A. (1977). Self-efficacy: Toward a unifying theory of behavioral change. *Psychological Review, 84,* 191–215. doi:10.1037/0033-295X.84.2.191

Bandura, A. (1986). *Social foundations of thought and action: A social cognitive theory.* Englewood Cliffs, NJ: Prentice Hall.

Bandura, A. (1991). Social cognitive theory of self-regulation. *Organizational behavior and human decision processes, 50,* 248–287. doi:10.1016/0749-5978(91)90022-L

Bandura, A. (1997). *Self-efficacy: The exercise of control.* New York, NY: Freeman.

Bandura, A. (2006). Toward a psychology of human agency. *Perspectives on Psychological Science, 1,* 164–180. doi:10.1111/j.1745-6916.2006.00011.x

Bandura, A., Barbaranelli, C., Caprara, C. V., & Pastorelli, C. (1996). Multifaceted impact of self-efficacy beliefs on academic functioning. *Child Development, 67*(3), 1206–1222. doi: 10.2307/1131888

Benware, C. A., & Deci, E. L. (1984). Quality of learning with an active versus passive motivational set. *American Educational Research Journal, 21*(4), 755–765. Retrieved from http://www.jstor.org/stable/1162999

Bruning, R., & Horn, C. (2000). Developing motivation to write. *Educational Psychologist, 35*(1), 27–35. doi:10.1207/s15326985ep3501_4

Bruning, R. H., & Kauffman, D. F. (2016). Self-efficacy beliefs and motivation in writing development. In C. A. MacArthur, S. Graham, & J. Fitzgerald (Eds.), *Handbook of writing research* (pp. 160–173). New York: NY: Guilford Press.

Deci, E. L., & Ryan, R. M. (1985). Intrinsic motivation and self-determination in human behavior. New York, NY: Plenum.

De Naeghl, J., Valcke, M., De Meyer, I., Warlop, N., van Braak. J., & Van Keer, H. (2014). The role of teacher behavior in adolescents' intrinsic reading motivation. *Reading and Writing, 27*, 1547–1565. doi:10.1007/s11145-014-9506-3

Duda, J. L., & Nicholls, J. G. (1992). Dimensions of achievement motivation in schoolwork and sport. *Journal of Educational Psychology, 84*(3), 290–299. doi:10.1037/0022-0663.84.3.290

Dweck, C. S., & Leggett, E. L. (1988). A social-cognitive approach to motivation and personality. *Psychological Review, 95*, 256–327. doi:10.1037/0033-295X.95.2.256

Eccles, J. S. (1984). Sex differences in achievement patterns. In T. Sonderegger (Ed.), *Nebraska Symposium on Motivation* (Vol. 32, pp. 97–132). Lincoln, NE: University of Nebraska Press.

Eccles, J. S., Adler, T. F., Futterman, R., Goff, S. B., Kaczala, C. M., Meece, J. L. & Midgley, C. (1983). Expectancies, values, and academic behaviors. In J. T. Spence (Ed.), *Achievement and achievement motivation* (pp. 75–146). San Francisco, CA: W. H. Freeman.

Elliot, A. J. (1999). Approach and avoidance motivation and achievement goals. *Educational Psychologist, 34*(3), 169–189. doi:10.1207/s15326985ep3403_3

Ferguson, Y. L., Kasser, T., & Jahng, S. (2010). Differences in life satisfaction and school satisfaction among adolescents from three nations: The role of perceived autonomy support. *Journal of Research on Adolescence, 21*, 649–661. doi:10.1111/j.1532-7795.2010.00698.x

Fredricks, J. A., Blumenfeld, P. C., & Paris, A. H. (2004). School engagement: Potential of the concept, state of the evidence. *Review of Educational Research, 74*, 59–109. doi:10.3102/00346543074001059

Graham, S. (1990). The role of production factors in learning disabled students' compositions. *Journal of Educational Psychology, 82*, 781–791. doi:10.1037/0022-0663.82.4.781

Grant H., & Dweck, C. (2003). Clarifying achievement goals and their impact. *Journal of Personality and Social Psychology, 85*, 541–553. doi:10.1037/0022-3514.85.3.541

Greene, B. A., Miller, R. B., Crowson, H. M., Duke, B. L., & Akey, K. L. (2004). Predicting high school students' cognitive engagement and achievement: Contributions of classroom perceptions and motivation. *Contemporary Educational Psychology, 29*, 462–482. doi:10.1016/j.cedpsych.2004.01.006

Guthrie, J. T., Cox, K. E., Knowles, K. T., Buehl, M., Mazzoni, S. A., & Fasulo, L. (2000). Building toward coherent instruction. In L. Baker, M. J. Dreher, & J. T. Guthrie (Eds.), *Engaging young readers: Promoting achievement and motivation* (pp. 209–237). New York: Guilford Press.

Guthrie, J. T., & Klauda, S. L. (2014). Effects of classroom practices on reading comprehension, engagement, and motivations for adolescents. *Reading Research Quarterly, 49*(4), 387–416. doi:10.1002/rrq.81

Guthrie, J. T., & Klauda, S. L. (2016). Engagement and motivational processes in reading. In P. Afflerbach (Ed.), *Handbook of individual differences in reading* (pp. 41–53). New York: Routledge.

Guthrie, J. T., Klauda, S. L., & Ho, A. N. (2013). Modeling the relationships among reading instruction, motivation, engagement, and achievement for adolescents. *Reading Research Quarterly, 48*, 9–26. doi:10.1002/rrq.035

Guthrie, J. T., Mason-Singh, A., & Coddington, C. S. (2012). Instructional effects of Concept-Oriented Reading Instruction on motivation for reading information text in middle school. In J. T. Guthrie, A. Wigfield, & S. L. Klauda (Eds.), *Adolescents' engagement in academic literacy* (pp. 155–215). University of Maryland, College Park. Retrieved from http://www.corilearning.com/research-publications

Guthrie, J. T., McRae, A. C., & Klauda, S. L. (2007). Contributions of Concept-Oriented Reading Instruction to knowledge about interventions for motivations in reading. *Educational Psychologist, 42*, 237–250. doi:10.1080/00461520701621087

Guthrie, J. T., & Wigfield, A. (2000). Engagement and motivation in reading. In M. L. Kamil, P. B. Mosenthal, P. D. Pearson, & R. Barr (Eds.), *Reading research handbook* (Vol. 3, pp. 403–424). Mahwah, NJ: Erlbaum.

Guthrie, J. T., Wigfield, A., Barbosa, P., Perencevich, K. C., Taboada, A., Davis, M. H., & Tonks, S. (2004). Increasing reading comprehension and engagement through Concept-Oriented Reading Instruction. *Journal of Educational Psychology, 96*, 403–423. doi:10.1037/0022-0663.96.3.403

Guthrie, J. T., Wigfield, A., Metsala, J. L., & Cox, K. E. (1999). Motivational and cognitive predictors of text comprehension and reading amount. *Scientific Studies of Reading, 3*(3), 231–256. doi:10.1207/s1532799xssr0303_3

Guthrie, J. T., Wigfield, A., & You, W. (2012). Instructional contexts for engagement and achievement in reading. In S. J. Christenson, A. L. Reschly, & C. Wylie (Eds.), *Handbook of Research on Student Engagement* (pp. 601–634). New York, NY: Springer.

Harris, K. R., & Graham, S. (1996). Making the writing process work: Strategies for composition and self-regulation. Cambridge, MA: Brookline.

Harris, K. R., & Graham, S. (1999). Programmatic intervention research: Illustration from the evolution of self-regulated strategy development. *Learning Disability Quarterly, 22,* 251–262. doi:10.2307/1511259

Harris, K. R., Graham, S., & Mason, L. H. (2006). Improving the writing, knowledge, and motivation of struggling young writers: Effects of self-regulated strategy development with and without peer support. *American Educational Research Journal, 43*(2), 295–340. doi:10.3102/00028312043002295

Hidi, S., and Anderson, V. (1992). Situational interest and its impact on reading and expository writing. In A. Renninger, S. Hidi, and A. Krapp (Eds.), *The role of interest in learning and development* (pp. 215–238). Hillsdale, NJ: Erlbaum.

Hidi, S., & Boscolo, P. (2006). Motivation and writing. In C. A. MacArthur, S. Graham, & J. Fitzgerald (Eds.), *Handbook of writing research* (pp. 144–157). New York: Guilford.

Hidi, S., and McLaren J. (1991). Motivational factors and writing: The role of topic interestingness. *European Journal of Psychology of Education 6*(2): 187–197. doi:10.1007/BF03191937

Hulleman, C. S., Godes, O., Hendricks, B. L., & Harackiewicz, J. M. (2010). Enhancing interest and performance with a utility value intervention. *Journal of Educational Psychology, 102,* 880–895. doi:10.1037/a0019506

Hulleman, C. S., & Harackiewicz, J. M. (2009). Promoting interest and performance in high school science classes. *Science, 326,* 1410–1412. doi:10.1126/science.1177067

Jang, H., Kim, E. J., & Reeve, J. (2012). Longitudinal test of self-determination theory's motivation mediation model in a naturally occurring classroom context. *Journal of Educational Psychology, 104,* 1175–1188. doi:10.1037/a0028089

Jang, H., Reeve, J., & Deci, E. L. (2010). Engaging students in learning activities: It is not autonomy support or structure but autonomy support and structure. *Journal of Educational Psychology, 102,* 588–600. doi:10.1037/a0019682

Jang, H., Reeve, J., Ryan, R. M., & Kim, A. (2009). Can self-determination theory explain what underlies the productive, satisfying learning experiences of collectivistically oriented Korean students? *Journal of Educational Psychology, 101,* 644–661. doi:10.1037/a0014241

Krashen, S. D., Lee, S-Y., Lao, C. (2018). *Comprehensible and compelling: The causes and effects of free and voluntary reading.* Santa Barbara, CA: Libraries Unlimited.

Lam, S., & Law, Y. (2007). The roles of instructional practices and motivation in writing performance. *The Journal of Experimental Education, 75*(2), 145–164. doi:10.3200/JEXE.75.2.145-164

Linnenbrink, E. A. (2005). The dilemma of performance-approach goals: The use of multiple goal contexts to promote students' motivation and learning. *Journal of Educational Psychology, 97,* 197–213. doi:10.1037/0022-0663.97.2.197

Linnenbrink-Garcia, L. & Patall, E. A. (2015). Motivation. In L. Corno & E. Anderson (Eds.), *Handbook of Educational Psychology* (3rd ed., pp. 91–103). New York: Routledge.

Maehr, M. L., & Midgley, C. (1996). *Transforming school cultures.* Boulder, CO: Westview Press.

Meece, J. L., Anderman, E. M., & Anderman, L. H. (2006). Classroom goal structure student motivation, and academic achievement. *Annual Review of Psychology, 57,* 487–503. doi:10.1146/annurev.psych.56.091103.070258

Meece, J. L., Blumenfeld, P. C., & Hoyle, R. (1988). Students' goal orientations and cognitive engagement in classroom activities. *Journal of Educational Psychology, 80,* 514–523. doi:10.1037/0022-0663.80.4.514

Meece, J. L., & Miller, S. D. (2001). A longitudinal analysis of elementary school students' achievement goals in literacy activities. *Contemporary Educational Psychology, 26,* 454–480. doi:10.1006/ceps.2000.1071

Midgley, C., Kaplan, A., Middleton, M., Maehr, M. L., Urdan, T., Hicks Anderman, L., & Roeser, R. (1998). The development and validation of scales assessing students' achievement goal orientations. *Contemporary Educational Psychology, 23,* 113–131. doi:10.1006/ceps.1998.0965

Mucherah, W., & Yoder, A. (2008). Motivation for reading and middle school students' performance on standardized testing in reading. *Reading Psychology, 29,* 214–235. doi:10.1080/02702710801982159

Multon, K. D., Brown, S. D., & Lent, R.W. (1991). Relation of self-efficacy beliefs to academic outcomes: A meta-analytic investigation. *Journal of Counseling Psychology, 38,* 30–38. doi:10.1080/02702710801982159

Newby, T. J. (1991). Classroom motivation: Strategies of first-year teachers. *Journal of Educational Psychology, 86,* 195–200. doi:10.1037/0022-0663.83.2.195

Ng, M. M., Guthrie, J. T., Van Meter, P., McCann, A., & Alao, S. (1998). How do classroom characteristics influences intrinsic motivations for literacy? *Reading Psychology, 19,* 319–398. doi:10.1177/0013124510380418

Pajares, F. (2003). Self-efficacy beliefs, motivation, and achievement in writing: A review of the literature. *Reading and Writing Quarterly, 19,* 139–158. doi:10.1080/10573560308222

Pajares, F., Johnson, M. J., & Usher, E. L. (2007). Sources of writing self-efficacy beliefs of elementary, middle, and high school students. *Research in the Teaching of English*, 104–120.

Pajares, F., & Kranzler, J. (1995). Self-efficacy beliefs and general mental ability in mathematical problem-solving. *Contemporary Educational Psychology, 20*, 426–443. doi:10.1006/ceps.1995.1029

Pajares, F., Miller, M. D., & Johnson, M. J. (1999). Gender differences in writing self-beliefs of elementary school students. *Journal of Educational Psychology, 91*, 50–61. doi:10.1037/0022-0663.91.1.50

Pajares, F., & Valiante, G. (2006). Self-efficacy beliefs and motivation in writing development. In C. MacArthur, S. Graham, & J. Fitzgerald (Eds.), Handbook of writing research (pp. 158–170). New York, NY: Guilford Press.

Patall, E. A. (2012). The motivational complexity of choosing: A review of theory and research. In R. Ryan (Ed.), *Oxford handbook of human motivation* (pp. 249–279). New York, NY: Oxford University Press.

Patall, E. A. (2013). Constructing motivation through choice, interest, and interestingness. *Journal of Educational Psychology, 105,* 522–534. doi:10.1037/a0030307

Pekrun, R. (2006). The control-value theory of achievement emotions: Assumptions, corollaries, and implications for educational research and practice. *Educational Psychology Review, 18*(4), 315–341. doi:10.1007/s10648-006-9029-9

Pekrun, R. (2000). A social-cognitive, control-value theory of achievement emotions. In J. Heckhausen (Ed.), *Advances in psychology, 131. Motivational psychology of human development: Developing motivation and motivating development* (pp. 143–163). New York, NY: Elsevier Science.

Pekrun, R., Elliot, A. J., & Maier, M. A. (2006). Achievement goals and discrete achievement emotions: A theoretical model and prospective test. *Journal of Educational Psychology, 98*(3), 583–597. doi:10.1037/0022-0663.98.3.583

Pekrun, R., & Perry, R. P. (2014). Control-value theory of achievement emotions. In R. Pekrun & L. Linnenbrink-Garcia (Eds.), *International handbook of emotions in education* (pp. 120–141). New York, NY: Taylor & Francis.

Pintrich, P. R. (2003). A motivational science perspective on the role of student motivation in learning and teaching contexts. *Journal of Educational Psychology, 95*(5), 667–686. doi:10.1037/0022-0663.95.4.667

Pintrich, P. R. (2000). Multiple goals, multiple pathways: The role of goal orientation in learning and achievement. *Journal of Educational Psychology, 93*(3), 544–555. doi:10.1037/0022-0663.92.3.544

Reeve, J., Bolt, E., & Cai, Y. (1999). Autonomy-supportive teachers: How they teach and motivate students. *Journal of Educational Psychology, 91*, 537–548. doi:10.1037/0022-0663.91.3.537

Reeve, J., & Jang, H. (2006). What teachers say and do to support students' autonomy during a learning activity. *Journal of Educational Psychology, 98,* 209–218. doi:10.1037/0022-0663.98.1.209

Ryan, R. M., & Deci, E. L. (2000). Intrinsic and extrinsic motivations: Classic definitions and new directions. *Contemporary Educational Psychology, 25,* 54–67. doi:10.1006/ceps.1999.1020

Schaffner, E., & Schiefele, U. (2007). Auswirkungen habitueller Lesemotivation auf die situative Textreprasentation [Effects of habitual reading motivation on the situational representation of text]. *Psychologie in Erziehung und Unterricht, 54*(4), 268–286.

Schiefele, U., & Schaffner, E. (2016). Factorial and construct validity of a new instrument for the assessment of reading motivation. *Reading Research Quarterly, 51,* 221–237. doi:10.1002/rrq.134

Schiefele, U., Schaffner, E., Möller, J., & Wigfield, A. (2012). Dimensions of reading motivation and their relation to reading behavior and competence. *Reading Research Quarterly, 47*(4), 427–463. Retrieved from http://www.jstor.org.proxy um.researchport.umd.edu/stable/23317751

Schunk, D. H. (2003). Self-efficacy for reading and writing: Influence of modeling, goal setting and self-evaluation. *Reading and Writing Quarterly, 19,* 159–172. doi:10.1080/10573560308219

Schunk, D. H., Pintrich, P. R., & Meece, J. L. (2008). *Motivation in education: Theory, research and application* (3rd ed.). Upper Saddle River, NJ: Pearson/Merrill Prentice Hall.

Schunk, D. H., & Swartz, C. W. (1993). Goals and progress feedback: Effects on self-efficacy and writing achievement. *Contemporary Educational Psychology, 18,* 337–354. doi:10.1006/ceps.1993.1024

Schunk, D. H., & Zimmerman, B. J. (2007). Influencing children's self-efficacy and self-regulation of reading and writing through modeling, *Reading & Writing Quarterly, 23*(1), 7–25, doi:10.1080/10573560600837578

Shell, D. F., Colvin, C., & Bruning, R. H. (1995). Self-efficacy, attributions, and outcome expectancy mechanisms in reading and writing achievement: Grade-level and achievement-level differences. *Journal of Educational Psychology, 87,* 386–398. doi:10.1037/0022-0663.87.3.386

Shell, D. F., Murphy, C., & Bruning, R. (1989). Self-efficacy and outcome expectancy mechanisms in reading and writing performance. *Journal of Educational Psychology, 81,* 91–100. doi:10.1037/0022-0663.81.1.91

Stipek, D., Givvin, K., Salmon, J., & MacGyvers, V. (1998). Can a teacher intervention improve classroom practices and student motivation in mathematics? *Journal of Experimental Education, 66,* 319–337. doi:10.1080/00220979809601404

Taboada Barber, A. M. (2016). Reading to learn for ELs: Motivation practices and comprehension strategies for informational texts. Portsmouth, NH: Heinemann.

Taboada Barber, A., Buehl, M. M., Kidd, J. K., Sturtevant, E. G., Richey Nuland, L., & Beck, J. (2015). Reading engagement in social studies: Exploring the role of a social studies literacy intervention on reading comprehension, reading self-efficacy, and engagement in middle school students with different language backgrounds. *Reading Psychology, 36*, 31–85. doi:10.1080/02702711.2013.815140

Taylor, B. M., Pearson, R. D., Clark, K., & Walpole, S. (2000). Effective schools and accomplished teachers: Lessons about primary-grade reading instruction in low-income schools. *Elementary School Journal, 101*, 121–165. Retrieved from http://www.jstor.org/stable/1002340

Troia, G. A., Harbaugh, A. G., Shankland, R. K., Wolbers, K. A., & Lawrence, A. M. (2012a). Relationships between writing motivation, writing activity, and writing performance: Effects of grade, sex, and ability. *Reading and Writing, 26*, 17–44. doi:10.1007/s11145-012-9379-2

Troia, G. A., Shankland, R. K., & Wolbers (2012b). Motivation research in writing: Theoretical and empirical considerations. *Reading and Writing Quarterly, 28*, 5–28.

Turner, J. C., Midgley, C., Meyer, D. K., Gheen, M., Anderman, A. M., Kang, Y., & Patrick, H. (2002). The classroom environment and students' reports of avoidance strategies in mathematics: A multimethod study. *Journal of Educational Psychology, 94*, 88–106. doi:10.1037/0022-0663.94.1.88

Urdan, T., & Schoenfelder, E. (2006). Classroom effects on student motivation: Goal structures, social relationships, and competence beliefs. *Journal of School Psychology, 44*, 331–349. doi:10.1016/j.jsp.2006.04.003

Weiner, B. (1985). An attributional theory of achievement motivation and emotion. *Journal of Educational Psychology, 92*, 548–573. doi:10.1037/0033-295X.92.4.548

Wigfield, A. (1994). Expectancy-value theory of achievement motivation: A developmental perspective. *Educational Psychology Review, 6*, 49–78.

Wigfield, A., & Eccles, J. S. (1992). The development of achievement task values: A theoretical analysis. *Developmental Review, 12*, 265–310.

Wigfield, A., & Eccles, J. S. (2000). Expectancy-value theory of achievement motivation. *Contemporary Educational Psychology, 25*, 68–81. doi:10.1006/ceps.1999.1015

Wigfield, A., & Guthrie, J. T. (1997). Relations to children's motivation for reading to the amount and breadth of their reading. *Journal of Educational Psychology, 89*, 420–432. doi:10.1037/0022-0663.89.3.420

Wigfield, A., Mason-Singh, A., Ho, A. N., & Guthrie, J. T. (2014). Intervening to improve children's reading motivation and comprehension: Concept-Oriented Reading Instruction. In S. A. Karabenick & T. C. Urdan (Eds.), *Motivational interventions (Advances in motivation and achievement, Volume 18)* (pp. 37–70). Bingley: Emerald Group Publishing Limited.

Wigfield, A., Rosenzweig, E. Q., & Eccles, J. (2017). Achievement values: Interactions, interventions, and future directions. In A. Elliot, C. Dweck, & D. Yeager (Eds.), *Handbook of Competence and Motivation: Theory and Application* (2nd ed., pp. 116–134). New York, NY: Guilford Press.

Wigfield, A., Tonks, S. T., & Klauda, S. L. (2016). Expectancy-value theory. In K. R. Wentzel & D. B. Miele (Eds.), *Handbook of motivation at school* (pp. 55–74). New York, NY: Routledge.

13

EDUCATIONAL NEUROSCIENCE FOR READING RESEARCHERS

George G. Hruby and Usha Goswami

This chapter is adapted from "Neuroscience and Reading: A Review for Reading Education Researchers," *Reading Research Quarterly, 46*(2); 156–172. Copyright © 2011 by the International Reading Association.

For the past 30 years, research on the brain has advanced impressively. This work, from fields known collectively as the neurosciences, has expanded our understanding of the neural chemistry, physiology, and growth processes that support behavior, cognition, language, emotion, sociality, and their development. It has also cast considerable light on the nature of individual differences and relatable disabilities, from genetic to behavioral levels of analysis. As these areas of research have expanded, attempts to relate insights from the neurosciences to education have been numerous, although the quality of these attempts have been variable and often, perhaps, premature or overexuberant, as many have commented (e.g., Bruer, 1997; Goswami, 2006; Hirsh-Pasek et al., 2007; Willis, 2007). Nonetheless, of all the areas addressed by the emerging field of educational neuroscience, Varma, McCandliss, and Schwartz (2008) have suggested that the neuroscience of reading processes has proven the most impressive in its sophistication.

In this review of the neuroscience literature on reading, we briefly describe the current state of the science regarding neural correlates of acknowledged and potential reading processes and reading development. Specifically, we briefly review the neural correlates of decoding and language comprehension and relate such findings to current models of reading, reading instruction, and reading disability. We then discuss what neuroscience research might mean for researchers and practitioners in education. We conclude by suggesting that the field has a clear need for literacy education scholars who are knowledgeable about the developmental and life sciences—individuals who could make use of insights from disciplines such as neuroscience to help inform reading theory, policy, and research.

Although our theme is the relationship of brain research to reading education, we do not devote extended paragraphs here to the research methods used in neuroscience, except as this may be necessary to clarify issues for scholars of literacy. This more technical information is interesting in its own right, of course, but it is readily available in previously published reviews and introductory texts (e.g., Gazzaniga, 2010; Hruby, 2009; Huettel, Song, & McCarthy, 2009; Luck, 2005; Mody, 2004; Willis, 2007). We allude to these details where helpful. (Refer to Table 13.1 for a helpful glossary of terms used throughout this article.) As in all experimental science, the findings and innovative techniques employed by neuroscience are still developing and are regularly subject to revision and critique, a point we elaborate on in this review.

Nevertheless, integrating findings from neuroscience research with other research perspectives on literacy offers exciting opportunities for education (Szücs & Goswami, 2007; Willingham &

Table 13.1 Glossary

Terms	Definition
	Orientation
anterior	Portion of a brain area most toward the front of the brain (e.g., anterior temporal = the area of the temporal lobe most toward the front of the head)
bilateral	On both sides of the brain in relatively the same hemispheric location
central	Toward the center of the brain
dorsal	Toward the top or top back of the brain
inferior	Portion of a brain area most toward the bottom of the brain
posterior	Portion of a brain area most toward the back of the brain
superior	Portion of a brain area most toward the top of the brain
ventral	Toward the underside of the brain
	Anatomical
amygdala	Almond-shaped area near the hippocampus for rapid identification of danger associations; regulates fear response
cerebellum	Bunlike lobe beneath the occipital cortex; processes automatic or repetitive motor movements
cerebrum	Sitting atop the brain stem; the most evolutionarily advanced of the major brain divisions; folded into gyri and sulci
cingulate cortex; anterior/posterior	Located in the middle of the cortex; processes input from the thalamus and neocortical areas; part of the limbic system regulating memory, emotion, and executive function
cortex, cortical, cerebral cortex	The folded sheet of neural tissue outermost to the cerebrum
encephalon	All the higher areas of the nervous system contained within the skull; the brain
frontal cortex/lobe	Forwardmost of the four major lobes of the cortex; associated with executive function, decision making, planning, building novel situation models, analyzing structure, motor associations, and motor control
gyrus (pl. *gyri*)	A ridge on the brain surface formed by the folding of brain tissue in the cortex
hemisphere	Halves of the neocortex; left and right
hippocampus	Part of the limbic system situated below the brain; somewhat wishbone shaped and extending into both hemispheres beneath the temporal lobes; related to memory formation and retrieval
lobe	A major anatomical region of the brain
neocortex	Outermost layers of the cerebral cortex
occipital cortex/lobe	Posteriormost cortical lobe; processes visual input
orbitofrontal cortex/lobe	Area of the prefrontal lobe directly over the eye sockets; associated with decision making, emotional control, and reward monitoring
parietal cortex/lobe	Posterior area of the brain between the sensory-motor and occipital lobes; integrates various sensory modalities from both the sensory cortex and occipital lobe; processes spatial relationship and coordinates of the body, maps, and so forth (generally in the right hemisphere), and symbolic functions in language and math; cross-modal associations allowing for categorization and categorical interrelationship

(*continued*)

Table 13.1 (Continued)

Terms	Definition
	Anatomical
prefrontal cortex/lobe	Anterior area of the frontal lobe; associated with social behaviors, personality, and complex cognitive processes such as planning
sensory-motor cortex	Saddling across the middle of the cerebral cortex; the posterior strip devoted to sensory input, the anterior strip devoted to motor movements; arranged somatotopically (i.e., located in an anatomically coherent sequence; e.g., motor area for the hand is near the motor area for the arm not the feet)
sulcus (pl. sulci)	The fissures between gyri on the brain surface
temporal cortex/lobe	Located in the vicinity of the temple, just over and anterior to the ears, on either side of the brain; processes auditory input, word forms, word meanings, sign meanings, and faces and is related to episodic and declarative memory as well as long-term memory thanks to its proximity to the hippocampus
	Methods of Brain Study
EEG	Electroencephalography; measuring activity of the brain through fluctuations in electrical charge at the surface of the scalp
encephalographic	Measuring activity in the brain through monitoring of electromagnetic fluctuations at the surface of the scalp
fMRI	Functional magnetic resonance imaging; color-coded indications of differences in blood flow (or other correlates, e.g., glucose or oxygen) between two conditions mapped onto an MRI image of the brain; because neurons require glucose and oxygen to function, the more glucose and oxygen taken up in an area of the brain, the greater the activity presumed to occur in the area
hemodynamic	Literally, blood flow; tracks blood flow in the brain, glucose concentrations, oxygen concentrations, or radioactive isotopes injected into the blood stream
MEG	Magnetoencephalography; measuring activity of the brain through fluctuations in magnetic charge at the surface of the scalp
MRI	Magnetic resonance imaging; imaging brain structure through detected differences in water density using magnetic current to align the water molecules in the brain
PET	Positron emission tomography; images the brain with radioactive isotopes, typically of glucose, which are taken up by brain cells when they are active, indicating areas of the brain that are relatively more active than others

Lloyd, 2007). Even though it is currently premature to make grand claims for the value of neuro-science research for application in literacy education practice, research, or policy, it is already clear that promising advances are being made. To give an example, the auditory neuroscience of basic speech processing is transforming our understanding of how the speech signal is coded neurally, foregrounding the importance of syllables and speech rhythm over phonemes (see Goswami & Szücs, 2011). Such basic research has implications for educational debates about teaching phonics and the educational value of oral language instruction, nursery rhymes, and poetry for reading acquisition. As another example, it will soon be possible to explore the impact of learning metrical poetry on the neural structures that are active during speech processing (see Goswami & Szücs, 2011). Hence, basic research in neuroscience may enable the development of a complementary evidence base to social and cultural perspectives for emphasizing oral language activities in early literacy programs.

Neural Correlates of Reading: An Overview

Studies of neural activation during reading can show us where and when reading processes occur in the brain. Neural imaging does not indicate that there are areas of the brain dedicated from birth to those reading processes; rather, most imaging indicates the anatomical result of development in response to successful instructional experiences. Thus, when brain images of struggling readers or nonreaders show different patterns of neural activation compared with competent readers, we cannot immediately determine from these data alone whether the difference is neurological/genetic or environmental/instructional. A reader with a genetically based neurological malformation preventing typical reading development may show the same atypical activation as a reader who did not receive quality reading instruction, a reader who received quality instruction but who was not developmentally ready for it, a reader who has linguistic and cognitive deficiencies because of limited early childhood language experiences, or a reader who has emotional problems because of an abusive home environment disruptive of his or her schooling. A brain chart, therefore, is not prima facie evidence for an innate deficiency.

The two most noted areas of brain research relatable to reading are correlational imaging studies that localize functional brain activity anatomically and correlational studies of neural activity that localize it in the time course of a reading event. A host of investigative technologies have been brought to bear in this work, and devising valid research designs is an ongoing challenge, as the sophistication of the facilitating technologies continues to advance rapidly. The results, too, are often highly variable and conflicting (Ross, 2010), and literacy educators should not get too caught up in the neophrenology—or less optimistically, "blobology" (Lieberman, 2006, p. 173)—wherein areas of dedicated function are mapped to precise locations in the brain.

More promising, brain imaging research may help alert us to disparities among the categories of reading subprocess demonstrated in the neurological research and those variously employed in models of reading (see examples in Ruddell & Unrau, 2004). As an example, a commonly employed phrase such as "sounding out the text" might suggest a singular text-to-sound decoding mechanism localized to a single brain area. However, brain-imaging studies have demonstrated several quite distinct areas of the brain that are active during sounding out (e.g., sensory visual processing of letters and visual word forms, perceptual processing of speech sounds, speech motor processing, spatial orientation). That being noted, we cannot yet dependably match specific brain areas to categories of function that may be impaired in a struggling decoder (e.g., visual crowding of letters). Similarly, many areas of the brain are devoted to the processing of word meaning, syntax, and sentence-level semantics. Yet, imaging techniques are not at the point where we can identify a particular area as a potential locus of confound for a struggling comprehender.

At first, it might not be clear why anyone would even wish to do so. As a practical matter, there is no reason to employ multimillion-dollar brain-imaging technology as a literacy assessment when much simpler and affordable behavioral assessments, coherently constructed and reasonably well tested for reliability and validity, are readily available. As a pedagogical matter, the ultimate objective of reading instruction is not to mediate brain activity or anatomy for its own sake but to facilitate the development of functional and assessable reading behaviors and remediate severe instances of dysfunction. Another objective is to foster an appreciation in students for the value of rewarding reading experiences, both individual and shared.

Conversely, the neuroscience research on reading and language processes suggests more generally that certain categories of function correlate with unique, if varied, activation of human brains. Models of decoding, comprehension, or reading that overlook any of these subprocesses, or stress some at the expense of others, may run the risk of failing to address the individual needs of developing or struggling readers, as some behavioral research already has suggested. We argue that the broader theoretical implications of neuroscience for understanding the vagaries and variability of literacy learning and development may prove of greater value for literacy education scholars than the still uncertain anatomical loci and biochemical processes of the brain.

Additionally, future work in educational neuroscience could lead to biomarkers for flagging future developmental and instructional difficulties in certain children, which could be helpful for providing those children with closer behavioral assessments and early interventions (Beddington et al., 2008; Goswami, 2009). However, as with any clinical assessment, guarding against false positives and premature tracking will be crucial for credibility. Early childhood is a notoriously pliant time, neurologically as well as behaviorally. Although the promise of biomarkers to confirm less precise behavioral assessments of cognitive or developmental difficulties is great, neuroscience is not yet at the point where it can help educators pick out particular subprocesses for intensive remediation of a struggling child. Given the immense functional variation of human brains and human beings, it is uncertain that it will ever do so in any but an ancillary fashion.

The anatomical localization of reading processes outlined in this review is based largely on hemodynamic correlation studies (i.e., studies of blood flow, glucose, or oxygen uptake in the brain) as biochemical correlates of neural activation, employing methods such as functional magnetic resonance imaging (fMRI) or positron emission tomography (PET). These studies do not, as is often misconstrued, provide a photograph of an individual brain in action. The colorful images are, in fact, statistical charts, indicating the difference between an experimental and a comparison condition averaged over a group of participants and trials. Because of the necessary use of subtractive methods between active conditions, the neural localization indicated in the charts are as much the result of the comparison condition chosen as the target condition being investigated (Caplan, 2004). In other words, the indicated result is the averaged difference between the two conditions, indicating the activity of the target condition relative to the activity of a selected comparison condition. Change the comparison condition, and you may well change the area of activation for a target behavior (e.g., Price & Mechelli, 2005).

Although results may indicate necessary areas of neural activation that exceed a particular, if conventional, signal–noise threshold, brain images do not provide a guide as to what would be comprehensively sufficient for a cognitive or behavioral function. Indications of localized activity may also indicate the particular degree of difficulty or familiarity of a task, which will vary between subjects and over trials, rather than the average baseline activity necessary for it, and the potential for meaningless positives is greater than appreciated by the nonspecialist (Bennett, Wolford, & Miller, 2009; Brown, 2007; Oakes et al., 2007). Finally, localized correlates of neural activity may indicate convergence zones for networks of necessary activation that may extend across the brain (Patterson, Nestor, & Rogers, 2007), which may be particularly true of complex or higher order tasks (Bennett & Miller, 2010). For instance, the simpler subprocesses involved in decoding are relatively easy to map to particular locations (e.g., visual processing in the occipital lobe) and, as a result, can be mapped as trajectories of typical sequence, of which some have argued there are two: a dorsal for sounding out and a ventral for word form (Dehaene, 2009). By contrast, the more complex subprocesses in readers' meaning construction seem to tap areas that process word meaning, syntax, semantics, text and narrative structure, tone, prior knowledge, emotion, and more in a multidirectional fashion and with great variability between subjects and readings (Boulenger, Hauk, & Pulvermüller, 2009; Hagoort, Hald, Bastiaansen, & Petersson, 2004; Patterson et al., 2007).

Lesion studies of stroke and accident victims, brain stimulation studies (e.g., transcranial magnetic stimulation), direct electrode assay studies, and imaging of functionally dedicated neural tracts (e.g., single photon emission computed tomography) have added to this anatomical data with ever greater detail and sophistication. However, hemodynamic studies typically span the neural activity of two to three seconds, which is an enormous amount of time for neural activity. For this reason, studies of direct electrical activity, known as event-related potential (ERP) studies, may be of more interest to reading process theorists because they provide a more precise tracking of when in the time course of a reading certain correlates of reading subprocess occur. These studies, tracking either neural action potentials (i.e., cascades of membrane depolarization running the length of thousands of neurons at a go; e.g., electroencephalography [EEG], direct electrode assays) or the fluctuation of electro-magnetic radiation at different points across the scalp (e.g., magnetoencephalography [MEG]) can distinguish the timing of events with millisecond precision. Newer MEG techniques are also much more precise in terms of anatomical location, although many technical and interpretive challenges still persist. As with the anatomical data, the hope is that this time-course data may eventually enable the identification and location of distinct subprocesses in reading.

The following review of the neural correlates of reading is quite condensed. The research base in this area is not only relatively large but also relatively new, highly varied, and growing exponentially (Cabeza & Nyberg, 2000). Replication and meta-analysis are limited. We have therefore restricted our review to studies and findings illustrative of less controversial claims, with only occasional nota-tion of exciting but uncertain evidence.

Decoding Processes in the Brain

What does the brain do when engaged in decoding or decoding-related processes? The simplest way to approach this question is to review imaging studies in which participants are given either real or nonsense words (i.e., unfamiliar letter strings that can be decoded; e.g., *tegwop*) and asked to read them. Early studies compared brain activation during single-word reading, using fMRI or PET with brain activation in a resting condition with eyes closed. For example, Rumsey et al. (1997) used this experimental design with skilled adult readers and PET, whereas Brunswick, McCrory, Price, Frith, and Frith (1999) used this experimental design with skilled adult readers and fMRI. As might be expected, a very large number of brain areas are activated in such experimental designs. There is extensive activation bilaterally (i.e., in both hemispheres) in brain areas related to audi-tion, vision, spatial and cross-modal processing, and spoken-language areas (e.g., posterior superior temporal cortex, occipitotemporal cortex, temporal and parietal areas, frontal cortex). Experiments using EEG that have contrasted real words and nonsense words, thereby keeping the visual–spatial demands associated with text processing constant and varying only whether the decoding target is a lexical word form, have shown that the brain responds differently to real versus nonsense words within one fifth of a second. This implies that lexical access (i.e., contact between the visual word form and its meaning) occurs very rapidly during reading. The speed of this differentiation has been shown to be similar for both children and adults across languages, suggesting that the time course of visual word recognition is very rapid (160–180 ms; see Csépe, Szücs, & Honbolygó, 2003; Sauseng, Bergmann, & Wimmer, 2004).

Implicit Reading Tasks

Comparing brain activity during visual identification of words with a subject's having his or her eyes closed cannot tell us anything specific about reading or its development, which has led the field to develop the implicit reading task. Implicit reading tasks try to dissociate reading, as the making of meaning from strings of printed symbols, from the associated requirements of processing visual sequences of such symbols. The implicit reading task uses false fonts (i.e., meaningless hieroglyphic-type symbols matched to letters for visual features like the ascenders in the letters *b, d, k*) and asks participants to pick out target visual features, such as ascenders. Brain activity for this visual search task is then compared with the same task based on words (i.e., picking the number of ascenders in a word such as *bubble*). In adults, such fMRI and PET studies (e.g., Price et al., 2003) have shown activation that is usually left-lateralized and focused on the occipitotemporal and posterior superior temporal cortices (see Figure 13.1; Price & McCrory, 2005). These left-hemisphere areas have hence been described as the core areas for letter identification in word reading. These areas are also active during spoken-language tasks (in the left superior temporal cortex) and visual tasks involving spoken language, such as picture naming (in the left occipitotemporal cortex).

Studies of children have generally supported the claim that a left-lateralized set of occipital and temporal areas are core to the word reading network. For example, Eden and colleagues used fMRI and the false-font task to compare brain activation during implicit reading in children and college students ages 7–22 years (Turkeltaub, Gareau, Flowers, Zeffiro, & Eden, 2003). First, the experimenters established that the 7-year-olds could perform the false-font task as competently as the college students, which was important, as the researchers hoped to attribute any changes in reading-related neural activity to developmental differences rather than differences in expertise. Comparisons of children with adults for word reading are always confounded by the inevitably greater familiarity that adults have with written words. Adults have read more words than children have, and this experiential factor will be reflected in brain activation; the same difference in word reading experience affects comparisons between children with and without dyslexia. Turkeltaub et al. reported that adults performing the implicit reading task activated the usual left-lateralized sites, including the left posterior temporal and left inferior frontal cortices.

However, when they restricted their analyses to children below 9 years of age, the main area engaged was the left posterior superior temporal cortex. This neural area is also active when participants perform phonological tasks in the scanner, such as rhyme judgment. Turkeltaub et al. (2003) thus suggested that activity in this area could be the neural correlate of grapheme–phoneme translation. When they looked at changes in activation with age, they found that activity in left temporal and frontal areas increased, while activity previously observed in right posterior areas declined. This pattern was interpreted as showing that reading-related activity becomes more left-lateralized with development.

The Visual Word Form Area

The left occipitotemporal cortex is involved in object recognition and is an area of interest in research on decoding because it has been suggested to house a word form area. This area is in essence a part of the visual cortex specialized for recognizing print, although there is some debate about this (see Démonet, Thierry, & Cardebat, 2005; Price & Devlin, 2003; Price & Mechelli, 2005). Labeled the visual word form area (VWFA), this neural region shows activity whenever printed words are shown to the adult brain, even if the words are only shown in the left visual field, which means that they first activate visual areas in the right hemisphere (see Cohen & Dehaene, 2004). The VWFA is also active when children are shown printed words.

However, expertise clearly plays a role in brain activation, as the VWFA becomes more active as children get older and become better readers (Pugh, 2006). Pugh and others have suggested that the amount of activity in the VWFA is the best neural correlate that we have of reading expertise. However, the VWFA is also active when one is shown nonsense words, which suggests that it is not purely an area responsive to word forms. Rather, it appears responsive to any sequence of printed letters. Nevertheless, activity in the VWFA increases when orthographic strings are more familiar, such that nonsense words that contain large fragments of real words elicit greater brain activity. Again, this supports a role for expertise in print–sound connections in modulating this brain activation, and as might be expected, the VWFA shows reduced activation in developmental dyslexia (e.g., B.A. Shaywitz et al., 2002).

Recently, a number of developmental studies have analyzed how neural activity in the VWFA tunes itself to print and becomes specialized for letter strings that are real words. In a study conducted in Switzerland, Maurer, Brandeis, and their colleagues (e.g., Maurer, Brem, Bucher, & Brandeis, 2005; Maurer et al., 2007) followed longitudinally, from the very beginning of learning to read in German, a sample of children who either were at risk for developmental dyslexia or had no risk for it in terms of family history. The researchers used EEG to measure millisecond-level

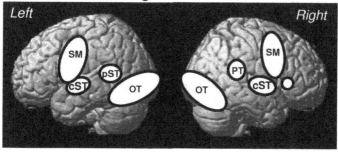

Reading aloud - Rest

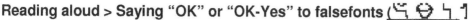

Feature detection on Words - falsefonts

Mid-fusiform *Anterior fusiform*

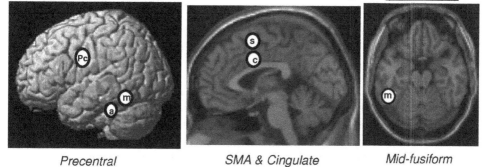

Reading aloud > Saying "OK" or "OK-Yes" to falsefonts

Precentral *SMA & Cingulate* *Mid-fusiform*

Figure 13.1 Cortical Areas Activated During the Reading of Single Words

Note. cST = central superior temporal cortex. OT = occipitotemporal cortex. pST = posterior superior temporal cortex. PT = posterior temporal cortex. SM = sensory-motor cortex. From "Functional Brain Imaging Studies of Skilled Reading and Developmental Dyslexia," by C.J. Price and E. McCrory, 2005, in M.J. Snowling and C. Hulme (Eds.), *The Science of Reading: A Handbook*, Malden, MA: Blackwell, p. 483.

changes in the electrical activity associated with the recognition of word forms. The task was to detect the repetition of either real words or meaningless symbol strings. As noted earlier, the brain registers a difference in activity to words versus nonsense words by about 160–180 milliseconds after the letter string is presented, hence the N170 (i.e., a negative deflection in brain electrical activity approximately 170 ms after stimulus onset) was the main measure of word-specific neural processing. Brain activity was recorded in kindergarten, before the children had received any instruction in reading, and again in second grade. Before any reading instruction had commenced, the children did not show an N170 to printed words, despite having considerable knowledge about individual letters. After approximately 1.5 years of reading instruction, the typically developing children showed a reliable N170 to words, described by the authors as evidence for a coarse tuning to print. The children at risk for dyslexia showed no significant differences in their brain activation compared with control children during the kindergarten measurements, but they did show a significantly reduced N170 to word forms in second grade. This response was reduced rather than absent. Maurer et al. (2007) suggested that the reduced N170 response was a clear neural correlate of a visual word-processing deficit.

Integrating Letters and Sounds

Since we know from behavioral work that visual word recognition is not a purely visual task, imaging studies showing neural activation when letters are associated with speech sounds are also required to interpret this word–symbol string difference. Blomert, Blau, and their colleagues have been carrying out a series of such studies using fMRI with adults who read in Dutch. For example, Blau, Van Atteveldt, Formisano, Goebel, and Blomert (2008) asked participants to decide whether they heard the vowel sound /a/ or /e/ in a forced-choice auditory task using degraded stimuli to avoid ceiling effects. Participants either heard just the speech sounds or heard the speech sounds in the presence of visually presented letters. The letters were either congruent (e.g., letter *A* for sound /a/) or incongruent (e.g., letter *A* for sound /e/).

Participants were significantly better at recognizing the target speech sound in the auditory–visual condition compared with the auditory–alone condition for the congruent letters and significantly worse for the incongruent letters. The fMRI data showed that brain activity in the auditory–visual condition differed in speech recognition areas of the brain and not in occipital areas, such as the VWFA. When the letters were congruent with the speech sounds, activity increased, and when the letters were incongruent with the speech sounds, activity decreased. However, an area very close to the VWFA was also modulated by auditory–visual congruency. Thus, although this study demonstrated that visual letters have a clear effect on the neural activity in areas classically active during speech processing, it did not demonstrate changes in neural activity in areas classically active during word decoding, but rather in closely associated areas.

Similar studies with children would be of interest in helping to pinpoint where, or perhaps when and where, neural activity correlated with letter–sound integration is situated. Meanwhile, Blau and colleagues have used the same task with adults with dyslexia and shown that incongruent letter–sound pairs (e.g., *A* and /e/) do not suppress neural activity in these speech-processing areas compared with the auditory-alone condition. The adults with dyslexia showed an enhancement in processing for the congruent condition (i.e., *A* and /a/), however, although it was weaker than in controls. Therefore, imaging data have shown similar neural processing in this task in typically reading adults and adults with dyslexia when letters and sounds are congruent, with decreased activity accompanying decreased decoding skill. Letter–sound integration as indexed by this particular neural correlate is, however, different in dyslexia, such that when letters and sounds do not match (e.g., *A* and /e/), incongruency does not change activity in this brain region for adults with dyslexia. This might be expected given the behavioral phenotype, but it is nonetheless interesting.

Time Course of Activation During Decoding

The neuroimaging studies discussed so far have shown systematic correlations between visual and auditory brain areas and word decoding, which will not be surprising to educators. However, one area in which neuroimaging has the potential to go beyond the correlations expected from behavioral studies is the measurement of the time course of activation. The sequence in which different brain areas become activated during reading is of interest, given different developmental models of how decoding skills become established. Such sequential information enables a test of developmental stage theories, such as the assumption that there is an early logographic stage in visual word recognition (Frith, 1985). In the logographic stage, it is assumed that holistic visual stimuli are associated with whole spoken words in the same way as familiar symbols like £ and $ are associated with the spoken words *pound* and *dollar*. If children can really go directly from print to meaning without recoding the print into sound first, then we might expect that neural structures active when viewing text and understanding meaning should show activation in very young readers, whereas neural structures that are active during phonological recoding should not.

Although imaging methods can track the time course of the activation of different neural structures, such methods are not easy to use with children, and relevant studies are currently rare. One technique, magnetic source imaging (MSI), depends on a combination of MEG and MRI (Simos et al., 2005). MEG measures the tiny magnetic fields generated by the electrical activity in the brain, rather than the electrical activity itself, and combines this information with MRI scans to localize the activity. The magnetic fields are tiny, estimated to be 1 billion times smaller than the magnetic field generated by the electricity in a lightbulb, and the technique is very expensive. Nevertheless, Simos and colleagues were able to conduct a longitudinal MSI study of 33 English-speaking children, measuring brain activity at the end of kindergarten and again at the end of first grade. The children completed a letter–sound task (i.e., the child saw a letter and had to provide its sound) and a simple nonsense-word reading task based on easy items with many analogies (e.g., *lan*).

A total of 33 children were studied, and half the group (16 children) were thought to be at risk of developmental dyslexia. This high-risk group showed significantly delayed neural activity in response to both letters and nonsense words in kindergarten in the occipitotemporal region, showing activation on average after 320 milliseconds compared with 210 milliseconds for children who were not at risk. The high-risk group also showed atypical activation in the left inferior frontal gyrus when performing the letter–sound task. For the high-risk children, the onset of neural activity in this region actually increased, from 603 milliseconds in kindergarten to 786 milliseconds in first grade. The typically developing children did not show this processing time increase. Comparing the onset of activity of the three core neural networks for reading, Simos et al. (2005) reported that low-risk children showed early activity in left occipitotemporal regions, followed by activity in temporoparietal regions, predominantly in the left hemisphere, and then bilateral activity in inferior frontal regions, which were also active during the production of speech. In contrast, high-risk children showed little differentiation in terms of the time course of activation between the occipitotemporal and temporoparietal regions. Nevertheless, temporoparietal activation is usually correlated with recoding print to sound, questioning the necessity of an early logographic stage in the development of decoding skills.

Analyses of Brain Structures

Another method for exploring how different neural areas are related during word decoding is to analyze structural differences in the neural areas known to be important for reading words. One available method, diffusion tensor imaging (DTI), can be used to measure white matter tracts, the "information highways" of the brain; white matter is the axons connecting different neurons in the brain and appears white because of the fatty myelin sheaths that speed up electrical signal transmission along the axons. In DTI, the diffusion of water in brain tissue is measured, enabling axonal fibers to be tracked because water diffuses more readily along the orientation of these fibers than in other directions.

Niogi and McCandliss (2006) used DTI to study white matter tracts in 31 children ages 6–10 years, 11 of whom were reading impaired. The children were also given standardized measures of reading, such as the Woodcock–Johnson word identification and word attack subscales. White matter integrity (i.e., axonal coherence and density) in two regions of the left temporoparietal cortex, the superior corona radiata in the left temporal lobe and the centrum semiovale, was correlated with performance in the word identification task. Therefore, the microstructure of white matter in these regions was correlated with individual differences in word reading. There was no similar correlation for homologous areas in the right hemisphere, and the relationships remained significant even after controlling for working memory, age, and nonverbal IQ in multiple regression equations.

Longitudinal investigation of the development of the microstructure of these areas could throw light on which developmental factors promote this structure–function relationship. Although such studies are not yet in the literature, we will mention one recent connectivity study notable for its ingenuity, which also illustrates how correlations, even correlations between brain structure rather than function (i.e., neural activity), are very far at present from throwing light on developmental mechanisms.

Carreiras et al. (2009) compared Colombian "guerrillas" (p. 983) reintegrating into Colombian society and belatedly learning to read as adults (i.e., late literates) with carefully matched adult illiterates, who had never learned to read in spite of having grown up in more typical social contexts, as well as typically reading adults (i.e., early literates). In this study, the structural brain differences shown using MRI and DTI between the late literates relative to the illiterates contradicted the classical version of the neural model of word reading, which assumes that information flows from the visual areas of the brain to the speech-related areas when visual word forms are encountered. Instead, the authors found that the angular gyrus, a classical spoken-language area, modulated dorsal occipital activity (i.e., the activation patterns suggested that spoken language areas controlled the amount of activation in visual areas). Carreiras and colleagues suggested that the oft-reported reduction in gray matter in the left temporoparietal areas in developmental dyslexia and associated reduced neural activity may be completely linked to reading expertise and have nothing to do functionally with having developmental dyslexia.

Synthesis

At present, there are still relatively few neuroimaging studies of word decoding by typically developing children. There are more studies of word decoding by children with dyslexia, but these have only been mentioned in passing here, as there are many difficulties in linking neural activation levels in these children with word reading per se. Nevertheless, there are some very consistent patterns of correlation in the neuroimaging studies of decoding that are available. Word processing appears to correlate with left-hemisphere activity. There is more neural activation in the left temporoparietal and occipitotemporal areas as reading skill increases.

The studies discussed earlier suggest that these correlations depend both on developing visual expertise (i.e., experience with the special visual stimuli that are words) and developing skills in letter–sound integration. When children have to read words aloud, there is also left-lateralized activity in the frontal areas of the brain that are associated with speech production and possibly articulatory codes, even when speech is not overtly produced in the scanner. None of these studies can as yet give us insights into developmental causal mechanisms. Nevertheless, the careful documentation of the neural networks that are active during decoding, their connectivity, and the time sequence of their activation are important first steps in using neuroimaging techniques to ask educationally relevant questions.

Language Comprehension Processes in the Brain

To date, most efforts at educational neuroscience matching neuroscience research to reading education have focused on brain processes and structures related to decoding instruction and its impairments, as in dyslexia (e.g., Hudson, High, & Otaiba, 2007; S. Shaywitz, 2003). This contrasts greatly with the nature of scholarship on reading and literacy education in general, including on reading disabilities, in which an emphasis on comprehension, as well as learner motivation, sociocultural context, identity, and other factors, is well developed (e.g., Israel & Duffy, 2009; Kamil, Pearson, Moje, & Afflerbach, 2010; McGill-Franzen & Allington, 2011). For the larger reading education field, then, educational neuroscience literature reviews that omit available research on language comprehension and other global processes fail to address many issues typically treated in literacy scholarship. More important, they fail to paint a comprehensive picture of the neuroscience research on reading as well. Attention to how comprehension is understood by neurolinguists demonstrates the possible value of this work.

Aside from vocabulary knowledge and cognitive strategies for content understanding, what reading education scholars and teacher educators presume language comprehension to entail is less than clear. Where the term *comprehension* is not circularly defined as understanding or meaning making, it is typically defined by the nature of what researchers can dependably measure. In essence, comprehension becomes what comprehension tests test, but the underlying subprocesses that present difficulties for struggling comprehenders/readers are often poorly articulated (cf. Lesaux & Kieffer, 2010). Syntax and semantics are alluded to irregularly and with great definitional variation (e.g., National Governors Association Center for Best Practices & Council of Chief State School Officers [NGA & CCSSO], 2010a).

English language arts instruction, in addition to word study, typically emphasizes instruction in the rules of grammar as well as style and, to a lesser extent, the nature of genre, tone, and discourse. Yet, the tracking of sentence- and paragraph-level semantic analysis, apart from syntax, is weak to nonexistent in most reading assessments (e.g., NGA & CCSSO, 2010b) and even in scholarship on the importance of language ability in literacy (e.g., Dickinson, Golinkoff, & Hirsh-Pasek, 2010). Attention by reading researchers and teacher educators to how neuroscientists parse the floating signifier of language comprehension may provide an alternative and possibly fuller map of necessary comprehension subprocesses. We group these here in terms of (a) word meaning processes, (b) syntactic and sentence-level meaning processes (semantics), (c) emotional signification, and (d) higher order cognitive and text feature processes.

What's in a Word?

In the neurolinguistic research base, comprehension is presumed to begin with relating an identified word form to its possible meanings through association as an item of vocabulary. As a result, research on word form recognition, morphological analysis, and word meaning, or semantics at the single-word level, is abundant (see the review in Osterhout, Kim, & Kuperberg, 2006). As already noted, word form identification may correlate with activity in the left inferior occipitotemporal area along the fusiform gyrus.

Word meaning has been commonly correlated with activation in the left medial, superior, and superior posterior temporal areas. In the early work along these lines, it was prematurely claimed that particular categories and classes of word meanings could be located in distinct areas of the left temporal lobe. With each new category studied (e.g., tools, machines, buildings, domestic animals, farm animals, wild animals), strong claims were made for distinct areas of activation. There seemed to be no end to the possible categorical distinctions that could be mapped, assuring a steady stream of such studies. However, eventual follow-up work found a lack of replication for these findings, indicating (a) individual but perfectly functional differences in localization, (b) a lack of clarity about what *encoding in the brain* might mean, and (c) overconfidence in the reliability of the early imaging techniques (Heim, 2005). Periodic improvements in imaging precision have inspired similar claims regarding word localization in the temporal lobe and elsewhere, but unless well replicated, they should be taken with caution (Ross, 2010).

More current work has suggested that areas across the brain dedicated to basic sensory, motor, emotional, analytic, or social processing converge in the left temporal lobe for word meanings (Frishkoff, Perfetti, & Westbury, 2009; Patterson et al., 2007). For instance, verbs that indicate physical actions activate areas in the motor or premotor cortex that link to categorical identification and word representation convergence zones in the left inferior anterior temporal area (Willems, Hagoort, & Casasanto, 2010).

The relationship of word identification ability to comprehension is now well known, but the relationship of word identification to subprocesses for identifying association patterns of spelling, sound, and meaning is ongoing. Building on Perfetti's lexical quality hypothesis (Perfetti & Hart, 2002), which asserts that the richness or abundance of semantic associations with a word is a correlate of comprehension of the text, Balass, Nelson, and Perfetti (2010) asked participants in an ERP study to make meaning judgments about newly learned, familiar, and unlearned words. This was done in three different conditions: (1) orthography to meaning (i.e., no phonology), wherein the participants were required to learn the spelling and meaning of rare words; (2) orthography to phonology (i.e., no meaning), wherein participants were required to learn the spelling and pronunciation of rare words; and (3) phonology to meaning (i.e., no orthography), wherein participants were required to learn the pronunciation and meaning of rare words. After being tested to demonstrate their knowledge of these new words, subjects were given a semantic-relatedness judgment task, matching related and non-related words, for rare words, known words, and unknown words not included in the previous learning task. ERP measurements were taken to determine novelty effects (P600) and meaning effects (N400).

The results suggested that the degree of word knowledge, specifically phonological, orthographic, and semantic knowledge, developed at the time of word learning influenced subsequent recognition of the word in new contexts, a finding with implications for vocabulary instruction. Although there were no comprehension differences in the behavioral data, the ERP data found the orthography–meaning condition produced a more powerful recognition effect than the orthography–phonology and phonology–meaning conditions. This is significant for vocabulary learning because incremental knowledge development about a word over time, primarily through print encounters, relies on recognizing past encounters with the word in print.

To study the role of morphological processing of words, Bozic, Marslen-Wilson, Stamatakis, Davis, and Tyler (2007) used fMRI to examine areas of activation by contrasting priming of word pairs that shared either an opaque morphological relationship (e.g., *archer, arch*) or a transparent morphological relationship (e.g., *bravely, brave*) with meaning-only (e.g., *stop, halt*), form-only (e.g., *catalog, cat*), and identity-priming (e.g., *cat, cat*) word pairs. The results suggested that morphological analysis is a subprocess involving left frontal areas of the brain distinct from word form recognition or word meaning identification processes located elsewhere. This finding may be of potential significance for educational research on vocabulary instruction considering the role of morphological analysis in word identification. Interestingly, this area of the brain is also activated in syntactic processing of sentences, a process known to often rely on morphemic indicators of grammatical relationship.

Occasionally, words must be parsed in terms of their syntactic or semantic function before they can be definitively identified or sounded out correctly as words (e.g., the noun or verb form of *progress*, the present or past tense verb form of *read*). Reading researchers already know that word processing is highly adaptive on behalf of comprehension satisfaction, and strict linearity of processing is absent, even at the word form level. Neuroscience studies have confirmed that syntactic and semantic processes can have a top-down effect on word meaning processes, and this effect may play a variable role even for words that are not ambiguous (Kuperberg, 2007). These results indicate that models of language that assume language meaning derives only from word meanings linked with grammatical markers are inadequate for representing authentic language processing (Boulenger et al., 2009; Friederici & Weissenborn, 2007; Hagoort & van Berkum, 2007; Rimrodt et al., 2009).

Syntax and Semantics

Research on vocabulary has been complemented by a substantial body of studies on syntactic processing (i.e., identification of grammatical function, grammatical interrelationship of words in a clause or sentence) and semantic processing (i.e., identification of indicative intention of words, phrases, and idioms, and their intentional relationship at a clausal, sentence, or passage level). The anatomical areas and time-course involvement of these two general domains appear distinct yet overlapping, and much more work on these processes can be expected. It could be that the traditional distinction between these domains is not easily disentangled at the level of neural function.

Typically, syntactic or semantic anomalies are used in comparisons to distinguish the relevant neural correlates. For instance, semantically anomalous sentences (e.g., "When peanuts fall in love . . .") elicit an exaggerated N400 signature, a peaking of negative charge approximately 400 milliseconds after the lexical anomaly, in the central parietal region (van Berkum, Hagoort, & Brown, 1999; see the review in Kutas, Van Petten, & Kluender, 2006). By contrast, anomalous syntactic structure elicits an abnormal early positive charge in the left anterior region, followed by an exaggerated P600 signature, a peaking of positive charge 600 milliseconds after onset, either in the central parietal region (Friederici & Kotz, 2003; Friederici, von Cramon, & Kotz, 1999), as with the N400, or in more anterior (i.e., frontal) areas of the brain (Osterhout et al., 2006). These unique time-course signatures suggest that semantic and syntactic processing of anomalies are neurologically distinct operations. The research further suggests that semantic and syntactic processing of correct or typical sentences is similarly timed (Kaan, Harris, Gibson, & Holcomb, 2000). In other words, ERP studies indicate that on a word-by-word basis, early brain activation is for word and morphosyntactic identification, followed at the N400 by semantic identification and at the P600 by a sentence-level syntactic recheck (Friederici & Kotz, 2003).

Such findings can support linear theories of syntactic processing (e.g., Friederici, 2002), although alternative distributed processing theories have been suggested (e.g., Hagoort, 2003) and supported by studies (Cooke et al., 2006; Hald, Bastiaansen, & Hagoort, 2006). Other studies suggest that traditional notions of syntax and semantics are ill matched to the processing indicated by ERP evidence, and alternative explanations of meaning elaboration are required to make sense of the data (Kuperberg, 2007). In spite of the uncertainties, timing of process is clearly of importance (Perfetti & Bolger, 2004), and when matched to more spatially precise imaging techniques, such as the newer MEG or fMRI techniques, ERP methods may give a more reliable indication of the order and structure of synactic and semantic processing of texts during comprehension (Heim, 2005).

Turning to the hemodynamic research (e.g., fMRI, PET), syntactic processes have been found to dependably associate with activity in the left frontal gyrus, or Broca's area (Sakai, Noguchi, Takeuchi, & Watanabe, 2002). Semantic processes are more variably located, depending on whether they are at the word level (posterior superior temporal and temporoparietal; e.g., Wernicke's area and related basal language areas, such as the supramarginal gyrus and temporal sulcus, as well as in left inferior frontal areas, at least for articulatory rehearsal; Rogalsky, Matchin, & Hickok, 2008), sentence level (left inferior frontal areas proximal to Broca's area), or text/discourse level (more distributed and bilateral frontal and parietal areas depending on task complexity or degree of abstraction; Binder, Desai, Graves, & Conant, 2009).

These areas of dedicated activation in response to syntactic and semantic demands develop over time in individually variable ways, possibly as a result of differing experience. Berl and colleagues (2010) used fMRI to study the effects of task, age, neuropsychological skill, and posttask performance in the reading versus listening of developmentally appropriate paragraph-length texts by subjects ranging from early childhood through preadolescence. The researchers found a consistent activation across ages and modality (i.e., reading, listening) in the left superior temporal sulcus, dubbing it the "comprehension cortex" (p. 115) because of its involvement in lexical-level syntactic and semantic tasks.

However, they also noted developmental differences in text-comprehension processing, with younger children demonstrating a more diffusely distributed activation pattern that included the right temporal pole and right cerebellum. Older children and adolescents showed increased activation in the left inferior frontal cortex while listening to stories, suggesting an increased recruitment of this area for more structurally complex texts, and this activation correlated positively with comprehension results. Reading was shown to require activation across a greater number of cortical areas than listening was (see Figure 13.2; Berl et al., 2010), including the right temporal and right inferior frontal lobes, possibly suggesting that children require this additional activation to construct meaning from the more difficult semantic structures typical of written texts compared with the age-typical semantic structures of children's oral language (cf. Yeatman, Ben-Shachar, Glover, & Feldman, 2010).

The Role of Emotion in Meaning

Emotional valence seems intuitively to be integral in tracking the meaning and/or meaningfulness of language and what it represents, and the neurolinguistic literature supports this (Ferstl, Rinck, &

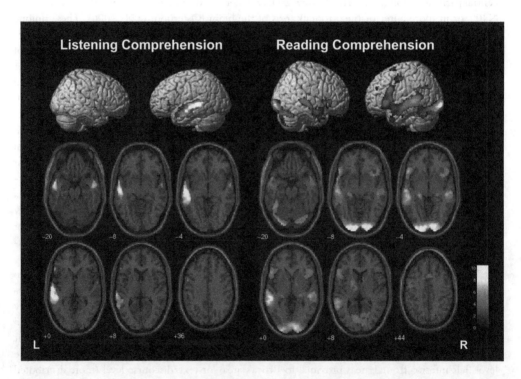

Figure 13.2 Cortical Areas Active in Listening Comprehension Versus Reading Comprehension in 4–12-Year-Old Children

Note. There was greater activation in the reading condition because of visual, letter-identification, and word form processing, but also possible verbal rehearsal and/or more syntactic–semantic processing. The comparison indicates a common language comprehension cluster in the superior to medial left temporal cortex similar to that found in adults. From "Functional Anatomy of Listening and Reading Comprehension During Development," by M.M. Berl, E.S. Duke, J. Mayo, L.R. Rosenberger, E.N. Moore, J. VanMeter, et al., 2010, *Brain and Language, 114*(2), p. 120.

von Cramon, 2005; Havas, Glenberg, & Rinck, 2007), with corresponding neural activity found in the anterior temporal and inferior prefrontal areas adjacent to the orbitofrontal cortex. These cortical areas are known to develop early in childhood for affect regulation and socioemotional response (for introductions to social neuroscience of early childhood, see Cozolino, 2006; Schore, 1994). They connect to subcortical areas in the basal ganglia that comodulate the endocrine system, and thereby the individual's emotional state, and are closely tied, both neurologically and hormonally, to subcortical areas involved in memory formation and its reconstruction, such as in the hypothalamus, anterior cingulate, and amygdala. There is also a fair degree of overlap between areas of the brain active during both emotional control and semantic memory (Binney, Embleton, Jefferies, Parker, & Ralph, 2010).

It should be acknowledged that the neurological basis for the relationship of emotion and sociality to language comprehension development is not yet well understood theoretically (cf. Immordino-Yang & Damasio, 2007). Nonetheless, these subcortical areas, and loci in the orbitofrontal and anterior temporal cortices, may prove a crucial link between language and meaning and could provide another front in the growing appreciation for the importance of early childhood social, emotional, and language development for subsequent literacy achievement (Beaucousin et al., 2007; Kuhl & Rivera-Gaxiola, 2008), as well as for the emotional quality of classroom environments.

Higher Order Cognitive and Discourse-Level Processes in Reading

Research is accumulating on the neural correlates of text genre identification, action tracking, processing of expository and narrative text structures, determining the appropriateness of tone or trope (e.g., irony, metaphor), identification and processing of idiom, and the use of appropriate discourse forms (for an intriguing review of some of these processes, see Perfetti & Frishkoff, 2008). For instance, the importance of basic cognitive functions, such as inference in relating textual information to prior world knowledge, is treated at some length (Friese, Rutschmann, Raabe, & Schmalhofer, 2008; Mason & Just, 2011). Executive skills in text tracking (Sesma, Mahone, Levine, Eason, & Cutting, 2009) and reader's analysis of metaphor (Mashal, Faust, Hendler, & Jung-Beeman, 2009) are additional examples of such work.

Making sense of decoded text symbols affords less of the contextual information provided during auditory processing of speech from, for instance, the visual tracking of facial movements to help identify ambiguous phonemes, as in the McGurk effect (Beauchamp, Nath, & Pasalar, 2010), or integrating the semantic content of hand gestures (Dick, Goldin-Meadow, Hasson, Skipper, & Small, 2009). Higher order context effects, such as those associated with linguistic environment, appear to have a developmental, not just functional, effect on language comprehension processes, particularly regarding syntax and higher order semantics and idioms (Raizada, Richards, Meltzoff, & Kuhl, 2008). All of these issues will likely become important as educational neuroscience further explores the effects of home and classroom discourse participation on language development.

Neuroscience research on the processing of text content in terms of subjects' prior knowledge is in its infancy; as an example of this research, Speer, Reynolds, Swallow, and Zacks (2009) have suggested that processing scenes and actions described in narrative texts involves sensory and motor processing areas of the brain. The importance of prior knowledge for text comprehension is well documented, with a distinction being made between declarative and procedural knowledge and between prior knowledge of the world and prior knowledge specific to language (e.g., prior knowledge of vocabulary, prior knowledge of dialect- and discourse-specific syntactic and semantic patterns, prior knowledge of domain-specific discourses and genres). There is the possibility that insofar as this prior knowledge of language or even of social protocols is the result of overlearned and thus automatized pattern recognition (e.g., syntactic and idiomatic pattern recognition), it would be more appropriately categorized as a form of developed skill rather than as explicit knowledge.

(Rule application models of language processing blur this distinction.) Still, the difference between prior knowledge that is specific to language comprehension rather than content comprehension is worth noting.

Also worth noting is the distinction between the tapping of developed processing skills and long-term memory with working memory's role in the construction of situation models from text. The construction of summary memories of a passage for retelling, for instance, requires the compression of details on the basis of significance. Lillywhite and colleagues (2010) used fMRI to contrast subjects' processing of passages read to them repeatedly and found a marked difference in neural activation between the first and subsequent hearing of the texts. The neural activation between the iterations of the passages extended from chiefly auditory and language comprehension areas in the initial reading to include areas in the frontal, parietal, and subcortical areas during subsequent readings, suggesting areas for modeling, memory, and recognition processes beyond basic language comprehension processes. When the analyses were extended to subjects' retelling or summarizing of the text, a strong correlation was discovered with activity in the right parietal cortex, suggesting its role in discourse representation.

Such discourse processing research may be of interest to reading professionals. However, it is rarely the case that the term *discourse* in neurolinguistics means what it does in psycho- or sociolinguistics (e.g., Gee, 2008), sources that have been highly influential in reading education scholarship. For the relevant neurolinguistic research, discourse is simply extended, usually narrative, text, with all of the micro- and macrostructural elements of such texts intact (e.g., Lillywhite et al., 2010). The point of such research is to determine the neural activity that correlates with the processing of such features and, as a result, determine whether structure-related categories of mental process have a tangible neural signature.

For instance, Yarkoni, Speer, and Zacks (2008) used fMRI to distinguish sentence-level comprehension processing from passage-level comprehension processing. Presuming that the reading of a narrative requires the building of mental representations of the narrative, which are then employed constructively to process subsequent narrative elements, they tracked the reading of cohesive narratives contrasted to paragraphs comprised of unrelated sentences. They found that similar areas of the brain were involved for comprehending the content of sentences, but distinct areas were tapped for the processing of the situation model, with the posterior parietal cortex implicated in the construction of such models, and anterior temporal areas implicated in their maintenance. Taking a different approach, Whitney and colleagues (2009) explored the distributed neural network underlying story comprehension. They contrasted the processing of sentence boundaries with content-substantive narrative shifts and were thereby able to demonstrate the role of the medial parietal cortex in narrative structure comprehension, and the apparent role of the precuneus and posterior cingulate in updating story representations. The role of the precuneus, tucked into the medial parietal fissure, for higher order processing is particularly intriguing, given its potential contribution to self-awareness and self-monitoring (Cavanna & Trimble, 2006).

As literacy scholars have long appreciated, reading is more than just the mental processes inside the head of a reader. Social, linguistic, and cultural factors all play a role both during a reading event and in reading development over time. Current developmental science has suggested that these contextual factors do not just happen to a reader but are aspects of a developing child's social and cultural environment, a symbolic landscape that the child learns to appropriate, represent, and negotiate in a generally functional and eventually strategic fashion (see the reviews in Eisenberg, 2006). Insofar as a reader perceives and responds, mentally or behaviorally, to representational elements of his or her sociocultural landscape, there will be correlated neurological activity and development to study (e.g., monitoring the intentions of others as distinguishable from physical causality; Mason & Just, 2011). The neurological correlates of such perceptions and responses are the focus of study for researchers in developmental cognitive neuroscience, the neuroscience of affect regulation, personality neuroscience, and social neuroscience.

Synthesis

The anatomical areas of the brain that correlate with the foundational language comprehension functions (i.e., vocabulary, syntax, semantics) are generally more active in the left hemisphere of the neocortex, although homologous areas in the right hemisphere are typically activated as well, especially for reading, possibly for related but distinct discourse processing or textual representations (Ferstl, Neumann, Bogler, & von Cramon, 2008). Higher order comprehension processes and strategic analysis involve a much more distributed set of brain loci.

The ERP time-course studies of syntactic and semantic processing during text comprehension in competent adult readers have indicated that syntactic processing begins in the left frontal and anterior temporal lobes with phrase-structure monitoring at approximately 150–250 milliseconds (Segalowitz & Zheng, 2009); expanding to verb–subject or syntactic/thematic processing around 300–350 milliseconds in the left inferior gyrus; an assessment of the semantic intention within the sentence at approximately 400 milliseconds (Marinkovic et al., 2003); and culminating, especially in cases of more complex syntactic structures, with a syntactic recheck or incongruity/novelty effect, peaking at approximately 600 milliseconds (Hagoort, 2003). Integration of syntactic and semantic processes occur at approximately 400–600 milliseconds (Friederici & Weissenborn, 2007). More global-level processing of text features occur subsequently. Although anatomical localization of these events in time-course studies does not always precisely match that suggested by functional anatomical studies, both types of studies are in agreement regarding the distinctive nature of word meaning, syntax, and semantic processes.

The neuroscience work on comprehension is far more variable than that on decoding processes in part because it ranges over a more extended and theoretically variable set of subprocesses. There is great theoretical uncertainty about the role these subprocesses play in text comprehension, and clearly the role would vary depending on the nature of the text, the culturally specific representational system employed, the purpose and context of the reading, and the ability and educational level of the reader. The same challenges to reliability posed to reading inventories at higher grade levels is at work here as well. For these reasons, constructing more ecologically valid studies of brain activation during comprehension would be helpful. In the future, this research may require a more substantial contribution from educational researchers than they have provided in the past.

Issues in the Educational Neuroscience of Reading

Methodological Issues in Neuroscience Research

Recent technological advances in the neurosciences have been rapid, and the number of cognitive neuroscience studies has expanded exponentially (Cabeza & Nyberg, 2000). Nevertheless, the majority of imaging findings are less than a decade old and are thus unreplicated. Meta-analyses are scarce (Maisog, Einbinder, Flowers, Turkeltaub, & Eden, 2008). Because of the novelty of the technological advances, many brain-imaging studies are often as much about a method's appropriate use, research design, and implementation as they are about the object of investigation, which has made for some engaging debates within the neuroscience literature. At first blush, reading education researchers may find these debates impenetrably technical.

Yet, most of the critique revolves around the fundamentals of research design and the logic of interpretation, issues with which well-prepared literacy researchers are familiar. Debates about such conceptual fundamentals as the difference between necessary and sufficient conditions, between correlation and causation, between reliability and validity, between constrained and unconstrained variables, and the use of circular reasoning and other fallacies in research design and interpretation have all made appearances in the history of reading research. Literacy researchers will find these familiar motifs evident in the critical neuroscience literature as well.

Among the technical and interpretive concerns recently treated, Vul, Harris, Winkielman, and Pashler (2009) noted that correlations in brain-imaging studies may have been seriously overstated. Bennett, Baird, Miller, and Wolford (2009) noted that the reliability of brain–behavior correlates varies widely depending on the type of behavior being correlated, and they reviewed many of the challenges that remain regarding reliability in brain-imaging studies. One possible issue has been inadequate attention to the need for multiple-comparisons correction, given the extensive number of calculations between conditions required in neuroimaging techniques (Bennett, Baird, et al., 2009). Other methodological issues have been suggested as well (see Brown, 2007; Oakes et al., 2007). All of this should caution educators and educational researchers from taking any particular brain study finding at face value, particularly when disseminated through the popular media, let alone as a definitive form of evidence for a reading program, method, policy, or theory.

Conceptual Frameworks for Bridging Neuroscience and Reading Research

At present, there is an emerging interdisciplinary neurocognitive perspective that is seeking to integrate brain, cognitive, social, and cultural perspectives on learning and activity (Fischer, Bernstein, & Immordino-Yang, 2007; Hall, Goswami, Harrison, Ellis, & Soler, 2010; Varma et al., 2008). Neuroscience research, research on educational processes, and research on learning can be mutually informing. For example, recent advances in neuroscience link directly to long-standing models in cognitive educational psychology, enabling the rigorous analysis of such models from a new evidence base. Unfortunately, this computational-brain framework is the one most often garbled in the popular media and brain-based education materials.

At the same time, an alternative theoretical framework is emerging that is organic rather than mechanistic, biological rather than representational, built on the motif of learning as growth (not merely conceptual growth but actual neurophysiological development), and powered by the bio-ecological dynamics of organisms as agents growing functionally in response to their ecological contingencies, environments to which they adapt through behavioral, developmental, epigenetic, and even evolutionary processes (e.g., Mareschal et al., 2007). An awareness of complex dynamical effects over time and across scales of analysis is certainly relevant to research in literacy education, particularly to research on sociocultural factors and on situated cognition.

Other theoretical frameworks are also possible (see Meltzoff, Kuhl, Movellan, & Sejnowski, 2009). Given the relatively advanced state of educational neuroscience on reading, literacy education seems to be an ideal field within which to forge and field-test new theoretical frameworks informed by, and coherent with, research in the neurosciences (Hruby, 2009). Such work could have significant implications for educational policy, theory, and practice.

Topical Focus and Level of Analysis

Remembering that research is about what it is about and not something else is almost too obvious to elaborate on, yet this fundamental observation has already been underscored by cognitive and neuroscience researchers alike (e.g., Bruer, 1997; Hirsh-Pasek et al., 2007). If we require research-based evidence on effective classroom practices, we should first attend to the copious research on effective classroom practices. If we are dissatisfied with this research, or the implications of its findings, we ought to attempt to improve on it. There is a kind of natural hierarchy to what kind of research is most relevant to a problem, and research on the problem itself should come first. Cognitive and social aspects of learning should probably come next, with cognitive neuroscience and educational neuroscience playing a more distant role. Yet, crucially, all of these research perspectives will eventually be important in achieving a full understanding of, for instance, the efficacy of classroom practices. All of these different levels of analysis and explanation have mutually supportive roles to play in an integrated understanding of how to improve classroom practices for literacy development. Reduction of cause to a single level of analysis when researching the complex nature of bioecological systems is unwarrantable and unlikely to be helpful for finding connections to efficacious educational practice.

The reading education research base, taken at large, indicates that the answer to the simplistic question, What works?, is it depends—on student variability, teacher efficacy, material resources, curricular objectives, and numerous other contextual factors. As experienced teachers know, no method will work for everyone in a given class, and nothing works for anyone all the time. Given that, the question should probably be rephrased as, What works for particular kinds of students, under particular circumstances, to particular ends, with particular dependability? Reading researchers have developed many useful methods and theoretical frameworks for investigating elements of this larger question. Yet, neuroscience also offers us methods for studying these questions within an educational context. Neuroscientists are trying to achieve an understanding of how learning occurs at neurosystemic, neurocytological, neurochemical, and neurogenomic levels of analyses. At these levels of analysis, learning will depend on physiological processes that may come to be phrased as general laws of learning. As we discover what these processes are, we can then use them to examine learning at the physiological level in response to various contexts and situations of learning. It is critical to be aware that neuroscience will not replace understandings arising from social science. Rather, neuroscience can complement the understandings derived from educational research and reinforce and refine our understanding of the processes involved in discourse comprehension and its development.

Research from ancillary domains, when coherently theorized as pertinent to classroom evidence, can be very illuminating and help us expand or reframe our thinking, as the history of reading education research has suggested (Alexander & Fox, 2004). As more is understood about the neurological processes and development that correlate with reading and its instruction, educational neuroscience on reading processes will likely begin to influence our theoretical constructs about reading education across the life span and, thereby, inform public discourse and policy formation. It therefore would be helpful if reading education scholars developed expertise in the research, philosophy, and limitations of neuroscience, and the developmental sciences more broadly, to help inform the public debate.

Biology and Complexity

Current life science has provided us with a much more complex understanding of developmental processes than popular views of genetic determinism may suggest. Physiological and genetic propensities are realized through interaction with an environment, be it nucleic, biochemical, cytological, systemic, organic, social, or symbolic (Gottlieb, 2007). Given the severely limited number of genes in the human genome that distinguish us from other species, much of the necessary information for behavior and learning is not actually encoded in the genome but off-loaded in the environment in which the genome has historically and developmentally functioned; the same also may be true of the putative need for the knowledge representations required for adaptive behavior (Clancey, 1997; Hendriks-Jansen, 1996).

This insight lies at the heart of the promise of neuroscience for literacy education. Literacy educators are creating the contexts within which children's brains develop, enabling them to perform increasingly demanding reading tasks and develop capacities for comprehension, understanding, and lifelong learning across many situations and domains. Reading and literacy development involve relationships among social, cultural, biological, cognitive, and developmental processes. The need to incorporate all research perspectives in constructing optimal policy and pedagogy means that the impact of bringing neuroscience into the traditions in reading education and literacy research may be profound.

Final Comments

In this review of the neuroscience research related to reading and literacy, we briefly reviewed findings on neurological correlates of decoding and comprehension, as well as some higher order processes in reading. We also elaborated on several issues regarding neuroscience methodology and theoretical framing for bringing neuroscience and literacy education research into an interdisciplinary conversation. We discussed some general cautions and mistaken assumptions.

As we hope we have made clear, the potential of neuroscience to help expand our understanding of reading processes, their development, and their occasional dysfunction is profound. We hope that our review of the research provides a helpful overview of the terrain and the issues confronting any attempt at an interdisciplinary conversation between literacy education research and neuroscience research. A successful interdisciplinary conversation could helpfully address many questions about literacy and its instruction and development. Until such time as knowledgeable literacy education scholars prepare themselves to engage in such a conversation, the full promise of the biological sciences for analyzing educational issues will remain obscure.

Note

Goswami, supported by the Medical Research Council (Grant G0400574) and a major research fellowship from the Leverhulme Trust, took the lead on the decoding processes section of this article. The authors thank Carl Frederiksen, Chuck Perfetti, and the *Reading Research Quarterly* editors for helpful comments and advice.

References

Alexander, P.A., & Fox, E. (2004). A historical perspective on reading research and practice. In R.B. Ruddell & N.J. Unrau (Eds.), *Theoretical models and processes of reading* (5th ed., pp. 33–68). Newark, DE: International Reading Association. doi:10.1598/0872075028.2

Balass, M., Nelson, J.R., & Perfetti, C.A. (2010). Word learning: An ERP investigation of word experience effects on recognition and word processing. *Contemporary Educational Psychology, 35*(2), 126–140. doi:10.1016/j.cedpsych.2010.04.001

Beauchamp, M.S., Nath, A.R., & Pasalar, S. (2010). fMRI-guided transcranial magnetic stimulation reveals that the superior temporal sulcus is a cortical locus of the McGurk effect. *The Journal of Neuroscience, 30*(7), 2414–2417. doi:10.1523/JNEUROSCI.4865-09.2010

Beaucousin, V., Lacheret, A., Turbelin, M., Morel, M., Mazoyer, B., & Tzourio-Mazoyer, N. (2007). FMRI study of emotional speech comprehension. *Cerebral Cortex, 17*(2), 339–352. doi:10.1093/cercor/bhj151

Beddington, J., Cooper, C.L., Field, J., Goswami, U., Huppert, F.A., Jenkins, R., et al. (2008). The mental wealth of nations. *Nature, 455*(7216), 1057–1060. doi:10.1038/451057a

Bennett, C.M., Baird, A.A., Miller, M.B., & Wolford, G.L. (2009). Neural correlates of interspecies perspective taking in the post-mortem Atlantic salmon: An argument for multiple comparisons correction. *Prefrontal. org.* Retrieved November 26, 2010, from prefrontal.org/files/posters/Bennett-Salmon-2009.pdf

Bennett, C.M., & Miller, M.B. (2010). How reliable are the results from functional magnetic resonance imaging? *Annals of the New York Academy of Sciences, 1191*, 133–155. doi:10.1111/j.1749-6632.2010.05446.x

Bennett, C.M., Wolford, G.L., & Miller, M.B. (2009). The principled control of false positives in neuroimaging. *Social Cognitive and Affective Neuroscience, 4*(4), 417–422. doi:10.1093/scan/nsp053

Berl, M.M., Duke, E.S., Mayo, J., Rosenberger, L.R., Moore, E.N., VanMeter, J., et al. (2010). Functional anatomy of listening and reading comprehension during development. *Brain and Language, 114*(2), 115–125. doi:10.1016/j.bandl.2010.06.002

Binder, J.R., Desai, R.H., Graves, W.W., & Conant, L.L. (2009). Where is the semantic system? A critical review and meta-analysis of 120 functional neuroimaging studies. *Cerebral Cortex, 19*(12), 2767–2796. doi:10.1093/cercor/bhp055

Binney, R.J., Embleton, K.V., Jefferies, E., Parker, G.J.M., & Ralph, M.A.L. (2010). The ventral and inferolateral aspects of the anterior temporal lobe are crucial in semantic memory: Evidence from a novel direct comparison of distortion-corrected fMRI, rTMS, and semantic dementia. *Cerebral Cortex, 20*(11), 2728–2738. doi:10.1093/cercor/bhq019

Blau, V., Van Atteveldt, N., Formisano, E., Goebel, R., & Blomert, L. (2008). Task-irrelevant visual letters interact with the processing of speech sounds in heteromodal and unimodal cortex. *European Journal of Neuroscience, 28*(3), 500–509. doi:10.1111/j.1460-9568.2008.06350.x

Boulenger, V., Hauk, O., & Pulvermüller, F. (2009). Grasping ideas with the motor system: Semantic somatotopy in idiom comprehension. *Cerebral Cortex, 19*(8), 1905–1914. doi:10.1093/cercor/bhn217

Bozic, M., Marslen-Wilson, W.D., Stamatakis, E.A., Davis, M.H., & Tyler, L.K. (2007). Differentiating morphology, form, and meaning: Neural correlates of morphological complexity. *Journal of Cognitive Neuroscience, 19*(9), 1464–1475. doi:10.1162/jocn.2007.19.9.1464

Brown, G.G. (2007). Functional magnetic resonance imaging in clinical practice: Look before you leap. *Neuropsychology Review, 17*(2), 103–106. doi:10.1007/s11065-007-9027-9

Bruer, J.T. (1997). Education and the brain: A bridge too far. *Educational Researcher, 26*(8), 4–16.

Brunswick, N., McCrory, E., Price, C.J., Frith, C.D., & Frith, U. (1999). Explicit and implicit processing of words and pseudowords by adult developmental dyslexics: A search for Wernicke's Wortschatz. *Brain, 122*(10), 1901–1917. doi:10.1093/brain/122.10.1901

Cabeza, R., & Nyberg, L. (2000). Imaging cognition II: An empirical review of 275 PET and fMRI studies. *Journal of Cognitive Neuroscience, 12*(1), 1–47. doi:10.1162/08989290051137585

Caplan, D. (2004). Functional neuroimaging studies of written sentence comprehension. *Scientific Studies of Reading, 8*(3), 225–240. doi:10.1207/s1532799xssr0803_3

Carreiras, M., Seghier, M.L., Baquero, S., Estévez, A., Lozano, A., Devlin, J.T., et al. (2009). An anatomical signature for literacy. *Nature, 461*(7266), 983–986. doi:10.1038/nature08461

Cavanna, A.E., & Trimble, M.R. (2006). The precuneus: A review of its functional anatomy and behavioural correlates. *Brain, 129*(3), 564–583. doi:10.1093/brain/awl004

Clancey, W.J. (1997). *Situated cognition: On human knowledge and computer representations.* New York: Cambridge University Press.

Cohen, L., & Dehaene, S. (2004). Specialization within the ventral stream: The case for the visual word form area. *NeuroImage, 22*(1), 466–476. doi:10.1016/j.neuroimage.2003.12.049

Cooke, A., Grossman, M., DeVita, C., Gonzalez-Atavales, J., Moore, P., Chen, W., et al. (2006). Large-scale neural network for sentence processing. *Brain and Language, 96*(1), 14–36. doi:10.1016/j.bandl.2005.07.072

Cozolino, L. (2006). *The neuroscience of human relationships: Attachment and the developing social brain.* New York: W.W. Norton.

Csépe, V., Szücs, D., & Honbolygó, F. (2003). Number-word reading as challenging task in dyslexia? An ERP study. *International Journal of Psychophysiology, 51*(1), 69–83. doi:10.1016/S0167-8760(03)00154-5

Dehaene, S. (2009). *Reading in the brain: The science and evolution of a human invention.* New York: Penguin.

Démonet, J.-F., Thierry, G., & Cardebat, D. (2005). Renewal of the neurophysiology of language: Functional neuroimaging. *Physiological Reviews, 85*(1), 49–95. doi:10.1152/physrev.00049.2003

Dick, A.S., Goldin-Meadow, S., Hasson, U., Skipper, J.I., & Small, S.L. (2009). Co-speech gestures influence neural activity in brain regions associated with processing semantic information. *Human Brain Mapping, 30*(11), 3509–3526. doi:10.1002/hbm.20774

Dickinson, D.K., Golinkoff, R.M., & Hirsh-Pasek, K. (2010). Speaking out for language: Why language is central to reading development. *Educational Researcher, 39*(4), 305–310. doi:10.3102/0013189X10370204

Eisenberg, N. (Vol. Ed.). (2006). *Handbook of child psychology: Vol. 3. Social, emotional, and personality development* (6th ed.). New York: John Wiley & Sons.

Ferstl, E.C., Neumann, J., Bogler, C., & von Cramon, D.Y. (2008). The extended language network: A meta-analysis of neuroimaging studies on text comprehension. *Human Brain Mapping, 29*(5), 581–593. doi:10.1002/hbm.20422

Ferstl, E.C., Rinck, M., & von Cramon, D.Y. (2005). Emotional and temporal aspects of situation model processing during text comprehension: An event-related fMRI study. *Journal of Cognitive Neuroscience, 17*(5), 724–739. doi:10.1162/0898929053747658

Fischer, K.W., Bernstein, J.H., & Immordino-Yang, M.H. (Eds.). (2007). *Mind, brain and education in reading disorders.* New York: Cambridge University Press.

Friederici, A.D. (2002). Towards a neural basis of auditory sentence processing. *Trends in Cognitive Sciences, 6*(2), 78–84. doi:10.1016/S1364-6613(00)01839-8

Friederici, A.D., & Kotz, S.A. (2003). The brain basis of syntactic processes: Functional imaging and lesion studies. *NeuroImage, 20*(Suppl. 1), S8–S17. doi:10.1016/j.neuroimage.2003.09.003

Friederici, A.D., von Cramon, D.Y., & Kotz, S.A. (1999). Language related brain potentials in patients with cortical and subcortical left hemisphere lesions. *Brain, 122*(6), 1033–1047. doi:10.1093/brain/122.6.1033

Friederici, A.D., & Weissenborn, J. (2007). Mapping sentence form onto meaning: The syntax–semantic interface. *Brain Research, 1146*, 50–58. doi:10.1016/j.brainres.2006.08.038.

Friese, U., Rutschmann, R., Raabe, M., & Schmalhofer, F. (2008). Neural indicators of inference processes in text comprehension: An event-related functional magnetic resonance imaging study. *Journal of Cognitive Neuroscience, 20*(11), 2110–2124. doi:10.1162/jocn.2008.20141

Frishkoff, G.A., Perfetti, C.A., & Westbury, C. (2009). ERP measures of partial semantic knowledge: Left temporal indices of skill differences and lexical quality. *Biological Psychology, 80*(1), 130–147. doi:10.1016/j.biopsycho.2008.04.017

Frith, U. (1985). Beneath the surface of developmental dyslexia. In K.E. Patterson, J.C. Marshall, & M. Coltheart (Eds.), *Surface dyslexia: Neuropsychological and cognitive studies of phonological reading* (pp. 301–330). Hillsdale, NJ: Erlbaum.

Gazzaniga, M.S. (Ed.). (2010). *The cognitive neurosciences* (4th ed.). Cambridge, MA: MIT Press.

Gee, J.P. (2008). *Social linguistics and literacies: Ideology in discourses* (3rd ed.). New York: Routledge.

Goswami, U. (2006). Neuroscience and education: From research to practice? *Nature Reviews Neuroscience, 7*(5), 406–413. doi:10.1038/nrn1907

Goswami, U. (2009). Mind, brain, and literacy: Biomarkers as usable knowledge for education. *Mind, Brain, and Education, 3*(3), 176–184. doi:10.1111/j.1751-228X.2009.01068.x

Goswami, U., & Szücs, D. (2011). Educational neuroscience: Developmental mechanisms towards a conceptual framework. *NeuroImage, 57*(3), 651–658.

Gottlieb, G. (2007). Developmental neurobehavioral genetics: Development as explanation. In B.C. Jones & P. Mormède (Eds.), *Neurobehavioral genetics: Methods and applications* (2nd ed., pp. 17–27). Boca Raton, FL: CRC.

Hagoort, P. (2003). Interplay between syntax and semantics during sentence comprehension: ERP effects of combining syntactic and semantic violations. *Journal of Cognitive Neuroscience, 15*(6), 883–899. doi:10.1162/089892903322370807

Hagoort, P., Hald, L., Bastiaansen, M., & Petersson, K.M. (2004). Integration of word meaning and world knowledge in language comprehension. *Science, 304*(5669), 438–441. doi:10.1126/science.1095455

Hagoort, P., & van Berkum, J. (2007). Beyond the sentence given. *Philosophical Transactions of the Royal Society B: Biological Sciences, 362*(1481), 801–811. doi:10.1098/rstb.2007.2089

Hald, L.A., Bastiaansen, M.C., & Hagoort, P. (2006). EEG theta and gamma responses to semantic violations in online sentence processing. *Brain and Language, 96*(1), 90–105. doi:10.1016/j.bandl.2005.06.007

Hall, K., Goswami, U., Harrison, C., Ellis, S., & Soler, J. (Eds.). (2010). *Interdisciplinary perspectives on learning to read: Culture, cognition and pedagogy.* New York: Routledge.

Havas, D.A., Glenberg, A.M., & Rinck, M. (2007). Emotion simulation during language comprehension. *Psychonomic Bulletin & Review, 14*(3), 436–441. doi:10.3758/BF03194085

Heim, S. (2005). The structure and dynamics of normal language processing: Insights from neuroimaging. *Acta Neurobiologiae Experimentalis, 65*(1), 95–116.

Hendriks-Jansen, H. (1996). *Catching ourselves in the act: Situated activity, interactive emergence, evolution, and human thought.* Cambridge, MA: MIT Press.

Hirsh-Pasek, K., Bruer, J., Kuhl, P., Goldin-Meadow, S., Stern, E., Galles, N.S., et al. (2007). *The Santiago declaration.* Retrieved November 26, 2010, from www.jsmf.org/santiagodeclaration/

Hruby, G.G. (2009). Grounding reading comprehension theory in the neuroscience literatures. In S.E. Israel & G.G. Duffy (Eds.), *Handbook of research on reading comprehension* (pp. 189–223). New York: Routledge.

Hudson, R.F., High, L., & Otaiba, S.A. (2007). Dyslexia and the brain: What does current research tell us? *The Reading Teacher, 60*(6), 506–515. doi:10.1598/RT.60.6.1

Huettel, S.A., Song, A.W., & McCarthy, G. (2009). *Functional magnetic resonance imaging* (2nd ed.). Sunderland, MA: Sinauer.

Immordino-Yang, M.H., & Damasio, A. (2007). We feel, therefore we learn: The relevance of affective and social neuroscience to education. *Mind, Brain, and Education, 1*(1), 3–10. doi:10.1111/j.1751-228X.2007.00004.x

Israel, S.E., & Duffy, G.G. (Eds.). (2009). *Handbook of research on reading comprehension.* New York: Routledge.

Kaan, E., Harris, A., Gibson, E., & Holcomb, P. (2000). The P600 as an index of syntactic integration difficulty. *Language and Cognitive Processes, 15*(2), 159–201. doi:10.1080/016909600386084

Kamil, M.L., Pearson, P.D., Moje, E.B., & Afflerbach, P.P. (Eds.). (2010). *Handbook of reading research* (Vol. 4). New York: Routledge.

Kuhl, P., & Rivera-Gaxiola, M. (2008). Neural substrates of language acquisition. *Annual Review of Neuroscience, 31*, 511–534. doi:10.1146/annurev.neuro.30.051606.094321

Kuperberg, G.R. (2007). Neural mechanisms of language comprehension: Challenges to syntax. *Brain Research, 1146*, 23–49. doi:10.1016/j.brainres.2006.12.063

Kutas, M., Van Petten, C.K., & Kluender, R. (2006). Psycholinguistics electrified II (1994–2005). In M.J. Traxler & M.A. Gernsbacher (Eds.), *Handbook of psycholinguistics* (2nd ed., pp. 659–724). Burlington, MA: Academic. doi:10.1016/B978-012369374-7/50018-3

Lesaux, N.K., & Kieffer, M.J. (2010). Exploring sources of reading comprehension difficulties among language minority learners and their classmates in early adolescence. *American Educational Research Journal, 47*(3), 596–632. doi:10.3102/0002831209355469

Lieberman, P. (2006). *Toward an evolutionary biology of language.* Cambridge, MA: Belknap.

Lillywhite, L.M., Saling, M.M., Demutska, A., Masterton, R., Farquharson, S., & Jackson, G.D. (2010). The neural architecture of discourse compression. *Neuropsychologia, 48*(4), 873–879. doi:10.1016/j. neuropsychologia.2009.11.004

Luck, S.J. (2005). *An introduction to the event-related potential technique.* Cambridge, MA: MIT Press.

Maisog, J.M., Einbinder, E.R., Flowers, D.L., Turkeltaub, P.E., & Eden, G.F. (2008). A meta-analysis of functional neuroimaging studies of dyslexia. *Annals of the New York Academy of Sciences, 1145*, 237–259. doi:10.1196/ annals.1416.024

Mareschal, D., Johnson, M.H., Sirois, S., Spratling, M.W., Thomas, M.S.C., & Westermann, G. (2007). Neuro-constructivism: *Vol. 1. How the brain constructs cognition.* New York: Oxford University Press.

Marinkovic, K., Dhond, R.P., Dale, A.M., Glessner, M., Carr, V., & Halgren, E. (2003). Spatiotemporal dynamics of modality-specific and supramodal word processing. *Neuron, 38*(3), 487–497. doi:10.1016/ S0896-6273(03)00197-1

Mashal, N., Faust, M., Hendler, T., & Jung-Beeman, M. (2009). An fMRI study of processing novel metaphoric sentences. *Laterality: Asymmetries of Body, Brain and Cognition, 14*(1), 30–54.

Mason, R.A., & Just, M.A. (2011). Differentiable cortical networks for inferences concerning people's intentions versus physical causality. *Human Brain Mapping, 32*(2), 313–329. doi:10.1002/hbm.21021

Maurer, U., Brem, S., Bucher, K., & Brandeis, D. (2005). Emerging neurophysiological specialization for letter strings. *Journal of Cognitive Neuroscience, 17*(10), 1532–1552. doi:10.1162/089892905774597218

Maurer, U., Brem, S., Bucher, K., Kranz, F., Benz, R., Steinhausen, H., et al. (2007). Impaired tuning of a fast occipito-temporal response for print in dyslexic children learning to read. *Brain, 130*(12), 3200–3210. doi:10.1093/brain/awm193

McGill-Franzen, A., & Allington, R.L. (Eds.). (2011). *Handbook of reading disability research.* New York: Routledge.

Meltzoff, A.N., Kuhl, P.K., Movellan, J., & Sejnowski, T.J. (2009). Foundations for a new science of learning. *Science, 325*(5938), 284–288. doi:10.1126/science.1175626

Mody, M. (2004). Neurobiological correlates of language and reading impairments. In C.A. Stone, E.R. Silliman, B.J. Ehren, & K. Apel (Eds.), *Handbook of language and literacy: Development and disorders* (pp. 49–72). New York: Guilford.

National Governors Association Center for Best Practices & Council of Chief State School Officers. (2010a). *Common core state standards for English language arts and literacy in history/social studies, science, and technical subjects.* Retrieved June 1, 2010, from www.corestandards.org/assets/CCSSI_ELA%20Standards.pdf

National Governors Association Center for Best Practices & Council of Chief State School Officers. (2010b). *Common core state standards for English language arts and literacy in history/social studies, science, and technical subjects: Appendix B: Text exemplars and sample performance tasks.* Retrieved June 1, 2010, from www.core standards.org/assets/Appendix_B.pdf

Niogi, S.N., & McCandliss, B.D. (2006). Left lateralized white matter microstructure accounts for individual differences in reading ability and disability. *Neuropsychologia, 44*(11), 2178–2188. doi:10.1016/j. neuropsychologia.2006.01.011

Oakes, T.R., Fox, A.S., Johnstone, T., Chung, M.K., Kalin, N., & Davidson, R.J. (2007). Integrating VBM into the general linear model with voxel-wise anatomical covariates. *NeuroImage, 34*(2), 500–508. doi:10.1016/j. neuroimage.2006.10.007

Osterhout, L., Kim, A., & Kuperberg, G. (2006). *The neurobiology of sentence comprehension.* Unpublished manuscript, University of Washington, Seattle; Tufts University, Medford, MA; Massachusetts General Hospital, Boston. Retrieved May 9, 2009, from psych.colorado.edu/~aakim/osterhout_handbook_of_psycho linguistics_chapter_v2.pdf

Patterson, K., Nestor, P.J., & Rogers, T.T. (2007). Where do you know what you know? The representation of semantic knowledge in the human brain. *Nature Reviews Neuroscience, 8,* 976–987. doi:10.1038/nrn2277

Perfetti, C.A., & Bolger, D.J. (2004). The brain might read that way. *Scientific Studies of Reading, 8*(3), 293–304. doi:10.1207/s1532799xssr0803_7

Perfetti, C.A., & Frishkoff, G.A. (2008). The neural bases of text and discourse processing. In B. Stemmer & H.A. Whitaker (Eds.), *Handbook of the neuroscience of language* (pp. 165–174). Burlington, MA: Academic. doi:10.1016/B978-0-08-045352-1.00016-1

Perfetti, C.A., & Hart, L. (2002). The lexical quality hypothesis. In L. Verhoeven, C. Elbro, & P. Reitsma (Eds.), *Precursors of functional literacy* (pp. 189–213). Philadelphia: John Benjamins.

Price, C.J., & Devkubm J.T. (2003). The myth of the visual word form area. *NeuroImage, 19*(3), 473–481. doi:10.1016/S1053-8119(03)00084-3

Price, C.J., Gorno-Tempini, M.L., Graham, K.S., Biggio, N., Mechelli, A., Patterson, K., et al. (2003). Normal and pathological reading: Converging data from lesion and imaging studies. *NeuroImage, 20*(Suppl. 1), S30–S41. doi:10.1016/j.neuroimage.2003.09.012

Price, C.J., & McCrory, E. (2005). Functional brain imaging studies of skilled reading and developmental dyslexia. In M.J. Snowling & C. Hulme (Eds.), *The science of reading: A handbook* (pp. 473–496). Malden, MA: Blackwell. doi:10.1002/9780470757642.ch25

Price, C.J., & Mechelli, A. (2005). Reading and reading disturbance. *Current Opinion in Neurobiology, 15*(2), 231–238. doi:10.1016/j.conb.2005.03.003

Pugh, K. (2006). A neurocognitive overview of reading acquisition and dyslexia across languages. *Developmental Science, 9*(5), 448–450. doi:10.1111/j.1467-7687.2006.00528.x

Raizada, R.D.S., Richards, T.L., Meltzoff, A., & Kuhl, P.K. (2008). Socioeconomic status predicts hemispheric specialisation of the left inferior frontal gyrus in young children. *NeuroImage, 40*(3), 1392–1401. doi:10.1016/j.neuroimage.2008.01.021

Rimrodt, S.L., Clements-Stephens, A.M., Pugh, K.R., Cortney, S.M., Gaur, P., Pekar, J.J., et al. (2009). Functional MRI of sentence comprehension in children with dyslexia: Beyond word recognition. *Cerebral Cortex, 19*(2), 402–413. doi:10.1093/cercor/bhn092

Rogalsky, C., Matchin, W., & Hickok, G. (2008). Broca's area, sentence comprehension, and working memory: An fMRI study. *Frontiers in Human Neuroscience, 2.* doi:10.3389/neuro.09.014.2008

Ross, E.D. (2010). Cerebral localization of functions and the neurology of language: Fact versus fiction or is it something else? *The Neuroscientist, 16*(3), 222–243. doi:10.1177/1073858409349899

Ruddell, R.B., & Unrau, N.J. (Eds.). (2004). *Theoretical models and processes of reading* (5th ed.). Newark, DE: International Reading Association.

Rumsey, J.M., Horwitz, B., Donohue, B.C., Nace, K., Maisog, J.M., & Andreason, P. (1997). Phonological and orthographic components of word recognition: A PET-rCBF study. *Brain, 120*(5), 739–759. doi:10.1093/brain/120.5.739

Sakai, K.L., Noguchi, Y., Takeuchi, T., & Watanabe, E. (2002). Selective priming of syntactic processing by event-related transcranial magnetic stimulation of Broca's area. *Neuron, 35*(6), 1177–1182. doi:10.1016/S0896-6273(02)00873-5

Sauseng, P., Bergmann, J., & Wimmer, H. (2004). When does the brain register deviances from standard word spelling? An ERP study. *Cognitive Brain Research, 20*(3), 529–532. doi:10.1016/j.cogbrainres.2004.04.008

Schore, A.N. (1994). *Affect regulation and the origin of the self: The neurobiology of emotional development.* Hillsdale, NJ: Erlbaum.

Segalowitz, S.J., & Zheng, X. (2009). An ERP study of category priming: Evidence of early lexical semantic access. *Biological Psychology, 80*(1), 122–129. doi:10.1016/j.biopsycho.2008.04.009

Sesma, H.W., Mahone, E.M., Levine, T., Eason, S.H., & Cutting, L.E. (2009). The contribution of executive skills to reading comprehension. *Child Neuropsychology, 15*(3), 232–246. doi:10.1080/09297040802220029

Shaywitz, B.A., Shaywitz, S.E., Pugh, K.R., Mencl, W.E., Fulbright, R.K., Skudlarski, P., et al. (2002). Disruption of posterior brain systems for reading in children with developmental dyslexia. *Biological Psychiatry, 52*(2), 101–110. doi:10.1016/S0006-3223(02)01365-3

Shaywitz, S. (2003). *Overcoming dyslexia: A new and complete science-based program for reading problems at any level.* New York: Alfred A. Knopf.

Simos, P.G., Fletcher, J.M., Sarkari, S., Billingsley, R.L., Francis, D.J., Castillo, E.M., et al. (2005). Early development of neurophysiological processes involved in normal reading and reading disability: A magnetic source imaging study. *Neuropsychology, 19*(6), 787–798. doi:10.1037/0894-4105.19.6.787

Speer, N.K., Reynolds, J.R., Swallow, K.M., & Zacks, J.M. (2009). Reading stories activates neural representations of visual and motor experiences. *Psychological Science, 20*(8), 989–999. doi:10.1111/j.1467-9280.2009.02397.x

Szücs, D., & Goswami, U. (2007). Educational neuroscience: Defining a new discipline for the study of mental representations. *Mind, Brain, and Education, 1*(3), 114–127. doi:10.1111/j.1751-228X.2007.00012.x

Turkeltaub, P.E., Gareau, L., Flowers, D.L., Zeffiro, T.A., & Eden, G.F. (2003). Development of neural mechanisms for reading. *Nature Neuroscience, 6*(7), 767–773. doi:10.1038/nn1065.

van Berkum, J., Hagoort, P., & Brown, C. (1999). Semantic integration in sentences and discourse: Evidence from the N400. *Journal of Cognitive Neuroscience, 11*(6), 657–671. doi:10.1162/089892999563724

Varma, S., McCandliss, B.D., & Schwartz, D.L. (2008). Scientific and pragmatic challenges for bridging education and neuroscience. *Educational Researcher, 37*(3), 140–152. doi:10.3102/0013189X08317687

Vul, E., Harris, C., Winkielman, P., & Pashler, H. (2009). Puzzlingly high correlations in fMRI studies of emotion, personality, and social cognition. *Perspectives on Psychological Science, 4*(3), 274–290. doi:10.1111/j.1745-6924.2009.01125.x

Whitney, C., Huber, W., Klann, J., Weis, S., Krach, S., & Kircher, T. (2009). Neural correlates of narrative shifts during auditory story comprehension. *NeuroImage, 47*(1), 360–366. doi:10.1016/j.neuroimage.2009.04.037

Willems, R.M., Hagoort, P., & Casasanto, D. (2010). Body-specific representations of action verbs: Neural evidence from right- left-handers. *Psychological Science, 21*(1), 67–74. doi:10.1177/0956797609354072

Willingham, D.T., & Lloyd, J.W. (2007). How educational theories can use neuroscientific data. *Mind, Brain, and Education, 1*(3), 140–149. doi:10.1111/j.1751-228X.2007.00014.x

Willis, J. (2007). Which brain research can educators trust? *Phi Delta Kappan, 88*(9), 697–699.

Yarkoni, T., Speer, N.K., & Zacks, J.M. (2008). Neural substrates of narrative comprehension and memory. *NeuroImage, 41*(4), 1408–1425. doi:10.1016/j.neuroimage.2008.03.062

Yeatman, J.D., Ben-Shachar, M., Glover, G.H., & Feldman, H.M. (2010). Individual differences in auditory sentence comprehension in children: An exploratory event-related functional magnet resonance imaging investigation. *Brain and Language, 114*(2), 72–79. doi:10.1016/j.bandl.2009.11.006

SECTION THREE

Sociocultural

In "Toward a More Anatomically Complete Model of Literacy Development: A Focus of Black Male Students and Texts" (Chapter 14), Alfred Tatum describes an approach to literacy instruction that he has expanded since its original framing ten years ago. Using a sociohistorical orientation as its guide, the model aims to move African American boys in grades 3–12 toward advanced levels of reading and writing. Numerous strands informed the design of Tatum's model: extant reading research, research on Black males, research on boys and literacy, studies of Black males in schools and society, and an exploration of the texts that influenced Black males over the past 300 years. The model being advanced presents multiple theoretical, instructional, and professional strands of development that are omitted in many literacy reform endeavors. Tatum's model of literacy instruction attends to four categories of literacy vital signs: those of reading, readers, literacy instruction, and educators. The ultimate purpose for the model is to provide Black males with support and resources as they progress through school and move through life. Tatum believes that a model such as that he proposes can shape educational research so that researchers focus more intently on advanced levels of reading and writing while recognizing different types of literacy.

In Karen Wohlwend's "Play as the Literacy of Children: Imagining Otherwise in Contemporary Early Childhood Education" (Chapter 15), the author acknowledges that time for play in the world of early childhood development is vanishing because of severe pressure to get down to business, address accountability measures, and improve multinational standings. In response, she explores the sociocultural foundations for re-establishing play as a form of natural literacy of children. She examines play's renewed importance in times of absorbing technologies and argues for the recasting of play to a central role in the preschool and kindergarten curricula. While asserting that play provides a central place for children's engagement across digital spaces and diverse cultures, she believes that play is a literacy "in its own right." It may be untidy, but children elect it and use it to begin to make sense of the worlds in which they live and find meaning with their friends and childhood playmates.

In a dual theory of new literacies, Donald Leu, Charles Kinzer, Julie Coiro, Jill Castek, and Laurie Henry (Chapter 16) describe how the educational challenges presented by shifting social needs and forces influence how people communicate with one another. Literacy today is deictic, multiple, multimodal, and multifaceted. The popularity of the Internet and social media has changed how we think about knowledge. For example, transmission of knowledge is no longer top-down, thus allowing for the enrichment of lives and exploration of new domains and perspectives. The ability to navigate relatively unregulated founts of information to construct new knowledge is available to those who can afford access to the Internet, which in turn creates a need for new forms of critical literacy.

14

TOWARD A MORE ANATOMICALLY COMPLETE MODEL OF LITERACY DEVELOPMENT

A Focus on Black Male Students and Texts

Alfred W. Tatum

Discussions about the literacy development of Black male students are largely disconnected from the rapid changes and significant advances occurring in the world and from the benefits of Black male contributions and participation. Instead, discussions are anchored by societal and personal challenges connected to race, poverty, and systemic oppression. Researchers, essayists, journalists, and novelists are writing about Black male students' literacy development ignoring the former, but not the latter. This results in a limited framing for students' literacy development and contributes to the challenges of moving these young males to advanced levels of literacy out of necessity, rather than limiting them to poorly conceptualized literacy practices that work to their detriment.

Similarly, educators in the United States are not enacting literacy practices that yield advanced levels of reading and writing in grades 3–12 for a large majority of Black male students. In fact, a focus on advanced levels of reading among Black males has not been part of our nation's literacy discourse at the elementary, middle, and high school levels (Ford, Harris, Tyson, & Trotman, 2001; Howard, 2008, 2013; Howard, Flennaugh, & Terry, 2012; Matthews, Kizzie, Rowley, & Cortina, 2010). Black males have been discussed more as cultural beings than intellectual beings (Delpit & Dowdy, 2002; Gay, 2000; Kinloch, 2011; Lazar, 2004; Lee, 2007). More attention has been given to addressing basic literacy skills or supporting students to become proficient readers. There has been a shift in the research literature away from a focus on traditional reading achievements of Black boys toward types of literacies—critical, hip-hop, contested—as a part of a movement to redefine what counts as literacy among them and explain why these literacies need to be honored (Johnson, 2015; Kirkland, 2013; Kirkland & Jackson, 2009; Morrell, 2002, 2008; Morrell & Duncan-Andrade, 2002; Paris & Alim, 2017).

Suggested pathways for advancing the literacy development of Black male students continue to experience theoretical and conceptual shifts as efforts are made to address documented achievement outcomes and honor the range of literacies these young males enact inside and outside of schools. In efforts to reverse trends of Black male students being underserved during reading instruction, the multiple in-school and out-of-school contexts that they negotiate are often overemphasized or ignored when planning instruction and selecting curricula. Researchers who focus on the literacy development of Black male students often describe the complex, nuanced, and layered complexities of their experiences, identities, and literacy development (Newkirk, 2002; Staples, 2008). More attention is given to Black males who underperform or who are disengaged than to high-performing Black male students (Ford, 2011; Harris & Graves, 2010; Husband, 2012; Winsler, Karkhanis, Kim, & Levitt, 2013). This leads to a concern that many Black male students are not having their talents nurtured.

Over the past decade, literacy researchers have challenged deficit discourses and framings with the aim of revising a long-standing failure narrative dating back hundreds of years (Anderson, 1988; Du Bois, 2001; Mays, 1971; Williams, 2005; Woodson, 1933) and influenced by structural inequities and systemic oppression (Haddix, 2009 Johnson, 2015; Paris & Alim, 2017; Wood & Jocius, 2013). Considering the prevalence of documented struggles that have shaped a dominant narrative, the extant research literature is quantitatively thin and lacks critical historical analysis. Few recommendations based on empirical data that have moved Black male students in the aggregate to advanced levels of reading exist. I could not identify one school-based or district-based quantitative or qualitative research study in the United States in which an intervention or program moved Black male students across the academic spectrum in grades 3–12 (n > 1 classroom) to advanced levels of reading (Tatum, 2012).

Recent research has yielded recommendations such as focusing on critical teaching of popular culture, place pedagogies, reading preferences, verbal and visual literacies, multicultural children's literature, or using culturally responsive approaches to literacy teaching to incite Black boys' engagement in literacy tasks or help them navigate school and society. Researchers have also recommended having students produce counter-narratives to texts or scripts that depict Black boys in a negative light (Jenkins, 2009; Moeller, 2011; Sarafini, 2013; Staples, 2008). The shifts in research have led to a call for a new theory of Black masculine literacies that focuses on the unique and dynamic forces influencing literacy in the lives of Black males (Kirkland & Jackson, 2009). Still, there is an absence of interdisciplinary depth, theoretical grounding, and focus on the type of pedagogy necessary to provide literacy instruction that tilts academically high-performing and low-performing Black males toward intellectual power and reading experiences that they find significant to their personal and academic trajectories while simultaneously improving their reading and writing achievement.

An apparent linkage across the more recent studies of Black male students in grades 3–12 is the identity discourses of race and masculinity in the U.S. racial hierarchy (Kirkland & Jackson, 2009; Staples, 2008; Young, 2007). Several scholars are now focusing on literacy in relationship to Black male masculinity and how race and gender are represented or misrepresented and the effect these representations have on gender consciousness (Staples, 2012; Young, 2000; Young, 2007). Discussions of race and social class and their influences on literacy instruction and outcomes create tensions and entanglements in schools and are often devoid of the critical analysis such conversations deserve. However, there is an urgent need to make sense of the tensions in research and practice. It has become perfunctory to describe Black males using descriptive statistics about their educational, economic, and societal outcomes without also providing the careful analysis done by social scientists and economists to unearth or provide a balanced perspective of cultural and structural explanations that influence these outcomes (Roderick, 1994; Wilson, 2009). An imbalanced view is often provided. Black male students are either described as having brilliant and exceptional literacies that are not valued or described as persistent occupiers of the lowest rung of academics. These incomplete portrayals often yield a misalignment between what is needed and what is offered.

In this chapter, I describe a more anatomically complete model of literacy instruction. The model has been expanded since its original framing ten years ago to capture shifts and growth in literacy research during the past decade. For example, the focus on disciplinary literacies or nurturing discipline habits of mind (Cervetti, Barber, Dorph, Pearson, & Goldschmidt, 2012; Fang, 2013; Moje, 2007; Varelas, Kane, & Wylie, 2012) was not as prominent in the literature ten years ago as it is today. Disciplinary literacies, however, have been the focus of Black education for centuries, a history that has been largely ignored in the literacy research (e.g., Federer, 2002; Fouche, 2003; Manning, 1983; Moses & Cobb, 2001). Using a sociohistorical orientation as the guide, my more anatomically complete model aims to move African American boys in grades 3–12 toward advanced levels of reading and writing.

My research focused on Black males began as an eighth-grade social studies teacher on Chicago's South Side. In trying to improve the reading and writing achievement of the Black male students with whom I worked, I was confronted with a myriad of challenges, including students' accumulation of failure in the middle grades, poor concepts of reading, lack of self-efficacy stemming from years of ineffective instruction, and a narrow conceptualization of the roles of literacy and texts. Four of the eighth-grade boys I taught during my third year of teaching simply refused to embrace print text as a significant source of their academic and personal development. I began to engage their voices as a teacher researcher to find ways to break down barriers that disenfranchised these boys who had been assigned to my classroom (Tatum, 2000). Over time, I realized that the four barriers to their engagement were the fear of being publicly embarrassed if they failed in front of their peers, their limited vocabulary knowledge, the lack of attention their teachers placed on reading books, and their perceptions that teachers expected them to fail.

Since that time, I have conducted multiple qualitative case studies; led school-wide literacy reform efforts in a large, racially diverse high school; taught Black male students ages 11 to 17 in writing institutes; created and taught a post-release education pathway institute for 16- to 19-year-old court-involved youth; and designed an early literacy impact research project for Black boys in grades 3–5. Additionally, my own status as a Black male who has deep relationships with texts informs the call I make to move toward a more anatomically complete model of literacy instruction and to examine the roles of texts in the lives of Black males.

The more anatomically complete model of literacy instruction that I propose integrates effective instructional practices informed by numerous strands:

- the extant reading research (Duke & Carlise, 2011; Fisher & Frey, 2012; Rasinski, Rikli, & Johnston, 2009);
- research on Black males (Akbar, 1991; E. Anderson, 2008; Blassingame, 1979 Fashola, 2005; Franklin, 2004; Haas, 2010; Harding, 1981; Hine & Jenkins; 1999; Hutchinson, 1994; Manning, 1983; Polite & Davis, 1999);
- research on boys and literacy (Brozo, 2010; Kirkland, 2013; Smith & Wilhelm, 2002; Tatum, 2009, 2014);
- general education and sociological texts focused on Black males in schools and society (Alexander, 2010; E. Anderson, 2008; Harding, 1981; Laura, 2014); and
- an examination of the writings and texts that influenced Black males over the past three hundred years (Mullane, 1993; Porter, 1995).

The model also gives attention to multiple conceptualizations of literacies and identities, some of which are situated within power structures such as class, gender, and race (Collins & Blot, 2003; Street, 1995). Finally, it aims to support teachers in structuring their students' day-to-day experiences in a way that leads to meaningful literacy exchanges with texts (Tatum, 2014).

As displayed in Figure 14.1, the model I am advancing has multiple theoretical, instructional, and professional development strands. Theoretical components constitute the head of the model and focus on defining the role of literacy instruction for students in their present-day contexts, creating empowering curriculum orientations, and using responsive approaches to literacy teaching. Each of these strands is glaringly omitted in many school literacy reform efforts. The instructional elements compose the body of the model and focus on research-based reading practices. The professional development aspects serve as the legs of the model and focus on in-school teacher professional development and teacher preparation.

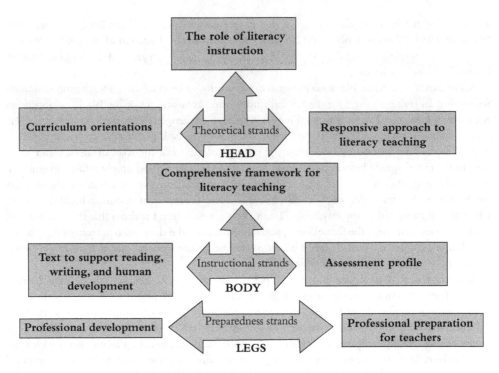

Figure 14.1 An Anatomically Complete Framework

Literacy reform efforts focus primarily on the instructional strands. While reading strategies offer much-needed support for struggling and non-struggling readers, the corpus of these strategies aimed at moving Black male students to advanced levels of reading and writing remains insufficient. Many teachers who have strong foundational knowledge for teaching reading still have trouble teaching Black boys who attend schools in high-poverty communities (Au, 2011; Edwards, McMillon, & Turner, 2010; Neuman, 2008; Payne, 2008). During an e-mail exchange that captures this challenge, a veteran educator of more than 25 years of experience informed me that she was ineffective with African American ninth-grade students in her classes. She acknowledged that she did not have competence with other components of literacy instruction, which I refer to as "vital signs" that could contribute to her effectiveness with Black male adolescents.

Multiple Vital Signs of Literacy Instruction

A more anatomically complete model of literacy instruction pays attention to four categories of literacy vital signs—vital signs of reading, of readers, of literacy instruction, and of educators—all essential elements for moving students toward advanced levels of reading and shaping meaningful literacy exchanges with texts. The vital signs refer to aspects of instruction that should be cultivated in classrooms and tailored to the characteristics of educators and students. As shown in Table 14.1, the categories of the vital signs correspond to four parallel factors affecting students' literacy- and life-related outcomes: reading achievement, relationships, rigor, and responsiveness.

The vital signs of reading provide the necessary working tools (e.g., decoding, comprehension monitoring, fluency, and other skills and strategies) that students need to read and understand texts independently, and they constitute a necessary minimum for all literacy efforts. Attending to the vital signs of reading by focusing on students' reading and writing skills is important in accelerating students' reading, writing, and intellectual development.

Table 14.1 Multiple Vital Signs of Literacy Instruction

	Reading	*Readers*	*Reading Instruction*	*Educators*
Rationale	Provide the working tools (What)	Improving the human condition (Why)	Refining the significance of literacy teaching (How)	Interacting with students, not scorecards of achievement (Who)
Vital Signs	Word knowledge	Home life	Quality instructional support	Competence
		Culture		Caring
	Fluency		Text	
		Environment		Commitment
	Strategy knowledge		Context	
		Language		Culpability
			Assessment	
	Writing	Economics		Courage
			Technology	
	Language development			
Aims to Advance	Reading and writing	Relationships	Rigor	Responsiveness

The vital signs of readers direct educators' attention to students' identities and lived experiences, both in school and outside of school, and are useful for considering ways to improve the human condition. When educators attend to the vital signs of readers—the everyday lives of the students they teach and the unlimited possibilities for students—they begin to build supportive relationships with their students.

The third set of vital signs, those of literacy instruction, are intimately related to the significance of literacy teaching. In other words, they are useful for conceptualizing the rationale for literacy teaching and enhancing academic rigor in the classroom to benefit struggling and non-struggling readers. Attention to the vital signs of reading instruction should cause educators to reflect on texts, quality instructional supports, assessments, and potential use of technology to shape rigorous and meaningful learning experiences in challenging academic environments.

The vital signs of educators are related to shaping educational contexts characterized by caring, commitment, competence, culpability, and courage. Students benefit when they know that they belong in the learning environment, when they experience psychological membership and kinship, and when they feel they are in the presence of an adult advocate who is not going to give up on them (Goodenow, 1993; Price, 2000). In this sense, attention to the vital signs of educators is a critical step toward providing literacy instruction that yields advanced levels of reading and writing, high levels of engagement with a wide range of texts across disciplines, and intellectual and personal growth and development. Moving toward a more anatomically complete model of literacy instruction that pays attention to these vital signs requires an understanding of the current state of their literacy instruction.

Underperformance Crisis: Overview of Literacy Landscape of African American Males

The Council of Great City Schools (CGCS), with 67-member districts comprising large school districts located in cities with populations over 250,000 and student enrollment over 35,000, reports that the percentages of CGCS districts performing at or above state proficiency rates in reading in

2011 in grades 4 and 8 were 17% and 19%, respectively. The percentage at fourth grade reflects a decline of five percentage points since the previous NAEP assessment in 2008. In 2011, there were no states with more than 19% of Black male students reading at a proficient level (National Assessment of Educational Progress, 2012). The absence of an approach that accelerates the reading achievement of Black male students while aiming to address the cultural, linguistic, and racial complexities perpetuates inequities in schools and society.

Reading achievement in the United States is clearly marked along economic, ethnic, and gender lines when basic and proficient levels of reading are reported. The confluence of historical antecedents, social class, community membership, language, race, ethnicity, and gender and their interplay with institutional structures have contributed to a crisis in literacy education that is difficult to unravel. However, national data indicate that 12% or fewer students across all ethnic groups are reading at advanced levels. The basic-proficient orientation to data reporting, as reflected in the following statement that appears above a National Assessment of Educational Progress (NAEP) reading data table, influences literacy reform efforts and program adoptions at the school and district levels as well as instructional and assessment practices:

> The percentages of White, Black, Hispanic and Asian-Pacific Islander fourth-grade students *who performed at or above the Proficient level in 2015* were not significantly different in comparison to 2013, but higher than in 1992. The percentages of *male and female students performing at or above the Proficient and Basic levels* were not significantly different from 2013, but higher than in 1992. In comparison to 2013, a higher percentage of fourth-grade students eligible for free/reduced-price school lunch performed at or above Proficient in 2015.
>
> *(National Assessment of Educational Progress, 2015)*

Discussing advanced levels of reading is not part of the national discourse. However, it should be deeply concerning that only 8% and 2% of boys are reading at advanced levels in grades 4 and 8, respectively. According to NAEP (2015), the advanced level denotes superior performance. NAEP defines this achievement level as follows:

> Fourth-grade students performing at the *Advanced* level should be able to make complex inferences and construct and support their inferential understanding of the text. Students should be able to apply their understanding of a text to make and support a judgment.
>
> When reading literary texts such as fiction, poetry, and literary nonfiction, fourth-grade students performing at the *Advanced* level should be able to identify the theme in stories and poems and make complex inferences about characters' traits, feelings, motivations, and actions. They should be able to recognize characters' perspectives and evaluate character motivation. Students should be able to interpret characteristics of poems and evaluate aspects of text organization.
>
> When reading informational texts such as articles and excerpts from books, fourth-grade students performing at the *Advanced* level should be able to make complex inferences about main ideas and supporting ideas. They should be able to express a judgment about the text and about text features and support the judgment with evidence. They should be able to identify the most likely cause given an effect, explain an author's point of view, and compare ideas across two texts.
>
> *(National Assessment of Educational Progress, 2015)*

Accelerating the reading achievement of Black male students in the United States is critically important for nurturing the next generation of leaders across fields and disciplines in the sciences and social sciences and professions in which Black men are underrepresented. Reading at basic and even proficient levels throughout the elementary and secondary years can foreclose academic, professional, and economic opportunities in the long term.

Advanced readers have more experiences with texts that inaugurate ideas, strengthen vocabulary, shape the identity or personality, and heighten consciousness that allows them to critically engage with fiction and nonfiction texts. Conceptually, it is difficult for many educators to embrace the possibility of advanced reading as the new normal for Black boys. Becoming an advanced reader also requires an *internalizing* among Black boys and teens that is often signaled by something or someone outside of them. James Baldwin's self-assessment as a young negro boy recorded in *The Fire Next Time*, first published in 1962, illustrates this point:

> For when I tried to assess my capabilities, I realized that I almost had none. In order to achieve the life I wanted, I had been dealt, it seemed to me, the worst possible hand . . . I could not sing. I could not dance. *I did not yet dare take the idea of becoming a writer seriously* [emphasis added].
>
> *(Baldwin, 1962/1990, p. 24)*

The idea of being or becoming a writer was foreign to him as a *Negro* because the world taught him to despise himself "from the moment [his] eyes [opened] on the world" (p. 25). The social and psychological costs that affected Baldwin's psyche continue today as some young Black male students try to make sense of harassment and discrimination as they negotiate public spaces, or as they try to meet the challenge of staying alive in urban areas such as Chicago, where my research occurs (Coates, 2015; Tatum, 2005). On balance, poorly conceptualized reading instruction can feel infinitesimally small in comparison to the magnitude of their lives. This can cause many Black male adolescents to lose confidence in reading as a tool of human development or protection. Loss of confidence in reading is greater for young boys who struggle early in their school years and have difficulty moving beyond their struggles, which leads to disengagement with reading. A rejection of reading or a failure to acquire strong literacy skills has disproportionately higher collateral consequences (Laura, 2014; Upchurch, 1996; Wilson, Quane, & Rankin, 1998). High-achieving Black male students also lose confidence in reading and writing in schools if the instruction misses the mark by failing to provide academic challenges or if it is poorly paced. Black male students, high academically performing adolescents in particular, do not want to be slow-walked through school as they move between their school world and the world outside of school (Cose, 2002; Hobbs, 2014).

Reading classrooms have become sites of marginalization for Black male students, and the reading and writing instruction that occurs within these sites need social transformation and reconstruction—namely, redefining what counts as legitimate reading and writing experiences and practices that yield exponential growth. Exponential growth in a reasonable period is needed to move the lowest performing readers to advanced levels. The large number of Black boys reading at below basic and basic levels in grades 3–8 is an underperformance crisis that cannot be ignored or mitigated by simply honoring their literacies that play out across multiple contexts or adopting a slow-growth orientation of literacy development based on multiyear school improvement plans.

The landscape of literacy development and proposed solutions to improve students' reading achievement in the United States are influenced by, at minimum, seven elements (see Table 14.2).

The market economy, advances in technology, and globalization have a gripping influence on the political discourse about literacy. The roles of reading and writing are viewed in direct relationship with the economy and college and career readiness. According to a report by the National Center on Education and the Economy (2006):

> This is a world in which a very high level preparation of reading, writing, speaking, mathematics, science, literature, history, and the arts will be an indispensable foundation

for everything that comes after for most members of the workforce. It is a world in which comfort with ideas and abstractions is the passport to a good job, in which creativity and innovation are the key to a good life, in which levels of education—a very different kind of education than most of us have had—are going to be the only security there is.

(p. 6)

Although an economic focus and attention to 21st-century literacy skills have become paramount in the national dialogue, we lack a clear definition of literacy instruction for all students in the United States that translates into classroom practices that lead to advanced levels of reading and writing. Without this clear definition, overwhelming and embarrassing inconsistency in literacy instruction occurs and can be expected to continue across schools. For example, an elementary principal recently informed me that the school's literacy model for the year was *individualized learning* (Alexander & Fox, see chapter 2 in this volume) that would be followed with fidelity.

Table 14.2 Seven Critical Elements Shaping the Landscape of Literacy Instruction in the United States

Accountability	Accountability has a gripping influence on the national dialogue about reading instruction. Discussions and literacy reform efforts are framed by formal assessment data, career- and college-readiness measures, school improvement plans, and National Assessment of Educational Progress outcomes.
Standards • Professional organizations • States • Content areas	Professional organizations such as the International Literacy Association and individual U.S. states have developed standards to shape literacy practices. The Common Core State Standards have influenced instruction, curriculum, and assessment. These standards are often found in lesson plans and are made visible in classrooms during instruction, as mandated by school and/or district administrators.
Teacher Preparation and Teacher Professional Development	Teacher education programs are increasingly held accountable for poor literacy instruction, while at the same time there has been a proliferation of teacher professional development focused on literacy instruction across the United States. Increasingly, there are more literacy coaches or teacher leaders assigned to elementary, middle, and high schools to support struggling readers. However, literacy coaches are not hired to advance the literacy development of non-struggling readers with the aim of moving the large majority of students to advanced levels of reading.
Gap Focus • Reading achievement gap • Racial achievement gap • Opportunity gap • Preparation gap	Closing the reading achievement gap between White students and students of color, except for Asian students, has been discussed for the past 50 years. Increasingly, schools are gauging their success by their ability to close the reading achievement gap. The gap is often discussed in terms of race, opportunity, or preparation.
Diversity • Shifting demographics • English language learners (ELLs)	Schools continue to experience major shifts in their demographics: Urban areas become destabilized as students move to surrounding suburban districts, and growing numbers of immigrants to the United States have led to a significant increase in the number of ELLs in U.S. classrooms.
Social Class • Race • Poverty	Reading data are aggregated to examine the performance of students from homes with low socioeconomic status. Research also looks at the effect parents' levels of education have on students' literacy.
Race • Impact • Dialogue	Although the dialogue is not robust in literacy reform efforts, there is a racialized component to the gap in reading achievement between high-performing readers and low-performing readers across economic levels.

Literacy experiences and the ways that literacy instruction is conceptualized and practiced can be characteristically different in environments with a large percentage of underperforming readers and for students attending schools with a comparatively smaller number of underperforming readers. Students' literacy experiences and academic schedules are governed by reading achievement data. Arguably, shortsighted or quick-fix solutions to address the crisis of underperformance among Black male students will continue to result in different literacy experiences and life-outcome trajectories for students along the economic and academic continuum.

Beyond an Economic Focus

The focus on economic projections oversimplifies the role of literacy education in the lives of Black male students. First, an economic focus fails to account for the day-to-day realities of Black males, particularly the young males living in high-poverty communities where long-term economic projections are overshadowed by immediate concerns like violence, classism, and punitive schooling practices—conditions that cause many of them to feel dehumanized and devalued. Literacy education should have a strong gravitational pull for Black males in their present-day context. Externally driven rationales for literacy instruction rooted in macrosociological concerns—such as taking on the challenges of life in a global economy or stabilizing communities that are imploding because of concentrated poverty—fail to interrupt students' existing "maladaptive" solutions" (Spencer, 1999; Spencer, Dupree, & Hartmann; 1997) or shape developmentally appropriate agendas that students can execute immediately because of literacy practices. I am reminded of a literacy lesson I taught to a group of third- and fourth-grade boys in which I used two texts that focused on the benefits of antioxidants and green tea. One young boy shared, "I think I am going to start drinking green tea" after learning about its health benefits. The literacy lesson led to intellectual development and planned personal development, two key components for engaging Black male students with texts (Tatum, Everett, Allen, Gyimah, & Moten, 2018a).

Unfortunately, the Black male presence in reading research is dismal (Lindo, 2006). Up to this point, studies involving Black male students have focused on factors that characterize these young males as *at-risk*. These studies have focused on comparing their academic outcomes to those of other students (Davis, 2001; Gilbert & Gilbert, 1998; Price, 2000). A meta-analysis is needed that examines how instructional practices, texts, and classroom contexts can be shaped to advance the literacy development of Black male students, both for low- and high-performing readers (Tatum, 2014; Tatum & Fisher, 2008). The current absence of a sociohistorical theorization is contributing to policy, curricular, and pedagogical misalignments that are not effective for these young males on a large scale. The lack of research informed by a sociohistorical theorization contributes to three major issues:

1. Many educators are failing to increase Black male students' engagement with a wide range of texts across disciplines, and subsequently the percentage reading at advanced levels is not growing.
2. Specific texts and text characteristics that engage Black male students are strikingly absent from the curriculum, or texts for Black male students are viewed from a limited lens that focuses on the boys' cultural characteristics, leading to default texts with Black male characters, beating-the-odds texts, boys' books, or social and racial justice texts to incite engagement, without a full complement of other texts that will benefit Black males.
3. Educators find it difficult to use texts to counter in-school and out-of-school context-related issues that heighten the vulnerability level of Black males.

A limited view of text for Black boys results in observable practical and theoretical vacillations among educators, policy makers, and educational publishers. The search for solutions to address the underperformance crisis of Black male students remains scattered; teachers of Black male students lack clarity about the other competencies outside of their disciplines they need to develop, and the support provided by teacher educators and professional developers remains as varied as the teacher educators and professional developers. The lives of many Black males are treated as expendable, both within and outside of schools.

In the remaining sections of this chapter, I draw from a sociohistorical orientation that supports the proposed anatomically complete model of literacy instruction. Choosing texts is central to the model and for moving Black male students to advanced levels of reading and writing. I will illustrate the importance of meaningful literacy exchanges for Black males and how these exchanges should focus on their intellectual and personal development.

Black Males and Texts: A Sociohistorical Orientation

Which texts should Black males be reading? Can you provide a list of texts for Black males? These are the easiest and most difficult questions to answer. In general, I respond, *all* texts belong to Black males, but we don't want to teach from *any* text. The demands of texts are great for Black males living in tough and safe neighborhoods, for Black males interested in expanding their knowledge and developing personally, and for Black males who want to read the best texts available on a topic (e.g., biology, artificial intelligence). Text selection requires serious consideration.

The impact of texts on the lives of Black males cannot be underestimated. Historically, texts have been central to their literacy development, with eminently clear connections among reading, speaking, writing, and action (Tatum, 2005, 2008). Although Black male students' relationships with texts are being severed in schools, Black males' strong relationships and engagement with texts are well established and have deep roots. Historical accounts of the lives of Black men are laden with references to enabling texts. An enabling text is one that moves beyond a solely cognitive focus—such as skill or strategy development—to include a social, cultural, political, spiritual, or economic focus. Enabling texts lead Black men and boys to become, act, or think differently because of what they read (Tatum, 2009). A sociohistorical orientation of literacy development offers guidance for selecting and mediating texts to promote intellectual and personal development and helps to explain how educators miss the mark when failing or refusing to select intellectually stimulating texts across disciplines. Misguided text selection can lead to disengagement or stagnant reading and writing outcomes.

To learn from and link Black male literacy development from the past to their literacy development in the present, I engaged in archival research (Bretell, 2000) to identify (a) texts central to their overall development, (b) how they engaged with the texts, and (c) the roles texts played in their lives. I was seeking implications for advancing the literacy development of Black male students. I also examined the archives for evidence of advanced literacies as characterized by voluminous reading and skilled, sophisticated writing.

As part of my examination, I constructed textual lineages (Tatum, 2007, 2009) of Black male archetypes' literary experiences. Textual lineages are diagrams of texts that individuals found meaningful and significant as described in documents written by or about them. I constructed the lineages by placing the first pivotal text the archetype identified at the top of the diagram. I then recorded other texts in the order they were discussed in the individual's biographical and autobiographical narratives. For example, Eldridge Cleaver, who wrote the memoir *Soul on Ice* (1968), shared how he "devoured [the book *Negroes with Guns* by Robert Williams] and let a few friends read it, before the [prison] library dug it and put it on the blacklist" (p. 71) (see Figure 14.2). He described other texts as "books that one wants to read—so bad that it [causes] a taste [in] the mouth" that only the books can satisfy (p. 70). Cleaver also complained that he could not get his hands on texts that were satisfactory to a man trying to function in the society and time in which he lived.

Stimulated by my reading of Dr. Martin Luther King Jr.'s autobiography (Carson, 1998) in 2003, when I first scribbled the term *textual lineages* in the margins of a book, I analyzed 94 biographical and autobiographical documents written by or about Black male archetypes from

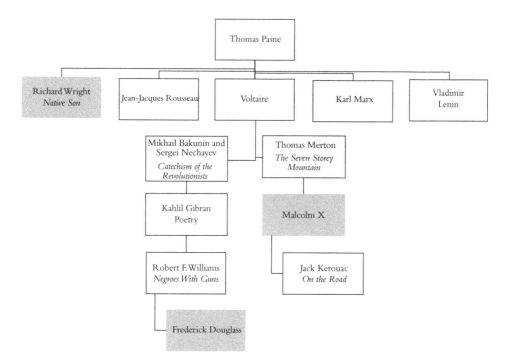

Figure 14.2   Eldridge Cleaver's Textual Lineage, Constructed from Reading Cleaver's *Soul on Ice* (1968)

Note: The shaded boxes denote texts that recur in the textual lineages of African American males from the 1960s onward

across the past three centuries. Among them were Nat Turner, Frederick Douglass, Martin Luther King Jr., Malcolm X, James Baldwin, and Huey Newton. I concluded that meaningful experiences with texts caused Black males to view themselves or others differently or moved them to some action in their current time and space (Tatum, 2008, 2014). The texts had an agenda-building quality, both small-scale and personal (i.e., I am going to change myself) or large-scale (i.e., I am going to change society).

In his political autobiography (1969), H. Rap Brown's words capture an enabling quality of texts. He wrote, "Other people enter Black America because of some experience they had in their childhood. Still others, because of something they may have read that was written by someone in Black America" (p. 10). The entering America is an example of being and doing something differently because of the reading. During the late 1960s and early 1970s, several Black males changed their names to reflect their emerging identities connected to reading and writing religious, political, or literary texts. Don Lee became Haki Madhubuti. H. Rap Brown became Jamil Abdullah Al-Amin. Leroi Jones became Amiri Baraka. Lew Alcindor became Kareem Abdul-Jabbar. Abdul-Jabbar offered:

> Much of my early awakening came from reading "The Autobiography of Malcolm X" as a freshman. I was riveted by Malcolm's story of how he came to realize that he was the victim of institutional racism that had imprisoned him long before he landed in an actual prison. That's exactly how I felt: imprisoned by an image of who I was supposed to be.
>
> *(Abdul-Jabbar, 2015, para. 9)*

After constructing the textual lineages of Black male archetypes, I constructed my own textual lineage using texts that were significant to me in middle and high school (see Figure 14.3).

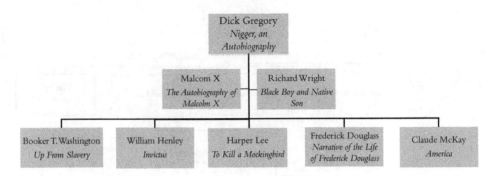

Figure 14.3 Tatum's Textual Lineage from Middle and High School

I recently noticed that scientific texts are glaringly absent from my personal textual lineage. There is no reasonable explanation other than that I had limited exposure to these texts in school despite being an avid, high-achieving reader who loved mathematics and the sciences as much as I loved literature and history. The texts in my lineage, all with a sociological bent, may have been the reason I minored in sociology as an undergraduate finance major. The texts in my lineage left an imprint on my psyche and became my signature texts when I taught language arts and social studies to my seventh- and eighth-grade students.

I also collected 243 textual lineages from Black male middle school and high school students to identify the characteristics of texts they found meaningful and significant to compare these characteristics with those identified in the examination of the textual lineages of Black male archetypes and myself (Tatum, 2009). I found that there are four characteristics of texts that Black males find meaningful in the present and significant over time:

1. They contribute to a healthy psyche.
2. They focus on collective struggle.
3. They provide a road map for being, doing, and acting in the world.
4. They provide modern awareness of the world. (Tatum, 2007).

Unfortunately, many Black boys and teens are unable to identify texts they find significant. As evidenced by the blank lineage submitted by an eighth-grade boy in an urban middle school (see Figure 14.4), these young Black male students often lack a growing textual lineage resulting from

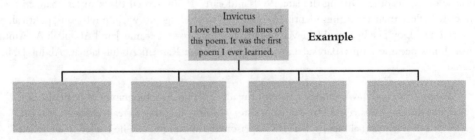

Directions: In each box above, place the title of a book, essay, or poem that you think you will always remember. Place only one title in a box. Explain why you think you will always remember the book, essay, or poem. Look at the example.

Figure 14.4 Textual Lineage of an Eighth-Grade Boy Attending an Urban Middle School Kaeson

in-school literacy practices. Instead, they generally encounter texts that are disabling—texts that reinforce their perceptions of being struggling readers if they are struggling readers, or stereotypical texts and associated literacy activities that do not capture Black male students' multiple identities and full range of potentially trajectory-shaping texts. Or, they encounter very few texts.

Currently, there is a consistent focus on texts relevant to the lives of Black male students with Black male images that speak in poignant and powerful ways to issues of identity development to address the virtual absence of a Black male presence in the curriculum (Meier, 2015). A focus on critical literacy that involves Black male students in conversations and critiques about power, race, gender, and privileges or in questioning the role of power in society is also reemerging (Coates, 2015; Hall & Piazza, 2008). Discussions on the types of texts that engage Black boys have focused on themes, preferences, lengths of texts, and more recently, new media texts for engagement. There is an absence of attention to how these texts connect to academic, personal, and reading development or influence writing.

The absence of text or textual lineage also has a profound impact on Black males. Benjamin Mays, who became president of Morehouse College, recounted the following in his autobiography:

> There are many things that one must learn and read in elementary and high school; otherwise it is too late, for each passing day makes its own new demands. Even if one had time to catch up on the reading he missed as a child, the end result would be different. I am sure I would have read many books in my childhood had they been available. They were not.
> *(Mays, 1971, p. 40)*

Limiting or curtailing Black male students' exposure to and experiences with texts is a form of coal mining or dwarfing. Booker T. Washington (1901) captured this in the early part of the 20th century when he wrote:

> Many children of the tenderest years were compelled then, as is now true, I fear, in most coal-mining districts, to spend a large part of their lives in these coal-mines, with little opportunity to get an education; and, what is worse, I have often noted that, as a rule, young boys who begin life in a coal-mine are often physically and mentally dwarfed. They soon lose ambition to do anything else than to continue as a coal-miner.
> *(p. 19)*

The absence of trajectory-shaping texts can forever limit one's vision and ambitions. This is the most damaging aspect of underexposure to texts, not the associated reading and writing outcomes. Other elements will compete for the minds of Black male students. In *Die Nigger Die!*, written in 1969, H. Rap Brown observed:

> You grow up in Black America and it's like living in a pressure cooker. Babies become men without going through childhood. And when you become a man, you got nothing to look forward to and nothing to look back on. So what do you make it on? The wine bottle, the reefer or Jesus. A taste of grape, the weed or the cross. These are the painkillers.
> *(p. 17)*

Taking a sociohistorical orientation that frames the significance of texts in the lives of Black males, the range of texts Black males read across the disciplines, and the impact of the presence or absence of texts in their early years led me to shift my focus to Black male students in the elementary grades. This also led me to think about the need to develop social and scientific consciousness as part of the literacy development for these students in grades 3–12. Dr. King's *Strength to Love* (1963) and James Baldwin's *The Price of the Ticket* (1985) became the two prototypical texts that keep the focus on advanced levels of reading and writing. Because of space, I will end by only discussing King's writings and how they capture all the components of a more anatomically complete model of literacy instruction.

Social and Scientific Consciousness and Interdisciplinary Writing

Dr. Martin Luther King Jr. is rightfully recognized as an icon of the civil rights movement and one of the world's most celebrated humanitarians. It would be equally judicious to recognize him as an icon for literacy. I observed visitors at the Martin Luther King Jr. Memorial along the National Mall in Washington, DC, marveling at many of his quotes pulled from the speeches and texts he wrote. Dr. King has one of the most far-ranging and far-reaching textual lineages. His writings also serve as a model of interdisciplinary writing. This is evident in the except below:

> I am thankful that we worship a God who is both toughminded and tenderhearted. If God were only toughminded, he would be a cold, passionless despot sitting in some far-off heaven "contemplating all," as Tennyson puts it in "The Palace of Art." He would be Aristotle's "unmoved mover," self-knowing, but not other-loving. But if God were only tenderhearted, he would be too soft and sentimental to function when things go wrong and incapable of controlling what he has made. He would be like H.G. Wells' lovable God in *God, the Invisible King*, who is strongly desirous of making a good world, but finds himself helpless before the surging powers of evil. God is neither hardhearted nor softminded; he is toughminded enough to transcend the world; he is tenderhearted enough to live in it.
>
> *(King, 1963, pp. 19–20)*

In the 133-word except above, King refers to authors or texts across several disciplines and genres—Tennyson (poetry), Aristotle (philosophy), and H. G. Wells (theology). King's writing signals consciousness and awareness of social and scientific literatures. He writes fluently across the disciplines, and there is evidence that he has encountered many texts that informed and shaped his writings. This more anatomically complete model aims to move Black males in this direction as they progress through school and move through life.

I analyzed King's text *Strength to Love* as a case study of the writing of a Black male archetype to extend my interests in examining Black males' relationship with texts.

The criteria for selecting texts for the analysis of writing were as follows:

- The book was written between 50 and 100 years ago.
- The author was a U.S. public figure with name recognition and accorded a place in American history.
- The author wrote at least one seminal text.
- The text had a minimum of 100 pages or 200 discernable paragraphs.
- The author was involved with critical issues contemporary to his time.
- The text was nonfiction or autobiographical.

In preparation for analysis, I identified author references, explicit text references, and referenced subjects (see Table 14.3). The analysis focused on two questions:

1. What do the author's writings suggest about his engagement with texts?
2. How was the author's engagement with texts reflected in his writings?

Paragraphs were the unit of analysis. Several examples of the unit of analysis are below:

EXAMPLE 1

Religion and the Bible were cited to crystallize the status quo. Science was commandeered to prove the biological inferiority. Even philosophical logic was manipulated to give intellectual credence to the system of oppression. Someone formulated the argument of inferiority according to the framework of an Aristotelian syllogism:

All men are made in the image of God;
God, as everyone knows, is not a Negro;
Therefore, the Negro is not a man.
So men conveniently twisted the insights of religion, science, and philosophy.

(King, 1963, pp. 44–45)

EXAMPLE 2

A persistent civil war rages within all of our lives. Something within us causes us to lament Ovid, the Latin Poet, "I see and approve the better things, but follow the worse," or to agree with Plato that human personality is like a charioteer having two headstrong horses, each wanting to go in a different direction, or to repeat with the Apostle Paul, "The good that I would I do not: but the evil which I would not, that I do."

(King, 1963, p. 51)

Table 14.3 King's References in *Strength to Love*

Explicit Author References	Explicit Text References	Subjects Referenced
Hegel	*Mein Kampf*	Greek mythology
Shakespeare	*God the Invisible King* by H. G. Wells	History
Aristotle	*Self-Reliance* by Emerson	Anthropology
Longfellow	*The Pathology of Race Prejudice—*	Science
Thomas Jefferson	essay by Dr. E. Franklin Frazier	Philosophy
John Bunyan	*Man Against Himself*	Psychology &
Dr. Harry Emerson Fosdick	*The Neurotic Personality of Our Times*	modern psychology
Ruth Benedict	*Modern Man in Search of a Soul*	Economics
Margaret Mead	*Peace of Mind*	Religion
Melville J. Herskovits	*Peace of Soul*	Law
John Bowring	*New York Times* article written	Military
Nietzsche	by Harrison Salisbury	Politics
Schopenhauer	*The Communist Manifesto*	Physics
Sir James Jeans	by Karl Marx	Sociology
Arthur Balfour		Technology
Rousseau		Art
Herbert Spencer		Geography
Darwin		Medicine
Alfred the Great		
G. K. Chesterton		
William Cullen Bryant		
Thomas Carlyle		
Lowell (poet)		
Tennyson		
Frederick Douglass		
Charles A. Beard (historian)		
Paul Tillich		
William Temple (Archbishop of Canterbury)		
T. R. Glover		

There is evidence that King engaged in a textual feast and wrote on a significant topic with people across a broad swath of humanity as his audience. He had deep engagement with texts and ideas. His writings at minimum capture his social and scientific consciousness and his high levels of literacy in both reading and writing. He wrote about God, the Copernican revolution, and Darwin in the same paragraph.

> The Christians who engaged in infamous persecutions and shameful inquisitions were not evil men but misguided men. The churchmen who felt that they had an edict from God to withstand the progress of science, whether in the form of a *Copernican revolution* or a *Darwinian theory* of natural selection, were not mischievous men but misinformed men. And so Christ's words from the cross are written in sharp-etched terms across some of the most inexpressible tragedies of history: "They know not what they do."
>
> *(King, 1963, p. 43)*

The examination of historical texts and of sociohistorical orientation are leading me to reconceptualize the role of literacy instruction, curriculum orientations, and the relationships among reading, writing, and texts for Black male students in grades 3–12. I am now working on a model that moves students to become interdisciplinary readers, writers, and thinkers. A sociohistorical orientation has also led me to increase Black male students' exposure to texts, to engage them in a textual feast across the academic disciplines in grades 3–12. Supporting Black male students to enact literacy this way will not occur without paying attention to the vital signs of reading, readers, reading instruction, and educators.

To nurture advanced reading and writing, avoid a slow-growth model of literacy instruction, and address the crisis of underperformance, I am now in the third year of a three-year study designed to have Black male third-, fourth-, and fifth-grade students read and write across two texts during every hour of instruction. They read and write across agenda-building texts across ten academic disciplines. The texts are selected to honor their multiple identities—academic, community, cultural, developmental, economic, gender, personal. The texts are also selected to nurture their intellectual and personal development. The reading components are designed to strengthen their concept of reading and decoding, nurture reading fluency and comprehension monitoring, engage them in close readings, and provide support for interdisciplinary writing (Tatum, Everett, Allen, Gyimah, & Moten, 2018b). The boys are reading and writing about cutting-edge developments across the globe, complemented by more local and personal texts to learn about themselves and their communities. This is proving to be a powerful combination.

Concluding Thoughts

Strengthening Black male students' engagement with written texts is still a perplexing phenomenon for many who are deeply concerned about their personal welfare and hierarchical arrangements in schools and society in the United States and abroad. I have argued that the challenges remain because literacy instruction for Black male students has been and continues to be poorly conceptualized and the roles of texts have been underexamined. To move in the right direction, I discussed the need for a more anatomically complete model of literacy for Black male students in grades 3–12 as well as the need for a sociohistorical orientation that gives guidance for selecting and mediating texts. It is imprudent to ignore the sociohistorical records of reading and writing among Black males when attempting to move them toward advanced levels of literacy achievement and advance their intellectual development. I assert that literacy instruction can serve as a mechanism to shape a more egalitarian society if more students have meaningful literacy exchanges with trajectory-shaping texts that increase their confidence in reading and writing as tools of intellectual, personal, and human development.

Educators and policy makers must assiduously question how policy, literacy mandates, pedagogical practices, and research will benefit and advance the literacy development of both the poorest and the most economically privileged students in the nation. A small percentage among both groups are reading and writing at advanced levels. The economically privileged and economically disadvantaged students of today will be bound together to solve the world's social, political, economic, and environmental challenges. Literacy development should be conceptualized in such a way that it addresses the needs of all students. It also should be conceptualized to nurture social and scientific consciousness that allows students to flourish in or shape a world experiencing seismic technological advances and shifts, but unable to break the yoke of racial and religious intolerance.

It may be helpful to adopt a life-course perspective (Mizell, 1999) that aligns neatly with cultural-ecological theories addressing out-of-school and in-school contexts, students' identities, and the structural barriers that exist in a highly stratified class-based and race-based society. But taking on such a perspective requires a broader conceptualization of literacy instruction for Black male students, who can be resilient and vulnerable at the same time. I suggest that educators and school reformers adopt a more anatomically complete model of literacy that integrates theoretical, instructional, and professional development strands as a comprehensive approach to advancing the literacy development of Black male students. Moving toward such a model can inform and shape the direction of educational research that focuses on advanced levels of reading and writing while acknowledging different types of literacy. Both will benefit Black male students in school and society.

References

Abdul-Jabbar, K. (2015, March 29). Why I converted to Islam. *Al Jazeera America.* Retrieved from http://america.aljazeera.com/opinions/2015/3/why-i-converted-to-islam.html

Akbar, N. (1991). *Visions for Black men.* Tallahassee, FL: Mind Productions.

Alexander, M. (2010). *The new Jim Crow: Mass incarceration in the age of colorblindness.* New York, NY: New Press.

Anderson, E. (Ed.). (2008). *Against the wall: Poor, young, Black, and male.* Philadelphia, PA: University of Pennsylvania Press.

Anderson, J. (1988). *The education of Blacks in the South, 1860–1935.* Chapel Hill, NC: The University of North Carolina Press.

Au, K. (2011). *Literacy achievement and diversity: Keys to success for students, teachers, and schools.* New York, NY: Teachers College Press.

Baldwin, J. (1985). *The price of the ticket. Collected nonfiction 1948–1985.* New York, NY: St. Martin's Press.

Baldwin, J. (1990). *The fire next time.* New York, NY: Vintage International. (Original work published 1962)

Blassingame, J. (1979). *The slave community: Plantation life in the antebellum South.* New York, NY: Oxford University Press.

Bretell, C. B. (2000). Fieldwork in the archives: Methods and sources in historical anthropology. In H. Russell Bernard (Ed.), *Handbook of methods in cultural anthropology* (pp. 513–546). Lanham, MD: Altamira Press.

Brown, H. R. (1969). *Die nigger die!* Chicago, IL: Lawrence Hill Books.

Brozo, W. (2010). *To be a boy, to be a reader: Engaging teen and preteen boys in active literacy.* Newark, DE: International Reading Association.

Carson, C. (Ed.). (1998). *The autobiography of Martin Luther King, Jr.* New York, NY: Warner Books.

Cervetti, G. N., Barber, J., Dorph, R., Pearson, P. D., & Goldschmidt, P. G. (2012). The impact of an integrated approach to science and literacy in elementary school classrooms. *Journal of Research in Science Teaching, 49*(5), 631–658.

Cleaver, E. (1968). *Soul on ice.* New York, NY: A Delta Book.

Coates, T. (2015). *Between the world and me.* New York, NY: Spiegel & Grau.

Collins, J., & Blot, R. (2003). *Literacy and literacies: Texts, power, and identity.* Cambridge: Cambridge University Press.

Cose, E. (2002). *The envy of the world: On being a Black man in America.* New York, NY: Washington Square Press.

Davis, J. (2001). Transgressing the masculine: African American boys and the failure of schools. In W. Martino & B. Meyann (Eds.), *What about the boys?* (pp. 140–153). Philadelphia, PA: Open University Press.

Delpit, L., & Dowdy, J. K. (2002). *The skin we speak: Thoughts on language and culture in the classroom*. New York, NY: The New York Press.

Du Bois, W. E. B. (2001). *The education of Black people: Ten critiques, 1906–1960*. New York, NY: Monthly Review Press.

Duke, N., & Carlise, J. (2011). The development of comprehension. In M. Kamil, P. D. Pearson, E. Moje, & P. Afflerbach (Eds.), *Handbook of reading research* (Vol. 4, pp. 199–228). New York, NY: Routledge.

Edwards, P., McMillon, G., & Turner, J. (2010). *Change is gonna come: Transforming literacy education for African American students*. New York, NY: Teachers College Press.

Fang, Z. (2013). Disciplinary literacy in science: Developing science literacy through trade books. *Journal of Adolescent & Adult Literacy, 57*(4), 274–278.

Fashola, O. (Ed.). (2005). *Educating African American males: Voices from the field*. Thousand Oaks, CA: Corwin Press.

Federer, W. J. (2002). *George Washington Carver: His life and faith in his own words*. St. Louis, MO: Amerisearch.

Fisher, D., & Frey, N. (2012). Close reading in elementary schools. *The Reading Teacher, 66*(3), 179–188.

Ford, D. Y. (2011). *Multicultural gifted education: Rationale, models, strategies, and resources* (2nd ed.). Waco, TX: Prufrock Press.

Ford, D. Y., Harris, J. J. III, Tyson, C. A., & Trotman, M. F. (2001). Beyond deficit thinking: Providing access for gifted African American students. *Roeper Review, 24*(2), 52–58.

Fouche, R. (2003). *Black inventors in the age of segregation: Granville T. Woods, Lewis H. Latimer, and Shelby J. Davidson*. Baltimore, MD: Johns Hopkins University Press.

Franklin, A. (2004). *From brotherhood to manhood*. Hoboken, NJ: Wiley.

Gay, G. (2000). *Culturally responsive teaching: Theory, research, and practice*. New York, NY: Teachers College Press.

Gilbert R., & Gilbert, P. (1998). *Masculinity goes to school*. New York, NY: Routledge.

Goodenow, C. (1993). The psychological sense of school membership among adolescents: Scale development and educational correlates. *Psychology in the Schools, 30*, 79–91.

Haas, J. (2010). *The assassination of Fred Hampton: How the FBI and the Chicago police murdered a Black Panther*. Chicago, IL: Lawrence Hill Books.

Haddix, M. (2009). Black boys can write: Challenging dominant framings of African American males in literacy research. *Journal of Adolescent & Adult Literacy, 53*(4), 341–343.

Hall, L. A., & Piazza, S. (2008). Critically reading texts: What students do and how teachers can help. *The Reading Teacher, 62*(1), 32–41.

Harding, V. (1981). *There is a river: The Black struggle for freedom in America*. New York, NY: Vintage.

Harris, T. S., & Graves, S. L. (2010). The influence of cultural capital transmission on reading achievement in African American fifth grade boys. *The Journal of Negro Education, 79*(4), 447–457.

Hine, D. C., & Jenkins, E. (Eds.). (1999). *A question of Black manhood: A reader in U.S. Black men's history and masculinity, Volume 1, "Manhood rights": The construction of Black male history and manhood, 1750–1870*. Bloomington, IN: Indiana University Press.

Hobbs, J. (2014). *The short and tragic life of Robert Peace: A brilliant young man who left Newark for the Ivy League*. New York, NY: Scribner.

Howard, T. (2008). Who really cares? The disenfranchisement of African American males in preK–12 schools. A critical race theory perspective. *Teachers College Record, 110*(5), 954–985.

Howard, T. C. (2013). *Black male(d): Peril and promise in the education of African American males*. New York, NY: Teachers College Press.

Howard, T. C., Flennaugh, T. K., & Terry, C. L. Sr. (2012). Black males, social imagery, and the disruption of pathological identities: Implications for research and teaching. *Educational Foundations, 26*(1), 85–102.

Husband, T. H. (2012). Addressing reading underachievement in African American boys through a multi-contextual approach. *Reading Horizons, 52*(1), 1–24.

Hutchinson, E. O. (1994). *The assassination of the Black male image*. Los Angeles, CA: Middle Passage Press.

Jenkins, S. (2009). How to maintain school reading success: Five recommendations from a struggling male reader. *The Reading Teacher, 63*(2), 159–162.

Johnson, L. (2015). The writing on the wall: Enacting place pedagogies in order to reimagine schooling for Black male youth. *Discourse Studies in the Cultural Practices of Education, 36*(6), 908–919.

King, M. L. (1963). *Strength to love*. Philadelphia, PA: Fortress Press.

Kinloch, V. (2011). *Urban literacies: Critical perspectives on language, learning, and community*. New York, NY: Teachers College Press.

Kirkland, D. E. (2011). Listening to echoes: Teaching young Black men literacy and the problem of ELA standards. *Language Arts, 88*(5), 373–380.

Kirkland, D. E. (2013). *A search past silence: The literacy of young Black men*. New York, NY: Teachers College Press.

Kirkland, D. E., & Jackson, A. (2009). "We real cool": Toward a theory of Black masculine literacies. *Reading Research Quarterly, 44*(3), 278–297.

Laura, C. (2014). *Being bad: My baby brother and the school-to-prison pipeline.* New York, NY: Teachers College Press.

Lazar, A. (2004). *Learning to be literacy teachers in urban schools: Stories of growth and change.* Newark, DE: International Reading Association.

Lee, C. (2007). *Culture, literacy, and learning: Taking bloom in the midst of the whirlwind.* New York, NY: Teachers College Press.

Lindo, E. (2006). The African American presence in reading intervention experiments. *Remedial and Special Education, 27*(3), 148–153.

Manning, K. (1983). *Black Apollo of science: The life of Ernest Everett Just.* New York, NY: Oxford University Press.

Matthews, J. S., Kizzie, K. T., Rowley, S. J., & Cortina, K. (2010). African Americans and boys: Understanding the literacy gap, tracing academic trajectories, and evaluating the role of learning-related skill. *Journal of Educational Psychology, 102*(3), 757–771.

Mays, B. (1971). *Born to rebel: An autobiography.* Athens, GA: The University of Georgia Press.

Meier, T. (2015). "The brown face of hope": Reading engagement and African American boys. *The Reading Teacher, 68*(5), 335–343.

Mizell, C. A. (1999). Life course influences of African American men's depression: Adolescent parental composition, self-concept, and adult earnings. *Journal of African American Studies, 29*(4), 467–490.

Moeller, R. (2011). "Aren't these boy books?": High school students' readings of gender in graphic novels. *Journal of Adolescent & Adult Literacy, 54*(7), 476–484.

Moje, E. (2007). Developing socially just subject-matter instruction: A review of the literature on disciplinary literacy teaching. *Review of Research in Education, 31,* 1–44.

Morrell, E. (2002). Toward a critical pedagogy of popular culture: Literacy development among urban youth. *Journal of Adolescent & Adult Literacy, 46*(1), 72–77.

Morrell, E. (2008). *Critical literacy and urban youth: Pedagogies of access, dissent, and liberation.* New York: Routledge.

Morrell, E., & Duncan-Andrade, J. M. R. (2002). Promoting academic literacy with urban youth through engaging hip-hop culture. *The English Journal, 91*(6), 88–92.

Moses, R., & Cobb, C. (2001). *Radical equations: Civil rights from Mississippi to the algebra project.* Boston, MA: Beacon.

Mullane, D. (1993). *Crossing the danger water: Three hundred years of African-American writing.* New York, NY: Anchor.

National Assessment of Educational Progress. (2012). *2012 Long-term trend reading assessment.* Retrieved from https://www.nationsreportcard.gov/ltt_2012/

National Assessment of Educational Progress. (2015). *The nation's report card: 2015 mathematics and reading assessments.* Retrieved from https://www.nationsreportcard.gov/reading_math_2015/#reading/acl?grade=4

National Center on Education and the Economy. (2006). *Tough choices or tough times: The report of the New Commission on the Skills of the American Workforce.* San Francisco, CA: Jossey-Bass.

Neuman, S. (2008). *Educating the other America: Top experts tackle poverty, literacy, and achievement in our schools.* Baltimore, MD: Brooks.

Newkirk, T. (2002). *Misreading masculinity: Boys, literacy, and popular culture.* Portsmouth, NH: Heinemann.

Paris, D., & Alim, S. (Eds.). (2017). *Culturally sustaining pedagogies: Teaching and learning for justice in a changing world.* New York, NY: Teachers College Press.

Payne, C. (2008). *So much reform, so little change: The persistence of failure in urban schools.* Cambridge, MA: Harvard Education Press.

Polite, V., & Davis, J. (Eds.). (1999). *African American males in school and society: Practices and policies for effective education.* New York, NY: Teachers College Press.

Porter, D. (1995). *Early negro writing, 1760–1837.* Baltimore, MD: Black Classic Press.

Price, J. (2000). Peer (dis)connections, school, and African American masculinities. In N. Lesko (Ed.), *Masculinities at school* (pp. 127–159). Thousand Oaks, CA: Sage.

Rasinski, T., Rikli, A., & Johnston, S. (2009). Reading fluency: More than automaticity? More than a concern for the primary grades? *Literacy Research and Instruction, 48*(4), 350–361.

Roderick, M. (1994). Grade retention and school dropout: Investigating the association. *American Educational Research Journal, 31*(4), 729–759.

Sarafini, F. (2013). Supporting boys as readers. *The Reading Teacher, 67*(1), 40–42.

Smith, M., & Wilhelm, J. (2002). *"Reading don't fix no Chevys": Literacy in the lives of young men.* Portsmouth, NH: Heinemann.

Spencer, M. B. (1999). Social and cultural influence on school adjustment: The application of an identity-focused cultural ecological perspective. *Educational Psychologists, 34*(1), 43–57.

Spencer, M. B., Dupree, D., & Hartmann, T. (1997). A phenomenological variant of ecological systems theory (PVEST): A self-oganization perspective in context. *Development and Psychopathology, 9*(4), 817–833.

Staples, J. (2008). Hustle & Flow: A critical student and teacher-generated framework for re-authoring a representation of Black masculinity. *Educational Action Research, 16*(3), 377–390.

Staples, J. (2012). "Niggaz dyin' don't make no news": Exploring the intellectual work of an African American urban adolescent boy in an after-school program. *Educational Action Research, 20*(1), 55–73.

Street, B. (1995). *Social literacies: Critical approaches to literacy in development, ethnography and education.* London: Longman.

Tatum, A. W. (2000). Breaking down barriers that disenfranchise African American adolescents in low-level reading tracks. *Journal of Adolescent & Adult Literacy, 44*, 52–64.

Tatum, A. W. (2005). *Teaching reading to African American adolescent males: Closing the achievement gap.* Portland, ME: Stenhouse.

Tatum, A. W. (2007). Building the textual lineages of African American male adolescents. In K. Beers, R. Probst, & L. Rief (Eds.), *Adolescent literacy: Turning promise into practice* (pp. 81–85). Portsmouth, NH: Heinemann.

Tatum, A. W. (2008). African American males at risk: A researcher's study of endangered males and literature that works. In S. Lehr (Ed.), *Shattering the looking glass: Issues, controversy, and trends in children's literature* (pp. 137–153). Norwood, MA: Christopher Gordon.

Tatum, A. W. (2009). *Reading for their life: (Re)building the textual lineages of African American adolescent males.* Portsmouth, NH: Heinemann.

Tatum, A. W. (2012). *Literacy practices for African-American male adolescents: The Students at the Center Series.* Washington, DC: Policy Report of Jobs for the Future.

Tatum, A. W. (2014). Orienting African American male adolescents toward meaningful literacy exchanges with texts. *Journal of Education, 194*(1), 35–47.

Tatum, A. W., Everett, S., Allen, S., Gyimah, M., & Moten, T. (2018a). *African American boys' writing in the elementary grades.* Manuscript in preparation.

Tatum, A. W., Everett, S., Allen, S., Gyimah, M., & Moten, T. (2018b). *Advancing the literacy development of African American boys in the elementary grades using an exponential growth model.* Manuscript in preparation.

Tatum, A. W., & Fisher, T. A. (2008). Nurturing resilience among adolescent readers. In S. Lenski & J. Lewis (Eds.), *Addressing the needs of struggling middle level and high school readers* (pp. 58–73). New York, NY: Guilford.

Upchurch, C. (1996). *Convicted in the womb.* New York, NY: Bantam Books.

Varelas, M., Kane, J. M., & Wylie, C. D. (2012). Young Black children and science: Chronotopes of narratives around their science journals. *Journal of Research in Science Teaching, 49*(5), 568–596.

Washington, B. T. (1901). *Up from slavery.* Garden City, NY: Doubleday.

Williams, H. A. (2005). *Self-taught: African American education in slavery and freedom.* Chapel Hill, NC: The University of North Carolina Press.

Williams, R. F. (1962). *Negroes with guns.* Detroit, MI: Wayne Street University Press.

Wilson, W. J. (2009). *More than just race: Being Black and poor in the inner city.* New York, NY: W. W. Norton.

Wilson, W. J., Quane, J. M., & Rankin, G. H. (1998). The new urban poverty: Consequences of the economic and social decline of inner-city neighborhoods. In F. R. Harris & L. A. Curtis (Eds.), *Locked in the poorhouse: Cities, race, and poverty in the United States* (pp. 57–94). Lanham, MD: Rowman & Littlefield.

Winsler, A., Karkhanis, D. G., Kim, Y. K., & Levitt, J. (2013). Being Black, male, and gifted in Miami: Prevalence and predictors of placement in elementary school gifted education programs. *Urban Review, 45*, 416–447.

Wood, S., & Jocius, R. (2013). Combatting "I hate this stupid book!": Black males and critical literacy. *The Reading Teacher, 66*(8), 661–669.

Woodson, C. G. (1933). *The miseducation of the Negro.* Washington, DC: The Associated Publishers.

Young, J. P. (2000). Boy talk: Critical literacy and masculinities. *Reading Research Quarterly, 35*(3), 312–337.

Young, V. (2007). *Your average nigga: Performing race, literacy, and masculinity.* Detroit, MI: Wayne State University Press.

15

PLAY AS THE LITERACY OF CHILDREN

Imagining Otherwise in Contemporary Childhoods

Karen E. Wohlwend

In this chapter, I examine play as a literacy of children—made by children for children—and argue for early childhood research and teaching that attends to the meanings children make for themselves and one another in contemporary times. First, a definition: Play is a set of imaginative practices through which players voluntarily engage to suspend the conventional meanings in the surrounding physical context and agree to replace these with pretend meanings for their own purposes, with transformative potential for their participation in home, peer, school, media, and digital cultures (Wohlwend, 2013). During play, children produce action-based stories and imaginary scenarios by enacting pretend identities with bodies or by animating toys, props, and other materials that enable players to virtually inhabit a shared pretend context.

But in this century, play researcher Vivian Paley (2004) cautions, "We have forgotten what it is like to be a child" (p. 3). Again. Early childhood educators have historically called for curriculum and instruction that honors the unique abilities and interests of the young child in order to provide appropriate learning. Over 150 years ago, Frederick Froebel conceptualized early schooling as a children's garden—*kindergarten*—and established a space for children to play, learn, and grow (Froebel, 1887/2005). But by the late 20th century, the garden had often devolved into a factory with children as the raw material (DeVries & Zan, 1994). Emergent literacy (Teale & Sulzby, 1986; Harste, Woodward, & Burke, 1984) provided a respite by showing children are capable of actively constructing literacy from a very early age and prompting a move toward a more developmentally appropriate curriculum (Bredekamp, 1987; Whitmore & Goodman, 1995; Whitmore et al., 2004). However, today early childhood teachers are again under intense pressure to stop playing around and to get down to the business of turning out better products. Time for play is vanishing from preschools and kindergartens, a casualty of demands to get ahead on governmental accountability benchmarks and multinational rankings (Bassok et al., 2016; Christakis, 2016).

In this chapter, I explore the sociocultural foundation for re-establishing play as a natural literacy of children, to examine its renewed significance in times of increasingly immersive and lifelike technologies, and to argue for the restoration of play to a central place in the preschool and kindergarten curricula. My argument aligns with a New Literacy Studies (Gee, 1996; Street, 1995) view of play as a key practice for engaging digital spaces and participatory cultures (Jenkins et al., 2009), but takes a new tack: rebooting play as first and foremost, a literacy in its own right; an untidy, just-fine-as-is literacy that young children choose and use to make sense of their worlds, reworking meanings with their friends for their own immediate social and cultural purposes.

The chapter is organized in four parts, each introduced and illustrated with a vignette of play excerpted from video data that I collected in a preschool classroom with children ages 3 to 5 years old. The first part sketches the foundation for theorizing children's play as natural and powerful storytelling. The second part theorizes and unpacks an episode of *imagining otherwise* in a preschool house corner, showing how children use play to construct action texts—action by action—as they quickly pivot among imaginary contexts to try on commonplace social practices such as book reading or online shopping. The third part moves from the house corner to the preschool's technology table to examine iPad play with an animation app, identifying multiple dimensions of play that shape young children's participation in digital cultures. The concluding part situates this action-oriented perspective on play in early literacy research and the realities of teaching in early childhood education, raising questions and implications for preparing young children for playing, reading, writing, and making in this century.

Play as Natural Storytelling

A conflict erupts in the preschool classroom library corner when 4-year-old Joshua sits down to read on a double row of sturdy wooden benches, which Evan and Ahmed have just pushed together and are now industriously pounding with small hammers. The pair of 5-year-old boys are pretending to build a fort and Joshua has unknowingly plopped down on its roof, hampering their construction work.

Evan warns Joshua, "We're working here. You can't, you can't, you can't, you can't, you can't, you can't—," but Joshua is already engrossed in the book and doesn't look up. Exasperated, Evan shouts, "Dude! I need to talk to you!" waving his hammer in circles to emphasize his frustration. "You can't trick us."

Joshua glances up at Evan, but continues calmly paging through *The Complete Book of the Flower Fairies,* a thick compilation of short poems written and illustrated in the 1920s by Cecily Mary Barker. Joshua slides his finger over each page, studying the naturalistic botanical watercolors of wildflowers paired with a matching fairy.

Giving up on talk, Evan and Ahmed drop to their hands and knees. Growling softly, they crawl around Joshua, up on the chairs and wooden benches and down on the floor again: two dragons lumbering along, circling their prey. Suddenly standing upright, Evan stretches in front of both boys and rotates his arms in large circles, unfurling imaginary wings. "I'm a bigger version of Toothless [a main character from DreamWorks' *How to Train Your Dragon*]. And I can both breathe ice AND blow fire. That's what I can do. Okay?" He disappears into the fort and quickly emerges again, flapping his wings in slow motion and breathing fire and ice, "Heeessssssh."

Joshua remains immersed in the fairy book, but Ahmed wonders, "Why do you like dragons so much?" When Evan ignores him and continues on his flight path, Ahmed realizes the pretense is live again and shifts into his dragon character to ask a question, "Why do dragons scare them, Toothless?" Evan's response is lost in the droning hum of 20 preschoolers at play as the pair glide away across the classroom, occasionally jumping on and off the low furniture and hissing at the populace.

My theorization of play as a literacy in its own right builds on a large established research base in play theory and early childhood education, which defines play as a symbol-making system (Vygotsky, 1935/1978) that reframes physical reality (Bateson, 1955/1972) as pretend scenarios that generate fluid, ambiguous meanings (Sutton-Smith, 1997) and express the whims and desires of players (Paley, 1992). For example, Vivian Paley (1984, 1986, 1988, 1990, 2010) listened carefully to 3-, 4-, 5-, and 6-year-olds in her classroom at the University of Chicago lab nursery school to uncover the intellectual, emotional, and social work that very young children accomplish during play. A teacher with an ethnographer's openness to uncertainty and willingness to challenge her own assumptions, Paley regarded herself as much a learner as the preschoolers and kindergartners she taught. She looked at play as a chance not only to learn *about* children but to learn *from* them, recognizing children's considerable expertise in play. Researchers who take an anthropological "sideways glance" at play (Schwartzman, 1976; Kendrick, 2005) look closely at play from a 4-year-old's eye level in order to understand the pretense from a child's perspective. This viewpoint provides answers to questions like "Why do you like dragons so much?" and uncovers the rich storytelling, emotional understanding, and social connection that emerge organically during play.

From this perspective, play is a first literacy, a child-friendly tool for meaning-making that has had and should continue to have a central place in the early childhood curriculum. Play produces a highly accessible "action text" made with moving bodies in familiar worlds that young children know best (Wohlwend, 2011b, p. 17). In other words, a play text does not need to be transcribed and pinned down with words on a page in order to mean and to matter deeply to children, as the dragon scene clearly shows. The action is already the text. Multimodality, or the interplay of sensory and semiotic aspects of language (Kress, 1997), conveys the enacted meanings of young children's play interactions through the low pitch of a rumbly growl (sound effects), the plodding speed of slow-moving bodies (movement), or the upright torso and undulating arms that indicate a dragon in flight (posture). Players actively manipulate the material environment to convey the meanings of their action texts using *modes*, which are the culturally shaped meanings of sensory and material properties of objects and space (Kress, 2010). Modes can be embodied (e.g., body movement, posture, facial expressions, gaze, voiced sound effects, proximity among players) or environmental (e.g., costumes, props, physical layout of furniture, music). Children can craft quite sophisticated action texts with modes and bodies before they can write with print and paper in a way that conveys much meaning to others (Kress, 1997). They naturally play to comprehend, develop, and represent their ideas about their worlds (Göncü, 1999), making play an early literacy that is a strong foundation for—and complement to—reading, writing, and making.

Extending work by early childhood researchers who carefully transcribed children's retellings of stories pretended in dollhouses, block corners, and play kitchens, I argue for valuing the narratives that children create as they play, but with a twist: I reconceptualize play as an always/already literacy that does not need to be translated into speech or captured in print on a page. From early childhood through the lifespan, play is a literacy that makes meanings with bodies and stuff, resemiotizing physical objects by detaching a conventional meaning and reattaching an alternate one (Vygotsky, 1935/1978). Players produce action-based stories and imaginary scenarios by *imagining otherwise*: by pretending to be someone else, someplace else, or something else to provide an imagined reality that is not available or possible in the immediate location of a home, playground, or classroom. In short, play is already enough on its own, made for children by children, in no need of the literacy evidence—dictated stories, drawn storyboards, written scripts, or filmed videos—that satisfy school benchmarks and state standards. Rather than confining play to an artificially compartmentalized subject area, my view of literacy suggests early childhood instruction should build on the situated literacies in children's lived experiences. We need to see and understand children's play in ways that capture the depth of meaning in their pretending and designing and that notice unspoken social meanings as well as unwritten literacies. In the next section, I theorize an action-oriented view of literacy to see the complexity and purpose in children's play and the literate and social meanings in their imaginative production.

Theorizing Play as a Literacy for Imagining Otherwise

Three girls are having a picnic, sipping from empty teacups and nibbling on an assortment of plastic cakes and tarts strewn on the floor of the preschool's play kitchen. Four-year-old Maeve approaches the group, fingering a small hinged plastic ladder, abstractedly opening and shutting it.

Five-year-old Angel waves her off, saying, "No one can play with us. We already have too much people. And we don't want to really play with those [ladders]." But a moment later, Angel abruptly changes her mind and decides the ladder will be a cell phone, telling Maeve, "You need to get the Barbie Game. . . . Close it up and turn it on and now press Barbie Game."

Obediently, Maeve closes the ladder. "I did press Barbie Game."

Abandoning the picnic, Maeve and Angel concentrate on the toy-ladder-turned-cell-phone to select objects for their Barbie Game. Maeve pushes on its rungs to type letters on its imaginary keyboard while Angel helpfully pronounces, "A-P-S-T—that's how you spell Barbie. Now what clothes you want?"

Maeve replies, "I want sparkly clothes."

Five-year-old Erin leaves the picnic area and joins the Barbie Game too. "Sparkly clothes? I can help you do it." Erin guides Maeve to the nearby rack of princess gowns, superhero capes, firefighter coats, and plush animal costumes. Maeve pulls out a pink satin dress with a fluffy, tulle skirt. "Yes, and Barbie has her own baby," she explains, picking up a baby doll in a denim infant front-pack carrier.

Erin responds, "You can download the clothes or download the things you want for your Barbie. You want the same clothes that you want to wear today for your Barbie doll?" Maeve nods yes and Erin heads off to the dollhouse area to find Barbie clothes to match Maeve's dress-up choices while Maeve intently untangles the straps of the baby carrier, snapping it into place around her waist.

Moments later, Erin returns with a thick hardcover library book, "They didn't have any Barbies at all . . . but I did buy a fairy book because I know you like fairies."

Delighted, Maeve holds out the book, "I love—my favorite fairy book! Does this one have chapters too?"

Taking the book and opening it on the small kitchen table in front of her, Erin smiles, "Yes, Chapter Two."

"I love Chapter Two."

"And there's even Chapter Three, and Chapter Four, and Chapter Five. There's each chapter you ever wanted."

Straightening the baby doll in the infant carrier, Maeve sits down at the table and turns the book so that it's open and squarely in front of her: "I get to read a chapter in my fairy book!"

Erin repositions the book, tilting it up, but careful to keep it facing Maeve. She stands beside the book, ready to read from the side so that Maeve can better see the pages. "Ok, how about I read Chapter Two?"

Maeve is puzzled by Erin's proposal to skip ahead in the chapter sequence: "Is that Chapter One?" When Erin ignores her question, Maeve turns to Angel and asks, "Is that Chapter One?" But Angel sniffs, "It's a fairy book," and walks away to stir the pots on the play stove.

"Chapter Two." Erin begins pretend reading at a random point about halfway through the book. She holds the book up slightly off the table, steadying it with her right hand while using her left hand as a pointer. Inventing the words, she places her index finger at the top of the right-hand page and moves it side to side and down the page, tracking across the print, left to right. "'People don't believe in fairies. And here's some of the fairies we have.'" She pauses to sweep her hand across the illustrations, noting, "'Cause there's some new fairies in there." She resumes her pretend reading, "'People think that people don't really like fairies. But that's not really true. Fairies are most best.'" Placing the book flat on the table, Erin turns the page.

On one level, this instance of reading a fairy book in the dramatic play center illustrates *playing to read*, a mixture of play and emergent literacy practices through which children learn to read by pretending to be readers (Wohlwend, 2007). Play allows children to learn how to read through exploration and approximation as they apply and imitate the reading demonstrations they've observed to coordinate conventions for tracking print, page-turning, voicing the cadence of storybooks, and creating story meanings (Whitmore & Goodman, 1995). Just as important, players who are pretending to read also explore who they can become as they try on identities as skillful readers. In this instance, Erin explored roles as reader and teacher while approximating the actions of her preschool teacher who reads from the side or upside down in order to display a picture book's illustrations as she reads aloud and demonstrates the left-to-right directionality of text by tracking print with a finger running under the words. At the same time, Maeve explored roles of avid reader and careful listener by expressing excitement for reading the book and by questioning Erin's skipping ahead to the second chapter.

On another level, the Barbie Game and fairy book reading vignette illustrates a different kind of reading-playing merger—*reading to play*—where emergent reading practices support children's pretend-play practices and make their performances as reader, teacher, app user, and online shopper more credible and more easily understood by coplayers. Children's pretend-play performances draw on their lived experiences: for example, knowledge of digital literacies enables the players to collaboratively change the meaning and use of a toy from plastic ladder to cell phone. This resemiotization is contingent on their mutual agreement to accept the ladder's revised meaning, and their corecognition of a repertoire of hand actions based on their shared knowledge of cell phones, apps, and digital cultures. These tacit understandings coordinate their joint agreement to open a pretend "Barbie Game," manipulate a pretend keyboard, and download pretend clothing.

Play and Mediated Action

In this vignette, the preschoolers poring over the illustrations of a thick book about fairies are coordinating several *mediated actions* that make up a common emergent literacy practice: pretend reading (Wohlwend, 2007). Rather than decoding the printed content of a text, pretend reading enacts the embodied actions of book handling: holding an open book, turning pages, tracking print, interpreting an illustration, inventing phrases that fit an illustration, pronouncing phrases with book-reading intonation, and so on. Mediated actions (Wertsch, 1991) occur as physical handling of objects that make meanings more accessible for participation in a cultural context. Said another way, mediated actions are small body movements with tools and artifacts that are used to make meanings for a particular time, place, and purpose. Mediation materializes abstract cultural tools such as language and literacy systems through concrete mediated actions that combine physical bodies, tools, and action to alter some aspect of the surrounding environment (Vygotsky, 1935/1978; Wertsch, 1991).

Within ordinary events such as a picnic, online shopping, or a read-aloud, mediated actions cluster into social practices (Bourdieu, 1977), the accepted ways of cooperating, belonging, and getting things done within a particular culture. Mediated actions are performed in sequenced patterns that make up social practices; and everyday events are made up of multiple social practices such as sipping tea, browsing through a rack of clothing, or reading a book. At times, social practices come together in ways that integrate and strengthen one another with significant impact on individual social and cultural participation, such as the development of literacy abilities or the strengthening of peer friendships.

When a mediated action is recognized as part of a valued social practice, it can become a marker of membership in its particular cultural group and members are then expected to be familiar and fluent in performing the action, in the correct sequence, and with other expected practices (Bourdieu, 1977). When a valued practice is performed, other members read and almost automatically respond with a sequence of expected mediated actions in the typical patterns of interacting in that culture. These interactions cluster in what Scollon (2001) termed *nexus of practice*—prevalent ways of reading and responding through action—that become familiar and unthinkingly enacted because they are ingrained into our bodies through everyday routines. For example, when people meet, they enact ingrained cultural expectations for pausing, nodding, and making eye contact (or not) during greeting exchanges. The appropriate response to "Hi, how are you?" might not be to answer with a report of one's current health status but to ignore the content of the question and correctly read the action as a perfunctory politeness that expects an echoing "Fine, how are you?" to close the greeting ritual.

Joining a preschool play group in progress is just as tricky and fraught with unspoken rules as entering an adult cocktail party conversation (Corsaro, 2003). In the vignette, for example, Maeve approached the group tentatively, waiting for acknowledgment. Angel read Maeve's hovering physical presence and the mediated action *holding a toy* as an unspoken bid to join the play group. She then rejected Maeve's request to play and also rejected the toy ladder as an unsatisfactory entry vehicle, "No one can play with us. We already have too much people. And we don't want to really play with those [ladders]." Fernie, Madrid, and Kantor (2011) define entry vehicles as prized classroom objects, which can be any object that is highly valued in a particular preschool peer culture (e.g., a new paintbrush, a weirdly shaped rock, a Mario Brothers figurine). Entry vehicles provide children with the material capital to enter play groups if the toy is highly popular or suggests a role in an in-progress play scenario. In this instance, Maeve's toy ladder is neither a prized possession nor a sensible object to bring to a pretend picnic.

But in a quick reversal, Angel uses the fluidity of play to rescind her rejection, to resemiotize the ladder, and to reclaim it as a workable entry vehicle. The ladder becomes a cell phone, a ubiquitous object that could easily be found at a picnic. Not only is this a reasonable prop, it also represents a scarce desirable object in the players' materially rich but technology-scarce classroom. Cell phones are an adult-only technology in this preschool; cell phones are restricted artifacts that children see teachers using all day but can rarely get their hands on. Elsewhere, I've found similar improvisations in early childhood classrooms where children cannot access or use the technologies they want to play with; instead children imagine otherwise to invent their own pretend technologies from the things that *are* readily available: toys, paper, and tape (Wohlwend, 2009b). In one elegant move, Angel not only transforms the ladder into an out-of-reach technology, she also elevates it with an imaginary Barbie Game app that gives it even more cachet for this group of Barbie and Disney Princess media fans. Finally, her directive ends with a mediated action that will bring Maeve as well as the toy ladder into the play action, "You need to get the Barbie Game. . . . Close it up and turn it on and now press Barbie Game." With amazing economy of words and action, Angel creates a pivot that transforms the play scenario from family picnic to online video game.

Pivots and Contexts

A pivot is an object that players use to trigger a shift from the here-and-now meanings of a physical space to the imaginary meanings of a play scenario. Vygotsky's (1935/1978) well-known example of a pivot is a stick that becomes a horse through pretense, enabling a new set of actions in the move from stick to steed. A pivot changes the meaning of the immediate object but it also changes the surrounding context so that new meanings, actions, and identities are suddenly available for players to try on. In this way, the pivot from toy ladder to cell phone changes not only the toy's meaning but also the underlying shared agreements among players that ground where they are and what they can do. Although Angel's pivot to the Barbie Game changed the context for pretense, the initial imaginary picnic was already a recontextualization of the physical space and its meaning as "classroom." The play kitchen area was furnished with a wooden stove, cupboard, refrigerator, and table, pots and pans, dishware, plastic food of every ilk, clothing, baby dolls, blankets, and pillows. These materials provide pivots that invite children to shift the frame from tangible experienced space to play frame (Goffman, 1974) so the meanings they create within this space are framed as occurring in imaginary elsewheres and "not real" (Bateson, 1955/1972). Maeve's doll and baby carrier are pivots that invite her to draw from her repertoire of mediated actions and identities. For example, the mediated actions of cradling the doll with one arm as she straps on the front pack transforms Maeve into a nurturing mother. When children play, their instant corecognition of the familiar meanings that the toys represent allows them to easily recontextualize their classroom into family dramas and replayings of mealtime, bedtime, and housekeeping rituals as children care for their dolls and stuffed animal pets. In this way, cultural histories of shared meanings for a common context are key to turning here-and-now action into meaningful social practice.

Angel's suggestion that Maeve select clothes indexed a mediated action in *online shopping*, a social practice typical in Barbie digital doll play where players purchase clothing and accessories to dress an online avatar. The mention of clothes draws Erin into the action as well. First, Erin guides Maeve to the rack of dress-up clothes to select a "sparkly" dress, then she elaborates on the Barbie Game and brings it into the world of action by suggesting that Maeve "download" clothes. Erin seamlessly blurs digital and classroom spaces by offering to find/download avatar clothes for the imaginary game, rummaging through the dollhouse accessories for miniature clothing. Unsuccessful in her clothing quest, she brings back an improvised substitute for Maeve, the fairy book, which serves as a new pivot to transform the context from digital game back to the classroom. The hyperflexibility of play has renewed importance for children growing up in a world where the boundaries between here and there, material and immaterial are evermore blurred. Such distinctions are nonexistent in the world of pretend play where you can pull a dress off the rack and hold it in your hands while you download a miniaturized copy for your doll that can be instantly fetched by your personal shopper.

Erin's mediated action of handing a book to Maeve is an opening move in the social practice of *gift giving* (even though the "gift" is from the classroom bookshelf and already belongs to any child in the classroom). Maeve read Erin's action and responded with a mediated action of instant acceptance, eagerly taking the book in her hands and holding it out to admire its dull green library cloth cover, "I love—my favorite fairy book!" Maeve placed the book on the table in front of her. The handing of a book also conveys an embodied invitation to read. In this way, Erin also initiated the social practice of *book reading*. Maeve read and responded to Erin's handing action by placing the book on the table. But there was silent contestation over who would be the reader in the repositioning that took place at the level of mediated action. As Maeve pulled up a chair to the table, Erin turned the book so that its print pages were facing her. This orientation made Erin the expected reader. When Maeve sat down, she turned the book on the table so that it faced her and opened it, "I get to read a chapter in my fairy book." Smoothly, Erin stepped to the side of the table and lifted just the top of the book off the table, "Okay, how about I read Chapter Two?" Her enactment of a read-aloud with teacherly hand actions further strengthened her position as play leader and cemented her appropriation of the role as reader. Erin's posture and body actions with the book and its meanings mediated the context slightly to reposition herself as a teacher-reader and Maeve as a student-listener. This action orientation to reading and writing reveals how literacy practices are made up of mediated actions that do not occur as isolated decontextualized behaviors or skills, but powerfully assemble bodies, tools, materials, meanings, cultures, places, histories, and identity expectations.

Action text describes the meanings produced by the interactive assemblages among moving bodies and objects when children act out an unfolding play narrative. In an action text, verbal language is just one of many means for communicating a story. At times—such as when children talk to clarify the pretend meaning of a toy or prop—verbal language carries the semiotic load. This kind of clarifying talk can be explicit or implicit. For example, an explicit proposition to pretend that a toy is something else would sound something like "Let's pretend the plastic ladder is a cell phone and its rungs are the keys on the keyboard." But Angel relied on implicit expectations to convey an invitation to pretend through her directive "You need to get the Barbie Game. . . . Close it up and turn it on and now press Barbie Game." Children often remain in character and use implicit clarifications to avoid interruptions that can break a fragile play frame (Sawyer, 1997). However, meanings can also be communicated through actions, rather than words, as in the stationary pause at the edge of the group that silently requests a chance to join the play in progress, a dismissive wave that rejects an unwelcome applicant, or the smile and outstretched hand with a book that means *gift*.

In the fairy book reading in this short vignette, early literacy educators can easily recognize the emergent literacy learning in book handling and pretend reading (Owocki & Goodman, 2002).

The mediated actions of holding the book, showing the illustrations, and tracking lines of print are interpreted as a literacy practice, according to shared expectations in this school culture. In the literacy-play nexus identified in this chapter, the imaginative meaning-making of play intertwines with emergent reading and digital literacy practices, emotional responses to favorite media themes, and social work in deciding who can join, who will lead, and who will follow. Play is built from constant proposals and agreements among players to pretend together, to imagine otherwise, and to adhere to a shared set of rules to govern their imagined world. This makes play both flexible and fragile as the rules for shared pretense bend and break to accommodate each player's ideas for the evolving narrative that shifts with every improvisation.

Using play to develop literacies or the young child's ability to read, write, and design is a commonplace strategy in developmentally appropriate literacy instruction. For decades, early childhood teachers have added print materials to classroom learning centers to encourage children to read bedtime stories to dolls, to write grocery lists in the play kitchen, or to design structures inspired by blueprints in the block corner. In this way, play is an inducement for practicing emergent literacy skills. As these are clearly appropriate and useful ways to encourage young children to engage literacy, the early childhood literature from the 1980s and 1990s is replete with research and teaching strategies on literacy-infused play centers (e.g., Owocki, 1999; Whitmore & Goodman, 1995). Additionally, an extensive body of literature also shows the value of encouraging a playful social environment for writing and encouraging dramatic enactments of children's written stories (Dyson, 1989, 1997, 2003, 2013; Genishi & Dyson, 2009), dramatizing a book with toys (Rowe, 2000), or digitally composing e-books (Burnett, Merchant, Simpson, & Walsh, 2017; Kucirkova & Falloon, 2017; Rowe & Miller, 2016). My work focuses on an aspect that is far less studied: play as a literacy that writes with bodies rather than print to produce an action text, whether dragon flights, family picnics, or imaginary video games.

Methods for Researching Action Texts

To examine children's play as action texts, I use mediated discourse analysis (Scollon, 2001; Scollon & Scollon, 2004) to look at play as a set of meaning-making practices with bodies, tools, and materials that players use to mediate and remake their worlds. Ron Scollon developed mediated discourse analysis by integrating ethnographic methods in linguistic anthropology with sociocultural theories of mediated action (Vygotsky, 1935/1978; Wertsch, 1991) and sociological theories of everyday interactions (Bourdieu, 1977; Goffman, 1974) that explain how a community's expectations for actions are ingrained into bodies and embedded into materials through social practices and cultural histories of use.

A filtering process in mediated discourse analysis provides an organizing framework for searching through the buzz of classroom activity to determine which of the countless moments of children's mediated actions with literacy materials produce transformations in meanings and social participation. The funnel design in this process progressively narrows the focus to find rich moments for microanalysis of mediated action. A six-step process unpacked the play interactions in the last vignette by providing a set of filters that guided data collection and analysis.

1. **Locations, players, and materials:** Where are the places that children choose to gather in play groups and which materials do they use to create play scenarios and build friendships (e.g., play kitchen, princess/Barbie play group, baby dolls, tea sets, fairy book)? Video analysis software enables examination of situated activity in each play center location in preschool classrooms and comparisons of groups to identify those who choose to play together frequently and their preferred play themes and materials.

2. **Prominent play practices:** In the focal locations, how do players wield materials to imagine new meanings for things in the physical environment? In other words, what are their *ways with*

things in these places (e.g., ways of handling a picture book that make credible Maeve's and Erin's performances of pretend readers and teachers)? The notion of ways with things is similar to Gee's (1999) characterization of discourse as "ways of doing and being" in critical discourse analysis, but with more emphasis on how artifacts and modes are used to produce meanings and shape participation in the group. Clips of key play practices are tagged in the video data and all practices are compared for their frequency and foregrounding by players.

3. **Nexus of practice:** For each key practice, what shared tacitly held expectations for particular combinations of practices are enacted during collaborative play? Which portrayals are easily recognized and implicitly agreed upon without much need for explanation (e.g., the instant recognition and use of a nexus of expected digital literacy and consumer practices with a smartphone: tapping on an imaginary screen to open an app and browsing to shop for clothing)? Video analysis of dense places where practices cluster are examined for patterns of interaction among players that can reveal their shared expectations for nexus (e.g., Erin's and Maeve's turn-taking and collaborative coordination of reader roles and actions with the fairy book). Looking at a practice across the entire video corpus and data set reveals how these nexus form and fit (or do not fit) with a group's shared play histories.

4. **Transformational moments:** Within a focal nexus, which moments produce collective transformations in the meanings in a play text that also substantially affect children's social relationships? Multiple passes across the video data set identify changes in play scenario meanings and players' participation in the context of each group's play histories (e.g., changing the meaning of the ladder to a cell phone pivots the nexus of practice from tea party propriety to online shopping but also shifts the pattern of participation so a child on the periphery of the group is able to take up a central role. It also expands the toy's potential play meanings for future play sessions).

5. **Mediated action:** Within these moments, how do actions, modes, and materials intersect in mediated action to enable transformation of story meanings and group participation? Children's pretend play, however fluid and fleeting, produces an immediate and concrete text, packed with shared meanings that become embedded in toys and ingrained in the actions of participants. Although play texts do not always involve tangible and durable literacy artifacts such as books or films, their actions, modes, and meanings are visible in context in the moment of imaginative production. Multimodal analysis (Wohlwend, 2011a) enables microanalysis of interaction (i.e., mapping movements and uses of actions, modes, and materials on video of children during play tracks shifts in meaning and participation). Close analysis reveals the mediated actions that hold the most potential for changing the nexus of practice—that is, a group's usual ways with things—with implications for early childhood teachers who seek to mediate children's play to offer more equitable participation.

6. **Circulations of discourse**. Throughout the process, mediated discourse analysis zooms out from video analysis or microanalysis of situated activity to trace the global histories and emanations of mediated action. The goal is to understand how a tiny physical action (e.g., tapping a cell phone screen or running a finger under print on the page) becomes a powerful site for circulating discourses and possibly changing expectations for appropriate ways of reading, writing, playing, and so on. Mediated discourse analysis looks closely at mediated action but also looks globally to trace mediated actions in the swirl of media, policy, current events, commercial motives, and other scapes across time and space. This mapping is informed by discourse analyses and cultural studies that connect these circulations to discourses that govern the availability and use of materials, modes, and actions in a particular space.

Elsewhere, I have argued that play is not only a literacy but also a tactic (Wohlwend, 2011b), a way of transforming power relations by making alternative spaces through pretend "as-if worlds" where children "learn to detach themselves from their reactions to their immediate surroundings, to enter a play world—a conceptual world that differs from the everyday—and to react to the imagined objects and events of that world" (Holland, Lachicotte, Skinner, & Cain, 1998, p. 50). Action texts can be transformative in the moment, as in Maeve's shift from fidgeting bystander to included player and pretend online shopper. Such transformation means and matters deeply to the players, whether or not it is dictated to a teacher, captured in a photo or film, or saved in a video game. Instead, the action text is ingrained in the group's shared histories and embedded into toys and other play materials. For example, the transformation in the vignette expands not only the accepted pretend meanings for a toy ladder to include cell phone but also expands player expectations for roles for Maeve.

The next vignette illustrates how the multimodality of actions with things shapes play texts and contexts, moving beyond here-and-now classroom pretense into digital worlds and media imaginaries, bounded by a nine-inch iPad screen.

Multiple Dimensions of Play Imaginaries

At the movie-making center, Erin arranges two tiny yarn dolls—superheroes Superman and The Flash—side by side on the table. Using the animation app *Puppet Pals*, she photographs the dolls with her iPad and then carefully traces around the dolls' image to make a cutout of the pair for her film (Figure 15.1).

Sitting nearby, Ahmed notices an orange-and-green yarn doll across the table. "Aquaman!"

"Huh?" Startled, Erin looks up and quickly tosses Aquaman to Ahmed and resumes tracing around the dolls on her screen with a deliberate forefinger. "Perfect!" She saves the cutout and scrolls through the next screen, browsing the assorted images of superheroes, princesses, ponies,

Figure 15.1 Tracing Flash and Superman

classroom toys, and selfies that other children have similarly photographed, cut out, and saved in the app. Erin taps the box to select the image she just created and then pauses expectantly—"What do you want?"—inviting Ahmed to choose a character and join the filmmaking.

Ahmed points to a photo cutout of a classmate, Lakin, and Erin selects the character by tapping its image. Ahmed adds, "I want Batman. Because he's your favorite superhero. And Superman. There. That's enough."

Erin notes that they are below the app's eight-character maximum: "We have four of 'em."

Ahmed points to additional characters. "Do Captain America, I mean, Green Lantern. Aquaman. Wonder Woman. That's enough now."

Erin turns the iPad slightly so that it is angled between the children and they agree on a castle and a forest as backdrops for their video. Erin taps Next on an arrow at the bottom of the screen and the screen populates with characters scattered around the forest backdrop. She slides the tablet a few inches toward Ahmed and he squares up the screen, presses the red Record button, and begins animating the characters with both thumbs. Erin twirls the Aquaman doll in her fingers as she watches.

Ahmed first resizes Lakin's image so that his classmate's face outgrows the entire screen and both children giggle. Using the same two-thumb resizing motion, he shrinks Green Lantern, then enlarges the Batman image until the Bat emblem fills the screen. Lowering his voice, he sings "Batmaaaan" as he repeatedly resizes the image so that it appears that the camera is zooming in and out on the logo.

Shrinking the Batman character to its original size, he next jiggles it furiously by rapidly rubbing a finger back and forth over the image, then repeats this shaking action with Wonder Woman. After dragging the remaining characters onto the backdrop, he saves the film by typing his name in the title bar and chooses Play to view the animation.

A few films later, Erin leaves and five-year-old Jane sits down next to Ahmed. "Do you like Wonder Woman?" he asks, offering Jane the Wonder Woman yarn doll in his outstretched hand. "You can be Wonder Woman," Ahmed assigns Jane a role in his superhero film. He slides a crooked arm around the other seven dolls, scooping them together to create a bounded and unavailable group of dolls. "These are the boys."

Jane accepts the Wonder Woman doll but what she really wants is a chance to trace on the iPad to make a character cutout like Erin just did. "I want to cut."

Ahmed replies, "I don't know what that is."

"I want to CUT." Jane repeats her request, louder.

"Oh! I know what you mean." Realizing what Jane wants, Ahmed returns to the home screen and begins a new film. On the character selection screen, he chooses Add Actor from Photo, then taps Take a Photo to launch the iPad's camera function. Jane places Wonder Woman on the table as Ahmed lifts the iPad off the table, frames the shot with the camera tool, centers the doll on the screen, and taps a button icon to snap the photo. The next screen displays the doll image with the cutting-tracing tool and Ahmed hands the iPad over to Jane. Happily, she begins to trace around the edges of Wonder Woman's image.

The photography, animation, and digital puppetry in this vignette are examples of technology-mediated literacy practices that are alive with modally rich movement and multiplied meanings that blur material-immaterial boundaries. In digital contexts, new kinds of interactions with emerging technologies stretch Vygotsky's (1935/1978) play as a leading activity to include personal sense-making (Edwards, 2011) with the wide range of global imaginaries that converge in contemporary everyday life (Medina & Wohlwend, 2014). This vignette illustrates how media imaginaries such as superhero film franchises intersect with the nexus of play and belonging in peer, school, and consumer cultures (Pugh, 2009; Wohlwend, 2009a). Such convergences make dense sites of engagement where the interplay of actions, meanings, modes, and materials can be tracked through four interdependent dimensions of play: multiplayer interaction, multilinear storying, multimodal production, and multimedia passions.

Multiplayer Interaction, Actions, and Bodies

Play enables multiplayer collaboration that requires children to jockey for storytelling space, whether in a child-sized kitchen or on a crowded touchscreen where they maneuver avatar characters on the same virtual landscape. To keep the action text going and the imaginary context intact, players smooth over contradictory meanings of character actions as they remix their disparate story ideas to create a mutually engaging, though not always sensible, text. Children also negotiate who will lead and who will follow, and the logistics of holding props and operating cameras. Erin's subtle hand movements and slight turns of the screen determined who was directing the story, but this authority quickly shifted from one moment to the next. Positioning the iPad so that the screen was squarely in front of her body meant Erin had sole control; tilting it slightly so that is was at a 45-degree angle between them opened an invitation for Ahmed to touch the screen and add a character.

Multilinear Storying, Meanings, and Collaboration

The improvisations of play unfold in unpredictable ways, facilitated by available materials such as touchscreens where the instant interactivity of a touch or a slide of a fingertip produces an immediate response, which allowed Ahmed and Erin to quickly shift direction and add three more superheroes. A child's desire to hold and create his own favorite superhero ("Aquaman!") as well as accommodate a friend's likes ("I want Batman. Because he's your favorite superhero.") produced multilinear storylines. Play creates an untidy tapestry, matted with abrupt stops and restarts, repetitions, and overlapping and looping plot threads that reflect the mix of players' literary knowledge, their cultural experiences, their friendships, their histories of negotiations and commitments to their shared play scenario, and their individual creative visions of how the story should unfold.

Multimodal Accessibility, Modes, and Action Texts

Ahmed's film is more an exploration of multimodal effects than a superhero story: a testing of the effects of fingertips sliding across a glass screen, images swelling beyond recognition, or movements zigzagging to create the appearance of vibration. The multiple modes in action texts thicken them and support collaboration by providing easily understood texts that allow children to quickly and clearly express ideas to one another through movements, props, voices, and sound effects. In this way, the multimodality of dramatic play action texts make them accessible and easy for very young children to make and to read. The lifelike multimodality of play also makes it a highly effective tool for collaboration. As children enact scenes, they instantly read and respond to one another's movements, facial expressions, postures, and gestures.

Multimedia Passions, Materials, and Transmedia

Children's play and digital engagements often involve commercial transmedia like *How to Train Your Dragon*, Barbie, and the DC Universe of superheroes in the three vignettes in this chapter. Transmedia are franchises of character-based multimedia that combine toys, games, and consumer goods distributed across video, gaming, shopping, and social media platforms. Children form passionate attachments to the appealing characters in films and video games that ground a line of consumer goods (Marsh, 2005; Marsh & Bishop, 2014). It might appear at first glance that children's media are benign and decorative with little power to do more that sprinkle character illustrations on themed products like toothbrushes, snacks, clothing, and video games. However, transmedia are designed to grow a brand and to incent young consumers to buy, guided by corporate profit motives rather than educational goals.

Children's transmedia play is both empowering and problematic. The extensive range and pervasive availability of transmedia products linked to everyday practices creates a widely recognized imaginary that peers recognize and value, creating capital that children can use to access play groups and strengthen friendships but to also enforce insider-outsider boundaries. Children's media knowledge can confer insider status in fan play groups where everyone can recite scripts or instantly recognize the difference between Captain America's and Green Lantern's costumes. In children's transmedia, the catchy songs and memorable snippets of dialogue in formulaic plots make it easy for very young children to recall and enact popular bits of media narrative—along with stereotypical characters and implied boy-only or girl-only player identities (Marsh, 1999, 2000; Wohlwend, 2009a, 2012). For example, there was obvious and uncontested boundary work in this vignette around gender: "These are the boys" and its unspoken subtext "and not for girls." Identities, desires, and attachments to beloved characters get tangled with highly available transmedia products, making it possible to consume, play, and live in character on a daily basis.

Immersive Imaginaries

The multiplicity of play—multiplayer, multilinear, multimodal, and multimedia—creates an immersive context that invites players to step in and imagine. It is important to emphasize that the product of play, with or without technology, is as much a context as a text, a space that frames a physical location, which all players agree to occupy and have a stake in maintaining through shared imagining (Corsaro, 2003). Children enact a storyline but the multimodality of their production also creates a tangible space that other players can see, touch, manipulate, and resemiotize, always contingent on the continued agreement of other players. These spaces are *collective cultural imaginaries* (Medina & Wohlwend, 2014), coconstructed improvisational pretend contexts that players collaboratively create, narrate, and inhabit. Like figured worlds (Holland et al., 1998), imaginaries are populated with identities, expectations, and prevailing cultural models for how things should be done in this space. When players share an understanding of an imaginary, they draw on their individual (and sometimes conflicting) knowledges and repertoires of cultural practices to guide their use of their bodies as they interpret, negotiate, and respond through their shared performance. This context, thickened with modes, meanings, bodies, and things, both supports and weakens a play context: by making it more lifelike and recognizable and by making breakdowns, ruptures, and tangents more likely as multiple players' ideas diverge and add more texture.

Imagining Otherwise in Early Literacy Education

Situating Play as Literacy in Early Childhood Education

Play and literacy have been extensively theorized and studied in early childhood research, both in relationship to one another and separately as distinct bodies of knowledge, sets of behaviors, systems of stages, and ways of enacting identity. Literacy research on early childhood play tends to study ways to leverage play to foster reading, writing, or language development. Such research produces justifications for play (as a means to produce literacy) by showing how symbolic play supports the development of narrative storytelling and writing (Fein, 1981; Pellegrini, 1985) or how dramatic play produces more and better interactions with print (Owocki, 1999; Strickland & Morrow, 1989). However, these approaches subsume play as an instructional strategy for developing literacy skills, defending time for play in terms of its deferred benefits on later achievement tests. We need critical approaches that recognize children as always/already cultural producers who play to express their diversity and engage inequity in their worlds: in language and written stories (Genishi & Dyson, 2009), in action texts on playgrounds (Thiel, 2015), or in repurposed artifacts in community makerspaces (Thiel & Jones, 2017).

Recent literacy research on new technologies, popular media, and digital cultures opens a new pathway for valuing play as a literacy in its own right, within user engagements with multimedia and social media in participatory cultures on global networks (Jenkins et al., 2009). In this view, playing apps on a phone or posting videos on Facebook or Twitter are contemporary ways of interacting with, producing, and sharing action texts. The ability to instantly create and wield live-action videos on social media has global impact. Video sharing is a powerful means of political participation that has launched recent social justice movements through raw video posted from bystanders' cell phones or police dash cams and body cams. Recent calls for critical media literacy have focused on the need for civic education that includes critical reading and consumption of news, websites, or social media silos. However, critical consumption is a partial answer. There is an equally urgent need to prepare students as media *producers* who communicate effectively and persuasively through action texts and immersive imaginaries (Sefton-Green, Marsh, Erstad & Flewitt, 2016; Marsh et al., 2015). Play offers a way for children to learn to engage the same challenges that filmmakers and app designers face as they anticipate the moves and intentions of viewers/players/users; coordinate or code sequences of potential actions; manipulate the effects of sound, light, and camera framing in digital tools; and negotiate and collaborate in a team of designers, actors, animators, coders, and other media production crew members.

However, educational innovations in technologies and social media have largely focused on older youth and adults while early literacy education is increasingly focused on print-and-paper tasks, often at the expense of playtime. In addition, developmental and safety concerns about screen time are constricting young children's access to mobile devices and computers in early childhood settings (Bassok & Rorem, 2016), not only shutting down learning through digital literacies but also further foreclosing classroom opportunities for developmentally appropriate play that might arise through filmmaking and video games. The iPad filmmaking center described in this chapter gave preschoolers in this classroom a rare opportunity to make original content and produce their own videos. As is the case in many early childhood classrooms, these young children did not usually read, write, create, or play with computers and iPads; instead the preschool teachers used their smartphones to photograph and document student learning or communicate with families (Blackwell, Wartella, Lauricella, & Robb, 2015; Wartella, Blackwell, Lauricella, & Robb, 2013). At best, this represents a significant underutilization of a widely available child-friendly technology. For example, the touchscreens and digital apps on smartphones and tablets have intuitive interfaces and fingertip operations that enable the youngest children to easily take photos of favorite toys, edit and animate the images, and produce short films to replay and share with friends, as they did with the puppetry app play in this chapter. In response to the chilling effect of screentime warnings (e.g., American Academy of Pediatrics, 2016), the National Association for the Education of Young Children in partnership with the Fred Rogers Center for Early Learning and Children's Media (2012) and other multinational research initiatives (Marsh et al., 2015; Sefton-Green et al., 2016) have called for more nuanced research that recognizes the productive value of interactive screens and the need for digital literacy and media literacy in early childhood education.

Raising Questions and Imagining Possibilities

Why does recentering play in early childhood education matter? It is easy to see that ensuring play in school is a matter of social justice by reframing this question: Who gets to play in school? Play is rapidly becoming a perquisite of affluence, only for children whose families can afford to send them to progressive schools where pretending, exploration, and child-directed inquiry are welcomed at an early age (Thiel & Jones, 2017; Wohlwend, 2017). Early opportunities to play provide young children with open-ended, peer-scaffolded spaces where learners can explore literacy practices in innovative ways. Play experiences allow children to collaboratively test the limits of their shared meanings and to develop ingrained actions, expectations, and dispositions toward evolving literacies in use in their worlds.

Why does teaching through play matter for early childhood teachers? Key to the reinstitution of play in preschool and kindergarten is allowing teachers the flexibility to create curricular space as well as time and physical space for children to explore. Teaching through play is a small change that can have a big impact on opportunities to teach in more culturally responsive ways since it allows children to bring in their families' cultural resources and enact their personal areas of expertise (Lewis-Ellison & Solomon, 2017).

What would happen if we dreamed big and redesigned early childhood spaces for a reconceptualization of children's play and making as action texts and imaginaries? What new tools and spaces would emerge if we designed classrooms as playscapes and makerspaces? Children's pretending is world-sized, too large to be contained in a script or even an animated film and already equipped for the emerging literacy practices and virtual realities that mold and mobilize materials, bodies, and artifacts.

What would happen if we dreamed concretely and imagined what could be done Monday morning? What if we expanded our expectations from reading and writing print to include play, toys, and iPad cameras as valid literacy tools? What would happen if we put play first on Monday's agenda? This could be as simple as letting go of the idea that children should write scripts or put words on paper before they can play a story.

Finally, there is power in allowing children to play and play and play. Repeated and regular opportunities to play in school allow children to deeply engage and work out the meanings of their stories through their imagining, to hold hands and learn about their worlds, and to find new paths forward to otherwises and elsewheres within the safety of pretense.

References

AAP (American Academy of Pediatrics). (2016). American Academy of Pediatrics announces new recommendations for children's media use. Retrieved from https://www.aap.org/en-us/about-the-aap/aap-press-room/pages/american-academy-of-pediatrics-announces-new-recommendations-for-childrens-media-use.aspx#sthash.2u6V3UQu.dpuf

Bassok, D., Latham, S., & Rorem, A. (2016). Is kindergarten the new first grade? *AERA Open, 1*(4), 1–31. doi:10.1177/2332858415616358

Bateson, G. (1955/1972). A theory of play and fantasy. In G. Bateson (Ed.), *Steps to an ecology of mind* (pp. 177–193). Chicago, IL: University of Chicago Press.

Blackwell, C. K., Wartella, E., Lauricella, A. R., & Robb, M. (2015). *Technology in the lives of educators and early childhood programs: Trends in access, use, and professional development from 2012 to 2014.* Evanston, IL: Center on Media and Human Development at Northwestern University and The Fred Rogers Center.

Bourdieu, P. (1977). *Outline of a theory of practice.* Cambridge: Cambridge University Press.

Bredekamp, S. (1987). *Developmentally appropriate practice in early childhood programs serving children from birth through age 8.* Washington, DC: National Association for the Education of Young Children.

Burnett, C., Merchant, G., Simpson, A., & Walsh, M. (Eds.). (2017). *The case of the iPad: Mobile literacies in education.* New York, NY: Springer.

Christakis, E. (2016, January/February). The new preschool is crushing kids. *The Atlantic.* Retrieved from http://www.theatlantic.com/magazine/archive/2016/01/the-new-preschool-is-crushing-kids/419139/

Corsaro, W. A. (2003). *We're friends right? Inside kids' culture.* Washington, DC: Joseph Henry Press.

DeVries, R., & Zan, B. (1994). *Moral classrooms, moral children: Creating a constructivist atmosphere in early education.* New York, NY: Teachers College Press.

Dyson, A. H. (1989). *Multiple worlds of child writers: Friends learning to write.* New York, NY: Teachers College Press.

Dyson, A. H. (1997). *Writing superheroes: Contemporary childhood, popular culture, and classroom literacy.* New York, NY: Teachers College Press.

Dyson, A. H. (2003). *The brothers and sisters learn to write: Popular literacies in childhood and school cultures.* New York, NY: Teachers College Press.

Dyson, A. H. (2013). *Rewriting the basics: Literacy learning in children's cultures.* New York, NY: Teachers College Press.

Edwards, S. (2011). Lessons from "a really useful engine"™: Using Thomas the Tank Engine™ to examine the relationship between play as a leading activity, imagination and reality in children's contemporary play worlds. *The Cambridge Journal of Education, 41*(2), 195–210. doi:10.1080/0305764X.2011.572867

Fein, G. G. (1981). Pretend play in childhood: An integrative review. *Child Development, 52*(4), 1095–1118. doi:10.2307/1129497

Fernie, D., Madrid, S., & Kantor, R. (Eds.). (2011). *Educating toddlers to teachers: Learning to see and influence the school and peer cultures of classrooms.* Cresskill, NJ: Hampton Press.

Froebel, F. (1887/2005). *The education of man* (W. N. Hailmann, Trans.). Mineola, NY: Dover.

Gee, J. P. (1996). *Social linguistics and literacies: Ideology in discourses* (2nd ed.). London: Taylor & Francis.

Gee, J. P. (1999). *An introduction to discourse analysis: Theory and method.* London: Routledge.

Genishi, C., & Dyson, A. H. (2009). *Children, language, and literacy: Diverse learners in diverse times.* New York and Washington, DC: Teachers College Press and the National Association for the Education of Young Children.

Goffman, E. (1974). *Frame analysis: An essay on the organization of experience.* Cambridge, MA: Harvard University Press.

Göncü, A. (1999). *Children's engagement in the world: Sociocultural perspectives.* Cambridge: Cambridge University Press.

Harste, J. C., Woodward, V., & Burke, C. (1984). *Language stories and literacy lessons.* Portsmouth, NH: Heinemann.

Holland, D., Lachicotte, W., Skinner, D., & Cain, C. (1998). *Identity and agency in cultural worlds.* Cambridge, MA: Harvard University Press.

Jenkins, H., Purushotma, R., Weigel, M., Clinton, K., & Robison, A. J. (2009). *Confronting the challenges of participatory culture: Media education for the 21st century.* Cambridge, MA: MIT Press.

Kendrick, M. (2005). Playing house: A "sideways" glance at literacy and identity in early childhood. *Journal of Early Childhood Literacy, 5*(1), 5–28. doi:10.1177/1468798405050592

Kress, G. (1997). *Before writing: Rethinking the paths to literacy.* London: Routledge.

Kress, G. (2010). *Multimodality: A social semiotic approach to contemporary communication.* London: Routledge.

Kucirkova, N., & Falloon, G. (Eds.). (2017). *Apps, technology and younger learners: International evidence for teaching.* New York: Routledge.

Lewis-Ellison, T., & Solomon, M. (2017). Digital play as purposeful productive literacies in African American boys. *The Reading Teacher, 71*(4), 495–500. doi:10.1002/trtr.1657

Marsh, J. (1999). Batman and Batwoman go to school: Popular culture in the literacy curriculum. *International Journal of Early Years Education, 7*(2), 117–131. doi:10.1080/0966976990070201

Marsh, J. (2000). "But I want to fly too!" Girls and superhero play in the infant classroom. *Gender and Education, 12*(2), 209–220. doi:10.1080/09540250050010018

Marsh, J. (2005). Ritual, performance, and identity construction: Young children's engagement with popular cultural and media texts. In J. Marsh (Ed.), *Popular culture, new media and digital literacy in early childhood* (pp. 28–50). London: Routledge.

Marsh, J., & Bishop, J. C. (2014). *Changing play: Play, media, and commercial culture from the 1950s to the present day.* Maidenhead: Open University Press.

Marsh, J., Plowman, L., Yamada-Rice, D., Bishop, J. C., Lahmar, J., Scott, F., . . . Winter, P. (2015). Exploring play and creativity in pre-schoolers' use of apps. *Final Project Report.* Sheffield: University of Sheffield. Retrieved from www.techandplay.org

Medina, C. L., & Wohlwend, K. E. (2014). *Literacy, play, and globalization: Converging imaginaries in children's critical and cultural performances.* New York, NY: Routledge.

National Association for the Education of Young Children & The Fred Rogers Center for Early Learning and Children's Media. (2012). *Technology and interactive media as tools in early childhood programs serving children from birth through age 8.* Washington, DC: Author.

Owocki, G. (1999). *Literacy through play.* Portsmouth, NH: Heinemann.

Owocki, G., & Goodman, Y. M. (2002). *Kidwatching: Documenting children's literacy development.* Portsmouth, NH: Heinemann.

Paley, V. G. (1984). *Boys and girls: Superheroes in the doll corner.* Chicago, IL: University of Chicago Press.

Paley, V. G. (1986). *Mollie is three: Growing up in school.* Chicago, IL: University of Chicago Press.

Paley, V. G. (1988). *Bad guys don't have birthdays: Fantasy play at four.* Chicago, IL: University of Chicago Press.

Paley, V. G. (1990). *The boy who would be a helicopter: The uses of storytelling in the classroom.* Cambridge, MA: Harvard University Press.

Paley, V. G. (1992). *You can't say you can't play.* Cambridge, MA: Harvard University Press.

Paley, V. G. (2004). *A child's work: The importance of fantasy play.* Chicago, IL: University of Chicago Press.

Paley, V. G. (2010). *The boy on the beach.* Chicago, IL: University of Chicago Press.

Pellegrini, A. D. (1985). The relations between symbolic play and literate behavior: A review and critique of the empirical literature. *Review of Educational Research, 55*(1), 107–121.

Pugh, A. J. (2009). *Longing and belonging: Parents, children, and consumer culture.* Berkeley, CA: University of California Press.

Rowe, D. W. (2000). Bringing books to life: The role of book-related dramatic play in young children's literacy learning. In K. A. Roskos & J. F. Christie (Eds.), *Play and literacy in early childhood: Research from multiple perspectives* (pp. 3–25). Mahwah, NJ: Lawrence Erlbaum Associates.

Rowe, D. W., & Miller, M. E. (2016). Designing for diverse classrooms: Using iPads and digital cameras to compose eBooks with emergent bilingual/biliterate four-year-olds. *Journal of Early Childhood Literacy, 16*(4), 425–472. DOE: 10.1177/1468798415593622

Sawyer, R. K. (1997). *Pretend play as improvisation: Conversation in the preschool classroom.* Mahwah, NJ: Lawrence Erlbaum Associates.

Schwartzman, H. B. (1976). The anthropological study of children's play. *Annual Review of Anthropology, 5*(289–328). doi:10.1146/annurev.an.05.100176.001445

Scollon, R. (2001). *Mediated discourse: The nexus of practice.* New York, NY: Routledge.

Scollon, R., & Scollon, S. W. (2004). *Nexus analysis: Discourse and the emerging Internet.* New York, NY: Routledge.

Sefton-Green, J., Marsh, J., Erstad, O., & Flewitt, R. (2016). Establishing a research agenda for the digital literacy practices of young children: A white paper for COST Action IS1410. Brussels, Belgium: European Cooperation in Science and Technology Association. Retrieved from http://digilitey.eu/wp-content/uploads/2015/09/DigiLitEYWP.pdf

Street, B. V. (1995). *Social literacies: Critical approaches to literary development.* Cambridge: Cambridge University Press.

Strickland, D., & Morrow, L. M. (1989). Environments rich in print promote literacy behavior during play. *The Reading Teacher, 43*, 178–179.

Sutton-Smith, B. (1997). *The ambiguity of play.* Cambridge, MA: Harvard University Press.

Teale, W. H., & Sulzby, E. (1986). *Emergent literacy: Writing and reading.* Norwood, NJ: Ablex.

Thiel, J. J. (2015). Bumblebee's in trouble: Embodied literacies during imaginative superhero play. *Language Arts, 93*(1), 38–49.

Thiel, J. J., & Jones, S. (2017). The literacies of things: Reconfiguring the material-discursive production of race and class in an informal learning center. *Journal of Early Childhood Literacy, 17*(3), 315–335. doi:10.1177/1468798417712066

Vygotsky, L. (1935/1978). *Mind in society: The development of higher psychological processes* (A. Luria, M. Lopez-Morillas, & M. Cole, Trans.). Cambridge, MA: Harvard University Press.

Wartella, E., Blackwell, C. K., Lauricella, A. R., & Robb, M. B. (2013). *Technology in the lives of educators and early childhood programs: 2012 survey of early childhood educators.* Evanston, IL: Center on Media and Human Development at Northwestern University & The Fred Rogers Center for Early Learning and Children's Media at Saint Vincent College.

Wertsch, J. V. (1991). *Voices of the mind: A sociocultural approach to mediated action.* Cambridge, MA: Harvard University Press.

Whitmore, K. F., & Goodman, Y. M. (1995). Transforming curriculum in language and literacy. In S. Bredekamp & R. Teresa (Eds.), *Reaching potentials: Transforming early childhood curriculum and assessment* (pp. 145–166). Washington, DC: National Association for the Education of Young Children.

Whitmore, K. F., Goodman, Y. M., Martens, P., & Owocki, G. (2004). Critical lessons from the transactional perspective on early literacy research. *Journal of Early Childhood Literacy, 4*(3), 291–325. doi:10.1177/1468798404047291

Wohlwend, K. E. (2007). Reading to play and playing to read: A mediated discourse analysis of early literacy apprenticeship. In D. W. Rowe, R. Jimenez, D. Compton, D. K. Dickinson, Y. Kim, K. M. Leander, & V. Risko (Eds.), *Fifty-sixth Yearbook of the National Reading Conference* (pp. 377–393). Oak Creek, WI: National Reading Conference.

Wohlwend, K. E. (2009a). Damsels in discourse: Girls consuming and producing identity texts through Disney Princess play. *Reading Research Quarterly, 44*(1), 57–83. doi:10.1598/rrq.44.1.3

Wohlwend, K. E. (2009b). Early adopters: Playing new literacies and pretending new technologies in print-centric classrooms. *Journal of Early Childhood Literacy, 9*(2), 117–140. doi:10.1177/1468798409105583

Wohlwend, K. E. (2011a). Mapping modes in children's play and design: An action-oriented approach to critical multimodal analysis. In R. Rogers (Ed.), *An introduction to critical discourse analysis in education* (2nd ed., pp. 242–266). New York: Routledge.

Wohlwend, K. E. (2011b). *Playing their way into literacies: Reading, writing, and belonging in the early childhood classroom.* New York, NY: Teachers College Press.

Wohlwend, K. E. (2012). "Are you guys girls?": Boys, identity texts, and Disney Princess play. *Journal of Early Childhood Literacy, 12*(3), 3–23. doi:10.1177/1468798411416787

Wohlwend, K. E. (2013). Play, literacies, and the converging cultures of childhood. In J. Larson & J. Marsh (Eds.), *The SAGE handbook of early childhood literacy* (2nd ed., pp. 80–95). London: Sage.

Wohlwend, K. E. (2017). Who gets to play? Access, popular media and participatory literacies. *Early Years: An International Research Journal, 37*(1), 62–76. doi:10.1080/09575146.2016.1219699

16

NEW LITERACIES

A Dual-Level Theory of the Changing Nature of Literacy, Instruction, and Assessment

Donald J. Leu, Charles K. Kinzer, Julie Coiro,
Jill Castek, and Laurie A. Henry

This chapter is adapted from "Toward a Theory of New Literacies Emerging From the Internet and Other Information and Communication Technologies," by D.J. Leu Jr., C.K. Kinzer, J.L. Coiro, & D.W. Cammack, in *Theoretical Models and Processes of Reading* (5th ed., pp. 1570–1613), edited by R.B. Ruddell and N.J. Unrau, 2004, Newark, DE: International Reading Association. Copyright © 2004 by the International Reading Association.

Literacy as Deixis

Today, the nature of literacy has become deictic. This simple idea carries important implications for literacy theory, research, and instruction that our field must begin to address. *Deixis* is a term used by linguists (Fillmore, 1966; Murphy, 1986; Traut & Kazzazi, 1996) to define words whose meanings change rapidly as their context changes. *Tomorrow*, for example, is a deictic term; the meaning of "tomorrow" becomes "today" every 24 hours. The meaning of literacy has also become deictic because we live in an age of rapidly changing information and communication technologies, each of which requires new literacies (Leu, 1997, 2000). Thus, to have been literate yesterday, in a world defined primarily by relatively static book technologies, does not ensure that one is fully literate today where we encounter new technologies such as Google docs, Skype, iMovie, Contribute, Basecamp, Dropbox, Facebook, Google, foursquare, Chrome, educational video games, or thousands of mobile apps. To be literate tomorrow will be defined by even newer technologies that have yet to appear and even newer discourses and social practices that will be created to meet future needs. Thus, when we speak of new literacies, we mean that literacy is not just new today; it becomes new every day of our lives.

How should we theorize the new literacies that will define our future, when literacy has become deictic? The answer is important because our concept of literacy defines both who we are and who we shall become. But there is a conundrum here. How can we possibly develop adequate theory when the object that we seek to study is itself ephemeral, continuously being redefined by a changing context? This is an important theoretical challenge that our field has not previously faced. The purpose of this chapter is to advance theory in a world where literacy has become deictic. It suggests that a dual-level theory of New Literacies is a useful approach to theory building in a world where the nature of literacy continuously changes.

We begin by making a central point: Social contexts have always shaped both the function and form of literate practices and been shaped by them in return. We discuss the social context of the current period and explain how this has produced new information and communication technologies (ICTs), and the new literacies that these technologies demand. Second, we explore several lowercase new literacies perspectives that are emerging. We argue that a dual-level New Literacies theory is essential to take full advantage of this important and diverse work. Third, we identify a set of principles, drawn from research, that inform an uppercase theory of New Literacies. Then, we present one lowercase theory of new literacies, the new literacies of online research and comprehension, to illustrate how a dual-level theory of New Literacies can inform new literacies research that takes related but different theoretical perspectives. We conclude by considering the implications of a dual-level theory of New Literacies for both research and practice.

Literacy in Today's Social Context

Literacy has always changed. Historical analyses demonstrate that both the forms and functions of literacy have been largely determined by the continuously changing social forces at work within any society and the technologies these forces often produce (Boyarin, 1993; Diringer, 1968; Gee, 2007b; Illera, 1997; Manguel, 1996; Mathews, 1966; N.B. Smith, 1965). This story began in Sumeria with the invention of cuneiform tablets, the first system of writing, during the fourth century B.C. (Boyarin, 1993; Diringer, 1968; Manguel, 1996). It continues to the present day.

Often, we lose sight of these historic roots. We need to remember that social forces, and the technologies they produce, often define the changing nature of literacy today just as they have in the past. Clearly, the social forces in the present context will exert similar changes. Thus, attempts to develop any theory of literacy must begin by exploring the critical social forces at work today.

What are the important social forces at work today that frame, and are framed by, the changes to literacy we are experiencing? We believe they include the following:

1. Global economic competition within economies based increasingly on the effective use of information and communication.
2. The rapid appearance of the Internet in both our professional and personal lives.
3. Public policy initiatives by nations that integrate literacy and the Internet into instruction.

Global Economic Competition Within Economies Based Increasingly on the Effective Use of Information and Communication

The world of work has been undergoing fundamental transformation (Kirsch, Braun, Yamamoto, & Sum, 2007; Organisation for Economic Co-operation and Development & the Centre for Educational Research and Innovation, 2010; Rouet, 2006; M.C. Smith, Mikulecky, Kibby, Dreher, & Dole, 2000). Indeed, it is this social context that prompts many of the changes to ICTs and to literacy that we experience, making the effective use of Internet technologies a central component of the literacy curriculum.

Traditionally, industrial-age organizations were organized in a vertical, top-down fashion where most decisions were made at the highest levels and then communicated to lower levels (see Figure 16.1). This wastes large amounts of intellectual capital within an organization and results in lower productivity. Today, global economic competition requires organizations to abandon these traditional command and control structures to leverage all of their intellectual capital, operate more productively, and become more competitive.

In a postindustrial economy (Reich, 1992), organizations seeking to achieve greater productivity and become more competitive reorganize themselves horizontally. Instead of all decisions emanating from the top of an organization, teams within lower levels of organizations are empowered to identify and solve important problems that generate new knowledge and lead to better ways of producing goods or providing services. These high-performance workplaces seek to use the intellectual

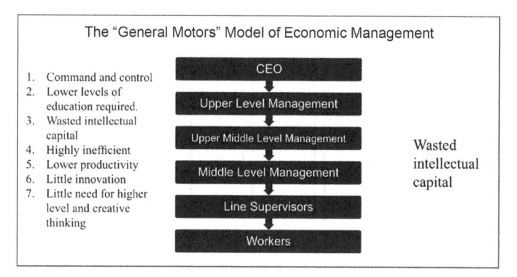

Figure 16.1 The Typical Organizational Structure of Industrial-Age Workplaces

capital of every employee to increase effective decision making and increase productivity. The effective use of information to solve problems allows a horizontally organized workplace to become much more productive and competitive (see Figure 16.2).

This change has had a fundamental effect on the nature of literacy within organizations. At the broadest level, members of these teams must:

- Quickly identify important problems in their work
- Locate useful information related to the problems they identify
- Critically evaluate the information they find
- Synthesize multiple sources of information to determine a solution
- Quickly communicate the solution to others so everyone within an organization is informed
- Monitor and evaluate the results of their solutions and decisions and modify these as needed

How do teams do this? Often they rely upon the Internet. Many economists have concluded that productivity gains realized during the past several decades have been due to the rapid integration of the Internet into the workplace, enabling units to better share information, communicate, and solve problems (Matteucci, O'Mahony, Robinson, & Zwick, 2005; van Ark, Inklaar, & McGuckin, 2003). Internet use in U.S. workplaces, for example, increased by nearly 60% during a single year (2002) among all employed adults 25 years of age and older (U.S. Department of Commerce, Economic and Statistics Administration & National Telecommunications and Information Administration, 2002).

The Rapid Appearance of the Internet in Our Professional and Personal Lives

It is not surprising that the Internet and other ICTs have appeared and become such a prominent part of our lives during the transition from an industrial to a postindustrial society. These new information and communication tools allow horizontally organized workplaces to identify important problems, address them, and nimbly modify and customize solutions as contexts and technologies change. In many cases, all of this is accomplished with team members situated in different locations around the globe.

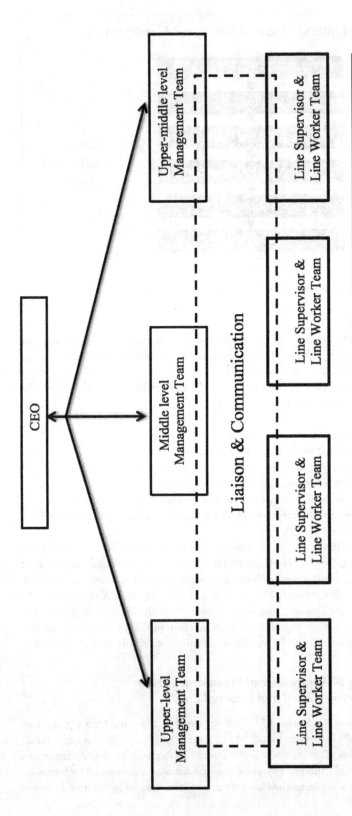

The figure shows new management and communication structures. Communication occurs in both directions at all levels, both horizontally and vertically, as indicated by the dashed box that shows teams communicate and work with one another across teams within a horizontal level but can also draw team members and communicate with teams vertically. Teams are often composed of members from all levels through liaison and communication, which occurs largely through information and communication technologies. The importance of communication and cross-team liaison/membership shows that new literacies are required for this structure to occur.

Figure 16.2 The Typical Organizational Structure of Postindustrial Workplaces

Source: Chuck K. Kinzer

This analysis suggests that competence with the new literacies required by the Internet and other ICTs is a crucial determinant of an engaged life in an online age of information and communication. However, it is important to recognize that these skills are not limited to simply creating more productive workers and workplaces. Even more important, the information resources and opportunities available on the Internet provide individuals with opportunities to make their personal lives richer and more fulfilling. This happens while advocating for social justice, refinancing a home, selecting a university to attend, managing a medical question, purchasing books, or any one of the hundreds of other tasks important to daily life. We also see this happening as citizens in some parts of the world use these skills and new technologies to overthrow corrupt and undemocratic political systems. Preparation in the new literacies required to use the internet and other ICTs enables individuals to have more fulfilling personal as well as professional lives.

Public Policy Initiatives by Nations That Integrate Literacy and the Internet Into Instruction

Previously, we reported on public policies in nations beginning to recognize how the Internet was changing the nature of literacy (Leu & Kinzer, 2000; Leu, Kinzer, Coiro, & Cammack, 2004). At that point, however, public policies about literacy and the Internet often traveled on separate but parallel tracks. Today, we are beginning to see the evolution of these parallel public policies as they slowly become more integrated in nations such as Australia, Canada, and the United States.

In Australia, for example, the Australian Curriculum, Assessment and Reporting Authority (ACARA; n.d.) has developed the Australian Curriculum. This Australian initiative integrates literacy and the Internet *within* the English curriculum, not outside of it as it had been previously. As indicated in the Australian Curriculum:

> ICT competence is *an important component of the English curriculum* [italics added]. Students develop the skills and understanding required to use a range of contemporary technologies. In particular, they explicitly develop increasingly sophisticated word-processing skills to enhance text construction. Students also progressively develop skills in using information technology when conducting research, a range of digital technologies to create, publish and present their learning, and communication technologies to collaborate and communicate with others both within and beyond the classroom. (ACARA, n.d., General Capabilities, Information and Communication Technology Competence section, para. 2)

The English curriculum integrates this capability into each year's statement of the content standards. Evidence of this integration also appears in the "Elaborations" of the English curriculum such as this one from Year 4 English (ELBE900): "Participating in online searches for information using navigation tools and discussing similarities and differences between print and digital information." In Australia, literacy and the Internet are becoming integrated with new literacies.

In another example, this time from Canada, the province of Manitoba has developed an educational framework called Literacy With ICT Across the Curriculum (Minister of Manitoba Education, Citizenship, and Youth, 2006). This initiative outlines skills and includes standards required in the 21st century in all aspects of their curriculum:

> Identifying appropriate inquiry questions; navigating multiple *information networks* [italics added] to locate relevant information; applying critical thinking skills to evaluate information sources and content; synthesizing information and ideas from multiple sources and networks; representing information and ideas creatively in visual, aural, and textual

formats; crediting and referencing sources of information and intellectual property; and communicating new understandings to others, both face to face and over distance.

(p. 18)

In the United States, the Common Core State Standards Initiative (National Governors Association Center for Best Practices & Council of Chief State School Officers, 2010) has sought to establish more uniform standards across states to prepare students for college and careers in the 21st century. One of their key design principles, research and media skills, shows that literacy and new technologies are beginning to be considered together:

> To be ready for college, workforce training, and life in a technological society, students need the ability to gather, comprehend, evaluate, synthesize, and report on information and ideas, to conduct original research in order to answer questions or solve problems, and to analyze and create a high volume and extensive range of print and non-print texts in media forms old and new. The need to conduct research and to produce and consume media is embedded into every aspect of today's curriculum.

(p. 4)

This design principle, however, is implemented most directly in the Common Core State Standards for writing than for reading (Leu et al., 2011). Consider, for example, these two (of 10) Anchor Standards (A.S.) in Writing:

> A.S. 6. Use technology, including the Internet, to produce and publish writing and to interact and collaborate with others.
> A.S. 8. Gather relevant information from multiple print and digital sources, assess the credibility and accuracy of each source, and integrate the information while avoiding plagiarism.

> *(National Governors Association Center for Best Practices &*
> *Council of Chief State School Officers, p. 41)*

In the Anchor Standards in Reading, we find a focus on the higher level thinking skills required while reading and conducting research online (Leu, Forzani, et al., in press).

Although these changes are more evolutionary than revolutionary, it is clear that literacy and Internet use are beginning to slowly become more integrated into the public policies and curricula of nations in ways that have a direct impact on literacy education. Because of global economic competition, even nations with a long tradition of local school control, such as Australia and the United States, are beginning to develop important national initiatives to raise literacy levels and prepare students for the use of the Internet.

A Dual-Level Theory of New Literacies

That the Internet changes the nature of literacy can be seen in the common ways that nations are trying to prepare students for these changes. It can also be seen by the fact that many scholars recently have been attracted to studying this problem and have sought to describe the changes taking place (e.g., Gee, 2007c; Kress, 2003; Lankshear & Knobel, 2006; Lemke, 2002; New London Group, 1996; Street, 1995, 2003). Many use the term *new literacies* to describe their work. *New literacies*, however, means many different things to many different people.

Some people use the term *new literacies* to capture the new social practices of literacy that are emerging (Street, 1995, 2003). Rather than seeing new social practices emerging from new technologies, they tend to see new technologies emerging from new social practices. Others use the term *new literacies* to describe important new strategies and dispositions that are essential for online research and comprehension (Castek, 2008; Coiro, 2003; Henry, 2006; International Reading Association, 2009). Still others see new literacies as new discourses (Gee, 2007b) or new semiotic contexts (Kress, 2003; Lemke, 2002). Others see literacy as differentiating into multiliteracies (Cope & Kalantzis, 1999; New London Group, 1996) or multimodal contexts (Hull & Schultz, 2002), and some see a construct that juxtaposes several of these orientations (Lankshear & Knobel, 2006). When one includes terms such as *ICT literacy* (International ICT Literacy Panel, 2002) or *informational literacy* (Hirsh, 1999; Kuiper & Volman, 2008), the construct of new literacies becomes even broader.

How are we to solve the conundrum posed earlier, where the nature of literacy changes even faster than we can develop adequate theory, especially within a context where there are so many competing theoretical perspectives that have emerged to direct separate lines of research? We believe the answer to this question is not to privilege one theoretical framework over another, but rather to take advantage of multiple perspectives, and new ones that will ultimately emerge, to capture the full range of the complexities defining literacy during a period in which literacy continually changes. In short, we see the separate lines of work taking place within a context that rapidly changes as an opportunity and not as a problem.

Lowercase and Uppercase New Literacies

Just as economic units have found it more productive to restructure from a command and control mentality to take advantage of everyone's intellectual capital, we must do the same in the literacy research community. We must find ways to bring all of our intellectual capital to the important task of understanding the extraordinary complexities that now define literacy as it continually changes and becomes richer and more complex. We can no longer afford to work in separate theoretical worlds, ignoring others and privileging our own. Recognizing that changes to literacy are taking place at many levels, and being dissatisfied with isolated attempts to capture those changes, we believe that a collaborative approach to theory building is essential, one that takes advantage of the power of multiple perspectives (Labbo & Reinking, 1999). This approach suggests that the best solutions result from collaborative groups who bring diverse, multiple perspectives to problems (Page, 2007). New Literacies theory takes an "open-source" approach, inviting everyone who studies the Internet's impact to contribute to theory development and to benefit from others' contributions. This includes more traditional theoretical and research traditions as well as those specific to new literacies because both old and new elements of literacy are layered in complex ways, and the nature of this layering and commingling is yet to be understood.

To account for the continuous changes taking place to literacy as well as the growing multiplicity of perspectives that are emerging, we frame new literacies theory on two levels: lowercase (new literacies) and uppercase (New Literacies). Lowercase theories explore a specific area of new literacies and/or a new technology, such as the social communicative transactions occurring with text messaging (e.g., Lewis & Fabos, 2005). Lowercase theories also include those that explore a focused disciplinary base, such as the semiotics of multimodality in online media (e.g., Kress, 2003) or a distinctive conceptual approach such as new literacy studies (Street, 1995, 2003). These lowercase theories are better able to keep up with the rapidly changing nature of literacy in a deictic world because they are closer to the specific types of changes that are taking place and interest those who study them within a particular heuristic. Lowercase theories also permit our field to maximize the lenses we use and the technologies and contexts we study. Every scholar who studies new literacy issues is generating important insights for everyone else, even if we do not share a particular lens, technology, or context. How, though, do we come to understand these insights, taking place in many different fields from many different perspectives? For this, we require a second level of theory, an uppercase New Literacies theory.

What defines this broader theory of New Literacies? New Literacies, as the broader, more inclusive concept, includes those common findings emerging across multiple, lowercase theories. New

Literacies theory benefits from work taking place in the multiple, lowercase dimensions of new literacies by looking for what appear to be the most common and consistent patterns being found in lowercase theories and lines of research. This approach permits everyone to fully explore their unique, lowercase perspective of new literacies, allowing scholars to maintain a close focus on many different aspects of the shifting landscape of literacy during a period of rapid change. At the same time, each of us also benefits from expanding our understanding of other, lowercase, new literacies perspectives. By assuming change in the model, everyone is open to a continuously changing definition of literacy, based on the most recent data that emerges consistently, across multiple perspectives, disciplines, and research traditions. Moreover, areas in which alternative findings emerge are identified, enabling each to be studied again, from multiple perspectives. From this process, common patterns emerge and are included in a broader, common, New Literacies theory.

This process enables the broader theory of New Literacies to keep up with consistent elements that will always define literacy on the Internet while it informs each of the lowercase theories of new literacies with patterns that are being regularly found by others. We believe that when literacy is deictic and multifaceted, a dual-level theory of New Literacies is not only essential but also provides a theoretical advantage over any single-dimensional approach to theory building and research. We are richer for working together and engaging in common research and theoretical conversations, something we believe happens too rarely.

Central Principles of an Uppercase Theory of New Literacies

Although it is too early to define a complete uppercase theory of New Literacies emerging from the Internet and other ICTs, we are convinced that it is time to begin this process by identifying the central principles upon which it should be built. Our work is pointing us to these principles of New Literacies that appear to be common across the research and theoretical work currently taking place:

1. The Internet is this generation's defining technology for literacy and learning within our global community.
2. The Internet and related technologies require additional new literacies to fully access their potential.
3. New literacies are deictic.
4. New literacies are multiple, multimodal, and multifaceted.
5. Critical literacies are central to new literacies.
6. New forms of strategic knowledge are required with new literacies.
7. New social practices are a central element of New Literacies.
8. Teachers become more important, though their role changes, within new literacy classrooms.

The Internet Is This Generation's Defining Technology for Literacy and Learning Within Our Global Community

From a sociolinguistics perspective, Gee (2007b) and the New London Group (2000) have argued that literacy is embedded in and develops out of the social practices of a culture. We agree. We have argued that the Internet and related technologies now define the new literacies that increasingly are a part of our literacy lives. Put simply, a central principle of New Literacies theory is that the Internet has become this generation's defining technology for literacy in our global community.

We can see this in several data points. More than a decade ago, 90% of adolescent students in the United States with home access to the Internet reported using the Internet for homework (Pew Internet & American Life Project, 2001). Over 70% of these students used the Internet as the primary source for information on their most recent school report or project, while only 24% of these students reported using the library for the same task. Four years later, in 2005, we reached the "tipping point year" for online reading among adolescents in the United States. For the first time, students ages 8–18 reported spending more time reading online, 48 minutes per day, than reading offline, 43 minutes per day (Kaiser Family Foundation, 2005). More recently, the first international assessment of online reading among 15-year-olds took place in 2009. The PISA International Assessment of Reading (Organisation for Economic Co-operation and Development, 2011) provided important information about online research and comprehension to public policymakers around the world who were demanding it (see also R.E. Bennett, Persky, Weiss, & Jenkins, 2007).

Perhaps the most compelling evidence, though, for this claim may be found in usage. According to one of the most systematic evaluations of worldwide Internet use, over 2.4 billion individuals now use the Internet—more than one third of the world's population (Internet World Stats, 2011). Moreover, at the current rate of growth, Internet use will be ubiquitous in the world within the next decade. Never in the history of civilization have we seen a new technology adopted by so many, in so many different places, in such a short period of time, with such powerful consequences for both literacy and life.

The Internet and Related Technologies Require Additional New Literacies to Fully Access Their Potential

New technologies such as the Internet and other ICTs require additional social practices, skills, strategies, and dispositions to take full advantage of the affordances each contains. Typically, new literacies build upon foundational literacies rather than replace them completely. Foundational literacies include those traditional social practices of literacy and the elements of literacy required for traditional text reading and writing, such as word recognition, vocabulary, comprehension, inferential reasoning, the writing process, spelling, response to literature, and others required for the literacies of the book and other printed material. However, foundational literacies will be insufficient if one is to make full use of the Internet and other ICTs (Hartman, Morsink, & Zheng, 2010; International Reading Association, 2009). Reading, writing, and communication will take new forms as text is combined with new media resources and linked within complex information networks requiring new literacies for their use (Dalton & Proctor, 2008; Wyatt-Smith & Elkins, 2008). During this process, new online and traditional offline literacies are often layered in rich and complex ways.

New Literacies Are Deictic

We began this chapter by suggesting that literacy has become deictic. The rapid transformations in the nature of literacy caused by technological change is a primary source for the deictic nature of literacy; new technologies regularly and repeatedly transform previous literacies, continually redefining what it means to become literate.

The deictic nature of literacy is also caused by a second source: the envisionments we construct as we create new social practices with new technologies. Envisionments take place when individuals imagine new possibilities for literacy and learning, transform existing technologies and practices to construct this vision, and then share their envisionment with others (Knobel & Wilber, 2009; Lankshear & Knobel, 2006; Leu, Karchmer, & Leu, 1999).

Finally, rapid transformations in the nature of literacy are produced because the Internet and other ICTs permit the immediate exchange of new technologies and social practices. Because we can immediately download a new technology from the Internet or send it to millions of individuals with just a keystroke, the changes to literacy derived from new technologies happen at a pace faster than ever before. In short, the Internet and other ICTs not only change themselves but also provide the central vehicle for exchanging new technologies for information and communication and new social practices. Thus, the already rapid pace of change in the forms and functions of literacy is exacerbated by the speed with which new technologies and new social practices are communicated (Leu, 2000).

New Literacies Are Multiple, Multimodal, and Multifaceted

New literacies are multiple, multimodal, and multifaceted, and as a result, our understanding of them benefits from multiple points of view. From a sociolinguistic perspective, the New London Group (2000) has defined *multiliteracies* as a set of open-ended and flexible multiple literacies required to function in diverse social contexts and communities. We believe the same multiplicity of literacy has also emerged because of multiple technological contexts. The Internet and other ICTs require that we develop a systematic understanding of the multiple literacies that exist in both new literacies practices (Lankshear & Knoble, 2006) and in the skills, strategies, and dispositions that are required with new technologies (Leu et al., 2004). This multiplicity of new literacies is apparent on at least three levels.

First, meaning is typically represented with multiple media and modalities. Unlike traditional text forms that typically include a combination of two types of media—print and two-dimensional graphics—Internet texts integrate a range of symbols and multiple-media formats, including icons, animated symbols, audio, video, interactive tables, and virtual reality environments (Callow, 2010; Lemke, 2002; Walsh, 2010). As a result, we confront new forms and combinations of texts and images that challenge our traditional understandings of how information is represented and shared with others (Jewitt & Kress, 2003; Unsworth, 2008). Semiotic perspectives on new literacies (e.g., Kress, 2003) allow an especially rich understanding of changes taking place in these areas.

Second, the Internet and other ICTs also offer multiple tools. Literate individuals will be those who can effectively determine, from the Internet's multiple offerings, a combination of tool(s) and form(s) that best meet their needs (American Association of School Librarians, 2007). Thus, New Literacies theory includes research that is taking place with multiple forms of online meaning and content construction. It assumes that proficient users of the Internet must understand how to construct meaning in new ways as well as construct, design, manipulate, and upload their own information to add to the constantly growing and changing body of knowledge that defines the Internet.

A final level of multiplicity consists of the new social practices and skills that are required as we encounter information with individuals from a much wider range of social contexts (Hull, Stornaiuolo, & Sahni, 2010; Hull, Zacher, & Hibbert, 2009). The global sharing of information permitted by the Internet introduces new challenges as we interpret and respond to information from multiple social and cultural contexts that share profoundly different assumptions about our world (Fabos & Young, 1999; Flanagin, Farinola, & Metzger, 2000). These multiple contexts for new literacies have important implications for educators preparing students to critically understand and interpret the meanings they find on the Internet and to communicate with others (see Hull et al., 2010).

In a world of exploding technologies and literacy practices, it becomes increasingly difficult to think of literacy as a singular construct that applies across all contexts. As a result, we benefit from the complexity that multiple theoretical perspectives provide (Labbo & Reinking, 1999). Any research study in new literacies benefits when multiple theoretical frameworks inform the research questions and results. It also suggests that new literacies are best studied in interdisciplinary teams as questions become far too complex for the traditional single-investigator model.

Critical Literacies Are Central to New Literacies

New Literacies demand new forms of critical literacy and greater dependency on critical thinking and analysis. Open networks, such as the Internet, permit anyone to publish anything; this is one of the opportunities this technology presents. It is also one of its limitations; information is much more widely available from people who have strong political, economic, religious, or ideological stances that profoundly influence the nature of the information they present to others. As a result, we must assist students to become more critical consumers of the information they encounter (Bråten, Strømsø, & Britt, 2009; Clemitt, 2008; Flanagin & Metzger, 2010; Metzger & Flanagin, 2008). Although the literacy curriculum has always included items such as critical thinking and separating fact from propaganda, more instructional time devoted to more complex analytic skills will need to be included in classrooms where the Internet and other ICTs play a more prominent role (Hobbs, 2010). As we begin to study the new literacies of the Internet, we will depend greatly on work from the communities of critical literacy and media literacy to provide us with the best research in this area.

New Forms of Strategic Knowledge Are Required With New Literacies

New technologies for networked information and communication are complex and require many new strategies for their effective use. Hypertext technologies, embedded with multiple forms of media and unlimited freedoms of multiple navigational pathways, present opportunities that may seduce some readers away from important content unless they have developed strategies to deal with these seductions (Lawless & Kulikowich, 1996; Lawless, Mills, & Brown, 2002). Other cognitive and aesthetic changes to text on the Internet presents additional strategic challenges to comprehension (Afflerbach & Cho, 2010; Coiro, 2003; Hartman et al., 2010; Spires & Estes, 2002), inquiry (Eagleton, 2001), and information seeking (Rouet, Ros, Goumi, Macedo-Rouet, & Dinet, 2011; Sutherland-Smith, 2002). Thus, new literacies will often be defined around the strategic knowledge central to the effective use of information within rich and complexly networked environments.

New Literacy Practices Are a Central Element of New Literacies

It is increasingly clear that new literacy practices are a central feature of New Literacies. Work by Lankshear and Knobel (2006) show us how two important elements of the changing nature of literacy generate additional, new literacies practices. First, new digital technologies enable new ways of constructing, sharing, and accessing meaningful content. Second, the collaborative, distributed, and participatory nature of these digital spaces enable the generation of what Lankshear and Knobel call a *distinctive ethos* and what Jenkins (2006) refers to as *engagement in participatory culture*. As a result, continuously new social practices of literacy will emerge, often within new discourse communities, and serve to redefine literacy and learning.

New social practices will be needed in classrooms to interact within increasingly complex technologies for information and communication (Jonassen, Howland, Moore, & Marra, 2003; Kiili, Laurinen, Marttunen, & Leu, 2011). Models of literacy instruction, for example, have often focused on an adult whose role was to teach the skills he or she possessed to a group of students who did not know those skills. This is no longer possible, or even appropriate, within a world of multiple new literacies. No one person can hope to know everything about the expanding and ever-changing technologies of the Internet and other ICTs. In fact, today, many young students possess higher levels of knowledge about some of these new literacies than most adults.

Consequently, effective learning experiences will be increasingly dependent upon new social practices, social learning strategies, and the ability of a teacher to orchestrate literacy learning opportunities between and among students who know different new literacies (Erstad, 2002). This will distribute knowledge about literacy throughout the classroom, especially as students move above the stages of foundational literacy. One student, for example, may know how to edit digital video scenes, but another may know how best to compress the video so it can function optimally in a Web-based environment. This social learning ability may not come naturally to all students, however, and many will need to be supported in learning *how* to learn about literacy from one another (Labbo, 1996; Labbo & Kuhn, 1998).

Teachers Become More Important, Though Their Role Changes, Within New Literacy Classrooms

The appearance of the Internet and other ICTs in school classrooms will increase the central role that teachers play in orchestrating learning experiences for students. Teachers will be challenged to thoughtfully guide students' learning within information environments that are richer and more complex than traditional print media, presenting richer and more complex learning opportunities for both themselves and their students (Coiro, 2009).

In a world of rapidly changing new literacies, it will be common for some students to be more literate with some technologies than their teacher is (Erstad, 2002; Harper, 2006). As a result, teachers will increasingly become orchestrators of learning contexts rather than dispensers of literacy skills. By orchestrating opportunities for the exchange of new literacies, both teachers and students may enhance their literacy skills and their potential for effective communication and information use (O'Brien, Beach, & Scharber, 2007; Schulz-Zander, Büchter, & Dalmer, 2002). Because teachers become even more important to the development of literacy and because their role changes, an expanded focus and greater attention will need to be placed on teacher education and professional development in new literacies.

The New Literacies of Online Research and Comprehension: A Lowercase Theory of New Literacies

The new literacies of online research and comprehension (Leu, Everett-Cacopardo, Zawilinski, McVerry, & O'Byrne, in press; Leu, Forzani, et al., in press) is one example of a lowercase new literacies theory. This frames online reading comprehension as a process of problem-based inquiry and includes the new skills, strategies, dispositions, and social practices that take place as we use information on the Internet to conduct research to solve problems and answer questions. It describes how students conduct research and read online to learn. A more formal definition is as follows:

> The new literacies of online research and comprehension include the skills, strategies, dispositions, and social practices necessary to successfully use and adapt to the rapidly changing information and communication technologies and contexts that continuously emerge and influence all areas of our personal and professional lives. Online research and comprehension is a self-directed process of constructing texts and knowledge while engaged in several online reading practices: identifying important problems, locating information, critically evaluating information, synthesizing information, and communicating information. Online research and comprehension can take place individually, but often appears to be enhanced when it takes place collaboratively.

What do we know about the new literacies of online research and comprehension? We are beginning to uncover many elements of this aspect of new literacies. They include the following:

1. Online research and comprehension is a self-directed process of text construction and knowledge construction.
2. Five practices appear to define online research and comprehension processing: (1) identifying a problem and then (2) locating, (3) evaluating, (4) synthesizing, and (5) communicating information.

3. Online research and comprehension is not isomorphic with offline reading comprehension; additional skills and strategies appear to be required.
4. Online contexts may be especially supportive for some struggling readers.
5. Adolescents are not always very skilled with online research and comprehension.
6. Collaborative online reading and writing practices appear to increase comprehension and learning.

Online Research and Comprehension Is a Self-Directed Process of Text Construction and Knowledge Construction

Readers choose the online texts that they read through the links that they follow as they gather information and construct the knowledge needed to solve a problem. Each reader typically follows a unique informational path, selecting a unique sequence of links to information and sampling unique segments of information from each location (see, e.g., Canavilhas, n.d.; McEneaney, Li, Allen, & Guzniczak, 2009). Thus, in addition to constructing knowledge in their minds, readers also physically construct the texts they read online (Afflerbach & Cho, 2008; Coiro & Dobler, 2007). While this is also possible during offline reading, of course, it always takes place during online reading (see Hartman et al., 2010). As a result, seldom do two readers read the same text to solve the same problem during online reading.

Five Processing Practices Appear to Define Online Research and Comprehension Processing

At least five processing practices occur during online research and comprehension: (1) reading to identify important questions, (2) reading to locate information, (3) reading to evaluate information critically, (4) reading to synthesize information, and (5) reading to communicate information. Within these five practices reside the skills, strategies, and dispositions that are distinctive to online reading comprehension as well as to others that are also important for offline reading comprehension (Leu, Reinking, et al., 2007).

Reading to Identify Important Questions

We read on the Internet to solve problems and answer questions. How a problem is framed or how a question is understood is a central aspect of online research and comprehension. Work by Taboada and Guthrie (2006) within traditional texts suggests that reading initiated by a question differs in important ways from reading that is not.

Reading to Locate Information

A second component of successful online research and comprehension is the ability to read and locate information that meets one's needs (Broch, 2000; Eagleton, Guinee, & Langlais, 2003; Guinee, Eagleton, & Hall, 2003; International ICT Literacy Panel, 2002; Sutherland-Smith, 2002). The reading ability required to locate information on the Internet may very well serve as a gatekeeping skill; if one cannot locate information, one will be unable to solve a given problem. New online reading skills and strategies may be required, for example, to generate effective keyword search strategies (Bilal, 2000; Guinee et al., 2003; Kuiper & Volman, 2008), to read and infer which link may be most useful within a set of search engine results (Henry, 2006), and to efficiently scan for relevant information within websites (McDonald & Stevenson, 1996; Rouet, 2006; Rouet et al., 2011).

Reading to Evaluate Information Critically

Critically evaluating online information includes the ability to read and evaluate the level of accuracy, reliability, and bias of information (Center for Media Literacy, 2005). Although these skills have always been necessary to comprehend and use offline texts, the proliferation of unedited information and the merging of commercial marketing with educational content (Fabos, 2008; Federal Trade Commission, 2002) present additional challenges that are quite different from traditional print and media sources. Tillman (2003), for example, contends that promotional efforts and related advertising may be more difficult to differentiate on the Internet than in print and other mass media forms (see also Fabos, 2008). Others (Britt & Gabrys, 2001) cite the lack of uniform standards and cues regarding document type in online text environments as necessitating a renewed interest in how students evaluate online information. Without explicit training in these new literacy skills, many students become confused and overwhelmed when asked to judge the accuracy, reliability, and bias of information they encounter in online reading environments (Graham & Metaxas, 2003; Sanchez, Wiley, & Goldman, 2006; Sundar, 2008). Consequently, as more students turn primarily to the Internet for their information (Pew Internet & American Life Project, 2005), these critical evaluation strategies become more relevant than ever before (Bråten et al., 2009; Bråten, Strømsø, & Salmerón, 2011).

Reading to Synthesize Information

Successful Internet use also requires the ability to read and synthesize information from multiple online sources (Jenkins, 2006). Synthesis requires the reader to bring together an awareness of the reading processes and an underlying understanding of the text. The Internet introduces additional challenges to coordinate and synthesize vast amounts of information presented in multiple media formats, from a nearly unlimited and disparate set of sources (Gilster, 1997; Jenkins, 2006; Rouet, 2006). This presents important challenges to online readers as they determine what to include and what to exclude.

Reading to Communicate Information

A fifth component of successful online research and comprehension is the ability to communicate via the Internet to seek information or share what one has learned (Britt & Gabrys, 2001). The interactive processes of reading and writing have become so intertwined on the Internet that they often happen simultaneously during communication. Moreover, each specific communication tool on the Internet is constituted differently and presents a range of new skills, strategies, and social practices to use them effectively (Coiro, Knobel, Lankshear, & Leu, 2008). New types of strategic knowledge are required, for example, to effectively participate and communicate in social networking environments such as e-mail, blogs, wikis, and instant messaging (Castek, 2008; Lewis & Fabos, 2005).

Online Research and Comprehension Is Not Isomorphic With Offline Reading Comprehension

Findings from several studies suggest that online research and comprehension appears not to be isomorphic with offline reading comprehension; additional reading comprehension skills seem to be required (Coiro, 2011; Coiro & Dobler, 2007; Leu et al., 2005; Leu, Zawilinski, et al., 2007). One study, among sixth-grade students proficient at using the Internet (Coiro & Dobler, 2007), found that online research and comprehension shared a number of similarities with offline reading comprehension but was also more complex and included notable differences. A second study found no statistically significant correlation between scores on a state reading comprehension assessment and an assessment of online research and comprehension with good psychometric properties (Leu et al., 2005). A third study (Coiro, 2011) found that offline reading comprehension and prior knowledge contributed a statistically significant amount of variance to the prediction of online research and comprehension, but an additional 16% of independent variance was contributed by knowing students' online research and comprehension ability. These data suggest that additional skills are required for online research and comprehension beyond those required for offline reading comprehension.

Similarly, Afflerbach and Cho's (2010) review of 46 studies involving thinkaloud protocols that focused on reading strategy use during Internet and hypertext reading found evidence of strategies that "appeared to have no counterpart in traditional reading" (p. 217). Many of these strategies clustered around a reader's ability to apply new strategies to reduce levels of uncertainty while navigating and negotiating appropriate reading paths in a shifting problem space (see also Afflerbach & Cho, 2008; Cho, 2010; Zhang & Duke, 2008). Hartman et al. (2010) also offer examples of how Internet research and comprehension places many more processing demands on the reader that amount to a host of new cognitive reading challenges for comprehending online texts. Finally, case studies and videos of online research show that students who perform at a low level on state reading assessments sometimes perform at unexpectedly high levels on tasks of online research and comprehension (Castek, Zawilinski, McVerry, O'Byrne, & Leu, 2011; Leu, Zawilinski, et al., 2007). Together, these results support the claim that additional skills and strategies may be required during online research and comprehension beyond those required for offline reading and comprehension.

Although differences appear to exist, we do not fully understand how and why offline reading comprehension and online research and comprehension are not isomorphic. Several explanations are possible. Current results, showing a lack of correlation between the two, may be because online research and comprehension is a problem-based task, while offline reading includes a wider range of comprehension tasks (cf. Taboada & Guthrie, 2006). Or it may be that the reading skills required to locate information online are such "bottleneck" skills that students who lack this ability perform poorly online, even though they may be highperforming offline readers. Or the fact that greater levels of critical evaluation are typically required online may be the source of the difference. Finally, differences may be due to the new communication tools that are often used.

It is also likely that we can increase or decrease statistical relationships between offline reading comprehension and online research and comprehension by simply varying the nature of the online research task. Online assessments that require richer, more complex use of online tools (search engines, e-mail attachments, blogs, wikis), or more complex information spaces, may generate less of a relationship with offline reading comprehension compared with online assessments that simply require the reader to read information on a single website. So it is still early to claim that the lack of isomorphism between online and offline reading is either strong or weak. That it can be demonstrated appears to be the case, but we require much more work to be able to fully understand the conditions under which the two contexts for reading require different skills and strategies.

We also do not know very much about the relative contribution of various elements of online research and comprehension to successful online research outcomes. It is likely that skill areas often required earlier in the process (defining a problem, locating information, and evaluating information) may be more determinative of successful performance than other areas are, but we have not yet evaluated this claim.

Online Contexts May Be Especially Supportive for Some Struggling Readers

It is surprising to find that some struggling readers do very well with online research and comprehension. Why might this be the case? Units of text are typically shorter online as readers follow informational links from one location to another, seeking information that will help them solve their informational problem. Shorter units of text are easier for struggling readers to process. In addition, online readers construct their own texts to read, as they choose different paths to follow. This increases engagement and makes it more likely that readers find their way to texts appropriate for their abilities. Also, online texts contain multimedia, a traditionally supportive context for struggling readers. Finally, each webpage is really a graphic image, and struggling readers are often quite skilled readers of information presented graphically. Sometimes, too, these readers use a new literacies skill, the use of Command + F, to quickly scan for information on a webpage with extensive amounts of text.

Adolescents Are Not Always Very Skilled With Online Research and Comprehension

Although adolescent "digital natives" may be skilled with social networking, texting, video downloads, MP3 downloads, or mash-ups, they are not always as skilled with online research and comprehension, including locating (Bilal, 2000; Eagleton et al., 2003) and critically evaluating information (S. Bennett, Maton, & Kervin, 2008; Sutherland-Smith, 2002; Wallace, Kupperman, Krajcik, & Soloway, 2000). In fact, adolescents tend to overgeneralize their ability to read online information effectively, informed by their ability to engage successfully with online social networking, texting, and video games (Kuiper, 2007).

Collaborative Online Reading and Writing Practices Appear to Increase Comprehension and Learning

Emerging work suggests that collaborative online reading and writing may yield important gains in literacy and learning. Work by Kiili et al. (2011) suggests that collaborative reading of online information about a controversial issue can lead to important learning gains. Comparing individual reading (Kiili, Laurinen, & Marttunen, 2008) with collaborative online reading (Kiili et al., 2011), individual readers concentrated on gathering facts, whereas the collaborative reading context offered additional opportunities for deeper exploration of ideas and different perspectives. Greater collaborative online reading also appears to lead to greater meaning construction and knowledge construction (Kiili et al., 2011).

Work by Everett-Cacopardo (2011), Zawilinski (2011), O'Byrne (2011), and Coiro, Castek, and Guzniczak (2011) also explores the importance of framing online research and comprehension as a collaborative, social practice. Everett-Cacopardo discovered that a number of teachers find it highly effective to have their students engage in collaborative, online projects with students in other nations. Zawilinski found that collaborative blogging in social studies between students in first and fifth grades led to important gains in understanding and communication. O'Byrne found that collaborative development of spoof sites led to greater skill with the critical evaluation of information related most closely to the elements students focused on in the creation of their webpages. Coiro et al. found that opportunities to co-construct meaning and responses to prompts that require students to read on the Internet may foster more efficient and productive comprehension of online informational texts—even among readers who are skilled at comprehending online texts independently. Thus, we are beginning to see this area of new literacies research consider more fully the important collaborative dimensions of online research and comprehension.

New Literacies Theory: Implications

New Literacies theory tells us that the Internet and other continuously emerging ICTs will be central to both our personal and professional lives and that these technologies require new literacies to effectively exploit their potential (International Reading Association, 2009; Kinzer & Leander, 2002). It also suggests that we must begin to integrate these new literacies into classrooms if we hope to prepare all students for the literacy futures they deserve. Most important, it suggests that continuous change will define the new literacies of the Internet and other ICTs (Cammack, 2002; Leu,

2000). Because of this rapid and continuous change, misalignments in assessment and instruction are likely to appear until we begin to recognize that literacy has become deictic, and take action not to fall behind the more contemporaneous realities of literacy. These misalignments are likely to create important problems for any educational system unable to keep up with the changes.

Consider, for example, the consequences that result from our current literacy assessments, such as the National Assessment of Educational Progress or any of the state assessments of reading in the United States. None of these assessments include any elements of new literacies. This misalignment with the contemporaneous realities of literacy may result in increasing existing gaps in reading achievement between rich and poor. How does this happen? The poorest students in any nation have the least access to the Internet at home (Cooper, 2004). Unfortunately, it is often the case that the poorest schools are also under the greatest pressure to raise scores on reading tests that have nothing to do with new literacies (cf. Henry, 2007). In poorer schools, there is often little incentive to teach the new literacies of online research and comprehension simply because they are not tested (Leu, O'Byrne, Zawilinski, McVerry, & Everett-Cacopardo, 2009). Thus, students in our poorest schools become doubly disadvantaged; they have less access to the Internet at home, and schools do not prepare them for new literacies at school.

In contrast, most children from advantaged communities have broadband Internet connections at home. As a result, teachers feel greater freedom to integrate the Internet into their curricula (Henry, 2007). Thus, students in richer districts become doubly privileged: They have greater access to the Internet at home, and they integrate it more often at school. It is a cruel irony that students who most need to be prepared at school for an online age of information are precisely those who are being prepared the least. This situation must change. We cannot afford to help the rich get richer and the poor get poorer through misalignments in our assessment instruments.

During a period of rapidly changing new literacies, we will need to adapt to the continuously changing nature of literacy in several areas. These include research, assessment, and professional development and teacher education.

Research

Research might begin by focusing on two major issues: (1) What are the social practices, skills, strategies, and dispositions essential to the acquisition of new literacies? and (2) How might we best support the development of these aspects of new literacies within both real and virtual learning contexts? As we develop answers to the first question, we should keep in mind that any answers will be in continuous evolution, as even newer technologies will require additional skills, strategies, dispositions, and social practices for their effective use. We should begin now to conceptualize this problem from a deictic perspective, perhaps with a research focus on how students and teachers continually adapt to the changes that will be a part of our lives. Research on how students and teachers learn how to learn may be far more important than a listing of specific skills and strategies within the continuously changing landscape of literacy that will define our future.

Answers to the second question are likely to take place within a context of problem-based learning (see Dochy, Segers, Van den Bossche, & Gijbels, 2003; Hmelo-Silver, 2004) because we have argued that new literacies are often used to solve problems and communicate solutions with online information. One instructional model has been developed for 1:1 computing classrooms in the Teaching Internet Comprehension to Adolescents project (Leu & Reinking, 2005) and described by Leu et al. (2008).

This project focused on inquiry-based learning around diverse informational texts that students encountered on the Internet while engaged in a series of curriculum-based information challenges. A three-phase approach to instruction was designed, called Internet reciprocal teaching (IRT). Over a 20-week period, with about 40 hours of instruction, this approach resulted in significant effects on online research and comprehension among typically low-achieving readers in seventh-grade language arts classrooms in rural South Carolina and urban Connecticut school districts (Leu & Reinking, 2009).

There is some indication that a more sustained period of IRT instruction can yield an even greater effect size. Castek (2008) found positive effects for fourth and fifth graders who were instructed using IRT and laptops. Students in the experimental group showed significantly greater gains in online research and comprehension than did control students: $t(52) = 5.79, p < .001$, with a large effect size (Cohen's $d = 1.58$). This study took place in self-contained classrooms rather than the rotating, 40-minute classes typical of middle schools, providing more time each day for instruction. From these results, it appears that a longer period of time, more than 40 hours, may be necessary to generate high levels of online research and comprehension.

Another area in which important research is taking place is online gaming. Several people have noted that literacy practices and literacy-related learning activities occur within online game play (Gee, 2007a; Squire, 2008, 2011; Steinkuehler, 2006). Leander and Lovvorn (2006), for example, note how an adolescent from the United States learned Finnish and various communication strategies as a result of collaborative video game play experiences. Yet, schools continue to emphasize traditional text-based literacy practices while doing little to integrate the potentials of gaming into the school curriculum.

We also need to consider broader sources of meaning beyond text. Work by Kress, Hull, and others (Hull & Schultz, 2002; Jewitt & Kress, 2003; Kress, 2003) tell us that we must understand more fully the roles of semiotics and multimodal forms if our students are to use the affordances of tools now required in informal as well as high-performance workplace and academic settings. We must begin to shift from a focus mainly on text comprehension strategies to the interaction among text, graphics, and other content (Kinzer, Hoffman, Turkay, Gunbas, & Chantes, 2011; Kinzer et al., in press), especially during out-of-school contexts (Kleifgen & Kinzer, 2009).

These and other areas of research that need to be explored may not be able to keep up with the rapidly changing landscape of literacy if traditional research paradigms are used; important aspects of literacy are likely to change before a body of consistent research findings can be gathered. Because new literacies continuously change, we require new epistemologies and research practices that keep up with the rapid changes we anticipate. How, for example, can we keep up with new ideas about what to teach and how to teach within research and dissemination paradigms that require five years or more between the conception of a research problem and the wide dissemination of results through research journals? How can we assess students on their ability to use the Internet and other ICTs when the very skills we assess will change as soon as new technologies appear? While a New Literacies perspective does not provide complete answers to these questions, it suggests that these are critical questions to ask.

The answers may emerge in the new models of research likely to appear among those who understand the changes we are experiencing. Those who develop digital curricula, for example, may come to realize that their most important resource is not the digital curriculum they provide to schools but rather the data they obtain from students who use the curriculum. With a network that both delivers curricular activities and assesses learning each day, data could be used to conduct immediate research on the design of lesson activities, revising a different element each night to obtain immediate results on the effects of that change the next day. Anyone with access to these data, and with the appropriate resources, will be able to conduct research on a scale and with a speed that we have not previously experienced. It is quite possible that the assumptions we currently have about how, when, where, and why instructional research is conducted will change rapidly in an age of new literacies.

Assessment

We currently lack valid, reliable, and practical assessments of new literacies to inform instruction and help students become better prepared for an online age of information and communication.

As a result, new literacies are not often integrated into reading or language arts instruction (Hew & Brush, 2007) and are, instead, typically viewed as an optional add-on rather than a vital component (O'Brien & Scharber, 2008). Until we develop valid, reliable, and practical assessments of new literacies to inform instruction, their integration into the classroom will always be delayed. Developing these assessments will be an important challenge in the years ahead.

Dynamic, online texts and their associated literacy practices require dynamic assessments that are sensitive to the diverse, multiple, and rapidly changing ways in which learners read, write, learn, and communicate information in the 21st century (Churches, 2009; International Reading Association & National Council of Teachers of English, 2010; Knobel & Wilber, 2009). Similarly, a range of social networking and information-sharing tools (e.g., Facebook, Twitter, Skype) continue to emerge and give rise to new means of communication and ways of connecting and sharing with wider and more diverse groups of individuals than ever before (Greenhow, Robelia, & Hughes, 2009; Johnson, Levine, Smith, & Smythe, 2009). Consequently, authentic assessments of new literacies should incorporate the information and communication tools used in the workforce and in students' daily lives (e.g., interactive blogs, wikis, e-mail) to pose and answer questions, reflect on and synthesize new learning, and collaborate across classrooms.

Assessments of new literacies should also document students' evolving dispositions toward participation in globally networked communities (Coiro, 2009; Popham, 2009). This includes assessments that document the ability to work productively as a team, appreciate differences in cultural practices and work patterns, demonstrate flexibility and perseverance during online inquiry, and respond appropriately to peer feedback (Afflerbach, 2007; American Association of School Librarians, 2007; O'Byrne & McVerry, 2009). Finally, we require better assessments of online research and comprehension, ones that are both reliable and valid and also practical. The ones we currently have appear to be valid and reliable but require extensive time to reliably score (Castek & Coiro, 2010).

Current work taking place in the Online Research and Comprehension Assessment (ORCA) project seeks this broader objective (Leu, Kulikowich, Sedransk, & Coiro, 2009). This project has developed 24 assessments that present authentic problems to students in science with text messages and collects data on both process and product aspects of the research they conduct online. The task concludes with students using their result to revise a classroom wiki or e-mailing a school board president about the results they discovered. A video of one assessment may be viewed by linking to this URL: neag.uconn.edu/orca-video-ira/. The ORCAs are currently being piloted and validated with representative state samples of nearly 2,800 seventh-grade students in Connecticut and Maine.

The most prominent challenge, perhaps, is that literacy assessments, to date, are always assessments of an individual working alone. Given the importance of social learning and collaborative meaning construction on the Internet and other ICTs, we will need to assess how well students can learn new literacies from others and how well they can co-construct meaning and collaborate in constructing written information with others. Learning how to learn from others and learning how to collaboratively construct meaning will be increasingly important in the years ahead. It seems clear that new technologies will require new approaches to both what is assessed and how we go about doing so (Coiro & Castek, 2010; Kinzer, 2010; National Research Council, 2001).

Professional Development and Teacher Education

Perhaps the greatest challenge that we face lies in professional development. It is safe to say that our educational systems have never before faced the professional development needs that will occur in our future. Current professional development models are often short in duration, with a focus on technology as a tool (Warschauer, 2006), despite the fact that studies of laptop integration universally conclude that extensive professional development on higher level learning with technology is required before gains can be realized (Penuel, 2006; Silvernail & Buffington, 2009;

Silvernail & Gritter, 2007; Silvernail & Lane, 2004; Warschauer, 2006). The continuous changes that lie ahead for literacy will require continuous professional development.

It is likely that new models of professional development will require more extended commitments from school leadership teams, over longer periods of time, than we are used to. It is well established that professional development with technology integration takes longer than other areas of classroom instruction do, as much as two to three times as long to produce the expected effects (Becta, 2003; McKenzie, 2001; Saylor & Kehrhahn, 2003). This is because training requires teachers to develop more than new instructional strategies. They also have to develop proficiency with new technologies, an even greater challenge for some.

Emerging work (Spires, Hervey, & Watson, 2012; Spires, Zheng, & Pruden, 2011) has found Mishra and Koehler's (2006) TPACK model to be a useful framework for helping educators understand the complex relationships among technology, content, and pedagogy to facilitate teacher growth in new literacies (see also Lohnes Watulak & Kinzer's, 2013, argument for an extension of this model). However, we need more research and clear data on the efficacy of these and other new models to direct us in this area.

Our colleagues who conduct research on teacher education also need to apply their finest heuristics, helping us to better understand how to prepare new and experienced teachers to support children in the new literacies of ICTs in the classroom. This will require an understanding of new literacies by academic institutions and teacher educators, who will need to implement changes in our college and university preservice programs.

What seems certain is that Internet resources will increase, not decrease, the central role teachers play in orchestrating learning experiences for students as literacy instruction converges with Internet technologies. The richer and more complex information environments of the Internet will challenge teachers to thoughtfully support student learning in these new literacies contexts (Coiro & Fogleman, 2011). This alone should make professional development and teacher education important priorities.

The Challenges of Change: Theory Building in a Deictic World of New Literacies

We believe that we are on the cusp of a new era in literacy theory, research, and practice, one in which the nature of reading, writing, and communication is being fundamentally transformed by the Internet. It will be up to each of us to recognize these changes and develop a richer understanding of them as we seek to prepare students for the new literacies of the Internet and other ICTs that define their future. They deserve nothing less.

To help us begin this journey, we have argued that one way to understand the changes taking place to literacy is to build theoretical models around change itself. We have outlined a dual-level theory of New Literacies, a perspective that provides a useful starting point to inquiry in this area and one that is both close to the continuous changes taking place at the lowercase level and also provides an understanding of the generalized principles that are common to all of the many contexts at the uppercase level.

Our own work tells us that each of us will be challenged in many ways as we enter this new world of new literacies. We will be challenged to conduct and publish research before the very issues that we study have changed as even newer literacies have appeared. We will be challenged to use collaborative models of research because so many of us work in institutions that still privilege the single-investigator model for dissertations, tenure, and promotion. We will be challenged to gain access to school classrooms when schools are under intense pressure to raise test scores, with assessments that exclude the new literacies we seek to study, and have little time for anything other than what is on their test. We will be challenged by the shift to centers of research where curriculum developers have access to massive amounts of daily data and rapidly change the classroom contexts for instruction in literacy and learning.

The most important challenge for each of us, though, may be of looking beyond our own lower-case theoretical framework to include findings taking place in other, related, new literacies work. We must begin to think in ways that do not simply privilege our own work but embrace the many other perspectives that can enrich our own understanding. By looking across multiple, lowercase, new literacies, we will develop a far richer understanding of the important work that each of us is conducting.

This chapter has explored emerging theoretical perspectives in new literacies and explained why we believe a dual-level, New Literacies theory is especially useful to understand the changes that are taking place. We hope that by sharing this perspective and the many challenges that we face, you will be encouraged to bring your own expertise to the important research that lies ahead. Nothing is more important to our collective future.

Notes

Portions of this material are based on work supported by the U.S. Department of Education under Award Nos. R305G050154 and R305A090608. Opinions expressed herein are solely those of the authors and do not necessarily represent the position of the U.S. Department of Education, Institute of Educational Sciences.

References

Afflerbach, P. (2007). *Understanding and using reading assessment.* Newark, DE: International Reading Association.

Afflerbach, P.A., & Cho, B.Y. (2008). Identifying and describing constructively responsive comprehension strategies in new and traditional forms of reading. In S. Israel & G. Duffy (Eds.), *Handbook of reading comprehension research* (pp. 69–90). Mahwah, NJ: Erlbaum.

Afflerbach, P.A., & Cho, B.Y. (2010). Determining and describing reading strategies: Internet and traditional forms of reading. In H.S. Waters & W. Schneider (Eds.), *Metacognition, strategy use, and instruction* (pp. 201–255). New York: Guilford.

American Association of School Librarians. (2007). *Standards for the 21st-century learner.* Retrieved from www.ala.org/ala/mgrps/divs/aasl/guidelinesandstandards/learningstandards/standards.cfm

Australian Curriculum, Assessment and Reporting Authority. (n.d.). *The Australian Curriculum* (Version 1.2). Retrieved from www.australian curriculum.edu.au/Home

Becta. (2003). *What the research says about barriers to the use of ICT in teaching.* Retrieved October 29, 2012 from www.mmiweb.org.uk/publications/ict/Research_Barriers_TandL.pdf

Bennett, R.E., Persky, H., Weiss, A.R., & Jenkins, F. (2007). *Problem solving in technology-rich environments: A report from the NAEP technology-based assessment project.* Retrieved from nces.ed.gov/pubsearch/pubsinfo.asp?pubid=2007466

Bennett, S., Maton, K., & Kervin, L. (2008). The digital natives debate: A critical review of the evidence. *British Journal of Educational Technology, 31*(9), 775–786.

Bilal, D. (2000). Children's use of the Yahooligans! Web search engine: Cognitive, physical, and affective behaviors on fact-based search tasks. *Journal of the American Society for Information Science, 51*(7), 646–665. doi:10.1002/(SICI)10974571(2000)51:7<646::AID-ASI7>3.0.CO;2-A

Boyarin, J. (Ed.). (1993). *The ethnography of reading.* Berkeley: University of California Press. doi:10.1525/california/9780520079557.001.0001

Bråten, I., Strømsø, H.I., & Britt, M.A. (2009). Trust matters: Examining the role of source evaluation in students' construction of meaning within and across multiple texts. *Reading Research Quarterly, 44*(1), 6–28. doi:10.1598/RRQ.44.1.1

Bråten, I., Strømsø, H.I., & Salmerón, L. (2011). Trust and mistrust when students read multiple information sources about climate change. *Learning and Instruction, 21*(2), 180–192. doi: 10.1016/j.learninstruc.2010.02.002

Britt, M.A., & Gabrys, G.L. (2001). Teaching advanced literacy skills for the World Wide Web. In C.R. Wolfe (Ed.), *Learning and teaching on the World Wide Web* (pp. 73–90). San Diego, CA: Academic. doi:10.1016/B978-012761891-3/50007-2

Broch, E. (2000). Children's search engines from an information search process perspective. *School Library Media Research*, 3. Retrieved from www.ala.org/arasl/aaslpubsandjournals/slmrb/slmrcontents/volume32000/childrens

Callow, J. (2010). Spot the difference: The changing nature of page-based and screen-based texts. *Screen Education, 58*, 106–110.

Cammack, D. (2002). Literacy, technology, and a room of her own: Analyzing adolescent girls' online conversations from historical and technological literacy perspectives. In D. Shallert, C. Fairbanks, J. Worthy, B. Maloch, & J. Hoffman (Eds.), *Fifty-first yearbook of the National Reading Conference* (pp. 129–141). Chicago: National Reading Conference.

Canavilhas, J. (n.d.). *Web journalism: From the inverted pyramid to the tumbled pyramid*. Retrieved from www.bocc.ubi.pt/pag/canavilhas-joao -inverted-pyramid.pdf

Castek, J. (2008). *How do 4th and 5th grade students acquire the new literacies of online reading comprehension? Exploring the contexts that facilitate learning.* Unpublished doctoral dissertation, University of Connecticut, Storrs.

Castek, J., & Coiro, J. (2010, April). *Measuring online reading comprehension in open networked spaces: Challenges, concerns, and choices.* Alternative poster session presented at the annual meeting of the American Educational Research Association, Denver, CO.

Castek, J., Zawilinski, L., McVerry, G., O'Byrne, I., & Leu, D.J. (2011). The new literacies of online reading comprehension: New opportunities and challenges for students with learning difficulties. In C. Wyatt-Smith, J. Elkins, & S. Gunn (Eds.), *Multiple perspectives on difficulties in learning literacy and numeracy* (pp. 91–110). New York: Springer.

Center for Media Literacy. (2005). *Literacy for the 21st century: An overview and orientation guide to media literacy education. Part 1 of the CML medialit kit: Framework for learning and teaching in a media age.* Retrieved from www.medialit.org/cml-medialit-kit

Cho, B.-Y. (2010, December 3). *A study of adolescents' constructive strategy use in a critical Internet reading task.* Paper presented at the annual meeting of the Literacy Research Association, Fort Worth, TX.

Churches, A. (2009). *Bloom's digital taxonomy.* Retrieved from edorigami.wikispaces.com/Bloom%27s+Digital+Taxonomy

Clemitt, M. (2008). Internet accuracy. *CQ Researcher, 18*(27), 625–648.

Coiro, J. (2003). Reading comprehension on the Internet: Expanding our understanding of reading comprehension to encompass new literacies. *The Reading Teacher, 56*(5), 458–464.

Coiro, J. (2009). Promising practices for supporting adolescents' online literacy development. In K.D. Wood & W.E. Blanton (Eds.), *Literacy instruction for adolescents: Research-based practice* (pp. 442–471). New York: Guilford.

Coiro, J. (2011). Predicting reading comprehension on the Internet: Contributions of offline reading skills, online reading skills, and prior knowledge. *Journal of Literacy Research, 43*(4), 352–392.

Coiro, J., & Castek, J. (2010). Assessment frameworks for teaching and learning English language arts in a digital age. In D. Lapp & D. Fisher (Eds.), *Handbook of research on teaching the English language arts* (3rd ed., pp. 314–321). New York: Routledge.

Coiro, J., Castek, J., & Guzniczak, L. (2011). Uncovering online reading comprehension processes: Two adolescents reading independently and collaboratively on the Internet. In P.J. Dunston, L.B. Gambrell, K. Headley, S.K. Fullerton, & P.M. Stecker (Eds.), *60th yearbook of the Literacy Research Association* (pp. 354–369). Oak Creek, WI: Literacy Research Association.

Coiro, J., & Dobler, E. (2007). Exploring the online comprehension strategies used by sixth-grade skilled readers to search for and locate information on the Internet. *Reading Research Quarterly, 42*(2), 214–257. doi:10.1598/RRQ.42.2.2

Coiro, J., & Fogleman, J. (2011). Capitalizing on Internet resources for content-area teaching and learning. *Educational Leadership, 68*(5), 34–38.

Coiro, J., Knobel, M., Lankshear, C., & Leu, D.J. (2008). Central issues in new literacies and new literacies research. In J. Coiro, M. Knobel, C. Lankshear, & D.J. Leu (Eds.), *Handbook of research on new literacies* (pp. 1–22). Mahwah, NJ: Erlbaum.

Cooper, M. (2004). *Expanding the digital divide and falling behind on broadband: Why telecommunications policy of neglect is not benign.* Washington, DC: Consumer Federation of America. Retrieved from www.consumerfed.org/pdfs/digitaldivide.pdf

Cope, B., & Kalantzis, M. (Eds.). (1999). *Multiliteracies: Literacy learning and the design of social futures.* New York: Routledge.

Dalton, B., & Proctor, P. (2008). The changing landscape of text and comprehension in the age of new literacies. In J. Coiro, M. Knobel, C. Lankshear, & D.J. Leu (Eds.), *Handbook of research on new literacies* (pp. 297–324). Mahwah, NJ: Erlbaum.

Diringer, D. (1968). *The alphabet: A key to the history of mankind.* New York: Funk & Wagnalls.

Dochy, F., Segers, M., Van den Bossche, P., & Gijbels, D. (2003). Effects of problem-based learning: A meta-analysis. *Learning and Instruction, 13*(5), 533–568. doi:10.1016/S0959-4752(02)00025-7

Eagleton, M. (2001). *Factors that influence Internet inquiry strategies: Case studies of middle school students with and without learning disabilities.* Paper presented at the annual meeting of the National Reading Conference, San Antonio, TX.

Eagleton, M., Guinee, K., & Langlais, K. (2003). Teaching Internet literacy strategies: The hero inquiry project. *Voices From the Middle, 10*(3), 28–35.

Erstad, O. (2002). Norwegian students using digital artifacts in project-based learning. *Journal of Computer Assisted Learning, 18*(4), 427–437. doi:10.1046/j.0266-4909.2002.00254.x

Everett-Cacopardo, H. (2011). *Classrooms without borders: How online collaboration can connect adolescents to literacy and learning around the world.* Manuscript submitted for publication.

Fabos, B. (2008). The price of information: Critical literacy, education, and today's Internet. In J. Coiro, M. Knobel, C. Lankshear, & D.J. Leu (Eds.), *Handbook of research on new literacies* (pp. 839–870). Mahwah, NJ: Erlbaum.

Fabos, B., & Young, M.D. (1999). Telecommunications in the classroom: Rhetoric versus reality. *Review of Educational Research, 69*(3), 217–259.

Federal Trade Commission. (2002, April). *Protecting children's privacy under COPPA: A survey on compliance.* Retrieved from www.ftc.gov/os/2002/04/coppasurvey.pdf

Fillmore, C. (1966). Deictic categories in the semantics of 'come.' *Foundations of Language, 2*(3), 219–227.

Flanagin, A.J., Farinola, W.J., & Metzger, M.J. (2000). The technical code of the Internet/World Wide Web. *Critical Studies in Media Communication, 17*(4), 409–428. doi:10.1080/15295030009388411

Flanagin, A.J., & Metzger, M.J. (2010). *An empirical examination of youth, digital media use, and information credibility.* Cambridge, MA: MIT Press.

Gee, J.P. (2007a). *Good video games and good learning: Collected essays on video games, learning and literacy.* New York: Peter Lang.

Gee, J.P. (2007b). *Social linguistics and literacies: Ideology in discourses.* London: Routledge.

Gee, J.P. (2007c). *What video games have to teach us about learning and literacy* (2nd ed.). New York: Macmillan. doi:10.1145/950566.950595

Gilster, P. (1997). *Digital literacy.* New York: John Wiley.

Graham, L., & Metaxas, P.T. (2003). Of course it's true: I saw it on the Internet! *Communications of the ACM, 46*(5), 71–75.

Greenhow, C., Robelia, B., & Hughes, J. (2009). Web 2.0 and classroom research: What path should we take now? *Educational Researcher, 38*(4), 246–259. doi:10.3102/0013189X09336671

Guinee, K., Eagleton, M.B., & Hall, T.E. (2003). Adolescents' Internet search strategies: Drawing upon familiar cognitive paradigms when accessing electronic information sources. *Journal of Educational Computing Research, 29*(3), 363–374. doi:10.2190/HD0A-N15L-RTFH-2DU8

Harper, D. (2006). *Generation YES (Youth and Educators Succeeding)—Vision to action: Adding student leadership to your technology plan.* Retrieved from www.genyes.com/media/programs/how_to_include_students_in_tech_plan.pdf

Hartman, D.K., Morsink, P.M., & Zheng, J. (2010). From print to pixels: The evolution of cognitive conceptions of reading comprehension. In E.A. Baker (Ed.), *The new literacies: Multiple perspectives on research and practice* (pp. 131–164). New York: Guilford.

Henry, L. (2006). SEARCHing for an answer: The critical role of new literacies while reading on the Internet. *The Reading Teacher, 59*(7), 614–627. doi:10.1598/RT.59.7.1

Henry, L.A. (2007). *Exploring new literacies pedagogy and online reading comprehension among middle school students and teachers: Issues of social equity or social exclusion?* Unpublished doctoral dissertation, University of Connecticut, Storrs.

Hew, K.F., & Brush, T. (2007). Integrating technology into K–12 teaching and learning: Current knowledge gaps and recommendations for future research. *Educational Technology Research and Development, 55*(3), 223–252. doi:10.1007/s11423-006-9022-5

Hirsh, S.G. (1999). Children's relevance criteria and information seeking on electronic resources. *Journal of the American Society for Information Science, 50*(14), 1265–1283. doi:10.1002/(SICI)1097-4571(1999)50:14<1265::AID-ASI2>3.0 .CO;2-E

Hmelo-Silver, C.E. (2004). Problem-based learning: What and how do students learn? *Educational Psychology Review, 16*(3), 235–266. doi:10.1023/B:EDPR.0000034022.16470.f3.

Hobbs, R. (2010). *Digital and media literacy: A plan of action. A white paper on the digital and media literacy recommendations of the Knight Commission on the information needs of communities in a democracy.* Washington, DC: The Aspen Institute. Retrieved from www.knightcomm. org/digital-and-media-literacy/

Hull, G., & Schultz, K. (2002). *School's out: Bridging out-of-school literacies with classroom practice.* New York: Teachers College Press.

Hull, G., Stornaiuolo, A., & Sahni, U. (2010). Cultural citizenship and cosmopolitan practice: Global youth communicate online. *English Education, 42*(4), 331–367.

Hull, G., Zacher, J., & Hibbert, L. (2009). Youth, risk, and equity in a global world. *Review of Research in Education, 33*(1), 117–159. doi:10.3102/0091732X08327746

Illera, J.L.R. (1997). De la lectura en papel a la lectura de multimedia [From reading on paper to reading multimedia]. In Fundalectura (Ed.), *Lectura y nuevas tecnologías: 3er congresso nacional de lectura* [Reading and new technologies: 3rd National Congress of Reading] (pp. 69–88). Bogotá, Colombia: Fundación para el Fomento de la Lectura.

International ICT Literacy Panel. (2002, May). *Digital transformation: A framework for ICT literacy.* Retrieved from www.ets.org/Media/Tests/Information_and_Communication_Technology_Literacy/ictreport.pdf.

International Reading Association. (2009). *New literacies and 21st century technologies* (Position statement). Newark, DE: Author. Available from: www.reading.org/General/AboutIRA/Position Statements/21stCenturyLiteracies.aspx

International Reading Association & National Council of Teachers of English. (2010). *Standards for the assessment of reading and writing* (Rev. ed.). Newark, DE, & Urbana, IL: Authors. Retrieved from www.reading.org/General/CurrentResearch/Standards/AssessmentStandards.aspx.

Internet World Stats. (2011). *Internet users in the world: Distribution by world regions.* Retrieved July 1, 2011, from www.internetworldstats.com/stats.htm

Jenkins, H. (2006). *Convergence culture: Where old and new media collide.* New York: New York University Press.

Jewitt, C., & Kress, G.R. (2003). *Multimodal literacy.* New York: Peter Lang.

Johnson, L., Levine, A., Smith, R., & Smythe, T. (2009). *Horizon report: 2009 K–12 edition.* Austin, TX: The New Media Consortium.

Jonassen, D.H., Howland, J., Moore, J., & Marra, R.M. (2003). *Learning to solve problems with technology: A constructivist perspective* (2nd ed.). Columbus, OH: Merrill/Prentice-Hall.

Kaiser Family Foundation. (2005). *Generation M: Media in the lives of 8–18 year-olds.* Retrieved from www.kff.org/entmedia/7251.cfm

Kiili, C., Laurinen, L., & Marttunen, M. (2008). Students evaluating Internet sources: From versatile evaluators to uncritical readers. *Journal of Educational Computing Research, 39*(1), 75–95. doi:10.2190/EC.39.1.e

Kiili, C., Laurinen, L., Marttunen, M., & Leu, D. J. (2011). *Working on understanding: Collaborative reading patterns on the Web.* Manuscript submitted for publication.

Kinzer, C.K. (2010). Considering literacy and policy in the context of digital environments. *Language Arts, 88*(1), 51–61.

Kinzer, C.K., Hoffman, D.L., Turkay, S., Gunbas, N., & Chantes, P. (2011). Exploring motivation and comprehension of a narrative in a video game, book and comic book format. In P.J. Dunston, L.B. Gambrell, K. Headley, S.K. Fullerton, & P.M. Stecker (Eds.), *60th Yearbook of the Literacy Research Association Yearbook* (pp. 263–278). Oak Creek, WI: Literacy Research Association.

Kinzer, C.K., Turkay, S., Hoffman, D.L., Gunbas, N., Chantes, P., Chaiwinij, A., et al. (in press). Examining the effects of text and images on story comprehension: An eye tracking study of reading in games and comics. In P.J. Dunston & S.K. Fullerton (Eds.), *61st yearbook of the Literacy Research Association.* Chicago: Literacy Research Association.

Kinzer, C.K., & Leander, K. (2002). Technology and the language arts: Implications of an expanded definition of literacy. In J. Flood, D. Lapp, J.R. Squire, & J.M. Jensen (Eds.), *Handbook of research and teaching the English language arts* (pp. 546–566). Mahwah, NJ: Erlbaum.

Kirsch, I., Braun, H., Yamamoto, K., & Sum, A. (2007). *America's perfect storm: Three forces changing our nation's future.* Princeton, NJ: Educational Testing Service. Retrieved from www.ets.org/Media/Research/pdf/PIC STORM.pdf.

Kleifgen, J., & Kinzer, C.K. (2009). Alternative spaces for education with and through technology. In H. Varenne & E. Gordon (Eds.), *Comprehensive education explorations, possibilities, challenges* (pp. 139–186). Lewiston, NY: Ewin Mellen.

Knobel, M., & Wilber, D. (2009). Let's talk 2.0. *Educational Leadership, 66*(6), 20–24.

Kress, G. (2003). *Literacy in the new media age.* London: Routledge. doi:10.4324/9780203164754

Kuiper, E. (2007). *Teaching Web literacy in primary education.* Retrieved from dare.ubvu.vu.nl/bitstream/1871/10836/1/7533.pdf.

Kuiper, E., & Volman, M. (2008). The Web as a source of information for students in K–12 education. In J. Coiro, M. Knobel, C. Lankshear, & D.J. Leu (Eds.), *Handbook of research on new literacies* (pp. 241–246). Mahwah, NJ: Erlbaum.

Labbo, L. (1996). A semiotic analysis of young children's symbol making in a classroom computer center. *Reading Research Quarterly, 31*(4), 356–385. doi:10.1598/RRQ.31.4.2

Labbo, L., & Kuhn, M. (1998). Electronic symbol making: Young children's computer-related emerging concepts about literacy. In D. Reinking, M. McKenna, L.D. Labbo, & R. Kieffer (Eds.), *Handbook of literacy and technology: Transformations in a post-typographic world* (pp. 79–92). Mahwah, NJ: Erlbaum.

Labbo, L.D., & Reinking, D. (1999). Negotiating the multiple realities of technology in literacy research and instruction. *Reading Research Quarterly, 34*(4), 478–492. doi:10.1598/RRQ.34.4.5

Lankshear, C., & Knobel, M. (2006). *New literacies* (2nd ed.). Maidenhead, UK: Open University Press.

Lawless, K.A., & Kulikowich, J.M. (1996). Understanding hypertext navigation through cluster analysis. *Journal of Educational Computing Research, 14*(4), 385–399. doi:10.2190/DVAP-DE23-3XMV-9MXH

Lawless, K.A., Mills, R., & Brown, S.W. (2002). Children's hypermedia navigational strategies. *Journal of Research on Computing in Education, 34*(3), 274–284.

Leander, K.M., & Lovvorn, J.F. (2006). Literacy networks: Following the circulation of texts, bodies, and objects in the schooling and online gaming of one youth. *Cognition and Instruction, 24*(3), 291–340. doi:10.1207/s1532690xci2403_1

Lemke, J.L. (2002). Travels in hypermodality. *Visual Communication, 1*(3), 299–325. doi:10.1177/147035720200100303

Leu, D.J., Jr. (1997). Caity's question: Literacy as deixis on the Internet. *The Reading Teacher, 51*(1), 62–67.

Leu, D.J., Jr. (2000). Literacy and technology: Deictic consequences for literacy education in an information age. In M.L. Kamil, P. Mosenthal, P.D. Pearson, & R. Barr (Eds.), *Handbook of reading research* (Vol. 3, pp. 743–770). Mahwah, NJ: Erlbaum.

Leu, D.J., Castek, J., Hartman, D., Coiro, J., Henry, L., Kulikowich, J., et al. (2005). *Evaluating the development of scientific knowledge and new forms of reading comprehension during online learning.* Final report presented to the North Central Regional Educational Laboratory/Learning Point Associates. Retrieved from www.newliteracies.uconn.edu/ncrel.html

Leu, D.J., Coiro, J., Castek, J., Hartman, D., Henry, L.A., & Reinking, D. (2008). Research on instruction and assessment in the new literacies of online reading comprehension. In C.C. Block & S. Parris (Eds.), *Comprehension instruction: Research-based best practices* (pp. 321–345). New York: Guilford.

Leu, D.J., Everett-Cacopardo, H., Zawilinski, L., McVerry, J.G., & O'Byrne, W.I. (in press). The new literacies of online reading comprehension. In C.A. Chapelle (Ed.), *The encyclopedia of applied linguistics.* Oxford, UK: Wiley-Blackwell.

Leu, D.J., Forzani, E., Burlingame, C., Kulikowich, J., Sedransk, N., Coiro, J., et al. (in press). The new literacies of online research and comprehension: Assessing and preparing students for the 21st century with Common Core State Standards. In S.B. Neuman, L.B. Gambrell (Eds.), & C. Massey (Assoc. Ed.), *Reading instruction in the age of Common Core Standards.* Newark, DE: International Reading Association.

Leu, D.J., Jr., Karchmer, R., & Leu, D.D. (1999). The Miss Rumphius effect: Envisionments for literacy and learning that transform the Internet. *The Reading Teacher, 52*(6), 636–642.

Leu, D.J., Jr., & Kinzer, C.K. (2000). The convergence of literacy instruction and networked technologies for information and communication. *Reading Research Quarterly, 35*(1), 108–127. doi:10.1598/RRQ.35.1.8

Leu, D.J., Jr., Kinzer, C.K., Coiro, J., & Cammack, D. (2004). Toward a theory of new literacies emerging from the Internet and other information and communication technologies. In R.B. Ruddell & N.J. Unrau (Eds.), *Theoretical models and processes of reading* (5th ed., pp. 1570–1613). Newark, DE: International Reading Association. doi:10.1598/0872075028.54

Leu, D.J., Kulikowich, J., Sedransk, N., & Coiro, J. (2009). *Assessing online reading comprehension: The ORCA project.* Research grant funded by the U.S. Department of Education, Institute of Education Sciences.

Leu, D.J., McVerry, J.G., O'Byrne, W.I., Kiili, C., Zawilinski, L., Everett-Cacopardo, H., et al. (2011). The new literacies of online reading comprehension: Expanding the literacy and learning curriculum. *Journal of Adolescent & Adult Literacy, 55*(1), (pp. 5–14). doi:10.1598/JAAL.55.1.1

Leu, D.J., O'Byrne, W.I., Zawilinski, L., McVerry, J.G., & Everett-Cacopardo, H. (2009). Expanding the new literacies conversation. *Educational Researcher, 38*(4), 264–269. doi:10.3102/0013189X09336676

Leu, D.J., & Reinking, D. (2005). *Developing Internet comprehension strategies among adolescent students at risk to become dropouts.* Research grant project funded by the U.S. Department of Education, Institute of Education Sciences.

Leu, D.J., & Reinking, D. (2009). *Final report: Developing Internet comprehension strategies among poor, adolescent students at risk to become dropouts.* Research grant funded by the U.S. Department of Education, Institute of Education Sciences.

Leu, D.J., Reinking, D., Carter, A., Castek, J., Coiro, J., & Henry, L.A. (2007, April 9). *Defining online reading comprehension: Using think-aloud verbal protocols to refine a preliminary model of Internet reading comprehension processes.* Paper presented at the American Educational Research Association, Chicago. Available from: docs.google.com/Doc?id=dcbjhrtq_10djqrhz

Leu, D.J., Zawilinski, L., Castek, J., Banerjee, M., Housand, B., & Liu, Y. (2007). What is new about the new literacies of online reading comprehension? In L. Rush, J. Eakle, & A. Berger (Eds.), *Secondary school literacy: What research reveals for classroom practices* (pp. 37–68). Urbana, IL: National Council of Teachers of English.

Lewis, C., & Fabos, B. (2005). Instant messaging, literacies, and social identities. *Reading Research Quarterly, 40*(4), 470–501. doi:10.1598/RRQ.40.4.5

Lohnes Watulak, S., & Kinzer, C.K. (2013). Beyond technology skills: Toward a framework for critical digital literacies in pre-service technology education. In J. Ávila & J.Z. Pandya (Eds.), *Critical digital literacies as social praxis: Intersections and challenges* (pp. 127–153). New York: Peter Lang.

Manguel, A. (1996). *A history of reading.* New York: Viking.

Mathews, M. (1966). *Teaching to read: Historically considered.* Chicago: University of Chicago Press.

Matteucci, N., O'Mahony, M., Robinson, C., & Zwick, T. (2005). Productivity, workplace performance and ICT: Industry and firm-level evidence for Europe and the US. *Scottish Journal of Political Economy, 52*(3), 359–386. doi:10.1111/j.0036-9292.2005.00349.x

McDonald, S., & Stevenson, R.J. (1996). Disorientation in hypertext: The effects of three text structures on navigation performance. *Applied Ergonomics, 27(1),* 61–68. doi:10.1016/0003-6870(95)00073-9

McEneaney, J.E., Li, L., Allen, K., & Guzniczak, L. (2009). Stance, navigation, and reader response in expository hypertext. *Journal of Literacy Research, 41*(1), 1–45. doi:10.1080/10862960802695081

McKenzie, J. (2001). *Planning good change with technology and literacy.* Bellingham, WA: FNO.

Metzger, M.J., & Flanagin, A.J. (Eds.). (2008). *Digital media, youth, and credibility.* Cambridge, MA: MIT Press.

Minister of Manitoba Education, Citizenship, and Youth. (2006). *A continuum model for literacy with ICT across the curriculum: A resource for developing computer literacy.* Retrieved from www.edu.gov.mb.ca/k12/tech/lict/resources/handbook/index.html

Mishra, P., & Koehler, M.J. (2006). Technological pedagogical content knowledge: A framework for teacher knowledge. *Teachers College Record, 108*(6), 1017–1054. doi:10.1111/j.1467-9620.2006.00684.x

Murphy, S.M. (1986). Children's comprehension of deictic categories in oral and written language. *Reading Research Quarterly, 21*(2), 118–131. doi:10.2307/747840

National Governors Association Center for Best Practices & Council of Chief State School Officers. (2010). *Common Core State Standards for English language arts and literacy in history/social studies, science, and technical subjects.* Washington, DC: Authors.

National Research Council. (2001). *Knowing what students know: The science and design of educational assessment.* Washington, DC: National Academy Press.

New London Group. (1996). A pedagogy of multiliteracies: Designing social futures. *Harvard Educational Review, 66*(1), 60–92.

New London Group. (2000). *Multiliteracies: Literacy learning and the design of social futures.* London: Routledge.

O'Brien, D., Beach, R., & Scharber, C. (2007). "Struggling" middle schoolers: Engagement and literate competence in a reading writing intervention class. *Reading Psychology, 28*(1), 51–73. doi:10.1080/02702710601115463

O'Brien, D., & Scharber, C. (2008). Digital literacies go to school: Potholes and possibilities. *Journal of Adolescent & Adult Literacy, 52*(1), 66–68. doi:10.1598/JAAL.52.1.7

O'Byrne, W.I. (2011). *Facilitating critical evaluation skills through content creation: Empowering adolescents as readers and writers of online information.* Unpublished doctoral dissertation, University of Connecticut, Storrs.

O'Byrne, W.I., & McVerry, J.G. (2009). Measuring the dispositions of online reading comprehension: A preliminary validation study. In K.M. Leander, D.W. Rowe, D.K. Dickinson, M.K. Hundley, R.T. Jimenez, & V.J. Risko (Eds.), *58th yearbook of the National Reading Conference Yearbook* (pp. 362–375). Oak Creek, W: National Reading Conference.

Organisation for Economic Co-operation and Development. (2011). PISA 2009 results: Students on line. *Digital technologies and performance* (Volume VI). Available from dx.doi.org/10.1787/9789264112995-en

Organisation for Economic Co-operation and Development & the Centre for Educational Research and Innovation. (2010). *Trends shaping education 2010.* Paris: OECD.

Page, S.E. (2007). *The difference: How the power of diversity creates better groups, firms, schools and societies.* Princeton, NJ: Princeton University Press.

Penuel, W.R. (2006). Implementation and effects of one-to-one computing initiatives: A research synthesis. *Journal of Research on Technology in Education, 38*(3), 329–348.

Pew Internet & American Life Project. (2001). *The Internet and education: Findings of the Pew Internet & American Life Project.* Retrieved from www.pewInternet.org/reports

Pew Internet & American Life Project. (2005). *Teens and technology.* Retrieved from www.pewinternet.org/topics.asp?c=4

Popham, W.J. (2009). Assessing student affect. *Educational Leadership, 66*(8), 85–86.

Reich, R. (1992). *The work of nations.* New York: Vintage.

Rouet, J.-F. (2006). *The skills of document use: From text comprehension to Web-based learning.* Mahwah, NJ: Erlbaum.

Rouet, J.-F., Ros, C., Goumi, A., Macedo-Rouet, M., & Dinet, J. (2011). The influence of surface and deep cues on primary and secondary school students' assessment of relevance in Web menus. *Learning and Instruction, 21*(2), 205–219. doi:10.1016/j.learninstruc.2010.02.007

Sanchez, C.A., Wiley, J., & Goldman, S.R. (2006). Teaching students to evaluate source reliability during Internet research tasks. In S.A. Barab, K.E. Hay, & D.T. Hickey (Eds.), *Proceedings of the seventh international conference on the learning sciences* (pp. 662–666). Bloomington, IN: International Society of the Learning Sciences.

Saylor, P., & Kehrhahn, M. (2003). Teacher skills get an upgrade. *Journal of Staff Development, 24*(14), 48–53.

Schulz-Zander, R., Büchter, A., & Dalmer, R. (2002). The role of ICT as a promoter of students' cooperation. *Journal of Computer Assisted Learning, 18*(4), 438–448. doi:10.1046/j.0266-4909.2002.002.x

Silvernail, D.L., & Buffington, P.J. (2009). *Improving mathematics performance, using laptop technology: The importance of professional development for success.* Retrieved from www.usm.maine.edu/cepare/pdf/Mathematics_Final_cover.pdf

Silvernail, D.L., & Gritter, A.K. (2007). *Maine's middle school laptop program: Creating better writers.* Gorham: Maine Education Policy Research Institute, University of Southern Maine.

Silvernail, D.L., & Lane, D. (2004). *The impact on Maine's one-to-one laptop program on middle school teachers and students.* Gorham: Maine Education Policy Research Institute, University of Southern Maine.

Smith, M.C., Mikulecky, L., Kibby, M.W., Dreher, M.J., & Dole, J.A. (2000). What will be the demands of literacy in the workplace in the next millennium? *Reading Research Quarterly, 35*(3), 378–383. doi:10.1598/RRQ.35.3.3

Smith, N.B. (1965). *American reading instruction.* Newark, DE: International Reading Association.

Spires, H.A., & Estes, T.H. (2002). Reading in Web-based learning environments. In C.C. Block & M. Pressley (Eds.), *Comprehension instruction: Research-based best practices* (pp. 115–125). New York: Guilford.

Spires, H.A., Hervey, L., & Watson, T. (2012). Scaffolding the TPACK framework in reading and language arts: New literacies, new minds. In C.A. Young & S. Kadjer (Eds.), *Research on technology in English education* (pp. 33–61). Charlotte, NC: Information Age.

Spires, H.A., Zheng, M., & Pruden, M. (2011). New technologies, new horizons: Graduate student views on creating their technological pedagogical content knowledge (TPACK). In K. Moyle & G. Wijngaards (Eds.), *Student reactions to learning with technologies: Perceptions and outcomes* (pp. 23–41). Hershey, PA: IGI Global.

Squire, K. (2008). Open-ended video games: A model for developing learning for the interactive age. In K. Salen (Ed.), *The ecology of games: Connecting youth, games, and learning* (pp. 167–198). Cambridge, MA: MIT Press.

Squire, K. (2011). *Video games and learning: Teaching and participatory culture in the digital age.* New York: Teachers College Press.

Steinkuehler, C. (2006). Massively multiplayer online videogaming as participation in a Discourse. *Mind, Culture, and Activity, 13*(1), 38–52. doi:10.1207/s15327884mca1301_4

Street, B. (1995). *Social literacies.* London: Longman.

Street, B. (2003). What's new in new literacy studies? *Current Issues in Comparative Education, 5*(2), 1–14.

Sundar, S.S. (2008). The MAIN model: A heuristic approach to understanding technology effects on credibility. In M.J. Metzger & A.J. Flanagin (Eds.), *Digital media, youth, and credibility* (pp. 73–100). Cambridge, MA: MIT Press.

Sutherland-Smith, W. (2002). Weaving the literacy web: Changes in reading from page to screen. *The Reading Teacher, 55*(7), 662–669.

Taboada, A., & Guthrie, J. (2006). Contributions of student questioning and prior knowledge to construction of knowledge from reading information text. *Journal of Literacy Research, 38*(1), 1–35. doi:10.1207/s15548430jlr3801_1

Tillman, H.N. (2003). *Evaluating quality on the Net.* Retrieved September 14, 2009, from www.hopetillman.com/findqual.html

Traut, G., & Kazzazi, K. (1996). *Dictionary of language and linguistics.* New York: Routledge.

Unsworth, L. (2008). Multiliteracies and meta-language: Describing image/text relations as a resource for negotiating multimodal texts. In J. Coiro, M. Knobel, C. Lankshear, & D.J. Leu (Eds.), *Handbook of research on new literacies* (pp. 377–405). Mahwah, NJ: Erlbaum.

U.S. Department of Commerce, Economic and Statistics Administration & National Telecommunications and Information Administration. (2002). *A nation online: How Americans are expanding their use of the Internet.* Washington, DC: Author.

van Ark, B., Inklaar, R., & McGuckin, R.H. (2003). ICT productivity in Europe and the United States: Where do the differences come from? *CESifo Economic Studies, 49*(3), 295–318. doi:10.1093/cesifo/49.3.295

Wallace, R.M., Kupperman, J., Krajcik, J., & Soloway, E. (2000). Science on the Web: Students on-line in a sixth-grade classroom. *Journal of the Learning Sciences, 9*(1), 75–104. doi:10.1207/s15327809jls0901_5

Walsh, M. (2010). Multimodal literacy: What does it mean for classroom practice? *The Australian Journal of Language and Literacy, 33*(3), 211–239.

Warschauer, M. (2006). *Laptops and literacy: Learning in the wireless classroom.* New York: Teachers College Press.

Wyatt-Smith, C., & Elkins, J. (2008). Multimodal reading and comprehension in online environments. In J. Coiro, M. Knobel, C. Lankshear, & D.J. Leu (Eds.), *Handbook of research on new literacies* (pp. 899–942). Mahwah, NJ: Erlbaum.

Zawilinski, L. (2011). *An exploration of a collaborative blogging approach to literacy and learning: A mixed method study.* Unpublished doctoral dissertation, University of Connecticut, Storrs.

Zhang, S., & Duke, N.K. (2008). Strategies for Internet reading with different reading purposes: A descriptive study of twelve good Internet readers. *Journal of Literacy Research, 40*(1), 128–162. doi:10.1080/10862960802070491

SECTION FOUR

Critical

This is the first time in the history of *Theoretical Models and Processes of Literacy* that a section titled "Critical" has appeared. Allan Luke leads off with Chapter 17, which addresses two major approaches to critical literacy: namely, critical pedagogy and critical text analysis. Both theoretical and practical at the same time, "Regrounding Critical Literacy: Representation, Facts and Reality" works with the theoretical tension between cultural systems of representation and the social, economic, material, and environmental realities of the world in which we live. This tension underscores the importance of answering two key educational questions: "What are the real and material consequences of texts and discourses? How can and, more importantly, how *should* we reshape them" (italics in the original). Answers to these questions are germane to the other five chapters in this section.

For instance in "A Relational Model of Adolescent Literacy Instruction: Disrupting the Discourse of 'Every Teacher a Teacher of Reading'," Donna Alvermann and Elizabeth Moje (Chapter 18) use Michel Foucault's concept of genealogy to analyze conditions that have enabled such a discourse to exist for nearly a century, but without widespread implementation in U.S.A. secondary schools. Their analysis touches first on key individuals and events that have influenced models of adolescent literacy instruction for more than a century before disclosing how potential disruptions of "every teacher a teacher of reading" have been buffered. The chapter concludes with a call for a model of adolescent literacy instruction that uses both a theory *of* action and a theory *in* action.

In "Positioning Theory" (Chapter 19), Mary McVee, Katarina Silvestri, Nichole Barrett, and Katherine Haq report on how seeing the world singularly from one's own vantage point has implications for how others in that sphere are situated. They also examine common misconceptions and critiques of positioning theory that have kept it on the periphery of literacy research until now. To sideline positioning theory, however, is to ignore the ways in which researchers from other fields of inquiry have successfully used it as a critical lens. This observation plus a careful tracing of the conceptual and historical roots of positioning theory have enabled McVee and her coauthors to suggest methodological areas in which contemporary literacy researchers can expect to make significant contributions to the theory.

"Gender Identity WOKE: A Theory of Trans★+ness for Animating Literacy Practices" (Chapter 20) by sj Miller raises critical consciousness by building on the intersections of spatial and hybridity theories. Social positioning theories, according to Miller, are still other examples of how the theory of Trans★+ness intersects with the broader literature on critical consciousness. Once embodied, the concept of WOKE, according to Miller, can alert literacy educators to the fact they "are summoned to understand, unpack, and unveil how school systems, literacy researchers, and teacher educators reinforce gender identity normativity" (e.g., by resorting to the male/female binary). The chapter concludes with a strategy for pushing back on essentializations posited by the author in *fourth space*.

Maneka Brooks in "Untapped Possibilities: Intersectionality Theory and Literacy Research" (Chapter 21) captures how her initial brush with intersectionality became a stepping stone toward theorizing what goes awry when literacy researchers depend on a concept Kimberlé Crenshaw calls "a single-axis analysis." In addition to unpacking this concept through an example drawn from research on long-term English learners, Brooks examines three theoretical principles that are key to understanding intersectionality theory. She then uses those principles to explore how embracing an intersectional lens can deepen literacy researchers' thinking about the design of their studies and hence, what they will be able to say about their findings. The chapter concludes with a section that addresses among other issues "the mythical limited scope of intersectionality theory."

"Reimagining Teacher Education" (Chapter 22) authored by Misty Sailors is what some might recognize as a book-end effect, of sorts, for the chapters that preceded it in this section. Indeed, the author's opening scenario suggests that discovering the potential for including imagination in theorizing teacher education has been a part of our field for quite some time—a potential just not acted upon until now. Sailors begins with a summarization of theories that have driven teacher education since behaviorism onward, including but not limited to humanism and adult learning, communities of practice, and liberation theory. In the second half of the chapter, she focuses on theories of imagination and imagining, which historically have derived from works on philosophy, psychology, sociology, phenomenology, and neuroscience. She explores the ways in which those theories can inform teacher education.

17

REGROUNDING CRITICAL LITERACY

Representation, Facts and Reality

Allan Luke

Introduction

Since the turn towards language and discourse in the social sciences in the past three decades, it has become increasingly rare for writers to refer to 'reality' or 'facts' without using single or double quote marks. For the conventional wisdom is, indeed, that realities are socially constructed by human beings through discourse. This has been complicated historically by the degree to which new media and expressive forms managed to blur, simulate, and disrupt Aristotelian distinctions between art and life, between image and object, between sign and signified, between discourse and representation. The concept of *mimesis* introduced in Aristotle's *Poetics* (1997), after all, depended on the independent existence of the object to be artistically represented. The risk always has been that bloggers and journalists, political and civic leaders, teachers and students alike are left unmoored to social or material reality, to work in a relativist universe of competing significations with no fixed epistemological grounds – with education reduced to a hall of intertextual mirrors.

Reality still looms large in everyday life, despite insistent and ongoing attempts to theoretically and pharmacologically eradicate it, to technologically overwrite it, to publicly misrepresent it as 'false' or 'fake', or, at the least, to place a large philosophic asterisk next to it. Consider the debate over climate change. However, this might appear to be a competition between contending versions of scientific knowledge, contending media representations of the debate, and economic doctrines and political ideologies at work – few human beings would doubt that there is a biosphere out there with some degree of actual facticity.

We might argue about how to name it, about the relative calibrations of change, and about causes. All appellations would indeed be discourse representations of 'truth'. But the alteration of an ecosystem; the loss of species; the emergence of new biological, meterological, atmospheric and geological phenomena and interactions are substantive and material, real, and consequential. All things may be constructed or construed through discourse and, indeed, all discourses are subject to variable and idiosyncratic interpretations – but some phenomena kill you; others just do not matter much. So even if we acknowledge the discourse construction of possible worlds, we need to make a parallel acknowledgement that all discourses are *not* the things of which they speak, nor do they have equivalent or comparable consequences, effects, and impacts in diverse worlds of material and social relations, human and non-human place and environment, interaction and action.

Perhaps the key philosophical and political issue in this millennium is *this* relationship between cultural systems of representation – traditional print texts, writing, mass media, journalism, advertisements, web pages, texts, visual arts and images, instant messages, digital communications – and social and economic, material and environmental realities. These 'modes of information' (Poster, 1990) stand in complex and dynamic relation to the material world, human technologies and labour, and social relations. In this philosophical, historical and theoretical chapter, I make the case that this relationship is the key educational question and curriculum issue facing educational systems. For education systems are, inter alia, systems of cultural representation (Luke, 2019)—institutions that both represent possible worlds and their cultural scripts, norms and practices and teach successive generations ways of using communication technologies to mediate this relationship. If indeed literacy remains a tool of cultural and social mediation (Cole, 1996), then critical literacies begin from the ethical scrutiny and analysis of modes of information with an orientation towards normative cultural and political analysis, action and interaction.

In regions with advanced urban information infrastructure, young people and adults live in a mediasphere that surrounds them with a seemingly endless and limitless flow of talk, broad and narrowcast media, visual images and texts of all modalities, and instant and digitally enabled communication. This sits alongside a robust transnational industry in the provision of the printed word, whether through books, newspapers, or screens. It is in relationship to this transnational political economy that governments, corporations, and educational institutions strive to mediate these flows – that is, to control and censor, tax, regulate, and capitalise upon who gets access to flows of information, and which texts and discourses are translatable into cultural and economic value and status, power and functionality. In these milieux, critical literacy involves a normative analysis of the relationship between contents, designs, shapes, and features of texts *and* their consequences in material and social contexts.

The rapidity of technological development, of media shift and crossover and the unruliness of users, designers, and developers have generated a volatility without precedent. Digital media (Google, Facebook, WeChat), hardware and software (Microsoft, Samsung, Apple, Oracle), digital infotainment and media (Sony, Dreamworks, Disney, Fox), and more traditional mixed-information corporations (Thomson/Reuters, Pearson, Newscorp) vie to manage and capitalise upon information, consolidate corporate control and ownership, regulate intellectual property and overtly shape its ideological and cultural content and uses (Castells, 2011). Further, there is substantial evidence now of a longstanding, extensive stealth infrastructure of mass surveillance, propaganda, and control. This includes policing and military institutions, state-sponsored and corporate intelligence agencies, and underground criminal organisations. It now extends to the activist communities that have arisen for the purposes of resistance and concerted action against these same developments and a range of organisations representing diverse political, cultural and social movements (Graham, 2017; Greenwald 2014).

The control, ownership, and ideological uses of these new flows are volatile and dynamic – yielding new forms of activism and social agency; anarchist, libertarian, secular and non-secular, and, depending on whose point of view you take, criminal action, while courts struggle to establish the parameters of legality, libel, and criminality in systems designed to govern print and face-to-face social relations, and to regulate commerce based on the exchange of material goods. In the past two years, the norms and conventions of political life, electoral politics, and legislation have been destabilised by social media, instant messaging, and an omniscient 24/7 multimedia news cycle. Powerful underground and grassroots communities of hackers, bloggers, and users work to establish their own procedural rules and protocols, with many destabilising and attacking state and corporate governance over communications, intellectual property, proprietary access and pay-per cost structures. If indeed the alchemy created by Gutenberg and Luther in 15th-century Europe led to assaults on canonical knowledge and, ultimately, book burnings on all sides – this universe of hacking of corporate and state security servers, intellectual property and copyright lawsuits, data mining for surveillance, marketing and criminal exploitation, and Wikileaks is the new battleground for the social and economic regulation of the value of textual representation. If this is indeed a version of the 'simultaneous universe' and 'electronic retribalization' envisioned by Marshall McLuhan (McLuhan & Fiore, 1968), the new information order increasingly resembles a combination of the surveillance state described by George Orwell and the hedonistic, narcissistic culture anticipated by Aldous Huxley.

There are worlds outside of this mediasphere where issues of access to writing and basic print literacy still persist. Autocratic and theocratic states attempt to maintain strict ideological control and censorship over information – Burma, North Korea, and Saudi Arabia, for example.[1] But the ongoing bids to censor the Internet and instant messaging in, for example, China and the Middle East point to the difficulties that ubiquitous and instant information flows pose for governments and multinational corporations that rely upon the control of who knows what and what will count as factual, truthful, and of significance (Lagerkvist, 2010). In a country like Singapore, for example, the public gained uncensored access to CNN and other global media after the first Gulf War. While the government maintains indirect and direct regulatory influence and control over print and broadcast media, and monitors and partially filters Internet traffic, it relies strongly on self-censorship by users (Lee, 2010). There are parallel lessons to be learned from Wikileaks and recent high-profile hackings of government and corporate servers about the fragility of control that government institutions, corporations, and individuals have over their proprietary information and texts.

Many countries are still engaged in the developmental struggle to establish functional school systems for the universal proliferation of basic literacy. There remain major populations, communities, and cultures that are not part of global information flows – either by spatial/technological isolation (e.g., Indigenous peoples in the Amazon, West Java, Central Africa, the South Pacific); by economic marginalisation (e.g., parts of Africa, West Asia, North and Western China); as the result of civil war and conflict (e.g., Yemen, Syria, Libya); or by deliberate cultural choice (e.g., Amish communities in Pennsylvania). As economies of scale shift, there are more cases of, for instance, the expanded use of mobile phone technology or satellite-based laptops amongst rural and remote populations to enhance trade and exchange, crop productivity or medical and community infrastructure. The effects of this spread remain mixed, often disrupting traditional knowledge, vernacular languages, and ways of life. But at the same time the spread of communications media historically has and continues to provide tools for the shaping and reshaping of material, social, and eco-biological relations (Innis, 1950).

While it is increasingly rare to refer to reality as a freestanding, non-problematic phenomenon, this new information and semiotic order is, in and of itself, a compelling social fact and reality. The theoretical and practical questions at the core of critical literacy programs is simple: Do changing media images, political statements, news reports, Internet websites, the language of laws, workplaces and everyday face-to-face talk have material effects upon peoples' lives, their work, the quality of social and civic relationships and their access to and use of resources? Certainly, communications technologies have changed the way many people work and learn; they have reshaped consumption and leisure, politics, and commerce, and what might count as public and private expression and experience. How they shape and can be used to reshape everyday lives and experience and knowledge are certainly things that, as critical literacy educators have already demonstrated, are viable with eight-year-olds developmentally in early print acquisition (e.g., Comber & Simpson, 2001; Vasquez, 2004); with disengaged, minority youth who have turned away from traditional print literacy pathways (e.g., Morrell, 2007); with second-language learners (Canagarajah, 2013; Kubota & Lin, 2009; Norton & Toohey, 2004); with college and university students from a range of socioeconomic and cultural backgrounds (cf. Tinberg, 2001); and with adults who have been economically and politically marginalised (e.g., Kumishiro & Ngo, 2007; Wallace, 2013).

Educational work in the field of critical literacy provides a key opportunity for the debating, unpacking, and learning about this family of questions: How does language, text, discourse and information make a difference? For whom? In what material, social, and consequential ways? In whose interests? According to what patterns, rules, and in what institutional and cultural sites?

These, I want to argue, are not fringe or boutique concerns of an elite literary, cultural studies or political education. Nor should these be elective of advanced options in an education system that is locked into the production of its human subjects as competitive capital for these new economies. Critical literacy is now old news. We can document four decades of diverse approaches to critical literacy that have arisen in the contexts of schooling, university study, adult basic and vocational education, second-language education, and, indeed, informal community-based education. In education systems in the United States and Commonwealth countries, and in other English-speaking countries, critical literacy has taken different developmental paths in a range of curriculum areas: English, second-language study, literature study, college composition, language arts, arts and visual education, technology and design education, and indeed, crossovers to numeracy and mathematics, social studies and history, and science education (e.g., Vasquez, 2016). Unlike many other educational developments, critical literacy did not originate or initially flourish in the countries of the English-speaking North and West. It originated in what was then called the 'third world', in regions undergoing decolonization, through languages other than English, with prototypical work in Portuguese and Spanish – and applications under way in Putonghua, Cantonese, Filipino, Farsi, Arabic, Slovenian, Japanese, Bahasa Malaysia, Bahasa Indonesia and other languages. This should be indicative of the current spread of research and development work on critical literacy globally; across nation states, education systems, cultures and political economies; and often directly in response to pressure from state authorities to monitor, censor, and control the work of citizens and scholars, teachers, and students.

This chapter has two purposes. It provides a brief introductory overview of the two major approaches to critical literacy: critical pedagogy and critical text analysis. This review is both theoretical and practical, covering the foundational assumptions of each approach and its historical genealogies and linking these to practical strategies for the teaching and learning of literacy. They are well established and documented (e.g., Kubota & Miller, 2017; Morgan & Ramanathan, 2005). My purpose here is *not* to make the case for them as an original, innovative, or radical alternatives yet again.

Instead, my second task is to make the case that all approaches of critical literacy attempt to practically bring together two distinct philosophies of text and representation: historical materialist critique of the state and political economy on the one hand, and poststructuralist and postmodern theories of discourse on the other. Various pedagogic languages are used to bridge the two, including literary and cultural studies text analysis, functional and critical linguistics. But the theoretical tension is a central practical pivot for approaches to critical literacy: understanding how the representation of possible worlds through language and image, texts and discourses shapes and alters the material and social, bio-ecological and economic realities and facts of these worlds. This tension leads to core educational questions: What are the real and material consequences of texts and discourses? How can and, more importantly, how *should* we reshape them?

Literacy and the Production of the Subject

Literacies – in traditional print and multimodal forms, on paper and screen – are malleable social and cultural practices with communications technologies. While there may indeed be particular cognitive, semiotic, and social 'affordances' (Kress, 2003) and cultural and economic 'biases' (Innis, 1949) affiliated with particular technologies – the specific practices, functions, and uses of texts and discourses that are prescribed and transmitted in any particular literacy education model are not given by the linguistic or technical features of the medium per se. They are instead specific selections from a theoretically infinite array of possible practices. Consider, for example, what schools typically teach six- and seven-year-olds to 'do' with print texts: that they are stories, that stories are for pleasure and fun, that we can think and talk about they mean, about individual affect and so forth. Far from these practices being natural or intrinsic to the medium of print – we could as readily teach children that texts are for memorization and chanting, that they are never to be contested, indeed as some communities already do. That is, we could assign very different sociocultural functions, discourse contents, and cognitive affordances to the medium and text in question. Such are the normative choices that all schemes for literacy education must make, whether deliberately or by default. As curriculum decisions, these are 'selective traditions of literacy' (Luke, 1988), motivated selections from a corpus of texts and discourses, skills, and practices that build and sustain particular cultural, social class and political ideologies, forces and interests.

When we refer to the social practices of reading, then, we refer to particular psychological skills, linguistic competences, cognitive strategies and so forth, but we also refer to specific preferred text types and conventionally affiliated discourses, particular social ideologies, particular cultural scripts for what people should do with text, when, where and to what social, political, economic and cultural – intellectual and spiritual – purposes and ends. To reiterate: these are normative cultural decisions – not technical scientific ones. The curriculum decisions about how to shape literate practices are based on a longitudinal and developmental vision of a fully-fledged literate subject using texts and discourses for particular forms of social and cultural action in identifiable social, cultural and institutional fields.

That the range of possible human practices with text is virtually infinite does not mean that these are, in a Saussurean sense, altogether 'arbitrary'. The relationships between signs and signifiers, between words and objects, between grammar and action may indeed be theoretically arbitrary, and the institutional selection of one text, disposition, or practice over another may, in a purely descriptive sense, be arbitrary vis à vis particular textual features or characteristics to be assigned cultural capital (cf. Bourdieu & Passeron, 1990). But they are not arbitrary in the sense that literate practices make up repertoires of conventional social and intellectual functions (Halliday, 1978) with exchange value in specific institutional, disciplinary and social fields (e.g., in universities, public fora, particular workplaces or specific disciplinary fields). Depending on the rules of exchange in given social and cultural fields of use, specific ways of doing things with text have 'exchange value' (cf. Bourdieu, 1991).

My point, then, is that *all* models of literacy education are bids to intergenerationally reproduce particular forms of disciplined tool use with the technologies of print and other media. It is not surprising, then, that those who approach the definition and study of literacy from particular disciplinary and foundational perspectives tend to normatively argue for the production of a literate subject who embodies that specific discipline. For example, literary poststructuralists advocate the production of specialised skills of deconstruction; cultural anthropologists argue for students to study language in use in the community; those who define literacy as a cognitive, scientific process define higher-order literacy in terms of recall, taxonomic analysis and falsification; feminist poststructuralists argue for the deconstruction of gendered speaking positions and representations; functional linguists argue for students to acquire a detailed and explicit knowledge of lexicogrammatical system and choice – and, indeed, various religions define and align the reading of sacred texts tautologically as evidence of having mastered a particular spiritual discipline (Kapitzke, 1995).

Models of critical literacy are not exempt. That is, they are not 'true' or 'untrue' but rather they are normative bids to construct a particular kind of cultural and political subject, to shape and produce particular ethical stances and practices with text (Muspratt, Luke, & Freebody, 1998). They are tethered to particular political bids to reconstruct what is done with the technology of writing in specific social class, cultural and political interests; under the auspices of broad principles of social and economic justice, freedom of expression and political self-determination, human rights and emancipation. Note that these are principles developed from Western and Anglo/European ethics, critical theory and philosophy, and liberal political theory (Luke, Sefton-Green, Graham, Kellner, & Ladwig, 2017). They are not necessarily locally generated cultural principles and may constitute, in themselves, forms of external cultural imposition. In consequence, models of critical literacy select and shape particular practices for students, and general claims about, for example, 'empowerment' make broad assumptions about the political and cultural efficacy of specific textual practices. The most rudimentary models of functional literacy make the case that the acquisition of basic skills generates improved pathways to employment. Similarly, models of critical literacy are predicated upon the assumption that particular approaches to reading (e.g., identifying social class ideologies underlying text messages; critiquing the economic or political motives of authors of particular texts) or writing (e.g., developing online digital art, digitally archiving community elders' stories) can generate both individual (e.g., identity, affiliation, agency) and collective effects (e.g., participation in larger social institutions and movements).

Critical Pedagogy

The term 'critical' has a distinctive etymology in Western philosophy and science. It is derived from the Greek adjective *kriticos*, meaning 'the ability to argue and judge'. Paulo Freire's (1970) revolutionary educational philosophy defined *critical literacy* as the capacity to analyse, critique and transform social, cultural, and political texts and contexts. Working in indigenous and peasant communities in Brazil, Freire had an approach to critical literacy that was grounded in dialectical materialist, phenomenological and contemporary Christian existentialist philosophies. It stands as a major contribution to a then emergent school of Catholic thought and political activism, liberation theology (Kirylo, 2011). Freire argued that the literacy transmitted in conventional schooling was based on a 'banking model' of education, wherein learners' lives, cultures, knowledge, and aspirations were taken as irrelevant. He advocated a dialogical approach to literacy based on ethical principles of reciprocal exchange. This dialectical move would critique, negate, and transform binary relationships of oppressed and oppressor, teacher and learner. 'Cultural circles' would begin with an analysis of participants' specific contexts, problems, struggles and aspirations. This problematicisation of the world can then lead on to engagement with the relevant technical, specialist, or expert knowledge required to address specific problems or taking on affiliated tasks (cf. Escobar, Fernandez, Guevara-Niebla, & Freire, 1994).

The acquisition of literacy entails the naming and renaming, narrating and analysing of life worlds as part of a problem-posing and problem-solving pedagogy. Accordingly, Freire's work focuses literacy educators on the transitivity and teleology of reading and writing: that they are always about substantive lives and material realities; and that they are always goal- and problem-directed. 'Reading the word', then, entails 'reading the world' (Freire & Macedo, 1987), enlisting one's power to critique and supplant dominant ideologies and false consciousness. Technical mastery of written language and other codes, then, is a means to broader social and cultural agency, individual and collective transformation – not an end in itself.

There is an extensive literature that extends Freire's principles and approaches in a broad project of 'critical pedagogy' (e.g., Darder, Baltodano, & Torres, 2003; Kincheloe, 2008; Lankshear & McLaren, 1993). Freire's work draws from Marx the key concept that ruling-class ideology defines school knowledge and ideology. By this view, conventional and uncritical approaches to literacy are expressions of dominant, ruling-class ideology that succeed in creating a receptive literacy, involving passive reproduction of systematically distorted views of the world. The alternative is to begin from learners' worldviews, in effect turning learners into teachers and inventors of the curriculum. By this account, the process of critical literacy entails a renaming of the world and an undoing of forms of 'false consciousness', supplanting these with 'critical consciousness'. The focus then of critical literacy is on students' engaging in forms of ideology critique: exposing and reconstructing misleading ideological versions of the world provided in media, literature, textbooks, and everyday texts (Shor & Freire, 1987).

Critical analyses of competing ideologies and economic conditions were central to literacy campaigns initiated by Freire and colleagues in Mozambique, and they are the focus of current efforts at explicitly political pedagogies in countries like Brazil, Venezuela, Peru, and Mexico (Kukendall, 2010). In such curricula, students are involved in analysis of the effects of colonialism, imperialism, autocracy, class and racial division, and unequal economic relations. In Freirian terms, this analysis entails working with learners to use language to name and *problematicise* the world – that is to take everyday ideological constructions of class, race, gender, sexuality, war, peace, conflict and so forth, and to make them problematic through dialogic exchange. In such a setting, traditional author- ity and epistemic knowledge relations of teachers and student shift: learners become teachers of their understandings and experiences, and teachers become learners of these same contexts. This shift might entail setting open, dialogic conditions of exchange by establishing a cultural circle amongst adult learners. In school classrooms, it might entail establishing democratic conditions where authentic exchange can occur around social, political, and cultural issues (Lewison, Leland, & Harste, 2007). Note that these approaches are based on a key assumption from Marxist ideology critique: that once ruling-class ideology is named and cleared out of the way, undistorted, accurate, and factual versions of history, community formation, and social and economic conditions can be brought to the table for analysis and action. Again, and as noted at the onset of this chapter, critical pedagogy raises the very practical pedagogical and curriculum question of the relationship between representation and truth, objectivity, reality, facticity and lived experience. But ultimately in and of itself it is unable to resolve the question without recourse to specific normative philosophical and political claims and doctrines about the nature and character of liberation and freedom, human rights, equality, sustainability and an ethics of care, and, indeed, justice – and indeed, without empir- ical, experiential and interpretive evidence about actual social, material and ecological conditions, relations and the degree to which these are affiliated with the actions, policies and interests of the state, its communities and interests, and those of specific social and economic institutions and agents. That is, approaches to critical pedagogy are dependent upon the mobilisation of specific critical social and political theories – typically these are derived, variously from neomarxian social theory, Frankfurt School sociology and pragmatics, postcolonial and critical race theories, and indeed, liberal democratic models of social justice.

Current critical literacy practices also draw from British and American cultural studies. Land- mark work by Richard Hoggart (1957) and Raymond Williams (1958) set the directions for approaches to critical literacy: (1) the expansion of textual and cultural objects beyond canonical and literary texts to include the everyday cultural forms and practices; (2) a focus on critical literacy as a counter-hegemonic form of critique that might, in turn, (3) enable a revoicing of marginalised class culture. Practical approaches to critical literacy advocated in US schools start from a focus on community relations or political events, moving towards agentive, alternative analyses (e.g., Morrell, 2007; Vasquez, 2007). In schools and universities, these approaches also focus literacy on forms of community study, the analysis of social movements, and political activism (e.g., Kumishiro & Ngo, 2007; Ávila & Pandya, 2014). Drawing from cultural studies, they have also involved the devel- opment of a critical 'media literacy', focusing on the analysis of popular cultural texts including advertising, news, broadcast media, and the Internet (e.g., Alvermann & Hagood, 2000; Ávila & Pandya, 2014; Kellner & Share, 2005; Share, 2015). Finally, there is a broad focus in these models on the development of alternative versions of history, altering dominant and hegemonic descriptions of national history, colonialism, and political processes. This is viewed as a process of 'recognitive justice' (Fraser, 1997), whereby marginalised histories, epistemological stances, vernacular languages and cultural knowledges from minority cultures are enlisted to revise, alter, and reconstruct the curriculum and school knowledge.

In this context, various marginalised groups have staked the grounds for approaches that require the aforementioned political ideology critique but also set the grounds for a strong focus on the sig- nificance of culture, broadly construed as shared value systems, interactional patterns, and forms of affiliation. This was part of the major critique of critical pedagogy that emerged in the early 1990s, when feminist scholars began to argue that the model risked ideological imposition that was con- trary to its ethos and did not adequately consider issues of gendered standpoint. In everyday practice, there was, and is, a parallel risk of pedagogic imposition given the complex forms of gendered and raced voice and power, identity, and subjectivity at work in the interactional contexts of classrooms and cultural circles (Luke, 2018; Luke & Gore, 1991). The critiques raised by poststructuralist feminists have had a major impact on critical pedagogy. Especially in Australia and Canada, approaches to school reading entail a critique of textual and media representations of women and girls as ideological and patriarchal – that is, as projecting dominant constructions of gender and sexuality and inequitable patterns of face-to-face interaction (Mellor, O'Neill, & Patterson, 2000). Relatedly, it has led to a stronger focus on standpoint and agency in critical educational theory, including a critique of critical pedagogy itself as a potential form of patriarchal or ethnocentric practice.

A parallel development draws upon postcolonial and critical race theory. American approaches to critical literacy have developed a strong focus on the 'politics of voice' (Darder et al., 2003); on building interaction around the distinctive cultural histories, identities and contexts faced by groups marginalised on the basis of difference of gender, language, culture and race, and sexual orientation. A critical approach to language and literacy education requires the setting of culturally appropriate and generative contexts for enactment of identity and solidarity (Kubota & Lin, 2009; Toohey & Norton, 2004). It extends a focus of critique on the political economy to examine everyday practices of patriarchy, racism, and sexism. There the enhancement of voice, speaking position and standpoint, and the practices of 'translanguaging' (Lau, Juby-Smith, & Desbiens, 2016; cf. Horner & Tetreault, 2017) become central pedagogical foci, with the assumption that these can be translated into forms of self-determination, agency, and social activism.

Discourse Analytic Approaches

The last three decades of ethnographic research on the social contexts and practices of literacy have established the cultural, social, cognitive, and linguistic complexity of its development and acquisition. This raises substantive educational challenges for critical pedagogy approaches. First, it is largely synchronic, advocating and practicing particular approaches to literacy pedagogy without a broader longitudinal template for developmental acquisition and use. While Freirian models provide a pedagogical approach, a political stance, and an orientation towards voice and ideology critique, they also raise difficult and persistent questions of how interpretive communities resolve issues of which cultural representations; which versions of truth and objectivity, political ideologies and ethical positions will be made to count in educational contexts (Muspratt et al., 1998). We will return to this issue momentarily. Further, Freirian models lack specificity in terms of how teachers and students can engage with the detailed and complex structures of texts, both traditional and multimodal. The acquisition of language, text and discourse requires the developmental engagement with levels of linguistic and discourse complexity (e.g., Gee, 1992; Lemke, 1996). Later models of critical literacy developed in Australia and the UK – conceptually and practically differentiated from critical pedagogy – attempt to come to grips with these key theoretical and practical issues.

An initial major critique of critical pedagogy approaches was that they overlooked the pressing need for students to master a range of textual genres, including those scientific forms that constitute powerful understandings of the social, physical, and material world (Halliday & Martin, 1995). The mastery of these same genres marks out a curricular glass ceiling in middle school, high school, and university study. Without the requisite mastery of expository writing, nominalization, intransitive and passive sentence-level syntax, specialised technical vocabulary, students may confront what David Corson (1985) termed a 'lexical bar'. According to systemic functional linguists, the mastery of genre entails a grasp of the social functions of lexical and syntactic functions, and an understanding of their relationships with affiliated discourses and ideologies (Hassan & Williams, 1996). Equitable access to how texts work, they argue, is an essential component to redistributive social justice (Fraser, 1997) in literacy education, and cannot be achieved through a principal focus on voice or ideology critique. The affiliated approach to critical literacy, then, makes the case for explicit instruction and direct access to 'Secret English' and 'genres of power' (Kalantzis & Cope, 1996). This is, indeed, a strong and explicit emphasis on a redistributive model that emphasises equality of access to dominant forms of cultural and linguistic capital. Yet there are unresolved issues about what balance of direct access to canonical and culturally significant text forms, on the one hand, and critique, on the other, might constitute an enfranchising and politically activist approach to critical literacy.

The alternative approach is based upon critical discourse analysis, an explicitly political derivative of systemic functional linguistics. Bringing together ideology critique with an explicit instructional focus on teaching how texts work, Fairclough (1990) argues for the teaching of 'critical language awareness'. This entails teaching students the analysis of a range of texts – functional, academic, literary – attending to both their lexicogrammatical structure, their ideological contents and discourses, and their identifiable conditions of production and use. Drawing from Halliday (1978), critical linguistics makes broad distinctions between ideological formations in texts (field), their social functions (tenor), and their distinctive features (mode). This enables teachers and students to focus on how words, grammar, and discourse choices shape a representation or version of material, natural and sociopolitical worlds (Janks, 2010). It also enables a focus on how words and grammar attempt to establish relations of power between authors and readers, speakers and addressees. Furthermore, it enables a critical engagement with the accessibility, rules of exchange, and relations of control and power within those social fields where texts are used, by whom, and in whose interests. It may also entail discussion of silence, absence, and the 'unsaid' in texts and contexts (Luke, 2018).

While the Freirian model argued that the dialogic process of critical pedagogy was 'empowering', the discourse analytic approach has encountered two principal critiques. The first is that a concentration on the explicit teaching of text types or 'genres' runs the risk of treating these historical, diachronic cultural forms as static, synchronic phenomena. The risk is that pedagogy will entail a formalization and reification of the propositional structures and lexicogrammatical choices of particular genres (Freedman & Medway, 2005). This is a particularly interesting linguistic/semiotic and curriculum problem in light of the rapid development and, indeed, instant obsolescence of digital and multimodal forms of writing and composition (Bowen & Whithaus, 2014). The practical risk here is that reproduction of genre and lexicogrammatical convention by students can reinforce and consolidate the hegemony of dominant cultures, institutions, and discourses, even as it attempts to enhance access for learners from marginalised communities. That is, that the attempt to achieve redistributive justice through access to dominant texts and their systems of exchange might be undertaken at the expense of a recognitive justice that sets out to critique and reconstruct these same texts and institutions.

The other affiliated theoretical move in critical discourse analysis is to turn attention towards the social and institutional fields where literacy is used, deployed, and generates value. Literate competence and capacity in both critical pedagogy and discourse analytic approaches is taken as affiliated with cultural, social, economic and political power that is potentially generalisable and transferable across contexts. Yet any instance of the use and value of literate practice is sociologically contingent on the rules of exchange in specific social and institutional fields (Luke, 2018). That is, whether, how and in what ways literacy might count depends on where it is deployed and by whom, and whether it is deployed in combination with the availability of various other forms of social, economic, and cultural capital. To address this, the critical discourse analysis approach extends the analysis of text and discourses to include dialogue on the institutional fields where they are written, used, read, and interpreted. Here the focus is on identifying and theorizing the rules of exchange that enable 'symbolic power' (Bourdieu, 1991) to be realised. This entails engaging students in the analysis and critique of those sites where texts are used and put to work, ranging from media, bureaucracies, corporations, businesses and worksites, civic and public institutions, and, of course, schools and universities. Hence, the discourse analytic approach sets the grounds for a fuller sociological, cultural, and political analysis of institutions, the state and corporation, and their operational relations of knowledge and power.

Critical literacy – by this account – entails the developmental engagement by learners with the major texts, discourses and modes of information, and, importantly, with the critical analyses of those social institutions and cultural sites where texts are used and exchanged. It attempts to attend to the ideological and hegemonic functions of texts, as in critical pedagogy models. But it augments this by providing students with technical resources for analysing how texts and discourses work – where, how, and in whose interests. For example, this might entail the analysis of a textbook or media representation of political or economic life. But in addition to questions of how a text might reflect learners' life worlds and experiences, it might also engage in dialogue about how the structure of specific clauses and sentences attempts to define the world and situate the reader in relation to that definition (Wallace, 2003; Janks, 2010). Finally, it sets out to extend the study of texts to critically examine institutional and cultural codes, rules and norms and whose interests these serve.

The Theoretical and Practical Problem: Representation and Reality

Critical literacy approaches view language, texts, and discourses as the principal means for representing and reshaping possible worlds. The aim is the development of human capacity to use texts to analyse and transform social relations and material conditions in their human interests and those of their communities and cultures. As a cultural and linguistic practice, then, critical literacy entails an understanding of how increasingly sophisticated texts and discourses can be manipulated to represent and, indeed, alter the world. As an educational philosophy, then, critical literacy education is premised on an ethical imperative for freedom of dialogue and the need to critique all texts, discourses, and ideologies as a means for equity and social justice.

Yet it is inevitably confronted with the problem of normativity: of whose reading of a text will count, of whose version of the world will count, and on what grounds. Freirian models begin from an explicit focus on authenticity of voice of participants in cultural circles, and in practice have moved to stress cultural standpoint and speaking rights. Critical discourse analysis models have tended to focus on the ideological contents and social relations coded in texts. The broad premise is that reality is constructed socially through discourse; that all texts are potentially ideological, and hence should be the subject of critical analysis and scrutiny.

But both approaches raise a core practical question: How do we ascertain truth and fact? This requires an acknowledgement of the existence of 'truth' and 'reality' outside of the particular texts in question and, indeed, realities outside the complex web of intertextual descriptions and relations formed by multiple available texts.

Consider this current example. With the support of the Tea Party and religious and conservative groups, the *Louisiana Science Education Act of 2008* set new grounds for curriculum debate. It argued that the discussion of intelligent design and 'alternative' views of science was necessary to ensure academic freedom in schools. But are we to treat the texts of evolutionary theory, for example, as ideological representations or as scientific truths? The move towards critical discourse analysis and text deconstruction may place discourse-based models of critical literacy at odds with traditional Marxist ideology critique. Does critical literacy mean, for example, that texts about the Holocaust or slavery, or about global warming, constitute yet further or more textual representations of the world? To be critiqued and deconstructed in terms of their rhetorical positioning devices or hidden ideological assumptions? What about truths, facts about history, social and material reality that they purport to represent?

My point here is that models of critical literacy in and of themselves require a commitment to the existence and accessibility of 'truth', 'facts', and 'realities' outside of the texts in question and, potentially, as having an existence independent of their immediate discursive construction. Freirian approaches typically resolve this through the mobilisation of reading and writing as part of a broader investigation of issues and facts, histories and cultures, as a means for 'reading the world' (Freire & Macedo, 1987; cf. Lankshear & Lawler, 1987). Critical discourse analytic approaches focus on the 'conditions of production' and 'conditions of reception' of the text (Fairclough, 1990): that is, the historical, cultural and political conditions of authorship and audience interpretation. In practical terms, this suggests the epistemological and educational strengths and limits of an exclusive focus on text analysis without broader cross-curricular scientific, social scientific, and aesthetic inquiry. Simply, while authentic 'voice' *and* close textual analysis may be necessary elements of critical literacy education, neither in itself provides sufficient empirical or ethical grounds for social and cultural action. Both must then turn to explore other texts and the facts, other material and social realities, and other epistemological, disciplinary and cultural frameworks for ethical and political judgement and action. Critical literacies depend upon an engagement with critical theories of society and culture, knowledge and power, economy and politics, and, indeed, ecology and place, biosphere and environment.

The concept of ideology sits at the foundation of approaches to critical pedagogy, critical literacy, and, indeed, critical educational theories. The term was developed by French philosopher Antoine Destutt de Tracy (1754–1836) to outline a system of liberal ideas in the aftermath of the French Revolution. It was reappropriated and redefined by Karl Marx to refer to the forms of false consciousness that were propagated by ruling classes. For Marx (1978), those classes that controlled the means of production had further extended their control to the 'means of mental production'. In this way, Marx argued, ideology worked like 'camera obscura', literally turning reality on its head and distorting vision (Marx & Engels, 1845/1970). Given the ongoing connection between ownership of the traditional means of production and the emergence of powerful new information/media/technology corporations which define and control the 'modes of information' (Poster, 1990), questions of ideology, critique, false consciousness and our capacity to ascertain, weigh and determine issues of truth, knowledge, human interests and power remain focal, troubling and unfinished theoretical and practical business. But while Marx and his 19th-century colleagues had recourse and belief in the possibility of non-ideological, objective truths – those of a still ascendant empirical science, of the emergent fields of economics, and of a philosophic 'scientific socialism' – we have arrived in a different historical moment, one of contending knowledge systems and diverse epistemological and historical stances. Conflict over what might count as science, and whether and how science and ideology, both classically defined, stand in relation to 'truth' arguably constitutes a threat to the social contract of liberal democracy. This era of radical scepticism, of intellectual and public heteroglossia and polysemy, while not historically unprecedented, raises central challenges which are at once epistemic and cognitive, political, and cultural – and, indeed, educational and pedagogical.

Particularly in the new mediasphere, the relationship between discourse and material biosocial worlds, between representation and historical/empirical reality remains the focal issue in critical pedagogy and critical literacy education. Far from being a conceptual or theoretical flaw or contradiction, it provides teachers and learners, curriculum developers, and educational researchers with a practical starting point and overall goal for teaching and learning. Unpacking the relationship between discourse representation and reality remains *the* core question of critical literacy as theory and practice.

Note

1 See the *Freedom House* updated reports on national internet censorship: https://freedomhouse.org/report/freedom-net/2016/saudi-arabia

References

Alvermann, D. E., & Hagood, M. C. (2000). Critical media literacy: Research, theory, and practice in "new times." *Journal of Educational Research, 93*(3), 193–205.
Aristotle (1997). *Poetics* (M. Heath, Trans.). London: Penguin.
Ávila, J., & Pandya, J. (Eds.). (2014). *Critical digital literacies as social praxis.* Berlin: Peter Lang.

Bourdieu, P. (1991). *Language and symbolic power.* J. Thompson (Ed.). (G. Raymond, M. Adamson, Trans.). Cambridge, MA: Harvard University Press.

Bourdieu, P., & Passeron, J. C. (1990). *Reproduction.* 2nd ed. (R. Nice., Trans.). London: Sage.

Bowen, T., & Whithaus, C. (Eds.). (2014). *Multimodal literacies and emerging genres.* Pittsburgh, PA: University of Pittsburgh Press.

Canagarajah, S. A. (2013). *Critical academic writing and multilingual students.* Ann Arbor, MI: University of Michigan Press.

Castells, M. (2011). *Communication power.* Oxford: Oxford University Press.

Cole, M. (1996). *Cultural psychology.* Cambridge: Cambridge University Press.

Comber, B., & Simpson, A. (Eds.). (2001). *Negotiating critical literacies in classrooms.* Mahwah, NJ: Lawrence Erlbaum.

Corson, D. (1985). *The lexical bar.* London: Pergamon.

Darder, A., Baltodano, M., & Torres, R. (Eds.). (2003) *The critical pedagogy reader.* New York, NY: Routledge.

Escobar, M., Fernandez, A. L., Guevara-Niebla, G., & Freire, P. (1994). *Paulo Freire on higher education.* Albany, NY: State University of New York Press.

Fairclough, N. (Ed.). (1990). *Critical language awareness.* London: Longman.

Fraser, N. (1997). *Justice interruptus.* New York: Routledge.

Freedman, A., & Medway, P. (2005). *Genre and the new rhetoric.* London: Taylor & Francis.

Freire, P. (1970). *Pedagogy of the oppressed* (M. Ramos, Trans.) New York, NY: Continuum.

Freire, P., & Macedo, D. (1987). *Literacy: Reading the word and the world.* South Hadley, MA: Bergin & Garvey.

Gee, J. P. (1992). *Social linguistics and literacies.* London: Taylor & Francis.

Graham, P. (2017). *Strategic communication, corporatism and eternal crisis: The Creel century.* New York, NY: Routledge.

Greenwald, G. (2014). *No place to hide: Edward Snowden, the NSA and the surveillance state.* New York, NY: Metropolitan.

Halliday, M. A. K. (1978). *Language as social semiotic.* London: Edward Arnold.

Halliday, M. A. K., & Martin, J. R. (1995). *Writing science.* London: Taylor & Francis.

Hassan, R., & Williams G. (Eds.). (1996) *Literacy in society.* London: Longman.

Hoggart, R. (1957). *The uses of literacy.* Harmondsworth: Penguin.

Horner, B., & Tetreault, L. (Eds.). (2017). *Crossing divides: Translingual writing pedagogies and programs.* Logan, UT: Utah State University Press.

Innis, H. (1949). *The bias of communications.* Toronto: University of Toronto Press.

Innis, H. (1950). *Empire and communications.* Toronto: University of Toronto Press.

Janks, H. (2010). *Literacy and power.* London: Routledge.

Kalantzis, M., & Cope, B. (Eds.). (1996). *The powers of literacy.* London: Taylor & Francis.

Kapitzke, C. (1995). *Literacy and religion.* Amsterdam: John Benjamins.

Kellner, D., & Share, J. (2005). Toward critical media literacy: Core concepts, debates, organisation and policy. *Discourse* 3, 369–386.

Kincheloe, J. (2008). *Critical pedagogy primer* (4th ed.). New York, NY: Peter Lang.

Kirylo, J. D. (2011). Liberation theology and Paulo Freire. *Counterpoints,* 385, 167–193.

Kress, G. (2003). *Literacy in the new media age.* London: Routledge.

Kubota, R., & Lin, A. (Eds.). (2009). *Race, culture and identities in second language learning.* New York, NY: Routledge.

Kubota, R. & Miller. E. (2017). Re-examining and re-envisioning criticality in language studies: Theories and practice. *Critical Inquiry in Language Studies, 14,* 129–157.

Kukendall, A. J. (2010). *Paulo Freire and the cold war politics of literacy.* Chapel Hill, NC: University of North Carolina Press.

Kumishiro, K., & Ngo, B. (Eds.). (2007). *Six lenses for anti-oppressive education.* New York, NY: Peter Lang.

Lagerkvist, J. (2010) *After the internet, before democracy: Competing norms in Chinese media and society.* Berlin: Peter Lang.

Lankshear, C., & Lawler, M. (1987). *Literacy, schooling and revolution.* London: Falmer.

Lankshear, C., & McLaren, P. (Eds.). (1993). *Critical literacy.* Albany, NY: State University of New York Press.

Lau, S., Juby-Smith, B., & Desbiens, I. (2016). Translanguaging as transgressive practice: Promoting critical literacy in a multi-age bilingual classroom. *Critical Inquiry in Language Studies, 14,* 99–127.

Lee, T. (2010). *The media, cultural control and government in Singapore.* London: Routledge.

Lemke, J. (1996). *Textual politics.* London: Taylor & Francis.

Lewison, M., Leland, C., & Harste, J. (2008). *Creating critical classrooms.* Mahwah, NJ: Lawrence Erlbaum.

Luke, A. (1988) *Literacy, textbooks and ideology.* London: Falmer Press.

Luke, A. (2018). *Critical literacy, schooling and social justice.* New York, NY: Routledge.

Luke, A. (2019). *Educational policy, narrative and discourse.* New York, NY: Routledge.

Luke, A., Sefton-Green, J., Graham, P., Kellner, D. & Ladwig, J. (2017) Digital ethics, political economy and the curriculum: This changes everything. In K. Mills, A. Stournaiuolo & J. Pandya-Zacher, Eds., *Handbook of writing, literacies and education in digital culture* (pp. 251–262). New York, NY: Routledge.

Luke, C., & Gore, J. (Eds.). (1991) *Feminisms and critical pedagogy.* London: Routledge.

McLuhan, M., & Fiore, Q. (1968). *War and peace in the global village.* New York, NY: Bantam.

Marx, Karl (1978). The civil war in France. In R. C. Tucker (Ed.). *The Marx-Engels reader.* (2nd ed, pp. 618–652). New York: Norton.

Marx, K., & Engels, F. (1845/1970). *The German ideology* (C. J. Arthur, ed.). New York, NY: New World.

Mellor, B., O'Neill, M., & Patterson, A. (2000) *Reading stories.* Perth, WA: Chalkface Press/National Council of Teachers of English.

Morgan, B., & Ramanathan, V. (2005) Critical literacies and language education: Global and local perspectives. *Annual Review of Applied Linguistics, 25,* 151–169.

Morrell, E. (2007) *Critical literacy and urban youth.* New York, NY: Routledge.

Muspratt, S., Luke, A., & Freebody, P. (1998) *Constructing critical literacies.* New York, NY: Hampton Press.

Norton, B., & Toohey, K. (Eds.). (2004). *Critical pedagogies and language learning.* Cambridge: Cambridge University Press.

Pandya, J., & Ávila, J. (Eds.). (2014). *Moving critical literacies forward.* New York, NY: Routledge.

Poster, M. (1990). *The mode of information.* Chicago, IL: University of Chicago Press.

Share, J. (2015). *Media literacy is elementary.* New York, NY: Peter Lang.

Shor, I., & Freire, P. (1987). *A pedagogy for liberation.* South Hadley, MA: Bergin & Garvey.

Tinberg, H. (2001). Review: Are we good enough? Critical literacy and the working class. *College English, 63,* 353–360.

Vasquez, V. (2004). *Negotiating critical literacies with young children.* Mahwah, NJ: Lawrence Erlbaum.

Vasquez, V. (2016). *Critical literacy across the K-6 curriculum.* New York, NY: Routledge.

Wallace, C. (2003). *Critical reading in language education.* London: Palgrave Macmillan.

Wallace, C. (2013). *Literacy and the bilingual learner.* London: Palgrave Macmillan.

Williams, R. (1958). *Culture and society: 1780–1950.* London: Chatto & Windus.

Williams, R. (1977). *Marxism and literature.* Oxford: Oxford University Press.

18

A RELATIONAL MODEL OF ADOLESCENT LITERACY INSTRUCTION

Disrupting the Discourse of "Every Teacher a Teacher of Reading"

Donna E. Alvermann and Elizabeth Birr Moje

In this chapter, we examine conditions that have enabled the discourse of "every teacher a teacher of reading" to exist for nearly a century, yet without widespread implementation in American secondary schools. We examine this phenomenon in three ways: first, through an overview of the key issues and individuals that have influenced models of adolescent literacy instruction in the past; second, through the use of Michel Foucault's (1984/1988) concept of genealogy, a historical analytic that makes possible the disruption of assumptions about the naturalness or inevitability of discourses, such as "every teacher a teacher of reading"; and finally, through a call for a relational model of adolescent literacy instruction that uses both a theory *of* action and a theory *in* action.

First, however, three terms need clarifying: *discourse, adolescent,* and *adolescent literacy.*

Bové (1995), a noted authority on Foucauldian concepts, defined *discourse* in terms of its functions:

> Discourses produce knowledge about humans and their society. But since the "truths" of these discourses are relative to the disciplinary structures, the logical framework in which they are institutionalized, they can have no claim upon us except that derived from the authority and legitimacy, the power, granted to or acquired by the institutionalized discourses in question.
>
> *(p. 56)*

Theoretically, then, the discourse of "every teacher a teacher of reading" produces its own truth value and its subjects (content area teachers) to the extent that the logical framework in which adolescent literacy instruction resides has the institutional authority to make that discourse seem natural and inevitable—as if the discourse itself is indispensable to adolescent literacy instruction.

Regarding the parameters of *adolescent* and *adolescent literacy*, we reject definitions that position young people as belonging to a group determined largely by chronological age and loosely associated age-driven factors (e.g., irresponsibility, emotionality). Rather than view adolescents as isolatable from the adult population, we favor arguments in the literature that show how claims of hierarchical positioning and sameness often preclude accounting for generational interdependency. For example, Hagood, Stevens, and Reinking's (2002) review of the cross-generational literature revealed concrete instances in which adolescents' proficiencies in some literacy practices exceeded those of adults engaged in the same practices (see also Barton, 2000; Green, Reid, & Bigum, 1998). The sameness principle, which would attribute to all youths the coming-of-age syndrome portrayed in numerous books and popular media, is both limiting and regularly challenged by scholars who view adolescence as a culturally constructed concept (Lesko, 2001; Vadeboncoeur & Stevens, 2005). Building on this concept, we view adolescent literacy not solely as a label that depends on arbitrary age categorizations but rather as a descriptor for the vast array of literate practices that young people bring to, and take away from, schooled learning.

Key Influences on Models of Adolescent Literacy Instruction

Historically, theoretical and practical implications of policies aimed at improving adolescent literacy instruction have garnered the attention of literacy educators, researchers, and policy makers both in the USA (e.g., Every Student Succeeds Act, 2015) and internationally (e.g., Garbe, Holle, & Weinhold, 2010). In an era marked by today's neoliberal perspectives on how literacy should function in a society—as a form of accumulated capital to be leveraged for competitive purposes—no discourse (or way of doing life) is left untouched, politically, educationally, or otherwise.

Two overarching and competing models of literacy instruction have dominated the field of adolescent literacy instruction since its inception: the autonomous and the ideological (Street, 1984, 1995). The autonomous model assumes that reading and writing are neutral processes, irrespective of context and larger social, historical, cultural, and political influences. It also assumes that a universal set of cognitive skills, when properly taught, can account for individual variations in a person's literacy achievement and interpretations of texts. By contrast, the ideological model, which draws from Street's (1984) anthropological fieldwork in Iran in the 1970s and from Scribner and Cole's (1981) research among the Vai in Liberia, assumes that reading and writing processes, while locally situated, are simultaneously subject to relations of power and ideological struggle regardless of how hidden or absent that struggle may seem. For example, Heath's (1983) early work in the Carolina Piedmont demonstrated that it is *how* children are socialized into different familial and community literacy practices (what she called "ways with words") and whether those ways match their schools' approaches to literacy instruction that influence, at least partially, their opportunities for future learning and choice of career paths.

To varying degrees, both the autonomous and ideological models have influenced the field of adolescent literacy instruction (Alvermann, 2009). What this impact looks like, time-wise, is captured here in a brief overview of adolescent literacy instruction with its focus on teaching text comprehension that culminated in the reader-text-activity-context (RTAC) model (RAND Reading Study Group, 2002), which is critiqued at length in a later section of this chapter.

Specific influences of the autonomous model are visible in the transition from oral reading and rote drills to silent reading instruction, which marked what Nila Banton Smith (1934/2002) viewed as the field's initial "emphasis on scientific investigation in reading" (p. 149). Smith attributed the impetus for this transition to Huey's (1908) influential research on reading for meaning (comprehension). From the start of the 20th century onward, theories supporting instructional models for teaching adolescents to comprehend teacher-assigned texts in subject area classrooms have sorted students on the grounds of test performance. Concern for students' welfare on such tests led Gray as early as 1925 to advise that "each teacher who makes reading assignments is responsible for the direction and supervision of the reading and study activities that are involved" (p. 71); hence, the timeworn expression "every teacher a teacher of reading."

Approximately six decades later, in a groundbreaking review of the literature on teaching adolescents to read in the disciplines, Moore, Readence, and Rickelman (1983) identified a major issue for 20th-century progressivist educators: namely, whether reading skills would continue to be taught separately from the subject area in which they were embedded or as an integrated part of that instruction. Although Laura Zirbes, an early progressivist educator from Columbia University, did not develop an instructional model per se, it is worth noting that her 1928 comparative analysis of techniques for improving the teaching of reading yielded support for simultaneous instruction in reading skills and subject matter. Like Zirbes, Ruth Strang was also instrumental in identifying ways of improving adolescent reading instruction in the content areas (Lapp, Guthrie, & Flood, 2007). However, it was likely Lou LaBrant's influence as president of the National Council of Teachers of English in the mid-1950s and her tireless advocacy for teaching reading as a part of all subject area courses (Alvermann, 2010) that prompted Hal Herber to instigate a federally funded research program involving cohorts of doctoral students at Syracuse University. Research from that program resulted in two editions of *Teaching Reading in Content Areas* (Herber, 1970, 1978). For the first time, secondary school teachers and teacher educators had access to a research-based curricular model for teaching adolescents to use reading skills and strategies while simultaneously learning subject matter.

Concurrent with this development in the field of adolescent literacy, the Center for the Study of Reading (CSR) at the University of Illinois, Urbana-Champaign received funding from the U.S. Department of Education in 1976 to study the underlying cognitive processes involved in text comprehension, including prior knowledge activation, metacognitive monitoring, and vocabulary development. Despite producing a significant body of basic research conducted mainly on college-age students' comprehension processing of researcher-prepared texts, which is still relevant today, the CSR's findings had limited ecological validity for addressing adolescent literacy instruction in secondary schools (Alvermann, Fitzgerald, & Simpson, 2006; Alvermann & Moore, 1991; Bean, 2000; Moje, Dillon, & O'Brien, 2000; Moore, 1996) as well as in teacher preparation programs (Anders, Hoffman, & Duffy, 2000).

Taking issue with the assumption that a universal set of cognitive skills, even when taught explicitly, can fully account for adolescents' motivation to read and their reading achievement, literacy researchers at the University of Georgia and University of Maryland collaborated on a grant proposal that led to a five-year (1992–1997) federally funded National Reading Research Center (NRRC) aimed at studying students' motivation to read in varying contexts both in and out of school. NRRC's mission benefited from the added perspectives of theorists working in cultural anthropology (Heath, 1983; Street, 1984), critical sociology of reading pedagogy (Baker & Luke, 1991; Luke, 2004), social linguistics (Gee, 1988), and sociocultural theory (Vygotsky, 1986; Wertsch, del Río, & Alvarez, 1995). It was the beginning of what Alexander and Fox (see chapter 2 this volume) refer to as the era of sociocultural learning (1986–1995), a time when focusing on the individual reader gave way to studying the contextual factors and group dynamics in which reading occurs. A parallel of this turn toward a more ideologically grounded model for studying adolescent reading instruction was a noticeable spike in the number of publications by researchers, teacher educators, and theorists who found reason to examine critically the larger historical, social, cultural, and political forces that were shaping the literacy practices of adolescents more generally, in and out of school (Alvermann, 2009; Moje, 2007; Vadeboncoeur, & Stevens, 2005).

Guided by sociocultural theories of learning and literacy that were prevalent at the time, the National Academy of Science charged the RAND Corporation, working in collaboration with the U.S. Department of Education's Office of Educational Research and Improvement, to appoint a panel of literacy experts whose goal would be to develop a definition of reading comprehension and set a national research agenda for improving classroom instruction in text comprehension (RAND Reading Study Group (RRSG), 2002). The panel was initially tasked with conducting an extensive review of the literature on reading comprehension that covered three previous decades of mostly experimental and quasi-experimental research related to cognitive processing in higher order learning. Based on their review, the RRSG panel reached a consensus on a model of reading comprehension that consisted of three elements: "the reader who is doing the comprehending, the text that is to be comprehended, and the activity in which comprehension is a part" (p. 11).

Notably, the resulting RTAC model of reading comprehension has continued to dominate the adolescent literacy field despite major reviews of the research literature (Dillon, O'Brien, Sato, & Kelly, 2011; Moje, 2007) that challenge the notion of generic literacy strategies being more important than the underlying structures of pedagogies originating within the separate disciplines (history, mathematics, chemistry, literature, the fine arts, and so on). Especially from the view of teachers in those disciplines, the call for "every teacher a teacher of reading" is often perceived as an unfair demand on teachers' time given their lack of training and expertise in teaching reading. Moreover, the call runs counter to institutionalized practices within disciplines (Bean, 2000; O'Brien, Stewart, & Moje, 1995). Prompted by this seeming impasse in the field of adolescent literacy instruction, we conducted a genealogical analysis of the "every teacher a teacher of reading" discourse to learn what enabling conditions (if any) might exist that make this discourse tenable from a rhetorical perspective, yet largely unacceptable to most subject area teachers. We chose Michel Foucault's (1976/1980) concept of genealogy as our analytic for discerning possible relations of power inherent in any such conditions.

Genealogy of the Discourse of "Every Teacher a Teacher of Reading"

Foucault (1971/1998) described genealogy as "gray, meticulous, and patiently documentary" (p. 569)—a description befitting an analytic that depends on an accumulation of historical source material written in words that take on slightly different meanings meant to appeal to different ways of thinking over time and context. Genealogy requires relentless attention to details that might otherwise escape notice when reading documents such as scholarly arguments, essays, research reports, legislative records, and policy statements. Unlike history's chronological listing of events in time-order fashion, Foucault's genealogy is not a search for the origin of a concept, discourse, or the like. Instead, in Foucault's words (1984/1988), a genealogy begins with "a question posed in the present" (p. 262). Engaging in a genealogical analysis of potentially enabling conditions that might make the discourse of "every teacher a teacher of reading" seem commonsensical and inevitable did not assume an originating event; nor did it assume that the discourse as it presently exists is the logical result of a series of events that followed a cause-effect order without discontinuities, errors, or chance.

It is equally important to bear in mind that a genealogy's focus on how something functions in the present does not preclude looking to the past (Foucault, 1971/1998); it merely negates, as noted previously, the existence of a single originating event and a lock-step progression of events that explain the present. In distinguishing his historical analytic from traditional historiography, Foucault employed a heuristic that he called *descent*. This heuristic guided us to seek multiple events (external to any cause-effect progression toward an ending point) and to remain "sensitive to their recurrence, not in order to trace the gradual curve of their evolution but to isolate the different scenes where they engaged in different roles" (p. 569). While analyzing descents in the literature on adolescent literacy instruction (e.g., through reviews of research, institutional and organizational reports, and policy documents), we remained open to *emergences*, a concept derived from the German word *entstehung*, which means "the moment of arising" (Foucault, 1971/1998, p. 576). Emergences typically show themselves in a network of events, such as those accompanying a paradigm change or more commonly those in which pressing social, political, and/or economic concerns shroud an issue to the point that it becomes part of everyday discourse channeled through multimodal ways of knowing (e.g., linguistic, visual imagery, sounds, memes, and performances).

Worth keeping in mind is that just as it is incorrect to search for uninterrupted continuity in descent, so too it is wrong to associate emergences with origins (Bové, 1995). Indeed, as we searched education reform documents, scholarly essays, legislative records, research reports, and policy statements for patterns of repetition and adjacency of events—that is, "their simultaneity within ostensibly different fields" (Bové, 1995, p. 60)—we did not seek causal influences among events. Instead, we noted relations of power involving domination, submission, and resistance that were embedded in networked events. Analyzing those relations of power made visible several potential disruptions of perceived ideas about the naturalness or inevitable progression of the discourse of "every teacher a teacher of reading."

That power relations are important in conducting a genealogy is made explicit in Prado's (2000) portrayal of emergence as "an appearance or advent enabled by a collision of forces, some of which enhance, nullify, or redirect others, and some of which combine with others to form new forces" (p. 37). By attending to the relations of power made visible during emergences and discontinuities in the literature on adolescent literacy instruction, we were able to disrupt some of our own assumptions about the inevitability of the discourse of "every teacher a teacher of reading." We did so not with the intent of bringing a century-old discourse to its knees, but instead to explore possibilities for its future. That goal is in keeping with a genealogy's interest in neither beginnings nor endings—only becomings. Analyzing such becomings produced the following insights into the persistence of "every teacher a teacher of reading."

Perceived Crises in Adolescent Literacy Instruction

The discourse of "every teacher a teacher of reading" appears in times of crisis and then fades into relative obscurity until the next crisis is declared. One such crisis was signaled in ACT's (2010) call for subject area teachers to provide literacy instruction in their disciplines that would build students' capacity to comprehend and respond to complex texts. ACT, a nonprofit organization that produces standardized high school achievement/college admission tests, joined the organizers of the Common Core State Standards Initiative to issue a report in 2010 titled "A First Look at the Common Core and College and Career Readiness." The report specified: "States must ensure that teachers in [all] subject areas use their unique content knowledge to foster students' ability to read, write, and communicate in the various disciplines" (p. 5). In 2012, the National Governors Association Center for Best Practice and the Council of Chief State School Officers (NGA/CCSSO) collaborated in designing a webpage titled "Myths vs. Facts" to address frequently asked questions in states considering adoption of the Common Core. An example drawn from this webpage, reads:

> *Myth*: English teachers will be asked to teach science and social studies reading materials.
> *Fact*: With the Common Core ELA Standards, English teachers will still teach their students literature as well as literary non-fiction. However, because college and career readiness overwhelmingly focuses on complex texts outside of literature, these standards also ensure students are being prepared to read, write, and research across the curriculum, including in history and science. These goals can be achieved by ensuring that teachers in other disciplines are also focusing on reading and writing to build knowledge within their subject areas.
>
> *(paras. 26–27)*

In this example, phrases such as "college and career readiness," "complex texts outside of literature," and "these standards also ensure" were presumably thought to carry sufficient weight and rationale for requiring teachers in disciplines other than the English language arts to also focus on reading and writing as knowledge-building processes within their subject areas.

Networked Events

The fact that ACT (2011), by its own admission, played a significant role in the wording of the Common Core standards and that it regularly provides benchmarks on the students it tests—for example, nationwide only 30% of the high school students tested in 2011 met the College Readiness Benchmark in science—points to an adjacency of networked events (Bové, 1995). In this way, a claimed crisis in adolescent literacy achievement in science (ACT, 2011) that aligned with both the Common Core State Standards Initiative and a specially designed webpage for deterring potential criticism of the Common Core could be viewed as supporting the naturalness or inevitability of "every teacher a teacher of reading." Yet, irrespective of any perceived seamlessness in these alignments, it is the case that networked events are prone to accidents.

Emergences and "Accidents"

Unlike the Common Core's (NGA/CCSSO, 2010) weighty documentation and online resources that spelled out specific guidelines for teaching the English language arts, the 2010 ACT report barely mentioned the role of non-English language arts teachers. In this collision of forces, or what Foucault (1971/1998) called "accidents" (p. 574), there was room for potential misinterpretation or dismissal of contradictory information. At the very least, confusion arising from these two reports could ostensibly have been viewed as destabilizing aspects of the discourse of "every teacher a teacher of reading." However, that appears not to have happened.

Nor did the widely distributed report of the Trends in International Mathematics and Science Study (TIMSS, 1999) make inroads into the literacy education community. In 1999, TIMSS showed that U.S. eighth-grade students' mathematics and science performance ranked significantly below their peers in other nations. A year later, the Program for International Student Assessment (PISA, 2000) report showed that 15-year-olds in the U.S. ranked 15th among their peers from OECD countries on three literacy scales: retrieving texts, interpreting texts, and reflecting on texts. Data from these international assessments also included information on the educational contexts in which the teaching and learning of subject-specific content took place. In both instances (ACT and the TIMSS/PISA comparisons), the "accidents" that occurred in Foucault's sense of the term (1971/1998) were perceived as issues not directly threatening to the maintenance of "every teacher a teacher of reading."

Rival Views of the Subject Area Teacher and the Teaching Process

Although important to our genealogy, a perceived crisis mentality did not account fully for historical discontinuities, which in our case were small "accidents" of insufficient force to disrupt the discourse of "every teacher a teacher of reading." If anything, they pointed to the enabling conditions that make the maintenance of such a discourse possible. Not so, however, when we consider the rival views of subject area teachers. But first, definitions are in order for two Foucauldian concepts: *power* and *discursive practice*. According to Foucault (1976/1980), "Power is neither given, nor exchanged, nor recovered, but rather exercised, and . . . it only exists in action" (p. 89). By noting such action in discursive practices common to adolescent literacy instruction—or what Foucault defined as "historically and culturally specific set[s] of rules for organizing and producing different forms of knowledge" (O'Farrell, 2007, para. 18)—we were able to document instances in which "every teacher a teacher of reading" seemed neither natural nor an inevitable fit with disciplinary teachers' instructional intentions.

The first of several "accidents" made visible the deviations in communicating the discursive practices that regulate a subject area teacher's sense of professional identity. For example, there is a discourse that implies all teachers can be teachers of reading simply by using their expertise and focusing on language that is meaningful to their disciplines. Then, there is another discourse that suggests subject area teachers can double as reading teachers if they simply commit to using a repertoire of comprehension strategies that focus students' attention on the course content (e.g., close reading). These two discourses are oppositional, and worse, neither is that appealing to subject area teachers who wonder why they should focus on language and literacy skills when lecturing or using multimediated learning activities can accomplish the same goal in far less time.

A second "accident" of considerable significance for subject area teachers' sense of identity arises each time administrative staff, researchers, or policy makers support curricular decisions that will ultimately affect teachers without meaningfully involving them in the decision-making process. Expecting teachers' cooperation at the implementation stage under such conditions is often fruitless. By choosing to delegate to teachers the responsibility for orchestrating and enacting the method suggested by the research on reading comprehension in 2002, the designers of the RTAC model arguably misjudged disciplinary teachers' sense of professional identity, and thus the degree to which they would willingly (or not) take up the discourse of "every teacher a teacher of reading." Through its inattention to the role of teachers as human actors—complete with their own domain-specific and socioculturally mediated discourses, knowledges, identities, and practices—the RTAC model likely further undermined the inevitability of the discourse of "every teacher a teacher of reading." Still, nothing appeared in the way of an alternative to that model.

A third "accident" was the reversal of what Alexander and Fox (see chapter 2 this volume) refer to as the era of engaged learning. Lasting from 1996 to 2005, the period witnessed the rise of hypermedia applications (Alexander & Jetton, 2003; Leu, Kinzer, Coiro, & Cammack, 2004), post-typographic texts (Reinking, McKenna, Labbo, & Kieffer, 1998), and dialogical discussions in subject area classrooms (Alvermann, Commeyras, Young, Randall, & Hinson, 1997; Guzzetti & Hynd, 1998). However, according to Alexander and Fox (2013), a rival stance that focused on identifying, teaching, and remediating comprehension subskills prevailed. Still prevalent in the era of performance-oriented learning (2006–2015), this remedial subskill approach continues, aided and abetted by personalized learning (see Alexander & Fox, chapter 2 this volume). This collision of forces, when represented as a move away from the sociocultural era and toward discursive practices that value individualized and personalized learning over group learning, would seem to have dealt a serious blow to whatever aspirations remain for subject area teachers to take up the mantra of "every teacher a teacher of reading."

Further Disruption

A parallel disruption of the discourse of "every teacher a teacher of reading" is reflected in Moje's (2007) review of the literature on disciplinary literacy teaching. In that review, she offered a critique of the practice of relying primarily on generic comprehension strategies in teacher education programs at both the undergraduate and graduate level. Despite support for such strategies by both the National Reading Panel (National Institute of Child Health and Human Development, 2000) and the RRSG (2002), Moje contended that they do not align well with the disciplinary structures underlying subject matter expertise. Examples of such structures include the forms of reasoning a history teacher might employ (as contrasted to those a mathematics teacher might use), or the themes and devices that an English teacher might favor (as contrasted to those a teacher of drama might find acceptable). These structural differences, coupled with a need for increased awareness of how symbolic representations vary by discipline, are but two realities that supporters of "every teacher a teacher of reading" have yet to address fully. This is not to claim that earlier models of adolescent literacy instruction have little or no value to the field. It is, however, an invitation to recognize the potential of a disciplinary literacy teaching model for reconceptualizing "every teacher a teacher of reading."

Call for an Adolescent Literacy Model That Uses Theory *of* and *in* Action

With the genealogical analysis of the discourse of "every teacher a teacher of reading" in mind, we now turn to an analysis of the prevailing adolescent literacy instruction model for reading comprehension— the reader-teacher-activity-context (RTAC) model—to examine how it has both supported and undermined a discourse of "every teacher a teacher of reading"—and in doing so, has made it difficult for teachers to take action in implementing it. In the process of examining the prevailing model, we offer new ways to think about literacy theories and models in general, and the RTAC model in particular.

For all its dominance, the RTAC model has fallen short of being carried into practice in sustained or systematic ways. Although the model is a powerful representation of the interactive process of meaning making for a given individual in a given activity at a given moment in time within a given context (see Figure 18.1), it does not translate to adolescent literacy teaching practice. That is, nothing in the model provides a theory of action for teachers who would seek to engage a range of students across a range of subject area classes focused on reading for meaning in different disciplines, which is the task of secondary school teachers across multiple disciplines.

Because the RTAC model overlooks the complex roles of subject area teachers, their goals, and the contexts in which they work, the model fails to guide their practice. If we can build a model that more completely specifies the complex and dynamic nature of adolescent literacy, then we might be better able to engage in translational work that guides the teaching of adolescent literacy by inviting teachers from a range of disciplines to see themselves as doing the work of literacy teaching to enhance learning in their subject domains.

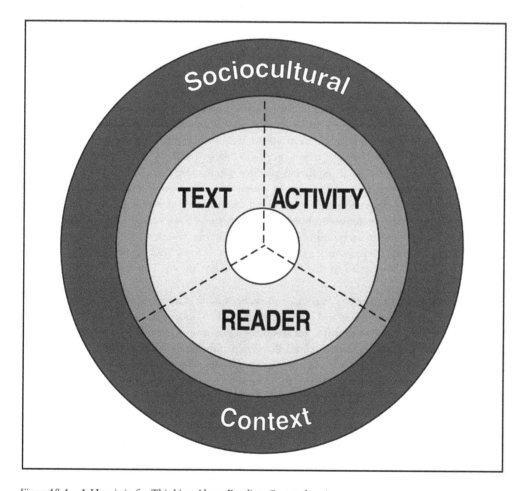

Figure 18.1   A Heuristic for Thinking About Reading Comprehension

Source: Reprinted from *Reading for Understanding: Toward an R&D Program in Reading Comprehension* (p. 12), by RAND Reading Study Group, 2002, Santa Monica, CA: RAND. Copyright by RAND. Reprinted with permission.

We unpack these ideas in more detail in the following sections of the chapter, beginning with the idea of making a more dynamic and activity-based representation of the current learning model of reading comprehension. Throughout this analysis, we offer variations on the RTAC model and suggest a possible, metaphoric model to guide the building of a theory in action. The theory in action is not, in itself, enough to inform the translation of adolescent literacy theory and research in the practice of "every teacher a teacher of reading." However, clarifying the dynamic nature of adolescent literacy could help to generate a theory *of* action for adolescent literacy teaching.

Building a Theory in Action of Adolescent Literate Practice/Literacy Learning

Theory and model building focused on human activity needs to recognize and situate the dynamic and context-bound nature of that activity. Readers bring something to text comprehension, but that interaction is immersed in, indeed mediated by, the activities and purposes for which acts of reading are engaged and the particular contexts in which those activities occur (Moje et al., 2000; Scribner & Cole, 1981). Readers employ their skills and knowledge from various past experiences as mediating tools (Vygotsky, 1978; Wertsch, del Río, & Alvarez, 1995) for certain goals and in particular ways that are dependent on the activities for which the reading task is being carried out. Activities, moreover, are mediated by the multiple and intersecting contexts in which they are carried out. These differences produce reading, or literacy, *practices*—that is, ways of reading and writing—together with ways of using reading and writing skills to achieve particular goals in those practices. For example, the literacy practices of an academic writing a research paper demand that basic skills of word knowledge and syntax be framed by knowledge of audience, appropriate register, and purpose of the written text. When that same academic turns to write a press release about a new high school program and must appeal to youths and their parents who live in an economically depressed urban setting, that writer must engage (or learn) different word-level and rhetorical skills because the textual and literate practice is embedded in an interaction with people engaged in a particular activity and context. As hinted at in the example, texts serve as tools that can further mediate activities and invoke or demand certain kinds of practices. The point here is that literacy skills are never autonomously engaged (see Street, 1984), but are always embedded in and motivated by the need to carry out certain literacy practices, which are socially and culturally produced and mediated. Thus, we offer this modification of the RTAC model (see Figure 18.2) to further specify the complexity of the dynamic relationship among a reader, a text, an activity, and a context.

Even this representation, however, is inadequate, because the model represents the process of *one* reader's interactions with text and activity, all situated in dimensions represented as discrete examples of context. However, multiple readers inhabit classrooms and other learning spaces, and multiple dimensions of context are in play and overlap, inform, and contest one another in any given literacy event. Moreover, readers bring contexts into spaces based on their different histories of participation in other contexts. Finally, those various contexts that are both actively present in classrooms and brought into classrooms as students' histories of participation can intersect in powerful ways. For example, consider that reading an article from *Science* on genetic therapies would be experienced differently by a student who loves to read anything related to life sciences, reads regularly with parents, works in a hospital part time, and whose family medical history includes a genetically transmitted disorder. That student brings contextual knowledge based on histories of participation to the act of reading the *Science* passage. Now consider how the context of the classroom itself might interact with those varied contextual histories of the student by imagining the difference between a context in which the *Science* article is read as preparation for a debate on a controversial gene therapy prior to a visit from a geneticist at a nearby university. That in-classroom context would set up a very different reading experience from that of a context

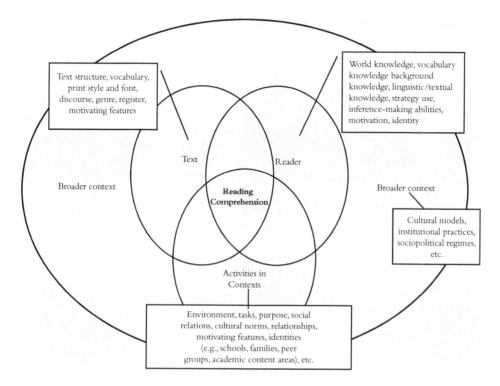

Figure 18.2 Expanded Reader-Text-Activity-Context Model

in which the students are assigned to read the article and write summaries to be submitted to a teacher. Although that student might possess the agency to extract necessary information from the article as a result of her various histories and passions, she is likely to make very different meanings from the two different reading interactions. That same student's reading experiences would also be shaped by the particular text on genetic therapies (e.g., the difference between the text of a *Science* article and one from a ten-line textbook callout) designed to engage and interest ninth-grade readers whose Lexile scores range from 1000 to 1200.

The reader's experiences would be mediated by the purpose for and activity in which they were reading any given text, whether the *Science* article or the textbook callout. Additionally, that purpose could shift not only from day to day but also from hour to hour. Students preparing for mandated state tests or college entrance examinations during one part of the school year might engage with classroom literacy experiences differently from the way they engage when the test pressure is diminished. Students might read a piece on gene therapy in a particular way if they heard a news report on the ethics of gene therapy on the way to school that morning. Students might read an article on gene therapy, or any other subject, in yet again a different way if they had a fight with a friend just before entering the classroom.

Finally, the same individual student might read the *Science* article on gene therapy differently in science class from the way she reads it in language arts or civics class: In part because the student may recognize the disciplinary or classroom differences at work; or in part because the teacher may have set different reading purposes or have developed different activities (e.g., a debate on the ethics of gene therapy vs. a follow-up laboratory activity on genetic mutations). Moje et al. (2004) attempted to link these ideas together with a model of skilled content literacy practice, as illustrated in Figure 18.3.

Funds of Knowledge and Discourse

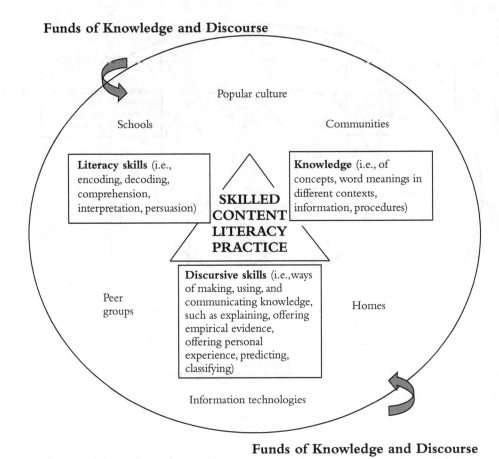

Figure 18.3 Skilled Content Literacy Practice: A Model

Source: Moje et al., 2004

Although this model attempts to signal the critical nature of disciplinary knowledge and the role of contexts and activity systems outside of school (via Moll, Veléz-Ibañez, & Greenberg's [1989] terminology of funds of knowledge), it falls short of providing a theory *in* or *of* action because it remains a static representation of a single reader's process. It cannot model the enactment of content literacy teaching practice, only what is happening as a single reader engages with a single text in a single classroom activity embedded in a nebulously identified context.

This kind of dynamic difference is certainly hinted at in the model, but the complexity of those various possible interactions is implicit and depends on the interpreter of the model having either extensive teaching experience or expertise in reading research and theory. Moreover, the model is not adequate to the task of representing or theorizing the experience of even a single secondary student, who moves through all of those spaces in a given day. Specifically, the experience of secondary school students could be conceptualized as one of navigating (Moje, 2013) different learning spaces as they move across the school day. These learning spaces are circumscribed by multiple differences in both physical and social spaces, including subject area/discipline, learning goals, teacher qualities, physical location of the classroom, student-student relationships, and time of day. Successful students appear to navigate these spaces with relative ease, picking up on cues regarding the literacy practices (among other social practices) necessary to be successful in each space, whereas less successful students appear to struggle to adapt their literacy and other social practices to the requirements of the space. These navigational acts require not only the ability to move across and integrate (or distill) many different subject area classroom demands (which are more or less informed by disciplinary practices, depending on the teacher) but also the integration or distillation of the many contexts, activity systems, and activities of everyday life (see Figure 18.4).

The model in Figure 18.4 may be useful in indexing the contexts at play in adolescent literacy practice and reading comprehension and also in terms of understanding the navigating acts that secondary school students must engage in, but it does not necessarily make a tight connection to the RTAC model. One is a model of the navigating work of a student, a representation of social practice; the other is a model of the act of reading comprehension of a student, a cognitive process. Each hints at the other, but neither makes clear the relationship between the social practices of a student navigating multiple everyday and school contexts and the cognitive processes of reading comprehension. Additionally, both models leave out the role of the teacher. We need to develop a model that integrates these aspects of reading comprehension and, more to the point of adolescent literacy teaching, of how to teach literate practice across a range of domains. Whatever new model we develop needs also to move past the linearity of relationship and activity represented in these past models.

Indeed, all the one-dimensional models (i.e., flat drawings on paper) that we consulted or constructed fell short of our goal of representing a dynamic theory in action, because they were unable to capture the dynamic and multilayered/multiactor nature of adolescent reading processes and practices, let alone represent the complexity necessary to guide a theory of action for secondary school literacy teaching.

It may be more productive, then, to employ an analogy or metaphor as a way of theorizing a dynamic theory in action of adolescent literacy. What better metaphor for a 21st-century model than one drawn from the recent advances in technology, the smartphone? In particular, we invoke

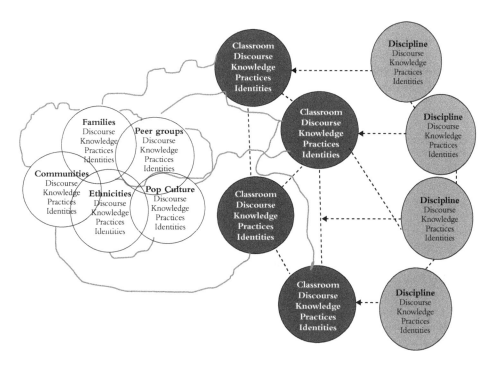

Figure 18.4 A Navigating Model of Secondary School Literacy

Source: Moje, 2008a

the image of Apple's iPhone, whose interface makes a particularly useful metaphor for the dynamic nature of reading comprehension. Any one of the apps is present and available at all times. With a swipe of a finger, one enters the world of a particular application, whether music, e-mail, maps, or even phone calling. Each application has the potential to intersect with another application. The calendar feature allows users to place phone numbers on appointment times, thus allowing them to simply tap the links to the phone numbers when the iPhone's clock signals that the appointed times have arrived. The phone numbers can be easily downloaded into the contacts list. Contacts can be shared, tagged, liked, and even memorialized with a photo taken by the phone's camera. These multiple and interacting applications are like the many features that routinely connect, overlap, and at times, interfere with one another in young people's reading practices. Indeed, all systems are dynamically interacting and ever changing. Thus, what is especially compelling about the iPhone metaphor is that when one application is in focus, the other applications still exist, and users can access them simultaneously. Moreover, when one zeroes in on an icon, new tools, ideas, images, and information are available that could not be seen on the original interface. This representation, when used as a model for envisioning the practice of literacy, helps push the way we think about the RTAC model because it provides a way to consider the multiple and intersecting variables in the operation of any dynamic system.

A question arises in employing this metaphor, however, when considering the way one changes applications on the iPhone. For those unfamiliar with the device, to add an application, the user installs it with a click of a button (and a swipe of a credit card, as applicable) from the iTunes store or some other source. To delete the application, the user presses and holds the on/off button until the icons begin to wiggle and an X shows up in the corner of each one. A simple tap of the X makes the icon disappear. What is the parallel in a model of reading comprehension? Is it possible to delete an aspect of reading practice? A more likely scenario is that the applications or variables in the reading comprehension/literate practice equation never disappear but that they do shift, change, or grow. They can certainly be updated, but rarely would the variables of literate practice simply disappear. Thus, the iPhone model of comprehension/literate practice has limitations in the sense that iPhone applications/variables are either present or absent rather than dynamically evolving.

The iPhone metaphor is a useful one for breaking free from one-dimensional modeling and allows for a representation that takes the ever-changing nature of the multiple variables of reading into account. Like the models that preceded it, however, this metaphor remains a representation of a single system and does not translate the representation into the work of a teacher who would be responsible for supporting students in navigating the different applications (texts, activities, and contexts). Thus, we turn to the second part of our theory and model-building work in this chapter: the task of expanding a working model of adolescent literacy.

Building a Theory of Action for Adolescent Literacy Teaching

Although useful work for expanding a working model of adolescent literacy, reconceptualizing the RTAC model to more fully account for the cognitive processes and social practices involved in literate practice did not help translate what we know from the model into a model for teaching practice. One key principle is critical to crafting a model of adolescent literacy teaching: Everything changes. Reading and literate practice are dynamic and relational, and the dynamism is magnified in secondary school settings across multiple knowledge/practice domains. People change, conditions of reading and learning change, activities change, and activity systems change.

To ground these points in the empirical world, recall from the previous section the example of the adolescent reader of the *Science* article on genetic therapies. Imagine adding a second student to the adolescent literacy model, in this case one who loves to read about the life sciences but has little background or personal motivation and whose previous biology teachers taught biology as a lecture with no assigned print text reading of any kind. The student's meaning making of the article would be shaped in particular and very different ways even before knowing what the teacher expected him to do with the text in the classroom.

The translational challenge to the RTAC model is that those two types of readers featured are two among an average of 30 (or more) in a typical secondary school classroom. Each of those readers draws from histories of participation in communities, families, ethnic groups, popular cultures, and peer groups to bring knowledge, identities, and discursive and literacy skills into a given classroom. Additionally, the class is likely to be one among five or six class periods a student attends every day. Moreover, the social relationships of those two students, and of all 30 students and their one teacher (who rightly remains invisible in the RTAC model because it is a model of comprehension or learning, not a model of teaching), will also mediate the ways the students and the teacher engage in the activity, the purposes for which they read, and the sense they make of the texts they are given or choose to read. These complexities are not represented in any way in the RTAC model or the variants we have considered. Finally, when considering the larger picture of secondary school reading or literacy development, all of this is further complicated by the fact that those 30 students are one set of many that subject area teachers will see each day while trying to ensure that they meet all the subject area content standards demanded in state and national guidelines. In sum, the RTAC model, although exceedingly useful for thinking about a moment of the reading process for one person situated in one context, is not as useful for translational research that seeks to encourage every teacher to be a teacher of reading content.

A translational model for adolescent literacy teaching, then, needs to recognize the dynamic nature of the RTAC model and apply the singular RTAC model to a site in which hundreds of readers come together in multiple spaces with varied goals and purposes to read an enormous number of texts over roughly 180 days every year. The tentative—and messy—model offered in Figure 18.5 represents our first attempt at a one-dimensional treatment of the model.

In this model, we have tried to show, within the confines of the printed page, the complexity of teaching literate practice when multiple young people (represented by the smallest circles) bring histories of participation in varied contexts (only loosely represented by phrases such as *popular culture* or *ethnicities*) into classroom spaces. Each youth brings a slightly different variation of these discourse communities, which further complicates the matter. These youths walk into classrooms with teachers who craft their own discursive practices, disciplinary and world knowledge, and identities together with the discourses of teaching, the discipline, and schooling. Additionally, each different subject area is informed or shaped by a different discipline with its own traditions. Some are more aligned with classroom practice than are others (and the alignment can vary by particular school context or teacher knowledge/background). Thus, we have placed the circles that represent the disciplines in different places relative to the classroom circles. Some disciplines sit more on the fringes of classroom practice, whereas others are more central to the classrooms, depending on the kind of disciplinary knowledge and practice teachers bring to their teaching, the level of the subject, the timing and structures of the school day (e.g., block scheduling vs. shorter periods), and the views of the school in regard to what counts as valid pedagogical practice. Teachers are tasked with teaching the discursive practices, knowledge, and linguistic skills of the discipline to anywhere from 100 to 180 students a year, a task made even more critical with the adoption of the Common Core State Standards, which make valuable, but only vaguely defined, disciplinary practice demands on teachers. All the while, teachers, like their students, are navigating this multiplicity of discourses, practices, identities, and knowledge while working toward predetermined goals and outcomes. Not only must they navigate these discursive and other differences, but they must also navigate the reality of their students' distinctly varied literacy skills, subject matter knowledge, and stances, practices, and identities. Moreover, it is the subject matter teacher's obligation to teach youths the necessary discipline-specific knowledge, linguistic skills, discursive practices, stances, and identities signaled in Figure 18.5's boxes. Is it any wonder that few secondary school teachers are eager to take on the role of reading teacher in addition to everything else they must do?

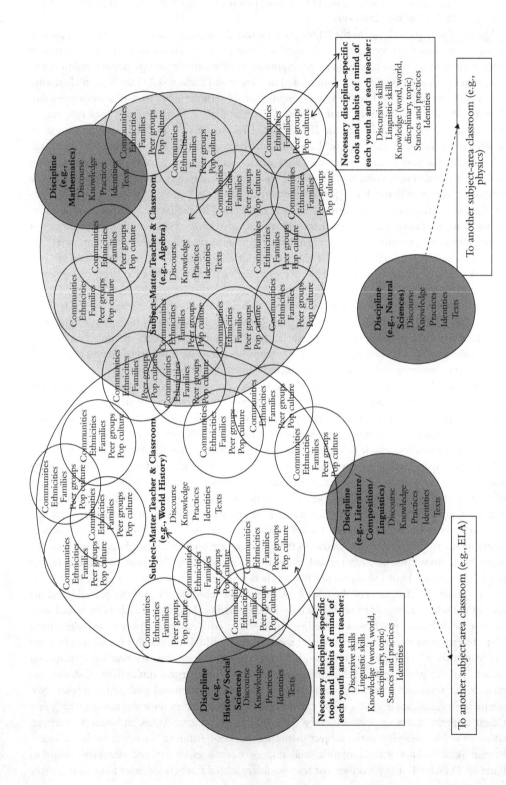

Figure 18.5 A Model of Adolescent Literacy Teaching (the ALT Model)

This model of adolescent literacy teaching may make the task of encouraging teachers to see themselves as teachers of reading seem hopeless, but we see the model as opening a space for informed action. No longer should policy be aimed solely at fixing a reader who measures below grade level on a single assessment, because the model of disciplinary literacy teaching represented in Figure 18.5, which draws from and extends the RTAC model and other models of comprehension we have reviewed, makes clear that far more than skill shapes the demonstration of comprehension or of literate practice writ large. No longer should secondary school teachers be asked to teach reading in any generic way, because the model situates reading inside particular disciplinary discourses, practices, knowledge domains, texts, and tools. No longer should teachers be expected to do this work armed with sets of cognitive strategies alone, because the model clarifies the role of multiple social practices in the work of teaching and the various discourse communities and funds of knowledge youths bring into secondary school subject area classrooms. In short, no longer should teachers be asked to be teachers of reading in simple terms, because the model makes clear that there is nothing simple about this work. The development of discipline-specific literacy practices, habits of mind, and skills needs to be situated not just in what one reader brings to one act of reading in one moment in time and in one classroom but also in the multiplicity of a reader's experience.

The act of teaching literate practice to adolescents at the secondary level, then, is as much about teaching youths to navigate the texts, discourses, identities, and knowledge of different subject areas, classrooms, and relationships (see Moje, 2013) as it is about teaching word-level skills, discipline-specific vocabulary, or even disciplinary habits of mind. This kind of teaching requires that teachers name discourse and practice in explicit ways (e.g., Bain, 2008; Lee, 2007; Warren, Ballenger, Ogonowski, Rosebery, & Hudicourt-Barnes, 2001; Wineburg & Martin, 2004), make visible how language functions to accomplish certain purposes (e.g., Coffin, 2004, 2006; Schleppegrell, Achugar, & Oteíza, 2004), and engage youths in practicing reading, writing, and speaking in the ways valued in the discipline (e.g., Lee & Spratley, 2006; Lemke, 1990; Moje, 2007, 2008b; Moje & Speyer, 2008). This kind of teaching requires that teachers begin such work with a recognition of many different histories of participation and the discourses and knowledge accompanying them that even one student may bring to a classroom, and to surface and discuss those discourses across the different students. The model we propose makes clear that a key next step in these efforts is to bring together the various interventions cited here (and many more like them) into a unified set of practices that guide teachers across and within disciplines. The model also demands that both researchers and policy makers take seriously the challenges of doing this work and call a halt to simplistic policy initiatives that demand practices from teachers without providing the resources of planning and teaching time, as well as sustained professional learning opportunities to support their learning to be teachers of literacy in their separate disciplines.

For some, the lack of a linear pathway in our model will call into question whether we have indeed outlined a theory of action. However, reading is among the most complex of human processes, situated in myriad human practices. No simple, linear model will explain it, and no simple, linear model will successfully guide its teaching. This kind of teaching is difficult. It is even more difficult to assess. Additionally, it is among the most essential of human endeavors. In the end, every teacher is a teacher of reading, but settling on what that discourse looks like is no simple matter; nor will it be accomplished in the same way, using the same steps, in different disciplines by different teachers interacting with different students in different classroom contexts having different social structures.

References

ACT. (2010). *A first look at the Common Core and college and career readiness.* Retrieved from www.act. org/content/dam/act/unsecured/documents/FirstLook.pdf

ACT. (2011). *The condition of college and career readiness.* Iowa City, IA: Author. Retrieved from www.ewa.org/sites/main/files/conditionofcollegeandcareerreadiness2011.pdf

Alexander, P. A., & Fox, E. (2013). A historical perspective on reading research and practice, redux. In D. E. Alvermann, N. J. Unrau, & R. B. Ruddell (Eds.), *Theoretical models and processes of reading* (6th ed., pp. 3–46). Newark, DE: International Reading Association.

Alexander, P. A., & Jetton, T. L. (2003). Learning from traditional and alternative texts: New conceptualization for an information age. In A. Graesser, M. Gernsbacher, & S. Goldman (Eds.), *Handbook of discourse processes.* Mahwah, NJ: Lawrence Erlbaum Associates.

Alvermann, D. E. (2009). Sociocultural constructions of adolescence and young people's literacies. In L. Christenbury, R. Bomer, & P. Smagorinsky (Eds.), *Handbook of adolescent literacy research* (pp. 14–28). New York, NY: Guilford Press.

Alvermann, D. E. (2010). The teaching of reading. In E. Lindemann (Ed.), *Reading the past, writing the future: A century of American literacy education the National Council of Teachers of English* (pp. 55–90). Urbana, IL: National Council of Teachers of English.

Alvermann, D. E., Commeyras, M., Young, J. P., Randall, S., & Hinson, D. (1997). Interrupting gendered discursive practices in classroom talk about texts: Easy to think about, difficult to do. *Journal of Literacy Research, 29*, 73–104.

Alvermann, D. E., Fitzgerald, J., & Simpson, M. (2006). Teaching and learning in reading. In P. A. Alexander & P. H. Winne (Eds.), *Handbook of educational psychology* (2nd ed., pp. 427–455). Mahwah, NJ: Lawrence Erlbaum Associates.

Alvermann, D. E., & Moore, D. W. (1991). Secondary reading. In R. Barr, M. L. Kamil, P. Mosenthal, & P. D. Pearson (Eds.), *Handbook of reading research* (Vol. 2, pp. 951–983). White Plains, NY: Longman.

Anders, P. L., Hoffman, J. V., & Duffy, G. G. (2000). Teaching teachers to teach reading: Paradigm shifts, persistent problems, and challenges. In M. L. Kamil, P. B. Mosenthal, P. D. Pearson, & R. Barr (Eds.), *Handbook of reading research* (Vol. 3, pp. 719–742). Mahwah, NJ: Lawrence Erlbaum Associates.

Bain, R. B. (2008). Into the breach: Using research and theory to shape history instruction. *Journal of Education, 189*(1/2), 159–168.

Baker, C. D., & Luke, A. (Eds.). (1991). *Towards a critical sociology of reading pedagogy: Papers of the XII World Congress on Reading.* Amsterdam: John Benjamins.

Barton, D. (2000). Researching literacy practices: Learning from activities with teachers and students. In D. Barton, M. Hamilton, & R. Ivanic (Eds.), *Situated literacies: Reading and writing in context* (pp. 167–179). New York, NY: Routledge.

Bean, T. W. (2000). Reading in the content areas: Social constructivist dimensions. In M. L. Kamil, P. B. Mosenthal, P. D. Pearson, & R. Barr (Eds.), *Handbook of reading research* (Vol. 3, pp. 629–644). Mahwah, NJ: Lawrence Erlbaum Associates.

Bové, P. A. (1995). Discourse. In F. Lentricchia & T. McLaughlin (Eds.), *Critical terms for literary study* (2nd ed., pp. 50–65). Chicago, IL: University of Chicago Press.

Coffin, C. (2004). Learning to write history: The role of causality. *Written Communication, 21*(3), 261–289. doi:10.1177/0741088304265476

Coffin, C. (2006). Learning the language of school history: The role of linguistics in mapping the writing demands of the secondary school curriculum. *Journal of Curriculum Studies, 38*(4), 413–429. doi:10.1080/00220270500508810

Dillon, D. R., O'Brien, D. G., Sato, M., & Kelly, C. M. (2011). Professional development and teacher education for reading instruction. In M. L. Kamil, P. D. Pearson, E. B. Moje, & P. P. Afflerbach (Eds.), *Handbook of reading research* (Vol. 4, pp. 629–660). New York, NY: Routledge.

Every Student Succeeds Act (ESSA). (2015). Retrieved from https://www.ed.gov/essa?src=rn

Foucault, M. (1980). *Power/knowledge: Selected interviews and other writings, 1972–1977* (C. Gordon, Ed., L. Marshall, J. Mepham, & K. Soper, Trans.). New York, NY: Pantheon. (Original work published 1976)

Foucault, M. (1988). Politics, philosophy, culture: Interviews and other writings, 1977–1984 (L. D. Kritzman, Ed., A. Sheridan, Trans.). New York, NY: Routledge. (Original interview published 1984)

Foucault, M. (1998). Nietzsche, genealogy, history (R. Hurley, Trans.). In J. D. Faubion (Ed.), *Aesthetics, method, and epistemology* (Vol. 2, pp. 369–391). New York, NY: New Press. (Reprinted from Hommage à Jean Hyppolite, pp. 145–172, D. F. Brouchard & S. Simon, Trans. 1971). Paris: Presses Universitaires de France)

Garbe, C., Holle, K., & Weinhold, S. (Eds.). (2010). *ADORE: Teaching struggling adolescent readers in European countries.* New York, NY: Peter Lang.

Gee, J. P. (1988). The legacies of literacy: From Plato to Freire through Harvey Graff. *Harvard Educational Review, 58*(2), 195–212.

Gray, W. S. (1925). A modern program of reading instruction for the grades and for the high school. In G. M. Whipple (Ed.), *24th Yearbook of the National Society for the Study of Education: Part 1. Report of the National Committee on Reading* (pp. 21–73). Bloomington, IL: Public School.

Green, B., Reid, J.-A., & Bigum, C. (1998). Teaching the Nintendo generation? Children, computer culture and popular technologies. In S. Howard (Ed.), *Wired-up: Young people and the electronic media* (pp. 18–40). London: UCL Press.

Guzzetti, B., & Hynd, C. (1998). *Theoretical perspectives on conceptual change.* Mahwah, NJ: Lawrence Erlbaum Associates.

Hagood, M. C., Stevens, L. P., & Reinking, D. (2002). What do THEY have to teach US? Talkin' 'cross generations! In D. E. Alvermann (Ed.), *Adolescents and literacies in a digital world* (pp. 68–83). New York, NY: Peter Lang.

Heath, S. B. (1983). *Ways with words: Language, life, and work in communities and classrooms.* New York, NY: Cambridge University Press.

Herber, H. L. (1970). *Teaching reading in content areas.* Englewood Cliffs, NJ: Prentice-Hall.

Herber, H. L. (1978). *Teaching reading in content areas* (2nd ed.). Englewood Cliffs, NJ: Prentice-Hall.

Huey, E. B. (1908). *The psychology and pedagogy of reading.* New York, NY: Macmillan.

Lapp, D., Guthrie, L. A., & Flood, J. (2007). Ruth May Strang (1895–1971): The legacy of a reading sage. In S. E. Israel & E. J. Monaghan (Eds.), *Shaping the reading field* (pp. 347–373). Newark, DE: International Reading Association.

Lee, C. D. (2007). *Culture, literacy, and learning: Taking bloom in the midst of the whirlwind.* New York, NY: Teachers College Press.

Lee, C. D., & Spratley, A. (2006). Reading in the disciplines: The challenges of adolescent literacy. New York: Carnegie Corporation of New York.

Lemke, J. L. (1990). *Talking science: Language, learning, and values.* Norwood, NJ: Ablex.

Lesko, N. (2001). Act your age! A cultural construction of adolescence. New York, NY: Routledge.

Leu, D. J., Kinzer, C. K., Coiro, J. L., & Cammack, D. W. (2004). Toward a theory of new literacies emerging from the Internet and other information and communication technologies. In R. B. Ruddell & N. J. Unrau (Eds.), *Theoretical models and processes of reading* (5th ed., pp. 1570–1613). Newark, DE: International Reading Association.

Luke, A. (2004). Two takes on the critical. In B. Norton & K. Toohey (Eds.), *Critical pedagogies and language learning* (pp. 21–31). Cambridge: Cambridge University Press.

Moje, E. B. (2007). Developing socially just subject-matter instruction: A review of the literature on disciplinary literacy teaching. In G. J. Kelly, A. Luke, & J. Green (Eds.), *Review of research in education* (Vol. 31, pp. 1–44). Washington, DC: American Educational Research Association. doi:10.3102/0091732X 07300046

Moje, E. B. (2008a, April). Developing disciplinary discourses and identities: What's knowledge got to do with it? Paper presented at the Conference on Discourse, Identity, and Educational Practices, Universidad Autónoma de Baja California, Ensenada, Mexico.

Moje, E. B. (2008b). Foregrounding the disciplines in secondary literacy teaching and learning: A call for change. *Journal of Adolescent & Adult Literacy, 52*(2), 96–107. doi:10.1598/JAAL.52.2.1

Moje, E. B. (2013). Hybrid literacies in a post-hybrid world: Making a case for navigating. In K. Hall, T. Cremin, B. Comber, & L. C. Moll (Eds.), *International handbook of research on children's literacy, learning and culture.* Oxford: Wiley-Blackwell.

Moje, E. B., Ciechanowski, K. M., Kramer, K. E., Ellis, L. M., Carrillo, R., & Collazo, T. (2004). Working toward third space in content area literacy: An examination of everyday funds of knowledge and discourse. *Reading Research Quarterly, 39*(1), 38–70.

Moje, E. B., Dillon, D. R., & O'Brien, D. G. (2000). Reexamining roles of learner, text, and context in secondary literacy. *Journal of Educational Research, 93*(3), 165–180.

Moje, E. B., & Speyer, J. (2008). The reality of challenging texts in high school science and social studies: How teachers can mediate comprehension. In K. A. Hinchman & H. K. Sheridan-Thomas (Eds.), *Best practices in adolescent literacy instruction* (pp. 185–211). New York: Guilford Press.

Moll, L. C., Veléz-Ibañez, C., & Greenberg, J. (1989). *Year one progress report: Community knowledge and classroom practice: Combining resources for literacy instruction.* Tucson, AZ: University of Arizona.

Moore, D. W. (1996). Contexts for literacy in secondary schools. In D. J. Leu, C. K. Kinzer, & K. A. Hinchman (Eds.), *Literacies for the 21st century: Research and practice* (pp. 15–46). Chicago, IL: National Reading Conference.

Moore, D. W., Readence, J. E., & Rickelman, R. J. (1983). An historical exploration of content area reading instruction. *Reading Research Quarterly, 18*(4), 419–438. doi:10.2307/747377

National Governors Association Center for Best Practices & Council of Chief State School Officers. (2010). *Common Core State Standards for English language arts and literacy in history/social studies, science, and technical subjects.* Washington, DC: Authors.

National Governors Association Center for Best Practices & Council of Chief State School Officers. (2012). Myths vs. facts. Retrieved from www.corestandards.org/about-the-standards/myths-vs-facts

National Institute of Child Health and Human Development. (2000). *Report of the National Reading Panel, Teaching children to read: An evidence-based assessment of the scientific research literature on reading and its implications for reading instruction* (NIH Publication No. 00–4769). Washington, DC: U.S. Government Printing Office.

O'Brien, D. G., Stewart, R. A., & Moje, E. B. (1995). Why content literacy is difficult to infuse into the secondary school: Complexities of curriculum, pedagogy, and school culture. *Reading Research Quarterly, 30*(3), 442–463.

O'Farrell, C. (2007). Key concepts. Retrieved from www.michel-foucault.com/concepts/index

PISA (2000). Highlights from the 2000 Program for International Student Assessment. Retrieved from https://nces.ed.gov/pubs2002/2002116.pdf

Prado, C. G. (2000). *Starting with Foucault: An introduction to genealogy* (2nd ed.). Boulder, CO: Westview.

RAND Reading Study Group (RRSG). (2002). *Reading for understanding: Toward an R&D program in reading comprehension.* Santa Monica, CA: Author.

Reinking, D., McKenna, M. C., Labbo, L. D., & Kieffer, R. D. (1998). *Handbook of literacy and technology: Transformations in a post-typographic world.* Mahwah, NJ: Lawrence Erlbaum Associates.

Schleppegrell, M. J., Achugar, M., & Oteíza, T. (2004). The grammar of history: Enhancing content-based instruction through a functional focus on language. *TESOL Quarterly, 38*(1), 67–93. doi:10.2307/3588259

Scribner, S., & Cole, M. (1981). *The psychology of literacy.* Cambridge, MA: Harvard University Press.

Smith, N. B. (2002). *American reading instruction.* Newark, DE: International Reading Association. (Original work published 1934 by Silver Burdett)

Street, B. V. (1984). *Literacy in theory and practice.* New York, NY: Cambridge University Press.

Street, B. V. (1995). *Social literacies: Critical approaches to literacy in development, ethnography and education.* London: Longman.

TIMSS. (1999). Trends in international mathematics and science study. Washington, DC: National Center for Education Statistics. Retrieved from https://nces.ed.gov/timss/results.asp

Vadeboncoeur, J. A., & Stevens, L. P. (Eds.). (2005). *Re/constructing "the adolescent": Sign, symbol, and body.* New York, NY: Peter Lang.

Vygotsky, L. S. (1978). *Mind in society: The development of higher psychological processes* (M. Cole, V. John-Steiner, S. Scribner, & E. Souberman, Eds. & Trans.). Cambridge, MA: Harvard University Press.

Vygotsky, L. S. (1986). *Thought and language* (Rev. ed., A. Kozulin, Ed.). Cambridge, MA: MIT Press.

Warren, B., Ballenger, C., Ogonowski, M., Rosebery, A. S., & Hudicourt-Barnes, J. (2001). Rethinking diversity in learning science: The logic of everyday sense-making. *Journal of Research in Science Teaching, 38*(5), 529–552. doi:10.1002/tea.1017

Wertsch, J. V., del Río, P., & Alvarez, A. (1995). Sociocultural studies: History, action, and mediation. In J. V. Wertsch, P. del Río, & A. Alvarez (Eds.), *Sociocultural studies of mind* (pp. 1–34). New York, NY: Cambridge University Press. doi:10.1017/CBO9781139174299.002

Wineburg, S. S., & Martin, D. (2004). Reading and rewriting history. *Educational Leadership, 62*(1), 42–45.

19

POSITIONING THEORY

Mary B. McVee, Katarina N. Silvestri, Nichole Barrett, and Katherine S. Haq

Overview

Despite the growing application of Positioning Theory (hereafter, PT) to literacy and language research, other than one edited volume (McVee, Brock, & Glazier, 2011), there have been few direct explications of PT for literacy researchers. Within this chapter, our goal is to introduce readers to the theoretical and conceptual history of PT and some of its basic precepts. We explore common misconceptions and critiques of PT and describe some ways that language and literacy researchers have effectively used PT as a critical lens. We conclude with theoretical and methodological areas in need of further elaboration or development where literacy researchers can make significant contributions to PT.

What is Positioning Theory?

Positions and Positioning Theory

With the publication of *Positioning: The Discursive Production of Selves*, Bronwyn Davies and Rom Harré (1990) introduced what has come to be known as Positioning Theory. Writing in *The Journal for the Theory of Social Behaviour (JTSB)*, Davies and Harré argued that *position* was "the appropriate expression with which to talk about the discursive production of a diversity of selves" (p. 47). In educational research studies, the following passage is often quoted:

> Once having taken up a particular position as one's own, a person inevitably sees the world from the vantage point of that position and in terms of the particular images, metaphors, story lines and concepts which are made relevant within the particular discursive practice in which they are positioned.
>
> *(Harré & Davies, 1990, p. 46)*

The quote provides a concise summary of the metaphor of position and positioning, a metaphor that is easily understood and taken up given its connection to everyday life. Despite this, we emphasize that PT involves a conceptual undertaking and is not merely a metaphorical representation. Because PT is a theory in its own right, and because the theory is sometimes conflated with the general metaphor of position, we capitalize the phrase "PT" throughout this chapter, although all quotes follow their original capitalization.

Positions in Contrast to Role

Harré has long contended that a reason to develop PT was as an alternative to the idea of *role* in social psychology. Harré and others have argued that roles are, or are perceived to be, more static or fixed, even in more interactive approaches such as Goffman's notion of footing or frames (see Davies & Harré, 1990, pp. 52–55). In contrast to models that view interlocutors performing prescribed roles, Davies and Harré (1990) posit that positions:

> permit us to think of ourselves as a choosing subject, locating ourselves in conversations according to those narrative forms with which we are familiar and bringing to those narratives our own subjective lived histories through which we have learnt metaphors, characters and plot.
>
> *(p. 52)*

Davies and Harré also stated that people understand positions in accordance with their own lived narrative experience—including beliefs, emotions, and subjective histories "*as well as* a knowledge of social structures (including roles) with their attendant rights, obligations and expectations" (Davies & Harré, 1990, p. 42). (For more on role and positioning, see McVee (2011, pp. 9–11)). In contrast to roles, positions are seen as fluid, dynamic, and immanent and are viewed as "a cluster of rights and duties to perform certain actions" (Harré & Moghaddam, 2003a, p. 5).

Storylines

Davies, Harré, and other positioning theorists embrace the metaphor of positioning but go beyond a superficial adoption of the metaphor:

> If we are to come close to understanding how it is that people actually interact in everyday life we need the metaphor of an unfolding narrative, in which we are constituted in one position or another within the course of one story, or even come to stand in multiple or contradictory positions, or to negotiate a new position by "refusing" the position that the opening rounds of a conversation have made available to us. With such a metaphor, we can begin to explain what it means to 'refuse' to accept the nature of the discourse through which particular conversation takes place.
>
> *(Davies & Harré, 1990, p. 53)*

Here, Davies and Harré speak not only of positions but of a "metaphor of an unfolding narrative" where discourses constitute one or more positions within a storyline or storylines. Davies and Harré acknowledge interactions as storylines or narratives unfold as they are enacted. Storylines are critical in PT, and as Davies and Harré (1990) acknowledge, there is a strong tie between PT and narratology, and they were "the first to bring 'positioning' to bear on interactive exchanges and to relate it to narratology" (Deppermann, 2013, p. 3). Storylines emphasize the "dynamics of social episodes" and how various individuals may contribute as they unfold (Harré & Moghaddam, 2003a, p. 6).

Basic Tenets of Positioning Theory Summarized

As the previous quotations demonstrate, Davies and Harré (1990) Harré and Van Langenhove (1991, 1999) drew upon the metaphor of positions to introduce key tenets of the theory of positioning. Major tenets of PT are summarized in Table 19.1 and will be addressed throughout the chapter. In its early iterations, Harré and co-founders of Positioning Theory argued that PT and position

Table 19.1 Principles of Positioning Theory Summarized by Foundational Texts

Positioning Theory as a Means for:

Positioning: The Discursive Production of Selves — Davies & Harré (1990)	Positioning Theory as a Means for:	Varieties of Positioning — Harré & Van Langenhove (1991)	Positioning theory: Moral Contexts of Intentional Action — Harré & Van Langenhove (1999)
Examining discursive acts, practices (p. 43)[a]	Considering subject positions as pertaining to rights, duties, and use of particular discourse (p. 46)	Considering positions within and in relation to moral orders [full article]	Emphasizing the immanentist perspective that positions are produced in the moment and are not bound by any one moment in time, as they can be oriented in past, located in the present, but also affected by future positions (p. 33, 45)
Providing a dynamic alternative of positioning to the more static concept of role (p. 43)	Understanding personhood, selfhood (pp. 46–47)	Identifying the following varieties of positions: First and second order positioning (p. 396) Performative and accountive positioning (p. 397) Moral and personal positioning (p. 397) Self and other positioning (p. 398) Tacit and intentional positioning (p. 398) Kinds of Intentional Positioning Deliberate self-positioning (p. 400) Forced self-positioning (p. 402) Deliberate positioning of others (p. 403) Forced positioning of others (p. 403)[b]	Considering subject positions as pertaining to rights, duties, and use of particular discourse (p. 35).
Studying speech acts and speech actions in conversational contexts (p. 45)	Investigating discursive practices, understandings of personhood in relation to self and others (pp. 46–47)		Introducing consideration of consequence and agency; rather than set roles, subject positions allow for individuals to locate themselves within or even resist narratives (pp. 40–41; 50–52)
Understanding language and other sign systems as dynamic, multi-faceted discourses (pp. 45–46)	Considering metaphors, storylines present in one's own discourses and subject positions (pp. 46–47)		
Considering metaphors, discourses present in the positions of others (p. 46)	Examining "jointly produced story lines" (p. 48)		
Recognizing the constitutive force of discourse as people exercise choice in discursive practices, dynamically taking up, rejecting, or changing subject positions (p. 46)			

The Self and Others — Harré & Moghaddam (2003)

Studying "performance style, the way people do things and the meanings ascribed to what they do" (p. 3) in social situations as alternative to reductionism and "performance capacity, how well individual humans do on specific tasks" (p. 3)

Examining power in social episodes, storylines, and positions (p. 10)

[a] Page numbers indicate specific areas where this topic is discussed within a work and has been summarized. Direct quotes are indicated with quotation marks.

[b] These varieties of positioning have been expanded upon in various works (e.g., McVee, Baldassarre, & Bailey, 2004; Sabat, 2008).

were introduced as a means for accomplishing those actions articulated in Table 19.1. Table 19.1 should not be construed as a complete representation of PT as the summaries rely primarily upon early work.

Over time, Harré and his colleagues, and occasionally his critics, have further explored, contested, or elaborated upon the basic ideas presented in early articles published in *JTSB*.

The Growth of Positioning Theory

The Emergence of Positioning Theory in Research

As noted above, the original Davies and Harré (1990) and Harré and Van Langenhove (1991) articles in the *JTSB* contained seeds of thought cultivated and explored across the 1990s as key collaborators continued to elaborate, expand, and apply principles of PT particularly through articles in *JTSB* (e.g., Howie & Peters, 1996; Tan & Moghaddam, 1995; Van Langenhove & Harré, 1994). Ideas pertaining to PT were also explored in a number of edited volumes, *Positioning Theory* (Harré & Van Langenhove, 1999) and *The Self and Others* (Harré & Moghaddam, 2003b), which contained articles predominantly by scholars from psychology, linguistics, and sociology. In addition, Harré and his colleagues have continued to apply Positioning Theory to specific domains (e.g., Harré & Moghaddam, 2013; Moghaddam, Harré, & Lee, 2008a; Moghaddam & Harré, 2010). These books by the primary co-founders of PT, working primarily in psychology, have been followed by discipline-specific volumes such as *Sociocultural Positioning in Literacy* (McVee, Brock, & Glazier, 2011) which focused on literacy-related educational studies and James (2014) in public relations.

As positioning theorists continued to publish articles in *JTSB* and in collections edited by Harré and his colleagues, scholars also began to apply PT to the interpretation and analysis of research data in a variety of fields. For example, to assist in articulating a transformative model of midwifery education, Phillips, Fawns, and Hayes (2002) applied PT to midwifery practices. In political relations, Slocum and Van Langenhove (2004) explored how PT could be used to consider regional integration and issues such as political collaboration or sovereignty. Utilizing positioning, Ritchie (2002) explored gender, status, and power relations in science education. Molloy and Clarke (2005) employed PT to study interviews with participants and video-taped feedback sessions between supervisors and students studying physiotherapy. Some scholars began explicating methodological concerns. For example, Redman and Fawns (2010) articulated how researchers could use pronoun grammar analysis (Mühlhaüsler & Harré, 1990) to help understand positions taken up within teacher meetings. Tirado and Gálvez (2007) have demonstrated how PT can be used to perform discourse analysis of virtual spaces.

While PT was being taken up across different disciplines, it had also begun surfacing in literacy and language education. In what is perhaps the earliest published uses of PT in a peer-reviewed education journal, Evans (1996) used PT to consider gender-related interactions and equity in peer-led book discussion groups. In the early 2000s, a number of literacy scholars also utilized PT for a diverse set of explorations. For example, Barone (2001) used PT to re-analyze existing findings and data to consider the relationships between a parent, student, and a researcher in classroom contexts, and Enciso (2001) drew upon PT in a discussion of reading assessments, equity, and policy. Drawing from Davies' (1993) work on gender, Anderson (2002) investigated gendered identities in a multi-age elementary classroom to look at how gender, identity, and literacy interactions were represented. McVee, Baldassarre, and Bailey (2004) extended Self-Other Positioning to a teacher's personal narrative and response to explorations of language, literacy, and culture. An exploration of privilege and its impact on English Language Arts teachers' developing practices in relation to literature read with their students was the context of Glazier's (2005) use of the theory.

Across the decades, additional articles elaborating or extending PT have been published, and PT has found its way into an increasingly diverse set of disciplines. In a recent literature review, McVee

(2017) identified more than 200 education related studies that used PT. Of studies using PT in education, more than 50% are related to literacy or language in classrooms, teacher education, or professional development. The growing interest in PT and the fact that a large subset of research studies using PT focus on some aspect of literacy and language indicate literacy scholars clearly find PT useful and applicable to their work.

Conceptual and Theoretical Roots of Positioning Theory

It can be helpful to think of PT using the analogy of a tree (Figure 19.1). The original article (Davies & Harré, 1990) has roots in a number of different fields—feminist poststructuralism, linguistics, philosophy, and social psychology. While the original publication has theoretical grounding in these fields, the connections to specific theorists and movements are not always immediately apparent. As early as 1983, Harré lamented that "excessive citation has become a vice in psychological writing" (p. x). While fewer citations make for less cluttered writing, it does make it challenging for novices to ferret out connections amongst theories. Theoretical influences become more apparent when considering the subsequent PT work led by Harré and collaborators (i.e., Van Langenhove and Moghaddam) who continued to publish works on PT after the original 1990 publication. For example, Harré (2015) and other positioning theorists (e.g., Harré & Van Langenhove, 1999; Howie & Peters, 1996; McVee, 2011; Moghaddam & Harré, 2010) delineated ideas pertaining to positioning that were rooted particularly in linguistics and speech-act theory (e.g., Searle, 1979); philosophy of language (e.g., Bakhtin, 1981; Wittgenstein, 1953), and social psychology (e.g., Vygotsky, 1978). Harré's writings around moral orders drew, in part, from Goffman (1963) (see Harré, 1983, pp. 236–242). Harré also suggested parallels between Goffman's notion of framing and position (e.g., Mühlhaüsler & Harré, p 229) and later more carefully delineated

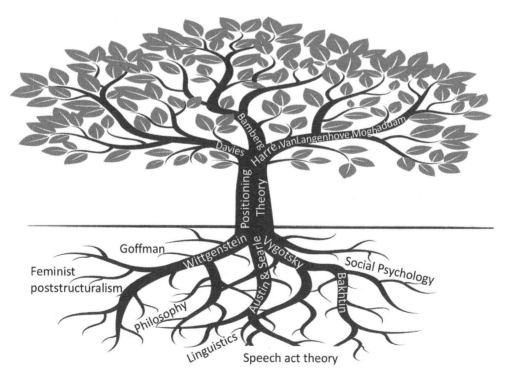

Figure 19.1   Positioning Theory Tree

Goffman's (1974, 1981) shift from dramaturgical models of interaction toward "footing" but also argued Goffman's work differed from positioning because footing and frames could "not escape the constraints of role theory" (Davies & Harré, 1990, p. 55).

The Bronwyn Davies Branch

Considering Figure 19.1, several distinct branches emerge from the trunk of the positioning tree. For example, there is a major branch of scholars, some citing the original Davies & Harré *JTSB* piece, but who primarily use theoretical frameworks built upon Davies' work on agency and gender (e.g., Davies, 1991, 2003). As such, this branch of the tree moves in a different direction than other publications that continued to build upon major precepts introduced in the original (Davies & Harré, 1990) and in early articles such as Harré and Van Langenhove (1991). It is beyond the scope of this chapter to review Davies' influential and important works encompassing agency, neoliberalism, feminism, gender and other topics, but at minimum, readers should be aware that her perspectives on agency and gender informed the earliest versions of PT. Davies also provided examples in the original work such as her critical analysis of boys' and girls' positions in response to the story *The Paper Bag Princess* (Davies & Harré 1990, pp. 59–61, 1999, pp. 50–52). While the critical lens employed by Davies is familiar to literacy researchers, it was not a perspective often taken up by early Positioning Theorists. Tirado and Gálvez (2007), for instance, have argued that PT owes a major debt to Foucault's discussion of subject positions and discourses (e.g., Foucault, 1972). This lens has resonated strongly with education scholars of gender and literacy who have employed positioning (e.g., Anderson, 2002; Earles, 2017). Davies' work is also important because it makes clear that agency and action were pivotal in PT from the beginning, which is important to stress as some have claimed PT does not adequately account for action and agency (e.g., Korobov, 2010; Peters & Appel, 1996). In discussing action and agency, Davies also drew from post-structuralist theory and feminist scholars to discuss subjectivity, storyline and narrative, all of which figure prominently in PT. There is also a very strong connection between Davies' interests and perspectives and those of Hollway, who is generally credited with introducing "position" and "positioning" in her work on gender relations and sexuality (Van Langenhove & Harré, 1999a, p. 16), influencing the writings of Davies and Harré (1990) and other positioning theorists.

The Michael Bamberg Branch

Another branch of positioning studies has emerged largely from Bamberg's work and articles published in *Narrative Inquiry* (formerly *Journal of Narrative and Life History*). While we cannot provide a full review of Bamberg's work, he has made major contributions to positioning analysis and PT, providing a clear methodological process for the analysis of narrative structure and performance. Bamberg (2004a, b) himself has attempted to articulate particular nuances of positioning and distinguish his approach from Davies and Harré (1990) (see Bamberg, 2004b, pp. 136–137). Perhaps the most important contribution of Bamberg's work was to provide a detailed, early illustration of positioning analysis methodology for narrative performance and structure (see Bamberg, 1997, p. 336). Bamberg's analytic approach addressed some limitations of early PT pieces that did not have detailed methodological sections, relying upon illustrations of dialogue rather than actual transcribed discourse. Bamberg's (2004b) three-tiered process can be replicated or adapted and has been integrated with PT (e.g., Hunt & Handsfield, 2013; Lofgren & Karlsson, 2016).

Bamberg has been placed on his own branch in Figure 19.1 rather than alongside other positioning theorists to reflect two elements of his work. First, Bamberg has pointed out some nuanced differences between his own thinking and his reading of Davies and Harré (1990). In addition, and more importantly, Bamberg catalyzed a line of research in narrative studies that address narrative positioning analysis. Significant areas of overlap with PT exist, but there are two major distinctions.

First, work on narrative positioning, often draws predominantly, and frequently exclusively, upon Bamberg's work. Also, of growing importance and influence is work by Bamberg (2006) and others (e.g., Bamberg & Georgakopoulou, 2008) on small stories, typically analyzed through Bamberg's previous approach to positioning analysis. While theoretical work and research studies in this area also have roots in social and discursive psychology, many of these scholars often do not cite Davies and Harré or other PT work, nor do they specifically attempt to further the work of Harré or other PT scholars. In this chapter, we focus on theoretical work that draws upon "Positioning Theory" in contrast to all forms of positioning analysis or theory. Bamberg's work is clearly useful and important to researchers of narrative, literacy, and language (Hunt, 2016; McVee, 2005), but, similar to Davies, there is a branch of research that has grown directly out of Bamberg's work that, even while having significant overlap, is often quite separate from Davies and Harré's PT.

Given the number of scholars involved in delineating PT, it is not possible to provide biographical insight to them all, but given Harré's influence, it is likely helpful to readers to learn about Harré's scholarly background. The next section presents a biography of Harré, followed by a more extended discussion of PT and storyline.

The Rom Harré Branch

Harré (2002) has referred to PT as "a relatively new branch of social psychology" (p. 160), and more than any other scholar, it is Harré who is associated with PT although as this branch of the tree indicates, Luk Van Langenhove and Ali Moghaddam have been his frequent collaborators. As a scholar with a prolific history, any overview in this chapter is quite brief when compared with Harré's biography (see Van Langenhove, 2010a). He first published a *Brief Introduction to Symbolic Logic* in 1954, and as he noted in author information for *The Self and Others* (2003b), by the early 2000s, he had authored or co-authored over 60 books. Several books have been devoted to collecting or commenting on Harré's work, for example, essays from Harré's collaborators and critics written in his honor (Bhaskar, 1990), a collection of his works related to scientific realism and modeling edited by Rothbart (2004), and a compendium of Harré's influential writings in social psychology edited by Van Langenhove (2010b). In addition, there is now a biennial conference where scholars present theoretical work, research studies, and literature reviews related to PT. Harré has authored and co-authored numerous articles on PT and a wide array of topics related to science, philosophy, linguistics, and psychology.

Some readers may be surprised to learn that Harré began his scholarly work in the sciences. He taught math and physics, and is well known for his works on scientific realism and the philosophy of physics (Van Langenhove, 2010a). Harré's interests in science and the philosophy of language were, in part, what led him to study at Oxford in the mid-1950s, influenced by J. L. Austin best known for his work in *speech-act theory*. Harré was a very early proponent of social psychology, which focused on developing a discursive approach to psychology. Given his interest in language and philosophy, it is unsurprising that he was one of the psychologists who understood early-on the importance of Vygotsky's thinking in developing social psychology. Readers of the sixth edition of *Theoretical Processes and Models of Reading* (Alvermann, Unrau, & Ruddell, 2013) may be familiar with the chapter revisiting schema theory and the Vygotsky Space model (McVee, Dunsmore, & Gavelek, 2013). This Vygotsky Space model was developed by Gavelek and Raphael (1996), adapted from Harré's writings (1983), and has been used by researchers in literacy, although usually separate from their use of PT (e.g., Pennington, Brock, Torrey, & Wolters, 2013). These connections to Vygotsky's work serve as a reminder that, while not always directly articulated in Harré's writings around PT, there are important theoretical underpinnings and intersections (e.g., Van Langenhove & Harré, 1999b, p. 131). Vygotskian influences will no doubt be areas of resonance for scholars of literacy and language where these perspectives are common. Because Vygotskian perspectives are well known, we will not address them here. (For more on Vygotsky and PT, see Howie & Peters, 1996; McVee, 2011.)

Positioning Theory as a Theoretical and Analytical Framework

Having roots in the work of speech–act theory, following Austin and Searle, and the language-based theories of Vygotsky, Wittgenstein, and others, it is not surprising that many writings about PT attend primarily to spoken language. Moghaddam and Harré (2010) have written: "It is with words that we ascribe rights and claim them for ourselves and place duties on others" (p. 3). Many of the original articles and edited volumes around PT do focus almost exclusively on words albeit in different domains (e.g., conversation, radio broadcasts, policy documents). At the same time, Harré and Moghaddam, and other positioning theorists, repeatedly observe that positioning theory is about "how people use words (*and discourse of all types*) to locate themselves and others" (p. 2, emphasis added). Theoretical writings and research studies related to positioning have most often foregrounded linguistic signs in acts of positioning, and very few researchers have attempted to explore multiple modalities (e.g., image, film, color, etc.) (For exceptions see McVee & Carse, 2016; Pinnow & Chval, 2015.) PT is about communicative practices of all kinds. As such, it is essential for readers to recognize that while many positioning theorists foreground spoken interaction, Harré and others recognize other symbolic representations and actions as means of positioning. Given this, scholars using PT can and should consider how symbols of all kinds, not only speech, can position people within or in relation to storylines.

The Positioning Triangle

In discussing storyline, the PT triad or triangle (Van Langenhove & Harré, 1993) has emerged as a key representation and analytic tool. In later versions, the label "Social Force" of discursive acts has often been replaced with "Speech Act" (e.g., Harré, Moghaddam, Cairnie, Rothbart, & Sabat, 2009, p. 18) or "Speech and Other Acts" (e.g., McVee, 2011, p. 6).

While adjusting labels to highlight speech and other acts can be particularly useful for use of the triangle as an analytic tool, removing the label "social force" somewhat masks the elements of power, and Austin's (1962) notion of illocutionary and perlocutionary force. *Illocutionary force* is "that which is achieved *in* saying something" (i.e., congratulating someone) and *perlocutionary force* "that which is achieved *by* saying something" (i.e., pleasing someone who received an award) (Van Langenhove

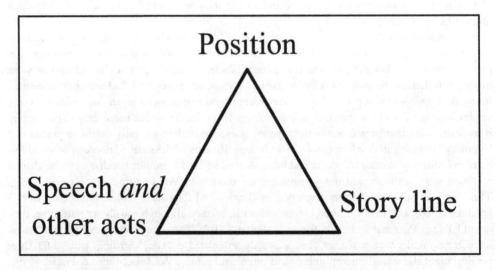

Figure 19.2   Positioning Triangle or Triad

Source: Adapted from Van Langenhove & Harre, 1999a, p. 18. Copyright by John Wiley & Sons, Ltd. Adapted with permission.

& Harré, 1999a, p. 17). In PT, communicative practices are comprised of social and individual elements that can be explored in the context of: position, speech and other acts, and storyline. Harré and Moghaddam (2003a) observe that, "The 'positioning triangle' can be entered empirically at any of the vertices, 'position,' 'speech act,' or 'storyline'" (p. 9). The intricacies of speech and actions whether they are person-to-person (e.g., a roll of the eyes) or person-to-social group (e.g., a white supremacist raising a poster of a Nazi swastika at a rally for free speech in the U.S.) can be investigated using the positioning triangle. Harré and Van Langenhove (1999) elaborate:

> Positioning theory focuses on understanding how psychological phenomena are produced in discourse. Its starting point is the idea that the constant flow of everyday life in which we all take part, is fragmented through discourse into distinct episodes that constitute the basic elements of both our biographies and the social world. The skills that people have to talk are not only based on capacities to produce words and sentences but equally on capacities to follow rules that shape the episodes of social life. Not only what we do but also what we can do is restricted by rights, duties and obligations we acquire, assume or which are imposed upon us in the concrete social contexts of everyday life.
>
> *(Harré & Van Langenhove, 1999, p. 4).*

Discourses are thus shaped by the symbol systems (words, images, and other acts) that people rely upon in their day-to-day life, and are also based upon the various moral orders that govern social interactions. One of the features of social interactions is "the moral positions of the participants and the rights and duties they have to say certain things" (Harré & Van Langenhove, 1999, p. 6). Moral orders and the rights and duties associated with them and our own lived experiences influence storylines that we can construct, or concomitantly, storylines we may refuse to enter, if we feel we have power to do so. In this way, interactants can refuse positions.

Moral orders are not merely local or personal. Moral orders exist at multiple levels, for instance, within institutions and nations. And, most often, moral orders are implicit. For example, in the United States, elected presidents have been expected to serve in the executive position of leadership by acting and speaking with restraint and decorum. When attending a global summit with others world leaders, it is a president's duty to put his own feelings aside and act for the greater good and with restraint. A president could refuse this storyline, and instead foreground his right to act and speak as he wishes. At a global summit, he might choose to push another world leader out of the way to get to the front in a photo or make off-the-cuff comments about the use of extreme military force, stepping out of sync with his policy advisors. Both examples demonstrate a democratically-elected president going against expected moral orders and storylines and positioning himself as having the right to do as he pleases. In these examples, the president creates a storyline wherein acts that are typically viewed as duties are replaced with personal rights.

The notion of rights and duties is important as Harré and Moghaddam (2003a) describe it in relation to position. We can think of a position as:

> a cluster of rights and duties to perform certain actions with a certain significance as acts, but which also may include prohibitions or denials of access to some of the local repertoire of meaningful acts. In a certain sense in each social milieu there is a kind of Platonic realm of positions, realized in current practices, which people can adopt, strive to locate themselves in, be pushed into, be displaced from or be refused access, recess themselves from and so on, in a highly mobile and dynamic way.
>
> *(pp. 5–6)*

In other cases, perceived rights and duties may also play into existing storylines that constrain the way that people position themselves. Students who are speaking Spanish in a classroom and who are told by a teacher that, "We speak English in this country," may feel powerless to reposition themselves, feeling that it is not their right to talk back to a teacher. The dynamic episodes or patterns created through speech acts and positions construct a storyline. "Each storyline is expressible in a loose cluster of narrative conventions" (Harré & Moghaddam, 2003a, p. 6). Examining and analyzing storylines draws attention to positions and to speech and other acts. Concomitantly, analyzing speech and other acts or positions results in attending to storylines. As noted earlier, analysis can begin from any point of the PT triangle. Several examples of analysis using the PT triangle can be found in Harré et al. (2009).

The Positioning Diamond

While most adaptations of the PT triangle involve minor changes, Slocum-Bradley (2009) proposed an adaptation to the PT triangle that includes rights and duties, identities, social forces, and storylines in the PT Diamond. Her purpose was to provide a conceptual framework that will "permit *systematic* analysis" (2009, p. 80, emphasis in the original) of discourse and positioning using a transdisciplinary framework. Her model has several advantages over the traditional PT triangle. It retains a visible marker for social forces, keeping analysts mindful of these and moral orders that shape rights and duties, positions, identities, and storylines. Slocum-Bradley also observes that the distinctions between rights, duties, and identities have often been glossed over whereas the positioning diamond, as an analytical framework, "makes this distinction explicit, thereby enabling a more refined analysis of meaning-making and more acute explanations of the unfolding of social episodes" (p. 91).

While Slocum-Bradley acknowledges the many facets that may be revealed through a positioning diamond, one limitation of many schematics of PT is the lack of representation across time. This limitation is problematic because "The distinction between past, present, and future does not go over neatly into psychological time, partly because the social and psychological past is not fixed. The social future can influence the social past" (Van Langenhove & Harré, 1999a, p. 15). We have thus adapted the PT Diamond to add the dimension of time as located within moral fields (see Figure 19.3). "Moral fields," writes Van Langenhove (2017), "are the invisible space in which persons live their lives" (p. 8).

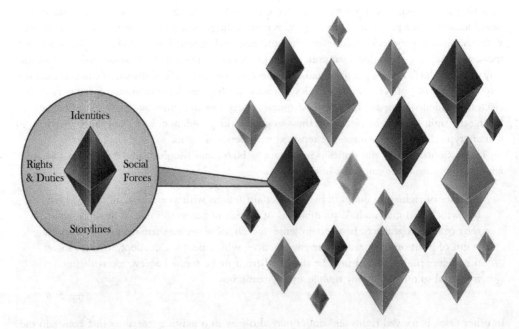

Figure 19.3 Positioning Theory Diamond in an Array of Relationships across Time
Source: Adapted from Slocum-Bradley, 2009. Copyright by John Wiley & Sons, Ltd. Adapted with permission.

Slocum-Bradley described her switch from triangle to a diamond as intentional. Figure 19.3 adapts her representation further to evoke the multifaceted nature of a gemstone. The metaphor is meant to intentionally convey to researchers that there may be other facets to discover even as they begin analysis. Slocum-Bradley's PT diamond relies upon a three-tiered level of examination predicated upon narrative analysis and small stories (e.g., Bamberg, 1997, 2004a, 20004b, 2006). In presenting her positioning diamond, Slocum-Bradley also attempted to disentangle "position" from "identity" (pp. 89–91), and attempted to demonstrate how identities could be evoked at all three levels of analysis, that is, within variety of moral fields (Van Langenhove, 2017). While time is often represented as linear—past, present, future—readers are reminded that social and psychological time can enfold not only what is happening in the present but can enfold the past and future as well. For instance, narrators may shift time through flash-ahead, flash-back, and in-the-moment sequences as a story is being narrated or a positioning episode unfolds (McVee, 2005), thus linking many of the "diamonds" in the social relationships represented in Figure 19.3.

Figure 19.3 attempts to capture this notion of positioning existing across the intersections of time but also in relation to moral orders or fields. "A powerful aspect of the use of positioning theory as an analytic tool is that not only persons and their identities both individual and social, but also societal issues on a cultural level can be tackled with the same conceptual apparatus" (Harré & Van Langenhove, 1999, pp. 11–12). This points to a compelling affordance of PT. At present, tensions around immigration, race, culture, and language use as related to identity are concerns and often flashpoints for disruption, contention, debate, and even violence in societies. PT offers an analytic lens to examine both local moral orders and how rights, duties, and storylines are constructed and represented, as well as how various individuals take up, contest, refuse, examine, question, participate in, construct, and interrogate these moral fields. Additionally, PT can be used to look across moral fields for individuals at the local, institutional, and/or societal level, considering how speech and other acts shape stories and position persons socially and individually. Positioning theorists thus have the opportunity to examine many storylines. In research as well as representation, positioning theorists can thus hopefully avoid falling into the "danger of the single story" (Adichie, 2009).

Misconceptions and Critiques of Positioning Theory

Positioning Theory as metaphor

Position or positioning is often used as a general metaphor in educational research, and scholars may draw upon various theoretical perspectives in their positioning analysis. For example, Souto-Manning (2010), Zacher (2008), and Mosley and Johnson (2007) all develop thoughtful scholarship around the general metaphor of position or positioning. These scholars use various theorists in their work (e.g., Bakhtin, Bourdieu, Vygotsky). In these examples, the researchers neither drew from nor intended to draw from PT in their analysis and discussion of positions. Such a stance is appropriate for scholars wishing to use general metaphors of positioning in their work. On the other hand, when choosing to apply PT, researchers should be deliberate and specific in their use of conceptual frameworks to avoid conflating generic discussions of position with PT.

Specificity is important because a common misconception of PT involves using it as a metaphor rather than theoretical framework. In a review of more than 200 educational research articles, McVee (2017) found that even when claiming explicitly to use PT, researchers often built upon a general metaphor of positioning rather than specific tenets of PT, missing opportunities for deeper and targeted analysis, additional theory building, or transdisciplinary connections. Additionally, several co-founders of PT (e.g., Moghaddam, 2017; Van Langenhove, 2017) have recently reiterated that PT is more than a metaphor—it is a set of theoretical principles that continues to emerge as a theory in its own right. PT should, Van Langenhove (2016) argues, "be seen as a starting point for reflecting upon the many different aspects of the social realm" (p. 66) and as a particular theory. The metaphorical pull of positioning is very strong. It is not only an abstract idea but an embodied experience for all people. Given the way in which embodied experiences ground our understanding of language and metaphor (Johnson, 2007; Lakoff & Johnson, 2003), it is not surprising that positioning has such resonance with researchers.

Positioning Theory and Empirical Analysis

One critique of PT has been that it has not relied upon empirical analysis of talk. Writing in the journal *Qualitative Research in Psychology*, Korobov (2010) argued, "Harré's positioning theory has *rarely been applied to actual empirical analyses of talk* (but rather has been occupied with a conceptual refutation of traditional psychology)" (p. 272, emphasis added). Harré, Van Langenhove, Moghaddam, and others have frequently introduced writings around PT as a critique of traditional cognitive psychology. They eschew information-processing models of mind associated with the first cognitive revolution, and emphasize how people use symbolic systems of all kinds within varied social contexts. Harré and his companions make clear they see PT as a challenge to traditional, experimental psychology, but constructing theoretical arguments against traditional perspectives in psychology is not the zenith of their work.

Examining only the first PT pieces in *JTSB* and introductions to their edited volumes, there may be weak support for Korobov's critique. However, across the edited volumes, it is clear that a larger agenda persists, and this includes development of PT in its own right (Van Langenhove, 2017), and also the analysis of conversational data or other data sources such as that represented across the edited volumes and research articles. In addition, there is no support for the assertion that PT is only rarely applied to the empirical study of discourse. For example, in a cross-disciplinary review of PT articles related to education of all levels and disciplines, McVee (2017) found that by 2010, there had been a minimum of 50 studies consisting mostly of talk across a variety of disciplines related to education in areas as diverse as midwifery, science, literacy, and library studies. (Keep in mind that this number does not include studies of talk or other communicative acts that drew on PT unrelated to education.)

Deppermann (2013) raised a related criticism:

> Harré's approach does not really sit well with the state of the art of fine-grained interactional and linguistic analysis of narrative and social interaction. *Studies by Harré and his co-workers rely on made-up examples and sketchy glosses, whose empirical basis in terms of data is unclear. They do neither use detailed sequential analysis of authentic social interaction based on audio and video recordings* nor do they attend to the precise linguistic and narrative choices and strategies employed to project and negotiate positions.
>
> *(pp. 4–5, emphasis added)*

By 2013, there had been more than 130 education related studies published across the disciplines using PT. Many of these studies, particularly those related to classroom discourse, used video and audio analyses and engage in detailed analysis of authentic discourse relying upon video, audio, and other artifacts.

Both critiques raised above are easily refutable and demonstrate a lack of awareness of how PT has been applied across the disciplines. Such critiques also issue a challenge for scholars who use PT. Given that a great deal of innovative application of PT happens outside of psychology or sociolinguistics, it is imperative that educational researchers move out of their comfort zones, presenting at conferences and publishing in journals outside their disciplines, targeting venues promoting interdisciplinary conversations.

Deppermann (2013) raises an additional criticism that is more easily justified regarding how positioning theorists fail to analyze narratives. Narrative positioning analysis is one area where, as noted earlier, some PT scholars have turned to methods developed by Michael Bamberg and others. There is a long tradition not only of narratology and analysis of narrative predicated upon literary analysis narratives (e.g., Burke, 1945; Herman, 2009), but also of sociolinguistic analysis of narrative (Bamberg, 2004a; De Fina & Georgakopoulou, 2015; Gee, 1986; Labov & Waletzky, 1967; Riessman, 1993). Because storyline figures so prominently in PT, it is surprising that more researchers have not drawn on specific forms of narrative analysis in their work. In storyline analysis, it would be helpful if more analytic procedures were included, and if researchers drew from narrative analysts. For example, chapters by McVee (2013) and Brock and Gavelek (2013) do not include a description of the narrative analysis and procedures used to identify the storylines. It is thus difficult for readers to access the specific forms of analysis used by the researchers. Particularly in peer-reviewed journals, authors should be clear about analytical procedures (Smagorinsky, 2008). For those new to narrative research, the journal of *Narrative Inquiry* provides many examples of theory, methods, and research articles, allowing for more discussion of methodological procedures than does the typical book chapter (cf. McVee, 2005, 2013).

Positioning Theory in Research on Literacy and Language

In this section, we describe a few exemplary studies that: 1) use PT as a theoretical framework, not merely a metaphor; 2) rely upon empirical data from a variety of sources and analyzed using various methodologies; and 3) provide useful models for applying PT.

Engaging Dialectically with Theory

Dressman (2008) explains that a strong relationship between theory, methodology, and data can be used to question, extend, and lead to evolution of theories over time. He writes, that "testing of both findings and theory . . . result[s] in a finer-grained and more complicated analysis and presentation of findings" (p. 135). In the evolution of PT, there are studies which use not only data but also frameworks (e.g., identity theories, Vygotsky's zone of proximal development, narrative inquiry) to push against or elaborate the foundational elements of PT (see Table 19.1) laid down by positioning theorists to construct an analytical framework (e.g., Anderson, 2009; Bomer & Laman, 2004). In other cases, PT is used to elaborate and extend other social theories and conceptualizations (e.g., McEntarfer & McVee, 2014).

Bomer and Laman (2004) use a recursive, dialectical relationship between theory and their immersion in data collected in naturalistic classroom settings to construct "a theoretical framework for the study of positioning and its significance in understanding children's literacy development" (p. 421). Grounded in the PT work of Davies and Harré (1990) as well as Harré and Van Langenhove (1999), the sociocultural identity work of Holland, Lachicotte, Skinner, and Cain (1998), and Vygotsky's zone of proximal development (1986), Bomer and Laman (2004) spent a year observing children's interactional discourse (as well as other sources, such as interviews and field notes) during writing. The methodology is explicit and tied inextricably with PT, particularly the developed analytical framework. Going beyond simply defining the kinds of positioning (e.g., reflexive and interactive) and storylines common to PT studies, Bomer and Laman (2004) additionally describe how children's composed texts as well as "discursive resources" (p. 439) are implicated in constructing positions, storylines, and identities in classroom contexts. As such, PT extends through their observations and ensuing understandings about how children positioned themselves and each other during extensive time spent in the literacy classroom under study. This exemplifies that back-and-forth relationship between theory and data described by Dressman (2008) as a way to build social theory, particularly related to reading and writing.

Instead of elaborating on concepts laid down by foundational positioning theorists to create a new analytical framework, McEntarfer and McVee (2014) build upon Wortham's (2001) interactional and representational positioning in narrative through the use of Davies & Harré's (1990) notion of subject positions plus their associated socially-shaped rights, duties, and obligations. The authors argue that these subject positions and Wortham's (2001) understanding of role in narrative are complementary, providing a broadening of scope for what roles and positions can be considered when analyzing narrative as action. Multiple kinds of positioning are defined with associated examples from the data, exploring the written, performed, and subsequently recontextualized narratives constructed by LGBTQ+ college students, linking participants' stories to power and agency. This study illustrates how PT can serve to complementarily expand understandings of narrative research frequently used in studies of literacy in classrooms or teacher education.

Both studies (Bomer & Laman, 2004; McEntarfer & McVee, 2014) demonstrate how literacy researchers can take up PT while engaging in dialectical arguments. As such, researchers engage in dialogue with theorists and researchers who have conducted previous literacy work constructing arguments with and through data to help further explain, elaborate, or even challenge particular theoretical elements or to extend theories in particular ways.

Applying and Extending Varieties of Positioning

Multiple studies address varieties of positioning, delineate the analytical methods used to identify such positions across the data set, and explicitly name these positions (and their corresponding theoretical citations) using illustrative examples while presenting findings (Bomer & Laman, 2004; Evans, 1996; McEntarfer & McVee, 2014; McVee, Baldassarre, & Bailey, 2004). For example, Evans (1996) examines student-led literature discussions in a fifth-grade classroom. She uses specific examples of speech and other acts to demonstrate how *first* and *second order positioning*, as well as *moral* and *personal* positioning, contribute to students' positioning of themselves and others. Findings show that students rely largely upon gender, cultural background, and status to position themselves, resist *intentional* or *forced* positions, or to position others in the group. This influences the nature and quality of their interactions around texts they read and raises questions concerning the ways that discourse practices in literature-based discussions influence student self-other positioning. As one of the earliest studies using PT in literacy, Evans questions assumptions about the democratic nature of student-led book discussions. Her study of specific positions is a model for literacy researchers and educators alike to investigate and understand dynamics in peer-to-peer literacy groups.

While Evans relied upon varieties of positions identified by Van Langenhove and Harré (1991), other scholars have used fine-grained discourse analysis to uncover new types of positioning (e.g., *intertextual positioning*) and to deepen understandings of previously identified positions (e.g., *Self-Other Positioning*). In the context of an ethnography of teachers' understandings and identity work related to literacy, language, and culture in a literacy teacher education course, McVee et al. (2004), analyzed written discourse and talk to consider Self-Other Positioning. In attempting to employ this previously theoretical category in actual analysis, they realized while coding that almost any statement could be coded as Self-Other. Ultimately, McVee et al., arrived at four new types of Self-Other Positioning "*Self-as-Other; Self-in-Other, Self-Opposed-to-Other, and Self-Aligned-with-Other*" (p. 285) which allowed them to engage in both a deeper level of analysis and theory building to explore how teachers understand the connections across culture and literacy.

These studies demonstrate that scholars have been using PT, sociolinguistic methods of analysis, and data of many kinds—not only transcripts—for many years. Additionally, because previous in-depth work has been carried out on types of positioning, those scholars wishing to employ PT in their studies, particularly in literacy and language research, should be aware of previous work related to varieties of positioning and build upon previous theoretical and methodological work, rather than relying upon only Davies & Harré (1990) or Van Langenhove and Harré (1991, 1999).

McVee et al., Evans, and others also share a common focus on attending to critical perspectives on race, language use, gender, and power as tied to practices of reading, writing, speaking, and listening.

Demonstrating Theoretical Tenets of Positioning through Data

Other studies make a point to use their data to illustrate how PT can be a means for understanding this relationship between speech acts, storylines, subject positions, and other constructs, such as identity, race, family dynamics, and further interactions (Barone, 2001; Kayi-Aydar, 2014). For example, Kayi-Aydar (2014) analyzes multiple points of data. She employs PT to analyze ESL classroom Discourse (i.e., student/teacher and student/student interactions, observations, interviews, student artifacts) and surface different kinds of identities present in the classroom. Ahmad and Tarek are presented as case studies of "talkative ESL students" (p. 693). Their cases illustrate key tenets of PT (i.e., subject positions, positional identities, rights, social expectations) and how these tenets work together. Kayi-Aydar (2014) reveals in her analysis that though both Ahmad and Tarek were deemed more proficient in English compared to their classmates. They were positioned differently at the intersection of theirs and others' speech acts, identities, and classroom social norms, which impacted their opportunities to learn. For example, Ahmad reflexively positioned himself as a proficient English speaker but was positioned interactively by his classmates as an "outsider" (p. 689).

Barone (2001) provides another exemplary illustration of how the components of PT work together as a theoretical-analytical tool. She conducts a recursive analysis or revisioning of how one child Billy was positioned in his literacy learning—along with his mother and herself as the researcher—over four years. This illustration provides the reader with a scope of what PT can accomplish when applied to an extensive data set including four years of field notes and interviews. Through PT, Barone uncovers storylines that counter dominant discourses about three kinds of people in relation to literacy and learning: "a) minority women, who are also poor and [are] foster mothers . . . b) minority children, who also were prenatally exposed to drugs . . . and c) the researcher" (p. 115). For example, the mother in this study, Lucille, held a power position over the researcher, Barone. Because Lucille was obviously more informed about her own neighborhood, she often spoke and acted from the position of a knowledgeable protector, positioning the researcher as naïve. This and other alternative storylines were derived by Barone using reflexive positioning through autobiographic telling (Moghaddam, 1999) over four years within conversations observed between Lucille, her son Billy, and Barone. Specifically, Barone's work can assist literacy researchers in thinking about positions as arrays set in a moral field across time (Van Langenhove, 2017) and also in focusing on literacy development but also researchers' subjectivities and positions.

Future Directions for Positioning Theory in Educational Research

As demonstrated by articles cited throughout this chapter, researchers of literacy and language have made significant contributions toward using PT as an analytical lens. Many educational researchers rely upon a combination of methods in their studies in ways that could provide useful examples for others using PT outside the field of education. Educational researchers routinely carry out qualitative studies that rely upon ethnographic techniques for data collection such as observation, interviews, and artifacts. This methodology results in rich data sets that may be comprised of written artifacts, images, video and audio recordings, transcription of spoken words, and increasingly, multimodal transcriptions which account for modes such as gaze, movement, image, color, and so on.

While positioning theorists, including Harré, acknowledge that positioning occurs through speech and *other acts*, illustrations that combine analysis of multiple modes of communication using social semiotics and PT are rare. Some articles do move beyond analysis of the spoken word to intentionally investigate other accompanying actions. For instance, Vetter (2013**)** investigates "non-verbal actions" that accompany speech using a PT framework (p. 184). Kayi-Aydar (2014) included analysis of gesture, gaze, facial expression. However, many researchers (e.g., Shanahan, 2013; Smith, 2016) have engaged in deep, analysis across literacy data sources through a social semiotic and multimodal lens in what has been called the "semiotic turn" (e.g., Siegel & Panofsky, 2009, p. 99). While many literacy researchers have applied PT and some have begun looking beyond speech and across various artifacts, we identified only two studies that directly used PT and social semiotics as theoretical frameworks and as analytic perspectives (McVee & Carse, 2016; Pinnow & Chval, 2015). Clearly, the connection between social semiotics, multimodality, and PT is an area where literacy scholars can make a significant contribution.

As a relatively young theory, literacy scholars can also make significant contributions to PT by building upon theoretical work that is familiar within educational research. As noted previously, significant theoretical intersections related to Vygotsky and Wittgenstein exist that could be further developed. Connections exist to theorists such as Bakhtin, Foucault, and even Critical Race Theory that could be further explored. In addition to the methods of multimodal analysis (Jewitt, 2009) mentioned above, theoretical connections could readily be developed between positioning and social semiotics (Hodge & Kress, 1988). Education is already by nature interdisciplinary and pulls from a variety of theories, and there are many examples of PT being used in conjunction with other theories. For example, Linehan and McCarthy (2000) draw upon the familiar theory of situated learning and communities of practice (Lave & Wenger, 1991) in conjunction with PT within enacted classroom storylines. Literacy and language researchers are also well poised to craft these types of data-based theoretical arguments to advance PT. One key, however, is that literacy and language researchers must share their work with a transdisciplinary audience, requiring scholars to move beyond their disciplinary circles to publish and present their work.

Conclusion

PT offers numerous affordances for social science researchers including those who are primarily interested in literacy and language. The following are adapted from an exposition of affordances in McVee (2011). PT provides:

- a dynamic alternative to dramaturgical metaphors of interaction (i.e., role)
- an extension of Vygotsky's work by attending to meditational tools (i.e., speech and other actions) which can be variably applied to social situations, with positioning understood as a meditational, social activity
- a theory and analytical tools (e.g., varieties of positions, positioning diamond) useful in:
  - examining how people position themselves and others
  - excavating identities of self in moment-by-moment interactions wherein identities are fluid
- a means to identify and theorize about moral orders and how they influence actions through creation or implication of rights and duties and who is assigned rights or duties
- opportunities to seek and investigate complexity in educational research
- opportunities to explore culturally situated practices in ways that highlight complexity through critical analysis of discourse, not just speech but all modalities (e.g., image, color, etc.)
- a means to attend to power dynamics inherent in particular positions while attending to agency and action

We encourage scholars who desire to use PT to read broadly across Harré and his colleagues' writings in discursive psychology, linguistics, sociology, and philosophy as well as to read across disciplines where PT is applied. For educational researchers, this means looking not only to fields like psychology, but also looking for work being carried out in the sub-disciplines within education. Such an approach will lead to a familiarity and knowledge of PT that captures the breadth and depth that Positioning Theory has developed in the last decades.

References

Adichie, C. N. (July, 2009). The danger of a single story. Retrieved from http://www.ted.com/talks/chimamanda_adichie_the_danger_of_a_single_story

Alvermann, D. E., Unrau, N., & Ruddell, R. B. (2013). *Theoretical models and processes of reading* (6th ed.). Newark, DE: International Reading Association.

Anderson, D. (2002). Casting recasting gender: Children constituting social identities through literacy. *Research in the Teaching of English, 36*(3), 391–427.

Anderson, K. (2009). Applying positioning theory to the analysis of classroom interactions: Mediatiing micro-identities, macro-kinds, and ideologies of knowing. *Linguistics and Education, 20*, 291–310.

Austin, J. L. (1962). *How to do things with words.* Oxford: Clarendon Press.

Bakhtin, M. M. (1981). *The dialogic imagination: Four essays.* Austin, TX: University of Texas Press.

Bamberg, M. (1997). Positioning between structure and performance. *Journal of Narrative and Life History, 7*(1–4), 335–342.

Bamberg, M. (2004a). Form and functions of 'slut bashing' in male identity constructions in 15–year-olds. *Human Development, 47*(6), 331–353. doi:10.1159/000081036

Bamberg, M. (2004b). Positionings with Davie Hogan: Stories, tellings, and identities. In C. Daiute & C. Lightfoot (Eds.), *Narrative analysis: Studying the development of individuals in society* (pp. 135–157). Thousand Oaks, CA: Sage.

Bamberg, M. (2006). Stories: Big or small why do we care? *Narrative Inquiry, 16*(1), 139–147.

Bamberg, M., & Georgakopoulou, A. (2008). Small stories as a new perspective in narrative and identity analysis. *Text and Talk, 28*(3), 377–396.

Barone, D. (2001). Revisioning: Positioning of a parent, student, and researcher in response to classroom context. *Reading Research and Instruction, 40*(2), 101–120.

Bhaskar, R. (Ed.). (1990). *Harré and his critics: Essays in honour of Rom Harré with his commentary on them.* Oxford: Blackwell.

Bomer, R., & Laman, T. (2004). Positioning in a primary writing workshop: Joint action in the discursive production of writing subjects. *Research in the Teaching of English*, 38(4), 420–466.

Brock, C. H., & Gavelek, J. (2013). "Mean girls" go to college: Conflicting storylines of friendship and enmity among young adults. In R. Harré & F. M. Moghaddam (Eds.), *The psychology of friendship and enmity: Relationships in love, work, politics, and war* (Vol. 1, pp. 179–194). Santa Barbara, CA: Praeger.

Burke, K. (1945). *A grammar of motives.* New York, NY: Prentice Hall.

Davies, B. (1991). The concept of agency: A feminist post-structuralist analysis. *Social Analysis: The International Journal of Social and Cultural Practice, 30*, 42–53.

Davies, B. (1993/2003). *Shards of glass.* Cresskill, NJ: Hampton Press.

Davies, B., & Harré, R. (1990). Positioning: The discursive production of selves. *Journal for the Theory of Social Behaviour, 20*(1), 43–63.

De Fina, A., & Georgakopoulou, A. (Eds.). (2015). *The handbook of narrative analysis.* Malden MA: Wiley Blackwell.

Deppermann, A. (2013). Editorial: Positioning in narrative interaction. *Narrative Inquiry, 23*(1), 1–15.

Dressman, M. (2008). *Using social theory in educational research: A practical guide.* New York, NY: Routledge.

Earles, J. (2017). Reading gender: a feminist, queer approach to children's literature and children's discursive agency. *Gender and Education, 29*(3), 369–388.

Enciso, P. E. (2001). Taking our seats: The consequences of positioning in reading assessments. *Theory into Practice, 40*(3), 166–174.

Evans, K. S. (1996). Creating spaces for equity? The role of positioning in peer-led literature discussions. *Language Arts, 73*(3), 194–202.

Foucault, M. (1972). *The archeology of knowledge* (A. M. S. Smith, Trans.). New York: Pantheon Books.

Gavelek, J. R., & Raphael, T. E. (1996). Changing talk about text: New roles for teachers and students. *Language Arts, 73*(3), 182–192.

Gee, J. (1986). Units in the production of narrative discourse. *Discourse Processes, 9*, 391–422.

Glazier, J. A. (2005). Talking and teaching through a positional lens: Recognizing what and who we privilege in our practice. *Teaching Education, 16*(3), 231–243.

Goffman, E. (1963). *Stigma.* New York, NY: Simon & Schuster.

Goffman, E. (1974). *Frame analysis.* New York, NY: Harper.

Goffman, E. (1981). *Forms of talk.* Philadelphia, PA: University of Pennsylvania Press.

Harré, R. (1954). *Brief introduction to symbolic logic.* Lahore: Anarkali Press.

Harré, R. (1983). *Personal being: A theory for individual psychology.* Oxford: Blackwell.

Harré, R. (2002). *Cognitive science: A philosophical introduction.* Thousand Oaks, CA: Sage.

Harre, R., & Moghaddam, F. M. (Eds.) (2003a). Introduction: The self and others in traditional psychology and in positioning theory. In R. Harré & F. Moghaddam (Eds.), *The self and others* (pp. 1–11). Westport, CT: Praeger.

Harré, R., & Moghaddam, F. M. (Eds.). (2003b). *The self and others.* Westport, CT: Praeger.

Harré, R., & Moghaddam, F. M. (Eds.). (2013). *The psychology of friendship and enmity: Relationships in love, work, politics, and war* (Vol. 1 & 2). Santa Barbara, CA: Praeger.

Harré, R., Moghaddam, F. M., Cairnie, T. P., Rothbart, D., & Sabat, S. R. (2009). Recent advances in positioning theory. *Theory & Psychology, 19*(5), 5–31.

Harré, R., & Van Langenhove, L. (1991). Varieties of positioning. *Journal for the Theory of Social Behaviour, 21*(4), 393–407.

Harré, R., & Van Langenhove, L. (Eds.). (1999). *Positioning theory: Moral contexts of intentional action.* Malden, MA: Blackwell.

Herman, D. (2009). *Basic elements of narrative.* Malden, MA: Wiley-Blackwell.

Hodge, R., & Kress, G. (1988). *Social semiotics.* Ithaca, NY: Cornell University Press.

Holland, D., Lachicotte, W., Skinner, D. C., & Cain, C. C. (1998). *Identity and agency in cultural worlds.* Cambridge, MA: Harvard University Press.

Howie, D., & Peters, M. (1996). Positioning theory: Vygotsky, Wittgenstein and social constructionist psychology. *Journal for the Theory of Social Behaviour, 26*(1), 51–64.

Hunt, C. S. (2016). Getting to the heart of the matter: Discursive negotiations of emotions within literacy coaching interactions. *Teaching and Teacher Education, 60,* 331–343.

Hunt, C. S., & Handsfield, L. J. (2013). The emotional landscapes of literary coaching: Issues of identity, power, and positioning. *Journal of Literary Research, 45*(1), 47–86.

James, M. (2014). *Positioning theory and strategic communication: A new approach to public relations.* New York, NY: Routledge.

Jewitt, C. (Ed.). (2009). *The Routledge handbook of multimodal analysis.* London: Routledge.

Johnson, M. (2007). *The meaning of the body: Aesthetics of human understanding.* Chicago, IL: University of Chicago Press.

Kayi-Aydar, H. (2014). Social positioning, participation, and second language learning: Talkative students in an academic ESL classroom. *TESOL international Association, 48*(4), 686–714.

Korobov, N. (2010). A discursive psychological approach to positioning. *Qualitative research in Psychology, 7*(3), 263–277.

Labov, W., & Waletzky, J. (1967). Narrative analysis: Oral versions of personal experience. In J. Helm (Ed.), *Essays on the verbal and visual arts* (pp. 12–44). Seattle, WA: University of Washington Press.

Lakoff, G., & Johnson, M. (2003). *Metaphors we live by.* Chicago, IL: University of Chicago Press.

Lave, J., & Wenger, E. (1991). *Situated learning: Legitimate peripheral participation.* Cambridge: Cambridge University Press.

Linehan, C., & McCarthy, J. (2000). Positioning in practice: Understanding participation in the social world. *Journal for the Theory of Social Behaviour, 30*(4), 435–453.

Lofgren, H., & Karlsson, M. (2016). Emotional aspects of teacher collegiality: A narrative approach. *Teaching and Teacher Education, 60,* 270–280.

McEntarfer, H. K., & McVee, M. B. (2014). "What are you, gay?" Positioning in monologues written and performed by members of a gay-straight alliance. *Linguistics and Education, 25,* 78–89.

McVee, M. B. (2005). Revisiting the Black Jesus: Re-emplotting a narrative through multiple retellings. *Narrative Inquiry, 15*(1), 161–195.

McVee, M. B. (2011). Positioning Theory and sociocultural perspectives: Affordances for educational researchers. In M. B. McVee, C. H. Brock, & J. A. Glazier (Eds.), *Sociocultural positioning in literacy: Exploring culture, discourse, narrative, and power in diverse educational contexts* (pp. 1–22). Cresskill, NJ: Hampton Press.

McVee, M. B. (2013). Interracial friendship and enmity between teachers and students: Lessons of urban schooling from a 'cracker girl'. In R. Harré & F. M. Moghaddam (Eds.), *The psychology of friendship and enmity: Relationships in love, work, politics, and war* (pp. 205–218). Santa Barbara, CA: Praeger.

McVee, M. B. (2017, July). *Positioning Theory and education: A call for a trans-disciplinary approach.* A keynote presented at the 2017 Positioning Theory Conference, Oxford.

McVee, M. B., Baldassarre, M., & Bailey, N. M. (2004). Positioning theory as lens to explore teachers' beliefs about literacy and culture. In C. M. Fairbanks, J. Worthy, B. Maloch, J. V. Hoffman, & D. L. Schallert (Eds.), *53rd National Reading Conference Yearbook* (pp. 281–295). Oak Creek, WI: National Reading Conference.

McVee, M. B., Brock, C. H., & Glazier, J. A. (Eds.). (2011). *Sociocultural positioning in literacy: Exploring culture, discourse, narrative, and power in diverse educational contexts.* Cresskill, NJ: Hampton Press.

McVee, M. B., & Carse, C. (2016). A multimodal analysis of storyline in 'The Chinese Professor' political advertisement: narrative construction and positioning in economic hard times. *Visual Communication, 15*(4), 403–427.

McVee, M. B., Dunsmore, K. L., Gavelek, J. (2013). Schema theory revisited. In D. E. Alvermann, N. J. Unrau, & R. B. Ruddel (Eds.), *Theoretical processes and models of reading* (6th ed., pp. 489–524). Newark, DE: International Reading Association.

Moghaddam, F. M. (1999). Reflexive positioning: Culture and private discourse. In R. Harré & Van Langenhove, L. (Eds.), *Positioning theory: Moral contexts of intentional action* (pp. 74–86). Malden, MA: Blackwell.

Moghaddam, F. M. (2017, July). *Positioning and political plasticity.* A keynote presented at the 2017 Positioning Theory Conference, Oxford.

Moghaddam, F. M., & Harré, R. (2010). *Words of conflict words of war.* Santa Barbara, CA: Praeger.

Moghaddam, F. M., Harré, R., & Lee, N. (Eds.). (2008a). *Global conflict resolution through positioning analysis.* New York, NY: Springer.

Molloy, E., & Clarke, D. (2005). The positioning of physiotherapy students and clinical supervisors in feedback sessions. *Health Professional Education, 7*(1), 79–90.

Mosley, M., & Johnson, A. S. (2007, November). Examining literacy teaching stories for racial positioning: Pursuing multimodal approaches. In *The 56th annual yearbook of the National Reading Conference.* Oak Creek, WI: National Reading Conference.

Mühlhaüsler, P., & Harré, R. (1990). *Pronouns and people: The linguistic construction of social and personal identity.* Oxford: Blackwell.

Pennington, J. L., Brock, C. H., Torrey, P., & Wolters, L. (2013). Opportunities to teach: Confronting the deskilling of teachers through the development of teacher knowledge of multiple literacies. *Teachers and Teaching, 19*(1), 63–77.

Peters, M., & Appel, S. (1996). Positioning theory: Discourse, the subject and the problem of desire. *Social Analysis: The International Journal of Social and Cultural Practice,* (40), 120–141.

Phillips, D., Fawns, R., & Hayes, B. (2002). From personal reflection to social positioning: The development of a transformational model of professional education in midwifery. *Nursing Inquiry, 9*(4), 239–249.

Pinnow, R. J., & Chval, K. B. (2015). "How much You wanna bet?": Examining the role of positioning in the development of L2 learner interactional competencies in the content classroom. *Linguistics and Education, 30,* 1–11.

Redman, C., & Fawns, R. (2010). How to use pronoun grammar analysis as a methodological tool for understanding the dynamic lived space of people. In S. Rodrigues (Ed.), *Using analytical frameworks for classroom research: Collecting data and analysing narrative* (pp. 163–182). New York, NY: Routledge.

Riessman, C. K. (1993). *Narrative analysis.* Newbury Park, CA: Sage Publications.

Ritchie, S. M. (2002). Student positioning within groups during science activities. *Research in Science Education, 32*(1), 35–54.

Rothbart, D. (Ed.) (2004). *Modeling: Gateway to the unknown a work by Rom Harré.* Amsterdam, The Netherlands: Elsevier.

Sabat, S. (2008). Positioning and conflict involving a person with dementia: A case study. In F. M. Moghaddam, R. Harré, & N. Lee (Eds.), *Global conflict resolution through positioning analysis* (pp. 81–94). New York: Springer.

Searle, J. R. (1979). *Expression and meaning.* Cambridge: Cambridge University Press.

Shanahan, L. E. (2013). Composing "kid-friendly" multimodal text: When conversations, instruction, and signs come together. *Written Communication, 30*(2), 194–227.

Siegel, M., & Panofsky, C. P. (2009). Designs for multimodality in literacy studies: Explorations in analysis. *Literacy Research Association Yearbook, 58,* 99–111.

Slocum, N., & Van Langenhove, L. (2004). The meaning of regional integration: Introducing positioning theory in regional integration. *Journal of European Integration, 26*(3), 227–252.

Slocum-Bradley, N. (2009). The Positioning Diamond: A trans-disciplinary framework for discourse analysis. *Journal for the Theory of Social Behaviour, 40*(1), 79–107.

Smagorinsky, P. (2008). The method section as conceptual epicenter in constructing social science reports. *Written Communication, 25*(3), 389–411. doi:10.1177/0741088308317815.

Smith, B. E. (2016): Composing across modes: A comparative analysis of adolescents' multimodal composing processes. *Learning, Media and Technology,* 1–20.

Souto-Manning, M. (2010). Challenging ethnocentric literacy practices: [Re] positioning home literacies in a Head Start classroom. *Research in the Teaching of English, 45,* 150–178.

Tan, S. L., & Moghaddam, F. M. (1995). Reflexive positioning and culture. *Journal for the Theory of Social Behaviour, 25*(4), 387–400.

Tirado, F., & Gálvez, A. (2007). Positioning theory and discourse analysis: Some tools for social interaction analysis. *Forum: Qualitative Social Research, 8*(2), np.

Van Langenhove, L. (2010a). Rom Harré and the exploration of the human umwelt. In L. Van Langenhove (Ed.), *People and societies* (pp. 1–6). New York: Routledge.

Van Langenhove, L. (Ed.) (2010b). *People and societies: Rom Harré and designing the social sciences.* New York Routledge.

Van Langenhove, L. (2016). Positioning theory as a framework for analyzing idiographic studies. In G. Sammut, J. Foster, S. Salvatore, & R. Andrisano-Ruggieri (Eds.), *Methods of psychological intervention* (pp. 55–70). Charlotte, NC: Information Age Publishing.

Van Langenhove, L. (2017). Varieties of moral orders and the dual structure of society: A perspective from positioning theory. *Frontiers in Society, 2.* http://doi.org/10.3389/fsoc.2017.00009

Van Langenhove, L., & Harré, R. (1993). Positioning and autobiography: Telling your life. In N. Coupland & J. F. Nussbaum (Eds.), *Discourse and lifespan identity* (pp. 81–99). Newbury Park, CA: Sage Publications.

Van Langenhove, L., & Harré, R. (1994). Cultural stereotypes and positioning theory. *Journal for the Theory of Social Behaviour, 24*(4), 359–372.

Van Langenhove, L., & Harré, R. (1999a). Introducing positioning theory. In R. Harré & L. Van Langenhove (Eds.), *Positioning theory: Moral contexts of intentional action* (pp. 14–31). Malden, MA: Blackwell.

Van Langenhove, L., & Harré, R. (1999b). Positioning as the production and use of stereotypes. In R. Harré & L. Van Langenhove (Eds.), *Positioning theory: Moral contexts of intentional action* (pp. 127–177). Malden, MA: Blackwell.

Vetter, A. (2013). "You need some laugh bones!": Leveraging AAL in a high school English classroom. *Journal of Literary Research, 45*(2), 173–206.

Vygotsky, L. S. (1978). *Mind in society: The development of higher psychological processes.* Cambridge, MA: Harvard University Press.

Wittgenstein, L. (1953). *Philosophical investigations.* Oxford: Blackwell.

Wortham, S. (2001). *Narratives in action: A strategy for research and analysis.* New York, NY: Teachers College Press.

Zacher, J. C. (2008). Analyzing children's social positioning and struggles for recognition in a classroom literacy event. *Research in the Teaching of English, 43*(1) 12–41.

20

GENDER IDENTITYWOKE

A Theory of Trans*+ness for Animating Literacy Practices

sj Miller

This work evolved out of observing, speaking to, and reading about how students are self-determining their gender identities. I cannot claim this work to be original because they are the ones who are original. Instead, this work is a map created to find and understand them, while simultaneously a place for them to locate themselves. A hope for this work is that students will continue to create maps, to carve out new contexts to mine meaning from and within, and to keep co-crafting new identities for continued growth and socio-emotional expansion. They are the guides that have paved ways for this work to be made possible . . . for infinite terrains to be traversed, and for new knowledges to be generated.

Gender Identity Awakening

Identities are shaped and informed by language: Language shapes and informs identities. In particular, uses of inflammatory and bullying language within political climates that police gender identity and regulate bodies in different school contexts position nonbinary gender identities to be vulnerable for social isolation and marginalization. Such is unfortunately front-facing, as evidenced by shifts in the U.S. political climate that have brought trans*+ identities into critical focus, warranting immediate attention in classroom practice[1]—these are not just local issues, they are of increasingly global concern. Of importance is how to draw from coded literacy practices used by *gender identityWOKE*[2] students as they safeguard themselves within their own peer networks. Gender identityWOKE is the self-awareness about one's gender identity that simultaneously questions its construction, the impacts of its social positioning, and its ties to ideological beliefs while staying engaged and ready to participate in its reinvention. Since language helps locate and find gender identities, such WOKENESS can help to imagine, invent, and reinvent language. Seen this way, language becomes a critical agentive nexus for self-identification, legitimization, and recognition and its inimitable qualities call on others to form a community dedicated (even unknowingly) to discursive and dialogical processes of language affirmation.

Resultant from such WOKENESS, literacy educators are summoned to understand, unpack, and unveil how school systems, literacy researchers, and teacher educators reinforce gender identity normativity and contribute to gender identity violence in schools and beyond, in order to open up spaces for opportunities and new knowledges to be activated and recognized. To disrupt reinscription of a gender identity binary (i.e., male/female as the only ways to identify gender), this work cannot live siloed or tokenized in books, texts, poems, art, songs, math problems, policies, scientific rationalizations, pictures, the media, or individuals; it has to be embodied by all as an agentive mediator that can bring about social change and galvanize a gender identityWOKE society. This chapter puts the emerging terminology of gender identityWOKE in conversation with the growing field of trans*+ and a pedagogy of refusal as a strategy for literacy practices across all grade levels and disciplines.

Rhizomatic Constructions of Gender Identity and Language

The word *trans*+ is hardly novel. As a prefix, it infers to cut across or go between, to go over or beyond or away from and/or to return to. Building from this definition, I conceive that *trans*+ can also be a noun, verb, adverb, or adjective, and is part of the family of the ever-expanding vernacular to identify a non-cisgender[3] person. It is about a constant integration of new ideas and concepts and new knowledges. *Trans*+ is composed of multitudes—a moving away from or a refusal to accept essentialized constructions of spaces, binaries, ideas, genders, bodies, or identities, and so on. Thereby, it is similar to the concept of rhizomatic. Rhizomatic or rhizome (Miller, 2016b) is an unpredictable pattern of concepts, spaces, that are interconnected by the indeterminate.

As *transgender* is derived from the Latin word meaning "across from" or "on the other side of," many consider *trans*+ with the asterisk and the plus sign to reference a continuum of evolving self-identifications and a useful umbrella term that signifies myriad identity categories. It has also been argued that *trans*+ is a reification of gender identity categories, yet other studies show that it is about a life that is ever-changing, moving forward, and refusing to be located in any binary. While some activists draw on the use of *trans* (without the asterisk and/or the plus sign), which is most often applied to trans men/women, the asterisk with the plus sign more broadly references ever-evolving non-cisgender gender identities, which are identified as, but certainly not limited to, (a)gender, cross-dresser, bigender, genderfluid, genderf**k, genderless, genderqueer, nonbinary, non-gender, third gender, trans man, trans woman, transgender, transsexual, gender expansive, gender dynamic, gender creative, gender fluid, two-spirit, and others. How the term continues to take form will evolve as identities and theories morph in indeterminate ways.

A Theory of Trans+

A theory of trans*+ *is* a critical consciousness about how people read and are read by the world (Freire, 1970) and a refusal and divesting from essentializations (Miller, 2016a, 2016b). A theory of trans*+ is built upon the intersections of spatiality and hybridity theories (Deleuze & Guattari, 1987; Miller, 2014a; Soja, 2010); geospatial theories (Nespor, 1997; Slattery, 1992, 1995; Soja, 2010); and social positioning theories (Butler, 1990; Foucault, 1990; Latour, 1996; Leander & Sheehy, 2004; McCarthey & Moje, 2002). Arising from this rhizome of theories, then, trans*+ as a theoretical concept not only is the connective tissue for these studies but uniquely suggests that students have agency in how they invite in, embody, and can be recognized by the self and others as they travel across contexts embodied by multitudinous identities that can be perpetually reinvented. Trans*+ as rhizome, situated within this understanding, then, is a networked space where relationships intersect; are concentric; do not intersect; can be parallel, nonparallel, perpendicular, obtuse, and fragmented. It is both an invisible and visible space, which embodies all of the forces co-constructing identities. Such spaces cut across borders of space, time, and technology and generate pathways into different contexts. It also recognizes that histories have spatial dimensions that are normalized with inequities hidden in bodies whereby bodies become contested sites that experience social justice and injustice both temporally and spatially (Miller, 2014a; Miller & Norris, 2007; Nespor, 1997; Slattery, 1992, 1995).

Pedagogy of Refusal

Situated within, and stemming from the theory of trans*+, a pedagogy of refusal emerges as a mediator and practice for literacy learning. As a literacy practice, a pedagogy of refusal is an enactment and engagement of learning that opens up space for ideas, concepts, and the indeterminate to be part of the process of learning. It proffers that answers are not compartmentalized into the binary of the *yes* or *no*, and that answers can shift back and forth, can be between, imagined, futuristic, and fragmented. Refusal can be thought of as a strategy to push back on essentializations, posited vis-à-vis *fourthspace* (Miller, 2008, 2014b, 2016a, 2016b). Fourthspace is a process taught as an enactment, as a critical pause or wait time before responding to a situation. It is a space that is only maintained and sustained by the person alone where they ("they" is used as first person singular pronoun) can eschew and traverse conventional norms or expectations and consider possibilities for radicalization and even transformation. Ongoing embodiments, long-term practice, and applications of fourthspace in and across schools can deepen human awareness and provide meaningful and intentional opportunities to shift deeply entrenched binary understandings of highly nuanced complexities about gender identity.

Animated as a literacy practice, a pedagogy of refusal supports and encourages a moving back and forth, between, over, beyond, away from, into, back to, and fragmented throughout learning. As students come to understand and recognize these possibilities through participation and practice, a pedagogy of refusal can grant bodied communications to both be made legible and become legible to others. Thought of this way in unison, their bodies and minds become emerging forms of and for understanding and teaching. Therefore, this theory of trans★⁺ suggests that for new knowledges to emerge, classrooms must be thought of and taught rhizomatically, or as a networked space where relationality and one's relationship to relationality are continually reinvented based on where both students and *educators* are in their awareness about gender identity (Miller, 2014a).

Gender identityWOKE

Gender identityWOKE is an indication of self-awareness about one's gender identity that questions simultaneously its construction, the impacts of its social positioning, and its ongoing state of readiness to participate in its reinvention. As noted, writing gender identityWOKE[4] as is, is intentional. It is both a signifier and an acknowledgment that language can change in form and shape. Attention to gender identityWOKENESS is still limited in practice and yet to be anchored across pedagogy, curriculum, and/or policy. Resultant, students, whose gender identities may seem incongruous with schools' practices, policies, and beliefs, are vulnerable to the ways negative representations of gender identity impact mind-sets and beliefs. In search of positive sources of recognition, these students turn to social media (Adams, 2017; Gieseking, 2015) to educate and gain validation and recognition of and from each other. Their social media networks, as a primary medium, are ushering in a *gender identity self-determination* (Miller, 2016a), where the individual is the ultimate authority on their own gender identity. These networks galvanize grassroots advocacy and activism across and within different social contexts. The impact of their gender identityWOKENESS is spatializing change as they educate their peers and adults about the ways in which they self-identify. Folding this WOKENESS into literacy learning means that educators stay engaged, stay WOKE to the ways that students self-identify, build from and on those assets for learning, and affirm and recognize that gender expression is flexible, is on a continuum, and can shift over time and in context.

Gender Identity Coproduction

Gender identity is how someone wants to be seen and legitimated through the eyes of another in the world—just as someone *is* (Federal Interagency Working Group, 2016; Herbert, 2016).[5] Selves are illuminated by their identities within specific social spaces and yet can be outcast, excluded, and then erased when their identities are not defined by their relationship to that space. Understood this way, then, gender identity is the soul and spirit of a person: It is how an individual feels about themselves (Levine, 2008), intuits, and then writes themselves into the world (Perl, 2004). Fashioned in these ways, gender identity can be the embodiment of gender, or lack thereof, and any expressions of the self are reinforced by how people want others to see and think about oneself. Gender identity can therefore be the physical, emotional, and/or psychological embodiment that rejects gender (agender)[6] altogether.

Understood through a theory of trans★+, agender/gender identity is a dynamic expander of an ever-evolving continuum of gender identity that—like trans★+—also cuts across; goes between, over, or beyond or away from; refuses or accepts; and/or returns to different embodiments (Federal Interagency Working Group, 2016; Miller, 2016b). It is also about a constant integration of new ideas and concepts and new knowledges, comprising multitudes, and a moving away from or a refusal to accept essentialized constructions of binaries, genders, and bodies (Miller, 2017).

A view of gender identity is bound and tied to dynamisms of structural and institutionalized manifestations of power; identity is not immune from the desire to be recognized or even assimilated, and power relations illuminate presence, absence, and futurity (Bordo, 1993). For instance, Foucault (1980) and Bourdieu (1980) suggested that the effects of power and surveillance construct identities, and that the embodiment of identities is vulnerable as a result of power. To this Bordo (1993) attested: "The human body is itself a politically inscribed entity, its physiology and morphology shaped by histories and practices of containment and control" (p. 21). Seen in this way, social spaces—for example, schools—are central to understanding gender identity because they shape "engagements in spatial tactics of power and in everyday social, cultural and literacy practices" (McCarthey & Moje, 2002, pp. 234–235). Because social spaces are defined in relationship to power, selves are illuminated by their identities within specific social spaces and yet can be excluded when they are not defined or readily identified by their relationship to that space. Identities can therefore destabilize when a social space excludes a particular identity and how identities have been defined in relationship to that space (or society). Identities, when not affirmed or recognized, face erasure and thereby extinction when a social space fails to positively illuminate them. For all this noted, addressing and supporting schools and all of their stakeholders to recognize and affirm a continuum of students' self-determined gender identities is prudent: If not, the consequences will be deleterious.

Movement Toward Inventing Language

Connecting to and locating trans★+ within the field of sociolinguistics advances an understanding of its usage and possible uses across different genres of literacy practices (e.g., reading, writing, speaking, modes of communication) in classrooms. Sociolinguistics is commonly understood as the effect of how cultural norms, expectations, and contexts intersect and impact the way language is used and generated. Drawing and agreeing, then, that language imprints on, and is embodied by a people, language can spatialize into pathways out of which language can flow. This process is asymmetrical and rhizomatic and opens up spaces for locating and finding selves in language while simultaneously co-constructing it.

For many trans★+ and gender-identified people, naming one's identity is an inherently embodied principle of gender self-determination, in which each individual is the ultimate authority on their own gender identity. According to Stanley (2014), gender self-determination constitutes "a collective praxis against the brutal pragmatism of the present, the liquidation of the past, and the austerity of the future" (p. 89). In this sense, "it is a form of resistance to normative structures of genital-based gender assignment. As a radical alternative to those normative systems, gender self-determination is realized first and foremost through the linguistic practice of self-identification" (Zimman, in press). Observed, then, is a refusal to be essentialized, reified, codified, and trapped by institutionalized structures that impose an identity algorithm. While policies certainly guide and shape mainstream practices and offer important protections, within these communities, there is a common (but not for all people) desire and need to self-identify in such a way that naming becomes imaginative and inventive. This act of resistance, vis-à-vis a refusal, mediates locating the self in second-space (the imagined) and thirdspace (the coming together of the real and the imagined) (Soja, 1996, p. 10) sanctuaries where language can emerge as preservationist and coded and provide opportunities for bodies to invent and reinvent language. In these spaces, what arises is "something new and unrecognizable, a new area of negotiation of meaning and representation" (Bhabha, 1994, qtd. in Soja, 1996, p. 11). What *arises* is that each person determines how they want to be spoken about and understood.

Seen this way, what manifests is a resistance to the mind/body split. In the spirit of Spinoza's work on neutral monism that pushes back on Descartes's Cartesian dualism (which divides the self into compartments, rendering people helpless against combating sociopolitical agendas), the unison of mind to body prepares individuals to have agency and empowerment. It is a refusal to be cast as objects, and instead, realized as purposeful and conscientious about the power in constructing identities. This state of being challenges and posits the power structures within hegemony as dysfunctional and recasts people as agents capable of acting on and transforming the worlds in which they live. Bhabha (1994) would concur that to not challenge the status quo reseats discourses of dominant culture. In this thirdspace, then, counter-hegemonic principles can serve as a political project that may shift into a different type of democracy (Soja, 1996, p. 111) and can lift out of binary identifiers and relocate to a space where ideas can "co-exist concurrently and in contradiction" (deLauretis, 1987, p. 26).

A Theory of Trans+ Applied to Identity and the Production of Indeterminate Language*

Stemming from the field of sociolinguistics, Lakoff, as interviewed on Gladstone and Garfield's (2016) podcast, described language imprinting as cyclical. He offered that when something is practiced, it activates neural connectors that make them easier to fire. As language is repeated, it then activates certain neuro-circuits, and every time a neuro-circuit is activated, it becomes stronger to whoever hears it. Foucault (1978) strengthened this perspective by noting that an internalization of language becomes routinized as self-regulatory.

In Lakoff's (1975) seminal work on differences between gendered speech, *Language and Woman's Place*, he described the "dominance" model. Lakoff theorized that women's divergent speech patterns are a by-product of male dominance, and this includes "all speakers who are in some way disenfranchised from institutionalized male power" (Hall, 2014, p. 220). In the 1980s, the field shifted to a "difference or two-cultures model" (Maltz & Borker, 1982), which suggests that "children are socialized into divergent interactional patterns within single-sex playgroups" (Hall, 2014, p. 220). Though not new to the field, as it links back to neo-Indo-European gendered language when crossing genders was perceived as deviant (Chamberlain, 1912; Flannery, 1946; Sapir, 1929), words such as *sissy* and *tomboy* resurfaced, evincing that when a child crossed gender boundaries for other-sex play, they were ridiculed.

Deborah Tannen (1990) in *You Just Don't Understand: Women and Men in Conversation* built from these models and brought into scholarship how the distinction between men's and women's speech must be unhinged from patriarchy and refocused onto same-sex peer relationships. These enduring perspectives bookend the foundation for what came to be seen as the "dominance" and "difference" models that have informed contemporary work on gender and language. The shift in models came to be known as the "discursive turn." Set into renewed motion, as research on language and sex certainly predates Tannen's, germane to her work was the unveiling of intersectional awareness about how language was not predetermined by sex; rather, it was informed by myriad identity categories, such as class, race, ethnicity, sexuality, and age (Zimman & Hall, 2016). Tannen's findings provided an illuminating and generative spark to recognize that prior research on gender and language was shaped by heteronormativity and thus, became foundational to the growth and continued expansion of queer theory. Tannen's work has helped set into motion the idea that individuals should have identity self-determination, or the ability to assert agency over naming their identities.

Drawing from these prior frames to understand how meaning is attached to language, I draw from different domains noted by the work of Bucholtz and Hall (2005). Building from a sociocultural linguistics perspective, they asserted that identity formation relies heavily on ideological structures, rooted in cultural beliefs and values as indexical (Ochs, 1992; Silverstein, 1985). This *indexical principle* relies on how meaning is discursively produced through identity categories and labels, implicatures and presuppositions about one's or another's identity, evaluative positioning toward someone else's talk and their social roles, and use of linguistic structures that are associated with specific people and groups (Bucholtz & Hall, 2005, p. 594). In other words, when someone positions another's identity, it demonstrates one's positioning animated by (difficult to sever) indissoluble ties to a heteronormative, patriarchal, hegemonic, cisgender/cissexual, ableistic, classed (and so on) system that has maintained and structured lives.

Identities seen through the intersection of cultural anthropology and feminist theory suggest that "any given construction of identity may be in part deliberate and intentional, in part habitual and hence often less than fully conscious" (Bucholtz & Hall, 2005, p. 606). This idea, known as the *partialness principle*, holds that identity construction is relational, interactional, and social and cannot be individually negotiated if it is socially negotiated. Bucholtz and Hall argued that (a) identity construction cannot be fully intentional if it is produced by practices and ideologies that may exceed conscious awareness, and (b) it may be formed through contestation and negotiation because of others' preexisting perceptions that are linked to larger ideological and held beliefs. In summation, when a person chooses to identify, be named, or be pronouned, those choices are rooted in prior defaults connected to ideological seatings, and conceived through negotiation and the desire to be gender self-determined.

Gender identity, then, situated within a trans*+ theory, as noted previously, is not static, and is always in perpetual construction and deconstruction (Miller, 2016b, p. 4). Confirming this, Barrett's (2002) work in queer linguistics asserts that even the word *trans*+* is a term in "which identity categories are not accepted as a priori entities, but are recognized as ideological constructs produced by social discourse" (p. 28). Hence, while an individual may invent a term that provides a lens to be seen and to see others through, it is nonetheless intersubjectively connected to hegemonic structures. So, the question is, how can naming the self be truly an act of empowerment and freedom from institutional constructs?

Naming. Power. Literacy.

Self-knowledge depends on an understanding of an internally felt self—"a discrete, invisible entity that may not be predictable based on external presentation" (Zimman, in press). Bakhtin (1981) would refer to this type of struggle as the power struggle of a dialogical relationship and the tension between an *authoritative discourse*, the voice of authority, and an *internally persuasive discourse*, or one's own voice. Drawing from Bakhtin, Britzman (1991) said that an authoritative discourse is a discourse that

> operates within a variety of social contexts and partly determines our "symbolic practices," or the normative categories that organize and disorganize our perceptions. It is "received" as static knowledge, dispensed in a style that eludes the knower, but dictates, in some ways, the knower's frames of references and the discursive practices that sustain them. Bakhtin termed such discourse the "word of the father, adult, teacher, etc." in that these positions already have the power to authorize subjects.

(pp. 20–21)

On the other hand, an internally persuasive discourse is similar to an authoritative discourse except that it is "denied all privilege" (Bakhtin, 1981, p. 342). An internally persuasive discourse

> pulls one away from norms and admits a variety of contradictory social discourses. As renegade knowledge, internally persuasive discourse has no institutional privilege, because its practices are in opposition to socially sanctioned views and normative meanings. It is the discourse of subversion. Internally persuasive discourse is, as Bakhtin argues, "half ours," and with the struggle to own it, and as it clashes with other internally persuasive discourses, "this discourse is able to reveal ever newer ways to mean."
>
> *(Britzman, 1991, p. 21)*

While gender identity can be self-determined, it is a negotiation between an internally persuasive discourse and authoritative discourse. Such understanding reflects a connection for so many students who turn to social media as spaces to find meaning in their identities—a space to turn from others attempting to author their lives. On this, Bucholtz and Hall's (2005) *emergence principle* suggests that "self-conceptions enter the social world via some form of discourse" (p. 587) and that some identities that do not conform to the social category they were assigned demonstrate diverse ways of self-awareness. Such identities can "sever the ideologically expected mapping between language, biology or culture; that is they subvert essentialist preconceptions of linguistic ownership" (p. 588).

Connecting to this, Zimman (in press) saw a parallel to *trans*★+ self-identification. They[7] argued that struggles over self-identification between language and sexuality are enduring and have gained more salience since the turn of the century (Bucholtz & Hall, 2004, 2005; Cameron & Kulick, 2003; Kulick, 2000). Notably, identity is not static and is coproduced through dialogue and co-constructed by understanding how someone self-identifies. Such self-identification helps another come to different ways of self-knowing and even in expanding or inventing terms based on new-found knowledge. As individuals continue to interact, such definitions can evolve, shift, and be (re)formed. While gender identity is personal, when shared publicly, it is not only legitimated (though up for scrutiny) but it also takes on social validation while it simultaneously produces new meaning and new knowledge. Such found meaning expands social awareness, and it can generate new opportunities for others to locate themselves within or beyond a gender identity. Trans★+ is thereby both authoritatively and internally reflexive. Students are indeed finding validation and recognition about their gender identities from each other and within these spaces of discoursed interaction.

Gender IdentityWOKE: Implications for Literacy Practice

Certainly, topics about and related to gender identity are hardly "new" or "niche," as these conversations have historical bases across the world. People have experienced gender fluidity and expansiveness since the dawn of recorded history, and it has always looked different or been labeled differently in other times and places (e.g., the mahus of Hawaii, muxes of Mexico, Fa'afafines of Samoa, two-spirited and berdache Native Americans of North America, warias of Indonesia, kathoeys of Thailand, Kocek of the Ottoman Empire, and hijras of India). While people do not change as much as language does, a handful of pioneers in the latter half of the 20th century paved the way for youth to be visible in their expressions of gender identity (personal communication with Jamison Green, March 23, 2017). The recognition and visibility of various communities have generated spaces for gender identity politics to move into a time where gender identity is accentuated vis-à-vis and attributed through self-expression. By no means did young people today invent gender fluidity, androgyny, bigender, agender, and so on, but their arrival into society now has been created for them as an opening for gender identity self-determination to be made more possible. Their imaginings, reinterpretations, and constant integrations of new forms to express their gender, and their willingness to step outside the binary and the boxes of cultural beliefs that have been forced upon all human beings in Western, Judeo-Christian-colonized (or heavily influenced) societies, have signaled to the adults in their spheres of influence that a new group of youth has arrived and will continue to do so. Such expansiveness about expressions of gender identity that have moved and that are moving from the margins into a multitude of social sites indicates that they must be folded into teaching and learning.

Staying Gender IdentityWOKE

To stay gender identityWOKE, educators can remain open to the gender identities students narrate as well as to others in their lives and the surrounding world (e.g., staying open to what they hear and learn from the world around will inform their thinking and discourse). This relationship to their students' gender identities, as a literacy practice, not only demonstrates a refusal to be reified and constrained by top-down policies and beliefs, but it allows for an indeterminacy to co-construct the learning environment. It also signifies that a teacher cares and recognizes that students' gender identities matter to them and can impact their motivation to learn. While many of the examples provided below can be applied to classroom practice, these activities require spaces to develop "repertoires of practice" (Gutiérrez & Rogoff, 2003) mediated by fourthspace. This might mean working with administration to create professional development opportunities, creating a peer or parent group to work through some of the language and one's understanding, and/or networking with others who are also seeking learning.

As a mediator for literacy learning, to be gender identityWOKE means that educators stay engaged with the ways that students self-identify and build on those assets for learning. It also means that educators affirm and recognize that gender expression is flexible, on a continuum, and can shift over time and in context. For instance, educators might design a lesson that unpacks and analyzes different representations of gender identity in the media and social media (i.e., newspapers, TV, news, websites they frequent, etc.). They might give an assignment that asks students over a week to log different representations of gender identity—who expresses the identity and in which genre (even if they watch the same person twice, how the identity might shift), how they self-identify, and the possible age (additional research might be necessary). As a class, they can unpack those representations and learn from each other's findings. They can then discuss the language they observed and how it manifested in different contexts. They can discuss how the person using the language was perceived by others, and if the person's age made any difference. With their students, educators can then build a class appendix that can be updated and drawn upon to develop lessons from the students' findings.

Accounting for students' findings, educators can build positively focused lessons around language and representations that both describe and show gender identities through math problems, writing assignments, images, art/ists, media representations, trailblazers, political movements, musicians, poets, key figures, and so on. Educators, along with students, can also engage in ongoing research about the histories of the individuals who have and who generate these genres. Over time and through prolonged engagement, students and educators alike develop emboldened capacities for a positive psychosocial-affective awareness that can support their own and others' qualities of life. While some schools around the country are taking up gender identity work, it is far from enough, let alone representative—cisgender and cissexual lessons continue to be the default. To stay gender identityWOKE and to expand representations and the gaze onto diverse gender identities, educators can fold self-determination[8] strategies into their classes that account for (a) recognizing a continuum of gender identities, (b) inviting in claimed names and pronouns, and (c) creating spaces for co-constructing meaning.

Literacy as Gender Identity

The self constitutes itself in discourse with the assistance of another's presence and speech. When educators mediate literacy by supporting students to be recognized by self and other, they mediate gender identity self-determination. Literacy, thereby, is co-constitutive of gender identity. Each coproduces the other. When educators ask students how they self-identify, students are set in an authoritative place and positioned with high value in the production of knowledge.

When students are affirmed and recognized (Miller, 2016a) in their claimed gender identities, the empowerment they may experience can generate and invent new knowledges. As Butler (2004) suggested, "the body gives rise to language and that language carries bodily aims, and performs bodily deeds" even when "not always understood by those who use language to accomplish certain conscious aims" (p. 199). When students do feel empowered in school, it can lead to an agentive spatialization both across and out-of-school contexts. This act of social justice has great possibility to rupture dangerous dichotomies and myths about gender identity while educating others about how all students (and others) can be made legible, credible, and recognizable.

Claimed Names and Pronouns

Each person has the right to author their lives. Sadly, schools often position people to author themselves through a neoliberal lens and substitutes claimed identities for positioned identities. This conscription is, more often than not, the norm. Educators can disrupt this positioning by inviting students to self-identify with claimed names and pronouns. While many people are beginning to use this strategy, they may not realize the larger positive impact this has on people.

A norm that has been established in the trans★+ community has been to directly ask someone how they self-identify, how they would like to be referred to, and what their claimed names and pronouns are or are not (some people are (a)pronounced, meaning they choose to not to use a pronoun). When someone changes their names or pronouns and asks others to use a particular name or pronoun, it marks a major milestone in one's identity transition, and being named or pronounced "correctly marks the moment in which a gender identity leaves the mind of a trans person and enters a new reality on the lips of an interlocutor" (Zimman, in press).

Pronouns

On occasions, when someone uses a pronoun that reveals *they* understand identity, it can have a powerful impact because it helps the person to whom they are speaking or referring to feel legitimated and recognized (Miller, 2016a). A direct index, according to Ochs (1992), is a way to identify gendered language in English. The third person singular pronouns *he/him/his* and *she/her/hers* signify reflect how speakers read genders. Recently, the entrance into the lexicon (in the *AP Stylebook*) of the singular *they* and its derivative forms *them/their/theirs*, or *themselves* as demarcation of a wide range of identities (Andrews, 2017), marks a movement away from the presumption of how one self-identifies into a gender-neutral state. One of the main rationales for this move was that when deciding on a pronoun for one's identity, defaulting to a male pronoun was sexist.[9] For example, "The child stood up and went to her desk" infers the child was a girl without knowing the gender. Stating this as "The child stood up and went to her or his (or his or her) desk" moves into a more objective state. Yet, when constructed as "The child stood up and went to *their* desk," a gender-neutral solution is generated.

To understand the use of the singular *they*, I provide a few other examples.

A. "<u>Somebody</u> got in their car, but <u>they</u> did not know where to drive."
B. "When I hugged my <u>friend</u>, <u>they</u> hugged me back."

For some trans★+ people and those who choose not to use *he/him/his* or *she/her/hers*, if they choose to use *they*, a sentence might read:

• "Sam stood up and <u>they</u> went out the door."
• "Kaneesha decided that <u>they'd</u> had enough and they left."

The lexicon is changing, and with the evolution and ever-growing identified pronouns, it is important to ask people how they self-identify. I suggest that educators should allow for claimed pronouns to be folded into assignments and classroom discourse. While society may have yet to catch up to such uses of writing or speech, classrooms are spaces for growth, legitimization, and affirmation. Students may have to explain their claimed pronouns in a college essay or in other formal types of writing, *but so be it*—at least to fold this work into some classes is a hearty beginning.

Drawing from the discussion about claimed names and pronouns, I provide some practices that have proven effective and dialogical-building in my own secondary, university, and nonuniversity experiences. Each example demonstrates powerful ways that affirm and recognize students, and that have generated rich discussions.

First is the "Get to Know Me," which allows students to privately reveal their *current*[10] claimed name, (a)gender (i.e., gender identity or absence of), and (a)pronouns (i.e., pronouns or absence of), and with an option to note if they want these identities publicly acknowledged (see Figure 20.1). For the student who does not want others to know about particular identities but is comfortable sharing that part of the self with the educator, the educator can respond on assignments with comments that recognize the student's true name, (a)gender, and (a)pronoun.

Another way educators can affirm and recognize students is to post placards in the classroom that affirm gender identity and inclusivity (see Figures 20.2 and 20.3) and make gender/agender identity recognition part of the ordinary classroom experience.

Another practice that has proven effective is to provide sentence starters that ask students to co-create other ones. For example, during daily interactions, when introducing yourself to someone, say:

> *Hi, nice to meet you. My current claimed name is* ___ *and my current claimed pronoun (or, in some cases, (a)pronoun) is/are* ___ .

Depending on one's familiarity with another, they might add:

> *My current claimed gender identity (or, in some cases, (a)gender) is/are* ___ .

Names, gender identity, and pronouns (please fill in the blanks in the sentences below, using the following prompts)

My assigned name is _____ and my claimed name (leave blank if they are the same) is _____. My assigned sex is _____, but my CURRENT, claimed (a)gender identity (leave blank if they are the same) is _____. The pronouns people use when referring to me include _____, but my CURRENT, claimed (a)pronoun(s) is/are _____.

In class I prefer you to use (please circle) *assigned* or *claimed* <u>name</u> and *assigned* or *claimed* <u>(a)pronouns</u>, but on my assignments, you can use (please circle) *assigned* or *claimed* <u>name</u> and *assigned* or *claimed* <u>(a)pronouns</u>.

Figure 20.1 Get to Know Me

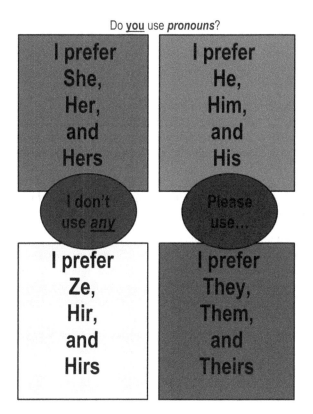

Figure 20.2   Pronoun Chart

Inclusive Space

This space
RESPECTS
all aspects of people, including age, gender, race,
ethnicity, religion/no religion, national origin,
immigration status, language, education, marital
status, body size, political affiliation/philosophy,
(a)sexual orientation, (a)gender identity/expression
and creativity, physical and mental ability,
socioeconomic status, genetic information, HIV
status, and veteran status.

Figure 20.3   Inclusive Space Sign

Students can also practice sentence starters for different social settings. These interactions may invite a conversation around gender identity that both recognizes and signals to others that gender identity is on an ever-expanding spectrum. For instance:

Currently, I am a heteroflexible, cisgender female.

Fill in important sexual orientation and gender/gender identity identifiers—for example, for *sexual orientation*, heterosexual, bisexual, pansexual, asexual, omnisexual; for *gender identity*, nonbinary, gender queer, agender, gender fluid, gender dynamic.

The Queer Literacy Framework: A Queer Literacy Framework Promoting (A)gender and Self-determination and Justice

My prior research based on the queer literacy framework (QLF) (Miller, 2015, 2016a, 2016b) supports educators to construct lessons that account for different perspectives about gender identity. This version of the framework comprises ten principles with subsequent commitments for educators to queer literacy practices from pre-K-12th grade and university classrooms. The framework is underscored by the notion that lives have been structured through an inheritance of a political, gendered, economic, social, religious, linguistic system with indissoluble ties to cis/heteropatriarchy. This is not to suggest a dismissal from (a)gender categories altogether, but to move into an expansive and open-ended paradigm that refuses to close itself or be narrowly defined, and that strives to shift and expand views that can account for a continuum of evolving (a)gender identities and differential bodied realities.

The framework is intended to be an autonomous, ongoing, nonhierarchical tool within a teaching repertoire; it is not something someone does once and moves away from. Rather, the principles and commitments should work alongside other tools and perspectives within a teacher's disposition and curriculum. An intention of the framework is that it can be applied and taken up across multiple grades, genres, and disciplines within literacy acquisition, and its sociospatialization—that is, its spreading across different contexts—can expand awareness.

Moving into the framework, axioms underscore the beliefs that guide the principles and commitments. These axioms are as follows:

- We live in a time we never made; gender norms predate our existence;
- Non-gender and sexual "differences" have been around forever, but norms operate to pathologize and delegitimize them;
- Children's self-determination is taken away early when gender is inscribed onto them. Their bodies/minds become unknowing participants in a roulette of gender norms;
- Children have rights to their own (a)gender legibility;
- Binary views on gender are potentially damaging;
- Gender must be dislodged/unhinged from sexuality;
- Humans have agency;
- We must move away from pathologizing beliefs that police humanity;
- Humans deserve positive recognition and acknowledgment for who they are;
- We are all entitled to the same basic human rights; and
- Life should be livable for all.

Discussing these axioms and unpacking the language with students can cultivate a deeper awareness about how some people embody prejudice. Building from these axioms, then, educators can practice this framework and generate assignments based on various principle(s) identified in Table 20.1.[11]

Table 20.1 The Queer Literacy Framework: A Queer Literacy Framework Promoting (a)gender Self-Determination and Justice. Modified version. (Copyright 2015 by the National Council of Teachers of English. Reprinted with permission.)

Principles	Commitments of Educators Who Queer Literacy
1. Refrains from possible presumptions that students ascribe to a gender	Educators who use queer literacy never presume that students have a gender.
2. Understands gender as a construct that has been and continues to be impacted by intersecting factors (e.g., social, historical, material, cultural, economic, religious)	Educators who employ queer literacy are committed to classroom activities that actively push back against gender constructs and provide opportunities to explore, engage, and understand how gender is constructed.
3. Recognizes that masculinity and femininity constructs are assigned to gender norms and are situationally performed	Educators who engage with queer literacy challenge gender norms and gender stereotypes and actively support students' various and multiple performances of gender.
4. Understands gender as flexible	Educators who engage with queer literacy are mindful about how specific discourse(s) can reinforce gender and norms, and purposefully demonstrate how gender is fluid, or exists on a continuum, shifting over time and in different contexts.
5. Opens up spaces for students to self-define with claimed (a) genders, (a)pronouns, or names	Educators who engage with queer literacy invite students to self-define and/or reject claimed or preferred gender, name, and/or pronoun.
6. Engages in ongoing critique of how gender norms are reinforced in literature, media, technology, art, history, science, math, etc.	Educators who use queer literacy provide ongoing and deep discussions about how society is gendered, and thus invite students to actively engage in analysis of cultural texts and disciplinary discourses.
7. Understands how neoliberal principles reinforce and sustain compulsory heterosexism, which secures homophobia; and how gendering secures bullying and transphobia	Educators who employ queer literacy understand and investigate structural oppression and how heterosexism sustains (a)gendered violence, and then generate meaningful opportunities for students to become embodied change agents, to be proactive against or to not engage in bullying behavior.
8. Understands that (a)gender trans-sects with other identities (e.g., sexual orientation, culture, language, age, religion, social class, body type, accent, height, ability, disability, and national origin) that inform students' beliefs and, thereby, actions	Educators who engage with queer literacy do not essentialize students' identities, but recognize how trans-sections of sexual orientation, culture, language, age, religion, social class, body type, accent, height, ability, disability, and national origin inform students' beliefs and, thereby, actions.
9. Advocates for equity across all categories of (a)gender performances	Educators who employ queer literacy do not privilege one belief or stance, but advocate for equity across all categories of (a)gender performances.
10. Believes that students who identify on a continuum of gender identities deserve to learn in environments free of bullying and harassment	Educators who use queer literacy make their positions known, when first hired, to students, teachers, administrators, and school personnel and take a stance when any student is bullied or marginalized, whether explicitly or implicitly, for their (a)gender identities.

Educators Can Draw on Students to Lead Gender IdentityWOKE Movements

Beyond what literacy educators can do to teach, affirm, and recognize their students' gender identities, what is different since the 1950s is electronic and digital forms of communication involving visual images. The media still shapes what people see, and in the 20th century, the story the media wanted to tell was the binary, male/female transition story inspired in the United States by Christine Jorgensen. In the 1990s, people like Kate Bornstein, Sandy Stone, and Jamison Green were on the forefront of the effort to break down that paradigm, and the media was finally beginning to notice (personal communication with Jamison Greene, March 23, 2017). Then, with rapid inventions of technology and social media in the 21st century, with its affordable computers and wider access to technology, social media, and YouTube, young people began documenting their transitions and recording their gender expressions in ways that were never available to previous generations.

Today, then, the fortification and impacts of these multiple trajectories are realized by students who are turning to each other for affirmation and recognition. Beyond what is commonly heard and seen within youth culture, students are revealing that their engagements with advocacy, peer groups, and social media provide spaces in which they are developing and understanding their gender identities and creating archives of pronoun configurations (Adams, 2017; Miller, 2016a, in press). While there are dozens of gender identity youth advocacy movements in existence and springing up around the country, the Trans Student Educational Resources (TSER; transstudent. org) is a comprehensive resource run by youth. The TSER informs educators about advocacy and empowerment, and the public and trans activists about how to be effective organizers. Their site includes resources (e.g., websites, publications, workshops, topic issues, policies, graphics, etc.) and information about topical issues.

While students are turning to video gaming and apps for kinship about gender identity, Tumblr is one of the most active, trafficked, and contagious of all youth movements (as are Facebook, Instagram, and Snapchat; Adams, 2017). It contains categories about protections; gender identity positivity; evolving language and terminology, including different types of romantic attraction; camps; genres that show positive representations; youth movements; video archives of youth speaking to each other; feminism; anarchy; and self-help, among other categories. It is a coded and safe space for them to call home. If teachers build upon and integrate these youth spaces into their lessons, it would likely increase engagement, motivation, and agency. When the education system fails to attend to this work, rationales are reproduced that can lead to gender identity violence and misunderstandings, and diminished capacities to create change. Staying gender identityWOKE contributes to equity for students.

Gender Identity Awakening

Drawing upon a theory of trans★⁺ness and a pedagogy of refusal, varying structural dimensions of policy, theory, pedagogy, and space can help to reposition students as gender identity self-determined. When students are understood to come to school with bodies that are "trans-sectional"—that is, bodies and identities are not limited to any single identity, but rather, their (gender identity) essentializations are always in question—the generation and integration of new knowledges and recognitions of self-awareness create a state of gender identity awakening. The work of educators, then, is to diminish the discontinuities between out-of-school and in-school literacy learning by moving this gender identity awakening across schools. Viewed this way, the embodied literacies students carry are sources for potential spatial-justice self-determination (i.e., the movement of gender identity justice across and within contexts). In other words, as students begin to understand that they have agency to determine how they want to be recognized and legitimized in and by their gender identities, and as they move from one context to another, they have the potential to shift and change mind-sets. A gender identity, when affirmed within school practices, positions students with increased capacities for a stronger livelihood.

A Reframed Schooling That Realizes Gender IdentityWOKENESS

This work entails a long-term commitment to move into the space of awakening *and* into a state of WOKENESS. To realize this, the work should be started pre-K so that its impact can be seen, felt, and sustained over time. These changes will require levels of commitment from a collective of various stakeholders, such as teachers, administrators, staff and school personnel (anyone who has contact with students), parents, communities, teacher education programs (deans, professors, preservice students), researchers, students, and policy makers who work in, for, and on behalf of schools. Much of this shift should begin in teacher education programs and through professional development so these key stakeholders can discuss what this would mean and can look like in practice. While the work is still nascent but increasingly more visible, the profession of education has rich and powerful opportunities to hit "refresh" and work toward sustainable changes about gender identityWOKENESS.

A hope for this work is that a theory of trans★⁺ness and a pedagogy of refusal are part of the ordinary and daily schooling practices. A folding in of these approaches removes the burden from students to have to "define" or self-explain their identities to others. These approaches open up spaces where their trans-sectional and ever-evolving, indeterminate gender identities are understood and recognized to be rich sources for learning literacy and literacy learning; where trans-sectionality is recognized as the core approach to students' lived experiences and the basis for learning and teaching; and where people are accepted in whichever gender identity presentation they are in, in situ. School can still become a place for every student and educator to just exist in a state of identityWOKENESS, free of question or surveillance, and a place where new foundations about gender identity can be a location for changing how gender identity is perceived in society.

Although the United States has been "pulled out" of UNESCO, UNESCO's 2016 report is a reminder about the criticality and urgency of attending this work globally, and especially now, locally. Sustainable Development Goal 4 states that countries cannot achieve sustainable development "to ensure inclusive and equitable quality education and promote lifelong learning opportunities for all—if students are discriminated against or experience violence because of their actual or perceived sexual orientation and gender identity." Students *are* treasure maps, and learning with and from them is gender identityWOKENESS, which not only animates opportunities for literacy practices but can galvanize and realize a gender identity justice for all.

Notes

1 *Trans★⁺* written with an asterisk and superscript plus sign denotes transgender identities that continue to emerge as indeterminate. *Trans★* with an asterisk denotes a segment of the transgender population that was inclusive of only some trans people's identities, while excluding others. In my writing, I use the superscript plus sign + to symbolize the ever-expanding and indeterminate ways of self-identifying, and the asterisk to honor those who fought for gender identity self-determination, which paved the way for new identities to emerge.

2 Writing *gender identityWOKE* as is, is intentional. It signifies that language can change in form and shape, and uppercasing WOKE emphasizes the importance of the state of alertness.

3 Cisgender means that one's gender identity and the sex assigned at birth align.

4 *Woke* or *wokeness* is a slang term, derivative of a state of being socially awake and self-aware. Its etymology is elusive, but it is rooted in Black culture. Arguably, it became a word of social awareness sparked by Erykah Badu's 2008 song "Master Teacher." In 2014, after the death of Michael Brown, "Stay woke" became a watchword hallmark reminding people of color to question all things hegemonic. See www.merriam-webster.com/words-at-play/woke-meaning-origin for an in-depth discussion. I recognize that some may consider this term appropriated; I recognize and respectfully acknowledge that. I am drawing

upon it for its significance and symbolic power that is rooted in a history of trauma and pain, its identified recognition of social and cultural empowerment, and its assertion in ongoing political battles. It is my hope that a gender identityWOKENESS can transform gender identity subjugation—and, always acknowledging the interconnectedness to the history of the term.

5 Scientific arguments have been made for how gender identity is informed (see Henig, 2017), but there is no concrete proof about how and why someone thinks or sees themselves to be a particular (a)gender identity.

6 I use *agender* or *(a)gender* (depending on its use in a sentence) to refer to a continuum of possibilities for self-identification.

7 This topic on the use of *they* as first person singular will be discussed in the section on pronouns.

8 For a lengthier dive into a discussion about how to generate lessons that account for self-determination, see Miller (2016a).

9 The singular *they* had emerged by the 14th century and was common in everyday spoken English, but its use has been the target of criticism since the late 19th century (see www.merriam-webster.com/words-at-play/singular-nonbinary-they). For further discussion of inflected forms and derivative pronouns, see https://en.wikipedia.org/wiki/Singular_they#Inflected_forms_and_derivative_pronouns.

10 The use of the word *current* signifies that gender identity and naming are on a continuum and demonstrates the awareness that it can shift depending on time, context, and circumstances.

11 It is important to consider how to build internal and external safety when designing lessons. Safety impacts students' willingness to engage in work and with each other. For a detailed discussion about how to design lessons that draw from the queer literacy framework and account for safety, see Miller (2016a, 2016b). Miller's work is built from prior research on safety by Moses (2002), Raz (1979), Kymlicka (1991), and Leonardi and Saenz (2014).

References

Adams, C. (2017, March 25). Social media, celebrities, and transgender youth. *CBSNews*. Retrieved from http://www.cbsnews.com/news/social-media-celebrities-and-transgender-youth/

Andrews, T. M. (2017, March 28). The singular, gender-neutral "they" added to the Associated Press Stylebook. *Washington Post*. Retrieved from https://www.washingtonpost.com/news/morning-mix/wp/2017/03/28/the-singular-gender-neutral-they-added-to-the-associated-press-stylebook/?utm_term=.4118be1b9296

Bakhtin, M. M. (1981). *The dialogical imagination: Four essays by M. M. Bakhtin* (M. Holquist & C. Emerson, Trans.). Austin, TX: University of Texas Press.

Barrett, R. (2002). Is queer theory important for sociolinguistic theory? In K. Campbell-Kibler et al. (Eds.), *Language and sexuality: Contesting meaning in theory and practice* (pp. 25–43). Stanford, CA: CSLI Press.

Bhabha, H. A. (1994). *The location of culture.* New York, NY: Routledge.

Bordo, S. (1993). *Unbearable weight: Feminism, western culture and the body.* Berkeley, CA: University of California Press.

Bourdieu, P. (1980). *The logic of practice.* Stanford, CA: Stanford University Press.

Britzman, D. (1991). *Practice makes practice.* Albany, NY: State University of New York.

Bucholtz, M., & Hall. K. (2004). Theorizing identity in language and sexuality research. *Language in Society, 33*(4), 501–547.

Bucholtz, M., & Hall, K. (2005). Identity and interaction: A sociocultural linguistic approach. *Discourse Studies, 7*(4–5), 585–614.

Butler, J. (1990). *Gender trouble: Feminism and the subversion of identity.* New York, NY: Routledge.

Butler, J. (2004). *Undoing gender.* New York, NY: Routledge.

Cameron, D., & Kulick, D. (2003). *Language and sexuality.* Cambridge: Cambridge University Press.

Chamberlain, A. F. (1912). Women's languages. *American Anthropologist, 14*(3), 579–581. deLauretis, T. (1987). *Technologies of gender: Essays on theory, film, and fiction.* Bloomington, IN: Indiana University Press.

Deleuze, G., & Guattari, F. (1987). *A thousand plateaus: Capitalism and schizophrenia.* Minneapolis, MN: University of Minnesota Press.

Federal Interagency Working Group on Improving Measurement of Sexual Orientation and Gender Identity in Federal Surveys. (2016). *Toward a research agenda for measuring sexual orientation and gender identity in federal surveys: Findings, recommendations, and next steps.* Washington, DC: Author.

Flannery, R. (1946). Men's and women's speech in Gros Ventre. *International Journal of American Linguistics, 12*(3), 133–135.

Foucault, M. (1978). *The history of sexuality.* New York, NY: Pantheon Books.

Foucault, M. (1980). *Power-knowledge: Selected interviews and other writings, 1972–1977.* New York, NY: Pantheon Books.

Foucault, M. (1990). *The history of sexuality.* New York, NY: Vintage.

Freire, P. (1970). *Pedagogy of the oppressed.* New York, NY: Continuum.

Gieseking, J. J. (2015). *For Leelah: Queering+ spaces of education.* Presentation in Presidential Plenary "Toward What Justice? Describing Diverse Dreams of Justice in Education," with M. Dumas, N. Erevelles, L. Patel, E. Tuck, & K. W. Yang. American Educational Research Association, Chicago, IL.

Gladstone, D., & Garfield, B. (Producers). (2016, December 2). Normalize this! [Audio podcast]. Retrieved from http://www.wnyc.org/story/on-the-media-2016-12-02/

Gutiérrez, K. D., & Rogoff, B. (2003). Cultural ways of learning: Individual traits or repertoires of practice. *Educational Researcher, 32*(5), 19–25.

Hall, K. (2014). Exceptional speakers: Contested and problematized gender identities. In M. Meyerhoff & J. Holmes (Eds.), *The handbook of language, gender, and sexuality* (2nd ed., pp. 220–239). Malden, MA: Blackwell.

Henig, R. M. (2017, January). How science is helping us understand gender. *National Geographic.* Retrieved from http://www.nationalgeographic.com/magazine/2017/01/how-science-helps-us-understand-gender-identity/

Herbert, J. (2016, August 10). Gender identity is in the brain. What does this tell us? *Psychology Today.* Retrieved from https://www.psychologytoday.com/blog/hormones-and-the-brain/201608/gender-identity-is-in-the-brain-what-does-tell-us

Kulick, D. (2000). Gay and lesbian language. *Annual Review of Anthropology, 29*(1), 243–285.

Kymlicka, W. (1991). *Liberalism, community, and culture.* New York, NY: Oxford University Press.

Lakoff, R. T. (1975). *Language and woman's place.* New York, NY: Harper & Row.

Latour, B. (1996). On interobjectivity (G. Bowker, Trans.). *Mind, Culture, and Activity: An International Journal, 3*(4), 228–245.

Leander, K., & Sheehy, M. (Eds.). (2004). *Spatializing literacy research and practice.* New York, NY: Peter Lang.

Leonardi, B., & Saenz, L. (2014). Conceptualizing safety from the inside out: Heteronormative spaces and their effects on students' sense of self. In L. Meyer & D. Carlson (Eds.), *Gender and sexualities in education: A reader* (pp. 202–229). New York, NY: Peter Lang.

Levine, P. (2008). *Healing trauma: A pioneering program for restoring the wisdom of your body.* Louisville, KY: Sounds True.

Maltz, D., & Borker, R. (1982). A cultural approach to male-female miscommunication. In J. Gumperz (Ed.), *Language and social identity* (pp. 196–216). New York, NY: Cambridge University Press.

McCarthey, S., & Moje, E. (2002). Identity matters. *Reading Research Quarterly, 37*(2), 228–238.

Miller, s. (2008). Fourthspace—Revisiting social justice in teacher education. In s. Miller, L. Beliveau, T. DeStigter, D. Kirkland, & P. Rice, *Narratives of social justice teaching: How English teachers negotiate theory and practice between preservice and inservice spaces* (pp. 1–21). New York, NY: Peter Lang.

Miller, s. (2014a). English is "not just about teaching semi-colons and Steinbeck": Instantiating dispositions for socio-spatial justice in English education. *Scholar-Practitioner Quarterly, 8*(3), 212–240.

Miller, s. (2014b). Spatializing social justice research in English education. In C. Compton-Lilly & Erica Halverson (Eds.), *Time and space in literacy research* (pp. 122–133). New York, NY: Routledge.

Miller, s. (2015). A queer literacy framework promoting (a)gender and (a)sexuality self-determination and justice. *English Journal, 104*(5), 37–44.

Miller, s. (Ed.). (2016a). *Teaching, affirming, and recognizing trans and gender creative youth: A queer literacy framework.* New York, NY: Palgrave Macmillan.

Miller, s. (2016b). Trans★+ing Classrooms: The pedagogy of refusal as mediator for learning. *Social Sciences, 5*(34), 1–17.

Miller, s. (2017). *Why (a)gender identity matters now, more than ever: Perspectives during a Trump era.* New York, NY: NYU's Metro Center.

Miller, s. (2018). Reframing schooling to liberate gender identity. *Multicultural Perspectives, 20*(2), 70–80.

Miller, s., & Norris, L. (2007). *Unpacking the loaded teacher matrix: Negotiating space and time between university and secondary English classrooms.* New York, NY: Peter Lang.

Moses, M. S. (2002). *Embracing race: Why we need race-conscious education policy.* New York, NY: Teachers College Press.

Nespor, J. (1997). *Tangled up in school: Politics, space, bodies and signs in the educational process.* Mahwah, NJ: Lawrence Erlbaum Associates.

Ochs, E. (1992). Indexing gender. In D. Alessandro & C. Goodwin (Eds.), *Rethinking context: Language as an interactive phenomenon* (pp. 335–358). Cambridge: Cambridge University Press.

Perl, S. (2004). *Felt sense: Writing with the body.* New York, NY: Heinemann.

Raz, J. (1979). *The morality of freedom.* New York, NY: Oxford University Press.

Sapir, E. (1929). The status of linguistics as a science. *Language, 5*(4), 207–214.

Silverstein, M. (1985). On the pragmatic "poetry" of prose. In D. Schiffrin (Ed.), *Meaning, form and use in context* (pp. 181–199). Washington, DC: Georgetown University Press.

Slattery, P. (1992). Toward an eschatological curriculum theory. *JCT: An Interdisciplinary Journal of Curriculum Studies, 93*(3), 7–21.

Slattery, P. (1995). *Curriculum development in the postmodern era.* New York, NY: Garland.

Soja, E. (1996). *Thirdspace: Journeys to Los Angeles and other real-and-imagined places.* Malden, MA: Blackwell.

Soja, E. (2010). *Seeking spatial justice.* Minneapolis, MN: University of Minnesota Press.

Stanley, E. A. (2014). Gender self-determination. *Transgender Studies Quarterly,* 1(1–2), 89–91.

Tannen, D. (1990). *You just don't understand: Women and men in conversation.* New York, NY: Morrow.

UNESCO. (2016). Homophobic and transphobic violence in education. Retrieved from https://en.unesco.org/themes/school-violence-and-bullying/homophobic-transphobic-violence

Zimman, L. (in press). Trans identification, agency, and embodiment in discourse: The linguistic construction of gender and sex. *International Journal of the Sociology of Language.*

Zimman, L., & Hall, K. (2016). Language, gender, and sexuality. In M. Aronoff (Ed.), *Oxford bibliographies online.* Retrieved from http://www.oxfordbibliographies.com/view/document/obo-9780199772810/obo-9780199772810-0109.xml

21

UNTAPPED POSSIBILITIES

Intersectionality Theory and Literacy Research

Maneka Deanna Brooks

As soon as I began to read the directions for the English language proficiency assessment, Alex shouted, "I know English. I don't wanna take this fucking test! I take this test every year!" He threw his unopened exam booklet onto the floor. Since he was being disruptive, I asked him to spend the rest of the class in the office. While he sat in the office, his classmates finished the reading and writing portions of the test. Later on that day, I spoke with Alex about his behavior during the test that constituted part of the criteria upon which a determination about his English proficiency would be based. He explained to me that he was incorrectly classified as an English learner (EL) because (among other reasons) he was an English speaker. He then waited for my justification of his categorization. I told him what I had learned about language proficiency in my teacher education program. I drew on Cummins's (2000) popular theoretical distinction between Basic Interpersonal Communicative Skills (BICS) and Cognitive Academic Language Proficiency (CALP). I explained to him that his English abilities were "surface fluency" (Cummins, 1979, p. 231). I shared that if he had *academic English proficiency*, his performance on the requisite standardized assessments would be sufficient to be reclassified as English proficient.

After I shared the information with Alex about BICS/CALP and his test scores, I grew uncomfortable. Initially, I did not understand the origin of the discomfort. I was merely sharing with Alex what I had learned by reading books based on peer-reviewed research about people "like him." Then it occurred to me: in order to call Alex's English language abilities *surface fluency*, I had to ignore what I knew about Alex's life history and linguistic abilities. I had to ignore that this 15-year-old had been speaking English and Spanish for all of his life. I had to erase the existence of his monolingual English-speaking classmates who also experienced difficulties on standardized assessments of English literacy. In order to be able to justify his ongoing classification as an EL, I had to erase any part of Alex or the broader social context that challenged his positioning as an EL. I had to subscribe to the definition of English proficiency that was enshrined in educational policy and supported by a dichotomous conception of language popularized through research.

I was uncomfortable because I was engaging in what Crenshaw (1989, p. 139) termed a "single-axis analysis." In the context of antidiscrimination law and advocacy, Crenshaw noted that the single-axis analysis "theoretically erases" Black women because there is no possibility for the existence of someone who is both Black and a woman. Race and gender are treated as mutually exclusive. As a result, antidiscrimination efforts that rely on this type of analysis cannot address the unique experiences of Black women. In a similar manner, my single-axis analysis required that I *theoretically erase* Alex's existence as an English-speaking bilingual. The EL identification was the sole lens through which I forced myself to understand Alex. This single-axis perspective only allowed me to conceive of him as someone who did not know English. This interpretation foreclosed possibilities for literacy education that entailed building upon Alex's identity as an English speaker.

Whether in the classroom, the courtroom, or some other social space, theories have power. The introductory vignette about Alex highlights the necessity of theories that make visible those individuals and groups who are erased through single-axis analyses. As Anzaldúa (1990) wrote, "*necesitamos teorías* that will rewrite history using race, class, gender and ethnicity as categories of analysis, theories that cross borders, that blur boundaries—new kinds of theories with new theorizing methods" (p. xxv). Intersectionality is the type of border-crossing and boundary-blurring theory for which Anzaldúa advocated. In this chapter, I argue that literacy researchers should engage with intersectionality theory. However, authentic engagement with intersectionality theory extends beyond sprinkling a few well-known citations into the theoretical framework section of a journal article or using the term *intersectional* to describe an analysis. Therefore, I wrote this chapter for literacy researchers who have yet to explore the implications of intersectionality theory for their own work. In the first section of the chapter, I examine three theoretical principles of intersectionality. In the second section, I examine how intersectionality theory can enhance research within literacy studies and the significance of literacy researchers engaging directly with the work of those who write and study about intersectionality, whom I refer to as intersectional theorists. Finally, I close by addressing perceptions that intersectionality has a limited theoretical scope. As a whole, this chapter provides an overview that encourages more literacy researchers to deeply engage with intersectionality.

What Is Intersectionality?

Intersectionality is now a frequently used term within multiple settings. For example, it can be found in academic journals, on social media platforms, and within various community organizing spaces. The multifaceted nature of intersectionality makes it difficult to define. For instance, May (2015) wrote that intersectionality is "an *epistemological practice*," "an *ontological project*," and an invitation to assume "a radical *coalitional political orientation*"; it "functions as a kind of *resistant imaginary*" (p. 34). Definitions offered by other intersectionality theorists mirror similar levels of complexity (Collins & Bilge, 2016 Crenshaw, 1991; Hancock, 2007a). Given the multilayered nature of intersectionality, it is necessary to define how I conceptualize intersectionality theory in this chapter. Rather than providing a brief definition of intersectionality theory, I identify and discuss three key theoretical principles of intersectionality.

In using the term *theoretical principles*, I draw on Anyon's (2009) definition of theory. Anyon described theory as "an architecture of ideas—a coherent structure of interrelated concepts—whose contemplation and application (1) helps us to understand and explain discursive and social phenomena and (2) provides a model of the way that discourse and social systems work and can be worked upon" (p. 3). Therefore, the theoretical principles that I describe are sets of building blocks that together form the "architecture of ideas" that is intersectionality theory. In order to explain these theoretical principles, I primarily rely on sources that were published post-2000. I selected these authors because their work captures recent advancements and debates. In addition, these texts situate themselves within the rich, diverse, and deep history of intersectionality. This strategic choice facilitated an examination that is neither ahistorical nor trapped in dated analyses.

Given this context, the cross-cutting principles that I describe below were those positioned across multiple texts as essential to intersectionality. The focus on what intersectionality does is characteristic of the work of many intersectionality theorists (e.g., Carbado, Crenshaw, Mays, & Tomlinson, 2013; Cho, Crenshaw, & McCall, 2013). Moreover, it allows for a diversity of ways in which intersectionality theory could be enacted in research and practice. However, these principles do not represent the totality of thinking of any one person or all of intersectionality theory. They serve to create an insightful introduction to an expansive field.

Theoretical Principle 1: Reject the Single-Axis Analyses

One of the most clearly identifiable aspects of an intersectional analysis is that it rejects a single-axis lens to examine social inequality. The single-axis analysis (as demonstrated through the introductory vignette with Alex and detailed in Crenshaw, 1989) makes one specific identity marker the most salient. Returning to my interaction with Alex, it required his official English learner classification to become the single most important way in which I understood him as a student. Scholars and practitioners of intersectionality recognize that the fundamental danger of this type of analysis is erasure (May, 2015). For example, Muhammad and Haddix (2016) in their review of Black girls' literacies noted that solely focusing on the racial identity of Black girls is incomplete. They high- lighted that engaging with this group of young people's dual positioning as Black and female is necessary for an authentic understanding of the multiplicity of their literacy practices. Specifically, the authors contended that "an intersectional lens is required to understand the literacy experiences of Black girls" (p. 304).

The erasure facilitated by the single-axis lens has real-life consequences for the everyday lives of human beings. For instance, Crenshaw's (1991) oft-cited article illustrates how gender-focused and race-blind policies around violence toward women in the United States serve solely to protect White women. She emphasized how they marginalize Black women and other women of color. In the context of violence toward women, this erasure means death or being the target of ongoing violence. In a more recent publication, Patton, Crenshaw, Haynes, and Watson (2016) pointed out that this lack of attention to the unique experiences of Black women and girls has not been rele- gated to the halls of history in the United States. They discussed how even within newer movements (both inside and outside of academia) for U.S. Black racial equality, the needs and issues of Black women are downplayed to those that impact Black men. They pointed out that this results in "an asymmetrical solidarity . . . perpetuated among Black people, relegating the lived experiences of Black women and girls to the margins" (p. 194). Intersectionality theory rejects the marginalization that is inherent to single-axis analyses.

The rejection of the single-axis analysis in and of itself is of little utility. It is necessary to artic- ulate another way in which to make sense of the social world. The second theoretical principle of intersectionality provides a pathway forward.

Theoretical Principle 2: Categories of Difference Are Mutually Constitutive

The second theoretical principle is that "categories of difference" are mutually constitutive. Within this theoretical principle, I chose to use the terminology put forth by Hancock (2007a) because the more commonly used term *identity* has a disputed meaning and status within intersectionality theory (Grzanka, 2014). The nature of this dispute lies in the fact that identity can be conceptualized in many different manners both across and within areas of study.

Grzanka's (2014) analysis of the status of identity in intersectionality research examined the nature of its disputed status. Specifically, he examined different disciplinary interpretations of iden- tity. He discussed how those who engage in intersectional work in the fields of sociology and legal studies take an approach to intersectionality where identity is secondary. The focus of intersec- tionality from this perspective is on social structures. He wrote, "If identity matters, it is because social identity categories are the products of these systems, such as racism, sexism, heterosexism, and capitalism, and are one especially efficacious way of recognizing and measuring the inequal- ities produced by such systems" (p. 68). On the other end of the spectrum, Grzanka argued that fields such as psychology and much of the humanities place a greater emphasis on subjectivity and agency. Grzanka acknowledged that his dichotomous representation of identity does not accurately reflect how it is most frequently enacted within intersectionality theory. He recognized that certain scholars attend more to societal or individual factors; yet, intersectional theorists were among the vanguard in recognizing how identity is impacted by both sets of factors.

Given the multiple ways in which the term *identity* can be interpreted, I draw on Hancock's (2007a) conceptualization of "categories of difference" because it challenges the representation of identity as essentialist and static. "Categories of difference are conceptualized as dynamic productions of individual and institutional factors. Such categories are simultaneously contested and enforced at the individual and institutional levels of analysis. Intersectionality research demands attentiveness to these facts" (p. 251). Categories of difference are situated in a conception of power that allows for the interface between context, structures, and individual agency. This conceptualization of categories of difference represents the kind of thinking that Grzanka argued is a hallmark of intersectionality. Henceforth, when a quotation uses the term *identity*, the reader should consider its meaning as equivalent to *category of difference*.

Defining categories of difference does not explain how intersectionality theory makes meaning of the interrelationship of these categories. Therefore, it is necessary to be explicit about how intersectionality engages with categories of difference. Intersectionality does not encompass an additive approach to categories of difference. Bowleg (2008) noted that additive approaches postulate "that social inequality increases with each additional stigmatized identity" (p. 314). Drawing on the work of scholars like Collins (2000), Cuadraz and Uttal (1999), and Weber and Parra-Medina (2003), Bowleg (2008) explicated two key problems with this approach. First, it assumes that categories of difference are "separate, independent, and summative" (p. 314). Second, it suggests that it is possible to rank categories of differences and correspondent experiences of discrimination or privilege. The additive approach is antithetical to intersectionality because it assumes that categories of difference can be disaggregated.

Collins and Bilge's (2016) definition of intersectionality provides insight as to how the relationships between categories of difference can be understood in a way that is neither additive nor subtractive. Instead of using the term *categories of difference* or *identity*, they talked about social divisions. In this context, these social divisions are what produce categories of differences. Collins and Bilge (2016) wrote:

> When it comes to social inequality, people's lives and the organization of power in a given society are better understood as being shaped not by a single axis of social division, be it race or gender or class, but by *many axes that work together and influence each other* [emphasis added].
>
> *(p. 2)*

The italicized part of the quotation illustrates the second key theoretical principle of intersectionality theory, which contests claims that intersectionality entails an additive approach to categories of difference. In fact, Hancock (2016) argued that one of the fundamental intellectual projects of intersectionality is that the "ontological relationships between categories are mutually constitutive" (p. 113). In other words, conceptualizing categories of difference as mutually constitutive is central to intersectionality.

Clarke and McCall (2013) illustrated how conceptualizing categories of difference as mutually constitutive can result in empirical work that challenges predominant understandings within a field. These authors began by highlighting that the traditional analytical approach within fertility research conceptualizes race/ethnicity, class, and gender as discrete. The subsequent findings generated from research within this tradition suggest that class matters more than race in discussions of women's fertility. For example, they noted that racial differences decrease when socioeconomic status is held constant. However, Clarke and McCall discussed how Clarke's (2011) study challenged this predominant interpretation through conceptualizing race, class, and gender as mutually constitutive. Clarke's work illustrated that the causes of college-educated Black women's fertility rates in the United States were different from those of their White and Latina compatriots. This type of explanation was only possible because Clarke's research

> 1) explore[d] connections between elite Black women's educational, occupational, romantic, and reproductive decision-making and their family formation outcomes, and 2) compare[d] their process of family formation to those of less educated Black women and degreed White and Hispanic women
>
> *(Clarke & McCall, 2013, p. 352).*

Clarke's research was guided by the intersectional theoretical principle that categories of differences are mutually constitutive. In other words, it recognized that the experience of class for women is also racialized. To draw on Clarke and McCall's terminology, this intersectional analysis facilitated a distinct type of "social explanation" for differences in fertility rates.

Theoretical Principle 3: Explicitly Challenge Inequality

The first two theoretical principles illustrate the basis of what Dill and Kohlman (2012) termed "strong intersectionality." They wrote: "'Strong intersectionality' seeks to ascertain how phenomena are mutually constituted and interdependent, how we must understand one phenomenon in deference to understanding another" (p. 169). The third theoretical principle pushes the previous two theoretical principles to a different level. It emphasizes that intersectionality theory should explicitly challenge inequality. Carbado et al. (2013) returned to the early and oft-cited work of Crenshaw to illustrate the centrality of challenging inequality to intersectionality theory. They wrote that the goal of intersectionality has always moved beyond description and analysis to social transformation. In this way, intersectionality theory is about generating both social explanations and normative solutions (Clarke & McCall, 2013). As a result, Collins and Bilge (2016) recognized that intersectionality theory is often used within fields that are explicitly connected to practice. For example, they noted the proliferation of intersectionality within criminal justice, education, public health, and social work.

Despite this explicit focus on social transformation, scholars note that intersectionality's theoretical utility is often challenged because it is perceived as overly divisive (e.g., Cole, 2009). This critique focuses on the underlying necessity of rejecting single-axis analysis and viewing categories of difference as mutually constitutive. For instance, Hancock (2007b) noted that in the context of political science research, the recognition of intracategory diversity is seen by some as a call for nuance that can continue ad infinitum, to the point at which it offers little utility in terms of social explanations of political phenomena (e.g., poverty, discrimination, etc.). In other words, intersectionality theory is positioned as leading away from social change that theorists argue is central to intersectionality.

In the face of these types of critiques of divisiveness, it is important to return to the initial discussion of the consequences of single-axis analysis, which highlights a single category of difference as being the most salient: erasure. As May (2015) reminded us: "Single-axis thinking perpetuates systemic privilege, obscures the interplay of systems of inequality, and masks within-group differences via homogenization: it rationalizes inequality and fractures or impedes cross-categorical coalitions for social change" (p. 81). Single-axis analysis facilitates the reproduction of inequality for those who are erased. In other words, single-axis analysis can reproduce inequitable power structures. Intersectionality theory provides a different orientation that recognizes differences and similarities across and within categories of difference (Cole, 2009; Spade, 2013; Weber & Parra-Medina, 2003).

Instead of seeding division, intersectionality theory calls upon researchers to reconceptualize how both research and change are enacted.

The Importance of Intersectionality Theory for Literacy Research

Intersectionality theory is important for literacy research because it requires researchers to explicitly engage with power. I am not implying that intersectionality will bring a new focus on power dynamics to literacy research, as researchers from a variety of perspectives have highlighted how power functions in literacy theory, literacy policy, and literacy practice (e.g., Martínez, Hikida, & Durán, 2015; Street, 1984; Willis & Harris, 2000). Rather, intersectionality provides a theoretical lens that offers a distinctive way to engage with power. Rejecting the single-axis analysis requires researchers to challenge the dominance of a group whose needs are best met by highlighting a single category of difference. Then, the conceptualization of categories of difference as being mutually constitutive (which is fundamental to intersectionality theory) provides a theoretical framework to engage in different types of analyses that can call attention to those individuals and groups who are rendered invisible, or to draw on the words of Lugones (1994), "fragmented," through nonintersectional analyses. Again, power is central to this analysis because it highlights the ways in which the intersection of institutional and individual factors interface in the lives of individuals and groups. Lastly, intersectionality theory requires the explicit challenging of inequality. In essence, it challenges existing power relations. Intersectionality theory is not about being critical for the sake of criticality. It provides a way to imagine new possibilities for challenging inequality through literacy research, practice, and policy.

While I argue that intersectionality theory is important for literacy research, it cannot be integrated into just any theoretical framework. Intersectionality theory necessitates a social perspective on literacy. This social conceptualization of literacy could be theorized through multiple lenses, including those that can be identified as sociocognitive or sociocultural (e.g., Alvermann et al., 2012; Gee, 2001; Gutiérrez, Morales, & Martinez, 2009; Perry, 2012). For the purposes of this chapter, the particular social conceptualization used is not important. The vital understanding is the recognition of literacy (however it is defined) as more than a purely cognitive endeavor. As described above, intersectionality theory highlights the significance of robust understandings of the people, the practices, and the sociopolitical world in which literacy is enacted. The conceptualization of literacy as distinct from the social and political world erases the possibilities of unique contributions of intersectionality theory to the study of literacy.

The Consequences of the Absence of Intersectionality Theory

Although I have made an argument for the necessity of intersectionality theory for literacy research, it has been absent in my own scholarship. I have not explicitly drawn on intersectionality theory or cited intersectional theorists (e.g., Brooks, 2015, 2016, 2017). My failure to draw on the work of intersectional theorists was in spite of the fact that Dr. Salina Gray, who was a member of my doctoral cohort, introduced me to the term and to the work of Kimberlé Crenshaw early in my doctoral program. I was so captivated by Dr. Gray's explanation of intersectionality that I sought out Crenshaw's (1989, 1991) early publications. As I read these texts, I was amazed by the way in which Crenshaw so accurately articulated my life experiences. However, I did not read any additional scholarship about intersectionality. As I began to focus on my dissertation research about bilingualism, language proficiency, and literacy, intersectionality did not appear fundamental to this project. Intersectionality seemed like something that was more relevant for my personal life experiences as an African American and Sri Lankan woman.

In my work since that time, I have used the theoretical perspectives that reflected the scholarship with which I was familiar. However, the previously described theoretical principles of intersectional theory did underscore the theoretical framing of my work: I rejected single-axis analysis, I treated categories of difference as mutually constitutive, and I explicitly challenged inequality. If I was able to engage in this type of framing without intersectional theorists, then why am I making an argument that I and other literacy researchers should use it? First, it is important to note that many intersectional scholars contend that it is not necessary to draw on intersectionality theorists explicitly to engage in intersectional thinking (e.g., Cho et al., 2013; Clarke & McCall, 2013). I agree with these scholars' description of the importance of intersectionality research holding firm with implementing key theoretical principles—that is, demonstrating intersectional ways of thinking and application. They argue that this is more important than referencing specific names or using the term *intersectionality* within the theoretical framework. However, as a literacy researcher who engaged in intersectional analysis without engaging with the scholarship on intersectionality, I want to highlight the shortcomings of this type of practice.

The Necessity of Reading About Intersectionality Theory

In order to illustrate how reading intersectionality theory can impact the way in which literacy research takes place, I turn to a piece that I recently published (Brooks, 2017). In this article, I examined English language spelling practices of an adolescent Latina named Jamilet Lopez. At the time of the study, Jamilet was in tenth grade. However, she had been classified as an EL since kindergarten. Although I did not frame this work using intersectionality theory, my literature review illustrated the previously described cross-disciplinary theoretical principles. Unlike other literacy research that begins with the premise that English literacy difficulties are evidence of students' "limited English proficiency," the recognition of the dynamic institutional and ideological processes that produce the EL category of difference allowed me to reject the single-axis explanation. Instead, it facilitated an analysis that was not situated within the ideological and institutional dynamics of the public school system in which Jamilet was enrolled. This framing allowed me to document how Jamilet's "spelling mistakes" demonstrated the depth of her English proficiency.

It was not until I read multiple texts about intersectionality theory that I realized areas in which my analysis could have gone deeper. Specifically, my reading of the work of Artiles (2013) highlighted shortcomings within the way I engaged with dynamic processes that produced specific categories of difference. Although Artiles (2013) was not discussing literacy research, his discussion of intracategorical complexity within the research on disability and race pushed my thinking. He argued that scholars who take up a social model of disability "start with a compelling critique of disability as historically and bureaucratically situated, showing how definitions evolve over time, ultimately reminding us of the ways in which race, class, gender, and disability have entangled histories" (p. 339). However, he noted that these approaches often overlook "comparable in-depth critiques of race, social class, and gender—in other words, critiques of other difference markers are proffered only to the extent that they inform disability" (p. 339). The research that Artiles discussed in the previous quotation did not follow the second principle that I previously described: categories of difference are mutually constitutive. After reading Artiles (2013) and examining my own work with Jamilet, I can see how I engaged in this kind of practice in my earlier piece (Brooks, 2017).

While I theorized a number of salient categories of difference as they explicitly related to conceptions of English language proficiency (e.g., race, language background, etc.), I did not explicitly demonstrate a similarly nuanced theoretical framing to examine Jamilet's classed-raced-gendered experiences of schooling. I did document her experiences with schooling in the findings, which had important implications for contextualizing her English language spelling practices. My point in highlighting the absence of this framing is to illustrate that directly engaging with intersectionality theory would have required that I explicitly name the documented inequities that shaped her broader schooling experiences outside of English language proficiency and literacy (e.g., overcrowded schools, zero-tolerance policies, and uncertified teachers) as structural and systemic. In the piece under discussion (Brooks, 2017), these connections exist within the findings but are not pushed to the forefront. Direct engagement with intersectionality theory would have allowed for the theoretical strengths of this work (and its evolutions) to impact my literacy research. Through engaging deeply with past and current intersectional theorists, I would have been able to reap the full benefits of this theory.

Literacy Theory and Intersectionality: Possibilities and Roadblocks

I have made an argument that literacy researchers should engage with intersectionality theory. However, I acknowledge that some researchers may be concerned about whether or not intersectionality is appropriate for their research. Therefore, in this final section, I respond to potential questions as they relate to the scope of intersectionality theory.

The Mythical Limited Scope of Intersectionality

Scholars of intersectionality (Carbado, 2013; Carbado et al., 2013; Cho et al., 2013; May, 2015) have documented a reoccurring critique that attempts to limit the utility of intersectionality to certain types of individuals and groups. The limitations ascribed to intersectionality vary. The most narrow iteration is that intersectionality is only relevant for U.S. Black women, and the most expansive is that it is only focused on individuals and groups with marginalized identities. However, there is no particular category of difference that is required of intersectional work (May, 2015). The focus on women and girls of color within the intersectionality literature reflects the origins of the work, the salience of these social categories within various societies, the centrality of inequality, and the importance of centering those who have been erased. It does not represent the only way in which intersectionality has been or will be used. Nevertheless, it is important to investigate how intersectionality has come to be viewed in such a narrow way.

The Prominence of U.S. Black Women

Intersectional scholars (Cooper, 2016; Hancock, 2016; May, 2015) point to the prominent role of U.S. Black women in the development of intersectionality as indelibly linked (explicitly and implicitly) to its positioning as "limited" and "parochial." For example, Carbado (2013) contended that underlying this critique of intersectionality is the idea that "Black women cannot . . . function as the backdrop for the genesis and articulation of a generalizable framework about power and marginalization" (p. 813). It is important to note that Carbado (2013) did not talk about a generalizable experience of power and marginalization. This type of claiming of generalizable experience would be enacting the type of erasure that intersectionality theory seeks to challenge. Instead, he talked about a "generalizable framework" from which the examination of the experiences of many different groups of people and individuals can occur. To draw on Anyon's (2009) words, it is the *contemplation* and *application* of intersectionality theory that "(1) helps us to understand and explain discursive and social phenomena and (2) provides a model of the way that discourse and social systems work and can be worked upon" (p. 3). Therefore, intersectionality can be used in new and unforeseen ways in a variety of fields and contexts (Carbado et al., 2013).

In discussing the prominence of U.S. Black women within intersectionality, recognizing the fundamental role of their thinking to current articulations of intersectionality and highlighting their centrality to attempts to marginalize intersectionality, I do not want to position intersectionality as solely the product of U.S. Black feminist academics and community leaders. The various books about intersectionality that I read referenced the thinking of various scholars who were identified as U.S. Black women, women of color from various ethnic/racial backgrounds, and Third World

Feminists (Collins & Bilge, 2016; Grzanka, 2014; Hancock, 2016; May, 2015). Therefore, centering U.S. Black women intersectional theorists reflects the power dynamics that are relevant to this particular critique.

Unjust Citational Practices

The numerous texts that I read about intersectionality brought to my attention the importance of citational practices—specifically to the necessity to discuss which intersectionality theorists are cited, when they are cited, and how they are cited (e.g., Cooper, 2016). One of the reasons that citational practices are so frequently discussed within the literature about intersectionality is because citational practices are complicit in positioning intersectionality as having a limited theoretical scope. Most notably, scholars have recognized that many of the critiques of intersectionality reflect a narow understanding of intersectionality theory that indicates a limited engagement with the literature. For instance, Hancock (2016) noted that one of the ways in which this position is evidenced is that scholars describe intersectional thinking as something that began in the late 1980s and early 1990s, which ignores the extensive theoretical lineage of intersectionality. Among other influential thinkers, Hancock (2016) identified visionary thinkers such as Anna Julia Cooper, Maria Stewart, Sojourner Truth, and Cohambee River Collective as essential to what eventually became current instantiations of intersectionality theory. Another way in which Hancock identified scholars' limited engagement with intersectionality research is that they solely cite seminal texts from the 1980s and 1990s. She argued that this practice implies that they believe that no new theorizing has occurred since then. As a result, many critiques of intersectionality as being limited in scope have not thoroughly engaged with intersectional theory.

In my own journey as a literacy researcher, I have experienced the way in which reading intersectional scholarship has allowed for me to recognize its robust theoretical strengths. As I mentioned above, I had previously thought that intersectionality was only relevant for my personal life experiences as a woman of color. However, reading intersectional scholarship has allowed for its theoretical strength to impact my thinking about literacy research. It has facilitated a move beyond stereotypes about intersectionality and toward meaningful engagement with this theory. Therefore, I encourage others who are unfamiliar with this body of literature to embark on a similar journey. Moreover, I call attention to the importance of the way in which citational practices should illustrate an in-depth engagement with the who, what, and how of intersectionality theory. As May (2015) wrote, citations "offer a way to mark collectivity, delineate historical precedence, and claim legacies of struggle" (p. 55). Unfortunately, as Bilge (2013) documented, attempts to broaden the origins and focus of intersectionality can result in the erasure of fundamental thinkers (specifically, Black women and other women of color). Therefore, literacy researchers who use intersectionality theory must be conscious of how their citational practices can function to exacerbate or ameliorate this problem.

Conclusion

In her book, May (2015, p. 53) highlighted three important aspects of intersectionality: unlearning (dominant) social imaginaries, attending to alternative world views, and centering the disremembered. May's description emphasizes that intersectionality goes beyond making visible the people and experiences that are hidden by a single-axis analysis. Intersectionality provides a distinct way of understanding the lives of individuals at the intersection of multiple categories of difference. Notably, these categories of differences are not static—but produced by social dynamics. Rather than being discrete or additive, intersectionality envisions these differences as operating in a mutually constitutive way. Intersectionality theory provides a way of challenging dominant ways of thinking about the relationship between categories of differences. However, considering categories as mutually co-constructed is not sufficient. Collins (2003, p. 212) cautioned us that this interpretation of intersectionality can be used as a tool to hide injustice. As stated above, intersectionality must explicitly engage with a multifaceted conception of power. It is this type of intersectional lens that is important for literacy research because it can facilitate distinct social explanations and create space for new ways of challenging social inequality.

References

Alvermann, D. E., Marshall, J. D., McLean, C. A., Huddleston, A. P., Joaquin, J., & Bishop, J. (2012). Adolescents' web-based literacies, identity construction, and skill development. *Literacy Research and Instruction*, *51*(3), 179–195. doi:10.1080/19388071.2010.523135

Anyon, J. (2009). Introduction: Critical social theory, educational research, and intellectual agency. In J. Anyon with M. J. Dumas, D. Linville, K. Nolan, M. Pérez, E. Tuck, & J. Weiss (Eds.), *Theory and educational research: Toward critical social explanation* (pp. 1–24). New York, NY: Routledge.

Anzaldúa, G. (1990). Haciendo caras, una entrada. In G. Anzaldúa (Ed.), *Making face, making soul: Haciendo caras: Creative and critical perspectives by feminists of color* (pp. xv–xxviii). San Francisco, CA: aunt lute books.

Artiles, A. J. (2013). Untangling the racialization of disabilities. *Du Bois Review: Social Science Research on Race*, *10*(2), 329–347. doi:10.1017/S1742058X13000271

Bilge, S. (2013). Intersectionality undone: Saving intersectionality from feminist intersectionality studies. *Du Bois Review: Social Science Research on Race*, *10*(2), 405–424. doi:10.1017/S1742058X13000283

Bowleg, L. (2008). When Black lesbian woman ≠ Black lesbian woman: The methodological challenges of qualitative and quantitative intersectionality research. *Sex Roles*, *59*(5–6), 312–325. doi:10.1007/s11199-008-9400-z

Brooks, M. D. (2015). "It's like a script.": Long-term English learners' experiences with and ideas about academic reading. *Research in the Teaching of English*, *49*(4), 383–406.

Brooks, M. D. (2016). Notes and talk: An examination of a long-term English learner reading-to -learn in a high school biology classroom. *Language and Education*, *30*(3), 235–251. doi:10.1080/09500782.2015.1102275

Brooks, M. D. (2017). "She doesn't have the basic understanding of a language": Using spelling research to challenge deficit conceptualizations of adolescent bilinguals. *Journal of Literacy Research*, *49*(3), 342–370. doi:10.1177/1086296X17714016

Carbado, D. W. (2013). Colorblind intersectionality. *Signs: Journal of Women in Culture and Society*, *38*(4), 811–845. doi:10.1086/669666

Carbado, D. W., Crenshaw, K. W., Mays, V. M., & Tomlinson, B. (2013). Intersectionality. *Du Bois Review: Social Science Research on Race*, *10*(2), 303–312. doi:10.1017/S1742058X13000349

Cho, S., Crenshaw, K. W., & McCall, L. (2013). Toward a field of intersectionality studies: Theory, applications, and praxis. *Signs: Journal of Women in Culture and Society*, *38*(4), 785–810. doi:10.1086/669608

Clarke, A. Y. (2011). *Inequalities of love: College-educated Black women and the barriers to romance and family*. Durham, NC: Duke University Press.

Clarke, A. Y., & McCall, L. (2013). Intersectionality and social explanation in social science research. *Du Bois Review: Social Science Research on Race*, *10*(2), 349–363. doi:10.1017/S1742058X13000325

Cole, E. R. (2009). Intersectionality and research in psychology. *American Psychologist*, *64*(3), 170. doi:10.1037/a0014564

Collins, P. H. (2000). *Black feminist thought*. New York, NY: Routledge.

Collins, P. H. (2003). Some group matters: Intersectionality, situated standpoints, and Black feminist thought. In T. L. Lott & J. P. Pittman (Eds.), *A companion to African-American philosophy* (pp. 205–229). Malden, MA: Blackwell.

Collins, P. H., & Bilge, S. (2016). *Intersectionality*. Cambridge: Polity.

Cooper, B. (2016). Intersectionality. In L. J. Disch, & M. E. Hawkesworth (Eds.), *The Oxford handbook of feminist theory* (pp. 385–406). New York, NY: Oxford University Press.

Crenshaw, K. (1989). Demarginalizing the intersection of race and sex: A Black feminist critique of antidiscrimination doctrine, feminist theory and antiracist politics. *University of Chicago Legal Forum*, *1*, 139–167.

Crenshaw, K. (1991). Mapping the margins: Intersectionality, identity politics, and violence against women of color. *Stanford Law Review*, *43*(6), 1241–1299. Retrieved from http://www.jstor.org/stable/1229039

Cuadraz, G. H., & Uttal, L. (1999). Intersectionality and in-depth interviews: Methodological strategies for analyzing race, class, and gender. *Race, Gender & Class*, *6*, 156–186. Retrieved from http://www.jstor.org/stable/41674900

Cummins, J. (1979). Linguistic interdependence and the educational development of bilingual children. *Review of Educational Research*, *49*(2), 222–251. doi:10.3102/00346543049002222

Cummins, J. (2000). *Language, power, and pedagogy: Bilingual children in the crossfire.* Clevedon: Multilingual Matters.

Dill, T. B., & Kohlman, M. H. (2012). Intersectionality: A transformative paradigm in feminist theory and social justice. In S. N. Hesse-Biber (Ed.), *Handbook of feminist research: Theory and praxis* (pp. 154–174). Thousand Oaks, CA: Sage.

Gee, J. P. (2001). Reading as situated language: A sociocognitive perspective. *Journal of Adolescent & Adult Literacy, 44*(8), 714–725. Retrieved from http://www.jstor.org/stable/40018744

Grzanka, P. R. (2014). Introduction: The (intersectional) self and society. In P. R. Grzanka (Ed.), *Intersectionality: A foundations and frontiers reader* (pp. 67–73). Boulder, CO: Westview Press.

Gutiérrez, K. D., Morales, P. Z., & Martinez, D. C. (2009). Re-mediating literacy: Culture, difference, and learning for students from nondominant communities. *Review of Research in Education, 33*(1), 212–245. doi:10.3102/0091732X08328267

Hancock, A. (2007a). Intersectionality as a normative and empirical paradigm. *Politics & Gender, 3*(2), 248–254. doi:10.1017/S1743923X07000062

Hancock, A. (2007b). When multiplication doesn't equal quick addition: Examining intersectionality as a research paradigm. *Perspectives on Politics, 5*(1), 63–79. doi:10.1017/S1537592707070065

Hancock, A. (2016). *Intersectionality: An intellectual history.* New York, NY: Oxford University Press.

Lugones, M. (1994). Purity, impurity, and separation. *Signs: Journal of Women in Culture and Society, 19*(2), 458–479. doi:10.1086/494893

Martínez, R. A., Hikida, M., & Durán, L. (2015). Unpacking ideologies of linguistic purism: How dual language teachers make sense of everyday translanguaging. *International Multilingual Research Journal, 9*(1), 26–42. doi:10.1080/19313152.2014.977712

May, V. M. (2015). *Pursuing intersectionality, unsettling dominant imaginaries.* New York, NY: Routledge.

Muhammad, G. E., & Haddix, M. (2016). Centering Black girls' literacies: A review of literature on the multiple ways of knowing of Black girls. *English Education, 48*(4), 299–336.

Patton, L. D., Crenshaw, K., Haynes, C., & Watson, T. N. (2016). Why we can't wait: (Re)examining the opportunities and challenges for Black women and girls in education [Guest editorial]. *The Journal of Negro Education, 85*(3), 194–198. doi:10.7709/jnegroeducation.85.3.0194

Perry, K. H. (2012). What is literacy?—A critical overview of sociocultural perspectives. *Journal of Language and Literacy Education, 8*(1), 50–71.

Spade, D. (2013). Intersectional resistance and law reform. *Signs: Journal of Women in Culture and Society, 38*(4), 1031–1055. doi:10.1086/669574

Street, B. V. (1984). *Literacy in theory and practice.* New York, NY: Cambridge University Press.

Weber, L., & Parra-Medina, D. (2003). Intersectionality and women's health: Charting a path to eliminating health disparities. *Advances in Gender Research, 7*, 181–230.

Willis, A. I., & Harris, V. J. (2000). Political acts: Literacy learning and teaching. *Reading Research Quarterly, 35*(1), 72–88. doi:10.1598/RRQ.35.1.6

22

RE-IMAGINING TEACHER EDUCATION

Misty Sailors

Imagine two first-grade teachers: one in rural Texas, with 22 learners;[1] another one, in rural Zomba (Malawi), with 150 learners.[2] These two teachers are engaged in different school-wide literacy transformation efforts, both including human and material support for changes to the curriculum, instruction, assessment, and education of these teachers and their colleagues. While both are willing to explore and enact practices in these unique, university–school partnerships, they used their imagination differently to embody the practices.

Take, for example, the day I visited the classroom of the Texas teacher. She and I had been working together for over a year; I had been serving as her coach. I was (frankly) surprised to see round-robin reading in her classroom. When I probed her about the lingering presence of this traditional instruction despite her commitment to be more innovative in her teaching, she looked me straight in the eye and said, "If you want me to do this, you have to *show* me what it looks like. From the start to the end of my school day, I need to *see* what this is before I can do it." Her comment stopped me short in my tracks.

Trying not to compare, I could not help but remember another classroom, two years earlier, in Zomba. As I entered that classroom, I gasped as I witnessed all 150 learners holding books in their hands—some were reading with partners, others with their teacher in a small reading groups (if you can consider 20 children around a teacher a small group). During our debriefing (and through an interpreter), I asked the teacher to talk with me about what I witnessed. "It's simple," she explained. "I just *imagined* what it might look like for all of them to be reading while I was working with my group and this"—pointing to the class—"is what I came up with."

I wondered about the differences in how the teachers approached the unknown. Both were newcomers to the practices we were growing in their classrooms. Both were eager to learn. And, both were receiving equal support. Yet, only one seemingly (and easily) drew on her imagination in her attempt to implement. These experiences led me to wonder where imagination is addressed in theories that inform teacher education. Interestingly, imagination seems to be often-ignored. In this chapter, I will argue for the inclusion of imagination (specifically the radical imagination) in teacher education and provide a path forward for doing so.

Introduction

Given the billions of dollars spent every year on "silver bullets" that promise "quick fixes" for teacher education, calls for more thorough examinations of teacher education are warranted. Literacy researchers have responded; the well-cited work of Anders, Hoffman, and Duffy (2000) seemingly launched the line of inquiry into teacher education, specifically the professional development of literacy teachers.[3] Anders and her colleagues focused their literature review on reading teachers to build toward what they called "features of quality" reading teacher education efforts (p. 730). In summary, those features centered on the need for teachers to volunteer to participate in and have choice over the content of their professional learning and be personally invested in their learning. Other features focused on intensive levels of support and opportunities and tools to reflect on their own practices. Still another set of features highlighted opportunities to converse and discuss their learning with other teachers. Finally, the last set of features emphasized teachers being part of a larger process of professional development, one that is inclusive of university-based researchers, school-based teacher educators, and teachers. In short, although the features are not described as theoretical, Anders and her colleagues were approaching a theory of teacher education. Their work contributed to a growing line of research on the professional development of literacy teachers, and the study is often cited as if it were a theory of teacher education (Sailors, Minton, & Villarreal, 2016).

Even with this seminal study firmly rooted and heavily cited, theories of teacher education remain on the back-burner of seminal literacy reference books. Case in point, this is the first edition of this book to address the theoretical framing of teacher education. This is very likely because the focus of the book was on theoretical models and processes of reading itself, rather than the education of teachers (preservice and serving) to teach reading (and in the case of this edition, literacy). Similarly, in a recent literature review of nine influential literacy research journals, Parsons and his team (2016) documented the appearance of only 52 studies dedicated to teacher education (pre- and in-service) out of the 1,238 studies they analyzed. Nearly 60% of the teacher education studies did not report their theoretical framing. There are two causes for concern: first (but not surprisingly), the number of studies representing teacher education was overall very low. In fact, only 4% of the studies examined by the team were represented in this database (personal communication with Parsons). And second, most of these studies were not framed theoretically. Upon closer examination of the 31 studies that explicitly stated their theory, the most widely used theories included constructivism, critical perspectives, and sociocultural. That said, while I appreciative the work of this team, they did not examine studies in other high-quality journals that may have further informed their findings.

My goal is not to argue for the need for theory in teacher education. Rather, I argue for the need for an additional theory, one that seemingly operates as implied in the underlying constructs of the theories used by many in teacher education—that of imagination. While imagination has been fully explored in the education of children and young people, the same is not true for teacher education. In exploring the role of imagination in teacher education, we might create spaces where professional learning nurtures teachers who can imagine themselves not only as "quality teachers" but also as those who engage as agents of change. And, if teacher education is about encouraging social change, we would do well to follow the words of Maxine Greene (1988): "If we are seriously interested in education for freedom. . . . For this to happen . . . [we must have] a new regard for imagination" (p. 126). I first summarize the theories that drive teacher education. I then turn my attention to theories of imagination and its role in teacher education.

Theories That Frame Teacher Education

The theories used to frame research on teacher education have varied over time and have drawn from a variety of learning theories. For example, in the early days of research on teacher education, researchers drew on theories of behaviorism (e.g., Thorndike, Bregman, Tilton, & Woodyard's 1928 seminal publication) that showed that adults can learn and that there was not a decline in learning as people age. While this research seems rather antiquated, those who work with teachers (pre- and serving) will recognize the ongoing impact of Thorndike's work in teacher education today. State and professional standards for professional preparation (which identify skills for beginning teachers and then prepare licensure assessments from those skills) draw heavily from notions of behaviorism. Professional development workshops (and teacher preparation courses) that use behavioral objectives to specify learning outcomes, notions of competency based teacher preparation curricula, and instructional design models continue to draw heavily from behaviorist notions of learning. Alive and well in the 21st century, these notions continue the long history of the "technocratization of teaching" (Goodlad, 1990). More contemporary theories have also contributed to the field of teacher education, including the ones that I summarize below. While this list is not to be considered exhaustive, it can be considered a starting place for thinking about the ways in which teacher education is currently framed.

Humanism and Theories of Adult Learning

Theories that draw from the philosophy of humanism (Merriam & Bierema, 2013) have guided the field of adult learning, including teacher education. These theories proposed that learners should be able to make their own choices during the learning process and were described in Maslow's (1970) early work. Knowles's (1973) work is considered part of this movement; it was his work that gave rise to the field of adult education at a time when theorists were attempting to study the differences between child and adult learning. Knowles's (1980) key concepts centered on what became known as andragogy, the notion that adult learners are self-directed in their learning, are internally motivated, and use previous experiences as resources for learning. In later years, Knowles's work expanded and described adult learners as driven by internally motivating factors (Knowles & Associates, 1984). Much of the earlier field of literacy teacher professional development draws heavily from the field of adult learning theories.

Situated Learning

More recent studies in teacher education draw heavily from theories that describe learning as ongoing, social, situated, and actively constructed (see the work of Putnam & Borko, 2000). These theories shifted the field from things done to teachers by outside "experts" to things done with or by teachers in response to their own pedagogical concerns and needs. This movement was guided by the work of Fullan and Hargreaves (1992), Guskey and Huberman (1995), Darling-Hammond and Sykes (1999), and Borko, Jacobs, and Koellner (2010). While not focused directly on literacy teacher education, their work influenced the field and included attention to a close link between professional learning and teacher practice, collaboration between teachers, and the links among knowledge, belief, and practice. Teacher learning, from this perspective, is guided by a set of activities that are multifaceted and personally and socially meaningful to the learner (teacher), and that were dubbed "authentic" in some circles (Brown, Collins, & Duguid, 1989). Teachers (as learners) must have access to learning experiences that are socially situated, inclusive of tools of their practice, and built around discussions with knowledgeable others (Putnam & Borko, 2000). Growing out of this movement were experiences offered to teachers as part of professional learning, including peer coaching, cognitive coaching, study groups, and professional learning communities.

Reflection

During this same period, the works of Donald Schön (1983, 1987) became extremely influential in the field of teacher education. Known as the epistemology of practice (Munby & Russell, 1997), Schön's work stressed practical professional knowledge, which he called "knowledge-in-action." Repositioning practice (e.g., teacher practice and the resulting knowledge that resides within practice) to be as rigorous as the development of theory in scientific research, Schön's work highlighted the privileging of Western culture's technical rationality. Arguably, one of his most important concepts, "reflection-in-action" (Schön, 1987, p. 72), refers to what happens when a practice is presented with a novel problem. The struggle with the problem is resolved when it is reframed within the context of action and happens when the practitioner engages in a cycle of inquiry, thinking about intuitive understanding of the problem, exploring, and testing a hypothesis about how to solve the problem. Thus, this professional cycle of inquiry models the "distinctive character of experimenting in practice" (p. 72).

Schön (1987) refers to the cycle as "experimenting in practice" (p. 72) and refers to reflection-in-action as central to the "art" of dealing with situations of "uncertainty, instability, uniqueness, and value conflict" (Schön, 1983, p. 50). In one of the few places where he wrote about teacher education, Schön noted an account of reflective practicum for beginning teachers (presumably in a teacher preparation program) that was grounded in providing differing experiences (grounded in practice) for teacher interns so they could "think of their teaching as a process of reflective experimentation in which they try to make sense of the sometimes puzzling things children say and do, asking themselves as it were, 'How must the children be thinking about this thing in order to ask the questions, or give the answers they do?'" (Schön, 1987, p. 323).

Communities of Practice

Extremely pragmatic and appreciative of teachers as professionals, there was a larger transformation taking place in literacy teacher education, with the work of Jean Lave and Etienne Wenger playing a prominent role. Often, teacher learning was situated as participants within what is known as a community of practice (Lave & Wenger, 1991). Learning, from this theory, occurs as members of the practice fine-tune their enterprise (what it means to be a participant in this community), create evolving forms of engagement (as the individual's identity in the community is dependent on alignment with others in the community), and develop shared repertoires, styles, and discourses (appropriate ways of thinking about their practice). At the heart of this theory is how newcomers are inducted into socially enduring and complex social activities.

For example, the theory was used in one teacher education study conducted by Coskie and Place (2008). In their study, the research team examined the ways in which teachers who participated in the National Board for Professional Teaching Standards certification process integrated their learning from that process into their practice. Using a multiyear, multiple case study design, the study demonstrated that the teachers appropriated the propositions, standards, and conceptual tools espoused in the National Board certification process. The identity of the teachers during the process of appropriation was complex, as they had to negotiate their identity as members of the National Board with those of their school identities. Those multiple identities allowed the teachers to act as "brokers" and opened new possibilities for learning for other teachers at their campuses.

Sociolinguistics

Others used theories from sociolinguistics to examine teacher education through the language of teaching and learning. This work (as seen through the lens of sociolinguistics) proposes that language has a function in societies and that the way we speak and write is shaped by structures of power associated with knowledge. In one study that employed this framework, literacy researchers Wetzel and her colleagues (Wetzel et al., 2015) used responsive critical discourse analysis with cooperating teachers while viewing and discussing videos of conversations with their preservice teachers. Framed through a sociolinguistics (Fairclough, 2013) perspective, the team examined how power circulated through the social interactions of the teachers while coaching their preservice teachers. The team found their use of critical discourse analysis provided agentive opportunities for the teams (cooperating teacher and university facilitator) to deconstruct coaching conversations, noticing, naming, appreciating, and critically evaluating the language (talk and nonverbal) of both their preservice teachers' and their own. The team argued that it was in this process of deconstruction of the coaching conversations that the cooperating teachers were able to reconstruct or engage in what is called positive discourse analysis (PDA). By engaging in PDA, cooperating teachers were able to "generate and rehearse new ways of engaging in mentoring conversations, and in mentoring relationships, with their [preservice teachers]" (Wetzel et al., 2015, p. 372).

Identity Theory

Even though there has been an increase in the number of studies examining coaching as one model of professional development of classroom teachers (Sailors & Shanklin, 2010), there have been only a few that examined the education of coaches (Sailors et al., 2016). Those that have explored issues of power within relationships between coaches and teachers (Sailors et al., 2016). Much of this work draws from theories of identity, which address the plurality and shifting of identities that are drawn from social contexts, such as race, class, gender, age, religion, job, family status, sexual orientation, and nationality (to name a few). These identities are socially constructed and reconstructed through negotiations of everyday life (Gee, 2012) and represent the "mediation of powerful discourses and their artifacts" (Holland, Lachicotte, Skinner, & Cain, 1998, p. 26).

In one such study, Hunt and Handsfield (2013) studied the ways in which first-year literacy coaches negotiated issues of power, positioning, and identity during professional development provided by the local university. The authors framed their study using positioning theory and de Certeau's theories of power and cultural production in everyday life. Their findings illustrated how the coaches both shaped and were shaped by the spaces of the institutions through which they negotiated conflicting expectations and discourses about coaching. Through their work, Hunt and Handsfield highlighted the emotional nature of the work of the coaches as they co-constructed their identities and negotiated their understandings of the purposes of literacy coaching and the spaces of school. In summary, the team called on the field to recognize the complexity of coaching and to offer more meaningful learning opportunities for coaches.

Liberation Theory

Still others have turned to anticolonial theories to guide their work in teacher education, following closely the work of Brazilian philosopher Paulo Freire. Arguing that the essence of the human condition is the struggle to be free, Freire lays the source of that condition on the laps of educators. Those who espouse liberation theory claim that teaching for humanity is more than just preparing students to be "good citizens" and "participate in the democratic process." Liberation education centers on the notion that teaching is a political act (Freire, 1971) and that teachers must engage in pedagogies that disrupt the status quo and denounce systems of social oppression. Drawing from anti-oppressive pedagogies and pedagogies of hope (Freire, 1994), liberation theorists would argue that teachers must be willing and able to participate in change and must have political clarity about their work (Bartolomé, 1994). Liberation education is dialogic in nature and is built on the concept of praxis. Praxis can only be accomplished when people who are oppressed are able to "decodify" or defamiliarize the "known" (Freire, 1985) in order to grow in their *conscientização* (Freire & Freire, 1994). It is through this decodification that people begin to uncover the social, political, and economic contradictions in their lives and in society.

In one such study that employed this theory, my colleagues and I engaged in a self-study of our reading specialist program (master's degree with advanced credentialing) to examine how teachers enrolled in our program talked about liberatory teaching, serving as a mirror of our program (Sailors, Martinez, et al., 2018). Our findings suggested that teachers grappled with conceptions of what it meant and looked like to teach toward freedom. Our findings offered a snapshot of two trajectories. The first was related to teacher development toward praxis. The second was the way in which we realized the need to dismantle hegemonic practices within our program. As a result, not only did we reframe our entire reading specialist program (see Sailors, Martinez, et al., 2018, for a description of those changes), we also worked together to develop a clearer sense of self-awareness of our (faculty in the program) ideologies and how our ideologies informed our practice. We worked (programmatically) to develop "political and ideological clarity" (Bartolomé & Balderrama, 2001, p. 54), which allowed us to identify institutional structures and dominant ideologies of cultural deficiency (DeNicolo & García, 2014).

Imagination in Theories that Inform Teacher Education

In summary, teacher education (research and practice) is supported by theory. However, in my examination of the theories that frame teacher education, there were only a few that (at least) made mention of imagination within the theory. For example, imagination was a source of creativity, according to Maslow (2014), but there was seemingly no place in his theory to describe the role of imagining in learning or how to build upon imagination for learning with teachers. Likewise, although inherent in Schön's call for the professions to be more 'artistic' (and thus, draw upon the use of imagination), there was no direct line to the imagination in Schön's work. And, although some have made the connection between sociocultural theories and imagination in classrooms (see the work of Vygotsky and the Holland et al., team), there has been no explicit link between teacher education and imagination within this theoretical frame. Finally, while Freire's work mentions the need for imagination, his work does not provide an avenue to understand how to tap into or develop it. In short, I could find very little attention to imagination within theories that inform teacher education, the role it plays within these theories, or how to facilitate the growth of the imagination of teachers. Because of this lack of explicit attention, I shifted my explorations toward to the study of imagination, looking at both historical and contemporary theories of imagination as potential sources for understanding the development of the imagination of teachers.

Imagination and Imagining

In this section, I present varying ways in which imagination and imagining have been approached historically, drawing on the works of philosophy, psychology, sociology, phenomenology, and neuroscience. As others have done, I reject a complete theory of imagination since there is no singular function of the imagination that can be used to make sense of its meaning and functions in human existence (Steeves, 2004). Rather, I defer to what Wittgenstein described as "family resemblances" (qtd. in Steeves, 2004, p. 5), or those theories and philosophies that share commonalities, thus allowing for a generalized theory.

Historical Perspectives on Imagination and Imagining

Historically, imagination has been studied since the beginning of Western philosophy. Aristotle recognized the imagination as distinct from perception[4] and mind, arguing that imagination produces images when there is no perception (as in dreams); that it is lacking in "lower animals"; and that it can be false, where perception is always "true" (Shields, 2016). He argued that "imagination remains largely a reproductive rather than a productive activity, a servant rather than a master of meaning, imitation rather than origin" (Kearney, 1988, p. 113). In short, Aristotle argued that imagination was a middle-range faculty (Casey, 2000).

Aristotle's ideas were reiterated and embellished during the Middle Ages (Engell, 1981) and were used to explain physical deformation in children. Seemingly, the imagination of women was deemed to be more likely influenced by impressions and thus, more easily corrupted by external images. In other words, if a pregnant woman encountered something disturbing (e.g., a snake), or if her desires were too strong (e.g., she craved apples), or if she gazed too long at an image (e.g., a portrait on a wall), representative images would seep into her womb and impact the baby (Asma, 2017).

The imagination fell out of favor as a contributing factor to perception during the Enlightenment period by those who ascribed to rationalism, such as Descartes. Scholars during this time period argued that the imagination was not an essential part of the mind, since it dealt with images in the brain whose existence could be doubted (Open University, 2016). Others during this time (such as Hume) insisted that the imagination allowed us to separate and combine ideas in new ways, but all the materials of thinking were derived from our impressions or the stimuli we receive directly through our senses (Engell, 1981).

Still others (e.g., Kant) described imagination as the root of human cognition and said it was one way knowledge was obtained, in what Kant called "transcendent imagination" (Engell, 1981, p. 130). German Romantic thinkers presented imagination as a superordinate faculty of the human mind and argued that imagination was the source that unified perception and creativity. Aligned with this thinking, Coleridge (as explained in Warnock, 1976) identified what he called primary imagination (which is not subject to human control) and secondary imagination (re-creation of new born out of the perceived world). Because the secondary imagination coexists with the primary, it is limited in its ability to create the ideal (e.g., can never reach it, such as perfection). While Coleridge believed that the primary was universal, he believed that only artists possessed a secondary imagination (Engell, 1981). Even though the imagination was lauded during this period, the Romantic imagination was unable to deliver on its promises as it was seemingly relegated to forming only images, never realities. Unfortunately, this definition of a secondary romantic imagination is what lingers today in popular definitions of imagination (Johnson, 1987). This dualism has plagued the Western world since the 17th century, and it "insists on an absolute division between the substance or nature of thought and the stance or nature of physical being" (McGee, 2016, p. 7).

Contemporary Theories of Imagination and Imagining

However, the work of 20th- and 21st-century philosophers would suggest that such a dualism is erroneous. Contemporary theories suggest that perception and imagination exist not only within the individual, but among people. That is, images are formed in a social context, as individual minds only arise in contexts where other minds exist (Chambliss, 1991). I address basic tenets of contemporary theories of imagination in this section.

Imagining as the Basis of Human Activity

Imagination and imagining are a significant part of the human experience (Heath, 2008) and an integral part of what it means to be human—a "completely essential condition for all human mental activity" (Vygotsky, 2004, p. 17). Imagination, as the "basis of all creative activity" (Vygotsky, 2004, p. 9), is the fundamental mode of human existence, and through it humans are able to experience the freedom of consciousness. In fact, Vygotsky (2004) credits the creation of "absolutely everything around us that was created by the hand of [humankind], the entire world of culture, as distinct from the world of nature" as a product of human imagination (p. 10).

Likewise, Dewey (1934/1986) recognized that "all possibilities reach us through the imagination" (p. 30). In many ways, the imagination is a playground where anything is possible, for it allows us to engage in realities that cannot be captured through our senses alone and allows us "clear insight into the remote, the absent, the obscure" (Dewey, 1910, p. 244). Lyons (2005) argued that through our imagination we can "create an infinite number of alternative and past realities" (p. 21) and thus, the world inside our mind is richer than the world outside our mind. While there is an intentionality aspect to imagination (sometimes it is intentional, other times it is not), imagination is necessitated by the desire for something different or new or because of an "aversion to the given state of things caused by the blocking of successful activity" (Dewey, 1916, p. 348). Because imagining is remarkably easy to enter into (e.g., we have near unlimited access to this capacity), it is easier to succeed at imagining than to fail at it (Casey, 2000).

Imagination as Experientially Based

Theorists who grapple with imagination seem to agree: all imaginative events can only be created by what we explicitly or implicitly know about an event (Casey, 2000). In other words, imagined events are created from elements drawn from our reality (or physical world) through our previous experiences. Those experiences can be lived, vicarious, or drawn from our understanding of the scientific world (Stevenson, 2003). Consequently, the "richer" and greater variety of experiences a person has, the "richer" the imagination (Vygotsky, 2004, p. 14).

However, for the experiences to inform our imagination, there must be an incubation period after the "accumulation of experience" (Ribot, qtd. in Vygotsky, 2004, p. 15). During incubation, inner meaning about the experience (including the artifacts, people, and goals) is created first with the "deformation" or "unforming" (Benjamin, 2004) of the experience itself. That is, we must dissociate (or break up the complex whole into a set of individual parts) from the previous experience so that we can associate those experiences with the new (imagination) (Vygotsky, 2004, pp. 25–26). This process of dissociation (called dismemberment by Sartre, 1972) moves to re-association; the materials might be re-associated subjectively or objectively (conceptually). In some cases, there is a change in the materials under the influence of imagination, such as exaggeration.

Once the incubation period is complete—that is, once the experience (and its associated images) is loosed from its perceptual context—imagining can begin (Sepper, 2013). The act of imagination (or creation) is a "climactic moment" following this long and internal process of incubation. The full cycle of the process will be completed only when imagination is embodied (or crystallized/fossilized) in external images (Vygotsky, 2004, p. 28). That is, we no longer require the external form; instead, we rely on inner means that we can reproduce. As our expertise grows with the experience, the parts that we learned as recognizable (and the cultural forms that mediated their learning) lose their ability to be separated and fall from awareness, and we no longer think about what or how we do what we do when we imagine (Holland et al., 1998, p. 117).

The Circular Nature of Imagining

Recent work would suggest that there is a circular nature between imagination and the perceived world (Varela & Depraz, 2003). The physical materials that make up our realities play a large role in the making of our imagination and our imaginings. Likewise, our imagination supplements and deepens our perceptions. In addition to our direct experiences in past realities, our imagination can be directed by someone else's lived experiences (e.g., those events we experience vicariously). One's perceptions of the physical world are impacted by one's vicarious experiences (imagined). Thus, those vicarious experiences become part of our lived worlds. Because of this, imagination takes on a very important function in societies—it becomes "the means by which a person's experience is broadened, because [s]he can imagine what [s]he has not seen, can conceptualize something from another person's narration and description of what [s]he [her]himself has never experienced" (Vygotsky, 2004, p. 17). While the roots of experience are found in the interactions of people with others and their environment, that experience becomes a matter of perception (or consciousness) when meanings from previous experiences enter into the experience (Dewey, 1934, p. 283). As such, the products of imagination consist of "transformed and reworked elements of reality" (Vygotsky, 2004, p. 16). From a neurological perspective, this process of recombining elements of past experiences into "simulations of novel future events" is an "adaptive" process (Schacter et al., 2012, p. 688) and one that has helped humans develop over time.

As an example of this adaptive practice, Dewey (1934/1986) observed that an invention "did not exist before [its inventor] . . . but the conditions for [its] existence were there in the physical material and energies and in human capacity" (pp. 33–34), or in the imaginings of the "inventor." Once an imaginary event materializes into the physical world (as did the locomotive in Dewey's example or the smartphone as a more contemporary example), it becomes the product of imaginings as well as a lived experience by others. In many ways (and from a socioconstructivist perspective), material objects are artifactual representations of not only the singular person but of the teams credited with their invention (e.g., Steve Jobs and his teams), as individual creativity is no longer significant. Rather, the sheer amount of what has been created in the human world is an "anonymous collective creative work of unknown inventors," making creativity (and imaginings) "the rule, rather than the exception" (Vygotsky, 2004, p. 11). To that end, all conscious experience has (out of necessity) some degree of imaginative quality as our lived experiences in the physical world are of the imaginings of someone else.

In this way, our imagination becomes the way our experiences are broadened as we are "not limited to the narrow circle and boundaries of [our] own experience but venture far beyond these boundaries, assimilating, with the help of [our] imagination someone else's historical or social experience" (Vygotsky, 2004, p. 17). It is through this circular nature of lived and imagined events that our physical world is in a constant state of being transformed by our imaginings and the imaginings of those around us. And, because of the onset of globalized literacy practices that are driven by technology, the recursive nature of imagination and our perceptions have the potential to grow exponentially.

Imagining Bodies, Figured Worlds, and Imagined Communities

It has been argued that what we typically think about in education is what is called the "inventive imagination" (Heath, 2008), a naive approach at best that represents imagination as the cognitive capacity to bring before the mind an image that is not physically present. Even though one might think of the notion of our "mind's eye" as an archaic phrase, it continues to be used in contemporary theory (see Holland et al., p. 139). Additionally, Heath (2008) believed that the model of imagination from which the field of education draws points to a largely structured and regimented imagination, one that derives from images of what we have "seen" or "done" (p. 120). In this section, I explore the ways in which imagination and imagining might expand theories that are used in teacher education.

Imagining Bodies

Merleau-Ponty, a French philosopher, rejected behaviorism (which saw the body as a passive recipient of stimuli) and intellectualism (which saw the body as an extension of the mind) and according to Steeves (2004) believed that the body possesses "inner communication with the world" (p. 17). That is, the world presents itself to the body in terms of possibilities. According to Merleau-Ponty, our bodies are governed at two levels. The first, our "body at this moment," are those experiences that occur below our level of conscious and voluntary action (Steeves, 2004, p. 19). The second, the "customary body," is the level where we have a tacit sense of our body's abilities and of its relation to the world (p. 20). As such, humans have what Merleau-Ponty called "body schema" (p. 19). This body schema is not just a mental image (as others have proposed) but is an immediate and affective sense of the body. Our body schema is how we are aware of what our bodies can and cannot do. Our body schema develops as our interactions in the world grow more complex and out of "the momentum of existence" (p. 22).

Essential to the development of the body schema is what Merleau-Ponty called the "virtual body," or our imaginative ability to consider alternative uses of our bodies and to assume various perspectives from which we can observe a situation (Steeves, 2004, p. 22). Our body schema is extended, through combined habits of the body, on the "basis of an imaginative level of embodied existence" (p. 22). Our virtual body affords us "a new use of [our] body" so as to "enrich and recast the body schema" (p. 22). The virtual body allows us to consider new ways of being in the world and affords us the opportunity to establish a plan of action to acquire the needed skills to carry that plan out. These adaptations of the body schema grow out of the need for alternative experiences and movements. In other words, as we encounter problems, our virtual bodies provide us with the space to rehearse and create (and re-create) our way toward solutions to those problems.

Merleau-Ponty argued that the realm of possibilities for humans exists only through the virtual body, which is an "embodied mode of the imagination" (Steeves, 2004, pp. 23–24). It is our virtual body that allows us to assume alternative positions within particular contexts because it provides an imaginative basis for embodied experiences. Our virtual body allows us to extend our habitual behavior beyond the bodily experience to the limitless realm of the imaginary (Steeves, 2001, pp. 376–377). According to Merleau-Ponty, the body schema and the virtual body are "two poles of a dialectic" that exist in an "imperceptible twist" in which they become integrated over time but never "quite coincide" (Steeves, 2004, p. 26). Together, they constitute the "imagining body" (p. 27).

Human perception plays an important part in our imagining bodies. Current theories of imagination define perception as a mode of existence that gives us access to objects so that we can experience them (Steeves, 2001). Our perception contains two essential aspects of an experience: the logic of the sensible world (which is oftentimes ambiguous to humans) as it appears to the observer, and the role of the observer (and most importantly of the body) in the interpretation of that experience (Steeves, 2004, p. 37). Synaesthetics, or the intertwining of the various sense qualities with a common synaesthetic experience, is at the heart of our bodily experience of the world. Objects appear to humans as "intersensory entities" (Steeves, 2004, p. 40); the texture of an object is revealed to us when we pick it up, its sound when we squeeze it. In that way, objects reveal themselves to us. Aligned with Merleau-Ponty's notion of reversibility, objects do not "see" us; rather, they look at us in such a way that they make themselves be "seen" by us (Steeves, 2001). But the synaesthetic qualities are not revealed to us all at one time. Rather, they are revealed one by one, unfolding in their qualities as the others reside in the "background" waiting to be uncovered by our senses. To perceive is to engage with the receding backgrounds as much as the appearing foregrounds in a virtually reversed way. In short, we must resort to synaesthetics to discover the essence of perceptual objects. It is only then that we can embody the perceived world into our imaginary bodies.

The virtual body, then, is an imaginative dimension of embodied existence. Thus, to perceive is to "engage with virtual qualities that are essentially virtual modes of embodiment" (Steeves, 2004, p. 48). Perception provides the body with "vital communication" of how to project itself onto the world, live the world, and occupy space in the world (Steeves, 2001, p. 375). As such, imagination is "at the heart of perception, so that the primacy of perception is simultaneously the primacy of the imaginary" (p. 378). In short, it is the imagining body that allows for the development of our unique and personal styles of existence.

Figured Worlds and Imagined Identities

In addition to imagining bodies, other scholars write of imagination as sociohistorical, contrived interpretations of the "figured worlds" in which we live (Holland et al., 1998, p. 52). Figured worlds are "socially produced, culturally constituted activities" (pp. 40–41) that are not so much things or objects to be perceived but processes and traditions that "gather us up and give us form as our lives intersect them" (p. 41). Our figured worlds include those spaces in which people learn to recognize each other as a particular kind of actor. The actors in those spaces share values for certain outcomes (over other outcomes) and attach significance to certain acts (over other acts). It is through these social interactions that people "figure" how to relate to each other over time, space, and place, through the organization of these figured worlds grow the identities and agency of the people who participate in them (p. 49). These identities—a concept that combines the intimate world with the collective space of the cultural forms and social relations in the figured worlds (p. 5)—are an imagining of "self" and, as such, are developed conceptually within social practice. Similarly, sense of self is enacted in day-to-day performances that provide relative positions of influence and prestige in and across figured worlds (Urrieta, 2007).

Identities in figured worlds are formed through the negotiation of positionality, where positions are "offered" to people in figured worlds and those positions can be accepted, rejected, or negotiated. Identities in figured worlds are authored and are made through world making, or "serious play" (Holland et al., 1998). This notion of "serious play" is most directly related to imagination, as play draws upon recognized genres of inner speech (which Holland said is an element of imagination) and activity. Holland argued that "serious play" takes the player beyond the immediate setting and happens through the world in which it is set (p. 236). It is through play that we learn to "act otherwise," and "think otherwise"; thus, "mastery . . . over our play is mastery over our imagination" (pp. 236–237). It is through our capacity to formulate social scenes in imagination that we develop a sense of self and agency, and ultimately, our play becomes embodied. The creation of "imagined worlds" opens spaces that are affordances for humans and are "potentiary, cultural resources that help us envision new identities that could give shape to the affiliations and disaffiliations we live by day to day" (pp. 249–250). And, as such, imagined worlds "can oppose the positions assigned to us by other powers . . . and they give content and form to the positions we seek for ourselves" (pp. 249–250). In doing so, we can dis-embody the authoring done to us by others and disrupt notions of power and authority.

Imagined Communities

While some figured worlds are located in the physical world, others are located in the abstract. Dubbed "imagined communities" by political scientist and historian Benedict Anderson (1983), these social spaces represent a utopian community—one in which there is a strong sense of commonality among the members of the social body even though this social body exists in the "image of their collectiveness" (p. 49). That is, many of the members will never know most of the other members of an imagined community or ever meet or even hear about them. As such, these groups are formed through the rise of cultural artifacts that have acquired deictic values, and the modular activities that are performed by members are done so separate from other members of the group. In fact, Anderson argued that all communities that exist beyond the immediate face-to-face contact (or "primordial villages") are imagined (p. 49). Members of these abstract communities have figured identities through the kinship they share with others imagined to be engaged in the same modular activity, and as such, these communities invite others into a space "where one does not exist" (p. 49). Nearly a virtual community, Anderson described imagined communities as imaginatively projected before they are realized; they are imagined through language and the way the community presents itself as both open ("welcome") and closed ("we"). Once the community formulates from the imagined to the concrete, the process of proliferation has begun; this notion is in keeping with the circular nature of imagination I described earlier.

This movement from the imaged to the concrete is dependent on the mass circulation of cultural resources. For example, Anderson (1983) described the origins and growth of nationalism as an outgrowth of what he called "print-capitalism"—books and media printed in vernacular generated through the use of the printing press that was proliferated by capitalist marketplaces. As a result of mass production, readers who spoke local dialects found a common discourse, forming what

Anderson called "national print-languages" (p. 224). Anderson's work has important implications for identities that are both positional and figured (Holland et al., 1998).

Radical Imaginings and Teacher Education

Examining recent theories used in literacy teacher education, it would appear that while some allude to notions of imagination and imagining, very few explicitly discuss it or how to develop it. Vygotsky (2004) not only promoted the need of imagination in learning for young children, he also claimed there is no evidence that this is any less true for adults; he believed that adults do use their imagination in learning (p. 32). What happens as people age, he contended, is that imagination "does not disappear completely in anyone, it merely becomes incidental" (p. 35). The only difference between the play of children and that of adults is the types of materials in which the imagination is "occupied" (Dewey, 1916, p. 236). In this section, I argue for the inclusion of imagination in teacher education.

Shifting From "Technocrats" to Radical Imaginings

Understanding imagination in teacher education can be done when it is placed "in opposition to the narrowing effects of habituation" (Dewey, 1934, p. 280). While there are certainly nonconforming models of teacher education to be found, many models of teacher education continue to "produce" teachers who are technocrats, or "slaves to the text, fearful of taking a risk," who "fail to make any concrete connections between what they have read and what is happening in the world, the country, or the local community," and who "rarely teach anything of personal value" and "speak correctly about dialectical thought but think mechanistically" (Freire, 1994, p. 34). The same might be said of many teacher educators operating within teacher education programs and people who "do" staff development. I am not suggesting that there is no longer a need for technical expertise of teachers and teacher educators. Rather, I align my work with Freire's notion of "specialist"—one whose role is not to deposit knowledge, but to facilitate the decodification of hegemonic practices found in many classrooms and schools today.

One way to decodify hegemonic practices is to decenter the realities of teacher education; that decentering is done by a sociological process the French-Greek philosopher Castoriadis called the "radical imagination" (1997). The notion of the "radical" inherits its most powerful meaning from the Latin *radix*, or "root," in the sense that radical ideas, ideologies, or perspectives are informed by the understanding that social, political, economic, and cultural problems are outcomes of deeply rooted tensions, contradictions, power imbalances, and forms of oppression and exploitation in societies. On one level, the radical imagination is the ability to imagine the world, life, and social institutions not as they are but as they might otherwise be (Haiven & Khasnabish, 2017). At a deeper level, the radical imagination can bring into experience that which is not just novel to the world of experience; it can actually create new experiences not represented in any other experience. Thus, our radical imagination has the potential to change our personal lives and the society in which we exist.

As part of our consciousness, the radical imagination allows us to explore the possibility of experiencing the world as different than what is present or that on which we have reflected. Heath (2008) described this as the more advanced levels of consciousness (where consciousness can become intentional) that transcendental reflection (levels of experiences that transcend the experience and provide the condition for experience and, ultimately, being) takes place. Thus, the radical imagination allows us to move from "seeing as" to "being as" (p. 122). In order to move to imagining teacher education as a place for the development of the radical imagination, there are several points teacher educators must consider, including critical inquiry, embodied practices, and reflexivity. Together, they allow for teachers and teacher educators to teach from an anti-hegemonic imperative.

Cultures of Critical Inquiry

If teachers are to be anti-hegemonic in their teaching, they have to draw upon their radical imagination. But, what about teachers who claim to not be able to use their imagination? Perhaps it is not that they have "lost" their imagination. It may be that their imagination (and their imagining) has been suppressed by the very institution of school in which they actively participate. Because they never saw imagination celebrated in school as learners themselves, they do not have a model of teaching that encourages and grows imagination as part of their repertoire of teaching practices. This may also be true of some teacher educators. Because inquiry convokes the imagination (Freire, 1998), framing teacher education from an inquiry perspective may be the first entry into growing a teacher's imagination, especially for those who claim not to have or be able to use their imagination. And, to go one step further, inquiry convokes not only imagination but also our very *raison d'être* (Freire, 1998, p. 82). To say it differently: critical inquiry convokes radical imagination.

Critical inquiry to grow the radical imagination is supported in complex learning environments. If teachers live their professional life in stasis (or equilibrium), there is no reason for imagination. However, the lack of adaptation to an environment gives rise to needs and motives, which in turn give rise to the imagination (Vygotsky, 2004). Because humans thrive in complex environments, the simpler the environment, the stronger the desire to create (and imagine). Thus, teacher education programs that emphasize complex learning environments and engage in reflexive thinking build an environment where imagination is encouraged and fostered.

If the precondition of the imagination is autonomy (Kaplan, 1972), then the only way for the radical imagination of teachers to grow is for teachers to decide what it is they want to learn about within their practice. As such, relevancy is at the heart of critical inquiry. Evidence from neurology indicates that imagined future events that were relevant to research participants were associated with stronger "feelings of experiencing" than those imagined future events that were irrelevant (Schacter et al., 2012, p. 679). This notion that relevancy matters reinforces what teachers have been telling researchers for years—teacher education has to be relevant to the lives of teachers. This becomes more than just a "professionalization" versus "de-professionalization" argument in teacher education. It becomes about growing the radical imagination of teachers so they can potentially grow the radical imagination of the children and young people with whom they work.

Embodied Practices Within Imagined Communities

But what happens if a teacher has not experienced critical inquiry or her radical imagination? Evidence from neurology indicates that people have greater vividness for future events that are in familiar settings than in unfamiliar settings (Schacter et al., 2012, pp. 678–679). This has implications for how we approach helping teachers imagine a different type of classroom. What does this mean for teachers who have never "seen" critical inquiry? If they are attempting to envision their classroom and it is extremely different from the classrooms in which they were engaged in past experiences (think Lortie, 1975), then they are going to have difficulty with the experience. Unless they live in an area that has easy access to concrete communities of practice (e.g., Teachers for Social Justice), teachers remain in the imagined community. Thus, those communities have to be available in their radical imagination.

If the imagining body allows for our personal style of existence (see earlier section), then it would make sense that our imagining bodies allow for a professional style of existence, since according to Freire, the personal is the professional and vice versa. And, to grow a professional style of existence, teacher education must take into consideration the development of the virtual body of teacher candidates and teachers who are growing their practice. That is, we must build into teacher education programs opportunities that foster the body schema of beginning teachers to develop, and not just in a banal way (e.g., mechanical teaching). Developing the body schema of teachers would allow them to imagine themselves in a classroom that convokes dialogic spaces, a classroom that allows and encourages dissent, and one that celebrates humanity. Perhaps teachers cannot rehearse and create solutions to problems they encounter in their classrooms because teacher educators are not developing virtual bodies early in their professional lives.

Similarly, to embody anti-hegemonic practices requires that teachers be afforded opportunities to synaesthetically engage with objects, tools, and people while they actively create who they are as actors inside the practice. And, their engagement must involve "serious play" (Holland et al., 1998). Through the imagined worlds created with teachers, they can then create similar imagined worlds with the children and young people in their classrooms. If the radical imagination is predicated on experiences (both lived and vicarious), then it only makes sense that teachers need to be provided with more (and richer) professional experiences and not just workshops where someone "tells" them what to do. For example, what if professional development involved traveling with teachers to other classrooms that embodied critical inquiry and radical imagination? To "see" others engaging in anti-hegemonic practices allows for teachers to imagine their own body schema and imagine what their own classroom might look like. What if teacher study groups were grounded in teachers sharing their narrative experiences? Because stories told by others find their way into our vicarious experiences, it would make sense (after some incubation period) that teachers would draw upon those experiences as part of their imaginative/lived cycles. As a result, teachers might have more productive imaginations (Vygotsky, 2004), and thus more opportunities to embody anti-hegemonic practices.

Reflection versus Reflexivity

Arguably, most attempts at teacher education rely heavily on teachers reflecting on their practices through the various forms of coaching and other support systems. Compared to reflection, which is described as an objective and analytical process in which we test "intuitive understandings of experienced phenomena" (Schön, 1983, p. 241), critical reflexive practice (or praxis) is different. Praxis involves exposing contradictions as a way of highlighting constructed realities. It is through the highlighting of tacit assumptions that people learn to read their word worlds and thus, decodify structures of oppressive power and authority.

Reflection *may* not be enough to move teachers toward anti-hegemonic practices since reflection maintains an objective view of the world, one in which "I'm not responsible for [X]" because "I can only do so much." When engaged in praxis, one is thinking critically about hegemony, including those behaviors, assumptions, values, and theories that influence our actions and interactions and the role we play in maintaining oppressive practices in our personal and professional lives. It is through reflexivity that we realize that our presuppositions and foundations are not something that belongs to us; they were furnished to us by our social institutions, and genuine reflexivity is therefore, "ipso facto, a challenging of the given institution of society, the putting into question of socially instituted representations" (Castoriadis, 1997, p. 267). Reflexivity should be at the center of teacher education if our goal is to grow anti-hegemonic teachers. And, reflexivity is only possible through the radical imagination since it is in the radical imagination that reflexive thought interrogates itself, its particular context, and its presuppositions and foundations.

Theoretically Shifting Research Within Teacher Education

If research within literacy teacher education is one more component of the radical imagination, then it must also have its proper attention in this chapter as research within teacher education remains largely unexplored and underrepresented in quality research journals (Sailors, Martinez, Davis,

Goatley, & Willis, 2017). That said, I purposely use the phrase "research within" (rather than on) teacher education as a way of disrupting the commonplace and bringing light to the need for radical imagination. As radical imagination plays a role in anti-hegemonic teaching, it can also play a role in decolonizing research within teacher education.

Redirecting the Focus

In many ways, research within literacy teacher education has followed the larger field of educational research and explored ways for teachers to be more efficient and effective with their instruction. Such bodies of work, known as the "beating the odds" and "what works, for whom" studies (e.g., see the works of Langer, 2000; the CIERA change model by Taylor, Pearson, Clark, & Walpole, 2000; and international work such as Sailors, Hoffman, & Matthee, 2007), have surely contributed to what we know about practice. Subsequently, those notions (based on effectiveness) have permeated not only teacher education but research on (used intentionally) teacher education. To that end, these notions of what become known as "best practices" remain grounded in a technocratic model of teaching and teacher education. This is a far cry from the kind of research we might be doing with teachers that is aligned with anti-hegemony, especially if we (as teacher educators and researchers within teacher education) have not historically and radically re-imagined teacher education.

What if we shifted the focus of our work toward growing our own radical imaginations and those of the teachers with whom we work as we engage in critical inquiry cycles of our teacher education programs? Earlier I mentioned a self-study that was an eye-opener for the program in which my work is focused. While my colleagues and I thought we were doing right by our teachers (and the children and young people with whom they work), we were shocked that our teachers were only marginally able to talk about liberatory education. However, when we engaged in praxis, we realized the need for a radical imagining of our program. We presented our work at the annual meeting of the Literacy Research Association (Manning, Sailors, Davis, Martinez, & Stortz, 2014), and others voiced similar concerns with their own programs, such as, "If you collected the same data at my institution, you would probably get similar results." So how do we, as a field, move away from technical expertise with our teachers and toward anti-hegemonic practices? It starts with our own radical imaginings of the research in which we engage. In keeping with Castoriadis's theory, if our imagination acts as part of our praxis, then our programs will be different when our consciousness is transformed, as will we as people. The field must consider self-critical study (rather than just self-study) as a way of engaging in radical imaginings of teacher education.

Decolonizing Who We Are

Merleau-Ponty wrote of the imaginary as a "decentering of the sensible" (qtd. in Morris, 2008, p. 140) and, as such, a way to rethink research within teacher education. In addition to questioning our assumptions and actions, challenging our own conceptions of reality, and exploring new possibilities for teacher education, our radical imagination allows us to work with others in achieving our collaborative goals. Such is the case for praxis related to theory and research within teacher education. Both "theory" and "research" are terms that are often monopolized by academia, which presumably holds the rights to production, distribution, consumption (although academia is willing to "share" with teachers), and exchange. Presumably when academics "do" it, the product is called "theory" and/or "research". When "others" (teachers) do it, the product sometimes gets caveats put around it ("action research" and "teacher research"). In addition to the lack of recognition of the contributions teachers make to the field of research, we also do not hear of "teacher theory." That is not to say that teachers do not theorize. They do. They may very well be engaged in what

Gee (2012) called tacit theories (see Unrau, Alvermann, & Sailors, chapter 1 this volume). What might it be like if we engaged teachers in using their radical imaginations to create research and their own theories of literacy teaching and learning?

Haiven and Khasnabish (2017) described three ways of thinking about research within social movements; I will borrow and apply their notions to teacher education. They argued that research can involve invocation, where research methods mobilize the researcher into the movement. It can involve avocation, where the researcher passes power to the movement and retreats within the movement. Or, it can involve convocation, the imagined form of research that convokes spaces of dialogue, debate, reflection, questioning, and empowerment. From this perspective, research is viewed as a collaborative venture aimed at reducing the gulf between theory and the problem to be solved in practice. Thus, convocations put the privilege and power into the hands of the movement. If we were (as part of our radical imagining within teacher education) to imagine a form of research that convokes such spaces, the processes and products of research may convoke the radical imagination with those with whom we work—teachers. What if we invited teachers into research with us, rather than "doing" research on (or about) them? What if we used the process of "critical inquiry" to engage them in research? Likewise, what if we used research with teachers to convoke their radical imagination about theory—their own and that of others? Especially noteworthy might be discourse and critical inquiry with teachers related to theories that have been used to oppress them and the children and youth with whom they work. Together we could re-imagine research and theory as part of an evolving social process, one in which the teacher educator/researcher convenes and convokes the social processes of research (Haiven & Khasnabish, 2017).

Concluding Thoughts

I began this chapter with a scenario that was the impetus for my inquiry into the role of imagination as an underlying theory in teacher education. Without belaboring my point of its importance, I will close with a quote from Dewey, drawn from his work on the ways in which beliefs find their way into our lives through religious practices and the way our imagination can free us of those practices. The quote is applicable to teacher education, as often theories and practices in teacher education are held as if they were from the spoken Word themselves. In the quote below, I substitute the word "practices" for Dewey's "religion" to denote the connection to theories in teacher education. He wrote, "The logic involved in getting rid of inconvenient aspects of past religions [practices] compels us to inquire how much in religion [practices] now accepted are survivals from outgrown cultures" (qtd. in Boydston, 1934, p. 7). Dewey (qtd. in Boydston, 1934) went on to suggest that it is through our imagination that we "wipe the slate clean and start afresh by asking what would be the idea of the unseen, of the manner of its control over us and the ways in which reverence and obedience would be manifested, if whatever is basically religious in experience had the opportunity to express itself free from all historic encumbrances" (p. 7). Dare we allow our radical imaginations and the radical imagination of teachers (preservice and serving) to challenge and thus change who we are as teachers and teacher educators, researchers within teacher education, and people? Dare we not? For if not, we deny ourselves and the teachers and children and youth with whom we work opportunities to grow in our creativity and humanity.

Notes

1 Described in Sailors, Villarreal, et al., 2018.
2 Described in Sailors et al., 2013.
3 This term refers to initial certification (e.g., preservice teacher education) and in-service teacher professional development, including workshops, graduate school, and advanced credentialing. I use the word "teacher"

to refer to the lifespan of the professional, from the onset in a teacher preparation program to retirement (and beyond).

4 Defined as a conscious awareness of something that is actually before us in the spatiotemporal world.

References

Anders, P. L., Hoffman, J. V., & Duffy, G. G. (2000). Teaching teachers to teach reading: Paradigm shifts, persistent problems, and challenges. In M. L. Kamil, P. B. Mosenthal, P. D. Pearson, & R. Barr (Eds.), *Handbook of reading research* (Vol. 3, pp. 719–742). Mahwah, NJ: Erlbaum.

Anderson, B. (1983). *Imagined communities: Reflections on the origin and spread of nationalism.* London: Verso.

Asma, S. T. (2017). *The evolution of imagination.* Chicago, IL: University of Chicago Press.

Bartolomé, L. I. (1994). Beyond the methods fetish: Toward a humanizing pedagogy. *Harvard Educational Review, 64*(2), 173–195.

Bartolomé, L. I., & Balderrama, M. V. (2001). The need for educators with political and ideological clarity: Providing our children with "The Best." In M. de la Luz Reyes and J. J. Halcón (Eds.), *The best for our children: Critical perspectives on literacy for Latino students* (pp. 48–64). New York, NY: Teachers College Press.

Benjamin, W. (2004). *Selected writings, vol. 1: 1913–1926.* Boston, MA: Beacon Press.

Borko, H., Jacobs, J., & Koellner, K. (2010). Contemporary approaches to teacher professional development. In E. Baker, B. McGaw, & P. Peterson (Eds.), *International encyclopedia of education* (3rd ed., vol. 7, pp. 548–555). Oxford: Elsevier.

Brown, J. S., Collins, A., & Duguid, P. (1989). Situated cognition and the culture of learning. *Educational Researcher, 18*(1), 32–42.

Casey, E. S. (2000). *Imagining: A phenomenological study* (2nd ed.). Bloomington, IN: Indiana University Press.

Castoriadis, C. (1997). *World in fragments: Writings on politics, society, psychoanalysis, and the imagination* (D. A. Curtis, Trans. and Ed.). Stanford, CA: Stanford University Press.

Chambliss, J. J. (1991). John Dewey's idea of imagination in philosophy and education. *The Journal of Aesthetic Education, 25*(4), 43–49.

Coskie, T. L., & Place, N. A. (2008). The National Board certification process as professional development: The potential for changed literacy practice. *Teaching and Teacher Education, 24*, 1893–1906.

Darling-Hammond, L., & Sykes, G. (Eds.). (1999). *Teaching as the learning profession: Handbook of policy and practice.* San Francisco, CA: Jossey-Bass.

DeNicolo, C. P., & García, G. E. (2014). Examining policies and practices: Two districts' responses to federal reforms and their use of language arts assessments with emergent bilinguals (K–3). In P. Dunston, S. K. Fullerton, M. W. Cole, D. Herro, J. A. Malloy, P. M. Wilder, & K. N. Headley (Eds.). *63rd yearbook of the Literacy Research Association* (pp. 229–242). Altamonte Springs, FL: Literacy Research Association.

Dewey, J. (1910). *How we think.* Boston, MA: D. C. Heath.

Dewey, J. (1916). *Democracy and education.* New York, NY: Free Press.

Dewey, J. (1934). *Art as experience.* New York, NY: Perigee Book.

Dewey, J. (1986). *A common faith. The collected works of John Dewey, 1882–1953.* In J. A. Boydston (Ed.). Carbondale, IL: Southern Illinois University Press.

Engell, J. (1981). *The creative imagination: Enlightenment to romanticism.* Cambridge, MA: Harvard University Press.

Fairclough, N. (2013). *Critical discourse analysis: The critical study of language* (2nd ed.). London: Routledge.

Freire, P. (1971). *Pedagogy of the oppressed.* New York, NY: Continuum.

Freire, P. (1985). *The politics of education: Culture power and liberation.* South Hadley, MA: Bergin & Garvey.

Freire, P. (1994). *Pedagogy of hope.* London: Continuum.

Freire, P. (1998). *Pedagogy of freedom: Ethics, democracy, and civic courage.* New York, NY: Rowman & Littlefield.

Freire, P., & Freire, A. M. A. (1994). *Pedagogy of hope: Reliving pedagogy of the oppressed.* New York, NY: Continuum.

Fullan, M., & Hargreaves, A. (Eds.). (1992). *Teacher development and educational change.* London: Falmer.

Gee, J. P. (2012). *Social linguistics and literacies: Ideology in discourses.* New York, NY: Routledge.

Goodlad, J. (1990). Better teachers for our nation's schools. *Phi Delta Kappan, 72*(3), 184–194.

Greene, M. (1988). *The dialectic of freedom.* New York, NY: Teachers College Press.

Guskey, T. R., & Huberman, M. (Eds.). (1995). *Professional development in education: New paradigms and practices.* New York, NY: Teachers College Press.

Haiven, M., & Khasnabish, A. (2017). *The radical imagination: Social movement research in the age of austerity.* London: Zed Books.

Heath, G. (2008). Exploring the imagination to establish frameworks for learning. *Studies in Philosophical Education, 27*, 115–123.

Holland, D., Lachicotte, W., Skinner, D., & Cain, C. (1998). *Identity and agency in cultural worlds.* Cambridge, MA: Harvard University Press.

Hunt, C. S., & Handsfield, L. J. (2013). The emotional landscapes of literacy coaching: Issues of identity, power, and positioning. *Journal of Literacy Research, 45*(1), 47–86.

Johnson, M. (1987). *The body in the mind: The bodily basis of meaning, imagination, and reason.* Chicago, IL: The University of Chicago Press.

Kaplan, E. K. (1972). Gaston Bachelard's philosophy of imagination: An introduction. *Philosophy and Phenomenological Research, 33,* 1–24.

Kearney, R. (1988). *The wake of imagination: Toward a postmodern culture.* London: Routledge.

Knowles, M. S. (1973). *The adult learner: A neglected species.* Houston, TX: Gulf.

Knowles, M. S. (1980). *The modern practice of adult education: From pedagogy to andragogy.* (2nd ed.). New York, NY: Cambridge Books.

Knowles, M. S., & Associates (1984). *Andragogy in action: Applying modern principles of adult learning.* San Francisco, CA: Jossey-Bass.

Langer, J. A. (2000). *Beating the odds: Teaching middle and high school students to read and write well* (Report Series 12014). Albany, NY: University at Albany State University of New York, National Research Center on English Language Learning and Achievement.

Lave, J., & Wenger, E. (1991). *Situated learning: Legitimate peripheral participation.* Cambridge: Cambridge University Press.

Lortie, D. C. (1975). *School teacher* (2nd ed.). Chicago, IL: University of Chicago Press.

Lyons, J. D. (2005). *Before imagination: Embodied thought from Montaigne to Rousseau.* Stanford, CA: Stanford University Press.

Manning, L., Sailors, M., Davis, D., Martinez, M., & Stortz, R. (2014). *Equalizing educational experiences: A critical look at teacher disposition and their stances toward social justice.* Paper presented at the annual meeting of the Literacy Research Association, Marco Island, FL.

Maslow, A. H. (1970). *Motivation and personality* (2nd ed.). New York, NY: HarperCollins.

Maslow, A. H. (2014). *Toward a psychology of being.* Floyd, VA: Rediscovered Books.

McGee, P. (2016). *Political monsters and democratic imaginations.* New York, NY: Bloomsbury Academic.

Merriam, S. B., & Bierema, L. L. (2013). *Adult learning: Linking theory and practice.* Retrieved from http://ebookcentral.proquest.com

Morris, D. (2008). Reversibility and ereignis: On being as Kantian imagination in Merleau-Ponty and Heidegger. *Philosophy Today, 52,* 135–143.

Munby, H., & Russell, T. (1997). Educating the reflective teacher: An essay review of two books by Donald Schön. *Journal of Curriculum Studies, 21*(1), 71–80.

Open University. (2016). *Imagination: The missing mystery of philosophy.* Milton Keynes: Author.

Parsons, S. A., Gallagher, M. A., & the George Mason University Content Analysis Team. (2016). A content analysis of nine literacy journals, 2009–2014. *Journal of Literacy Research, 48*(4), 476–502.

Putnam, R. T., & Borko, H. (2000). What do new views of knowledge and thinking have to say about research on teacher learning? *Educational Researcher, 29,* 4–15.

Sailors, M., Hoffman, J. V., & Matthee, B. (2007). South African schools that promote literacy learning with students from low-income communities. *Reading Research Quarterly, 42,* 364–387.

Sailors, M., Martinez, M., Davis, D., Goatley, V., & Willis, A. (2017). Interrupting and disrupting literacy research. *Journal of Literacy Research, 49*(1), 6–9.

Sailors, M., Martinez, M., Manning, L., Davis, D., Stortz, R., & Sellers, T. (2018). When effective instruction is not enough: A critical look at emergent understandings of liberatory pedagogy by teachers in a master's program. In A. E. Lopez & E. L. Olan (Eds.), *Transformative pedagogies for teacher education: Moving towards critical praxis in an era of change* (pp. 15–30). Charlotte, NC: Information Age.

Sailors, M., Minton, S., & Villarreal, L. (2016). Literacy coaching and comprehension instruction. In S. Israel (Ed.), *Handbook of research on comprehension instruction* (pp. 601–625). New York, NY: Routledge.

Sailors, M., & Shanklin, N. L. (2010). Growing evidence to support coaching in literacy and mathematics. *The Elementary School Journal, 111*(1), 1–6.

Sailors, M., Villarreal, A., Sellers, T., Schutz, P., Minton, S., & Wilburn, M. (2018). Curricular materials for children and young people who struggle with learning to read: The case of Roadrunner Reader Inquiry Kits. In P. O. Garcia & P. B. Lind (Eds.), *Reading achievement and motivation in boys and girls* (pp. 201–218). New York, NY: Springer.

Sailors, M., Hoffman, J. V., Wilson, T., Villarreal, L., Peterson, K., Chilora, H., Phiri, L., & Saka, T. (2013). Implementing a school-wide reading program in Malawi: A case study. In P. J. Dunston, S. K. Fullerton, C. C. Bates, K. Headley, & P. M. Stecker (Eds.), *62nd yearbook of the Literacy Research Association* (pp. 220–232). Altamonte Springs, FL: Literacy Research Association.

Sartre, J. (1972). *Imagination*. Ann Arbor, MI: University of Michigan Press.

Schacter, D. L., Addis, D. R., Hassibis, D., Martin, V. C., Spreng, R. N., & Szpunar, K. (2012). The future of memory: Remembering, imagining, and the brain. *Neuron Review, 76*, 677–694.

Schön, D. A. (1983). *The reflective practitioner: How professionals think in action*. New York, NY: Basic Books.

Schön, D. A. (1987). *Educating the reflective practitioner: Toward a new design for teaching and learning in the professions*. San Francisco, CA: Jossey-Bass.

Sepper, D. L. (2013). *Understanding imagination: The reason of images*. New York, NY: Springer.

Shields, C. (2016). Aristotle's psychology. In E. N. Zalta (Ed.), *The Stanford encyclopedia of philosophy* (Winter 2016 ed.). Retrieved from https://plato.stanford.edu/archives/win2016/entries/aristotle-psychology/

Steeves, J. B. (2001). The virtual body: Merleau-Ponty's early philosophy of imagination. *Philosophy Today, 45*(4), 370–380.

Steeves, J. B. (2004). *Imagining bodies: Merleau-Ponty's philosophy of imagination*. Pittsburgh, PA: Duquesne University Press.

Stevenson, L. (2003). Twelve conceptions of imagination. *British Journal of Aesthetics, 43*, 238–259.

Taylor, B. M., Pearson, P. D., Clark K. F., & Walpole, S. (2000). Effective schools and accomplished teachers: Lessons about primary-grade reading instruction in low-community schools. *The Elementary School Journal, 101*, 121–165.

Thorndike, E. L., Bregman, E. O., Tilton, J. W., & Woodyard, E. (1928). Adult learning. New York: Macmillan.

Urrieta, L. (2007). Figured worlds and education: An introduction to the special issue. *The Urban Review, 39*(2), 107–116.

Varela, F. J., & Depraz, N. (2003). In B. A. Wallace (Ed.), *Buddhism and science: Breaking new ground* (pp. 195–232). New York, NY: Columbia Press.

Vygotsky, L. S. (1978). *Mind in society: The development of higher psychological processes* (M. Cole, V. John-Steiner, S. Scribner, & E. Souberman, Eds.). Cambridge, MA: Harvard University Press.

Vygotsky, L. S. (2004). Imagination and creativity in childhood. *Journal of Russian and East European Psychology, 42*(1), 7–97.

Warnock, M. (1976). *Imagination*. Berkeley, CA: University of California Press.

Wetzel, M. M., Maloch, B., Hoffman, J. V., Taylor, L. A., Vlach, S. K., & Greeter, E. (2015). Developing mentoring practices through video-focused responsive discourse analysis. *Literacy Research: Theory, Method, and Practice, 64*, 359–378.

SECTION FIVE

Looking Back, Looking Forward

The final section of this volume offers eight chapters (plus an email correspondence associated with one of the chapters) that explore theoretical models and processes in literacy in ways that are both canonical and contemporary. For example, in chapter 23, "The Transactional Theory of Reading," Louise Rosenblatt illustrates some of the assumptions and concepts that undergird the transactional theory of the reading process. Rosenblatt applies the concept of transaction to transacting with texts, the reader's stance, and the efferent-aesthetic continuum. She also applies the concept of transaction to writing in similar ways, including the writer's stance and writing about texts. Rosenblatt illustrates authorial reading and discusses the role of communication between authors and readers.

Following Rosenblatt's chapter is a brief email correspondence between Jonathan Ratner (the son of Louise M. Rosenblatt) and Donna Alvermann, who in her duties as one of the editors responsible for securing permission to reprint his mother's chapter in *TMPL7*, serendipitously learned of Jonathan Ratner's perspectives on why "'transaction'. . . matters critically today, given the prevalence of confabulation and spin in articles on political subjects—and of tribal readings within group-based bubbles of communication."

Mark Dressman's (chapter 24), "Transactional Reading in Historical Perspective," extends Rosenblatt's work. Dressman carefully traces the historical roots of Rosenblatt's work, illustrating the influences on her work. He demonstrates the ways in which Rosenblatt's work focuses on the individuality and autonomy of readers rather than the sociocultural influences on readers. Dressman concludes his chapter with a call for classroom instruction that would lead to students who are savvy readers rather than just people who love to read literature without the awareness of why or how they have come to love literature.

Leketi Makalela's work (chapter 25), "Multilanguaging and Infinite Relations of Dependency: Re-theorizing Reading Literacy from Ubuntu," presents an alternative framework for literacy theory and practice, one that is based on the African value system of Ubuntu. Ubuntu translanguaging, referred to as multilanguaging, valorizes versatile, mobile, and fluid interactions between languages and literacies. It shows that language and literacy are bound in infinite relations of dependency where there is a constant disruption of orderliness and simultaneous recreation of new discursive resources in the complex process of meaning making.

Allison Skerrett's work (chapter 26), "Advancing Theoretical Perspectives on Transnationalism in Literacy Research," explains and expands upon concepts embedded in transnational theory to illuminate the potential it offers for the field of literacy. She begins the chapter with an explanation of sending and receiving nations, moves into notions of cross-border flows, and then examines hybridity. The chapter identifies key domains in the field of literacy whose knowledge bases stand to be strengthened from applications of transnational theories. The chapter also discusses transnationally inclusive approaches to literacy education.

In chapter 27, "The Social Practice of Multimodal Reading: A New Literacy Studies–Multimodal Perspective on Reading," Jennifer Rowsell, Gunther Kress, Kate Pahl, and Brian Street situate reading within two approaches, the New Literacy Studies and social semiotic approach to multimodality. They present a view of reading through these two lenses and various stages of reading (from early childhood and youth literacies to adult academic literacies), accounting for reading in various contexts. They conclude their chapter with a discussion of the future of literacy, pedagogy, and policy.

Mira-Lisa Katz, Nancy Brynelson, and John R. Edlund's chapter (28), "Enacting Rhetorical Literacies: The Expository Reading and Writing Curriculum in Theory and Practice," makes the case for integrating multiple theories from the fields of reading comprehension, rhetoric, literacy, and composition to foster college readiness, academic literacy development, and literate identity formation at the high school level. They write about the use of the Expository Reading and Writing Curriculum (ERWC) to establish a classroom environment where all opinions are empowered and enacted. Practices within the ERWC support the development of academic identities and civic literacies and cultivate literate habits of mind.

In chapter 29, "Propositions from Affect Theory for Feeling Literacy through the Event," Christian Ehret argues for the necessity of reconceptualizing affect in relation to emotion for literacy studies. He illustrates his theory of feeling literacy through his experiences writing with one adolescent, Ella, while she was hospitalized for leukemia treatment. Ehret contrasts the history of representational and constructivist logic for interpreting emotion in literacy studies with the non-representational perspectives of affect theory developed from the process philosophies of Whitehead, Deleuze, and Massumi.

Deborah R. Dillon and David G. O'Brien's work, "Pragmatism [not just] Practicality as a Theoretical Framework in Literacy Research" (chapter 30) completes this section. In their chapter, Dillon and O'Brien explore ways that work in literacy has taken up the framework of pragmatism. They offer a brief review of how pragmatism has been defined and used and how it is sometimes overused and misconstrued by educational researchers. They conclude with a call for academics and communities of inquiry to adopt pragmatism as a way of engaging in research that is meaningful and credible.

23

THE TRANSACTIONAL THEORY OF READING AND WRITING

Louise M. Rosenblatt

This chapter is reprinted from *Theoretical Models and Processes of Reading* (4th ed., pp. 1057–1092), edited by R.B. Ruddell, M.R. Ruddell, & H. Singer, Newark, DE: International Reading Association. Copyright © 1994 by the International Reading Association.

Terms such as *the reader* are somewhat misleading, though convenient, fictions. There is no such thing as a generic reader or a generic literary work; there are in reality only the potential millions of individual readers of individual literary works. . . . The reading of any work of literature is, of necessity, an individual and unique occurrence involving the mind and emotions of some particular reader.

(Rosenblatt, 1938/1983)

That statement, first published in *Literature as Exploration* in 1938, seems especially important to reiterate at the beginning of a presentation of a "theoretical model" of the reading process. A theoretical model by definition is an abstraction, or a generalized pattern devised in order to think about a subject. Hence, it is essential to recognize that, as I concluded, we may generalize about similarities among such events, but we cannot evade the realization that there are actually only innumerable separate transactions between readers and texts.

As I sought to understand how we make the meanings called novels, poems, or plays, I discovered that I had developed a theoretical model that covers all modes of reading. Ten years of teaching courses in literature and composition had preceded the writing of that statement. This had made possible observation of readers encountering a wide range of "literary" and "nonliterary" texts, discussing them, keeping journals while reading them, and writing spontaneous reactions and reflective essays. And decades more of such observation preceded the publication of *The Reader, the Text, the Poem* (Rosenblatt, 1978), the fullest presentation of the theory and its implications for criticism.

Thus, the theory emerges from a process highly appropriate to the pragmatist philosophy it embodies. The problem arose in the context of a practical classroom situation. Observations of relevant episodes led to the hypotheses that constitute the theory of the reading process, and these have in turn been applied, tested, confirmed, or revised in the light of further observation.

Fortunately, while specializing in English and comparative literature, I was in touch with the thinking on the forefront of various disciplines. The interpretation of these observations of readers' reading drew on a number of different perspectives—literary and social history, philosophy, aesthetics, linguistics, psychology, and sociology. Training in anthropology provided an especially important point of view. Ideas were developed that in some instances have only recently become established.

451

It seems necessary, therefore, to begin by setting forth some of the basic assumptions and concepts that undergird the transactional theory of the reading process. This in turn will involve presentation of the transactional view of the writing process and the relationship between author and reader.

The Transactional Paradigm

Transaction

The terms *transaction* and *transactional* are consonant with a philosophic position increasingly accepted in the 20th century. A new paradigm in science (Kuhn, 1970) has required a change in our habits of thinking about our relationship to the world around us. For 300 years, Descartes' dualistic view of the self as distinct from nature sufficed, for example, for the Newtonian paradigm in physics. The self, or "subject," was separate from the "object" perceived. "Objective" facts, completely free of subjectivity, were sought, and a direct, immediate perception of "reality" was deemed possible. Einstein's theory and the developments in subatomic physics revealed the need to acknowledge that, as Neils Bohr (1959) explained, the observer is part of the observation—human beings are part of nature. Even the physicists' facts depend to some extent on the interests, hypotheses, and technologies of the observer. The human organism, it became apparent, is ultimately the mediator in any perception of the world or any sense of "reality."

John Dewey's pragmatist epistemology fitted the new paradigm. Hence, Dewey joined with Arthur F. Bentley to work out a new terminology in *Knowing and the Known* (1949). They believed the term *interaction* was too much associated with the old positivistic paradigm, with each element or unit being predefined as separate, as "thing balanced against thing," and their "interaction" studied. Instead, they chose *transaction* to imply "unfractured observation" of the whole situation. Systems of description and naming "are employed to deal with aspects and phases of action, without final attribution to 'elements' or presumptively detachable or independent 'entities,' 'essences,' or 'realities'" (p. 108). The knower, the knowing, and the known are seen as aspects of "one process." Each element conditions and is conditioned by the other in a mutually constituted situation (cf. Rosenblatt, 1985b).

The new paradigm requires a break with entrenched habits of thinking. The old stimulus–response, subject–object, individual–social dualisms give way to recognition of transactional relationships. The human being is seen as part of nature, continuously in transaction with an environment—each one conditions the other. The transactional mode of thinking has perhaps been most clearly assimilated in ecology. Human activities and relationships are seen as transactions in which the individual and social elements fuse with cultural and natural elements. Many current philosophy writers may differ on metaphysical implications but find it necessary to come to terms with the new paradigm.[1]

Language

The transactional concept has profound implications for understanding language. Traditionally, language has been viewed as primarily a self-contained system or code, a set of arbitrary rules and conventions that is manipulated as a tool by speakers and writers or imprints itself on the minds of listeners and readers. Even when the transactional approach has been accepted, this deeply ingrained way of thinking continues to function, tacitly or explicitly, in much theory, research, and teaching involving texts.[2] The view of language basic to the transactional model of reading owes much to the philosopher John Dewey but even more to his contemporary Charles Sanders Peirce, who is recognized as the U.S. founder of the field of semiotics or semiology, the study of verbal and nonverbal signs. Peirce provided concepts that differentiate the transactional view of language and reading from structuralist and poststructuralist (especially deconstructionist) theories. These reflect the influence of another great semiotician, the French linguist Ferdinand de Saussure (Culler, 1982).

Saussure (1972) differentiated actual speech (*parole*) from the abstractions of the linguists (*langue*), but he stressed the arbitrary nature of signs and minimized the referential aspect. Even more important was his dyadic formulation of the relationship between "signifier and signified," or between words and concept. These emphases fostered a view of language as an autonomous, self-contained system (Rosenblatt, 1993).

In contrast, Peirce (1933, 1935) offered a triadic formulation. "A sign," Peirce wrote, "is in conjoint relation to the thing denoted and to the mind. . . ." The "sign is related to its object only in consequence of a mental association, and depends on habit" (Vol. 3, p. 360). The triad constitutes a symbol. Peirce repeatedly refers to the human context of meaning. Because he evidently did not want to reinforce the notion of "mind" as an entity, he typically phrased the "conjoint" linkage as among sign, object, and "interpretant," which should be understood as a mental operation rather than an entity (Vol. 6, p. 347). Peirce's triadic model firmly grounds language in the transactions of individual human beings with their world.

Recent descriptions of the working of the brain by neurologists and other scientists seem very Peircean. Although they are dealing with a level not essential to our theoretical purposes, they provide an interesting reinforcement. "Many leading scientists, including Dr. Francis Crick, think that the brain creates unified circuits by oscillating distant components at a shared frequency" (Appenzeller, 1990, pp. 6–7). Neurologists speak of "a third-party convergence zone [which seems to be a neurological term for Peirce's interpretant] that mediates between word and concept convergence zones" (Damasio, 1989, pp. 123–132). Studies of children's acquisition of language support the Peircean triad, concluding that a vocalization or sign becomes a word, a verbal symbol, when the sign and its object or referent are linked with the same "organismic state" (Werner & Kaplan, 1962, p. 18).

Though language is usually defined as a socially generated system of communication—the very bloodstream of any society—the triadic concept reminds us that language is always internalized by a human being transacting with a particular environment. Vygotsky's recognition of the social context did not prevent his affirming the individual's role: The "sense of a word" is

> the sum of all the psychological events aroused in our consciousness by the word. It is a dynamic, fluid, complex whole, which has several zones of unequal stability. Meaning [i.e., reference] is only one of the zones of sense, the most stable and precise zone. A word acquires its sense from the context in which it appears; in different contexts, it changes its sense.
>
> *(1962, p. 46)*

Vygotsky postulated "the existence of a dynamic system of meaning, in which the affective and the intellectual unite." The earliest utterances of children evidently represent a fusion of "processes which later will branch off into referential, emotive, and associative part processes" (Rommetveit, 1968, pp. 147, 167). The child learns to sort out the various aspects of "sense" associated with a sign, decontextualize it, and recognize the public aspect of language, the collective language system. This does not, however, eliminate the other dimensions of sense. A language act cannot be thought of as totally affective or cognitive, or as totally public or private (Bates, 1979, pp. 65–66).

Bates provides the useful metaphor of an iceberg for the total sense of a word to its user: The visible tip represents what I term the public aspect of meaning, resting on the submerged base of private meaning. *Public* designates usages or meanings that dictionaries list. Multiple meanings indicated for the same word reflect the fact that the same sign takes on different meanings at different times and in different linguistic or different personal, cultural, or social contexts. In short, *public* refers to usages that some groups of people have developed and that the individual shares.

Note that *public* and *private* are not synonymous with *cognitive* and *affective*. Words may have publicly shared affective connotations. The individual's private associations with a word may or may not agree with its connotations for the group, although these connotations must also be individually acquired. Words necessarily involve for each person a mix of both public and private elements, the base as well as the tip of the semantic iceberg.

For the individual, then, the language is that part, or set of features, of the public system that has been internalized through that person's experiences with words in life situations. "Lexical concepts must be shared by speakers of a common language . . . yet there is room for considerable individual difference in the details of any concept" (Miller & Johnson-Laird, 1976, p. 700). The residue of the individual's past transactions—in particular, natural and social contexts—constitutes what can be termed a linguistic–experiential reservoir. William James especially suggests the presence of such a cumulative experiential aura of language.

Embodying funded assumptions, attitudes, and expectations about language and about the world, this inner capital is all that each of us has to draw on in speaking, listening, writing, or reading. We "make sense" of a new situation or transaction and make new meanings by applying, reorganizing, revising, or extending public and private elements selected from our personal linguistic–experiential reservoirs.

Linguistic Transactions

Face-to-face communication—such as a conversation in which a speaker is explaining something to another person—can provide a simplified example of the transactional nature of all linguistic activities. A conversation is a temporal activity, a back-and-forth process. Each person has come to the transaction with an individual history, manifested in what has been termed a linguistic–experiential reservoir. The verbal signs are the vibrations in the air caused by a speaker. Both speaker and addressee contribute throughout to the spoken text (even if the listener remains silent) and to the interpretations that it calls forth as it progresses. Each must construct some sense of the other person. Each draws on a particular linguistic–experiential reservoir. The specific situation, which may be social and personal, and the setting and occasion for the conversation in themselves provide clues or limitations as to the general subject or framework and hence to the references and implications of the verbal signs. The speaker and addressee both produce further delimiting cues through facial expressions, tones of voice, and gestures. In addition to such nonverbal indications of an ongoing mutual interpretation of the text, the listener may offer questions and comments. The speaker thus is constantly being helped to gauge and to confirm, revise, or expand the text. Hence, the text is shaped transactionally by both speaker and addressee.

The opening words of a conversation, far from being static, by the end of the interchange may have taken on a different meaning. And the attitudes, the state of mind, even the manifest personality traits, may have undergone change. Moreover, the spoken text may be interpreted differently by each of the conversationalists.

But how can we apply the conversation model of transaction to the relationship between writers and readers, when so many of the elements that contribute to the spoken transaction are missing—physical presence, timing, actual setting, nonverbal behaviors, tones of voice, and so on? The signs on the page are all that the writer and the reader have to make up for the absence of these other elements. The reader focuses attention on and transacts with an element in the environment, namely the signs on the page, the text.

Despite all the important differences noted above, speech, writing, and reading share the same basic process—transacting through a text. In any linguistic event, speakers and listeners and writers and readers have only their linguistic–experiential reservoirs as the basis for interpretation. Any interpretations or new meanings are restructurings or extensions of the stock of experiences of language, spoken and written, brought to the task. In Peircean terms, past linkages of sign, object, and interpretant must provide the basis for new linkages, or new structures of meaning. Instead of an interaction, such as billiard balls colliding, there has been a transaction, thought of rather in terms of reverberations, rapid oscillations, blendings, and mutual conditionings.

Selective Attention

William James's concept of "selective attention" provides an important insight into this process. During the first half of this century, a combination of behaviorism and positivism led to neglect of the concept, but since the 1970s psychologists have reasserted its importance (Blumenthal, 1977; Myers, 1986). James (1890) tells us that we are constantly engaged in a "choosing activity," which he terms "selective attention" (Vol. I, p. 284). We are constantly selecting out of the stream, or field, of consciousness "by the reinforcing and inhibiting agency of attention" (Vol. I, p. 288). This activity is sometimes termed "the cocktail party phenomenon": In a crowded room where many conversations are in progress, we focus our attention on only one of them at a time, and the others become a background hum. We can turn our selective attention toward a broader or narrower area of the field. Thus, while language activity implies an intermingled kinesthetic, cognitive, affective, associational matrix, what is pushed into the background or suppressed and what is brought into awareness and organized into meaning depend on where selective attention is focused.

The transactional concept will prevent our falling into the error of envisaging selective attention as a mechanical choosing among an array of fixed entities rather than as a dynamic centering on areas or aspects of the contents of consciousness. The linguistic reservoir should not be seen as encompassing verbal signs linked to fixed meanings, but as a fluid pool of potential triadic symbolizations. Such residual linkages of sign, signifier, and organic state, it will be seen, become actual symbolizations as selective attention functions under the shaping influence of particular times and circumstances.

In the linguistic event, any process will be affected also by the physical and emotional state of the individual, for example, by fatigue or stress. Attention may be controlled or wandering, intense or superficial. In the discussion that follows, it will be assumed that such factors enter into the transaction and affect the quality of the process under consideration.

The paradoxical situation is that the reader has only the black marks on the page as the means of arriving at a meaning—and that meaning can be constructed only by drawing on the reader's own personal linguistic and life experiences. Because a text must be produced by a writer before it can be read, logic might seem to dictate beginning with a discussion of the writing process. It is true that the writer seeks to express something, but the purpose is to communicate with a reader (even if it is only the writer wishing to preserve some thought or experience for future reference). Typically, the text is intended for others. Some sense of a reader or at least of the fact that the text will function in a reading process is thus implicit in the writing process. Hence, I shall discuss the reading process first, then the writing process. Then, I shall broach the problems of communication and validity of interpretation before considering implications for teaching and research.

The Reading Process

Transacting With the Text

The concepts of transaction, the transactional nature of language, and selective attention now can be applied to analysis of the reading process. Every reading act is an event, or a transaction involving a particular reader and a particular pattern of signs, a text, and occurring at a particular time in a particular context. Instead of two fixed entities acting on one another, the reader and the text are two aspects of a total dynamic situation. The "meaning" does not reside readymade "in" the text or "in" the reader but happens or comes into being during the transaction between reader and text.

The term *text* in this analysis denotes, then, a set of signs capable of being interpreted as verbal symbols. Far from already possessing a meaning that can be imposed on all readers, the text actually remains simply marks on paper, an object in the environment, until some reader transacts with it.

The term *reader* implies a transaction with a text; the term *text* implies a transaction with a reader. "Meaning" is what happens during the transaction—hence the fallacy of thinking of them as separate and distinct entities instead of factors in a total situation.

The notion that the marks in themselves possess meaning is hard to dispel. For example, *pain* for a French reader will link up with the concept of bread and for an English reader with the concept of bodily or mental suffering. A sentence that Noam Chomsky (1968, p. 27) made famous can help us realize that not even the syntax is inherent in the signs of the text but depends on the results of particular transactions: *Flying planes can be dangerous.*

Actually, only after we have selected a meaning can we infer a syntax from it. Usually, factors entering into the total transaction, such as the context and reader's purpose, will determine the reader's choice of meaning. Even if the reader recognizes the alternative syntactic possibilities, these factors still prevail. This casts doubt on the belief that the syntactical level, because it is lower or less complex, necessarily always precedes the semantic in the reading process. The transactional situation suggests that meaning implies syntax and that a reciprocal process is going on in which the broader aspects guiding choices are actively involved.

Here we see the difference between the physical text, defined as a pattern of signs, and what is usually called "the text," a syntactically patterned set of verbal symbols. This actually comes into being during the transaction with the signs on the page.

When we see a set of such marks on a page, we believe that it should give rise to some more or less coherent meaning. We bring our funded experience to bear. Multiple inner alternatives resonate to the signs. Not only the triadic linkages with the signs but also certain organismic states, or certain ranges of feeling, are stirred up in the linguistic–experiential reservoir. From these activated areas, selective attention—conditioned, as we have seen, by multiple physical, personal, social, and cultural factors entering into the situation—picks out elements that will be organized and synthesized into what constitutes "meaning." Choices have in effect probably been made simultaneously, as the various "levels" transact, conditioning one another, so to speak.

Reading is, to use James's phrase, a "choosing activity." From the very beginning, and often even before, some expectation, some tentative feeling, idea, or purpose, no matter how vague at first, starts the reading process and develops into the constantly self-revising impulse that guides selection, synthesis, and organization. The linguistic–experiential reservoir reflects the reader's cultural, social, and personal history. Past experience with language and with texts provides expectations. Other factors are the reader's present situation and interests. Perusing the unfolding text in the light of past syntactic and semantic experience, the reader seeks cues on which to base expectations about what is forthcoming. The text as a verbal pattern, we have seen, is part of what is being constructed. Possibilities open up concerning the general kind of meaning that may be developing, affecting choices in diction, syntax, and linguistic and literary conventions.

As the reader's eyes move along the page, the newly evoked symbolizations are tested for whether they can be fitted into the tentative meanings already constructed for the preceding portion of the text. Each additional choice will signal certain options and exclude others, so that even as the meaning evolves, the selecting, synthesizing impulse is itself constantly shaped and tested. If the marks on the page evoke elements that cannot be assimilated into the emerging synthesis, the guiding principle or framework is revised; if necessary, it is discarded and a complete rereading occurs. New tentative guidelines, new bases for a hypothetical structure, may then present themselves. Reader and text are involved in a complex, nonlinear, recursive, self-correcting transaction. The arousal and fulfillment—or frustration and revision—of expectations contribute to the construction of a cumulative meaning. From a to-and-fro interplay between reader, text, and context emerges a synthesis or organization, more or less coherent and complete. This meaning, this "evocation," is felt to correspond to the text.

Precisely because for experienced readers so much of the reading process is, or should be, automatic, aspects of the reading process tend to be described in impersonal, mechanistic terms.

Psychologists are rightfully concerned with learning as much as possible about what goes on between the reader's first visual contact with the marks on the page and the completion of what is considered an interpretation of them. A number of different levels, systems, and strategies have been analytically designated, and research has been directed at clarifying their nature. These can be useful, but from a transactional point of view, it is important to recognize their potentialities and their limitations. A mechanistic analogy or metaphor lends itself especially to analyses of literal reading of simple texts. Results need to be cautiously interpreted. Recognizing the essential nature of both reader and text, the transactional theory requires an underlying metaphor of organic activity and reciprocity.

The optical studies of Adelbert Ames (1955) and the Ames–Cantril "transactional psychology" (Cantril & Livingston, 1963), which also derived its name from Dewey and Bentley's *Knowing and the Known* (1949), deserve first mention in this regard. These experiments demonstrated that perception depends much on the viewer's selection and organization of visual cues according to past experience, expectations, needs, and interests. The perception may be revised through continued transactions between the perceiver and the perceived object.

F.C. Bartlett's theory of *Remembering* (1932; which I regret having discovered even later than did his fellow scientists) and his term *schema* are often called on to explain psychological processes even broader than his special field. It is not clear, however, that those who so readily invoke his schema concept are heeding his fears about a narrow, static usage of the term. Rejecting the image of a warehouse of unchanging items as the metaphor for schemata, he emphasized rather "active, developing patterns"—"constituents of living, momentary settings belonging to the organism" (Bartlett, 1932, p. 201). His description of the "constructive character of remembering," his rejection of a simple mechanical linear process, and his concepts of the development and continuing revision of schemata all have parallels in the transactional theory of linguistic events. His recognition of the influence of both the interests of the individual and the social context on all levels of the process also seems decidedly transactional.

The Reader's Stance

The broad outline of the reading process sketched thus far requires further elaboration. An important distinction must be made between the operations that produce the meaning, say, of a scientific report and the operations that evoke a literary work of art. Neither contemporary reading theory nor literary theory has done justice to such readings, nor to the fact that they are to be understood as representing a continuum rather than an opposition. The tendency generally has been to assume that such a distinction depends entirely on the texts involved. The character of the "work" has been held to inhere entirely in the text. But we cannot look simply at the text and predict the nature of the work. We cannot assume, for instance, that a poem rather than an argument about fences will be evoked from the text of Frost's *Mending Wall* or that a novel rather than sociological facts about Victorian England will be evoked from Dickens's *Great Expectations*. Advertisements and newspaper reports have been read as poems. Each alternative represents a different kind of selective activity, a different kind of relationship, between the reader and the text.

Essential to any reading is the reader's adoption, conscious or unconscious, of what I have termed a *stance* guiding the "choosing activity" in the stream of consciousness. Recall that any linguistic event carries both public and private aspects. As the transaction with the printed text stirs up elements of the linguistic–experiential reservoir, the reader adopts a selective attitude or stance, bringing certain aspects into the center of attention and pushing others into the fringes of consciousness. A stance reflects the reader's purpose. The situation, the purpose, and the linguistic–experiential equipment of the reader, as well as the signs on the page, enter into the transaction and affect the extent to which public and private meanings and associations will be attended to.

The Efferent–Aesthetic Continuum

The reading event must fall somewhere in a continuum, determined by whether the reader adopts what I term a *predominantly aesthetic* stance or a *predominantly efferent* stance. A particular stance determines the proportion or mix of public and private elements of sense that fall within the scope of the reader's selective attention. Or, to recall Bates's metaphor, a stance results from the degree and scope of attention paid respectively to the tip and to the base of the iceberg. Such differences can be represented only by a continuum, which I term the *efferent–aesthetic continuum*.

The Efferent Stance

The term *efferent* (from the Latin *efferre,* to carry away) designates the kind of reading in which attention is centered predominantly on what is to be extracted and retained after the reading event. An extreme example is a man who has accidentally swallowed a poisonous liquid and is rapidly reading the label on the bottle to learn the antidote. Here, surely, we see an illustration of James's point about selective attention and our capacity to push into the periphery of awareness or ignore those elements that do not serve our present interests. The man's attention is focused on learning what is to be done as soon as the reading ends. He concentrates on what the words point to, ignoring anything other than their barest public referents, constructing as quickly as possible the directions for future action. These structured ideas are the evocation felt to correspond to the text.

Reading a newspaper, textbook, or legal brief would usually provide a similar, though less extreme, instance of the predominantly efferent stance. In efferent reading, then, we focus attention mainly on the public "tip of the iceberg" of sense. Meaning results from abstracting out and analytically structuring the ideas, information, directions, or conclusions to be retained, used, or acted on after the reading event.

The Aesthetic Stance

The predominantly aesthetic stance covers the other half of the continuum. In this kind of reading, the reader adopts an attitude of readiness to focus attention on what is being lived through during the reading event. The term *aesthetic* was chosen because its Greek source suggested perception through the senses, feelings, and intuitions. Welcomed into awareness are not only the public referents of the verbal signs but also the private part of the "iceberg" of meaning: the sensations, images, feelings, and ideas that are the residue of past psychological events involving those words and their referents. Attention may include the sounds and rhythms of the words themselves, heard in "the inner ear" as the signs are perceived.

The aesthetic reader pays attention to—savors—the qualities of the feelings, ideas, situations, scenes, personalities, and emotions that are called forth and participates in the tensions, conflicts, and resolutions of the images, ideas, and scenes as they unfold. The lived-through meaning is felt to correspond to the text. This meaning, shaped and experienced during the aesthetic transaction, constitutes "the literary work," the poem, story, or play. This "evocation," and not the text, is the object of the reader's "response" and "interpretation," both during and after the reading event.

Confusion about the matter of stance results from the entrenched habit of thinking of the *text* as efferent or aesthetic, expository or poetic, literary or nonliterary, and so on. Those who apply these terms to texts should realize that they actually are reporting their interpretation of the writer's intention as to what kind of reading the text should be given. The reader is free, however, to adopt either predominant stance toward any text. *Efferent* and *aesthetic* apply, then, to the writer's and the reader's selective attitude toward their own streams of consciousness during their respective linguistic events.

To recognize the essential nature of stance does not minimize the importance of the text in the transaction. Various verbal elements—metaphor, stylistic conventions or divergence from linguistic or semantic norms, even certain kinds of content—have been said to constitute the "poeticity" or "literariness" of a text. Such verbal elements, actually, do often serve as cues to the experienced reader to adopt an aesthetic stance. Yet it is possible to cite acknowledged literary works that lack one or all of these elements. Neither reading theorists nor literary theorists have given due credit to the fact that none of these or any other arrangements of words could make their "literary" or "poetic" contribution without the reader's prior shift of attention toward mainly the qualitative or experiential contents of consciousness, namely, the aesthetic stance.

The Continuum

The metaphorical nature of the term *the stream of consciousness* can be called on further to clarify the efferent-aesthetic continuum. We can image consciousness as a stream flowing through the darkness. Stance, then, can be represented as a mechanism lighting up—directing the attention to— different parts of the stream, selecting out objects that have floated to the surface in those areas and leaving the rest in shadow. Stance, in other words, provides the guiding orientation toward activating particular areas and elements of consciousness, that is, particular proportions of public and private aspects of meaning, leaving the rest at the dim periphery of attention. Some such play of attention over the contents of what emerges into consciousness must be involved in the reader's multifold choices from the linguistic–experiential reservoir.

Efferent and aesthetic reflect the two main ways of looking at the world, often summed up as "scientific" and "artistic." My redundant usage of "predominantly" aesthetic or efferent underlines rejection of the traditional, binary, either–or tendency to see them as in opposition. The efferent stance pays more attention to the cognitive, the referential, the factual, the analytic, the logical, the quantitative aspects of meaning. And the aesthetic stance pays more attention to the sensuous, the affective, the emotive, the qualitative. But nowhere can we find on the one hand the purely public and on the other hand the purely private. Both of these aspects of meaning are attended to in different proportions in any linguistic event. One of the earliest and most important steps in any reading event, therefore, is the selection of either a predominantly efferent or a predominantly aesthetic stance toward the transaction with a text. Figure 23.1 indicates different readings by the same reader of the same text at different points on the efferent–aesthetic continuum. Other readers would probably produce readings that fall at other points on the continuum.

Although many readings may fall near the extremes, many others, perhaps most, may fall nearer the center of the continuum. Where both parts of the iceberg of meaning are more evenly balanced, confusion as to dominant stance is more likely and more counterproductive. It is possible to read efferently and assume one has evoked a poem, or to read aesthetically and assume one is arriving at logical conclusions to an argument.

Also, it is necessary to emphasize that a predominant stance does not rule out fluctuations. Within a particular aesthetic reading, attention may at times turn from the experiential synthesis to efferent analysis, as the reader recognizes some technical strategy or passes a critical judgment. Similarly, in an efferent reading, a general idea may be illustrated or reinforced by an aesthetically lived-through illustration or example. Despite the mix of private and public aspects of meaning in each stance, the two dominant stances are clearly distinguishable. No two readings, even by the same person, are identical. Still, someone else can read a text efferently and paraphrase it for us in such a way as to satisfy our efferent purpose. But no one else can read aesthetically—that is, experience the evocation of—a literary work of art for us.

Because each reading is an event in particular circumstances, the same text may be read either efferently or aesthetically. The experienced reader usually approaches a text alert to cues offered by the text and, unless another purpose intervenes, automatically adopts the appropriate predominant stance. Sometimes the title suffices as a cue. Probably one of the most obvious cues is the arrangement of broad margins and uneven lines that signals that the reader should adopt the aesthetic stance and undertake to make a poem. The opening lines of any text are especially important from this point of view, for their signaling of tone, attitude, and conventional indications of stance to be adopted.

Louise M. Rosenblatt

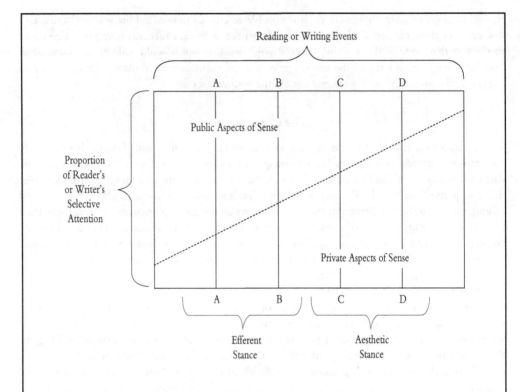

Any linguistic activity has both public (lexical, analytic, abstracting) and private (experiential, affective, associational) components. Stance is determined by the proportion of each component admitted into the scope of selective attention. The efferent stance draws mainly on the public aspect of sense; the aesthetic stance includes proportionally more of the experiential, private aspect.

Reading or writing events A and B fall into the efferent part of the continuum, with B admitting more private elements. Reading or writing events C and D both represent the aesthetic stance, with C according a higher proportion of attention to the public aspects of sense.

Figure 23.1   The Efferent–Aesthetic Continuum

Of course, the reader may overlook or misconstrue the cues, or they may be confusing. And the reader's own purpose, or schooling that indoctrinates the same undifferentiated approach to all texts, may dictate a different stance from the one the writer intended. For example, the student reading *A Tale of Two Cities* who knows that there will be a test on facts about characters and plot may be led to adopt a predominantly efferent stance, screening out all but the factual data. Similarly, readings of an article on zoology could range from analytic abstracting of factual content to an aesthetic savoring of the ordered structure of ideas, the rhythm of the sentences, and the images of animal life brought into consciousness.

Evocation, Response, Interpretation

The tendency to reify words is frequently represented by discussions centering on a title, say, *Invisible Man* or *The Bill of Rights*. These titles may refer to the text, as we have been using the word, that

460

is, to the pattern of inscribed signs to be found in physical written or printed form. More often, however, the intended reference is to "the work." But the work—ideas and experiences linked with the text—can be found only in individual readers' reflections on the reading event, the evocation and responses to it during and after the reading event.

Evocation

Thus far, we have focused on the aspects of the reading process centered on organizing a structure of elements of consciousness construed as the meaning of the text. I term this *the evocation* to cover both efferent and aesthetic transactions. The evocation, the work, is not a physical "object," but, given another sense of that word, the evocation can be an object of thought.

The Second Stream of Response

We must recognize during the reading event a concurrent stream of reactions to, and transactions with, the emerging evocation. Even as we are generating the evocation, we are reacting to it; this may in turn affect our choices as we proceed with the reading. Such responses may be momentary, peripheral, or felt simply as a general state, for example, an ambiance of acceptance or perhaps of confirmation of ideas and attitudes brought to the reading. Sometimes something unexpected or contrary to prior knowledge or assumptions may trigger conscious reflection. Something not prepared for by the preceding organization of elements may cause a rereading. The attention may shift from the evocation to the formal or technical traits of the text. The range of potential reactions and the gamut of degrees of intensity and articulateness depend on the interplay among the character of the signs on the page (the text), what the individual reader brings to it, and the circumstances of the transaction.

The various strands of response, especially in the middle ranges of the efferent–aesthetic continuum, are sometimes simultaneous, interacting, and interwoven. They may seem actually woven into the texture of the evocation itself. Hence, one of the problems of critical reading is differentiation of the evocation corresponding to the text from the concurrent responses, which may be projections from the reader's a priori assumptions. Drawing the line between them is easier in theory than in the practice of any actual reading. The reader needs to learn to handle such elements of the reading experience. The problem takes on different forms in efferent and aesthetic reading.

Expressed Response

"Response" to the evocation often is designed as subsequent to the reading event. Actually, the basis is laid during the reading, in the concurrent second stream of reactions. The reader may recapture the general effect of this after the event and may seek to express it and to recall what in the evocation led to the response. Reflection on "the meaning" of even a simple text involves the recall, the reactivation of some aspects of the process carried on during the reading. "Interpretation" tends to be a continuation of this effort to clarify the evocation.

The account of the reading process thus far has indicated an organizing, synthesizing activity, the creation of tentative meanings, and their modification as new elements enter into the focus of attention. In some instances, the reader at some point simply registers a sense of having completed a sequential activity and moves on to other concerns. Sometimes a sense of the whole structure crystallizes by the close of the reading.

Expressed Interpretation

Actually, the process of interpretation that includes arriving at a sense of the whole has not been given enough attention in theories of reading, perhaps because reading research has typically dealt with simple reading events. For the term *interpret*, dictionaries list, among others, several relevant meanings. One is "to set forth the meaning of; to elucidate, to explain." Another is "to construe, or understand in a particular way." A third is "to bring out the meaning of by performance (as in music)." These tend to reflect the traditional notion of "the meaning" as inherent in the text.

The transactional theory requires that we draw on all three of these usages to cover the way in which the term should be applied to the reading process. The evocation of meaning in transaction with a text is indeed interpretation in the sense of performance, and transactional theory merges this with the idea of interpretation as individual construal. The evocation then becomes the object of interpretation in the sense of elucidating or explaining. The expressed interpretation draws on all these aspects of the total transaction.

Interpretation can be understood as the effort to report, analyze, and explain the evocation. The reader recalls the sensed, felt, thought evocation while at the same time applying some frame of reference or method of abstracting in order to characterize it, to find the assumptions or organizing ideas that relate the parts to the whole. The second stream of reactions will be recalled, and the reasons for them sought, in the evoked work or in prior assumptions and knowledge. The evocation and the concurrent streams of reaction may be related through stressing, for example, the logic of the structure of ideas in an efferent evocation or the assumptions about people or society underlying the lived-through experience of the aesthetic reading.

Usually, interpretation is expressed in the efferent mode, stressing underlying general ideas that link the signs of the text. Interpretation can take an aesthetic form, however, such as a poem, a painting, music, dramatization, or dance.

Interpretation brings with it the question of whether the reader has produced a meaning that is consonant with the author's probable intention. Here we find ourselves moving from the reader–text transaction to the relationship between author and reader. The process that produces the text will be considered before dealing with such matters as communication, validity of interpretation, and the implications of the transactional theory for teaching and research.

The Writing Process

The Writing Transaction

Writers facing a blank page, like readers approaching a text, have only their individual linguistic capital to draw on. For the writer, too, the residue of past experiences of language in particular situations provides the material from which the text will be constructed. As with the reader, any new meanings are restructurings or extensions of the stock of experiences the writer brings to the task. There is a continuing to-and-fro or transactional process as the writer looks at the page and adds to the text in the light of what has been written thus far.

An important difference between readers and writers should not be minimized, however. In the triadic sign–object–interpretant relationship, the reader has the physical pattern of signs to which to relate the symbolizations. The writer facing a blank page may start with only an organismic state, vague feelings and ideas that require further triadic definition before a symbolic configuration—a verbal text—can take shape.

Writing is always an event in time, occurring at a particular moment in the writer's biography, in particular circumstances, under particular external as well as internal pressures. In short, the writer is always transacting with a personal, social, and cultural environment. Thus, the writing process must be seen as always embodying both personal and social, or individual and environmental, factors.

Given the Peircean triadic view of the verbal symbol, the more accessible the fund of organismically linked words and referents, the more fluent the writing. This helps us place in perspective an activity such as free writing. Instead of treating it as a prescriptive "stage" of the writing process, as some seem to do, it should be seen as a technique for tapping the linguistic reservoir without being hampered by anxieties about acceptability of subject, sequence, or mechanics. Especially for those inhibited by unfortunate past writing experiences, this can be liberating, a warm-up exercise for starting the juices flowing, so to speak, and permitting elements of the experiential stream, verbal components of memory, and present concerns to rise to consciousness. The essential point is that the individual linguistic reservoir must be activated.

No matter how free and uninhibited the writing may be, the stream of images, ideas, memories, and words is not entirely random; William James reminds us that the "choosing activity" of selective attention operates to some degree. Like the reader, the writer needs to bring the selective process actively into play, to move toward a sense of some tentative focus for choice and synthesis (Emig, 1983).

This directedness will be fostered by the writer's awareness of the transactional situation: the context that initiates the need to write and the potential reader or readers to whom the text will presumably be addressed. Often in trial-and-error fashion, and through various freely flowing drafts, the writer's sensitivity to such factors translates itself into an increasingly clear impulse that guides selective attention and integration. For the experienced writer, the habit of such awareness, monitoring the multifold decisions or choices that make up the writing event, is more important than any explicit preliminary statement of goals or purpose.

The Writer's Stance

The concept of stance presented earlier in relation to reading is equally important for writing. A major aspect of the delimitation of purpose in writing is the adoption of a stance that falls at some point in the efferent–aesthetic continuum. The attitude toward what is activated in the linguistic–experiential reservoir manifests itself in the range and character of the verbal symbols that will "come to mind," and to which the writer will apply selective attention. The dominant stance determines the proportion of public and private aspects of sense that will be included in the scope of the writer's attention (see Figure 23.1).

In actual life, the selection of a predominant stance is not arbitrary but is a function of the circumstances, the writer's motives, the subject, and the relation between writer and prospective reader or readers. For example, someone who had been involved in an automobile collision would need to adopt very different stances in writing an account of the event for an insurance company and in describing it in a letter to a friend. The first would activate an efferent selective process, bringing into the center of consciousness and onto the page the public aspects, such as statements that could be verified by witnesses or by investigation of the terrain. In the letter to the friend, the purpose would be to share an experience. An aesthetic stance would bring within the scope of the writer's attention the same basic facts, together with feelings, sensations, tensions, images, and sounds lived through during this brush with death. The selective process would favor words that matched the writer's inner sense of the felt event and that also would activate in the prospective reader symbolic linkages evoking a similar experience. Given different purposes, other accounts might fall at other points of the efferent–aesthetic continuum.

Purpose or intention should emerge from, or be capable of constructively engaging, the writer's actual experiential and linguistic resources. Past experience need not be the limit of the writer's scope, but the writer faced with a blank page needs "live" ideas—that is, ideas having a strongly energizing linkage with the linguistic–experiential reservoir. Purposes or ideas that lack the capacity to connect with the writer's funded experience and present concerns cannot fully activate the linguistic reservoir and provide an impetus to thinking and writing.

A personally grounded purpose develops and impels movement forward. Live ideas growing out of situations, activities, discussions, problems, or needs provide the basis for an actively selective and synthesizing process of making meaning. The quickened fund of images, ideas, emotions, attitudes, and tendencies to act offers the means of making new connections, for discovering new facets of the world of objects and events, in short, for thinking and writing creatively.

Louise M. Rosenblatt

Writing About Texts

When a reader describes, responds to, or interprets a work—that is, speaks or writes about a transaction with a text—a new text is being produced. The implications of this fact in terms of process should be more fully understood. When the reader becomes a writer about a work, the starting point is no longer the physical text, the marks on the page, but the meaning or the state of mind felt to correspond to that text. The reader may return to the original text to recapture how it entered into the transaction but must "find words" for explaining the evocation and the interpretation.

The reader-turned-writer must once again face the problem of choice of stance. In general, the choice seems to be the efferent stance. The purpose is mainly to explain, analyze, summarize, and categorize the evocation. This is usually true even when the reading has been predominantly aesthetic and a literary work of art is being discussed. However, the aesthetic stance might be adopted in order to communicate an experience expressing the response or the interpretation. An efferent reading of, for example, the U.S. Declaration of Independence might lead to a poem or a story. An aesthetic reading of the text of a poem might also lead, not to an efferently written critical essay, but to another poem, a painting, or a musical composition.

The translator of a poem is a clear example of the reader-turned-writer, being first a reader who evokes an experience through a transaction in one language and then a writer who seeks to express that experience through a writing transaction in another language. The experiential qualities generated in a transaction with one language must now be communicated to—evoked by—readers who have a different linguistic–experiential reservoir, acquired in a different culture.

Authorial Reading

Thus far, we have been developing parallels between the ways in which readers and writers select and synthesize elements from the personal linguistic reservoir, adopt stances that guide selective attention, and build a developing selective purpose. Emphasis has fallen mainly on similarities in composing structures of meaning related to texts. If readers are in that sense also writers, it is equally—and perhaps more obviously—true that writers must also be readers. At this point, however, some differences within the parallelisms begin to appear.

The writer, it is generally recognized, is the first reader of the text. Note an obvious, though neglected, difference: While readers transact with a writer's finished text, writers first read the text as it is being inscribed. Because both reading and writing are recursive processes carried on over a period of time, their very real similarities have masked a basic difference. The writer will often reread the total finished text, but, perhaps more important, the writer first reads and carries on a spiral, transactional relationship with the very text emerging on the page. This is a different kind of reading. It is authorial—a writer's reading. It should be seen as an integral part of the composing process. In fact, it is necessary to see that writing, or composing, a text involves *two* kinds of authorial reading, which I term *expression oriented* and *reception oriented*.

Expression-Oriented Authorial Reading

As a reader's eyes move along a printed text, the reader develops an organizing principle or framework. The newly evoked symbolizations are tested for whether they can be fitted into the tentative meanings already constructed for the preceding portion of the text. If the new signs create a problem, this may lead to a revision of the framework or even to a complete rereading of the text and restructuring of the attributed meaning.

The writer, like readers of another's text, peruses the succession of verbal signs being inscribed on the page to see whether the new words fit the preceding text. But this is a different, expression-oriented

464

reading, which should be seen as an integral part of the composing process. As the new words appear on the page, they must be tested, not simply for how they make sense with the preceding text but also against an inner gauge—the intention, or purpose. The emerging meaning, even if it makes sense, must be judged as to whether it serves or hinders the purpose, however nebulous and inarticulate, that is the motive power in the writing. Expression-oriented authorial reading leads to revision even during the earlier phases of the writing process.

The Inner Gauge

Most writers will recall a situation that may illustrate the operation of an "inner gauge." A word comes to mind or flows from the pen and, even if it makes sense, is felt not to be right. One word after another may be brought into consciousness and still not satisfy. Sometimes the writer understands what is wrong with the word on the page—perhaps that it is ambiguous or does not suit the tone. But often the writer cannot articulate the reason for dissatisfaction. The tension simply disappears when "the right word" presents itself. When it does, a match between inner state and verbal sign has happened.

Such an episode manifests the process of testing against an inner touchstone. The French writer Gustave Flaubert with his search for *le mot juste*, the exact word, offers the analogy of the violinist who tries to make his fingers "reproduce precisely those sounds of which he has the inward sense" (1926, pp. 11, 47). The inner gauge may be an organic state, a mood, an idea, perhaps even a consciously constituted set of guidelines.

For the experienced writer, this kind of completely inner-oriented reading, which is integral to the composing process, depends on and nourishes an increasingly clear though often tacit sense of purpose, whether efferent or aesthetic. The writer tries to satisfy a personal conception while also refining it. Such transactional reading and revision can go on throughout the writing event. There are indeed times when this is the *only* reading component—when one writes for oneself alone, to express or record an experience in a diary or journal, or perhaps to analyze a situation or the pros and cons of a decision.

Reception-Oriented Authorial Reading

Usually, however, writing is felt to be part of a potential transaction with other readers. At some point, the writer dissociates from the text and reads it through the eyes of potential readers; the writer tries to judge the meaning *they* would make in transaction with that pattern of signs. But the writer does not simply adopt the "eyes" of the potential reader. Again, a twofold operation is involved. The emerging text is read to sense what others might make of it. But this hypothetical interpretation must also be checked against the writer's own inner sense of purpose.

The tendency has been to focus on writing with an eye on the anticipated reader. My concern is to show the interplay between the two kinds of authorial reading and the need, consciously or automatically, to decide the degree of emphasis on one or the other. The problem always is to find verbal signs likely to activate linkages in prospective readers' linguistic reservoirs matching those of the writer. A poet may be faced with the choice between a personally savored exotic metaphor and one more likely to be within the experience of prospective readers. Or a science writer may have to decide whether highly detailed precision may be too complex for the general reader.

Writers must already have some hold on the first, expression-oriented kind of inner awareness if they are to benefit from the second reading-through-the-eyes-of-others. The first becomes a criterion for the second. The experienced writer will probably engage in a synthesis, or rapid alternation, of the two kinds of authorial reading to guide the selective attention that filters out the verbal elements coming to mind. When communication is the aim, revision should be based on such double criteria in the rereading of the text.

Communication Between Author and Readers

The reader's to-and-fro process of building an interpretation becomes a form of transaction with an author persona sensed through and behind the text. The implied relationship is sometimes even termed "a contract" with the author. The closer their linguistic–experiential equipment, the more likely the reader's interpretation will fulfill the writer's intention. Sharing at least versions of the same language is so basic that it often is simply assumed. Other positive factors affecting communication are contemporary membership in the same social and cultural group, the same educational level, and membership in the same discourse community, such as academic, legal, athletic, literary, scientific, or theological. Given such similarities, the reader is more likely to bring to the text the prior knowledge, acquaintance with linguistic and literary conventions, and assumptions about social situations required for understanding implications or allusions and noting nuances of tone and thought.

Yet, because each individual's experience is unique, differences due to social, ethnic, educational, and personal factors exist, even with contemporaries. The reading of works written in another period bespeaks an inevitable difference in linguistic, social, or cultural context. Here, especially, readers may agree on interpretations without necessarily assuming that their evocations from the text fit the author's intention (Rosenblatt, 1978, p. 109ff).

Differences as to the author's intention often lead to consultation of extra-textual sources. For works of the past especially, scholars call on systematic methods of philological, biographical, and historical research to discover the personal, social, and literary forces that shaped the writer's intention. The contemporary reception of the work also provides clues. Such evidence, even if it includes an author's stated intention, still yields hypothetical results and cannot dictate our interpretation. We must still read the text to decide whether it supports the hypothetical intention. The reader is constantly faced with the responsibility of deciding whether an interpretation is acceptable. The question of validity of interpretation must be faced before considering implications for teaching and research.

Validity of Interpretation

The problem of validity of interpretation has not received much attention in reading theory or educational methodology. Despite the extraordinary extent of the reliance on testing in our schools, there seems to be little interest in clarifying the criteria that enter into evaluation of "comprehension." Actual practice in the teaching of reading and in the instruments for testing of reading ability has evidently been tacitly based on, or at least has indoctrinated, the traditional assumption that there is a single determinate "correct" meaning attributable to each text. The stance factor, the efferent–aesthetic continuum, has especially been neglected; operationally, the emphasis has been on the efferent, even when "literature" was involved.

The polysemous character of language invalidates any simplistic approach to meaning, creating the problem of the relationship between the reader's interpretation and the author's intention. The impossibility of finding a single absolute meaning for a text or of expecting any interpretation absolutely to reflect the writer's intention is becoming generally recognized by contemporary theorists. "Intention" itself is not absolutely definable or delimitable even by the writer. The word *absolute,* the notion of a single "correct" meaning inherent "in" the text, is the stumbling block. The same text takes on different meanings in transactions with different readers or even with the same reader in different contexts or times.

Warranted Assertibility

The problem of the validity of any interpretation is part of the broader philosophical problem cited at the beginning of this chapter. Perception of the world is always through the medium of individual human beings transacting with their worlds. In recent decades, some literary theorists, deriving their arguments from poststructuralist Continental writers and taking a Saussurean view of language as an autonomous system, have arrived at an extreme relativist position. They have developed a reading method that assumes all texts can be "deconstructed" to reveal inner contradictions. Moreover, the language system and literary conventions are said to completely dominate author and reader, and agreement concerning interpretation simply reflects the particular "interpretive community" in which we find ourselves (Fish, 1980; Rosenblatt, 1991).

Such extreme relativism is not, however, a necessary conclusion from the premise that absolutely determinate meaning is impossible. By agreeing on criteria of evaluation of interpretations, we can accept the possibility of alternative interpretations yet decide that some are more acceptable than others.

John Dewey, accepting the nonfoundationalist epistemological premises and foregoing the quest for absolutes, solved the scientists' problem by his idea of "warranted assertibility" as the end of controlled inquiry (1938, pp. 9, 345). Given shared criteria concerning methods of investigation and kinds of evidence, there can be agreement concerning the decision as to what is a sound interpretation of the evidence, or "a warranted assertion." This is not set forth as permanent, absolute truth, but leaves open the possibility that alternative explanations for the same facts may be found, that new evidence may be discovered, or that different criteria or paradigms may be developed.

Although Dewey used primarily scientific interpretation or knowledge of the world based on scientific methods to illustrate warranted assertibility, he saw the concept as encompassing the arts and all human concerns. It can be applied to the problem of all linguistic interpretation (Rosenblatt, 1978, Chap. 7; 1983, p. 151ff). Given a shared cultural milieu and shared criteria of validity of interpretation, we can, without claiming to have the single "correct" meaning of a text, agree on an interpretation. Especially in aesthetic reading, we may find that alternative interpretations meet our minimum criteria, and we can still be free to consider some interpretations superior to others.

In contrast to the notion of readers locked into a narrow "interpretive community," the emphasis on making underlying or tacit criteria explicit provides the basis not only for agreement but also for understanding tacit sources of disagreement. This creates the possibility of change in interpretation, acceptance of alternative sets of criteria, or revision of criteria. Such self-awareness on the part of readers can foster communication across social, cultural, and historical differences between author and readers, as well as among readers (Rosenblatt, 1983).

In short, the concept of warranted assertibility, or shared criteria of validity of interpretation in a particular social context, recognizes that some readings may satisfy the criteria more fully than others. Basic criteria might be (1) that the context and purpose of the reading event, or the total transaction, be considered; (2) that the interpretation not be contradicted by, or not fail to cover, the full text, the signs on the page; and (3) that the interpretation not project meanings which cannot be related to signs on the page. Beyond these items arise criteria for interpretation and evaluation growing out of the whole structure of shared cultural, social, linguistic, and rhetorical assumptions.

Thus, we can be open to alternative readings of the text of *Hamlet*, but we also can consider some readings as superior to others according to certain explicit criteria, for example, complexity of intellectual and affective elements and nature of implicit value system. Such considerations permit comparison and "negotiation" among different readers of the same text as well as clarification of differences in assumptions concerning what constitutes a valid interpretation (Rosenblatt, 1978, 1983). On the efferent side of the continuum, current discussions of alternative criteria for interpretation of the U.S. Constitution provide another complex example.

Criteria for the Efferent–Aesthetic Continuum

Precisely because, as Figure 23.1 indicates, both public and private elements are present in all reading, the criteria of validity of interpretation differ for readings at various points on the efferent–aesthetic continuum. Because the predominantly efferent interpretation must be publicly verifiable or justifiable, the criteria of validity rest primarily on the public, referential aspects of meaning and require that any affective and associational aspects not dominate. The criteria for the predominantly aesthetic reading call for attention to the referential, cognitive aspects, but only as they are interwoven and colored by the private, affective, or experiential aspects generated by the author's patterns of signs. Especially in the middle ranges of the efferent–aesthetic continuum, it becomes important for writers to provide clear indications as to stance and for readers to be sensitive to the writer's purpose and the need to apply relevant criteria.

"Literary" Aspects of Efferent Reading

In recent decades, in one scientific field after another, the opposition between scientific and "literary" writing has been found to be illusory. Writers in the natural and social sciences have become aware of the extent to which they engage in semantic and syntactic practices that have usually been considered "literary" and that they, too, have been using narrative, metaphor, and other rhetorical devices. Examples are the importance of metaphor in writings about economics or the idea that the historian writes narrative and that he can never be completely objective in selecting his facts. Sensitivity to sexist and racist tropes has increased awareness of the extent to which metaphor permeates all kinds of texts and, indeed, all language. Sometimes the efferent–aesthetic distinction seems to be completely erased (for example, the historian is sometimes said to write "fiction").

It becomes necessary to recall that the stance reflecting the aesthetic or efferent purpose, not the syntactic and semantic devices alone, determines the appropriate criteria. For example, in a treatise on economics or a history of the frontier, the criteria of validity of interpretation appropriate to their disciplines, which involve primarily verifiability and logic, would still apply. When an economist remarks that "the scientists had better devise good metaphors and tell good stories" (McCloskey, 1985), the concept of a dominant stance becomes all the more essential. The criteria for "good" should be not only how vivid and appealing the stories are but also how they gibe with logic and facts and what value systems are implied.

The relevance of the efferent–aesthetic continuum (Figure 23.1) may be illustrated by the example of metaphor: The scientist speaks of the "wave" theory of light, and we focus on the technical concept at the extreme efferent end of the continuum. Shakespeare writes, "Like as the wave makes toward the pebbled shore/So do our minutes hasten to their end," and our aesthetic attention to the feeling of inevitability of the succeeding waves enhances the feeling of the inevitability of the passage of time in our lives. A political analysis suggested surrendering to the inevitability of fascism by calling it "the wave of the future. . . . There is no fighting it" (Lindbergh, 1940, p. 934). Despite the vividness of the metaphor, efferent attention should have remained dominant, applying the efferent criterion. Did logic and factual evidence support the persuasive appeal?

Implications for Teaching

Reading and Writing: Parallelisms and Differences

Parallelisms between reading and writing processes have raised questions concerning their connections, especially in the classroom. The reading and writing processes both overlap and differ. Both reader and writer engage in constituting symbolic structures of meaning in a to-and-fro, spiral transaction with the text. They follow similar patterns of thinking and call on similar linguistic habits. Both processes depend on the individual's past experiences with language in particular life situations. Both reader and writer therefore are drawing on past linkages of signs, signifiers, and organic states in order to create new symbolizations, new linkages, and new organic states. Both reader and writer develop a framework, principle, or purpose, however nebulous or explicit, that guides the selective attention and the synthesizing, organizing activities that constitute meaning. Moreover, every reading and writing act can be understood as falling somewhere on the efferent–aesthetic continuum and as being predominantly efferent or aesthetic.

The parallels should not mask the basic differences—the transaction that starts with a text produced by someone else is not the same as a transaction that starts with the individual facing a blank page. To an observer, two people perusing a typed page may seem to be doing the same thing (namely, "reading"). But if one of them is in the process of writing that text, different activities will be going on. The writer will be engaged in either expression-oriented or reception-oriented authorial reading. Moreover, because both reading and writing are rooted in mutually conditioning transactions between individuals and their particular environments, a person may have very different experiences with the two activities, may differ in attitudes toward them, and may be more proficient in one or the other. Writing and reading are sufficiently different to defeat the assumption that they are mirror images: The reader does not simply reenact the author's process. Hence, it cannot be assumed that the teaching of one activity automatically improves the student's competence in the other.

Still, the parallels in the reading and writing processes described above and the nature of the transaction between author and reader make it reasonable to expect that the teaching of one can affect the student's operations in the other. Reading, essential to anyone for intellectual and emotional enrichment, provides the writer with a sense of the potentialities of language. Writing deepens the reader's understanding of the importance of paying attention to diction, syntactic positions, emphasis, imagery, and conventions of genre. The fact that the sign–interpretant–object triad is, as Peirce said, dependent on habit indicates an even more important level of influence. Cross-fertilization will result from reinforcement of linguistic habits and thinking patterns resulting from shared transactional processes of purposive selective attention and synthesis. How fruitful the interplay between the individual student's writing and reading will be depends largely on the nature of the teaching and the educational context.

The Total Context

Here we return to our basic concept that human beings are always in transaction and in a reciprocal relationship with an environment, a context, a total situation. The classroom environment, or the atmosphere created by the teacher and students transacting with one another and the school setting, broadens out to include the whole institutional, social, and cultural context. These aspects of the transaction are crucial in thinking about education and especially the "literacy problem." Because each individual's linguistic–experiential reservoir is the residue of past transactions with the environment, such factors condition the sense of possibilities, or the potential organizing frameworks or schema and the knowledge and assumptions about the world, society, human nature, that each brings to the transactions. Socioeconomic and ethnic factors, for example, influence patterns of behavior, ways of carrying out tasks, even understanding of such concepts as "story" (Heath, 1983). Such elements also affect the individual's attitude toward self, toward the reading or writing activity, and toward the purpose for which it is being carried on.[3]

The transactional concept of the text always in relation either to author or reader in specific situations makes it untenable to treat the text as an isolated entity or to overemphasize either author or reader. Recognizing that language is not a self-contained system or static code on the one hand avoids the traditional obsession with the product—with skills, techniques, and conventions, essential though they are—and, on the other, prevents a pendulum swing to overemphasis on process or on the personal aspects.

Treatment of either reading or writing as a dissociated set of skills (though both require skills) or as primarily the acquisition of codes and conventions (though both involve them) inhibits sensitivity to the organic linkages of verbal signs and their objects. Manipulating syntactic units without a sense of a context that connects them into a meaningful relationship may in the long run be counterproductive.

Nor can the transactional view of the reading and writing processes be turned into a set of stages to be rigidly followed. The writer's drafts and final texts—or the reader's tentative interpretations, final evocation, and reflections—should be viewed as stopping points in a journey, as the outward and visible signs of a continuing process in the passage from one point to the other. A "good" product, whether a well-written paper or a sound textual interpretation, should not be an end in itself—a terminus—but should be the result of a process that builds the strengths for further journeys or, to change the metaphor, for further growth. "Product" and "process" become interlocking concerns in nurturing growth.

Hence, the teaching of reading and writing at any developmental level should have as its first concern the creation of environments and activities in which students are motivated and encouraged to draw on their own resources to make "live" meanings. With this as the fundamental criterion, emphasis falls on strengthening the basic processes that we have seen to be shared by reading and writing. The teaching of one can then reinforce linguistic habits and semantic approaches useful in the other. Such teaching, concerned with the ability of the individual to generate meaning, will permit constructive cross-fertilization of the reading and writing (and speech) processes.

Enriching the individual's linguistic–experiential reservoir becomes an underlying educational aim broader than the particular concern with either reading or writing. Especially in the early years, the linkage between verbal sign and experiential base is essential. The danger is that many current teaching practices may counteract the very processes presumably being taught. The organization of instruction, the atmosphere in the classroom, the kinds of questions asked, the ways of phrasing assignments, and the types of tests administered should be scrutinized from this point of view.

The importance of a sense of purpose, of a guiding principle of selection and organization in both writing and reading, is being increasingly recognized. The creation of contexts that permit purposive writing and reading can enable the student to build on past experience of life and language, to adopt the appropriate stance for selective attention, and to develop inner gauges or frameworks for choice and synthesis that produce new structures of live meaning.

Collaborative Interchange

In a favorable educational environment, speech is a vital ingredient of transactional pedagogy. Its importance in the individual's acquisition of a linguistic–experiential capital is clear. It can be an extremely important medium in the classroom. Dialogue between teacher and students and interchange among students can foster growth and cross-fertilization in both the reading and writing processes. Such discussion can help students develop insights concerning transactions with texts as well as metalinguistic understanding of skills and conventions in meaningful contexts.

Students' achievement of insight into their own reading and writing processes can be seen as the long-term justification for various curricular and teaching strategies. For example, writers at all levels can be helped to understand their transactional relationship to their readers by peer reading and discussion of texts. Their fellow students' questions, varied interpretations, and misunderstandings dramatize the necessity of the writer's providing verbal signs that will help readers gain required facts, share relevant sensations or attitudes, or make logical transitions. Such insights make possible the second, reader-oriented authorial reading.

Similarly, group interchange about readers' evocations from texts, whether of their peers or adult authors, can in general be a powerful means of stimulating growth in reading ability and critical acumen. Readers become aware of the need to pay attention to the author's words in order to avoid preconceptions and misinterpretations. When students share responses to transactions with the same text, they can learn how their evocations from the same signs differ, can return to the text to discover their own habits of selection and synthesis, and can become aware of, and critical of, their own processes as readers. Interchange about the problems of interpretation that a particular group of readers encounters and a collaborative movement toward self-critical interpretation of the text can lead to the development of critical concepts and interpretive criteria. Such metalinguistic awareness is valuable to students as both readers and writers.

The teacher in such a classroom is no longer simply a conveyor of ready-made teaching materials and recorder of results of ready-made tests or a dispenser of ready-made interpretations. Teaching becomes constructive, facilitating interchange, helping students make their spontaneous responses the basis for raising questions and growing in the ability to handle increasingly complex reading transactions (Rosenblatt, 1983).[4]

The Student's Efferent–Aesthetic Repertory

The efferent–aesthetic continuum, or the two basic ways of looking at the world, should be part of the student's repertory from the earliest years. Because both stances involve cognitive and affective as well as public and private elements, students need to learn to differentiate the circumstances that call for one or the other stance. Unfortunately, much current practice is counterproductive, either failing to encourage a definite stance or implicitly requiring an inappropriate one. Favorite illustrations are the third-grade workbook that prefaced its first poem with the question "What facts does this poem teach you?," and the boy who complained that he wanted information about dinosaurs, but his teacher only gave him "storybooks." Small wonder that graduates of our schools (and colleges) often read poems and novels efferently or respond to political statements and advertisements with an aesthetic stance.

Despite the overemphasis on the efferent in our schools, failure to understand the matter of the public–private "mix" has prevented successful teaching even of efferent reading and writing. Teaching practices and curricula, from the very beginning, should include both efferent and aesthetic linguistic activity and should build a sense of the different purposes involved. Instruction should foster the habits of selective attention and synthesis that draw on relevant elements in the semantic reservoir and should nourish the ability to handle the mix of private and public aspects appropriate to a particular transaction.

Especially in the early years, this should be done largely indirectly, through, for example, choice of texts, contexts for generating writing and reading, or implications concerning stance in the questions asked. In this way, texts can serve dynamically as sources from which to assimilate a sense of the potentialities of the English sentence and an awareness of strategies for organizing meaning and expressing feeling. Emphasis on analysis of the evocations, or terminology for categorizing and describing them have no value if they overshadow or substitute for the evoked work. Such activities acquire meaning and value when, for example, they answer a writer's own problems in expression or explain for a reader the role of the author's verbal strategies in producing a certain felt response.

The developmental sequence suggested here is especially important in aesthetic reading. Much teaching of poetry at every level, including high school and college, at present takes on a continuously repeated remedial character because of the continued confusion about stance through emphasis on efferent analysis of the "literary" work. Students need to be helped to have unimpeded aesthetic experiences. Very young children's delight in the sound and rhythms of words, their interest in stories, and their ability to move easily from verbal to other modes of expression too often fade. They need to be helped to hold on to the experiential aspect. When this can be taken for granted, efferent, analytical discussions of form or background will not be substitutes for the literary work but become a means of enhancing it. Discussion then can become the basis for assimilating criteria of sound interpretation and evaluation appropriate to the various points on the continuum and to the student's developmental status.

Implications for Research

Research based on the transactional model has a long history (Applebee, 1974; Farrell & Squire, 1990). Until fairly recently, it has generated research mainly by those concerned with the teaching of literature in high schools and colleges, rather than by those concerned with reading per se in the elementary school (Beach & Hynds, 1990; Flood et al., 1991; Purves & Beach, 1972). It is not possible here to survey this already considerable body of research, much of it exploring aspects of response to literature; nor does space allow discussion of recent volumes dealing with applications of transactional theory in elementary school, high school, and college (Clifford, 1991; Cox & Many, 1992; Hungerford, Holland, & Ernst, 1993; Karolides, 1992). I shall instead suggest some general considerations concerning research topics and theoretical and methodological pitfalls.

The transactional model of reading, writing, and teaching that has been presented constitutes, in a sense, a body of hypotheses to be investigated. The shift it represents from the Cartesian to the post-Einsteinian paradigm calls for removal of the limitations on research imposed by the dominance of positivistic behaviorism. Instead of mainly treating reading as a compendium of separate skills or as an isolated autonomous activity, research on any aspect should center on the human being speaking, writing, reading, and continuously transacting with a specific environment in its broadening circles of context. And as Bartlett (1932) reminds us, any secondary theoretical frameworks, such as schemata or strategies, are not stable entities but configurations in a dynamic, changing process. Although the focus here will be on reading research, the interrelationship among the linguistic modes, especially reading and writing, broadens the potential scope of problems mentioned.

The view of language as a dynamic system of meaning in which the affective and the cognitive unite raises questions about the emphasis of past research. Researchers' preoccupation with the efferent is exemplified by their focus on Piaget's work on the child's development of mathematical and logical concepts and the continuing neglect of the affective by behaviorist, cognitive, and artificial intelligence psychologists. This is slowly being counterbalanced by growing interest in the affective and the qualitative (e.g., Deese, 1973; Eisner & Peshkin, 1990; Izard, 1977). We need to understand more fully the child's growth in capacity for selective attention to, and synthesis of, the various components of meaning.

Research in reading should draw on a number of interrelated disciplines, such as physiology, sociology, and anthropology, and should converge with the general study of human development. The transactional theory especially raises questions that involve such broad connections. Also, the diverse subcultures and ethnic backgrounds represented by the student population and the many strands that contribute to a democratic culture present a wide range of questions for research about reading, teaching, and curriculum.

Developmental Processes

The adult capacity to engage in the tremendously complex process of reading depends ultimately on the individual's long developmental process, starting with "learning how to mean" (Halliday, 1975; Rosenblatt, 1985b). How does the child move from the earliest, undifferentiated state of the world to "the referential, emotive, and associative part processes" (Rommetveit, 1968, p. 167)? Developmental research can throw light on the relation of cognitive and emotional aspects in the growth of the ability to evoke meaning in transactions with texts.

Research is needed to accumulate systematic understanding of the positive environmental and educational factors that do justice to the essential nature of both efferent and aesthetic linguistic behavior, and to the role of the affective or private aspects of meaning in both stances. How can children's sensorimotor explorations of their worlds be reinforced, their sensitivity to the sounds and qualitative overtones of language be maintained? In short, what can foster their capacity to apprehend in order to comprehend, or construct, the poem, story, or play? Much also remains to be understood about development of the ability to infer, or make logical connections, or, in short, to read efferently and critically.

How early in the child's development should the context of the transaction with the text create a purpose for one or the other dominant stance, or help the reader learn to adopt a stance appropriate to the situation? At different developmental stages, what should be the role or roles of reflection on the reading experience through spoken comments, writing, and the use of other media?

An overarching question is this: How can skills be assimilated in a context that fosters understanding of their relevance to the production of meaning? How can the young reader acquire the knowledge, intellectual frameworks, and sense of values that provide the connecting links for turning discrete verbal signs into meaningful constructs? The traditional methods of teaching and testing recognize the important functions of the symbolic system, the alphabetic and phonological elements (the "code"), and linguistic conventions by fragmenting processes into small quantifiable units. These are quantitatively and hence economically assessable. But do such methods set up habits and attitudes toward the written word that inhibit the process of inferring meaning, or organizing and synthesizing, that enters into even simple reading tasks? How can we prepare the way for increasingly rich and demanding transactions with texts?

Performance

Assessment of performance level is usually required as a means of assuring the accountability of the school. Whether standardized tests accurately measure the student's ability is currently being called into question. Research on correlation of reading ability with factors such as age, gender, ethnic and socioeconomic background, and so on has confirmed the expectation that they are active factors. However, such research reports a state of affairs that is interpreted according to varying assumptions, not all conducive to the development of mature readers and writers. The transactional emphasis on the total context of the reading act reinforces the democratic concern with literacy and supports the call for vigorous political and social reform of negative environmental factors. At the same time teachers must recognize that the application of quantitatively based group labels to individual students may unfairly create erroneous expectations that become self-fulfilling prophecies.

Teaching Methods

In the current transition away from traditional teaching methods, there is the danger that inappropriate research designs may be invoked to evaluate particular teaching methods. What criteria of successful teaching and what assumptions about the nature of linguistic processes underlie the research design and the methods of measurement? Any interpretations of results should take into account the various considerations concerning reader, text, and context set forth in the transactional model.

Results of research assessing different teaching methods raise an important question: Did the actual teaching conform to the formulaic labels attached to the methods being compared? The vagueness of a term such as *reader-response method* can illustrate the importance of more precise understanding of the actual teaching processes being tested in a particular piece of research. The same term has been applied to teachers who, after eliciting student responses to a story, fall back on habitual methods of demonstrating the "correct" interpretation and to teachers who make the responses the beginning of a process of helping students grow in their ability to arrive at sound, self-critical interpretations.

Much remains to be done to develop operational descriptions of the approaches being compared. Studies are needed of how teachers lead, or facilitate, without dominating or dictating. Ethnographic study of classroom dynamics, records of interchange among teacher and students, videotapes of classrooms, and analyses of text give substance to test results.

Response

Students' empirical responses to a text (mainly written protocols) form the basis of much of the research on methods generally referred to as reader response or transactional. (The term *response* should be understood to cover multiple activities.) Protocols provide indirect evidence about the students' evocation, the work as experienced, and reactions to it. Such research requires a coherent system of analysis of students' written or oral reports. What evidence, for example, is there that the reading of a story has been predominantly aesthetic?

The problem of empirical assessment of the student's aesthetic reading of a text offers particular difficulties, especially because no single "correct" interpretation or evaluation is posited. This requires setting up criteria of interpretation that reflect not only the presence of personal feelings and associations, which are only one component, but also their relationship to the other cognitive and attitudinal components. In short, the assessment must be based on clearly articulated criteria as to signs of growing maturity in handling personal response, relating to the evoked text, and use of personal and intertextual experience vis-à-vis the responses of others.

In order to provide a basis for statistical correlation, content analysis of protocols has been used largely to determine the components or aspects of response. The purpose is to distinguish personal feelings and attitudes from, for example, efferent, analytic references to the sonnet form. This requires a systematic set of categories, such as *The Elements of Writing About a Literary Work* (Purves & Rippere, 1968), which has provided a common basis for a large number of studies. As the emphasis on process has increased, refinements or alternatives have been devised. The need is to provide for study of the relationship among the various aspects of response, or the processes of selecting and synthesizing activities by which readers arrive at evocations and interpretations (Rosenblatt, 1985a). Qualitative methods of research at least should supplement, or perhaps should become the foundation for, any quantitative methods of assessing transactions with the written word.

Experimental designs that seek to deal with the development of the ability to handle some aspect of literary art should avoid methodologies and experimental tasks that instead serve to test efferent metalinguistic capacities. For example, levels of ability to elucidate metaphor or to retell stories may not reflect children's actual sensing or experiencing of metaphors or stories so much as their capacity to efferently abstract or categorize (Verbrugge, 1979).

The dependence on single instances of reading in assessing an individual's abilities is currently being called into question. The previous reminder that we are dealing with points in a continuing and changing developmental process is especially relevant. Habits are acquired and change slowly; it may be found that the effects of a change, for example, from traditional to response methods of teaching literature, cannot be assessed without allowing for a period of transition from earlier approaches and the continuation of the new approaches over time.

Basal readers have in the past offered especially clear examples of questions and exercises tacitly calling for an efferent stance toward texts labeled stories and poems. There has been little to help students assimilate and make automatic the aesthetic mode of relating to a text. Here, preparations for reading, the teacher's questions both before and after reading, and the mode of assessment, which powerfully influences teaching, should be scrutinized.

Studies that seek to generalize about the development of abilities by simultaneous testing of the different age levels have the problem of taking into account the factor of schooling. To what extent do changes in children's ability to retell or comment on the grammar of a story reflect schooling in the appropriate way to talk about a story? Similarly, to what extent are reported changing literary interests in the middle years not a reflection of personality changes but of too narrow definitions of *literary*?

Research Methodologies

The preceding discussion has centered on suggesting problems for research implied by the transactional model. Research methods or designs have been mentioned mainly in reference to their potentialities and limitations for providing kinds of information needed and to criteria for interpretation of data. Quantitatively based generalizations about groups are usually called for, but currently there is interest in clarifying the potentialities and limitations of both quantitative and qualitative research. Empirical experimental designs are being supplemented or checked by other research approaches, such as the case study (Birnbaum & Emig, 1991), the use of journals, interviews during or after the linguistic event, portfolios, and recordings in various media. Because the single episode test has various limitations, research in which researcher and teacher collaborate, or carefully planned research carried on by the teacher, provides the opportunity for extended studies. The transactional model especially indicates the value of ethnographic or naturalistic research because it deals with problems in the context of the ongoing life of individuals and groups in a particular cultural, social, and educational environment (Kantor, Kirby, & Goetz, 1981; Zaharlick & Green, 1991). The developmental emphasis also supports the call for longitudinal studies (Tierney, 1991). Interdisciplinary collaboration, desirable at any time, seems especially so for longitudinal studies. Research will need to be sufficiently complex, varied, and interlocking to do justice to the fact that reading is at once an intensely individual and an intensely social activity, an activity that from the earliest years involves the whole spectrum of ways of looking at the world.

Acknowledgments

I want to thank June Carroll Birnbaum and Roselmina Indrisano for reading this manuscript, and Nicholas Karolides and Sandra Murphy for reading earlier versions.

Notes

1 The 1949 volume marks Dewey's choice of *transaction* to designate a concept present in his work since 1896. My own use of the term after 1950 applied to an approach developed from 1938 on.

2 By 1981, *transactional theory, efferent stance,* and *aesthetic stance* were sufficiently current to be listed and were attributed to me in *A Dictionary of Reading and Related Terms* (Harris & Hodges, 1981). But the often confused usage of the terms led me to write "Viewpoints: Transaction Versus Interaction—A Terminological Rescue Operation" (1985).

3 The transactional model of reading presented here covers the whole range of similarities and differences among readers and between author and reader. Always in the transaction between reader and text, activation of the reader's linguistic–experiential reservoir must be the basis for the construction of new meanings and new experiences; hence, the applicability to bilingual instruction and the reading of texts produced in other cultures.

4 *Literature as Exploration* emphasizes the instructional process that can be built on the basis of personal evocation and response. Illustrations of classroom discussions and chapters such as "Broadening the Framework," "Some Basic Social Concepts," and "Emotion and Reason" indicate how the teacher can democratically moderate discussion and help students toward growth not only in ability to handle increasingly complex texts but also in personal, social, and cultural understanding.

References

Ames, A. (1955). *The nature of our perceptions, prehensions and behavior.* Princeton, NJ: Princeton University Press.

Appenzeller, T. (1990, November/December). Undivided attention. *The Sciences.*

Applebee, A.N. (1974). *Tradition and reform in the teaching of English*. Urbana, IL: National Council of Teachers of English.

Bartlett, F.C. (1932). *Remembering: A study in experimental and social psychology*. London: Cambridge University Press.

Bates, E. (1979). *The emergence of symbols*. New York: Academic.

Beach, R., & Hynds, S. (1990). Research on response to literature. In E. Farrell & J.R. Squire (Eds.), *Transactions with literature* (pp. 131–205). Urbana, IL: National Council of Teachers of English.

Birnbaum, J., & Emig, J. (1991). Case study. In J. Flood, J.M. Jensen, D. Lapp, & J.R. Squire (Eds.), *Handbook of research on teaching the English language arts* (pp. 195–204). New York: Macmillan.

Blumenthal, A.L. (1977). *The process of cognition*. Englewood Cliffs, NJ: Prentice Hall.

Bohr, N. (1959). Discussion with Einstein. In P.A. Schilpp (Ed.), *Albert Einstein, Philosopher-Scientist* (p. 210). New York: HarperCollins.

Cantril, H., & Livingston, W.K. (1963). The concept of transaction in psychology and neurology. *Journal of Individual Psychology, 19*, 3–16.

Chomsky, N. (1968). *Language and mind*. New York: Harcourt Brace.

Clifford, J. (Ed.). (1991). *The experience of reading: Louise Rosenblatt and reader response theory*. Portsmouth, NH: Boynton/Cook.

Cox, C., & Many, J.E. (Eds.). (1992). *Reader's stance and literary understanding*. Norwood, NJ: Ablex.

Culler, J. (1982). *On deconstruction*. Ithaca, NY: Cornell University Press.

Damasio, A.R. (1989). The brain binds entities by multilingual activities for convergence zones. *Neural Computation, 1*.

Deese, J. (1973). Cognitive structure and affect in language. In P. Pliner & T. Alloway (Eds.), *Communication and affect*. New York: Academic.

Dewey, J. (1938). *Logic: The theory of inquiry*. New York: Henry Holt.

Dewey, J., & Bentley, A.F. (1949). *Knowing and the known*. Boston: Beacon.

Eisner, E.W., & Peshkin, A. (1990). *Qualitative inquiry in education: The continuing debate*. New York: Teachers College Press.

Emig, J. (1983). *The web of meaning*. Portsmouth, NH: Boynton/Cook.

Farrell, E., & Squire, J.R. (Eds.). (1990). *Transactions with literature*. Urbana, IL: National Council of Teachers of English.

Fish, S. (1980). *Is there a text in this class?* Cambridge, MA: Harvard University Press.

Flaubert, G. (1926). *Correspondance* (Vol. 2). Paris: Louis Conard.

Flood, J., Jensen, J.M., Lapp, D., & Squire, J.R. (Eds.). (1991). *Handbook of research on teaching the English language arts*. New York: Macmillan.

Halliday, M.A.K. (1975). *Learning how to mean*. New York: Elsevier.

Harris, T.L., & Hodges, R.E. (Eds.). (1981). *A dictionary of reading and related terms*. Newark, DE: International Reading Association.

Heath, S.B. (1983). *Ways with words: Language, life, and work in communities and classrooms*. Cambridge, UK: Cambridge University Press.

Hungerford, R., Holland, K., & Ernst, S. (Eds.). (1993). *Journeying: Children responding to literature*. Portsmouth, NH: Heinemann.

Izard, C.E. (1977). *Human emotions*. New York: Plenum.

James, W. (1890). *The principles of psychology* (2 vols.). New York: Henry Holt.

Kantor, K.J., Kirby, D.R., & Goetz, J.P. (1981). Research in context: Ethnographic studies in English education. *Research in the Teaching of English, 15*(4), 293–309.

Karolides, N.J. (Ed.). (1992). *Reader response in the classroom: Evoking and interpreting meaning in literature*. White Plains, NY: Longman.

Kuhn, T. (1970). *The structure of scientific revolutions* (2nd ed.). Chicago: University of Chicago Press.

Lindbergh, A.M. (1940). *The wave of the future*. New York: Harcourt Brace.

McCloskey, D. (1985). *The rhetoric of economics*. Madison: University of Wisconsin Press.

Miller, G.A., & Johnson-Laird, P.N. (1976). *Language and perception*. Cambridge, MA: Harvard University Press.

Myers, G. (1986). *William James: His life and thought*. New Haven, CT: Yale University Press.

Peirce, C.S. (1933, 1935). *Collected papers* (Vol. 3, Vol. 6) (P. Weiss & C. Hartshorne, Eds.). Cambridge, MA: Harvard University Press.

Purves, A.C., & Beach, R. (1972). *Literature and the reader: Research in response to literature*. Urbana, IL: National Council of Teachers of English.

Purves, A.C., & Rippere, V. (1968). *Elements of writing about a literary work: A study of response to literature*. Urbana, IL: National Council of Teachers of English.

Rommetveit, R. (1968). *Words, meanings, and messages*. New York: Academic.

Rosenblatt, L.M. (1978). *The reader, the text, the poem: The transactional theory of the literary work.* Carbondale: Southern Illinois University Press.

Rosenblatt, L.M. (1983). *Literature as exploration* (4th ed.). New York: Modern Language Association. (Original work published 1938).

Rosenblatt, L.M. (1985a). The transactional theory of the literary work: Implications for research. In C. Cooper (Ed.), *Researching response to literature and the teaching of literature.* Norwood, NJ: Ablex.

Rosenblatt, L.M. (1985b). Viewpoints: Transaction versus interaction—A terminological rescue operation. *Research in the Teaching of English, 19*, 96–107.

Rosenblatt, L.M. (1991). Literary theory. In J. Flood, J.M. Jensen, D. Lapp, & J.R. Squire (Eds.), *Handbook of research on teaching the English language arts* (pp. 57–62). New York: Macmillan.

Rosenblatt, L.M. (1993). The transactional theory: Against dualisms. *College English, 55*(4), 377–386.

Saussure, F. (1972). *Cours de linguistique générale.* Paris: Payot.

Tierney, R.J. (1991). Studies of reading and writing growth: Longitudinal research on literacy development. In J. Flood, J.M. Jensen, D. Lapp, & J.R. Squire (Eds.), *Handbook of research on teaching the English language arts* (pp. 176–194). New York: Macmillan.

Verbrugge, R.R. (1979). The primacy of metaphor in development. In E. Winner & H. Gardner (Eds.), *Fact, fiction, and fantasy in childhood.* San Francisco: Jossey-Bass.

Vygotsky, L.S. (1962). *Thought and language* (F. Hanmann & G. Vakar, Eds. & Trans.). Cambridge, MA: MIT Press.

Werner, H., & Kaplan, B. (1962). *Symbol formation.* New York: Wiley.

Zaharlick, A., & Green, J. (1991). Ethnographic research. In J. Flood, J.M. Jensen, D. Lapp, & J.R. Squire (Eds.), *Handbook of research on teaching the English language arts* (pp. 205–223). New York: Macmillan.

Appendix: The Vale of Email(s)

On Thu, Apr 26, 2018 at 3:50 PM, Jon Ratner <JonRatner@westat.com> wrote:

Donna,

It's gratifying to me that my mom's chapter will appear in the new edition, and that you assign the chapter in your doctoral seminars. Professional life after death is usually vanishingly short. Thirteen years after her death—that's practically an epoch, given the changes in the world and in the professional sphere of literary theory, reading, and literacy. May her work come alive in the thinking and work of the field for another thirteen years.

I think she'd have interesting things to say about the transactional experience in regards to the ever-present screen and the role of the index finger in moving readers from text to Instagram to text. (I'm not talking about what her judgment or comments would be on the new modes that bring texts to readers and whisk them away as well. I'm talking about what her attempt to describe and understand those new modes would be.)

I know she'd have interesting things to say about why "transaction" rather than "reader-response" matters critically today, given the prevalence of confabulation and spin in articles on political subjects—and of tribal readings within group-based bubbles of communication.[1] The efferent-aesthetic continuum has great relevance to this flowering of articles and media content that is created to (mis)*inform*—an efferent dimension, *entertain*—an aesthetic dimension, and *persuade*—an aspect of efferent activity that she didn't emphasize (if I recall correctly). All this is interesting to me, in part because she was interested in but critical of S. I. Hayakawa's book, *Language in Thought and Action*. I only wish I remembered more about what she said about this book and topic!

In any case, getting your email picked my spirits up. If there's any way I can be of further help, please tell me.

Best regards,
Jonathan

---

[1]Forwarded message ——————
From: **Jon Ratner** <JonRatner@westat.com>
Date: Fri, Apr 27, 2018 at 10:46 AM
Subject: RE: Request of The Estate of Louise M. Rosenblatt (Contributor)
To: Donna Alvermann <dalverma@uga.edu>

Donna,

Thanks for your wonderful response. It made my day! So we're even!

I'd be glad to have you include my email message following the Louise chapter. It's gratifying and totally unexpected to have you, your co-editors, and the editor at Routledge like what I wrote so much and suggest that it be included with her chapter.

I probably should reread what I wrote. Since it wasn't written for the wider world, it's conceivable there's something I might want to tweak. After writing the preceding sentence, I just reread the first email quickly. One thought is that the lead sentence about "transaction" versus "reader-response" might be cryptic to many readers.

My point was, in part, that the text matters as the anchor for communication among readers. (If Jill says that a tweet from President Trump makes her think of Nietzsche's superman, that thought begs the question, what in the text leads you to say that?)

In part, though, LMR said that our discussion as readers can not only be a path out of solipsism ("my reading is the only reality"), and not only a venue for developing shared understandings of texts ("our reading of the text is X"). Our discussion can be an opportunity for readers *in an efferent mode* to ground their reading in evidence *outside the text*.

A poem-text that alludes to Einstein's love of arcs (the nonlinear form as a thing of beauty) does not compel the reader to rush to physics articles in order to test the accuracy of the text of the poem about Einstein's physics. (In one of her articles, my mother criticized the common English class question, "What Does This Poem Mean?" (BTW, in the article's first paragraph, I make an appearance as the unnamed boy who listened to the poem. ☺)) The poem-text can easily stand on its own. (Though once the text leaves the poet's pen, the reader rules in terms of what he or she chooses to do with it.)

But a tweet, a news article, and a polemic on TV or the internet, do understandably lead readers to ask for evidence beyond the text. These texts, these "arti-facts," resemble the instruction sheet for a piece of electronics. However we respond to these texts aesthetically and in terms of adrenaline, we might also want to know whether, if we follow them, we can (figuratively or literally) turn the new TV on. That leads us to search for evidence. In 2018, "evidence" is highly contested and, I'm confident Louise would say, vitally important to get right, or as right as available information allows us to be.

My rendering of all this harkens back to her philosophical pragmatism. A friend of my parents, the American philosopher Abraham Kaplan, once explained pragmatism's approach to truth as involving "grounded intersubjectivity." Intersubjectivity, in that we must recognize that each of us sees what he or she sees, and that to function in a social world we rely on shared perceptions and understandings—hence the "inter" in "intersubjectivity." But, Kaplan says, my say-so isn't good enough, and our shared say-so isn't good enough. We must demand of ourselves and each other to know what the "grounds" are for my belief or our belief. So: "grounded intersubjectivity." My mother liked to put things her own way. She might not approve entirely of what I've just written. Nonetheless, I'd have to say to her, "Mom, this is my reading of your texts. Show me in those texts where I went astray."

I think she'd be pleased that the conversation, this type of conversation, continues.

Many thanks for making my morning much more interesting than I ever anticipated.

Best regards,
Jonathan

24

TRANSACTIONAL READING IN HISTORICAL PERSPECTIVE

Mark Dressman

Let me give full credit at the outset of this chapter to Louise Rosenblatt's legacy as an educator. No one in the history of literature education—not James F. Hosic, not Arthur Appleby, not Mortimer Adler or Alan Purves or Judith Langer or Deborah Appleman or my mentor, Julie Jensen—has had a more positive influence on the teaching of literature than Louise Rosenblatt. If her only accomplishment had been to cause English teachers around the world to ask students what *they* thought a text meant and then to use those ideas as material in the building of understanding within a class, that alone would be enough to assure her place in history, and to thank her.

As literacy researchers and educators, we owe Rosenblatt a great debt, but we do not owe her work or her ideas uncritical acceptance. Her theory of reading is no more than a theory, an unproven account of how something happens, and like all theories, especially in the humanities and social sciences, it is one grounded in its creator's transactions with the world, mediated by long-held, deep-rooted, and often unacknowledged systems of belief. Theories are thus as ideological as they are empirical: They express both a vision of how the world is and of how that world should be.

The Historical Account

As Rosenblatt herself has explained, her writing about reading began with the first edition of *Literature as Exploration*, published in New York City in 1938. In Europe in the mid-1930s, fascism was on the rise and in New York intellectuals grew increasingly worried. A meeting was called by John Dewey, Ruth Benedict, and other leading figures, and Louise Rosenblatt, then a young professor at New York University, was commissioned to write a book about the role of literature in promoting democratic values. Dewey had published *Art as Experience* in 1934, and its focus on the power of art as a catalyst for social discourse and development was a clear influence on Rosenblatt's arguments, as were psychoanalysis and anthropological views of culture and society.

But the first addition of *Literature as Exploration* was not a very theoretical book in that it did not attempt to describe how students read but rather how teachers should teach. Rosenblatt wrote in the first-person plural, beginning many paragraphs with "We teachers," and her tone was, in contemporary terms, one of "advocacy" for engaging students in discussions of texts that focused on issues of economic and social inequality in addition to literary themes around plot, character, setting, and theme. New Criticism—a literary movement advocating for "close reading" of texts without any attention to the context of their authorship—was then ascendant within the academy, but she barely discussed its implications directly. However, her sensitivity to the backgrounds of students and concern for engaging them in discussions on their own terms might have constituted an indirect critique, not of close reading but of New Criticism's pedagogy, which typically focused on the instructor's presentation of his/her close reading of a literary text to the exclusion of student perspectives.

Thirty years later, in 1968, Rosenblatt published the second, revised edition of *Literature as Exploration*. As Joan Parker Webster and I (Dressman & Webster, 2001) have documented and for reasons that cannot be fully explained, this edition systematically removed most of its references to societal influences on students' reading and shifted its authorial stance from one of solidarity with teachers to one of writing about teachers in the third person. It emphasized an image of readers as individuals making conscious choices in their interpretations and downplayed the role of the classroom as a location for discussion about societal issues, although it retained its focus on classroom discussion as a means of developing textual experience.

In 1949, Arthur Bentley and John Dewey published *Knowing and the Known*, in which for the first time they described human experience and understanding of the world as a *transactional* process and contrasted it to two previous historical views, *self-action* and *interaction*. However, in the 1968 edition of *Literature as Exploration*, Rosenblatt continued to describe relations between a reader and a text as an *interaction*. It was not until 1976 in the third edition of *Literature as Exploration* that *transaction* was substituted for the earlier term as nearly its only revision.

These two moves—the removal of references to the societal value of literature and the simple substitution of one word for another—signaled the beginning of the end of any Deweyan influence on Rosenblatt's work, despite continued references to Dewey as her source of inspiration in later publications. The central provision of Dewey's aesthetics is the power of works of art, and especially of popular art, to provoke discussions within society about beauty, power, injustice, politics, and so on; he likely would have rejected the progressive privatization of the literary experience in Rosenblatt's later work as detrimental to art's societal purpose. Similarly, the simple substitution of *transaction* for *interaction* with no further revision strongly suggests that Rosenblatt missed the full implications of Dewey and Bentley's argument. For them, a transaction was a far-ranging event, one that included historical, physical, and sociocultural consequences for both sides of the transaction. The difference between their definition of transaction and the one assumed by Rosenblatt is the difference between the way a shopkeeper might view a transaction—as a local exchange of goods for money—and the way an economist might view the same transaction—as an exchange created and enabled by complex systems of manufacture and trade, and whose consequences would ripple throughout the entire economy with multiplicative effect.

Rosenblatt codified her views as a theory of reading with the publication of *The Reader, the Text, the Poem: The Transactional Theory of the Literary Work*, which, in keeping with other theories of reader response at the time (e.g., Bleich, 1975; Holland, 1975; Iser, 1978), focused on the reader as central to textual interpretation. Like the second and third (1976) editions of *Literature as Exploration*, reading was described as an act involving a "transaction" between an individual reader and a text to create an interpretation, or "poem." Rosenblatt insisted that the background and life experiences of the reader were central to the reading act and implied that these experiences were more personal than sociocultural, in keeping with her focus on the individuality and autonomy of readers. The main innovation of this book was her description of how a reader's purpose determined what a reader took from the text, which was described "as an object of paper and ink until some reader responds to the marks on the page as verbal symbols" (1978, p. 23). These purposes were described as falling along a continuum, with aesthetic purposes associated with pleasure and the contemplation of the literary work for its own sake on one end, and efferent, or more practical purposes such as seeking information as the means to a goal beyond the text, on the other end.

The publication of *The Reader, the Text, the Poem* marked the end of any association with Dewey's aesthetics, for two reasons. For Dewey, a transaction involved an exchange between two entities, each with its own agency; but Rosenblatt's characterization of a text as "paper and ink" brought to life by a reader virtually eliminated any active role for texts in the reading process. Second, despite continued warnings "against dualisms" to the end of her career (Rosenblatt, 1993), *RTP* fairly swam in binary distinctions, between aesthetic and efferent reading; between literature and "trash"; between the reader and the text; between the reader and the poem; between the text and the poem; and so on.

Between the publication of *RTP* in 1978 and the fifth and last edition of *Literature as Exploration* in 1995 (the fourth edition in 1983 was essentially a reprint of the third), a revolution in literary criticism took place, driven by a series of Continental literary and social critics. Althusser (1971) had earlier introduced the concept of *interpellation* to describe how readers were "hailed" by a text and drawn into ideological alignment with it; Bakhtinian concepts such as *heteroglossia, dialogism,* and *chronotope* (Bakhtin, 1981) demonstrated the role of linguistic history and of time-space in shaping the meaning of texts for readers; and Derrida (1976) demonstrated how the always-already deconstruction of texts lays bare their internal contradictions in active ways that challenged the authority of any individual reading of a text. At the same time, multiple ethnographies of reading (e.g., Christian-Smith, 1993; Radway, 1983) documented the gender politics of "leisure reading," and historians of the novel (e.g., Armstrong, 1987; Baym, 1978) documented its role in the ongoing emancipation of women from the home. In 1995, the same year that the final edition of *Literature as Exploration* was published, Hartman published "Eight readers reading: The intertextual links of proficient readers reading multiple passages." The implications of this empirical work were that readers' purposes and the stances they took within and across texts were multiple and far more complex than any scheme placing reading along a single continuum.

Rosenblatt resisted all these developments and their implications. In the fifth and last edition of *Literature as Exploration* (1995), she aligned critics of the 1980s and 1990s "with the New Critics and the traditionalists in overemphasizing the text." Her concern was to preserve the primacy of the "personal aesthetic experience" over critics "concerned with abstracting the underlying systems of codes and conventions that the text possesses for a particular 'interpretive community'" (p. 294). Only after a text had been *"aesthetically evoked* (her italics)" could it "become the object of reflection and analysis, according to the various critical and scholarly approaches" (p. 295). Despite having progressively deleted nearly every reference to social, cultural, economic, and historic influences on readers over five editions of *Literature as Exploration,* she still insisted that her theory took these macrostructural influences into account, but only as they might contribute to individuals' readings of a text: "The importance of the culture is recognized (here, *Literature as Exploration* is especially pertinent), but, I point out, personal choice and variety derive from the fact that cultural conventions are individually internalized" (p. 295). By insisting that "culture" is something individual and subject to "personal choice," she dismisses culture as a collective force in society and societal, cultural influences on both individual and collective readings of texts.

Perspective: Reader, Text, and Historical/Sociocultural Context

Of course, reading is a transaction between a reader and a text. However, scholarship of the last 40 years has also demonstrated that texts are never simply ink on paper, and that readers are not simply individuals whose private lives and experiences help to shape the meanings they build when they read. In sum, the evidence points to a definition of a transaction more in line with Dewey and Bentley's in 1949 and with an economist's concept of a transaction than with a shopkeeper's, and to a vision of reading more aligned with Dewey's aesthetics in *Art as Experience* in 1934 and with Rosenblatt's 1938 edition of *Literature as Exploration* than with the 1995 edition. The evidence also suggests that the binary of reader/text is itself untenable, given that each is the product of human transactions historically, economically, linguistically, culturally, and so on, so that in the moment of their coming together, the two become essentially one.

This is not to say that readers in the same social class, gender, culture, linguistic group, religion, or other category will all have the same reading of a text; but the preponderance of the research evidence strongly demonstrates that their readings will likely share common insights and points of view, and that these cumulative readings can have a profound effect on history. This is not as insidious or as negative as it seems; in fact, it may often prove quite central to the aims of social progress; take, for example, Baym's (1978) account of how the plots of "woman's fiction" in the nineteenth century provided readers with a template and encouragement to break away from virtual domestic enslavement, laying the grounds for woman's suffrage and feminism in the twentieth century. Nor does recognition of the agency of texts degrade the agency of readers; it only means that the less readers are aware of how history, language, an author's intentions, and influences in their own sociocultural backgrounds help to shape their response to a text, the greater and more unconscious these effects are likely to be. Ironically, then, savvy readers who are aware of these forces on their reading are more likely to take greater control of their own responses (and to have far deeper and more complex aesthetic experiences) than readers who approach literature imagining that they are autonomous individuals in a free encounter with ink on a page.

But, doesn't an awareness of how one's own background and the history of a literary work shape the reader's response interfere with, even destroy, its pleasure, the sense of being "lost" in it, and move it from the "aesthetic" side of the continuum to the "efferent," making its reading into work? That has never been my experience. After 40 years as an educator and devotee of social theory, I still find myself caught up in a good story or great poetry, be it in a jingle, a rap, or a more traditional form. But now, my initial response to a literary text is almost immediately followed by my wondering about exactly how that text worked its "magic" on me, for I know it wasn't magic; it was something within the transaction. That wondering leads to discussion with others and to more reflection, to remembrance of research and theory I've read, and sometimes to additional research, and it all in the end enriches and makes my experience of that text *even more aesthetic and pleasurable.*

As a secondary English teacher, this was also my experience. I never taught literary theory, nor would I ever advocate making historical and theoretical research the centerpiece of an English class, or even "frontloading" the reading of a text with notes and lectures about history or literary form. But as we read and as students became engaged with characters, plot, setting, and themes, I would introduce historical facts about the author or the social context in which the work was written, and I might point out that the girls in the class were having a different reaction than the boys, and ask why that might be so. We would go to the library to do research about an unfamiliar setting and I would even introduce some Marxist or Darwinian concepts into class discussion. In other words, while our reading would begin with students' initial responses to a text, it would quickly move to a more analytical project, one in which the story *in* the text—that is, its basic or "literal" meaning— was reread and reinterpreted against the story *of* the text, or the story of the text's composition placed within an accounting of its historical, sociocultural, and authorial context. Far from interrupting or corrupting students' pleasure, I consistently found that these well-placed external facts and ideas dramatically enriched students' understanding and appreciation of the text as a work of art.

In conclusion, I can sympathize with teachers who are thrilled if their students become "lost" in a text and can't wait to discuss a book or poem in class. But I find it difficult to accept if this is as far as they feel they need to take their students, and I am very concerned if they cite Rosenblatt as their reason for stopping there. Readers of this chapter may dispute whether that was Rosenblatt's intention or not, but I hope that they will not dispute that it is far better to teach students to become savvy readers—readers who appreciate the beauty of a text in all its facets but at the same time have the skills and awareness to know how and why that text is having its effect—than to become lovers of literature without knowing how or why that has happened.

References

Althusser, L. (1971). *Lenin and philosophy and other essays* (B. Brewster, Trans.). London: New Left Books.
Armstrong, N. (1987). *Desire and domestic fiction.* Minneapolis, MN: University of Minnesota Press.

Bakhtin, M. M. (1981). *The dialogic imagination: Four essays by M. M. Bakhtin* (M. Holquist, Ed., C. Emerson & M. Holquist, Trans.). Austin, TX: University of Texas Press.

Baym, N. (1978). *Woman's fiction: A guide to novels by and about women in America, 1820–70.* Urbana, IL: University of Illinois Press.

Bleich, D. (1975). *Readings and feelings: An introduction to subjective criticism.* Urbana, IL: National Council of Teachers of English.

Christian-Smith, L. (1993). *Texts of desire: Essays on fiction, femininity, and schooling.* New York, NY: Falmer.

Derrida, J. (1976). *Of grammatology* (G. C. Spivak, Trans.). Baltimore, MD: Johns Hopkins University Press.

Dewey, J. (1934). *Art as experience.* New York, NY: Minton, Balch, & Co.

Dewey, J., & Bentley, A. F. (1949). *Knowing and the known.* Boston, MA: Beacon Press.

Dressman, M., & Webster, J. P. (2001). Retracing Rosenblatt: A textual archaeology. *Research in the Teaching of English, 36*(1), 110–145.

Hartman, D. K. (1995). Eight readers reading: The intertextual links of proficient readers reading multiple passages. *Reading Research Quarterly, 30*(3), 520–561.

Holland, N. (1975). *The dynamics of literary response.* New York, NY: W. W. Norton and Co.

Iser, W. (1978). *The implied reader: Patterns of communication in prose from Bunyan to Beckett.* Baltimore, MD: Johns Hopkins University Press.

Radway, J. (1983). *Reading the romance: Women, patriarchy, and popular literature.* Chapel Hill, NC: University of North Carolina Press.

Rosenblatt, L. M. (1938). *Literature as exploration* (1st ed.). New York, NY: D. Appleton-Century.

Rosenblatt, L. M. (1968). *Literature as exploration* (2nd ed.). New York, NY: Noble & Noble.

Rosenblatt, L. M. (1976). *Literature as exploration* (3rd ed.). New York, NY: Noble & Noble.

Rosenblatt, L. M. (1978). *The reader, the text, the poem: The transactional theory of the literary work.* Carbondale, IL: Southern Illinois University Press.

Rosenblatt, L. M. (1983). *Literature as exploration* (4th ed.). New York, NY: Modern Language Association of America.

Rosenblatt, L. (1993). The transactional theory: Against dualisms. *College English, 55*(4), 377–386.

Rosenblatt, L. M. (1995). *Literature as exploration* (5th ed.). New York, NY: Modern Language Association.

25

MULTILANGUAGING AND INFINITE RELATIONS OF DEPENDENCY

Re-theorizing Reading Literacy from Ubuntu

Leketi Makalela

Introduction

It goes without question that the introduction of the multilingual turn movement has exponentially challenged monolingual practices in language and literacy education worldwide. The past ten years have seen a proliferation of arguments for translanguaging as an alternative framework to transform and decolonize classroom pedagogies and increase knowledge access for multilingual learners in literacy instruction (e.g., Canagarajah, 2011; Garcia, 2009; Makalela, 2015a, 2015b). Despite its promises for change, the view of multilingualism in sub-Saharan Africa still reflects Western conceptions of knowing and invariably promotes monolingual bias, with its inherent logic of one strong language equalling one strong nation and the orthodox metanarrative that using more than one language creates mental confusion (Baker, 2011; Brock-Utne, 2000, 2015; Makalela, 2015a; Ricento, 2000). These ideological orientations are to date still influential in national language policies, language planning discourses, and literacy practices throughout the world.

Multilingual regions such as sub-Saharan Africa, which makes 13% of the world's population and 30% of the world's languages, become major casualties of monolingual and epistemic biases (Makalela, 2016; UNESCO, 2010). With no conclusive findings on the actual number of languages spoken in the region, there is very little theorization on the super-fluid status of these languages and overlapping usage across a wider spectrum of their speech communities. As a result, monolingual bias, where African languages are viewed as sealed entities capable of being placed in boxes (Makalela, 2015a; Makoni, 2003), has become a major force that entrenches ex-colonial languages as *sine qua non* for educational success, political activity, and upward social mobility. Yet the educational challenges faced by many African children have continued to deepen, with UNESCO reports constantly indicating that sub-Saharan Africa represents about 70% of the people deemed to be illiterate in the world (Bamgbose, 2000; Makalela, 2017).

In this chapter, I question the validity of Western-based theories of literacy acquisition and argue that monolingual bias in literacy instruction practices plays a role in failing multilingual students, especially in the Global South. Through an analysis of linguistic and cultural history on Limpopo Valley in South Africa, I propose *Ubuntu translanguaging*, also described as *multilanguaging*, as an alternative conceptual framework to understand infinite relations, where literacy practices should not be viewed as a conglomeration of autonomous skills, and how the Ubuntu transliteracy model can be harnessed as a pedagogic strategy to increase access to knowledge and to affirm the identity positions of multilingual children. Recommendations for using Ubuntu translanguaging pedagogy as a heuristic for complex multilingual classrooms are considered at the end of the chapter for adaptation in comparable contexts.

Temporal Fluidity: Looking Back to Fetch

One of the theoretical treasures in African philosophy is the value of historical consciousness and the need to constantly refer back while stretching forward. As an example, it is useful here to evoke the Akan metaphor that is mainly dominant in West Africa regarding the power of looking back in order to stretch ahead with vigour and determination. A mythical bird called Sankofa is instructive about temporal fluidity, where the past and the present are a confluent continuum, living in the same cosmological order without clear boundaries (Makalela, in press). This mythical bird resembles strategic engagement with backward and forward movements. Literally speaking, the head goes into the past while the feet are stretching into the future so that the present, past and future become a continuum whole. I have written separately (Makalela, 2005) about how this logic of time is reflected in the languages spoken where temporal difference is not distinctive or bounded.

Using Sankofa as a heuristic to understand language and literacy patterns in pre-colonial Africa, there is evidence of civilization that was developed before the European colonial invasion. In particular, scholars have documented successful trade between forest, southern lakes, and the Congo kingdoms (e.g., Carruthers, 2006). The Southern African kingdom of Mapungubwe under Emperor Monomotapa is an example of a civilization that spread to other parts of the world. Mapungubwe, which borders South Africa, Botswana, and Zimbabwe, emerged as a result of the confluence of the rivers of Sashe and Limpopo and eventually came to be known as the Limpopo Valley.

Archaeologists in the 1930s brought substantial evidence of successful trade between the city of Mapungubwe,[1] Egypt, India, and China, among others (see Foucher, 1937 for a full appraisal). Relevant to this chapter is that more than one language was used to communicate complex ideas that resulted in one of the civilization centres of the early medieval period. These languages included variants of Shona or Kalanga, Sotho, Khoe-San, and Nguni languages that were spread all over the kingdom (Makalela, 2015b).

Evidence from ceramic pots and indigenous games such as morabaraba[2] suggest a multi-ethnic, multicultural, and multilingual community (e.g., Carruthers, 2006). The people of Mapungubwe practised Ubuntu – their humanist approach to life where it was believed that human beings come from the reed and that they belong together (Khoza, 2013). In their cultural ethos, they believed in the collective, and Ubuntu became a way of life, as found in today's versions of *umuntu ngumuntu ngabantu* (a version for the Nguni languages) or *motho ke motho ka batho* (a version for the Sotho languages), which translate into "you are because we are" or "I am because you are". The "I × We" logic permeates the philosophical orientation of most of speakers of Bantu languages in sub-Saharan Africa, with versions of this saying available in almost all the languages. Because of this belief in interdependence, the Mapungubwe inhabitants achieved one of the greatest civilization centres in the region. Their ways of being and knowing show an infinite relation of dependency.

One Classroom – One Language: Introducing Monolingual Literacies in a Multilingual World

While it was a popular belief stemming from the Enlightenment period that using more than one language would be the source of chaos and confusion for nation-states (Ricento, 2000), this logic was foreign in African communities (Khoza, 2013; Makalela, 2017). Loss of the predominance of African languages as fluid entities in Africa can be traced as far back as the Berlin convention of 1884. Britain, France, Italy, Germany, Portugal, and Spain divided Africa into colonial states where the languages of the colonized countries were subverted in order to provide a pathway for linguistic and cultural domination from the colonial countries. As observed earlier, a key imperative for colonization was to control the thoughts and identity positions of the local people by means of linguistic regimentation (Davidson, 1992). To convert the local people into subjects of the empires, funded commissions were created in order to oversee linguistic imperialism and total control of how the local people used languages. The latest in a series of commissions is the Phelps-Stokes Commission of the 1920s (Makalela, 2017). The commission made several recommendations on language management, which still have a bearing on language policies:

- The tribal language should be used in the lower elementary standards or grades.
- A *lingua franca* of African origin should be introduced in the middle classes of the school if the area is occupied by large Native groups speaking diverse languages.
- The language of the European nation in control should be taught in the upper standards. (King, 1971, p. 56)

The recommendation of the Phelps Commission was sought to explain and clarify a linguistic programme that was put in place almost a century earlier (i.e., in 1884). What is very striking in this commission report is the packaging of language literacies in a sequence and hierarchy. Separation of languages here reflects the dominant monolingual view of separate development. The outcome of the commission, as also reported in Makalela (2017), affirmed an Africa-wide immersion programme that has four categories:

1. Delayed immersion found in former British and Belgian colonies;
2. Total assimilation in former French, Portuguese, and Spanish colonies;
3. Double assimilation in Tanzania and Eritrea; and
4. Retention of local languages in primary schools (Somalia, Ethiopia, Comoros, Madagascar, and Tanzania).

In the first category, the British and the Belgians preferred a delayed immersion policy where the first three years of education were conducted through the medium of African languages and followed by a transition into the language of the colonizer. The result of this sequential model has been a systematic loss of confidence in the local languages for education in higher grades. The second model of language, or word control, is total assimilation, where the French, Portuguese, and Spanish insisted on the use of the colonial language from preschool as a reasonable option to prepare children for colonial immersion.

Third, there were countries that were shared by different colonial powers successively due to trade-offs of the world wars. Tanzania and Eritrea are typical countries that had successive transitions. The former colonizing countries, Germany and Italy, respectively, lost the First World War and as part of the treaty, Tanzania and Eritrea were signed off to become British colonies. The local languages such as Kiswahili had already taken root and nationalized by the time the British took power, and in line with the British model of delayed immersion, the national languages of these countries were used for the whole of primary school education as the concentration was on replacing the former colonial culture and language in the upper standards.

The last category of language control reflects countries that were allowed to use local languages in primary school education for a number of reasons. One of these was that the countries were so small that having a local language would not have large-scale consequences in changing the colonial hierarchy and domination in the upper levels. First, Italian colonization style was loose, reflecting on their own history (Davidson, 1992). According to Davidson (1992), Italy was the last country that was under the siege of foreign states and therefore all forms of external control were not consistent with their cultural disposition. For this reason, they did not retain colonial control in African colonies like Libya, Eritrea, and Somalia. Finally, small islands like Madagascar and the Comoros were left to their own devices to use local languages for primary school education as long as the languages of higher grades were those of the colonial powers.

So far, the language control models described above explain the dominance of language separation and the use of one language at a given time or phase of schooling. Evidently, none of these has been successful despite the ministers of education swinging pendulums between the monolingual models without realizing that any of these systems neglected the cultural competence of fluidity and simultaneity. What is evident is that all these monolingual (one language at a time) policy options create a linguistic curtain where Africans are separated from knowledge, from deeper understanding of the world they inhabit and from their sense of being.

Developing Alternative Literacy Theories From Cultural Competence

One of the ways to upset monolingual bias and allow multiple voices to come into contact is to look back at the sociolinguistic background of the African people prior to colonialism. The history of Mapungubwe, as described earlier, and its linguistic repertoire become a cardinal point for Southern Africa to reclaim African linguistic and cultural competence. I have elsewhere (Makalela, 2016) shown that the African value system of Ubuntu is a heuristic for African multilingualism where the use of more than one language through fluid and porous interaction is a norm that can be cultivated strategically in African classrooms. I have coined the concept *Ubuntu translanguaging* to account for a combined understanding of communicative practices where input and output are exchanged in different languages and one language is incomplete without the other in conjunction with the Ubuntu mantra of "*I am because we are*".

Translanguaging as a pedagogical strategy has been studied elsewhere in the world as a discourse where linguistic input and output are alternated in different languages (Creese & Blackledge, 2010; Garcia, 2009, 2011; Garcia & Wei, 2014). In African situations, the notion of alternation is complex in that alternation within and between languages could involve more than two named languages in the same communicative event. My colleague and I have shown that there are both vertical and horizontal translanguaging discourse practices in classrooms (Nkadimeng & Makalela, 2015). For example, teachers who teach different subjects have a tendency of using languages of their preferences to a similar group of learners who interact and respond in any of the named languages preferred by teachers. In other words, six teachers who choose six different named languages are giving an input in these languages, but the classroom interaction dynamics require them to respond to questions that may come in any of the learners' preferred languages. At the same time, learners share information and discuss the content using a variety of languages where they give an input and receive outputs in different languages. This is a typical school where complex translingual interactions are the norm and this is the only way these learners and teachers make sense of the world and of who they are (see Nkadimeng & Makalela, 2015 for a full appraisal of the situation).

Viewing multilingualism from this experience of complex translanguaging provides opportunities for an epistemological shift from what languages look like to what speakers do with languages. Research is constant that orthographical work of the missionary linguists who moved in different directions, often without a central coordination system, mis-invented artificial languages (e.g., Makoni, 2003). For example, a language variety called Sesotho was written down by three different missionary groups who devised the spelling systems differently according to their own languages. In northern South Africa, a German missionary group founded and developed an orthography of the language they called Northern Sotho (which later became Sepedi). The London Missionary group worked in the western part of the country and named their language Western Sotho (which later became Setswana) and then a Roman Catholic missionary group in the south, wrote down a language they called Southern Sotho (which is known today as Sesotho). Here, one language that should have one writing system and more readers was divided into three different languages.

Application of the translanguaging approach in the context of Ubuntu provides policy makers with measures to question the validity of language boundaries and redraw the linguistic map from a fluid position. Within the logic of Ubuntu translanguaging, notions such as first language, mother tongue, and second language are questioned as these do not account for complex translingual discourse practices in many African contexts. Instead, they suggest a sequential view of language acquisition (i.e., one language at a time) and they tend to favour a monoglossic curriculum. Garcia (2009) avers that neither additive bilingual nor subtractive bilingual programmes are useful ways in which multilingual children need to be educated. Both programmes begin with monolingual orientation and result in monolingual output and use of languages in the society, thus perpetuating a multilingual but separate nation. I refer to this linguistic output as *monolingual multilingualism*, where multilingualism is viewed as separate languages, as is the case with the South African language policy of 11 official languages. Put differently, multilingualism from the translanguaging point of view does not place emphasis on enumeration of languages; rather, it is the degree to which simultaneous use of the languages in line with the linguistic competence of the speakers is valorized. Below is a description of current literacy practices in South Africa

Current Literacy Status in South Africa

For approximately 42 years of Apartheid South Africa, indigenous African languages have always been systematically excluded as languages for learning (i.e., used as the medium of learning and teaching) beyond grade 3. At the dawn of the new sociopolitical dispensation that began in 1994, there was a guarantee for parity of esteem and full realization of literacy opportunities through these languages. The South African Constitution in 1996 decreed 11 languages an official status: Sepedi, Sesotho, Setswana, isiZulu, SiSwati, isiXhosa, isiNdebele, Tshivenda, Xitsonga, English and Afrikaans (Republic of South Africa, 1996). In addition, the Bill of Rights made a provision for every child to be taught in languages of his or her choice:

> Every child has the right to receive education in the official language of their choice in public educational institutions where that education is reasonably practicable.
>
> *(Republic of South Africa, 1996, 29[2])*

The school governing bodies were given powers to determine school-based language policy where, among other considerations, at least 40 or more learners should be available for a language to be granted status of medium of instruction in public schools. The Language-in-Education Policy devolved the powers to these bodies as follows:

> Subject to any law dealing with language in education and the constitutional rights of the learners, in determining the language policy of the school, the governing body must stipulate how the school will promote multilingualism through using more than one language of learning and teaching, and/or applying special immersion or language maintenance programmes.
>
> *(Republic of South Africa, 1997, p. 8)*

I have observed elsewhere that this provision is interpreted from a monolingual perspective where subtractive bilingual tendencies become the norm (Makalela, 2017). In most primary schools, the first three years are still in one's home language and then the transition into the medium of English begins at grade 4. A very few schools opted for a "straight-for-English" policy where English is introduced as the language of literacy and learning from grade 1. In effect, the Apartheid status quo remains as these practices have not changed and they do not offer a learning environment where multilingual literacies are employed simultaneously as resources for identity affirmation and epistemic access.

Unequal Access to Literacy

While the South African Constitution commits to 11 official languages, the language-in-education practices still reflect domination of Afrikaans and English, and by extension they put speakers of these languages at an advantage. In addition, the national examination at grade 12 is still exclusively conducted in these two languages. Neville Alexander observed this pattern of literacy inequality and poignantly reflected as follows:

> It is an amazing fact that South Africa, in spite of its modernist pretensions, is one of the few countries worldwide where at least primary school children are not taught through the medium of the mother tongue or a language of immediate community. . . . It is an equally amazing fact that within the South African context the only children who receive mother tongue medium education virtually from cradle to the tertiary level are the minority English and Afrikaans-speaking children of the country. Children born to parents whose home language is one or other African language; i.e., the vast majority of our children, are doomed to be taught through a medium of the second language (mostly English) from the third or fourth year of school, mostly by teachers for whom this medium is at best a second language but often only a third language.
>
> *(Alexander, 2001, pp. 16–17)*

Alexander was unequivocal that the maintenance of Afrikaans- and English-medium education system repeats many years of linguistic discrimination, not only from the inception of Apartheid in 1948 but also from the onset of colonial contact where local languages were excluded and mocked as "clucking of turkeys" (Alexander, 1989). This maintenance is also seen at tertiary institutions where either English monolingualism or Afrikaans-English bilingualism is the norm while the majority of the students in these institutions have no opportunity to learn in any of the African languages. The grand challenge to sub-Saharan Africa, however, is the domination of monolingual ideologies, which to date limits literacy access to the majority of students. Below is a model of multilingualism that offers an alternative pathway to educating multilingual students.

Ubuntu Translanguaging Model

A translanguaging model based on Ubuntu principles, referred to here as Ubuntu translanguaging, shifts the gaze from language divisions to complex repertoires that are fluid in everyday meaning-making interactions. More importantly, it reflects a dialectic disruption of linguistic boundaries and simultaneous re-creation of new ones.

The Ubuntu translanguaging (UT) model denotes a fluid and porous relationship where in the first instance languages operate within the humanity logic of the "I × We", which is translated from the African value system of Ubuntu with its basic tenet: "*I am because you are; you are because I am*". The binding of "I" with "We" through a multiplication sign suggests an existential and complex relationship between these entities that look separate, yet are tied together by a sense of co-existence. This ontological matrix of self and others is at the root of Ubuntu, where forces of humaneness bind an infinite bond of collectivity (Khoza, 2013; Makalela, 2015a). In this connection, languages are a representation of this human cultural logic of being together as opposed to being separate entities that are capable of being placed in sealed boxes (Makalela, 2015a). Because of their endowment with Ubuntu, language encounters in multilingual communities show a constant process of disruption and eruption – dialectic processes that occur simultaneously. As they do this, they overlap into one another to the extent that boundaries between them become blurred and irrelevant to the meaning-making processes.

The next point worth noting in this model is the notion of *incompletion*. Drawn from the Ubuntu logic, it denotes the realization that no language is complete without the other in complex multi-lingual encounters. As shown with the "I × We", both the "I"-ness and "We"-ness do not form a coherent whole in their identity matrix. The second principle of incompletion comes from the experience of treating visitors. Expressions of this are found in idiomatic phrases such as "*moeng etla ka geso re je ka wena*", or "visitor, please come to my place so that I am complete". As in this human need for companionship, feeling of incompletion and the genetic make-up, languages that were acquired simultaneously would always create this space of incompletion in meaning making. It is in the desire to be complete that linguistic repertoires for meaning making come closer to one another in multilingual communication.

The third aspect of Ubuntu translanguaging is *interdependence,* which follows naturally from incompletion. Interdependence refers to co-existence of two or more language entities in the pro-cess of meaning making. Because these languages were acquired at the same time, the worldview and self-concept of the speakers were formed from this plural nexus of one language depending on another for full expression in sense making: the world around one and the self. The consistent state of being incomplete becomes a pre-requisite for completing the cycle of meaning making. This means that multilingual speakers have to use repertoires from different varieties to make sense of the world and have deeper understanding of realities around them. Both aspects of incompletion and interdependence relate to the mobile status of the 21st-century features and the resultant view of languages as in a constant state of transition. The languages of the world have responded to this new sociolinguistic reality of interdependent multilingualism as opposed to monolingual multilin-gualism described earlier. Interdependence is, therefore, the outcome of an infinite relationship of dependency as opposed to independence.

The fourth tenet of UT is the complexity of information flow where both horizontal and ver-tical mobility of information in communicative events take place *simultaneously*. This flow has a push-pull with backward and forward movements that render the terminal end of information flow unpredictable, uncertain, and indefinite. Whereas it is common worldwide for interlocutors to hear input in one language and give out a response (output) in a different language, many African soci-olinguistic realities allow for input in more than one named language and output in more than one language in speech events. As reported earlier, the secondary school classroom multilingual encoun-ters in South African townships like Soweto, Tembisa, Alexandra, and Katlehong (Nkadimeng & Makalela, 2015) offer a unique space to define complexities of how information flows between the learners and their teachers, on the one hand, and between the learners themselves where input and output are exchanged in at least six named languages. Most children growing in these contexts will have communicative proficiency in more than three languages by the time they are 6 (an optimal age for full mastery of one's home language).

As stated earlier, the notions of mother tongue and first language are problematic since they do not reflect the acquisition and proficiency modalities of these contexts. For convenience of the school choice of languages, these children often mention any language they perceive to be preferred either by the teacher or indeed their parents at home. Their choices therefore do not represent linguistic proficiencies, but historical identities largely based on ethnicities rather than languages. Teachers who grow up in these contexts also develop similar linguistic ability where they choose at any given point to give an output in more than one language while teaching. I have consistently observed that different teachers assigned to a variety of subjects use different language varieties to the extent that each teacher may be associated with about three named language varieties for classroom communication. Learners, on the other hand, communicate with one another in a vari-ety of language forms to make sense of the content as they would normally communicate in their communities.

The teachers talking to students in a variety of languages represent a vertical flow of informa-tion, while students talking to one another to cross-pollinate the ideas learned through a variety of language represent a horizontal flow of information. Either stream of information flow is incomplete for multilingual speakers in these complex encounters and will need to depend on each other for a complete sense of meaning making and self-affirmation. It is in this connection of flow complexity that the pillars of Ubuntu translanguaging, namely: "I × We", *incompletion, interdependence, vertical* and *horizontal* axis create discontinuous continuity, constant disruption of language and literacy boundaries and simultaneous re-creation of new ones. In everyday speech, the journey of multilingual speakers is to cross boundaries of named languages, overlap and disrupt features of one language by constantly drawing from and replacing them with features of other languages without losing focus on the meaning-making process – making sense of the world around them and of who they are. This fluid mobility that is unrestricted by boundaries of named languages is best described as discontinuous continuity within the Ubuntu translanguaging model.

Ubuntu Translanguaging/Multilanguaging Pedagogy

For classroom interactions, translanguaging allows teachers to use this cultural competence of Ubuntu to create opportunities for complex information flow where input and output are exchanged porously for meaning making. Garcia's (2009) notion of dynamic bilingualism is useful for considering alternative models for literacy in schools:

> What is needed today are practices firmly rooted in the multilingual and multimodal language and literacy practices of children in schools of the twenty-first century, practices that would be informed by a vision starting from the sum: an integrated plural vision.
>
> *(Garcia, 2009, p. 8)*

This vision, espoused in Ubuntu, requires pedagogical strategies where more than one language is used for instruction. I have shown elsewhere what the Ubuntu translanguaging pedagogy process is (Makalela, 2014, 2015a, 2015b) and it is repeated in detail below:

Turn and Talk: "I Learn Because You Learn"

Although turn and talk is considered a brain-based learning technique, it is used in Ubuntu Translanguaging Pedagogy (UTP) as a social activity focusing on an Ubuntu principle of inclusive learning, "I learn because you learn". Community or group learning, often found in traditional African societies, allows students to model or demonstrate their learning with the teacher taking the role of a facilitator or enabler. Instead of approaching learning as an individual brain activity, UTP allows for extended opportunities to create groups to solve new problems or reinforce learning. During the group tasks, the instructor facilitates moments for students to listen and answer in a variety of languages understood within the small group. Students who struggle to understand the content taught have this opportunity to learn from peers who may have grasped different parts of the lesson. The instructor will set time limits for the first set of interactions and then allow students to move to the next group ("visitor, come to my 'house'") till a saturation point is reached, which is typically followed by reports to the whole group. The main tenet of "I learn because you learn" is that all possible languages and non-verbal communication cues are used to deepen understanding.

Phonological Awareness Contrasts

Teaching non-cognate languages often creates phonological gaps that can only be detected once both languages are used simultaneously in speaking and listening tasks. The UTP approach is to contrast sound patterns for a selected group of languages. For example, the English vowel system and syllabic structure require explicit attention to phonological awareness because its orthographic system is not transparent. Pronunciation of /s/, for example, in words such as *cat*s, *dog*s and *horse*s, varies significantly, whereas most Bantu languages are highly predictable, with more transparent orthography. Another example is syllabic variation where no one syllable carries a full meaning segment in African languages of Bantu origin, whereas English uses monosyllabic words as a starting point for word comprehension (e.g., *speak*, *like*, *eat*). The idea here is to compare and contrast sound systems in different languages as a basis for further acquisition.

Read-Aloud Contrasts

The rhythm of reading aloud is often found to be influenced by languages that the student is already familiar with. Although the outcome is oral reading proficiency in a specific language, the teacher encourages students to bring samples of reading texts to be read in class so that oral reading fluency from the familiar language/s can be directly transferred or identified as the source of reading challenges in the target language/s. Texts in different languages and pre-recorded readings in these languages can be sourced for use in the classrooms.

Word/Sentence Walls in Different Languages

A UTP teacher would put up words, phrases and sentences on the walls or writing board for students to see the similarities and differences at the same time. Versions in other languages can be developed by the teacher or students after having read texts in the target language/s. This side-by-side approach can be used to teach from words to word order (morphosyntax).

Writing Sections in Different Languages for Scaffolding

At various stages of students' draft written prose, different languages known to the students are leveraged to promote deep thinking over the subject matter. This language mix could be within and between paragraphs or whole texts. The principle here is that students tend to produce a high-quality writing system if their familiar languages are used as resources for meaning making. They do not only develop a voice but also metalinguistic awareness of the different rhetorical structures that they navigate through to produce the final product.

Input and Output Exchange: The Four Macro-Skills

This task is a classical translanguaging view of input and output exchange via different languages. The students read a text in one language and then write about the text in a different language. This, however, assumes that languages other than the medium of learning and teaching have writing systems and that the students have a basic understanding of the written forms. For oral conversations, students receive input in one or more languages and then give a spoken output in different languages and vice-versa.

Multilingual Literacy Corners

Students read stories and are asked to reconstruct the stories in different languages in their own way and in the target language. At the end of this activity, each student will have an opportunity to "own" versions of the same story in different languages. These are published in one selected corner in the classroom for incidental rehearsal in the future.

Reading Walls in Different Languages

Students read texts in a target language and then are asked to re-tell the story in any or a combination of their familiar languages. The classroom walls are used as text reconstruction space where different pieces of the story are pasted in a sequence of the original text.

The UTP approaches described above carry the Ubuntu principle of "I am because you are" and its extended application of "one language is because another is" and "I learn because you learn". While most of the processes explained are found broadly in pedagogical models for best practices worldwide, the UTP brings the human approach based on the real language practices of speakers of Bantu languages and their ways of knowing and being. These processes, used in combination or singly, take away the central role of the teacher and provide a disruptive classroom situation where both the students and teachers go there daily to learn. While the UTP approach has more of a language and literacy focus, it is applicable in other content areas of learning. A plethora of studies conducted on the effectiveness of this pedagogy has shown that this practice improves access to knowledge and affirms students' identities (e.g., Madiba, 2014; Makalela, 2015b, 2017). One of the reasons translanguaging practices succeed in classrooms is that multilingual students are already involved in the process of linguistic exchange despite the fact that their curriculum privileges monolingualism. Garcia makes this salient point explicit:

> Despite curricular arrangements that separate languages, the most prevalent bilingual practice in the bilingual education classrooms is that of translanguaging. Because of the increased recognition of the bilingual continuum that is present in schools and communities that are revitalizing their languages, or schools where more than one language group is present, linguistically integrated group work is prevalent in many bilingual classrooms. Here, students appropriate the use of language, and although teachers may carefully plan when and how languages are to be used, children themselves use their entire linguistic repertoires flexibly. Often this language use appropriation by students is done *surreptitiously*.
>
> *(Garcia, 2009, p. 304, emphasis original)*

One would add that even though some classrooms may police language use and punish children for using more than just the language of learning and teaching, languages co-exist in their phonological loop – a mental lexicon where words and sentences are generated. In other words, translanguaging is a representation of cognitive linguistic fluidity where language repertoires co-exist either before or after speech interactions. Attempts to avoid this cognitive process are not tenable and often prove counterproductive. The cognitive benefits of translanguaging, on the other hand, surpass those of monolingual readers and writers in literacy encounters. Baker (2011) put this in perspective:

> It is possible in a monolingual teaching situation, for students to answer questions or write an essay about a subject without fully understanding it. Processing for meaning may not have occurred. Whole sentences or paragraphs can be copied or adapted out of a textbook, from the internet or from dictation by the teacher without real understanding. It is less easy to do this with "translanguaging". To read and discuss a topic in one language, and then to write about it in another language, means that the subject matter has to be processed and "digested".
>
> *(Baker, 2011, p. 289)*

Research in South Africa on translanguaging in recent years (Madiba, 2014; Makalela, 2013, 2014, 2015a, 2015b) all point to the successful use of translanguaging strategies to improve traditional and academic literacy as well as to dispel myths that African languages are multiple and unintelligible. These studies point out that there are social literacy benefits of involving African languages in English classrooms where parents who become empowered to interact with their children and contribute to knowledge construction. Specific work on grade 4 learners (Makalela 2015b) shows that after bringing the use of an African language, Sepedi, in the English classroom for reading, writing, speaking and listening purposes, learners developed deeper levels of comprehension in both languages. The translanguaging practice then became a routine, which enabled the early readers to have an agency of their learning and parents to be actively involved in their children's education.

Concluding Remarks

In this chapter, I have sought to propose a translanguaging model that is based on the African cultural competence of Ubuntu: *I am because you are; you are because I am* as an alternative heuristic to monolingual bias that accounts for failing trends in the sub-Saharan education systems. I have described dominant monolingual orientations that stem from the Enlightenment period of nation statism to show that these colonial practices of one language at a time in African classrooms are not normative to the sub-Saharan sociocultural milieus. The argument launched is that monolingual bias has resulted in students being disconnected from real words and, by implication, from authentic existence due to linguistic deprivation to mediate epistemic access and identity affirmation: the whole reason they go to school. To disconnect monolingual narratives and ideologies of oneness, it was necessary to look back at the African value system of Ubuntu, which in its plurality mediated best forms of civilization such as Mapungubwe in Southern Africa.

The notion of translanguaging, when connected with Ubuntu, provides a heuristic to develop a theory of interdependent multilingualism. Here, we learn that the Ubuntu pillars of incompletion, interdependence and overlap (vertical and horizontal flow) epitomize the complex multilingual encounters found in many African sociolinguistic spaces. The chapter provides an argument that an alternative system based on the African cultural competence, Ubuntu translanguaging pedagogy, also known as multilanguaging, is a useful framework to guide literacy development for knowledge access. Examples of how multilanguaging works to increase reading performance and positive school experiences from primary and secondary schools confirm the utility of moving beyond monolingual biases in literacy theories to relying on what students know best: translingual competence.

In *multilanguaging*, we discover a plural vision of interdependence of the language systems and their fluid, overlapping and discursive nature to match the everyday ways of communicating where the use of one language is incomplete without the other. Taken together, there is a need for more research to explore various modalities of the multilanguaging framework and the need for a gravitation from monolingual multilingualism to the fluid, porous word view and the logic of "I × We" in multilingual literacy teaching contexts.

Notes

1 Mapungubwe is a historical name of the Limpopo Valley, an area that stretches the surroundings of Limpopo and Sashe rivers in what is today the border of Botswana, Zimbabwe and South Africa.
2 Morabaraba is an indigenous African board game, played originally on engraved stones. It is shared across a wider spectrum of the speakers of indigenous African languages.

References

Alexander, N. (1989). *Language policy and national unity in South Africa/Azania*. Cape Town: Buchu Books.
Alexander, N. (2001). The state of nation building in the New South Africa. *Pretexts: literary and cultural studies*, 10 (1) published online.

Baker, C. (2011). *Foundations of bilingual education and bilingualism* (4th ed.). Clevedon: Multilingual Matters.

Bamgbose . (2000). *Language and exclusion: The consequences of language policies in Africa.* Hamburg: LIT.

Brock-Utne, B. (2000). *Whose education for all? The recolonization of the African mind.* New York, NY: Falmer Press.

Brock-Utne, B. (2015). Language, literacy and democracy in Africa. In L. Makalela (Ed.), *New directions on language and literacy education for multilingual classrooms in Africa* (pp. 15–33). Cape Town, SA: CASAS.

Canagarajah, S. (2011). Codemeshing in academic writing: identifying teachable strategies of translanguaging. *Modern Language Journal,* 95: 401–417.

Carruthers, J. (2006). Mapungubwe: An historical and contemporary analysis of a hybrid heritage cultural landscape. *Koedoe, 49*(1), 1–13.

Creese, A., & Blackledge, A. (2010). Translanguaging in the bilingual classroom: A pedagogy for learning and teaching? *The Modern Language Journal, 94,* 103–115.

Davidson, B. 1992. *The black man's burden: Africa and the curse of the Nation-State.* Oxford: James Currey.

Foucher, P. (1937). *Mapungubwe: Ancient Bantu civilization on the Limpopo.* Cambridge: Cambridge University Press.

Garcia, O. (2009). *Bilingual education in the 21st century: A global perspective.* Malden, MA: Wiley/Blackwell.

Garcia, O. (2011). From language garden to sustainable languaging: Bilingual education in a global world. *Perspectives, 34*(1), 5–9.

Garcia, O., & Li Wei. (2014). *Translanguaging: Language, bilingualism and education.* London: Palgrave Pivot.

Khoza, R. (2013). *Let Africa lead: African transformational leadership for 21st century business.* Johannesburg: Vezubuntu.

King, K. J. (1971). *Pan-Africanism and Education: A Study of Race, philanthropy and education in the southern states of America and East Africa.* Oxford: Clarendon Press.

Madiba, M. (2014). Promoting concept literacy through multilingual glossaries: A translanguaging approach. In C. Van der Walt & L. Hibbert (Eds.), *Multilingual teaching and learning in higher education in South Africa* (pp. 68–87). Clevedon: Multilingual Matters.

Makalela, L. (2005). We speak eleven tongues: Reconstructing multilingualism in South Africa. In B. Brock-Utne & R. Hopson (Eds.), *Languages of instruction for African emancipation: Focus on postcolonial contexts and considerations* (pp. 147–174). Cape Town: CASAS and Mkuki n Nyota.

Makalela, L. (2013). Translanguaging in Kasi-taal: Rethinking old language boundaries for new language planning. *Stellenbosch Papers in Linguistics Plus, 42,* 111–125.

Makalela, L. (2014). Teaching indigenous African languages to speakers of other African languages: The effects of translanguaging for multilingual development. In C. Van der Walt & L. Hibbert (Eds.), *Multilingual teaching and learning in higher education in South Africa* (pp. 88–104). Clevedon: Multilingual Matters.

Makalela, L. (2015a). Moving out of linguistic boxes: The effects of translanguaging for multilingual classrooms. *Language and Education, 29*(3), 200–127.

Makalela, L. (Ed.). (2015b). *New directions in language and literacy education for multilingual classrooms in Africa.* Cape Town: CASAS.

Makalela, L. (2016). Ubuntu translanguaging: An alternative framework for complex multilingual encounters. *Southern African Linguistics and Applied Language Studies, 34*(3), 187–196.

Makalela, L. (2017). Bilingualism in South Africa: Reconnecting with Ubuntu translanguaging. In *Bilingual and Multilingual Education* (pp. 297–309). Springer International Publishing.

Makalela, L. (in press). *From cloning African children to translanguaging: Language, literacy and multilingual return in sub-Saharan Africa.* Dar es Salaam, Tanzania: Nkuki n' Nyota.

Makoni, S. (2003). From misinvention to disinvention of language: Multilingualism and the South African Constitution. In S. Makoni, G. Smithermann, A. Ball, & A. Spears (Eds.), *Black linguistics: Language, society and politics in Africa and the Americas* (pp. 132–149). London: Routledge.

Nkadimeng, S. P., & Makalela, L. (2015). Identity negotiation in a superdiverse community: The fuzzy languaging logic of high school students in Soweto. *International Journal of the Sociology of Language, 234,* 7–26.

Republic of South Africa. (1996). *The Constitution of the Republic of South Africa.* Pretoria. Government Printers.

Republic of South Africa. (1997). *The language in education policy document.* Pretoria: Government Printers.

Ricento, T. (2000). Historical and theoretical perspectives in language policy and planning. *Journal of Sociolinguistics, 4*(2), 196–213.

UNESCO. (2010). *Why and how Africa should invest in African languages and multilingual education: An evidence- and practice-based policy advocacy brief.* Hamburg, Germany: UNESCO Institute for Lifelong Learning.

26

ADVANCING THEORETICAL PERSPECTIVES ON TRANSNATIONALISM IN LITERACY RESEARCH

Allison Skerrett

Monica (pseudonym) was a 17-year-old young woman when I first met her in 2013 on the internationally diverse island of Dutch Sint Maarten, where she was born. Her mother immigrated from Curacao, another Caribbean island, to Sint Maarten, where she met Monica's father, a native-born citizen of Sint Maarten. Monica completed a portion of elementary education in Sint Maarten. Dutch, one of the nation's official languages, is a required curriculum subject. However, English is the dominant lingua franca of the Caribbean—the language in use in everyday social life and in most Sint Maarten schools. Accordingly, Monica was fluent in English and Dutch as well as her mother's native Papiamento.

Monica's father lived a transnational lifestyle to maximize the family's economic opportunities. He lived and worked across Sint Maarten and Connecticut and Florida, in the United States. Monica moved to the United States to live with her father at the age of 9 when he secured long-term employment there, and she attended U.S. schools until the age of 16. She spent summer holidays and other extended school breaks in Sint Maarten with her mother and their extended family and community, with digital literacies keeping kin closely connected across two nation-states for several years.

During the middle of Monica's 11th-grade year in Florida, her father announced that he had taken a new job in Sint Maarten and that the entire family would be moving back to that island. Monica was "pretty mad" about this decision "because I was going in my last year [of high school]." Yet she felt little agency or power to change this decision. "It wasn't really something I could say about it. It was like, 'We are going.' . . . [and] my judgment wasn't really [worth] anything."

Monica experienced significant educational challenges due to this transnational move. One of these setbacks occurred because she arrived into an educational system in the middle of the school year with limited available seats in public schools. Monica was subsequently enrolled in a vocational school designed for students who were not expected to pursue higher education upon graduating. Another very literal setback was that Monica was placed in the equivalent of U.S. ninth grade because she had lost fluency in Dutch, a subject students needed to pass in a school-leaving examination in order to earn a high school diploma.

Monica became increasingly frustrated and discouraged with the unevenness of her academic experience. As she put it: "They pushed me back to ninth grade [because] the Dutch is very hard for me. The other classes are very easy." Monica articulated her emergent theorizing of educational policies and practices that would better account for the educational experiences of transnational students like herself. She proposed that in cases like hers, education officials "should have let it [the language requirement] slide because I am coming back."

At the onset of her second year on Sint Maarten, Monica found her way to a low-cost private school that did not bear the Dutch language requirement. This school offered a curriculum developed by a U.S.-based curriculum provider. Academic content in math, language arts, social studies, and other school subjects reflected the content matter that U.S. students learn. Yet instruction at this school was organized in an individual, self-paced approach with teachers serving as tutors to students as needed. Monica noted that "it is really hard when you are focusing by yourself" and that the curriculum lacked challenge; it was "pretty much the same" as what she had experienced at the vocational school.

Moreover, the family increasingly suffered from the economic strain of paying for secondary education, requiring Monica to start working, which negatively affected her school attendance. These circumstances led to Monica progressively dropping out of school, a process that was complete by January 2015. It would be another year, under the counseling and promises of financial support from family and friends, that Monica agreed to pursue the high school General Equivalency Diploma that she eventually earned.

Transnationalism refers to the phenomenon wherein people, through a mix of necessity and choice, live their lives across two or more countries. This lifestyle generates cross-national familial, social, educational, cultural, economic, sociopolitical, and other networks, with their associated benefits and challenges (DeJaeghere & Vu, 2015; Levitt, 2001; Skerrett, 2015; Vertovec, 2009). This chapter first unpacks and expands upon key analytic concepts employed across diverse academic disciplines concerned with transnationalism and illuminates these concepts' as-yet-unrealized potential for the field of literacy. These theoretical concepts include sending and receiving nations, cross-border flows, and hybridity (DeJaeghere & Vu, 2015; Levitt, 2001; Skerrett, 2015; Smith & Guarnizo, 1998; Vertovec, 2009).

The chapter then explores two areas in literacy research that can be more thoroughly examined through theoretical perspectives that include these analytic concepts associated with transnationalism: literacy education in K-12 schools and transnational educational policy making and practices. This focus on formal schooling directly implicates the role of nation-states and their educational institutions and agents in the experiences and outcomes of school-age transnational people, as vividly illustrated in Monica's vignette above, and as theorized in other scholarship and research on transnationalism (Appadurai, 2013; Skerrett, 2015, 2018; Skerrett & Bomer, 2013; Stornaiuolo, Smith, & Phillips, 2017).

Key Theoretical Concepts Within Transnationalism

Transnationalism has a relatively short, though potent, presence in literacy research. Transnationalism and its theoretical concepts and perspectives developed across fields such as anthropology, sociology, and political science; migration, ethnic, and diaspora studies; and comparative and international development education (CIDE) (DeJaeghere & Vu, 2015). The expansive study of transnational phenomena across diverse fields has led to multiple theoretical perspectives and a plethora of analytic concepts—as well as varied definitions, understandings, and applications of them across studies of transnationalism (DeJaeghere & Vu, 2015). Yet, the concepts of sending and receiving nations, cross-border flows, and hybridity have maintained high currency in studies of transnationalism.

Sending and Receiving Nations

Transnationalism involves two or more nation-states, with the transnational person's place of origin called the sending nation. Living across sending and receiving nations gives rise to cross-national networks; flows of people, ideas, and resources; and the generation of transnational identities and competencies (DeJaeghere & Vu, 2015). These understandings about sending and receiving nations hold for literacy research as well—see, for example, Lam and Warriner's (2012) comprehensive review of the mobilities of people and their literacies. All studies of transnationalism implicitly or explicitly invoke the constructs of sending and receiving nations. However, the extent to which one or more nation-states is given consideration, and the construction of nation-states as active or passive entities in transnationalism, affects the nature of research knowledge that is produced.

A diminished focus on nation-states or constructions of nation-states as passive entities is often found in studies of the transnational individual or community and their processes of generating and sustaining transnational identities and practices, including social relations across borders. In literacy research, such studies often delve into people's uses, development, and transformation of their language, literacy, and cultural practices to effectively navigate and optimize transnational life (e.g., Lam & Rosario-Ramos, 2009; Skerrett, 2012). For example, in a study of a Mexican American transnational youth (Skerrett, 2012), I examined how a young woman negotiated with different languages and literacy practices as she participated across life in Mexico and the United States over a three-year period. Vanesa (pseudonym) and her family's transnational arrangement was that Vanesa, her two siblings, and mother resided in the United States while her father lived in Mexico to maintain a small but productive family business. Vanesa's father made periodic extended trips to the United States to be with the family, and Vanesa, her siblings, and her mother would also spend extended time, such as summers and Christmas breaks, at their home in Mexico.

In that analysis, I focused on how Vanesa experienced shifts in her language and literacy practices as she participated in increasingly diverse social settings, including school. Vanesa described how her U.S. middle school was filled with "very White people" (Skerrett, 2012, p. 382), and so when she entered a high school serving primarily Latina/o and African American students, she noted distinctions among English language varieties,

> [The high school has] like different people and stuff and they speak like another language. Well, not another language but a slang language, and I didn't know those words. And like, well, people in my other school, like White kids and stuff, they didn't speak like that.
> *(Skerrett, 2012, pp. 382–383)*

Vanesa also noted that being tracked into English as a second language (ESL) classes limited her friendships with other dominant-Spanish-speaking youths. Gaining greater fluency in English as well as entering mainstream classes created new social relations with linguistically diverse students: "And then I started talking English, and I have a lot of friends." Friendships with Mexican American students generated Spanish-English code-switching language practices for Vanesa; her affinity for hip-hop music and dance styles grew at this school, where this music was the most popular genre. Acquiring affinity for hip-hop music and dance encouraged another shift in Vanesa's language practices. She began to appreciate, understand, and learn to use African American English as she participated in the social worlds of her high school, including the school's dance team. Vanesa expressed pride as she told me she had been selected for a coveted role as one of three performers in the only hip-hop dance routine of one of the school's theater arts shows. The overall analysis thus indicated a trend of Vanesa shifting her language and literacy practices and values toward those of the dominant social and official literacy worlds she inhabited in the United States.

While this analysis illuminated the social processes of a transnational youth's language and literacy shifts, I undertook a more limited analysis pertinent to the role of the nation-state in Vanesa's language and literacy shifts. Analyzing these shifts in consideration of the role of nation-states would have allowed me to highlight and critique institutional practices sanctioned by the nation-state, such as the total segregation of newcomer students from the broader school population according to determinations about their prowess with the language of power. I would have explored more deeply whether and to what extent Vanesa felt able to maintain strong values and practices relative to the languages, literacies, and cultural practices associated with her Mexican background as she pursued broader acceptance and status in the official and unofficial social worlds of U.S. schools. Furthermore, I would have dwelled more deeply on how a literacy curriculum could be designed for transnational and other linguistically diverse students to equip them to be more conscious, questioning, and intentional with language as they understood their language practices in relation to national linguistic ideologies and systems of power.

Yet one aspect of this analysis (Skerrett, 2012) represented an emergent focus on the role of the nation-state in Vanesa's experience of transnational life. Because the intent of the analysis was to explore Vanesa's experiences of transnationalism, including its intersections with her language, literacy, and cultural practices both in and out of school, I examined a piece of writing that Vanesa produced in her literacy class. The purpose of examining this text was part of the analysis's overall effort to understand the processes through which transnational youths develop their varied perspectives on transnational life. Vanesa's text, entitled "Dad & Me," was a story about a time when she very sick in the United States while her father was in Mexico. I discovered through analyzing this text that Vanesa employed an academic literacy practice, written composition in school, to generate economic and sociopolitical perspectives on transnationalism.

For example, in "Dad & Me," Vanesa theorized that when families undertake border crossings, they continuously weigh the economic benefits of transnational life against its significant emotional costs. "The fact that my dad is not with us . . . it's hard for me but I know he is making a sacrifice for me, for us to be better persons and to be prepare[d] for the future" (Skerrett, 2012, p. 378). Vanesa further produced a sociopolitical perspective on transnational people's agency in crossing borders if not always physically, then emotionally and spiritually, including as facilitated by digital literacies. The turning point of Vanesa's story is a phone conversation with her father that greatly lifts her emotional and physical well-being.

Reexamination of this study begins to illuminate what is missed or underemphasized with the extraction or dilution of the role of the nation-state in studies of transnational people. Attention to the role of the nation-state in this reanalysis presented above illuminates how hegemonic hierarchies of cultural and linguistic practices, values, and beliefs among nations, their institutions, and citizens impact the language and literacy practices, identities, and beliefs that individuals generate in transnational life (Appadurai, 2013; Blommaert, 2010; Skerrett, 2018). Accordingly, future literacy research on transnationalism can attempt to situate the activities and outcomes of transnational individuals and communities within the sociopolitical, cultural, economic, and ideological relationships, beliefs, values, and activities of their different nation-states.

Reformulations of Sending and Receiving Nations

Although each nation-state is its own entity, the distinction between sending and receiving nations is being challenged in reformulations of transnational theoretical perspectives. Based on their review of studies of transnationalism across diverse disciplines, DeJaeghere and Vu (2015) spoke of a generally accepted understanding of a "metaphorical overlap between sending and receiving nation-states" (p. 271) that is anchored in active social, cultural, economic, and other ties and maintenance activities. Transnational processes occur in this middle space—they are anchored in and span two or more nation-states (Faist, 2000, qtd. in DeJaeghere & Vu, 2015), and transnational theories refuse the idea of essentialized national borders (DeJaeghere & Vu, 2015). The activities within the overlapping space align with the concept of transnationalism from below (Smith & Guarnizo, 1998).

Transnationalism from below (Smith & Guarnizo, 1998) emphasizes the activities of transnational individuals and communities to achieve their aspirations of transnational living. Attaining their goals requires transnational people to make sense of, and respond to, their nation-states' relations with and perspectives on one another. Literacy studies working within the middle space examine the language and literacy practices people employ or generate to develop and maintain transnational identities, remain connected to their communities of origin, and achieve their goals in their receiving nations while supporting (e.g., with remittances) those left behind in the sending nation (see Lam & Warriner's 2012 review). In studies of this nature, the focal geography necessarily leans toward people's practices within their receiving nation, thus emphasizing ideas of physical and political borders that separate nations and peoples.

Yet scholars of transnationalism and globalization express concern that positioning individual and community processes within this overlapping space does not adequately highlight the role and influences of nation-states on these "middle space" processes and activities (Appadurai, 2013; Skerrett, 2018; Stornaiuolo et al., 2017). Clearer articulation of the workings of the nation-state in transnational phenomena signals another important concept, transnationalism from above (Smith, 1994; Smith & Guarnizo, 1998). Transnationalism from above addresses nation-states in relation to one another—for example, transnational comparisons of economic, educational, technological, and other resources between and among nations, and global practices and policy making in these areas.

I conducted a recent analysis that examined the role of nation-states in the development of music literacy practices and perspectives of a Caribbean-U.S. transnational youth (Skerrett, 2018). Cameron (pseudonym) was born on French Saint Martin into a musical and transnational family. He attended schools in Saint Martin until the age of 16, all of which offered music education as an official curriculum subject. His family augmented these curriculum offerings with outside-school voice and instrument training for him. Cameron developed into a talented and well-known musician on the island who performed frequently at high-profile social events as well as in more intimate settings like church and family events. Cameron's transnational family extended into New York City, and several of these kin were also theater arts performers. With frequent and extended stays in New York City, Cameron noted that the broader social context of New York held more expansive social opportunities and technological and media infrastructures to build and showcase his talents, thus priming him for a flourishing musical future. For Cameron, the music world of New York City "was much bigger than what I saw here in St. Martin. What I was seeing when I did travel to New York . . . I felt it was open hands to, you know, bigger opportunities . . . a bigger way to showcase [my talents]" (Skerrett, 2018, p. 42).

Thus Cameron presented his thinking in ways that indicated his cognizance of how unequal distributions of technologies of literacies across world nations (Appadurai, 2013) affected the quality of literacies one could develop, depending on the national geography in which one lived. Reporting on a visit to a performing arts high school, Cameron compared the Saint Martin schools he had attended with this school, explaining: "It [the New York school] was more organized in the States than it was in St. Martin. The classes were more built for like music. They had the stands, the risers, and the classes, the levels for the different singing parts" (Skerrett, 2018, p. 43). Thus Cameron convinced his parents to allow him to complete his secondary education at this performing arts high school in New York.

Yet at this school, global ideologies of the cultures that were of most worth (Appadurai, 2013) resulted in a form of music education that was dominated by American and Eurocentric musical forms, with no emphasis on Caribbean or other musical cultural forms. Analyzing these data with a dedicated interest in the role the nation-state and its institutions played in Cameron's development of particular competencies and preferences in music literacies, I found that not just schools, but media and other institutions of the United States were important actors in his development of musical practices and views of a particular nature. Cameron's musical practices and preferences developed in ways that represented a greater privileging of Ameri-Eurocentric musical forms than those of his original culture or other world nations' performance styles.

Cross-Border Flows

Cameron's music education in a U.S. educational institution did not encourage pathways wherein musical cultures of different nations could enter and be engaged with by students and teachers. Nonetheless, cross-border flows is another analytic concept that is germane to transnational theories and naturally linked to the concepts of sending and receiving nations. Transnational people can activate and participate in flows with or without engaging in physical movements of their bodies, for example by moving capital and ideas through the technological, financial, and other global infrastructures of their nation-states. Flows also occur within nations as transnational people create and connect to communities who share in their national or ethnic origins or who share the experience of being transnational. These within-nation flows and the networks they create also facilitate cross-national flows, as described in the section above about sending and receiving nations.

As with the concept of sending and receiving nations, retheorizations of transnational viewpoints jointly consider the roles and activities of the transnational individual or community *and* the nation-state in cross-border flows. Scholars of globalization and transnationalism express concerns that the processes by which nation-states and their institutions may be transformed by the cultural, linguistic, and literacy practices of their transnational citizens remain largely invisible in studies that do not spotlight and critically examine the actor and activities of the nation-state (Appadurai, 2013; Skerrett, 2018).

Literacy research has employed the concept of cross-border flows to illuminate how transnational individuals and communities maintain or adapt their cultural ways of being and their language and literacy practices after crossing into new nation-states; how they create and maintain social networks and pathways to facilitate flows of knowledge and capital across borders; and how they develop robust communities within the receiving nation filled with resources for successfully navigating transnational life (see Lam and Warriner's 2012 review). Such studies convey implicit or generalized understandings that transnational individual and community cross-border flows are occurring within the larger construct of nation-states but do not deeply examine the nature and outcome of those interactions.

Globalization theorist Appadurai (1996) originally conceptualized global cultural flows characterized by disjunctures between economics, culture, and politics. His work speaks to the interconnections, interrelationships, and political positionality of different actors, including the nation-state, diasporic communities (communities of people who share a historical racial/ethnocultural background), religious subgroups, bounded neighborhoods, and individual actors. Paying closer attention to the circulation of cultural flows, Appadurai (2013) theorized that certain forms of culture that do not have well-established global circulatory pathways experience "bumps and blocks" (p. 68) as they seek to create new circulatory pathways amidst existing networks. This creates a dual structure in which new and established cultural forms do not mutually transform one another but instead "are forced to co-exist in uneven and uneasy combinations" (Appadurai, 2013, p. 67). Nations and their institutions, as powerful cultural agents in a globalized world of flows, may not be as accommodating of unfamiliar cultural forms being introduced to them by their transnational citizens. Thus, it is the "incessant effort" of human imagination and agency to produce a transformed local culture (Appadurai, 2013, p. 68).

Often, literacy research has examined how transnational individuals or communities of diverse people share in, create, and adapt cultural practices in physical and virtual transnational communities (e.g., see Alim, 2011 for an extensive review of hip-hop as a global literacy practice). Yet the type of cultural flows explored by Alim (2011) and others fits within the category of transnationalism from below (Smith & Guarnizo, 1998), with little attention to how cultures enter or are allowed to flow into and transform the nation-state and its institutions. For example, upon noticing the predominantly U.S.- and Eurocentric practices that Cameron was learning in his U.S. school, I interviewed his U.S. music teacher about whether she or Cameron attempted to bring in musical styles from the Caribbean or other geographies (Skerrett, 2018). Her response was no, that she had selected and was focusing primarily on the show choir genre, and that since Cameron was so talented, she directed his artistry into a musical genre that she, as an educational agent of the nation-state (Appadurai, 2013), had selected as the official curriculum. Literacy research must move in a direction that affords more precise understandings of flows as they relate to institutions such as schools, because such sites of power are the nexus at which mutual transformation of the individual's and the nation-state's cultural identities, beliefs, values, and practices occur (Appadurai, 2013; Skerrett, 2018).

Blommaert's (2010) theoretical and empirical work stands as an example of the kind of knowledge transnational theory can generate in literacy research if joint consideration is given to cultural flows that involve individuals and communities as well as the nation-state. Blommaert's work in the field of language and literacy considers the interrelations between linguistic practices in transnational communities and in formal institutions of the nation-state. Blommaert accounted for the mobility and significance of the sociolinguistic resources of transnational individuals and communities within this world of flows. An emphasis on linguistic repertoires rather than "language" allowed Blommaert (2010) to display the range of semiotic resources available for making meaning: "concrete accents, language varieties, registers, modalities such as writing . . . and language ideologies" (p. 102). Blommaert presented a theory of sociolinguistics of mobility that "focuses not on language-in-place but language-in-motion" (p. 5) and vertically organized sociolinguistic "scales" in which concrete linguistic resources are deployed in sociocultural, historical, and political contexts. Issues of linguistic power and inequality across different contexts through which language is deployed are at the center of Blommaert's work.

Access to scales involves issues of power and inequality, given that different language practices are organized hierarchically in terms of their sophistication and value across nonsituational scales. "Scales [involve] a sophisticated standard language variety or advanced multimodal or multilingual literacy skills" (Blommaert, 2010, p. 5). Each horizontal space, such as a neighborhood, region, or country, is also a vertical space in which scales operate to index language and literacy differences along the scalar "patterns of social, cultural, and political value-attribution" (p. 5), what Blommaert (2010) called "orders of indexicality" (p. 21). Using the idea of "superdiversity," Blommaert described neighborhoods where people possess and deploy densely diverse linguistic resources through individual and collaborative work. Blommaert (2010) illuminated these elements at work in a diverse Belgian neighborhood. In this Dutch context, particular African languages maintained currency within the home and particular kin and social relations. However, these African languages, mixed with varieties of English and Dutch, allowed speakers to access higher scales and interactions with others beyond their intimate communities and achieve broader social and economic goals (such as purchasing goods and traveling across space). Moreover, the African languages offered far less mobility for their speakers than standard Dutch or English across scale levels and situations at the top rungs, such as interactions with schools.

Very new work in literacy research is beginning to explore flows of transnational literacies and other practices with a framing of nation-states as active cultural and political actors in these processes. Such studies are intentionally conceptually framed within a global landscape of increasing—and increasingly policed—borders. For example, the intersections among and impacts of local, global, and national policies on the mobility of people's literacy practices, or their transliteracies, are central ideas in Stornaiuolo et al.'s (2017) work. These researchers called for greater theoretical and methodological attention to the ideological and sociopolitical factors that enable or constrain youths' multiliteracy practices within and across different social contexts, including spaces governed by the nation-state such as schools. They described the present times as representing the "paradox of mobility [that] invites close analysis of how people's literacy practices can be differentially valued and recognized, in turn reproducing, exacerbating, or challenging existing social inequities" (Stornaiuolo et al., 2017, p. 70).

Cross-Border Flows Across Virtual and Physical Geographies

Within Stornaiuolo et al.'s (2017) and other studies of cross-border flows lies a key observation of how research on transnational literacies often represents a split between an emphasis on virtual worlds and an emphasis on physical geographies (Leander, Phillips, & Taylor, 2010). For example, literacy researchers have conceptualized virtual spaces as ones in which transnationalism is experienced and transnational literacies and identities are developed, employed, and displayed. Findings include how online worlds enable transnational youths to develop valuable social, cultural, and linguistic and literacy capital, such as strong writing skills; build their original languages while developing new ones; and access transnational communities and identities while maintaining local connections (Black, 2009; Lam & Rosario-Ramos, 2009; McLean, 2010). For the youths in these studies, little attention is paid to physical flows of their bodies across nations and flows of their literacy activities within and across nations. Yet research that attends jointly to physical and virtual border crossing and language and literacy practices within and across the physical worlds of different nations would raise important questions about the role of the nation-state, for example, how policing of transborder movements contributes to how some people enact transnational lives and literacies. Without bringing explicit attention to the influence of nation-states in transnational people's negotiation of their literacies in virtual worlds, especially when the youths of interest are physically anchored in just one nation, research risks celebrating particular processes of transnational literacy development while veiling understandings of the sociopolitics undergirding them.

Some literacy studies do investigate how transnational youths' physical—though not in conjunction with virtual—movements across space and place shape their learning (Sánchez, 2009). Sánchez (2009) inquired into how the adolescent children in working-class Mexican American transnational families experienced and negotiated various positions of capital advantage and disadvantage between themselves and their Mexican counterparts within and across the social fields of their families' Mexican communities of origin and their U.S. worlds. Within their Mexican communities, the U.S.-born transnational adolescents were positioned more favorably than those born in Mexico due to their political capital of U.S. citizenship and economic resources. However, within this same social field, the U.S.-born youths occupied positions of cultural and linguistic disadvantage in comparison to their Mexican family members and community, who were more knowledgeable of Mexican culture and the Spanish language. Sánchez (2009) concluded that the transnational youths developed valuable intercultural knowledge, multilingual skills, and cosmopolitan identities and worldviews that allowed them to understand and negotiate these political, linguistic, cultural, and economic differences and connections between themselves and their Mexican associates.

Overall, literacy scholars possess strong understandings of how virtual spaces facilitate transnational youths' learning, and the knowledge base on how physical sojourning across transnational geographies affects transnational people's literacy learning is slowly growing. Yet little is known about the interrelations among virtual and physical spaces across which transnational people continuously move (or wish to move) and how those mobilities affect their learning processes, including their development of transnational literacies (Leander et al., 2010). This agenda is an important one to take up in literacy research. Enhanced understandings and applications of the construct of cross-border flows would be helpful in crafting such research inquiries.

My analysis of transnational youth Cameron's literacy learning across borders illuminated how physical mobility and sojourning were directly implicated in the nature of his perspectives on music literacies and his music literacy development (Skerrett, 2018). In my broader analysis of Cameron's case, I also paid analytic attention to the role of virtual worlds in the music literacy learning processes, identities, and practices, although the role of virtual worlds in Cameron's development of transnational music literacy practices and perspectives was not included in the published analysis. However, my broader analysis revealed that virtual worlds and digital literacies played a significant role in Cameron sustaining a transnational musician literacy identity and associated practices, even though his school experience did not create space for doing so.

For example, Cameron owned an active Facebook page filled with a compilation of musical genres and performance styles that represented his simultaneous situatedness in the physical musical worlds and practices of New York, French Saint Martin, and Dutch Sint Maarten. Thus, virtual worlds and digital literacies presented greater agency and opportunities for Cameron to develop and consequently participate in a transnational musical space. This space was one in which

Cameron could bring together his U.S. musical practices and peers as well as his music and broader social community from Sint Maarten, Saint Maarten, and other parts of the world. Considering jointly Cameron's physical as well as virtual music literacy life created a more complete view of Cameron as a transnational learner and user of cross-national and cross-cultural music literacies. This example of Cameron's case illustrates the need for and value of pursuing literacy research that examines conjunctively the roles of virtual and physical worlds in the development of transnational literacies and identities.

Hybridity

As illustrated above, Cameron's virtual musical world allowed him to maintain a more representative display of his transnational music identity, literacies, and preferences that spanned national cultures and included his musical activities in physical geographies of different nation-states. This coexistence or blending of different musical performance cultures, or other language and literacy practices, is often described in literacy research with the term *hybridity* (Alim, 2011; Lam & Warriner, 2012; Skerrett, 2015). Literacy scholars have indicated, through their theoretical framings and analysis of data, that hybridity manifests in how transnational people draw upon multiple cultures and cultural forms, world knowledges and experiences, and semiotic tools (such as language, visual images, and gestures) that reflect those of the nations to which they have ties to engage with literacy activities or produce literacy artifacts. This conception of hybridity is useful for framing transnational living and transnational people in appreciative, agentive, and innovative ways, and illuminating essential competencies that are useful for all people, notwithstanding their transnational status, in an increasingly globalized world.

Although the term *hybridity* is an essential concept in transnational theory, it is rarely defined and thoroughly analyzed (Appadurai, 2013; DeJaeghere & Vu, 2015). Implicit in the uses of the term *hybridity* across literacy research and other fields are notions of generativity, innovation, integration, admixtures, multiplicity, change, and transformation. Yet hybrid identities and language and literacy practices do not emerge or occur only through social interactions and activities at the level of transnationalism from below (Smith & Guarnizo, 1998)—meaning through the interactions among individuals and communities that are rich with diverse repertoires. Hybridity must be understood as occurring through individual, social, and sociopolitical processes that involve the nation-state and its institutions, and dominant ideologies at work about the nations and associated language, cultural, and literacy practices that are of most worth (Appadurai, 2013; DeJaeghere & Vu, 2015; Skerrett, 2018; Stornaiuolo et al., 2017). My discussions of research findings related to transnational youths such as Monica, Vanesa, and Cameron (Skerrett, 2012, 2015, 2018, respectively) all illustrate how the development of hybrid identities and language and literacy practices are influenced both by the individual and her or his local communities as well as the nation-states to which they belong.

Appadurai (2013) made careful distinctions in how the term *hybridity* is understood and applied. He called on scholars "to move decisively beyond existing models of . . . hybridity . . . and the like which have largely been about mixture at the level of content" (p. 67). He proposed an enhanced agenda in which scholars probe into the cohabitation of forms, such as the genre of material culture itself and the nation, as it is at this nexus that mutual transformation occurs. Examples of material culture include language, literacy, and cultural knowledge and practices with their associated artifacts, such as particular performance genres, and the values assigned to them. Thus hybridity, in keeping with Appadurai's (2013) thinking, can be understood in two ways. One definition refers to evidence of a commingling of different cultural, linguistic, and other practices and knowledge culled from different national contexts within a particular cultural form. This is the most common framing of hybridity in current literacy research, as seen, for example, in expansive literature reviews of the globalized or transnational language and literacy practices of transnational peoples (Alim, 2011; Lam & Warriner, 2012).

An alternative understanding of hybridity, less easily achieved but highly significant, is the emergence of a cultural form that represents a *reconstitution* of knowledge, relationships, practices, values, and the like among nations and their people who share in a given cultural form. Applications of these clear, and in the second case, more complex, definitions of hybridity in literacy research can lead to more sophisticated knowledge and understandings about the identities, knowledge, and practices that transnational people develop in relationship to the activities and influences of their nation-states. Returning to the case of Cameron (Skerrett, 2018) illuminates Appadurai's meaning of a hybridity that represents reconstitutions of both nation-states' and people's knowledge, relationships, practices, and values.

After completing his first year at the performing arts high school in New York, Cameron experienced a politically enforced yearlong sojourn on Saint Martin and Sint Maarten. This was due to problems with his immigration paperwork that resulted in the United States refusing him reentry to the country after a summer stay on the islands. This incidence allowed deep exploration of the ways in which nations, their institutions and agents, and a transnational citizenry may engage in mutual transformation of knowledge, values, beliefs, and cultural practices (Appadurai, 2013). Analyzing Cameron's interview data, I observed his initial deep despair about having to remain indefinitely in the Caribbean: "Do I really have to be back *here*?" Yet, as a resilient youth who also continued to view New York as "my destiny," Cameron reframed this event as a "setback" and encouraged himself to "be patient. The world is not over and good things come to those who wait."

Nevertheless, upon enrolling in a high school on Dutch Sint Maarten without a music performing arts program, Cameron became unhappy with the curriculum, and he advocated for beginning such a program at the school and offered to teach it himself. Hybridity at the level of reconstitution of relationships, values, and practices among the individual and the nation-state, including its institutions (Appadurai, 2013), manifested with the school administration providing generous support for Cameron, such as time and space on the official curriculum, to implement this music program. Furthermore, Cameron shaped the high school performing arts program, as well as influenced the existing elementary program, by incorporating into them the musical style of show choir that he learned in New York.

However, this was a transformed version of the show choir Cameron had learned; this new cultural form was not solely a blending of show choir elements and musical culture of the Caribbean, which would reflect hybridity at the level of content (Appadurai, 2013). Cameron instead reconstituted the show choir performance genre to accommodate the language practices, local and global cultural knowledge, and musical literacy competencies that his student-peers possessed while also insisting that his peers acquire competency in the core features of show choir. This analysis stands as an example of the kind of theorizing in literacy research that can generate more complex knowledge about the processes of mutual transformation of the identities, values, beliefs, and cultural practices of nation-states and their institutions in relationship to those of their transnational peoples.

Theoretical Perspectives on Transnationalism for Literacy Education in Schools

The description above of how a transnational student-citizen and educational agents worked together to reconstitute the school curriculum in ways that enhanced student learning as well as the curriculum indicates the importance of theorizing what transnationalism can mean for literacy education in schools. As the discussions above have been indicating, much of what is known in the field of literacy about the nature of the identities and cultural, linguistic, and literacy practices generated and deployed by transnational people has been produced from research in contexts outside of school (Lam & Warriner, 2012; Skerrett, 2015). Indeed, the literature on the sociopolitical circumstances (including educational needs) of transnational students lives primarily in the fields of sociology and CIDE (DeJaeghere & Vu, 2015). A United Nations Department of Economic and Social Affairs policy brief (2016) reported that as of 2013, 28.2 million migrants worldwide are between the ages of 15 and 24, and ongoing data collection by UNICEF (2017) reveals that as of 2015, 31 million children worldwide are migrants. These numbers represent a substantial demographic of school-age youths.

In an era when world nations are populated by the greatest numbers of transnational youths that they ever have been (Hamann & Zúñiga, 2011; Soong, 2016; UNICEF, 2017; United Nations Department of Economic and Social Affairs, 2016), it is critical that literacy research take up the agenda of how formal literacy education in school can be enhanced for transnational youths and all students. In calling for greater attention to the literacy education of transnational youths who populate many classrooms today, this chapter suggests a direction for literacy research that merges the personal and social lives of transnational individuals and communities and the institutions and activities of the nation-state. Application of the theoretical concepts related to transnationalism treated in this chapter can bridge the knowledge base on transnational youths' language and literacy practices, developed largely in outside-school contexts, with the formal processes of literacy instruction and learning in schools (Skerrett, 2015).

A few literacy studies do bring transnational students' literacies into relationship with the institution of school. For example, Jiménez, Smith, and Teague (2009) studied the transnational literacies within a particular community and conceptualized how teachers could draw upon that knowledge to promote transnational students' learning. My colleague and I (Skerrett & Bomer, 2013) worked closely for a year and a half with a reading teacher in the United States as she implemented a reading curriculum that we collaboratively made increasingly responsive to the multicultural, multilingual, and multiliterate students she taught, some of whom led transnational lives. Our study illustrated, in part, how this teacher's literacy instruction facilitated transnational students' drawing upon their transnational repertoires for interpreting and composing multilingual and multimodal academic texts that contained transnational themes. In my longitudinal work on transnationalism and literacy education, I have spoken and spent time with transnational youths and their teachers whose lives span the United States, Canada, the Caribbean, Mexico, and Asia. I have interviewed students extensively about their educational experiences in schools across nations. I have interviewed teachers of these students as well, and analyzed the curriculum they have designed or have been assigned to work with diverse populations that include transnational students (e.g., Skerrett, 2015, 2016).

The sum of these research experiences and the insights I have gleaned from these students and educators have allowed me to generate a theoretical perspective on transnationalism that I call a transnationally inclusive approach to literacy education (Skerrett, 2015, 2016). Transnationally inclusive literacy education principles extend existing conceptual models for promoting teaching and learning in diverse classrooms to make them intentionally inclusive of transnational students. For example, Ball's (2009) theory of generativity addresses teachers in classrooms that serve students from two or more cultural and linguistic groups. The theory begins with a stance and set of practices that require teachers to learn with and from their students about their own and their communities' resources and conceptualize how that knowledge can be used for curriculum planning and pedagogical problem solving. Transnationally inclusive literacy education principles theorizes how teachers can identify and learn about transnational students who compose part of the diversity of classrooms and incorporate that knowledge into curricular planning and instruction. Likewise, the New London Group's (1996) theory of a pedagogy of multiliteracies outlines a process through which teachers can create curricular and pedagogical bridges between the multiple language and literacy skills students develop in outside-school contexts and academic literacies. Transnationally inclusive literacy education principles explicitly conceptualize how teachers can create curriculum and instructional bridges between the transnational language and literacy practices, spanning multiple national settings in school and outside-school contexts, in which transnational youths engage.

Transnationally inclusive literacy education principles (Skerrett, 2015) include three dimensions. The first dimension entails teachers actively inquiring with their students into students' social, cultural, and educational experiences in one or more countries, and students' language and literacy practices spanning local and transnational contexts. These inquiries are student-led, requiring students' self-reflection; research into their families' and communities' resources; and production, sharing, and critical analysis of the knowledge they produce with their classroom community.

The second dimension of transnationally inclusive literacy education entails teachers using the knowledge acquired about students to guide their design of curriculum and instructional methods that uniquely respond to students' educational and social histories, academic strengths, and learning needs. In enacting dimension two, teachers' curriculum and pedagogical practices consistently emphasize reading, writing, and critical thinking skills to enable all students, including transnational students, to strengthen skills that are useful in global educational and social contexts.

Reading and writing instruction and learning tasks encourage students to draw upon their multicultural, multilingual, and multiliterate competencies, as well as their world knowledge and perspectives in the learning process. Critical inquiry into issues of social injustice affecting their local communities and world nations is also a key component of the literacy curriculum. So is fostering students' metacognitive awareness of how the literacy skills and competencies they are developing are important for all educational contexts and all areas of life. Accordingly, a transnationally inclusive approach to literacy education can assist *all* students in developing identities as globally literate citizens who read, write, and consider significant problems across local and global geographies.

The third dimension of transnationally inclusive literacy education calls for teachers and students to document and share students' academic development and ongoing educational needs with other educational partners. This dimension is especially critical for transnational students because it enables teachers in different countries, and across schools in a particular nation, to gain deeper understandings of the learning experiences their transnational students have had and the areas in which they need specific supports. A transnationally inclusive approach to literacy education necessitates building transnational professional networks among teachers who share in the academic development of particular transnational students. This dimension of building knowledge-sharing networks puts students and families in leadership positions alongside teachers in fostering the development of these professional networks and facilitating students' ongoing education, even when a transnational move results in interrupted schooling. For example, armed with an academic plan and learning resources for staying on course with literacy development (Skerrett, 2015), students will keep learning in any transnational locale and reenter schools feeling more confident in their identities and strengths as literacy learners. This third dimension of supporting transnational students' education across nations will be taken up more fully in the following section, which applies the theoretical perspective of a transnationally inclusive approach to policy making and practices relative to transnational students.

Teachers who take a transnationally inclusive approach to literacy education will provide greater opportunities for their transnational students to achieve academic success. However, *all* students, notwithstanding their transnational status, who engage with this instructional approach can become stronger readers, writers, and critical thinkers, who possess social justice stances of a global character. Teachers and students who undertake a transnationally inclusive approach to literacy education will acquire specialized knowledge, dispositions, and capacities for participating effectively in a globalized world. These include:

- Understandings and appreciation of how transnational students and their repertoires compose part of the diverse and valuable resources for teaching and learning available in classrooms;
- Greater knowledge and capabilities pertaining to using and strengthening languages, literacies, and sociocultural knowledge to participate productively in and across transnational literacy contexts, including schools;

- A more comprehensive knowledge base related to the educational, cultural, political, and other aspects of different nations, or particular regions within them, to which transnational students have ties; and
- Identities of global citizenship that include expertise and capacities to identify, care about, critically analyze, and develop potential solutions to social justice concerns of all people and all nations.

Literacy research must acknowledge the very real learning opportunities and challenges within formal schooling for transnational youths. Literacy research can make stronger theoretical and instructional knowledge contributions about transnational students' literacy learning processes by attending to their learning in school. Literacy theorizing can apply and expand upon literacy learning process theories such as a transnationally inclusive approach to literacy education, as well as innovate new theories, to study the literacy learning processes of transnational youths and teachers in classrooms (for teachers, too, will be learning while teaching). Nation-states have no romantic notions about border-crossing people and their literacies (Appadurai, 2013; Stornaiuolo et al., 2017). Cases like Monica's, which began this chapter, make this point abundantly clear. Thus, the field of literacy needs to respond with seriousness and vigor to develop knowledge that will positively impact the educational experiences and outcomes of transnational youths in institutions of the nation-state.

Advancing Transnational Theories of Literacy Education Into Policy and Practice

Schools function as agents of socialization for students into the beliefs, practices, values, and identities of the nation-state (Lesko, 2012; Tyack & Tobin, 1994). Thus, theories such as a transnationally inclusive approach to literacy education (Skerrett, 2015) are not necessarily conducive to nation-states' perspectives on, and goals for, their transnational peoples. The literacy learning processes and relational ties activated by undertaking any form of transborder literacy pedagogy can thus be understood within the category of transnationalism from below (Smith & Guarnizo, 1998), operating beneath and sometimes in contest with the practices and priorities of national educational systems. Nations and their educational institutions, though their official discourses may be accepting of diversity—as signaled with terminology such as the U.S. *melting pot* and the Canadian *mosaic*—have their upper limits in terms of how diversity is encouraged and allowed to affect the nation-state, its institutions, and practices (Porter, 1965; Skerrett, 2008; Torres, 1995). Nation-states are ultimately concerned with cultural homogeneity, fearing that cultural diversity will lead to social and political weakening of their national fabrics. Students' acquisition of the official language(s) of the nation-state; students' development of the literacy skills that will advance the nation's financial, political, and educational status on the global stage; and a sense of national rather than transnational citizenry are viewed as ways to protect and pursue national progress (Lesko, 2012; Skerrett, 2008).

DeJaeghere and Vu (2015) reviewed a range of studies in CIDE that illustrate these conflicts between the needs of transnational learners and the concerns of the nation-state. As they put it: "Education may not only be reactive to students with transnational experience but . . . it may also be a mode through which certain forms of transnationalism are fostered" (p. 278). Zúñiga and Hamann (2009), based on their study of how transnational educational networks of support for Mexican American student border-crossers could be developed, concluded that national school systems "are not deliberately designed to consider the needs . . . of an increasingly international, mobile population" (p. 329).

Furthermore, when world nations participate in international educational organizations that seek to address global educational concerns, it is often the nations holding the least power who face the greatest economic and other sanctions for not implementing those policies (George & Lewis, 2011;

Moutsios, 2009). Given the often large differential in economic and political might between sending and receiving nations, it is an impressive challenge to consider how cross-national educational policies may be developed that would be judiciously employed across world nations that share in the education of transnational students. In the area of curriculum policy, nations on the bottom rungs of global educational and economic systems often ascribe to a perspective that employing the curricular content and assessment practices of powerful world nations in their schools will favorably position their students to access and succeed at education in those nations (Sperandio, Hobson, Douglas, & Pruitt, 2009; Wagner, 2010).

The irony of such perspectives and practices is that such students fail to receive a form of education that sufficiently engages them with their own histories, cultures, languages, and literacies for successfully navigating life in their countries of origin (George & Lewis, 2011; Skerrett, 2015, 2016). At the same time, the real or imagined curriculum of other world nations that teachers are asked to implement in their own national contexts often results in a fragmented copy of that exulted curriculum as these educational and social contexts frequently lack the technological, economic, cultural, and other resources to implement it fully (Skerrett, 2015, 2016; Sperandio et al., 2009).

Given the nature of this highly politicized landscape in which transnational educational policy making and implementation occurs, how may transnational theories for literacy education advance educational policies and practices that are educationally and socially just for transnational students? Transnationalism from above (Smith, 1994; Smith & Guarnizo, 1998) addresses the activity of nation-states in relation to one another—through transnational economic, educational, and other policy making and practices; the creation of national institutions to address mobile populations; and nation-states' participation in international organizations concerned with transnational populations. I (Skerrett, 2015, 2016) have theorized how identifying the multiple actors involved in the education of transnational students and positioning them in agentive roles as educational partners and brokers can form the foundation for transnationally connected professional learning communities. These actors include transnational students, families, and communities that can serve as informants to teachers across nations about the educational practices in use across the schools students attend. Transnational students and families can serve as cultural and linguistic brokers to sponsor relationships among teachers and schools across borders.

Herein can begin professional conversations that involve a learning-oriented and respectful stance by all parties about the curricular and instructional similarities and differences a transnational student will have to navigate across different nations' schools. In this sociopolitical overlapping space, teachers can share the literacy curriculum and instructional practices in use across different national classrooms, and teachers may decide how they can learn from and share one another's practices for the benefit of easing the educational disjunctures that transnational students so often experience. For example, in my book (Skerrett, 2015), I outlined a number of practical strategies, including individualized academic plans for transnational students about to enter a new national educational system, plans that are created jointly by a language, literacy, or other teacher or educational agent in both the sending and receiving nation. I have suggested the use of teaching and learning journals by both transnational students and their teachers so that teaching practices and literacy development and challenges are well documented and can be shared with teachers in and across the different national contexts in which transnational students receive education. I have further suggested sharing mechanisms, for example, through digital affordances such as e-mail and Facebook, traditional postal mail services, or physical transport by the transnational student across nations.

These sorts of activities represent educational practices and teacher policy making in the realm of transnationalism from below. However, as I have theorized (Skerrett, 2015, 2016), by enlarging these relationships and conversations to include school leaders, multiple schools, community leaders, and institutions in particular geographies across nations, larger policy-making conversations and considerations may begin that advance into the nation-state's activities at the level of transnationalism from above (Smith & Guarnizo, 1998). The support and involvement of those with policy-making power at local (such as school and district leaders) through national and international levels are critical for funding, affirming, protecting, and expanding these practices and forming officially recognized policies around them. The United Nations (2016) concurs with this kind of policy-making process to address the circumstances of transnational youths:

> Promoting cooperation at all levels—local, national, regional and international—as well as strengthening meaningful youth participation in the migration policy debate and programmes will be critical to managing migration to harness the development potential of youth migration while mitigating associated risks.
>
> *(p. 2)*

The work of Zúñiga and Hamann (2009) is exemplary in this regard, as they mapped the geographies that most of their Mexican-U.S. border-crossing student participants traversed from a region in California to several focal regions in some Mexican states and began fostering networks and policy conversations among schools, school leaders, and teachers.

In my current work in the Caribbean, I am focusing on building professional learning networks among teachers and schools in the transnational nation-state of St. Maarten to cultivate cultural and sociopolitical educational spaces where teachers and school leaders can share their practices, challenges, and efforts at educating a highly diverse and mobile transnational student population (Skerrett, 2016). As the numbers of actors within these networks multiply and spread across different schools on that island and schools in other countries that share in the education of some of their students, the hope is to enter national policy conversations about promoting the teaching expertise of educators and transnational students' learning, thus also satisfying national educational priorities. In this work, I lean on scholarship in the field of educational change—theoretical constructs such as systems learning and professional learning networks that span global educational systems (e.g., Hargreaves & Shirley, 2014). The goal of projects such as this is the mutual transformation of the educational lives and practices of transnational students, their teachers, and the nation-states they inhabit, what Appadurai (2013) referenced as a form of hybridity that represents reconstitution and mutual transformations of relationships, values, interactions, and practices among nation-states and their citizens.

There is a body of literacy research concerned with promoting the generation of critical knowledge by marginalized social groups and employing literacy tools and practices to address and redress social problems spanning schools and local and national communities (e.g., Kinloch, 2010; Souto-Manning, 2010). This body of work aligns with studies in fields such as CIDE and sociology pertaining to the activism of transnational students and the networks they build to address sociopolitical problems within and across their nation-states (Plaza, 2009; Smith, 1994). Literacy scholars can draw from traditions of literacy and social justice activism to guide future theorizing and advocacy for nation-states' implementation of educational policies and practices that are supportive of the literacy learning and progress of transnational students. Monica's own nascent theorizing is an example of how transnational youths themselves are understanding the particularities of their national educational contexts and how their home nations may begin to reconsider their existing educational policies in light of the experiences and needs of their transnational student populations.

References

Alim, H. S. (2011). Global ill-literacies: Hip hop cultures, youth identities, and the politics of literacy. *Review of Research in Education*, *35*(1), 120–147.

Appadurai, A. (1996). *Modernity at large: Cultural dimensions of globalization*. Minneapolis, MN: University of Minnesota Press.

Appadurai, A. (2013). *The future as cultural fact: Essays on the global condition*. London: Verso.

Ball, A. F. (2009). Toward a theory of generative change in culturally and linguistically complex classrooms. *American Educational Research Journal*, *46*(1), 45–72.

Black, R. W. (2009). English-language learners, fan communities, and 21st century skills. *Journal of Adolescent and Adult Literacy, 52*(8), 688–697.

Blommaert, J. (2010). *The sociolinguistics of globalization.* New York, NY: Cambridge University Press.

DeJaeghere, J., & Vu, L. (2015). Transnationalism and its analytic possibilities for CIDE. In J. C. Weidman & W. J. Jacob (Eds.), *Beyond the comparative: Advancing theory and its application to practice* (pp. 269–291). Rotterdam: Sense.

George, J., & Lewis, T. (2011). Exploring the local/global boundary in developing countries: The case of the Caribbean. *Compare: A Journal of Comparative and International Education, 41*(6), 721–734.

Hamann, E. T., & Zúñiga, V. A. (2011). Schooling and the everyday ruptures transnational children encounter in the United States and Mexico. In C. Coe, R. R. Reynolds, D. A. Boehm, J. M. Hess, & H. Rae-Espinoza (Eds.), *Everyday ruptures: Children, youth, and migration in global perspective* (pp. 141–160). Nashville, TN: Vanderbilt University Press.

Hargreaves, A., & Shirley, D. (2014). *The global fourth way: The quest for educational excellence.* Thousand Oaks, CA: Corwin Press.

Jiménez, R. T., Smith, P. H., & Teague, B. L. (2009). Transnational and community literacies for teachers. *Journal of Adolescent and Adult Literacy, 53*(1), 16–26.

Kinloch, V. (2010). *Harlem on our minds: Place, race, and the literacies of urban youth.* New York, NY: Teachers College Press.

Lam, W. S. E., & Rosario-Ramos, E. (2009). Multilingual literacies in transnational digitally mediated contexts: An exploratory study of immigrant teens in the United States. *Language and Education, 23*(2), 171–190.

Lam, W. S. E., & Warriner, D. S. (2012). Transnationalism and literacy: Investigating the mobility of people, languages, texts, and practices in contexts of migration. *Reading Research Quarterly, 47*(2), 191–215.

Leander, K., Phillips, N., & Taylor, K. (2010). The changing social spaces of learning: Mapping new mobilities. *Review of Research in Education, 34*, 329–394.

Lesko, N. (2012). *Act your age! A cultural construction of adolescence* (2nd ed.). New York, NY: Routledge.

Levitt, P. (2001). *The transnational villagers.* Berkeley, CA: University of California Press.

McLean, C. (2010). A space called home: An immigrant adolescent's digital literacy practices. *Journal of Adolescent & Adult Literacy, 54*(1), 13–22.

Moutsios, S. (2009). International organisations and transnational education policy making. *Compare: A Journal of Comparative and International Education, 39*(4), 467–478.

New London Group. (1996). A pedagogy of multiliteracies: Designing social futures, *Harvard Educational Review, 66*(1), 60–92.

Plaza, D. (2009). Transnational identity maintenance via the Internet: A content analysis of the websites constructed by second generation Caribbean-origin students in post-secondary institutions. *Human Architecture: Journal of the Sociology of Self-Knowledge, 7*(4), Article 5. Retrieved from http://scholarworks.umb.edu/humanarchitecture/vol7/iss4/5

Porter, J. (1965). *The vertical mosaic: An analysis of social class and power in Canada.* Toronto, ON: University of Toronto Press.

Sánchez, P. (2009, April/May). Even beyond the local community: A close look at Latina youth's return trips to Mexico. *The High School Journal, 92*(4), 49–66.

Skerrett, A. (2008). Racializing educational change: Melting pot and mosaic influences on educational policy and practice. *Journal of Educational Change, 9*(3), 261–280.

Skerrett, A. (2012). Languages and literacies in translocation: Experiences and perspectives of a transnational youth. *Journal of Literacy Research, 44*(4), 364–395.

Skerrett, A. (2015). *Teaching transnational youth: Literacy and education in a changing world.* New York, NY: Teachers College Press.

Skerrett, A. (2016). Refiguring a Caribbean school within and across local and global communities. *Journal of Professional and Community Capital, 1*(4), 254–269.

Skerrett, A. (2018). Learning music literacies across transnational settings. *Journal of Literacy Research, 50*(1), 31–51.

Skerrett, A., & Bomer, R. (2013). Recruiting languages and lifeworlds for border-crossing compositions. *Research in the Teaching of English, 47*(3), 313–337.

Smith, M. P. (1994). "Can you imagine?" Transnational migration and globalization of grassroots politics. *Social Text, 39*, 15–33.

Smith, M. P., & Guarnizo, L. E. (Eds.). (1998). *Transnationalism from below.* New Brunswick, NJ: Transaction.

Soong, H. (2016). *Transnational students and mobility: Lived experiences of migration.* London: Routledge.

Souto-Manning, M. (2010). *Freire, teaching and learning: Culture circles across contexts.* New York, NY: Peter Lang.

Sperandio, J., Hobson, D., Douglas, R., & Pruitt, R. (2009). Does context matter?: Importing US educational programs to schools overseas. *Compare: A Journal of Comparative and International Education, 39*(6), 707–721.

Stornaiuolo, A., Smith, A., & Phillips, N. C. (2017). Developing a transliteracies framework for a connected world. *Journal of Literacy Research*, *49*(1), 68–91.

Torres, A. (1995). *Between melting pot and mosaic: African Americans and Puerto Ricans in New York's political economy.* Philadelphia, PA: Temple University Press.

Tyack, D., & Tobin, W. (1994). The "grammar" of schooling: Why has it been so hard to change? *American Educational Research Journal*, *31*(3), 453–479.

UNICEF. (2017). Child migration and displacement. Retrieved from https://data.unicef.org/topic/child-migration-and-displacement/migration/

United Nations Department of Economic and Social Affairs. (2016). Youth issue briefs 2016: Youth and migration. Retrieved from http://www.un.org/esa/socdev/documents/youth/fact-sheets/youth-migration.pdf

Vertovec, S. (2009). *Transnationalism*. New York, NY: Routledge.

Wagner, D. A. (2010). Quality of education, comparability and assessment choice in developing countries. *Compare: A Journal of Comparative and International Education*, *40*(6), 741–760.

Zúñiga, V., & Hamann, E. T. (2009). Sojourners in Mexico with US school experience: A new taxonomy for transnational students. *Comparative Education Review*, *53*(3), 329–353.

27

THE SOCIAL PRACTICE OF MULTIMODAL READING

A New Literacy Studies–Multimodal Perspective on Reading

Jennifer Rowsell, Gunther Kress, Kate Pahl, and Brian Street

The aim of this chapter is to situate reading within two complementary approaches: New Literacy Studies (NLS) and a social semiotic approach to multimodality (SSMM). We use the term *reading* both as a fairly neutral description of an activity (as in, "what are you reading now?") and as a topic for theoretical attention (as in, "how can we understand reading in contemporary environments?"). In the latter sense, we argue that *reading* appears differently when it is viewed in the frame of social practices and environments and in the perspective of modally complex compositions than it does in other approaches. As concepts, reading and writing—making meaning in and with texts—name practices and processes today that differ in many respects from those some 30 or 40 years ago. At the same time, there are constants about reading and about writing as composition that provide a strong enough reason for us to look at reading from these two fields of research and theory, both of which focus on meaning making as located in social environments. Whereas the emphasis of NLS leans more toward an attention to understanding and describing social environments (where meaning is made and by whom), that of SSMM leans more toward semiotic factors (how meaning is made, by what agents, with what principles of and resources for making meaning), or in other words, toward the (material) realization of meanings.

This chapter is organized in five parts. First, we develop a view of reading through the lens of NLS and SSMM and show how these two approaches may be integrated. In the second, third, and fourth parts, we present ages and stages of reading, from early childhood literacies to youth literacies to adult academic literacies, and try to account for reading in different social settings. In the final section, we conclude with a discussion of ways forward with literacy, pedagogy, and policy. Throughout the chapter, we offer an integrated model of reading and of the reading process rooted in an epistemology that draws on both NLS and SSMM as a viable frame for thinking about reading in new times.

Why Reading Is Different Today

Children read—that is, make meaning from an engagement with—a vast range of aspects of the tangible world long before they are drawn into schooling and schooled practices, when, for instance, from a young age, they make what they regard as texts in what seems to be drawing more than writing (Kress, 1997). It is also the case when children make meaning in representing their world in any number of other ways: enacting aspects of the world in mimed movement, in gesture and facial expression, or combining existing or newly made three-dimensional objects with verbal commentary and movement in complex, sequentially staged tableaux. Such meaning making tends to be named play, and that naming acts as a potent means of deterring serious investigation of the relation of principles of composition in one domain—say, of drawing or building—with those in another, in this case with writing or reading in a conventional sense.

Such bracketing out of specific, early composition and reading has led to a profound, unrecognized problem in studies of early meaning making and its relation to reading and writing. This problem is compounded when we add, as we must, even at the earliest stages of more formal reading, the need to understand the communicational practices that form the taken-for-granted mainstream of children's communicational world. The possibilities that have arisen with the media of digital technologies, such as browsing screens, scrolling and scanning multiple websites, clicking, following and reading hyperlinks, communicating through social networks, and the associated forms of producing texts, present potentials for making meaning in both reading and writing, which are quite unlike those that existed until, say, 30 or 40 years ago. Given that, it becomes essential to consider what reading and writing involve now, what they are, and how they can be thought about and theorized.

While learning to read in its more narrow sense has always meant learning to make sense of texts, making sense of texts has always been multimodal. Even traditional books, of whatever kind, have pictures, gutters, trim sizes, fonts, and illustration styles with color or in black and white. Choices from among these meaningful resources—modes for making meaning—signal decisions to match a message and the practices used to make a message meaningful to an audience and, at the same time, to signal aesthetic choices related to audience and purpose. In what follows, we look at how NLS perspectives came into being and how they challenge the efficacy of such reading processes as shared reading, picture books, and other common reading interventions.

Reading Perspectives in NLS

NLS combines such disparate fields as anthropology, semiotics, sociology, and linguistics to look at situated language as value-laden and shaped by contexts. NLS was and is rooted in issues of power and differentials in power. It has not explicitly focused on reading and reading processes, but rather on oral and written languages and the tools used for social practices within diverse settings.

Thinking about NLS in terms of reading demands revisiting researchers who are associated with the field as a domain of theory and practice. Anthropologist and folklorist Hymes (1974) looked at oral narratives within Native American communities, acknowledging and documenting how language shifts across cultural practices. During his career, he formulated an ethnography of speaking to account for poetic structures and narratives within languages as signaling communicative competence existing within communities as opposed to a universalized notion of communicative competence.

A student of Hymes, Heath (1983) similarly documented a 10-year ethnography of literacy practices in the homes of children and their families living in three different communities. Her book *Ways With Words: Language, Life, and Work in Communities and Classrooms* describes the different language and literacy practices of two rural communities and one urban community in the Piedmont Carolinas in the 1970s. Heath contrasted a black community (Trackton) to a working-class community (Roadville), paying close attention to the ways parents in these two communities spoke to their children and raised them and how the children interacted with their parents. Then she looked at what happened when the children went to school. In the cases of both Trackton and Roadville children, there was a disjuncture between their home literacy practices and their school literacy practices.

This was in sharp contrast to the children from the third community, a town Heath called Maintown. The children in Maintown were primarily teachers' children, who had been raised and talked to in ways that echoed the norms of school literacy. To understand how different ways of interacting contributed to different outcomes in literacy, Heath (1983) focused her study around the concept of literacy events, which she defined as "any action sequence, involving one or more persons, in which the production and/or comprehension of print plays a role" (p. 92). This concept enabled Heath to understand in a contrastive way by isolating specific instances of the different events and practices around literacy.

Heath (2012) has since published a follow-up to her *Ways With Words* study, in which she tracks three generations of families from Trackton and Roadville as they moved across the United States in search of work, responding to the larger economic and social changes in the country across this period. She documents the older generation's responses to her accounts of their earlier literacy practices and relates these to the current practices of their children and grandchildren in their new environments.

Shortly after Heath's original study, Brian Street (1984) examined literacy practices in different parts of the same community in Iran, finding correspondingly that literacy practices are shaped by context and identity. He introduced an ideological view of literacy that takes into account not only practices, concepts, texts, identities, and the contexts in which they take place but also how these relate to issues of power. His study demonstrated how Standard English, which was seen as happening in school, had rendered outside literacy practices as less powerful and less relevant.

Since that time, Street has extended the NLS perspective to accounts of literacy practices in other settings, such as the United States (B. Street, 1993; J.C. Street & Street, 1991), Ethiopia (Gebre, Openjuru, Rogers, & Street, 2009), and the United Kingdom (B. Street, 1997, 2011). With regard to how NLS might apply to the actual practices of education at both school and university levels, Street and colleagues (Ivanič, 1998; Jones, Turner, & Street, 1999; Lea, 2004; Lea & Street, 1998, 2006; Lillis & Scott, 2008; B. Street, 1996, 2009; Wingate, 2009; Wingate & Tribble, 2012) have developed the notion of academic literacies as a way of both analyzing what is going on in these contexts and proposing strategies for pedagogy that take account of these new perspectives. The academic literacies approach has been applied particularly in higher education in the United Kingdom but also has relevance to schooling and links with debates in the United States regarding writing across the curriculum and writing in the disciplines and rhetoric (see Prior, 1998; Russell, 1991; Russell, Lea, Parker, Street, & Donahue, 2009).

On the whole, NLS signified a social turn away from a focus on minds and a psychology of reading to a focus on social practice and interaction. Born out of several movements, from the ethnography of speaking (Gumperz, 1982; Hymes, 1974) to sociohistorical psychology with the work of Vygotsky (1978), to cultural models (Holland, Lachicotte, Skinner, & Cain, 1998), to linguistics (Gee, 1996), to composition theory (Bazerman, 1988) and sociological theory (Bourdieu, 1991), NLS offers literacy education broadly and reading specifically an alternative way of viewing reading processes and theoretical models. Stemming from different disciplines, NLS has pushed the field of literacy education to view literacy practices, such as reading a basal reader, as always situated within specific social practices and within specific Discourses (Gee, 1996). NLS has enabled researchers to think about the social practices and interactions that take place around reading events in ways that take account of all the modes involved in an increasingly complex and varied semiotic landscape.

Reading in the Perspective of Multimodal Social Semiotics

The contemporary textual landscape is marked by intense diversity. There is the relatively well-understood, hitherto usual plethora of textual (written and spoken) genres, reflecting social organizations of a more traditional kind. Additionally, there is now an increasing and increasingly normalized diversity of means for making texts due to the ever more insistent appearance of multimodality.

More and more, contemporary texts draw on a number of modes: speech, image (still or moving), writing, music, and action. More and more, the dominant site of appearance for texts is the screen, or rather, screens of all kinds.

These factors are giving rise to a pronounced difference in kinds of text linked to generations. Those below, say, the age of 30 tend to have a distinctly different position in social organization and arrangements and hence a different stance toward texts, compared with those above that age group. That is the case both in the production of texts and in practices of reading. In other words, the present communicational landscape is one of a seemingly considerable confusion: traditional texts coexist with texts produced with different means of production, digital being foremost; with different resources for representation, one major factor being that of multimodality; and last, using different principles of composition, with one prominent change being a move from linearly organized texts to texts organized on principles of modular composition. All of these can be traced back to different assumptions and givens about the social order, power, hierarchy, authority, and therefore, rights and forms of authorship.

Given the differences in stance in and to the social, there are correspondingly different genres. All of these features mark a social, generational, technological, and semiotic/representational divide. Traditional texts are typified by the means and technologies of their production, usually involving single authorship and print with its various means of dissemination as collections of pages, such as newspapers, magazines, and books. The more recent, but also now contemporary, texts are likewise typified by the means and technologies of their production, involving often multiple, continuously fluid authorship; word processing; the potential to be open and unconstrained (by comparison with print media such as the book); unlimited digital means of dissemination as screens (rather than as pages) of various kinds; and new or transformed genres, such as e-mail, websites, blogs, and so forth. These texts are based on differently organized and differently (un)constrained social arrangements and on digital technologies as the means of production and dissemination and as the sites of display.

This contrast of traditional and contemporary can be described in many ways: socially and semiotically. Socially, the major change is about structures of authority/power, leading to changes in the position of readers and forms and practices of reading. Other major changes involve the fraying of formerly firm frames and the move to quite different kinds of framing, a change in notions of canonicity, and changes in forms of subjectivity and identity in line with these changes. Semiotically, the change can be described in terms of, as mentioned earlier, a contrast of traditional pages to contemporary screens, as a shift from linearity to modularity, by a move from the centrality of speech and writing to multimodal arrangements, by changes in sites of appearance, and by the different principles of composition. All of these differences add up to distinct kinds of textual organization that habituate readers to distinct forms of reading.

NLS and Multimodality as Complementary Perspectives

Possibilities for the shaping of identity are completely interlinked with textual features, whether in making text for disseminations (outward production) or in engaging with texts in transformation (inward production). In each case, there is an accommodation to the principles that are evident in the shape of the text and, over time, a habituation to the social and semiotic characteristics that have given rise to the features of texts in their ontological and epistemological potentials and in their affordances for access to and participation in social life. Consequently, practices of reading, forms of readership, and kinds of readers—just three of the many possible aspects of identity—are shaped in encounters with texts in production through the possibilities of their dissemination and in the encounters of reading.

In the frame of SSMM, as much as in that of NLS, these factors are taken to be the effects of social organizations and practices. For example, different kinds of textual coherence can be taken as pointing to different kinds of social organization. Cohesion and coherence are signs, or semiotic indicators, of social phenomena. A tightly organized social group with strong social framing is likely to produce tightly framed, integrated, cohesive and coherent texts. A society that is less tightly integrated, that is characterized by porous boundaries and frames, is likely to produce texts that are less integrated, with fewer and weaker cohesive markers and hence less or differently coherent (Bezemer & Kress, 2008, 2009; Halliday & Hasan, 1976).

As one example, we might point to what is by now a quite common shift from presenting some material—say, an introduction to a text—in an integrated, syntactically and textually coherent paragraph to the appearance of similar material now as a bullet-point list of items, to do what might be regarded as a similar task. In the paragraph, the author provides the ordering and integration of the material; in the bullet-point list, the maker of the text provides relevant material but leaves it up to the reader to establish his or her sense of coherence from the items in the list. In the paragraph, one cannot take the sentences that make up the paragraph and put them in a different order. In the bullet-point list, it often does not make a great difference to change the order of the points.

In Figure 27.1a, for example, is the introductory and framing paragraph for a poem, John Milton's "L'Allegro," from an English textbook of the 1930s. In Figure 27.1b is a similar introductory and framing textual element for Denise Levertov's "What Were They Like?," a poem about the war in Vietnam, from an English textbook from the year 2000. Examples of this kind can be multiplied in relation to different features—continuous, running text replaced now by layout devices of various kinds, by the use of color, and so on.

Habitual and extended engagement with texts leads to settled expectations of what different texts are like and to assumptions and practices of how they are to be read. These assumptions in turn lead to dispositions that respond to and enact the characteristics and organization of the texts, overtly or implicitly. A text organized linearly suggests that the reader should follow the ordering of the textual entities as established by an author: an order of words in sequence; the order of syntax, which in writing becomes the ordering of sentences; of paragraphs, themselves an ordered arrangement of sentences; and of whole texts, in which all of these elements find their overall order. A temporally sequenced text, or a narrative, such as an Agatha Christie murder mystery, is best read in the linear order of the genre set out by the author.

By contrast, the text of a website, as a modular arrangement, suggests no such reading. In that case, it is the interest of the individual that determines the order of reading the text. The generic features of the website text itself are, as with all texts, the expression of the larger level social order, although one entirely different to that of the narrative. While the narrative strongly insists on one kind of reading and, in that, implicitly suggests a particular social order, the website is the product of a rhetorician's assumptions about the varied interests of a diverse audience, and it is designed to allow the interest of any one reader to shape the coherence of the text resulting from his or her interested engagement. Texts, if read as they are meant to be, habituate their readers to a certain stance to text, to reading practices and to meaning, to authorial authority or to the reader's exercise of individual interested agency, and to the social writ large.

The characteristics of a text are the effect of a closely integral relation of reading, readership, and identity, which forms the basis of the SSMM approach to reading. Active semiotic work—the agency of individuals—is entailed in producing texts, whether in outward or inward production. The production is the semiotic work of engaging with an aspect of the world seen as text. That work entails selection of what is to be attended to and an interpretation/transformation of that, as shaped by resources brought by the reader to the text. An NLS approach complements this semiotic work in that it functions as a constant reminder that reading practices cannot be separated from the social, cultural, and ideological contexts that give rise to them.

What follows from our integrated approach is that the first step in reading is to frame what is to be read and then locate that in the wider social landscape: Where in the textual landscape does this text have its origins? Where does it belong? Answers will determine the reader's approach and engagement with the text. Of course, this does not assume that the reader is similarly located in the textual landscape as is the maker of the text. Nor does it determine whether, having made such an assessment, the (potential) reader will actually engage with the text, that is, that he or she will become a reader.

NLS, with its focus on situated concepts of literacy in homes and communities, has opened up a much broader concept of what literacy and, thereby, reading is as a social practice (Barton & Hamilton, 1998; B. Street, 1993). This perspective has enabled researchers to provide alternative languages of description for literacy. These alternative scripts enable a postmodern understanding of literacy practices that acknowledges diversity and builds on existing multilingual and multimodal literacy practices within families (Compton-Lilly et al., 2012; Gregory, 2008). In particular, much of the research on reading has not fully recognized the impact of digital technologies on reading development (Levy, 2011). Given that many research studies of home literacy practices have acknowledged the importance of the digital in the communicational landscape of young children, it is urgent and important to develop a theoretical model of the processes and practices of reading that acknowledges these changes (Marsh, 2011).

Young children do not have access to a community's principles of recognition and so establish their own, and these in turn are constantly checked by them against the world engaged with or

---

(a) For John Milton's "L'Allegro" in the 1930s

> 'L'Allegro.'
> The Elizabethan age was succeeded by a period of religious and political strife, which culminated in the triumph of Puritanism under Oliver Cromwell. Therefore the expansive development of literature was restricted, and thought mainly concentrated on one particular book—the Bible. The dominating figure of this age is John Milton, the great Puritan poet; but he is so supremely an artist that he blends the perfection of ancient art, as learnt from the Renaissance, with the religious turmoil of his time, which has had so profound an effect on his work. His most famous poem is the epic *Paradise Lost*, which relates the story of 'man's first disobedience and its fruit.' He also wrote many shorter poems, of which the following is an example.

(b) For Denise Levertov's "What Were They Like?" in 2000

> *Some details:*
> * The war lasted from 1959 to 1975.
> * Communist North Vietnam was fighting South Vietnam.
> * Fearing the growth of Communism, the US supported the South for the last ten years.
> * 543 000 American troops were there at the height of the conflict.
> * The war involved ferocious jungle fighting. intense air strikes and civilian casualties.
> * 3–4 million Vietnamese died.
> * 58 000 Americans died, and anti-war protests at home eventually contributed to the American withdrawal and defeat.

Figure 27.1   English Textbook Introductions to Poetry

represented. The process of socialization can be seen, in that way, as a constant process of increasing approximation to a community's principles of recognition, or to put it a different way, its rules. In what follows, we demonstrate how an NLS–multimodal perspective allows us to analyze instantiations of these processes in reading events in the early years. In the next two sections, the author team singles out the voices of researchers who conducted the research, but the chapter is very much a jointly authored piece.

Reading and Early Childhood Literacies

In this section, I (Kate) describe the contexts for young children's experience of reading. I particularly look at the landscapes of the home (Pahl, 2002, 2004) in constructing particular affordances for reading. I focus on the idea of reading as an interpretative social practice that is at once cultural, that is, making something meaningful and effective; critical, that is, understanding that reading is situated within relations of power; and operational—that is, reading is something that requires "knowing what to do to make 'it' work" (Green, 1998, p. 43). Aligning myself with early researchers, such as Ferreiro and Teberosky (1982), who recognized the plethora of print that lies outside schooling, I consider how this landscape of print constructs reading practices and how these practices can be understood as culturally located. I also recognize the layered nature of reading. Mackey (2010) has described how early reading can be understood in relation to affect (the emotion associated with being read to or reading) and location (e.g., home, church, play) when reading. These factors have to be understood as critical when considering young children's reading.

Landscapes of Home Reading Practices

By landscapes of the home, I mean the materially situated world in which young children are immersed, as described by anthropologists such as Miller (2008, 2010). This landscape includes the sensory and the embodied, which is where, as Heath (1983) observed, children learn their "ways with words." This landscape, however, has changed radically since Heath's research and now includes the digital and, increasingly, a situation in which print seeps across a wide range of technological and immaterial practices. I therefore acknowledge, with researchers such as Marsh (2011), the ways in which young children's literacy practices in the home are both embodied and situated and then flickered across the screens of the home in ways that defy a situated concept of literacy. Reading is a practice that can involve scanning a game as it comes up on the screen, locating print within a message coming up on the screen, and then composing a reply.

Levy (2011) suggests that the concept of reading as solely being associated with books can be critiqued. She draws on the work of Carrington (2005) and Marsh (2005), who have identified the plethora of new media and popular cultural literacy resources in home settings. Many scholars (e.g., Compton-Lilly et al., 2012; Marsh, 2005) have critiqued the assumption that literacy practices in the home can be mapped onto a largely middle-class model of literacy, which equates early literacy with sharing picture books. Instead, many researchers have identified a number of literacy practices that are much more diverse, including oral storytelling, multilingual storytelling, using different languages and scripts, engaging in digital and popular-culture texts, and employing different modalities for reading and writing script. For example, in her study of Hispanic families and their home literacy practices, Zentella (2005) offers the following:

> My sister and I never saw our parents read a full-length book in English or Spanish, although they read letters from Puerto Rico and Mexico, the *New York Daily News* and *El Diario,* and *mami* had prayer books. But there were no novels, no bookshelves, no magazines on coffee tables, and least of all cookbooks. I did not get books as gifts, nor did I consider a book a desirable present, and was not read to. The library books I brought home

were never the topic of family discussions, and I did my homework alone. *Mami* used to yell at me to stop reading late into the night. She said that so much reading was bad for me; it could *volverme loca,* that is, drive me crazy.

(p. 14)

Researchers of intergenerational home literacy practices in multilingual households have identified, much as Heath (1983) did in the Trackton and Roadville communities, a plethora of practices associated with print and with reading that are incongruent with the reading practices offered in school settings (González, Moll, & Amanti, 2005; Gregory, Long, & Volk, 2004; Kenner, 2004). Keating (2005) has described the ways in which Portuguese women who were migrants in London used popular magazines in Portuguese to support their identities. She considered how their engagement with these magazines offered an escape to other worlds and represented a "complex interaction between people's inner motivations and the ways they handle the ideologies at play in the contexts in which they have been socialized" (p. 116). Moreover, Keating argues, "When relating to social practices of literacy, these women seemed to *repeat,* to *recognise,* to *reflect* upon and to *recombine* ways with literacy and, in this process, *reinvent* these practices for themselves" (p. 114). These processes of reflecting, recombining, and ultimately transforming, as applied to reading, require also a radical rethinking of the concept of reading as a culturally available trope that often calls up the image of the book, the story, and the home with books as a signifier for cultural capital.

Learning to Read in New Worlds

In her book *Young Children Reading: At Home and at School,* Levy (2011) identifies the study of reading with a number of different perspectives, including a cognitive-psychological perspective that focuses on reading as a staged process with phonics as the central focus of research and practice. However, there are concerns voiced by early years' educators that this approach can be reductive and lead to an assumption that reading is simply a matter of decoding letters. In a recent study of eight families in Sheffield, England, funded by Book Trust, different constructs associated with a variety of perspectives were identified in relation to home reading practices (Pahl, Lewis, & Ritchie, 2010). One type of perspective, which we called skills focused, was associated with families who saw reading as being about decoding and the acquisition of the skills used to read a book independently. However, these families often missed the connectivity and emotional depth of sharing home literacy practices across a range of modalities. Levy's own study identified how all the children in her research came to associate reading as being the ability to decode words in books, despite their home literacy practices including a much wider range of literacies (p. 109).

Levy (2011) also suggests that there are a number of researchers who focus on reading and use a more psycholinguistic perspective, which considers the context of reading and the whole-language approach as involving reading for meaning. However, she argues that both this approach and the cognitive-psychological perspective "fail to acknowledge the complexity of issues surrounding the ways in which children learn to read and become readers of a variety of different texts" (p. 13). Part of the difficulty of using these approaches for a conceptualization of reading is that the concept of reading is associated primarily with printed texts rather than texts on-screen. Kress (2003) argues that the concept of "reading path" is important in locating a concept of reading across modalities:

Reading paths in writing (as in speech) are set with very little or no leeway; in the image they are open. Reading across modes is a different concept and something that requires a close analysis of both image and text.

(p. 157)

Levy (2011) argues for a sociopolitical perspective of reading and maintains that schools have the power to determine what is meant by *reading*. She combines this perspective with a sociocultural perspective that argues for the importance of broadening a conception of literacy and print to include a variety of text types and modalities. This might also include extending the reach of how reading can be defined. If reading is understood as being a culturally situated social practice, young children's engagement with reading can be differently mapped, and the sites and spaces where young children experience print and engage with reading can be understood as pertaining to the activity that is called reading.

In the study of home book-sharing practices, described previously, young children experienced reading differently according to how parents understood reading. Some parents, who were identified as skills focused, saw reading as a skill that young children could acquire through reading on their own, separately, away from parents. This model, like many school-based models of print, focuses on how children would acquire reading as an independent skill. Other parents in the study equated book sharing with connectivity, including emotional closeness, oral storytelling, and the use of gesture and drama to make stories come alive. Book sharing could take place in many different places, including on the bus and in outdoor settings. As mentioned earlier, the cultural and interpretative schemata that accompanied the concept of a picture book is embedded within cultural frames of reference (Rogoff, 2003) and can be understood to be something that varies across cultures.

However, certain reading practices have become more culturally salient in Western cultures than in others. Just as Kress (2003) argues that print literacy is more salient than other multimodal communicative practices, home reading practices have become mapped onto the concept of home book sharing rather than considering the role of reading in a number of other complex cultural practices. For example, Rosowsky (2008) describes how children learn to decode text in Arabic while learning the Koran at mosque school in quite different ways to the way children are taught to read at school. Much of the Koran learning involved recitation and pure phonics without reading for meaning. Other forms of reading involve constructing oral stories, but using script to capture the stories so they could be read later. Oral storytelling can involve writing a story that is new so it may be read aloud to younger siblings.

Reading can involve reading the messages in the online role-playing game Club Penguin (Marsh, 2011) and also learning the instructions on a computer. As Marsh elaborates in her study of children's interaction with Club Penguin, "The ability to navigate a complex multimodal screen was . . . a primary skill required to engage in Club Penguin" (p. 108). The affordances of the screen require an attention to multimodality, that is, an awareness of the way in which meaning is represented in a multiplicity of modes on-screen. A multimodal approach means that all aspects of the screen combine together to make meaning (Kress, 2003). The concept of multimodality can aid an understanding of situated reading practices. Marsh argues, therefore, that a multiplicity of modes is involved when looking at children's reading practices online, including the importance of sound and animation. By understanding reading as embedded within a wider frame of interaction, it becomes a social practice with complex links across domains of practice.

Looking Closely at Home Reading Practices

In my own study of home writing practices, called "Writing in the Home and in the Street," funded by the Arts and Humanities Research Council (U.K.), I considered the range of reading materials available in two homes: a British Asian family whose grandparents migrated from Pakistan to the north of England and a white workingclass family. Both families lived in Rotherham in northern England. The families made films and took photographs of their home reading practices over the period of one year. In the case of the British Asian household, which involved a study of two girls, ages 8 and 12 at the time of the data described here, I logged a range of literacy practices, including Arabic script as inscriptions on walls and within Koranic literature, script embedded in toys and within decorations, embroidery, and script within books and reading matter, such as notebooks in which the young girls wrote. Their images of home reading practices reflected this range. In Figure 27.2 we see this instantiated within an image taken by the eldest girl of her home literacy practices.

These practices include a toy keyboard, a globe, a set of books, toys, and other small objects that include aspects of print. Ethnographic work in this home revealed that the girls wrote stories in

Figure 27.2   A 12-Year-Old British Asian Girl's Photograph of Her Home Literacy Practices

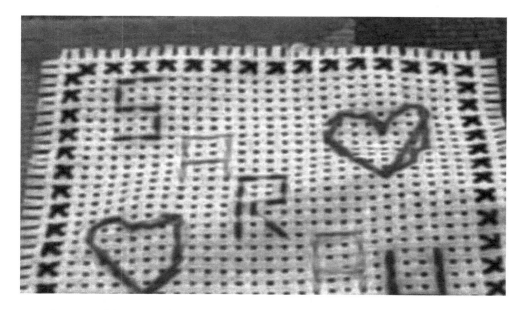

Figure 27.3   A Still from a British Asian Girl's Video of Embroidery Making

notebooks to read to their younger sibling at night. Writing was therefore undertaken in order to produce read-alouds. The production of writing was also intertwined with the family's cultural heritage across generations. Making textiles was a strong part of this family's heritage. The girls recorded a video of the making of a piece of embroidery with the youngest child's name on it (see Figure 27.3). I asked the girls' aunt, with whom I was also in contact, about this, and she e-mailed me back (August 2010):

> The textile side of our heritage comes from the women in the family. We have older rel-
> atives that do appliqué, crochet, embroidery, sewing and knitting (from the girls' mother's
> side their grandmother's sister and cousin and from their father's side, his two cousins who
> live close by). My younger sister loves craft type of activities and buys the girls a lot of
> resources to do sewing and fabric work especially on birthdays, Christmas and Eid.

Here, reading is a process of depicting meaning embedded within wider cultural practices of using embroidery and as an example of an identity, or name.

Reading in the Street

The process of learning to read is about understanding the reading ecologies that exist in homes and communities. When investigating writing in the home and in the street, these ecologies are found to be linked to the play spaces, both inside and outside the home and both online and off-line, that create a sense of affect for the child. Ingold (2007) discusses the entanglements that occur when making pathways through the worlds. These can be understood as lines and traces of real knowledge. Mackey (2010) talks about "reading the city" (p. 326) as being a process of coming to know that could also be mapped onto her process of coming to read the signs and symbols around her. In a series of community walks as part of the "Writing in the Home and in the Street" research project, a group of 10–11-year-old children described the experience of reading the neighborhood to me. The children talked about how they felt when they encountered graffiti in their homes and surroundings:

Kate: When you see a nasty word, do you think it is good or bad?
Marianne: Bad. We have got one on our gates someone wrote it! When I first moved into my
           house, there was graffiti all over the wall, and they had had a paintball fight. You can
           still see it. It were black, and it were white, and it was hard to get off. Me granddad had
           to do that. (audio recording, June 2011)

Marianne lived in a home where what she read on the walls constructed her experience of home literacy practices.

Literacies in community contexts are nested within the cultural, economic, and social forces that surround them. In poor neighborhoods, literacy is often less visible, as shops are closed down and resources withheld because of economic constraints (Neuman & Celano, 2001). Local literacies are linked to the sounds, the accents, and the smells of a neighborhood. Reading a community is about reading the social worlds of the children brought up in that neighborhood. It is also about the lay-ered nature of experience and the ways in which children come to experience the world through print. For example, a conversation with Luke showed a layered quality to his experience:

Kate: I want to know what you think of the graffiti on this slide?
Luke: It's all rude! We should spray it. It's not fair on young children.

Reading signs in the community can be hurtful and problematic. The children commented on the racist nature of some graffiti and how the everyday reading matter in the environment was damag-ing their sense of their community (see Figure 27.4).

Figure 27.4   Image by a Child of a Community Artwork Damaged by Graffiti

Reading the linguistic landscape is a process of acquiring what Mackey (2010) calls "an embodied understanding of the local world" (p. 329), a world that is discovered through pathways, through walls and boundaries, through the lines that are taken, from home to school and back again, and also through the lines that are presented to children in the form of words and symbols on the street. For young children, reading is sensory and embodied (Pink, 2009). Letters and print are inscribed within material objects (Miller, 2010). The small embodiments that are present in everyday cultural life (Hoggart, 1957) make up the experience of reading. Reading can be about following the lines of graffiti on the street (Ingold, 2007), and it is also about the feeling a child gets when he or she notices some racist graffiti or an obscene word. Reading is a process that is in place (Comber, 2010) and linked to the landscape of childhood in ways that are profound and highly local (Barton & Hamilton, 1998). In the next section, we contrast this landscape of early childhood reading to the landscape of adolescent and teenage reading practices.

Reading and Youth Literacies

In this section, I (Jennifer) explore adolescents and teenagers and their reading practices. I begin with some facts about high school students and reading. Approximately two-thirds of 8th- and 12th-grade students read at less than the proficient level on the National Assessment of Educational Progress (Rampey, Dion, & Donahue, 2009). About 1.2 million U.S. students drop out of school annually, and their literacy skills are lower than most industrialized nations (Laird, Kienzl, DeBell, & Chapman, 2007). These statistics miss out on so many subtleties and idiosyncrasies of readers, but they do tell a story.

Adolescent literacies refer to the literacy practices of youths "who act provisionally at particular times" (Alvermann, 2006, p. 40). Alvermann talks about the everyday lives of adolescents as encompassing "the performative, visual, aural, and semiotic understandings necessary for constructing and reconstructing print and nonprint-based texts" (Alvermann, 2002, p. viii). Research in the area of adolescents' out-of-school digital literacy practices (Davies, 2006; Williams & Merten, 2008; Yi, 2008) is a growing area of research and inquiry. One of the most cited articles in this area is by Lewis and Fabos (2005), who examined the ways in which students manipulate and play with vernacular conventions, Standard English grammar, and electronic typography in sophisticated ways when they communicate. The researchers interviewed teenagers about their private instant-messaging practices and observed teens while they were engaged in this practice. Lewis and Fabos's research demonstrates the level of sophisticated rhetorical and discursive devices exhibited by students: "The young people we interviewed were conscious of choosing different tones and language styles depending on whom they were IMing" (p. 484). When students felt free to play with language code, they were not only more willing to write, but they also organically understood the significance of tone and syntax. Although their texts may not have satisfied the requirements of an English assignment, they demonstrated a reflective understanding of the nuances of language and, more specifically, situated language.

In my observations, interviews, and work with youths, reading is a fluid practice that involves movement across multiple genres of texts and that draws on multiple modes to comprehend texts. To gather information today demands reading across hybrid texts and finding the information in a sea of words, visuals, and hyperlinks. First of all, the production and reception of texts, as well as the possibility of moving between different genres of texts, is more fluid and frequent than it has ever been. Digital domains facilitate such mobility across time and space to understand a concept or to complete a text. To create mobility in digital texts, reading relies on converged texts in multimedia formats.

When the adolescents and teenagers with whom I work read, they read for interest, purpose, function, and perhaps the strongest reading practice of all, so they can remake a text into something else. Contemporary readers often read in snippets of information from multiple genres on multiple devices (mostly mobile devices for quick information). Adolescent and teenage readers expect hyperlinks, they expect color and images, they expect to go through different kinds of texts to find different kinds of information, and they expect to remix such information into another reading text. Nevertheless, a key ingredient often missing from their consumption of texts is comprehension and critical framing.

To illustrate, I draw on a two-year study in an urban, highly diverse secondary school in Toronto where the grade 11 teacher, Evelyn (pseudonym) is taking a design approach to the teaching of literature and media. In the study, funded by an IRA Elva Knight Research Grant and entitled "The Producers: Design Literacies in Action," I examine the literacy practices of the 11th-grade students. The study approaches English teaching and learning from a design perspective by asking students as rhetoricians to choose the best possible mode for a task.

By *design*, I am referring to a view of communication as designed compositions made up of visual, audio, spatial, and linguistic modes. The New London Group (1996) argues for a pedagogy based on the notion of design, claiming that to be literate today, meaning makers draw on multimodal resources as available designs that can be redesigned. The classroom teacher and I teach together, and we adopt a design-based epistemology for our study of English literature and media studies. A component of the study deals with comprehending and critically framing student reading practices. One unit of study in the research focuses on media and popular culture. For each lesson within the unit, students are presented with media and popular-culture texts. The example I offer here to illustrate teenage reading is a lesson on analyzing and critically framing language and visual features in gossip magazines, such as *Life & Style* and *Us*. To read these genres of texts critically entails a degree of scrutinizing, interrogating, and generally calling information into question, as well as actively identifying and elucidating stereotypes.

A key reading practice for a good reader of a gossip magazine is to analyze pictures, read, and critically frame written text. To promote critical reading strategies, Evelyn and I spent an hour and a half on oppositional readings of gossip magazines and popular-culture texts. We asked the students to read each gossip magazine in stages. For the first 15 minutes, the students read for information, locating new information and listing it on sticky notes that they placed throughout the print media.

Then, Evelyn and I interrogated different examples of print media to illustrate what it means to do an oppositional reading of a text. We drew on media studies theory and practices that interrogate and challenge content for stereotypes, embedded assumptions, and preferred readings. After modeling the process of oppositional reading, the students selected one gossip magazine to interrogate for meanings and stereotypes. In Figure 27.5 are two examples of their readings of photographs and their commentaries.

The third stage in the lesson moved from oppositional readings of print media to moving-image media to foster a differentiation between mediums and media. The class watched YouTube videos of advertising that exhibit similar stereotypes and hidden messages. During viewing, the class completed a chart that asked them to comment on preferred reading of text and oppositional reading of text. We watched the commercial once with sound and then another time without sound to offer different versions of the reading experience. For the final stage of the lesson, the students were asked to create their own gossip, popular-culture text and then critically frame the process of composition and the completed text.

The 90-minute lesson identified students' perceived understandings of stereotypes and subliminal messages, and we provided some ways to critically frame these readings. Moving across genres from print to moving-image media compelled students to think about how different media converge messages through common and different techniques. For instance, some students noted that vectors (Kress & van Leeuwen, 1996) are present in both print and moving images, but sound, voice, and melody modulate the tone of the message in subtle and nuanced—or as we said earlier, modular—ways. In other words, the students recognized that increasing the number and quality of modes within a text shifted its meaning. The students could only identify that shift by reading/viewing moving-image texts in different ways: with sound, without visuals and with sound, and so forth.

When they produced their own vernacular, print media texts, students were able to layer language and visuals with more connotations and discursive devices and with vectors to elicit a preferred

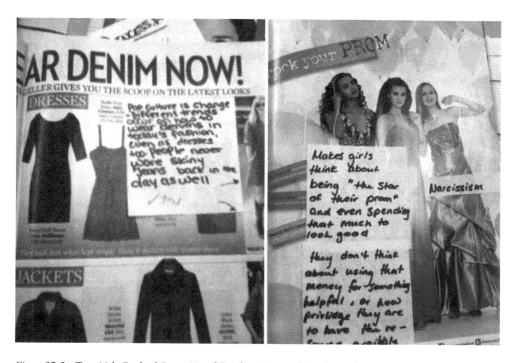

Figure 27.5   Two 11th Graders' Oppositional Reading Notes of Popular-Culture Texts

reading. By moving from neutral readings to oppositional readings to remixing these texts into their own versions and then demonstrating the converging of different values, stereotypes, and hidden messages in visuals and written text, the students acquired a meta-awareness of rhetorical devices and visual and discursive strategies that influence readings of texts. As we demonstrate in the next section, reading shifts yet again as readers move into adulthood and institutions of higher learning, or what Lea and Street (1998) call an academic literacies model.

Reading and Adult, Academic Literacies

The academic literacies model was developed by Lea and Street (1998), drawing on the theoretical framework of NLS (Gee, 1990; B. Street, 1984; Lea & Street, 1998). The model recognizes academic writing as a set of social practices within a given institutional and disciplinary context and (perhaps more than the U.S. writing-in-the-disciplines approach) highlights the influence of factors such as power and authority on student reading and writing. In the development of this model, Lea and Street conducted an empirical research project in two very different universities in the United Kingdom, in which they examined student writing against a background of institutional practices, power relations, and identities. Rather than frame their work in terms of good and poor writing, they suggested that any explanation needed to examine faculty and student expectations around writing without making any judgments about which practices were deemed most appropriate. Findings from the research suggested fundamental gaps between student and faculty understandings of the requirements of student writing, providing evidence of conflicts of understanding at the level of epistemology and authority and contestation over knowledge, rather than at the level of technical skill, surface linguistic competence, and cultural assimilation.

Based on analysis of their research data, Lea and Street (1998) explicate three models of student writing, which they term study skills, academic socialization, and academic literacies. The study skills model is primarily concerned with the surface features of text and is based on the assumption that mastery of the correct rules of grammar and syntax, coupled with attention to punctuation and spelling, will ensure student competence in academic writing. By contrast, the academic socialization model assumes that students need to be acculturated into the discourses and genres of particular disciplines and that making the features and requirements of these explicit to students will result in their becoming successful writers. The third model, academic literacies, is concerned with meaning making, identity, and power and authority, and it foregrounds the institutional nature of what counts as knowledge in any particular academic context.

The academic literacies model is similar in many ways to the academic socialization model except that the former views the processes involved in acquiring appropriate and effective uses of literacy as more complex, dynamic, nuanced, situated, and involving both epistemological issues and social processes, including power relations among people and institutions and social identities. In some respects, the third model, academic literacies, subsumes many of the features of the other two. Lea and Street (1998) point out that the models are not mutually exclusive and that each should be seen as encapsulating the other. Nevertheless, the researchers argue that the academic literacies model is best able to take account of the nature of student writing in relation to institutional practices, power relations, and identities—in short, to consider the complexity of meaning making that the other two models fail to provide.

The explication of the three models proposed by Lea and Street (1998) has been drawn on in the literature on teaching and learning across a range of higher education contexts (e.g., Thesen & van Pletzen, 2006, on South Africa) and calls for a more in-depth understanding of student reading and writing, and their relationship to learning across the academy, thus offering an alternative to deficit models of learning and literacy based on autonomous models of literacy. Academic literacies, for instance, has been a useful critical framework for identifying shortcomings in the current provision at U.K. universities (Lea & Street, 2006; Lillis, 2006, p. 33). However, there is still much to do in developing the pedagogic implications of these research and theoretical approaches (cf. Lillis, 2006; Lillis & Scott, 2008; Wingate, 2006, 2008), including developing the reading dimension of such approaches given that they have tended to focus mainly on writing. A social practice perspective on both writing and reading, then, moves outside of school and reconceptualizes school as itself a specific social practice among many, rather than a single uniform skill.

NLS and Multimodal Reading: Implications for Literacy, Pedagogy, and Policy

How all of this applies specifically to reading is an issue currently being debated in the field. As we indicated in this chapter, adopting a social perspective on reading draws attention to the fact that reading in the contemporary era may involve more and different semiotic skills than it has traditionally, when the emphasis was more on decoding skills. For instance, as we noted, attention to the social practices associated with reading leads us to recognize that children read long before they engage in schooling practices. Children engage in social relations around reading that include their parents, notably the bedtime story as Heath (1983) has indicated; with peers as they listen to and repeat readings that they hear in their own and others' homes; in their everyday exposure to public signage, posters, and shopping; and in their involvement in communicative technologies, such as browsing screens, scrolling and scanning multiple websites, clicking, following and reading hyperlinks, communicating through social networks, and so forth.

Although the main goal of this chapter was to view reading through an integrated NLS and multimodal social semiotic lens, we might also begin to move beyond just the theoretical and methodological implications that a chapter in such an important volume highlights and also develop pedagogical principles. The theory and method that we have outlined certainly lead us to recognize that current reading processes and theoretical models need to broaden definitions of reading, which are quite narrow at present, and expand these definitions beyond the word and book-sharing notions of reading. What is clear from observing any student in school, or person on the street, is that reading has gone through a transformation since the last century. There is the sheer vastness of technology and digital worlds that have dramatically shifted what we read (modes) and how we read (practices), not to mention dramatic shifts in cultural and linguistic diversity. Although there are larger debates about new approaches and methodologies for reading, the field of reading demands radical changes in policy and pedagogy so extant research and innovations can inform current accepted reading processes and theoretical models.

What might be the implications of these broader accounts of reading for pedagogy, for how teachers work to help their students acquire the reading (and writing) practices needed at different stages of the education system? If we take Heath's (1983) starting point in *Ways With Words* and her new rich account of the experience of subsequent generations in the contemporary world of diversity in social and communicative practices (Heath, 2012), then we might as educationalists take more account of how people actually make use of reading and writing in their everyday lives—the local communities and interpersonal relations of parents, children, peers, and then those in community organizations associated with them, such as the churches, second-hand stores, and dance clubs that Heath described. This could then lead policymakers in education as well as teachers to build into their pedagogy the growing literature that applies such a social practice perspective in educational contexts.

We might, then, begin to bring together the fields reviewed here, combining New Literacy Studies and multimodality with the standard views of education that, as we have suggested, have not always recognized these new developments so continue to focus on narrower conceptions of reading, text, grammar, and so on. Such a bridging position would argue that social literacy practices learned in the world of work and play are what learners at school need to know about as they enter formal education and that teachers could and should build on these in their classroom practice. Yet, at the same time, schooling can help articulate these everyday literacies and perhaps bring together a greater variety of them than students are likely to encounter in their own everyday lives. Moreover, perhaps some explicit marking of the features of the different genres and modes, following the directions pointed out previously, can be helpful in learning and enhancing these practices, notably those features that remain hidden partly because of the narrow view of literacy frequently adopted in educational contexts. If this chapter helps us move in this direction, as both theorists and as practitioners, then it will, we hope, have fulfilled the main aims of this volume as a whole.

Note

Thank you to Tara McGowan for her assiduous editorial skills and reading of the manuscript.

References

Alvermann, D.E. (Ed.). (2002). *Adolescents and literacies in a digital world.* New York: Peter Lang.
Alvermann, D.E. (2006). Ned and Kevin: An online discussion that challenges the 'not-yet-adult' cultural model. In K. Pahl & J. Rowsell (Eds.), *Travel notes from the new literacy studies: Instances of practice* (pp. 19–38). Tonawonda, NY: Multilingual Matters.
Barton, D., & Hamilton, M. (1998). *Local literacies: Reading and writing in one community.* New York: Routledge.
Bazerman, C. (1988). *Shaping written knowledge: The genre and activity of the experimental article in science.* Madison: University of Wisconsin Press.
Bezemer, J., & Kress, G. (2008). Writing in multimodal texts: A social semiotic account of designs for learning. *Written Communication, 25*(2), 166–195. doi:10.1177/0741088307313177
Bezemer, J., & Kress, G. (2009). Visualizing English: A social semiotic history of a school subject. *Visual Communication, 8*(3), 247–262. doi:10.1177/1470357209106467
Bourdieu, P. (1991). *Language and symbolic power* (J.B. Thompson, Ed.; G. Raymond & M. Adamson, Trans.). Cambridge, UK: Polity Press.
Carrington, V. (2005). New textual landscapes, information and early literacy. In J. Marsh (Ed.), *Popular culture, new media and digital literacy in early childhood* (pp. 10–20). New York: RoutledgeFalmer.
Comber, B. (2010). Critical literacies in *place*: Teachers who work for just and sustainable communities. In J. Lavia & M. Moore (Eds.), *Cross-cultural perspectives on policy and practice: Decolonizing community contexts* (pp. 43–57). New York: Routledge.
Compton-Lilly, C., Rogers, R., & Lewis, T.Y. (2012). Analyzing epistemological considerations related to diversity: An integrative critical literature review of family literacy scholarship. *Reading Research Quarterly, 47*(1), 33–60.
Davies, J. (2006). Escaping to the borderlands: An exploration of the Internet as a cultural space for teenaged Wiccan girls. In K. Pahl & J. Rowsell (Eds.), *Travel notes from the new literacy studies: Instances of practice* (pp. 57–71). Tonawonda, NY: Multilingual Matters.
Ferreiro, E., & Teberosky, A. (1982). *Literacy before schooling* (K.G. Castro, Trans.). Exeter, NH: Heinemann.
Gebre, A.H., Openjuru, G., Rogers, A., & Street, B. (2009). *Everyday literacies in Africa: Ethnographic studies of literacy and numeracy practices in Ethiopia.* Addis Ababa, Ethiopia: Fountain.
Gee, J.P. (1990). *Social linguistics and literacies: Ideology in Discourses.* New York: Falmer.
Gee, J.P. (1996). *Social linguistics and literacies: Ideology in Discourses* (2nd ed.). New York: Falmer.
González, N., Moll, L.C., & Amanti, C. (2005). *Funds of knowledge: Theorizing practices in households, communities, and classrooms.* Mahwah, NJ: Erlbaum.
Green, B. (1998). The new literacy challenge? *Literacy Learning: Secondary Thoughts, 7*(1), 36–46.
Gregory, E. (2008). *Learning to read in a new language: Making sense of words and worlds.* Thousand Oaks, CA: Sage.
Gregory, E., Long, S., & Volk, D. (Eds.). (2004). *Many pathways to literacy: Young children learning with siblings, grandparents, peers and communities.* New York: RoutledgeFalmer.
Gumperz, J.J. (1982). *Discourse strategies.* New York: Cambridge University Press.
Halliday, M.A.K., & Hasan, R. (1976). *Cohesion in English.* London: Longman.
Heath, S.B. (1983). *Ways with words: Language, life, and work in communities and classrooms.* New York: Cambridge University Press.
Heath, S.B. (2012). *Words at work and play: Three decades in family and community life.* New York: Cambridge University Press.
Hoggart, R. (1957). *The uses of literacy.* London: Penguin.

Holland, D., Lachicotte, W., Jr., Skinner, D., & Cain, C. (1998). *Identity and agency in cultural worlds.* Cambridge, MA: Harvard University Press.

Hymes, D. (1974). *Foundations in sociolinguistics: An ethnographic approach.* Philadelphia: University of Pennsylvania Press.

Ingold, T. (2007). *Lines: A brief history.* New York: Routledge.

Ivanič, R. (1998). *Writing and identity: The discoursal construction of identity in academic writing.* Philadelphia: John Benjamins.

Jones, C., Turner, J., & Street, B. (Eds.). (1999). *Students writing in the university: Cultural and epistemological issues.* Philadelphia: John Benjamins.

Keating, M.C. (2005). The person in the doing: Negotiating the experience of self. In D. Barton & K. Tusting (Eds.), *Beyond communities of practice: Language, power and social context* (pp. 105–138). New York: Cambridge University Press.

Kenner, C. (2004). *Becoming biliterate: Young children learning different writing systems.* Sterling, VA: Trentham.

Kress, G. (1997). *Before writing: Rethinking the paths to literacy.* New York: Routledge.

Kress, G. (2003). *Literacy in the new media age.* New York: Routledge.

Kress, G., & van Leeuwen, T. (1996). *Reading images: The grammar of visual design.* New York: Routledge.

Laird, J., Kienzl, G., DeBell, M., & Chapman, C. (2007). Dropout rates in the United States: 2005 (NCES 2007–059). Washington, DC: National Center for Education Statistics, Institute of Education Sciences, U.S. Department of Education.

Lea, M.R. (2004). Academic literacies: A pedagogy for course design. *Studies in Higher Education, 29*(6), 739–756. doi:10.1080/0307507042000287230

Lea, M.R., & Street, B.V. (1998). Student writing in higher education: An academic literacies approach. *Studies in Higher Education, 23*(2), 157–172.

Lea, M.R., & Street, B.V. (2006). The "academic literacies" model: Theory and applications. *Theory Into Practice, 45*(4), 368–377.

Levy, R. (2011). *Young children reading: At home and at school.* Thousand Oaks, CA: Sage.

Lewis, C., & Fabos, B. (2005). Instant messaging, literacies, and social identities. *Reading Research Quarterly, 40*(4), 470–501. doi:10.1598/RRQ.40.4.5

Lillis, T. (2003). Student writing as "academic literacies": Drawing on Bakhtin to move from "critique" to "design." *Language and Education, 17*(3), 192–207.

Lillis, T., & Scott, M. (2008). Defining academic literacies research: Issues of epistemology, ideology and strategy. *Journal of Applied Linguistics, 4*(1), 5–32.

Mackey, M. (2010). Reading from the feet up: The local work of literacy. *Children's Literature in Education, 41*(4), 323–339. doi:10.1007/s10583-010-9114-z

Marsh, J. (2005). Introduction: Children of the digital age. In J. Marsh (Ed.), *Popular culture, new media and digital literacy in early childhood* (pp. 1–8). New York: RoutledgeFalmer.

Marsh, J. (2011). Young children's literacy practices in a virtual world: Establishing an online interaction order. *Reading Research Quarterly, 46*(2), 101–108. doi:10.1598/RRQ.46.2.1

Miller, D. (2008). *The comfort of things.* Malden, MA: Polity.

Miller, D. (2010). *Stuff.* Malden, MA: Polity.

Neuman, S.B., & Celano, D. (2001). Access to print in low-income and middle-income communities: An ecological study of four neighborhoods. *Reading Research Quarterly, 36*(1), 8–26. doi:10.1598/RRQ.36.1.1

New London Group. (1996). A pedagogy of multiliteracies: Designing social futures. *Harvard Educational Review, 66*(1), 60–92.

Pahl, K. (2002). Ephemera, mess and miscellaneous piles: Texts and practices in families. *Journal of Early Childhood Literacy, 2*(2), 145–166. doi:10.1177/14687984020022002

Pahl, K. (2004). Narratives, artifacts and cultural identities: An ethnographic study of communicative practices in homes. *Linguistics and Education, 15*(4), 339–358. doi:10.1016/j.linged.2005.07.002

Pahl, K., Lewis, M., & Ritchie, L. (2010). *Book sharing in the home: An ethnographic study.* Unpublished report, Book Trust.

Pink, S. (2009). *Doing sensory ethnography.* Thousand Oaks, CA: Sage.

Prior, P.A. (1998). *Writing/disciplinarity: A sociohistoric account of literate activity in the academy.* Mahwah, NJ: Erlbaum.

Rampey, B.D., Dion, G.S., & Donahue, P.I. (2009). *NAEP 2008 trends in academic progress* (NCES 2009–479). Washington, DC: National Center for Education Statistics, Institute of Education Sciences, U.S. Department of Education.

Rogoff, B. (2003). *The cultural nature of human development.* New York: Oxford University Press.

Rosowsky, A. (2008). *Heavenly readings: Liturgical literacy in a multilingual context.* Tonawanda, NY: Multilingual Matters.

Russell, D.R. (1991). *Writing in the academic disciplines, 1870–1990: A curricular history*. Carbondale: Southern Illinois University Press.

Russell, D.R., Lea, M., Parker, J., Street, B., & Donahue, T. (2009). Exploring notions of genre in "academic literacies" and "writing across the curriculum": Approaches across countries and contexts. In C. Bazerman, A. Bonini, & D. Figueiredo (Eds.), *Genre in a changing world: Perspectives on writing* (pp. 395–423) Fort Collins, CO: WAC Clearinghouse; West Lafayette, IN: Parlor.

Street, B.V. (1984). *Literacy in theory and practice*. New York: Cambridge University Press.

Street, B.V. (1993). *Cross-cultural approaches to literacy*. New York: Cambridge University Press.

Street, B.V. (1996). Academic literacies. In D. Baker, J. Clay, & C. Fox (Eds.), *Challenging ways of knowing: In English, maths and science* (pp. 96–122). London: Falmer.

Street, B. (1997). The implications of the "new literacy studies" for literacy education. *English in Education, 31*(3), 45–59.

Street, B.V. (2009). "Hidden" features of academic paper writing. *Working Papers in Educational Linguistics, 24*(1), 1–17.

Street, B. (2011). NLS1 and NLS2: Implications of a social literacies perspective for policies and practices of literacy education. In A. Goodwyn & C. Fuller (Eds.), *The great literacy debate: A critical response to the Literacy Strategy and the Framework for English* (pp. 106–116). New York: Routledge.

Street, J.C., & Street, B. (1991). The schooling of literacy. In D. Barton & R. Ivanič (Eds.), *Writing in the community* (pp. 143–166). Thousand Oaks, CA: Sage.

Thesen, L., & van Pletzen, E. (Eds.). (2006). *Academic literacy and the languages of change*. New York: Continuum.

Vygotsky, L.S. (1978). *Mind in society: The development of higher psychological processes* (M. Cole, V. John-Steiner, S. Scribner, & E. Souberman, Eds. & Trans.). Cambridge, MA: Harvard University Press.

Williams, A.L., & Merten, M.J. (2008). A review of online social networking profiles by adolescents: Implications for future research and intervention. *Adolescence, 43*(170), 253–274.

Wingate, U. (2006). Doing away with "study skills." *Teaching in Higher Education, 11*(4), 457–469.

Wingate, U. (2009). Enhancing students' transition to university through online preinduction courses. In R. Donnelly & F. McSweeney (Eds.), *Applied e-learning and e-teaching in higher education* (pp. 178–200). Hershey, PA: Information Science Reference.

Wingate, U., & Tribble, C. (2012). The best of both worlds? Towards an EAP/academic literacies writing pedagogy. *Studies in Higher Education, 37*(5), 157–172.

Yi, Y. (2008). Relay writing in an adolescent online community. *Journal of Adolescent & Adult Literacy, 51*(8), 670–680. doi:10.1598/JAAL.51.8.6

Zentella, A.C. (Ed.). (2005). *Building on strength: Language and literacy in Latino families and communities*. New York: Teachers College Press; Covina: California Association for Bilingual Education.

28

ENACTING RHETORICAL LITERACIES

The Expository Reading and Writing Curriculum in Theory and Practice

Mira-Lisa Katz, Nancy Brynelson, and John R. Edlund

This chapter analytically describes a promising high school English course, the Expository Reading and Writing Curriculum (ERWC), that effectively integrates multiple theories from the fields of reading comprehension, rhetoric, literacy, and composition to foster college readiness, academic literacy development, and literate identity formation at the high school level. Following a discussion of the policy context that spawned this statewide educational initiative in California, authors describe the curriculum, discuss significant theoretical influences, and explain how the ERWC puts these theories into practice in diverse instructional contexts. The chapter subsequently explains how the ERWC establishes a classroom environment in which the opinions of both students and teachers are actively sought and respected; provides strategic instructional scaffolding that enables students at varying levels of proficiency to more effectively read, think critically about, and compose sophisticated expository texts; integrates literacy pedagogies with concepts and practices from Aristotelian rhetoric to promote principled debates about ideas and texts that both students and teachers find highly engaging; and flexibly supports teachers' development of generative pedagogies that enable students to acquire high-level rhetorical literacies. Blending effective practices based on research in reading comprehension, rhetoric, literacy, and composition, the ERWC supports the development of young people's academic identities and civic literacies and strengthens teachers' capacities to further cultivate the deeply literate habits of mind that students need to be successful in college, career, and community.

Policy Context

In 2009, President Barack Obama announced the American Graduation Initiative and its goal of achieving "the highest proportion of college graduates in the world" by 2020 (Office of the Press Secretary, 2009, para. 3). Although calls for increased rates of college completion are louder today than ever before (Bill & Melinda Gates Foundation, 2010; J.M. Lee, Edwards, Menson, & Rawls, 2011; Lumina Foundation, 2010; National Governors Association [NGA], 2010; NGA & Council of Chief State School Officers [CCSSO], 2010c; U.S. Department of Education, 2011), they are hardly new, and the factors contributing to the lack of college completion have been well documented over time (Adelman, 1999, 2006; Lewis & Farris, 1996; Mansfield & Farris, 1991; Parsad & Lewis, 2003). The debate regarding the purpose of higher education and the role of remedial education within it—quality versus equity—began after World War II and the G.I. Bill, rose a second time in response to Sputnik, and escalated yet again in the 1970s after the Vietnam War and the Civil Rights movement (Parker, Bustillos, & Behringer, 2010), as higher education experienced increasing shifts in student demographics. The current debate regarding remediation has shifted yet again; now the choice is access versus efficiency due to the enormous costs of remediation.[1] The view that remedial programs are largely ineffective (based on college completion rates) heads the list of reasons why remediation during college should be prevented and eliminated (Alliance for Excellent Education, 2006, 2011c; Strong American Schools, 2008).

As readers of this volume are well aware, critiques of elementary and secondary education in general, and literacy education in particular, were brought into sharp focus with the publication of *A Nation at Risk: The Imperative for Educational Reform* (National Commission on Excellence in Education, 1983) and *Becoming a Nation of Readers: The Report of the Commission on Reading* (Anderson, Hiebert, Scott, & Wilkinson, 1984) and with the results of the 1994 National Assessment of Educational Progress in reading (Williams, Reese, Campbell, Mazzeo, & Phillips, 1995). Initially, the concern regarding the decline in levels of reading proficiency centered on the early elementary grades; attention turned, however, from the wars surrounding beginning reading to the crisis of adolescent literacy in the 2000s (ACT, 2006; Biancarosa & Snow, 2006; Committee to Improve Reading and Writing in Middle and High Schools, 2009; Kamil, 2003; Kamil et al., 2008; NASBE Study Group on Middle and High School Literacy, 2005; National Commission on Writing in America's Schools and Colleges, 2003; Torgesen et al., 2007) and the disconnect between high school curricula and college expectations (ACT, 2005; American Diploma Project, 2004; Conley, 2003; Intersegmental Committee of the Academic Senates of the California Community Colleges, the California State University, and the University of California [ICAS], 2002; Joftus, 2002; Kirst, 2004).

It was within this policy context that the board of trustees of the California State University (CSU) enacted Executive Order 665 in 1997, establishing criteria for determining proficiency in mathematics and English and the consequences for failing to meet the criteria. The board also established a goal for 90% of the CSU's incoming students to be proficient according to the 1997 criteria in both mathematics and English by 2007. Several years into the policy, it became clear that achieving the goal of 90% proficient was not realistic (Mills, 2004). Consistent with the move to align high school and college curricula, the CSU embarked on an initiative to align the K–16 assessment systems so students could be identified as ready or not ready for college-level courses in mathematics and English much earlier in their school careers, making college readiness something they could pursue while still in high school. The CSU's Early Assessment Program was established in 2002 in collaboration with the California Department of Education and the California State Board of Education to accomplish this goal. The Early Assessment Program consists of five components: the test administered in 11th grade in conjunction with the mandated California Standards Test; high school preparation in English and mathematics; teacher and administrator professional development; parent and family communication; and preservice teacher preparation. Starting in 2004, students who were identified as ready for college-level courses were exempted from the requirement to take placement tests in English and/or mathematics and were moved directly into credit-bearing coursework upon enrollment in the CSU. Students who were identified as not ready for college-level courses were encouraged to do additional preparation during their senior year of high school.

The ERWC Curriculum

In response to the call for additional preparation, a task force comprised of CSU and high school educators collaborated to create the ERWC. Designed to prepare college-bound seniors for the literacy demands of higher education and civic life, the ERWC guides students through a sequence of 14 rigorous instructional units organized into a yearlong, rhetoric-based course that develops advanced proficiency in expository, analytical, and persuasive reading and writing. The course helps students read, comprehend, respond to, talk, and write about nonfiction and literary texts and provides instruction in research methods and documentation conventions. Through long-term, deep engagement with texts from varied genres throughout the course, students increase their awareness of and ability to employ the rhetorical strategies and stylistic devices of published authors. They read closely to examine the relationship between an author's argument or theme and the audience and purpose; to analyze the impact of linguistic and rhetorical devices; and to examine the social, political, philosophical, and ideological assumptions that underlie each text. Students who successfully complete the course can effectively use these strategic approaches independently when reading unfamiliar texts and writing in response to them.

Throughout the course, students explore and analyze a wide range of texts, including contemporary essays, newspaper and magazine articles, editorials, reports, memos, biographies, online materials, and assorted public documents, as well as other nonfiction and fiction texts. Written assignments, formative assessments, and holistic scoring guides constitute part of each of the 71 instructional units or modules (most are based on multiple texts) organized across two semesters.[2] Each module is built around a high-interest topic discussed from multiple perspectives, sometimes across genres. All modules include instruction in critical reading, metacognitive and rhetorical analyses, vocabulary, grammar, research methods, documentation conventions, and analytical writing based on information learned from, and in response to, the assigned texts.

A balanced and comprehensive 11th-12th-grade English language arts course (see Figure 28.1), the ERWC performs two different but strategically related functions:

1. It prepares college-bound students to take on the methodical academic reading and writing practices expected by college faculty across the disciplines.
2. It prepares teachers to more advantageously support their high school students' development of the textual practices that they will need to succeed in college and beyond while meeting California's recently adopted Common Core State Standards (CCSS) for teaching informational texts and rhetorical analysis.

In addition to helping students develop the literacies and competencies expected in postsecondary contexts (as outlined by ICAS, 2002), the ERWC materials are designed to embody the following key principles of an effective expository reading and writing curriculum:

- The integration of interactive reading and writing processes
- A rhetorical approach to texts that fosters critical thinking
- Materials and themes that engage students and provide a foundation for principled debate and argument
- Classroom activities, language routines, and interactional patterns designed to model and foster successful practices of fluent readers and writers
- Research-based methodologies with a consistent relationship between theory and practice
- Built-in flexibility to allow teachers to respond to varied students' needs and diverse instructional contexts
- Alignment with California's CCSS for English language arts (California Department of Education, 2010)

These principles (California State University, 2008, p. xi) are instantiated in the ERWC's assignment template (a patterned process through which each of the curricular units is flexibly structured), which outlines the important moves that students make as they read and interact with texts, connect the texts they read to the writing they plan to do, and talk and write about the ideas and issues contained in and inspired by the texts. Throughout the instructional process, students read and revisit readings with different purposes. They discuss and write about the texts and their own thinking numerous times—each time with a different purpose. As a result of this relentless focus on the text, students construct deep understandings of what the texts say, mean, and do, and are

Module Order	Module Summary & Final Writing Assignment	Texts
1. Fast Food: Who's to Blame?	Based on four newspaper articles and several letters to the editor, this module engages students in analyzing various perspectives on who is to blame for the rise in childhood obesity. Final Writing: timed writing, rhetorical evaluation of the letters to the editor, or textbased argumentative essay.	• Barboza, David. "If You Pitch It, They Will Eat." *New York Times* 3 Aug. 2003, late ed., sec. 3: 1. • Brownlee, Shannon. "It's Portion Distortion That Makes America Fat." *Sacramento Bee* 5 Jan. 2003: E1+. • Weintraub, Daniel. "The Battle Against Fast Food Begins in the Home." *Sacramento Bee* 17 Dec. 2002: B7. • Zinczenko, David. "Don't Blame the Eater." *New York Times* 23 Nov. 2002, late ed.: A19.
2. Going for the Look	After analyzing an article on the lawsuit accusing Abercrombie & Fitch of discriminatory hiring practices, *Going for the Look* concludes with a timed writing or an argumentative essay.	• Greenhouse, Steven. "Going for the Look, but Risking Discrimination." *New York Times* 13 July 2003, sec. 1: 12.
3. The Rhetoric of the Op-Ed Page: Ethos, Logos, and Pathos	This module introduces the Aristotelian concepts of ethos, logos, and pathos and applies them to a rhetorical analysis of an op-ed piece by Jeremy Rifkin. The culminating writing assignment is a letter to the editor responding to the Rifkin piece.	• Edlund, John. "Three Ways to Persuade." *Expository Reading and Writing Course: Semester One.* Long Beach: CA State UP, 2008. (29–32) • Rifkin, Jeremy. "A Change of Heart About Animals." *Los Angeles Times* 1 Sept. 2003: B15.
4. The Value of Life	*The Value of Life* asks students to synthesize and critically respond to four pieces: Hamlet's "To be, or not to be" soliloquy; an excerpt from Lance Armstrong's It's Not About the Bike; an article by Amanda Ripley on the aftermath of 9/11; and a life insurance tool, the Human Life Value Calculator. The unit concludes with an academic essay responding to all sources.	• Armstrong, Lance, with Sally Jenkins. It's *Not About the Bike: My Journey Back to Life.* New York: Putnam, 2000. (1–5) • Life and Health Insurance Foundation for Education. "The Human Life Value Calculator." • Ripley, Amanda. "What Is a Life Worth?" *Time* 11 Feb. 2002: 22–27. • Shakespeare, William. Hamlet, Act III, Sc. 1, Hamlet's "To be, or not to be" soliloquy.
5. Racial Profiling	After reading an argumentative essay by Bob Herbert on racial profiling, students write their own argumentative piece on a similar topic.	• Herbert, Bob. "In America; Hounding the Innocent." *New York Times* 13 July 1999, late ed., sec. 4: 17.
6. Juvenile Justice	Drawing on four newspaper articles about whether juveniles who commit serious crimes should be tried and sentenced as adults, *Juvenile Justice* asks students to evaluate authors' rhetorical stances and synthesize their arguments in a text-based academic essay.	• Krikorian, Greg. "Many Kids Called Unfit for Adult Trial." *Sacramento Bee* 3 Mar. 2003: A6. • Liptak, Adam. "Ruling is Awaited on Death Penalty for Young Killers." *New York Times* 4 Jan. 2005, late ed.: A1+. • Lundstrom, Marjie. "Kids Are Kids—Until They Commit Crimes." *Sacramento Bee* 1 Mar. 2001: A3.

Figure 28.1 Expository Reading and Writing Curriculum Matrix of Modules

		• Thompson, Paul. "Startling Finds on Teenage Brains." *Sacramento Bee* 25 May 2001: B7.
7. The Last Meow	Focusing on a reflective essay about recent developments in veterinary medicine, *The Last Meow* asks students to infer the writer's argument and then compose a piece in one of the following genres: persuasive or academic summary, letter to the editor, I-Search or research paper, or other options.	• Bilger, Burkhard. "The Last Meow." *New Yorker* 8 Sept. 2003: 46–53.
8. Into the Wild	Based on *Into the Wild*, a full-length non-fiction work by Jon Krakauer (1996), this module offers students extended opportunities to think deeply about human motivation and maturation and includes excerpts from the American Transcendentalists and Russian novelists who influenced the main character's thinking. Students conclude with a text-based academic essay on one of a number of themes.	• Krakauer, Jon. *Into the Wild*. New York: Doubleday, 1996.
9. Bring a Text to Class	Introducing the second semester of the ERWC, *Bring a Text to Class* builds on out-of-school texts, broadly conceived, that students bring in to share. The module enables students to make their textual expertise explicit and connects out-of-school and in-school reading. Students conclude by reflecting on classmates' chosen texts and reflecting metacognitively on their own reading practices.	• "Hip-Hop Becoming Worldwide Language for Youth Resistance." *USA Today Magazine* Sept. 2000: 7.
10. Language, Gender, and Culture	Drawing on readings in literature and sociolinguistics, *Language, Gender, and Culture* invites students to explore how language conveys cultural values and gender-based communication styles. Students conclude with a textbased academic essay.	• Ehrlich, Gretel. "About Men." *The Solace of Open Spaces*. New York: Penguin, 1985. 49–53. • Kingston, Maxine Hong. *The Woman Warrior: Memoirs of a Childhood Among Ghosts*. New York: Random House, 1976. 165–82. • Tannen, Deborah. "His Politeness Is Her Powerlessness." *You Just Don't Understand: Women and Men in Conversation*. New York: William Morrow/HarperCollins, 1990. 203–05.
11. Left Hand of Darkness	*The Left Hand of Darkness* is a multi-genre science fiction novel that includes field reports, folktales, and other genre-bending texts.	• Le Guin, Ursula K. *The Left Hand of Darkness*. New York: Penguin, 1969.

Figure 28.1 (Continued)

	Students extend the rhetorical techniques of the ERWC to a full-length literary work and conclude with a text-based academic essay.	
12. The Politics of Food	*The Politics of Food* is based on two articles that ask readers to consider connections between science, agriculture, and politics as they relate to human health and well-being. Students conclude the module with a text-based academic essay.	• Berry, Wendell. "The Pleasures of Eating." *What Are People For? Essays.* New York: North Point/Farrar, Straus and Giroux, 1990. 145–52. • Pollan, Michael. "When a Crop Becomes King." *New York Times* 19 July 2002, late ed.: A17.
13. Justice: Childhood Love Lessons	Based on an argumentative essay by bell hooks, *Childhood Love Lessons* examines the relationship between parental discipline and expressions of love. Students respond with a persuasive essay.	• hooks, bell. "Justice: Childhood Love Lessons." *All About Love: New Visions.* New York: William Morrow, 2000. 17–30.
14. Bullying at School: Research Project	In *Bullying at School,* students read widely from refereed journal articles and conduct primary and secondary research on their own, deepening their understanding of how to find, evaluate, and document sources. The unit concludes with students writing a School Code of Conduct on bullying.	• In addition to a number of other texts, articles from the following journals constitute the reading: *ERIC Digests; Curriculum Review; Current Health; Our Children; Time; Intervention in School and Clinic; Journal of the American Medical Association; Education World; Educational Leadership; Educational Research.*

Figure 28.1 (Continued)

subsequently able to use those understandings to craft and support their own arguments in both speaking and writing (see Figure 28.2). Throughout the ERWC course, the texts students read become progressively more complex, and what students do with texts, in terms of both reading and writing, becomes increasingly challenging.

The notion of text complexity has garnered national attention of late. In the national CCSS, text complexity is determined according to three factors:

> Qualitative evaluation of the text: Levels of meaning, structure, language conventionality and clarity, and knowledge demands
> Quantitative evaluation of the text: Readability measures and other scores of text complexity
> Matching reader to text and task: Reader variables (such as motivation, knowledge, and experiences) and task variables (such as purpose and the complexity generated by the task assigned and the questions posed)
>
> *(NGA & CCSSO, 2010a, p. 12)*

In addition to increasing comprehension demands over time, the ERWC's rhetorical approach engages students in extended and challenging composing processes. Although a given text may be fairly simple to read (at the levels of quantitative and possibly qualitative complexity, as defined earlier), what one does with a text may involve multiple and nuanced analyses. In conjunction with varied analytical reading, writing that involves negotiating and weaving together the voices of others and crafting one's own stance in response to multiple texts constitutes equally complex textual work.

Such notions of text and task complexity have recently converged in the context of conversations about the emphasis on argument in the CCSS for writing. Literacy educator Gerald Graff

Reading Rhetorically	
To "read rhetorically" means to focus not only on what the text says, but also on the purposes it serves, the intentions of the author, and the effects on the audience. This section is designed to scaffold the practices of fluent academic readers for students who are developing as academic readers, writers, and thinkers.	
Prereading • Getting Ready to Read • Exploring Key Concepts • Surveying the Text • Making Predictions and Asking Questions • Understanding Key Vocabulary	Prereading describes the processes that readers use as they prepare to read a new text. It involves surveying the text and considering what they know about the topic and the text itself, including its purpose, content, author, form, and language. This process helps readers to develop a rationale for reading, anticipate what the text will discuss, and establish a framework for understanding the text when reading begins.
Reading • Reading for Understanding • Considering the Structure of the Text • Noticing Language • Annotating and Questioning the Text • Analyzing Stylistic Choices	The reading process involves using the knowledge developed during prereading to understand the text and to confirm, refine, or refute the predictions that the reader has made about the text. This section begins by asking students to read "with the grain," also called "playing the believing game." Once they have established their understanding of the text, they then read "against the grain," also called "playing the doubting game." Both processes help students comprehend a text more deeply.
Postreading • Summarizing and Responding • Thinking Critically • Reflecting on Your Reading Process	Postreading describes the process that readers follow once they have read and reread the text. It can involve restating the central ideas of the text and responding to them from a personal perspective, but it also often includes questioning the text and noting its rhetorical strategies, evaluating its arguments and evidence, and considering how it fits into the larger conversation about the topic.
Connecting Reading to Writing	
Although the writing process can be divided into stages, writing—like reading—is essentially a recursive process that continually revisits previous moments. Up until this point students have been "writing to learn" by using writing for taking notes, making marginal notations, mapping the text, making predictions, and asking questions. At this point they are ready to build on the ongoing dialogue they have had with sources, peers, and teachers, producing their own texts by using the words, ideas, and arguments that have been raised in readings and class discussion. In this transitional moment, their reading will inform, inspire, and guide their writing as they shift from being an audience for the writing of others to addressing their own audience as writers themselves.	
Discovering What You Think • Considering the Writing Task • Taking a Stance • Gathering Evidence to Support Your Claims • Getting Ready to Write	Allowing time for students to consider and process what they have read helps them establish a connection to the writing assignment. It promotes information gathering and idea generation as students begin to craft a response to a writing task. This transition from reading to writing provides opportunities for students to analyze information gathered during reading, assess its value, and begin to imagine the trajectory their own argument might take as they develop their thinking and attempt to convince readers of their stance.
Writing Rhetorically	
Thinking of writing as a rhetorical activity invites students to consider the importance of audience, purpose, ethos, situation, message, and genre as they write to affect readers in particular ways. The rhetorical approach calls on them to consider the circumstances that inform a particular occasion for writing before deciding on an argument and how it might give shape to their writing. Thus writing rhetorically emphasizes contextualized thinking, sense making, and persuasion as prerequisites for considerations about form or genre. At this point as students begin to compose a first draft, they are about to make an active contribution to the conversation among voices and between texts with which they have been interacting while reading. It can be helpful to think of the writing at this stage is "reading-based" in that it synthesizes the viewpoints and information of various sources for the writer's own purposes.	

Figure 28.2 Expository Reading and Writing Curriculum Assignment Template Overview

Entering the Conversation	Writing can be a way of discovering what we think and working
• Composing a Draft • Considering Structure • Using the Words of Others (and Avoiding Plagiarism) • Negotiating Voices	through our personal concerns (as described above in "Discovering What You Think"), for example in diaries and journals, but most often we write to express our ideas to others; writing is communication. In addition to forms of print and electronic media, such as letters, newspaper articles, memos, posters, reports, online forums, and websites, writing broadly conceived also includes texting, emailing, posting to a blog or submitting a message to a discussion board, tweeting, or using social media sites like Facebook. All of these forms of writing, as well as the more formal academic essay privileged in schools and universities, involve writers in entering an ongoing conversation in order to communicate thoughts, ideas, and arguments.
Revising and Editing	Most students equate revising with editing, but more advanced
• Revising Rhetorically • Considering Stylistic Choices • Editing the Draft • Responding to Feedback • Reflecting on Your Writing Process	writers understand that revision involves "re-evaluating" the concepts of the paper: the use of information, the arrangement and structure of arguments, and the development and significance of ideas. Revision—as both a reading activity and a writing activity—is based on an assessment of how well the writing has communicated the writer's intentions—the argument or ideas of the text. Revising for rhetorical effectiveness invites writers to address issues of content and structure before addressing sentence-level concerns such as word choice and grammatical accuracy.

Figure 28.2 (Continued)

asserts, "The university is largely an 'argument culture,' . . . therefore, K–12 schools should 'teach the conflicts' so that students are adept at understanding and engaging in argument (both oral and written) when they enter college" (NGA & CCSSO, 2010b, p. 24). In some circles in education (where rhetoric is not, perhaps, as commonly understood), we have observed that the term *argument* is sometimes used to refer only to logos. Although some educators around the nation have voiced concern about the emphasis on logical argument (logos) the ERWC teaches all three categories of appeals, or forms of persuasion that constitute Aristotelian rhetoric: ethos, the presentation of the character and authority of the speaker; logos, the use of words and arguments; and pathos, the appeal to the emotions of the audience. Logos may be privileged in academic circles in general, and in the Common Core in particular, but the ERWC goes beyond the CCSS, apprenticing students to ways of analyzing the texts they read by using rhetoric and then applying those understandings to their writing. Because single texts often use multiple forms of persuasion, text analysis in the ERWC requires that students have a broad knowledge of rhetorical appeals. Although the ERWC embraces the CCSS in terms of teaching students to write effective logical arguments (as evidenced by the elements of the assignment template "Taking a Stance" and "Gathering Evidence to Support Your Claims"), the ERWC goes beyond the CCSS to include a broader range of stances and appeals that students may need to generate as writers themselves.

However, if students participating in the ERWC analyze and produce the kinds of texts envisioned by the curriculum, they will have gone well beyond the Common Core, and as well they should because they will need such skills and habits of mind to participate fully not only in college and career but also in many spheres beyond them. As the CCSS aptly assert:

> The value of effective argument extends well beyond the classroom or workplace. . . . As Richard Fulkerson (1996) puts it in *Teaching the Argument in Writing*, the proper context for thinking about argument is one "in which the goal is not victory but a good decision, one in which all arguers are at risk of needing to alter their views, one in which a

participant takes seriously and fairly the views different from his or her own" (pp. 16–17). Such capacities are broadly important for the literate, educated person living in the diverse, information-rich environment of the twenty-first century.

(NGA & CCSSO, 2010b, p. 25)

Disseminated via professional development jointly sponsored by the CSU system and county offices of education throughout California, to date more than 14,000 educators have participated in the 20-hour ERWC professional development program (usually spread over four days across a period of several months) to learn about the course, receive free copies of the curriculum, and join the statewide ERWC Online Community, an online forum that supports ERWC teachers and teacher educators throughout the state. The arc of professional learning for most teachers begins with use of ERWC modules integrated within their existing literature-based curriculum; as they teach more of the curriculum and witness the impact it has on their students' reading and writing, many teachers move into advocacy roles, working to persuade their school administrators to offer the ERWC as a dedicated 12th-grade English course. Approved by the University of California and the CSU as a yearlong college-preparatory English course in 2006, the ERWC has been formally adopted by over 1,000 California high schools. Originally aligned with California's English–language arts content standards (California Department of Education, 1998) and currently aligned with the recently adopted CCSS (California Department of Education, 2010), the ERWC lends itself to flexible use: Teachers can shape it to meet varied students' needs in diverse instructional contexts.

The policy context today is not very different from when the project began, except that a new urgency has crept into the dialogue as international comparisons of academic performance reveal ever-worsening rankings for U.S. students (Organisation for Economic Co-operation and Development, 2010). Calls for international benchmarking from the Education Commission of the States and many of the organizations cited earlier urge educators to do a better job of preparing students not just for college but also for global competition (Education Commission of the States, 2008; Thompson, 2009). The Alliance for Excellent Education (2011b) asserts, "now more than ever, the nation's education system is being challenged by a technology-driven global economy that requires a skilled and deeply literate workforce" (p. 1).

The CCSS are a response to the call for increased competitiveness and the desire for more consistent and coherent assessment data nationwide. The CCSS place an even greater emphasis on reading and writing complex informational text and argumentation than do the 1997 California English–language arts content standards (NGA & CCSSO, 2010c). Because of its focus on expository text and rhetoric, the ERWC aligns well with the new standards and is viewed by many as a model of effective and engaging curriculum that has the advantage of also addressing the CCSS (A.R. Vaughn, personal communication, October 26, 2011). Moreover, current teachers of the ERWC have been identified as potential leaders in the transition to California's CCSS (N.S. Brownell, personal communication, November 3, 2011).

The ERWC was designed to help students develop the literate dispositions and habits of mind necessary for academic success by building task persistence and competence through engaging topics and research-based instructional methodologies (Alvermann & Moore, 1991; Langer, 1995, 2000; Nystrand, 1997). Coupled with the focus on rhetoric and critical thinking—the real work of adults in college, careers, and communities—the ERWC enables students to develop agency in academic contexts, cultivate identities as potentially successful college-going students, and become active participants in the varied literacies woven throughout all facets of life.

Integrating the Teaching of Reading and Writing: A Brief History

Although we have known for some time that reading and writing are best taught together (Duke, Pearson, Strachan, & Billman, 2011; Shanahan, 2006; Tierney & Shanahan, 1991), the effective integration of reading and writing instruction remains largely a recommendation rather than an artful practice, while historically, many models of literacy have foregrounded the teaching of either reading (Anderson & Pearson, 1984; Kintsch, 2004; Rosenblatt, 1978/1994; Ruddell & Unrau, 2004) or writing (Flower & Hayes, 1981). The ERWC fully integrates reading and writing through sustained and recursive blending of comprehension, rhetoric, literacy, and composition processes and practices (Pressley, 2000, 2002; Wilkinson & Son, 2011).

Between the 1960s and 1980s, researchers began exploring the beneficial consequences of integrating the teaching of reading and writing (see Tierney & Shanahan, 1991, for an extensive review of the early work in this area). Very early studies (Loban, 1963, 1964, as cited in Tierney & Shanahan, 1991) have suggested that proficient writers read well, whereas less proficient writers are less successful at reading; however, later research (e.g., Martin, as cited in Tierney & Shanahan, 1991; Tierney, 1983, as cited in Tierney & Shanahan, 1991) has suggested that previous claims were overstated and somewhat misleading (Tierney & Shanahan, 1991). Shanahan and Lomax argued in 1986 that "reading influences writing, *and* writing influences reading," which suggests "that reading and writing should be taught in ways that maximize the possibility of using information drawn from both reading and writing. (p. 208)" (as quoted in Tierney & Shanahan, p. 249). Although such thinking is no longer new, blending rhetorically based reading and writing as the ERWC does in service of fostering deep academic learning and literacy embodies instantiations and combinations of reading and writing pedagogies that are novel.

Since the 1980s, there has been considerable interest in the similarities "between the cognitive *processes* underlying reading and writing" (Tierney & Shanahan, 1991, p. 250). Summaries of this research appear elsewhere (Langer & Flihan, 2000; Tierney & Shanahan, 1991), but for the purposes of the present review, Wittrock's 1984 claim remains noteworthy: "Reading and writing are generative cognitive processes in which readers and writers 'create meanings by building relations between the text and what they know, believe, and experience' (p. 77)" (as quoted in Tierney & Shanahan, 1991, p. 251). Other researchers suggest that reading and writing—both creative acts of composing—share underlying processes, such as goal setting, projection, perspective taking, and review (Tierney & Pearson, as cited in Tierney & Shanahan, 1991, p. 251). Kucer's (1985, 2009) research additionally highlights the salience of context and background knowledge in the production of textual worlds—a critically important idea that has been expanded on by other researchers.

Although process-oriented studies in recent decades have done much to enhance our understanding of the similarities and differences between reading and writing processes, and indeed, they confirm the benefits of integrated reading and writing instruction, studies to date have not yet gone far enough in helping us understand "the transactional nature of reading and writing, of intertextuality, of how interpersonal factors influence meaning-making" (Tierney & Shanahan, 1991, p. 255), nor has most research to date helped us understand the complex interpersonal factors that influence meaning making, or negotiations of voice, self, and other in the context of academic reading and writing. Also of importance to understanding the ERWC is the research on readers' and writers' transactions with texts (e.g., RAND Reading Study Group, 2002; Smith, 1983, 1984).

> To read and write, as Augustine and Winterowd (1986); Beach and Liebman-Kleine (1986); Bruce (1980); Tierney, LaZansky, Raphael, and Cohen (1987); Pratt (1977); Pearson and Tierney (1984); and Shanklin (1981) have suggested, requires authors who expect meaning-making on the part of readers *and* readers who do the meaning-making. Writers, as they produce text, consider their readers—or at least the transactions in which readers are likely to engage. . . . [W]riters try to address and satisfy what they project as the response of the reader to that speech act that underlies the surface structure of the communication. . . . Readers, as they read text, respond to what they perceive writers are trying to get them to think of, as well as what readers themselves perceive they need to do.
> *(Tierney & Shanahan, 1991, p. 259)*

Shanahan's (2006) review of research conducted between 1985 and 2000 claims that "reading and writing are dependent upon common cognitive substrata of abilities (e.g., visual, phonological, and semantic systems or short- and long-term memory), and anything that improves these abilities may have implications for both reading and writing development" (p. 174). Building on his research with Fitzgerald (Fitzgerald & Shanahan, as cited in Shanahan, 2006), he suggests that "readers and writers rely on four common knowledge bases" (p. 174): domain or content knowledge; metaknowledge; knowledge of specific features of writing (from phonemic, orthographic, and morphological to lexical, syntactic, and discursive); and procedural knowledge. Citing research spanning a century (from Dejerine's pioneering work in the 1890s on word blindness and agraphia to neuroscientific research from the late 1990s and early 2000s), Shanahan notes the importance of the "overlapping but separable nature of reading and writing at a neurological level" (p. 177).

This overlap, it turns out, is at the root of the two basic reasons it is beneficial to integrate reading and writing instructionally: The first has to do with what is shared across reading and writing domains, and the second has to do with what is different about them. Shanahan (2006) explains,

> One learning theory holds that learning is achieved through examining and reexamining information from a variety of cognitive perspectives (McGinley & Tierney, 1989). . . . Within this theory, each reconsideration of information [whether via reading or writing] is deepened, not from repetition (that is a memory issue), but from thinking about the information in a new way. Since reading and writing have a somewhat different cognitive footprint, . . . it is possible that reading and writing can provide these separate vantages for learning.
>
> *(p. 177)*

This explains why it is not enough to teach both reading and writing in the same class (as has so often been done during the past three decades in the name of 'integrating reading and writing'). "Research suggests that individuals combine reading and writing in different ways for various [real-world] tasks" (p. 177). Their usage must be truly woven together in ways that resonate deeply with authentic uses of reading and writing in the worlds of school, work, and civic life.

How we employ texts at school, at work, and in our communities determines, reflects, and supports the varied social and cultural purposes for which they are used. Shanahan (2006) concludes that a "rich empirical research base" demonstrates how

> reading and writing depend upon a common base of cognitive processes and knowledge, and we have a particularly fertile understanding of what kinds of linguistic knowledge are shared between reading and writing, how the patterns of this knowledge sharing change with development, and how reading and writing influence each other. These studies have revealed even closer relations between reading and writing than those previously found and have extended our understanding of the bidirectionality of these relations. . . .
>
> Studies have shown that it is possible to teach reading so that it improves writing and to teach writing so that it improves reading, but we do not know how to do this consistently.
>
> *(p. 179)*

We suggest that the ERWC—which is both a curriculum and a method that puts rhetorical, sociocultural, composition, and comprehension theories of language and learning simultaneously into practice—is moving in this promising direction.

Comprehension: Where Reading Research Has Taken Us

Chronicling the development of over 50 years of reading research, Pearson (2011a) states that "most models of reading have tried to explain how reader factors, text factors and context factors interact when readers make meaning" (slide 25). Citing Richards, Pearson suggests that the scholarship of the mid-20th century, although focused on "new criticism" in literature (during the 1940s and 1950s), tended in the 1960s to follow bottom-up cognitive models, which he notes were very "text-centric" (slide 26). In the 1970s, cognitive models became more schema-based, "and the reader response models (Rosenblatt) of the 80s focused more on reader factors—knowledge or interpretation mattered most" (Pearson, 2011a, slide 28). The sociocultural models of the 1990s widened the scope of study to include social, socioeconomic, and cultural influences alongside purpose, situation, and the ways values of discourse communities inevitably collide in the context of literacy teaching and learning.

Tracing a parallel trajectory of scholarship on comprehension strategies instruction since the 1970s, Wilkinson and Son (2011) outline four waves of reading research (following the three described by Pressley). In the 1970s and early 1980s, research "focused on the effects of teaching students individual comprehension strategies" (p. 362). Although specific strategies (e.g., activating background knowledge, questioning, summarizing, picturing the text) proved effective, the second wave of research in the 1980s focused on multiple-strategies instruction (e.g., reciprocal teaching).

> During the second wave, the direct explanation approach to strategy instruction came to the fore (Duffy, et al., 1987). Teachers explained to students . . . how to use a small repertoire of strategies, modeled the use of the strategies, and engaged students in guided and independent practice of the strategies.
>
> *(p. 362)*

Studies of this approach yielded "fairly robust benefits for students' comprehension" (p. 362).

The third wave of research, Wilkinson and Son (2011) suggest, "focused on a more flexible approach . . . called 'transactional strategies instruction' (TSI), so called because it emphasized transactions between readers and text, transactions among participants (students and teacher), and joint construction of understanding" (p. 363). In TSI, there is more emphasis on conversation among students— "on dialogue, on giving students more control over their own learning, and on collaborative inquiry as a mean [*sic*] of constructing knowledge and understanding" (p. 367). Based on the evolution of this research, there is now "no doubt that instruction in small repertoires of comprehension strategies, when implemented well, produces robust effects on measures of comprehension, including standardized tests (e.g., Anderson, 1992; Brown et al., 1996; Collins, 1991)" (p. 364).

In their review of comprehension strategies instruction, Wilkinson and Son (2011) describe the final and fourth wave as dialogic. Central to such

> approaches is the juxtaposition of relative perspectives or discourses that gives rise to tension and sometimes conflict among different voices. From a dialogic perspective, it is from the interaction and struggle among different, even competing, voices that meaning and understanding emerge.
>
> *(p. 367)*

Programs that fall within this fourth wave include Concept-Oriented Reading Instruction (CORI), in-depth expanded applications of science, and Reading Apprenticeship (Greenleaf, Schoenbach, Cziko, & Mueller, 2001; Schoenbach & Greenleaf, 2009; Schoenbach, Greenleaf, Cziko, & Hurwitz, 1999). What these programs share is a focus on teaching comprehension within specific subject areas. Of particular note is the ability of programs like Reading Apprenticeship to help educators teach reading comprehension in middle and high school contexts where subject matter demands are more complex.

Unsurprisingly, classroom discussion plays a critical role in promoting comprehension. Although this idea is not new, its implementation is now based on more robust research and theory from sociocognitive, sociocultural, and other approaches to teaching and learning.

> From a sociocognitive perspective, discussion enables students to make public their perspectives on issues arising from the text, consider alternative perspectives proposed by peers, and attempt to reconcile conflicts among opposing points of view (Almasi, 1995). From a sociocultural perspective, discussion enables students to co-construct knowledge and understandings about the text and internalize ways of thinking that foster the knowledge, skills, and dispositions needed to transfer to the reading of new texts (Wells, 2007). And from a dialogic perspective, the tension and conflict between relative perspectives and competing voices in discussion about a text helps shape the discourse and students' comprehension (Nystrand, 2006).
>
> *(Wilkinson & Son, 2011, p. 369)*

As we might expect, the quality and types of talk matter; open discussion, authentic questions, and uptake of learners' ideas "in the context of academically challenging tasks" correlate positively with students' reading comprehension and academic performance (p. 370). Citing research by Anderson and colleagues, Wilkinson and Son (2011) posit that learning to make rhetorical moves in conversation (taking a position on an issue and using evidence to support it) transfers from group discussion to "written argumentation performed individually and independently" (p. 372). Intertextuality (cf. Lemke, 1992)—learning to make sense of multiple texts in conversations with one another—"might be regarded as the sine qua non of dialogic approaches to teaching comprehension" (Wilkinson and Son, 2011, p. 374). The bottom line is that high-quality discussion creates authentic opportunities "for students to develop the automatic, fluid articulation of strategies necessary for generative and flexible comprehension" (p. 376).

Enacting Rhetorical Literacies

A particularly critical element of the ERWC—the integration of Aristotelian rhetoric—is not considered fully enough (if at all) in the many studies cited earlier, nor is it considered more generally in most research on literacy and reading comprehension. We believe a greater focus on the rhetorical dimension could greatly enhance young people's academic literacies as well as their abilities to successfully engage in meaningful and principled civic debate. Originally inspired by Bean, Chappell, and Gillam (2004), the ERWC authors view both reading and writing as rhetorical processes. Essentially a dialogic approach to literacy (Bakhtin, 1981; Vygotsky, 1978; Wilkinson & Son, 2011), the ERWC is well positioned within Wilkinson and Son's fourth wave of dialogic research on comprehension instruction for its use of discussion, argumentation, and intertextuality (discussed in more detail in the next section). Also congruent with theories of engagement and motivation (Ainley, 2006; Bandura, 1997; Csikszentmihalyi, 1990, 1997; Deci, 1980; Hidi & Harackiewicz, 2000; Pajares, 2003; Reed, Schallert, Beth, & Woodruff, 2004; Ryan & Deci, 2000, 2002; Schunk, 2003), the ERWC echoes the key structures in CORI, including "1) goals for learning; 2) autonomy support; 3) social collaboration; 4) strategy instruction; 5) interesting texts; and 6) real-world interaction" (Swan, 2004, p. 285; see also Guthrie, McRae, & Klauda, 2007; Guthrie, Wigfield, Barbosa, et al., 2004; Guthrie, Wigfield, & Klauda, 2012; Guthrie, Wigfield, & Perencevich, 2004). The rhetorical literacies enacted through the ERWC promote textual and conversational processes and dispositions that aid comprehension, engagement, and transfer.

Such dialogical back-and-forth—what Bakhtin calls the reciprocal relationship between speaker and listener—is central to the rhetorical approach of the ERWC. As Bakhtin suggests, "a word is territory *shared* by both addresser and addressee, by the speaker and his interlocutor. (pp. 85–86)" (as quoted in Tierney & Shanahan, 1991, p. 259). Texts made up of words amplify this fundamental relationship. Drawing on Bakhtin's ideas, Nystrand (1986) describes what he calls the reciprocity principle, by which readers and writers orient their actions to others based on social rules of conduct. As readers and writers become more familiar with such rules and as habits of mind develop, the expectations for reciprocity in discourse shape ongoing dialogue. While the ERWC draws on concepts and research from the fields of composition, reading theory, and pedagogy as well as literacy studies, we posit that one of the most powerful dimensions of the ERWC curriculum is the strategic blending of Aristotelian rhetoric with research-based approaches to secondary and postsecondary literacies—in particular, the teaching of reading and composition.

Aristotle's practical and teachable system is an integral part of the ERWC reading process. For each reading, students are asked questions related to ethos about who the writer is, what authority the writer has to talk about the subject, what biases (social, cultural, political) the writer might have, and how the writer presents him- or herself. They are also asked pathos-related questions about how the writer is engaging their emotions and whether these strategies influence their response to the arguments of the piece. These questions inspire modes of response that are crucial to an academic assessment of the worth of a text: Is it logical, rational, reliable, and credible? They also teach students that authors deploy rhetorical and linguistic strategies designed to persuade readers and that they are the object of these strategies. These realizations cause students to feel that they have some power over the text, as they begin to see the rhetorical machinery in action, and to feel that they are personally part of the conversation. These dual effects increase students' engagement with the reading and, subsequently, with the writing.

Although the ERWC is deeply influenced by Aristotle, like some of the other fourth-wave dialogic approaches (Wilkinson & Son, 2011), it is also informed by concepts from Bakhtin (1981). His basic unit of analysis for understanding discourse is the utterance. He says, "Any utterance—the finished, written utterance not excepted—makes response to something and is calculated to be responded to in turn. It is but one link in a continuous chain of speech performances" (p. 35).

From this viewpoint, with anything we hear or read, the first act is a response; we agree, we disagree, we take offense, or we are puzzled, baffled, incredulous, or stunned. For Bakhtin (1981), understanding and response are one:

> In the actual life of speech, every concrete act of understanding is active: it assimilates the word to be understood into its own conceptual system filled with specific objects and emotional expressions, and is indissolubly merged with the response, with a motivated agreement or disagreement. . . . Understanding comes to fruition only in the response. Understanding and response are dialectically merged and mutually condition each another; one is impossible without the other.
>
> *(p. 282)*

In most current models of reading comprehension, such as Kintsch's (2004), the reader processes the semantic, syntactical, and grammatical relationships in the text to form a textbase that interacts with prior knowledge (the knowledge base) to create a situational model of the meaning of the text. Such models are concerned primarily with how readers make meaning from text (rather than with the purposes of the author, the designs of the author on the reader, the reasons the reader has for reading a text, or what actions the reader may be inspired to take after reading). However, if we replace "knowledge base" with "conceptual system" (and Bakhtin would probably say "ideological system"), we get closer to what Bakhtin (1981) is getting at here. The knowledge base is not neutral; some meanings can be integrated more easily than others. Thus, there is always a response, a motivated agreement or disagreement. The ERWC curriculum deploys strategies for making meaning out of the text but importantly, we think, goes beyond the text and knowledge base to create a contextualized or situational model that includes rhetorical concerns.

Rhetoric, in fact, can be seen as strategies for influencing the way a text is received, what Bakhtin (1981) calls the response. For rhetorical models to work, however, an author or author concept must exist. We argue that blending rhetoric with reading comprehension strategies enhances students' abilities to accomplish one of the most distinctive features of academic discourse: the weaving together of others' words for the writer's own purposes. As students make the shift from readers to writers, they will need to quote, paraphrase, and summarize their sources. Bakhtin's notions about language are also useful for understanding and theorizing this process.

In "Discourse in the Novel," Bakhtin (1981) introduces the concept of doublevoiced discourse, or heteroglossia. He defines *heteroglossia* as *"another's speech in another's language*, serving to express authorial intentions but in a refracted way" (p. 324). In other words, the novelist takes words and phrases from different social strata in society and puts them in the mouths of characters, where they resonate with the voices of the actual people who spoke them—the voice of the character, the voice of the narrator, and the voice of the author—each voice meaning something different. For Bakhtin, heteroglossia is a linguistic given; it constitutes the basic building material of the novel. The ERWC likewise treats academic texts as heteroglossic responses to other texts, other voices.

From a Bakhtinian point of view, an academic paper can be seen as a documented heteroglossic utterance. The ERWC teaches strategies that rhetorical writers use to control the effects of heteroglossia, to arrange the multiple voices into a unified choir. The student writer must indicate a stance toward each text that he or she uses in the piece and orchestrate how the different texts relate to one another. All of these practices of representing texts and voices are commonplace in academic writing, part of the appropriation and assimilation of the words and ideas of others. Building these kinds of textual dispositions, the ERWC enables students to enact rhetorical literacies with a sense of agency and engagement.

The Fifth Wave: Achieving Deeper Learning Through Rhetorical Literacies

To recap the research on comprehension strategies instruction as outlined earlier and elsewhere, Wilkinson and Son's (2011) first wave focused on single-strategy instruction, the second wave centered on multiple-strategies instruction, the third wave fostered transactional strategies instruction (the right tool at the right time), and the fourth wave attended additionally to the dialogue about— and with—texts and their authors. Pearson (2011b) proposes a fifth wave, "Something in between explicit lessons, opportunistic teaching, and mini-lessons" (slide 70). This imagined fifth wave of instruction uses authentic examples, a good deal of group problem solving, and genuine puzzling examples to help students distinguish between "Nike Reading: Just do it!" and "Sherlock Holmes Reading: Deliberate puzzle resolution, Reading Like a Detective" (slide 70). The goal is what the Alliance for Excellent Education (2011a, 2011b) calls deeper learning, which combines critical thinking and critical literacy. The first comes out of the "Liberal Humanist Tradition of Rhetoric and Argumentation," and the second emerges from a blend of "post-modern traditions, all of which begin with the assumption that language is inherently political, never neutral, [and] laden with purpose, intention, and action" (Pearson, 2011b, slide 132). The ERWC embodies this convergence, going beyond what text *says*, to help students examine not only what it *means* and *does* but also how it *achieves effects on readers*—that is, how an author wields language rhetorically and structurally to accomplish and convey meaning and intention or action. With regard to enhancing students' reading abilities, Pearson (2011b) suggests that we can improve students' comprehension when:

- We engage students in rich *discussions* that allow [them] to integrate knowledge, experience, strategies, and textual insights
- We recognize that talk is our most important vehicle for gaining a rich and highly differentiated/integrated vocabulary/conceptual knowledge base
- We engage kids in reading a variety of texts that vary in challenge, genre, and discipline

- We teach strategies and routines explicitly and in as contextualized a manner as we can muster!
- We provide lots of opportunities for just plain reading
- We aim for critical analysis of ideas:

  - From what the text Says → Means → Does

- We provide teachers with *real support* in PD (slide 136)

It is this rich and complex blending of reading comprehension, literacy, and rhetorical and composition processes and practices that constitutes rhetorical literacies.

Enhancing Reading Comprehension and Academic Literacies Through Discussion

Extending the tradition of research conducted since the 1970s and 1980s, Applebee, Langer, Nystrand, and Gamoran (2003) summarize 64 studies (from the fields of anthropology, linguistics, psychology, literary theory, and English education) documenting the effects of discussion on literacy performance in middle and high school English classes. These authors review the work of a variety of scholars who

> have argued that high-quality discussion and exploration of ideas—not just the presentation of high-quality content by the teacher or text—are central to the developing understandings of readers and writers (Alvermann et al., 1996; Eeds & Wells, 1989; Gambrell & Almasi, 1996; Guthrie, Schafer, Wang, & Afflerbach, 1995).
>
> *(p. 688)*

Applebee et al. assert that "students whose classroom literacy experiences emphasize discussion-based approaches in the context of high academic demands internalize the knowledge and skills necessary to engage in challenging literacy tasks on their own" (p. 685). Although their study looks more broadly at the effects of discussion-based approaches on literacy development, Applebee et al. found that "the approaches that contributed most to student performance on . . . complex literacy tasks . . . were those that used discussion to develop comprehensive understanding, encouraging exploration and multiple perspectives rather than focusing on correct interpretations and predetermined conclusions" (p. 722). They note that typically, research on comprehension strategy instruction "has focused on an array of specific techniques for structuring discussion and embedding comprehension strategies" (p. 722). In contrast, their measures of discussion-based activities focused,

> [m]ore generally, on the presence and extent of discussion and related activities designed to involve students in the exploration of ideas. The positive results that we obtained suggest that the spontaneous scaffolding or support for developing ideas that are generated during open discussions is a powerful tool for learning. This conclusion parallels one from the National Reading Panel review of comprehension strategy instruction (Langenberg, 2000), which found particular strength in approaches that involved a variety of strategies embedded in the natural flow of classroom discussion of difficult texts, because skilled reading "involves an ongoing adaptation of multiple cognitive processes" (p. 4.47).
>
> *(p. 722)*

A recent meta-analysis of classroom studies that more specifically examines the capacity of discussion-based approaches to promote "high-level comprehension of text (i.e., critical literacy)" (Murphy, Wilkinson, Soter, Hennessey, & Alexander, 2009, p. 741) suggests that a variety of discussion-based approaches, whether critical-analytic, efferent, or aesthetic/expressive, can specifically improve reading comprehension:

High-level comprehension requires that students engage with text in an epistemic mode to acquire not only knowledge of the topic but also knowledge about how to think about the topic and the capability to reflect on one's own thinking (cf. Chang-Wells & Wells, 1993). . . .

. . . In the context of discussion, students make public their perspectives on issues arising from the text, consider alternative perspectives proposed by peers, and attempt to reconcile conflicts among opposing points of view.

(p. 741)

Much literacy research to date that draws on sociocognitive and sociocultural work of theorists such as Vygotsky (1978) and Bakhtin (1981) assumes a strong link between talk and learning, and some have extended this idea to consider how talk about text specifically improves reading comprehension, thinking, and reasoning (Murphy et al., 2009). Echoing Bakhtin, Murphy et al. point out that "reasoning is necessarily a response to what has been said or experienced as well as an anticipation of what will be said in response. The underlying presupposition is that reasoning is dynamic and relational" (p. 741). Despite differing goals across discussion formats and approaches, Murphy and colleagues conclude "that discussions about and around text have the potential to increase student comprehension, metacognition, critical thinking, and reasoning, as well as students' ability to state and support arguments" (p. 743). Although less teacher talk and more student talk are not guarantees of enhanced student comprehension, Murphy et al. note that successful discussion approaches encourage "teachers to yield the floor to students . . . while mindfully attending to the nature of the discourse" (p. 761). It is this last point that we think is in part responsible for the ERWC's success. The curriculum inspires deep engagement through a wide range of literacy practices centered on high-interest texts from varied genres while simultaneously scaffolding sophisticated conversational practices (cf. Applebee, 1996; Applebee et al., 2003; Cazden, 2001; Langer, 1995; Nystrand, 1997) about text that are eventually taken up by students, informing and shaping their subsequent reading and writing.

How do talking, thinking, and writing shape one another? Collins and Madigan's (2010) Writing Intensive Reading Comprehension (WIRC) research suggests that

comprehension and expression happen together and coconstructively—comprehension contributes to expression, and expression contributes to comprehension. This is true of all language activities; talking and writing and even thinking in words help to construct meaning by capturing ideas and images in language. In this manner, comprehension and communication of meaning happen together because meaning is actively constructed as we use words to understand ideas and images.

(p. 106)

Like many of the ERWC's rhetorical literacy activities, Collins and Madigan's interactive think-sheets (see also Englert & Raphael, 1989) engage students in what these authors call "'two-handed reading.' [Students] write with one hand on the book they are writing about and one hand on the thinksheet they are using" (p. 110). Such "targeted reading"—efferent, scaffolded reading for a particular purpose (or a series of different purposes)—focuses students' "attention on specific areas of text to answer a question or respond to a writing task" (p. 110). Importantly, thinksheets, graphic organizers, and other questioning and annotation strategies externalize the reading process, making assistance, modeling, and scaffolding easier for teachers to design. As Collins and Madigan astutely point out, "Having students write their way through reading comprehension problems may be better than only talking them through the same problems because [writing about reading] records the effects of the dialogue students have with teacher, peers, and text"; such writing also ensures "that every student contributes to the work of building an understanding of the selection; this is often not the case with class discussion" occurring minus any writing (p. 114).

Like the work of Collins and Madigan (2010), the kinds of questions that the ERWC poses are not solely content based (nor are they typical test questions); students are regularly invited to reflect on their own rhetorical purposes for writing and organizing responses to text that attend to language structure and disciplinary discourse conventions. The ERWC goes a significant step further by asking students of varied proficiency levels to carefully examine and explain the rhetorical tools employed by a text's author. The collaborative unpacking of rhetorical literacies that regularly and repeatedly occurs throughout the ERWC (through both talk and writing in conjunction with reading guided by teacher modeling and assistance from classmates) ultimately enables students to understand how texts are constructed (considering not only what they say, mean, and do but also how they do it) at a level of detail that fosters reading comprehension on the one hand and students' writing on the other. As students become more skilled at integrating complex rhetorical purposes and linguistic structures into their own prose, they gain rhetorical strength and literate independence.

The ERWC creates structured yet open-ended conversational and textual opportunities for students to become deeply engaged in the content, meaning, and structure of varied genres, gradually releasing responsibility (Duke et al., 2011; Fisher & Frey, 2008; Pearson & Gallagher, 1983) to students, who then make independent, strategic choices about which rhetorical tools to deploy based on their own judgment of a given text's particular characteristics. This is authentic and deep learning in action.

The Roles of Engagement and Motivation in the ERWC's Rhetorical Literacy Approach

Increasing student motivation and engagement to improve adolescent literacy achievement has become a frequent recommendation offered by policy reports and research syntheses (Biancarosa & Snow, 2006; Duke et al., 2011; Kamil et al., 2008; Torgesen et al., 2007). The need to improve motivation and engagement to enhance reading comprehension, literacy, and academic achievement are well established, and various frameworks for fostering motivation and engagement have emerged (Brozo & Flynt, 2008; Gambrell, 2011; Guthrie, Hoa, et al., 2007; Guthrie, McRae, & Klauda, 2007; Kamil et al., 2008; Naceur & Schiefele, 2005; Reed et al., 2004; Schoenbach & Greenleaf, 2009; Turner & Paris, 1995). Evaluation studies of the ERWC cite increases in motivation and engagement as common responses to questions on the effects of the ERWC in student, teacher, and administrator surveys and interviews. Teachers and administrators report that the course effects changes in students' attitudes about their own academic identities, as well as about literacy learning more generally, and their desire to pursue postsecondary education.

> It is rare in the world of evaluation research on classroom teaching to encounter such terms as *"passion," "excitement," "desire," "motivation," "enjoyment,"* or *"engagement"* when describing how a professional development program has impacted students (Box 28.1). When asked what benefits the ERWC course had on their students' reading and writing skills and on their enjoyment of English, the teacher respondents described common student responses to the ERWC experience as *"liking"* or *"loving"* the course. Teachers reported that students displayed higher interest in the subject matter of the course.
>
> *(Hafner, Joseph, & McCormick, 2010, p. 15)*

Grassroots support for the ERWC from high school teachers is due in large part, we believe, to the response of high school students to the reading selections and themes of the course modules. Teachers at ERWC professional development workshops comment that their students "like" and "succeed" with the materials in ways they have not experienced with other programs. Although the module themes and texts were deliberately selected to be interesting to adolescents, other features of the curriculum support student motivation and engagement as well.

The ERWC fits well with several constructs and frameworks for motivation and engagement. Two programs with documented records of success, which emphasize engagement, are CORI and Reading Apprenticeship. CORI employs six key instructional practices: goals for learning, hands-on or real-world learning, interesting texts, choices or autonomy support, social collaboration, and strategy instruction (Guthrie, McRae, & Klauda, 2007; Swan, 2004). The Reading Apprenticeship model, grounded in the learning theories of Vygotsky, incorporates four dimensions (social, personal, cognitive, and knowledge-building) that intersect through metacognitive conversations, which cultivate adolescent reading development (Schoenbach et al., 1999). More recently, Schoenbach and Greenleaf (2009) discuss learning opportunities that help students develop the following:

> **Box 28.1: Student Attitudes**
>
> Enjoy = 27
> Interest = 20
> Engaged = 18
> Like = 7
> Connection = 7
> Love = 5
> Relate to = 5
> More confident = 4
> Comfort = 2
> Less threat = 2
> Motivation = 2
> Buy-in = 2

1. Dispositions for engagement in academic tasks.
2. Text-based problem-solving capacities.
3. Discipline-based literacy practices.
4. Resilient learner identities. (p. 99)

Interest and intrinsic motivation can lead to long-term and deeper levels of text-based learning (Naceur & Schiefele, 2005) and, like the ERWC, both CORI and Reading Apprenticeship harness authentic interest and inquiry to encourage students to invest personally in literacy tasks (Alexander & Fox, 2011; Alexander & Murphy, 1998; Schiefele, 1999).

The reading selections for the ERWC modules represent topics or themes of interest to adolescents (e.g., fast food and obesity, workplace discrimination based on looks, racial profiling, juveniles charged as adults) and powerful rhetorical strategies and models of language that students can discuss and analyze deeply. Most importantly, the issues addressed in the modules are relevant to the lives of young adults and are truly debatable—a fact that is reflected by the inclusion of multiple perspectives in the readings. By not promoting one right answer or a particular position, the modules provide autonomy support. Students choose their positions relative to the topic at hand and interact in many different ways with the text, their peers, and the teacher to establish their thinking. Using Aristotelian rhetoric to analyze, discuss, and write about the readings, students gain insight into how authors use language strategically and subtly to convey not only ideas (content) but also their positions about those ideas (purpose). Students learn to discern how authors shape the text to accomplish particular results (e.g., building logical arguments, establishing author's credibility, appealing to the emotions of the reader). By analyzing text in this fashion (through annotation, questioning, predicting, summarizing, and many other reading–writing activities), over time, students develop a sense of power over the text, moving from understanding what a particular text says to what it does and deciding how they will respond.

As students come to exert greater control over the reading process as well as the writing they do in response to the readings, their perceptions of themselves as autonomous learners and thinkers grow. In the writing rhetorically stage of the ERWC, students "consider the importance of audience, purpose, ethos, message, and genre to affect readers in particular ways, and they . . . make an active contribution to the conversation of voices and texts they have been interacting with while reading" (California State University, in press). As the tables turn and students come to understand how writers exert control over their readers, students in turn begin to understand how to exert control over their readers. Importantly, we think, the power dynamics in the class room also shift as students collaborate with peers and the teacher to genuinely discover what they think and, subsequently, negotiate and elaborate their positions. Valued now as coconstructors in thinking and analysis, students eventually become more autonomous in the teaching–learning exchange, enabling teachers to gradually step back, releasing responsibility for learning to students.

Many literacy researchers have distilled the research on engagement and motivation into lists of key practices. For example, Gambrell (2011) offers seven rules of engagement for reading: relevance, wide range, sustained reading, choices, social interaction, strategies for success with challenging texts, and appropriate incentives. Brozo and Flynt (2008) propose six principles for motivating students to read: self-efficacy, interest in new learning, out-of-school literacies connected with in-school literacies, abundance of interesting texts, expanded choices and options, and structured collaboration.

Most of the items in these lists are integral to the ERWC; specifically, the prior discussion illustrates the roles of interest and autonomy in the course. Another important component in motivating and engaging students in the ERWC is self-efficacy (Bandura, 1997; Pajares, 2003; Schunk, 2003). Schunk describes self-efficacy as "beliefs about [one's] capabilities to learn or perform behaviors at designated levels" (p. 159). Because of the historical and traditional focus on narrative forms, many students and teachers have few strategies for accessing expository text and analyzing it at deeper levels. The ERWC structures the reading of texts by giving students reasons to return to the text many times for various purposes. Students learn to dissect the text in terms of organizational structure and rhetorical purpose, understand new vocabulary, analyze stylistic choices, consider grammatical features, and evaluate arguments. Often without realizing it, students read a text multiple times, come to understand both its content and purpose, and critically analyze the writing's rhetorical and linguistic features. Although considerable flexibility exists within the course to adjust instruction according to the needs of students, the structure of the curriculum, as outlined in the assignment template (see Figure 28.2), moves students to competence at high levels of cognitive complexity while simultaneously engaging them through interest, autonomy support, and self-efficacy.

In addition to enthusiasm and interest, engagement also involves persistence, effort, and attention (National Research Council & Institute of Medicine, 2004), and persistence and effort are susceptible to students' perceptions of self-efficacy (Dweck, 2006). In the ERWC, students must sustain effort to read and analyze texts, establish a position based on evidence, negotiate their own position in relation to those of the authors they have read, and construct an effective argument in writing. Sustained attentiveness or cognitive engagement, described by Csikszentmihalyi (1990) as flow, is the ideal state; whether or not students in the ERWC achieve flow, they have opportunities to sustain effort over time to accomplish high-level literacy tasks and goals. Although some may contend that autonomy support and teacher-provided structure are incompatible, Jang, Reeve, and Deci (2010) argue otherwise, suggesting

> that teachers might want to initiate learning activities by involving students' inner motivational resources, communicating in noncontrolling and informational ways and acknowledging students' perspectives and negative feelings when motivational (e.g., listlessness) and behavioral (e.g., disrespectful language) problems arise. For the provision of structure, we suggest that teachers might want to initiate learning activities by offering clear and detailed expectations and instructions, offering helpful guidance and scaffolding as students try to

profit from the lesson, and providing feedback to enhance perceptions of competence and perceived personal control during a reflective postperformance period.

(p. 598)

The ERWC modules support teachers as they attempt to balance deep literacy learning with matters of interest, autonomy, and self-efficacy in promoting student engagement and motivation.

As students enact rhetorical literacies in the ERWC, they are often led to new conceptions of themselves as real players in the academic conversation. Given the high-stakes testing context from which the ERWC emerged, it is significant that students, who are preparing for college, and their teachers have the tools to improve secondary academic literacy so success in postsecondary education becomes a possible reality. Our Reading Apprenticeship colleagues describe this process of developing readerly and writerly identities well:

> As adolescents explore, or try on, possible selves, teachers encourage them to try on new reader identities, to explore and expand their visions of who they are and who they can become (Davidson & Koppenhaver, 1993). . . .
> Lave and Wenger (1991) describe the process of identity formation as a negotiation of the meaning of "participative experiences" and social interpretations of these experiences; through this negotiation, we construct who we are. Feldman (2004) reminds us that "learning not only changes what we know and do, but it changes who we are" (p. 144). When we ask students to learn something new, we are asking them to become someone new. When teachers are able to provide consistent support for students to try on new ways of acting, thinking, and interacting, we have seen evidence of significant shifts in academic identity over the course of an academic year(Litman & Greenleaf, 2008).
> *(Schoenbach & Greenleaf, 2009, p. 105)*

Existing Research on the ERWC

The research support for the rhetorical literacy practices in the ERWC and the promising results of earlier nonexperimental studies suggest that effective implementation of the curriculum would yield significant benefits for students preparing for college English. Over the past seven years, the CSU has conducted a series of evaluations of the ERWC, beginning to build a research base for summative program evaluation. The studies to date have been a rich source of formative feedback to the program design team and have informed ongoing refinement of curricular design; however, summative findings of these initial studies (described next) suggest that more formal and systematic study is needed. To that end, an Investing in Innovation development grant from the federal government is helping fund a large-scale quasi-experimental study, currently underway. Next, we briefly summarize the findings of the three studies conducted between 2005 and 2010 and provide a basic overview of the Investing in Innovation grant's study design.

First Study

In 2005, a nonexperimental pilot study was conducted with a small sample of participating ERWC teachers ($n = 10$) in representative schools in California to assess the Early Assessment Program's "Professional Development in English" (California State University, 2005). The ERWC teachers were asked to identify colleagues in their schools who had not yet participated in ERWC professional development to serve as a comparison group. All teachers (ERWC and non-ERWC) administered a Reading and Composing Skills Test at the end of their students' senior year. The results indicated a positive impact for students who participated in the ERWC on the skills associated with college readiness in English. Survey results also revealed the students' enthusiasm for the course, suggesting that strong positive attitudes toward rhetorical reading, writing, and thinking and high levels of engagement in course content were additionally associated with the course.

Second Study

In 2008, a larger study was conducted to assess implementation and associated student gains in a series of implementation designs. The Reading Institute for Academic Preparation[3] was an 80-hour program of professional learning conducted over a 12-month period that also incorporated professional learning for the ERWC. In this study, 37 schools were identified and matched on characteristics of school size, socioeconomic status, and percentage of English learners. The authors reported that in the highest implementing ERWC schools, an increase in the percentage of students who gained proficiency in English was 5 times the state average and 10 times the rate found in the comparison group. The outcome measure was the grade 11 California Standards Test. Participating teachers reported high levels of satisfaction with the curriculum and the related professional development (Program Evaluation and Research Collaborative, 2008).

Third Study

In 2010, a mixed-methods evaluation of the ERWC was released (Hafner et al., 2010). The study captured a variety of survey-based findings indicating broad support for the curriculum. For example, participating teachers reported that the course had a positive impact on students' reading and writing skills, motivation, and increased time on task associated with improvements in English proficiency. Quantitative student outcomes were collected to measure the percentage of students identified as proficient in English by the CSU upon entry. The authors reported that the improvement of scores on the California Standards Test in English Language Arts from 2006 to 2010 (rate of gain) was higher for schools implementing the ERWC than the statewide average (a 7 percentage-point gain versus a 4-point gain statewide).

Taken together, these studies illustrate strong support from educational professionals on the content richness of the ERWC and the associated engagement of students. These initial nonexperimental studies and opportunistic matched-case designs suggest some promising indications of student gains associated with the intervention; however, only with a rigorous quasi-experimental or experimental design could an inferential statement on the gains associated with the ERWC curriculum be made. Such a study, currently underway, is described next.

Current Research

An Investing in Innovation development grant from the U.S. Department of Education is currently funding additional research on the efficacy of the ERWC. The project, "From Rhetoric to College Readiness: The Expository Reading and Writing Course," is a collaborative effort of the Fresno County Office of Education, the CSU, and WestEd and aims to (1) expand, update, and refine the curriculum; (2) increase the scope and effectiveness of professional development; (3) establish intensive implementation classrooms; and (4) investigate the effectiveness of the ERWC using a rigorous, quasi-experimental research design. Approximately 6,000 students will be included in the study (3,000 in the intensive implementation classrooms). The study will follow students from their senior year of high school through their first year of college and into their second year of college. The regression–discontinuity analysis proposed for the study will permit us to reach conclusions regarding the effectiveness of the curriculum during high school and its lasting effects into college.

Anticipated outcomes include the following: (1) Approximately 3,000 students will demonstrate college readiness at the end of 12th grade and subsequent success in their first and second years of college; (2) approximately 75 teachers will demonstrate the capacity to teach the ERWC effectively; and (3) district, county, and university English language arts specialists will successfully support implementing teachers through professional development and coaching. Plans for other qualitative research efforts are being developed as well. What is learned about the efficacy of the curriculum and its optimum methods of implementation will allow us to consider how the curriculum and its professional learning programs might be scaled up to support students beyond California.

Future Directions: Multimedia, Multigenre, and Multimodal Practices in the ERWC

Readers may wonder about the roles of multimedia and multimodal texts in the ERWC. In their book *Multimodal Literacy*, Jewitt and Kress (2003) define *media* as the *"technologies for making and distributing meanings as messages"* (p. 4), including print and online books, newspapers, journals, magazines, videos, films, podcasts, musical recordings, blogs, message boards, images, and social media. Such forms are used in many of the ERWC modules (and appear with greater frequency within the classrooms of many individual teachers). Although not currently addressed explicitly in the curriculum itself, we also feel that more attention should be given to representational modes, "the resources that a culture makes available as *the means for making representations and meaning*" (p. 4), which include but are not limited to image, gaze, movement, gesture, speech, music, rhythm, and sound. Jewitt and Kress explain that "modes are broadly understood to be the effect of the work of culture in shaping material into resources for representation" (p. 1). They suggest that although all modes are in some sense equal—that is, potentially "significant for meaning and communication" (p. 2)—modes are also partial: Depending on context and communicative purpose as well as on the nature of the content itself, different modes may become foregrounded.

This is certainly the case in schools and universities, where particular kinds of texts tend to be highly privileged, whereas others go largely unstudied or even acknowledged. In light of that, the heavy focus on print-based textual analysis and rhetorical reading, writing, and thinking in the ERWC accomplishes three things:

1. It provides a rigorous yet highly accessible and engaging way for high school students to become more proficient at wielding critical 21st-century literacies.
2. It offers extended professional learning opportunities for high school teachers, builds a shared sense of community, and enhances their capacity to foster the literate competencies outlined by the CCSS.
3. It exemplifies a scalable model of a statewide initiative to increase college-going readiness for high school youths in one of the world's most linguistically, socioeconomically, and culturally diverse nations.

Some of the current ERWC units (e.g., module 9: "Bring a Text to Class," described in Figure 28.1) invite students to explore personally meaningful out-of-school texts of their own choosing (e.g., song lyrics and spoken word, poetry, video game instructions, car or bicycle repair manuals, articles from popular magazines, online blog and social network postings). Like many other literacy scholars, we believe that if teachers can become more familiar with the texts students read voluntarily outside of school, these literacies can in turn help create connections to the types of reading and writing that are highly prized within schools.[4] The reality, though, is that because we live in an increasingly technologically complex and textually demanding world, it is imperative that we do a better job of preparing young people for colleges, universities, workplaces, civic institutions, and community organizations where it will be taken for granted that they are highly conversant with a wide range of media and able to seamlessly toggle between multiple modes of expression, including formal academic or academic-like reading and writing. It is our intention to maintain a strong—some might even say relentless—emphasis on print modalities because students taking the ERWC are preparing for a freshman year of college in which print may be the symbolic domain with which they interact and create texts most intensely. Nevertheless, the ERWC's rhetorical underpinnings also naturally lend themselves to analyzing and authoring an extremely broad range of texts, including multimodal, multimedia, and multigenre texts. In future years, we will remain committed to continuing to expand students' access to myriad literacies through the ERWC.

To date, multimodal research has contributed considerably to helping language and literacy educators and researchers reconceptualize learning in a number of crucial ways. For example, we are now aware that (1) modes almost always occur in concert, rarely alone; (2) meanings are distributed across modes in distinctive ways at different times according to social contexts and purposes; (3) modes of representation interact with media; (4) modes shape what is represented and learners' uptake of those representations; and (5) varied forms of representation and learners' abilities to take them up are greatly affected by teachers' strategic pedagogical choices, hence their vital importance (Katz, in press). We will continue to reflect on these aspects of the ERWC pedagogically and theoretically.

Also of great interest to the ERWC design team are the arguments of genre theorists who have debated for years about the best ways for individuals to gain access to academic discourse (Frankel, 2010). In Frankel's review of the competing perspectives on the place of genre in academic literacy instruction, she points to models that support explicit genre instruction as "necessary in order for traditionally underserved students to gain access to the cultures and genres of power" (p. 46). She also claims that "knowledge of the textual markers that correspond to genres of power provides access to the cultures of power to which they belong" (pp. 46–47). As it is used in the ERWC (in concert with research-based approaches to reading comprehension, composition, and literacy), a rhetorical stance constitutes a powerful tool for analyzing the textual markers and cultural dimensions of genre and other critical characteristics of texts. The curriculum's second edition will include more multigenre writing and further explore the connections between rhetoric and genre theories and practices.

The ERWC is sufficiently broad and flexible to integrate new and multiple media, modes, and genres, as well as many forms of instruction and thinking. Linking popular culture and adolescents' out-of-school interests with the rhetorical literacies of academia and power via pedagogically sound and thematically engaging curriculum, the ERWC promises to support students' development of deep literacies and literate identities—the skills, dispositions, and habits of mind that will expand young people's opportunities to engage fully, and meaningfully, in the 21st century.

Notes

1 Even though sometimes presented as new concerns, debates regarding efficiency have haunted education reform movements since the Industrial Revolution (Ravitch, 2010).
2 A 3rd edition of ERWC is forthcoming in 2019.
3 The CSU's Early Assessment Program is a major collaborative effort by three California agencies, the CSU, the California Department of Education, and the California State Board of Education. Under the program's umbrella are several components, including a professional development effort called the Reading Institute for Academic Preparation, which has operated since 2002–2003 and has provided professional learning to thousands of California high school teachers in all disciplines.
4 See Alvermann, 2002, 2010, 2011; Alvermann, Young, Green, & Wisenbaker, 1999; Duncan-Andrade & Morrell, 2008; Dyson, 1997; Hinchman, Alvermann, Boyd, Brozo, & Vacca, 2003; Hull & Katz, 2006; Hull & Schultz, 2002; Jiménez, 2000; Jordan, Jensen, & Greenleaf, 2001; Kamil, Intrator, & Kim, 2000; Katz, 2008, in press; C.D. Lee, 1995; Mahiri & Sablo, 1996; Moje, Dillon, & O'Brien, 2000; Moll, Amanti, Neff, & Gonzalez, 1992; Morrell, 2004; Skilton-Sylvester, 2002; and Vasudevan, DeJaynes, & Schmier, 2010.

References

ACT. (2005). *Crisis at the core: Preparing all students for college and work*. Iowa City, IA: Author. Retrieved October 26, 2012, from www.act.org/research/policymakers/pdf/crisis)report.pdf

ACT. (2006). *Reading between the lines: What the ACT reveals about college readiness in reading*. Iowa City, IA: Author. Retrieved October 26, 2012, from www.act.org/research/policymakers/reports/reading.html

Adelman, C. (1999). *Answers in the tool box: Academic intensity, attendance patterns, and bachelor's degree attainment*. Washington, DC: U.S. Department of Education. Retrieved October 26, 2012, from www2.ed.gov/pubs/Toolbox/index.html

Adelman, C. (2006). *The toolbox revisited: Paths to degree completion from high school through college*. Washington, DC: U.S. Department of Education. Retrieved October 26, 2012, from www2.ed.gov/rschstat/research/pubs/toolboxrevisit/toolbox.pdf

Ainley, M. (2006). Connecting with learning: Motivation, affect and cognition in interest processes. *Educational Psychology Review, 18*(4), 391–405. doi:10.1007/s10648-006-9033-0

Alexander, P.A., & Fox, E. (2011). Adolescents as readers. In M.L. Kamil, P.D. Pearson, E.B. Moje, & P.P. Afflerbach (Eds.), *Handbook of reading research* (Vol. 4, pp. 157–176). New York: Routledge.

Alexander, P.A., & Murphy, P.K. (1998). Profiling the differences in students' knowledge, interest, and strategic processing. *Journal of Educational Psychology, 90*(3), 435–447.

Alliance for Excellent Education. (2006). *Paying double: Inadequate high schools and community college remediation* [Issue brief]. Washington, DC: Author. Retrieved October 26, 2012, from www.all4ed.org/files/remediation.pdf

Alliance for Excellent Education. (2011a). *Assessing deeper learning* [Policy brief]. Washington, DC: Author. Retrieved October 26, 2012, from www.all4ed.org/files/AssessingDeeperLearning.pdf

Alliance for Excellent Education. (2011b). *A time for deeper learning: Preparing students for a changing world* [Policy brief]. Washington, DC: Author. Retrieved October 26, 2012, from www.all4ed.org/files/DeeperLearning.pdf

Alliance for Excellent Education. (2011c). *Saving now and saving later: How high school reform can reduce the nation's wasted remediation dollars* [Issue brief]. Washington, DC: Author. Retrieved October 26, 2012, from www.all4ed.org/files/SavingNowSavingLaterRemediation.pdf

Alvermann, D.E. (2002). Effective literacy instruction for adolescents. *Journal of Literacy Research, 34*(2), 189–208.

Alvermann, D.E. (Ed.). (2010). *Adolescents' online literacies: Connecting classrooms, digital media, and popular culture*. New York: Peter Lang.

Alvermann, D.E. (2011). Popular culture and literacy practices. In M.L. Kamil, P.D. Pearson, E.B. Moje, & P.P. Afflerbach (Eds.), *Handbook of reading research* (Vol. 4, pp. 541–560). New York: Routledge.

Alvermann, D.E., & Moore, D.W. (1991). Secondary school reading. In R. Barr, M.L. Kamil, P. Rosenthal, & P.D. Pearson (Eds.), *Handbook of reading research* (Vol. 2, pp. 951–983). New York: Longman.

Alvermann, D.E., Young, J.P., Green, C., & Wisenbaker, J.M. (1999). Adolescents' perceptions and negotiations of literacy practices in after-school read and talk clubs. *American Educational Research Journal, 36*(2), 221–264.

American Diploma Project. (2004). *Ready or not: Creating a high school diploma that counts*. Washington, DC: Achieve. Retrieved October 26, 2012, from www.achieve.org/readyornot

Anderson, R.C., Hiebert, E.H., Scott, J.A., & Wilkinson, I.A.G. (1984). *Becoming a nation of readers: The report of the Commission on Reading*. Washington, DC: National Institute of Education, U.S. Department of Education.

Anderson, R.C., & Pearson, P.D. (1984). A schematheoretic view of basic processes in reading comprehension. In P.D. Pearson, R. Barr, M.L. Kamil, & P. Mosenthal (Eds.), *Handbook of reading research* (pp. 255–291). New York: Longman.

Applebee, A.N. (1996). *Curriculum as conversation: Transforming traditions of teaching and learning*. Chicago: University of Chicago Press.

Applebee, A.N., Langer, J.A., Nystrand, M., & Gamoran, A. (2003). Discussion-based approaches to developing understanding: Classroom instruction and student performance in middle and high school English. *American Educational Research Journal, 40*(3), 685–730. doi:10.3102/00028312040003685

Bakhtin, M.M. (1981). Discourse in the novel (C. Emerson & M. Holquist, Trans.). In M. Holquist (Ed.), *The dialogic imagination: Four essays* (pp. 259–422). Austin: University of Texas Press.

Bandura, A. (1997). *Self-efficacy: The exercise of control*. New York: W.H. Freeman.

Bean, J.C., Chappell, V.A., & Gillam, A.M. (2004). *Reading rhetorically*. New York: Longman.

Biancarosa, G., & Snow, C.E. (2006). *Reading next—a vision for action and research in middle and high school literacy: A report to Carnegie Corporation of New York* (2nd ed.). Washington, DC: Alliance for Excellent Education.

Bill & Melinda Gates Foundation. (2010). *Why college completion?* Seattle, WA: Author. Retrieved October 26, 2012, from www.gatesfoundation.org/postsecondaryeducation/Pages/why-collegecompletion.aspx

Brozo, W.G., & Flynt, E.S. (2008). Motivating students to read in the content classroom: Six evidence-based principles. *The Reading Teacher, 62*(2), 172–174. doi:10.1598/RT.62.2.9

California Department of Education. (1998). *English–language arts content standards for California public schools: Kindergarten through grade twelve.* Sacramento, CA: Author.

California Department of Education. (2010). *California's common core state standards for English language arts, literacy in history/social studies, science, and technical subjects.* Sacramento, CA: Author. Retrieved October 26, 2012, from www.cde.ca.gov/re/cc

California State University, Task Force on Expository Reading and Writing. (2008). *Expository Reading and Writing Course assignment template.* Long Beach, CA: Author.

California State University, Task Force on Expository Reading and Writing. (in press). *Expository Reading and Writing Course assignment template.* Long Beach, CA: Author.

California State University, Teacher Education and Public School Programs. (2005). *Pilot study evaluation of the Early Assessment Program's professional development in English 2004–05 report.* Long Beach, CA: Author. Retrieved October 26, 2012, from www.calstate.edu/teacherED/docs/EAP_ReportFinalA.pdf

Cazden, C.B. (2001). *Classroom discourse: The language of teaching and learning* (2nd ed.). Portsmouth, NH: Heinemann.

Collins, J.L., & Madigan, T.P. (2010). Using writing to develop struggling learners' higher level reading comprehension. In J.L. Collins & T.G. Gunning (Eds.), *Building struggling students' higher level literacy: Practical ideas, powerful solutions* (pp. 103–124). Newark, DE: International Reading Association.

Committee to Improve Reading and Writing in Middle and High Schools. (2009). *A critical mission: Making adolescent reading an immediate priority in SREB states.* Atlanta, GA: Southern Regional Education Board. Retrieved October 31, 2012, from publications.sreb.org/2009/09301_Critical_Mission_Reading_.pdf

Conley, D. (2003). *Mixed messages: What state high school tests communicate about student readiness for college.* Eugene: Center for Educational Policy Research, University of Oregon.

Csikszentmihalyi, M. (1990). *Flow: The psychology of optimal experience.* New York: Harper & Row.

Csikszentmihalyi, M. (1997). *Finding flow: The psychology of engagement with everyday life.* New York: Basic.

Deci, E.L. (1980). *The psychology of self-determination.* Lexington, MA: Heath.

Duke, N.K., Pearson, P.D., Strachan, S.L., & Billman, A.K. (2011). Essential elements of fostering and teaching reading comprehension. In S.J. Samuels & A.E. Farstrup (Eds.), *What research has to say about reading instruction* (4th ed., pp. 51–93). Newark, DE: International Reading Association.

Duncan-Andrade, J.M.R., & Morrell, E. (2008). *The art of critical pedagogy: Possibilities for moving from theory to practice in urban schools.* New York: Peter Lang.

Dweck, C.S. (2006). *Mindset: The new psychology of success.* New York: Random House.

Dyson, A.H. (1997). *Writing superheroes: Contemporary childhood, popular culture, and classroom literacy.* New York: Teachers College Press.

Education Commission of the States. (2008). *From competing to leading: An international benchmarking blueprint.* Denver, CO: Author. Retrieved October 26, 2012, from www.ecs.org/html/meetingsEvents/NF2008/resources/ECS-InternationalBenchmarking.pdf

Englert, C.S., & Raphael, T.E. (1989). Developing successful writers through cognitive strategy instruction. In J.E. Brophy (Ed.), *Advances in research on teaching* (Vol. 1, pp. 105–153). Greenwich, CT: JAI.

Fisher, D., & Frey, N. (2008). *Better learning through structured teaching: A framework for the gradual release of responsibility.* Alexandria, VA: Association for Supervision and Curriculum Development.

Flower, L., & Hayes, J.R. (1981). A cognitive process theory of writing. *College Composition and Communication, 32*(4), 365–387. doi:10.2307/356600

Frankel, K.K. (2010). *Rethinking the role of explicit genre instruction in the classroom.* Unpublished manuscript, University of California, Berkeley.

Gambrell, L.B. (2011). Seven rules of engagement: What's most important to know about motivation to read. *The Reading Teacher, 65*(3), 172–178. doi:10.1002/TRTR.01024

Greenleaf, C.L., Schoenbach, R., Cziko, C., & Mueller, F.L. (2001). Apprenticing adolescent readers to academic literacy. *Harvard Educational Review, 71*(1), 79–129.

Guthrie, J.T., Hoa, A.L.W., Wigfield, A., Tonks, S.M., Humenick, N.M., & Littles, E. (2007). Reading motivation and reading comprehension growth in the later elementary years. *Contemporary Educational Psychology, 32*(3), 282–313. doi:10.1016/j.cedpsych.2006.05.004

Guthrie, J.T., McRae, A., & Klauda, S.L. (2007). Contributions of Concept-Oriented Reading Instruction to knowledge about interventions for motivations in reading. *Educational Psychologist, 42*(4), 237–250. doi:10.1080/00461520701621087

Guthrie, J.T., Wigfield, A., Barbosa, P., Perencevich, K.C., Taboada, A., Davis, M.H., et al. (2004). Increasing reading comprehension and engagement through Concept-Oriented Reading Instruction. *Journal of Educational Psychology, 96*(3), 403–423. doi:10.1037/0022-0663.96.3.403

Guthrie, J.T., Wigfield, A., & Klauda, S.L. (2012). *Adolescents' engagement in academic literacy* (Report No. 7). College Park: University of Maryland, College Park. Retrieved October 26, 2012, October 31, 2012, from www.corilearning.com/research-publications/2012_adolescents_engagement_ebook.pdf

Guthrie, J.T., Wigfield, A., & Perencevich, K.C. (Eds.). (2004). *Motivating reading comprehension: Concept-Oriented Reading Instruction.* Mahwah, NJ: Erlbaum.

Hafner, A., Joseph, R., & McCormick, J. (2010). *Assessing the impact of English professional development on teaching practices, student learning and readiness for college: An evaluation of the Expository Reading and Writing Course: FIPSE final report.* Los Angeles: California State University.

Hidi, S., & Harackiewicz, J.M. (2000). Motivating the academically unmotivated: A critical issue for the 21st century. *Review of Educational Research, 70*(2), 151–179.

Hinchman, K.A., Alvermann, D.E., Boyd, F.B., Brozo, W.G., & Vacca, R.T. (2003). Supporting older students' in- and out-of-school literacies. *Journal of Adolescent & Adult Literacy, 47*(4), 304–310.

Hull, G.A., & Katz, M.-L. (2006). Crafting an agentive self: Case studies of digital storytelling. *Research in the Teaching of English, 41*(1), 43–81.

Hull, G., & Schultz, K. (Ed.). (2002). *School's out! Bridging out-of-school literacies with classroom practice.* New York: Teachers College Press.

Intersegmental Committee of the Academic Senates of the California Community Colleges, the California State University, and the University of California. (2002). *Academic literacy: A statement of competencies expected of students entering California's public colleges and universities.* Sacramento, CA: Author.

Jang, H., Reeve, J., & Deci, E.L. (2010). Engaging students in learning activities: It is not autonomy support or structure but autonomy support and structure. *Journal of Educational Psychology, 102*(3), 588–600. doi:10.1037/a0019682

Jewitt, C., & Kress, G. (2003). *Multimodal literacy.* New York: Peter Lang.

Jiménez, R.T. (2000). Literacy and the identity development of Latina/o students. *American Educational Research Journal, 37*(4), 971–1000.

Joftus, S. (2002). *Every child a graduate: A framework for an excellent education for all middle and high school students.* Washington, DC: Alliance for Excellent Education.

Jordan, M., Jensen, R., & Greenleaf, C. (2001). "Amidst familial gatherings": Reading apprenticeship in a middle school classroom. *Voices From the Middle, 8*(4), 15–24.

Kamil, M.L. (2003). *Adolescents and literacy: Reading for the 21st century.* Washington, DC: Alliance for Excellent Education.

Kamil, M.L., Borman, G.D., Dole, J., Kral, C.C., Salinger, T., & Torgesen, J. (2008). *Improving adolescent literacy: Effective classroom and intervention practices* (NCEE 2008–4027). Washington, DC: National Center for Education Evaluation and Regional Assistance, Institute of Education Sciences, U.S. Department of Education.

Kamil, M.L., Intrator, S.M., & Kim, H.S. (2000). The effects of other technologies on literacy and literacy learning. In M.L. Kamil, P.B. Mosenthal, P.D. Pearson, & R. Barr (Eds.), *Handbook of reading research* (Vol. 3, pp. 771–788). Mahwah, NJ: Erlbaum.

Katz, M.-L. (2008). Growth in motion: Supporting young women's embodied identity and cognitive development through dance after school. *Afterschool Matters, 7*(Spring), 12–22.

Katz, M.-L. (Ed.). (in press). *Moving ideas: Multimodality and embodied learning in communities and schools.* New York: Peter Lang.

Kintsch, W. (2004). The construction–integration model of text comprehension and its implications for instruction. In R.B. Ruddell & N.J. Unrau (Eds.), *Theoretical models and processes of reading* (5th ed., pp. 1270–1328). Newark, DE: International Reading Association. doi:10.1598/0872075028.46

Kirst, M.W. (2004). The high school–college disconnect. *Educational Leadership, 62*(3), 51–55.

Kucer, S.B. (1985). The making of meaning: Reading and writing as parallel processes. *Written Communication, 2*(3), 317–336. doi:10.1177/0741088385002003006

Kucer, S.B. (2009). *Dimensions of literacy: A conceptual base for teaching reading and writing in school settings* (3rd ed.). New York: Routledge.

Langer, J.A. (1995). *Envisioning literature: Literary understanding and literature instruction.* New York: Teachers College Press.

Langer, J.A. (2000). *Beating the odds: Teaching middle and high school students to read and write well* (CELA Research Report No. 12014; 2nd ed. rev.). Albany: National Research Center on English Learning & Achievement, University at Albany, State University of New York.

Langer, J.A., & Flihan, S. (2000). Writing and reading relationships: Constructive tasks. In R. Indrisano & J.R. Squire (Eds.), *Perspectives on writing: Research, theory, and practice* (pp. 112–139). Newark, DE: International Reading Association.

Lee, C.D. (1995). A culturally based cognitive apprenticeship: Teaching African American high school students skills in literary interpretation. *Reading Research Quarterly, 30*(4), 608–630. doi:10.2307/748192

Lee, J.M., Jr., Edwards, K., Menson, R., & Rawls, A. (2011). *The college completion agenda: 2011 progress report: Executive summary.* New York: College Board. Retrieved October 31, 2012, from completionagenda.collegeboard.org/sites/default/files/reports_pdf/Progress_Executive_Summary.pdf

Lemke, J.L. (1992). Intertextuality and educational research. *Linguistics and Education, 4*(3/4), 257–267. doi:10.1016/0898-5898(92)90003-F

Lewis, L., & Farris, E. (1996). *Remedial education in higher education institutions in fall 1995* (NCES 97–584). Washington, DC: National Center for Education Statistics, Office of Educational Research and Improvement, U.S. Department of Education.

Lumina Foundation. (2010). *Raising the bar on college completion.* Indianapolis, IN: Author. Retrieved October 26, 2012, from www.luminafoundation. org/newsroom/newsletter/archives/2010–10.html

Mahiri, J., & Sablo, S. (1996). Writing for their lives: The non-school literacy of California's urban African American youth. *The Journal of Negro Education, 65*(2), 164–180. doi:10.2307/2967311

Mansfield, W., & Farris, E. (1991). *College-level remedial education in the fall of 1989* (NCES 91–191). Washington, DC: National Center for Education Statistics, Office of Educational Research and Improvement, U.S. Department of Education.

Mills, K. (2004). Preparing for success in college: California State University is working closely with high schools to improve English and math skills. *National CrossTalk, 12*(4). Retrieved October 26, 2012, from www.highereducation.org/crosstalk/ct0404/news0404–preparing.shtml

Moje, E.B., Dillon, D.R., & O'Brien, D. (2000). Reexamining roles of learner, text, and context in secondary literacy. *The Journal of Educational Research, 93*(3), 165–180. doi:10.1080/00220670009598705

Moll, L.C., Amanti, C., Neff, D., & Gonzalez, N. (1992). Funds of knowledge for teaching: Using a qualitative approach to connect homes and classrooms. *Theory Into Practice, 31*(2), 132–141. doi:10.1080/00405849209543534

Morrell, E. (2004). *Linking literacy and popular culture: Finding connections for lifelong learning.* Norwood, MA: Christopher-Gordon.

Murphy, P.K., Wilkinson, I.A.G., Soter, A.O., Hennessey, M.N., & Alexander, J.F. (2009). Examining the effects of classroom discussion on students' comprehension of text: A meta-analysis. *Journal of Educational Psychology, 101*(3), 740–764. doi:10.1037/a0015576

Naceur, A., & Schiefele, U. (2005). Motivation and learning—the role of interest in construction of representation of text and long-term retention: Inter- and intraindividual analyses. *European Journal of Psychology of Education, 20*(2), 155–170. doi:10.1007/BF03173505

NASBE Study Group on Middle and High School Literacy. (2005). *Reading at risk: The state response to the crisis in adolescent literacy.* Alexandria, VA: National Association of State Boards of Education.

National Commission on Excellence in Education. (1983). *A nation at risk: The imperative for educational reform.* Washington, DC: Author.

National Commission on Writing in America's Schools and Colleges. (2003). *The neglected "R": The need for a writing revolution.* New York: College Entrance Examination Board. Retrieved October 26, 2012, from www.nwp.org/cs/public/print/resource/2523

National Governors Association. (2010). *Complete to compete.* Washington, DC: Author. Retrieved October 26, 2012, from www.nga.org/files/live/sites/NGA/files/pdf/10GREGOIREBROCHURE.PDF

National Governors Association Center for Best Practices & Council of Chief State School Officers. (2010a). *Common core state standards for English language arts and literacy in history/social studies, science, and technical subjects.* Washington, DC: Authors. Retrieved October 26, 2012, from www.corestandards.org

National Governors Association Center for Best Practices & Council of Chief State School Officers. (2010b). *Common core state standards for English language arts and literacy in history/social studies, science, and technical subjects: Appendix A: Research supporting key elements of the standards.* Washington, DC: Authors. Retrieved October 26, 2012, from www.corestandards.org/assets/Appendix_A.pdf

National Governors Association Center for Best Practices & Council of Chief State School Officers. (2010c). *Mission statement.* Washington, DC: Authors. Retrieved October 26, 2012, from www.corestandards.org

National Research Council & Institute of Medicine. (2004). *Engaging schools: Fostering high school students' motivation to learn.* Washington, DC: National Academies Press.

Nystrand, M. (1986). Introduction. In *The structure of written communication: Studies in reciprocity between writers and readers* (pp. 1–20). Orlando, FL: Academic.

Nystrand, M. (with Gamoran, A., Kachur, R., & Prendergast, C.). (1997). *Opening dialogue: Understanding the dynamics of language and learning in the English classroom.* New York: Teachers College Press.

Office of the Press Secretary, The White House. (2009, July 14). *Excerpts of the president's remarks in Warren, Michigan and a fact sheet on the American Graduation Initiative.* Retrieved October 26, 2012, from www.whitehouse.gov/the_press_office/Excerpts-of-the-Presidents-remarks-in-Warren-Michigan-and-fact-sheet-on-the-American-Graduation-Initiative

Organisation for Economic Co-operation and Development. (2010). *PISA 2009 results: What students know and can do: Vol. I. Student performance in reading, mathematics and science.* Paris: Author. Retrieved October 26, 2012, from dx.doi.org/10.1787/9789264091450-en

Pajares, F. (2003). Self-efficacy beliefs, motivation, and achievement in writing: A review of the literature. *Reading & Writing Quarterly, 19*(2), 139–158. doi:10.1080/10573560308222

Parker, T.L., Bustillos, L.T., & Behringer, L.B. (2010). *Remedial and developmental education policy at a crossroads.* Boston: Policy Research on Preparation Access and Remedial Education, Getting Past Go, University of Massachusetts Boston. Retrieved October 26, 2012, from www.gettingpastgo.org/docs/Literature-Review-GPG.pdf

Parsad, B., & Lewis, L. (2003). *Remedial education at degree-granting postsecondary institutions in fall 2000: Statistical analysis report* (NCES 2004–010). Washington, DC: National Center for Education Statistics, Institute of Education Sciences, U.S. Department of Education. Retrieved October 26, 2012, from www.nces.ed.gov/pubs2004/2004010.pdf

Pearson, P.D. (2011a, November). *What will the future bring? A narrow window of opportunity to get comprehension instruction right!!! (A confluence of opportunity).* PowerPoint presentation presented at the annual meeting of the California Reading Association, Vacaville. Retrieved October 30, 2012, from www.scienceandliteracy.org/research/pdavidpearson

Pearson, P.D. (2011b, December). *Supporting reading comprehension: Transforming reading comprehension: 10 research-based principles.* PowerPoint presentation presented to elementary principals and literacy coaches from Providence, RI. Retrieved March 28, 2012, from www.scienceandliteracy.org/research/pdavidpearson

Pearson, P.D., & Gallagher, M.C. (1983). The instruction of reading comprehension. *Contemporary Educational Psychology, 8*(3), 317–344. doi:10.1016/0361-476X(83)90019-X

Pressley, M. (2000). What should comprehension instruction be the instruction of? In M.L. Kamil, P.B. Mosenthal, P.D. Pearson, & R. Barr (Eds.), *Handbook of reading research* (Vol. 3, pp. 545–561). Mahwah, NJ: Erlbaum.

Pressley, M. (2002). *Reading instruction that works: The case for balanced teaching* (2nd ed.). New York: Guilford.

Program Evaluation and Research Collaborative. (2008). *Evaluating the impact of reading and writing professional development on student reading and writing outcomes: Evaluation report.* Los Angeles: Charter College of Education, California State University.

RAND Reading Study Group. (2002). *Reading for understanding: Toward an R&D program in reading comprehension.* Santa Monica, CA: RAND.

Ravitch, D. (2010). *The death and life of the great American school system: How testing and choice are undermining education.* New York: Basic.

Reed, J.H., Schallert, D.L., Beth, A.D., & Woodruff, A.L. (2004). Motivated reader, engaged writer: The role of motivation in the literate acts of adolescents. In T.L. Jetton & J.A. Dole (Eds.), *Adolescent literacy research and practice* (pp. 251–282). New York: Guilford.

Rosenblatt, L.M. (1994). *The reader, the text, the poem: The transactional theory of the literary work.* Carbondale: Southern Illinois University. (Original work published 1978)

Ruddell, R.B., & Unrau, N.J. (2004). Reading as a meaning-construction process: The reader, the text, and the teacher. In R.B. Ruddell & N.J. Unrau (Eds.), *Theoretical models and processes of reading* (5th ed., pp. 1462–1521). Newark, DE: International Reading Association.

Ryan, R.M., & Deci, E.L. (2000). Intrinsic and extrinsic motivations: Classic definitions and new directions. *Contemporary Educational Psychology, 25*(1), 54–67. doi:10.1006/ceps.1999.1020

Ryan, R.M., & Deci, E.L. (2002). An overview of self-determination theory: An organismic-dialectical perspective. In E.L. Deci & R.M. Ryan (Eds.), *Handbook of self-determination research* (pp. 3–33). Rochester, NY: University of Rochester Press.

Schiefele, U. (1999). Interest and learning from text. *Scientific Studies of Reading, 3*(3), 257–279. doi:10.1207/s1532799xssr0303_4

Schoenbach, R., & Greenleaf, C. (2009). Fostering adolescents' engaged academic literacy. In L. Christenbury, R. Bomer, & P. Smagorinsky (Eds.), *Handbook of adolescent literacy research* (pp. 98–112). New York: Guilford.

Schoenbach, R., Greenleaf, C., Cziko, C., & Hurwitz, L. (1999). *Reading for understanding: A guide to improving reading in middle and high school classrooms.* San Francisco: Jossey-Bass & WestEd.

Schunk, D.H. (2003). Self-efficacy for reading and writing: Influence of modeling, goal setting, and self-evaluation. *Reading & Writing Quarterly, 19*(2), 159–172. doi:10.1080/10573560308219

Shanahan, T. (2006). Relations among oral language, reading, and writing development. In C.A. MacArthur, S. Graham, & J. Fitzgerald (Eds.), *Handbook of writing research* (pp. 171–183). New York: Guilford.

Skilton-Sylvester, E. (2002). Literate at home but not at school: A Cambodian girl's journey from playwright to struggling writer. In G. Hull & K. Schultz (Eds.), *School's out! Bridging out-of-school literacies with classroom practice* (pp. 61–90). New York: Teachers College Press.

Smith, F. (1983). Reading like a writer. *Language Arts, 60*(5), 558–567.

Smith, F. (1984). Reading like a writer. In J.M. Jensen (Ed.), *Composing and comprehending* (pp. 47–56). Urbana, IL: ERIC Clearinghouse on Reading and Communication Skills & National Conference on Research in English.

Strong American Schools. (2008). *Diploma to nowhere.* Washington, DC: Author. Retrieved October 26, 2012, from www.deltacostproject.org/resources/pdf/DiplomaToNowhere.pdf

Swan, E.A. (2004). Motivating adolescent readers through Concept-Oriented Reading Instruction. In T.L. Jetton & J.A. Dole (Eds.), *Adolescent literacy research and practice* (pp. 283–303). New York: Guilford.

Thompson, B.A. (2009). *International benchmarking toolkit.* Denver, CO: Education Commission of the States. Retrieved October 26, 2012, from www.ecs.org/IB/IBtoolkit3-26-09.pdf

Tierney, R.J., & Shanahan, T. (1991). Research on the reading–writing relationship: Interactions, transactions, and outcomes. In R. Barr, M.L. Kamil, P. Mosenthal, & P.D. Pearson (Eds.), *Handbook of reading research* (Vol. 2, pp. 246–280). Mahwah, NJ: Erlbaum.

Torgesen, J.K., Houston, D.D., Rissman, L.M., Decker, S.M., Roberts, G., Vaughn, S., et al. (2007). *Academic literacy instruction for adolescents: A guidance document from the Center on Instruction.* Portsmouth, NH: RMC Research Corporation, Center on Instruction.

Turner, J., & Paris, S.G. (1995). How literacy tasks influence children's motivation for literacy. *The Reading Teacher, 48*(8), 662–673.

U.S. Department of Education. (2011). *College completion tool kit.* Washington, DC: Author. Retrieved October 26, 2012, from www.whitehouse.gov/sites/default/files/college_completion_tool_kit.pdf

Vasudevan, L., DeJaynes, T., & Schmier, S. (2010). Multimodal pedagogies: Playing, teaching and learning with adolescents' digital literacies. In D.E. Alvermann (Ed.), *Adolescents' online literacies: Connecting classrooms, digital media, and popular culture* (pp. 5–25). New York: Peter Lang.

Vygotsky, L.S. (1978). *Mind in society: The development of higher psychological processes* (M. Cole, V. John-Steiner, S. Scribner, & E. Souberman, Eds. & Trans.). Cambridge, MA: Harvard University Press.

Wilkinson, I.A.G., & Son, E.H. (2011). A dialogic turn in research on learning and teaching to comprehend. In M.L. Kamil, P.D. Pearson, E.B. Moje, & P.P. Afflerbach (Eds.), *Handbook of reading research* (Vol. 4, pp. 359–387). New York: Routledge.

Williams, P.L., Reese, C.M., Campbell, J.R., Mazzeo, J., & Phillips, G.W. (1995). *NAEP 1994 reading: A first look: Findings from the National Assessment of Educational Progress* (Rev. ed.). Washington, DC: National Center for Education Statistics, Institute of Education Sciences, U.S. Department of Education. Retrieved October 26, 2012, from nces.ed.gov/nationsreportcard/pubs/main1994/rchpt1.asp

29

PROPOSITIONS FROM AFFECT THEORY FOR FEELING LITERACY THROUGH THE EVENT

Christian Ehret

Introduction

> Problems in general are often well posed in terms of language and language remains a handy tool for explaining them. But the actual process of thinking—in any discipline—is largely an unconscious affair.

(McCarthy, 2017, para. 5)

At first it may feel jarring to read Cormac McCarthy, a contemporary author of highly stylized literary novels, describing language as subordinate to a largely unconscious process of thought. And unconscious thought? Paradoxical. Quintessential of "high" intellectual achievements, writing novels must first be considered a rigorous, logical, well-planned, and recursive process of research, drafting, editing, and revision, moment by moment, month by month, year by year. Certainly, this is part of the story. But McCarthy would be quick to quip with an often-overlooked chapter: "If you believe that you actually use language in the solving of problems I wish that you would write to me and tell me how you go about it" (para. 5). What would it mean to take McCarthy's proposition seriously? To ask where writing comes from if thinking is largely an unconscious affair? What would it mean for our understanding of literacy events, and of literacy research, were we to take seriously that they are both partly unconscious, felt activities with and around texts?

One need only look to McCarthy's slightly younger contemporary, George Saunders, a renowned short story writer, MacArthur 'genius grant' recipient, and himself a professor of writing, who describes the process of writing his first novel, *Lincoln in the Bardo*, as largely "intuitive," "mysterious," and a "pain in the ass." Searching for some semblance of his method, Saunders speculates. He writes an essay in which he imagines himself as "a guy (Stan)" who "constructs a model railroad town in his basement" (Saunders, 2017, para. 4). In the essay, Stan bends over the model town to see a hobo warming himself under plastic railroad tracks. He notices how he had previously arranged the hobo in what feels like a wistful posture, gazing back at the city. Why is he looking there?

> Stan notes a plastic woman in the window, then turns her a little, so she's gazing out. Over at the railroad bridge, actually. Huh. Suddenly, Stan has made a love story. Oh, why can't

563

they be together? If only "Little Jack" would just go home. To his wife. To Linda. [. . .] What did Stan (the artist) just do? Well, first, surveying his little domain, he noticed which way his hobo was looking. Then he chose to change that little universe, by turning the plastic woman. Now, Stan didn't exactly decide to turn her. It might be more accurate to say that it occurred to him to do so; in a split-second, with no accompanying language, except maybe a very quiet internal "Yes."

(paras. 4–5)

Of course, Saunders is not Stan, and his novel did not emerge from tinkering with a model train set. Neither is his approach to writing directly represented in this story. And yet through his speculative writing the reader feels something of Saunders's process, one that Saunders himself needed to reimagine obliquely in order to know again and express the feeling of a very quiet internal "Yes" as it emerges through the writing event.

What might Saunders's speculative description reveal about the dimensions of a writing event that come before and after language? About writing as an "unconscious affair"? The potentials for the hobo's story are not limitless. Rather, they seem to grow from affective relations with the plastic town: the arbitrariness of his gaze toward the blue Victorian house; the way the basement light reflects on the faded black ink of the plastic woman's left eye, resembling a human glint that, in an instant and irrationally, makes her Linda. Linda is ambivalent about Little Jack's situation beneath the tracks. She is hurt by his actions and their young son is becoming more distant the longer Jack is away, but she still loves him. Seemingly without language, the story grows in light glinting off chips in a painted eye. The story emerges in a relational process wherein Stan moves the plastic woman, and the plastic woman moves Stan. There are no definable linkages, no direct resemblance between this narrative that emerges and the various movements of Saunders and the model town pieces. Just the same, the objects Saunders imagines moving share no discernible resemblance to the story they generate through the coming together of their movements throughout the writing event. And yet they come together to produce a qualitative composition, a feeling of something happening, a story. As Massumi (2011) puts it, "the linkage is what the objects share *through* their combination: implication in the same *event*" (p. 107, emphasis in original).

In this semblance of a writing event, writing emerges through an experience of bodies moving and being moved, affecting and being affected, whether or not the feeling of movement is recognized consciously. Beyond language, affect is a force in the social field that moves writing forward. The discernible moments of this forward motion are relational (Stan moving model; model moving Stan) transformations (model becoming Linda) of the story becoming different (if only "Little Jack" would just go home) in an imminently material process across the surface of things (Ingold, 2017), where material works on mind and mind on material. Massumi (2011) is helpful again here on how affect produces this surface sense of motion in a story coming to be: "The felt perception of continuing movement is *qualitative* because it directly grasps the changing nature of the shared event 'behind,' 'across,' or 'through' its objective ingredients and their observable combinations. It is, simply: relationship. Directly perceptually-felt 'nonsensuously' perceived" (p. 107, emphasis in original). The relationship between semblance and event evokes the nonsensuous, or amodal, perception of something happening that is beyond description in any single bodily sense or semiotic mode, which themselves are a resemblance of something, a representation of experience materialized. The moment-to-moment felt-sense of change between both Saunders and models—and models and models—affects a sense of motion in the story's becoming that, for readers of Saunders's essay, becomes a new event in coming to know a writing process. Events are the singular, amodal feeling of something happening produced through emergent relations between bodies, human and nonhuman. Events feel like something, "the direct perception of what happens between the senses, in no one mode" (Massumi, 2011, p. 110).

Overview

By evoking its affects rather than representing his writing process explicitly, Saunders brings readers—and himself—closer to how writing is, in part, an unconscious affair that sometimes provokes the feeling of a very quiet internal "Yes." The "Yeses" of relational transformations are "quiet" because they are the affects, conscious or not, that come immediately before naming the feeling "Yes," "That's it!," or simply smiling to oneself. These "Yeses" are the feeling of writing *through the event,* the amodal feeling of something happening. But they are also "quiet" in the sense that such affective dimensions of literacy events as they are felt, lived, and experienced beyond language and representation have been muffled by the representational theories pervading the humanities, social sciences, and literacy studies through the beginning of the 21st century. Indeed, Saunders's speculative act of creation as both analysis and expression of an event in his writing process is a far more intuitive approach than is common in literacy research. Even beyond cognitive or positivist experimental approaches, researchers working in the wake of the New Literacy Studies (NLS) have theorized alphabetic and multimodal writing events almost exclusively in relation to social practices (e.g., Bezemer & Kress, 2015; Street, 2014) distributed across local-global ecologies (Stornaiuolo, Smith, & Phillips, 2017). And this theorization of events in relation both to local patterns of activity and to broader social and cultural practices follows the larger epistemology of social constructivism that apprehends and delimits the social field through a preoccupation with representation or epiphenomenal meanings and concepts "cited by and projected on bodies, habits, practices, behaviors, and environments" (Anderson & Harrison, 2010, p. 5).

Studies of culture, social life, and literacy through such representations have provided powerful, field-changing insights into the discursive, ideological influences on literate activity (Gee, 2015); into the modes of power that generate inequities through social constructions of whose literacies count where (Alvermann, 2009); and even into whose feelings count in classroom literacy events (Lewis & Tierney, 2013). But the epistemological constraint of coming to know literacy events only in their relation to durable practices (including their potential to become such or not), Discourses, codes, and conventions has meant that the feeling of social life that resists such representations has remained a powerfully unknown force flowing outside the logic of the field's representationally bound theoretic tools. Emotion has been analyzed primarily as a mediator or a meditational means, turning feeling into a representation that can be analyzed outside of immediate, embodied experience. Feeling, emotion, and bodies become representations, mere resemblances of their living movements. Although these are the primary theoretic tools literacy researchers have developed thus far to describe events, they certainly are not all events are. You can feel it.

Without eschewing the essential insights that have developed, and are still developing, from the NLS and the related social and discursive turns in the humanities and social sciences, how might we look beyond representations and discursive constructions of bodies in order to know literacy events as living bodies actually feel and experience them? How can we come to know literacy events beyond language alone? How would a nonrepresentational theory of literacy events come to know and to express, as in Saunders's speculative analysis, the affective intensities that course under the surface of code and convention? And if addressing these problems is largely an unconscious affair, then what theoretic tools are necessary in provoking our unconscious? What theoretic tools could attune our bodies, as researchers, to the affective intensities of literacy events that give them their feeling of "lifeness," of actually existing through the constant onflow of time as we experience it?

To address these questions and to develop new theoretic tools for feeling literacies in process, for listening for the quiet internal "Yes," this chapter follows what has been termed the affect turn in the social sciences and humanities, and asks: How might literacy events be conceptualized in a minor key in order to better know and feel them as they happen? Scholars working in the interdisciplinary area of affect studies (Gregg & Seigworth, 2009) have theorized their form of critique variously as "minor" (Manning, 2016) or "weak" (Stewart, 2008) in part to distinguish their work from "strong" representational theories that stabilize events in the social field, in order to, for example, "code" and know them as, and through, representations. Lived and thought carefully, nonrepresentational theory in any discipline is nothing if not an admission of frailty that wonders at the same. It is a rigorous refusal to code, categorize, tame, and overexplain human desire, admitting that this is neither possible nor desirable, while at the same time meeting that desire in the moment, feeling for what modulates it and moves it toward more or less just becomings. If nonrepresentational theory is "post"human, then, it is not because it focuses on matter and materiality above the human, but because it thinks of the human as always already in relation to its world, not as the strong, prime knower over, above, and outside of what is in fact a co-constitutive becoming.

Coming to know and feel literacy events through nonrepresentational theory therefore requires techniques of analysis and expression that turn from epistemology, representation, and postmodern forms of critique, arguing that these strong theories enact a negative form of constructivism that diagnoses problems of mediation and power in social life as if it were only, and blanketly, "formatted and regulated by a master code" (Braidotti, 2011, p. 3). Coming to know and feel the dimensions of literacy events that resist representation, and that escape McCarthy's and Saunders's words, requires orientating inquiry with ontologies of becoming that meet affect through its emergence in immanent social fields. Affect studies therefore draws on the relational, process philosophies of Spinoza (1985), Whitehead (1927–1928/1985), Deleuze (1990), and Massumi (2002, 2011), of whom the latter three are particularly concerned with the concept of emergence, or unfolding time. In ontologies of becoming, the present emerges because it is never *present*. The past is always becoming the future. There is no stopping it. This moving sense of time forces a dramatic reorientation to the notion of the "event" as something that can never be known from above or beyond its own unfolding.

I develop this philosophical lineage in a weak, emergent theory of literacy events that operates in parallel to the strong representational theories of the NLS. To do so, I produce theoretic propositions through revisiting my experiences of literacy events with 12-year-olds Cole and Ella in a children's hospital. I begin with Cole, feeling through our experiences of writing together in order to produce a nonrepresentational and nonlinear alternative to the more common teleological theorization of literacy events and practices. This nonrepresentational theory of literacy events develops through the concepts of *relational transformation*, *affective tonality*, *event-time*, and *desire*.

Following, I articulate three propositions for feeling literacy *through the event* from experiences writing with Ella after Cole had left the hospital. Over about three months, Ella and I wrote together and developed ideas for a novel she wanted to write. Like Cole, Ella was hospitalized for leukemia treatment, and I was spending time with youth like her as part of an anthropological inquiry into how adolescents used their literacies while hospitalized in the American Southeast. Knowing and feeling affective dimensions of literacies as they emerge through the moment, as they did through moments with Ella, require speculative propositions that lure us into grasping relational transformations as they happen. The propositions I develop emerge from my own refeeling of writing with Ella.

Relational transformations, such as Saunders's quiet "Yes," are differences that make a difference in writing, reading, speaking, and media making. They are differences that make a difference in who writers, readers, speakers, and media makers are becoming. They are differences in a minor key, floating under the solid surfaces of representationally trained inquiry. Feeling these differences that feel like something beyond language, requires *becoming a proposition* as a technique for affirming a more fully embodied and felt response to literacy events in our own lives and the lives with whom we research. For me, in relation now to Ella, becoming a proposition means feeling forward to how I might live and think differently in the events of my future work. They operate as lures intensifying, in the moment of their happening, the experiences to which they only weakly refer. Becoming a proposition therefore attunes us to change happening in the mundane makings of ordinary events that feel like something more than they are. It affirms change that is often only felt, if powerfully, through minor gestures in the course of living and learning with texts.

Literacy through the Event

In a way, Manning writes about distinctions of value between what tends to be at stake in representational and nonrepresentational theorizations of literacy events:

> The major is the structural tendency that organizes itself according to predetermined definitions of value. The minor is a force that courses through it, unmooring its structural integrity, problematizing its normative standards. The unwavering belief in the major as the site where events occur, where events make a difference, is based on accepted accounts of what registers as change as well as existing parameters for gauging the value of that change. . . . The grand is given the status it has not because it is where the transformative power lies, but because it is easier to identify major shifts than to catalogue the nuanced rhythms of the minor.
>
> *(Manning, 2016, p. 1)*

What is major in a literacy event is most familiar for those working from sociocultural perspectives. Studying literacy events through the major orients inquiry toward a linear teleology of human development in relation to social practices. For instance, a researcher might ask, how is this "occasion in which a piece of writing is integral to the nature of the participants' interactions and their interpretive processes" (Heath, 1982, p. 93) related to a human being's development toward the "general cultural ways of utilizing written language" (Barton & Hamilton, 2000, p. 8) within a specific discursive field (Gee, 2015)? This cultural-historical perspective on literacy through a linear construction of time, and through a teleological image of development, also aids in questioning relationships between literacy practices and identity development, as well as how specific literacy practices are more or less valued in specific social contexts, such as adolescents' "out-of-school literacies" and the hegemonic image of literacy most often valued in compulsory schooling (Vasudevan & Campano, 2009).

Although its analysis continues to produce essential insights for the field, the major proceeds through the structural tendency to critique value from abstractions preexisting, and on the outside of, the social field as it is lived and experienced through its own becoming. Known from outside of an event's unfolding, the major tends to what has already been culturally determined and can therefore be used to analyze whose literacies count where and when, and in what direction they might go. The critique of social life through the mediation of culturally determined, representational units of analysis such as texts, practices, agency, artifacts, and contexts, therefore remains essential for literacy research, especially in challenging pervasive educational inequities across the globe. Yet, these strong theories can overlook the everyday embodied experience of change that cannot be predicted or remediated through such representational units alone, units which are culturally determined a priori. Specifically, the analysis of emotion as a form or representation of cultural mediation can overlook the idiosyncratic, irrational affects that give events the very feeling of mattering, and that generate and sustain the human desiring that makes reading, writing, and social change *feel* essential (Ehret & Hollett, 2016).

Major Theories of Emotion in Literacy Events

Take emotion as analyzed in the major key of cultural-historical theory. From a cultural-historical perspective, emotion is located in mediated action, a dialectical relationship between body and social context (Vadeboncoeur & Collie, 2013). Emotion, unified with cognition, generates a frame for experience, or the experience of one's experience. This emotional valence "provides the means through which people render their socially and culturally situated activity into meaningful texts, not as individuals surrounded and affected by context but as people acting in conjunction with context through their employment of mediational tools" (Smagorinsky & Daigle, 2012, p. 295). Students in a high school English classroom may therefore frame writing tasks through various affective dispositions that have developed over time in relation to, for example, the discursive expectations of certain writing genres or specific school and classroom cultures. In a classroom, for instance, a student might render into a "text" the situation of having to take on an academic voice as "hard" or even inimical to their personal experiences outside of the classroom (Smagorinsky & Daigle, 2012). The cultural tools for meaning-making this student employs in her writing are framed through—and from an analyst's perspective seemingly determined by—her linear, situated development of emotional responses to writing in school, how she reads the situation as a sort of culturally constructed text.

Beyond the perspective of situated, emotional framing, others have described how emotion mediates and mobilizes meaning-making in response to texts (e.g., Lewis & Tierney, 2013; Thein, Sloan, & Guise, 2015). In this view, emotion is tied to mediated action, and thus becomes known, and later analyzed, through its appearance in language or other sign systems, such as multimodal texts (Kress, 2009), or bodily action, such as gesture, read textually (Streeck, Goodwin, & LeBaron, 2011). For example, Vadeboncoeur and Collie (2013) developed a cultural-historical theory of feeling via Vygotsky's argument for the unity of intellectual and affective processes. They described "feeling" (using the term interchangeably with "emotion" and "affect") as dialectically linked to what they call "verbal feeling" (p. 210), including cultural semiotic systems other than language in their use of "verbal." In their view, "feeling is mediated by social relationships and language and cultural semiotic systems and develops in relation to changes in the development of thinking toward verbal thinking as dialectically related verbal feeling" (p. 221). Here, there is a "logic" to feeling as it develops *through language* over time. The felt intensities of social life are always fed back into language for sense-making. Human feeling is known as verbal feeling. Not only is it therefore most salient when it comes to consciousness and is rationalized, but feeling is subordinated to language, as if its nonsensical quality demands strong sense-making to be of use.

Through such strong theories, a researcher may then make sense of affect in literacy events as it appears in language or other sign systems, such as embodied action read textually, wherein there is evidence of how "changes in the development of thinking toward verbal thinking as dialectically related to verbal feeling" mediates action and meaning-making in relation to texts. This form of analysis takes place outside of the event itself, through experience reduced to representations. The unit of analysis, although theoretically unified with social and cultural context, is emotion as it is represented in linguistic and textual artifacts of previously lived experience. Outside of the immediate moment of the event's feeling, the major is easier to identify in experience as it comes to be reduced to textual units of previously mediated action. The transformative power of the quiet internal "Yes" relinquishes its status to emotion as it makes itself known through more emphatic, and more *reason*ably analyzable, representations.

Minor Theories of Affect and Literacy through the Event

Coming to know the minor requires meeting experience at a different point in time, through its emergence (Leander & Ehret, 2019). This is one reason why ontologies of becoming destabilize affect and disentangle it from major theories that conflate affect and emotion and analyze affect only when it is stabilized and qualified in language and representation. In ontologies of becoming, affect is a social force that precedes or never comes to language, consciousness, or representation (Massumi, 2002). Coming to know affect as it moves through literacy events requires, therefore, a sort of bodily attunement from within the social field of the event unfolding. It requires thinking-feeling literacy *through the event*. Through the event, what moves across surfaces seemingly without language, what solves McCarthy's problems and invigorates them anew resonates in the minor key. What is minor is mutable and creates its own value in relation to the singularity of the event unfolding. It is desire desiring. Desire is the feeling of social production that keeps literate activity moving through the event. Desire keeps the feeling of the event feeling. A properly weak concept, desire as known through nonrepresentational theory does not have an object (Deleuze & Guattari, 1977/2009); that is, desire is not void or deficit-centered, the longing for something one lacks. Rather, desire is the impersonal force of producing, of bringing into being the set of sociomaterial relations that keep production going. Desire thus has profound consequences for literate production, and for how we continuously come to know ourselves as human through literate activity.

Here is a literacy event wherein desiring and writing feel not only indistinguishable, but also necessary to each other's production—an example of literacy becoming through the event. During my anthropological inquiry of adolescents' literacies in a children's hospital, I tutored Cole, a 12-year-old boy, who like Ella was hospitalized for leukemia treatment (see Ehret, 2018). Cole's school labeled him as "struggling" with literacy, a label that followed him into the hospital through the chart sent by his school counselor. According to the chart, Cole had never written a composition longer than three paragraphs. My charge, in consultation with the career hospital school teachers, was to write with Cole a "significant" composition to submit to his English teacher back at school in order to show his progress while away. Because Cole would get hung up building an argument or narrative over multiple paragraphs, we codeveloped a strategy for composing longer pieces that drew on one of his many talents. Cole was a loquacious storyteller, especially of time spent camping and swimming with his family in the Smokies. Histrionically, while wearing his camouflage University of Tennessee cap, he would relate adventures driving by black bears and stopping by swimming holes.

We developed a pedagogic rhythm: He would tell me a story about a special experience he had with his family before his hospitalization, and I would video-record the story on my iPad. When he was finished, I would ask him questions that drew out additional details about what seemed liked important scenes: Cole's dad illicitly feeding a bear (Cole play-laughing nervously simulating peeking out from the car window); the special camping trip his family took after his first hospitalization for extended treatment, before the three-month stay during which I first met him. We would use these videos to draw storyboards from which to write out essays of about one to three prose paragraphs. After a few weeks developing our rhythm of storytelling, video-recording, storyboarding, and writing short pieces, Cole decided he wanted to "just write." Cole was already working with hospital social workers and art therapists to create his "journey journal," a sort of therapeutic memory book in which patients record their "journey" with cancer from diagnosis through treatment. Because the "journey journal" genre had already done some scaffolding in narrative chronology, I thought it would make sense for Cole to write one paragraph for each page of his journal, numbering those paragraphs in chronological order. There were more than enough pages in the journal for us to craft a "significant" essay to send to Cole's English teacher.

About a week into our project, when we reached the fourth paragraph, Cole got stuck trying to write about an intense moment just after his admission to the hospital. "I was really sick that one time and they thought I might was gonna die and they was all around my bed," Cole said. At least nine doctors, nurses, and hospital staff comprised the "they" all around his bed, and it was the need to put this complex spatial arrangement into prose that caused Cole's struggle. Instead of prose, Cole decided to insert a drawing of the moment into his fourth paragraph. During the event (Cole struggling to compose this scene), I felt the major tendency to produce a teachable moment that reached outside of the event itself and toward the development of Cole's writing practice, specifically the ability to compose compound sentences to describe spatially complex settings. This constructed notion of writing development was the major tendency of pedagogical relations defining, from the outside, the value of a pedagogical moment. This value defined through the structural tendencies of the major was not simply a pedagogical feeling related to writing development in general, but it was also a major tendency of theory and research. In strong theory, this literacy event is related to, for example, the definable cultural practices of valuing varied sentence structures. And as a researcher, I felt that I owed evidence of Cole's progress in writing to the hospital school teachers allowing me to work with their students. The major's tendencies are strong not only in their representational logics, but also in their pulls on bodies through the moment.

Desire, however, escapes such grand notions of what constitutes development, change, or outcome. As we talked over the picture, Cole told me for the first time about his Aunt Emily. Only three years older than he, Emily had been admitted to the same children's hospital only one day after Cole, and also for cancer treatment. "She's like my best friend, you know? Since I'm the one she listens to most and I know what she's sayin' when no one else don't," the latter being especially important given that her own treatment was not as successful as Cole's, resulting in her losing the ability to speak. While Cole and I were writing his journey essay, she was admitted to intensive care and there was talk of moving her to palliative treatment. "We have a special relationship," Cole said, "Once we was swimming on a camping trip and she didn't want to get in the water and they all was like, 'Get in there it's fun,' and all. But she would only get in swimming once I was. I was the only one could get'er in there."

In the next turn of talk, Cole decided that he wanted to abandon the journey journal and write a story about this special connection with his aunt. Although I felt ambivalent letting go of this teachable moment for writing, as well as of the lengthy essay and the learning outcomes it would evidence, I moved forward with Cole to write the piece for his Aunt Emily. We followed a desiring literate activity qualitatively different from literate activity imagined as motivated through major tendencies. We moved through an event that *produced its own value*, a value immanent to the event itself but that made possible the value of events that followed, as Cole produced his story and read it to his aunt at her bedside. As Manning (2016) argued, "A process must determine its own reason" (p. 34), and the writing process is no exception.

Feeling Literacy Through the Event

Four concepts developed from process philosophy help to feel the nuanced rhythms of the minor flowing through this event with Cole and on to the events that followed: *relational transformation*, *affective tonality*, *event-time*, and *desire*. Thinking-feeling these concepts through my own and Cole's experiences with literacy through this moment further evinces how the event generated its own value qualitatively different from a priori conceptualizations that otherwise may have turned it toward different potentials: sentence structure, essay length, proof of research and teaching efficacy therein, for example. After developing these concepts below, I use them to inform propositions for feeling literacies through emergent moments, where ebbs and flows of major and minor come into perceptible tension and where the event's potential could still tend this way or that, but also where the potential for minor gestures to push the event toward more just, affective futures for literacy learning are just as urgent as Cole's desiring writing for his aunt. Specifically, by thinking through similar, though singular, events with Ella, I expand these concepts in propositions for becoming emergent as researchers, for living the propositions themselves as a technique for feeling literacies in process and coming to know potentials for educational change differently.

Relational Transformations

The moment in which I felt ambivalent in the event's unfolding—the push and pull of major and minor tendencies registering in a feeling of uncertainty—was an index of the event's becoming. This indexical feeling provides not a unit of analysis for eventual critique, but a registering on the body of something happening, a feeling of relations between human bodies, materials, time, and space becoming different. In this sense, the event is not *in* any one thing, but quality or a sense of the relationship of things coming to be: "The event is not identical to the bodies which it affects, but neither is it transcendent to what happens to them or what they do, such that it cannot be said any longer that they are (ontologically) different to bodies" (Badiou, 2007, p.38). The event is of the material moment, immanent, an immediation of thought in the act that cannot be fully understood through reduced mediated units or representations (Manning & Massumi, 2014).

Up until this immanent, relational, indexical feeling of transformative potential, Cole had not told me about his aunt, someone I came to know he felt for very deeply and about whose experience of cancer he struggled to talk, often glancing down at his wringing hands while describing time spent next to her hospital bed. After both his telling me about her in this event and my moving forward with him to write the story, our relationship became different. Imbricated in the becoming of the event itself, there was therefore relational transformation of: (1) Cole's writing, wherein a quiet internal "Yes" produced desiring around writing about his aunt; (2) Cole's relationship with his aunt made different through the writing and through his reading of the writing to her; and (3) the pedagogical and personal relationship between myself and Cole.

About the latter, it would be easy to say he opened up to me after this moment, but it's much harder to describe the shift in tone and the sense of searching I felt in the experiences he began relating from this point forward. He told me more stories about his treatments, about the mouth sores those treatments caused, and dreaming about those sores spread over his entire body in a progression no one could stop. There was a sense of searching through these stories and conversations wherein we were not looking for reasons why these sores and this illness were happening, but why they happen at all to anyone. Relational transformations through the event are not simply a transformation of writing coming to be—Saunders-Stan moving the model who becomes Linda—but the transformations of human relationships, their tone, texture, and trajectories. Relational transformations produce relational desirings that cannot be predicted in advance.

Various process philosophies have developed language to feel alongside these moments of difference actualized, including Deleuze's (1990) notion of the break, or differences that makes a difference (Boldt & Leander, 2017). The break is itself an indexical moment in the event's becoming toward a relational transformation, where the major's tendency is broken through a minor gesture (Manning, 2016), such as the taking of a hand or turning to writing about an aunt because it feels right, a feeling that produces desiring in a new, more humane direction. Qualitatively different from the easier to identify major shifts in agency or identities culturally determined from outside the event (see also Leander & Boldt, 2013), the nuanced rhythms of the minor produce relational transformations that are primarily felt.

Through the event, literacy feels like *some*thing, not some*thing* that can be put into words, codes, or categories of emotion. For instance in this moment with Cole, the potential for relational transformation made itself known in what I can now qualify as a feeling of ambivalence, but that in the event was only a tense feeling of not knowing which way to go, the push and pull of major and minor tendencies in the event's emergence. In the social field, "the event intensifies bodies, concentrates their constitutive multiplicity" (Badiou, 2007, p. 38). Relational transformations are powerful moments of educational change in the everyday, moments that can break this way or that, toward more or less just futures. And this moment about to break, the moment before Cole and I felt which way to write, is an instance of literacy becoming through the event where bodies are intensified, where bodies feel like they are in *something* together. Attuning to these events' becoming therefore also means attuning to the felt potentials for educational change arising and being taken up, or not.

Affective Tonality within and Across Event-Times

Although the event is a becoming through time, event-time contributes to the feeling of that becoming. That is, if literacy through the event is known through the feeling of a potential for relational transformation, then this feeling includes the feeling of time. Through the event, time feels different from its constructed, linear representations. On a different level of experience from chronologies or clocks, event-time is a durational fold in experience texturing the event coming-to-be. Event-time is a durational fold in experience because it is a "non-linear lived duration of experience in the making" (Manning, 2016, p. 15) that comprises the lived dimension of experience as such. Event-time feels like an expansion or contraction, a pulsing or a rhythm, or neither but something other than straight, linear, or measured. Time standing still or rushing past opens a relational field in which transformations become possible outside of the constructed time where the major imagines something happening: between the bells, in the meeting, on time. In this relational field that event-time opens, something becomes possible in the tension between major and minor. The relational coming-to-be of my ambivalence—all the factors that made me feel ambivalent, that made time expand—also made the event's tending this way or that feel like it took forever. In this material complexity of event-time, there is no pure continuity between cause and effect (Manning, 2016, p. 23). I did not cause Cole to consider his aunt any more than the decision to move in the direction of writing for her was all my own, Cole's, or the memory of being with her coming to Cole's mind, or the worry for her future. The event's tending to desiring writing for his aunt was a relational moment between *all of this* and more in which minor gestures—Cole's sharing his stories about Emily and my moving toward those stories, for example—shifted the major toward pedagogy and writing in the minor key. And this took forever, producing sweat, not just because hospital rooms feel tense for healthy bodies. Event-time makes itself known immanently and through the body.

Moments known through event-time are singularities that cannot be understood from outside of the "'just-so' of *this* event" (Massumi, 2011, p. 112, emphasis in original). These "singularities are turning points and points of inflection; bottlenecks, knots, foyers, and centers; points of fusion, condensation, and boiling; points of tears and joy, sickness and health, hope and anxiety, 'sensitive' points" (Deleuze, 1990, p. 52), which I have described in relation to the event with Cole as also the tensions between major and minor tendencies of teaching, learning, and literacy theories and methodologies intensifying in experience. But although always singular, events also take on a sensuous identity, an amodal, lived quality that marks the "just-so" of an event. Via Stern (1985), Massumi (2011) gives the example of parent rocking an infant in his arms as an event of soothing. In Massumi's theorization, the process of soothing is a singular, relational event between parent and child with a felt quality that marks its relation to other singular moments of soothing: "The infant is not a passive recipient of the parent's soothing. In a young child, every experience is a whole-body [amodal] experience. The child's being vibrates with the parent's movements. Mouth gurgles, toes curl, eyes blink then close, arms flutter then still, in rhythm with the soothings. The child's movements have their own activation counter, across sense modalities of taste, vision, tactility, and proprioception" (pp. 111–112). This relational sharing distributes agency in the production of "soothing" across child-parent moving in rhythm with each other, and therefore locates the sensuous experience of soothing not "in" either parent or child but in the "life-experience that comes with the movements. . . . The relational quality of soothing . . . is like an affective atmosphere suffusing and surrounding the . . . affects involved. It is an *affective tonality*" (p. 112, emphasis in original). Affective tonality "expresses the *kind* of liveness that is this event's: its *generic* quality" (p. 112, emphasis in original).

The affective tonality of literacy through the event, within and across event-times, is therefore one way of dealing with the problem of continuity in process ontologies without succumbing to representational or linear images of time. And this conceptualization of affective tonality allows for the qualification of events—soothing, care, fright, embarrassment—while maintaining fidelity to each event's singularity. The genericness of affective tonality therefore "refers to a diversity of events, whose singular just-so's are directly, perceptually-felt to belong together, across any distance at which they might occur" (Massumi, 2011, p. 112). Similar to the parent-child experience of soothing, pedagogical encounters of literacy through the event include a differential involvement in the same moment, a relational sharing of perceived movements and rhythms between students, teachers, and their environments. Elsewhere, I have described how these moments of relational sharing produce affective atmospheres of care and boredom both within singular events and across events distributed across weeks (Hollett & Ehret, 2015, 2017).

With Cole, the affective tonality was only felt and never named, but I could loosely name our coproduced atmosphere as one of searching. Searching is the sense, when produced in tandem with another, that you are together doing something important, looking for answers to essential questions that can find no complete or ultimately satisfying answers through direct expression or pure logic: What makes my [Cole's] relationship with my Aunt Emily different from my relationship with other family members or her relationship with other family members? Why do I feel that writing this for her is vital, and how will it make her feel? How will I [Christian] mentor Cole through a piece of writing so necessary, yet so far removed from my own experience? Why do *I* feel that this writing is vital? Relational transformations produce affective tonalities that cannot be separated from event-time, or from the movements and rhythms of bodies and materials through the event. Thus, event-time is not separate from space, the affective tonality of the movement, but they both, relationally, produce each other's quality, here a quality of searching through moments that felt weakly connected to each other in a way no major theory could capture.

Desiring literacies: A life in the making

A life with literacy is, in part, a searching through relational transformations, feelings through event-time connected by their affective tonalities, and each with converging and diverging trajectories, lines of desire that send us searching for answers to unanswerable questions through writing, reading, speaking, and making media. Desiring literacies create their own value through the qualitative felt-sense of their searching. They are the uses of our literacies in the searching for something impossible to find, the searching for which marks our humanity: Cole's searching through his writing; my searching alongside him; the relational transformations in the writing, and through the writing together. These are the uses of literacy that give it the *sense* of mattering throughout a life, a sense beyond its purely representational uses, a quality of "lifeness" immanent to the event that doesn't produce meaning, but that makes it feel meaningful.

From a nonrepresentational perspective, there is therefore a distinction between *a* life and *the* life, a playful yet essential distinction Deleuze (2006) makes throughout his final work published before his suicide in 1995 at age 70. In the short piece "Immanence: A Life," Deleuze conceptualizes *a* life, as in Cole's or mine, as the emergent experience of self in relation to an event. In other words, *a* life is immanent to the event. *The* life is the composition of events of related affective tonalities . . . and also the intersecting of events of related affective tonalities . . . and also the desire to forge connections within and between these "world-lines" (Massumi, 2011), the sense of connection between events of related affective tonalities that are the word world*ing*, the world feeling alive. *The* life is therefore a "minorizing" of one's identity, an undercurrent to the major representation of self. *The* life is a musical composition, the feeling of having existed in this or that way, and the feeling of "this or that way" coming together in a composition, "somewhat as a musical composition is organised by its theme" (Badiou, 2007, p. 39). In this sense, what would it mean to think about a life with literacy through events traversing the life we experience?

If the subject—Cole, for example—is constantly becoming through events of relational transformation, then the problem for nonrepresentational inquiry in literacies studies is not how the subject has been constructed—Cole as "struggling" with school literacies—but rather how the life is becoming with literacies in a life of writing, reading, speaking, and media making, how a life is becoming more or less valued in relation to the spaces through which it moves. Desiring literacies therefore cannot be thought without considering power, or whose literacies count where and when. But process ontologies know power through how it comes to matter immanently (Ehret, Hollett, & Jocius, 2016), as onto-power (Massumi, 2015). Onto-power refers to how power *actually exists* (see for example, Anderson, 2016), how it makes itself felt materially and immanently—for example, power's affects registering in my body, pulling me toward an institutionally valuable form of writing with Cole.

For Deleuze and his frequent collaborator Guattari, power is not definable exclusively in relation to the panopticon of the state (cf., Foucault) or to capital (cf., Marx) or to the Oedipal (Deleuze & Guattari, 1977/2009). For Deleuze and Guattari (1977/2009), each of these conceptualizations of power force human desire and identity into a constant, intrinsic state of lack in relation to the desired object: the state's will, capital, parents. This is why for Deleuze desiring is a productive process, or force, without an object: "Desire constantly couples continuous flows and partial objects that are by nature fragmentary and fragmented. Desire causes the current to flow, itself flows in turn, and breaks the flows" (Deleuze & Guattari, 1977/2009, p. 5). Desire is the will to connect, to forge relations. For Deleuze and Guattari nothing can be known outside of its relationality—a relation to this and . . . and . . . and . . . Desire is the force of production that develops through relations.

What is at stake in coming to know desire through literacy events? The movements of a life that composes the life? In the event with Cole, the tension of major and minor tendencies were the play of power on potentially limiting desire, potentially tending it toward producing sameness: the "significant" essay as research and teaching "outcome." Desire, in this sense, is a neutral productive force that can be played in different keys, produced to move according to different rhythms. What was at stake in playing desire in the major or minor key through this literacy event with Cole? What would it mean differently to his identity as a writer were a significant essay to identify him as a successful writer in his school? What would it mean differently to his relationship with his aunt, with me, and with himself, to write for his aunt and not for the major? On the one hand, this is a false choice. Although we moved according to the latter, Cole was also able to submit his six-paragraph essay for Aunt Emily to his teacher, and I submitted it to the hospital teachers. But on the other hand, the minor gesture of desiring toward writing for his aunt enabled a relational transformation not otherwise possible, and it opened the potential for events of similar affective tonality between us as literacy teacher and learner. The minor gesture enabled not only a different life with writing, but also the life that became our pedagogical relationship over time.

What is at stake coming to know desire through literacy events is the meaningfulness of the life of literacy teaching and learning. Desire is a minor antidote to strong theories of emotion that reduce emotional responses in social and cultural contexts to linear development of emotional responses over time, or to rationalized, verbalized feeling in relation to verbal thinking—as in Cole's verbalized feeling of writing this hospital scene as "tough," or a student's verbalization of taking on an academic voice "hard" in a high school writing class. It was not the framing of this literacy event that reproduced an emotion, but the movement of desiring that opened the potential for a relational transformation, the very quiet internal "Yes" for Cole in the writing and for me in the teaching. What is at stake is dislocating educational change from majoritarian conceptualizations and feeling potentials for relational transformation in the mundane movements of the everyday.

Propositions for Feeling Literacies in Process

Feeling for these moments of relational transformation in the everyday requires becoming emergent as a researcher, and thereby allowing the flows of affect to be immanent to our encounters with literacy through the event. Through the event, the tensions of major and minor register through constant movements of affective intensities that open potentials for relational transformations, often in unpredictable moments like mine with Cole. The more familiar post hoc theoretic tools and units of analysis do not prepare us to work through the movements of such events, nor are they calibrated to feel the idiosyncratic value literacies develop in process, such as Cole's desiring writing for his aunt. This poses a significant challenge for literacy studies that I do not aim to resolve here. Rather, my goal is to open the challenge to the field by articulating modes of existence that do not impose method or other representational, analytic units onto the event from the outside. The rigor of this form of critique is therefore to attune to the possibility of experience, the affective excess of moments that escapes order, structures, and major theories. The possibilities to which this technique of poststructural inquiry attunes therefore include the potential for new concepts, knowledge, and experiences with literacies to create their own value immanently. As Manning (2016) put it: "The rigor must occur from within the occasion of experience, from the event's own stakes in its coming-to-be" (p. 38).

Becoming a Proposition: Emergence and Speculation through the Event

The technique of becoming emergent in education research develops from a speculative pragmatism. Following Stengers (2010), if speculative pragmatism is an emergent process of affirming the minor's potential for relational transformation, then it is also an essential process of educational change itself, a "learning to resist a future that presents itself as obvious, plausible, and normal . . . to gamble that the present still provides substance for resistance" (p. 10). In relation to affect, resisting the refrains of obvious futures requires developing theoretic propositions that lure the unconscious into action. Propositions in nonrepresentational literacy inquiry are speculative lures for feeling that, in the moment, actualize and become felt as a part of experience, thereby intensifying it. The intensification of experience through nonrepresentational propositions affirms "value as elements in feeling" (Whitehead, 1927–1928/1985, p. 185). Speculative propositions link feelings to possibilities in the minor key. Affirming value as elements in feeling meets the possibilities for change at a level of experience qualitatively different from the major, and therefore does not suggest a "life without politics or life with a different politics"; rather, speculative pragmatism through propositional lures is an invitation to feel life "with a politics of difference" (Boldt & Leander, 2017, p. 415).

In order to act as a lure for feeling without predicting feeling in advance, speculative propositions must themselves be articulated weakly. Whitehead (1927–1928/1985) describes the complexity of this weak theory:

> The point is that every proposition refers to a universe exhibiting some general systematic metaphysical character. Apart from this background, the separate entities which go to form the proposition, and the proposition as a whole, are without determinate character. Nothing has been defined, because every definite entity requires a systemic universe to supply its requisite status. Thus every proposition proposing a fact must, in its complete analysis, propose the general character of the universe required for that fact.
>
> *(p. 11)*

Without determinate character, speculative propositions do not designate a phenomenon or activity ahead of its own happening. Propositions do not describe matters-of-fact, nor are they representations of judgments (Stengers, 2011). Rather, it pertains to the proposition to evoke the "general character of the universe," the world-lines, that link singular events to each other without pre- or overdetermining the emergent value in those events' coming-to-be. In the context of literacy research, speculative propositions function to attune us to events-in-the-making, where the potentials for relational transformations that make a difference in where we might go with our literacies are only just becoming. Feeling ambivalent was an unarticulated proposition intensifying experience in the event with Cole, a proposition that was a tension between major and minor nudging the event this way or that.

Writing with Ella months after Cole had left the hospital forced me to reflect on how to do better in the moment, to move more quickly toward minor gestures that might open to desiring literacies. This is not sentimentalization of moments, but a desiring itself that resists major tendencies to define the sentiments of a life with literacy from constructed images of time and space imagined as existing above or beyond the event's unfolding. The sentiments becoming through moments with Ella resonated with events Cole and I shared, their affective tonalities weakly linked through tensions of major and minor and through a sense of searching through writing alone and together.

Refeeling through these weakly connected events and their resonating affects, I here develop propositions that express the affective tonalities of literacy events across these resonating moments. These propositions are weakly articulated as speculative lures for feeling literacies in process that create their own value, for intensifying experiences coming-to-be so as to resist the refrains of obvious futures and feel forward through relational transformations in a life of living and learning with texts.

Proposition 1: Literacy in the Event Determines its Own Value through Relational Transformations

I met Ella about two weeks into her hospitalization. As with Cole, I was nudged to develop a writing project with her to submit to her English teacher. We had a few weeks to complete our project, and Ella was the only student with whom I was working at the time. So at first we would just meet together in the hospital school room and talk about books, music, and popular culture, but mostly just possible names for all the funny hospital smells we could think of (there were so many . . .). Ella talked a lot about her mother and sole caregiver, with whom she had developed a passion for the fantasy romance genre, particularly in novels and television series. Ella described coming out of her room at night, unable to sleep, and just sitting on the love seat next to her mom, who would usually be reading a paperback. "The best ones'll have someone like Maleficent making spells and trouble and something," Ella related seriously in one early conversation.

The English teacher in me was already imagining the genre story she might produce, even before Ella told me that many nights on the love seat would turn into imaginative conversations between her and her mom. In these conversations, they would imagine how to improve storylines they thought could be made better, spinning new stories from shabby plots. Ella's mom lived and worked in a neighboring state, and although she was at the hospital more than seemed possible, she wasn't there every night. The emotional valence of previous experiences with literacy on the love seat, the cultural tools of genre reading and related oral literacies, and the mediation of pop culture media texts and mass market paperbacks, these and more were major theories coming into the event. And these major interpretations of the event were certainly conscious in my decision to move forward with Ella's choice to write a "fantasy romance novel," helping me to feel value in what we were able to work on outside of common curricular constraints. We were able to write through a piece whose material for meaning-making I could locate in the culture, history, and genres of reading with her mom, as well as in the emotional present where bringing that history close felt necessary.

We decided that Ella would write a page or two on the computer in her room, and then we would meet again to talk about what she had written. When we met a few days later in the hospital schoolroom, Ella showed me the structure she had decided upon. The story would move between (1) italicized dialogue of confrontations between a teen protagonist, Zena, and an evil Maleficent-like sorceress, Guinevere, making trouble in her life and (2) unitalicized prose depicting scenes around Zena's house where the trouble played out. This cycle became the narrative conceit driving the story forward, (1) confronting the trickster, (2) trickster trouble, and around again. The setting was always her home, with her mom, her bedroom, and the family den. After our second meeting, through which she had written six short scenes using this structure, a section of italicized dialogue and one of narrative action, I imagined the cycle continuing. I asked Ella where she thought the story was "going to go," trying to gently nudge her out of her cyclical refrain of setting and structure. I was unprepared for her response: "It's sometimes like bein' sick where it messes you up, I don't know." Ella said in describing her evil sorceress, Guinevere, "She's just gonna do stuff to her [Zena].".

Relational transformations do not make sense as rational, mediated action or meaning-making. Rather, they produce sense, the feeling that something is happening in *just this way*. And this sense of things infuses how relations become different—between writer and writing, mentor and student writer—as event-time opens to unforeseen potentials. Ella was not describing to me who she was as a writer, but how she was feeling, how she was desiring literacies to move through something that was simultaneously bringing us together and keeping us apart. I had no means of accessing her experience in the hospital or with leukemia, but the affective tonality of searching through the impossible-to-know registered across the life of our writing together from that moment on. The push and pull of a life coming together between lives impossibly apart is a feeling of relational transformation in the social field that, paradoxically, feels like closeness and care. The recognition of this paradox is empathy through the event: the desiring to feel another's singular, unfeelable experience.

How Ella used her literacies through the life of these writing experiences could not be disentangled from the nonrepresentational movements of desire, the production of affective tonalities, and the relational transformations between Ella and her writing, between Ella and myself. As with relations in the social field, relations between writer and writing—here Ella and her genre fiction—also produce a push and pull of paradoxical searching through togetherness-apart, the shared struggle of a meddling disease between writer and protagonist, and a separation between embodiment and fantasy. How would the proposition that literacy in the event determines its own value through relational transformations in the social field change our sense of possibilities in the movements of writing and social life? Of what writing can do, not as therapy to address a lack of understanding, a reflection, but as a production that generates deeper senses of what is continuing to happen? Of where teaching writing can go, and how the movements of teaching might create their own value? Of how the impossibility of knowing is a valuable reason to write?

Proposition 2: The Affective Tonality Produced and Modulated through an Event Contributes to the Sense of a Life that Composes the Life

This moment of relational transformation opened such speculative feeling between Ella and myself, and perhaps between Ella and her writing, had she not already felt it or put the feeling into words before expressing it aloud to me. Different from, but yet another semblance of, Saunders's "Yes," this relational transformation opened a life with writing between me and Ella, an emergent experience of self in relation to event. And this transformative event also opened the life of our writing together over a series of moments, wherein events of her writing alone and us talking about her writing together felt weakly connected through an affective tonality of close-separation and the care that feeling close-separation engendered.

As a writing mentor, I was still concerned about the cyclical nature of Ella's writing, however, and the lack of potential for conflict resolution between Guinevere and Zena. Suggesting a change of setting and thinking perhaps of Zena's high school, I asked Ella where Guinevere followed Zena outside of her house. Ella chewed on the question briefly, rocking her Eiffel Tower necklace between her index finger and thumb. "Maybe what would be real good is if Zena and Nalan [Zena's best guy friend appearing now for the first time] went places like New York and Guinevere was chasin' after them to where they had to be secret[ive] about where they were going."

Not unlike Saunders's Stan, perhaps, Ella rocking her necklace moved our writing together through Zena and Nalan's road trip. In order to imagine all the places they might go, we opened Google Maps, zooming into Google Street View in New York and Paris, seeing the places that I knew Ella herself wanted to visit. Across the coming weeks we moved through imagined settings together: Zena and Nalan's experiences in Kentucky, then Washington, DC, New York, and finally Europe. Although still making trouble, Guinevere appeared less often as the story became more about Zena and Nalan's budding, though implicit, romance. Ella's writing developed in the process, as she learned to move characters through different cities, cultures, and ways of speaking. She varied the structure of her chapter sections and broke out of her cyclical refrain between italicized confrontational dialogue and unitalicized narrative action.

But the composition of writing events also *felt* different from this linear development through writing practices. For one, Ella left the hospital and yet wanted to continue our conversations together. I agreed, and we Skyped to discuss her work every time she felt that she had made enough progress, about five times total after she was discharged. Importantly, the desire to forge connections within and between these world-lines—the sense of connection between events of related affective tonalities that are the word *worlding*—are inextricable from the production of the events themselves that only feel related. Like the nonrepresentational concept of affect, this desiring need not be conscious. The desiring to develop world-lines is an impersonal force that *produces* events of related affective tonalities. For Ella and myself, this meant the desiring of becoming through writing together, through closeness apart, and through searching in the movements of characters evading a meddling disease. There was no motivation to write. Only a desiring production of world-lines that, in their singularities and familiarities, felt like comfort and care.

Proposition 3: Known through the Event's Becoming, Literacies Produce Signs that are Generated through, and Generative of, Desire

In the first part of his book on Proust's *À la recherche du temps perdu* (hereafter, Search) Deleuze (2000/1972) describes his, and Proust's narrator's, encounters with signs. Deleuze's goal throughout the work is to challenge the common notion of memory and subjective association as the Search's structuring theme, and he begins this argument illustrating how signs in the Search, such as the iconic madeleine, are not representative of mere psychological states—the involuntary invocation of memory—but are rather parts of experience that mobilize the involuntary and unconscious toward searching for something unnamed and unnamable. In this way, Deleuze argues, "the Search is oriented to the future, not to the past" (p. 4). The Search is therefore an ongoing process of discovery, a narrative apprenticeship in signs, which hieroglyphically deny immediate understanding. In this sense, the "reading" of signs produces movement, or searching for meanings not immediately apprehensible. Beyond literal decoding, reading signs produces desire that itself produces signs, through reading new texts or through writing or making media in search of something not obviously, or even rationally, represented in the sign itself.

Moving again through the life of writing with Ella, I cannot help but return to Deleuze's reading of Proust, itself a proposition intensifying my experience of writing now, unconsciously activated, and forcing me to think differently. The major tendency to compel conflict, and conflict resolution, in Ella's narrative, or to break the setting out of her home, was perhaps an overdetermination of her writing process. Her desiring to write a fantasy romance was itself a searching through signs. A searching that brought us together and pushed us apart, a process that took her beyond what the writing she produced communicates.

If we come to know the world by how it moves us, and how we move in relation, then signs are not simply something that must be decoded. They also send us searching. This searching produces the life with literacy that is a composition of style, of a feeling of having lived and learned with texts in the minor key, a level of experience different from linear development through constructed time, communities, and cultures. Feeling literacy through the event, then, relates not only to how *a* life with literacy feels but also to how *the* life is composed.

The life is not only a birth-to-death feeling of having moved and been moved in relation to textual production and interpretation. It is also the nested continuities of event-times, weakly linked through their affective tonalities; nested continuities that are multiple and unpredictably many throughout a human existence. With Ella, this includes not only her own searching through the production of signs in the process of individual relational transformations, and through the production of a series of related scenes in her novel, but also the production of pedagogical moments of relational transformation between writer and writing mentor. In literacy research, feeling literacies in process requires an attunement to a life becoming the life, in textual, pedagogical, and social transformations.

Coda: A Propositional Literacy Studies

How might literacy inquiry continue in coming to know not only the major tendencies that impinge upon our experiences with literacy through the event, but also the affective movements of the minor that produce relational transformations between writer and writing, mentor and mentee; *a* life using literacies and *the* life with literacies? How might becoming a proposition lure our bodies into feeling the flows of the minor, and thereby allow literacy inquiry to become speculative and, literally, creative through the event? One element of this creation may be more nuanced propositions that aid researchers and other literacy professionals in making unforeseen change possible in everyday minor gestures. As the propositions in this chapter have expressed, unforeseen change happens through singular experiences of events that create their own value, and these moments of relational transformation develop on a level of experience qualitatively different from those on which the field's major theories operate.

With these questions, I conclude this chapter not with a retrospective discussion of points made, but with speculative movements proposing points to come. Here is a final proposition in lieu of a discussion: *Let literacy inquiry grow through neither the major nor the minor, but through both and-, through an ecology of practices attuned to the ethics the event demands of us.* One level of theory does not negate the other, major and minor. They are both always already happening on different planes of experience. As researchers, it is therefore important not to mix planes, to know the minor through the major and vice versa, but to bring them into relation through an ecology of practices in the field.

An ecology of practices, as Stengers (2010) might argue, does not place major above minor in a structural or hierarchical image of knowledge "types," but rather places them into an ecology of ways of coming to know how we use our literacies not only to achieve specific purposes in social context, but also to search for answers to unanswerable questions, the searching for which defines our shared humanity. Inquiry into literacy as social, cultural, political, and affective activity must therefore attune itself to the proposition that neither the major nor minor demands our full attention, but both and. This proposition is only an abstraction until it intensifies the experience of inquiry in which you feel it immanent and essential to the moment coming-to-be, the moment in which you feel "literacy through the event" as qualitatively different from "the literacy event," the event as strongly related to a practice. This is not therefore an argument to set up a new divide or binary choice between representational and nonrepresentational modes of inquiry and critique, but an affirming of how research comes to matter in the moment and how we feel our way forward with theoretic tools at hand.

And yet, the minor is particularly attuned to the level of experience on which literacy feels like the most humane of all human practices. The minor moves us importantly toward the knowledge that meaning-making is not only culturally and historically situated; it is also a moving production of desire for making meaning that generates relational transformations between human beings and texts and human beings, other human beings, and their social worlds. The minor attunes us to our idiosyncratic desirings to forge connections and form new relations through reading, writing, and making media. On another level from the linear notion of cultural-historical development, desire moves through the life of literacy, producing world-lines that (weakly) connect events of resonating affective tonalities. These events are the relational transformations of literacy through the event—between writer and writing, sign and signer, mentor and mentee— that index the becoming of a difference that makes a difference. These events are the mundane sense of change in the everyday.

Dislocating change, value, and knowing through an ecology of practices in literacy studies therefore affirms how change happens in mundane moments that are often only felt, but intensely so. Change happens most often in everyday moments and movements with literacy—as with Cole and Ella. These moments create their own value and set desiring forward on unpredictable paths with reading, writing, and media making. Change is transformational because it is unlocatable, always in movement, always only in relation to valued cultural practices and identities that preexist the event or that exist outside of it. The feeling of change is unlocatable because it exceeds these representations. The value of change can only be felt in propositions that provoke the unconscious toward feeling in process a very quiet internal "Yes."

References

Alvermann, D. E. (2009). Sociocultural constructions of adolescence and young people's literacies. In L. Christenbury, R. Bomer, R., & P. Smagorinsky (Eds.), *Handbook of adolescent literacy research* (pp. 14–28). New York, NY: Guilford Press.

Anderson, B. (2016). Neoliberal affects. *Progress in Human Geography, 40*(6), 734–753.

Anderson, B., & Harrison, P. (2010). The promise of non-representational theories. In B. Anderson & P. Harrison (Eds.), *Taking-place: Non-representational theories and geography* (pp. 1–36). London: Ashgate Publishing.

Badiou, A. (2007). The event in Deleuze. *Parrhesia, 2*, 37–44.

Barton, D., & Hamilton, M. (2000). Literacy practices. In D. Barton, M. Hamilton, & R. Ivanič (Eds.), *Situated literacies: Reading and writing in context* (pp. 7–15). New York, NY: Routledge.

Bezemer, J., & Kress, G. (2015). *Multimodality, learning and communication: A social semiotic frame.* New York, NY: Routledge.

Boldt, G. M., & Leander, K. M. (2017). Becoming through 'the break': A post-human account of a child's play. *Journal of Early Childhood Literacy, 17*(3), 409–425.

Braidotti, R. 2011. *Nomadic theory: The portable Rosi Braidotti.* New York, NY: Columbia University Press.

Deleuze, G. (1990). *The logic of sense.* New York, NY: Columbia University Press.

Deleuze, G. (2000/1972). *Proust and signs: The complete text.* Minneapolis, MN: University of Minnesota Press.

Deleuze, G. (2006). Immanence: A Life. In *Two regimes of madness: Texts and interviews 1975–1995.* New York, NY: Semiotext(e).

Deleuze, G., & Guattari, F. (1977/2009). *Anti-Oedipus: Capitalism and schizophrenia.* New York, NY: Penguin Books.

Ehret, C. (2018). Moments of teaching and learning in a children's hospital: Affects, textures, and temporalities. *Anthropology & Education Quarterly, 49*(1), 53–71.

Ehret, C., & Hollett, T. (2016). Affective dimensions of participatory design research in informal learning environments: Placemaking, belonging, and correspondence. *Cognition and Instruction, 34*(3), 250–258.

Ehret, C., Hollett, T., & Jocius, R. (2016). The matter of new media making: An intra-action analysis of adolescents making a digital book trailer. *Journal of Literacy Research, 48*(3), 346–377.

Gee, J. P. (2015). *Social linguistics and literacies: ideology in discourses* (5th ed.). New York, NY: Routledge.

Gregg, M., & Seigworth, G. J. (2009). *The affect theory reader.* Durham, NC: Duke University Press.

Heath, S. B. (1982). Protean shapes in literacy events: Ever-shifting oral and literate traditions. In D. Tannen (Ed.), *Spoken and written language: Exploring orality and literacy* (pp. 91–117). Norwood, NJ: Ablex.

Hollett, T., & Ehret, C. (2015). "Bean's world": (Mine) Crafting affective atmospheres of gameplay, learning, and care in a children's hospital. *New Media & Society, 17*(11), 1849–1866.

Hollett, T., & Ehret, C. (2017). Relational methodologies for mobile literacies: Intra-action, atmosphere, and rhythm. In C. Burnett, G. Merchant, A. Simpson & M. Walsh (Eds.), *The case of the iPad: Mobile literacies in education* (pp. 227–244). London: Springer.

Ingold, T. (2017). Surface visions. *Theory, Culture & Society, 34*(7–8), 99–108.

Kress, G. (2009). *Multimodality: A social semiotic approach to contemporary communication.* New York, NY: Routledge.

Leander, K. M., & Boldt, G. (2013). Rereading "A pedagogy of multiliteracies": Bodies, texts, and emergence. *Journal of Literacy Research, 45*(1), 22–46.

Leander, K. M., & Ehret, C. (Eds.). (2019). *Affect in literacy teaching and learning: Pedagogies, politics, and coming to know.* New York, NY: Routledge.

Lewis, C., & Tierney, J. D. (2013). Mobilizing emotion in an urban classroom: Producing identities and transforming signs in a race-related discussion. *Linguistics and Education, 24*(3), 289–304.

Manning, E. (2016). *The minor gesture.* Durham, NC: Duke University Press.

Manning, E., & Massumi, B. (2014). *Thought in the act: Passages in the ecology of experience*. Minneapolis, MN: University of Minnesota Press.

Massumi, B. (2002). *Parables for the virtual: Movement, affect, sensation*. Durham, NC: Duke University Press.

Massumi, B. (2011). *Semblance and event: Activist philosophy and the occurrent arts*. Cambridge, MA: MIT Press.

Massumi, B. (2015). *Ontopower: War, powers, and the state of perception*. Durham, NC: Duke University Press.

McCarthy, C. (2017, April 20). The Kekulé problem. *Nautilus, 47*. Retrieved from: http://nautil.us/issue/47/consciousness/the-kekul-problem

Saunders, G. (2017, March 4). What writers really do when they write. *The Guardian*. Retrieved from: https://www.theguardian.com/books/2017/mar/04/what-writers-really-do-when-they-write

Smagorinsky, P., & Daigle, E. A. (2012). The role of affect in students' writing for school. In E. Grigorenko, E. Mambrino, & D. Preiss (Eds.), *Writing: A mosaic of perspectives and views* (pp. 293–307). New York, NY: Taylor & Francis.

Spinoza, B. (1985). *The collected works of Spinoza* (E. Curley, trans.). Princeton, NJ: Princeton University Press.

Stern, D. N. (1985). *The interpersonal world of the infant: A view from psychoanalysis and developmental psychology*. New York, NY: Karnac Books.

Stengers, I. (2011). *Thinking with Whitehead: A free and wild creation of concepts*. Cambridge, MA: Harvard University Press.

Stengers, I. (2010). *Cosmopolitics I*. Minneapolis, MN: University of Minnesota Press.

Stewart, K. (2008). Weak theory in an ufinished world. *Journal of Folklore Research, 45*(1), 71–82.

Streeck, J., Goodwin, C., & LeBaron, C. (Eds.). (2011). *Embodied interaction: Language and body in the material world*. Cambridge: Cambridge University Press.

Stornaiuolo, A., Smith, A., & Phillips, N. C. (2017). Developing a transliteracies framework for a connected world. *Journal of Literacy Research, 49*(1), 68–91.

Street, B. V. (2014). *Social literacies: Critical approaches to literacy in development, ethnography and education*. New York, NY: Routledge.

Thein, A. H., Sloan, D. L., & Guise, M. (2015). Examining emotional rules in the English classroom: A critical discourse of one student's literary responses in two classroom contexts. *Research in the Teaching of English, 49*(3), 200–223.

Vadeboncoeur, J. A., & Collie, R. J. (2013). Locating social and emotional learning in schooled environments: A Vygotskian perspective on learning as unified. *Mind, Culture, and Activity, 20*(3), 201–225.

Vasudevan, L., & Campano, G. (2009). The social production of adolescent risk and the promise of adolescent literacies. *Review of Research in Education, 33*(1), 310–353.

Whitehead, A. N. (1927–1928/1985). *Process and reality*. New York, NY: The Free Press.

30

PRAGMATISM [NOT JUST] PRACTICALITY AS A THEORETICAL FRAMEWORK IN LITERACY RESEARCH

Deborah R. Dillon and David G. O'Brien

Our original discussion of this topic appeared in *Reading Research Quarterly* (Dillon, O'Brien, & Heilman, 2000) in response to the daunting task of predicting research trends as we ushered in the current millennium. Subsequent versions appeared in both the fifth and sixth editions of *Theoretical Models and Processes of Reading*. Now, since we first wrote on the topic of pragmatism and practicality, we have the advantage of looking back over nearly two decades of inquiry in the field to reflect upon what we have learned about pragmatism in the conduct of research.

In this chapter, against the backdrop of an increasing interest in pragmatism and aligning research methods with this perspective (Biesta & Burbules, 2003; Johnson et al., 2017; Morgan, 2007; Patton, 2002, 2014; Rosiek, 2013), we attempt to more clearly distinguish between pragmatism as a broad philosophical position, and its *practicality* component as it has been applied to inquiry. We comment on how research methodologists and researchers have leaned more toward practicality, and in doing so, missed our stance and other scholars' positions on why pragmatism, more broadly, is and will continue to be useful and necessary, even aside from the practicality arguments. We also critique the use of "pragmatism" as an umbrella term for research approaches like mixed methods and design-based research to the exclusion of other approaches that may also be grounded in both pragmatism and practicality. Finally, we offer a caution that pragmatism's very popularity as a way to address "practical" issues and answer "authentic" questions could also be its downfall. We see this happening if it is overused or inappropriately taken up due to its practical, flexible nature—with the end result being the essentializing of pragmatism as practicality.

Pragmatism and Inquiry: A Brief Overview

Pragmatism is a distinctive American branch of philosophy that began in the context of late-nineteenth-century critiques of both hard science and social science. William James described pragmatism as "an attitude of looking away from first things, principles, 'categories,' supposed necessities; and of looking towards last things, fruits, consequences, facts" (James, 1997, as cited in Menand, 1997, p. 98). In more current work, Juuti and Lavonen (2006) describe pragmatism as research "for education," rather than research "about education." Through the lens of pragmatism, knowledge and "research results" are simply those used and thoughtfully understood to be useful to real people in real contexts.

The label "pragmatism," like other vague terms, has been avoided by leading educational philosophers and researchers because it is an overused, misconstrued "terminological lightning rod" (Boisvert, 1998, p. 11). Even Dewey, who considered himself a pragmatist, did not use the word in his texts, noting, "Perhaps the word lends itself to misconception. . . . So much misunderstanding and relatively futile controversy have gathered about the word that it seemed advisable to avoid its use" (as cited in Boisvert, 1998, p. 11).

In this chapter we use pragmatism to support what Bernstein (1983) called "radical critiques of the intellectually imperialistic claims made in the name of method" (p. xi). In calling for pragmatism we are *not* advocating the approach of a particular methodology, method, or research design. Instead, we assert that conducting inquiry to useful ends should take precedence over finding ways to defend one's epistemology. It is important to remember, as Dewey noted, that pragmatism does not mean "if it works then it's true" (Boisvert, 1998, p. 31), even though the term had been so cast. We will further clarify this when we critique the practicality vs. other foundations of pragmatism arguments.

Dewey (1938/1981) noted that the value of scientific research must be considered in terms of the projected consequences of activities—*the end in view*. Dewey identified genuine problems that were part of actual social situations as those researchers should address. These problems (from practice), according to Dewey, should be identified and carefully defined before inquiry is undertaken. In fact, this latter point—the need to convert a problematic situation into a set of conditions forming a definite problem—was recognized by Dewey as a weakness of much inquiry. Researchers might select a set of preferred methods without an understanding of the problem. After the problem or subject matter (the phenomenon under study) was identified and the dimensions clearly defined, Dewey recommended that the issue be investigated from various perspectives, depending on the purpose or objective of the inquiry. Finally, as Dewey stated, "the ultimate end and test of all inquiry is the transformation of a problematic situation (which involves confusion and conflict) into a unified one" (p. 401). For Dewey, all inquiry should be focused on transformation and evaluation of the features of situations in which we find ourselves (Biesta & Burbules, 2003).

Thus, the pragmatism developed by Holmes, James, Peirce, and Dewey, according to Menand (2002), offers that "ideas are not 'out there' waiting to be discovered, but are tools—like forks and knives and microchips—that people devise to cope with the world in which they find themselves . . . [and] since ideas are provisional responses to particular and irreproducible circumstances, their survival depends not on their immutability but on their adaptability" (p. xi). In addition, the usefulness of pragmatic inquiry, as conceived by Dewey, also should be considered in terms of its capacity to contribute to a democratic life, broadly defined. Dewey observed that democracy "has not been adequately realized in any time" (as cited in Boisvert, 1998, p. 299), and the goal of democracy is the "creation of a freer and . . . more humane experience in which all contribute" (Dewey, 1939/1993a, p. 245).

In a more recent argument, Putnam (2017) contends that pragmatism interrogates a space outside of "paradigmatic" sciences like physics, in terms of scientific claims. In inquiry, we make claims, we express beliefs, we offer conjectures (e.g., Sandoval, 2014) and formulate warrants based on these claims or beliefs. However, "objective" data do not presuppose these warrants. Instead, "ethical" warranted claims address interests that stem from the common welfare determined by discussion among inquirers leading to a shared commitment to solving a problem. This is not just the practicality argument—pragmatism meaning that "the ends justify the means"—but posits that researchers have an *ethical* (rather than "objective" data–driven) responsibility to work on agreed-upon issues that are considered important by a collective. And ideas that are simply valuable are not ultimately *valued* without what Dewey (as cited in Putnam, 2017) has termed *criticism*, or the rigorous critique of a community that decides such issues are warranted for inquiry.

Because the problems that pragmatists address are to contribute to a more democratic way of life characterized by the creation of a freer and more humane experience, the identification of problems for inquiry is particularly important. Dewey emphasized the inherently social nature of all problem posing, and he believed that people cannot understand themselves, or develop their practical reasoning, in isolation from others (1932/1987a; 1929/1987b).

Therefore, problems need to be socially situated and identified to be legitimate foci of inquiry. Dewey believed that all inquiry is natural, situational, and grounded in problems, interrogations of theory and practice; and evaluative. The inquiry process suggested by a pragmatic stance is quite different from traditional inquiry in which a researcher establishes a question or problem and proceeds without the integration of nonexpert opinion. In fact, for some researchers the integration of nonexpert opinion, which was key to Dewey, is understood as a sign of methodological weakness. The importance of dialogue and listening in inquiry requires new roles for researchers and also for the community of learners and practitioners, or the "subjects," as traditional researchers would call them.

A pragmatic approach to knowledge in general and to research results in particular is completely different from the way in which research is usually understood. In fact, it "flips" generalizability and specificity upside down: Research should be focused toward the *useable* and the *specific* rather than the *generalizable* and *abstract*. As Biesta and Burbules (2003) explain, pragmatists see the point of doing educational research as "not only to find out what might be possible or achievable, but also to deal with the question of whether what is possible and achievable is *desirable*—and more specifically, whether it is desirable from an educational point of view" (p. 109).

Pragmatism explicitly critiques the dangers of decontextualized knowledge and of actions and ideological positions that stem from it. It calls for a personal commitment to revision, reflection, and inquiry, which is more important than the latest "scientific truth"; pragmatists argue that it leads to the only sort of truth that is both useful and justifiable. What is true in a democracy, and what is true in science, must always be considered, reconsidered, and viewed as contested. Yet, this isn't a hopeless or endless task. We always have existing grounds upon which to examine, explore, and reconsider. In the next section, we further explore the implications of these issues for literacy researchers.

Pragmatism as a Basis for Inquiry in Literacy

Our point in the first edition of this chapter in 2000 was that political agendas resulting in policy changes at the turn of the century had profound implications for what research was conducted in the field, what findings were valued and taken up by researchers and policy makers, and what impact both the research and policies had on practices associated with K-12 students' learning. We describe what we mean by this policy impact in the following sections of this chapter.

Scientifically Based Research

Pragmatism, which undergirded studies that attempted to solve important, immediate problems by enlisting collaborative stakeholders, came up against "scientifically based research"—a descriptor that was constructed to benchmark programs that could be used in compliance with the Reading Excellence Act (1999). This federal definition of research began a process in which policy shaped the educational services that could be funded under particular initiatives. In addition, the National Reading Panel report (NRP), published by the National Institute of Child Health and Human Development (NICHD, 2000), had a profound impact on what reading research was deemed worthy of being conducted, and included a policy document that eventually had tremendous bearing on practice in our nation's schools, and had a direct impact on the federally funded research projects that followed. The panel of experts who compiled the report made decisions to include research that met particular parametric and statistical standards for validity and generalizability, leaving out a large body of scholarship, much of which was qualitative research.

Research valued within that "scientifically based" policy climate included randomized controlled experiments for primary research studies, and meta-analyses as the standard for combining results and drawing conclusions across studies. It should be noted that the definition of "scientifically based research," included in the reauthorization of Office of Educational Research and Improvement (OERI; e.g., H.R. 4875 in 2000, H.R. 3801 in 2002, and ESRA in 2002) outlined the types of educational research that could be funded by the new Institute of Education Sciences (IES).

In our chapter in the sixth edition of *TMPR*, we examined some tenets of the National Research Council (NRC, 2002) report, not only to find the roots of scientifically based research as it was applied almost 20 years ago, but also to show how policy makers selectively picked some design features of it and ignored others when writing the No Child Left Behind Act (NCLB, 2001). In response to a request from the National Educational Research Policy and Priorities Board (NER-PPB), a National Research Council (NRC) committee was commissioned in 2000 by the National Academy of Sciences. The group engaged in work resulting in the Scientific Research in Education (SRE) study (National Research Council, 2002). The committee was given the charge to ". . . review and synthesize recent literature on the science and practice of scientific educational research and consider how to support high quality science in a federal education research agency" (see NRC Executive Summary, p.1, National Research Council, 2002).

The overall goal for this group of scholars and policy makers was to clarify the definition of scientific inquiry in education, and to speculate how the federal government could endorse and foster research that leads to "evidence-based" education policy and practice. The definition that emerged from the SRE report positioned research in education as akin to that in the sciences, noting that research "is a continual process of rigorous reasoning supported by a dynamic interplay among methods, theories, and findings . . . [that] builds understandings in the form of models or theories that can be tested . . . [and] progresses as a result of a not-so-invisible hand of professional skepticism and criticism" (p. 2). But the definition went on to state that "multiple methods, applied over time and tied to evidentiary standards, are essential to establishing a base of scientific knowledge" (p. 2) and the six guiding principles the group proposed *did not* restrict designs to traditional positivist approaches to empiricism, theory validation, or particular research methods or types of evidence.

In fact, the authors of this 2002 report acknowledged that the field of education is challenging to study because it has multiple layers, is always changing, is highly value laden, involves a number of people from different walks of life, and requires "attention to the physical, social, cultural, economic, and historical environments in the research process because these contextual factors often influence results in significant ways" (p. 5). The authors also made a crucially important statement that supports our current arguments: "The design of a study does not make the study scientific. A wide variety of legitimate scientific designs are available for education research. They range from randomized experiments of voucher programs to in-depth ethnographic case studies of teachers to neurocognitive investigations of number learning using positive emission tomography brain imaging" (p. 6). The goal of the authors was not to provide the federal government with a definition of what constitutes scientific research in education, but rather to provide design principles to foster a "scientific culture" within the agency (ironically, design principle 3 was to "insulate the agency from inappropriate political interference").

Despite the reasonable ideas expressed in the report, and the numerous and insightful critiques written in response to the call for a scientific culture as an alternative to the hard-and-fast narrow definition of research created by other reports and policy brokers (see the November 2002 issue of *Educational Researcher*), in January 2002, right after the SRE report was released, NCLB (2001) was passed into law. NCLB included a definition of scientifically based research that privileged testing hypotheses and using experimental and quasi-experimental designs only.

Research and Situated Literacy

Currently, the bulk of federal funding still supports mostly experimental research and other research wherein researchers' questions are answered with quantitative data. The Institute of Education Sciences still uses the same "gold standard" of randomized controlled studies that it initiated in 2002 to select studies for funding. But the interest in, and funding of, "scientifically based" research, particularly research focused on reading, has waned. In fact, the use of terms for subfields of literacy study like reading and writing and basic process research into these areas have been absorbed into the broader field of literacy, which is now researched mostly based in sociocultural theories and qualitative research methods (Beach & O'Brien, 2018).

Federal funding currently guides neither the focus nor bulk of research in the field of literacy. Rather, the trend that was originally marked by the "social turn" and New Literacy Studies (NLS (e.g., Gee, 1999; O'Brien & Rogers, 2015))—arguably started by the foundational work of Shirley Brice Heath (1983)—continues to undergird most of the inquiry. The social turn has given impetus to a host of socially and culturally based research. Although not heavily funded, this research is often designed to respond to authentic problems in schools and communities. NLS research is, by its definition of literacy, situated. It is defined by the sociocultural contexts, actors, and problems that are researched within it, and the work is driven by a need to achieve important, practical consequences.

So-called third paradigms (Johnson et al., 2017; Johnson & Onwuegbuzie, 2004) like mixed methods research (MMR) and design-based research approaches to inquiry (Design- Based Research Collective, 2003) have become increasingly popular in education as a whole as well as within the field of literacy education. These third paradigm approaches formally align themselves with pragmatism because researchers using them equate pragmatism with research designs that eschew epistemological purism (the pure interpretivists vs. the pure positivists) in favor of more reasonable, practical approaches and the use of qualitative and quantitative data to respond to research questions that are often situated within communities of collaborators.

However, many other research approaches that are labeled as qualitative or interpretive research and do not align themselves with pragmatism are clearly based in many of pragmatism's philosophical tenets including but not limited to practicality. It is at best unclear, or at worst ambiguous, what pragmatism means for inquiry when one looks at the American pragmatists—Dewey, James, and Peirce—over the corpus of their writings, and their changing positions over time (Macarthur, 2017). But it is clear that if one leans mostly toward pragmatism as practicality, one could make the case for a steady shift of literacy education toward pragmatism, even during the height of funding tied to the Reading Excellence Act at the turn of the last century, because the funding, and many of the state projects tied to it, were designed to collaboratively address an important, practical problem identified by the broad community. Even beyond the practicality position, the goal to better educate young students as part of the Reading Excellence Act and Reading First does include a core pragmatism position—as part of a shared moral stance (a Deweyan position). This position requires American educators to band together to improve young students' acquisition of early reading skills—in spite of the exclusion of an entire corpus of interpretive inquiry to reach the goal.

In the next section, we start to scrutinize the practicality argument to begin our effort to distinguish between practicality and other aspects of pragmatism. We point to the danger of using practicality arguments like "if it works, use it" or "the ends justify the means" with reference to pragmatic stances in inquiry.

Pragmatism and Practicality Revisited

There are two practicality perspectives that inform why some research is identified as being based in pragmatism and some is not: (1) the practicality of using research methods that best answer research questions toward useful outcomes; and (2) the practicality of connecting research directly to practice.

Pragmatism as Methodological Practicality

Many research methodologists are content with aligning some methods or designs with pragmatism by claiming practicality as the main feature. For example, Johnson and Onwuegbuzie (2004), after discussing briefly the paradigm wars between positivist and interpretivist researchers, call for a "third paradigm," mixed methods, and for "methodological pluralism" based on "paradigmatic and epistemological ecumenicalism," in which researchers select from a range of epistemological stances and use the data that complement those stances.

Why is this epistemological ecumenicalism so good? Supposedly because it provides more useful outcomes and offers the "best chance" to respond to increasingly complex interdisciplinary questions. To give an example, we are currently engaged in a five-year project in which a collaborative, interdisciplinary team of literacy and social studies educators, a historian, and five International Baccalaureate (IB) high school history and global politics teachers are working to better support high school students in the Minneapolis public schools as they learn advanced-level history and global politics with complex texts and discourse. The high school students in the courses are young people who do not often have access to IB coursework, but in the interest of social justice and access, the school wanted to open up these opportunities for advanced coursework. To figure out how to do this, we worked for two years just to understand one another's epistemological stances (O'Brien et al., 2017).

The educators in the history group focus on "command terms" that describe processes and purposes deemed important in thinking historically. They confound the complexity with multiple sets of thinking skills, some of which are specifically tied to reading and writing texts (e.g., The Stanford History Education Group) and more general thinking skills that give students access to ways to think historically (the five Cs). They want to know, and assume that we can figure out, how high school students can learn to think better historically. The literacy contingent wants to know about the intersection of this historical thinking with literacy. We believe that you can study or eventually understand how specific literacy processes and practices can be used to support specific kinds of historical thinking for a variety of youths in these classrooms. We logically figured that design-based research with mixed methods and a range of qualitative and quantitative data would help us address these complex questions. Our approach represents a clear case of researchers who take up a pragmatic stance to engage in challenging work in schools with school partners.

Johnson and Onwuegbuzie (2004) contend that pragmatism is a practical way for researchers to move beyond the positivist-interpretivist dualism so they can do research that draws from multiple data toward a "workable solution." This "best chance" for a "workable solution" (pp. 15–16) is the typical application of pragmatism to inquiry primarily due to a popular definition of practicality. These mixed methodologists state, "The bottom line is that research approaches should be mixed in ways that offer the best opportunities for answering important research questions" (p. 16). They cite a statement from pragmatist Charles Peirce (1878) wherein he notes that a "pragmatic method" implies that we should "consider what effects, that might conceivably have practical bearings. . . ." They then cite William James's (1907) argument: "The pragmatic method is primarily a method of settling metaphysical disputes that otherwise might be interminable. . . . The pragmatic method in such cases is to try to interpret each notion by tracing its respective practical consequences" (p. 18). By simple inference, we can conclude that Johnson and Onwuegbuzie consider epistemological purists as *impractical* because those purists stick with the assumption that knowledge is associated with "purely" positivist or interpretivist positions. They make a good case, although sometimes impracticality yields external funding or accolades from other scholars for advancing theoretical (albeit, impractical) ideas.

Pragmatism and the Practicality of Practice

There is a sense that research-to-practice inquiry like "participatory action research" is viewed as accessible to teachers and other practitioners. One approach to practicality in this sense is understanding how teachers integrate research knowledge into their repertoires of professional knowledge (e.g., Clandinin & Connelly, 1996) grounded in their experiences in the real-world contexts in which they practice. Research approaches that involve teachers collaborating with researchers in conceptualizing research based on actual problems that arise from practice, in the contexts in which teachers work, are more likely to be viewed as practical (Cochran-Smith & Lytle, 1993; Van Velze, 2013).

Nevertheless, in spite of this practicality of practice, there is little evidence that teachers can easily draw from such work (Henrick, Cobb, Penuel, Jackson, & Clark, 2017; Hiebert, Gallimore, & Stigler, 2002; Van Velze, 2013). Researchers often fail to attend to the ways in which practitioners understand research, particularly how they see it as solving important problems in their practice or responding to the immediate needs of their students. Research is often difficult to translate from the academic discourse. Researchers decide to collaborate with teachers and work together to formulate questions, design research, and collect data, but the professional knowledge and values of the two groups sometimes never quite intersect. Researchers nudge teachers toward research designs and the epistemological discourses that often privilege the researchers. Teachers are often disengaged from the inquiry due to the time demands of their practice and simply because they are not as intrigued by research in and of itself as researchers are.

We embrace Coburn, Penuel, and Geil's (2013) definition of research-practice partnerships (RPPs)—"Long-term, mutualistic collaborations between practitioners and researchers that are intentionally organized to investigate problems of practice and solutions for improving district outcomes." (p. 2). Henrick et al. (2017) discuss three types of RPPs, based on the work of Coburn et al., including (1) *research alliances*, which focus on long-term alliances between universities and the communities where they are located or the alliances between regional educational laboratories and various communities; (2) *design research partnerships* where researchers and practitioners collaborate to design, study, improve, and scale innovations in teaching and learning, usually with a focus on improving specific practices empirically linked to improved student learning; and (3) *networked improvement communities* (NICs), which are structured collaborations between education professionals, researchers, and designers that aim to support the development of networks that are organized around a shared problem of practice (Bryk et al., 2015). NICs often involve educational organizations using agreed-upon tools and designs to share results across a network, with the goal of adapting the findings to practices across a range of contexts. Henrick et al. contend that we know relatively little about how to gauge the effectiveness of these partnerships. But clearly all of them are grounded in the practicality aspect of pragmatism based on the assumption that collaborative groups working on mutually agreed-upon problems toward practical ends is a positive endeavor.

Approaches that are often touted as being based in pragmatism, such as mixed methods research (MMR) and design-based research (DBR), are by design tuned to the practicality of practice. But researchers using these methodologies and methods know well the pragmatism-practicality tensions and the lack of clear evidence of their success outlined above. Although teachers will alter aspects of their practice due to participation in collaborative research, they are likely to drift back to prior practices in the absence of ongoing collaboration. We have learned these lessons on a multitude of collaborative projects, many of them starting with questions from our practice-based colleagues.

Pragmatism, broadly speaking, *can* be the foundation of inquiry into practical issues outside of the constraints of the "exact sciences" (Putnam, 2017). The assumption is that if researchers collaborate with practitioners, unconstrained by the epistemological foundations of fixed hypotheses, validating theories, and collecting data representing previous validated constructs, collaborators are free to uncover "what works" in practice. Nevertheless, this exclusivity argument that aligns pragmatism with practicality falters when one realizes that neither theory testing, nor validation, nor reaching practical conclusions is tied to any one research approach or data type, be it positivism, post-positivism, or combinations of quantitative and interpretive approaches in mixed methods designs—an argument we already presented above.

In short, "scientific" studies require "non-scientific" knowledge (Putnam, 2017). Groups who take up certain beliefs and explain the plausibility of their theories do so often because of sets of values—and they may stick with these values in the absence of supporting data. Practicality can mean just deciding to answer a practical question with preconceptions about what the answer might be, or should be—or fitting data to values or theories that one prefers so as best to address the question.

Pragmatism Beyond Practicality

As noted, when research methodologists discuss the practicality arguments of pragmatism, they often cite the American pragmatists, Dewey, James, and Peirce as a unified, like-minded group. They tend to pull from these scholars arguments that align with one another with relation to issues like collaboration of researchers and others; they note that researchers guided by pragmatism tend to ask and answer questions that help solve important, authentic questions that have practical import for society. They also argue that all the American pragmatists avoid getting bogged down in typical, but unresolvable, epistemological arguments that sap both time and intellectual energy that would be better applied to doing the immediate work of inquiry that gets things done.

Yet things get more complicated when scholars who study these noted pragmatists unearth the discrepancies regarding their stances about inquiry, objectivity, and epistemologies, particularly on issues like truth over time, across writings and with reference to one another's positions (e.g., Putnam's [2017] scrutiny of James's morphing theory of truth) including how one's positions might influence the others (e.g., the extent to which James aligned his perspectives on truth with Peirce).

If you pick a particular pragmatist like Dewey, a philosopher who never actually referred to himself as a pragmatist, you might end up with more of a contemporary critique that varies considerably from more classical critiques—e.g., Kaldec's (2007) notion of Dewey's critical pragmatism that focuses on his idea of "democracy as a way of life." Inquiry within this range of positions can partially align with the practicality argument—i.e., you engage in inquiry in order to solve practical problems based on common concerns through collaborative work within democratic communities. This is an argument for pragmatism we have focused on in several versions of this chapter over almost 20 years of its existence. But the argument goes beyond the practical to notions of civic commitment, shared responsibility, democratic goals and mutually valued public agendas that might influence public policy.

Practicality does not necessarily align with the philosophical assumptions of pragmatism, other than the often overadopted notion of James that truth can be defined as what works—so success and wishful thinking can underlie pragmatic approaches (Macarthur, 2017). Instead, beyond this simple practicality of doing what works is the sense of the shared responsibility, through experience, of solving important problems for and with a broad community—problems that, if solved, benefit the larger public good. To solve a problem requires a collective moral conviction that it should be addressed. Collective, socially moral stances are important to Dewey (Putnam, 2017).

The current interest, or even revival of interest, in American pragmatism is the possible promise of moral solutions to problems identified and tackled by citizens—the faith that these members of communities will identify problems and take up the heavy lifting involved in solving them (see Throntveit, 2014). At the same time, these pragmatists are also morally responsible for using the results of their inquiry to critique aspects of institutions and their power structures that might actually sustain, reproduce, or amplify the problems (Kaldec, 2007). Such is the issue of researchers collaborating with school-based colleagues to address practical, agreed-upon problems, some of which are actually created and sustained by the institution of schooling and the people within and outside the system. Several years ago, our school-based colleagues wanted us to help them support high school students who were having trouble reading "complex" history texts in an advanced placement curriculum (VanDeventer, Lemanski, & O'Brien, 2016). Our initial practical response was to help equip the students with better skills and strategies in academic language and disciplinary literacy to tackle the texts (O'Brien & Ortmann, 2016). As we worked into year 3 of this five-year project, we were struck with the overall idea that these advanced curricula—in this case an IB program—represented, through their definition of "challenging" students through difficult curricula, a sort of de facto tracking, advertently excluding students who are typically not successful in these classes because they could not navigate the inaccessible texts and tasks presented to them. This essentially resulted in an equity and social justice issue sustained by institutionalized structures and practices (O'Brien et al., 2017).

As we continue to address the problem originally posed by the teachers, we have not only looked at how to make the curriculum more accessible (often by eliminating inaccessible texts), but we are also planning to use the work to present a case to the International Baccalaureate Programme and its network of 4,583 world schools to draw upon our results to help the organization better critique their overall goals, materials, and pedagogies with respect to social justice and educational access. This research approach does not shed the idea of the practicality of pragmatism. Instead it adds critical pragmatism (Kaldec, 2007) as part of our moral responsibility to attempt to change aspects of the institution that promote and sustain the problem that we are trying to collaboratively solve. What scholars choose to study is another moral responsibility. We discuss this next.

A Pragmatic Stance for Literacy Inquiry in the Future

Scrutiny from within and outside the field of literacy has for decades forced an internal examination of our research and the ways that we engage in inquiry. As Chall (1998) noted 20 years ago, the public "seems to place less confidence now than in the past in the power of research and analysis to find better solutions" (pp. 21–22). Chall commented on the unorganized plethora of research findings that seem to have little impact on pedagogy or on solving current literacy problems, whereas Marty Ruddell (1999) writing at about the same time, emphasized that in a time when our theoretical frameworks and methods were more diverse than at any time in our scholarly history in literacy, unfortunately policy makers, politicians, and advisors who inform them marginalize important forms of inquiry. Ruddell contended that this marginalization occurred because research often does not conform to the accepted, albeit narrow, politically correct paradigm, which was, at that time, a positivist stance that favored experimental research designs. Clearly, in many arenas, the privileging of particular knowledge has not changed.

Currently the field of literacy education has a diversity of research tribes as distinct as the research speech communities comprising research groups once described by Mosenthal (1985), which we discussed in our first version of this chapter in 2000. Many literacy researchers, particularly scholars associated with the Literacy Research Association (LRA) and the research groups or assemblies of the National Council of Teachers of English (e.g., NCTEAR; NCRLL), feel little allegiance to a scientific paradigm that was dominant in or just before the turn of the last century. The International Reading Association (IRA), which morphed into the International Literacy Association (ILA) in 2013, like most other professional organizations, now leans toward literacy more broadly defined.

Research into such basic processes in reading and more quantitatively based instructional research, which used to be prevalent in the National Reading Conference (renamed the Literacy Research Association), is now even more prevalent in the Society for the Scientific Study of Reading (SSSR). Started in the early 1990s, SSSR maintains a mostly positivist or postpositivist stance and continues to proliferate mostly quantitatively based "scientific" studies of reading as well as research in language and literacy and written discourse processing. Researchers who align themselves there have backgrounds in fields ranging from educational psychology with interests in language and learning to discourse processing and basic cognitive processes in reading, linguistics, and neurosciences.

In fact, there is now a sense among many within the field of literacy education that positivist stances and the methodologies aligned with them are neither acceptable for answering many of the questions posed in the field of literacy nor even *ethically* reasonable in terms of their sampling, their interventions, their approaches to validity and reliability, and their bases for generalization. Moreover, there is even sentiment among many researchers who ground themselves in sociocultural theories of literacy that if researchers choose to study constructs defined and operationalized in research by "psychological," scientific, or psychometric assumptions (e.g., research on "struggling readers" or closing the "achievement gap"), they are subscribing to notions of deficit discourses. Deficit discourses are grounded in the notion that standardized tests and other measures that objectify literacy processes in restrictive and biased ways are legitimized by doing research on those objectified, decontextualized constructs, and paradigmatic and epistemological stances that promote these are uncritical and potentially harmful to children and youth (Shapiro, 2014).

In terms of the practicality arguments, these tribes (e.g., the psychological or "scientism" researchers; the sociocultural researchers) can easily be labeled as impractical researchers who are more concerned with the purity of their paradigms and rigid adherence to their respective methods than researchers focused on solving important problems of concern to practitioners. On one side, we find positivism, experiments, and quantified variables representing constructs that reify psychological, decontextualized notions of literacy; on the other side we find a range of situated practices defined and grounded by an almost impossibly complex set of intersecting socially and culturally situated factors, viewed through so many theoretical lenses that they fail to clarify directions for future practice.

But we also affirm that many scholars avoid these paradigmatic allegiances and instead work collaboratively for the common good, meeting what they believe are their ethical and moral responsibilities to work side by side with community partners to improve the communities in which they reside and work. We discuss this further in the dimensions of literacy inquiry section.

Dimensions of Literacy Inquiry for the Future

Although it is difficult to change particular large systems or structures (e.g., university systems, government agencies) and their value systems, we can begin to make changes as individuals and as a research community. We believe that a pragmatism-based perspective offers literacy researchers a way to approach inquiry that will enable us to agree to disagree, address the important work of defining the literacy problems we need to solve, determine how best to solve these problems, and ensure that the results inform practice (Mosenthal, 1999). In the next section, we move in this direction by presenting dimensions of literacy inquiry that we believe must continue to be defined, articulated, put into practice, and evaluated.

Dimension #1: Building Communities of Inquiry

Dewey reminded us that from a pragmatism perspective it is critical that we reconceptualize how inquiry is conducted, whom we involve, and the roles assumed by various participants within the process. For example, the National Association of State Universities and Land-Grant Colleges published a report by the Kellogg Commission on the Future of State and Land-Grant Universities called *Returning to Our Roots: The Engaged Institution* (1999). This document presents a key issue relating to the reconceptualization of how inquiry is conducted, challenging university personnel to work toward organizing staff and resources to better serve local and national needs in meaningful and coherent ways. The Kellogg Commission noted that university personnel must go beyond traditional notions of outreach and service to what is termed engagement (for an extended discussion of these ideas see Dillon, O'Brien, & Heilman, 2000).

The idea of engagement is consonant with Dewey's conception of social inquiry. Clearly, a commitment to engagement is necessary in forming partnerships. Strong leadership coupled with support by administrators, promotion and tenure committees, and funding agencies is also necessary. Communities must be open to diverse solutions to problems and varying roles of persons involved in partnerships. Challenges to this new concept of engagement and social inquiry revolve around logistical and accountability issues: How will communities of inquiry come together and function? Who will ultimately be responsible for the success or failure of partnerships? Will personnel be supported and rewarded for their efforts in both the short and long term? How do we know that people in communities of inquiry have the critical skills needed to deliberate problems? How will we mediate power and get along?

These challenges of pragmatism highlight what Bernstein (1983) understood to be a "paradox of praxis": "The type of solidarity, communicative interaction, dialogue, and judgment required for the concrete realization of praxis already presupposes incipient forms of community life that such praxis seeks to foster" (p. 175). Similarly, Dewey (1927/1993b) observed, "A class of experts is inevitably so removed from common interests as to become a class with private interests and private knowledge, which in social matters is not knowledge at all" (p. 187). It is difficult to conduct pragmatic inquiry that relies on communication and dialogue when teachers, community members, and researchers are not accustomed to working together; when literacy researchers are often separated by paradigmatic boundaries reinforced by power interests; and when researchers are similarly unaccustomed to communicative dialogue and interaction across disciplines both within education and across the academy.

Dewey (1916) envisioned communities of inquiry as entities that internally reflect "numerous and varied interests" and "full and free interplay with other forms of association" (p. 83). This conception is opposite our usual one of independent research or academic communities in which interests and memberships are explicitly narrow. As Foucault (1975/1977, 1980) delineated, disciplinary practices with distinct types of knowledge and knowledge makers are disciplined and understood as systems of power and authority. The suggestion of a more inclusive notion of research participants and academic communities through pragmatism implicates deeply entrenched notions of power and authority.

Yet research partnerships are critical. A desire to work collaboratively to identify and solve problems is key to the formation of partnerships between school-based personnel, literacy researchers, and community members. This stance requires a form of advocacy by members of the partnership, or what Rorty (1982) called "loyalty to other human beings" (p. 162), in order to promote "the creation of a freer and more humane experience" (Dewey, 1939/1993a, p. 245). For instance, partners might take up the cause of students who have been tracked using limited assessment measures. As an example of the dynamics of such advocacy, which is often in stark contrast to education, one can turn to medical research, which often shows how a pragmatic perspective, with participants in the role of advocates for themselves and others, influences research and practice (see Dillon et al., 2000, for an elaborated example of this concept). A challenging question for educators is why we see little need for advocacy with such a large number of stakeholders, including researchers, teachers, parents, students, and citizens. Pragmatists would seek to develop partnerships in which engagement is central to the work, where university- and school-based educators as well as students and community members bring their respective expertise to bear during deliberations, and where all stakeholders advocate for themselves to identify educational problems and inquiry designs. Ultimately, all stakeholders would be advocates for student learning. An example of a project that adheres to several of these ideals focuses on preparing elementary reading teachers on-site in an urban school setting, where the principal, parents, and K-6 teachers are partnering with university literacy educators to identify key knowledge, dispositions, and skills needed by new teachers to work with the diverse learners in this urban neighborhood (Israelson, Brodeur, & Dillon, 2012; Israelson, Dillon, & Brodeur, 2013).

Dimension #2: Moral Obligation in the Selection of Research Problems

Currently, many educational researchers are stepping back from their inquiry projects and the philosophical debates about the conduct of research to ask themselves these questions: Why do I engage in educational research? How meaningful is my research? Who benefits from my work? Dewey (1938/1981) would urge literacy researchers to consider problems we face in light of the institutional, social, political, and contextual influences surrounding those problems. From this pragmatic perspective, more time must be spent talking about the problem with participants and other constituents, defining the contours and the ways that addressing one feature of it may contribute to understanding another, and thinking about the concerns and implications associated with our decisions. This stage is what Dewey characterized as "enjoying the doubtful" (p. 182). The effort at the inception of the study can result in stronger, richer efforts along the way. Particular discernment for identifying what might be a useful focus of inquiry or a problem to solve usually rests with the researcher, or what Dewey called "the expert."

A pragmatic perspective requires that researchers share this power with participants; researchers come to the table with expertise, but other stakeholders also bring their knowledge and experience. Within this context, researchers are charged with teaching community members about methodological options available to understanding and solving problems. And often community members also teach researchers about tools and methods that can enrich the inquiry process. The sort of democratic dialogue Dewey envisioned in such a setting helps foster both understanding and community. Dewey (1927/1993b) observed that "the essential need . . . is the improvement in methods and conditions of debate, discussion, and persuasion" (p. 187). Such dialogue is an important skill, which is equally appropriate for citizens, researchers, and students. Within this process, researchers lose some freedom in the formulation of problems, the way they are addressed, and what is reported from the research. However, sharing of power is worthwhile when inquiry is viewed as responsive, meaningful, and credible to all participants.

Along with broadening the collective of persons associated with inquiry and redefining the roles persons might assume within this process, there is a need to reconsider how we develop research agendas, identify problems, and craft studies. We propose a literacy inquiry agenda spanning three foci: (1) developing a set of critical problems generated by a diverse group of stakeholders, which are foundational to large-scale research projects with multiple sites and community inquiry teams; (2) developing a set of critical problems generated at the local level by community inquiry teams; (3) collectively identifying problems that interest individual researchers and can be parsed into various facets to be addressed by individual expertise. Consistent with a pragmatic stance, we believe that on an international, national, local, and personal level, researchers should consider Dewey's vision of inquiry as collectively generating research problems from actual social situations (practices) as identified by all stakeholders through practical discourse.

As we think about re-envisioning the conduct of research, we are faced with the realization that researchers themselves pose the biggest challenge to taking a pragmatic stance in developing multiple interconnected research foci. That is because these scholars often research issues they enjoy or feel passionately about, and/or because they want to position themselves professionally, socially, and culturally to fit into acknowledged trends and to be recognized by respectable communities. Dewey and other pragmatists oppose the perspective of research as a personal matter, noting that research agendas should be public and socially grounded in intent and process. Inquiry not so grounded fails to serve the purpose of democratic reconstruction. Embedded within the challenge of public vs. personal research agendas is the question of how the nature of research is influenced by the way researchers are positioned by the social, cultural, and historical contexts in which they conduct inquiry. For example, researchers are valued in university settings for the innovative knowledge they generate and, like it or not, for their productivity as quantified by the number of articles they've published in prestigious journals. Add to this narrow conceptualization of productivity the continuing institutional pressure to reform teacher education programs and a situation is created in which scholars actually have less time to be scholarly. In such a climate, research is often quickly conceived; small data sets are collected, analyzed, and interpreted in a cursory manner; and reports of research are written in bits and pieces when time permits in outlets that university promotion and tenure committees find acceptable (but persons engaged in practice may not read). Thus, much of this research may have little effect on the practices of K-12 educators or on learners' lives. There is evidence that this institutional culture continues to remain a formidable force that affects the character and quality of literacy inquiry. As a bright spot, many colleges of education have worked to expand tenure and promotion statements to include publicly engaged scholarship and honor a range of research methodologies including long-term research in community settings with a variety of partners.

In sum, few literacy scholars or prospective advocates of scholarship have clearly identified a broad set of issues that deserve unified, convergent efforts, despite the urging of scholars such as Dillon who argued that literacy scholars need to "work with school-based colleagues and other stakeholders to formulate pragmatic, important, and researchable questions and create appropriate research designs to collect data to address these questions—including mixed research designs" (Falk-Ross et al., 2007, pp. 225–243).

One positive example of a unified effort was a multi-site study that was designed and enacted to identify the characteristics of effective elementary reading teacher preparation programs (Hoffman & Roller, 2001; Hoffman, Roller, Maloch, Sailors, Duffy, & Beretvas, 2005). Funded by IRA, this study encouraged collaboration among literacy researchers, literacy leaders, and IRA for the purpose of crafting coherent researchable questions and initiating an appropriate design to answer them. This scholarship—and the spin-off studies launched from it—created the foundation for major teacher education reform in elementary reading teacher preparation in the U.S. It also illustrated how a pragmatic stance toward forming multiple yet connected research projects was facilitative of the participants' efforts.

Despite the identified need for a shared research agenda, most literacy researchers also believe that opportunities must be provided for innovative, unconventional research that advances the field. This tension between large-scale and local research agendas, shared and individual agendas, and the role of research paradigms can be managed productively with considerable thought, effort, dialogue, and organization.

Finally, in maintaining a pragmatic stance, the selection and design of studies in the literacy field should be developed with the end in view. Traditionally, this end in view is a post hoc entity we call implications or recommendations rather than an a priori design issue. Pragmatic research conversations would begin with these questions: What do we hope to achieve at the conclusion of the study? Why is this end important for learners? The conversation about the end result could help participants better define problems and improve the design of studies, and this conversation could help participants focus on the specific social, cultural, and other contextual aspects that affect a particular inquiry. Despite its apparent usefulness, an end-in-view perspective, grounded in social responsibility and democratic purposes, presents a challenge in conducting research. In beginning a study, researchers typically review related research, carefully crafting hypotheses or guiding research questions, developing a design that best addresses questions, collecting and analyzing data, theorizing, and interpreting the results. It is possible that the end-in-view fixation may cause researchers to lose sight of the research process, including methodological possibilities, or of certain structural considerations as a project unfolds (Thompson, 1997).

Dimension #3: Reconsidering Traditions, Methodologies and How We Communicate Findings

To move forward in the field of literacy research, we believe that scholars need to continue to think about the research traditions in which they operate and the rationale behind these choices. Technical expertise and theoretical and methodological purity have been the hallmarks of quality in paradigmatically driven research. Researchers believe that if they attend to these elements, more credible findings will result. From a pragmatic stance, using a variety of methodologies can either strengthen a study or lead to its downfall. The use of multimethodologies can add breadth and depth and numerical, pictorial, and narrative data to support themes, assertions, or findings. But these studies must still evidence the tenets of quality research. Many researchers are careful to ground their work in substantive theories from the field of literacy; nevertheless, these same scholars can sometimes be criticized for neglecting to use and exhibit understanding about the theoretical frameworks undergirding their methodologies. In addition, although the title Doctor of Philosophy is reminiscent of the days in which a broad education was more valued, academe, as already noted, currently does not support the development of broadly educated researchers. Neither does academe support the development of inquiry communities with school and community collaborators, or with the potentially diverse groups of colleagues that pragmatic inquiry needs to thrive. Again, Foucault (1975/1977, 1980) reminded us that the ways in which we structure knowledge in academe serve to create regimes of truth and structures of power and authority. Thus, a pragmatic turn in inquiry provides us with compelling challenges, not only to the ways in which ideas are conceived and pursued but also to the ways in which power and authority are structured among intellectuals and society in general. The change we suggest has both philosophical and political ramifications.

Concurrent with the need for new knowledge is an awareness of which knowledge bases we draw upon and which ones we inadvertently overlook. We urge literacy researchers to continue to consider new traditions and methodologies, even as they develop expertise (and a level of comfort) with a few. For example, many literacy researchers have now taken up Scheurich and Young's (1997) discussion of race-based paradigms constructed via cultural and historical contexts. These authors argue that all current epistemologies and accompanying tensions (e.g., issues of qualitative vs. quantitative methodologies, objective vs. subjective reality, validity and paradigmatic issues in general) rise out of the social history of the dominant White race, thus reflecting and reinforcing that social history and racial group. We need to continue to extend paradigms to address "epistemological racism," recognizing that dominant and subordinate racial groups "do not think and interpret realities in the same way as White people because of their divergent structural positions, histories, and cultures" (Stanfield, 1985, p. 400). Scheurich and Young (1997) argued that even critical approaches (critical theory, feminism, lesbian/gay orientations, and critical postmodernism), where racism has been a focus, have been racially biased. A pragmatic perspective beckons literacy researchers to attend to how various racial groups select issues for inquiry, conceptualize research, interpret phenomena, and record results. This is an epistemological issue that is critical to understanding literacy events currently and in the future (for a discussion of these issues see Parker, 2002; for examples of research in action, see the work of Kris Gutierrez, Carol Lee, Gloria Ladson-Billings).

Finally, a pragmatic stance requires that literacy researchers consider how we communicate the findings from our inquiry to other communities of inquirers, researchers within and across paradigmatic lines and disciplines, and individuals outside the research context (e.g., policy makers and the general public). Writing for multiple audiences and writing about ideas that others find useful (keeping the end in mind as one constructs a study) are important goals. The typical article format for sharing work should change to better illuminate complex concepts for a range of readers and to meet the needs of policy makers in terms of brevity (e.g., through the use of executive summaries), clarity, and elimination of jargon. A shift in the expectations of journal editors and editorial review boards is also needed to promote the publication of concise research reports while also recognizing the value of longer articles that detail theory and methodology.

Research in the Future: The Millennials Charge Themselves to Make a Difference

In a recent article by Jennifer Anikst (2015), a case is presented for "pragmatic idealism" as the millennials' basic approach to life and work. Anikst interviewed David Burstein, a millennial himself, who is the author of *Fast Future: How the Millennial Generation Is Shaping Our World* (2014) and the cofounder of Run for America, a political movement. Burstein argues that historically, pragmatism and idealism have been understood as opposite ends of the spectrum. He proposes that now more than ever we have to blend the two, because the challenges we face in our world are so great. And despite our enhanced abilities to take them on, we also need more individuals who strive to do just that, to change the world in positive ways by figuring out how to develop the strategies and tools to confront obstacles. He believes that millennials as a group espouse this way of thinking. They show it in their stance toward desiring a career vs. merely working at a job, and by engaging in tasks that foster the organization they work in while at the same time bettering the world. Burstein rejects the critique that millennials often exude an entitled stance or appear to not work hard at their jobs. Instead, he observes that they seek to take up difficult societal and global challenges. Yet he acknowledges that they require support to help them think about how they can channel their talent and contribute their intellectual and other considerable resources toward helping our world become a better place.

The charge for millennials will be to dig into what they are truly passionate about in their work and to use their energy to continually learn and grow for self-fulfillment, while simultaneously enhancing the world they care so deeply about. A challenge for them will be to develop depth in their work, particularly with community partners in one location over extended time periods, since their nature seems to be to move from one job to another to locate new challenges and learning opportunities. Leaders in educational institutions where millennials seek career paths will be required to reconsider structures, the nature of work, and build better organizations that foster the ways millennials engage in activities and the tasks they take up. Burstein also states that we have to support millennials by helping them remain focused on their responsibility for the future of our world.

We argue that this is a charge for all of us as literacy researchers. We must ground ourselves to envision the kinds of communities, schools, learning experiences, and lives we—and those who live in these communities—want for our current and future youth and children. Likewise, we must reaffirm our commitment and the work we will take up alongside our community partners to foster this enhanced vision.

Conclusions

Answers to complex questions related to how learners become and remain literate and how teachers can support this process await further investigation. An individual researcher's beliefs and expertise can no longer be the sole rationale for the research questions selected and pursued. Instead, the complexity of problems and social situations that affect practice and concern local constituents must be key to the creation of shared research agendas. Similar to the efforts of IRA and researchers from multiple institutions from around the country who participated in the elementary reading teacher education studies (Hoffman, Roller, Maloch, Sailors, Duffy, & Beretvas,

2005), we need literacy organizations and higher education literacy leaders to organize initiatives in which P-16 colleagues and community partners formulate pragmatic, important, and research-able questions and create appropriate research designs to collect data to address these questions. It is through these collaborations, and the findings from the studies, that our most robust and impactful solutions can arise.

We have proposed pragmatism as a stance that academics and communities of inquirers consider. In addition, we have introduced Burstein's concept of pragmatic idealism. Pragmatism is not a paradigm adapted from others that are currently popular; rather, it is a revolutionary break in our thinking and practice relating to inquiry. As a literacy community, we need to challenge ourselves to step back and think collectively and individually about the inquiry in which we are engaged. Is our research meaningful, credible, and prone to making a difference in students' learning and teachers' pedagogy? Does our inquiry work toward concrete alternatives for students and teachers? As Rorty (1982) explained, "For the pragmatists, the pattern of all inquiry—scientific as well as moral—is deliberation concerning the relative attractions of various concrete alternatives" (p. 164). We see the goal of research as practical rationality serving moral concerns with social justice at its core. Research grounded in pragmatism can be a practical and hopeful inquiry, one that avoids the arrogance of modernist empiricism and the angst of postmodern deconstructions. We believe this approach seeks to understand yet also to inform, change processes, and empower marginalized individuals. From both a practicality and a more elaborated pragmatic stance, we contend that persons holding positivist and postpositivist epistemological stances can and should collaborate with people holding sociocultural epistemological stances; this can be accomplished by using research designs like mixed methods and design-based research to address complex questions that cannot be addressed by any single group with its preferred epistemology.

In their column "What Can We, as Americans Do Together?" two politicians from different parties reflect on what's missing from solving today's social problems (Penny & Horner, 2012). We take a lesson from them: We need leadership to move forward. Embracing a pragmatic stance—one that unites not further divides—the field of literacy research is a call for courageous and responsible leadership. Many educational researchers are already taking personal and professional risks to step out of their comfort zones and up to the educational challenges of today's world. These leaders realize that solutions to vexing educational issues require finding common ground instead of polarizing positions to address the realities facing students, teachers, schools, families, and communities.

The question becomes: On the big issues facing us in education, where will you find common ground with those who have different ideologies and research perspectives? Are we ready to listen, to learn, to reflect, and to hold ourselves to a higher standard? The National Research Council Report (2002), offered a parting word of advice that is still relevant today: "Ultimately, policy makers and practicing educators will have to formulate specific policies and practices on the basis of values and practical wisdom as well as education research. Science-based education research will affect, but typically not solely determine, these policies and practices" (p. 17). Our recent history as educational researchers has been fraught with anxiety, anguish, and despair. But there have been moments of insight. Perhaps one might be an adaptation of playwright Eugène Ionesco's central idea: Ideologies *need not* separate us. Dreams *of what could be* bring us together.

References

Anikst, J. (2015, October 5). How millennials make "pragmatic idealism" work. *Globe and Mail*. Retrieved from https://beta.theglobeandmail.com/report-on-business/careers/leadership-lab/how-millennials-make-pragmatic-idealism-work-forthem/article26663877/?ref=http://www.theglobeandmail.com& Reprinted with permission from Rotman Management, the magazine of the University of Toronto's Rotman School of Management.

Beach, R., & O'Brien, D. (2018). Significant literacy research informing English language arts instruction. In D. Lapp & D. Fisher (Eds.), *Handbook of teaching the English language arts* (4th ed., pp. 30–56). New York, NY: Routledge.

Bernstein, R. (1983). *Beyond objectivism and relativism: Science, hermeneutics and practice*. Philadelphia, PA: University of Pennsylvania Press.

Biesta, G., & Burbules, N. C. (2003). *Pragmatism and educational research*. Lanham, MD: Rowman & Littlefield Publishers.

Boisvert, R. D. (1998). *John Dewey: Rethinking our time*. Albany, NY: State University of New York Press.

Bryk, A. S., Gomez, L., Grunow, A., & LeMahieu, P. (2015). *Learning to improve: How America's schools can get better at getting better*. Cambridge, MA: Harvard Education Publishing Group.

Burstein, D. (2014). *Fast future: How the millennial generation is shaping our world*. Boston, MA: Beacon Press.

Chall, J. S. (1998). My life in reading. In E. G. Sturtevant, J. A. Dugan, P. Linder, & W. M. Linek (Eds.), *Literacy and community* (pp. 12–24). Commerce, TX: College Reading Association.

Clandinin, D. J., & Connelly, F. M. (1996). Teachers' professional knowledge landscapes: Teacher stories—stories of teachers—school stories—stories of school. *Educational Researcher, 25*(3), 24–30.

Cochran-Smith, M., & Lytle, S. L (1993). *Inside/outside: Teacher research and knowledge*. New York, NY: Teachers College Press.

Coburn, C. E., Penuel, W. R., & Geil, K. E. (2013, January). Research-practice partnerships: A strategy for leveraging research for educational improvement in school districts. New York, NY: William T. Grant Foundation.

Design-Based Research Collective. (2003). Design-based research: An emerging paradigm for educational inquiry. *Educational Researcher, 31*(1), 5–8.

Dewey, J. (1916). *Democracy and education: An introduction to the philosophy of education*. New York, NY: Macmillan.

Dewey, J. (1981). Social Inquiry. In J. J. McDermott (Ed.), *The philosophy of John Dewey* (pp. 397–420). Chicago, IL: University of Chicago Press. (Original work published 1938)

Dewey, J. (1987a). Ethics revisited. In J. A. Boydson (Ed.), *The later works of John Dewey, 1925–1953* (Vol. 7). Carbondale, IL: Southern Illinois University Press. (Original work published 1932)

Dewey, J. (1987b). The quest for certainty. In J. A. Boydson (Ed.), *The later works of John Dewey, 1925–1953* (Vol. 4). Carbondale, IL: Southern Illinois University Press. (Original work published 1929)

Dewey, J. (1993a). Creative democracy—The task before us. In D. Morris & I. Shapiro (Eds.), *John Dewey: The political writings* (pp. 240–245). Indianapolis, IN: Hackett. (Original work published 1939)

Dewey, J. (1993b). The public and its problems. In D. Morris & I. Shapiro (Eds.), *John Dewey: The political writings* (pp. 173–191). Indianapolis, IN: Hackett. (Original work published 1927)

Dillon, D. R., O'Brien, D. G., & Heilman, E. E. (2000). Literacy research in the next millennium: From paradigms to pragmatism and practicality. *Reading Research Quarterly, 35*, 10–26.

Foucault, M. (1977). *Discipline and punish: The birth of the prison* (A. Sheridan, Trans.). New York, NY: Pantheon. (Original work published 1975)

Foucault, M. (1980). Truth and power. In C. Gordon (Ed.), *Power/knowledge: Selected interviews and other writings, 1972–77* (pp. 109–133). New York, NY: Pantheon.

Falk-Ross, F., Sampson, M. B., Fox, B. J., Berger, A., Lewis, J., Cassidy, J., . . . Dillon, D. R. (2007). Stepping forward together: Voicing the concerns of teacher educators through practical applications and collaborative actions. In *28th Yearbook of the College Reading Association* (pp. 225–243), Pittsburg, KS: College Reading Association.

Gee, J. P. (1999). Critical issues: Reading and the new literacy studies: Reframing the national academy of sciences report on reading. *Journal of Literacy Research, 31*(3), 355–374.

Heath, S. B. (1983). *Ways with words: Language, life and work in communities and classrooms*. New York, NY: Cambridge University Press.

Henrick, E. C., Cobb, P., Penuel, W. R., Jackson, K., & Clark, T. (2017). *Assessing research-practice partnerships: Five dimensions of effectiveness*. New York, NY: William T. Grant Foundation.

Hiebert, J., Gallimore, R., & Stigler, J. W. (2002). A knowledge base for the teaching profession: What would it look like and how can we get one? *Educational Researcher, 32*(5), 3–15.

Hoffman, J. V., & Roller, C. M. (2001). The IRA excellence in reading teacher preparation commission's report: Current practices in reading teacher education at the undergraduate level in the United States. In C. M. Roller (Ed.), *Learning to teach reading: Setting the research agenda* (pp. 32–79). Newark, DE: International Reading Association.

Hoffman, J. V., Roller, C., Maloch, B., Sailors, M., Duffy, G., & Beretvas, S. N. (2005). Teachers' preparation to teach reading and their expectations and practices in the first three years of teaching. *Elementary School Journal, 105*(3), 267–287.

Israelson, M. Brodeur, K., & Dillon, D. R. (2012). *A study of preservice elementary literacy teachers' development of culturally sustaining knowledge in practice*. Paper presented at the Literacy Research Association, San Diego, CA, November 29.

Israelson, M., Dillon, D. R., & Brodeur, K. (2013). *The impact of a parent panel on preservice teachers' self-efficacious beliefs about collaborating with parents and culturally sustaining knowledge in practice*. Paper presented at the annual meeting of the Literacy Research Association, Dallas, TX, December 6.

Johnson, R. B., & Onwuegbuzie, A. J. (2004). Mixed methods research: A research paradigm whose time has come. *Educational Researcher*, *33*(7), 14–26.

Johnson, R. B., Onwuegbuzie, A. J., de Waal, C., Stefurak, T., & Hildebrandt, D. (2017). Unpacking pragmatism for mixed methods research. In D. Wyse, N. Selwyn, E. Smith, & L. E. Suter (Eds.), *The Bera/Sage handbook of educational research* (pp. 259–279). Los Angeles, CA: Sage.

Juuti, K., & Lavonen, J. (2006). Design-based research in science education: One step towards methodology. *Nordic Studies in Science Education*, *2*(4), 54–68.

Kaldec, A. (2007). *Dewey's critical pragmatism*. New York, NY: Rowman and Littlefield Publishers.

Kellogg Commission on the Future of State and Land-Grant Universities. (1999). *Returning to our roots: The engaged institution*. Washington, DC: National Association of State Universities and Land-Grant Colleges.

Macarthur, D. (2017). Introduction. In D. Macarthur (Ed.), *Hilary Putnam and Ruth Anna Putnam: Pragmatism as a way of life*. Cambridge, MA: Belknap Press of Harvard University Press.

Menand, L. (1997). *Pragmatism: A reader*. New York: Knopf Doubleday Publishing Group.

Menand, L. (2002). *The metaphysical club: A story of ideas in America*. New York, NY: Farrar, Straus and Giroux.

Morgan, D. L. (2007). Paradigms lost and pragmatism regained: Methodological implications of combining qualitative and quantitative methods. *Journal of Mixed Methods Research*, *1*(1), 48–76.

Mosenthal, P. B. (1985). Defining progress in educational research. *Educational Researcher*, *14*(9), 3–9.

Mosenthal, P. B. (1999). Critical issues: Forging conceptual unum in the literacy field of pluribus: An agenda-analytic perspective. *Journal of Literacy Research*, *31*, 213–254.

National Institute of Child Health and Human Development. (2000). *Teaching children to read: An evidence-based assessment of the scientific research literature on reading and its implications for reading instruction* (NIH Publication No. 00-4769). Washington, DC: US Government Printing Office.

National Research Council. (2002). *Scientific research in education*. R. Shavelson & L. Towne (Eds.), Committee on Scientific Principles for Educational Research. Washington, DC: National Academy Press.

No Child Left Behind Act (2001). Pub. L. No. 107–110. Retrieved from http://www2.ed.gov/policy/elsec/leg/esea02/107-110.pdf

O'Brien, D., & Rogers, T. (2015). Sociocultural perspectives on literacy and learning. In E. Anderman & L. Corno (Eds.), *Handbook of educational psychology* (3rd ed.). American Psychological Association. New York, NY: Routledge.

O'Brien, D., & Ortmann, L. (2016). Disciplinary literacy: A multidisciplinary synthesis. In K. A. Hinchman and D. Appleman (Eds.), Adolescent *literacy: A handbook of practice-based research*. New York, NY: Guilford Press.

O'Brien, D. G., Dillon, D. R., Avery, P. G., Poch, R., Ortmann, L. L., VanDeventer, M. M., & Hylton, R. (2017). *A disciplinary literacy framework fostering equity, access, and agency in a history international baccalaureate curriculum*. Paper presented at the annual meeting of the American Educational Research Association, San Antonio, TX, April 29.

Parker, L. (2002). What's race got to do with it? Critical race theory's conflicts with and connections to qualitative research methodology and epistemology. *Qualitative Inquiry*, *8*(1), 7–22.

Patton, M. Q. (2002). *Qualitative evaluation and research methods* (3rd ed.). Newbury Park, CA: Sage.

Patton, M. Q. (2014). *Qualitative research and evaluation and methods: Integrating theory and practice* (4th ed.). Newbury Park, CA: Sage.

Penny, T., & Horner, T. (2012, May 20). What can we, as Americans do together? *Star Tribune*, p. OP3.

Putnam, H. (2017). Pragmatism and non-scientific knowledge. In H. Putnam and R. A. Putnam *Pragmatism as a way of life* (pp. 55–70). Cambridge, MA: Belknap Press of Harvard University Press.

Reading Excellence Act. Title VIII of the Departments of Labor, Health, and Human Services, and Education, and Related Agencies Appropriations Act (1999). The Omnibus Appropriations Bill, 1999. Public Law 105–277. Retrieved from http://www.gpo.gov/fdsys/pkg/PLAW-105publ277/pdf/PLAW-105publ277.pdf

Rorty, R. (1982). *Consequences of pragmatism*. Minneapolis, MN: University of Minnesota Press.

Rosiek, J. L. (2013). Pragmatism and post qualitative futures. *International Journal of Qualitative Studies in Education*, *26*(6), 692–705.

Ruddell, M. R. (1999). Of stand-up comics, statisticians, storytellers, and small girls walking backward: A new look at the discourses of literacy research. In T. Shanahan & F. V. Rodriguez-Brown (Eds.), *The forty-eighth yearbook of the national reading conference* (pp. 1–16). Oak Creek, WI: National Reading Conference.

Sandoval, W. (2014). Conjecture mapping: An approach to systematic educational design research. *Journal of the Learning Sciences, 23*(1), 18–36, doi: 10.1080/10508406.2013.778204

Scheurich, J. J., & Young, M. D. (1997). Coloring epistemologies: Are our research epistemologies racially biased? *Educational Researcher, 26*(4), 4–16.

Shapiro, S. (2014). "Words that you said got bigger": English language learners' lived experiences of deficit discourse. *Research in the Teaching of English, 48*(4), 386–406.

Stanfield, J. H., II. (1985). The ethnocentric basis of social science knowledge production. *Review of Research in Education, 12*, 387–415.

Thompson, A. (1997). Political pragmatism and educational inquiry. In F. Margonis (Ed.), *Philosophy of Education* (pp. 425–434). Urbana, IL: Philosophy of Education Society.

Throntveit, T. (2014). *William James and the quest for an ethical republic.* New York, NY: Palgrave Macmillan-St. Martin's Press.

VanDeventer, M., Lemanski, L., & O'Brien, D. (2016). Beyond the textbook: Reimagining disciplinary literacy in teacher education. Paper presented at the annual meeting of the Literacy Research Association, Nashville, TN, November 30–December 2.

Van Velze, J. H. (2013). Educational researchers and practicality. *American Educational Research Journal, 50*(4), 789–811.

EDITOR BIOGRAPHICAL SKETCHES

Donna E. Alvermann is a University of Georgia Appointed Distinguished Research Professor, and the Omer Clyde and Elizabeth Parr Aderhold Professor in Education. Formerly an editor of *Reading Research Quarterly* and the *Journal of Literacy Research* (with David Reinking), she received the Literacy Research Association's Oscar Causey Award and the International Literacy Association's William S. Gray Citation of Merit. While a 6th grader, Donna organized a James Dean fan club, perhaps leading to her interest in the literacies of popular culture. She is currently learning to play the acoustic guitar, no doubt her biggest challenge ever.

Norman J. Unrau is a Professor Emeritus of California State University, Los Angeles. After 25 years as a high school teacher, he completed his doctorate at University of California, Berkeley. Norm served as editor of the *Journal of Adolescent & Adult Literacy* and authored *Content Area Reading and Writing* and *Thoughtful Teachers, Thoughtful Learners*. He also published articles in *Review of Educational Research, Journal of Adolescent & Adult Literacy, Journal of Educational Research, Reading Psychology*, and elsewhere. Norm enjoys playing tennis and traveling with his wife, Cherene.

Misty Sailors is a Professor of Literacy Education and Director of the Center for the Inquiry of Transformative Literacies at the University of Texas at San Antonio. She is currently the lead editor for the *Journal of Literacy Research*. She is a member of the International Literacy Association's (ILA) Literacy Research Panel and ILA's Standards Revision Committee (Standards for Literacy Professionals 2017). Her research has been funded by the Institute of Education Sciences and the United States Agency for International Development. She reads, travels, gardens, and crochets.

Robert B. Ruddell began his teaching career in a one-room school in West Virginia. Now Professor Emeritus, University of California, Berkeley, Bob is a recipient of the International Literacy Association's William S. Gray Citation of Merit and the Literacy Research Association's Oscar S. Causey Award, both for exceptional research achievements. His work is published in *The Reading Teacher, Language Arts,* and a variety of research journals. Bob is the author of *How to Teach Reading to Elementary and Middle School Students: Practical Ideas from Highly Effective Teachers*. He relaxes with tantalizing mystery novels and a good round of golf.

CONTRIBUTOR BIOGRAPHICAL SKETCHES

Patricia A. Alexander is the Jean Mullan Professor of Literacy and Distinguished Scholar-Teacher in the Department of Development and Quantitative Methodology at the University of Maryland. She is editor of *Contemporary Educational Psychology* and Routledge's Educational Psychology Handbook series editor. Her research focuses primarily on learning from text within academic domains. She has published over 260 books, chapters, and articles and made over 400 keynotes, invited talks, and research presentations.

Richard C. Anderson is in his fifty-fifth year at the University of Illinois, where he is now Professor Emeritus, but still active in research and writing. Dick is currently excited about understanding how different approaches to classroom discussion shape children's social, emotional, and cognitive development.

Nichole Barrett is an English Education doctoral candidate at the University at Buffalo, SUNY. When she is not nose deep in a *Harry Potter* book or on an adventure with her brother, she is exploring the intersection between digital video composition, identity, and student voice, specifically among rural students. Her other research interests include finding ways to provide spaces for adolescents to explore who they are through literature and creation.

Maneka Deanna Brooks is an Assistant Professor at Texas State University where she teaches both undergraduate and graduate courses on language, literacy, and culture. Her research agenda centers on the literacy practices and educational experiences of bilingual adolescents who have been institutionally identified as experiencing difficulties with literacy. Her most recent publications about these topics can be found in the *Journal of Literacy Research*, *TESOL Quarterly*, and the *Journal of Adolescent & Adult Literacy*.

Nancy Brynelson co-directs the Center for the Advancement of Reading and Writing for the California State University, Office of the Chancellor. A former bilingual teacher, elementary principal, district administrator, and state language arts consultant, she co-wrote the *2015 English Language Arts/English Language Development Framework for California Public Schools*. Inducted into the California Reading Association Reading Hall of Fame in 2010, she received the California Association of Teachers of English Award of Merit in 2017.

Kelly B. Cartwright is a Professor at Christopher Newport University, near the Virginia coast where she enjoys walking the beach and climbing lighthouses with her children. Kelly is editor of *Literacy Processes: Cognitive Flexibility in Learning and Teaching* (Guilford, 2008) and author of *Word Callers: Small-Group and One-to-One Interventions for Children Who "Read" but Don't Comprehend* (Heinemann, 2010) and *Executive Skills and Reading Comprehension: A Guide for Educators* (Guilford, 2015).

Jill Castek is Associate Professor of New Literacies and Bi/Multilingual Immigrant Learners in the Department of Teaching, Learning, and Sociocultural Studies at the University of Arizona. Jill's research addresses digital literacy and learning across the lifespan and in classrooms and the community. Her interests include outdoor activities and travel, environmental sustainability, and citizen science. She co-edits the Digital Literacies for Disciplinary Learning column in the *Journal of Adolescent & Adult Literacy*.

Julie Coiro is Associate Professor in the School of Education at the University of Rhode Island, where she co-directs the Ph.D. in Education program and the Graduate Certificate in Digital Literacy. Julie conducts research on online reading comprehension, digital inquiry, and collaborative knowledge building. She also enjoys traveling and being outdoors with her husband Charlie and two daughters Meghan and Sarah.

Deborah R. Dillon is Senior Associate Dean for Graduate and Professional Programs and Guy Bond Chair in Reading at the University of Minnesota, Twin Cities. While associate "deaning" is rewarding, Deborah seeks balance in her life. She spends time with her parents who live in MN, travels to new places with her husband and daughter, and finds moments to recharge in her garden or cheer on the MN Twins baseball team.

Mary Anne Doyle, Professor of Reading, Neag School of Education, University of Connecticut, is the Consulting Editor for the Marie Clay Literacy Trust and assists with the ongoing revision and re-publication of Marie Clay's many texts. Her publications include numerous monographs, book chapters, and articles, and she currently serves as editor in chief of the *Journal of Reading Recovery*.

Mark Dressman is Professor of Secondary Education in the College of Education at the University of Illinois at Champaign-Urbana, where he teaches courses in English education, content area literacy, and qualitative research. He is the author of multiple articles in *Reading Research Quarterly, Journal of Literacy Research,* and *Curriculum Inquiry.* He is co-editor with Randall Sadler of the forthcoming *Handbook of Informal Language Learning* to be published by Wiley-Blackwell.

Nell K. Duke is a Professor at the University of Michigan in Ann Arbor, Michigan, where Nell was born and raised. Among her recent projects are continuing to raise her two beloved children, conducting a large-scale study of the impact of project-based instruction, publishing *Connect4Learning: The Pre-K Curriculum* (Kaplan Early Learning), and continuing to serve as co-editor of the *Not This But That* book series (Heinemann).

John R. Edlund currently teaches rhetoric and literature in the Department of English and Foreign Languages at California State Polytechnic University, Pomona. He chaired the task force that developed the original California State University Expository Reading and Writing Course (ERWC) in 2003 and chaired the steering committee for that program until 2018.

Christian Ehret is an assistant professor at McGill University, where he studies affective dimensions of learning and literacy across settings. A new Montrealer, he enjoys exploring the city's vibrant urban art scene on long walks through its diverse neighborhoods. Ehret received an NCTE Promising Researcher Award, and his book, Affect in Literacy Teaching and Learning: Pedagogies, Politics, and Coming to Know, co-edited with Kevin Leander, is forthcoming from Routledge.

Emily Fox has taught in-service teachers about reading for the University of Maryland and is now working (slowly) on a book about reading for Routledge's Educational Psychology Insights series. She has authored recent handbook chapters on learning to read, multiple source use in history, individual differences in reading, text and comprehension, and reading as an academic domain.

James Paul Gee is the Mary Lou Fulton Presidential Professor of Literacy Studies and a Regents' Professor at Arizona State University and a member of the National Academy of Education. He lives on a small farm in Northern Arizona amidst sheep, goats, donkeys, pigs, and chickens whose purpose is solely to live and thrive. He has written a lot about a lot of different things.

Kenneth S. Goodman changed our understanding of literacy processes, how they are learned, and how best to teach them. His theory of the reading process based on comprehensive theory is the most cited and demonstrates that reading is a unitary process in which readers actively construct meaning; they make sense of print. His theory is built on linguistic, psycholinguistic, and sociolinguistic concepts and is also practical theory because teachers who understand this view of reading and writing understand what it is that learners do as they develop literacy.

Yetta M. Goodman speaks, consults, and works with education departments and professional literacy organizations worldwide. She is active and has held leadership positions in major professional literacy organizations and is a member of the Reading Hall of Fame. She popularized the term kidwatching encouraging teachers at every level to become knowledgeable professional observers of the language and learning development of their students of all ages. Her whole language philosophy and extensive writing is focused on support for innovative classrooms, students, and teachers.

Usha Goswami is Professor of Cognitive Developmental Neuroscience at the University of Cambridge and Director of the Centre for Neuroscience in Education. Trained as a primary school teacher, she decided to pursue research in child psychology. Her current research examines developmental relations between phonology and basic auditory processing of amplitude modulation and amplitude rise time. In 2011, she received the Aspen Brain Forum Senior Investigator Prize in Neuroeducation.

Katherine S. Haq (University of Buffalo) is a literacy doctoral candidate and retired elementary school teacher. An award-winning gardener, experienced urban kayaker, and mother of three sons, Kate trolls libraries across New York and Pennsylvania reading young adult critical contemporary literature. Her research interests dove-tail with her activism work involving urban adolescent civic engagement, literacy, and homelessness. Other research interests include positioning theory, narrative inquiry, teacher identity, and ethnography.

Laurie A. Henry is a Professor in the Department of Doctoral Studies in Literacy and Dean of the Seidel School of Education, Salisbury University, Maryland. In addition to her research related to mobilizing learning and innovative instructional spaces, she enjoys kayaking, beachcombing, and international travel. In her previous position with the University of Kentucky, she collaborated with Fayette County Public Schools to design and launch the STEAM Academy High School.

George G. Hruby currently dons the persona of Executive Director for the Collaborative Center for Literacy Development and is an Associate Research Professor at the University of Kentucky's College of Education. A recent vita reveals he's published, gets grants, teaches well, and likes children and other small animals. The self behind the mask eschews entitlement, binaries, social media, and other forms of aggression.

Mira-Lisa Katz is Associate Director of WestEd's Strategic Literacy Initiative in San Francisco, California, and Professor Emerita of English at Sonoma State University. She is editor of *Moving Ideas: Multimodality and Embodied Learning in Communities and Schools* (Peter Lang, 2013), co-editor of the Leading Literacy Change department for the International Literacy Association's *Journal of Adolescent & Adult Literacy*, and writes about a broad range of topics in education, dance, and the arts.

Walter Kintsch is Professor Emeritus in the Department of Psychology and the Institute of Cognitive Science at the University of Colorado. His work has focused on text comprehension and memory. His construction-integration theory claims that discourse comprehension initially proceeds on the basis of inexact and context insensitive construction rules, followed by an integration process that suppresses contextually irrelevant material.

Charles (Chuck) K. Kinzer, Professor Emeritus, Communication, Media and Learning Technologies Design, Teachers College, Columbia University, is teaching online, writing, and photographing birds and wildlife on Washington's west coast. He has been the co-editor of the *National Reading Conference* (now LRA) *Yearbook*, and is co-author of *Interactive Literacy Education* (Erlbaum/Taylor Francis), *Metrics in Simulations and Games for Learning* (Springer), and *Effective Reading Instruction* and *Programmed Word Attack* (both, Prentice-Hall).

Susan Lutz Klauda is a Faculty Specialist at the University of Maryland and an Adjunct Professor at The Catholic University of America. When not reading, writing, or teaching about literacy and human development, she can be found exploring the DC area and beyond with her family. Her research has appeared in such journals as *Reading Research Quarterly, Journal of Educational Psychology,* and *Educational Psychology Review.*

Karen A. Krasny is Professor at York University and York-Massey Visiting Scholar at University of Toronto where she is investigating 19th-century advances in typography and illustration that contributed to the autonomy of the child reader. She authored *Gender and Literacy: A Handbook for Educators and Parents* (Praeger), and her recent work appears in *Semiotica*. She and Peter enjoy living near their twin sons and delighting in Toronto's rich cultural scene.

Gunther Kress, Professor of Semiotics and Education at UCL Institute of Education, London, is interested in meaning (-making) in contemporary environments, and developing social semiotic theory of multimodality in which communication, learning, and identity are interconnected. Indicative books: *Social Semiotics*; *Before Writing: Rethinking the Paths to Literacy*; *Reading Images: The Grammar of Graphic Design*; *Literacy in the New Media Age*; and (with Jeff Bezemer) *Multimodality, Communication, Learning: A Social Semiotic Frame.*

Don A. Leu is Professor of Education and Neag Chair of Literacy and Technology at the University of Connecticut. He captains the 47-foot vessel, *Change of Latitude* with Debbie Leu, cruising Pacific Northwest waters to Alaska. He edited the *Handbook of Research in New Literacies* with Julie Coiro, Michele Knobel, and Colin Lankshear. His research appears in *Reading Research Quarterly, Reading and Writing, Journal of Educational Psychology,* and *Computers and Education.*

Karen Levush is a graduate student in the Human Development and Quantitative Methodology Department at the University of Maryland, College Park. She coordinates the Language and Literacy Research Center in the College of Education. As a teacher in the District of Columbia public school system, Karen facilitated her school's response to intervention processes and led a year-long program of teacher professional development focused on self-regulation in the classroom.

Allan Luke taught at Queensland University of Technology and is now writing, recording, and playing music in Brisbane, Australia. He is author of *Critical Literacy, Schooling and Social Justice* (Routledge, 2018), *Educational Policy, Narrative and Discourse* (Routledge, 2018) and editor, with Guanglun M. Mu and Karen Dooley, of *Bourdieu and Chinese Education* (Routledge, 2018).

Leketi Makalela is professor and founding director of the Hub for Multilingual Education and Literacies, at the University of the Witwatersrand, South Africa. He is also a Distinguished Visiting Professor at City University of New York under the Advanced Research Collaborative program. His research interests include translanguaging, multilingual education, and indigenous literacies. His most recent book is *Shifting Lenses: Multilanguaging, Decolonization and Education in the Global South* (2018).

Sandra McCormick is Professor Emerita, The Ohio State University. She enjoys sitting on the deck of their home with her husband, Bob Ruddell, savoring views of the Golden Gate Bridge, skyline of San Francisco, and San Francisco Bay. She is co-author, with Jerry Zutell, of *Instructing Students Who Have Literacy Problems.* Her research appears in *Reading Research Quarterly, The Reading Teacher, Journal of Learning Disabilities,* and many other literacy-related journals.

Mary B. McVee (aka "theory girl," a nickname bestowed by former students) pursues interests in positioning, social and embodied learning, social semiotics, culture, and narrative. When not conducting research at the University of Buffalo, SUNY, Mary puts theory into practice by attempting to shift the positions of her three lovely children and husband toward enacted practices such as picking up their dirty socks.

sj Miller is a trans★+–disciplinary scholar whose research emphasis is on policy and schooling practices about gender identity. sj's award-winning book *Teaching, Affirming, and Recognizing Trans and Gender Creative Youth: A Queer Literacy Framework* (Palgrave Macmillan 2016), was recently translated in Spanish for use across Latin America.

Elizabeth Birr Moje is dean, George Herbert Mead Collegiate Professor of Education, and an Arthur F. Thurnau Professor of Literacy, Language, and Culture in the School of Education at the University of Michigan. Moje teaches courses in secondary and adolescent literacy, cultural theory, and research methods. A former high school history and biology teacher, Moje's research examines young people's navigations of culture, identity, and literacy learning in Detroit, Michigan.

David O'Brien is Professor of Literacy Education at the University of Minnesota, Twin Cities. When not working on his project related to disciplinary literacy in high schools or teaching research courses, he keeps busy re-learning the hobbies that he gave up early in his career (music, photography, armchair political science), all in an effort to jump start a more balanced life and future trajectory.

Kate Pahl is Professor of Arts and Literacy at Manchester Metropolitan University. She is the author, with Jennifer Rowsell, of Living Literacies (MIT press, forthcoming) and Materializing Literacies in Communities (2014). Her work is concerned with literacy in home and community contexts.

Jonathan Ratner, the son of the late Louise M. Rosenblatt, learned her theoretical perspective on texts through osmosis. A graduate of Harvard (B.A.) and Yale (Ph.D.), he taught economics at Wellesley College and SUNY at Albany. Later an associate director at the U.S. Government Accountability Office, he is now at a research firm. His "Six Stones for a Mosaic: Louise and Teaching from Her Son's Perspective" appeared in *Voices from the Middle* (3/2005).

Louise M. Rosenblatt was 100 years old at her death. Described as "an influential scholar of reading and the teaching of literature and an Emeritus Professor of English Education at New York University," she related the text to "the experience of personal engagement and involvement central to the reading experience." A little-known fact about Rosenblatt: fluent in French (her doctorate was from the Sorbonne), she worked during World War II for a U.S. intelligence agency, analyzing information from Nazi-occupied France.

Jennifer Rowsell is a Professor and Canada Research Chair in Multiliteracies at Brock University in Canada. She has written, co-written, and co-edited 23 books on such wide-ranging topics as New Literacy Studies, multimodality, youth and popular culture, digital literacies, multiliteracies, ethnography and the digital divide. Co-editor of the *Routledge Expanding Literacies in Education* series with Cynthia Lewis, Rowsell is also the Department Editor of Digital Literacies for *The Reading Teacher.*

Mark Sadoski, Professor Emeritus at Texas A&M University, authored (with Allan Paivio) two editions of *Imagery and Text: A Dual Coding Theory of Reading and Writing* (Erlbaum, 2001; Routledge, 2013), and chapters in previous editions of *Theoretical Models and Processes of Reading* (IRA, 1994, 2004, 2013). An award-winning landscape photographer, he is sometimes found in Hollywood visiting his actor son, Thomas Sadoski, his actress daughter-in-law, Amanda Seyfried, and his delightful granddaughter.

Katarina N. Silvestri (University at Buffalo) is a literacies doctoral candidate and teacher educator by day, progressive rock bass player and purveyor of lush vocal harmonies by night. She serves as research project manager for the Center for Literacy and Reading Instruction and researches student-centered inquiry learning; multimodal, artifactual, embodied perspectives; disciplinary literacies; and language, literacy, and culture. She begins as Assistant Professor of Literacy at SUNY Cortland in Fall 2018.

Allison Skerrett is Associate Professor in the Department of Curriculum and Instruction at The University of Texas at Austin. Her research focuses on adolescents' literacy practices, transnational literacies, and secondary English education in urban contexts. Her research appears in the *American Educational Research Journal, Journal of Literacy Research, Reading Research Quarterly, Research in the Teaching of English, Urban Education*; and in her book, *Teaching Transnational Youth* (Teachers College Press, 2015).

Anna Smith is an Assistant Professor at Illinois State University where she studies contemporary composition, writing development, and transliteracies. She is the co-author of Developing Writers: Teaching and Learning in the Digital Age with Richard Andrews. To support her own development as a writer, she enjoys geeking out about emerging technologies with the youth and teachers with whom she works.

Brian V. Street, Professor Emeritus at King's College London, University of London, Visiting Professor of Education in the Graduate School of Education, University of Pennsylvania, Visiting Professor in the School of Education and Professional Development, University of East Anglia and Visiting Professor at the School of Education, Universidade Federal de Minas Gerais, Brazil. In 2016, he received an honorary degree of Doctor of the University at Open University (OU, United Kingdom) in recognition of his academic and scholarly distinction and exceptional contribution to our understanding of the nature of literacy and its significance in people's lives.

Ana Taboada Barber is an Associate Professor at the University of Maryland, where she completed her PhD after emigrating to the United States from Buenos Aires, Argentina. Among her projects, she has written a book on how motivation and cognitive factors shape the reading comprehension of Spanish-speaking English learners. Ana enjoys raising her very curious 4-year-old boy who is teaching her more about bilingualism than she might have thought possible.

Alfred W. Tatum is the Dean of the College of Education and Professor of Literacy Education at the University of Illinois at Chicago. He conducts research in conceptually contested spaces in which he works directly with African American males ages 8–19 to move them toward high literacy achievement while advancing their intellectual development. He is the author of *Teaching Reading to Black Adolescent Males* (Stenhouse, 2005) and *Reading For Their Life* (Heinemann, 2009).

Karen Wohlwend is an Associate Professor at Indiana University, where she studies early childhood makerspaces and enjoys exploring Bloomington's wooded bike paths with her family. She is author of *Playing Their Way into Literacies* (Teachers College Press, 2011), *Literacy Playshop* (Teachers College Press, 2013), and co-author with Carmen Medina of *Literacy, Play, and Globalization* (Routledge, 2014).

INDEX